FOUNDATIONS OF
ARTIFICIAL INTELLIGENCE

Foundations of Artificial Intelligence

Series Editors

J. Hendler
H. Kitano
B. Nebel

ELSEVIER
AMSTERDAM–BOSTON–HEIDELBERG–LONDON–NEW YORK–OXFORD
PARIS–SAN DIEGO–SAN FRANCISCO–SINGAPORE–SYDNEY–TOKYO

Handbook of Knowledge Representation

Edited by

Frank van Harmelen
Vrije Universiteit Amsterdam
The Netherlands

Vladimir Lifschitz
University of Texas at Austin
USA

Bruce Porter
University of Texas at Austin
USA

ELSEVIER
AMSTERDAM–BOSTON–HEIDELBERG–LONDON–NEW YORK–OXFORD
PARIS–SAN DIEGO–SAN FRANCISCO–SINGAPORE–SYDNEY–TOKYO

Elsevier
Radarweg 29, PO Box 211, 1000 AE Amsterdam, The Netherlands
The Boulevard, Langford Lane, Kidlington, Oxford OX5 1GB, UK

First edition 2008

Library of Congress Cataloging-in-Publication Data
A catalog record for this book is available from the Library of Congress

British Library Cataloguing in Publication Data
A catalogue record for this book is available from the British Library

ISBN: 978-0-444-52211-5

For information on all Elsevier publications
visit our website at books.elsevier.com

Printed and bound in the United Kingdom

Transferred to Digital Print 2010

Working together to grow
libraries in developing countries

www.elsevier.com | www.bookaid.org | www.sabre.org

ELSEVIER   BOOK AID
International   Sabre Foundation

We dedicate this book
to the memory of Ray Reiter (1939–2002)

Preface

Knowledge Representation and Reasoning is at the heart of the great challenge of Artificial Intelligence: to understand the nature of intelligence and cognition so well that computers can be made to exhibit human-like abilities. As early as 1958, John McCarthy contemplated Artificial Intelligence systems that could exercise common sense. From this and other early work, researchers gained the conviction that (artificial) intelligence could be formalized as symbolic reasoning with explicit representations of knowledge, and that the core research challenge is to figure out how to represent knowledge in computers and to use it algorithmically to solve problems.

Fifty years later, this book surveys the substantial body of scientific and engineering insights that constitute the field of Knowledge Representation and Reasoning. Advances have been made on three fronts. First, researchers have explored general methods of knowledge representation and reasoning, addressing fundamental issues that cut across application domains. Second, researchers have developed specialized methods of knowledge representation and reasoning to handle core domains, such as time, space, causation and action. Third, researchers have tackled important applications of knowledge representation and reasoning, including query answering, planning and the Semantic Web. Accordingly, the book is divided into three sections to cover these themes.

Part I focuses on general methods for representing knowledge in Artificial Intelligence systems. It begins with background on classical logic and theorem proving, then turns to new approaches that extend classical logic—for example, to handle qualitative or uncertain information—and to improve its computational tractability.

- Chapter 1 provides background for many of the subsequent chapters by surveying classical logic and methods of automated reasoning.

- Chapter 2 describes the remarkable success of satisfiability (SAT) solvers. Researchers have found that this type of automated reasoning can be used for an ever increasing set of practical applications and that it can be made surprisingly efficient.

- Chapter 3 reviews research in Description Logics, which provides methods for representing and reasoning with terminological knowledge. Description logics are the core of the representation language of the Semantic Web.

- Chapter 4 describes constraint programming, a powerful paradigm for solving combinatorial search problems. This style of knowledge representation and reasoning draws together a wide range of techniques from artificial intelligence, operations research, algorithms and graph theory.

- Chapter 5 reviews the influential work on Conceptual Graphs. This structured representation provides an expressive language and powerful reasoning methods that are essential for applications such as Natural Language Understanding.

- Chapter 6 introduces nonmonotonic logics, which deal with complications related to handling exceptions to general rules. These logics are called "nonmonotonic" because they describe the retraction of information from a knowledge base when additional exceptions are taken into account.

- Chapter 7 builds on the previous one by describing Answer Set logic, which neatly handles default rules and exceptions, along with the nonmonotonic reasoning that they engender. This form of logic also supports reasoning about the causal effects of actions—another key feature of common sense.

- Chapter 8 continues this theme with a survey of techniques for Belief Revision, that is, how an agent changes its knowledge base in light of new information that contradicts a previous belief.

- Chapter 9 explains the role of qualitative models of continuous systems. These models enable another key feature of common sense: reasoning with incomplete information. This form of reasoning can compute, for example, the possible future states of a system, which is important for numerous tasks, such as diagnosis and tutoring.

- Chapter 10 demonstrates that these theories and techniques establish the basis for problem solvers that exploit an explicit model of the behavior of systems for tasks such as design, testing, and diagnosis. Being based on first principles knowledge and inference engines with a formal logical foundation, rather than experience tied to specific instances and situations, such model-based problem solvers achieve the competence and robustness needed for industrial applications of knowledge representation and reasoning techniques.

- Chapter 11 confronts the unavoidable problem of uncertainty in real world domains, and surveys the extensive research on Bayesian networks as a method for modeling and reasoning with uncertain beliefs.

Part II delves into the special challenges of representing and reasoning with some core domains of knowledge, including time, space, causation and action. These challenges are ubiquitous across application areas, so solutions must be general and composable.

- Chapter 12 discusses ways to represent the temporal aspects of an ever-changing world. In a theme that recurs throughout this section, this raises a variety of interesting ontological issues—such as whether time should be modeled with points or intervals, and at what level of granularity—along with the pragmatic consequences of these decisions.

- Chapter 13 surveys qualitative representations of space—including topology, orientation, shape, size and distance—as well as reasoning methods appropriate to each. Although no single theory covers these topics comprehensively, researchers have produced a powerful tool kit.

- Chapter 14 builds on the two previous chapters, and also on research on qualitative modeling, to tackle the general problem of physical reasoning. Two important domain theories are developed (for liquids and solid objects), and the key issue of shifting between alternative models is explored.

- Chapter 15 surveys representations of an agent's knowledge and beliefs, including propositions about the knowledge state of other agents (e.g., "Tom believes that Mary knows..."). This work nicely extends to handle common knowledge and distributed knowledge within a community of agents.

- Chapter 16 surveys the long history of the "situation calculus"—a knowledge representation designed to handle dynamic worlds. As first defined by McCarthy and Hayes, a situation is "a complete state of the universe at an instance of time". Because situations are first-order objects that can be quantified over, this framework has proven to be a strong foundation for reasoning about change.

- Chapter 17 describes the Event Calculus as an alternative to the Situation Calculus with some additional nice features. In particular, the event calculus facilitates representing continuous events, nondeterministic effects, events with duration, triggered events, and more.

- Chapter 18 continues the development of representation languages designed for dynamic worlds by introducing Temporal Action Logics. This family of languages is especially well suited for reasoning about persistence, i.e., features of the world that carry forward through time, unchanged, until an action affects them. It facilitates the representation of nondeterministic actions, actions with duration, concurrent actions and delayed effects of actions, partly due to its use of explicit time, and it tightly couples an automated planner to the formalism.

- Chapter 19 focuses on Nonmonotonic Causal Logic, which handles dynamic worlds using a strong solution to the frame problem. This logic starts with assumption that everything has a cause: either a previous action or inertia (persistence). This results in nice formalizations for key issues such as ramifications, implied action preconditions, and concurrent interacting effects of actions.

Part III surveys important applications of knowledge representation and reasoning. The application areas span the breadth of Artificial Intelligence to include question answering, the Semantic Web, planning, robotics and multi-agent systems. Each application draws extensively on the research results described in Parts I and II.

- Chapter 20 surveys research in question answering systems. These systems answer questions given a corpus of relevant documents and, in some cases, a knowledge base of common sense information. The system's challenge is to select relevant passages of text (an information retrieval task), interpret them (a natural language understanding task) and infer an answer to the question (a reasoning task).

- Chapter 21 reviews progress on the Semantic Web: an extension of the World Wide Web in which content is expressed in a formal language to enable software agents to find, integrate and reason with it. This raises numerous challenges, including scaling knowledge representation methods to the size of the Web.

- Chapter 22 surveys advances in automated planning, which make these systems considerably more powerful than "classical planners" from the early years of Artificial Intelligence. The new framework supports, for example, nondeterministic actions and partial observability, which are important attributes of real-world domains.

- Chapter 23 extends knowledge representation and reasoning in a new direction: cognitive robotics. The challenge in this application is that the robots' world is dynamic and incompletely known, which requires re-thinking traditional approaches to AI tasks, such as planning, as well as coupling high-level reasoning with low-level perception.

- Chapter 24 surveys research on multi-agent systems, in which it is important that each agent represent and reason about the other agents in the environment. This is especially challenging when the agents have different, or worse—conflicting—goals.

- Chapter 25 describes tools and techniques for knowledge engineering: how to acquire the knowledge that can be expressed in the formalisms described in the other chapters.

Together, these 25 chapters, organized in the three sections "General Methods", "Specialized Representations" and "Applications", provide a unique survey of the best that Knowledge Representation has achieved, written by researchers who have helped to shape the field. We hope that students, researchers and practitioners in all areas of Artificial Intelligence and Cognitive Science will find this book to be a useful resource.

Acknowledgement

Early drafts of each chapter were reviewed by authors of other chapters, and by these research colleagues: Krzysztof Apt, Paolo Ferraris, Enrico Giunchiglia, Joohyung Lee, Antonis Kakas, Benjamin Kuipers, David Poole, and Mary-Anne Williams. We are grateful to them all.

Frank Harmelen
Vrije Universiteit Amsterdam

Vladimir Lifschitz
University of Texas at Austin

Bruce Porter
University of Texas at Austin
July 2007

Editors

Frank van Harmelen
Vrije Universiteit Amsterdam
The Netherlands

Vladimir Lifschitz
University of Texas at Austin
USA

Bruce Porter
University of Texas at Austin
USA

Contributors

Franz Baader
Technische Universität Dresden
Germany

Marcello Balduccini
Texas Tech University
USA

Chitta Baral
Arizona State University
USA

Gerhard Brewka
University of Leipzig
Germany

Alessandro Cimatti
ITC/IRST
Italy

Anthony G. Cohn
University of Leeds
UK

Adnan Darwiche
University of California, Los Angeles
USA

Ernest Davis
New York University
USA

Patrick Doherty
Linköping University
Sweden

Michael Fisher
University of Liverpool
UK

Kenneth D. Forbus
Northwestern University
USA

Michael Gelfond
Texas Tech University
USA

Carla P. Gomes
Cornell University
USA

Jim Hendler
Rensselaer Polytechnic Institute
USA

Ian Horrocks
University of Oxford
UK

Henry Kautz
University of Rochester
USA

Jonas Kvarnström
Linköping University
Sweden

Gerhard Lakemeyer
RWTH Aachen University
Germany

Hector Levesque
University of Toronto
Canada

Yuliya Lierler
University of Texas at Austin
USA

Vladimir Lifschitz
University of Texas at Austin
USA

Fangzhen Lin
Hong Kong University of Science and
Technology
Hong Kong

Contributors

Leora Morgenstern
IBM Thomas J. Watson Research Center
USA

Yoram Moses
Technion, Israel Institute of Technology
Israel

Erik T. Mueller
IBM Thomas J. Watson Research Center
USA

Ilkka Niemelä
Helsinki University of Technology
Finland

Pavlos Peppas
University of Patras
Greece

Marco Pistore
Università di Trento
Italy

David Plaisted
University of North Carolina at Chapel
Hill
USA

Jochen Renz
The Australian National University
Australia

Francesca Rossi
University of Padova
Italy

Ashish Sabharwal
Cornell University
USA

Ulrike Sattler
University of Manchester
UK

Guus Schreiber
Vrije Universiteit Amsterdam
The Netherlands

Bart Selman
Cornell University
USA

John F. Sowa
VivoMind Intelligence, Inc.
USA

Peter Struss
Technische Universität München
Germany

Paolo Traverso
ITC/IRST
Italy

Mirosław Truszczyński
University of Kentucky
USA

Hudson Turner
University of Minnesota, Duluth
USA

Peter van Beek
University of Waterloo
Canada

Frank van Harmelen
Vrije Universiteit Amsterdam
The Netherlands

Wiebe van der Hoek
University of Liverpool
UK

Toby Walsh
University of New South Wales
Australia

Michael Wooldridge
University of Liverpool
UK

Contents

Contents

III   Knowledge Representation in Applications   777

Part I

General Methods in Knowledge Representation and Reasoning

Handbook of Knowledge Representation
Edited by F. van Harmelen, V. Lifschitz and B. Porter
© 2008 Elsevier B.V. All rights reserved
DOI: 10.1016/S1574-6526(07)03001-5

Chapter 1

Knowledge Representation and Classical Logic

Vladimir Lifschitz, Leora Morgenstern, David Plaisted

1.1 Knowledge Representation and Classical Logic

Mathematical logicians had developed the art of formalizing declarative knowledge long before the advent of the computer age. But they were interested primarily in formalizing mathematics. Because of the important role of nonmathematical knowledge in AI, their emphasis was too narrow from the perspective of knowledge representation, their formal languages were not sufficiently expressive. On the other hand, most logicians were not concerned about the possibility of automated reasoning; from the perspective of knowledge representation, they were often too generous in the choice of syntactic constructs. In spite of these differences, classical mathematical logic has exerted significant influence on knowledge representation research, and it is appropriate to begin this Handbook with a discussion of the relationship between these fields.

The language of classical logic that is most widely used in the theory of knowledge representation is the language of first-order (predicate) formulas. These are the formulas that John McCarthy proposed to use for representing declarative knowledge in his Advice Taker paper [171], and Alan Robinson proposed to prove automatically using resolution [230]. Propositional logic is, of course, the most important subset of first-order logic; recent surge of interest in representing knowledge by propositional formulas is related to the creation of fast satisfiability solvers for propositional logic (see Chapter 2). At the other end of the spectrum we find higher-order languages of classical logic. Second-order formulas are particularly important for the theory of knowledge representation, among other reasons, because they are sufficiently expressive for defining transitive closure and related concepts, and because they are used in the definition of circumscription (see Section 6.4).

Now a few words about the logical languages that are *not* considered "classical". Formulas containing modal operators, such as operators representing knowledge and belief (Chapter 15), are not classical. Languages with a classical syntax but a nonclassical semantics, such as intuitionistic logic and the superintuitionistic logic of strong equivalence (see Section 7.3.3), are not discussed in this chapter either. Nonmonotonic logics (Chapters 6 and 19) are nonclassical as well.

This chapter contains an introduction to the syntax and semantics of classical logic and to natural deduction; a survey of automated theorem proving; a concise overview of selected implementations and applications of theorem proving; and a brief discussion of the suitability of classical logic for knowledge representation, a debate as old as the field itself.

1.2   Syntax, Semantics and Natural Deduction

Early versions of modern logical notation were introduced at the end of the 19th century in two short books. One was written by Gottlob Frege [89]; his intention was "to express a content through written signs in a more precise and clear way than it is possible to do through words" [261, p. 2]. The second, by Giuseppe Peano [204], introduces notation in which "every proposition assumes the form and the precision that equations have in algebra" [261, p. 85]. Two other logicians who have contributed to the creation of first-order logic are Charles Sanders Peirce and Alfred Tarski.

The description of the syntax of logical formulas in this section is rather brief. A more detailed discussion of syntactic questions can be found in Chapter 2 of the *Handbook of Logic in Artificial Intelligence and Logic Programming* [68], or in introductory sections of any logic textbook.

1.2.1   Propositional Logic

Propositional logic was carved out of a more expressive formal language by Emil Post [216].

Syntax and semantics

A *propositional signature* is a nonempty set of symbols called *atoms*. (Some authors say "vocabulary" instead of "signature", and "variable" instead of "atom".) *Formulas* of a propositional signature σ are formed from atoms and the 0-place connectives $\perp$ and $\top$ using the unary connective $\neg$ and the binary connectives $\wedge$, $\vee$, $\rightarrow$ and $\leftrightarrow$. (Some authors write & for $\wedge$, $\supset$ for $\rightarrow$, and $\equiv$ for $\leftrightarrow$.)[1]

The symbols FALSE and TRUE are called *truth values*. An *interpretation* of a propositional signature σ (or an *assignment*) is a function from σ into {FALSE, TRUE}. The semantics of propositional formulas defines which truth value is assigned to a formula F by an interpretation I. It refers to the following truth-valued functions, associated with the propositional connectives:

x	$\neg(x)$
FALSE	TRUE
TRUE	FALSE

---

[1]Note that $\perp$ and $\top$ are not atoms, according to this definition. They do not belong to the signature, and the semantics of propositional logic, defined below, treats them in a special way.

x	y	$\wedge(x, y)$	$\vee(x, y)$	$\rightarrow(x, y)$	$\leftrightarrow(x, y)$
FALSE	FALSE	FALSE	FALSE	TRUE	TRUE
FALSE	TRUE	FALSE	TRUE	TRUE	FALSE
TRUE	FALSE	FALSE	TRUE	FALSE	FALSE
TRUE	TRUE	TRUE	TRUE	TRUE	TRUE

For any formula F and any interpretation I, the truth value F^I that is *assigned* to F by I is defined recursively, as follows:

- for any atom F, $F^I = I(F)$,

- $\bot^I = $ FALSE, $\top^I = $ TRUE,

- $(\neg F)^I = \neg(F^I)$,

- $(F \odot G)^I = \odot(F^I, G^I)$ for every binary connective $\odot$.

If the underlying signature is finite then the set of interpretations is finite also, and the values of F^I for all interpretations I can be represented by a finite table, called the *truth table* of F.

If $F^I = $ TRUE then we say that the interpretation I *satisfies* F, or is a *model* of F (symbolically, $I \models F$).

A formula F is a *tautology* if every interpretation satisfies F. Two formulas, or sets of formulas, are *equivalent* to each other if they are satisfied by the same interpretations. It is clear that F is equivalent to G if and only if $F \leftrightarrow G$ is a tautology.

A set Γ of formulas is *satisfiable* if there exists an interpretation satisfying all formulas in Γ. We say that Γ *entails* a formula F (symbolically, $\Gamma \models F$) if every interpretation satisfying Γ satisfies F.[2]

To represent knowledge by propositional formulas, we choose a propositional signature σ such that interpretations of σ correspond to states of the system that we want to describe. Then any formula of σ represents a condition on states; a set of formulas can be viewed as a knowledge base; if a formula F is entailed by a knowledge base Γ then the condition expressed by F follows from the knowledge included in Γ.

Imagine, for instance, that Paul, Quentin and Robert share an office. Let us agree to use the atom p to express that Paul is in the office, and similarly q for Quentin and r for Robert. The knowledge base $\{p, q\}$ entails neither r nor $\neg r$. (The semantics of propositional logic does not incorporate the closed world assumption, discussed below in Section 6.2.4.) But if we add to the knowledge base the formula

$$\neg p \vee \neg q \vee \neg r, \qquad (1.1)$$

expressing that at least one person is away, then the formula $\neg r$ (Robert is away) will be entailed.

Explicit definitions

Let Γ be a set of formulas of a propositional signature σ. To extend Γ by an *explicit definition* means to add to σ a new atom d, and to add to Γ a formula of the form

---

[2]Thus the relation symbol $\models$ is understood either as "satisfies" or as "entails" depending on whether its first operand is an interpretation or a set of formulas.

$d \leftrightarrow F$, where F is a formula of the signature σ. For instance, if

$$\sigma = \{p, q, r\}, \qquad \Gamma = \{p, q\},$$

as in the example above, then we can introduce an explicit definition that makes d an abbreviation for the formula $q \wedge r$ ("both Quentin and Robert are in"):

$$\sigma' = \{p, q, r, d\}, \qquad \Gamma' = \{p, q, d \leftrightarrow (q \wedge r)\}.$$

Adding an explicit definition to a knowledge base Γ is, in a sense, a trivial modification. For instance, there is a simple one-to-one correspondence between the set of models of Γ and the set of models of such an extension: a model of the extended set of formulas can be turned into the corresponding model of Γ by restricting it to σ. It follows that the extended set of formulas is satisfiable if and only if Γ is satisfiable. It follows also that adding an explicit definition produces a "conservative extension": a formula that does not contain the new atom d is entailed by the extended set of formulas if and only if it is entailed by Γ.

It is *not* true, however, that the extended knowledge base is *equivalent* to Γ. For instance, in the example above $\{p, q\}$ does not entail $d \leftrightarrow (q \wedge r)$, of course. This observation is related to the difference between two ways to convert a propositional formula to conjunctive normal form (that is, to turn it into a set of clauses): the more obvious method based on equivalent transformations on the one hand, and Tseitin's procedure, reviewed in Section 2.2 below, on the other. The latter can be thought of as a sequence of steps that add explicit definitions to the current set of formulas, interspersed with equivalent transformations that make formulas smaller and turn them into clauses. Tseitin's procedure is more efficient, but it does not produce a CNF equivalent to the input formula; it only gives us a conservative extension.

Natural deduction in propositional logic

Natural deduction, invented by Gerhard Gentzen [96], formalizes the process of introducing and discharging assumptions, common in informal mathematical proofs.

In the natural deduction system for propositional system described below, derivable objects are *sequents* of the form $\Gamma \Rightarrow F$, where F is a formula, and Γ is a finite set of formulas ("F under assumptions Γ"). For simplicity we only consider formulas that contain neither $\top$ nor $\leftrightarrow$; these connectives can be viewed as abbreviations. It is notationally convenient to write sets of assumptions as lists, and understand, for instance, $A_1, A_2 \Rightarrow F$ as shorthand for $\{A_1, A_2\} \Rightarrow F$, and $\Gamma, A \Rightarrow F$ as shorthand for $\Gamma \cup \{A\} \Rightarrow F$.

The axiom schemas of this system are

$$F \Rightarrow F$$

and

$$\Rightarrow F \vee \neg F.$$

The inference rules are shown in Fig. 1.1. Most of the rules can be can be divided into two groups—introduction rules (the left column) and elimination rules (the right column). Each of the introduction rules tells us how to *derive* a formula of some syntactic form. For instance, the conjunction introduction rule ($\wedge I$) shows that we can derive

$$(\wedge I)\ \frac{\Gamma \Rightarrow F \quad \Delta \Rightarrow G}{\Gamma, \Delta \Rightarrow F \wedge G} \qquad\qquad (\wedge E)\ \frac{\Gamma \Rightarrow F \wedge G}{\Gamma \Rightarrow F} \quad \frac{\Gamma \Rightarrow F \wedge G}{\Gamma \Rightarrow G}$$

$$(\vee I)\ \frac{\Gamma \Rightarrow F}{\Gamma \Rightarrow F \vee G} \quad \frac{\Gamma \Rightarrow G}{\Gamma \Rightarrow F \vee G} \qquad (\vee E)\ \frac{\Gamma \Rightarrow F \vee G \quad \Delta_1, F \Rightarrow H \quad \Delta_2, G \Rightarrow H}{\Gamma, \Delta_1, \Delta_2 \Rightarrow H}$$

$$(\rightarrow I)\ \frac{\Gamma, F \Rightarrow G}{\Gamma \Rightarrow F \rightarrow G} \qquad\qquad (\rightarrow E)\ \frac{\Gamma \Rightarrow F \quad \Delta \Rightarrow F \rightarrow G}{\Gamma, \Delta \Rightarrow G}$$

$$(\neg I)\ \frac{\Gamma, F \Rightarrow \bot}{\Gamma \Rightarrow \neg F} \qquad\qquad (\neg E)\ \frac{\Gamma \Rightarrow F \quad \Delta \Rightarrow \neg F}{\Gamma, \Delta \Rightarrow \bot}$$

$$(C)\ \frac{\Gamma \Rightarrow \bot}{\Gamma \Rightarrow F}$$

$$(W)\ \frac{\Gamma \Rightarrow \Sigma}{\Gamma, \Delta \Rightarrow \Sigma}$$

Figure 1.1: Inference rules of propositional logic.

a conjunction if we derive both conjunctive terms; the disjunction introduction rules ($\vee I$) show that we can derive a disjunction if we derive one of the disjunctive terms. Each of the elimination rules tells us how we can *use* a formula of some syntactic form. For instance, the conjunction elimination rules ($\wedge E$) show that a conjunction can be used to derive any of its conjunctive terms; the disjunction elimination rules ($\vee E$) shows that a disjunction can be used to justify reasoning by cases.

Besides introduction and elimination rules, the deductive system includes the contradiction rule (C) and the weakening rule (W).

In most inference rules, the set of assumptions in the conclusion is simply the union of the sets of assumptions of all the premises. The rules ($\rightarrow I$), ($\neg I$) and ($\vee E$) are exceptions; when one of these rule is applied, some of the assumptions from the premises are "discharged".

An example of a proof in this system is shown in Fig. 1.2. This proof can be informally summarized as follows. Assume $\neg p, q \rightarrow r$ and $p \vee q$. We will prove r by cases.

Case 1: p. This contradicts the assumption $\neg p$, so that r follows.

Case 2: q. In view of the assumption $q \rightarrow r$, r follows also.

Consequently, from the assumptions $\neg p$ and $q \rightarrow r$ we have derived $(p \vee q) \rightarrow r$.

The deductive system described above is sound and complete: a sequent $\Gamma \Rightarrow F$ is provable in it if and only if $\Gamma \models F$. The first proof of a completeness theorem for propositional logic (involving a different deductive system) is due to Post [216].

Meta-level and object-level proofs

When we want to establish that a formula F is entailed by a knowledge base Γ, the straightforward approach is to use the definition of entailment, that is, to reason about interpretations of the underlying signature. For instance, to check that the formulas $\neg p$ and $q \rightarrow r$ entail $(p \vee q) \rightarrow r$ we can argue that no interpretation of the signature $\{p, q, r\}$ can satisfy both $\neg p$ and $q \rightarrow r$ unless it satisfies $(p \vee q) \rightarrow r$ as well.

A sound deductive system provides an "object-level" alternative to this meta-level approach. Once we proved the sequent $\Gamma \Rightarrow F$ in the deductive system described above, we have established that Γ entails F. For instance, the claim that the formulas $\neg p$ and $q \rightarrow r$ entail $(p \vee q) \rightarrow r$ is justified by Fig. 1.2. As a matter of convenience, informal summaries, as in the example above, can be used instead of formal proofs.

1.	$\neg p \Rightarrow \neg p$	— axiom
2.	$q \rightarrow r \Rightarrow q \rightarrow r$	— axiom
3.	$p \vee q \Rightarrow p \vee q$	— axiom
4.	$p \Rightarrow p$	— axiom
5.	$p, \neg p \Rightarrow \bot$	— by $(\neg E)$ from 4, 1
6.	$p, \neg p \Rightarrow r$	— by (C) from 5
7.	$q \Rightarrow q$	— axiom
8.	$q, q \rightarrow r \Rightarrow r$	— by $(\rightarrow E)$ from 7, 2
9.	$p \vee q, \neg p, q \rightarrow r \Rightarrow r$	— by $(\vee E)$ from 3, 6, 8
10.	$\neg p, q \rightarrow r \Rightarrow (p \vee q) \rightarrow r$	— by $(\rightarrow I)$ from 9

Figure 1.2: A proof in propositional logic.

Since the system is not only sound but also complete, the object-level approach to establishing entailment is, in principle, always applicable.

Object-level proofs can be used also to establish general properties of entailment. Consider, for instance, the following fact: for any formulas $F_1, \ldots, F_n$, the implications $F_i \rightarrow F_{i+1}$ $(i = 1, \ldots, n-1)$ entail $F_1 \rightarrow F_n$. We can justify it by saying that if we assume F_1 then $F_2, \ldots, F_n$ will consecutively follow using the given implications. By saying this, we have outlined a method for constructing a proof of the sequent

$$F_1 \rightarrow F_2, \ldots, F_{n-1} \rightarrow F_n \quad \Rightarrow \quad F_1 \rightarrow F_n$$

that consists of $n-1$ implication eliminations followed by an implication introduction.

1.2.2   First-Order Logic

Syntax

In first-order logic, a *signature* is a set of symbols of two kinds—*function constants* and *predicate constants*—with a nonnegative integer, called the *arity*, assigned to each symbol. Function constants of arity 0 are called *object constants*; predicate constants of arity 0 are called *propositional constants*.

Object variables are elements of some fixed infinite sequence of symbols, for instance, $x, y, z; x_1, y_1, z_1, \ldots$. *Terms* of a signature σ are formed from object variables and from function constants of σ. An *atomic formula* of σ is an expression of the form $P(t_1, \ldots, t_n)$ or $t_1 = t_2$, where P is a predicate constant of arity n, and each t_i is a term of σ.[3] Formulas are formed from atomic formulas using propositional connectives and the quantifiers $\forall, \exists$.

An occurrence of a variable v in a formula F is *bound* if it belongs to a subformula of F that has the form $\forall v G$ or $\exists v G$; otherwise it is *free*. If at least one occurrence of v in F is free then we say that v is a *free variable* of F. Note that a formula can contain both free and bound occurrences of the same variable, as in

$$P(x) \wedge \exists x \, Q(x). \tag{1.2}$$

---

[3]Note that equality is not a predicate constant, according to this definition. Although syntactically it is similar to binary predicate constants, it does not belong to the signature, and the semantics of first-order logic, defined below, treats equality in a special way.

We can avoid such cases by renaming bound occurrences of variables:

$$P(x) \wedge \exists x_1 Q(x_1). \tag{1.3}$$

Both formulas have the same meaning: x has the property P, and there exists an object with the property Q.

A *closed* formula, or a *sentence*, is a formula without free variables. The *universal closure* of a formula F is the sentence $\forall v_1 \ldots v_n F$, where $v_1, \ldots, v_n$ are the free variables of F.

The result of the *substitution* of a term t for a variable v in a formula F is the formula obtained from F by simultaneously replacing each free occurrence of v by t. When we intend to consider substitutions for v in a formula, it is convenient to denote this formula by an expression like $F(v)$; then we can denote the result of substituting a term t for v in this formula by $F(t)$.

By $\exists! v F(v)$ ("there exists a unique v such that $F(v)$") we denote the formula

$$\exists v \forall w (F(w) \leftrightarrow v = w),$$

where w is the first variable that does not occur in $F(v)$.

A term t is *substitutable* for a variable v in a formula F if, for each variable w occurring in t, no subformula of F that has the form $\forall w G$ or $\exists w G$ contains an occurrence of v which is free in F. (Some authors say in this case that t is free for x in F.) This condition is important because when it is violated, the formula obtained by substituting t for v in F does not usually convey the intended meaning. For instance, the formula $\exists x (f(x) = y)$ expresses that y belongs to the range of f. If we substitute, say, the term $g(a, z)$ for y in this formula then we will get the formula $\exists x (f(x) = g(a, z))$, which expresses that $g(a, z)$ belongs to the range of f—as one would expect. If, however, we substitute the term $g(a, x)$ instead, the result $\exists x (f(x) = g(a, x))$ will *not* express that $g(a, x)$ belongs to the range of f. This is related to the fact that the term $g(a, x)$ is not substitutable for y in $\exists x (f(x) = y)$; the occurrence of x resulting from this substitution is "captured" by the quantifier at the beginning of the formula. To express that $g(a, x)$ belongs to the range of f, we should first rename x in the formula $\exists x (f(x) = y)$ using, say, the variable x_1. The substitution will produce then the formula $\exists x_1 (f(x_1) = g(a, x))$.

Semantics

An *interpretation* (or *structure*) of a signature σ consists of

- a nonempty set $|I|$, called the *universe* (or *domain*) of I,

- for every object constant c of σ, an element c^I of $|I|$,

- for every function constant f of σ of arity $n > 0$, a function f^I from $|I|^n$ to $|I|$,

- for every propositional constant P of σ, an element P^I of {FALSE, TRUE},

- for every predicate constant R of σ of arity $n > 0$, a function R^I from $|I|^n$ to {FALSE, TRUE}.

The semantics of first-order logic defines, for any sentence F and any interpretation I of a signature σ, the truth value F^I that is assigned to F by I. Note that the definition does not apply to formulas with free variables. (Whether $\exists x(f(x) = y)$ is true or false, for instance, is not completely determined by the universe and by the function representing f; the answer depends also on the value of y within the universe.) For this reason, stating correctly the clauses for quantifiers in the recursive definition of F^I is a little tricky. One possibility is to extend the signature σ by "names" for all elements of the universe, as follows.

Consider an interpretation I of a signature σ. For any element ξ of its universe $|I|$, select a new symbol ξ^*, called the *name* of ξ. By σ^I we denote the signature obtained from σ by adding all names ξ^* as object constants. The interpretation I can be extended to the new signature σ^I by defining $(\xi^*)^I = \xi$ for all $\xi \in |I|$.

For any term t of the extended signature that does not contain variables, we will define recursively the element t^I of the universe that is *assigned* to t by I. If t is an object constant then t^I is part of the interpretation I. For other terms, t^I is defined by the equation

$$f(t_1, \ldots, t_n)^I = f^I(t_1^I, \ldots, t_n^I)$$

for all function constants f of arity $n > 0$.

Now we are ready to define F^I for every sentence F of the extended signature σ^I. For any propositional constant P, P^I is part of the interpretation I. Otherwise, we define:

- $R(t_1, \ldots, t_n)^I = R^I(t_1^I, \ldots, t_n^I)$,

- $\perp^I = \text{FALSE}$, $\top^I = \text{TRUE}$,

- $(\neg F)^I = \neg(F^I)$,

- $(F \odot G)^I = \odot(F^I, G^I)$ for every binary connective $\odot$,

- $\forall w F(w)^I = \text{TRUE}$ if $F(\xi^*)^I = \text{TRUE}$ for all $\xi \in |I|$,

- $\exists w F(w)^I = \text{TRUE}$ if $F(\xi^*)^I = \text{TRUE}$ for some $\xi \in |I|$.

We say that an interpretation I *satisfies* a sentence F, or is a *model* of F, and write $I \models F$, if $F^I = \text{TRUE}$. A sentence F is *logically valid* if every interpretation satisfies F. Two sentences, or sets of sentences, are *equivalent* to each other if they are satisfied by the same interpretations. A formula with free variables is said to be *logically valid* if its universal closure is logically valid. Formulas F and G that may contain free variables are *equivalent* to each other if $F \leftrightarrow G$ is logically valid.

A set Γ of sentences is *satisfiable* if there exists an interpretation satisfying all sentences in Γ. A set Γ of sentences *entails* a formula F (symbolically, $\Gamma \models F$) if every interpretation satisfying Γ satisfies the universal closure of F.

Sorts

Representing knowledge in first-order languages can be often simplified by introducing sorts, which requires that the definitions of the syntax and semantics above be generalized.

Besides function constants and predicate constants, a many-sorted signature includes symbols called *sorts*. In addition to an arity n, we assign to every function constant and every predicate constant its *argument sorts* $s_1, \ldots, s_n$; to every function constant we assign also its *value sort* s_{n+1}. For instance, in the situation calculus (Section 16.1), the symbols *situation* and *action* are sorts; *do* is a binary function symbol with the argument sorts *action* and *situation*, and the value sort *situation*.

For every sort s, we assume a separate infinite sequence of variables of that sort. The recursive definition of a term assigns a sort to every term. Atomic formulas are expressions of the form $P(t_1, \ldots, t_n)$, where the sorts of the terms $t_1, \ldots, t_n$ are the argument sorts of P, and also expressions $t_1 = t_2$ where t_1 and t_2 are terms of the same sort.

An interpretation, in the many-sorted setting, includes a separate nonempty universe $|I|^s$ for each sort s. Otherwise, extending the definition of the semantics to many-sorted languages is straightforward.

A further extension of the syntax and semantics of first-order formulas allows one sort to be a "subsort" of another. For instance, when we talk about the blocks world, it may be convenient to treat the sort *block* as a subsort of the sort *location*. Let b_1 and b_2 be object constants of the sort *block*, let *table* be an object constant of the sort *location*, and let *on* be a binary function constant with the argument sorts *block* and *location*. Not only $on(b_1, table)$ will be counted as a term, but also $on(b_1, b_2)$, because the sort of b_2 is a subsort of the second argument sort of *on*.

Generally, a subsort relation is an order (reflexive, transitive and anti-symmetric relation) on the set of sorts. In the recursive definition of a term, $f(t_1, \ldots, t_n)$ is a term if the sort of each t_i is a subsort of the ith argument sort of f. The condition on sorts in the definition of atomic formulas $P(t_1, \ldots, t_n)$ is similar. An expression $t_1 = t_2$ is considered an atomic formula if the sorts of t_1 and t_2 have a common supersort. In the definition of an interpretation, $|I|^{s_1}$ is required to be a subset of $|I|^{s_2}$ whenever s_1 is a subsort of s_2.

In the rest of this chapter we often assume for simplicity that the underlying signature is nonsorted.

Uniqueness of names

To talk about Paul, Quentin and Robert from Section 1.2.1 in a first-order language, we can introduce the signature consisting of the object constants *Paul*, *Quentin*, *Robert* and the unary predicate constant *in*, and then use the atomic sentences

$$in(Paul), \quad in(Quentin), \quad in(Robert) \qquad (1.4)$$

instead of the atoms p, q, r from the propositional representation.

However some interpretations of this signature are unintuitive and do not correspond to any of the 8 interpretations of the propositional signature $\{p, q, r\}$. Those are the intepretations that map two, or even all three, object constants to the same element of the universe. (The definition of an interpretation in first-order logic does not require that c_1^I be different from c_2^I for distinct object constants c_1, c_2.) We can express that $Paul^I$, $Quentin^I$ and $Robert^I$ are pairwise distinct by saying that I satisfies the "unique name conditions"

$$Paul \neq Quentin, \quad Paul \neq Robert, \quad Quentin \neq Robert. \qquad (1.5)$$

Generally, the *unique name assumption* for a signature σ is expressed by the formulas

$$\forall x_1 \ldots x_m y_1 \ldots y_n (f(x_1, \ldots, x_m) \neq g(y_1, \ldots, y_n)) \tag{1.6}$$

for all pairs of distinct function constants f, g, and

$$\forall x_1 \ldots x_n y_1 \ldots y_n (f(x_1, \ldots, x_n) = f(y_1, \ldots, y_n)$$
$$\rightarrow (x_1 = y_1 \wedge \cdots \wedge x_n = y_n)) \tag{1.7}$$

for all function constants f of arity > 0. These formulas entail $t_1 \neq t_2$ for any distinct variable-free terms t_1, t_2.

The set of equality axioms that was introduced by Keith Clark [57] and is often used in the theory of logic programming includes, in addition to (1.6) and (1.7), the axioms $t \neq x$, where t is a term containing x as a proper subterm.

Domain closure

Consider the first-order counterpart of the propositional formula (1.1), expressing that at least one person is away:

$$\neg in(Paul) \vee \neg in(Quentin) \vee \neg in(Robert). \tag{1.8}$$

The same idea can be also conveyed by the formula

$$\exists x \neg in(x). \tag{1.9}$$

But sentences (1.8) and (1.9) are not equivalent to each other: the former entails the latter, but not the other way around. Indeed, the definition of an interpretation in first-order logic does not require that every element of the universe be equal to c^I for some object constant c. Formula (1.9) interprets "at least one" as referring to a certain group that includes *Paul*, *Quentin* and *Robert*, and may also include others.

If we want to express that every element of the universe corresponds to one of the three explicitly named persons then this can be done by the formula

$$\forall x (x = Paul \vee x = Quentin \vee x = Robert). \tag{1.10}$$

This "domain closure condition" entails the equivalence between (1.8) and (1.9); more generally, it entails the equivalences

$$\forall x F(x) \leftrightarrow F(Paul) \wedge F(Quentin) \wedge F(Robert),$$
$$\exists x F(x) \leftrightarrow F(Paul) \vee F(Quentin) \vee F(Robert)$$

for any formula $F(x)$. These equivalences allow us to replace all quantifiers in an arbitrary formula with multiple conjunctions and disjunctions. Furthermore, under the unique name assumption (1.5) any equality between two object constants can be equivalently replaced by $\top$ or $\bot$, depending on whether the constants are equal to each other. The result of these transformations is a propositional combination of the atomic sentences (1.4).

Generally, consider a signature σ containing finitely many object constants $c_1, \ldots, c_n$ are no function constants of arity > 0. The *domain closure assumption* for σ is the formula

$$\forall x (x = c_1 \vee \cdots \vee x = c_n).\tag{1.11}$$

The interpretations of σ that satisfy both the unique name assumption $c_1 \neq c_j$ $(1 \leqslant i < j \leqslant n)$ and the domain closure assumption (1.11) are essentially identical to the interpretations of the propositional signature that consists of all atomic sentences of σ other than equalities. Any sentence F of σ can be transformed into a formula F' of this propositional signature such that the unique name and domain closure assumptions entail $F' \leftrightarrow F$. In this sense, these assumptions turn first-order sentences into abbreviations for propositional formulas.

The domain closure assumption in the presence of function constant of arity > 0 is discussed in Sections 1.2.2 and 1.2.3.

Reification

The first-order language introduced in Section 1.2.2 has variables for people, such as Paul and Quentin, but not for places, such as their office. In this sense, people are "reified" in that language, and places are not. To reify places, we can add them to the signature as a second sort, add *office* as an object constant of that sort, and turn *in* into a binary predicate constant with the argument sorts *person* and *place*. In the modified language, the formula *in(Paul)* will turn into *in(Paul, office)*.

Reification makes the language more expressive. For instance, having reified places, we can say that every person has a unique location:

$$\forall x \exists! p\; in(x, p).\tag{1.12}$$

There is no way to express this idea in the language from Section 1.2.2.

As another example illustrating the idea of reification, compare two versions of the situation calculus. We can express that block b_1 is clear in the initial situation S_0 by writing either

$$clear(b_1, S_0)\tag{1.13}$$

or

$$Holds(clear(b_1), S_0).\tag{1.14}$$

In (1.13), *clear* is a binary predicate constant; in (1.14), *clear* is a unary function constant. Formula (1.14) is written in the version of the situation calculus in which (relational) fluents are reified; *fluent* is the first argument sort of the predicate constant *Holds*. The version of the situation calculus introduced in Section 16.1 is the more expressive version, with reified fluents. Expression (1.13) is viewed there as shorthand for (1.14).

Explicit definitions in first-order logic

Let Γ be a set of sentences of a signature σ. To extend Γ by an *explicit definition of a predicate constant* means to add to σ a new predicate constant P of some arity n, and to add to Γ a sentence of the form

$$\forall v_1 \ldots v_n (P(v_1, \ldots, v_n) \leftrightarrow F),$$

where $v_1, \ldots, v_n$ are distinct variables and F is a formula of the signature σ. About the effect of such an extension we can say the same as about the effect of adding an explicit definition to a set of propositional formulas (Section 1.2.1): there is an obvious one-to-one correspondence between the models of the original knowledge base and the models of the extended knowledge base.

With function constants, the situation is a little more complex. To extend a set Γ of sentences of a signature σ by an *explicit definition of a function constant* means to add to σ a new function constant f, and to add to Γ a sentence of the form

$$\forall v_1 \ldots v_n v (f(v_1, \ldots, v_n) = v \leftrightarrow F),$$

where $v_1, \ldots, v_n, v$ are distinct variables and F is a formula of the signature σ such that Γ entails the sentence

$$\forall v_1 \ldots v_n \exists! v F.$$

The last assumption is essential: if it does not hold then adding a function constant along with the corresponding axiom would eliminate some of the models of Γ.

For instance, if Γ entails (1.12) then we can extend Γ by the explicit definition of the function constant *location*:

$$\forall x p (location(x) = p \leftrightarrow in(x, p)).$$

Natural deduction with quantifiers and equality

The natural deduction system for first-order logic includes all axiom schemas and inference rules shown in Section 1.2.1 and a few additional postulates. First, we add the introduction and elimination rules for quantifiers:

$$(\forall I) \ \frac{\Gamma \Rightarrow F(v)}{\Gamma \Rightarrow \forall v F(v)} \qquad\qquad (\forall E) \ \frac{\Gamma \Rightarrow \forall v F(v)}{\Gamma \Rightarrow F(t)}$$

where v is not a free variable of any formula in Γ — where t is substitutable for v in $F(v)$

$$(\exists I) \ \frac{\Gamma \Rightarrow F(t)}{\Gamma \Rightarrow \exists v F(v)} \qquad\qquad (\exists E) \ \frac{\Gamma \Rightarrow \exists v F(v) \quad \Delta, F(v) \Rightarrow G}{\Gamma, \Delta \Rightarrow G}$$

where t is substitutable for v in $F(v)$ — where v is not a free variable of any formula in Δ, G

Second, postulates for equality are added: the axiom schema expressing its reflexivity

$$\Rightarrow t = t$$

and the inference rules for replacing equals by equals:

$$(Repl) \ \frac{\Gamma \Rightarrow t_1 = t_2 \quad \Delta \Rightarrow F(t_1)}{\Gamma, \Delta \Rightarrow F(t_2)} \qquad \frac{\Gamma \Rightarrow t_1 = t_2 \quad \Delta \Rightarrow F(t_2)}{\Gamma, \Delta \Rightarrow F(t_1)}$$

where t_1 and t_2 are terms substitutable for v in $F(v)$.

This formal system is sound and complete: for any finite set Γ of sentences and any formula F, the sequent $\Gamma \Rightarrow F$ is provable if and only if $\Gamma \models F$. The completeness of (a different formalization of) first-order logic was proved by Gödel [100].

1.	$(1.9) \Rightarrow (1.9)$	— axiom
2.	$\neg in(x) \Rightarrow \neg in(x)$	— axiom
3.	$x = P \Rightarrow x = P$	— axiom
4.	$x = P, \neg in(x) \Rightarrow \neg in(P)$	— by *Repl* from 3, 2
5.	$x = P, \neg in(x) \Rightarrow \neg in(P) \vee \neg in(Q)$	— by $(\vee I)$ from 4
6.	$x = P, \neg in(x) \Rightarrow (1.8)$	— by $(\vee I)$ from 5
7.	$x = Q \Rightarrow x = Q$	— axiom
8.	$x = Q, \neg in(x) \Rightarrow \neg in(Q)$	— by *Repl* from 7, 2
9.	$x = Q, \neg in(x) \Rightarrow \neg in(P) \vee \neg in(Q)$	— by $(\vee I)$ from 8
10.	$x = Q, \neg in(x) \Rightarrow (1.8)$	— by $(\vee I)$ from 9
11.	$x = P \vee x = Q \Rightarrow x = P \vee x = Q$	— axiom
12.	$x = P \vee x = Q, \neg in(x) \Rightarrow (1.8)$	— by $(\vee E)$ from 11, 6, 10
13.	$x = R \Rightarrow x = R$	— axiom
14.	$x = R, \neg in(x) \Rightarrow \neg in(R)$	— by *Repl* from 13, 2
15.	$x = R, \neg in(x) \Rightarrow (1.8)$	— by $(\vee I)$ from 14
16.	$(1.10) \Rightarrow (1.10)$	— axiom
17.	$(1.10) \Rightarrow x = P \vee x = Q$ $\vee x = R$	— by $(\forall E)$ from 16
18.	$(1.10), \neg in(x) \Rightarrow (1.8)$	— by $(\vee E)$ from 17, 12, 15
19.	$(1.9), (1.10) \Rightarrow (1.8)$	— by $(\exists E)$ from 1, 18

Figure 1.3: A proof in first-order logic.

As in the propositional case (Section 1.2.1), the soundness theorem justifies establishing entailment in first-order logic by an object-level argument. For instance, we can prove the claim that (1.8) is entailed by (1.9) and (1.10) as follows: take x such that $\neg in(x)$ and consider the three cases corresponding to the disjunctive terms of (1.10); in each case, one of the disjunctive terms of (1.8) follows. This argument is an informal summary of the proof shown in Fig. 1.3, with the names *Paul*, *Quentin*, *Robert* replaced by P, Q, R.

Since proofs in the deductive system described above can be effectively enumerated, from the soundness and completeness of the system we can conclude that the set of logically valid sentences is recursively enumerable. But it is not recursive [56], even if the underlying signature consists of a single binary predicate constant, and even if we disregard formulas containing equality [135].

As discussed in Section 3.3.1, most descriptions logics can be viewed as decidable fragments of first-order logic.

Limitations of first-order logic

The sentence

$$\forall xy(Q(x, y) \leftrightarrow P(y, x))$$

expresses that Q is the inverse of P. Does there exist a first-order sentence expressing that Q is the *transitive closure* of P? To be more precise, does there exist a sentence F of the signature $\{P, Q\}$ such that an interpretation I of this signature satisfies F if and only if Q^I is the transitive closure of P^I?

The answer to this question is no. From the perspective of knowledge representation, this is an essential limitation, because the concept of transitive closure is the mathematical counterpart of the important commonsense idea of reachability. As discussed in Section 1.2.3 below, one way to overcome this limitation is to turn to second-order logic.

Another example illustrating the usefulness of second-order logic in knowledge representation is related to the idea of domain closure (Section 1.2.2). If the underlying signature contains the object constants $c_1, \dots, c_n$ and no function constants of arity > 0 then sentence (1.11) expresses the domain closure assumption: an interpretation I satisfies (1.11) if and only if

$$|I| = \{c_1^I, \dots, c_n^I\}.$$

Consider now the signature consisting of the object constant c and the unary function constant f. Does there exist a first-order sentence expressing the domain closure assumption for this signature? To be precise, we would like to find a sentence F such that an interpretation I satisfies F if and only if

$$|I| = \{c^I, f(c)^I, f(f(c))^I, \dots\}.$$

There is no first-order sentence with this property.

Similarly, first-order languages do not allow us to state Reiter's foundational axiom expressing that each situation is the result of performing a sequence of actions in the initial situation ([225, Section 4.2.2]; see also Section 16.3 below).

1.2.3 Second-Order Logic

Syntax and semantics

In second-order logic, the definition of a signature remains the same (Section 1.2.2). But its syntax is richer, because, along with object variables, we assume now an infinite sequence of *function variables* of arity n for each $n > 0$, and an infinite sequence of *predicate variables* of arity n for each $n \geqslant 0$. Object variables are viewed as function variables of arity 0.

Function variables can be used to form new terms in the same way as function constants. For instance, if α is a unary function variable and c is an object constant then $\alpha(c)$ is a term. Predicate variables can be used to form atomic formulas in the same way as predicate constants. In non-atomic formulas, function and predicate variables can be bound by quantifiers in the same way as object variables. For instance,

$$\forall \alpha \beta \exists \gamma \forall x (\gamma(x) = \alpha(\beta(x)))$$

is a sentence expressing the possibility of composing any two functions. (When we say that a second-order formula is a sentence, we mean that all occurrences of all variables in it are bound, including function and predicate variables.)

Note that $\alpha = \beta$ is not an atomic formula, because unary function variables are not terms. But this expression can be viewed as shorthand for the formula

$$\forall x (\alpha(x) = \beta(x)).$$

Similarly, the expression $p = q$, where p and q are unary predicate variables, can be viewed as shorthand for

$$\forall x (p(x) \leftrightarrow q(x)).$$

The condition "Q is the transitive closure of P" can be expressed by the second-order sentence

$$\forall xy(Q(x, y) \leftrightarrow \forall q(F(q) \rightarrow q(x, y))), \tag{1.15}$$

where $F(q)$ stands for

$$\forall x_1 y_1(P(x_1, y_1) \rightarrow q(x_1, y_1))$$
$$\wedge \forall x_1 y_1 z_1((q(x_1, y_1) \wedge q(y_1, z_1)) \rightarrow q(x_1, z_1))$$

(Q is the intersection of all transitive relations containing P).

The domain closure assumption for the signature $\{c, f\}$ can be expressed by the sentence

$$\forall p(G(p) \rightarrow \forall x \; p(x)), \tag{1.16}$$

where $G(p)$ stands for

$$p(c) \wedge \forall x(p(x) \rightarrow p(f(x)))$$

(any set that contains c and is closed under f covers the whole universe).

The definition of an interpretation remains the same (Section 1.2.2). The semantics of second-order logic defines, for each sentence F and each interpretation I, the corresponding truth value F^I. In the clauses for quantifiers, whenever a quantifier binds a function variable, names of arbitrary functions from $|I|^n$ to I are substituted for it; when a quantifier binds a predicate variable, names of arbitrary functions from $|I|^n$ to {FALSE, TRUE} are substituted.

Quantifiers binding a propositional variable p can be always eliminated: $\forall p F(p)$ is equivalent to $F(\bot) \wedge F(\top)$, and $\exists p F(p)$ is equivalent to $F(\bot) \vee F(\top)$. In the special case when the underlying signature consists of propositional constants, second-order formulas (in prenex form) are known as *quantified Boolean formulas* (see Section 2.5.1). The equivalences above allow us to rewrite any such formula in the syntax of propositional logic. But a sentence containing predicate variables of arity > 0 may not be equivalent to any first-order sentence; (1.15) and (1.16) are examples of such "hard" cases.

Object-level proofs in second-order logic

In this section we consider a deductive system for second-order logic that contains all postulates from Sections 1.2.1 and 1.2.2; in rules ($\forall E$) and ($\exists I$), if v is a function variable of arity > 0 then t is assumed to be a function variable of the same arity, and similarly for predicate variables. In addition, we include two axiom schemas asserting the existence of predicates and functions. One is the axiom schema of comprehension

$$\Rightarrow \exists p \forall v_1 \ldots v_n(p(v_1, \ldots, v_n) \leftrightarrow F),$$

where $v_1, \ldots, v_n$ are distinct object variables, and p is not free in F. (Recall that $\leftrightarrow$ is not allowed in sequents, but we treat $F \leftrightarrow G$ as shorthand for $(F \rightarrow G) \wedge (G \rightarrow F)$.)

1.	$F \Rightarrow F$	— axiom
2.	$F \Rightarrow p(x) \rightarrow p(y)$	— by $(\forall E)$ from 1
3.	$\Rightarrow \exists p \forall z(p(z) \leftrightarrow x = z)$	— axiom (comprehension)
4.	$\forall z(p(z) \leftrightarrow x = z) \Rightarrow \forall z(p(z) \leftrightarrow x = z)$	— axiom
5.	$\forall z(p(z) \leftrightarrow x = z) \Rightarrow p(x) \leftrightarrow x = x$	— by $(\forall E)$ from 4
6.	$\forall z(p(z) \leftrightarrow x = z) \Rightarrow x = x \rightarrow p(x)$	— by $(\wedge E)$ from 5
7.	$\Rightarrow x = x$	— axiom
8.	$\forall z(p(z) \leftrightarrow x = z) \Rightarrow p(x)$	— by $(\rightarrow E)$ from 7, 6
9.	$F, \forall z(p(z) \leftrightarrow x = z) \Rightarrow p(y)$	— by $(\rightarrow E)$ from 8, 2
10.	$\forall z(p(z) \leftrightarrow x = z) \Rightarrow p(y) \leftrightarrow x = y$	— by $(\forall E)$ from 4
11.	$\forall z(p(z) \leftrightarrow x = z) \Rightarrow p(y) \rightarrow x = y$	— by $(\wedge E)$ from 10
12.	$F, \forall z(p(z) \leftrightarrow x = z) \Rightarrow x = y$	— by $(\rightarrow E)$ from 9, 11
13.	$F \Rightarrow x = y$	— by $(\exists E)$ from 1, 12
14.	$\Rightarrow F \rightarrow x = y$	— by $(\rightarrow I)$ from 13

Figure 1.4: A proof in second-order logic. F stands for $\forall p(p(x) \rightarrow p(y))$.

The other is the axioms of choice

$$\Rightarrow \forall v_1 \ldots v_n \exists v_{n+1} p(v_1, \ldots, v_{n+1})$$
$$\rightarrow \exists \alpha \forall v_1 \ldots v_n (p(v_1, \ldots, v_n, \alpha(v_1, \ldots, v_n)),$$

where $v_1, \ldots, v_{n+1}$ are distinct object variables.

This deductive system is sound but incomplete. Adding any sound axioms or inference rules would not make it complete, because the set of logically valid second-order sentences is not recursively enumerable.

As in the case of first-order logic, the availability of a sound deductive system allows us to establish second-order entailment by object-level reasoning. To illustrate this point, consider the formula

$$\forall p(p(x) \rightarrow p(y)) \rightarrow x = y,$$

which can be thought of as a formalization of "Leibniz's principle of equality": two objects are equal if they share the same properties. Its logical validity can be justified as follows. Assume $\forall p(p(x) \rightarrow p(y))$, and take p to be the property of being equal to x. Clearly x has this property; consequently y has this property as well, that is, $x = y$. This argument is an informal summary of the proof shown in Fig. 1.4.

1.3 Automated Theorem Proving

Automated theorem proving is the study of techniques for programming computers to search for proofs of formal assertions, either fully automatically or with varying degrees of human guidance. This area has potential applications to hardware and software verification, expert systems, planning, mathematics research, and education.

Given a set A of axioms and a logical consequence B, a theorem proving program should, ideally, eventually construct a proof of B from A. If B is not a consequence of A, the program may run forever without coming to any definite conclusion. This is the best one can hope for, in general, in many logics, and indeed even this is not always possible. In principle, theorem proving programs can be written just by enumerating all possible proofs and stopping when a proof of the desired statement is found, but this approach is so inefficient as to be useless. Much more powerful methods have been developed.

History of theorem proving

Despite the potential advantages of machine theorem proving, it was difficult initially to obtain any kind of respectable performance from machines on theorem proving problems. Some of the earliest automatic theorem proving methods, such as those of Gilmore [99], Prawitz [217], and Davis and Putnam [70] were based on Herbrand's theorem, which gives an enumeration process for testing if a theorem of first-order logic is true. Davis and Putnam used Skolem functions and conjunctive normal form clauses, and generated elements of the Herbrand universe exhaustively, while Prawitz showed how this enumeration could be guided to only generate terms likely to be useful for the proof, but did not use Skolem functions or clause form. Later Davis [66] showed how to realize this same idea in the context of clause form and Skolem functions. However, these approaches turned out to be too inefficient. The *resolution* approach of Robinson [229, 230] was developed in about 1963, and led to a significant advance in first-order theorem provers. This approach, like that of Davis and Putnam [70], used clause form and Skolem functions, but made use of a *unification* algorithm to find the terms most likely to lead to a proof. Robinson also used the resolution inference rule which in itself is all that is needed for theorem proving in first-order logic. The theorem proving group at Argonne, Illinois took the lead in implementing resolution theorem provers, with some initial success on group theory problems that had been intractable before. They were even able to solve some previously open problems using resolution theorem provers. For a discussion of the early history of mechanical theorem proving, see [67].

About the same time, Maslov [168] developed the *inverse method* which has been less widely known than resolution in the West. This method was originally defined for classical first-order logic without function symbols and equality, and for formulas having a quantifier prefix followed by a disjunction of conjunctions of clauses. Later the method was extended to formulas with function symbols. This method was used not only for theorem proving but also to show the decidability of some classes of first-order formulas. In the inverse method, substitutions were originally represented as sets of equations, and there appears to have been some analogue of most general unifiers. The method was implemented for classical first-order logic by 1968. The inverse method is based on forward reasoning to derive a formula. In terms of implementation, it is competitive with resolution, and in fact can be simulated by resolution with the introduction of new predicate symbols to define subformulas of the original formula. For a readable exposition of the inverse method, see [159]. For many extensions of the method, see [71].

In the West, the initial successes of resolution led to a rush of enthusiasm, as resolution theorem provers were applied to question-answering problems, situation calculus problems, and many others. It was soon discovered that resolution had serious inefficiencies, and a long series of refinements were developed to attempt to overcome them. These included the unit preference rule, the set of support strategy, hyper-resolution, paramodulation for equality, and a nearly innumerable list of other refinements. The initial enthusiasm for resolution, and for automated deduction in general, soon wore off. This reaction led, for example, to the development of specialized decision procedures for proving theorems in certain theories [190, 191] and the development of expert systems.

However, resolution and similar approaches continued to be developed. Data structures were developed permitting the resolution operation to be implemented much more efficiently, which were eventually greatly refined [222] as in the Vampire prover [227]. One of the first provers to employ such techniques was Stickel's Prolog Technology Theorem Prover [252]. Techniques for parallel implementations of provers were also eventually considered [34]. Other strategies besides resolution were developed, such as model elimination [162], which led eventually to logic programming and Prolog, the matings method for higher-order logic [3], and Bibel's connection method [28]. Though these methods are not resolution based, they did preserve some of the key concepts of resolution, namely, the use of unification and the combination of unification with inference in clause form first-order logic. Two other techniques used to improve the performance of provers, especially in competitions [253], are *strategy selection* and *strategy scheduling*. Strategy selection means that different theorem proving strategies and different settings of the coefficients are used for different kinds of problems. Strategy scheduling means that even for a given kind of problem, many strategies are used, one after another, and a specified amount of time is allotted to each one. Between the two of these approaches, there is considerable freedom for imposing an outer level of control on the theorem prover to tailor its performance to a given problem set.

Some other provers dealt with higher-order logic, such as the TPS prover of Andrews and others [4, 5] and the interactive NqTHM and ACL2 provers of Boyer, Moore, and Kaufmann [142, 141] for proofs by mathematical induction. Today, a variety of approaches including formal methods and theorem proving seem to be accepted as part of the standard AI tool kit.

Despite early difficulties, the power of theorem provers has continued to increase. Notable in this respect is Otter [177], which is widely distributed, and coded in C with very efficient data structures. Prover9 is a more recent prover of W. McCune in the same style, and is a successor of Otter. The increasing speed of hardware has also significantly aided theorem provers. An impetus was given to theorem proving research by McCune's solution of the Robbins problem [176] by a first-order equational theorem prover derived from Otter. The Robbins problem is a first-order theorem involving equality that had been known to mathematicians for decades but which no one was able to solve. McCune's prover was able to find a proof after about a week of computation. Many other proofs have also been found by McCune's group on various provers; see for example the web page http://www.cs.unm.edu/~veroff/MEDIAN_ALGEBRA/. Now substantial theorems in mathematics whose correctness is in doubt can be checked by interactive theorem provers [196].

First-order theorem provers vary in their user interfaces, but most of them permit formulas to be entered in clause form in a reasonable syntax. Some provers also permit the user to enter first-order formulas; these provers generally provide various ways of translating such formulas to clause form. Some provers require substantial user guidance, though most such provers have higher-order features, while other provers are designed to be more automatic. For automatic provers, there are often many different flags that can be set to guide the search. For example, typical first-order provers allow the user to select from among a number of inference strategies for first-order logic as well as strategies for equality. For equality, it may be possible to specify a termination ordering to guide the application of equations. Sometimes the user will select incomplete strategies, hoping that the desired proof will be found faster. It is also often possible to set a size bound so that all clauses or literals larger than a certain size are deleted. Of course one does not know in advance what bound to choose, so some experimentation is necessary. A *sliding priority* approach to setting the size bound automatically was presented in [211]. It is sometimes possible to assign various weights to various symbols or subterms or to variables to guide the proof search. Modern provers generally have term indexing [222] built in to speed up inference, and also have some equality strategy involving ordered paramodulation and rewriting. Many provers are based on resolution, but some are based on model elimination and some are based on propositional approaches. Provers can generate clauses rapidly; for example, Vampire [227] can often generate more than 40,000 clauses per second. Most provers rapidly fill up memory with generated clauses, so that if a proof is not found in a few minutes it will not be found at all. However, equational proofs involve considerable simplification and can sometimes run for a long time without exhausting memory. For example, the Robbins problem ran for 8 days on a SPARC 5 class UNIX computer with a size bound of 70 and required about 30 megabytes of memory, generating 49,548 equations, most of which were deleted by simplification. Sometimes small problems can run for a long time without finding a proof, and sometimes problems with a hundred or more input clauses can result in proofs fairly quickly. Generally, simple problems will be proved by nearly any complete strategy on a modern prover, but hard problems may require fine tuning. For an overview of a list of problems and information about how well various provers perform on them, see the web site at www.tptp.org, and for a sketch of some of the main first-order provers in use today, see http://www.cs.miami.edu/~tptp/CASC/ as well as the journal articles devoted to the individual competitions such as [253, 254]. Current provers often do not have facilities for interacting with other reasoning programs, but work in this area is progressing.

In addition to developing first-order provers, there has been work on other logics, too. The simplest logic typically considered is *propositional logic*, in which there are only predicate symbols (that is, Boolean variables) and logical connectives. Despite its simplicity, propositional logic has surprisingly many applications, such as in hardware verification and constraint satisfaction problems. Propositional provers have even found applications in planning. The general validity (respectively, satisfiability) problem of propositional logic is NP-hard, which means that it does not in all likelihood have an efficient general solution. Nevertheless, there are propositional provers that are surprisingly efficient, and becoming increasingly more so; see Chapter 2 of this Handbook for details.

Binary decision diagrams [43] are a particular form of propositional formulas for which efficient provers exist. BDD's are used in hardware verification, and initiated a tremendous surge of interest by industry in formal verification techniques. Also, the Davis–Putnam–Logemann–Loveland method [69] for propositional logic is heavily used in industry for hardware verification.

Another restricted logic for which efficient provers exist is that of temporal logic, the logic of time (see Chapter 12 of this Handbook). This has applications to concurrency. The model-checking approach of Clarke and others [48] has proven to be particularly efficient in this area, and has also stimulated considerable interest by industry.

Other logical systems for which provers have been developed are the theory of equational systems, for which term-rewriting techniques lead to remarkably efficient theorem provers, mathematical induction, geometry theorem proving, constraints (Chapter 4 of this Handbook), higher-order logic, and set theory.

Not only proving theorems, but finding counterexamples, or building models, is of increasing importance. This permits one to detect when a theorem is not provable, and thus one need not waste time attempting to find a proof. This is, of course, an activity which human mathematicians often engage in. These counterexamples are typically finite structures. For the so-called *finitely controllable* theories, running a theorem prover and a counterexample (model) finder together yields a decision procedure, which theoretically can have practical applications to such theories. Model finding has recently been extended to larger classes of theories [51].

Among the current applications of theorem provers one can list hardware verification and program verification. For a more detailed survey, see the excellent report by Loveland [164]. Among potential applications of theorem provers are planning problems, the situation calculus, and problems involving knowledge and belief.

There are a number of provers in prominence today, including Otter [177], the provers of Boyer, Moore, and Kaufmann [142, 141], Andrew's matings prover [3], the HOL prover [101], Isabelle [203], Mizar [260], NuPrl [62], PVS [201], and many more. Many of these require substantial human guidance to find proofs. The Omega system [240] is a higher order logic proof development system that attempts to overcome some of the shortcomings of traditional first-order proof systems. In the past it has used a natural deduction calculus to develop proofs with human guidance, though the system is changing.

Provers can be evaluated on a number of grounds. One is *completeness*; can they, in principle, provide a proof of every true theorem? Another evaluation criterion is their performance on specific examples; in this regard, the TPTP problem set [255] is of particular value. Finally, one can attempt to provide an analytic estimate of the efficiency of a theorem prover on classes of problems [212]. This gives a measure which is to a large extent independent of particular problems or machines. The *Handbook of Automated Reasoning* [231] is a good source of information about many areas of theorem proving.

We next discuss resolution for the propositional calculus and then some of the many first-order theorem proving methods, with particular attention to resolution. We also consider techniques for first-order logic with equality. Finally, we briefly discuss some other logics, and corresponding theorem proving techniques.

1.3.1   Resolution in the Propositional Calculus

The main problem for theorem proving purposes is given a formula A, to determine whether it is valid. Since A is valid iff $\neg A$ is unsatisfiable, it is possible to determine validity if one can determine satisfiability. Many theorem provers test satisfiability instead of validity.

The problem of determining whether a Boolean formula A is satisfiable is one of the NP-complete problems. This means that the fastest algorithms known require an amount of time that is asymptotically exponential in the size of A. Also, it is not likely that faster algorithms will be found, although no one can prove that they do not exist.

Despite this negative result, there is a wide variety of methods in use for testing if a formula is satisfiable. One of the simplest is *truth tables*. For a formula A over $\{P_1, P_2, \ldots, P_n\}$, this involves testing for each of the 2^n valuations I over $\{P_1, P_2, \ldots, P_n\}$ whether $I \models A$. In general, this will require time at least proportional to 2^n to show that A is valid, but may detect satisfiability sooner.

Clause form

Many of the other satisfiability checking algorithms depend on conversion of a formula A to *clause form*. This is defined as follows: An *atom* is a proposition. A *literal* is an atom or an atom preceded by a negation sign. The two literals P and $\neg P$ are said to be *complementary* to each other. A *clause* is a disjunction of literals. A formula is in *clause form* if it is a conjunction of clauses. Thus the formula

$$(P \vee \neg R) \wedge (\neg P \vee Q \vee R) \wedge (\neg Q \vee \neg R)$$

is in clause form. This is also known as *conjunctive normal form*. We represent clauses by sets of literals and clause form formulas by sets of clauses, so that the above formula would be represented by the following set of sets:

$$\{\{P, \neg R\}, \{\neg P, Q, R\}, \{\neg Q, \neg R\}\}.$$

A *unit clause* is a clause that contains only one literal. The *empty clause* $\{\}$ is understood to represent FALSE.

It is straightforward to show that for every formula A there is an equivalent formula B in clause form. Furthermore, there are well-known algorithms for converting any formula A into such an equivalent formula B. These involve converting all connectives to $\wedge$, $\vee$, and $\neg$, pushing $\neg$ to the bottom, and bringing $\wedge$ to the top. Unfortunately, this process of conversion can take exponential time and can increase the length of the formula by an exponential amount.

The exponential increase in size in converting to clause form can be avoided by adding extra propositions representing subformulas of the given formula. For example, given the formula

$$(P_1 \wedge Q_1) \vee (P_2 \wedge Q_2) \vee (P_3 \wedge Q_3) \vee \cdots \vee (P_n \wedge Q_n)$$

a straightforward conversion to clause form creates 2^n clauses of length n, for a formula of length at least $n2^n$. However, by adding the new propositions R_i which are defined as $P_i \wedge Q_i$, one obtains the new formula

$$(R_1 \vee R_2 \vee \cdots \vee R_n) \wedge ((P_1 \wedge Q_1) \leftrightarrow R_1) \wedge \cdots \wedge ((P_n \wedge Q_n) \leftrightarrow R_n).$$

When this formula is converted to clause form, a much smaller set of clauses results, and the exponential size increase does not occur. The same technique works for any Boolean formula. This transformation is satisfiability preserving but not equivalence preserving, which is enough for theorem proving purposes.

Ground resolution

Many first-order theorem provers are based on resolution, and there is a propositional analogue of resolution called *ground resolution*, which we now present as an introduction to first-order resolution. Although resolution is reasonably efficient for first-order logic, it turns out that ground resolution is generally much less efficient than Davis and Putnam-like procedures for propositional logic [70, 69], often referred to as DPLL procedures because the original Davis and Putnam procedure had some inefficiencies. These DPLL procedures are specialized to clause form and explore the set of possible interpretations of a propositional formula by depth-first search and backtracking with some additional simplification rules for unit clauses.

Ground resolution is a decision procedure for propositional formulas in clause form. If C_1 and C_2 are two clauses, and $L_1 \in C_1$ and $L_2 \in C_2$ are complementary literals, then

$$(C_1 - \{L_1\}) \cup (C_2 - \{L_2\})$$

is called a *resolvent* of C_1 and C_2, where the set difference of two sets A and B is indicated by $A - B$, that is, $\{x : x \in A, x \notin B\}$. There may be more than one resolvent of two clauses, or maybe none. It is straightforward to show that a resolvent D of two clauses C_1 and C_2 is a logical consequence of $C_1 \wedge C_2$.

For example, if C_1 is $\{\neg P, Q\}$ and C_2 is $\{\neg Q, R\}$, then one can choose L_1 to be Q and L_2 to be $\neg Q$. Then the resolvent is $\{\neg P, R\}$. Note also that R is a resolvent of $\{Q\}$ and $\{\neg Q, R\}$, and $\{\}$ (the empty clause) is a resolvent of $\{Q\}$ and $\{\neg Q\}$.

A *resolution proof* of a clause C from a set S of clauses is a sequence $C_1, C_2, \ldots, C_n$ of clauses in which each C_i is either a member of S or a resolvent of C_j and C_k, for j, k less than i, and C_n is C. Such a proof is called a (resolution) *refutation* if C_n is $\{\}$. Resolution is *complete*:

Theorem 1.3.1. *Suppose S is a set of propositional clauses. Then S is unsatisfiable iff there exists a resolution refutation from S.*

As an example, let S be the set of clauses

$$\{\{P\}, \{\neg P, Q\}, \{\neg Q\}\}.$$

The following is a resolution refutation from S, listing with each resolvent the two clauses that are resolved together:

    1. P given
    2. $\neg P, Q$ given
    3. $\neg Q$ given
    4. Q 1, 2, resolution
    5. $\{\}$ 3, 4, resolution

(Here set braces are omitted, except for the empty clause.) This is a resolution refutation from S, so S is unsatisfiable.

Define $\mathbf{R}(S)$ to be $\bigcup_{C1,C2 \in S}$ resolvents$(C1, C2)$. Define $\mathbf{R}^1(S)$ to be $\mathbf{R}(S)$ and $\mathbf{R}^{i+1}(S)$ to be $\mathbf{R}(S \cup \mathbf{R}^i(S))$, for $i > 1$. Typical resolution theorem provers essentially generate all of the resolution proofs from S (with some improvements that will be discussed later), looking for a proof of the empty clause. Formally, such provers generate $\mathbf{R}^1(S)$, $\mathbf{R}^2(S)$, $\mathbf{R}^3(S)$, and so on, until for some i, $\mathbf{R}^i(S) = \mathbf{R}^{i+1}(S)$, or the empty clause is generated. In the former case, S is satisfiable. If the empty clause is generated, S is unsatisfiable.

Even though DPLL essentially constructs a resolution proof, propositional resolution is much less efficient than DPLL as a decision procedure for satisfiability of formulas in the propositional calculus because the total number of resolutions performed by a propositional resolution prover in the search for a proof is typically much larger than for DPLL. Also, Haken [107] showed that there are unsatisfiable sets S of propositional clauses for which the length of the shortest resolution refutation is exponential in the size (number of clauses) in S. Despite these inefficiencies, we introduced propositional resolution as a way to lead up to first-order resolution, which has significant advantages. In order to extend resolution to first-order logic, it is necessary to add *unification* to it.

1.3.2 First-Order Proof Systems

We now discuss methods for partially deciding validity. These construct proofs of first-order formulas, and a formula is valid iff it can be proven in such a system. Thus there are *complete* proof systems for first-order logic, and Gödel's incompleteness theorem does not apply to first-order logic. Since the set of proofs is countable, one can partially decide validity of a formula A by enumerating the set of proofs, and stopping whenever a proof of A is found. This already gives us a theorem prover, but provers constructed in this way are typically very inefficient.

There are a number of classical proof systems for first-order logic: Hilbert-style systems, Gentzen-style systems, natural deduction systems, semantic tableau systems, and others [87]. Since these generally have not found much application to automated deduction, except for semantic tableau systems, they are not discussed here. Typically they specify inference rules of the form

$$\frac{A_1, A_2, \ldots, A_n}{A}$$

which means that if one has already derived the formulas $A_1, A_2, \ldots, A_n$, then one can also infer A. Using such rules, one builds up a proof as a sequence of formulas, and if a formula B appears in such a sequence, one has proved B.

We now discuss proof systems that have found application to automated deduction. In the following sections, the letters $f, g, h, \ldots$ will be used as *function symbols*, $a, b, c, \ldots$ as *individual constants*, x, y, z and possibly other letters as *individual variables*, and $=$ as the equality symbol. Each function symbol has an *arity*, which is a non-negative integer telling how many arguments it takes. A *term* is either a variable, an individual constant, or an expression of the form $f(t_1, t_2, \ldots, t_n)$ where f is a function symbol of arity n and the t_i are terms. The letters $r, s, t, \ldots$ will denote terms.

Clause form

Many first-order theorem provers convert a first-order formula to *clause form* before attempting to prove it. The beauty of clause form is that it makes the syntax of first-order logic, already quite simple, even simpler. Quantifiers are omitted, and Boolean

connectives as well. One has in the end just sets of sets of literals. It is amazing that
the expressive power of first-order logic can be reduced to such a simple form. This
simplicity also makes clause form suitable for machine implementation of theorem
provers. Not only that, but the validity problem is also simplified in a theoretical sense;
one only needs to consider the *Herbrand interpretations*, so the question of validity
becomes easier to analyze.

Any first-order formula A can be transformed to a clause form formula B such
that A is satisfiable iff B is satisfiable. The translation is not validity preserving. So
in order to show that A is valid, one translates $\neg A$ to clause form B and shows that
B is unsatisfiable. For convenience, assume that A is a *sentence*, that is, it has no free
variables.

The translation of a first-order sentence A to clause form has several steps:

- Push negations in.

- Replace existentially quantified variables by Skolem functions.

- Move universal quantifiers to the front.

- Convert the matrix of the formula to conjunctive normal form.

- Remove universal quantifiers and Boolean connectives.

This transformation will be presented as a set of rewrite rules. A rewrite rule $X \to Y$
means that a subformula of the form X is replaced by a subformula of the form Y.

The following rewrite rules push negations in:

$$(A \leftrightarrow B) \to (A \to B) \wedge (B \to A),$$
$$(A \to B) \to ((\neg A) \vee B),$$
$$\neg\neg A \to A,$$
$$\neg(A \wedge B) \to (\neg A) \vee (\neg B),$$
$$\neg(A \vee B) \to (\neg A) \wedge (\neg B),$$
$$\neg \forall x A \to \exists x (\neg A),$$
$$\neg \exists x A \to \forall x (\neg A).$$

After negations have been pushed in, we assume for simplicity that variables in the
formula are renamed so that each variable appears in only one quantifier. Existential quantifiers are then eliminated by replacing formulas of the form $\exists x A[x]$ by
$A[f(x_1, \ldots, x_n)]$, where $x_1, \ldots, x_n$ are all the universally quantified variables whose
scope includes the formula A, and f is a new function symbol (that does not already
appear in the formula), called a *Skolem function*.

The following rules then move quantifiers to the front:

$$(\forall x A) \vee B \to \forall x (A \vee B),$$
$$B \vee (\forall x A) \to \forall x (B \vee A),$$
$$(\forall x A) \wedge B \to \forall x (A \wedge B),$$
$$B \wedge (\forall x A) \to \forall x (B \wedge A).$$

Next, the matrix is converted to conjunctive normal form by the following rules:

$$(A \lor (B \land C)) \to (A \lor B) \land (A \lor C),$$

$$((B \land C) \lor A) \to (B \lor A) \land (C \lor A).$$

Finally, universal quantifiers are removed from the front of the formula and a conjunctive normal form formula of the form

$$(A_1 \lor A_2 \lor \cdots \lor A_k) \land (B_1 \lor B_2 \lor \cdots \lor B_m) \land \cdots \land (C_1 \lor C_2 \lor \cdots \lor C_n)$$

is replaced by the set of sets of literals

$$\{\{A_1, A_2, \ldots, A_k\}, \{B_1, B_2, \ldots, B_m\}, \ldots, \{C_1, C_2, \ldots, C_n\}\}.$$

This last formula is the clause form formula which is satisfiable iff the original formula is.

As an example, consider the formula

$$\neg \exists x (P(x) \to \forall y Q(x, y)).$$

First, negation is pushed past the existential quantifier:

$$\forall x (\neg (P(x) \to \forall y Q(x, y))).$$

Next, negation is further pushed in, which involves replacing $\to$ by its definition as follows:

$$\forall x \neg ((\neg P(x)) \lor \forall y Q(x, y)).$$

Then $\neg$ is moved in past $\lor$:

$$\forall x ((\neg\neg P(x)) \land \neg \forall y Q(x, y)).$$

Next the double negation is eliminated and $\neg$ is moved past the quantifier:

$$\forall x (P(x) \land \exists y \neg Q(x, y)).$$

Now, negations have been pushed in. Note that no variable appears in more than one quantifier, so it is not necessary to rename variables. Next, the existential quantifier is replaced by a Skolem function:

$$\forall x (P(x) \land \neg Q(x, f(x))).$$

There are no quantifiers to move to the front. Eliminating the universal quantifier yields the formula

$$P(x) \land \neg Q(x, f(x)).$$

The clause form is then

$$\{\{P(x)\}, \{\neg Q(x, f(x))\}\}.$$

Recall that if B is the clause form of A, then B is satisfiable iff A is. As in propositional calculus, the clause form translation can increase the size of a formula by an exponential amount. This can be avoided as in the propositional calculus by introducing new predicate symbols for sub-formulas. Suppose A is a formula with sub-formula B, denoted by $A[B]$. Let $x_1, x_2, \ldots, x_n$ be the free variables in B. Let P be a new predicate symbol (that does not appear in A). Then $A[B]$ is transformed to the formula $A[P(x_1, x_2, \ldots, x_n)] \wedge \forall x_1 \forall x_2 \ldots \forall x_n (P(x_1, x_2, \ldots, x_n) \leftrightarrow B)$. Thus the occurrence of B in A is replaced by $P(x_1, x_2, \ldots, x_n)$, and the equivalence of B with $P(x_1, x_2, \ldots, x_n)$ is added on to the formula as well. This transformation can be applied to the new formula in turn, and again as many times as desired. The transformation is satisfiability preserving, which means that the resulting formula is satisfiable iff the original formula A was.

Free variables in a clause are assumed to be universally quantified. Thus the clause $\{\neg P(x), Q(f(x))\}$ represents the formula $\forall x(\neg P(x) \vee Q(f(x)))$. A term, literal, or clause not containing any variables is said to be *ground*.

A set of clauses represents the conjunction of the clauses in the set. Thus the set $\{\{\neg P(x), Q(f(x))\}, \{\neg Q(y), R(g(y))\}, \{P(a)\}, \{\neg R(z)\}\}$ represents the formula $(\forall x(\neg P(x) \vee Q(f(x)))) \wedge (\forall y(\neg Q(y) \vee R(g(y)))) \wedge P(a) \wedge \forall z \neg R(z)$.

Herbrand interpretations

There is a special kind of interpretation that turns out to be significant for mechanical theorem proving. This is called a *Herbrand interpretation*. Herbrand interpretations are defined relative to a set S of clauses. The domain D of a Herbrand interpretation I consists of the set of terms constructed from function and constant symbols of S, with an extra constant symbol added if S has no constant symbols. The constant and function symbols are interpreted so that for any finite term t composed of these symbols, t^I is the term t itself, which is an element of D. Thus if S has a unary function symbol f and a constant symbol c, then $D = \{c, f(c), f(f(c)), f(f(f(c))), \ldots\}$ and c is interpreted so that c^I is the element c of D and f is interpreted so that f^I applied to the term c yields the term $f(c)$, f^I applied to the term $f(c)$ of D yields $f(f(c))$, and so on. Thus these interpretations are quite syntactic in nature. There is no restriction, however, on how a Herbrand interpretation I may interpret the predicate symbols of S.

The interest of Herbrand interpretations for theorem proving comes from the following result:

Theorem 1.3.2. *If S is a set of clauses, then S is satisfiable iff there is a Herbrand interpretation I such that $I \models S$.*

What this theorem means is that for purposes of testing satisfiability of clause sets, one only needs to consider Herbrand interpretations. This implicitly leads to a mechanical theorem proving procedure, which will be presented below. This procedure makes use of *substitutions*.

A *substitution* is a mapping from variables to terms which is the identity on all but finitely many variables. If L is a literal and α is a substitution, then $L\alpha$ is the result of replacing all variables in L by their image under α. The application of substitutions to terms, clauses, and sets of clauses is defined similarly. The expression $\{x_1 \mapsto t_1, x_2 \mapsto t_2, \ldots, x_n \mapsto t_n\}$ denotes the substitution mapping the variable x_i to the term t_i, for $1 \leqslant i \leqslant n$.

For example, $P(x, f(x))\{x \mapsto g(y)\} = P(g(y), f(g(y)))$.

If L is a literal and α is a substitution, then $L\alpha$ is called an *instance* of L. Thus $P(g(y), f(g(y)))$ is an instance of $P(x, f(x))$. Similar terminology applies to clauses and terms.

If S is a set of clauses, then a *Herbrand set* for S is an unsatisfiable set T of ground clauses such that for every clause D in T there is a clause C in S such that D is an instance of C. If there is a Herbrand set for S, then S is unsatisfiable.

For example, let S be the following clause set:

$$\{\{P(a)\}, \{\neg P(x), P(f(x))\}, \{\neg P(f(f(a)))\}\}.$$

For this set of clauses, the following is a Herbrand set:

$$\{\{P(a)\}, \{\neg P(a), P(f(a))\}, \{\neg P(f(a)), P(f(f(a)))\}, \{\neg P(f(f(a)))\}\}.$$

The *ground instantiation problem* is the following: Given a set S of clauses, is there a Herbrand set for S?

The following result is known as Herbrand's theorem, and follows from Theorem 1.3.2:

Theorem 1.3.3. *A set S of clauses is unsatisfiable iff there is a Herbrand set T for S.*

It follows from this result that a set S of clauses is unsatisfiable iff the ground instantiation problem for S is solvable. Thus the problem of first-order validity has been reduced to the ground instantiation problem. This is actually quite an achievement, because the ground instantiation problem deals only with syntactic concepts such as replacing variables by terms, and with propositional unsatisfiability, which is easily understood.

Herbrand's theorem implies the completeness of the following theorem proving method:

Given a set S of clauses, let $C_1, C_2, C_3, \ldots$ be an enumeration of all of the ground instances of clauses in S. This set of ground instances is countable, so it can be enumerated. Consider the following procedure **Prover**:

procedure Prover(S)
    for $i = 1, 2, 3, \ldots$ **do**
        if $\{C_1, C_2, \ldots, C_i\}$ is unsatisfiable **then** return "unsatisfiable" **fi**
    od
end **Prover**

By Herbrand's theorem, it follows that **Prover**(S) will eventually return "unsatisfiable" iff S is unsatisfiable. This is therefore a primitive theorem proving procedure. It is interesting that some of the earliest attempts to mechanize theorem proving [99] were based on this idea. The problem with this approach is that it enumerates many ground instances that could never appear in a proof. However, the efficiency of propositional decision procedures is an attractive feature of this procedure, and it may be possible to modify it to obtain an efficient theorem proving procedure. And in fact, many of the theorem provers in use today are based implicitly on this procedure, and thereby on Herbrand's theorem. The *instance-based* methods such as model evolution [23, 25], clause linking [153], the disconnection calculus [29, 245], and OSHL [213] are based fairly directly on Herbrand's theorem. These methods attempt to apply DPLL-like approaches [69] to first-order theorem proving. Ganzinger and Korovin [93] also study the properties of instance-based methods and show how redundancy elimination and decidable fragments of first-order logic can be incorporated into them. Korovin has continued this line of research with some later papers.

Unification and resolution

Most mechanical theorem provers today are based on unification, which guides the instantiation of clauses in an attempt to make the procedure **Prover** above more efficient. The idea of unification is to find those instances which are in some sense the most general ones that could appear in a proof. This avoids a lot of work that results from the generation of irrelevant instances by **Prover**.

In the following discussion $\equiv$ will refer to syntactic identity of terms, literals, etc. A substitution α is called a *unifier* of literals L and M if $L\alpha \equiv M\alpha$. If such a substitution exists, L and M are said to be *unifiable*. A substitution α is a *most general unifier* of L and M if for any other unifier β of L and M, there is a substitution γ such that $L\beta \equiv L\alpha\gamma$ and $M\beta \equiv M\alpha\gamma$.

It turns out that if two literals L and M are unifiable, then there is a most general unifier of L and M, and such most general unifiers can be computed efficiently by a number of simple algorithms. The earliest in recent history was given by Robinson [230].

We present a simple unification algorithm on terms which is similar to that presented by Robinson. This algorithm is worst-case exponential time, but often efficient in practice. Algorithms that are more efficient (and even linear time) on large terms have been devised since then [167, 202]. If s and t are two terms and α is a most general unifier of s and t, then $s\alpha$ can be of size exponential in the sizes of s and t, so constructing $s\alpha$ is inherently exponential unless the proper encoding of terms is used; this entails representing repeated subterms only once. However, many symbolic computation systems still use Robinson's original algorithm.

procedure **Unify**(r, s);
    [[return the most general unifier of terms r and s]]
       if r is a variable **then**
         if $r \equiv s$ **then** return { } **else**
        (**if** r occurs in s **then** return **fail else**
         return $\{r \mapsto s\}$) **else**
       if s is a variable **then**
        (**if** s occurs in r **then** return **fail else**
         return $\{s \mapsto r\}$) **else**
       if the top-level function symbols of r and s
        differ or have different arities **then** return **fail**
      else
        suppose r is $f(r_1 \ldots r_n)$ and s is $f(s_1 \ldots s_n)$;
        return(**Unify_lists**$([r_1 \ldots r_n], [s_1 \ldots s_n])$)
end **Unify**;

procedure Unify_lists($[r_1 \ldots r_n], [s_1 \ldots s_n]$);
  if $[r_1 \ldots r_n]$ is empty **then** return {}
    else
        $\theta \leftarrow$ **Unify**(r_1, t_1);
          if $\theta \equiv$ **fail then** return **fail fi**;
        $\alpha \leftarrow$ **Unify_lists**$([r_2 \ldots r_n]\theta, [s_2 \ldots s_n]\theta)$
          if $\alpha \equiv$ **fail then** return **fail fi**;
  return $\{\theta \circ \alpha\}$
end Unify_lists;

For this last procedure, $\theta \circ \alpha$ is defined as the composition of the substitutions θ and α, defined by $t(\theta \circ \alpha) = (t\theta)\alpha$. Note that the composition of two substitutions is a substitution. To extend the above algorithm to literals L and M, return **fail** if L and M have different signs or predicate symbols. Suppose L and M both have the same sign and predicate symbol P. Suppose L and M are $P(r_1, r_2, \ldots, r_n)$ and $P(s_1, s_2, \ldots, s_n)$, respectively, or their negations. Then return **Unify_lists**($[r_1 \ldots r_n], [s_1 \ldots s_n]$) as the most general unifier of L and M.

As examples of unification, a most general unifier of the terms $f(x, a)$ and $f(b, y)$ is $\{x \mapsto b, y \mapsto a\}$. The terms $f(x, g(x))$ and $f(y, y)$ are not unifiable. A most general unifier of $f(x, y, g(y))$ and $f(z, h(z), w)$ is $\{x \mapsto z, y \mapsto h(z), w \mapsto g(h(z))\}$.

One can also define unifiers and most general unifiers of *sets* of terms. A substitution α is said to be a unifier of a set $\{t_1, t_2, \ldots, t_n\}$ of terms if $t_1\alpha \equiv t_2\alpha \equiv t_3\alpha \cdots$. If such a unifier α exists, this set of terms is said to be unifiable. It turns out that if $\{t_1, t_2, \ldots, t_n\}$ is a set of terms and has a unifier, then it has a most general unifier, and this unifier can be computed as **Unify**$(f(t_1, t_2, \ldots, t_n), f(t_2, t_3, \ldots, t_n, t_1))$ where f is a function symbol of arity n. In a similar way, one can define most general unifiers of sets of literals.

Finally, suppose C_1 and C_2 are two clauses and A_1 and A_2 are nonempty subsets of C_1 and C_2, respectively. Suppose for convenience that there are no common variables between C_1 and C_2. Suppose the set $\{L: L \in A_1\} \cup \{\neg L: L \in A_2\}$ is unifiable, and let α be its most general unifier. Define the *resolvent* of C_1 and C_2 on the subsets A_1 and A_2 to be the clause

$$(C_1 - A_1)\alpha \cup (C_2 - A_2)\alpha.$$

A resolvent of C_1 and C_2 is defined to be a resolvent of C_1 and C_2 on two such sets A_1 and A_2 of literals. A_1 and A_2 are called *subsets of resolution*. If C_1 and C_2 have common variables, it is assumed that the variables of one of these clauses are renamed before resolving to insure that there are no common variables. There may be more than one resolvent of two clauses, or there may not be any resolvents at all.

Most of the time, A_1 and A_2 consist of single literals. This considerably simplifies the definition, and most of our examples will be of this special case. If $A_1 \equiv \{L\}$ and $A_2 \equiv \{M\}$, then L and M are called *literals of resolution*. We call this kind of resolution *single literal resolution*. Often, one defines resolution in terms of *factoring* and single literal resolution. If C is a clause and θ is a most general unifier of two distinct literals of C, then $C\theta$ is called a *factor* of C. Defining resolution in terms of factoring has some advantages, though it increases the number of clauses one must store.

Here are some examples. Suppose C_1 is $\{P(a)\}$ and C_2 is $\{\neg P(x), Q(f(x))\}$. Then a resolvent of these two clauses on the literals $P(a)$ and $\neg P(x)$ is $\{Q(f(a))\}$. This is because the most general unifier of these two literals is $\{x \mapsto a\}$, and applying this substitution to $\{Q(f(x))\}$ yields the clause $\{Q(f(a))\}$.

Suppose C_1 is $\{\neg P(a, x)\}$ and C_2 is $\{P(y, b)\}$. Then $\{\}$ (the empty clause) is a resolvent of C_1 and C_2 on the literals $\neg P(a, x)$ and $P(y, b)$.

Suppose C_1 is $\{\neg P(x), Q(f(x))\}$ and C_2 is $\{\neg Q(x), R(g(x))\}$. In this case, the variables of C_2 are first renamed before resolving, to eliminate common variables, yielding the clause $\{\neg Q(y), R(g(y))\}$. Then a resolvent of C_1 and C_2 on the literals $Q(f(x))$ and $\neg Q(y)$ is $\{\neg P(x), R(g(f(x)))\}$.

Suppose C_1 is $\{P(x), P(y)\}$ and C_2 is $\{\neg P(z), Q(f(z))\}$. Then a resolvent of C_1 and C_2 on the sets $\{P(x), P(y)\}$ and $\{\neg P(z)\}$ is $\{Q(f(z))\}$.

A *resolution proof* of a clause C from a set S of clauses is a sequence $C_1, C_2, \ldots, C_n$ of clauses in which C_n is C and in which for all i, either C_i is an element of S or there exist integers $j, k < i$ such that C_i is a resolvent of C_j and C_k. Such a proof is called a (resolution) *refutation* from S if C_n is $\{\}$ (the empty clause).

A theorem proving method is said to be *complete* if it is able to prove any valid formula. For unsatisfiability testing, a theorem proving method is said to be complete if it can derive **false**, or the empty clause, from any unsatisfiable set of clauses. It is known that resolution is complete:

Theorem 1.3.4. *A set S of first-order clauses is unsatisfiable iff there is a resolution refutation from S.*

Therefore one can use resolution to test unsatisfiability of clause sets, and hence validity of first-order formulas. The advantage of resolution over the **Prover** procedure above is that resolution uses unification to choose instances of the clauses that are more likely to appear in a proof. So in order to show that a first-order formula A is valid, one can do the following:

- Convert $\neg A$ to clause form S.

- Search for a proof of the empty clause from S.

As an example of this procedure, resolution can be applied to show that the first-order formula

$$\forall x \exists y (P(x) \rightarrow Q(x, y)) \wedge \forall x \forall y \exists z (Q(x, y) \rightarrow R(x, z))$$
$$\rightarrow \forall x \exists z (P(x) \rightarrow R(x, z))$$

is valid. Here $\rightarrow$ represents logical implication, as usual. In the refutational approach, one negates this formula to obtain

$$\neg[\forall x \exists y (P(x) \rightarrow Q(x, y)) \wedge \forall x \forall y \exists z (Q(x, y) \rightarrow R(x, z))$$
$$\rightarrow \forall x \exists z (P(x) \rightarrow R(x, z))],$$

and shows that this formula is unsatisfiable. The procedure of Section 1.3.3 for translating formulas into clause form yields the following set S of clauses:

$$\{\{\neg P(x), Q(x, f(x))\}, \{\neg Q(x, y), R(x, g(x, y))\}, \{P(a)\}, \{\neg R(a, z)\}\}.$$

The following is then a resolution refutation from this clause set:

1. $P(a)$ (input)
2. $\neg P(x), Q(x, f(x))$ (input)
3. $Q(a, f(a))$ (resolution, 1, 2)
4. $\neg Q(x, y), R(x, g(x, y))$ (input)
5. $R(a, g(a, f(a)))$ (3, 4, resolution)
6. $\neg R(a, z)$ (input)
7. false   (5, 6, resolution)

The designation "input" means that a clause is in S. Since **false** (the empty clause) has been derived from S by resolution, it follows that S is unsatisfiable, and so the original first-order formula is valid.

Even though resolution is much more efficient than the **Prover** procedure, it is still not as efficient as one would like. In the early days of resolution, a number of refinements were added to resolution, mostly by the Argonne group, to make it more efficient. These were the set of support strategy, unit preference, hyper-resolution, subsumption and tautology deletion, and demodulation. In addition, the Argonne group preferred using small clauses when searching for resolution proofs. Also, they employed some very efficient data structures for storing and accessing clauses. We will describe most of these refinements now.

A clause C is called a *tautology* if for some literal L, $L \in C$ and $\neg L \in C$. It is known that if S is unsatisfiable, there is a refutation from S that does not contain any tautologies. This means that tautologies can be deleted as soon as they are generated and need never be included in resolution proofs.

In general, given a set S of clauses, one searches for a refutation from S by performing a sequence of resolutions. To ensure completeness, this search should be *fair*, that is, if clauses C_1 and C_2 have been generated already, and it is possible to resolve these clauses, then this resolution must eventually be done. However, the order in which resolutions are performed is nonetheless very flexible, and a good choice in this respect can help the prover a lot. One good idea is to prefer resolutions of clauses that are small, that is, that have small terms in them.

Another way to guide the choice of resolutions is based on subsumption, as follows: Clause C is said to *subsume* clause D if there is a substitution Θ such that $C\Theta \subseteq D$. For example, the clause $\{Q(x)\}$ subsumes the clause $\{\neg P(a), Q(a)\}$. C is said to *properly subsume* D if C subsumes D and the number of literals in C is less than or equal to the number of literals in D. For example, the clause $\{Q(x), Q(y)\}$ subsumes $\{Q(a)\}$, but does not properly subsume it. It is known that clauses properly subsumed by other clauses can be deleted when searching for resolution refutations from S. It is possible that these deleted clauses may still appear in the final refutation, but once a clause C is generated that properly subsumes D, it is never necessary to use D in any further resolutions. Subsumption deletion can reduce the proof time tremendously, since long clauses tend to be subsumed by short ones. Of course, if two clauses properly subsume each other, one of them should be kept. The use of appropriate data structures [222, 226] can greatly speed up the subsumption test, and indeed term indexing data structures are essential for an efficient theorem prover, both for quickly finding clauses to resolve and for performing the subsumption test. As an example [222], in a run of the Vampire prover on the problem LCL-129-1.p from the

TPTP library of www.tptp.org, in 270 seconds 8,272,207 clauses were generated of which 5,203,928 were deleted because their weights were too large, 3,060,226 were deleted because they were subsumed by existing clauses (*forward subsumption*), and only 8053 clauses were retained.

This can all be combined to obtain a program for searching for resolution proofs from S, as follows:

procedure Resolver(S)
   $R \leftarrow S$;
     while false $\notin R$ **do**
        choose clauses $C_1, C_2 \in R$ fairly, preferring small clauses;
        if no new pairs C_1, C_2 exist **then** return "satisfiable" **fi**;
        $R' \leftarrow \{D: \ D$ is a resolvent of C_1, C_2 and D is not a tautology$\}$;
        for $D \in R'$ **do**
          if no clause in R properly subsumes D
           then $R \leftarrow \{D\} \cup \{C \in R: \ D$ does not properly subsume $C\}$ **fi**;
        od
     od
end **Resolver**

In order to make precise what a "small clause" is, one defines $\|C\|$, the *symbol size* of clause C, as follows:

$$\|x\| = 1 \quad \text{for variables } x$$
$$\|c\| = 1 \quad \text{for constant symbols } c$$
$$\|f(t_1, \ldots, t_n)\| = 1 + \|t_1\| + \cdots + \|t_n\| \quad \text{for terms } f(t_1, \ldots, t_n)$$
$$\|P(t_1, \ldots, t_n)\| = 1 + \|t_1\| + \cdots + \|t_n\| \quad \text{for atoms } P(t_1, \ldots, t_n)$$
$$\|\neg A\| = \|A\| \quad \text{for atoms } A$$
$$\|\{L_1, L_2, \ldots, L_n\}\| = \|L_1\| + \cdots + \|L_n\| \quad \text{for clauses } \{L_1, L_2, \ldots, L_n\}$$

Small clauses, then, are those having a small symbol size.

Another technique used by the Argonne group is the *unit preference strategy*, defined as follows: A *unit clause* is a clause that contains exactly one literal. A *unit resolution* is a resolution of clauses C_1 and C_2, where at least one of C_1 and C_2 is a unit clause. The *unit preference* strategy prefers unit resolutions, when searching for proofs. Unit preference has to be modified to permit non-unit resolutions to guarantee completeness. Thus non-unit resolutions are also performed, but not as early. The unit preference strategy helps because unit resolutions reduce the number of literals in a clause.

Refinements of resolution

In an attempt to make resolution more efficient, many, many refinements were developed in the early days of theorem proving. We present a few of them, and mention a number of others. For a discussion of resolution and its refinements, and theorem proving in general, see [53, 163, 45, 271, 87, 155]. It is hard to know which refinements will help on any given example, but experience with a theorem prover can help to give one a better idea of which refinements to try. In general, none of these refinements help very much most of the time.

A literal is called *positive* if it is an atom, that is, has no negation sign. A literal with a negation sign is called *negative*. A clause C is called *positive* if all of the literals in C are positive. C is called *negative* if all of the literals in C are negative. A resolution of C_1 and C_2 is called positive if one of C_1 and C_2 is a positive clause. It is called negative if one of C_1 and C_2 is a negative clause. It turns out that positive resolution is complete, that is, if S is unsatisfiable, then there is a refutation from S in which all of the resolutions are positive. This refinement of resolution is known as P_1 deduction in the literature. Similarly, negative resolution is complete. Hyper-resolution is essentially a modification of positive resolution in which a series of positive resolvents is done all at once. To be precise, suppose that C is a clause having at least one negative literal and $D_1, D_2, \ldots, D_n$ are positive clauses. Suppose C_1 is a resolvent of C and D_1, C_2 is a resolvent of C_1 and D_2, $\ldots$, and C_n is a resolvent of C_{n-1} and D_n. Suppose that C_n is a positive clause but none of the clauses C_i are positive, for $i < n$. Then C_n is called a *hyper-resolvent* of C and $D_1, D_2, \ldots, D_n$. Thus the inference steps in hyper-resolution are sequences of positive resolutions. In the hyper-resolution strategy, the inference engine looks for a complete collection $D_1 \ldots D_n$ of clauses to resolve with C and only performs the inference when the entire hyper-resolution can be carried out. Hyper-resolution is sometimes useful because it reduces the number of intermediate results that must be stored in the prover.

Typically, when proving a theorem, there is a general set A of axioms and a particular formula F that one wishes to prove. So one wishes to show that the formula $A \to F$ is valid. In the refutational approach, this is done by showing that $\neg(A \to F)$ is unsatisfiable. Now, $\neg(A \to F)$ is transformed to $A \land \neg F$ in the clause form translation. One then obtains a set S_A of clauses from A and a set S_F of clauses from $\neg F$. The set $S_A \cup S_F$ is unsatisfiable iff $A \to F$ is valid. One typically tries to show $S_A \cup S_F$ unsatisfiable by performing resolutions. Since one is attempting to prove F, one would expect that resolutions involving the clauses S_F are more likely to be useful, since resolutions involving two clauses from S_A are essentially combining general axioms. Thus one would like to only perform resolutions involving clauses in S_F or clauses derived from them. This can be achieved by the *set of support* strategy, if the set S_F is properly chosen.

The set of support strategy restricts all resolutions to involve a clause in the *set of support* or a clause derived from it. To guarantee completeness, the set of support must be chosen to include the set of clauses C of S such that $I \not\models C$ for some interpretation I. Sets A of axioms typically have standard models I, so that $I \models A$. Since translation to clause form is satisfiability preserving, $I' \models S_A$ as well, where I' is obtained from I by a suitable interpretation of Skolem functions. If the set of support is chosen as the clauses not satisfied by I', then this set of support will be a subset of the set S_F above and inferences are restricted to those that are relevant to the particular theorem. Of course, it is not necessary to test if $I \models C$ for clauses C; if one knows that A is satisfiable, one can choose S_F as the set of support.

The *semantic resolution* strategy is like the set-of-support resolution, but requires that when two clauses C_1 and C_2 resolve, at least one of them must not be satisfied by a specified interpretation I. Some interpretations permit the test $I \models C$ to be carried out; this is possible, for example, if I has a finite domain. Using such a semantic definition of the set of support strategy further restricts the set of possible resolutions over the set of support strategy while retaining completeness.

Other refinements of resolution include ordered resolution, which orders the literals of a clause, and requires that the subsets of resolution include a maximal literal in their respective clauses. Unit resolution requires all resolutions to be unit resolutions, and is not complete. Input resolution requires all resolutions to involve a clause from S, and this is not complete, either. Unit resulting (UR) resolution is like unit resolution, but has larger inference steps. This is also not complete, but works well surprisingly often. Locking resolution attaches indices to literals, and uses these to order the literals in a clause and decide which literals have to belong to the subsets of resolution. Ancestry-filter form resolution imposes a kind of linear format on resolution proofs. These strategies are both complete. Semantic resolution is compatible with some ordering refinements, that is, the two strategies together are still complete.

It is interesting that resolution is complete for *logical consequences*, in the following sense: If S is a set of clauses, and C is a clause such that $S \models C$, that is, C is a logical consequence of S, then there is a clause D derivable by resolution such that D subsumes C.

Another resolution refinement that is useful sometimes is *splitting*. If C is a clause and $C \equiv C_1 \cup C_2$, where C_1 and C_2 have no common variables, then $S \cup \{C\}$ is unsatisfiable iff $S \cup \{C_1\}$ is unsatisfiable and $S \cup \{C_2\}$ is unsatisfiable. The effect of this is to reduce the problem of testing unsatisfiability of $S \cup \{C\}$ to two simpler problems. A typical example of such a clause C is a ground clause with two or more literals.

There is a special class of clauses called *Horn clauses* for which specialized theorem proving strategies are complete. A *Horn clause* is a clause that has at most one positive literal. Such clauses have found tremendous application in logic programming languages. If S is a set of Horn clauses, then unit resolution is complete, as is input resolution.

Other strategies

There are a number of other strategies which apply to sets S of clauses, but do not use resolution. One of the most notable is *model elimination* [162], which constructs *chains* of literals and has some similarities to the DPLL procedure. Model elimination also specifies the order in which literals of a clause will "resolve away". There are also a number of *connection methods* [28, 158], which operate by constructing links between complementary literals in different clauses, and creating structures containing more than one clause linked together. In addition, there are a number of *instance-based* strategies, which create a set T of ground instances of S and test T for unsatisfiability using a DPLL-like procedure. Such instance-based methods can be much more efficient than resolution on certain kinds of clause sets, namely, those that are highly non-Horn but do not involve deep term structure.

Furthermore, there are a number of strategies that do not use clause form at all. These include the semantic tableau methods, which work backwards from a formula and construct a tree of possibilities; Andrews' matings method, which is suitable for higher order logic and has obtained some impressive proofs automatically; natural deduction methods; and sequent style systems. Tableau systems have found substantial application in automated deduction, and many of these are even adapted to formulas in clause form; for a survey see [106].

Evaluating strategies

In general, we feel that qualities that need to be considered when evaluating a strategy are not only *completeness* but also *propositional efficiency, goal-sensitivity* and *use of semantics*. By propositional efficiency is meant the degree to which the efficiency of the method on propositional problems compares with DPLL; most strategies do poorly in this respect. By goal-sensitivity is meant the degree to which the method permits one to concentrate on inferences related to the particular clauses coming from the negation of the theorem (the set S_F discussed above). When there are many, many input clauses, goal sensitivity is crucial. By use of semantics is meant whether the method can take advantage of natural semantics that may be provided with the problem statement in its search for a proof. An early prover that did use semantics in this way was the geometry prover of Gelernter et al. [94]. Note that model elimination and set of support strategies are goal-sensitive but apparently not propositionally efficient. Semantic resolution is goal-sensitive and can use natural semantics, but is not propositionally efficient, either. Some instance-based strategies are goal-sensitive and use natural semantics and are propositionally efficient, but may have to resort to exhaustive enumeration of ground terms instead of unification in order to instantiate clauses. A further issue is to what extent various methods permit the incorporation of efficient equality techniques, which varies a lot from method to method. Therefore there are some interesting problems involved in combining as many of these desirable features as possible. And for strategies involving extensive human interaction, the criteria for evaluation are considerably different.

1.3.3 Equality

When proving theorems involving equations, one obtains many irrelevant terms. For example, if one has the equations $x + 0 = x$ and $x * 1 = x$, and addition and multiplication are commutative and associative, then one obtains many terms identical to x, such as $1 * x * 1 * 1 + 0$. For products of two or three variables or constants, the situation becomes much worse. It is imperative to find a way to get rid of all of these equivalent terms. For this purpose, specialized methods have been developed to handle equality.

As examples of mathematical structures where such equations arise, for groups and monoids the group operation is associative with an identity, and for abelian groups the group operation is associative and commutative. Rings and fields also have an associative and commutative addition operator with an identity and another multiplication operator that is typically associative. For Boolean algebras, the multiplication operation is also idempotent. For example, set union and intersection are associative, commutative, and idempotent. Lattices have similar properties. Such equations and structures typically arise when axiomatizing integers, reals, complex numbers, matrices, and other mathematical objects.

The most straightforward method of handling equality is to use a general first-order resolution theorem prover together with the *equality axioms*, which are the following (assuming free variables are implicitly universally quantified):

$x = x,$

$x = y \rightarrow y = x,$

$x = y \wedge y = z \rightarrow x = z,$

$x_1 = y_1 \wedge x_2 = y_2 \wedge \cdots \wedge x_n = y_n \rightarrow f(x_1 \ldots x_n) = f(y_1 \ldots y_n)$
   for all function symbols f,

$x_1 = y_1 \wedge x_2 = y_2 \wedge \cdots \wedge x_n = y_n \wedge P(x_1 \ldots x_n) \rightarrow P(y_1 \ldots y_n)$
   for all predicate symbols P

Let **Eq** refer to this set of equality axioms. The approach of using **Eq** explicitly leads to many inefficiencies, as noted above, although in some cases it works reasonably well.

Another approach to equality is the *modification method* of Brand [40, 19]. In this approach, a set S of clauses is transformed into another set S' with the following property: $S \cup$ **Eq** is unsatisfiable iff $S' \cup \{x = x\}$ is unsatisfiable. Thus this transformation avoids the need for the equality axioms, except for $\{x = x\}$. This approach often works a little better than using **Eq** explicitly.

Contexts

In order to discuss other inference rules for equality, some terminology is needed. A *context* is a term with occurrences of $\square$ in it. For example, $f(\square, g(a, \square))$ is a context. A $\square$ by itself is also a context. One can also have literals and clauses with $\square$ in them, and they are also called contexts. If n is an integer, then an *n-context* is a term with n occurrences of $\square$. If t is an n-context and $m \leqslant n$, then $t[t_1, \ldots, t_m]$ represents t with the leftmost m occurrences of $\square$ replaced by the terms $t_1, \ldots, t_m$, respectively. Thus, for example, $f(\square, b, \square)$ is a 2-context, and $f(\square, b, \square)[g(c)]$ is $f(g(c), b, \square)$. Also, $f(\square, b, \square)[g(c)][a]$ is $f(g(c), b, a)$. In general, if r is an n-context and $m \leqslant n$ and the terms s_i are 0-contexts, then $r[s_1, \ldots, s_n] \equiv r[s_1][s_2] \ldots [s_n]$. However, $f(\square, b, \square)[g(\square)]$ is $f(g(\square), b, \square)$, so $f(\square, b, \square)[g(\square)][a]$ is $f(g(a), b, \square)$. In general, if r is a k-context for $k \geqslant 1$ and s is an n-context for $n \geqslant 1$, then $r[s][t] \equiv r[s[t]]$, by a simple argument (both replace the leftmost $\square$ in $r[s]$ by t).

Termination orderings on terms

It is necessary to discuss partial orderings on terms in order to explain inference rules for equality. Partial orderings give a precise definition of the complexity of a term, so that $s > t$ means that the term s is more complex than t in some sense, and replacing s by t makes a clause simpler. A partial ordering $>$ is *well-founded* if there are no infinite sequences x_i of elements such that $x_i > x_{i+1}$ for all $i \geqslant 0$. A *termination ordering* on terms is a partial ordering $>$ which is well founded and satisfies the *full invariance property*, that is, if $s > t$ and Θ is a substitution then $s\Theta > t\Theta$, and also satisfies the *replacement property*, that is, $s > t$ implies $r[s] > r[t]$ for all 1-contexts r.

Note that if $s > t$ and $>$ is a termination ordering, then all variables in t appear also in s. For example, if $f(x) > g(x, y)$, then by full invariance $f(x) > g(x, f(x))$, and by replacement $g(x, f(x)) > g(x, g(x, f(x)))$, etc., giving an infinite descending sequence of terms.

The concept of a *multiset* is often useful to show termination. Informally, a multiset is a set in which an element can occur more than once. Formally, a multiset S is a function from some underlying domain D to the non-negative integers. It is said to be finite if $\{x: S(x) > 0\}$ is finite. One writes $x \in S$ if $S(x) > 0$. $S(x)$ is called the *multiplicity* of x in S; this represents the number of times x appears in S. If S and T are multisets then $S \cup T$ is defined by $(S \cup T)(x) = S(x) + T(x)$ for all x. A partial ordering $>$ on D can be extended to a partial ordering $\gg$ on multisets in the following way: One writes $S \gg T$ if there is some multiset V such that $S = S' \cup V$ and $T = T' \cup V$ and S' is nonempty and for all t in T' there is an s in S' such that $s > t$. This relation can be computed reasonably fast by deleting common elements from S and T as long as possible, then testing if the specified relation between S' and T' holds. The idea is that a multiset becomes smaller if an element is replaced by any number of smaller elements. Thus $\{3, 4, 4\} \gg \{2, 2, 2, 2, 1, 4, 4\}$ since 3 has been replaced by $2, 2, 2, 2, 1$. This operation can be repeated any number of times, still yielding a smaller multiset; in fact, the relation $\gg$ can be defined in this way as the smallest transitive relation having this property [75]. One can show that if $>$ is well founded, so is $\gg$. For a comparison with other definitions of multiset ordering, see [131].

We now give some examples of termination orderings. The simplest kind of termination orderings are those that are based on size. Recall that $\|s\|$ is the symbol size (number of symbol occurrences) of a term s. One can then define $>$ so that $s > t$ if for all Θ making $s\Theta$ and $t\Theta$ ground terms, $\|s\Theta\| > \|t\Theta\|$. For example, $f(x, y) > g(y)$ in this ordering, but it is not true that $h(x, a, b) > f(x, x)$ because x could be replaced by a large term. This termination ordering is computable; $s > t$ iff $\|s\| > \|t\|$ and no variable occurs more times in t than s.

More powerful techniques are needed to get some more interesting termination orderings. One of the most remarkable results in this area is a theorem of Dershowitz [75] about simplification orderings, that gives a general technique for showing that an ordering is a termination ordering. Before his theorem, each ordering had to be shown well founded separately, and this was often difficult. This theorem makes use of simplification orderings.

Definition 1.3.5. *A partial ordering $>$ on terms is a* simplification ordering *if it satisfies the replacement property, that is, for 1-contexts r, $s > t$ implies $r[s] > r[t]$, and has the subterm property, that is, $s > t$ if t is a proper subterm of s. Also, if there are function symbols f with variable arity, it is required that $f(\ldots s \ldots) > f(\ldots\ldots)$ for all such f.*

Theorem 1.3.6. *All simplification orderings are well founded.*

Proof. Based on Kruskal's tree theorem [148], which says that in any infinite sequence $t_1, t_2, t_3, \ldots$ of terms, there are natural numbers i and j with $i < j$ such that t_i is embedded in t_j in a certain sense. It turns out that if t_i is embedded in t_j then $t_j \geqslant t_i$ for any simplification ordering $>$. □

The *recursive path ordering* is one of the simplest simplification orderings. This ordering is defined in terms of a *precedence* ordering on function symbols, which is a partial ordering on the function symbols. One writes $f < g$ to indicate that f is less than g in the precedence relation on function symbols. The recursive path ordering will be presented as a complete set of inference rules that may be used to construct proofs of $s > t$. That is, if $s > t$ then there is a proof of this in the system. Also, by using the inference rules backwards in a goal-directed manner, it is possible to construct a reasonably efficient decision procedure for statements of the form $s > t$. Recall that if $>$ is an ordering, then $\gg$ is the extension of this ordering to multisets. The ordering we present is somewhat weaker than that usually given in the literature.

$$\frac{f = g \qquad \{s_1 \ldots s_m\} \gg \{t_1 \ldots t_n\}}{f(s_1 \ldots s_m) > g(t_1 \ldots t_n)}$$

$$\frac{s_i \geqslant t}{f(s_1 \ldots s_m) > t}$$

$$\frac{true}{s \geqslant s}$$

$$\frac{f > g \qquad f(s_1 \ldots s_m) > t_i \text{ all } i}{f(s_1 \ldots s_m) > g(t_1 \ldots t_n)}$$

For example, suppose $* > +$. Then one can show that $x * (y + z) > x * y + x * z$ as follows:

$$\frac{\dfrac{\dfrac{\dfrac{\dfrac{true}{y \geqslant y}}{y + z > y}}{\{x, y + z\} \gg \{x, y\}}}{x * (y + z) > x * y} \qquad \dfrac{\dfrac{\dfrac{\dfrac{true}{y \geqslant y}}{y + z > z}}{\{x, y + z\} \gg \{x, z\}}}{x * (y + z) > x * z} \qquad * > +}{x * (y + z) > x * y + x * z}$$

For some purposes, it is necessary to modify this ordering so that subterms are considered lexicographically. In general, if $>$ is an ordering, then the lexicographic extension $>_{lex}$ of $>$ to tuples is defined as follows:

$$\frac{s_1 > t_1}{(s_1 \ldots s_m) >_{lex} (t_1 \ldots t_n)}$$

$$\frac{s_1 = t_1 \qquad (s_2 \ldots s_m) >_{lex} (t_2 \ldots t_n)}{(s_1 \ldots s_m) >_{lex} (t_1 \ldots t_n)}$$

$$\frac{true}{(s_1 \ldots s_m) >_{lex} (\ )}$$

One can show that if $>$ is well founded, then so is its extension $>_{lex}$ to bounded length tuples. This lexicographic treatment of subterms is the idea of the lexicographic path ordering of Kamin and Levy [136]. This ordering is defined by the following inference rules:

$$\frac{f = g \qquad (s_1 \ldots s_m) >_{lex} (t_1 \ldots t_n) \qquad f(s_1 \ldots s_m) > t_j, \text{ all } j \geqslant 2}{f(s_1 \ldots s_m) > g(t_1 \ldots t_n)}$$

$$\frac{s_i \geqslant t}{f(s_1 \ldots s_m) > t}$$

$$\frac{true}{s \geqslant s}$$

$$\frac{f > g \qquad f(s_1 \ldots s_m) > t_i \text{ all } i}{f(s_1 \ldots s_m) > g(t_1 \ldots t_n)}$$

In the first inference rule, it is not necessary to test $f(s_1 \ldots s_m) > t_1$ since $(s_1 \ldots s_m) >_{lex} (t_1 \ldots t_n)$ implies $s_1 \geqslant t_1$ hence $f(s_1 \ldots s_m) > t_1$. One can show that this ordering is a simplification ordering for systems having fixed arity function symbols. This ordering has the useful property that $f(f(x, y), z) >_{lex} f(x, f(y, z))$; informally, the reason for this is that the terms have the same size, but the first subterm $f(x, y)$ of $f(f(x, y), z)$ is always larger than the first subterm x of $f(x, f(y, z))$.

The first orderings that could be classified as recursive path orderings were those of Plaisted [208, 207]. A large number of other similar orderings have been developed since the ones mentioned above, for example the *dependency pair* method [7] and its recent automatic versions [120, 98].

Paramodulation

Above, we saw that the equality axioms **Eq** can be used to prove theorems involving equality, and that Brand's modification method is another approach that avoids the need for the equality axioms. A better approach in most cases is to use the *paramodulation rule* [228, 193] defined as follows:

$$\frac{C[t], r = s \vee D, r \text{ and } t \text{ are unifiable, } t \text{ is not a variable, } \mathbf{Unify}(r, t) = \theta}{C\theta[s\theta] \vee D\theta}$$

Here $C[t]$ is a clause containing a subterm t, C is a context, and t is a non-variable term. Also, $C\theta[s\theta]$ is the clause $(C[t])\theta$ with $s\theta$ replacing the specified occurrence of $t\theta$. Also, $r = s \vee D$ is another clause having a literal $r = s$ whose predicate is equality and remaining literals D, which can be empty. To understand this rule, consider that $r\theta = s\theta$ is an instance of $r = s$, and $r\theta$ and $t\theta$ are identical. If $D\theta$ is false, then $r\theta = s\theta$ must be true, so it is possible to replace $r\theta$ in $(C[t])\theta$ by $s\theta$ if $D\theta$ is false. Thus $C\theta[s\theta] \vee D\theta$ is inferred. It is assumed as usual that variables in $C[t]$ or in $r = s \vee D$ are renamed if necessary to insure that these clauses have no common variables before performing paramodulation. The clause $C[t]$ is said to be paramodulated *into*. It is also possible to paramodulate in the other direction, that is, the equation $r = s$ can be used in either direction.

For example, the clause $P(g(a)) \vee Q(b)$ is a paramodulant of $P(f(x))$ and $(f(a) = g(a)) \vee Q(b)$. Brand [40] showed that if **Eq** is the set of equality axioms given above and S is a set of clauses, then $S \cup \mathbf{Eq}$ is unsatisfiable iff there is a proof of the empty clause from $S \cup \{x = x\}$ using resolution and paramodulation as inference rules. Thus, paramodulation allows us to dispense with all the equality axioms except $x = x$.

Some more recent proofs of the completeness of resolution and paramodulation [125] show the completeness of restricted versions of paramodulation which considerably reduce the search space. In particular, it is possible to restrict this rule so that it is not performed if $s\theta > r\theta$, where $>$ is a termination ordering fixed in advance. So if one has an equation $r = s$, and $r > s$, then this equation can only be used to replace instances of r by instances of s. If $s > r$, then this equation can only be used in the reverse direction. The effect of this is to constrain paramodulation so that "big" terms are replaced by "smaller" ones, considerably improving its efficiency. It would be a disaster to allow paramodulation to replace x by $x * 1$, for example. Another complete refinement of ordered paramodulation is that paramodulation only needs to be done into the "large" side of an equation. If the subterm t of $C[t]$ occurs in an equation $u = v$ or $v = u$ of $C[t]$, and $u > v$, where $>$ is the termination ordering being used, then the paramodulation need not be done if the specified occurrence of t is in v. Some early versions of paramodulation required the use of the functionally reflexive axioms of the form $f(x_1, \ldots, x_n) = f(x_1, \ldots, x_n)$, but this is now known not to be necessary. When D is empty, paramodulation is similar to "narrowing", which has been much studied in the context of logic programming and term rewriting. Recently, a more refined approach to the completeness proof of resolution and paramodulation has been found [16, 17] which permits greater control over the equality strategy. This approach also permits one to devise resolution strategies that have a greater control over the order in which literals are resolved away.

Demodulation

Similar to paramodulation is the rewriting or "demodulation" rule, which is essentially a method of simplification.

$$\frac{C[t], r = s, r\theta \equiv t, r\theta > s\theta}{C[s\theta]}.$$

Here $C[t]$ is a clause (so C is a 1-context) containing a non-variable term t, $r = s$ is a unit clause, and $>$ is the termination ordering that is fixed in advance. It is assumed that variables are renamed so that $C[t]$ and $r = s$ have no common variables before this rule is applied. The clause $C[s\theta]$ is called a *demodulant* of $C[t]$ and $r = s$. Similarly, $C[s\theta]$ is a demodulant of $C[t]$ and $s = r$, if $r\theta > s\theta$. Thus an equation can be used in either direction, if the ordering condition is satisfied.

As an example, given the equation $x * 1 = x$ and assuming $x * 1 > x$ and given a clause $C[f(a) * 1]$ having a subterm of the form $f(a) * 1$, this clause can be simplified to $C[f(a)]$, replacing the occurrence of $f(a) * 1$ in C by $f(a)$.

To justify the demodulation rule, the instance $r\theta = s\theta$ of the equation $r = s$ can be inferred because free variables are implicitly universally quantified. This makes it possible to replace $r\theta$ in C by $s\theta$, and vice versa. But $r\theta$ is t, so t can be replaced by $s\theta$.

Not only is the demodulant $C[s\theta]$ inferred, but the original clause $C[t]$ is typically deleted. Thus, in contrast to resolution and paramodulation, demodulation replaces clauses by simpler clauses. This can be a considerable aid in reducing the number of generated clauses. This also makes mechanical theorem proving closer to human reasoning.

The reason for specifying that $s\theta$ is simpler than $r\theta$ is not only the intuitive desire to simplify clauses, but also to ensure that demodulation terminates. For example, there is no termination ordering in which $x * y > y * x$, since then the clause $a * b = c$ could demodulate using the equation $x * y = y * x$ to $b * a = c$ and then to $a * b = c$ and so on indefinitely. Such an ordering $>$ could not be a termination ordering, since it violates the well-foundedness condition. However, for many termination orderings $>$, $x * 1 > x$, and thus the clauses $P(x * 1)$ and $x * 1 = x$ have $P(x)$ as a demodulant if some such ordering is being used.

Resolution with ordered paramodulation and demodulation is still complete if paramodulation and demodulation are done with respect to the same simplification ordering during the proof process [125]. Demodulation is essential in practice, for without it one can generate expressions like $x * 1 * 1 * 1$ that clutter up the search space. Some complete refinements of paramodulation also restrict which literals can be paramodulated into, which must be the "largest" literals in the clause in a sense. Such refinements are typically used with resolution refinements that also restrict subsets of resolution to contain "large" literals in a clause. Another recent development is *basic paramodulation*, which restricts the positions in a term into which paramodulation can be done [18, 194]; this refinement was used in McCune's proof of the Robbins problem [176].

1.3.4 Term Rewriting Systems

A beautiful theory of *term-rewriting systems* has been developed to handle proofs involving *equational systems*; these are theorems of the form $E \models e$ where E is a collection of equations and e is an equation. For such systems, term-rewriting techniques often lead to very efficient proofs. The Robbins problem was of this form, for example.

An *equational system* is a set of equations. Often one is interested in knowing if an equation follows logically from the given set. For example, given the equations $x + y = y + x$, $(x + y) + z = x + (y + z)$, and $-(-(x + y) + -(x + -y)) = x$, one might want to know if the equation $-(-x + y) + -(-x + -y) = x$ is a logical consequence. As another example, one might want to know whether $x * y = y * x$ in a group in which $x^2 = e$ for all x. Such systems are of interest in theorem proving, programming languages, and other areas. Common data structures like lists and stacks can often be described by such sets of equations. In addition, a functional program is essentially a set of equations, typically with higher order functions, and the execution of a program is then a kind of equational reasoning. In fact, some programming languages based on term rewriting have been implemented, and can execute several tens of millions of rewrites per second [72]. Another language based on rewriting is MAUDE [119]. Rewriting techniques have also been used to detect flaws in security protocols and prove properties of such protocols [129]. Systems for mechanising such proofs on a computer are becoming more and more powerful. The Waldmeister system [92] is particularly effective for proofs involving equations and rewriting. The area of rewriting was largely originated by the work of Knuth and Bendix [144]. For a discussion of term-rewriting techniques, see [76, 11, 77, 199, 256].

Syntax of equational systems

A term u is said to be a *subterm* of t if u is t or if t is $f(t_1, \ldots, t_n)$ and u is a subterm of t_i for some i. An *equation* is an expression of the form $s = t$ where s and t are terms. An *equational system* is a set of equations. We will generally consider only unsorted equational systems, for simplicity The letter E will be used to refer to equational systems.

We give a set of inference rules for deriving consequences of equations.

$$\frac{t = u}{t\theta = u\theta}$$

$$\frac{t = u}{u = t}$$

$$\frac{t = u}{f(\ldots t \ldots) = f(\ldots u \ldots)}$$

$$\frac{t = u \qquad u = v}{t = v}$$

$$\frac{true}{t = t}$$

The following result is due to Birkhoff [30]:

Theorem 1.3.7. *If E is a set of equations then $E \models r = s$ iff $r = s$ is derivable from E using these rules.*

This result can be stated in an equivalent way. Namely, $E \models r = s$ iff there is a finite sequence $u_1, u_2, \ldots, u_n$ of terms such that r is u_1 and s is u_n and for all i, u_{i+1} is obtained from u_i by replacing a subterm t of u_i by a term u, where the equation $t = u$ or the equation $u = t$ is an instance of an equation in E.

This gives a method for deriving logical consequences of sets of equations. However, it is inefficient. Therefore it is of interest to find restrictions of these inference rules that are still capable of deriving all equational consequences of an equational system. This is the motivation for the theory of term-rewriting systems.

Term rewriting

The idea of a term rewriting system is to orient an equation $r = s$ into a rule $r \rightarrow s$ indicating that instances of r may be replaced by instances of s but not vice versa. Often this is done in such a way as to replace terms by simpler terms, where the definition of what is simple may be fairly subtle. However, as a first approximation, smaller terms are typically simpler. The equation $x + 0 = x$ then would typically be oriented into the rule $x + 0 \rightarrow x$. This reduces the generation of terms like $((x + 0) + 0) + 0$ which can appear in proofs if no such directionality is applied. The study of term rewriting systems is concerned with how to orient rules and what conditions guarantee that the resulting systems have the same computational power as the equational systems they came from.

Terminology

In this section, variables r, s, t, u refer to *terms* and $\rightarrow$ is a relation over terms. Thus the discussion is at a higher level than earlier.

A *term-rewriting system R* is a set of rules of the form $r \rightarrow s$, where r and s are terms. It is common to require that any variable that appears in s must also appear in r. It is also common to require that r is not a variable. The *rewrite relation $\rightarrow_R$* is defined by the following inference rules:

$$\frac{r \to s \qquad \rho \text{ a substitution}}{r\rho \to s\rho}$$

$$\frac{r \to s}{f(\ldots r \ldots) \to f(\ldots s \ldots)}$$

$$\frac{true}{r \to^* r}$$

$$\frac{r \to s}{r \to^* s}$$

$$\frac{r \to^* s \qquad s \to^* t}{r \to^* t}$$

$$\frac{r \to s}{r \leftrightarrow s}$$

$$\frac{s \to r}{r \leftrightarrow s}$$

$$\frac{true}{r \leftrightarrow^* r}$$

$$\frac{r \leftrightarrow s}{r \leftrightarrow^* s}$$

$$\frac{r \leftrightarrow^* s \qquad s \leftrightarrow^* t}{r \leftrightarrow^* t}$$

The notation $\vdash_r$ indicates derivability using these rules. The r subscript refers to "rewriting" (not to the term r). A set R of rules may be thought of as a set of logical axioms. Writing $s \to t$ is in R, indicates that $s \to t$ is such an axiom. Writing $R \vdash_r s \to t$ indicates that $s \to t$ may refer to a rewrite relation not included in R. Often $s \to_R t$ is used as an abbreviation for $R \vdash_r s \to t$, and sometimes the subscript R is dropped. Similarly, $\to_R^*$ is defined in terms of derivability from R. Note that the relation $\to_R^*$ is the reflexive transitive closure of $\to_R$. Thus $r \to_R^* s$ if there is a sequence $r_1, r_2, \ldots, r_n$ such that r_1 is r, r_n is s, and $r_i \to_R r_{i+1}$ for all i. Such a sequence is called a *rewrite sequence* from r to s, or a *derivation* from r to s. Note that $r \to_R^* r$ for all r and R. A term r is *reducible* if there is a term s such that $r \to s$, otherwise r is *irreducible*. If $r \to_R^* s$ and s is irreducible then s is called a *normal form* of r.

For example, given the system $R = \{x + 0 \to x, 0 + x \to x\}$, the term $0 + (y + 0)$ rewrites in two ways; $0 + (y + 0) \to 0 + y$ and $0 + (y + 0) \to y + 0$. Applying rewriting again, one obtains $0 + (y + 0) \to^* y$. In this case, y is a normal form of $0 + (y + 0)$, since y cannot be further rewritten. Computationally, rewriting a term s proceeds by finding a subterm t of s, called a *redex*, such that t is an instance of the left-hand side of some rule in R, and replacing t by the corresponding instance of the right-hand side of the rule. For example, $0 + (y + 0)$ is an instance of the left-hand side $0 + x$ of the rule $0 + x \to x$. The corresponding instance of the right-hand side x of this rule is $y + 0$, so $0 + (y + 0)$ is replaced by $y + 0$. This approach assumes that all variables on the right-hand side appear also on the left-hand side.

We now relate rewriting to equational theories. From the above rules, $r \leftrightarrow s$ if $r \to s$ or $s \to r$, and $\leftrightarrow^*$ is the reflexive transitive closure of $\leftrightarrow$. Thus $r \leftrightarrow^* s$ if there is a sequence $r_1, r_2, \ldots, r_n$ such that r_1 is r, r_n is s, and $r_i \leftrightarrow r_{i+1}$ for all i. Suppose R is a term rewriting system $\{r_1 \to s_1, \ldots, r_n \to s_n\}$. Define $R^=$ to be the associated equational system $\{r_1 = s_1, \ldots, r_n = s_n\}$. Also, $t =_R u$ is defined as $R^= \models t = u$, that is, the equation $t = u$ is a logical consequence of the associated equational system. The relation $=_R$ is thus the smallest congruence relation generated by R, in algebraic terms. The relation $=_R$ is defined semantically, and the relation $\to^*$ is defined syntactically. It is useful to find relationships between these two concepts in order to be able to compute properties of $=_R$ and to find complete restrictions of the inference rules of Birkhoff's theorem. Note that by Birkhoff's theorem, $R^= \models t = u$ iff $t \leftrightarrow^*_R u$. This is already a connection between the two concepts. However, the fact that rewriting can go in both directions in the derivation for $t \leftrightarrow^*_R u$ is a disadvantage. What we will show is that if R has certain properties, some of them decidable, then $t =_R u$ iff any normal form of t is the same as any normal form of u. This permits us to decide if $t =_R u$ by rewriting t and u to any normal form and checking if these are identical.

1.3.5 Confluence and Termination Properties

We now present some properties of term rewriting systems R. Equivalently, these can be thought of as properties of the rewrite relation $\to_R$. For terms s and t, $s \downarrow t$ means that there is a term u such that $s \to^* u$ and $t \to^* u$. Also, $s \uparrow t$ means that there is a term r such that $r \to^* s$ and $r \to^* t$. R is said to be *confluent* if for all terms s and t, $s \uparrow t$ implies $s \downarrow t$. The meaning of this is that any two rewrite sequences from a given term, can always be "brought together". Sometimes one is also interested in *ground confluence*. R is said to be ground confluent if for all ground terms r, if $r \to^* s$ and $r \to^* t$ then $s \downarrow t$. Most research in term rewriting systems concentrates on confluent systems.

A term rewriting system R (alternatively, a rewrite relation $\to$) has the *Church–Rosser property* if for all terms s and t, $s \leftrightarrow^* t$ iff $s \downarrow t$.

Theorem 1.3.8. *(See [192].) A term rewriting system R has the Church–Rosser property iff R is confluent.*

Since $s \leftrightarrow^* t$ iff $s =_R t$, this theorem connects the equational theory of R with rewriting. In order to decide if $s =_R t$ for confluent R it is only necessary to see if s and t rewrite to a common term.

Two term rewriting systems are said to be *equivalent* if their associated equational theories are equivalent (have the same logical consequences).

Definition 1.3.9. *A term rewriting system is* terminating (*strongly normalizing*) *if it has no infinite rewrite sequences. Informally, this means that the rewriting process, applied to a term, will eventually stop, no matter how the rewrite rules are applied.*

One desires all rewrite sequences to stop in order to guarantee that no matter how the rewriting is done, it will eventually terminate. An example of a terminating system is $\{g(x) \to f(x), f(x) \to x\}$. The first rule changes g's to f's and so can only be applied as many times as there are g's. The second rule reduces the size and so it can only be applied as many times as the size of a term. An example of a nonterminating system is $\{x \to f(x)\}$. It can be difficult to determine if a system is terminating. The intuitive idea is that a system terminates if each rule makes a term simpler in some sense. However, the definition of simplicity is not always related to size. It can be that a term becomes simpler even if it becomes larger. In fact, it is not even partially decidable whether a term rewriting system is terminating [128]. Termination orderings are often used to prove that term rewriting systems are terminating. Recall the definition of termination ordering from Section 1.3.3.

Theorem 1.3.10. *Suppose R is a term rewriting system and $>$ is a termination ordering and for all rules $r \to s$ in R, $r > s$. Then R is terminating.*

This result can be extended to quasi-orderings, which are relations that are reflexive and transitive, but the above result should be enough to give an idea of the proof methods used. Many termination orderings are known; some will be discussed in Section 1.3.5. The orderings of interest are computable orderings, that is, it is decidable whether $r > s$ given terms r and s.

Note that if R is terminating, it is always possible to find a normal form of a term by any rewrite sequence continued long enough. However there can be more than one normal form. If R is terminating and confluent, there is exactly one normal form for every term. This gives a decision procedure for the equational theory, since for terms r and s, $r =_R s$ iff $r \leftrightarrow^*_R s$ (by Birkhoff's theorem) iff $r \downarrow s$ (by confluence) iff r and s have the same normal form (by termination). This gives us a directed form of theorem proving in such an equational theory. A term rewriting system which is both terminating and confluent is called *canonical*. Some authors use the term *convergent* for such systems [76]. Many such systems are known. Systems that are not terminating may still be *globally finite*, which means that for every term s there are finitely many terms t such that $s \to^* t$. For a discussion of global finiteness, see [105].

We have indicated how termination is shown; more will be presented in Section 1.3.5. However, we have not shown how to prove confluence. As stated, this looks like a difficult property. However, it turns out that if R is terminating, confluence is decidable, from Newman's lemma [192], given below. If R is not terminating, there are some methods that can still be used to prove confluence. This is interesting, even though in that case one does not get a decision procedure by rewriting to normal form, since it allows some flexibility in the rewriting procedure.

Definition 1.3.11. *A term rewriting system is* locally confluent (weakly confluent) *if for all terms r, s, and t, if $r \to s$ and $r \to t$ then $s \downarrow t$.*

Theorem 1.3.12 *(Newman's lemma). If R is locally confluent and terminating then R is confluent.*

It turns out that one can test whether R is locally confluent using *critical pairs* [144], so that local confluence is decidable for terminating systems. Also, if R is not locally confluent, it can sometimes be made so by computing critical pairs between rewrite rules in R and using these critical pairs to add new rewrite rules to R until the process stops. This process is known as *completion* and was introduced by Knuth and Bendix [144]. Completion can also be seen as adding equations to a set of rewrite rules by ordered paramodulation and demodulation, deleting new equations that are instances of existing ones or that are instances of $x = x$. These new equations are then oriented into rewrite rules and the process continues. This process may terminate with a finite canonical term rewriting system or it may continue forever. It may also fail by generating an equation that cannot be oriented into a rewrite rule. One can still use *ordered rewriting* on such equations so that they function much as a term rewriting system [61]. When completion does not terminate, and even if it fails, it is still possible to use a modified version of the completion procedure as a semidecision procedure for the associated equational theory using the so-called *unfailing completion* [14, 15] which in the limit produces a ground confluent term rewriting system. In fact, Huet proved earlier [126] that if the original completion procedure does not fail, it provides a semidecision procedure for the associated equational theory.

Termination orderings

We give techniques to show that a term rewriting system is terminating. These all make use of well founded partial orderings on terms having the property that if $s \to t$ then $s > t$. If such an ordering exists, then a rewriting system is terminating since infinite reduction sequences correspond to infinite descending sequences of terms in the ordering. Recall from Section 1.3.3 that a termination ordering is a well-founded ordering that has the full invariance and replacement properties.

The termination ordering based on size was discussed in Section 1.3.3. Unfortunately, this ordering is too weak to handle many interesting systems such as those containing the rule $x * (y + z) \to x * y + x * z$, since the right-hand side is bigger than the left-hand side and has more occurrences of x. This ordering can be modified to weigh different symbols differently; the definition of $\|s\|$ can be modified to be a weighted sum of the number of occurrences of the symbols. The ordering of Knuth and Bendix [144] is more refined and is able to show that systems containing the rule $(x * y) * z \to x * (y * z)$ terminate.

Another class of termination orderings are the polynomial orderings suggested by Lankford [149, 150]. For these, each function and constant symbol is interpreted as a polynomial with integer coefficients and terms are ordered by the functions associated with them.

The recursive path ordering was discussed in Section 1.3.3. In order to handle the associativity rule $(x * y) * z \to x * (y * z)$ it is necessary to modify the ordering so that subterms are considered lexicographically. This lexicographic treatment of subterms is the idea of the lexicographic path ordering of Kamin and Levy [136]. Using this ordering, one can prove the termination of Ackermann's function. There are also many orderings intermediate between the recursive path ordering and the lexicographic path ordering; these are known as orderings with "status". The idea of status is that for some function symbols, when $f(s_1 \ldots s_m)$ and $f(t_1 \ldots t_n)$ are compared, the subterms s_i and t_i are compared using the multiset ordering. For other function symbols, the subterms are compared using the lexicographic ordering. For other function symbols, the subterms are compared using the lexicographic ordering in reverse, that is, from right to left; this is equivalent to reversing the lists and then applying the lexicographic ordering. One can show that all such versions of the orderings are simplification orderings, for function symbols of bounded arity.

There are also many other orderings known that are similar to the above ones, such as the recursive decomposition ordering [132] and others; for some surveys see [75, 244]. In practice, *quasi-orderings* are often used to prove termination. A relation is a quasi-ordering if it is reflexive and transitive. A quasi-ordering is often written as $\geqslant$. Thus $x \geqslant x$ for all x, and if $x \geqslant y$ and $y \geqslant z$ then $x \geqslant z$. It is possible that $x \geqslant y$ and $y \geqslant x$ even if x and y are distinct; then one writes $x \approx y$ indicating that such x and y are in some sense "equivalent" in the ordering. One writes $x > y$ if $x \geqslant y$ but not $y \geqslant x$, for a quasi-ordering $\geqslant$. The relation $>$ is called the *strict part* of the quasi-ordering $\geqslant$. Note that the strict part of a quasi-ordering is a partial ordering. The multiset extension of a quasi-ordering is defined in a manner similar to the multiset extension of a partial ordering [131, 75].

Definition 1.3.13. *A quasi-ordering $\geqslant$ on terms satisfies the* replacement property (*is monotonic) if $s \geqslant t$ implies $f(\ldots s \ldots) \geqslant f(\ldots t \ldots)$. Note that it is possible to have $s > t$ and $f(\ldots s \ldots) \approx f(\ldots t \ldots)$.*

Definition 1.3.14. *A quasi-ordering $\geqslant$ is a* quasi-simplification ordering *if $f(\ldots t \ldots) \geqslant t$ for all terms and if $f(\ldots t \ldots) \geqslant f(\ldots \ldots) $ for all terms and all function symbols f of variable arity, and if the ordering satisfies the replacement property.*

Definition 1.3.15. *A quasi-ordering $\geqslant$ satisfies the* full invariance property (*see Section 1.3.5) if $s > t$ implies $s\Theta > t\Theta$ for all s, t, Θ.*

Theorem 1.3.16. (*See Dershowitz [74].*) *For terms over a finite set of function symbols, all quasi-simplification orderings have strict parts which are well founded.*

Proof. Using Kruskal's tree theorem [148]. □

Theorem 1.3.17. *Suppose R is a term rewriting system and $\geqslant$ is a quasi-simplification ordering which satisfies the full invariance property. Suppose that for all rules $l \rightarrow r$ in R, $l > r$. Then R is terminating.*

Actually, a version of the recursive path ordering adapted to quasi-orderings is known as the recursive path ordering in the literature. The idea is that terms that are identical up to permutation of arguments, are equivalent. There are a number of different orderings like the recursive path ordering.

Some decidability results about termination are known. In general, it is undecidable whether a system R is terminating [128]; however, for ground systems, that is, systems in which left and right-hand sides of rules are ground terms, termination is decidable [128]. For non-ground systems, termination of even one rule systems has been shown to be undecidable [63]. However, automatic tools have been developed that are very effective at either proving a system to be terminating or showing that it is not terminating, or finding an orientation of a set of equations that is terminating [120, 82, 145, 98]. In fact, one such system [145] from [91] was able to find an automatic proof of termination of a system for which the termination proof was the main result of a couple of published papers.

A number of relationships between termination orderings and large ordinals have been found; this is only natural since any well-founded ordering corresponds to some ordinal. It is interesting that the recursive path ordering and other orderings provide intuitive and useful descriptions of large ordinals. For a discussion of this, see [75] and [73].

There has also been some work on modular properties of termination; for example, if one knows that R_1 and R_2 terminate, what can be said about the termination of $R_1 \cup R_2$ under certain conditions? For a few examples of works along this line, see [258, 259, 182].

1.3.6 Equational Rewriting

There are two motivations for equational rewriting. The first is that some rules are nonterminating and cannot be used with a conventional term rewriting system. One example is the commutative axiom $x + y = y + x$ which is nonterminating no matter how it is oriented into a rewrite rule. The second reason is that if an operator like $+$ is associative and commutative then there are many equivalent ways to represent terms like $a + b + c + d$. This imposes a burden in storage and time on a theorem prover or term rewriting system. Equational rewriting permits us to treat some axioms, like $x + y = y + x$, in a special way, avoiding problems with termination. It also permits us to avoid explicitly representing many equivalent forms of a term. The cost is a more complicated rewriting relation, more difficult termination proofs, and a more complicated completion procedure. Indeed, significant developments are still occurring in these areas, to attempt to deal with the problems involved. In equational rewriting, some equations are converted into rewrite rules R and others are treated as equations E. Typically, rules that terminate are placed in R and rules for which termination is difficult are placed in E, especially if E unification algorithms are known.

The general idea is to consider E-equivalence classes of terms instead of single terms. The E-equivalence classes consist of terms that are provably equal under E. For example, if E includes associative and commutative axioms for $+$, then the terms $(a + b) + c, a + (b + c), c + (b + a)$, etc., will all be in the same E-equivalence class. Recall that $s =_E t$ if $E \models s = t$, that is, t can be obtained from s by replacing subterms using E. Note that $=_E$ is an equivalence relation. Usually some representation of the whole equivalence class is used; thus it is not necessary to store all the different terms in the class. This is a considerable savings in storage and time for term rewriting and theorem proving systems.

It is necessary to define a rewriting relation on E-equivalence classes of terms. If s is a term, let $[s]_E$ be its E-equivalence class, that is, the set of terms E-equivalent to s. The simplest approach is to say that $[s]_E \rightarrow [t]_E$ if $s \rightarrow t$. Retracting this back to individual terms, one writes $u \rightarrow_{R/E} v$ if there are terms s and t such that $u =_E s$ and $v =_E t$ and $s \rightarrow_R t$. This system R/E is called a *class rewriting system*. However, R/E rewriting turns out to be difficult to compute, since it requires searching through all terms E-equivalent to u. A computationally simpler idea is to say that $u \rightarrow v$ if u has a subterm s such that $s =_E s'$ and $s' \rightarrow_R t$ and v is u with s replaced by t. In this case one writes that $u \rightarrow_{R,E} v$. This system R, E is called the *extended rewrite system* for R modulo E. Note that rules with E-equivalent left-hand sides need not be kept. The R, E rewrite relation only requires using the equational theory on the chosen redex s instead of the whole term, to match s with the left-hand side of some rule. Such E-matching is often (but not always, see [116]) easy enough computationally to make R, E rewriting much more efficient than R/E rewriting. Unfortunately, $\rightarrow_{R/E}$ has better logical properties for deciding $R \cup E$ equivalence. So the theory of equational rewriting is largely concerned with finding connections between these two rewriting relations.

Consider the systems R/E and R, E where R is $\{a * b \rightarrow d\}$ and E consists of the associative and commutative axioms for $*$. Suppose s is $(a * c) * b$ and t is $c * d$. Then $s \rightarrow_{R/E} t$ since s is E-equivalent to $c * (a * b)$. However, it is not true that $s \rightarrow_{R,E} t$ since there is no subterm of s that is E-equivalent to $a * b$. Suppose s is $(b * a) * c$. Then $s \rightarrow_{R,E} d * c$ since $b * a$ is E-equivalent to $a * b$.

Note that if E equivalence classes are nontrivial then it is impossible for class rewriting to be confluent in the traditional sense (since any term E-equivalent to a normal form will also be a normal form of a term). So it is necessary to modify the definition to allow E-equivalent normal forms. We want to capture the property that class rewriting is confluent when considered as a rewrite relation on equivalence classes. More precisely, R/E is (*class*) *confluent* if for any term t, if $t \rightarrow^{*}_{R/E} u$ and $t \rightarrow^{*}_{R/E} v$ then there are E-equivalent terms u' and v' such that $u \rightarrow^{*}_{R/E} u'$ and $v \rightarrow^{*}_{R/E} v'$. This implies that R/E is confluent and hence Church–Rosser, considered as a rewrite relation on E-equivalence classes. If R/E is class confluent and terminating then a term may have more than one normal form, but all of them will be E-equivalent. Furthermore, if R/E is class confluent and terminating, then any $R^{=} \cup E$ equivalent terms can be reduced to E equivalent terms by rewriting. Then an E-equivalence procedure can be used to decide $R^{=} \cup E$ equivalence, if there is one. Note that E-equivalent rules need not both be kept, for this method.

R is said to be *Church–Rosser modulo E* if any two $R^{=} \cup E$-equivalent terms can be R, E rewritten to E-equivalent terms. This is not the same as saying that R/E is Church–Rosser, considered as a rewrite system on E-equivalence classes; in fact, it is a stronger property. Note that R, E rewriting is a subset of R/E rewriting, so if R/E is terminating, so is R, E. If R/E is terminating and R is Church–Rosser modulo E then R, E rewriting is also terminating and $R^{=} \cup E$-equality is decidable if E-equality is. Also, the computationally simpler R, E rewriting can be used to decide the equational theory. But Church–Rosser modulo E is not a local property; in fact it is undecidable in general. Therefore one desires decidable sufficient conditions for it. This is the contribution of Jouannaud and Kirchner [130], using confluence and "coherence". The idea of coherence is that there should be some similarity in the way all elements of an E-equivalence class rewrite. Their conditions involve critical pairs between rules and equations and E-unification procedures.

Another approach is to add new rules to R to obtain a logically equivalent system R'/E; that is, $R^{=} \cup E$ and $R'^{=} \cup E$ have the same logical consequences (i.e., they are equivalent), but R', E rewriting is the same as R/E rewriting. Therefore it is possible to use the computationally simpler R', E rewriting to decide the equality theory of R/E. This is done for associative–commutative operators by Peterson and Stickel [205]. In this case, confluence can be decided by methods simpler than those of Jouannaud and Kirchner. Termination for equational rewriting systems is tricky to decide; this will be discussed later. Another topic is completion for equational rewriting, adding rules to convert an equational rewriting system into a logically equivalent equational rewriting system with desired confluence properties. This is discussed by Peterson and Stickel [205] and also by Jouannaud and Kirchner [130]; for earlier work along this line see [151, 152].

AC rewriting

We now consider the special case of rewriting relative to the associative and commutative axioms $E = \{f(x, y) = f(y, x), f(f(x, y), z) = f(x, f(y, z))\}$ for a function symbol f. Special efficient methods exist for this case. One idea is to modify the term structure so that R, E rewriting can be used rather than R/E rewriting. This is done by *flattening*, that is a term $f(s_1, f(s_2, \ldots, f(s_{n-1}, s_n) \ldots))$, where none of the s_i have f as a top-level function symbol, is represented as $f(s_1, s_2, \ldots, s_n)$. Here f is a vary-adic symbol, which can take a variable number of arguments. Similarly, $f(f(s_1, s_2), s_3)$ is represented as $f(s_1, s_2, s_3)$. This represents all terms that are equivalent up to the associative equation $f(f(x, y), z) = f(x, f(y, z))$ by the same term. Also, terms that are equivalent up to permutation of arguments of f are also considered as identical. This means that each E-equivalence class is represented by a single term. This also means that all members of a given E-equivalence class have the same term structure, making R, E rewriting seem more of a possibility. Note however that the subterm structure has been changed; $f(s_1, s_2)$ is a subterm of $f(f(s_1, s_2), s_3)$ but there is no corresponding subterm of $f(s_1, s_2, s_3)$. This means that R, E rewriting does not simulate R/E rewriting on the original system. For example, consider the systems R/E and R, E where R is $\{a * b \rightarrow d\}$ and E consists of the associative and commutative axioms for $*$. Suppose s is $(a * b) * c$ and t is $d * c$. Then $s \rightarrow_{R/E} t$; in fact, $s \rightarrow_{R,E} t$. However, if one flattens the terms, then s becomes $*(a, b, c)$ and s no longer rewrites to t since the subterm $a * b$ has disappeared.

To overcome this, one adds *extensions* to rewrite rules to simulate their effect on flattened terms. The extension of the rule $\{a * b \rightarrow d\}$ is $\{*(x, a, b) \rightarrow *(x, d)\}$, where x is a new variable. With this extended rule, $*(a, b, c)$ rewrites to $d * c$. The general idea, then, is to flatten terms, and extend R by adding extensions of rewrite rules to it. Then, extended rewriting on flattened terms using the extended R is equivalent to class rewriting on the original R. Formally, suppose s and t are terms and s' and t' are their flattened forms. Suppose R is a term rewriting system and R' is R with the extensions added. Suppose E is associativity and commutativity. Then $s \rightarrow_{R/E} t$ iff $s' \rightarrow_{R',E} t'$. The extended R is obtained by adding, for each rule of the form $f(r_1, r_2, \ldots, r_n) \rightarrow s$ where f is associative and commutative, an extended rule of the form $f(x, r_1, r_2, \ldots, r_n) \rightarrow f(x, s)$, where x is a new variable. The original rule is also retained. This idea does not always work on other equational theories, however. Note that some kind of associative–commutative matching is needed for extended rewriting. This can be fairly expensive, since there are so many permutations to consider, but it is fairly straightforward to implement. Completion relative to associativity and commutativity can be done with the flattened representation; a method for this is given in [205]. This method requires associative–commutative unification (see Section 1.3.6).

Other sets of equations

The general topic of completion for other equational theories was addressed by Jouannaud and Kirchner in [130]. Earlier work along these lines was done by Lankford, as mentioned above. Such completion procedures may use E-unification. Also, they may distinguish rules with linear left-hand sides from other rules. (A term is *linear* if no variable appears more than once.)

AC termination orderings

We now consider termination orderings for special equational theories E. The problem is that E-equivalent terms are identified when doing equational rewriting, so that all E-equivalent terms have to be considered the same by the ordering. Equational rewriting causes considerable problems for the recursive path ordering and similar orderings. For example, consider the associative–commutative equations E. One can represent E-equivalence classes by flattened terms, as mentioned above. However, applying the recursive path ordering to such terms violates monotonicity. Suppose $* > +$ and $*$ is associative–commutative. Then $x*(y+z) > x*y+x*z$. By monotonicity, one should have $u*x*(y+z) > u*(x*y+x*z)$. In fact, this fails; the term on the right is larger in the recursive path ordering. A number of attempts have been made to overcome this. The first was the associative path ordering of Dershowitz, Hsiang, Josephson, and Plaisted [78], developed by the last author. This ordering applied to transformed terms, in which big operators like $*$ were pushed inside small operators like $+$. The ordering was not originally extended to non-ground terms, but it seems that it would be fairly simple to do so using the fact that a variable is smaller than any term properly containing it. A simpler approach to extending this ordering to non-ground terms was given later by Plaisted [209], and then further developed in Bachmair and Plaisted [12], but this requires certain conditions on the precedence. This work was generalized by Bachmair and Dershowitz [13] using the idea of "commutation" between two term rewriting systems. Later, Kapur [139] devised a fully general associative termination ordering that applies to non-ground terms, but may be hard to compute. Work in this area has continued since that time [146]. Another issue is the incorporation of status in such orderings, such as left-to-right, right-to-left, or multiset, for various function symbols. E-termination orderings for other equational theories may be even more complicated than for associativity and commutativity.

Congruence closure

Suppose one wants to determine whether $E \models s = t$ where E is a set (conjunction) of ground equations and s and t are ground terms. For example, one may want to decide whether $\{f^5(c) = c, f^3(c) = c\} \models f(c) = c$. This is a case in which rewriting techniques apply but another method is more efficient. The method is called *congruence closure* [191]; for some efficient implementations and data structures see [81]. The idea of congruence closure is essentially to use equality axioms, but restricted to terms that appear in E, including its subterms. For the above problem, the following is a derivation of $f(c) = c$, identifying equations $u = v$ and $v = u$:

1. $f^5(c) = c$ (given).

2. $f^3(c) = c$ (given).

3. $f^4(c) = f(c)$ (2, using equality replacement).

4. $f^5(c) = f^2(c)$ (3, using equality replacement).

5. $f^2(c) = c$ (1, 4, transitivity).

6. $f^3(c) = f(c)$ (5, using equality replacement).

7. $f(c) = c$ (2, 6, transitivity).

One can show that this approach is complete.

E-unification algorithms

When the set of axioms in a theorem to be proved includes a set E of equations, it is often better to use specialized methods than general theorem proving techniques. For example, if the binary infix operator $*$ is associative and commutative, many equivalent terms $x * (y * z)$, $y * (x * z)$, $y * (z * x)$, etc. may be generated. These cannot be eliminated by rewriting since none is simpler than the others. Even the idea of using unorderable equations as rewrite rules when the applied instance is orderable, will not help. One approach to this problem is to incorporate a general E-unification algorithm into the theorem prover. Plotkin [214] first discussed this general concept and showed its completeness in the context of theorem proving. With E unification built into a prover, only one representative of each E-equivalence class need be kept, significantly reducing the number of formulas retained. E-unification is also known as semantic unification, which may be a misnomer since no semantics (interpretation) is really involved. The general idea is that if E is a set of equations, an E-unifier of two terms s and t is a substitution Θ such that $E \models s\Theta = t\Theta$, and a most general E-unifier is an E-unifier that is as general as possible in a certain technical sense relative to the theory E. Many unification algorithms for various sets of equations have been developed [239, 9]. For some theories, there may be at most one most general E-unifier, and for others, there may be more than one, or even infinitely many, most general E-unifiers.

An important special case, already mentioned above in the context of term-rewriting, is associative–commutative (AC) unification. In this case, if two terms are E-unifiable, then there are at most finitely many most general E-unifiers, and there are algorithms to find them that are usually efficient in practice. The well-known algorithm of [251] essentially involves solving Diophantine equations and finding a basis for the set of solutions and finding combinations of basis vectors in which all variables are present. This can sometimes be very time consuming; the time to perform AC-unification can be double exponential in the sizes of the terms being unified [137]. Domenjoud [80] showed that the two terms $x + x + x + x$ and $y_1 + y_2 + y_3 + y_4$ have more than 34 billion different AC unifiers. Perhaps AC unification algorithm is artificially adding complexity to theorem proving, or perhaps the problem of theorem proving in the presence of AC axioms is really hard, and the difficulty of the AC unification simply reveals that. There may be ways of reducing the work involved in AC unification. For example, one might consider resource bounded AC unification, that is, finding all unifiers within some size bound. This might reduce the number of unifiers in cases where many of them are very large. Another idea is to consider "optional variables", that is, variables that may or may not be present. If x is not present in the product $x * y$ then this product is equivalent to y. This is essentially equivalent to introducing a new identity operator, and greatly reduces the number of AC unifiers. This approach has been studied by Domenjoud [79]. This permits one to represent a large number of solutions compactly, but requires one to keep track of optionality conditions.

Rule-based unification

Unification can be viewed as equation solving, and therefore is part of theorem proving or possibly logic programming. This approach to unification permits conceptual simplicity and also is convenient for theoretical investigations. For example, unifying two literals $P(s_1, s_2, \ldots, s_n)$ and $P(t_1, t_2, \ldots, t_n)$ can be viewed as solving the set of equations $\{s_1 = t_1, s_2 = t_2, \ldots, s_n = t_n\}$. Unification can be expressed as a collection of rules operating on such sets of equations to either obtain a most general unifier or detect non-unifiability. For example, one rule replaces an equation $f(u_1, u_2, \ldots, u_n) = f(v_1, v_2, \ldots, v_n)$ by the set of equations $\{u_1 = v_1, u_2 = v_2, \ldots, u_n = v_n\}$. Another rule detects non-unifiability if there is an equation of the form $f(\ldots) = g(\ldots)$ for distinct f and g. Another rule detects non-unifiability if there is an equation of the form $x = t$ where t is a term properly containing x. With a few more such rules, one can obtain a simple unification algorithm that will terminate with a set of equations representing a most general unifier. For example, the set of equations $\{x = f(a), y = g(f(a))\}$ would represent the substitution $\{x \leftarrow f(a), y \leftarrow g(f(a))\}$. This approach has also been extended to E-unification for various equational theories E. For a survey of this approach, see [133].

1.3.7 Other Logics

Up to now, we have considered theorem proving in general first-order logic. However, there are many more specialized logics for which more efficient methods exist. Such logics fix the domain of the interpretation, such as to the reals or integers, and also the interpretations of some of the symbols, such as "+" and "$*$". Examples of theories considered include Presburger arithmetic, the first-order theory of natural numbers with addition [200], Euclidean and non-Euclidean geometry [272, 55], inequalities involving real polynomials (for which Tarski first gave a decision procedure) [52], ground equalities and inequalities, for which congruence closure [191] is an efficient decision procedure, modal logic, temporal logic, and many more specialized logics. Theorem proving for ground formulas of first-order logic is also known as *satisfiability modulo theories* (SMT) in the literature. Description logics [8], discussed in Chapter 3 of this Handbook, are sublanguages of first-order logic, with extensions, that often have efficient decision procedures and have applications to the semantic web. Specialized logics are often built into provers or logic programming systems using *constraints* [33]. The idea of using constraints in theorem proving has been around for some time [143]. Another specialized area is that of computing polynomial ideals, for which efficient methods have been developed [44]. An approach to combining decision procedures was given in [190] and there has been continued interest in the combination of decision procedures since that time.

Higher-order logic

In addition to the logics mentioned above, there are more general logics to consider, including higher-order logics. Such logics permit quantification over functions and predicates, as well as variables. The HOL prover [101] uses higher-order logic and permits users to give considerable guidance in the search for a proof. Andrews' TPS prover is more automatic, and has obtained some impressive proofs fully automatically, including Cantor's theorem that the powerset of a set has more elements than the set. The TPS prover was greatly aided by a breadth-first method of instantiating matings described in [31]. In general, higher-order logic often permits a more natural formulation of a theorem than first-order logic, and shorter proofs, in addition to being more expressive. But of course the price is that the theorem prover is more complicated; in particular, higher-order unification is considerably more complex than first-order unification.

Mathematical induction

Without going to a full higher-order logic, one can still obtain a considerable increase in power by adding mathematical induction to a first-order prover. The mathematical induction schema is the following one:

$$\frac{\forall y[[\forall x((x < y) \to P(x))] \to P(y)]}{\forall y P(y)}.$$

Here $<$ is a well-founded ordering. Specializing this to the usual ordering on the integers, one obtains the following Peano induction schema:

$$\frac{P(0), \forall x(P(x) \to P(x+1))}{\forall x P(x)}.$$

With such inference rules, one can, for example, prove that addition and multiplication are associative and commutative, given their straightforward definitions. Both of these induction schemas are second-order, because the predicate P is implicitly universally quantified. The problem in using these schemas in an automatic theorem prover is in instantiating P. Once this is done, the induction schema can often be proved by first-order techniques. One way to adapt a first-order prover to perform mathematical induction, then, is simply to permit a human to instantiate P. The problem of instantiating P is similar to the problem of finding loop invariants for program verification.

By instantiating P is meant replacing $P(y)$ in the above formula by $A[y]$ for some first-order formula A containing the variable y. Equivalently, this means instantiating P to the function $\lambda z. A[z]$. When this is done, the first schema above becomes

$$\frac{\forall y[[\forall x((x < y) \to A[x])] \to A[y]]}{\forall y A[y]}.$$

Note that the hypothesis and conclusion are now first-order formulas. This instantiated induction schema can then be given to a first-order prover. One way to do this is to have the prover prove the formula $\forall y[[\forall x((x < y) \to A[x])] \to A[y]]$, and then conclude $\forall y A[y]$. Another approach is to add the first-order formula $\{\forall y[[\forall x((x < y) \to A[x])] \to A[y]]\} \to \{\forall y A[y]\}$ to the set of axioms. Both approaches are facilitated by using a structure-preserving translation of these formulas to clause form, in which the formula $A[y]$ is defined to be equivalent to $P(y)$ for a new predicate symbol P.

A number of semi-automatic techniques for finding such a formula A and choosing the ordering $<$ have been developed. One of them is the following: To prove that for all finite ground terms t, $A[t]$, first prove $A[c]$ for all constant symbols c, and then for each function symbol f of arity n prove that $A[t_1] \wedge A[t_2] \wedge \cdots \wedge A[t_n] \to A[f(t_1, t_2, \ldots, t_n)]$. This is known as *structural induction* and is often reasonably effective.

A common case when an induction proof may be necessary is when the prover is not able to prove the formula $\forall x A[x]$, but the formulas $A[t]$ are separately provable for all ground terms t. Analogously, it may not be possible to prove that $\forall x(\text{natural\_number}(x) \to A[x])$, but one may be able to prove $A[0]$, $A[1]$, $A[2]$, ... individually. In such a case, it is reasonable to try to prove $\forall x A[x]$ by induction, instantiating $P(x)$ in the above schema to $A[x]$. However, this still does not specify which ordering $<$ to use. For this, it can be useful to detect how long it takes to prove the $A[t]$ individually. For example, if the time to prove $A[n]$ for natural number n is proportional to n, then one may want to try the usual (size) ordering on natural numbers. If $A[n]$ is easy to prove for all even n but for odd n, the time is proportional to n, then one may try to prove the even case directly without induction and the odd case by induction, using the usual ordering on natural numbers.

The Boyer–Moore prover NqTHM [38, 36] has mathematical induction techniques built in, and many difficult proofs have been done on it, generally with substantial human guidance. For example, correctness of AMD Athlon's elementary floating point operations, and parts of IBM Power 5 and other processors have been proved on it. ACL2 [142, 141] is a software system built on Common Lisp related to NqTHM that is intended to be an industrial strength version of NqTHM, mainly for the purpose of software and hardware verification. Boyer, Kaufmann, and Moore won the ACM Software System Award in 2005 for these provers. A number of other provers also have automatic or semi-automatic induction proof techniques. Rippling [47] is a technique originally developed for mathematical induction but which also has applications to summing series and general equational reasoning. The *ground reducibility* property is also often used for induction proofs, and has applications to showing the completeness of algebraic specifications [134]. A term is *ground reducible* by a term rewriting system R if all its ground instances are reducible by R. This property was first shown decidable in [210], with another proof soon after in [138]. It was shown to be exponential time complete by Comon and Jacquemard [60]. However, closely related versions of this problem are undecidable. Recently Kapur and Subramaniam [140] described a class of inductive theorems for which validity is decidable, and this work was extended by Giesl and Kapur [97]. Bundy has written an excellent survey of inductive theorem proving [46] and the same handbook also has a survey of the so-called *inductionless induction* technique, which is based on completion of term-rewriting systems [59]; see also [127].

Set theory

Since most of mathematics can be expressed in terms of set theory, it is logical to develop theorem proving methods that apply directly to theorems expressed in set theory. Second-order provers do this implicitly. First-order provers can be used for set theory as well; Zermelo–Fraenkel set theory consists of an infinite set of first-order axioms, and so one again has the problem of instantiating the axiom schemas so that a first-order prover can be used. There is another version of set theory known as von Neumann–Bernays–Gödel set theory [37] which is already expressed in first-order logic. Quite a bit of work has been done on this version of set theory as applied to automated deduction problems. Unfortunately, this version of set theory is somewhat cumbersome for a human or for a machine. Still, some mathematicians have an interest in this approach. There are also a number of systems in which humans can construct proofs in set theory, such as Mizar [260] and others [26, 219]. In fact, there is an entire project (the QED project) devoted to computer-aided translation of mathematical proofs into completely formalized proofs [218].

It is interesting to note in this respect that many set theory proofs that are simple for a human are very hard for resolution and other clause-based theorem provers. This includes theorems about the associativity of union and intersection, for example. In this area, it seems worthwhile to incorporate more of the simple definitional replacement approach used by humans into clause-based theorem provers.

As an example of the problem, suppose that it is desired to prove that $\forall x((x \cap x) = x)$ from the axioms of set theory. A human would typically prove this by noting that $(x \cap x) = x$ is equivalent to $((x \cap x) \subseteq x) \wedge (x \subseteq (x \cap x))$, then observe that $A \subseteq B$ is equivalent to $\forall y((y \in A) \rightarrow (y \in B))$, and finally observe that $y \in (x \cap x)$ is equivalent to $(y \in x) \wedge (y \in x)$. After applying all of these equivalences to the original theorem, a human would observe that the result is a tautology, thus proving the theorem.

But for a resolution theorem prover, the situation is not so simple. The axioms needed for this proof are

$$(x = y) \leftrightarrow [(x \subseteq y) \wedge (y \subseteq x)],$$

$$(x \subseteq y) \leftrightarrow \forall z((z \in x) \rightarrow (z \in y)),$$

$$(z \in (x \cap y)) \leftrightarrow [(z \in x) \wedge (z \in y)].$$

When these are all translated into clause form and Skolemized, the intuition of replacing a formula by its definition gets lost in a mass of Skolem functions, and a resolution prover has a much harder time. This particular example may be easy enough for a resolution prover to obtain, but other examples that are easy for a human quickly become very difficult for a resolution theorem prover using the standard approach.

The problem is more general than set theory, and has to do with how definitions are treated by resolution theorem provers. One possible method to deal with this problem is to use "replacement rules" as described in [154]. This gives a considerable improvement in efficiency on many problems of this kind. Andrews' matings prover has a method of selectively instantiating definitions [32] that also helps on such problems in a higher-order context. The U-rules of OSHL also help significantly [184].

1.4 Applications of Automated Theorem Provers

Among theorem proving applications, we can distinguish between those applications that are truly automated, and those requiring some level of human intervention; between KR and non-KR applications; and between applications using classical first-order theorem provers and those that do not. In the latter category fall applications using theorem proving systems that do not support equality, or allow only restricted languages such as Horn clause logic, or supply inferential procedures beyond those of classical theorem proving.

These distinctions are not independent. In general, applications requiring human intervention have been only slightly used for KR; moreover, KR applications are more likely to use a restricted language, or to use special-purpose inferential procedures.

It should be noted that any theorem proving system that can solve the math problems that form a substantial part of the TPTP (Thousands of Problems for Theorem Provers) testbed [255] must be a classical first-order theorem prover that supports equality.

1.4.1 Applications Involving Human Intervention

Because theorem proving is in general intractable, the majority of applications of automated theorem provers require direction from human users in order to work. The intervention required can be extensive, e.g., the user may be required to supply lemmas to the proofs on which the automated theorem prover is working [84]. In the worst case, a user may be required to supply every step of a proof to an automated theorem prover; in this case, the automated theorem prover is functioning simply as a proof checker.

The need for human intervention has often limited the applicability of automated theorem provers to applications where reasoning can be done offline; that is, where the reasoner is not used as part of a real-time application. Even given this restriction, automated theorem provers have proved very valuable in a number of domains, including software development and verification of software and hardware.

Software development

An example of an application to software development is the Amphion system, which was developed by Stickel et al. [250] and uses the SNARK theorem prover [249]. It has been used by NASA to compose programs out of a library of FORTRAN-77 subroutines. The user of Amphion, who does not have to have any familiarity with either theorem proving or the library subroutines, gives a graphical specification; this specification is translated into a theorem of first-order logic; and SNARK provides a constructive proof of this theorem. This constructive proof is then translated into the application program in FORTRAN-77.

The NORA/HAMMR system [86] similarly determines what software components can be reused during program development. Each software component is associated with a *contract* written in a formal language which captures the essentials of the component's behavior. The system determines whether candidate components have compatible contracts and are thus potentially reusable; the proof of compatibility is carried out using an automated theorem prover, though with a fair amount of human guidance. Automated theorem provers used for NORA/HAMMR include Setheo [158], Spass [268, 269], and PROTEIN [24], a theorem prover based on Mark Stickel's PTTP [246, 248].

In the area of algorithm design and program analysis and optimization, KIDS (Kestrel Interactive Development System) [241] is a program derivation system that uses automated theorem proving technology to facilitate the derivation of programs from high-level program specifications. The program specification is viewed as a goal, and rules of transformational development are viewed as axioms of the system. The system, guided by the user, searches to find the appropriate transformational rules, the application of which leads to the final program. Both Amphion and KIDS require relatively little intervention from the user once the initial specification is made; KIDS, for example, requires active interaction only for the algorithm design tactic.

Hardware and software verification

Formal verification of both hardware and software has been a particularly fruitful application of automated theorem provers. The need for verification of program correctness had been noted as far back as the early 1960s by McCarthy [172], who suggested approaching the problem by stating a theorem that a program had certain properties—and in particular, computed certain functions—and then using an automated theorem prover to prove this theorem. Verification of cryptographic protocols is another important subfield of this area.

The field of hardware verification can be traced back to the design of the first hardware description languages, e.g., ISP [27], and became active in the 1970s and 1980s, with the advent of VLSI design. (See, e.g, [22].) It gained further prominence after the discovery in 1994 [108] of the Pentium FDIV bug, a bug in the floating point unit of Pentium processors. It was caused by missing lookup table entries and led to incorrect results for some floating point division operators. The error was widespread, well-publicized, and costly to Intel, Pentium's manufacturer, since it was obliged to offer to replace all affected Pentium processors.

General-purpose automated theorem provers that have been commonly used for hardware and/or software verification include the following:

- The Boyer–Moore theorem provers NqTHM and ACL2 [36, 142] were inspired by McCarthy's first papers on the topic of verifying program correctness. As mentioned in the previous section, these award-winning theorem provers have been used for many verification applications.

- The Isabelle theorem prover [203, 197] can handle higher-order logics and temporal logics. Isabelle is thus especially well-suited for cases where program specifications are written in temporal or dynamic logic (as is frequently the case). It has also been used for verification of cryptographic protocols [242], which are frequently written in higher order and/or epistemic logics [49].

- OTTER has been used for a system that analyzes and detects attacks on security APIs (application programming interfaces) [273].

Special-purpose verification systems which build verification techniques on top of a theorem prover include the following:

- The PVS system [201] has been used by NASA's SPIDER (Scalable Processor-Independent Design for Enhanced Reliability) to verify SPIDER protocols [206].

- The KIV (Karlsruhe Interactive Verifier) has been used for a range of software verification applications, including validation of knowledge-based systems [84].

The underlying approach is similar to that of the KIDS and Amphion projects in that first, the user is required to enter a specification; second, the user is entering a specification of a modularized system, and the interactions between the modules; and third, the user works with the system to construct a proof of validity. More interaction between the user and the theorem prover seems to be required in this case, perhaps due to the increased complexity of the problem. KIV offers a number of techniques to reduce the burden on the user, including reuse of proofs and the generation of counterexamples.

1.4.2 Non-Interactive KR Applications of Automated Theorem Provers

McCarthy argued [171] for an AI system consisting of a set of axioms and an automated theorem prover to reason with those axioms. The first implementation of this vision came in the late 1960s with Cordell Green's question-answering system QA3 and planning system [103, 104]. Given a set of facts and a question, Green's question-answering system worked by resolving the (negated) question against the set of facts. Green's planning system used resolution theorem proving on a set of axioms representing facts about the world in order to make simple inferences about moving blocks in a simple blocks-world domain. In the late 1960s and early 1970s, SRI's Shakey project [195] attempted to use the planning system STRIPS [85] for robot motion planning; automated theorem proving was used to determine applicability of operators and differences between states [232]. The difficulties posed by the intractability of theorem proving became evident. (Shakey also faced other problems, including dealing with noisy sensors and incomplete knowledge. Moreover, the Shakey project does not actually count as a non-interactive application of automated theorem proving, since people could obviously change Shakey's environment while it acted. Nonetheless, projects like these underscored the importance of dealing effectively with theorem proving's essential intractability.)

In fact, there are today many fewer non-interactive than interactive applications of theorem proving, due to its computational complexity. Moreover, non-interactive applications will generally use carefully crafted heuristics that are tailored and fine-tuned to a particular domain or application. Without such heuristics, the theorem-proving program would not be able to handle the huge number of clauses generated. Finally, as mentioned above, non-interactive applications often use ATPs that are not general theorem provers with complete proof procedures. This is because completeness and generality often come at the price of efficiency.

Some of the most successful non-interactive ATP applications are based on two theorem provers developed by Mark Stickel at SRI, PTTP [246, 248] and SNARK [249]. PTTP attempts to retain as much as possible the efficiency of Prolog (see Section 1.4.4 below) while it remedies the ways in which Prolog fails as a general-purpose theorem prover, namely, its unsound unification algorithm, its incomplete search strategy, and its incomplete inference system. PTTP was used in SRI's TACITUS system [121, 124], a message understanding system for reports on equipment failure, naval operations, and terrorist activities. PTTP was used specifically to furnish minimal-cost abductive explanations. It is frequently necessary to perform abduction—that is, to posit a likely explanation—when processing text. For example, to understand the sentence "The Boston office called", one must understand that the construct of metonymy (the use of a single characteristic to identify an entity of which it is an attribute) is being used, and that what is meant is *a person in the office* called. Thus, to understand the sentence we must posit an explanation of a person being in the office and making that call.

There are usually many possible explanations that can be posited for any particular phenomenon; thus, the problem arises of choosing the simplest non-trivial explanation. (One would not, for example, wish to posit an explanation consistent with an office actually being able to make a call.) TACITUS considers explanations of the form $P(a)$, where $\forall x P(x) \rightarrow Q(x)$ and $Q(a)$ are in the theory, and chooses the explanation that has minimal cost [247]. Every conjunct in the logical form of a sentence is given an assumability cost; this cost is passed back to antecedents in the Horn clause. Because of the way costs are propagated, the cost may be partly dependent on the length of the proofs of the literals in the explanation.

PTTP was also used in a central component of Stanford's Logic-Based Subsumption Architecture for robot control [1], which was used to program a Nomad-200 robot to travel to different rooms in a multi-story building. The system employed a multi-layered architecture; in each layer, PTTP was used to prove theorems from the given axioms. Goals were transmitted to layers below or to robot manipulators.

PTTP is fully automated; the user has no control over the search for solutions. In particular, each rule is used in its original form and in its contrapositive. In certain situations, such as stating principles about substituting equals, reasoning with a contrapositive form can lead to considerable inefficiency.

Stickel's successor theorem prover to PTTP, SNARK [249], gives users this control. It is more closely patterned after Otter; difficult theorems that are intractable for PTTP can be handled by SNARK. It was used as the reasoning component for SRI's participation in DARPA's High-Performance Knowledge Bases (HPKB) Project [58], which focused on constructing large knowledge bases in the domain of crisis management; and developing question-answering systems for querying these knowledge bases. SNARK was used primarily in SRI's question-answering portion of that system. SNARK, in contrast to what would have been possible with PTTP, allowed users to fine tune the question-answering system for HPKB, by crafting an ordering of predicates and clauses on which resolution would be performed. This ordering could be modified as the knowledge base was altered. Such strategies were necessary to get SNARK to work effectively given the large size of the HPKB knowledge base.

For its use in the HPKB project, SNARK had to be extended to handle temporal reasoning.

SNARK has also been used for consistency checking of semantic web ontologies [20].

Other general-purpose theorem provers have also been used for natural language applications, though on a smaller scale and for less mature applications. Otter has been used in PENG (Processable English) [236], a controlled natural language used for writing precise specifications. Specifications in PENG can be translated into first-order logic; Otter is then used to draw conclusions. As discussed in detail in Chapter 20, Bos and Markert [35] have used Vampire (as well as the Paradox model finder) to determine whether a hypothesis is entailed by some text.

The Cyc artificial intelligence project [157, 156, 169] is another widespread application of non-interactive automated theorem proving. The ultimate goal of Cyc is the development of a comprehensive, encyclopedic knowledge base of commonsense facts, along with inference mechanisms for reasoning with that knowledge. Cyc contains an ontology giving taxonomic information about commonsense concepts, as well as assertions about the concepts.

Cyc's underlying language, CycL, allows expression of various constructs that go beyond first-order logic. Examples include:

- The concept of contexts [50]: one can state that something is true in a particular context as opposed to absolutely. (E.g., the statement that vampires are afraid of garlic is true in a mythological context, though not in real life.)

- Higher-order concepts. (E.g., one can state that if a relation is reflexive, symmetric, and transitive, it is an equivalence relation.)

- Exceptions. (E.g., one can say that except for Taiwan, all Chinese provinces are part of the People's Republic of China.)

The Cyc knowledge base is huge. Nevertheless, it has been successfully used in real-world applications, including HPKB. (Cyc currently has over 3 million assertions; at the time of its use in HPKB, it had over a million assertions.) Theorem proving in Cyc is incomplete but efficient, partly due to various special-purpose mechanisms for reasoning with its higher-order constructs. For example, Cyc's reasoner includes a special module for solving *disjointWith* queries that traverses the taxonomies in the knowledge base to determine whether two classes have an empty intersection.

Ramachandran et al. [221, 220] compared the performance of Cyc's reasoner with standard theorem provers. First, most of ResearchCyc's knowledge base[4] was translated into first-order logic. The translated sentences were then loaded into various theorem provers, namely, Vampire, E [235], Spass, and Otter. The installations of Vampire and Spass available to Ramachandran et al. did not have sufficient memory to load all assertions, necessitating performing the comparison of Cyc with these theorem provers on just 10 percent of ResearchCyc's knowledge base. On sample queries—e.g., "Babies can't be doctors", "If the U.S. bombs Iraq, someone is responsible", –Cyc proved to be considerably more efficient. For example, for the query about babies and doctors, Cyc took 0.04 seconds to answer the query, while Vampire took 847.6 seconds.

Ramachandran and his colleagues conjecture that the disparity in performance partly reflects the fact that Cyc's reasoner and the standard theorem provers have been designed for different sets of problems. General automated theorem provers have been designed to perform deep inference on small sets of axioms. If one looks at the problems in the TPTP database, they often have just a few dozen and rarely have more than a few hundred axioms. Cyc's reasoner, on the other hand, has been designed to perform relatively shallow inference on large sets of axioms.

It is also worth noting that the greatest disparity of inference time between Cyc and the other theorem provers occurred when Cyc was using a special purpose reasoning module. In that sense, of course, purists might argue that Cyc is not really doing

---

[4]ResearchCyc [169] contains the knowledge base open to the public for research; certain portions of Cyc itself are not open to the public. The knowledge base of ResearchCyc contains over a million assertions.

theorem proving faster than standard ATPs; rather, it is doing something that is functionally equivalent to theorem proving while ATPs are doing theorem proving, and it is doing that something much faster.

1.4.3 Exploiting Structure

Knowledge bases for real-world applications and commonsense reasoning often exhibit a modular-like structure, containing multiple sets of facts with relatively little connection to one another. For example, a knowledge base in the banking domain might contain sets of facts concerning loans, checking accounts, and investment instruments; moreover, these sets of facts might have little overlap with one another. In such a situation, reasoning would primarily take place within a module, rather than between modules. Reasoning between modules would take place—for example, one might want to reason about using automated payments from a checking account to pay off installments on a loan—but would be limited. One would expect that a theorem prover that takes advantage of this modularity would be more efficient: most of the time, it would be doing searches in reduced spaces, and it would produce fewer irrelevant resolvents.

A recent trend in automated reasoning focuses on exploiting structure of a knowledge base to improve performance. This section presents a detailed example of such an approach. Amir and McIlraith [2] have studied the ways in which a knowledge base can be automatically partitioned into loosely coupled clusters of domain knowledge, forming a network of subtheories. The subtheories in the network are linked via the literals they share in common. Inference is carried out within a subtheory; if a literal is inferred within one subtheory that links to another subtheory, it may be passed from the first to the second subtheory.

Consider, from [2], the following theory specifying the workings of an espresso machine, and the preparation of espresso and tea: (Note that while this example is propositional, the theory is first-order.)

(1) $\neg$ okpump $\vee\neg$ onpump $\vee$ water

(2) $\neg$ manfill $\vee$ water

(3) $\neg$ manfill $\vee\neg$ onpump

(4) manfill $\vee$ onpump

(5) $\neg$ water $\vee\neg$ okboiler $\vee\neg$ onboiler $\vee$ steam

(6) water $\vee\neg$ steam

(7) okboiler $\vee\neg$ steam

(8) onboiler $\vee\neg$ steam

(9) $\neg$ steam $\vee\neg$ cofee $\vee$ hotdrink

(10) coffee $\vee$ teabag

(11) $\neg$ steam $\vee\neg$ teabag $\vee$ hotdrink

Intuitively, this theory can be decomposed into three subtheories. The first, *A1*, containing axioms 1 through 4, regards water in the machine; it specifies the relations between manually filling the machine with water, having a working pump, and having water in the machine. The second, *A2*, containing axioms 5 through 8, regards getting steam; it specifies the relations between having water, a working boiler, the boiler switch turned on, and steam. The third, *A3*, containing axioms 9 through 11, regards getting a hot drink; it specifies the relation between having steam, having coffee, having a teabag, and having a hot drink.

In this partitioning, the literal *water* links *A1* and *A2*; the literal *steam* links *A2* and *A3*. One can reason with logical partitions using forward message-passing of linking literals. If one asserts *okpump*, and performs resolution on the clauses of *A1*, one obtains *water*. If one asserts *okboiler* and *onboiler* in *A2*, passes *water* from *A1* to *A2*, and performs resolution in *A2*, one obtains *steam*. If one passes *steam* to *A3* and performs resolution in *A3*, one obtains *hotdrink*.

In general, the complexity of this sort of reasoning depends on the number of partitions, the size of the partitions, the interconnectedness of the subtheory graph, and the number of literals linking subtheories. When partitioning the knowledge base, one wants to minimize these parameters to the extent possible. (Note that one cannot simultaneously minimize all parameters; as the number of partitions goes down, the size of at least some of the partitions goes up.)

McIlraith et al. [165] did some empirical studies on large parts of the Cyc database used for HPKB, comparing the results of the SNARK theorem prover with and without this partitioning strategy. SNARK plus (automatically-performed) partitioning performed considerably better than SNARK with no strategy, though it was comparable to SNARK plus set-of-support strategies. When partitioning was paired with another strategy like set-of-support, it outperformed combinations of strategies without partitioning.

Clustering to improve reasoning performance has also been explored by Hayes et al. [115]. In a similar spirit, there has been growing interest in modularization of ontologies from the Description Logic and Semantic Web communities [267, 223, 102]. Researchers have been investigating how such modularization affects the efficiency of reasoning (i.e., performing subsumption and classification, and performing consistency checks) over the ontologies.

1.4.4 Prolog

In terms of its use in working applications, the logic programming paradigm [147] represents an important success in automated theorem proving. Its main advantage is its efficiency; this makes it suitable for real-world applications. The most popular language for logic programming is Prolog [41].

What makes Prolog work so efficiently is a combination of the restricted form of first-order logic used, and the particular resolution and search strategies that are implemented. In the simplest case, a Prolog program consists of a set of Horn clauses; that is, either atomic formulas or implications of the form $(P_1 \wedge P_2 \wedge \cdots) \rightarrow P_0$, where the P_i's are all atomic formulas. This translates into having at most one literal in the consequence of any implication. The resolution strategy used is linear-input resolution: that is, for each resolvent, one of the parents is either in the initial database or is an ancestor of the other parent. The search strategy used is backward-chaining; the reasoner backchains from the query or goal, against the sentences in the logic program.

The following are also true in the logic programming paradigm: there is a form of negation that is interpreted as negation-as-failure: that is, *not a* will be taken to be true if *a* cannot be proven; and the result of a logic program can depend on the ordering of its clauses and subgoals. Prolog implementations provide additional control mechanisms, including the cut and fail operators; the result is that few programs in Prolog are pure realizations of the declarative paradigm. Prolog also has an incomplete mechanism for unification, particularly of arithmetic expressions.

Prolog has been widely used in developing expert systems, especially in Europe and Japan, although languages such as Java and C++ have become more popular.

Examples of successful practical applications of logic programming include the HAPPS system for model house configuration [83] and the Munich Rent Advisor [90], which calculates the estimated fair rent for an apartment. (This is a rather complex operation that can take days to do by hand.) There has been special interest in the last decade on world-wide web applications of logic programming (see *Theory and Practice of Logic Programming*, vol. 1, no. 3).

What are the drawbacks to Prolog? Why is there continued interest in the significantly less efficient general theorem provers?

First, the restriction to Horn clause form is rather severe; one may not be able to express knowledge crucial for one's application. An implication whose conclusion is a disjunction is not expressible in Horn clause form. This means, for example, that one cannot represent a rule like

> *If you are diagnosed with high-blood pressure, you will either have to reduce your salt intake or take medication*

because that is most naturally represented as an implication with a disjunction in the consequent.

Second, Prolog's depth-first-search strategy is incomplete.

Third, because, in most current Prolog implementations, the results of a Prolog program depend crucially on the ordering of its clauses, and because it is difficult to predict how the negation-as-failure mechanism will interact with one's knowledge base and goal query, it may be difficult to predict a program's output.

Fourth, since Prolog does not support inference with equality, it cannot be used for mathematical theorem proving.

There has been interest in the logic programming community in addressing limitations or perceived drawbacks of Prolog. Disjunctive logic programming [6] allows clauses with a disjunction of literals in the consequent of a rule. Franconi et al. [88] discusses one application of disjunctive logic programming, the implementation of a clean-up procedure prior to processing census data.

The fact that logic programs may have unclear or ambiguous semantics has concerned researchers for decades. This has led to the development of answer set programming, discussed in detail in Chapter 7, in which logic programs are interpreted with the stable model semantics. Answer set programming has been used for many applications, including question answering, computational biology, and system validation.

1.5 Suitability of Logic for Knowledge Representation

The central tenet of logicist AI[5]—that knowledge is best represented using formal logic—has been debated as long as the field of knowledge representation has existed. Among logicist AI's strong advocates are John McCarthy [171, 175], Patrick Hayes [112, 114, 111], and Robert Moore [186]; critics of the logicist approach have included Yehoshua Bar-Hillel [21], Marvin Minsky [185], Drew McDermott [180], and Rodney Brooks [42]. (McDermott can be counted in both the logicist and anti-logicist camps, having advocated for and contributed to logicist AI [178, 181, 179] before losing faith in the enterprise.)

The crux of the debate is simply this: Logicists believe that first-order logic, along with its modifications, is a language particularly well suited to capture reasoning, due to its expressivity, its model-theoretic semantics, and its inferential power. Note [112] that it is not a particular syntax for which logicists argue; it is the notion of a formal, declarative semantics and methods of inference that are important. (See [95, 64, 233, 39] for examples of how AI logicism is used.) Anti-logicists have argued that the program, outside of textbook examples, is undesirable and infeasible. To paraphrase McDermott [180], You Don't Want To Do It, and You Can't Do It Anyway.

This handbook clearly approaches AI from a logicist point of view. It is nevertheless worthwhile examining the debate in detail. For it has not consisted merely of an ongoing sequence of arguments for and against a particular research approach. Rather, the arguments of the anti-logicists have proved quite beneficial for the logicist agenda. The critiques have often been recognized as valid within the logicist community; researchers have applied themselves to solving the underlying difficulties; and in the process have frequently founded productive subfields of logicist AI, such as nonmonotonic reasoning. Examining the debate puts into context the research in knowledge representation that is discussed in this Handbook.

1.5.1 Anti-logicist Arguments and Responses

In the nearly fifty years since McCarthy's Advice Taker paper first appeared [171], the criticisms against the logicist approach have been remarkably stable. Most of the arguments can be characterized under the following categories:

- Deductive reasoning is not enough.

- Deductive reasoning is too expensive.

- Writing down all the knowledge (the right way) is infeasible.

- Other approaches do it better and/or cheaper.

The argument: Deductive reasoning is not enough

McCarthy's original logicist proposal called for the formalization of a set of common-sense facts in first-order logic, along with an automated theorem prover to reason with

---

[5]The term *logicism* generally refers to the school of thought that mathematics can be reduced to logic [270], *logicists* to the proponents of logicism. Within the artificial intelligence community, however, a *logicist* refers to a proponent of logicist AI, as defined in this section [257].

those facts. He gave as an example the reasoning task of planning to get to the airport. McCarthy argued that starting out from facts about first, the location of oneself, one's car, and the airport; second, how these locations relate to one another; third, the feasibility of certain actions, such as walking and driving; fourth, the effects that actions had; and fifth, basic planning constructs, one could deduce that to get to the airport, one should walk to one's car and drive the car to the airport. There were, all together, just 15 axioms in this draft formalization.

Bar-Hillel argued:

> It sounds rather incredible that the machine could have arrived at its conclusion—which, in plain English, is "Walk from your desk to your car!"— by sound deduction! This conclusion surely could not possibly follow from the premise in any serious sense. Might it not be occasionally cheaper to call a taxi and have it take you over to the airport? Couldn't you decide to cancel your flight or to do a hundred other things?

The need for nonmonotonic reasoning

In part, Bar-Hillel was alluding to the many exceptions that could exist in any realistically complex situation. Indeed, it soon became apparent to AI researchers that exceptions exist for even simple situations and facts. The classic example is that of reasoning that a bird can fly. Birds typically can fly, although there are exceptions, such as penguins and birds whose wings are broken. If one wants to formalize a theory of bird flying, one cannot simply write

$$\forall x (Bird(x) \rightarrow Flies(x)) \tag{1.17}$$

because that would mean that all birds fly. That would be wrong, because it does not take penguins and broken-winged birds into account. One could instead write

$$\forall x (Bird(x) \land \neg Penguin(x) \land \neg Brokenwinged(x) \rightarrow Flies(x)) \tag{1.18}$$

which says that all birds fly, as long as they are not penguins or broken-winged, or better yet, from the representational point of view, the following three formulas:

$$\forall x (Bird(x) \land \neg Ab(x) \rightarrow Flies(x)), \tag{1.19}$$

$$\forall x (Penguin(x) \rightarrow Ab(x)), \tag{1.20}$$

$$\forall x (Brokenwinged(x) \rightarrow Ab(x)) \tag{1.21}$$

which say that birds fly unless they are abnormal, and that penguins and broken-winged birds are abnormal.

A formula in the style of (1.18) is difficult to write, since one needs to state all possible exceptions to bird flying in order to have a correct axiom. But even aside from the representational difficulties, there is a serious inferential problem. If one only knows that Tweety is a bird, one cannot use axiom (1.18) in a deductive proof. One needs to know as well that the second and third conjuncts on the left-hand side of the implication are true: that is, that Tweety is not a penguin and is not broken-winged. Something stronger than deduction is needed here; something that permits jumping to the conclusion that Tweety flies from the fact that Tweety is a bird and the absence of any knowledge that would contradict this conclusion. This sort of default reasoning would be *nonmonotonic* in the set of axioms: adding further information (e.g., that Tweety is a penguin) could mean that one has to retract conclusions (that is, that Tweety flies).

The need for nonmonotonic reasoning was noted, as well, by Minsky [185]. At the time Minsky wrote his critique, early work on nonmonotonicity had already begun. Several years later, most of the major formal approaches to nonmonotonic reasoning had already been mapped out [173, 224, 181]. This validated both the logicist AI approach, since it demonstrated that formal systems could be used for default reasoning, and the anti-logicists, who had from the first argued that first-order logic was too weak for many reasoning tasks.

Nonmonotonicity and the anti-logicists

From the time they were first developed, nonmonotonic logics were seen as an essential logicist tool. It was expected that default reasoning would help deal with many KR difficulties, such as the frame problem, the problem of efficiently determining which things remain the same in a changing world. However, it turned out to be surprisingly difficult to develop nonmonotonic theories that entailed the expected conclusions. To solve the frame problem, for example, one needs to formalize the *principle of inertia*—that properties tend to persist over time. However, a naive formalization of this principle along the lines of [174] leads to the *multiple extension* problem; a phenomenon in which the theory supports several models, some of which are unintuitive. Hanks and McDermott [110] demonstrated a particular example of this, the Yale shooting problem. They wrote up a simple nonmonotonic theory containing some general facts about actions (that loading a gun causes the gun to be loaded, and that shooting a loaded gun at someone causes that individual to die), the principle of inertia, and a particular narrative (that a gun is loaded at one time, and shot at an individual a short time after). The expected conclusion, that the individual will die, did not hold. Instead, Hanks and McDermott got multiple extensions: the expected extension, in which the individual dies; and an unexpected extension, in which the individual survives, but the gun mysteriously becomes unloaded. The difficulty is that the principle of inertia can apply either to the gun remaining loaded or the individual remaining alive. Intuitively we expect the principle to be applied to the gun remaining loaded; however, there was nothing in Hank's and McDermott's theory to enforce that.

The Yale shooting problem was not hard to handle: solutions began appearing shortly after the problem became known. (See [160, 161, 238] for some early solutions.) Nonetheless, the fact that nonmonotonic logics could lead to unexpected conclusions for such simple problems was evidence to anti-logicists of the infeasibility of logicist AI. Indeed, it led McDermott to abandon logicist AI. Nonmonotonic logic was essentially useless, McDermott argued [180], claiming that it required one to know beforehand what conclusions one wanted to draw from a set of axioms, and to build that conclusion into the premises.

In contrast, what logicist AI learned from the Yale shooting problem was the importance of a good underlying representation. The difficulty with Hanks and McDermott's axiomatization was not that it was written in a nonmonotonic logic; it was that it was devoid of a concept of causation. The Yale shooting problem does not arise in an axiomatization based on a sound theory of causation [243, 187, 237].

From today's perspective, the Yale shooting scenario is rather trivial. Over the last ten years, research related to the frame problem has concentrated on more elaborate kinds of action domains—those that include actions with indirect effects, nondeterministic actions, and interacting concurrently executed actions. Efficient implementations of such advanced forms of nonmonotonic reasoning have been used in serious industrial applications, such as the design of a decision support system for the Space Shuttle [198].

The current state of research on nonmonotonic reasoning and the frame problem is described in Chapters 6, 7, and 16–20 of this Handbook.

The need for abduction and induction

Anti-logicists have pointed out that not all commonsense reasoning is deductive. Two important examples of non-deductive reasoning are *abduction*, explaining the cause of a phenomenon, and *induction*, reasoning from specific instances of a class to the entire class. Abduction, in particular, is important for both expert and commonsense reasoning. Diagnosis is a form of abduction; understanding natural language requires abduction as well [122].

Some philosophers of science [215, 117, 118] have suggested that abduction can be grounded in deduction. The idea is to hypothesize or guess an explanation for a particular phenomenon, and then try to justify this guess using deduction. A well-known example of this approach is known as the deductive-nomological hypothesis.

McDermott [180] has argued against such attempts, pointing out what has been noted by philosophers of science [234]: the approach is overly simplistic, can justify trivial explanations, and can support multiple explanations without offering a way of choosing among candidates. But he was tilting at a straw man. In fact, the small part of logicist AI that has focused on abduction has been considerably more sophisticated in its approach. As discussed in the previous section, Hobbs, Stickel, and others have used theorem proving technology to support abductive reasoning [247, 122], but they do it by carefully examining the structure of the generated proofs, and the particular context in which the explanandum occurs. There is a deliberate and considered approach toward choosing among multiple explanations and toward filtering out trivial explanations.

There is also growing interest in *inductive logic programming* [189]. This field uses machine learning techniques to construct a logic program that entails all the positive and none of the negative examples of a given set of examples.

The argument: Deductive reasoning is too expensive

> The decisive question [is] how a machine, even assuming it will have somehow countless millions of facts stored in its memory, will be able to pick out those facts which will serve as premises for its deduction.
>
> *Yehoshua Bar-Hillel [21]*

When McCarthy first presented his Advice Taker paper and Bar-Hillel made the above remark, automated theorem proving technology was in its infancy: resolution theorem proving was still several years away from being invented. But even with relatively advanced theorem proving techniques, Bar-Hillel's point remains. General automated theorem proving programs frequently cannot handle theories with several hundred axioms, let alone several million.

This point has in fact shaped much of the AI logicist research agenda. The research has progressed along several fronts. There has been a large effort to make general theorem proving more efficient (this is discussed at length in Section 1.3); special-purpose reasoning techniques have been developed, e.g., by the description logic community [11] as well as by Cyc (see Section 1.4.2) to determine subsumption and disjointness of classes; and logic programming techniques (for both Prolog (see Section 1.4.4) and answer set programming (see Chapter 7)) have been developed so that relatively efficient inferences can be carried out under certain restricted assumptions. The HPKB project and Cyc demonstrate that at least in some circumstances, inference is practical even with massively large knowledge bases.

The argument: Writing down all the knowledge (the right way) is infeasible

> Just constructing a knowledge base is a major intellectual research problem
> ... The problem of finding suitable axioms—the problem of "stating the facts"
> in terms of always-correct, logical, assumptions—is very much harder than is
> generally believed.
>
> *Marvin Minsky [185].*

The problem is in fact much greater than Minsky realized, although it has taken AI logicists a while to realize the severity of the underlying issues. At the time that Minsky wrote his paper, his critique on this point was not universally appreciated by proponents of AI logicism. The sense one gets from reading the papers of Pat Hayes [113, 114, 111],[6] for example, is one of confidence and optimism. Hayes decried the paucity of existing domain formalizations, but at the time seemed to believe that creating the formalizations could be done as long as enough people actually sat down to write the axioms. He proposed, for the subfield of naive physics, that a committee be formed, that the body of commonsense knowledge about the physical world be divided into clusters, with clusters assigned to different committee members, who would occasionally meet in order to integrate their theories.

But there never was a concerted effort to formalize naive physics. Although there have been some attempts to formalize knowledge of various domains (see, e.g., [123], and the proceedings of the various symposia on Logical Formalizations of Commonsense Knowledge), most research in knowledge representation remains at the meta-level. The result, as Davis [65] has pointed out, is that at this point constructing a theory that can reason correctly about simple tasks like staking plants in a garden is beyond our capability.

What makes it so difficult to write down the necessary knowledge? It is not, certainly, merely the writing down of millions of facts. The Cyc knowledge base, as discussed in Section 1.4, has over 3 million assertions. But that knowledge base is still missing the necessary information to reason about staking plants in a garden, cracking eggs into a bowl, or many other challenge problems in commonsense reasoning and knowledge representation [183]. Size alone will not solve the problem. That is why attempts to use various web-based technologies to gather vast amounts of knowledge [170] are irrelevant to this critique of the logicist approach.

---

[6]Although [111] was published in the 1980s, a preliminary version was first written in the late 1970s.

Rather, formalizing domains in logic is difficult for at least the following reasons:

- First, it is difficult to become aware of all our implicit knowledge; that is, to make this knowledge explicit, even in English or any other natural language. The careful examination of many domains or non-trivial commonsense reasoning problems makes this point clear. For example, reasoning about how and whether to organize the giving of a surprise birthday present [188] involves reasoning about the factors that cause a person to be surprised, how surprises can be foiled, joint planning, cooperation, and the importance of correct timing. The knowledge involved is complex and needs to be carefully teased out of the mass of social protocols that unknowingly govern our behavior.

- Second, as Davis [65] has pointed out, there is some knowledge that is difficult to express in any language. Davis gives the example of reasoning about a screw. Although it is easy to see that a small bump in the surface will affect the functionality of a screw much more than a small pit in the surface, it is hard to express the knowledge needed to make this inference.

- Third, there are some technical difficulties that prevent formalization of certain types of knowledge. For example, there is still no comprehensive theory of how agents infer and reason about other agents' ignorance (although [109] is an excellent start in this direction); this makes it difficult to axiomatize realistic theories of multi-agent planning, which depend crucially on inferring what other agents do and do not know, and how they make up for their ignorance.

- Fourth, the construction of an ontology for a domain is a necessary but difficult prerequisite to axiomatization. Deciding what basic constructs are necessary and how to organize them is a tricky enterprise, which often must be reworked when one starts to write down axioms and finds that it is awkward to formalize the necessary knowledge.

- Fifth, it is hard to integrate existing axiomatizations. Davis gives as an example his axiomatizations of string, and of cutting. There are various technical difficulties—mainly, assumptions that have been built into each domain axiomatization—that prevent a straightforward integration of the two axiomatizations into a single theory that could support simple inferences about cutting string. The problem of integration, in simpler form, will also be familiar to anyone who has ever tried to integrate ontologies. Concepts do not always line up neatly; how one alters these concepts in order to allow subsumption is a challenging task.

There have nonetheless been many successes in writing down knowledge correctly. The best known are the theories of causation and temporal reasoning that were developed in part to deal with the frame and Yale shooting problems. Other successful axiomatizations, including theories of knowledge and belief, multiple agency, spatial reasoning, and physical reasoning, are well illustrated in the domain theories in this Handbook.

The argument: Other approaches do it better and/or cheaper

> Anyone familiar with AI must realize that the study of knowledge representation—at least as it applies to the "commonsense" knowledge required for reading typical text such as newspapers—is not going anywhere fast. This subfield of AI has become notorious for the production of countless non-monotonic logics and almost as many logics of knowledge and belief, and none of the work shows any obvious application to actual knowledge-representation problems.
>
> *Eugene Charniak [54]*

During the last fifteen years, statistical learning techniques have become increasingly popular within AI, particularly for applications such as natural language processing for which classic knowledge representation techniques had once been considered essential. For decades, for example, it had been assumed that much background domain knowledge would be needed in order to correctly parse sentences. For instance, a sentence like *John saw the girl with the toothbrush* has two parses, one in which the prepositional phrase *with the toothbrush* modifies the phrase *John saw*, and one in which it modifies the noun phrase *the girl*. Background knowledge, however, eliminates the first parse, since people do not see with toothbrushes. (In contrast, both parses are plausible for the sentence *John saw the girl with the telescope*.) The difficulty with KR-based approaches is that it requires a great deal of knowledge to properly process even small corpora of sentences.

Statistical learning techniques offers a different paradigm for many issues that arise in processing language. One useful concept is that of *collocation* [166], in which a program learns about commonly occurring collocated words and phrases, and subsequently uses this knowledge in order to parse. This is particularly useful for parsing and disambiguating phonemes for voice recognition applications. A statistical learning program might learn, for example, that *weapons of mass destruction* are words that are collocated with a high frequency. If this knowledge is then fed into a voice recognition program, it could be used to disambiguate between the words *math* and *mass*. The words in the phrase *Weapons of math destruction* are collocated with a low frequency, so that interpretation becomes less likely.

Programs using statistical learning techniques have become popular in text-retrieval applications; in particular, they are used in systems that have performed well in recent TREC competitions [262–266]. Statistical-learning systems stand out because they are often cheaper to build. There is no need to painstakingly build tailor-made knowledge bases for the purposes of understanding a small corpora of texts.

Nevertheless, it is unlikely that statistical-learning systems will ever obviate the need for logicist AI in these applications. Statistical techniques can go only so far. They are especially useful in domains in which language is highly restricted (e.g., newspaper texts, the example cited by Charniak), and for applications in which deep understanding is not required. But for many true AI applications, such as story understanding and deep question-answering applications, deep understanding is essential.

It is no coincidence that the rising popularity of statistical techniques has coincided with the rise of the text-*retrieval* competitions (TREC) as opposed to the message-*understanding* competitions (MUC). It is also worth noting that the successful participants in HPKB relied heavily on classical logicist KR techniques [58].

In general, this pattern appears in other applications. Statistical learning techniques do well with low cost on relatively easy problems. However, hard problems remain resistant to these techniques. For these problems, logicist-KR-based techniques appear to work best.

This may likely mean that the most successful applications in the future will make use of both approaches. As with the other critiques discussed above, the logicist research agenda is once again being set and influenced by non-logicist approaches; ultimately, this can only serve to strengthen the applicability of the logicist approach and the success of logicist-based applications.

Acknowledgements

The comments of Eyal Amir, Peter Andrews, Peter Baumgartner, Ernie Davis, Esra Erdem, Joohyung Lee, Christopher Lynch, Bill McCune, Sheila McIlraith, J. Moore, Maria Paola Bonacina, J. Hsiang, H. Kirchner, M. Rusinowitch, and Geoff Sutcliffe contributed to the material in this chapter. The first author was partially supported by the National Science Foundation under Grant IIS-0412907.

Bibliography

[1] E. Amir and P. Maynard-Reid. Logic-based subsumption architecture. *Artificial Intelligence*, 153(1–2):167–237, 2004.

[2] E. Amir and S. McIlraith. Partition-based logical reasoning for first-order and propositional theories. *Artificial Intelligence*, 162(1–2):49–88, 2005.

[3] P.B. Andrews. Theorem proving via general matings. *Journal of the ACM*, 28:193–214, 1981.

[4] P.B. Andrews, M. Bishop, S. Issar, D. Nesmith, F. Pfenning, and H. Xi. TPS: A theorem proving system for classical type theory. *Journal of Automated Reasoning*, 16:321–353, 1996.

[5] P.B. Andrews and C.E. Brown. TPS: A hybrid automatic-interactive system for developing proofs. *Journal of Applied Logic*, 4:367–395, 2006.

[6] C. Aravindan, J. Dix, and I. Niemelä. Dislop: A research project on disjunctive logic programming. *AI Commun.*, 10(3–4):151–165, 1997.

[7] T. Arts and J. Giesl. Termination of term rewriting using dependency pairs. *Theoretical Computer Science*, 236(1–2):133–178, 2000.

[8] F. Baader, D. Calvanese, D.L. McGuinness, D. Nardi, and P.F. Patel-Schneider. *The Description Logic Handbook: Theory, Implementation, Applications*. Cambridge University Press, Cambridge, UK, 2003.

[9] F. Baader and W. Snyder. Unification theory. In A. Robinson and A. Voronkov, editors. *Handbook of Automated Reasoning*, vol. I, pages 445–532. Elsevier Science, 2001 (Chapter 8).

[10] F. Baader, editor. *CADE-19, 19th International Conference on Automated Deduction*, Miami Beach, FL, USA, July 28–August 2, 2003. *Lecture Notes in Computer Science*, vol. 2741. Springer, 2003.

[11] F. Baader and T. Nipkow. *Term Rewriting and All That*. Cambridge University Press, Cambridge, England, 1998.

[12] L. Bachmair and D. Plaisted. Termination orderings for associative–commutative rewriting systems. *J. Symbolic Computation*, 1:329–349, 1985.

[13] L. Bachmair and N. Dershowitz. Commutation, transformation, and termination. In J.H. Siekmann, editor. *Proceedings of the Eighth International Conference on Automated Deduction*, pages 5–20, 1986.

[14] L. Bachmair, N. Dershowitz, and J. Hsiang. Orderings for equational proofs. In *Proceedings of the Symposium on Logic in Computer Science*, pages 346–357, 1986.

[15] L. Bachmair, N. Dershowitz, and D. Plaisted. Completion without failure. In H. Aït-Kaci and M. Nivat, editors. *Resolution of Equations in Algebraic Structures 2: Rewriting Techniques*, pages 1–30. Academic Press, New York, 1989.

[16] L. Bachmair and H. Ganzinger. Rewrite-based equational theorem proving with selection and simplification. *J. Logic Comput.*, 4(3):217–247, 1994.

[17] L. Bachmair and H. Ganzinger. Resolution theorem proving. In Robinson and Voronkov [231], pages 19–99.

[18] L. Bachmair, H. Ganzinger, C. Lynch, and W. Snyder. Basic paramodulation. *Information and Computation*, 121(2):172–192, September 1995.

[19] L. Bachmair, H. Ganzinger, and A. Voronkov. Elimination of equality via transformation with ordering constraints. *Lecture Notes in Computer Science*, 1421:175–190, 1998.

[20] K. Baclawski, M.M. Kokar, R.J. Waldinger, and P.A. Kogut. Consistency checking of semantic web ontologies. In I. Horrocks and J.A. Hendler, editors. *International Semantic Web Conference, Lecture Notes in Computer Science*, vol. 2342, pages 454–459. Springer, 2002.

[21] Y. Bar-Hillel, J. McCarthy, and O. Selfridge. Discussion of the paper: Programs with common sense. In V. Lifschitz, editor. *Formalizing Common Sense*, pages 17–20. Intellect, 1998.

[22] H.G. Barrow. Verify: A program for proving correctness of digital hardware designs. *Artificial Intelligence*, 24(1–3):437–491, 1984.

[23] P. Baumgartner. FDPLL—A first-order Davis–Putnam–Logemann–Loveland procedure. In D. McAllester, editor. *CADE-17—The 17th International Conference on Automated Deduction*, vol. 1831, pages 200–219. Springer, 2000.

[24] P. Baumgartner and U. Furbach. PROTEIN: A PROver with a theory extension INterface. In *Proceedings of the Conference on Automated Deduction*, 1994.

[25] P. Baumgartner and C. Tinelli. The model evolution calculus. In F. Baader, editor. *CADE-19: The 19th International Conference on Automated Deduction, Lecture Notes in Artificial Intelligence*, vol. 2741, pages 350–364. Springer, 2003.

[26] J.G.F. Belinfante. Computer proofs in Gödel's class theory with equational definitions for composite and cross. *Journal of Automated Reasoning*, 22:311–339, 1999.

[27] C.G. Bell and A. Newell. *Computer Structures: Readings and Examples*. McGraw-Hill, 1971.

[28] W. Bibel. *Automated Theorem Proving*. 2nd edition. Vieweg, Braunschweig/Wiesbaden, 1987.

[29] J.-P. Billon. The disconnection method. In P. Miglioli, U. Moscato, D. Mundici, and M. Ornaghi, editors. *Proceedings of TABLEAUX-96, Lecture Notes in Artificial Intelligence*, vol. 1071, pages 110–126. Springer, 1996.

[30] G. Birkhoff. On the structure of abstract algebras. *Proc. Cambridge Philos. Soc.*, 31:433–454, 1935.

[31] M. Bishop. A breadth-first strategy for mating search. In H. Ganzinger, editor. *CADE-16: Proceedings of the 16th International Conference on Automated Deduction Trento, Italy, 1999, Lecture Notes in Artificial Intelligence*, vol. 1632, pages 359–373. Springer-Verlag, 1999.

[32] M. Bishop and P.B. Andrews. Selectively instantiating definitions. In *Proceedings of the 15th International Conference on Automated Deduction*, pages 365–380, 1998.

[33] A. Bockmayr and V. Weispfenning. Solving numerical constraints. In A. Robinson and A. Voronkov, editors. *Handbook of Automated Reasoning*, vol. 1, pages 751–842. Elsevier, Amsterdam, The Netherlands, January 2001 (Chapter 12).

[34] M.P. Bonacina. On the reconstruction of proofs in distributed theorem proving: a modified clause-diffusion method. *J. Symbolic Comput.*, 21(4):507–522, 1996.

[35] J. Bos and K. Markert. Recognising textual entailment with logical inference. In *HLT/EMNLP*. The Association for Computational Linguistics, 2005.

[36] R. Boyer, M. Kaufmann, and J. Moore. The Boyer–Moore theorem prover and its interactive enhancement. *Computers and Mathematics with Applications*, 29(2):27–62, 1995.

[37] R. Boyer, E. Lusk, W. McCune, R. Overbeek, M. Stickel, and L. Wos. Set theory in first-order logic: Clauses for Gödel's axioms. *Journal of Automated Reasoning*, 2:287–327, 1986.

[38] R. Boyer and J. Moore. *A Computational Logic*. Academic Press, New York, 1979.

[39] R.J. Brachman and H.J. Levesque. *Knowledge Representation and Reasoning*. Morgan Kaufmann, 2004.

[40] D. Brand. Proving theorems with the modification method. *SIAM J. Comput.*, 4:412–430, 1975.

[41] I. Bratko. *Prolog Programming for Artificial Intelligence*. 3rd edition. Addison-Wesley, 2000.

[42] R.A. Brooks. Intelligence without representation. *Artificial Intelligence*, 47(1–3):139–159, 1991.

[43] R. Bryant. Symbolic boolean manipulation with ordered binary-decision diagrams. *ACM Computing Surveys*, 24(3):293–318, September 1992.

[44] B. Buchberger. Gröbner bases: An algorithmic method in polynomial ideal theory. In N.K. Bose, editor. *Multidimensional Systems Theory*, pages 184–232. Reidel, 1985.

[45] A. Bundy. *The Computer Modelling of Mathematical Reasoning*. Academic Press, New York, 1983.

[46] A. Bundy. The automation of proof by mathematical induction. In A. Robinson and A. Voronkov, editors. *Handbook of Automated Reasoning*, vol. I, pages 845–911. Elsevier Science, 2001 (Chapter 13).

[47] A. Bundy, D. Basin, D. Hutter, and A. Ireland. *Rippling: Meta-Level Guidance for Mathematical Reasoning. Cambridge Tracts in Theoretical Computer Science*, vol. 56. Cambridge University Press, 2005.

[48] J. Burch, E. Clarke, K. McMillan, D. Dill, and J. Hwang. Symbolic model checking: 10^{20} states and beyond. *Information and Computation*, 98(2):142–170, June 1992.

[49] M. Burrows, M. Abadi, and R.M. Needham. Authentication: A practical study in belief and action. In M.Y. Vardi, editor. *TARK*, pages 325–342. Morgan Kaufmann, 1988.

[50] S. Buvac. Resolving lexical ambiguity using a formal theory of context. In K. van Deemter and S. Peters, editors. *Semantic Ambiguity and Underspecification*. Center for the Study of Language and Information, Stanford, 1996.

[51] R. Caferra, A. Leitsch, and N. Peltier. *Automated Model Building*. Kluwer Academic Publishers, 2004.

[52] B.F. Caviness and J.R. Johnson, editors. *Quantifier Elimination and Cylindrical Algebraic Decomposition*. Springer-Verlag, New York, 1998.

[53] C. Chang and R. Lee. *Symbolic Logic and Mechanical Theorem Proving*. Academic Press, New York, 1973.

[54] E. Charniak. *Statistical Language Learning*. MIT Press, 1993.

[55] S.C. Chou and X.S. Gao. Automated reasoning in geometry. In A. Robinson and A. Voronkov, editors. *Handbook of Automated Reasoning*, vol. I, pages 707–749. Elsevier Science, 2001 (Chapter 11).

[56] A. Church. A note on the Entscheidungsproblem. *Journal of Symbolic Logic*, 1:40–41, 1936. Correction, ibid., 101–102.

[57] K. Clark. Negation as failure. In H. Gallaire and J. Minker, editors. *Logic and Data Bases*, pages 293–322. Plenum Press, New York, 1978.

[58] P.R. Cohen, R. Schrag, E.K. Jones, A. Pease, A. Lin, B. Starr, D. Gunning, and M. Burke. The DARPA high-performance knowledge bases project. *AI Magazine*, 19(4):25–49, 1998.

[59] H. Comon. Inductionless induction. In A. Robinson and A. Voronkov, editors. *Handbook of Automated Reasoning*, vol. I, pages 913–962. Elsevier Science, 2001 (Chapter 14).

[60] H. Comon and F. Jacquemard. Ground reducibility is EXPTIME-complete. In *Proc. 12th IEEE Symp. Logic in Computer Science (LICS'97)*, Warsaw, Poland, June–July 1997, pages 26–34. IEEE Comp. Soc. Press, 1997.

[61] H. Comon, P. Narendran, R. Nieuwenhuis, and M. Rusinowitch. Deciding the confluence of ordered term rewrite systems. *ACM Trans. Comput. Logic*, 4(1):33–55, 2003.

[62] R.L. Constable, et al. *Implementing Mathematics with the NuPrl Proof Development System*. Prentice-Hall, Englewood Cliffs, NJ, 1986.

[63] M. Dauchet. Simulation of Turing machines by a left-linear rewrite rule. In *Proceedings of the 3rd International Conference on Rewriting Techniques and Applications, Lecture Notes in Computer Science*, vol. 355, pages 109–120. Springer, 1989.

[64] E. Davis. *Representations of Commonsense Knowledge*. Morgan Kaufmann, San Francisco, CA, 1990.

[65] E. Davis. The naive physics perplex. *AI Magazine*, 19(3):51–79, 1998.

[66] M. Davis. Eliminating the irrelevant from mechanical proofs. In: *Proceedings Symp. of Applied Math.* vol. 15, pages 15–30, 1963.

[67] M. Davis. The prehistory and early history of automated deduction. In J. Siekmann and G. Wrightson, editors. *Automation of Reasoning*, vol. 1. Springer-Verlag, Berlin, 1983.

[68] M. Davis. First order logic. In D.M. Gabbay, C.J. Hogger, and J.A. Robinson, editors. *Handbook of Logic in AI and Logic Programming*, vol. 1, pages 31–65. Oxford University Press, 1993.

[69] M. Davis, G. Logemann, and D. Loveland. A machine program for theorem-proving. *Communications of the ACM*, 5:394–397, 1962.

[70] M. Davis and H. Putnam. A computing procedure for quantification theory. *Journal of the ACM*, 7:201–215, 1960.

[71] A. Degtyarev and A. Voronkov. The inverse method. In A. Robinson and A. Voronkov, editors. *Handbook of Automated Reasoning*, vol. I, pages 179–272. Elsevier Science, 2001 (Chapter 4).

[72] E. Deplagne, C. Kirchner, H. Kirchner, and Q.H. Nguyen. Proof search and proof check for equational and inductive theorems. In Baader [10], pages 297–316.

[73] N. Dershowitz. On representing ordinals up to γ_0. Unpublished note, 1980.

[74] N. Dershowitz. Orderings for term-rewriting systems. *Theoretical Computer Science*, 17:279–301, 1982.

[75] N. Dershowitz. Termination of rewriting. *Journal of Symbolic Comput.*, 3:69–116, 1987.

[76] N. Dershowitz and J.-P. Jouannaud. Rewrite systems. In J. van Leeuwen, editor. *Handbook of Theoretical Computer Science*. North-Holland, Amsterdam, 1990.

[77] N. Dershowitz and D.A. Plaisted. Rewriting. In A. Robinson and A. Voronkov, editors. *Handbook of Automated Reasoning*, vol. I, pages 535–610. Elsevier Science, 2001 (Chapter 9).

[78] N. Dershowitz, J. Hsiang, N. Josephson, and D.A. Plaisted. Associative–commutative rewriting. In *Proceedings of the Eighth International Joint Conference on Artificial Intelligence*, pages 940–944, August 1983.

[79] E. Domenjoud. AC-unification through order-sorted AC1-unification. In *Proceedings of the 4th International Conference on Rewriting Techniques and Applications*, *Lecture Notes in Computer Science*, vol. 488. Springer-Verlag, 1991.

[80] E. Domenjoud. Number of minimal unifiers of the equation $\alpha x_1 + \cdots + \alpha x_p =_{AC} \beta y_1 + \cdots + \beta y_q$. *Journal of Automated Reasoning*, 8:39–44, 1992.

[81] P.J. Downey, R. Sethi, and R. Tarjan. Variations on the common subexpression problem. *Journal of the ACM*, 27(4):758–771, 1980.

[82] J. Endrullis, J. Waldmann, and H. Zantema. Matrix interpretations for proving termination of term rewriting. In Furbach and Shankar [91], pages 574–588.

[83] R.S. Engelmore. Knowledge-based systems in Japan, 1993. http://www.wtec.org/loyola/kb/.

[84] D. Fensel and A. Schönegge. Specifying and verifying knowledge-based systems with KIV. In J. Vanthienen and F. van Harmelen, editors. *EUROVAV*, pages 107–116. Katholieke Universiteit Leuven, Belgium, 1997.

[85] R. Fikes and N.J. Nilsson. Strips: A new approach to the application of theorem proving to problem solving. *Artificial Intelligence*, 2(3–4):189–208, 1971.

[86] B. Fischer, J. Schumann, and G. Snelting. Deduction-based software component retrieval. In W. Bibeland and P.H. Schmitt, editors. *Automated Deduction: A Basis for Applications*, vol. 3. Kluwer Academic, 1998.

[87] M. Fitting. *First-Order Logic and Automated Theorem Proving*. Springer-Verlag, New York, 1990.

[88] E. Franconi, A.L. Palma, N. Leone, S. Perri, and F. Scarcello. Census data repair: a challenging application of disjunctive logic programming. In R. Nieuwenhuis and A. Voronkov, editors. *LPAR, Lecture Notes in Computer Science*, vol. 2250, pages 561–578. Springer, 2001.

[89] G. Frege. *Begriffsschrift, eine der arithmetischen nachgebildete Formelsch-prache des reinen Denkens*. Halle, 1879. English translation: [261, pp. 1–82].

[90] T.W. Frühwirth and S. Abdennadher. The Munich rent advisor: A success for logic programming on the Internet. *TPLP*, 1(3):303–319, 2001.

[91] U. Furbach and N. Shankar, editors. *Automated Reasoning, Third International Joint Conference, IJCAR 2006*, Seattle, WA, USA, August 17–20, 2006, Proceedings. *Lecture Notes in Computer Science*, vol. 4130. Springer, 2006.

[92] J.-M. Gaillourdet, T. Hillenbrand, B. Löchner, and H. Spies. The new Waldmeister loop at work. In Baader [10], pages 317–321.

[93] H. Ganzinger and K. Korovin. New directions in instantiation-based theorem proving. In *Proc. 18th IEEE Symposium on Logic in Computer Science, (LICS'03)*, pages 55–64. IEEE Computer Society Press, 2003.

[94] H. Gelernter, J.R. Hansen, and D.W. Loveland. Empirical explorations of the geometry theorem proving machine. In E. Feigenbaum and J. Feldman, editors. *Computers and Thought*, pages 153–167. McGraw-Hill, New York, 1963.

[95] M. Genesereth and N.J. Nilsson. *Logical Foundations of Artificial Intelligence*. Morgan Kaufmann, San Mateo, CA, 1987.

[96] G. Gentzen. Untersuchungen über das logische Schließen. *Mathematische Zeitschrift*, 39:176–210, 1935.

[97] J. Giesl and D. Kapur. Deciding inductive validity of equations. In Baader [10], pages 17–31.

[98] J. Giesl, P. Schneider-Kamp, and R. Thiemann. Automatic termination proofs in the dependency pair framework. In Furbach and Shankar [91], pages 281–286.

[99] P.C. Gilmore. A proof method for quantification theory. *IBM Journal of Research and Development*, 4:28–35, 1960.

[100] K. Gödel. Die Vollständigkeit fer Axiome des logischen Funktionenkalküls. *Monatshefte für Mathematik und Physik*, 37:349–360, 1930. English translation: [261, pp. 582–591].

[101] M.J. Gordon and T.F. Melham, editors. *Introduction to HOL: A Theorem-Proving Environment for Higher-Order Logic*. Cambridge University Press, 1993.

[102] B.C. Grau, B. Parsia, E. Sirin, and A. Kalyanpur. Automatic partitioning of owl ontologies using-connections. In I. Horrocks, U. Sattler, and F. Wolter, editors. *Description Logics*, volume 147 of *CEUR Workshop Proceedings*, 2005.

[103] C.C. Green. *The Applications of Theorem Proving to Question-Answering Systems*. Garland, New York, 1969.

[104] C.C. Green. Application of theorem proving to problem solving. In *IJCAI*, pages 219–240, 1969.

[105] J.V. Guttag, D. Kapur, and D. Musser. On proving uniform termination and restricted termination of rewriting systems. *SIAM J. Comput.*, 12:189–214, 1983.

[106] R. Hähnle. Tableaux and related methods. In A. Robinson and A. Voronkov, editors. *Handbook of Automated Reasoning*, vol. I, pages 100–178. Elsevier Science, 2001 (Chapter 3).

[107] A. Haken. The intractability of resolution. *Theoretical Computer Science*, 39:297–308, 1985.

[108] T.R. Halfhill. An error in a lookup table created the infamous bug in Intel's latest processor. *BYTE*, March 1995.

[109] J.Y. Halpern and G. Lakemeyer. Multi-agent only knowing. *J. Logic Comput.*, 11(1):41–70, 2001.

[110] S. Hanks and D.V. McDermott. Nonmonotonic logic and temporal projection. *Artificial Intelligence*, 33(3):379–412, 1987.

[111] P.J. Hayes. Naive physics I: Ontology for liquids. In J. Hobbs and R. Moore, editors. *Formal Theories of the Commonsense World*, pages 71–107. Ablex, Norwood, NJ, 1975.

[112] P.J. Hayes. In defence of logic. In *IJCAI*, pages 559–565, 1977.

[113] P.J. Hayes. The naive physics manifesto. In D. Michie, editor. *Expert Systems in the Microelectronic Age*. Edinburgh University Press, 1979.

[114] P.J. Hayes. The second naive physics manifesto. In J. Hobbs and R. Moore, editors. *Formal Theories of the Commonsense World*, pages 1–36. Ablex, Norwood, NJ, 1985.

[115] P.J. Hayes, T.C. Eskridge, R. Saavedra, T. Reichherzer, M. Mehrotra, and D. Bobrovnikoff. Collaborative knowledge capture in ontologies. In P. Clark and G. Schreiber, editors. *K-CAP*, pages 99–106. ACM, 2005.

[116] S. Heilbrunner and S. Hölldobler. The undecidability of the unification and matching problem for canonical theories. *Acta Informatica*, 24:157–171, 1987.

[117] C.G. Hempel. *Aspects of Scientific Explanation and Other Essays in the Philosophy of Science*. Free Press, 1965.

[118] C.G. Hempel and P. Oppeneheim. Studies in the logic of explanation. In C.G. Hempel, editor. *Aspects of Scientific Explanation and Other Essays in the Philosophy of Science*, pages 245–295. Free Press, 1965. Also includes 1964 postscript. Originally published in Philosophy of Science, 1948.

[119] J. Hendrix, J. Meseguer, and H. Ohsaki. A sufficient completeness checker for linear order-sorted specifications modulo axioms. In Furbach and Shankar [91], pages 151–155.

[120] N. Hirokawa and A. Middeldorp. Automating the dependency pair method. In Baader [10], pages 32–46.

[121] J.R. Hobbs. An overview of the TACITUS project. *Computational Linguistics*, 12(3), 1986.

[122] J.R. Hobbs, D.E. Appelt, J. Bear, D.J. Israel, M. Kameyama, M.E. Stickel, and M. Tyson. Fastus: A cascaded finite-state transducer for extracting information from natural-language text. *CoRR*, cmp-lg/9705013, 1997. Earlier version available as SRI Technical Report 519.

[123] J.R. Hobbs and R.C. Moore. *Formal Theories of the Commonsense World*. Ablex, 1985.

[124] J.R. Hobbs, M.E. Stickel, D.E. Appelt, and P.A. Martin. Interpretation as abduction. *Artificial Intelligence*, 63(1–2):69–142, 1993.

[125] J. Hsiang and M. Rusinowitch. Proving refutational completeness of theorem-proving strategies: the transfinite semantic tree method. *Journal of the ACM*, 38(3):559–587, July 1991.

[126] G. Huet. A complete proof of correctness of the Knuth–Bendix completion algorithm. *J. Comput. Systems Sci.*, 23(1):11–21, 1981.

[127] G. Huet and J.M. Hullot. Proofs by induction in equational theories with constructors. *Journal of Computer and System Sciences*, 25:239–266, 1982.

[128] G. Huet and D. Lankford. On the uniform halting problem for term rewriting systems. Technical Report Rapport Laboria 283, IRIA, Le Chesnay, France, 1978.

[129] F. Jacquemard, M. Rusinowitch, and L. Vigneron. Compiling and verifying security protocols. In *Logic Programming and Automated Reasoning*, pages 131–160, 2000.

[130] J.-P. Jouannaud and H. Kirchner. Completion of a set of rules modulo a set of equations. *SIAM J. Comput.*, 15:1155–1194, November 1986.

[131] J.-P. Jouannaud and P. Lescanne. On multiset orderings. *Information Processing Letters*, 15:57–63, 1982.

[132] J.-P. Jouannaud, P. Lescanne, and F. Reinig. Recursive decomposition ordering. In *Proceedings of the Second IFIP Workshop on Formal Description of Programming Concepts*, pages 331–348. North-Holland, 1982.

[133] J.-P. Jouannaud and C. Kirchner. Solving equations in abstract algebras: A rule-based survey of unification. In J.-L. Lassez and G. Plotkin, editors. *Computational Logic: Essays in Honor of Alan Robinson*. MIT Press, Cambridge, MA, 1991.

[134] J.-P. Jouannaud and E. Kounalis. Automatic proofs by induction in theories without constructors. *Inform. and Comput.*, 82(1):1–33, 1989.

[135] L. Kalmár. Zurückführung des Entscheidungsproblems auf den Fall von Formeln mit einer einzigen, bindren, Funktionsvariablen. *Compositio Mathematica*, 4:137–144, 1936.

[136] S. Kamin and J.-J. Levy. Two generalizations of the recursive path ordering. Unpublished, February 1980.

[137] D. Kapur and P. Narendran. Double-exponential complexity of computing a complete set of AC-unifiers. In *Proceedings 7th IEEE Symposium on Logic in Computer Science*, pages 11–21. Santa Cruz, CA, 1992.

[138] D. Kapur, P. Narendran, and H. Zhang. On sufficient completeness and related properties of term rewriting systems. *Acta Informatica*, 24:395–416, 1987.

[139] D. Kapur, G. Sivakumar, and H. Zhang. A new method for proving termination of AC-rewrite systems. In *Proc. of Tenth Conference on Foundations of Software Technology and Theoretical Computer Science, Lecture Notes in Comput. Sci.*, vol. 472, pages 133–148. Springer-Verlag, December 1990.

[140] D. Kapur and M. Subramaniam. Extending decision procedures with induction schemes. In D.A. McAllester, editor. *CADE-17: Proceedings of the 17th International Conference on Automated Deduction,* vol. 1831, pages 324–345. Springer-Verlag, London, UK, 2000.

[141] M. Kaufmann, P. Manolios, and J.S. Moore, editors. *Computer-Aided Reasoning: ACL2 Case Studies*. Kluwer Academic Press, Boston, MA, 2000.

[142] M. Kaufmann, P. Manolios, and J.S. Moore. *Computer-Aided Reasoning: An Approach*. Kluwer Academic Press, Boston, MA, 2000.

[143] C. Kirchner, H. Kirchner, and M. Rusinowitch. Deduction with symbolic constraints. *Revue Francaise d'Intelligence Artificielle*, 4(3):9–52, 1990.

[144] D.E. Knuth and P.B. Bendix. Simple word problems in universal algebras. In J. Leech, editor. *Computational Problems in Abstract Algebra*, pages 263–297. Pergamon Press, Oxford, 1970.

[145] A. Koprowski and H. Zantema. Automation of recursive path ordering for infinite labelled rewrite systems. In Furbach and Shankar [91], pages 332–346.

[146] K. Korovin and A. Voronkov. An AC-compatible Knuth–Bendix order. In Baader [10], pages 47–59.

[147] R.A. Kowalski. *Logic for Problem Solving*. North-Holland, Amsterdam, 1980.

[148] J.B. Kruskal. Well-quasi-ordering, the tree theorem, and Vazsonyi's conjecture. *Transactions of the American Mathematical Society*, 95:210–225, 1960.

[149] D. Lankford. Canonical algebraic simplification in computational logic. Technical Report Memo ATP-25, Automatic Theorem Proving Project. University of Texas, Austin, TX, 1975.

[150] D. Lankford. On proving term rewriting systems are Noetherian. Technical Report Memo MTP-3, Mathematics Department, Louisiana Tech., University, Ruston, LA, 1979.

[151] D. Lankford and A.M. Ballantyne. Decision problems for simple equational theories with commutative-associative axioms: Complete sets of commutative-associative reductions. Technical Report Memo ATP-39, Department of Mathematics and Computer Science, University of Texas, Austin, TX, 1977.

[152] D. Lankford, G. Butler, and A. Ballantyne. A progress report on new decision algorithms for finitely presented abelian groups. In *Proceedings of the 7th International Conference on Automated Deduction, Lecture Notes in Computer Science*, vol. 170, pages 128–141. Springer, May 1984.

[153] S.-J. Lee and D. Plaisted. Eliminating duplication with the hyper-linking strategy. *Journal of Automated Reasoning*, 9(1):25–42, 1992.

[154] S.-J. Lee and D. Plaisted. Use of replace rules in theorem proving. *Methods of Logic in Computer Science*, 1:217–240, 1994.

[155] A. Leitsch. *The Resolution Calculus. Texts in Theoretical Computer Science*. Springer-Verlag, Berlin, 1997.

[156] D.B. Lenat. Cyc: A large-scale investment in knowledge infrastructure. *Communications of the ACM*, 38(11):32–38, 1995.

[157] D.B. Lenat and R.V. Guha. *Building Large Knowledge Based Systems: Representation and Inference in the Cyc Project*. Addison-Wesley, Reading, MA, 1990.

[158] R. Letz and G. Stenz. Model elimination and connection tableau procedures. In A. Robinson and A. Voronkov, editors. *Handbook of Automated Reasoning*, vol. II, pages 2015–2114. Elsevier Science, 2001 (Chapter 28).

[159] V. Lifschitz. What is the inverse method? *J. Autom. Reason.*, 5(1):1–23, 1989.

[160] V. Lifschitz. Pointwise circumscription: Preliminary report. In *AAAI*, pages 406–410, 1986.

[161] V. Lifschitz. Formal theories of action (preliminary report). In *IJCAI*, pages 966–972, 1987.

[162] D. Loveland. A simplified format for the model elimination procedure. *Journal of the ACM*, 16:349–363, 1969.

[163] D. Loveland. *Automated Theorem Proving: A Logical Basis.* North-Holland, New York, 1978.

[164] D.W. Loveland. Automated deduction: looking ahead. *AI Magazine*, 20(1):77–98, Spring 1999.

[165] B. MacCartney, S.A. McIlraith, E. Amir, and T.E. Uribe. Practical partition-based theorem proving for large knowledge bases. In G. Gottlob and T. Walsh, editors. *IJCAI*, pages 89–98. Morgan Kaufmann, 2003.

[166] C. Manning and H. Schutze. *Foundations of Statistical Natural Language Processing.* MIT Press, 1999.

[167] A. Martelli and U. Montanari. An efficient unification algorithm. *Transactions on Programming Languages and Systems*, 4(2):258–282, April 1982.

[168] S.Ju. Maslov. An inverse method of establishing deducibilities in the classical predicate calculus. *Dokl. Akad. Nauk SSSR*, 159:1420–1424, 1964. Reprinted in SiekmannWrightson83a.

[169] C. Matuszek, J. Cabral, M.J. Witbrock, and J. DeOliviera. An introduction to the syntax and content of cyc. In *Proceedings of the AAAI 2006 Spring Symposium on Formalizing and Compiling Background Knowledge and its Applications to Knowledge Representation and Question Answering*, 2006.

[170] C. Matuszek, M.J. Witbrock, R.C. Kahlert, J. Cabral, D. Schneider, P. Shah, and D.B. Lenat. Searching for common sense: Populating cyc from the web. In M.M. Veloso and S. Kambhampati, editors. *AAAI*, pages 1430–1435. AAAI Press/The MIT Press, 2005.

[171] J. McCarthy. Programs with common sense. In *Proceedings of the Teddington Conference on the Mechanization of Thought Processes*, pages 75–91. London, 1959.

[172] J. McCarthy. A basis for a mathematical theory of computation. In *Computer Programming and Formal Systems*. North-Holland, 1963.

[173] J. McCarthy. Circumscription: A form of non-monotonic reasoning. *Artificial Intelligence*, 13(1–2):23–79, 1980.

[174] J. McCarthy. Applications of circumscription to formalizing common sense knowledge. *Artificial Intelligence*, 26(3):89–116, 1986.

[175] J. McCarthy and P.J. Hayes. Some philosophical problems from the standpoint of artificial intelligence. In B. Meltzer and D. Michie, editors. *Machine Intelligence 4*, pages 463–502. Edinburgh University Press, Edinburgh, 1969.

[176] W.W. McCune. Solution of the Robbins problem. *Journal of Automated Reasoning*, 19(3):263–276, December 1997.

[177] W. McCune and L. Wos. Otter—the CADE-13 competition incarnations. *J. Autom. Reason.*, 18(2):211–220, 1997.

[178] D.V. McDermott. Tarskian semantics, or no notation without denotation!. *Cognitive Science*, 2(3):277–282, 1978.

[179] D.V. McDermott. A temporal logic for reasoning about processes and plans. *Cognitive Science*, 6:101–155, 1982.

[180] D.V. McDermott. A critique of pure reason. *Computational Intelligence*, 3:151–160, 1987.

[181] D.V. McDermott and J. Doyle. Non-monotonic logic I. *Artificial Intelligence*, 13(1–2):41–72, 1980.

[182] A. Middeldorp. Modular properties of term rewriting systems. PhD thesis, Vrije Universiteit, Amsterdam, 1990.

[183] R. Miller and L. Morgenstern. The commonsense problem page, 1997. http://www-formal.stanford.edu/leora/commonsense.

[184] S. Miller and D.A. Plaisted. Performance of OSHL on problems requiring definition expansion. In R. Letz, editor. *7th International Workshop on First-Order Theorem Proving*, Koblenz, Germany, September 15–17, 2005.

[185] M. Minsky. A framework for representing knowledge. In P.H. Winston, editor. *The Psychology of Computer Vision*. McGraw-Hill, 1975. Also available as MIT-AI Lab Memo 306.

[186] R.C. Moore. The role of logic in knowledge representation and commonsense reasoning. In *AAAI*, pages 428–433, 1982.

[187] L. Morgenstern. The problems with solutions to the frame problem. In K.M. Ford and Z.W. Pylyshyn, editors. *The Robot's Dilemma Revisited*. Ablex, 1996.

[188] L. Morgenstern. A first-order axiomatization of the surprise birthday present problem: Preliminary report. In *Proceedings of the Seventh International Symposium on Logical Formalizations of Commonsense Reasoning*, 2005. Also published as Dresden Technical Report, ISSN 1430-211X.

[189] S. Muggleton and L. De Raedt. Inductive logic programming: Theory and methods. *J. Logic Program.*, 19/20:629–679, 1994.

[190] G. Nelson and D.C. Oppen. Simplification by cooperating decision procedures. *ACM TOPLAS*, 1(2):245–257, 1979.

[191] G. Nelson and D.C. Oppen. Fast decision procedures based on congruence closure. *Journal of the ACM*, 27(2):356–364, 1980.

[192] M.H.A. Newman. On theories with a combinatorial definition of 'equivalence'. *Annals of Mathematics*, 43(2):223–243, 1942.

[193] R. Nieuwenhuis and A. Rubio. Paramodulation-based theorem proving. In A. Robinson and A. Voronkov, editors. *Handbook of Automated Reasoning*, vol. I, pages 371–443. Elsevier Science, 2001 (Chapter 7).

[194] R. Nieuwenhuis and A. Rubio. Theorem proving with ordering and equality constrained clauses. *J. Symbolic Comput.*, 19(4):321–351, 1995.

[195] N.J. Nilsson. Shakey the robot. Technical Report 323. SRI International, 1984.

[196] T. Nipkow, G. Bauer, and P. Schultz. Flyspeck I: Tame graphs. In Furbach and Shankar [91], pages 21–35.

[197] T. Nipkow, L.C. Paulson, and M. Wenzel. *Isabelle/HOL: A Proof Assistant for Higher-Order Logic*. Springer-Verlag, 2003.

[198] M. Nogueira, M. Balduccini, M. Gelfond, R. Watson, and M. Barry. An A-Prolog decision support system for the Space Shuttle. In *Proceedings of International Symposium on Practical Aspects of Declarative Languages (PADL)*, pages 169–183, 2001.

[199] E. Ohlebusch. *Advanced Topics in Term Rewriting*. Springer, New York, 2002.

[200] D.C. Oppen. Elementary bounds for Presburger Arithmetic. In *STOC'73: Proceedings of the Fifth Annual ACM Symposium on Theory of Computing*, pages 34–37. ACM Press, New York, NY, USA, 1973.

[201] S. Owrie, J.M. Rushby, and N. Shankar. PVS: A prototype verification system. In D. Kapur, editor. *Proceedings of the Eleventh Conference on Automated Deduction, Lecture Notes in Artificial Intelligence*, vol. 607, pages 748–752. Springer, June 1992.

[202] M. Paterson and M.N. Wegman. Linear unification. *J. Comput. System Sci.*, 16(2):158–167, 1978.

[203] L.C. Paulson. *Isabelle: A Generic Theorem Prover. Lecture Notes in Comput. Sci.*, vol. 828. Springer-Verlag, New York, 1994.

[204] G. Peano. Arithmetices principia, nova methodo exposita. Turin, 1889. English translation: [261, pp. 83–97].

[205] G.E. Peterson and M.E. Stickel. Complete sets of reductions for some equational theories. *Journal of the ACM*, 28(2):233–264, 1981.

[206] L. Pike. Formal verification of time-triggered systems. PhD thesis, Indiana University, 2005.

[207] D. Plaisted. A recursively defined ordering for proving termination of term rewriting systems. Technical report R-78-943, University of Illinois at Urbana-Champaign, Urbana, IL, 1978.

[208] D. Plaisted. Well-founded orderings for proving termination of systems of rewrite rules. Technical report R-78-932, University of Illinois at Urbana-Champaign, Urbana, IL, 1978.

[209] D. Plaisted. An associative path ordering. In *Proceedings of an NSF Workshop on the Rewrite Rule Laboratory*, pages 123–136, April 1984.

[210] D. Plaisted. Semantic confluence tests and completion methods. *Information and Control*, 65(2–3):182–215, 1985.

[211] D. Plaisted and S.-J. Lee. Inference by clause matching. In Z. Ras and M. Zemankova, editors. *Intelligent Systems: State of the Art and Future Directions*, pages 200–235. Ellis Horwood, West Sussex, 1990.

[212] D. Plaisted and Y. Zhu. *The Efficiency of Theorem Proving Strategies: A Comparative and Asymptotic Analysis*. Vieweg, Wiesbaden, 1997.

[213] D.A. Plaisted and Y. Zhu. Ordered semantic hyperlinking. *Journal of Automated Reasoning*, 25(3):167–217, October 2000.

[214] G. Plotkin. Building-in equational theories. In *Machine Intelligence*, vol. 7, pages 73–90. Edinburgh University Press, 1972.

[215] K. Popper. *The Logic of Scientific Discovery*. Hutchinson, London, 1959.

[216] E. Post. Introduction to a general theory of elementary propositions. *American Journal of Mathematics*, 43:163–185, 1921. Reproduced in [261, pp. 264–283].

[217] D. Prawitz. An improved proof procedure. *Theoria*, 26:102–139, 1960.

[218] QED Group. The QED manifesto. In A. Bundy, editor. *Proceedings of the Twelfth International Conference on Automated Deduction, Lecture Notes in Artificial Intelligence*, vol. 814, pages 238–251. Springer-Verlag, New York, 1994.

[219] A. Quaife. Automated deduction in von Neumann–Bernays–Gödel set theory. *Journal of Automated Reasoning*, 8:91–147, 1992.

[220] D. Ramachandran, P. Reagan, and K. Goolsbey. First-orderized researchcyc: Expressivity and efficiency in a common-sense ontology. Working Papers of the *AAAI Workshop on Contexts and Ontologies: Theory, Practice, and Applications*, 2005.

[221] D. Ramachandran, P. Reagan, K. Goolsbey, K. Keefe, and E. Amir. Inference-friendly translation of researchcyc to first order logic, 2005. Unpublished.

[222] I.V. Ramakrishnan, R. Sekar, and A. Voronkov. Term indexing. In A. Robinson and A. Voronkov, editors. *Handbook of Automated Reasoning*, vol. II, pages 1853–1964. Elsevier Science, 2001 (Chapter 26).

[223] A.L. Rector. Modularisation of domain ontologies implemented in description logics and related formalisms including owl. In J.H. Gennari, B.W. Porter, and Y. Gil, editors. *K-CAP*, pages 121–128. ACM, 2003.

[224] R. Reiter. A logic for default reasoning. *Artificial Intelligence*, 13(1–2):81–132, 1980.

[225] R. Reiter. *Knowledge in Action: Logical Foundations for Specifying and Implementing Dynamical Systems*. MIT Press, 2001.

[226] A. Riazanov. Implementing an efficient theorem prover. PhD thesis, The University of Manchester, Manchester, July 2003.

[227] A. Riazanov and A. Voronkov. The design and implementation of VAMPIRE. *AI Communications*, 15(2–3):91–110, 2002.

[228] G. Robinson and L. Wos. Paramodulation and theorem-proving in first order theories with equality. In *Machine Intelligence*, vol. 4, pages 135–150. Edinburgh University Press, Edinburgh, Scotland, 1969.

[229] J. Robinson. Theorem proving on the computer. *Journal of the ACM*, 10:163–174, 1963.

[230] J. Robinson. A machine-oriented logic based on the resolution principle. *Journal of the ACM*, 12:23–41, 1965.

[231] J.A. Robinson and A. Voronkov, editors. *Handbook of Automated Reasoning (in 2 volumes)*. Elsevier/MIT Press, 2001.

[232] J.F. Rulifson, J.A. Derksen, and R.J. Waldinger. Qa4: A procedural calculus for intuitive reasoning. Technical Report 73, AI Center, SRI International, 333 Ravenswood Ave., Menlo Park, CA 94025, Nov. 1972.

[233] S. Russell and P. Norvig. *Artificial Intelligence: A Modern Approach*. 2nd edition. Prentice-Hall, 2003.

[234] W.C. Salmon. *Four Decades of Scientific Explanation*. University of Minnesota Press, 1989.

[235] S. Schulz. E—a brainiac theorem prover. *AI Communications*, 15(2):111–126, 2002.

[236] R. Schwitter. English as a formal specification language. In *DEXA Workshops*, pages 228–232. IEEE Computer Society, 2002.

[237] M. Shanahan. *Solving the Frame Problem*. MIT Press, Cambridge, MA, 1997.

[238] Y. Shoham. Chronological ignorance: Time, nonmonotonicity, necessity and causal theories. In *AAAI*, pages 389–393, 1986.

[239] J. Siekmann. Unification theory. *Journal of Symbolic Computation*, 7:207–274, 1989.

[240] J. Siekmann, C. Benzmüller, and S. Autexier. Computer supported mathematics with Omega. *Journal of Applied Logic*, 4(4):533–559, 2006.

[241] D.R. Smith. KIDS: A knowledge-based software development system. In M. Lowry and R. McCartney, editors. *Automating Software Design*, pages 483–514. MIT Press, 1991.

[242] C. Sprenger, M. Backes, D.A. Basin, B. Pfitzmann, and M. Waidner. Cryptographically sound theorem proving. In *CSFW*, pages 153–166. IEEE Computer Society, 2006.

[243] L.A. Stein and L. Morgenstern. Motivated action theory: A formal theory of causal reasoning. *Artificial Intelligence*, 71(1):1–42, 1994.

[244] J. Steinbach. Extensions and comparison of simplification orderings. In *Proceedings of the 3rd International Conference on rewriting techniques and applications, Lecture Notes in Computer Science*, vol. 355, pages 434–448. Springer, 1989.

[245] G. Stenz and R. Letz. DCTP—a disconnection calculus theorem prover. In R. Gore, A. Leitsch, and T. Nipkow, editors. *Proc. of the International Joint Conference on Automated Reasoning, Lecture Notes in Artificial Intelligence*, vol. 2083, pages 381–385. Springer, 2001.

[246] M.E. Stickel. A Prolog technology theorem prover: Implementation by an extended Prolog compiler. *Journal of Automated Reasoning*, 4(4):353–380, 1988.

[247] M.E. Stickel. A Prolog-like inference system for computing minimum-cost abductive explanation in natural-language interpretation. *Annals of Mathematics and Artificial Intelligence*, 4:89–106, 1991.

[248] M.E. Stickel. A Prolog technology theorem prover: A new exposition and implementation in Prolog. *Theoretical Computer Science*, 104:109–128, 1992.

[249] M.E. Stickel, R.J. Waldinger, and V.K. Chaudhri. A guide to SNARK. Technical report, SRI International, 2000.

[250] M.E. Stickel, R.J. Waldinger, M.R. Lowry, T. Pressburger, and I. Underwood. Deductive composition of astronomical software from subroutine libraries. In A. Bundy, editor. *CADE, Lecture Notes in Computer Science*, vol. 814, pages 341–355. Springer, 1994.

[251] M.E. Stickel. A unification algorithm for associative–commutative functions. *J. of the ACM*, 28:423–434, 1981.

[252] M.E. Stickel. A Prolog technology theorem prover: Implementation by an extended Prolog compiler. In *Proceedings of the 8th International Conference on Automated Deduction*, pages 573–587, 1986.

[253] G. Sutcliffe. CASC-J3: The 3rd IJCAR ATP system competition. In U. Furbach and N. Shankar, editors. *Proc. of the International Joint Conference on Automated Reasoning, Lecture Notes in Artificial Intelligence*, vol. 4130, pages 572–573. Springer, 2006.

[254] G. Sutcliffe. The CADE-20 automated theorem proving competition. *AI Communications*, 19(2):173–181, 2006.

[255] C.B. Suttner and G. Sutcliffe. The TPTP problem library (TPTP v2.0.0). Technical Report AR-97-01, Institut für Informatik, Technische Universität München, Germany, 1997.

[256] Terese. *Term Rewriting Systems. Cambridge Tracts in Theoretical Computer Science*, vol. 55. Cambridge University Press, 2003.

[257] R. Thomason. Logic and artificial intelligence. In *Stanford Encyclopedia of Philosophy*. Stanford University, 2003.

[258] Y. Toyama. On the Church–Rosser property for the direct sum of term rewriting systems. *Journal of the ACM*, 34(1):128–143, January 1987.

[259] Y. Toyama, J.W. Klop, and H.-P. Barendregt. Termination for the direct sum of left-linear term rewriting systems. In *Proceedings of the 3rd International Conference on Rewriting Techniques and Applications, Lecture Notes in Computer Science*, vol. 355, pages 477–491. Springer, 1989.

[260] A. Trybulec and H. Blair. Computer aided reasoning with Mizar. In R. Parikh, editor. *Logic of Programs, Lecture Notes in Comput. Sci.*, vol. 193. Springer-Verlag, New York, 1985.

[261] J. van Heijenoort, editor. *From Frege to Gödel: A Source Book in Mathematical Logic, 1879–1931*. Harvard University Press, 1967.

[262] E.M. Voorhees and L.P. Buckland, editors. *The Eleventh Text Retrieval Conference*, 2002.

[263] E.M. Voorhees and L.P. Buckland, editors. *The Twelfth Text Retrieval Conference*, 2003.

[264] E.M. Voorhees and L.P. Buckland, editors. *The Thirteenth Text Retrieval Conference*, 2004.

[265] E.M. Voorhees and L.P. Buckland, editors. *The Fourteenth Text Retrieval Conference*, 2005.

[266] E.M. Voorhees and L.P. Buckland, editors. *The Fifteenth Text Retrieval Conference*, 2006.

[267] Y. Wang, P. Haase, and J. Bao. A survey of formalisms for modular ontologies. In *Workshop on Semantic Web for Collaborative Knowledge Acquisition*, 2007.

[268] C. Weidenbach. Combining superposition, sorts and splitting. In Robinson and Voronkov [231], pages 1965–2013.

[269] C. Weidenbach, U. Brahm, T. Hillenbrand, E. Keen, C. Theobald, and D. Topic. S pass version 2.0. In A. Voronkov, editor. *CADE, Lecture Notes in Computer Science*, vol. 2392, pages 275–279. Springer, 2002.

[270] A.N. Whitehead and B. Russell. *Principia Mathematica*. University Press, 1957. Originally published 1910–1913.

[271] L. Wos, R. Overbeek, E. Lusk, and J. Boyle. *Automated Reasoning: Introduction and Applications*. Prentice-Hall, Englewood Cliffs, NJ, 1984.

[272] W.-T. Wu. On the decision problem and the mechanization of theorem proving in elementary geometry. *Scientia Sinica*, 21:159–172, 1978.

[273] P. Youn, B. Adida, M. Bon, J. Clulow, J. Herzog, A. Lin, R.L. Rivest, and R. Anderson. Robbing the bank with a theorem prover. Technical report 644, University of Cambridge Computer Laboratory, August 2005.

Edited by F. van Harmelen, V. Lifschitz and B. Porter
© 2008 Elsevier B.V. All rights reserved
DOI: 10.1016/S1574-6526(07)03002-7

Chapter 2

Satisfiability Solvers

Carla P. Gomes, Henry Kautz, Ashish Sabharwal, Bart Selman

The past few years have seen an enormous progress in the performance of Boolean satisfiability (SAT) solvers. Despite the worst-case exponential run time of all known algorithms, satisfiability solvers are increasingly leaving their mark as a general-purpose tool in areas as diverse as software and hardware verification [29–31, 228], automatic test pattern generation [138, 221], planning [129, 197], scheduling [103], and even challenging problems from algebra [238]. Annual SAT competitions have led to the development of dozens of clever implementations of such solvers (e.g., [13, 19, 71, 93, 109, 118, 150, 152, 161, 165, 170, 171, 173, 174, 184, 198, 211, 213, 236]), an exploration of many new techniques (e.g., [15, 102, 149, 170, 174]), and the creation of an extensive suite of real-world instances as well as challenging hand-crafted benchmark problems (cf. [115]). Modern SAT solvers provide a "black-box" procedure that can often solve hard structured problems with over a million variables and several million constraints.

In essence, SAT solvers provide a generic combinatorial reasoning and search platform. The underlying representational formalism is propositional logic. However, the full potential of SAT solvers only becomes apparent when one considers their use in applications that are not normally viewed as propositional reasoning tasks. For example, consider AI planning, which is a PSPACE-complete problem. By restricting oneself to polynomial size plans, one obtains an NP-complete reasoning problem, easily encoded as a Boolean satisfiability problem, which can be given to a SAT solver [128, 129]. In hardware and software verification, a similar strategy leads one to consider *bounded* model checking, where one places a bound on the length of possible error traces one is willing to consider [30]. Another example of a recent application of SAT solvers is in computing stable models used in the answer set programming paradigm, a powerful knowledge representation and reasoning approach [81]. In these applications—planning, verification, and answer set programming—the translation into a propositional representation (the "SAT encoding") is done automatically and is hidden from the user: the user only deals with the appropriate higher-level representation language of the application domain. Note that the translation to SAT generally leads to a substantial increase in problem representation. However, large SAT encodings are no longer an obstacle for modern SAT solvers. In fact, for many combinatorial search and reasoning tasks, the translation to SAT followed by the use of a modern SAT solver is often more effective than a custom search engine running on the original problem formulation. The explanation for this phenomenon is that SAT solvers have been engineered to such an extent that their performance is difficult to duplicate, even when one tackles the reasoning problem in its original representation.[1]

Although SAT solvers nowadays have found many applications outside of knowledge representation and reasoning, the original impetus for the development of such solvers can be traced back to research in knowledge representation. In the early to mid eighties, the tradeoff between the computational complexity and the expressiveness of knowledge representation languages became a central topic of research. Much of this work originated with a seminal series of papers by Brachman and Levesque on complexity tradeoffs in knowledge representation, in general, and description logics, in particular [36–38, 145, 146]. For a review of the state of the art in this area, see Chapter 3 of this Handbook. A key underling assumption in the research on complexity tradeoffs for knowledge representation languages is that the best way to proceed is to find the most elegant and expressive representation language that still allows for worst-case polynomial time inference. In the early nineties, this assumption was challenged in two early papers on SAT [168, 213]. In the first [168], the tradeoff between typical-case complexity versus worst-case complexity was explored. It was shown that most randomly generated SAT instances are actually surprisingly easy to solve (often in linear time), with the hardest instances only occurring in a rather small range of parameter settings of the random formula model. The second paper [213] showed that many satisfiable instances in the hardest region could still be solved quite effectively with a new style of SAT solvers based on local search techniques. These results challenged the relevance of the "worst-case" complexity view of the world.[2]

The success of the current SAT solvers on many real-world SAT instances with millions of variables further confirms that typical-case complexity and the complexity of real-world instances of NP-complete problems is much more amenable to effective general purpose solution techniques than worst-case complexity results might suggest. (For some initial insights into why real-world SAT instances can often be solved efficiently, see [233].) Given these developments, it may be worthwhile to reconsider

---

[1]Each year the International Conference on Theory and Applications of Satisfiability Testing hosts a SAT competition or race that highlights a new group of "world's fastest" SAT solvers, and presents detailed performance results on a wide range of solvers [141–143, 215]. In the 2006 competition, over 30 solvers competed on instances selected from thousands of benchmark problems. Most of these SAT solvers can be downloaded freely from the web. For a good source of solvers, benchmarks, and other topics relevant to SAT research, we refer the reader to the websites SAT Live! (http://www.satlive.org) and SATLIB (http://www.satlib.org).

[2]The contrast between typical- and worst-case complexity may appear rather obvious. However, note that the standard algorithmic approach in computer science is still largely based on avoiding any non-polynomial complexity, thereby implicitly acceding to a worst-case complexity view of the world. Approaches based on SAT solvers provide the first serious alternative.

the study of complexity tradeoffs in knowledge representation languages by not insisting on worst-case polynomial time reasoning but allowing for NP-complete reasoning sub-tasks that can be handled by a SAT solver. Such an approach would greatly extend the expressiveness of representation languages. The work on the use of SAT solvers to reason about stable models is a first promising example in this regard.

In this chapter, we first discuss the main solution techniques used in modern SAT solvers, classifying them as complete and incomplete methods. We then discuss recent insights explaining the effectiveness of these techniques on practical SAT encodings. Finally, we discuss several extensions of the SAT approach currently under development. These extensions will further expand the range of applications to include multi-agent and probabilistic reasoning. For a review of the key research challenges for satisfiability solvers, we refer the reader to [127].

2.1 Definitions and Notation

A propositional or Boolean formula is a logic expressions defined over variables (or atoms) that take value in the set {FALSE, TRUE}, which we will identify with {0, 1}. A *truth assignment* (or assignment for short) to a set V of Boolean variables is a map $\sigma : V \rightarrow \{0, 1\}$. A *satisfying assignment* for F is a truth assignment σ such that F evaluates to 1 under σ. We will be interested in propositional formulas in a certain special form: F is in *conjunctive normal form* (CNF) if it is a conjunction (AND, $\wedge$) of *clauses*, where each clause is a disjunction (OR, $\vee$) of *literals*, and each literal is either a variable or its negation (NOT, $\neg$). For example, $F = (a \vee \neg b) \wedge (\neg a \vee c \vee d) \wedge (b \vee d)$ is a CNF formula with four variables and three clauses.

The Boolean Satisfiability Problem (SAT) is the following: *Given a CNF formula F, does F have a satisfying assignment?* This is the canonical NP-complete problem [51, 147]. In practice, one is not only interested in this decision ("yes/no") problem, but also in finding an actual satisfying assignment if there exists one. All practical satisfiability algorithms, known as SAT solvers, do produce such an assignment if it exists.

It is natural to think of a CNF formula as a set of clauses and each clause as a set of literals. We use the symbol Λ to denote the *empty clause*, i.e., the clause that contains no literals and is therefore unsatisfiable. A clause with only one literal is referred to as a *unit* clause. A clause with two literals is referred to as a *binary* clause. When every clause of F has k literals, we refer to F as a k-CNF formula. The SAT problem restricted to 2-CNF formulas is solvable in polynomial time, while for 3-CNF formulas, it is already NP-complete. A *partial assignment* for a formula F is a truth assignment to a subset of the variables of F. For a partial assignment ρ for a CNF formula F, $F|_{\rho}$ denotes the *simplified* formula obtained by replacing the variables appearing in ρ with their specified values, removing all clauses with at least one TRUE literal, and deleting all occurrences of FALSE literals from the remaining clauses.

CNF is the generally accepted norm for SAT solvers because of its simplicity and usefulness; indeed, many problems are naturally expressed as a conjunction of relatively simple constraints. CNF also lends itself to the DPLL process to be described next. The construction of Tseitin [225] can be used to efficiently convert any given propositional formula to one in CNF form by adding new variables corresponding to its subformulas. For instance, given an arbitrary propositional formula G, one would first locally re-write each of its logic operators in terms of $\wedge$, $\vee$, and $\neg$ to obtain, say, $G = (((a \wedge b) \vee (\neg a \wedge \neg b)) \wedge \neg c) \vee d$. To convert this to CNF, one possibility is to add four auxiliary variables w, x, y, and z, construct clauses that encode the four relations $w \leftrightarrow (a \wedge b)$, $x \leftrightarrow (\neg a \wedge \neg b)$, $y \leftrightarrow (w \vee x)$, and $z \leftrightarrow (y \wedge \neg c)$, and add to that the clause $(z \vee d)$.

2.2 SAT Solver Technology—Complete Methods

A *complete* solution method for the SAT problem is one that, given the input formula F, either produces a satisfying assignment for F or proves that F is unsatisfiable. One of the most surprising aspects of the relatively recent practical progress of SAT solvers is that the best complete methods remain variants of a process introduced several decades ago: the DPLL procedure, which performs a backtrack search in the space of partial truth assignments. A key feature of DPLL is efficient pruning of the search space based on falsified clauses. Since its introduction in the early 1960's, the main improvements to DPLL have been smart branch selection heuristics, extensions like clause learning and randomized restarts, and well-crafted data structures such as lazy implementations and watched literals for fast unit propagation. This section is devoted to understanding these complete SAT solvers, also known as "systematic" solvers.[3]

2.2.1 The DPLL Procedure

The Davis–Putnam–Logemann–Loveland or DPLL procedure is a complete, systematic search process for finding a satisfying assignment for a given Boolean formula or proving that it is unsatisfiable. Davis and Putnam [61] came up with the basic idea behind this procedure. However, it was only a couple of years later that Davis, Logamann, and Loveland [60] presented it in the efficient top–down form in which it is widely used today. It is essentially a branching procedure that prunes the search space based on falsified clauses.

Algorithm 2.1, DPLL-recursive(F, ρ), sketches the basic DPLL procedure on CNF formulas. The idea is to repeatedly select an unassigned literal ℓ in the input formula F and recursively search for a satisfying assignment for $F|_\ell$ and $F|_{\neg\ell}$. The step where such an ℓ is chosen is commonly referred to as the *branching* step. Setting ℓ to TRUE or FALSE when making a recursive call is called a *decision*, and is associated with a *decision level* which equals the recursion depth at that stage. The end of each recursive call, which takes F back to fewer assigned variables, is called the *backtracking* step.

---

[3]Due to space limitation, we cannot do justice to a large amount of recent work on complete SAT solvers, which consists of hundreds of publications. The aim of this section is to give the reader an overview of several techniques commonly employed by these solvers.

Algorithm 2.1: DPLL-recursive(F, ρ)

Input : A CNF formula F and an initially empty partial assignment ρ
Output : UNSAT, or an assignment satisfying F
begin
    $(F, \rho) \leftarrow$ UnitPropagate(F, ρ)
    if F contains the empty clause **then return** UNSAT
    if F has no clauses left **then**
        Output ρ
        return SAT
    $\ell \leftarrow$ a literal not assigned by ρ // the branching step
    if DPLL-recursive($F|_\ell, \rho \cup \{\ell\}$) $= SAT$ **then return** SAT
    return DPLL-recursive($F|_{\neg\ell}, \rho \cup \{\neg\ell\}$)
end

sub UnitPropagate(F, ρ)
begin
    while F contains no empty clause but has a unit clause x **do**
        $F \leftarrow F|_x$
        $\rho \leftarrow \rho \cup \{x\}$
    return (F, ρ)
end

A partial assignment ρ is maintained during the search and output if the formula turns out to be satisfiable. If $F|_\rho$ contains the empty clause, the corresponding clause of F from which it came is said to be *violated* by ρ. To increase efficiency, unit clauses are immediately set to TRUE as outlined in Algorithm 2.1; this process is termed *unit propagation*. *Pure literals* (those whose negation does not appear) are also set to TRUE as a preprocessing step and, in some implementations, during the simplification process after every branch.

Variants of this algorithm form the most widely used family of complete algorithms for formula satisfiability. They are frequently implemented in an iterative rather than recursive manner, resulting in significantly reduced memory usage. The key difference in the iterative version is the extra step of *unassigning* variables when one backtracks. The naive way of unassigning variables in a CNF formula is computationally expensive, requiring one to examine every clause in which the unassigned variable appears. However, the *watched literals* scheme provides an excellent way around this and will be described shortly.

2.2.2 Key Features of Modern DPLL-Based SAT Solvers

The efficiency of state-of-the-art SAT solvers relies heavily on various features that have been developed, analyzed, and tested over the last decade. These include fast unit propagation using watched literals, learning mechanisms, deterministic and randomized restart strategies, effective constraint database management (clause deletion mechanisms), and smart static and dynamic branching heuristics. We give a flavor of some of these next.

Variable (and value) selection heuristic is one of the features that vary the most from one SAT solver to another. Also referred to as the *decision strategy*, it can have a significant impact on the efficiency of the solver (see, e.g., [160] for a survey). The commonly employed strategies vary from randomly fixing literals to maximizing a moderately complex function of the current variable- and clause-state, such as the MOMS (Maximum Occurrence in clauses of Minimum Size) heuristic [121] or the BOHM heuristic (cf. [32]). One could select and fix the literal occurring most frequently in the yet unsatisfied clauses (the DLIS (Dynamic Largest Individual Sum) heuristic [161]), or choose a literal based on its weight which periodically decays but is boosted if a clause in which it appears is used in deriving a conflict, like in the VSIDS (Variable State Independent Decaying Sum) heuristic [170]. Newer solvers like BerkMin [93], Jerusat [171], MiniSat [71], and RSat [184] employ further variations on this theme.

Clause learning has played a critical role in the success of modern complete SAT solvers. The idea here is to cache "causes of conflict" in a succinct manner (as learned clauses) and utilize this information to prune the search in a different part of the search space encountered later. We leave the details to Section 2.2.3, which will be devoted entirely to clause learning. We will also see how clause learning provably exponentially improves upon the basic DPLL procedure.

The watched literals scheme of Moskewicz et al. [170], introduced in their solver zChaff, is now a standard method used by most SAT solvers for efficient constraint propagation. This technique falls in the category of lazy data structures introduced earlier by Zhang [236] in the solver Sato. The key idea behind the watched literals scheme, as the name suggests, is to maintain and "watch" two special literals for each active (i.e., not yet satisfied) clause that are not FALSE under the current partial assignment; these literals could either be set to TRUE or be as yet unassigned. Recall that empty clauses halt the DPLL process and unit clauses are immediately satisfied. Hence, one can always find such watched literals in all active clauses. Further, as long as a clause has two such literals, it cannot be involved in unit propagation. These literals are maintained as follows. Suppose a literal ℓ is set to FALSE. We perform two maintenance operations. First, for every clause C that had ℓ as a watched literal, we examine C and find, if possible, another literal to watch (one which is TRUE or still unassigned). Second, for every previously active clause C' that has now become satisfied because of this assignment of ℓ to FALSE, we make $\neg\ell$ a watched literal for C'. By performing this second step, positive literals are given priority over unassigned literals for being the watched literals.

With this setup, one can test a clause for satisfiability by simply checking whether at least one of its two watched literals is TRUE. Moreover, the relatively small amount of extra book-keeping involved in maintaining watched literals is well paid off when one unassigns a literal ℓ by backtracking—in fact, one needs to do absolutely nothing! The invariant about watched literals is maintained as such, saving a substantial amount of computation that would have been done otherwise. This technique has played a critical role in the success of SAT solvers, in particular, those involving clause learning. Even when large numbers of very long learned clauses are constantly added to the clause database, this technique allows propagation to be very efficient—the long added clauses are not even looked at unless one assigns a value to one of the literals being watched and potentially causes unit propagation.

Conflict-directed backjumping, introduced by Stallman and Sussman [220], allows a solver to backtrack directly to a decision level d if variables at levels d or lower are the only ones involved in the conflicts in both branches at a point other than the branch variable itself. In this case, it is safe to assume that there is no solution extending the current branch at decision level d, and one may flip the corresponding variable at level d or backtrack further as appropriate. This process maintains the completeness of the procedure while significantly enhancing the efficiency in practice.

Fast backjumping is a slightly different technique, relevant mostly to the now-popular *FirstUIP* learning scheme used in SAT solvers `Grasp` [161] and `zChaff` [170]. It lets a solver jump directly to a lower decision level d when even one branch leads to a conflict involving variables at levels d or lower only (in addition to the variable at the current branch). Of course, for completeness, the current branch at level d is *not* marked as unsatisfiable; one simply selects a new variable and value for level d and continues with a new conflict clause added to the database and potentially a new implied variable. This is experimentally observed to increase efficiency in many benchmark problems. Note, however, that while conflict-directed backjumping is always beneficial, fast backjumping may not be so. It discards intermediate decisions which may actually be relevant and in the worst case will be made again unchanged after fast backjumping.

Assignment stack shrinking based on conflict clauses is a relatively new technique introduced by Nadel [171] in the solver `Jerusat`, and is now used in other solvers as well. When a conflict occurs because a clause C' is violated and the resulting conflict clause C to be learned exceeds a certain threshold length, the solver backtracks to almost the highest decision level of the literals in C. It then starts assigning to FALSE the unassigned literals of the violated clause C' until a new conflict is encountered, which is expected to result in a smaller and more pertinent conflict clause to be learned.

Conflict clause minimization was introduced by Eén and Sörensson [71] in their solver `MiniSat`. The idea is to try to reduce the size of a learned conflict clause C by repeatedly identifying and removing any literals of C that are implied to be FALSE when the rest of the literals in C are set to FALSE. This is achieved using the subsumption resolution rule, which lets one derive a clause A from $(x \vee A)$ and $(\neg x \vee B)$ where $B \subseteq A$ (the derived clause A subsumes the antecedent $(x \vee A)$). This rule can be generalized, at the expense of extra computational cost that usually pays off, to a sequence of subsumption resolution derivations such that the final derived clause subsumes the first antecedent clause.

Randomized restarts, introduced by Gomes et al. [102], allow clause learning algorithms to arbitrarily stop the search and restart their branching process from decision level zero. All clauses learned so far are retained and now treated as additional initial clauses. Most of the current SAT solvers, starting with `zChaff` [170], employ aggressive restart strategies, sometimes restarting after as few as 20 to 50 backtracks. This has been shown to help immensely in reducing the solution time. Theoretically, unlimited restarts, performed at the correct step, can provably make clause learning very powerful. We will discuss randomized restarts in more detail later in the chapter.

2.2.3 Clause Learning and Iterative DPLL

Algorithm 2.2 gives the top-level structure of a DPLL-based SAT solver employing clause learning. Note that this algorithm is presented here in the *iterative* format (rather than recursive) in which it is most widely used in today's SAT solvers.

Algorithm 2.2: `DPLL-ClauseLearning-Iterative`

Input   : A CNF formula
Output : UNSAT, or SAT along with a satisfying assignment
begin
    while TRUE **do**
        `DecideNextBranch`
        while TRUE **do**
            status $\leftarrow$ `Deduce`
            if status = CONFLICT **then**
                blevel $\leftarrow$ `AnalyzeConflict`
                if blevel = 0 **then return** UNSAT
                `Backtrack` (blevel)
            else if status = SAT **then**
                Output current assignment stack
                return SAT
            else break
end

The procedure `DecideNextBranch` chooses the next variable to branch on (and the truth value to set it to) using either a static or a dynamic variable selection heuristic. The procedure `Deduce` applies unit propagation, keeping track of any clauses that may become empty, causing what is known as a conflict. If all clauses have been satisfied, it declares the formula to be satisfiable.[4] The procedure `AnalyzeConflict` looks at the structure of implications and computes from it a "conflict clause" to learn. It also computes and returns the decision level that one needs to backtrack. Note that there is no explicit variable flip in the entire algorithm; one simply learns a conflict clause before backtracking, and this conflict clause often implicitly "flips" the value of a decision or implied variable by unit propagation. This will become clearer when we discuss the details of conflict clause learning and unique implication point.

In terms of notation, variables assigned values through the actual variable selection process (`DecideNextBranch`) are called *decision* variables and those assigned values as a result of unit propagation (`Deduce`) are called *implied* variables. *Decision* and *implied literals* are analogously defined. Upon backtracking, the last decision variable no longer remains a decision variable and might instead become an implied variable depending on the clauses learned so far. The *decision level of a decision variable x* is one more than the number of current decision variables at the time of branching on x. The *decision level of an implied variable y* is the maximum of the decision levels of decision variables used to imply y; if y is implied a value without using any decision variable at all, y has decision level zero. The *decision level* at any step of the underlying DPLL procedure is the maximum of the decision levels of all current decision variables, and zero if there is no decision variable yet. Thus, for instance, if the clause

---

[4]In some implementations involving lazy data structures, solvers do not keep track of the actual number of satisfied clauses. Instead, the formula is declared to be satisfiable when all variables have been assigned truth values and no conflict is created by this assignment.

learning algorithm starts off by branching on x, the decision level of x is 1 and the algorithm at this stage is at decision level 1.

A clause learning algorithm stops and declares the given formula to be unsatisfiable whenever unit propagation leads to a conflict at decision level zero, i.e., when no variable is currently branched upon. This condition is sometimes referred to as a *conflict at decision level zero*.

Clause learning grew out of work in artificial intelligence seeking to improve the performance of backtrack search algorithms by generating explanations for failure (backtrack) points, and then adding the explanations as new constraints on the original problem. The results of Stallman and Sussman [220], Genesereth [82], Davis [62], Dechter [64], de Kleer and Williams [63], and others proved this approach to be quite promising. For general constraint satisfaction problems the explanations are called "conflicts" or "no-goods"; in the case of Boolean CNF satisfiability, the technique becomes clause learning—the reason for failure is learned in the form of a "conflict clause" which is added to the set of given clauses. Despite the initial success, the early work in this area was limited by the large numbers of no-goods generated during the search, which generally involved many variables and tended to slow the constraint solvers down. Clause learning owes a lot of its practical success to subsequent research exploiting efficient lazy data structures and constraint database management strategies. Through a series of papers and often accompanying solvers, Bayardo Jr. and Miranker [17], Marques-Silva and Sakallah [161], Bayardo Jr. and Schrag [19], Zhang [236], Moskewicz et al. [170], Zhang et al. [240], and others showed that clause learning can be efficiently implemented and used to solve hard problems that cannot be approached by any other technique.

In general, the learning process hidden in `AnalyzeConflict` is expected to save us from redoing the same computation when we later have an assignment that causes conflict due in part to the same reason. Variations of such conflict-driven learning include different ways of choosing the clause to learn (different *learning schemes*) and possibly allowing multiple clauses to be learned from a single conflict. We next formalize the graph-based framework used to define and compute conflict clauses.

Implication graph and conflicts

Unit propagation can be naturally associated with an *implication graph* that captures all possible ways of deriving all implied literals from decision literals. In what follows, we use the term *known clauses* to refer to the clauses of the input formula as well as to all clauses that have been learned by the clause learning process so far.

Definition 2.1. *The implication graph G at a given stage of* DPLL *is a directed acyclic graph with edges labeled with sets of clauses. It is constructed as follows:*

Step 1: *Create a node for each decision literal, labeled with that literal. These will be the indegree-zero source nodes of G.*

Step 2: *While there exists a known clause $C = (l_1 \vee \cdots l_k \vee l)$ such that $\neg l_1, \ldots, \neg l_k$ label nodes in G,*

  (i) *Add a node labeled l if not already present in G.*

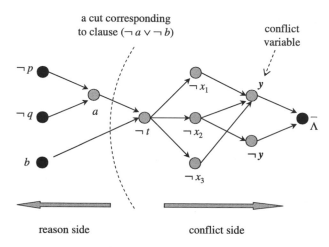

Figure 2.1: A conflict graph.

(ii) *Add edges (l_i, l), $1 \leqslant i \leqslant k$, if not already present.*

(iii) *Add C to the label set of these edges. These edges are thought of as grouped together and associated with clause C.*

Step 3: *Add to G a special "conflict" node $\overline{\Lambda}$. For any variable x that occurs both positively and negatively in G, add directed edges from x and $\neg x$ to $\overline{\Lambda}$.*

Since all node labels in G are distinct, we identify nodes with the literals labeling them. Any variable x occurring both positively and negatively in G is a *conflict variable*, and x as well as $\neg x$ are *conflict literals*. G contains a *conflict* if it has at least one conflict variable. DPLL at a given stage has a *conflict* if the implication graph at that stage contains a conflict. A conflict can equivalently be thought of as occurring when the residual formula contains the empty clause Λ. Note that we are using $\overline{\Lambda}$ to denote the node of the implication graph representing a conflict, and Λ to denote the empty clause.

By definition, the implication graph may not contain a conflict at all, or it may contain many conflict variables and several ways of deriving any single literal. To better understand and analyze a conflict when it occurs, we work with a subgraph of the implication graph, called the *conflict graph* (see Fig. 2.1), that captures only one among possibly many ways of reaching a conflict from the decision variables using unit propagation.

Definition 2.2. *A conflict graph H is any subgraph of the implication graph with the following properties:*

(a) *H contains $\overline{\Lambda}$ and exactly one conflict variable.*

(b) *All nodes in H have a path to $\overline{\Lambda}$.*

(c) *Every node l in H other than $\overline{\Lambda}$ either corresponds to a decision literal or has precisely the nodes $\neg l_1, \neg l_2, \ldots, \neg l_k$ as predecessors where $(l_1 \vee l_2 \vee \cdots \vee l_k \vee l)$ is a known clause.*

While an implication graph may or may not contain conflicts, a conflict graph always contains exactly one. The choice of the conflict graph is part of the strategy of the solver. A typical strategy will maintain one subgraph of an implication graph that has properties (b) and (c) from Definition 2.2, but not property (a). This can be thought of as a *unique inference* subgraph of the implication graph. When a conflict is reached, this unique inference subgraph is extended to satisfy property (a) as well, resulting in a conflict graph, which is then used to analyze the conflict.

Conflict clauses

For a subset U of the vertices of a graph, the *edge-cut* (henceforth called a cut) corresponding to U is the set of all edges going from vertices in U to vertices not in U.

Consider the implication graph at a stage where there is a conflict and fix a conflict graph contained in that implication graph. Choose any cut in the conflict graph that has all decision variables on one side, called the *reason side*, and $\overline{\Lambda}$ as well as at least one conflict literal on the other side, called the *conflict side*. All nodes on the reason side that have at least one edge going to the conflict side form a *cause* of the conflict. The negations of the corresponding literals forms the *conflict clause* associated with this cut.

Learning schemes

The essence of clause learning is captured by the *learning scheme* used to analyze and learn the "cause" of a failure. More concretely, different cuts in a conflict graph separating decision variables from a set of nodes containing $\overline{\Lambda}$ and a conflict literal correspond to different learning schemes (see Fig. 2.2). One may also define learning schemes based on cuts not involving conflict literals at all such as a scheme suggested by Zhang et al. [240], but the effectiveness of such schemes is not clear. These will not be considered here.

It is insightful to think of the *nondeterministic* scheme as the most general learning scheme. Here we select the cut nondeterministically, choosing, whenever possible, one whose associated clause is not already known. Since we can repeatedly branch on the same last variable, nondeterministic learning subsumes learning multiple clauses from a single conflict as long as the sets of nodes on the reason side of the corresponding cuts form a (set-wise) decreasing sequence. For simplicity, we will assume that only one clause is learned from any conflict.

In practice, however, we employ deterministic schemes. The *decision* scheme [240], for example, uses the cut whose reason side comprises all decision variables. Relsat [19] uses the cut whose conflict side consists of all implied variables at the current decision level. This scheme allows the conflict clause to have exactly one variable from the current decision level, causing an automatic flip in its assignment upon backtracking. In the example depicted in Fig. 2.2, the decision clause $(p \vee q \vee \neg b)$ has b as the only variable from the current decision level. After learning this conflict clause and backtracking by unassigning b, the truth values of p and q (both FALSE) immediately imply $\neg b$, flipping the value of b from TRUE to FALSE.

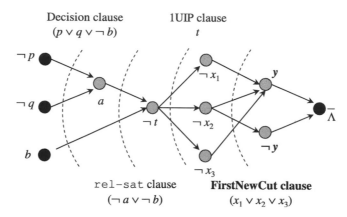

Figure 2.2: Learning schemes corresponding to different cuts in the conflict graph.

This nice flipping property holds in general for all *unique implication points* (UIPs) [161]. A UIP of an implication graph is a node at the current decision level d such that every path from the decision variable at level d to the conflict variable or its negation must go through it. Intuitively, it is a *single* reason at level d that causes the conflict. Whereas relsat uses the decision variable as the obvious UIP, Grasp [161] and zChaff [170] use *FirstUIP*, the one that is "closest" to the conflict variable. Grasp also learns multiple clauses when faced with a conflict. This makes it typically require fewer branching steps but possibly slower because of the time lost in learning and unit propagation.

The concept of UIP can be generalized to decision levels other than the current one. The *1UIP scheme* corresponds to learning the FirstUIP clause of the current decision level, the *2UIP scheme* to learning the FirstUIP clauses of both the current level and the one before, and so on. Zhang et al. [240] present a comparison of all these and other learning schemes and conclude that 1UIP is quite robust and outperforms all other schemes they consider on most of the benchmarks.

Another learning scheme, which underlies the proof of a theorem to be presented in the next section, is the *FirstNewCut* scheme [22]. This scheme starts with the cut that is closest to the conflict literals and iteratively moves it back toward the decision variables until a conflict clause that is not already known is found; hence the name FirstNewCut.

2.2.4 A Proof Complexity Perspective

Propositional proof complexity is the study of the structure of proofs of validity of mathematical statements expressed in a propositional or Boolean form. Cook and Reckhow [52] introduced the formal notion of a proof system in order to study mathematical proofs from a computational perspective. They defined a propositional proof system to be an efficient algorithm A that takes as input a propositional statement S and a purported proof π of its validity in a certain pre-specified format. The crucial property of A is that for all invalid statements S, it rejects the pair (S, π) for all π, and for all valid statements S, it accepts the pair (S, π) for some proof π. This notion of proof systems can be alternatively formulated in terms of unsatisfiable formulas—those that are FALSE for all assignments to the variables.

They further observed that if there is no propositional proof system that admits short (polynomial in size) proofs of validity of all tautologies, i.e., if there exist computationally hard tautologies for every propositional proof system, then the complexity classes NP and co-NP are different, and hence P $\neq$ NP. This observation makes finding tautological formulas (equivalently, unsatisfiable formulas) that are computationally difficult for various proof systems one of the central tasks of proof complexity research, with far reaching consequences to complexity theory and Computer Science in general. These hard formulas naturally yield a hierarchy of proof systems based on the sizes of proofs they admit. Tremendous amount of research has gone into understanding this hierarchical structure. Beame and Pitassi [23] summarize many of the results obtained in this area.

To understand current complete SAT solvers, we focus on the proof system called *resolution*, denoted henceforth as RES. It is a very simple system with only one rule which applies to disjunctions of propositional variables and their negations: (a OR B) and ((NOT a) OR C) together imply (B OR C). Repeated application of this rule suffices to derive an empty disjunction if and only if the initial formula is unsatisfiable; such a derivation serves as a proof of unsatisfiability of the formula.

Despite its simplicity, unrestricted resolution as defined above (also called *general resolution*) is hard to implement efficiently due to the difficulty of finding good choices of clauses to resolve; natural choices typically yield huge storage requirements. Various restrictions on the structure of resolution proofs lead to less powerful but easier to implement refinements that have been studied extensively in proof complexity. Those of special interest to us are *tree-like resolution*, where every derived clause is used at most once in the refutation, and *regular resolution*, where every variable is resolved upon at most one in any "path" from the initial clauses to the empty clause. While these and other refinements are sound and complete as proof systems, they differ vastly in efficiency. For instance, in a series of results, Bonet et al. [34], Bonet and Galesi [35], and Buresh-Oppenheim and Pitassi [41] have shown that regular, ordered, linear, positive, negative, and semantic resolution are all exponentially stronger than tree-like resolution. On the other hand, Bonet et al. [34] and Alekhnovich et al. [7] have proved that tree-like, regular, and ordered resolution are exponentially weaker than RES.

Most of today's complete SAT solvers implement a subset of the resolution proof system. However, till recently, it was not clear where exactly do they fit in the proof system hierarchy and how do they compare to refinements of resolution such as regular resolution. Clause learning and random restarts can be considered to be two of the most important ideas that have lifted the scope of modern SAT solvers from experimental toy problems to large instances taken from real world challenges. Despite overwhelming empirical evidence, for many years not much was known of the ultimate strengths and weaknesses of the two.

Beame, Kautz, and Sabharwal [22, 199] answered several of these questions in a formal proof complexity framework. They gave the first precise characterization of clause learning as a proof system called CL and began the task of understanding its power by relating it to resolution. In particular, they showed that with a new learning scheme called FirstNewCut, clause learning can provide exponentially shorter proofs than any proper refinement of general resolution satisfying a natural self-reduction property. These include regular and ordered resolution, which are already known to be much stronger than the ordinary DPLL procedure which captures most of the SAT solvers that do not incorporate clause learning. They also showed that a slight variant of clause learning with unlimited restarts is as powerful as general resolution itself.

From the basic proof complexity point of view, only families of unsatisfiable formulas are of interest because only proofs of unsatisfiability can be large; minimum proofs of satisfiability are linear in the number of variables of the formula. In practice, however, many interesting formulas are satisfiable. To justify the approach of using a proof system CL, we refer to the work of Achlioptas, Beame, and Molloy [2] who have shown how negative proof complexity results for unsatisfiable formulas can be used to derive run time lower bounds for specific inference algorithms, especially DPLL, running on satisfiable formulas as well. The key observation in their work is that before hitting a satisfying assignment, an algorithm is very likely to explore a large unsatisfiable part of the search space that results from the first bad variable assignment.

Proof complexity does not capture everything we intuitively mean by the power of a reasoning system because it says nothing about how difficult it is to *find* shortest proofs. However, it is a good notion with which to begin our analysis because the size of proofs provides a lower bound on the running time of any implementation of the system. In the systems we consider, a branching function, which determines which variable to split upon or which pair of clauses to resolve, guides the search. A negative proof complexity result for a system ("proofs must be large in this system") tells us that a family of formulas is intractable even with a perfect branching function; likewise, a positive result ("small proofs exist") gives us hope of finding a good branching function, i.e., a branching function that helps us uncover a small proof.

We begin with an easy to prove relationship between DPLL (without clause learning) and tree-like resolution (for a formal proof, see, e.g., [199]).

Proposition 2.1. *For a CNF formula F, the size of the smallest DPLL refutation of F is equal to the size of the smallest tree-like resolution refutation of F.*

The interesting part is to understand what happens when clause learning is brought into the picture. It has been previously observed by Lynce and Marques-Silva [157] that clause learning can be viewed as adding resolvents to a tree-like resolution proof. The following results show further that clause learning, viewed as a propositional proof system CL, is exponentially stronger than tree-like resolution. This explains, formally, the performance gains observed empirically when clause learning is added to DPLL based solvers.

Clause learning proofs

The notion of clause learning proofs connects clause learning with resolution and provides the basis for the complexity bounds to follow. If a given formula F is unsatisfiable, the clause learning based DPLL process terminates with a conflict at decision level zero. Since all clauses used in this final conflict themselves follow directly or indirectly from F, this failure of clause learning in finding a satisfying assignment constitutes a logical proof of unsatisfiability of F. In an informal sense, we denote by CL the proof system consisting of all such proofs; this can be made precise using the notion of a branching sequence [22]. The results below compare the sizes of proofs in CL with the sizes of (possibly restricted) resolution proofs. Note that clause learning algorithms can use one of many learning schemes, resulting in different proofs.

We next define what it means for a refinement of a proof system to be natural and proper. Let $C_S(F)$ denote the length of a shortest refutation of a formula F under a proof system S.

Definition 2.3. *(See [22, 199].) For proof systems S and T, and a function $f : \mathbb{N} \rightarrow [1, \infty)$,*

- *S is* natural *if for any formula F and restriction ρ on its variables, $C_S(F|_\rho) \leqslant C_S(F)$.*

- *S is a* refinement *of T if proofs in S are also (restricted) proofs in T.*

- *S is $f(n)$-proper as a refinement of T if there exists a witnessing family $\{F_n\}$ of formulas such that $C_S(F_n) \geqslant f(n) \cdot C_T(F_n)$. The refinement is exponentially-proper if $f(n) = 2^{n^{\Omega(1)}}$ and super-polynomially-proper if $f(n) = n^{\omega(1)}$.*

Under this definition, tree-like, regular, linear, positive, negative, semantic, and ordered resolution are natural refinements of RES, and further, tree-like, regular, and ordered resolution are exponentially-proper [34, 7].

Now we are ready to state the somewhat technical theorem relating the clause learning process to resolution, whose corollaries are nonetheless easy to understand. The proof of this theorem is based on an explicit construction of so-called "proof-trace extension" formulas, which interestingly allow one to translate *any* known separation result between RES and a natural proper refinement S of RES into a separation between CL and S.

Theorem 2.1. *(See [22, 199].) For any $f(n)$-proper natural refinement S of RES and for CL using the FirstNewCut scheme and no restarts, there exist formulas $\{F_n\}$ such that $C_S(F_n) \geqslant f(n) \cdot C_{CL}(F_n)$.*

Corollary 2.1. *CL can provide exponentially shorter proofs than tree-like, regular, and ordered resolution.*

Corollary 2.2. *Either CL is not a natural proof system or it is equivalent in strength to RES.*

We remark that this leaves open the possibility that CL may not be able to simulate all regular resolution proofs. In this context, MacKenzie [158] has used arguments similar to those of Beame et al. [20] to prove that a natural variant of clause learning can indeed simulate all of regular resolution.

Finally, let CL-- denote the variant of CL where one is allowed to branch on a literal whose value is already set explicitly or because of unit propagation. Of course, such a relaxation is useless in ordinary DPLL; there is no benefit in branching on a variable that does not even appear in the residual formula. However, with clause learning, such a branch can lead to an immediate conflict and allow one to learn a key conflict clause that would otherwise have not been learned. This property can be used to prove that RES can be efficiently simulated by CL-- with enough restarts. In this context, a clause learning scheme will be called *non-redundant* if on a conflict, it always learns a clause not already known. Most of the practical clause learning schemes are non-redundant.

Theorem 2.2. (*See [22, 199].*) CL-- *with any non-redundant scheme and unlimited restarts is polynomially equivalent to* RES.

We note that by choosing the restart points in a smart way, CL together with restarts can be converted into a *complete* algorithm for satisfiability testing, i.e., for all unsatisfiable formulas given as input, it will halt and provide a proof of unsatisfiability [16, 102]. The theorem above makes a much stronger claim about a slight variant of CL, namely, with enough restarts, this variant can always find proofs of unsatisfiability that are as short as those of RES.

2.2.5 Symmetry Breaking

One aspect of many theoretical as well as real-world problems that merits attention is the presence of *symmetry* or *equivalence* amongst the underlying objects. Symmetry can be defined informally as a mapping of a constraint satisfaction problem (CSP) onto itself that preserves its structure as well as its solutions. The concept of symmetry in the context of SAT solvers and in terms of higher level problem objects is best explained through some examples of the many application areas where it naturally occurs. For instance, in FPGA (field programmable gate array) routing used in electronics design, all available wires or channels used for connecting two switch boxes are equivalent; in our design, it does not matter whether we use wire #1 between connector X and connector Y, or wire #2, or wire #3, or any other available wire. Similarly, in circuit modeling, all gates of the same "type" are interchangeable, and so are the inputs to a multiple fan-in AND or OR gate (i.e., a gate with several inputs); in planning, all identical boxes that need to be moved from city A to city B are equivalent; in multi-processor scheduling, all available processors are equivalent; in cache coherency protocols in distributed computing, all available identical caches are equivalent. A key property of such objects is that when selecting k of them, we can choose, *without loss of generality*, any k. This without-loss-of-generality reasoning is what we would like to incorporate in an automatic fashion.

The question of symmetry exploitation that we are interested in addressing arises when instances from domains such as the ones mentioned above are translated into CNF formulas to be fed to a SAT solver. A CNF formula consists of constraints over different kinds of variables that typically represent tuples of these high level objects (e.g., wires, boxes, etc.) and their interaction with each other. For example, during the problem modeling phase, we could have a Boolean variable $z_{w,c}$ that is TRUE iff the first end of wire w is attached to connector c. When this formula is converted into DIMACS format for a SAT solver, the *semantic meaning* of the variables, that, say, variable 1324 is associated with wire #23 and connector #5, is discarded. Consequently, in this translation, the global notion of the obvious interchangeability of the set of wire objects is lost, and instead manifests itself indirectly as a symmetry between the (numbered) variables of the formula and therefore also as a symmetry within the set of satisfying (or unsatisfying) variable assignments. These sets of symmetric satisfying and unsatisfying assignments artificially explode both the satisfiable and the unsatisfiable parts of the search space, the latter of which can be a challenging obstacle for a SAT solver searching for a satisfying assignment.

One of the most successful techniques for handling symmetry in both SAT and general CSPs originates from the work of Puget [187], who showed that symmetries can be *broken* by adding one lexicographic ordering constraint per symmetry. Crawford et al. [55] showed how this can be done by adding a set of simple "lex-constraints" or *symmetry breaking predicates* (SBPs) to the input specification to weed out all but the lexically-first solutions. The idea is to identify the group of permutations of variables that keep the CNF formula unchanged. For each such permutation π, clauses are added so that for every satisfying assignment σ for the original problem, whose permutation $\pi(\sigma)$ is also a satisfying assignment, only the lexically-first of σ and $\pi(\sigma)$ satisfies the added clauses. In the context of CSPs, there has been a lot of work in the area of SBPs. Petrie and Smith [182] extended the idea to value symmetries, Puget [189] applied it to products of variable and value symmetries, and Walsh [231] generalized the concept to symmetries acting simultaneously on variables and values, on set variables, etc. Puget [188] has recently proposed a technique for creating dynamic lex-constraints, with the goal of minimizing adverse interaction with the variable ordering used in the search tree.

In the context of SAT, value symmetries for the high-level variables naturally manifest themselves as low-level variable symmetries, and work on SBPs has taken a different path. Tools such as Shatter by Aloul et al. [8] improve upon the basic SBP technique by using lex-constraints whose size is only linear in the number of variables rather than quadratic. Further, they use graph isomorphism detectors like Saucy by Darga et al. [56] to generate symmetry breaking predicates only for the generators of the algebraic groups of symmetry. This latter problem of computing graph isomorphism, however, is not known to have any polynomial time algorithms, and is conjectured to be strictly between the complexity classes P and NP (cf. [136]). Hence, one must resort to heuristic or approximate solutions. Further, while there are formulas for which few SBPs suffice, the number of SBPs one needs to add in order to break *all* symmetries can be exponential. This is typically handled in practice by discarding "large" symmetries, i.e., those involving too many variables with respect to a fixed threshold. This may, however, sometimes result in much slower SAT solutions in domains such as clique coloring and logistics planning.

A very different and indirect approach for addressing symmetry is embodied in SAT solvers such as PBS by Aloul et al. [9], pbChaff by Dixon et al. [68], and Galena by Chai and Kuehlmann [44], which utilize non-CNF formulations known as pseudo-Boolean inequalities. Their logic reasoning is based on what is called the Cutting Planes proof system which, as shown by Cook et al. [53], is strictly stronger than resolution on which DPLL type CNF solvers are based. Since this more powerful proof system is difficult to implement in its full generality, pseudo-Boolean solvers often implement only a subset of it, typically learning only CNF clauses or restricted pseudo-Boolean constraints upon a conflict. Pseudo-Boolean solvers may lead to purely syntactic representational efficiency in cases where a single constraint such as $y_1 + y_2 + \cdots + y_k \leqslant 1$ is equivalent to $\binom{k}{2}$ binary clauses. More importantly, they are relevant to symmetry because they sometimes allow implicit encoding. For instance, the single constraint $x_1 + x_2 + \cdots + x_n \leq m$ over n variables captures the essence of the pigeonhole formula PHP^n_m over nm variables which is provably exponentially hard to solve using resolution-based methods without symmetry considerations [108]. This implicit representation, however, is not suitable in certain applications such as clique coloring and planning that we discuss. In fact, for unsatisfiable clique coloring instances, even pseudo-Boolean solvers provably require exponential time.

One could conceivably keep the CNF input unchanged but modify the solver to detect and handle symmetries during the search phase as they occur. Although this approach is quite natural, we are unaware of its implementation in a general purpose SAT solver besides sEqSatz by Li et al. [151], which has been shown to be effective on matrix multiplication and polynomial multiplication problems. Symmetry handling during search has been explored with mixed results in the CSP domain using frameworks like SBDD and SBDS (e.g., [72, 73, 84, 87]). Related work in SAT has been done in the specific areas of automatic test pattern generation by Marques-Silva and Sakallah [162] and SAT-based model checking by Shtrichman [214]. In both cases, the solver utilizes global information obtained at a stage to make subsequent stages faster. In other domain-specific work on symmetries in problems relevant to SAT, Fox and Long [74] propose a framework for handling symmetry in planning problems solved using the planning graph framework. They detect equivalence between various objects in the planning instance and use this information to reduce the search space explored by their planner. Unlike typical SAT-based planners, this approach does not guarantee plans of optimal length when multiple (non-conflicting) actions are allowed to be performed at each time step in parallel. Fortunately, this issue does not arise in the SymChaff approach for SAT to be mentioned shortly.

Dixon et al. [67] give a generic method of representing and dynamically maintaining symmetry in SAT solvers using algebraic techniques that guarantee polynomial size unsatisfiability proofs of many difficult formulas. The strength of their work lies in a strong group theoretic foundation and comprehensiveness in handling all possible symmetries. The computations involving group operations that underlie their current implementation are, however, often quite expensive.

When viewing complete SAT solvers as implementations of proof systems, the challenge with respect to symmetry exploitation is to push the underlying proof system up in the weak-to-strong proof complexity hierarchy without incurring the significant cost that typically comes from large search spaces associated with complex proof systems. While most of the current SAT solvers implement subsets of the resolution proof system, a different kind of solver called SymChaff [199, 200] brings it up closer to *symmetric resolution*, a proof system known to be exponentially stronger than resolution [226, 139]. More critically, it achieves this in a time- and space-efficient manner. Interestingly, while SymChaff involves adding structure to the problem description, it still stays within the realm of SAT solvers (as opposed to using a constraint programming (CP) approach), thereby exploiting the many benefits of the CNF form and the advances in state-of-the-art SAT solvers.

As a structure-aware solver, SymChaff incorporates several new ideas, including simple but effective symmetry representation, multiway branching based on variable classes and symmetry sets, and symmetric learning as an extension of clause learning to multiway branches. Two key places where it differs from earlier approaches are in using high level problem description to obtain symmetry information (instead of trying to recover it from the CNF formula) and in maintaining this information dynamically but without using a complex group theoretic machinery. This allows it to overcome many drawbacks of previously proposed solutions. It is shown, in particular, that straightforward annotation in the usual PDDL specification of planning problems is enough to automatically and quickly generate relevant symmetry information, which in turn makes the search for an optimal plan several orders of magnitude faster. Similar performance gains are seen in other domains as well.

2.3　SAT Solver Technology—Incomplete Methods

An *incomplete* method for solving the SAT problem is one that does not provide the guarantee that it will eventually either report a satisfying assignment or prove the given formula unsatisfiable. Such a method is typically run with a pre-set limit, after which it may or may not produce a solution. Unlike the systematic solvers based on an exhaustive branching and backtracking search, incomplete methods are generally based on *stochastic local search*. On problems from a variety of domains, such incomplete methods for SAT can significantly outperform DPLL-based methods. Since the early 1990's, there has been a tremendous amount of research on designing, understanding, and improving local search methods for SAT (e.g., [43, 77, 88, 89, 104, 105, 109, 113, 114, 116, 132, 137, 152, 164, 180, 183, 191, 206, 219]) as well as on hybrid approaches that attempt to combine DPLL and local search methods (e.g., [10, 106, 163, 185, 195]).[5] We begin this section by discussing two methods that played a key role in the success of local search in SAT, namely GSAT [213] and Walksat [211]. We will then explore the phase transition phenomenon in random SAT and a relatively new incomplete technique called Survey Propagation. We note that there are also other exciting related solution techniques such as those based on Lagrangian methods [207, 229, 235] and translation to integer programming [112, 124].

The original impetus for trying a local search method on satisfiability problems was the successful application of such methods for finding solutions to large N-queens problems, first using a connectionist system by Adorf and Johnston [6], and then using greedy local search by Minton et al. [167]. It was originally assumed that this success simply indicated that N-queens was an *easy* problem, and researchers felt that such techniques would fail in practice for SAT. In particular, it was believed that local search methods would easily get stuck in local minima, with a few clauses remaining unsatisfied. The GSAT experiments showed, however, that certain local search strategies often do reach global minima, in many cases much faster than systematic search strategies.

GSAT is based on a randomized local search technique [153, 177]. The basic GSAT procedure, introduced by Selman et al. [213] and described here as Algorithm 2.3, starts with a randomly generated truth assignment. It then greedily changes ('flips') the assignment of the variable that leads to the greatest decrease in the total number of unsatisfied clauses. Such flips are repeated until either a satisfying assignment is found or a pre-set maximum number of flips (MAX-FLIPS) is reached. This process is repeated as needed, up to a maximum of MAX-TRIES times.

---

[5] As in our discussion of the complete SAT solvers, we cannot do justice to all recent research in local search solvers for SAT. We will again try to provide a brief overview and touch upon some interesting details.

Algorithm 2.3: GSAT(*F*)

Input   : A CNF formula *F*
Parameters : Integers MAX-FLIPS, MAX-TRIES
Output   : A satisfying assignment for *F*, or FAIL
begin
   for *i* ← 1 to MAX-TRIES **do**
      σ ← a randomly generated truth assignment for *F*
      for *j* ← 1 to MAX-FLIPS **do**
         if *σ* satisfies *F* **then return** *σ*   // success
         ν ← a variable flipping which results in the greatest decrease
            (possibly negative) in the number of unsatisfied clauses
         Flip *ν* in *σ*
   return FAIL   // no satisfying assignment found
end

Selman et al. showed that GSAT substantially outperformed even the best back-tracking search procedures of the time on various classes of formulas, including randomly generated formulas and SAT encodings of graph coloring problems [123]. The search of GSAT typically begins with a rapid greedy descent towards a better assignment, followed by long sequences of "sideways" moves, i.e., moves that do not increase or decrease the total number of unsatisfied clauses. In the search space, each collection of truth assignments that are connected together by a sequence of possible sideways moves is referred to as a *plateau*. Experiments indicate that on many formulas, GSAT spends most of its time moving from plateau to plateau. Interestingly, Frank et al. [77] observed that in practice, almost all plateaus do have so-called "exits" that lead to another plateau with a lower number of unsatisfied clauses. Intuitively, in a very high dimensional search space such as the space of a 10,000 variable formula, it is very rare to encounter local minima, which are plateaus from where there is no local move that decreases the number of unsatisfied clauses. In practice, this means that GSAT most often does not get stuck in local minima, although it may take a substantial amount of time on each plateau before moving on to the next one. This motivates studying various modifications in order to speed up this process [209, 210]. One of the most successful strategies is to introduce noise into the search in the form of uphill moves, which forms the basis of the now well-known local search method for SAT called Walksat [211].

Walksat interleaves the greedy moves of GSAT with random walk moves of a standard Metropolis search. It further focuses the search by always selecting the variable to flip from an unsatisfied clause *C* (chosen at random). If there is a variable in *C* flipping which does not turn any currently satisfied clauses to unsatisfied, it flips this variable (a "freebie" move). Otherwise, with a certain probability, it flips a random literal of *C* (a "random walk" move), and with the remaining probability, it flips a variable in *C* that minimizes the *break-count*, i.e., the number of currently satisfied clauses that become unsatisfied (a "greedy" move). Walksat is presented in detail as Algorithm 2.4. One of its parameters, in addition to the maximum number of tries and flips, is the *noise* $p \in [0, 1]$, which controls how often are non-greedy moves

---

Algorithm 2.4: Walksat(F)

Input   : A CNF formula F
Parameters : Integers MAX-FLIPS, MAX-TRIES; noise parameter $p \in [0, 1]$
Output   : A satisfying assignment for F, or FAIL
begin
    for $i \leftarrow 1$ to MAX-TRIES **do**
        $\sigma \leftarrow$ a randomly generated truth assignment for F
        for $j \leftarrow 1$ to MAX-FLIPS **do**
            if σ satisfies F **then return** σ `// success`
            $C \leftarrow$ an unsatisfied clause of F chosen at random
            if $\exists$ variable $x \in C$ with break-count $= 0$ **then**
                $v \leftarrow x$ `// freebie move`
            else
                With probability p: `// random walk move`
                    $v \leftarrow$ a variable in C chosen at random
                With probability $1 - p$:   `// greedy move`
                    $v \leftarrow$ a variable in C with the smallest break-count
            Flip v in σ
    return FAIL   `// no satisfying assignment found`
end

---

considered during the stochastic search. It has been found empirically that for various problems from a single domain, a single value of p is optimal.

The focusing strategy of Walksat based on selecting variables solely from unsatisfied clauses was inspired by the $O(n^2)$ randomized algorithm for 2-SAT by Papadimitriou [178]. It can be shown that for any satisfiable formula and starting from any truth assignment, there exists a sequence of flips using only variables from unsatisfied clauses such that one obtains a satisfying assignment.

When one compares the biased random walk strategy of Walksat on hard random 3-CNF formulas against basic GSAT, the simulated annealing process of Kirkpatrick et al. [131], and a pure random walk strategy, the biased random walk process significantly outperforms the other methods [210]. In the years following the development of Walksat, many similar methods have been shown to be highly effective on not only random formulas but on many classes of structured instances, such as encodings of circuit design problems, Steiner tree problems, problems in finite algebra, and AI planning (cf. [116]). Various extensions of the basic process have also been explored, such as dynamic search policies like adapt-novelty [114], incorporating unit clause elimination as in the solver UnitWalk [109], and exploiting problem structure for increased efficiency [183]. Recently, it was shown that the performance of stochastic solvers on many structured problems can be further enhanced by using new SAT encodings that are designed to be effective for local search [186].

2.3.1 The Phase Transition Phenomenon in Random k-SAT

One of the key motivations in the early 1990's for studying incomplete, stochastic methods for solving SAT problems was the finding that DPLL-based systematic solvers perform quite poorly on certain randomly generated formulas. Consider a random

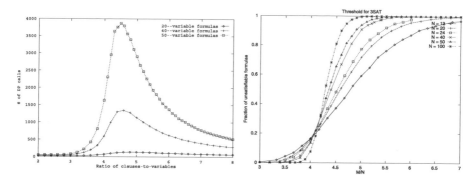

Figure 2.3: The phase transition phenomenon in random 3-SAT. Left: Computational hardness peaks at $\alpha \approx 4.26$. Right: Problems change from being mostly satisfiable to mostly unsatisfiable. The transitions sharpen as the number of variables grows.

k-CNF formula F on n variables generated by independently creating m clauses as follows: for each clause, select k distinct variables uniformly at random out of the n variables and negate each variable with probability 0.5. When F is chosen from this distribution, Mitchell, Selman, and Levesque [168] observed that the median hardness of the problems is very nicely characterized by a key parameter: the *clause-to-variable ratio*, m/n, typically denoted by α. They observed that problem hardness peaks in a critically constrained region determined by α alone. The left pane of Fig. 2.3 depicts the now well-known "easy-hard-easy" pattern of SAT and other combinatorial problems, as the key parameter (in this case α) is varied. For random 3-SAT, this region has been experimentally shown to be around $\alpha \approx 4.26$ (see [54, 132] for early results), and has provided challenging benchmarks as a test-bed for SAT solvers. Cheeseman et al. [45] observed a similar easy-hard-easy pattern in random graph coloring problems. For random formulas, interestingly, a slight natural variant of the above "fixed-clause-length" model, called the variable-clause-length model, does *not* have a clear set of parameters that leads to a hard set of instances [76, 92, 190]. This apparent difficulty in generating computationally hard instances for SAT solvers provided the impetus for much of the early work on local search methods for SAT. We refer the reader to [50] for a nice survey.

This critically constrained region marks a stark transition not only in the computational hardness of random SAT instances but also in their satisfiability itself. The right pane of Fig. 2.3 shows the fraction of random formulas that are unsatisfiable, as a function of α. We see that nearly all problems with α below the critical region (the under-constrained problems) are satisfiable. As α approaches and passes the critical region, there is a sudden change and nearly all problems in this over-constrained region are unsatisfiable. Further, as n grows, this phase transition phenomenon becomes sharper and sharper, and coincides with the region in which the computational hardness peaks. The relative hardness of the instances in the unsatisfiable region to the right of the phase transition is consistent with the formal result of Chvátal and Szemerédi [48] who, building upon the work of Haken [108], proved that large unsatisfiable random k-CNF formulas almost surely require exponential size resolution refutations, and thus exponential length runs of any DPLL-based algorithm proving unsatisfiability. This formal result was subsequently refined and strengthened by others (cf. [21, 24, 49]).

Relating the phase transition phenomenon for 3-SAT to statistical physics, Kirkpatrick and Selman [132] showed that the threshold has characteristics typical of phase transitions in the statistical mechanics of disordered materials (see also [169]). Physicists have studied phase transition phenomena in great detail because of the many interesting changes in a system's macroscopic behavior that occur at phase boundaries. One useful tool for the analysis of phase transition phenomena is called *finite-size scaling* analysis. This approach is based on rescaling the horizontal axis by a factor that is a function of n. The function is such that the horizontal axis is stretched out for larger n. In effect, rescaling "slows down" the phase-transition for higher values of n, and thus gives us a better look inside the transition. From the resulting universal curve, applying the scaling function backwards, the actual transition curve for each value of n can be obtained. In principle, this approach also localizes the 50%-satisfiable-point for any value of n, which allows one to generate the hardest possible random 3-SAT instances.

Interestingly, it is still not formally known whether there even exists a critical constant α_c such that as n grows, almost all 3-SAT formulas with $\alpha < \alpha_c$ are satisfiable and almost all 3-SAT formulas with $\alpha > \alpha_c$ are unsatisfiable. In this respect, Friedgut [78] provided the first positive result, showing that there exists a *function* $\alpha_c(n)$ depending on n such that the above threshold property holds. (It is quite likely that the threshold in fact does not depend on n, and is a fixed constant.) In a series of papers, researchers have narrowed down the gap between upper bounds on the threshold for 3-SAT (e.g., [40, 69, 76, 120, 133]), the best so far being 4.596, and lower bounds (e.g., [1, 5, 40, 75, 79, 107, 125]), the best so far being 3.52. On the other hand, for random 2-SAT, we do have a full rigorous understanding of the phase transition, which occurs at clause-to-variable ratio of 1 [33, 47]. Also, for general k, the threshold for random k-SAT is known to be in the range $2^k \ln 2 - O(k)$ [3, 101].

2.3.2 A New Technique for Random k-SAT: Survey Propagation

We end this section with a brief discussion of Survey Propagation (SP), an exciting new algorithm for solving hard combinatorial problems. It was discovered in 2002 by Mezard, Parisi, and Zecchina [165], and is so far the only known method successful at solving random 3-SAT instances with one million variables and beyond in near-linear time in the most critically constrained region.[6]

The SP method is quite radical in that it tries to approximate, using an iterative process of local "message" updates, certain marginal probabilities related to the set of satisfying assignments. It then assigns values to variables with the most extreme probabilities, simplifies the formula, and repeats the process. This strategy is referred to as SP-inspired decimation. In effect, the algorithm behaves like the usual DPLL-based methods, which also assign variable values incrementally in an attempt to find a satisfying assignment. However, quite surprisingly, SP almost never has to backtrack. In other words, the "heuristic guidance" from SP is almost always correct. Note that, interestingly, computing marginals on satisfying assignments is strongly believed

---

[6]It has been recently shown that by finely tuning the noise parameter, Walksat can also be made to scale well on hard random 3-SAT instances, well above the clause-to-variable ratio of 4.2 [208].

to be much harder than finding a single satisfying assignment (#P-complete vs. NP-complete). Nonetheless, SP is able to efficiently approximate certain marginals on random SAT instances and uses this information to successfully find a satisfying assignment.

SP was derived from rather complex statistical physics methods, specifically, the so-called *cavity method* developed for the study of spin glasses. The method is still far from well-understood, but in recent years, we are starting to see results that provide important insights into its workings (e.g., [4, 12, 39, 140, 159, 166]). Close connections to belief propagation (BP) methods [181] more familiar to computer scientists have been subsequently discovered. In particular, it was shown by Braunstein and Zecchina [39] (later extended by Maneva, Mossel, and Wainwright [159]) that SP equations are equivalent to BP equations for obtaining marginals over a special class of combinatorial objects, called covers. In this respect, SP is the first successful example of the use of a probabilistic reasoning technique to solve a purely combinatorial search problem. The recent work of Kroc et al. [140] empirically established that SP, despite the very loopy nature of random formulas which violate the standard tree-structure assumptions underlying the BP algorithm, is remarkably good at computing marginals over these covers objects on large random 3-SAT instances.

Unfortunately, the success of SP is currently limited to random SAT instances. It is an exciting research challenge to further understand SP and apply it successfully to more structured, real-world problem instances.

2.4 Runtime Variance and Problem Structure

The performance of backtrack-style search methods can vary dramatically depending on the way one selects the next variable to branch on (the "variable selection heuristic") and in what order the possible values are assigned to the variable (the "value selection heuristic"). The inherent exponential nature of the search process appears to magnify the unpredictability of search procedures. In fact, it is not uncommon to observe a backtrack search procedure "hang" on a given instance, whereas a different heuristic, or even just another randomized run, solves the instance quickly. A related phenomenon is observed in random problem distributions that exhibit an "easy-hard-easy" pattern in computational complexity, concerning so-called "exceptionally hard" instances: such instances seem to defy the "easy-hard-easy" pattern. They occur in the under-constrained area, but they seem to be considerably harder than other similar instances and even harder than instances from the critically constrained area. This phenomenon was first identified by Hogg and Willimans [111] in graph coloring and by Gent and Walsh in satisfiability problems [83]. An instance is considered to be exceptionally hard, for a particular search algorithm, when it occurs in the region where almost all problem instances are satisfiable (i.e., the under constrained area), but is considerably harder to solve than other similar instances, and even harder than most of the instances in the critically constrained area [83, 111, 217]. However, subsequent research showed that such instances are not inherently difficult; for example, by simply renaming the variables or by considering a different search heuristic such instances can be easily solved [212, 218]. Therefore, the "hardness" of exceptionally hard instances does not reside in the instances *per se*, but rather in the combination of the instance with the details of the search method. This is the reason why researchers studying the hardness of computational problems use the median to characterize search difficulty, instead of the mean, since the behavior of the mean tends to be quite *erratic* [95].

2.4.1 Fat and Heavy Tailed Behavior

The study of the full runtime distributions of search methods—instead of just the moments and median—has been shown to provide a better characterization of search methods and much useful information in the design of algorithms. In particular, researchers have shown that the runtime distributions of complete backtrack search methods reveal intriguing characteristics of such search methods: quite often complete backtrack search methods exhibit *fat* and *heavy-tailed* behavior [80, 95, 111]. Such runtime distributions can be observed when running a deterministic backtracking procedure on a distribution of random instances, and perhaps more importantly by repeated runs of a randomized backtracking procedure on a single instance.

The notion of *fat-tailedness* is based on the concept of *kurtosis*. The *kurtosis* is defined as μ_4/μ_2^2 (μ_4 is the fourth central moment about the mean and μ_2 is the second central moment about the mean, i.e., the variance). If a distribution has a high central peak and long tails, than the kurtosis is in general large. The *kurtosis* of the standard normal distribution is 3. A distribution with a *kurtosis* larger than 3 is *fat-tailed* or *leptokurtic*. Examples of distributions that are characterized by *fat-tails* are the exponential distribution, the lognormal distribution, and the Weibull distribution.

Heavy-tailed distributions have "heavier" tails than fat-tailed distributions; in fact they have some infinite moments, e.g., they can have infinite mean, infinite variance, etc. More rigorously, a random variable X with probability distribution function $F(\cdot)$ is heavy-tailed if it has the so-called Pareto like decay of the tails, i.e.:

$$1 - F(x) = \Pr[X > x] \sim Cx^{-\alpha}, \quad x > 0,$$

where $\alpha > 0$ and $C > 0$ are constants. When $1 < \alpha < 2$, X has infinite variance, and infinite mean and variance when $0 < \alpha \leqslant 1$. The log–log plot of $1 - F(x)$ of a Pareto-like distribution (i.e., the survival function) shows linear behavior with slope determined by α. Like *heavy*-tailed distributions, *fat*-tailed distributions have long tails, with a considerable mass of probability concentrated in the tails. Nevertheless, the tails of *fat*-tailed distributions are lighter than *heavy*-tailed distributions.

DPLL style complete backtrack search methods have been shown to exhibit heavy-tailed behavior, both in random instances and real-world instances. Example domains are QCP [95], scheduling [97], planning [102], model checking, and graph coloring [122, 230]. Several formal models generating heavy-tailed behavior in search have been proposed [46, 94, 122, 233, 234]. If the runtime distribution of a backtrack search method is heavy-tailed, it will produce runs spanning over several orders of magnitude, some extremely long but also some extremely short. Methods like randomization and restarts try to exploit this phenomenon [102].

2.4.2 Backdoors

Insight into heavy-tailed behavior comes from considering backdoor variables. These are variables which, when set, give us a polynomial subproblem. Intuitively, a small backdoor set explains how a backtrack search method can get "lucky" on certain runs, where backdoor variables are identified early on in the search and set the right way. Formally, the definition of a backdoor depends on a particular algorithm, referred to as *sub-solver*, that solves a tractable sub-case of the general constraint satisfaction problem [233].

Definition 2.4. *A* sub-solver *A given as input a CSP, C, satisfies the following*:

  (i) Trichotomy: *A either rejects the input C, or "determines" C correctly (as unsatisfiable or satisfiable, returning a solution if satisfiable)*,

 (ii) Efficiency: *A runs in polynomial time*,

(iii) Trivial solvability: *A can determine if C is trivially true (has no constraints) or trivially false (has a contradictory constraint)*,

(iv) Self-reducibility: *if A determines C, then for any variable x and value v, A determines $C[v/x]$.*[7]

For instance, A could be an algorithm that enforces arc consistency. Using the definition of sub-solver we can now formally define the concept of backdoor set. Let A be a sub-solver and C be a CSP. A nonempty subset S of the variables with domain D is a (weak) *backdoor* in C for A if for some $a_S : S \to D$, A returns a satisfying assignment of $C[a_S]$. Intuitively, the backdoor corresponds to a set of variables, such that when set correctly, the sub-solver can solve the remaining problem. A stronger notion of backdoors considers both satisfiable and unsatisfiable (inconsistent) problem instances. A nonempty subset S of the variables is a *strong backdoor* in C for A if for all $a_S : S \to D$, A returns a satisfying assignment or concludes unsatisfiability of $C[a_S]$.

Szeider [223] considered the parameterized complexity of the problem of determining whether a SAT instance has a weak or strong backdoor set of size k or less for DPLL style sub-solvers, i.e., subsolvers based on unit propagation and/or pure literal elimination. He showed that detection of weak and strong backdoor sets is unlikely to be fixed-parameter tractable. Nishimura et al. [172] provided more positive results for detecting backdoor sets where the sub-solver solves Horn or 2-CNF formulas, both of which are linear time problems. They proved that the detection of such a strong backdoor set is fixed-parameter tractable, while the detection of a weak backdoor set is not. The explanation that they offered for such a discrepancy is quite interesting: for strong backdoor sets one only has to guarantee that the chosen set of variables gives a subproblem within the chosen syntactic class; for weak backdoor sets, one also has to guarantee satisfiability of the simplified formula, a property that cannot be described syntactically.

Dilkina et al. [66] studied the tradeoff between the complexity of backdoor detection and the backdoor size. They proved that adding certain obvious inconsistency checks to the underlying class can make the complexity of backdoor detection jump from being within NP to being both NP-hard and coNP-hard. On the positive side, they showed that this change can dramatically reduce the size of the resulting backdoors. They also explored the differences between so-called deletion backdoors and strong backdoors, in particular, with respect to the class of renamable Horn formulas.

---

[7]We use $C[v/x]$ to denote the simplified CSP obtained by setting the value of variable x to v in C.

  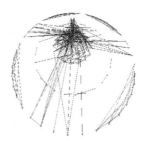

Figure 2.4: Constraint graph of a real-world instance from the logistics planning domain. The instance in the plot has 843 vars and 7301 clauses. One backdoor set for this instance w.r.t. unit propagation has size 16 (not necessarily the minimum backdoor set). Left: Constraint graph of the original instance. Center: Constraint graph after setting 5 variables and performing unit propagation. Right: Constraint graph after setting 14 variables and performing unit propagation.

Concerning the size of backdoors, random formulas do not appear to have small backdoor sets. For example, for random 3-SAT problems near the phase transition, the backdoor size appears to be a constant fraction (roughly 30%) of the total number of variables [119]. This may explain why the current DPLL based solvers have not made significant progress on hard randomly generated instances. Empirical results based on real-world instances suggest a more positive picture. Structured problem instances can have surprisingly small sets of backdoor variables, which may explain why current state-of-the-art solvers are able to solve very large real-world instances. For example, the logistics-d planning problem instance (log.d) has a backdoor set of just 12 variables, compared to a total of nearly 7000 variables in the formula, using the polynomial time propagation techniques of the SAT solver Satz [148]. Hoffmann et al. [110] proved the existence of *strong* backdoor sets of size just $O(\log n)$ for certain families of logistics planning problems and blocks world problems.

Even though computing minimum backdoor sets is worst-case intractable [223], if we bound the size of the backdoor, heuristics and techniques like randomization and restarts can often uncover a small backdoor in practice [130]. In fact, state-of-the-art SAT solvers are surprisingly effective in finding small backdoors in many structured problem instances. Figure 2.4 shows a visualization of the constraint graph of a logistics planning problem and how this graph is drastically simplified after only a few variables occurring in a small backdoor (found by SAT solvers) are set. In related work, Slaney and Walsh [216] studied the structural notion of "backbones" and Dequen and Dubois introduced a heuristic for DPLL based solvers that exploits the notion of backbone and outperforms other heuristics on random 3-SAT problems [65, 70].

2.4.3 Restarts

One way to exploit heavy-tailed behavior is to add restarts to a backtracking procedure. A sequence of short runs instead of a single long run may be a more effective use of computational resources (see Figure 2.5). Gomes et al. proposed randomized rapid restarts (RRR) to take advantage of heavy-tailed behavior and boost the efficiency of complete backtrack search procedures [102]. In practice, one gradually increases the cutoff to maintain completeness [16, 102]. Gomes et al. showed that a

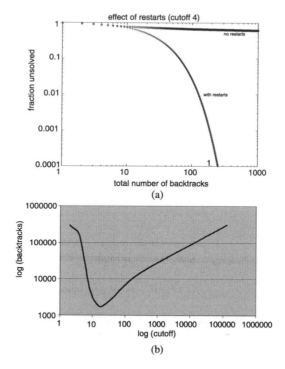

(a)

(b)

Figure 2.5: Restarts: (a) Tail $(1 - F(x))$ as a function of the total number of backtracks for a QCP instance, log–log scale; the lower curve is for a cutoff value of 4 and the upper curve is without restarts. (b) The effect of different cutoff values on solution cost for the logistics.d planning problem. Graph adapted from [95, 96].

restart strategy with a fixed cutoff eliminates heavy-tail behavior and has finite moments [96].

Prior to the discovery of heavy-tailed behavior and backdoor sets, randomized restart policies have been studied in the context of general randomized Las Vegas procedures. Luby et al. [155] showed that when the underlying runtime distribution of the randomized procedure is fully known, the optimal restart policy is a fixed cutoff. When there is no *a priori* knowledge about the distribution, they also provided a *universal strategy* which minimizes the expected cost. This consists of runs whose lengths are powers of two, and each time a pair of runs of a given length has been completed, a run of twice that length is immediately executed. The universal strategy is of the form: 1, 1, 2, 1, 1, 2, 4, 1, 1, 2, 4, 8, ... Although the universal strategy of Luby et al. is provably within a log factor of the optimal fixed cutoff, the schedule often converges too slowly in practice. Walsh [230] introduced a restart strategy, inspired by Luby et al.'s analysis, in which the cutoff value increases geometrically. The advantage of such a strategy is that it is less sensitive to the details of the underlying distribution. Following the findings of Gomes et al. [102] and starting with zChaff, state-of-the-art SAT solvers now routinely use restarts. In practice, the solvers use a default cutoff value, which is increased, linearly, every given number of restarts, guaranteeing the completeness of the solver in the limit [170]. Another important feature is that they retain learned clauses across restarts.

In reality, we will be somewhere between full and no knowledge of the runtime distribution. Horvitz et al. [117] introduced a Bayesian framework for learning predictive models of randomized backtrack solvers based on this situation. Extending that work, Kautz et al. [126] considered restart policies that can factor in information based on real-time observations about a solver's behavior. In particular, they introduced an *optimal* policy for dynamic restarts that considers observations about solver behavior. They also considered the dependency between runs. They gave a dynamic programming approach to generate the optimal restart strategy, and combined the resulting policy with real-time observations to boost performance of backtrack search methods.

Variants of restart strategies include randomized backtracking [156], and the random jump strategy [237] which has been used to solve a dozen previously open problems in finite algebra. Finally, one can also take advantage of the high variance of combinatorial search methods by combining several algorithms into a "portfolio", and running them in parallel or interleaving them on a single processor [100, 173].

2.5 Beyond SAT: Quantified Boolean Formulas and Model Counting

We end this chapter with a brief overview of two important problems that extend beyond propositional satisfiability testing and will lie at the heart of the next generation automated reasoning systems: Quantified Boolean Formula (QBF) reasoning and counting the number of models (solutions) of a problem. These problems present fascinating challenges and pose new research questions. Efficient algorithms for these will have a significant impact on many application areas that are inherently beyond SAT, such as adversarial and contingency planning, unbounded model checking, and probabilistic reasoning.

These problems can be solved, in principle and to some extent in practice, by extending the two most successful frameworks for SAT algorithms, namely, DPLL and local search. However, there are some interesting issues and choices that arise when extending SAT-based techniques to these harder problems. In general, these problems require the solver to, in a sense, be cognizant of *all solutions* in the search space, thereby reducing the effectiveness and relevance of commonly used SAT heuristics designed for quickly zooming in on a single solution. The resulting scalability challenge has drawn many satisfiability researchers to these problems.

2.5.1 QBF Reasoning

A Quantified Boolean Formula (QBF) is a Boolean formula in which variables are quantified as existential ($\exists$) or universal ($\forall$) (cf. [135]). We will use the term QBF for *totally quantified (also known as closed) Boolean formulas in prenex form* beginning (for simplicity) with $\exists$:

$$F = \exists x_1^1 \ldots \exists x_1^{t(1)} \forall x_2^1 \ldots \forall x_2^{t(2)} \ldots Q x_k^1 \ldots Q x_k^{t(k)} M,$$

where M is a Boolean formula referred to as the *matrix* of F, x_i^j above are distinct and include all variables appearing in M, and Q is $\exists$ if k is odd and $\forall$ if k is even. Defining $V_i = \{x_i^1, \ldots, x_i^{t(i)}\}$ and using associativity within each level of quantification, we can simplify the notation to $F = \exists V_1 \forall V_2 \exists V_3 \ldots Q V_k M$. A QBF solver is an algorithm that determines the truth value of such formulas F, i.e., whether there exist values of variables in V_1 such that for every assignment of values to variables in V_2 there exist values of variables in V_3, and so on, such that M is satisfied (i.e., evaluates to TRUE).

QBF reasoning extends the scope of SAT to domains requiring adversarial analysis, like conditional planning [192], unbounded model checking [26, 194], and discrete games [86]. As a simple applied example, consider a two-player game where each player has a discrete set of actions. Here a winning strategy for a player is a partial game tree that, for every possible game play of the opponent, indicates how to proceed so as to guarantee a win. This kind of reasoning is more complex than the single-agent reasoning that SAT solvers offer, and requires modeling and analyzing adversarial actions of another agent with competing interests. Fortunately, such problems are easily and naturally modeled using QBF. The QBF approach thus supports a much richer setting than SAT. However, it also poses new and sometimes unforeseen challenges.

In terms of the worst-case complexity, deciding the truth of a QBF is PSPACE-complete [222] whereas SAT is "only" NP-complete.[8] Even with very few quantification levels, the explosion in the search space is tremendous in practice. Further, as the winning strategy example indicates, even a solution to a QBF may require exponential space to describe, causing practical difficulties [25].

Nonetheless, several tools for deciding the truth of a given QBF (QBF solvers) have been developed. These include DPLL-style search based solvers like Quaffle [241], QuBE [90], Semprop [144], Evaluate [42], Decide [193], and QRSat [175]; local search methods like WalkQSAT [85]; skolemization based solvers like sKizzo [26]; q-resolution [134] based solvers like Quantor [28]; and symbolic, BDD based tools like QMRES and QBDD [176]. Most of these solvers extend the concepts underlying SAT solvers. In particular, they inherit conjunctive normal form (CNF) as the input representation, which has been the standard for SAT solvers for over a decade. Internally, some solvers also employ disjunctive normal form (DNF) to cache partial solutions for efficiency [242].

We focus here on DPLL-based QBF solvers. The working of these solvers is not very different from that of DPLL-based SAT solvers. The essential difference is that when the DPLL process branches on an universal variable x by setting it to TRUE and finds that branch to be satisfiable, it must also verify that the branch $x = $ FALSE is also satisfiable. The need to be able to do this "universal reasoning" and explore both branches of universal variables has, as expected, a substantial impact on the efficiency of the solver.

In a series of papers, Zhang and Malik [241], Letz [144], and Giunchiglia et al. [91] described how the clause learning techniques from SAT can be extended to *solution learning* for QBF. The idea is to not only cache small certificates of unsatisfiability of sub-formulas (as learned CNF clauses), but also to cache small certificates of satisfiability of sub-formulas (as learned DNF "terms", also referred to as *cubes*). This can, in principle, be very useful because not only does a QBF solver need to detect unsatisfiability efficiently, it needs to also detect satisfiability efficiently and repeatedly.

Another interesting change, which is now part of most QBF solvers, is related to unit propagation. This stems from the observation that if the variables with the

---

[8]PSPACE-complete problems are generally believed to be significantly harder than NP-complete problems; cf. [179].

deepest quantification level in a clause are universal, they cannot help satisfy that clause. The clause can effectively ignore these universal variables. This also plays a role in determining which clauses are learned upon reaching a conflict, and also has a dual counterpart about existential variables in a DNF term.

While the performance of QBF solvers has been promising, translating a QBF into a (much larger) SAT specification and using a good SAT solver is often faster in practice—a fact well-recognized and occasionally exploited [26, 28, 202]. This motivates the need for further investigation into the design of QBF solvers and possible fundamental weaknesses in the modeling methods used.

It has been recently demonstrated by Samulowitz et al. that the efficiency of QBF solvers can be improved significantly—much more so than SAT solvers—by employing certain pre-processing techniques on the formula at the very beginning [204] or using inference techniques, such as those based on binary clauses, on the fly [203]. These methods typically involve adding a certain type of easy-to-compute resolvents as redundant constraints to the problem, with the hope of achieving faster propagation. Results show that this works very well in practice.

Any QBF reasoning task has a natural game playing interpretation at a high level. Using this fact, Ansotegui et al. [11] described a general framework for modeling adversarial tasks as QBF instances. They view a problem P as a two-player game G with a bounded number of turns. This is different from the standard interpretation of a QBF as a game [179]; in their approach, one must formulate the higher level problem P as a game G *before* modeling it as a QBF. The sets of "rules" to which the existential and universal players of G are bound may differ from one player to the other. Ansotegui et al. [11] observed that typical CNF-based encodings for QBF suffer from the "illegal search space issue" where the solver finds it artificially hard to detect certain illegal moves made by the universal player. An example of an illegal move in, say, chess is to move a piece completely off the board or to move two pieces at a time. Recognizing such illegal moves of the universal player corresponds to deducing that the resulting formula can be easily satisfied by the existential player no matter what the universal player does next. Unlike a "local" violation of a clause, such detection involves *all* clauses of the formula and is non-trivial. In the standard QBF encodings, the solver is often be forced to explore an exponential number of such moves on multiple levels in the search tree. Ansotegui et al. proposed the use of special indicator variables that flag the occurrence of such illegal moves, which is then exploited by their solver to prune the search space.

Another recent proposal by Sabharwal et al. [201], implemented in the QBF solver `Duaffle` which extends `Quaffle`, is a new generic QBF modeling technique that uses a dual CNF-DNF representation. The dual representation considers the above game-theoretic view of the problem. The key idea is to exploit a dichotomy between the players: rules for the existential player are modeled as CNF clauses, (the negations of) rules for the universal player modeled as DNF terms, and game state information is split equally into clauses and terms. This symmetric dual format places "equal responsibility" on the two players, in stark contrast with other QBF encodings which tend to leave most work for the existential player. This representation has several advantages over pure-CNF encodings for QBF. In particular, it allows unit propagation *across quantifiers* and avoids the illegal search space issue altogether.

An independent dual CNF-DNF approach of Zhang [239] converts a full CNF encoding into a logically equivalent full DNF encoding and provides both to the solver. In contrast, `Duaffle` exploits the representational power of DNF to simplify the model and make it more compact, while addressing some issues associated with pure CNF representations. Both of these dual CNF-DNF approaches are different from fully non-clausal encodings, which also have promise but are unable to directly exploit rapid advances in CNF-based SAT solvers. Recently, Benedetti et al. [27] have proposed "restricted quantification" for pure-CNF encodings for QCSPs. This general technique addresses the illegal search space issue and is applicable also to QBF solvers other than those that are search based.

2.5.2 Model Counting

Propositional model counting or #SAT is the problem of computing the number of models for a given propositional formula, i.e., the number of distinct variable assignments for which the formula evaluates to TRUE. This problem generalizes SAT and is known to be a #P-complete problem, which means that it is no easier than solving a QBF with a fixed but unbounded number of "there exist" and "forall" quantification levels in its variables [224]. For comparison, notice that SAT can be thought of as a QBF with exactly one level of "there exist" quantification.

Effective model counting procedures would open up a range of new applications. For example, various probabilistic inference problems, such as Bayesian net reasoning, can be effectively translated into model counting problems (cf. [14, 58, 154, 196]). Another application is in the study of hard combinatorial problems, such as combinatorial designs, where the number of solutions provides further insights into the problem. Even finding a single solution can be a challenge for such problems: counting the number of solutions is much harder. Not surprisingly, the largest formulas we can solve for the model counting problem with state-of-the-art model counters are significantly smaller than the formulas we can solve with the best SAT solvers.

The earliest practical approach for counting models is based on an extension of systematic DPLL-based SAT solvers. The idea is to directly explore the complete search tree for an n-variable formula, associating 2^t solutions with a search tree branch if that branch leads to a solution at decision level $n - t$. By using appropriate multiplication factors and continuing the search after a single solution is found, `Relsat` [18] is able to provide incremental lower bounds on the model count as it proceeds, and finally computes the exact model count. Newer tools such as `Cachet` [205] often improve upon this by using techniques such as component caching [20].

Another approach for model counting is to convert the formula into a form from which the count can be deduced easily. The tool `c2d` [57] uses this knowledge compilation technique to convert the given CNF formula into decomposable negation normal form (DDNF) [59] and compute the model count.

Most exact counting methods, especially those based on DPLL search, essentially attack a #P-complete problem "head on"—by searching the raw combinatorial search space. Consequently, these algorithms often have difficulty scaling up to larger problem sizes. We should point out that problems with a higher solution count are not necessarily harder to determine the model count of. In fact, `Relsat` can compute the true model count of highly under-constrained problems with many "don't care" variables and a lot of models by exploiting big clusters in the solution space. The model counting problem is instead much harder for more intricate combinatorial problems where the solutions are spread much more finely throughout the combinatorial space.

Wei and Selman [232] use Markov Chain Monte Carlo (MCMC) sampling to compute an approximation of the true model count. Their model counter, ApproxCount, is able to solve several instances quite accurately, while scaling much better than both Relsat and Cachet as problem size increases. The drawback of Approx-Count is that one is not able to provide any hard guarantees on the model count it computes. To output a number close to the true count, this counting strategy requires near-uniform sampling from the set of solutions, which is generally difficult to achieve. Near-uniform sampling from the solution space is much harder than just generating a single solution. MCMC methods can provide theoretical convergence guarantees but only in the limit, which in the worst case may require an exponential number of Markov chain steps.

Interestingly, the inherent strength of most state-of-the-art SAT solvers comes actually from the ability to quickly narrow down to a certain portion of the search space the solver is designed to handle best. Such solvers therefore sample solutions in a highly non-uniform manner, making them seemingly ill-suited for model counting, unless one forces the solver to explore the full combinatorial space. An intriguing question is whether there is a way around this apparent limitation of the use of state-of-the-art SAT solvers for model counting.

MBound [98] is a new method for model counting, which interestingly uses any complete SAT solver "as is". It follows immediately that the more efficient the SAT solver used, the more powerful its counting strategy becomes. MBound is inspired by recent work on so-called "streamlining constraints" [99], in which additional, non-redundant constraints are added to the original problem to increase constraint propagation and to focus the search on a small part of the subspace, (hopefully) still containing solutions. This strategy was earlier shown to be successful in solving very hard combinatorial design problems, with carefully created, domain-specific streamlining constraints. In contrast, MBound uses a domain-independent streamlining technique.

The central idea of the approach is to use a special type of randomly chosen constrains as streamliners, namely XOR or parity constraints on the problem variables. Such constraints require that an odd number of the involved variables be set to TRUE. (This requirement can be translated into the usual CNF form by using additional variables [225].) MBound works by repeatedly adding a number s of such constraints to the formula and feeding the result to a state-of-the-art complete SAT solver. At a very high level, each random XOR constraint will cut the search space approximately in half. So, intuitively, if after the addition of s XOR's the formula is still satisfiable, the original formula must have at least of the order of 2^s models. More rigorously, it can be shown that if we perform t experiments of adding s random XOR constraints and our formula remains satisfiable in each case, then with probability at least $1 - 2^{-\alpha t}$, our original formula will have at least $2^{s-\alpha}$ satisfying assignments for any $\alpha > 0$. As a result, by repeated experiments or by weakening the claimed bound, one can arbitrarily boost the confidence in the lower bound count. Similar results can also be derived for the upper bound. A surprising feature of this approach is that it does not depend at all on how the solutions are distributed throughout the search space. It relies on the very special properties of random parity constraints, which in effect provide a good hash function, randomly dividing the solutions into two near-equal sets. Such constraints were first used by Valiant and Vazirani [227] in a randomized reduction from SAT to the related problem Unique SAT.

Bibliography

[1] D. Achlioptas. Setting 2 variables at a time yields a new lower bound for random 3-SAT. In *32st STOC*, pages 28–37, Portland, OR, May 2000.

[2] D. Achlioptas, P. Beame, and M. Molloy. A sharp threshold in proof complexity. In *33rd STOC*, pages 337–346, Crete, Greece, July 2001.

[3] D. Achlioptas, A. Naor, and Y. Peres. Rigorous location of phase transitions in hard optimization problems. *Nature*, 435:759–764, 2005.

[4] D. Achlioptas and F. Ricci-Tersenghi. On the solution-space geometry of random constraint satisfaction problems. In *38th STOC*, pages 130–139, Seattle, WA, May 2006.

[5] D. Achlioptas and G. Sorkin. Optimal myopic algorithms for random 3-SAT. In *41st FOCS*, pages 590–600, Redondo Beach, CA, Nov. 2000. IEEE.

[6] H. Adorf and M. Johnston. A discrete stochastic neural network algorithm for constraint satisfaction problems. In *Intl. Joint Conf. on Neural Networks*, pages 917–924, San Diego, CA, 1990.

[7] M. Alekhnovich, J. Johannsen, T. Pitassi, and A. Urquhart. An exponential separation between regular and general resolution. In *34th STOC*, pages 448–456, Montréal, Canada, May 2002.

[8] F.A. Aloul, I.L. Markov, and K.A. Sakallah. Shatter: Efficient symmetry-breaking for Boolean satisfiability. In *40th DAC*, pages 836–839, Anahein, CA, June 2003.

[9] F.A. Aloul, A. Ramani, I.L. Markov, and K.A. Sakallah. PBS: A backtrack-search pseudo-Boolean solver and optimizer. In *5th SAT*, pages 346–353, Cincinnati, OH, May 2002.

[10] Anbulagan, D.N. Pham, J.K. Slaney, and A. Sattar. Old resolution meets modern SLS. In *20th AAAI*, pages 354–359, Pittsburgh, PA, July 2005.

[11] C. Ansotegui, C.P. Gomes, and B. Selman. The Achilles' heel of QBF. In *20th AAAI*, pages 275–281, Pittsburgh, PA, July 2005.

[12] E. Aurell, U. Gordon, and S. Kirkpatrick. Comparing beliefs, surveys, and random walks. In *17th NIPS*, Vancouver, Canada, Dec. 2004.

[13] F. Bacchus. Enhancing Davis Putnam with extended binary clause reasoning. In *18th AAAI*, pages 613–619, Edmonton, Canada, July 2002.

[14] F. Bacchus, S. Dalmao, and T. Pitassi. Algorithms and complexity results for #SAT and Bayesian inference. In *44nd FOCS*, pages 340–351, Cambridge, MA, Oct. 2003.

[15] F. Bacchus and J. Winter. Effective preprocessing with hyper-resolution and equality reduction. In *6th SAT*, Santa Margherita, Italy, May 2003. *LNCS*, vol. 2919, pages 341–355. Springer, 2004.

[16] L. Baptista and J.P. Marques-Silva. Using randomization and learning to solve hard real-world instances of satisfiability. In *6th CP*, pages 489–494, Singapore, Sept. 2000.

[17] R.J. Bayardo Jr. and D.P. Miranker. A complexity analysis of space-bounded learning algorithms for the constraint satisfaction problem. In *13th AAAI*, pages 298–304, Portland, OR, Aug. 1996.

[18] R.J. Bayardo Jr. and J.D. Pehoushek. Counting models using connected components. In *17th AAAI*, pages 157–162, Austin, TX, July 2000.

[19] R.J. Bayardo Jr. and R.C. Schrag. Using CSP look-back techniques to solve real-world SAT instances. In *14th AAAI*, pages 203–208, Providence, RI, July 1997.

[20] P. Beame, R. Impagliazzo, T. Pitassi, and N. Segerlind. Memoization and DPLL: Formula caching proof systems. In *Proc., 18th Annual IEEE Conf. on Comput. Complexity*, pages 225–236, Aarhus, Denmark, July 2003.

[21] P. Beame, R. Karp, T. Pitassi, and M. Saks. On the complexity of unsatisfiability proofs for random k-CNF formulas. In *30th STOC*, pages 561–571, Dallas, TX, May 1998.

[22] P. Beame, H. Kautz, and A. Sabharwal. Understanding and harnessing the potential of clause learning. *J. Artificial Intelligence Res.*, 22:319–351, Dec. 2004.

[23] P. Beame and T. Pitassi. Propositional proof complexity: past, present, future. In *Current Trends in Theoretical Computer Science*, pages 42–70. World Scientific, 2001.

[24] P.W. Beame and T. Pitassi. Simplified and improved resolution lower bounds. In *37th FOCS*, pages 274–282, Burlington, VT, Oct. 1996. IEEE.

[25] M. Benedetti. Extracting certificates from quantified Boolean formulas. In *19th IJCAI*, pages 47–53, Edinburgh, Scotland, July 2005.

[26] M. Benedetti. sKizzo: a suite to evaluate and certify QBFs. In *20th CADE*, Tallinn, Estonia, July 2005. *LNCS*, vol. 3632, pages 369–376. Springer, 2005.

[27] M. Benedetti, A. Lallouet, and J. Vautard. QCSP made practical by virtue of restricted quantification. In *20th IJCAI*, pages 38–43, Hyderabad, India, Jan. 2007.

[28] A. Biere. Resolve and expand. In *7th SAT*, Vancouver, BC, Canada, May 2004. *LNCS*, vol. 3542, pages 59–70. Springer, 2005 (Selected papers).

[29] A. Biere, A. Cimatti, E.M. Clarke, M. Fujita, and Y. Zhu. Symbolic model checking using SAT procedures instead of BDDs. In *36th DAC*, pages 317–320, New Orleans, LA, June 1999.

[30] A. Biere, A. Cimatti, E.M. Clarke, and Y. Zhu. Symbolic model checking without BDDs. In *5th TACAS*, pages 193–207, Amsterdam, the Netherlands, Mar. 1999.

[31] P. Bjesse, T. Leonard, and A. Mokkedem. Finding bugs in an alpha microprocessor using satisfiability solvers. In *Proc. 13th Int. Conf. on Computer Aided Verification*, 2001.

[32] M. Böhm and E. Speckenmeyer. A fast parallel SAT-solver—efficient workload balancing. *Ann. of Math. AI*, 17(3–4):381–400, 1996.

[33] B. Bollobás, C. Borgs, J.T. Chayes, J.H. Kim, and D.B. Wilson. The scaling window of the 2-SAT transition. *Random Struct. Alg.*, 19(3–4):201–256, 2001.

[34] M.L. Bonet, J.L. Esteban, N. Galesi, and J. Johansen. On the relative complexity of resolution refinements and cutting planes proof systems. *SIAM J. Comput.*, 30(5):1462–1484, 2000.

[35] M.L. Bonet and N. Galesi. Optimality of size-width tradeoffs for resolution. *Comput. Compl.*, 10(4):261–276, 2001.

[36] R.J. Brachman and H.J. Levesque. The tractability of subsumption in frame based description languages. In *AAAI'84*, pages 34–37, 1984.

[37] R.J. Brachman and H.J. Levesque, editors. *Readings in Knowledge Representation*. Morgan Kaufmann, 1985.

[38] R.J. Brachman and J. Schmolze. An overview of the KL-ONE knowledge representation system. *Cognitive Science*, 9(2):171–216, 1985.

[39] A. Braunstein and R. Zecchina. Survey propagation as local equilibrium equations. *J. Stat. Mech.*, P06007, 2004. URL http://lanl.arXiv.org/cond-mat/0312483.

[40] A. Broder, A. Frieze, and E. Upfal. On the satisfiability and maximum satisfiability of random 3-CNF formulas. In *Proc., 4th SODA*, Jan. 1993.

[41] J. Buresh-Oppenheim and T. Pitassi. The complexity of resolution refinements. In *18th Annual IEEE Symp. on Logic in Comput. Sci.*, pages 138–147, Ottawa, Canada, June 2003.

[42] M. Cadoli, M. Schaerf, A. Giovanardi, and M. Giovanardi. An algorithm to evaluate quantified Boolean formulae and its experimental evaluation. *J. Automat. Reason.*, 28(2):101–142, 2002.

[43] B. Cha and K. Iwama. Adding new clauses for faster local search. In *13th AAAI*, pages 332–337, Portland, OR, Aug. 1996.

[44] D. Chai and A. Kuehlmann. A fast pseudo-Boolean constraint solver. In *40th DAC*, pages 830–835, Anahein, CA, June 2003.

[45] P. Cheeseman, B. Kenefsky, and W. Taylor. Where the really hard problems are. In *Proceedings of IJCAI-91*, pages 331–337. Morgan Kaufmann, 1991.

[46] H. Chen, C. Gomes, and B. Selman. Formal models of heavy-tailed behavior in combinatorial search. In *7th CP*, 2001.

[47] V. Chvátal and B. Reed. Mick gets some (the odds are on his side). In *33rd FOCS*, pages 620–627. IEEE, Pittsburgh, PA, Oct. 1992..

[48] V. Chvátal and E. Szemerédi. Many hard examples for resolution. *J. ACM*, 35(4):759–768, 1988.

[49] M. Clegg, J. Edmonds, and R. Impagliazzo. Using the Gröbner basis algorithm to find proofs of unsatisfiability. In *28th STOC*, pages 174–183, Philadelphia, PA, May 1996.

[50] S. Cook and D. Mitchell. Finding Hard Instances of the Satisfiability Problem: A Survey. In *DIMACS Series in Discrete Math. Theoret. Comput. Sci.*, vol. 35, pages 1–17. American Math. Society, 1997.

[51] S.A. Cook. The complexity of theorem proving procedures. In *Conf. Record of 3rd STOC*, pages 151–158, Shaker Heights, OH, May 1971.

[52] S.A. Cook and R.A. Reckhow. The relative efficiency of propositional proof systems. *J. Symbolic Logic*, 44(1):36–50, 1977.

[53] W. Cook, C.R. Coullard, and G. Turan. On the complexity of cutting plane proofs. *Discrete Appl. Math.*, 18:25–38, 1987.

[54] J.M. Crawford and L. Auton. Experimental results on the cross-over point in satisfiability problems. In *Proc. AAAI-93*, pages 21–27, Washington, DC, 1993.

[55] J.M. Crawford, M.L. Ginsberg, E.M. Luks, and A. Roy. Symmetry-breaking predicates for search problems. In *5th KR*, pages 148–159, Cambridge, MA, Nov. 1996.

[56] P.T. Darga, M.H. Liffiton, K.A. Sakallah, and I.L. Markov. Exploiting structure in symmetry detection for CNF. In *41st DAC*, pages 518–522, San Diego, CA, June 2004.

[57] A. Darwiche. New advances in compiling CNF into decomposable negation normal form. In *Proc., 16th Euro. Conf. on AI*, pages 328–332, Valencia, Spain, Aug. 2004.

[58] A. Darwiche. The quest for efficient probabilistic inference, July 2005. Invited Talk, IJCAI-05.

[59] A. Darwiche and P. Marquis. A knowledge compilation map. *J. Artificial Intelligence Res.*, 17:229–264, 2002.

[60] M. Davis, G. Logemann, and D. Loveland. A machine program for theorem proving. *Comm. ACM*, 5:394–397, 1962.

[61] M. Davis and H. Putnam. A computing procedure for quantification theory. *Comm. ACM*, 7:201–215, 1960.

[62] R. Davis. Diagnostic reasoning based on structure and behavior. *J. Artificial Intelligence*, 24(1–3):347–410, 1984.

[63] J. de Kleer and B.C. Williams. Diagnosing multiple faults. *J. Artificial Intelligence*, 32(1):97–130, 1987.

[64] R. Dechter. Learning while searching in constraint-satisfaction-problems. In *5th AAAI*, pages 178–185, Philadelphia, PA, Aug. 1986.

[65] G. Dequen and O. Dubois. Kcnfs: An efficient solver for random k-SAT formulae. In *6th SAT*, 2003.

[66] B. Dilkina, C.P. Gomes, and A. Sabharwal. Tradeoffs in the complexity of backdoor detection. In *13th CP*, Providence, RI, Sept. 2007.

[67] H.E. Dixon, M.L. Ginsberg, E.M. Luks, and A.J. Parkes. Generalizing Boolean satisfiability II: Theory. *J. Artificial Intelligence Res.*, 22:481–534, 2004.

[68] H.E. Dixon, M.L. Ginsberg, and A.J. Parkes. Generalizing Boolean satisfiability I: Background and survey of existing work. *J. Artificial Intelligence Res.*, 21:193–243, 2004.

[69] O. Dubois, Y. Boufkhad, and J. Mandler. Typical random 3-SAT formulae and the satisfiability threshold. In *Proc., 11th SODA*, pages 126–127, San Francisco, CA, Jan. 2000.

[70] O. Dubois and G. Dequen. A backbone search heuristic for efficient solving of hard 3-SAT formulae. In *18th IJCAI*, 2003.

[71] N. Eén and N. Sörensson. MiniSat: A SAT solver with conflict-clause minimization. In *8th SAT*, St. Andrews, UK, June 2005.

[72] T. Fahle, S. Schamberger, and M. Sellmann. Symmetry breaking. In *7th CP*, Paphos, Cyprus, Nov. 2001. *LNCS*, vol. 2239, pages 93–107. Springer, 2001.

[73] F. Focacci and M. Milano. Global cut framework for removing symmetries. In *7th CP*, Paphos, Cyprus, Nov. 2001. *LNCS*, vol. 2239, pages 77–92. Springer, 2001.

[74] M. Fox and D. Long. The detection and exploitation of symmetry in planning problems. In *16th IJCAI*, pages 956–961, July 1999.

[75] J. Franco. Probabilistic analysis of the pure literal heuristic for the satisfiability problem. *Ann. Oper. Res.*, 1:273–289, 1983.

[76] J. Franco and M. Paull. Probabilistic analysis of the Davis–Putnam procedure for solving the satisfiability problem. *Discrete Appl. Math.*, 5:77–87, 1983.

[77] J. Frank, P. Cheeseman, and J. Stutz. Where gravity fails: Local search topology. *J. Artificial Intelligence Res.*, 7:249–281, 1997.

[78] E. Friedgut. Sharp thresholds of graph properties, and the *k*-SAT problem. *J. Amer. Math. Soc.*, 12:1017–1054, 1999.

[79] A. Frieze and S. Suen. Analysis of two simple heuristics on a random instance of *k*-SAT. *J. Algorithms*, 20(2):312–355, 1996.

[80] D. Frost, I. Rish, and L. Vila. Summarizing CSP hardness with continuous probability distributions. In *Proceedings of the Fourteenth National Conference on Artificial Intelligence (AAAI-97)*, pages 327–334. AAAI Press, New Providence, RI, 1997.

[81] M. Gelfond. Answer sets. In F. van Harmelen, V. Lifschitz, and B. Porter, editors. *The Handbook of Knowledge Representation*. Elsevier, Oxford, 2006.

[82] M.R. Genesereth. The use of design descriptions in automated diagnosis. *J. Artificial Intelligence*, 24(1–3):411–436, 1984.

[83] I. Gent and T. Walsh. Easy problems are sometimes hard. *J. Artificial Intelligence*, 70:335–345, 1994.

[84] I.P. Gent, W. Harvey, T. Kelsey, and S. Linton. Generic SBDD using computational group theory. In *8th CP*, Kinsale, Ireland, Sept. 2003. *LNCS*, vol. 2833, pages 333–347. Springer, 2003.

[85] I.P. Gent, H.H. Hoos, A.G.D. Rowley, and K. Smyth. Using stochastic local search to solver quantified Boolean formulae. In *8th CP*, Kinsale, Ireland, Sept. 2003. *LNCS*, vol. 2833, pages 348–362. Springer, 2003.

[86] I.P. Gent and A.G. Rowley. Encoding Connect-4 using quantified Boolean formulae. In *2nd Intl. Work. Modelling and Reform. CSP*, pages 78–93, Kinsale, Ireland, Sept. 2003.

[87] I.P. Gent and B.M. Smith. Symmetry breaking in constraint programming. In *Proc., 14th Euro. Conf. on AI*, pages 599–603, Berlin, Germany, Aug. 2000.

[88] I.P. Gent and T. Walsh. Towards an understanding of hill-climbing procedures for SAT. In *11th AAAI*, pages 28–33, Washington, DC, July 1993.

[89] M.L. Ginsberg and D.A. McAllester. GSAT and dynamic backtracking. In *4th KR*, pages 226–237, Bonn, Germany, May 1994.

[90] E. Giunchiglia, M. Narizzano, and A. Tacchella. QUBE: A system for deciding quantified Boolean formulas satisfiability. In *1st IJCAR*, Siena, Italy, June 2001. *LNCS*, vol. 2083, pages 364–369. Springer, 2001.

[91] E. Giunchiglia, M. Narizzano, and A. Tacchella. Learning for quantified Boolean logic satisfiability. In *18th AAAI*, pages 649–654, Edmonton, Canada, July 2002.

[92] A. Goldberg. On the complexity of the satisfiability problem. Technical Report No. 16, Courant Computer Science, New York University, 1979.

[93] E. Goldberg and Y. Novikov. BerkMin: A fast and robust sat-solver. In *DATE*, pages 142–149, Paris, France, Mar. 2002.

[94] C. Gomes, C. Fernandez, B. Selman, and C. Bessiere. Statistical regimes across constrainedness regions. In *10th CP*, 2004.

[95] C. Gomes, B. Selman, and N. Crato. Heavy-tailed distributions in combinatorial search. In *3rd CP*, pages 121–135, 1997.

[96] C. Gomes, B. Selman, N. Crato, and H. Kautz. Heavy-tailed phenomena in satisfiability and constraint satisfaction problems. *J. Automat. Reason.*, 24(1–2):67–100, 2000.

[97] C. Gomes, B. Selman, K. McAloon, and C. Tretkoff. Randomization in back-track search: Exploiting heavy-tailed profiles for solving hard scheduling problems. In *4th Int. Conf. Art. Intel. Planning Syst.*, 1998.

[98] C.P. Gomes, A. Sabharwal, and B. Selman. Model counting: A new strategy for obtaining good bounds. In *21th AAAI*, pages 54–61, Boston, MA, July 2006.

[99] C.P. Gomes and M. Sellmann. Streamlined constraint reasoning. In *10th CP*, Toronto, Canada, Oct. 2004. *LNCS*, vol. 3258, pages 274–289. Springer, 2004.

[100] C.P. Gomes and B. Selman. Algorithm portfolios. *Artificial Intelligence*, 126(1–2):43–62, 2001.

[101] C.P. Gomes and B. Selman. Can get satisfaction. *Nature*, 435:751–752, 2005.

[102] C.P. Gomes, B. Selman, and H. Kautz. Boosting combinatorial search through randomization. In *15th AAAI*, pages 431–437, Madison, WI, July 1998.

[103] C.P. Gomes, B. Selman, K. McAloon, and C. Tretkoff. Randomization in back-track search: Exploiting heavy-tailed profiles for solving hard scheduling problems. In *4th Int. Conf. Art. Intel. Planning Syst.*, pages 208–213, Pittsburgh, PA, June 1998.

[104] J. Gu. Efficient local search for very large-scale satisfiability problems. *SIGART Bulletin*, 3(1):8–12, 1992.

[105] J. Gu, P.W. Purdom, J. Franco, and B.J. Wah. Algorithms for the satisfiability (SAT) problem: a survey. In *Satisfiability (SAT) Problem, DIMACS*, pages 19–151. American Mathematical Society, 1997.

[106] D. Habet, C.M. Li, L. Devendeville, and M. Vasquez. A hybrid approach for SAT. In *8th CP*, Ithaca, NY, Sept. 2002. *LNCS*, vol. 2470, pages 172–184. Springer, 2002.

[107] M. Hajiaghayi and G. Sorkin. The satisfiability threshold for random 3-SAT is at least 3.52, 2003. URL http://arxiv.org/abs/math/0310193.

[108] A. Haken. The intractability of resolution. *Theoret. Comput. Sci.*, 39:297–305, 1985.

[109] E.A. Hirsch and A. Kojevnikov. UnitWalk: A new SAT solver that uses local search guided by unit clause elimination. *Ann. Math. Artificial Intelligence*, 43(1):91–111, 2005.

[110] J. Hoffmann, C. Gomes, and B. Selman. Structure and problem hardness: Asymmetry and DPLL proofs in SAT-based planning. In *11th CP*, 2005.

[111] T. Hogg and C. Williams. Expected gains from parallelizing constraint solving for hard problems. In *Proceedings of the Twelfth National Conference on Artificial Intelligence (AAAI-94)*, pages 1310–1315, Seattle, WA, 1994. AAAI Press.

[112] J.N. Hooker. A quantitative approach to logical inference. *Decision Support Systems*, 4:45–69, 1988.

[113] H.H. Hoos. On the run-time behaviour of stochastic local search algorithms for SAT. In *Proceedings of AAAI-99*, pages 661–666. AAAI Press, 1999.

[114] H.H. Hoos. An adaptive noise mechanism for WalkSAT. In *18th AAAI*, pages 655–660, Edmonton, Canada, July 2002.

[115] H.H. Hoos and T. Stützle. SATLIB: An online resource for research on SAT. In I.P. Gent, H. van Maaren, and T. Walsh, editors. *SAT2000*, pages 283–292. IOS Press, 2000. URL http://www.satlib.org.

[116] H.H. Hoos and T. Stützle. *Stochastic Local Search: Foundations and Applications*. Morgan Kaufmann, San Francisco, CA, USA, 2004.

[117] E. Horvitz, Y. Ruan, C. Gomes, H. Kautz, B. Selman, and D. Chickering. A Bayesian approach to tackling hard computational problems. In *17th UAI*, 2001.

[118] M. Huele, J. van Zwieten, M. Dufour, and H. van Maaren. March-eq: Implementing additional reasoning into an efficient lookahead SAT solver. In *7th SAT*, Vancouver, BC, Canada, May 2004. *LNCS*, vol. 3542, pages 345–359. Springer, 2005.

[119] Y. Interian. Backdoor sets for random 3-SAT. In *6th SAT*, 2003.

[120] S. Janson, Y.C. Stamatiou, and M. Vamvakari. Bounding the unsatisfiability threshold of random 3-SAT. *Random Structures Algorithms*, 17(2):103–116, 2000.

[121] R.G. Jeroslow and J. Wang. Solving propositional satisfiability problems. *Ann. Math. Artificial Intelligence*, 1(1–4):167–187, 1990.

[122] H. Jia and C. Moore. How much backtracking does it take to color random graphs? Rigorous results on heavy tails. In *10th CP*, 2004.

[123] D. Johnson, C. Aragon, L. McGeoch, and C. Schevon. Optimization by simulated annealing: an experimental evaluation; part II. *Oper. Res.*, 39, 1991.

[124] A. Kamath, N. Karmarkar, K. Ramakrishnan, and M. Resende. Computational experience with an interior point algorithm on the satisfiability problem. In *Proceedings of Integer Programming and Combinatorial Optimization*, pages 333–349, Waterloo, Canada, 1990. Mathematical Programming Society.

[125] A.C. Kaporis, L.M. Kirousis, and E.G. Lalas. The probabilistic analysis of a greedy satisfiability algorithm. *Random Structures Algorithms*, 28(4):444–480, 2006.

[126] H. Kautz, E. Horvitz, Y. Ruan, C. Gomes, and B. Selman. Dynamic restart policies. In *18th AAAI*, 2002.

[127] H. Kautz and B. Selman. The state of SAT. *Discrete Appl. Math.*, 155(12):1514–1524, 2007.

[128] H.A. Kautz and B. Selman. Planning as satisfiability. In *Proc., 10th Euro. Conf. on AI*, pages 359–363, Vienna, Austria, Aug. 1992.

[129] H.A. Kautz and B. Selman. Pushing the envelope: Planning, propositional logic, and stochastic search. In *13th AAAI*, pages 1194–1201, Portland, OR, Aug. 1996.

[130] P. Kilby, J. Slaney, S. Thiebaux, and T. Walsh. Backbones and backdoors in satisfiability. In *20th AAAI*, 2005.

[131] S. Kirkpatrick, D. Gelatt Jr., and M. Vecchi. Optimization by simulated annealing. *Science*, 220(4598):671–680, 1983.

[132] S. Kirkpatrick and B. Selman. Critical behavior in the satisfiability of random boolean expressions. *Science*, 264:1297–1301, May 1994. Also p. 1249: "Math. Logic: Pinning Down a Trecherous Border in Logical Statements" by B. Cipra.

[133] L.M. Kirousis, E. Kranakis, and D. Krizanc. Approximating the unsatisfiability threshold of random formulas. In *Proceedings of the Fourth Annual European Symposium on Algorithms*, pages 27–38, Barcelona, Spain, Sept. 1996.

[134] H. Kleine-Büning, M. Karpinski, and A. Flögel. Resolution for quantified Boolean formulas. *Inform. and Comput.*, 117(1):12–18, 1995.

[135] H. Kleine-Büning and T. Lettmann. *Propositional Logic: Deduction and Algorithms*. Cambridge University Press, 1999.

[136] J. Köbler, U. Schöning, and J. Torán. *The Graph Isomorphism Problem: its Structural Complexity*. Birkhauser Verlag, ISBN 0-8176-3680-3, 1993.

[137] K. Konolige. Easy to be hard: Difficult problems for greedy algorithms. In *4th KR*, pages 374–378, Bonn, Germany, May 1994.

[138] H. Konuk and T. Larrabee. Explorations of sequential ATPG using Boolean satisfiability. In *11th VLSI Test Symposium*, pages 85–90, 1993.

[139] B. Krishnamurthy. Short proofs for tricky formulas. *Acta Inform.*, 22:253–274, 1985.

[140] L. Kroc, A. Sabharwal, and B. Selman. Survey propagation revisited. In *23rd UAI*, pages 217–226, Vancouver, BC, July 2007.

[141] D. Le Berre O. Roussel, and L. Simon (Organizers). SAT 2007 competition. URL http://www.satcompetition.org/2007, May 2007.

[142] D. Le Berre and L. Simon (Organizers). SAT 2004 competition. URL http://www.satcompetition.org/2004, May 2004.

[143] D. Le Berre and L. Simon (Organizers). SAT 2005 competition. URL http://www.satcompetition.org/2005, June 2005.

[144] R. Letz. Lemma and model caching in decision procedures for quantified Boolean formulas. In *Proc. of the TABLEAUX*, Copenhagen, Denmark, July 2002. *LNCS*, vol. 2381, pages 160–175. Springer, 2002.

[145] H.J. Levesque and R.J. Brachman. A fundamental tradeoff in knowledge representation and reasoning. In R.J. Brachman and H.J. Levesque, editors. *Readings in Knowledge Representation*, pages 41–70. Morgan Kaufmann, 1985.

[146] H.J. Levesque and R.J. Brachman. Expressiveness and tractability in knowledge representation and reasoning. *Computational Intelligence*, 3(2):78–93, 1987.

[147] L. Levin. Universal sequential search problems. *Problems of Information Transmission*, 9(3):265–266, 1973 (originally in Russian).

[148] C. Li and Anbulagan. Heuristics based on unit propagation for satisfiability problems. In *15th IJCAI*, 1997.

[149] C.M. Li. Integrating equivalency reasoning into Davis–Putnam procedure. In *17th AAAI*, pages 291–296, Austin, TX, July 2000.

[150] C.M. Li and Anbulagan. Heuristics based on unit propagation for satisfiability problems. In *15th IJCAI*, pages 366–371, Nagoya, Japan, Aug. 1997.

[151] C.M. Li, B. Jurkowiak, and P.W. Purdom. Integrating symmetry breaking into a DLL procedure. In *SAT*, pages 149–155, Cincinnati, OH, May 2002.

[152] X.Y. Li, M.F.M. Stallmann, and F. Brglez. QingTing: A local search sat solver using an effective switching strategy and an efficient unit propagation. In *6th SAT*, pages 53–68, Santa Margherita, Italy, May 2003.

[153] S. Lin and B. Kernighan. An efficient heuristic algorithm for the traveling-salesman problem. *Oper. Res.*, 21:498–516, 1973.

[154] M.L. Littman, S.M. Majercik, and T. Pitassi. Stochastic Boolean satisfiability. *J. Automat. Reason.*, 27(3):251–296, 2001.

[155] M. Luby, A. Sinclair, and D. Zuckerman. Optimal speedup of Las Vegas algorithms. *Inform. Process. Lett.*, 47:173–180, 1993.

[156] I. Lynce, L. Baptista, and J. Marques-Silva. Stochastic systematic search algorithms for satisfiability. In *4th SAT*, 2001.

[157] I. Lynce and J.P. Marques-Silva. An overview of backtrack search satisfiability algorithms. *Ann. Math. Artificial Intelligence*, 37(3):307–326, 2003.

[158] P.D. MacKenzie. Private communication, July 2005.

[159] E.N. Maneva, E. Mossel, and M.J. Wainwright. A new look at survey propagation and its generalizations. In *16th SODA*, pages 1089–1098, Vancouver, Canada, Jan. 2005.

[160] J.P. Marques-Silva. The impact of branching heuristics in propositional satisfiability algorithms. In *9th Portuguese Conf. on AI*, Sept. 1999. *LNCS*, vol. 1695, pages 62–74. Springer, 1999.

[161] J.P. Marques-Silva and K.A. Sakallah. GRASP—a new search algorithm for satisfiability. In *ICCAD*, pages 220–227, San Jose, CA, Nov. 1996.

[162] J.P. Marques-Silva and K.A. Sakallah. Robust search algorithms for test pattern generation. In *27th FTCS*, pages 152–161, Seattle, WA, June 1997.

[163] B. Mazure, L. Sais, and E. Gregoire. Boosting complete techniques thanks to local search methods. In *Proc. Math and AI*, 1996.

[164] D.A. McAllester, B. Selman, and H. Kautz. Evidence for invariants in local search. In *AAAI/IAAI*, pages 321–326, Providence, RI, July 1997.

[165] M. Mézard, G. Parisi, and R. Zecchina. Analytic and algorithmic solution of random satisfiability problems. *Science*, 297(5582):812–815, 2002.

[166] M. Mézard and R. Zecchina. Random k-satisfiability problem: From an analytic solution to an efficient algorithm. *Phys. Rev. E*, 66:056126, Nov. 2002.

[167] S. Minton, M. Johnston, A. Philips, and P. Laird. Solving large-scale constraint satisfaction an scheduling problems using a heuristic repair method. In *Proceedings AAAI-90*, pages 17–24, AAAI Press, 1990.

[168] D. Mitchell, B. Selman, and H. Levesque. Hard and easy distributions of SAT problems. In *Proc. AAAI-92*, pages 459–465, San Jose, CA, 1992.

[169] R. Monasson, R. Zecchina, S. Kirkpatrick, B. Selman, and L. Troyansky. Determining computational complexity from characteristic phase transitions. *Nature*, 400(8):133–137, 1999.

[170] M.W. Moskewicz, C.F. Madigan, Y. Zhao, L. Zhang, and S. Malik. Chaff: Engineering an efficient SAT solver. In *38th DAC*, pages 530–535, Las Vegas, NV, June 2001.

[171] A. Nadel. The Jerusat SAT solver. Master's thesis, Hebrew University of Jerusalem, 2002.

[172] N. Nishimura, P. Ragde, and S. Szeider. Detecting backdoor sets with respect to horn and binary clauses. In *7th SAT*, 2004.

[173] E. Nudelman, A. Devkar, Y. Shoham, K. Leyton-Brown, and H.H. Hoos. SATzilla: An algorithm portfolio for SAT, 2004. In conjunction with SAT-04.

[174] R. Ostrowski, E. Grégoire, B. Mazure, and L. Sais. Recovering and exploiting structural knowledge from CNF formulas. In *8th CP*, Ithaca, NY, Sept. 2002. *LNCS*, vol. 2470, pages 185–199. Springer, 2002.

[175] C. Otwell, A. Remshagen, and K. Truemper. An effective QBF solver for planning problems. In *Proc. MSV/AMCS*, pages 311–316, Las Vegas, NV, June 2004.

[176] G. Pan and M.Y. Vardi. Symbolic decision procedures for QBF. In *10th CP*, Toronto, Canada, Sept. 2004. *LNCS*, vol. 3258, pages 453–467. Springer, 2004.

[177] C. Papadimitriou and K. Steiglitz. *Combinatorial Optimization*. Prentice-Hall, Inc., 1982.

[178] C.H. Papadimitriou. On selecting a satisfying truth assignment. In *32nd FOCS*, pages 163–169, San Juan, Puerto Rico, Oct. 1991. IEEE.

[179] C.H. Papadimitriou. *Computational Complexity*. Addison-Wesley, 1994.

[180] A.J. Parkes and J.P. Walser. Tuning local search for satisfiability testing. In *13th AAAI*, pages 356–362, Portland, OR, Aug. 1996.

[181] J. Pearl. *Probabilistic Reasoning in Intelligent Systems: Networks of Plausible Inference*. Morgan Kaufmann, 1988.

[182] K.E. Petrie and B.M. Smith. Symmetry breaking in graceful graphs. In *8th CP*, Kinsale, Ireland, Sept. 2003. *LNCS*, vol. 2833, pages 930–934. Springer, 2003.

[183] D.N. Pham, J. Thornton, and A. Sattar. Building structure into local search for SAT. In *20th IJCAI*, pages 2359–2364, Hyderabad, India, Jan. 2007.

[184] K. Pipatsrisawat and A. Darwiche. RSat 1.03: SAT solver description. Technical Report D-152, Automated Reasoning Group, Computer Science Department, UCLA, 2006.

[185] S.D. Prestwich. Local search and backtracking vs non-systematic backtracking, 2001.

[186] S.D. Prestwich. Variable dependency in local search: Prevention is better than cure. In *10th SAT*, Lisbon, Portugal, May 2007.

[187] J.-F. Puget. On the satisfiability of symmetrical constrained satisfaction problems. In *Int. Symp. on Method. for Intel. Syst.*, Trondheim, Norway, June 1993. *LNCS*, vol. 689, pages 350–361. Springer, 1993.

[188] J.-F. Puget. Dynamic lex constraints. In *12th CP*, Nantes, France, Sept. 2006. *LNCS*, vol. 4204, pages 453–467. Springer, 2006.

[189] J.-F. Puget. An efficient way of breaking value symmetries. In *21th AAAI*, Boston, MA, July 2006.

[190] P.W. Purdom Jr. and C.A. Brown. Polynomial average-time satisfiability problems. *Inform. Sci.*, 41:23–42, 1987.

[191] M.G.C. Resende and T.A. Feo. A GRASP for satisfiability. In D.S. Johnson and M.A. Trick, editors. *Cliques, Coloring, and Satisfiability: the Second DIMACS Implementation Challenge, DIMACS Series in Discrete Mathematics and Theoretical Computer Science*, vol. 26, pages 499–520. American Mathematical Society, 1996.

[192] J. Rintanen. Constructing conditional plans by a theorem prover. *J. Artificial Intelligence Res.*, 10:323–352, 1999.

[193] J. Rintanen. Improvements to the evaluation of quantified Boolean formulae. In *16th IJCAI*, pages 1192–1197, Stockholm, Sweden, July 1999.

[194] J. Rintanen. Partial implicit unfolding in the Davis-Putnam procedure for quantified Boolean formulae. In *8th Intl. Conf. Logic for Prog., AI, and Reason.*, Havana, Cuba, Dec. 2001. *LNCS*, vol. 2250, pages 362–376. Springer, 2001.

[195] I. Rish and R. Dechter. To guess or to think? hybrid algorithms for SAT. In *Proceedings of the Conference on Principles of Constraint Programming (CP-96)*, pages 555–556, 1996.

[196] D. Roth. On the hardness of approximate reasoning. *J. Artificial Intelligence*, 82(1–2):273–302, 1996.

[197] S.J. Russell and P. Norvig. *Artificial Intelligence: A Modern Approach*. 2nd edition. Prentice-Hall, 2002.

[198] L. Ryan. Efficient algorithms for clause-learning SAT solvers. Master's thesis, Simon Fraser University, Vancouver, 2003.

[199] A. Sabharwal. Algorithmic applications of propositional proof complexity. PhD thesis, University of Washington, Seattle, 2005.

[200] A. Sabharwal. SymChaff: A structure-aware satisfiability solver. In *20th AAAI*, pages 467–474, Pittsburgh, PA, July 2005.

[201] A. Sabharwal, C. Ansotegui, C.P. Gomes, J.W. Hart, and B. Selman. QBF modeling: Exploiting player symmetry for simplicity and efficiency. In *9th SAT*, Seattle, WA, Aug. 2006. *LNCS*, vol. 4121, pages 353–367. Springer, 2006.

[202] H. Samulowitz and F. Bacchus. Using SAT in QBF. In *11th CP*, Sitges, Spain, Oct. 2005. *LNCS*, vol. 3709, pages 578–592. Springer, 2005.

[203] H. Samulowitz and F. Bacchus. Binary clause reasoning in QBF. In *9th SAT*, Seattle, WA, Aug. 2006. *LNCS*, vol. 4121, pages 353–367. Springer, 2006.

[204] H. Samulowitz, J. Davies, and F. Bacchus. Preprocessing QBF. In *12th CP*, Nantes, France, Sept. 2006. *LNCS*, vol. 4204, pages 514–529. Springer, 2006.

[205] T. Sang, F. Bacchus, P. Beame, H.A. Kautz, and T. Pitassi. Combining component caching and clause learning for effective model counting. In *7th SAT*, Vancouver, Canada, May 2004.

[206] D. Schuurmans and F. Southey. Local search characteristics of incomplete SAT procedures. In *Proc. of the 17th National Conf. on Artificial Intelligence (AAAI-2000)*, pages 297–302, 2000.

[207] D. Schuurmans, F. Southey, and R.C. Holte. The exponentiated subgradient algorithm for heuristic boolean programming. In *17th IJCAI*, pages 334–341, Seattle, WA, Aug. 2001.

[208] S. Seitz, M. Alava, and P. Orponen. Focused local search for random 3-satisfiability. *J. Stat. Mech.*, P06006:1–27, 2005.

[209] B. Selman and H. Kautz. Domain-independent extensions to GSAT: Solving large structured satisfiability problems. In *13th IJCAI*, pages 290–295, France, 1993.

[210] B. Selman, H. Kautz, and B. Cohen. Noise strategies for local search. In *Proc. AAAI-94*, pages 337–343, Seattle, WA, 1994.

[211] B. Selman, H. Kautz, and B. Cohen. Local search strategies for satisfiability testing. In D.S. Johnson and M.A. Trick, editors. *Cliques, Coloring, and Satisfiability: the Second DIMACS Implementation Challenge, DIMACS Series in Discrete Mathematics and Theoretical Computer Science*, vol. 26, pages 521–532. American Mathematical Society, 1996.

[212] B. Selman and S. Kirkpatrick. Finite-size scaling of the computational cost of systematic search. *Artificial Intelligence*, 81(1–2):273–295, 1996.

[213] B. Selman, H.J. Levesque, and D.G. Mitchell. A new method for solving hard satisfiability problems. In *10th AAAI*, pages 440–446, San Jose, CA, July 1992.

[214] O. Shtrichman. Accelerating bounded model checking of safety properties. *Form. Meth. in Sys. Des.*, 1:5–24, 2004.

[215] C. Sinz (Organizer). SAT-race 2006, Aug. 2006. URL http://fmv.jku.at/sat-race-2006.

[216] J.K. Slaney and T. Walsh. Backbones in optimization and approximation. In *17th IJCAI*, pages 254–259, Seattle, WA, Aug. 2001.

[217] B.M. Smith and S.A. Grant. Sparse constraint graphs and exceptionally hard problems. In *14th IJCAI*, vol. 1, pages 646–654, Montreal, Canada, Aug. 1995.

[218] B.M. Smith and S.A. Grant. Modelling exceptionally hard constraint satisfaction problems. In *3rd CP*, Austria, Oct. 1997. *LNCS*, vol. 1330, pages 182–195. Springer, 1997.

[219] W.M. Spears. Simulated annealing for hard satisfiability problems. In D.S. Johnson and M.A. Trick, editors. *Cliques, Coloring, and Satisfiability: the Second DIMACS Implementation Challenge, DIMACS Series in Discrete Mathematics and Theoretical Computer Science*, vol. 26, pages 533–558. American Mathematical Society, 1996.

[220] R.M. Stallman and G.J. Sussman. Forward reasoning and dependency-directed backtracking in a system for computer-aided circuit analysis. *J. Artificial Intelligence*, 9:135–196, 1977.

[221] P.R. Stephan, R.K. Brayton, and A.L. Sangiovanni-Vincentelli. Combinatorial test generation using satisfiability. *IEEE Trans. CAD and IC*, 15(9):1167–1176, 1996.

[222] L.J. Stockmeyer and A.R. Meyer. Word problems requiring exponential time. In *Conf. Record of 5th STOC*, pages 1–9, Austin, TX, Apr.–May 1973.

[223] S. Szeider. Backdoor sets for DLL solvers. *J. Auto. Reas.*, 2006 (Special issue on SAT 2005).

[224] S. Toda. On the computational power of PP and $\oplus$P. In *30th FOCS*, pages 514–519, 1989.

[225] G.S. Tseitin. On the complexity of derivation in the propositional calculus. In A.O. Slisenko, editor, *Studies in Constructive Mathematics and Mathematical Logic, Part II*. 1968.

[226] A. Urquhart. The symmetry rule in propositional logic. *Discrete Appl. Math.*, 96–97:177–193, 1999.

[227] L.G. Valiant and V.V. Vazirani. NP is as easy as detecting unique solutions. *Theoret. Comput. Sci.*, 47(3):85–93, 1986.

[228] M.N. Velev and R.E. Bryant. Effective use of Boolean satisfiability procedures in the formal verification of superscalar and VLIW microprocessors. *J. Symbolic Comput.*, 35(2):73–106, 2003.

[229] B.W. Wah and Y. Shang. A discrete Lagrangian-based global-search method for solving satisfiability problems. *J. of Global Optimization*, 12(1):61–99, 1998.

[230] T. Walsh. Search in a small world. In *16th IJCAI*, 1999.

[231] T. Walsh. General symmetry breaking constraints. In *12th CP*, Sept. 2006. *LNCS*, vol. 4204, pages 650–664. Springer, 2006.

[232] W. Wei and B. Selman. A new approach to model counting. In *8th SAT*, St. Andrews, UK, June 2005. *LNCS*, vol. 3569, pages 324–339. Springer, 2005.

[233] R. Williams, C. Gomes, and B. Selman. Backdoors to typical case complexity. In *18th IJCAI*, 2003.

[234] R. Williams, C. Gomes, and B. Selman. On the connections between backdoors, restarts, and heavy-tailedness in combinatorial search. In *6th SAT*, 2003.

[235] Z. Wu and B.W. Wah. Trap escaping strategies in discrete Lagrangian methods for solving hard satisfiability and maximum satisfiability problems. In *16th AAAI*, pages 673–678, Orlando, FL, July 1999.

[236] H. Zhang. SATO: An efficient propositional prover. In *14th CADE*, Townsville, Australia, July 1997. *LNCS*, vol. 1249, pages 272–275. Springer, 1997.

[237] H. Zhang. A random jump strategy for combinatorial search. In *International Symposium on AI and Math.*, Fort Lauderdale, FL, 2002.

[238] H. Zhang and J. Hsiang. Solving open quasigroup problems by propositional reasoning. In *Proceedings of the International Computer Symp.*, Hsinchu, Taiwan, 1994.

[239] L. Zhang. Solving QBF by combining conjunctive and disjunctive normal forms. In *21th AAAI*, pages 143–149, Boston, MA, July 2006.

[240] L. Zhang, C.F. Madigan, M.H. Moskewicz, and S. Malik. Efficient conflict driven learning in a Boolean satisfiability solver. In *ICCAD*, pages 279–285, San Jose, CA, Nov. 2001.

[241] L. Zhang and S. Malik. Conflict driven learning in a quantified Boolean satisfiability solver. In *ICCAD*, pages 442–449, San Jose, CA, Nov. 2002.

[242] L. Zhang and S. Malik. Towards a symmetric treatment of satisfaction and conflicts in quantified Boolean formula evaluation. In *8th CP*, pages 200–215, Ithaca, NY, Sept. 2002.

Handbook of Knowledge Representation
Edited by F. van Harmelen, V. Lifschitz and B. Porter
© 2008 Elsevier B.V. All rights reserved
DOI: 10.1016/S1574-6526(07)03003-9

Chapter 3

Description Logics

Franz Baader, Ian Horrocks, Ulrike Sattler

In this chapter we will introduce description logics, a family of logic-based knowledge representation languages that can be used to represent the terminological knowledge of an application domain in a structured way. We will first review their provenance and history, and show how the field has developed. We will then introduce the basic description logic $\mathcal{ALC}$ in some detail, including definitions of syntax, semantics and basic reasoning services, and describe important extensions such as inverse roles, number restrictions, and concrete domains. Next, we will discuss the relationship between description logics and other formalisms, in particular first order and modal logics; the most commonly used reasoning techniques, in particular tableau, resolution and automata based techniques; and the computational complexity of basic reasoning problems. After reviewing some of the most prominent applications of description logics, in particular ontology language applications, we will conclude with an overview of other aspects of description logic research, and with pointers to the relevant literature.

3.1 Introduction

Description logics (DLs) [14, 25, 50] are a family of knowledge representation languages that can be used to represent the knowledge of an application domain in a structured and formally well-understood way. The name *description logics* is motivated by the fact that, on the one hand, the important notions of the domain are described by concept *descriptions*, i.e., expressions that are built from atomic concepts (unary predicates) and atomic roles (binary predicates) using the concept and role constructors provided by the particular DL; on the other hand, DLs differ from their predecessors, such as semantic networks and frames, in that they are equipped with a formal, *logic*-based semantics.

We will first illustrate some typical constructors by an example; formal definitions will be given in Section 3.2. Assume that we want to define the concept of "A man that is married to a doctor, and all of whose children are either doctors or professors." This concept can be described with the following concept description:

Human ⊓ ¬Female ⊓ (∃married.Doctor) ⊓ (∀hasChild.(Doctor ⊔ Professor)).

This description employs the Boolean constructors *conjunction* (⊓), which is interpreted as set intersection, *disjunction* (⊔), which is interpreted as set union, and *negation* (¬), which is interpreted as set complement, as well as the *existential restriction* constructor (∃r.C), and the *value restriction* constructor (∀r.C). An individual, say Bob, belongs to ∃married.Doctor if there exists an individual that is married to Bob (i.e., is related to Bob via the married role) and is a doctor (i.e., belongs to the concept Doctor). Similarly, Bob belongs to ∀hasChild.(Doctor ⊔ Professor) if all his children (i.e., all individuals related to Bob via the hasChild role) are either doctors or professors.

Concept descriptions can be used to build statements in a DL knowledge base, which typically comes in two parts: a terminological and an assertional one. In the *terminological* part, called the TBox, we can describe the relevant notions of an application domain by stating properties of concepts and roles, and relationships between them—it corresponds to the *schema* in a database setting. In its simplest form, a TBox statement can introduce a name (abbreviation) for a complex description. For example, we could introduce the name HappyMan as an abbreviation for the concept description from above:

HappyMan ≡ Human ⊓ ¬Female ⊓ (∃married.Doctor) ⊓

(∀hasChild.(Doctor ⊔ Professor)).

More expressive TBoxes allow the statement of more general *axioms* such as

∃hasChild.Human ⊑ Human,

which says that only humans can have human children. Note that, in contrast to the abbreviation statement from above, this statement does not define a concept. It just constrains the way in which concepts and roles (in this case, Human and hasChild) can be interpreted.

Obviously, all the knowledge we have described in our example could easily be represented by formulae of first-order predicate logic (see also Section 3.3). The variable-free syntax of description logics makes TBox statements easier to read than the corresponding first-order formulae. However, the main reason for using DLs rather than predicate logic is that DLs are carefully tailored such that they combine interesting means of expressiveness with decidability of the important reasoning problems (see below).

The *assertional* part of the knowledge base, called the ABox, is used to describe a concrete situation by stating properties of individuals—it corresponds to the *data* in a database setting. For example, the assertions

HappyMan(BOB),   hasChild(BOB, MARY),   ¬Doctor(MARY)

state that Bob belongs to the concept HappyMan, that Mary is one of his children, and that Mary is not a doctor. Modern DL systems all employ this kind of restricted ABox formalism, which basically can be used to state ground facts. This differs from the use of the ABox in the early DL system KRYPTON [38], where ABox statements could be arbitrary first-order formulae. The underlying idea was that the ABox could then be used to represent knowledge that was not expressible in the restricted TBox formalism of KRYPTON, but this came with a cost: reasoning about ABox knowledge required the use of a general theorem prover, which was quite inefficient and could lead to non-termination of the reasoning procedure.

Modern description logic systems provide their users with reasoning services that can automatically deduce implicit knowledge from the explicitly represented knowledge, and always yield a correct answer in finite time. In contrast to the database setting, such inference capabilities take into consideration *both* the terminological statements (schema) *and* the assertional statements (data). The *subsumption* algorithm determines subconcept-superconcept relationships: C is subsumed by D if all instances of C are necessarily instances of D, i.e., the first description is always interpreted as a subset of the second description. For example, given the definition of HappyMan from above plus the axiom Doctor $\sqsubseteq$ Human, which says that all doctors are human, HappyMan is subsumed by ∃married.Human—since instances of HappyMan are married to some instance of Doctor, and all instances of Doctor are also instances of Human. The *instance* algorithm determines instance relationships: the individual i is an instance of the concept description C if i is always interpreted as an element of the interpretation of C. For example, given the assertions from above and the definition of HappyMan, MARY is an instance of Professor (because BOB is an instance of HappyMan, so all his children are either Doctors or Professors, MARY is a child of BOB, and MARY is not a Doctor). The *consistency* algorithm determines whether a knowledge base (consisting of a set of assertions and a set of terminological axioms) is non-contradictory. For example, if we add ¬Professor(MARY) to the three assertions from above, then the knowledge base containing these assertions together with the definition of HappyMan from above is inconsistent.

In a typical application, one would start building the TBox, making use of the reasoning services provided to ensure that all concepts in it are satisfiable, i.e., are not subsumed by the bottom concept, which is always interpreted as the empty set. Moreover, one would use the subsumption algorithm to compute the subsumption hierarchy, i.e., to check, for each pair of concept names, whether one is subsumed by the other. This hierarchy would then be inspected to make sure that it coincides with the intention of the modeler. Given, in addition, an ABox, one would first check for its consistency with the TBox and then, for example, compute the most specific concept(s) that each individual is an instance of (this is often called *realizing* the ABox). We could also use a concept description as a query, i.e., we could ask the DL system to identify all those individuals that are instances of the given, possibly complex, concept description.

In order to ensure a reasonable and predictable behavior of a DL system, these inference problems should at least be decidable for the DL employed by the system, and preferably of low complexity. Consequently, the expressive power of the DL in question must be restricted in an appropriate way. If the imposed restrictions are too severe, however, then the important notions of the application domain can no longer be expressed. Investigating this trade-off between the expressivity of DLs and the complexity of their inference problems has been one of the most important issues in DL research. This investigation has included both theoretical research, e.g., determining the worst case complexities for various DLs and reasoning problems, and practical research, e.g., developing systems and optimization techniques, and empirically evaluating their behavior when applied to benchmarks and used in various applications. The emphasis on decidable formalisms of restricted expressive power is also the reason why a great variety of extensions of basic DLs have been considered. Some of these extensions leave the realm of classical first-order predicate logic, such as DLs with modal and temporal operators, fuzzy DLs, and probabilistic DLs (see [22] for details), but the goal of this research was still to design decidable extensions. If an application requires more expressive power than can be supplied by a decidable DL, then one usually embeds the DL into an application program or another KR formalism (see Section 3.8) rather than using an undecidable DL.

In the remainder of this section we will first give a brief overview of the history of DLs, and then describe the structure of this chapter. Research in Description Logics can be roughly classified into the following phases.

Phase 0 (1965–1980) is the pre-DL phase, in which *semantic networks* [138] and *frames* [122] were introduced as specialized approaches for representing knowledge in a structured way, and then criticized because of their lack of a formal semantics [163, 35, 84, 85]. An approach to overcome these problems was Brachman's *structured inheritance networks* [36], which were realized in the system KL-ONE, the first DL system.

Phase 1 (1980–1990) was mainly concerned with implementation of systems, such as KL-ONE, K-REP, KRYPTON, BACK, and LOOM [41, 119, 38, 137, 118]. These systems employed so-called *structural subsumption algorithms*, which first normalize the concept descriptions, and then recursively compare the syntactic structure of the normalized descriptions [126]. These algorithms are usually relatively efficient (polynomial), but they have the disadvantage that they are complete only for very inexpressive DLs, i.e., for more expressive DLs they cannot detect all subsumption/instance relationships. During this phase, the first logic-based accounts of the semantics of the underlying representation formalisms were given [38, 39], which made formal investigations into the complexity of reasoning in DLs possible. For example, in [39] it was shown that seemingly small additions to the expressive power of the representation formalism can cause intractability of the subsumption problem. In [148] it was shown that subsumption in the representation language underlying KL-ONE is even undecidable, and in [127] it was shown that the use of a TBox formalism that allows the introduction of abbreviations for complex descriptions makes subsumption intractable if the underlying DL has the constructors conjunction and value restriction (these constructors were supported by all the DL systems available at that time). As a reaction to these negative complexity results, the implementors of the CLASSIC system (the first industrial-strength DL system) carefully restricted the expressive power of their DL [135, 37].

Phase 2 (1990–1995) started with the introduction of a new algorithmic paradigm into DLs, so-called *tableau based algorithms* [149, 63, 89]. They work on propositionally closed DLs (i.e., DLs with all Boolean operators), and are complete also for expressive DLs. To decide the consistency of a knowledge base, a tableau based algorithm tries to construct a model of it by structurally decomposing the concepts in the knowledge base, thus inferring new constraints on the elements of this model. The algorithm either stops because all attempts to build a model failed with obvious contradictions, or it stops with a "canonical" model. Since, in propositionally closed DLs, the subsumption and the instance problem can be reduced to consistency, a consistency algorithm can solve all the inference problems mentioned above. The first systems employing such algorithms (KRIS and CRACK) demonstrated that optimized implementations of these algorithms led to an acceptable behavior of the system, even though the worst-case complexity of the corresponding reasoning problems is no longer in polynomial time [18, 44]. This phase also saw a thorough analysis of the complexity of reasoning in various DLs [63, 64, 62], and the important observation that DLs are very closely related to modal logics [144].

Phase 3 (1995–2000) is characterized by the development of inference procedures for very expressive DLs, either based on the tableau approach [100, 92], or on a translation into modal logics [57, 58, 56, 59]. Highly optimized systems (FaCT, RACE, and DLP [95, 80, 133]) showed that tableau-based algorithms for expressive DLs led to a good practical behavior of the system even on (some) large knowledge bases. In this phase, the relationship to modal logics [57, 146] and to decidable fragments of first-order logic [33, 129, 79, 77, 78] was also studied in more detail, and applications in databases (like schema reasoning, query optimization, and integration of databases) were investigated [45, 47, 51].

We are now in *Phase 4*, where the results from the previous phases are being used to develop industrial strength DL systems employing very expressive DLs, with applications like the Semantic Web or knowledge representation and integration in medical- and bio-informatics in mind. On the academic side, the interest in less expressive DLs has been revived, with the goal of developing tools that can deal with very large terminological and/or assertional knowledge bases [6, 23, 53, 1].

The structure of the remainder of the chapter is as follows. In Section 3.2 we introduce the syntax and semantics of the prototypical DL $\mathcal{ALC}$, and some important extensions of $\mathcal{ALC}$. In Section 3.3 we discuss the relationship between DLs and other logical formalisms. In Section 3.4 we describe tableau-based reasoning techniques for $\mathcal{ALC}$, and in Section 3.5 we investigate the computation complexity of reasoning in $\mathcal{ALC}$. In Section 3.6 we introduce other reasoning techniques that can be used for DLs. In Section 3.7 we discuss the use of DLs in ontology language applications. Finally, in Section 3.8, we sketch important areas of DL research that have not been mentioned so far, and provide pointers to the literature.

Although we have endeavored to cover the most important areas of DL research, we have decided to treat some areas in more detail rather than giving a comprehensive survey of the whole field. Readers seeking such a survey are directed to [14].

3.2 A Basic DL and its Extensions

In this section we will define the syntax and semantics of the basic DL $\mathcal{ALC}$, and the most widely used DL reasoning services. We will also introduce important extensions to $\mathcal{ALC}$, including inverse roles, number restrictions, and concrete domains. The name $\mathcal{ALC}$ stands for "Attributive concept Language with Complements". It was first introduced in [149], where also a first naming scheme for DLs was proposed: starting from a basic DL $\mathcal{AL}$, the addition of a constructors is indicated by appending a corresponding letter; e.g., $\mathcal{ALC}$ is obtained from $\mathcal{AL}$ by adding the complement operator ($\neg$) and $\mathcal{ALE}$ is obtained from $\mathcal{AL}$ by adding existential restrictions ($\exists r.C$) (for more details on such naming schemes for DLs, see [10]).

3.2.1 Syntax and Semantics of $\mathcal{ALC}$

In the following, we give formal definitions of the syntax and semantics of the constructors that we have described informally in the introduction. The DL that includes just this set of constructors (i.e., conjunction, disjunction, negation, existential restriction and value restriction) is called $\mathcal{ALC}$.

Definition 3.1 ($\mathcal{ALC}$ syntax). *Let N_C be a set of* concept names *and N_R be a set of* role names. *The set of $\mathcal{ALC}$-concept descriptions is the smallest set such that*

1. $\top, \bot$, *and every concept name $A \in N_C$ is an $\mathcal{ALC}$-concept description,*

2. *if C and D are $\mathcal{ALC}$-concept descriptions and $r \in N_R$, then $C \sqcap D$, $C \sqcup D$, $\neg C$, $\forall r.C$, and $\exists r.C$ are $\mathcal{ALC}$-concept descriptions.*

In the following, we will often use "$\mathcal{ALC}$-concept" instead of "$\mathcal{ALC}$-concept description". The semantics of $\mathcal{ALC}$ (and of DLs in general) is given in terms of *interpretations*.

Definition 3.2 ($\mathcal{ALC}$ semantics). *An interpretation $\mathcal{I} = (\Delta^{\mathcal{I}}, \cdot^{\mathcal{I}})$ consists of a non-empty set $\Delta^{\mathcal{I}}$, called the* domain *of $\mathcal{I}$, and a function $\cdot^{\mathcal{I}}$ that maps every $\mathcal{ALC}$-concept to a subset of $\Delta^{\mathcal{I}}$, and every role name to a subset of $\Delta^{\mathcal{I}} \times \Delta^{\mathcal{I}}$ such that, for all $\mathcal{ALC}$-concepts C, D and all role names r,*

$$\top^{\mathcal{I}} = \Delta^{\mathcal{I}}, \qquad \bot^{\mathcal{I}} = \emptyset,$$

$$(C \sqcap D)^{\mathcal{I}} = C^{\mathcal{I}} \cap D^{\mathcal{I}}, \qquad (C \sqcup D)^{\mathcal{I}} = C^{\mathcal{I}} \cup D^{\mathcal{I}}, \qquad \neg C^{\mathcal{I}} = \Delta^{\mathcal{I}} \setminus C^{\mathcal{I}},$$

$$(\exists r.C)^{\mathcal{I}} = \{x \in \Delta^{\mathcal{I}} \mid \text{There is some } y \in \Delta^{\mathcal{I}} \text{ with } \langle x, y \rangle \in r^{\mathcal{I}} \text{ and } y \in C^{\mathcal{I}}\},$$

$$(\forall r.C)^{\mathcal{I}} = \{x \in \Delta^{\mathcal{I}} \mid \text{For all } y \in \Delta^{\mathcal{I}}, \text{if } \langle x, y \rangle \in r^{\mathcal{I}}, \text{then } y \in C^{\mathcal{I}}\}.$$

We say that $C^{\mathcal{I}}$ ($r^{\mathcal{I}}$) is the extension *of the concept C (role name r) in the interpretation $\mathcal{I}$. If $x \in C^{\mathcal{I}}$, then we say that x is an* instance *of C in $\mathcal{I}$.*

As mentioned in the introduction, a DL knowledge base (KB) is made up of two parts, a terminological part (called the TBox) and an assertional part (called the ABox), each part consisting of a set of axioms. The most general form of TBox axioms are so-called general concept inclusions.

Definition 3.3. *A* general concept inclusion *(GCI) is of the form $C \sqsubseteq D$, where C, D are $\mathcal{ALC}$-concepts. A finite set of GCIs is called a* TBox. *An interpretation $\mathcal{I}$ is a* model *of a GCI $C \sqsubseteq D$ if $C^{\mathcal{I}} \subseteq D^{\mathcal{I}}$; $\mathcal{I}$ is a* model *of a TBox $\mathcal{T}$ if it is a model of every GCI in $\mathcal{T}$.*

We use $C \equiv D$ as an abbreviation for the symmetrical pair of GCIs $C \sqsubseteq D$ and $D \sqsubseteq C$.

An axiom of the form $A \equiv C$, where A is a concept name, is called a *definition*. A TBox $\mathcal{T}$ is called *definitorial* if it contains only definitions, with the additional restriction that (i) $\mathcal{T}$ contains at most one definition for any given concept name, and (ii) $\mathcal{T}$ is acyclic, i.e., the definition of any concept A in $\mathcal{T}$ does not refer (directly or indirectly) to A itself. Definitorial TBoxes are also called *acyclic* TBoxes in the literature. Given a definitorial TBox $\mathcal{T}$, concept names occurring on the left-hand side of such a definition are called *defined* concepts, whereas the others are called *primitive* concepts. The name "definitorial" is motivated by the fact that, in such a TBox, the extensions of the defined concepts are uniquely determined by the extensions of the primitive concepts and the role names. From a computational point of view, definitorial TBoxes are interesting since they may allow for the use of simplified reasoning techniques (see Section 3.4), and reasoning with respect to such TBoxes is often of a lower complexity than reasoning with respect to a general TBox (see Section 3.5).

The ABox can contain two kinds of axiom, one for asserting that an individual is an instance of a given concept, and the other for asserting that a pair of individuals is an instance of a given role name.

Definition 3.4. *An* assertional axiom *is of the form* $x : C$ *or* $(x, y) : r$*, where C is an $\mathcal{ALC}$-concept, r is a role name, and x and y are individual names. A finite set of assertional axioms is called an* ABox*. An interpretation $\mathcal{I}$ is a model of an assertional axiom $x : C$ if $x^{\mathcal{I}} \in C^{\mathcal{I}}$, and $\mathcal{I}$ is a model of an assertional axiom $(x, y) : r$ if $\langle x^{\mathcal{I}}, y^{\mathcal{I}} \rangle \in r^{\mathcal{I}}$; $\mathcal{I}$ is a model of an ABox $\mathcal{A}$ if it is a model of every axiom in $\mathcal{A}$.*

Several other notations for writing ABox axioms can be found in the literature, e.g., $C(x)$, $r(x, y)$ and $\langle x, y \rangle : r$.

Definition 3.5. *A* knowledge base *(KB) is a pair $(\mathcal{T}, \mathcal{A})$, where $\mathcal{T}$ is a TBox and $\mathcal{A}$ is an ABox. An interpretation $\mathcal{I}$ is a model of a KB $\mathcal{K} = (\mathcal{T}, \mathcal{A})$ if $\mathcal{I}$ is a model of $\mathcal{T}$ and $\mathcal{I}$ is a model of $\mathcal{A}$.*

We will write $\mathcal{I} \models \mathcal{K}$ (resp. $\mathcal{I} \models \mathcal{T}, \mathcal{I} \models \mathcal{A}, \mathcal{I} \models a$) to denote that $\mathcal{I}$ is a model of a KB $\mathcal{K}$ (resp., TBox $\mathcal{T}$, ABox $\mathcal{A}$, axiom a).

3.2.2 Important Inference Problems

We define inference problems with respect to a KB consisting of a TBox and an ABox. Later on, we will also consider special cases where the TBox or/and ABox is empty, or where the TBox satisfies additional restrictions, such as being definitorial.

Definition 3.6. *Given a KB $\mathcal{K} = (\mathcal{T}, \mathcal{A})$, where $\mathcal{T}$ is a TBox and $\mathcal{A}$ is an ABox, $\mathcal{K}$ is called* consistent *if it has a model. A concept C is called* satisfiable *with respect to $\mathcal{K}$ if there is a model $\mathcal{I}$ of $\mathcal{K}$ with $C^{\mathcal{I}} \neq \emptyset$. Such an interpretation is called a* model of C *with respect to $\mathcal{K}$. The concept D* subsumes *the concept C with respect to $\mathcal{K}$ (written $\mathcal{K} \models C \sqsubseteq D$) if $C^{\mathcal{I}} \subseteq D^{\mathcal{I}}$ holds for all models $\mathcal{I}$ of $\mathcal{K}$. Two concepts C, D are* equivalent *with respect to $\mathcal{K}$ (written $\mathcal{K} \models C \equiv D$) if they subsume each other with* *respect to* $\mathcal{K}$. *An individual a is an* instance of a concept C with respect to $\mathcal{K}$ (*written* $\mathcal{K} \models a : C$) *if* $a^{\mathcal{I}} \in C^{\mathcal{I}}$ *holds for all models* $\mathcal{I}$ *of* $\mathcal{K}$. *A pair of individuals* (a, b) *is an* instance of a role name r with respect to $\mathcal{K}$ (*written* $\mathcal{K} \models (a, b) : r$) *if* $\langle a^{\mathcal{I}}, b^{\mathcal{I}} \rangle \in r^{\mathcal{I}}$ *holds for all models* $\mathcal{I}$ *of* $\mathcal{K}$.

For a DL providing all the Boolean operators, like $\mathcal{ALC}$, all of the above reasoning problems can be reduced to KB consistency. For example, $(\mathcal{T}, \mathcal{A}) \models a : C$ iff $(\mathcal{T}, \mathcal{A} \cup \{a : \neg C\})$ is inconsistent. We will talk about satisfiability (resp., subsumption and equivalence) with respect to a TBox $\mathcal{T}$, meaning satisfiability (resp., subsumption and equivalence) with respect to the KB $(\mathcal{T}, \emptyset)$. This is often referred to as *terminological* reasoning. In many cases (e.g., in the case of $\mathcal{ALC}$), the ABox has no influence on terminological reasoning, i.e., satisfiability (resp., subsumption and equivalence) with respect to $(\mathcal{T}, \mathcal{A})$ coincides with satisfiability (resp., subsumption and equivalence) with respect to $\mathcal{T}$, as long as the ABox $\mathcal{A}$ is consistent (i.e., has a model).

3.2.3 Important Extensions to $\mathcal{ALC}$

One prominent application of DLs is as the formal foundation for ontology languages. Examples of DL based ontology languages include OIL [69], DAML + OIL [97, 98], and OWL [134], a recently emerged ontology language standard developed by the W3C Web-Ontology Working Group.[1]

High quality ontologies are crucial for many applications, and their construction, integration, and evolution greatly depends on the availability of a well-defined semantics and powerful reasoning tools. Since DLs provide for both, they should be ideal candidates for ontology languages. That much was already clear ten years ago, but at that time there was a fundamental mismatch between the expressive power and the efficiency of reasoning that DL systems provided, and the expressivity and the large knowledge bases that users needed [67]. Through basic research in DLs over the last 10–15 years, as summarized in the introduction, this gap between the needs of ontologist and the systems that DL researchers provide has finally become narrow enough to build stable bridges. In particular, $\mathcal{ALC}$ has been extended with several features that are important in an ontology language, including (qualified) number restrictions, inverse roles, transitive roles, subroles, concrete domains, and nominals.

With *number restrictions*, it is possible to describe the number of relationships of a particular type that individuals can participate in. For example, we may want to say that a person can be married to at most one other individual:

$$\text{Person} \sqsubseteq \, \leqslant 1 \, \text{married},$$

and we may want to extend our definition of HappyMan to include the fact that instances of HappyMan have between two and four children:

$$\text{HappyMan} \equiv \text{Human} \sqcap \neg\text{Female} \sqcap (\exists\text{married.Doctor})$$
$$\sqcap (\forall\text{hasChild.}(\text{Doctor} \sqcup \text{Professor}))$$
$$\sqcap \, \geqslant 2 \, \text{hasChild} \sqcap \, \leqslant 4 \, \text{hasChild}.$$

---

[1] http://www.w3.org/2001/sw/WebOnt/.

With *qualified number restrictions*, we can additionally describe the type of individuals that are counted by a given number restriction. For example, using qualified number restrictions, we could further extend our definition of HappyMan to include the fact that instances of HappyMan have at least two children who are doctors:

$$\text{HappyMan} \equiv \text{Human} \sqcap \neg\text{Female} \sqcap (\exists\text{married}.\text{Doctor})$$

$$\sqcap (\forall\text{hasChild}.(\text{Doctor} \sqcup \text{Professor}))$$

$$\sqcap \geqslant 2\,\text{hasChild}.\text{Doctor} \sqcap \leqslant 4\,\text{hasChild}.$$

With *inverse roles*, *transitive roles*, and *subroles* [100] we can, in addition to hasChild, also use its inverse hasParent, specify that hasAncestor is transitive, and specify that hasParent is a subrole of hasAncestor.

Concrete domains [16, 115] integrate DLs with concrete sets such as the real numbers, integers, or strings, as well as concrete predicates defined on these sets, such as numerical comparisons (e.g., $\leqslant$), string comparisons (e.g., isPrefixOf), or comparisons with constants (e.g., $\leqslant 17$). This supports the modeling of concrete properties of abstract objects such as the age, the weight, or the name of a person, and the comparison of these concrete properties. Unfortunately, in their unrestricted form, concrete domains can have dramatic effects on the decidability and computational complexity of the underlying DL [17, 115]. For this reason, a more restricted form of concrete domain, known as *datatypes* [101], is often used in practice.

The *nominal* constructor allows us to use individual names also within concept descriptions: if a is an individual name, then $\{a\}$ is a concept, called a nominal, which is interpreted by a singleton set. Using the individual Turing, we can describe all those computer scientists that have met Turing by CScientist $\sqcap \exists$hasMet.$\{$Turing$\}$. The so-called "one-of" constructor extends the nominal constructor to a finite set of individuals. In the presence of disjunction, it can, however, be expressed using nominals: $\{a_1, \ldots, a_n\}$ is equivalent to $\{a_1\} \sqcup \cdots \sqcup \{a_n\}$. The presence of nominals can have dramatic effects on the complexity of reasoning [159].

An additional comment on the naming of DLs is in order. Recall that the name given to a particular DL usually reflects its expressive power, with letters expressing the constructors provided. For expressive DLs, starting with the basic DL $\mathcal{AL}$ would lead to quite long names. For this reason, the letter $\mathcal{S}$ is often used as an abbreviation for the "basic" DL consisting of $\mathcal{ALC}$ extended with transitive roles (which in the $\mathcal{AL}$ naming scheme would be called $\mathcal{ALC}_{R+}$).[2] The letter $\mathcal{H}$ represents subroles (role $\mathcal{H}$ierarchies), $\mathcal{O}$ represents nominals (n$\mathcal{O}$minals), $\mathcal{I}$ represents inverse roles ($\mathcal{I}$nverse), $\mathcal{N}$ represent number restrictions ($\mathcal{N}$umber), and $\mathcal{Q}$ represent qualified number restrictions ($\mathcal{Q}$ualified). The integration of a concrete domain/datatype is indicated by appending its name in parenthesis, but sometimes a "generic" **D** is used to express that some concrete domain/datatype has been integrated. The DL corresponding to the OWL DL ontology language includes all of these constructors and is therefore called $\mathcal{SHOIN}(\mathbf{D})$.

---

[2] The use of $\mathcal{S}$ is motivated by the close connection between this DL and the modal logic **S4**.

3.3   Relationships with other Formalisms

In this section, we discuss the relationships between DLs and predicate logic, and between DLs and Modal Logic. This is intended for readers who are familiar with these logics; those not familiar with these logics might want to skip the following subsection(s), since we do not introduce modal or predicate logic here—we simply use standard terminology. Here, we only describe the relationship of the basic DL $\mathcal{ALC}$ and some of its extensions to these other logics (for a more detailed analysis, see [33] and Chapter 4 of [14]).

3.3.1   DLs and Predicate Logic

Most DLs can be seen as fragments of first-order predicate logic, although some provide operators such as transitive closure of roles or fixpoints that require second-order logic [33]. The main reason for using Description Logics rather than general first-order predicate logic when representing knowledge is that most DLs are actually *decidable* fragments of first-order predicate logic, i.e., there are effective procedures for deciding the inference problems introduced above.

Viewing role names as binary relations and concept names as unary relations, we define two translation functions, π_x and π_y, that inductively map $\mathcal{ALC}$-concepts into first order formulae with one free variable, x or y:

$$\pi_x(A) = A(x), \qquad\qquad \pi_y(A) = A(y),$$
$$\pi_x(C \sqcap D) = \pi_x(C) \wedge \pi_x(D), \qquad \pi_y(C \sqcap D) = \pi_y(C) \wedge \pi_y(D),$$
$$\pi_x(C \sqcup D) = \pi_x(C) \vee \pi_x(D), \qquad \pi_y(C \sqcup D) = \pi_y(C) \vee \pi_y(D),$$
$$\pi_x(\exists r.C) = \exists y.r(x, y) \wedge \pi_y(C), \qquad \pi_y(\exists r.C) = \exists x.r(y, x) \wedge \pi_x(C),$$
$$\pi_x(\forall r.C) = \forall y.r(x, y) \Rightarrow \pi_y(C), \qquad \pi_y(\forall r.C) = \forall x.r(y, x) \Rightarrow \pi_x(C).$$

Given this, we can translate a TBox $\mathcal{T}$ and an ABox $\mathcal{A}$ as follows, where $\psi[x/a]$ denotes the formula obtained from ψ by replacing all free occurrences of x with a:

$$\pi(\mathcal{T}) = \bigwedge_{C \sqsubseteq D \in \mathcal{T}} \forall x.(\pi_x(C) \Rightarrow \pi_x(D)),$$

$$\pi(\mathcal{A}) = \bigwedge_{a:C \in \mathcal{A}} \pi_x(C)[x/a] \wedge \bigwedge_{(a,b):r \in \mathcal{A}} r(a, b).$$

This translation preserves the semantics: we can obviously view DL interpretations as first-order interpretations and vice versa, and it is easy to show that the translation preserves models. As an easy consequence, we have that reasoning in DLs corresponds to first-order inference:

Theorem 3.1. *Let $(\mathcal{T}, \mathcal{A})$ be an $\mathcal{ALC}$-knowledge base, C, D possibly complex $\mathcal{ALC}$-concepts, and a an individual name. Then*

1. *$(\mathcal{T}, \mathcal{A})$ is consistent   iff $\pi(\mathcal{T}) \wedge \pi(\mathcal{A})$ is consistent,*
2. *$(\mathcal{T}, \mathcal{A}) \models C \sqsubseteq D$ iff $(\pi(\mathcal{T}) \wedge \pi(\mathcal{A})) \Rightarrow (\pi(\{C \sqsubseteq D\}))$ is valid,*
3. *$(\mathcal{T}, \mathcal{A}) \models a : C$ iff $(\pi(\mathcal{T}) \wedge \pi(\mathcal{A})) \Rightarrow (\pi(\{a : C\}))$ is valid.*

This translation not only provides an alternative way of defining the semantics of $\mathcal{ALC}$, but also tells us that all the introduced reasoning problems for $\mathcal{ALC}$ knowledge bases are decidable. In fact, the translation of a knowledge base uses only variables x and y, and thus yields a formula in the *two variable fragment of first-order logic*, which is known to be decidable in non-deterministic exponential time [79]. Alternatively, we can use the fact that this translation uses quantification only in a restricted way, and therefore yields a formula in the *guarded fragment* [2], which is known to be decidable in deterministic exponential time [78]. Thus, the exploration of the relationship between DLs and first-order logics even gives us upper complexity bounds "for free". However, for $\mathcal{ALC}$ and also many other DLs, the upper bounds obtained this way are not necessarily optimal, which justifies the development of dedicated reasoning procedures for DLs.

The translation of more expressive DLs may be straightforward, or more difficult, depending on the additional constructs. Inverse roles can be captured easily in both the guarded and the two variable fragment by simply swapping the variable places; e.g., $\pi_x(\exists R^-.C) = \exists y.R(y, x) \land \pi_y(C)$. Number restrictions can be captured using (in)equality or so-called *counting quantifiers*. It is known that the two-variable fragment with counting quantifiers is still decidable in non-deterministic exponential time [130]. Transitive roles, however, cannot be expressed with two variables only, and the three variable fragment is known to be undecidable. The guarded fragment, when restricted carefully to the so-called *action guarded fragment* [75], can still capture a variety of features such as number restrictions, inverse roles, and fixpoints, while remaining decidable in deterministic exponential time.

3.3.2 DLs and Modal Logic

Description Logics are closely related to Modal Logics, yet they have been developed independently. This close relationship was discovered relatively late [144], but has since then been exploited quite successfully to transfer complexity and decidability results as well as reasoning techniques [145, 57, 90, 3]. It is not hard to see that $\mathcal{ALC}$-concepts can be viewed as syntactic variants of formulae of the (multi) modal logic **K**: Kripke structures can easily be viewed as DL interpretations and, conversely, DL interpretations as Kripke structures; we can then view concept names as propositional variables, and role names as modal parameters, and realize this correspondence through the rewriting $\longleftrightarrow$, which allows $\mathcal{ALC}$-concepts to be translated into modal formulae and conversely modal formulae into $\mathcal{ALC}$-concepts, as follows:

$\mathcal{ALC}$-concept		Modal **K** formula
A	$\longleftrightarrow$	a, for concept name A and propositional variable a,
$C \sqcap D$	$\longleftrightarrow$	$C \land D$,
$C \sqcup D$	$\longleftrightarrow$	$C \lor D$,
$\neg C$	$\longleftrightarrow$	$\neg C$,
$\forall r.C$	$\longleftrightarrow$	$[r]C$,
$\exists r.C$	$\longleftrightarrow$	$\langle r \rangle C$.

Let us use $\dot{C}$ for the modal formula obtained by rewriting the $\mathcal{ALC}$-concept C. The translation of DL knowledge bases is slightly more tricky: a TBox $\mathcal{T}$ is satisfied only in those structures where, for each $C \sqsubseteq D$, $\neg\dot{C} \lor \dot{D}$ holds *globally*, i.e., in each world of our Kripke structure (or, equivalently, in each element of our interpretation domain). We can express this using the universal modality, that is, a special modal parameter

U that is interpreted as the total relation in all Kripke structures. Before we discuss ABoxes, let us first state the properties of our correspondence so far.

Theorem 3.2. *Let $\mathcal{T}$ be an $\mathcal{ALC}$-TBox and E, F possibly complex $\mathcal{ALC}$-concepts. Then*

1. *F is satisfiable with respect to $\mathcal{T}$*   *iff* $\dot{F} \wedge \bigwedge_{C \sqsubseteq D \in \mathcal{T}} [U](\neg \dot{C} \vee \dot{D})$
    is satisfiable,

2. *$\mathcal{T} \models E \sqsubseteq F$*   *iff* $(\bigwedge_{C \sqsubseteq D \in \mathcal{T}} [U](\neg \dot{C} \vee \dot{D})) \wedge \dot{E} \wedge \neg \dot{F}$
    is unsatisfiable.

Like TBoxes, ABoxes do not have a direct correspondence in modal logic, but they can be seen as a special case of a modal logic constructor, namely *nominals*. These are special propositional variables that hold in exactly one world; they are the basic ingredient of *hybrid logics* [4], and usually come with a special modality, the @-operator, that allows one to refer to the (only) world in which the nominal a holds. For example, $@_a \psi$ holds if, in the world where a holds, ψ holds as well. Hence an ABox assertion of the form $a : C$ corresponds to the modal formula $@_a \dot{C}$, and an ABox assertion $(a, b) : r$ corresponds to $@_a \langle r \rangle b$. In this latter formula, we see that nominals can act both as a parameter to the @ operator, like a, and as a propositional variables, like b. Please note that the usage of individual names in ABoxes corresponds to formulae where nominals are used in a rather restricted form only—some DLs, such as $\mathcal{SHOIN}$ or $\mathcal{SHOIQ}$, allow for a more general use of nominals, which is normally indicated by the letter $\mathcal{O}$ in a DL's name.

As in the case of first-order logic, some DL constructors have close relatives in modal logics and some do not. Number restrictions correspond to so-called *graded modalities* [70], which in modal logic received only limited attention until the connection with DLs was found. In some variants of propositional dynamic logic [71], a modal logic for reasoning about programs, we find *deterministic programs*, which correspond to (unqualified) number restrictions of the form $\leqslant 1R.\top$ [29]. Similarly, we find there *converse programs*, which correspond to *inverse roles*, and *regular expressions of programs*, which correspond to roles built using transitive-reflexive closure, union, and composition.

3.4   Tableau Based Reasoning Techniques

A variety of reasoning techniques can be used to solve the reasoning problems introduced in Section 3.2. These include resolution based approaches [102, 104], automata based approaches [49, 161], and structural approaches (for sub-Boolean DLs) [6]. The most widely used technique, however, is the tableau based approach first introduced by Schmidt-Schauß and Smolka [149]. In this section, we described this technique for the case of our basic DL $\mathcal{ALC}$.

3.4.1   A Tableau Algorithm for $\mathcal{ALC}$

We will concentrate on knowledge base consistency because, as we have seen in Section 3.2, this is a very general problem to which many others can be reduced. For example, given a knowledge base $\mathcal{K} = (\mathcal{T}, \mathcal{A})$, a concept C is subsumed by a concept D with respect to $\mathcal{K}$ ($\mathcal{K} \models C \sqsubseteq D$) iff $(\mathcal{T}, \mathcal{A} \cup \{x : (C \sqcap \neg D)\})$ is not consistent, where x is a new individual name (i.e., one that does not occur in $\mathcal{K}$). For $\mathcal{ALC}$ with a general TBox, i.e., one where the TBox is not restricted to contain only definitorial axioms (see Section 3.2), this problem is known to be EXPTIME-complete [144].

The tableau based decision procedure for the consistency of general $\mathcal{ALC}$ knowledge bases sketched below (and described in more detail in [12, 14]), runs in worst-case *non-deterministic* double exponential time.[3] However, according to the current state of the art, procedures such as this work well in practice, and are the basis for highly optimized implementations of DL systems such as FaCT [95], FaCT++ [160], RACER [81] and Pellet [151].

Given a knowledge base $(\mathcal{T}, \mathcal{A})$, we can assume, without loss of generality, that all of the concepts occurring in $\mathcal{T}$ and $\mathcal{A}$ are in *negation normal form* (NNF), i.e., that negation is applied only to concept names. An arbitrary $\mathcal{ALC}$ concept can be transformed to an equivalent one in NNF by pushing negations inwards using a combination of de Morgan's laws and the duality between existential and universal restrictions ($\neg \exists r.C \equiv \forall r.\neg C$ and $\neg \forall r.C \equiv \exists r.\neg C$). For example, the concept $\neg(\exists r.A \sqcap \forall s.B)$, where A, B are concept names, can be transformed to the equivalent NNF concept $(\forall r.\neg A) \sqcup (\exists s.\neg B)$. For a concept C, we will use $\dot{\neg} C$ to denote the NNF of $\neg C$.

The idea behind the algorithm is that it tries to prove the consistency of a knowledge base $\mathcal{K} = (\mathcal{T}, \mathcal{A})$ by constructing (a representation of) a model of $\mathcal{K}$. It does this by starting from the concrete situation described in $\mathcal{A}$, and explicating additional constraints on the model that are implied by the concepts in $\mathcal{A}$ and the axioms in $\mathcal{T}$. Since $\mathcal{ALC}$ has a so-called forest model property, we can assume that this model has the form of a set of (potentially infinite) trees, the root nodes of which can be arbitrarily interconnected. If we want to obtain a decision procedure, we can only construct finite trees representing the (potentially) infinite ones (assuming that a model exists at all); this can be done such that the finite representation can be *unraveled* into an infinite forest model $\mathcal{I}$ of $(\mathcal{T}, \mathcal{A})$.

In order to construct such a finite representation, the algorithm works on a data structure called a *completion forest*. This consists of a labelled directed graph, each node of which is the root of a *completion tree*. Each node x in the completion forest (which is either a root node or a node in a completion tree) is labelled with a set of concepts $\mathcal{L}(x)$, and each edge $\langle x, y \rangle$ (which is either one between root nodes or one inside a completion tree) is labelled with a set of role names $\mathcal{L}(\langle x, y \rangle)$. If $\langle x, y \rangle$ is an edge in the completion forest, then we say that x is a predecessor of y (and that y is a successor of x); in case $\langle x, y \rangle$ is labelled with a set containing the role name r, then we say that y is an r-successor of x.

When started with a knowledge base $(\mathcal{T}, \mathcal{A})$, the completion forest $\mathcal{F}_{\mathcal{A}}$ is initialized such that it contains a root node x_a, with $\mathcal{L}(x_a) = \{C \mid a : C \in \mathcal{A}\}$, for each individual name a occurring in $\mathcal{A}$, and an edge $\langle x_a, x_b \rangle$, with $\mathcal{L}(\langle x_a, x_b \rangle) = \{r \mid (a, b) : r \in \mathcal{A}\}$, for each pair (a, b) of individual names for which the set $\{r \mid (a, b) : r \in \mathcal{A}\}$ is nonempty.

---

[3]This is due to the algorithm searching a tree of worst-case exponential depth. By re-using previously computed search results, a similar algorithm can be made to run in exponential time [66], but this introduces a considerable overhead which turns out to be not always useful in practice.

⊓-rule: if 1. $C_1 \sqcap C_2 \in \mathcal{L}(x)$, x is not blocked, and
           2. $\{C_1, C_2\} \not\subseteq \mathcal{L}(x)$
        then set $\mathcal{L}(x) = \mathcal{L}(x) \cup \{C_1, C_2\}$

⊔-rule: if 1. $C_1 \sqcup C_2 \in \mathcal{L}(x)$, x is not blocked, and
           2. $\{C_1, C_2\} \cap \mathcal{L}(x) = \emptyset$
        then set $\mathcal{L}(x) = \mathcal{L}(x) \cup \{C\}$ for some $C \in \{C_1, C_2\}$

∃-rule: if 1. $\exists r.C \in \mathcal{L}(x)$, x is not blocked, and
           2. x has no r-successor y with $C \in \mathcal{L}(y)$,
        then create a new node y with $\mathcal{L}(\langle x, y \rangle) = \{r\}$ and $\mathcal{L}(y) = \{C\}$

∀-rule: if 1. $\forall r.C \in \mathcal{L}(x)$, x is not blocked, and
           2. there is an r-successor y of x with $C \notin \mathcal{L}(y)$
        then set $\mathcal{L}(y) = \mathcal{L}(y) \cup \{C\}$

⊑-rule: if 1. $C_1 \sqsubseteq C_2 \in \mathcal{T}$, x is not blocked, and
           2. $C_2 \sqcup \dot{\neg} C_1 \notin \mathcal{L}(x)$
        then set $\mathcal{L}(x) = \mathcal{L}(x) \cup \{C_2 \sqcup \dot{\neg} C_1\}$

Figure 3.1: The tableau expansion rules for $\mathcal{ALC}$.

The algorithm then applies so-called *expansion rules*, which syntactically decompose the concepts in node labels, either inferring new constraints for a given node, or extending the tree according to these constraints (see Fig. 3.1). For example, if $C_1 \sqcap C_2 \in \mathcal{L}(x)$, and either $C_1 \notin \mathcal{L}(x)$ or $C_2 \notin \mathcal{L}(x)$, then the ⊓-rule adds both C_1 and C_2 to $\mathcal{L}(x)$; if $\exists r.C \in \mathcal{L}(x)$, and x does not yet have an r-successor with C in its label, then the ∃-rule generates a new r-successor node y of x with $\mathcal{L}(y) = \{C\}$. Note that the ⊔-rule is different from the other rules in that it is *non-deterministic*: if $C_1 \sqcup C_2 \in \mathcal{L}(x)$ and neither $C_1 \in \mathcal{L}(x)$ nor $C_2 \in \mathcal{L}(x)$, then it adds *either C_1 or C_2* to $\mathcal{L}(x)$. In practice this is the main source of complexity in tableau algorithms, because it may be necessary to explore all possible choices of rule applications.

The algorithm stops if it encounters a *clash*: a completion forest in which $\{A, \neg A\} \subseteq \mathcal{L}(x)$ for some node x and some concept name A. In this case, the completion forest contains an obvious inconsistency, and thus does not represent a model. If the algorithm stops without having encountered a clash, then the obtained completion forest yields a finite representation of a forest model, and the algorithm answers "$(\mathcal{T}, \mathcal{A})$ is consistent"; if none of the possible non-deterministic choices of the ⊔-rule leads to such a representation of a forest model, i.e., all of them lead to a clash, then the algorithm answers "$(\mathcal{T}, \mathcal{A})$ is inconsistent".

Please note that we have two different kinds of non-determinism in this algorithm. The non-deterministic choice between the two disjuncts in the ⊔-rule is "don't know" non-deterministic, i.e., if the first choice leads to a clash, then the second one must be explored. In contrast, the choice of which rule to apply next to a given completion forest is "don't care" non-deterministic, i.e., one can choose an arbitrary applicable rule without the need to backtrack and explore alternative choices.

It remains to explain the meaning of "blocked" in the formulation of the expansion rules. Without the ⊑-rule (i.e., in case the TBox is empty), the tableau algorithm for $\mathcal{ALC}$ would always terminate, even without blocking. In order to guarantee termination of the expansion process even in the presence of GCIs, the algorithm uses a technique called *blocking*.[4] Blocking prevents application of expansion rules when the construction becomes repetitive; i.e., when it is obvious that the sub-tree rooted in some node x will be "similar" to the sub-tree rooted in some predecessor y of x. To be more precise, we say that a node y is an *ancestor* of a node x if they both belong to the same completion tree and either y is a predecessor of x, or there exists a predecessor z of x such that y is an ancestor of z. A node x is *blocked* if there is an ancestor y of x such that $\mathcal{L}(x) \subseteq \mathcal{L}(y)$ (in this case we say that y blocks x), or if there is an ancestor z of x such that z is blocked; if a node x is blocked and none of its ancestors is blocked, then we say that x is *directly blocked*. When the algorithm stops with a clash free completion forest, a branch that contains a directly blocked node x represents an infinite branch in the corresponding model having a regular structure that corresponds to an infinite repetition (or "unraveling") of the section of the graph between x and the node that blocks it (see Section 3.6.1).

Theorem 3.3. *The above algorithm is a decision procedure for the consistency of* $\mathcal{ALC}$ *knowledge bases.*

A complete proof of this theorem is beyond the scope of this chapter, and we will only sketch the idea behind the proof: the interested reader can refer to [12, 14] for more details. Firstly, it is easy to see that the algorithm terminates: expansion rule applications always extend node labels or add new nodes, and we can fix an upper bound on the size of node labels (they can only contain concepts that are derivable from the syntactic decomposition of concepts occurring in the input KB), on the fan-out of trees in the completion forest (a node can have at most one successor for each existential restriction occurring in its label), and on the length of their branches (due to blocking). Secondly, soundness follows from the fact that we can transform a fully expanded and clash free completion forest into a model of the input KB by "throwing away" all blocked nodes and "bending" each edge from a non-blocked into a blocked node to the node it is blocked by.[5] Finally, completeness follows from the fact that, given a model of the input KB, we could use it to guide applications of the ⊔-rule so as to produce a fully expanded and clash free completion forest.

The procedure described above can be simplified if the TBox is definitorial, i.e., if it contains only unique and acyclic definitions (see Section 3.2). In this case, reasoning with a knowledge base can be reduced to the problem of reasoning with an ABox only (equivalently, a knowledge base with an empty TBox) by *unfolding* the concepts used in ABox axioms [126]: given a KB $(\mathcal{T}, \mathcal{A})$, where the definition $A \equiv C$ occurs in $\mathcal{T}$, all occurrences of A in $\mathcal{A}$ can be replaced with C. Repeated application of this procedure can be used to eliminate from $\mathcal{A}$ all those concept names for which there is a definition in $\mathcal{T}$. As mentioned above, when the TBox is empty the ⊑-rule is no longer required and blocking can be dispensed with. This is because the other rules only introduce concepts that are smaller than the concept triggering the rule application; we will come back to this in Section 3.5.1.

---

[4]In description logics, blocking was first employed in [8] in the context of an algorithm that can handle the transitive closure of roles, and was improved on in [13, 46, 12, 92].

[5]For $\mathcal{ALC}$, we can always construct a finite cyclical model in this way; for more expressive DLs, we may need different blocking conditions, and we may need to unravel such cycles in order to construct an infinite model.

It is easy to see that the above *static* unfolding procedure can lead to an exponential increase in the size of the ABox [126]. In general, this cannot be avoided since there are DLs where reasoning with respect to definitorial TBoxes is harder than without TBoxes [127, 114]. For $\mathcal{ALC}$, however, we can avoid an increase in the complexity of the algorithm by unfolding definitions not a priori, but only as required by the progress of the algorithm. This so-called *lazy* unfolding [15, 95, 114] is achieved by substituting the $\sqsubseteq$-rule by the following two $\equiv_i$-rules:

$\equiv_1$-rule: if 1. $A \equiv C \in \mathcal{T}$, $A \in \mathcal{L}(x)$, $\equiv_2$-rule: if 1. $A \equiv C \in \mathcal{T}$, $\neg A \in \mathcal{L}(x)$,
                2. and $C \notin \mathcal{L}(x)$,   2. and $\dot{\neg}C \notin \mathcal{L}(x)$,
        then set $\mathcal{L}(x) = \mathcal{L}(x) \cup \{C\}$;   then set $\mathcal{L}(x) = \mathcal{L}(x) \cup \{\dot{\neg}C\}$.

As in the case of static unfolding, blocking is not required: the acyclicity condition on the TBox means that if a concept C is added to $\mathcal{L}(x)$ as a result of an application of one of the $\equiv_i$-rules to the concept A or $\neg A$ and axiom $A \equiv C$, then further unfolding of C cannot lead to the introduction of another occurrence of A in the sub-tree below x.

The tableau algorithm can also be extended to deal with a wide range of other DLs, including those supporting, e.g., (qualified) number restrictions, inverse roles, transitive roles, subroles, concrete domains and nominals. Extending the algorithm to deal with such features is mainly a matter of adding expansion rules to deal with the new constructors (e.g., number restrictions), adding new clash conditions (e.g., to deal with obviously unsatisfiable number restrictions), and using a more sophisticated blocking condition in order to guarantee both termination and soundness when using the extended rule set.

3.4.2 Implementation and Optimization Techniques

Although reasoning in $\mathcal{ALC}$ (with respect to an arbitrary KB) is of a relatively high complexity (EXPTIME-complete), the pathological cases that lead to such high *worst case* complexity are rather artificial, and rarely occur in practice [127, 86, 154, 95]. Even in realistic applications, however, problems can occur that are much too hard to be solved by naive implementations of theoretical algorithms such as the one sketched in Section 3.4.1. Modern DL systems, therefore, include a wide range of optimization techniques, the use of which has been shown to improve *typical case* performance by several orders of magnitude [96]. These systems exhibit good typical case performance, and work well in realistic applications [15, 44, 95, 81, 133].

A detailed description of optimization techniques is beyond the scope of this chapter, and the interested reader is referred to Chapter 8 of [14] for further information. It will, however, be interesting to sketch a couple of the key techniques: absorption and dependency directed backtracking.

Absorption

Whereas definitorial TBoxes can be dealt with efficiently by using lazy unfolding (see Section 3.4.1 above), more general axioms are not amenable to this optimization technique. In particular, GCIs $C \sqsubseteq D$, where C is non-atomic, must be dealt with by explicitly making every individual in the model an instance of $D \sqcup \dot{\neg}C$ (see Fig. 3.1). Large numbers of such GCIs result in a very high degree of non-determinism due to the introduction of these disjunctions, and thus to catastrophic performance degradation [95].

Absorption is a rewriting technique that tries to reduce the number of GCIs in the TBox by absorbing them into axioms of the form $A \sqsubseteq C$, where A is a concept name. The basic idea is that an axiom of the form $A \sqcap D \sqsubseteq D'$ can be rewritten as $A \sqsubseteq D' \sqcup \neg D$ and absorbed into an existing $A \sqsubseteq C$ axiom to give $A \sqsubseteq C \sqcap (D' \sqcup \neg D)$ [93]. Although the disjunction is still present, lazy unfolding applied to this axiom (where only the $\equiv_1$ rule needs to be applied) ensures that the disjunction is only introduced for individuals that are already known to be instances of A.

Dependency directed backtracking

Inherent unsatisfiability concealed in sub-descriptions can lead to large amounts of unproductive backtracking search known as thrashing. For example, expanding the description $(C_1 \sqcup D_1) \sqcap \cdots \sqcap (C_n \sqcup D_n) \sqcap \exists R.(A \sqcap B) \sqcap \forall R.\neg A$ could lead to the fruitless exploration of 2^n possible expansions of $(C_1 \sqcup D_1) \sqcap \cdots \sqcap (C_n \sqcup D_n)$ before the inherent unsatisfiability of $\exists R.(A \sqcap B) \sqcap \forall R.\neg A$ is discovered. This problem is addressed by adapting a form of dependency directed backtracking called *backjumping*, which has been used in solving constraint satisfiability problems [27].

Backjumping works by labeling concepts with a dependency set indicating the non-deterministic expansion choices on which they depend. When a clash is discovered, the dependency sets of the clashing concepts can be used to identify the most recent non-deterministic expansion where an alternative choice might alleviate the cause of the clash. The algorithm can then jump back over intervening non-deterministic expansions *without* exploring any alternative choices. Similar techniques have been used in first-order theorem provers, e.g., the "proof condensation" technique employed in the HARP theorem prover [128].

3.5 Complexity

In this section, we discuss the computational complexity of some of the reasoning problems we have specified. Since introducing complexity classes and other notions of computational complexity would go beyond the scope of this chapter, we expect the reader to be familiar with the complexity classes PSpace and ExpTime, the notions of membership in and hardness for such a class, and what it means for a problem to be undecidable. Those readers who want to learn more about computational complexity are referred to [131], or any other textbook covering computational complexity.

3.5.1 $\mathcal{ALC}$ ABox Consistency is PSpace-complete

In Section 3.4.1, we have seen a tableau based algorithm that decides the consistency of $\mathcal{ALC}$ ABoxes with respect to TBoxes. Here, we will first consider ABoxes only and explain how this algorithm can be implemented to use polynomial space only; that is, we will show that consistency of $\mathcal{ALC}$ ABoxes is *in* PSpace. Then we will show that we cannot do better; that is, that consistency of $\mathcal{ALC}$ ABoxes is PSpace-*hard*.

For these considerations, we need to agree how to measure the size of the input. For $\mathcal{A}$ an ABox $\mathcal{A}$, intuitively its size $|\mathcal{A}|$ is the length required to write $\mathcal{A}$ down, where we assume that the length required to write concept and role names is 1. Formally, we define the size of ABoxes as follows:

$$|\mathcal{A}| = \sum_{a:C \in \mathcal{A}} (|C| + 1) + \sum_{(a,b):r \in \mathcal{A}} 3,$$

$|A| = 1$ for a concept name A (including $\top$, $\bot$),

$|\neg D| = |D| + 1,$

$|D_1 \sqcap D_2| = |D_1 \sqcup D_2| = |D_1| + |D_2| + 1,$

$|\exists R.D| = |\forall R.D| = |D| + 2.$

Next, let us look again at the tableau algorithm. First, note that, in the absence of a TBox, neither the $\sqsubseteq$-rule not the $\equiv_i$-rules is applicable. Second, observe that the tableau algorithm builds a completion forest in a monotonic way; that is, all expansion rules either add concepts to node labels or new nodes to the forest, but never remove anything. The forest it constructs consists of two parts: for each individual name in $\mathcal{A}$, the forest contains a root node, which we will call an *old node* in the following. The edges between old nodes all stem from role assertions in $\mathcal{A}$, and thus may occur without restrictions. Other nodes (i.e., the notes in the completion tress that are not root nodes) are generated by the $\exists$-rule, and we call them *new nodes*; we call the other rules *augmenting* rules, because they only augment the labels of existing nodes. In contrast to edges between old nodes, edges between new nodes are of a particular shape: each new node is found in a completion tree with an old node at its root.

Let us consider the node labels. Initially, for an old node x_a, $\mathcal{L}(x_a)$ contains the concepts C from the assertions $a : C \in \mathcal{A}$. Other concepts are added by the expansion rules, and we observe that these expansion rules only add subconcepts of the concepts occurring in $\mathcal{A}$. Since there are at most $|\mathcal{A}|$ such subconcepts, each node label can be stored in space polynomial in $|\mathcal{A}|$. Moreover, for each concept D in the label of a new node x, the (unique) predecessor of x contains a larger concept. Hence the maximum size of concepts in node labels strictly decreases along a path of new nodes, and thus the depth of each completion tree in our completion graph is bounded by $\max\{|C| \mid a : C \in \mathcal{A}\}$.

Finally, we note that the expansion rules can be applied in an arbitrary order: the correctness proof for the algorithm does not rely on a specific application order. Hence we can use the following order: first, all augmenting rules are exhaustively applied to old nodes. Next, we treat each old node in turn, and build the tree rooted at it in a depth first manner. That is, for an old node x_a, we deal in turn with each existential restriction $\exists r.C \in \mathcal{L}(x_a)$: we apply the $\exists$-rule in order to generate an r-successor x_0 with $\mathcal{L}(x_0) = \{C\}$, apply the $\forall$-rule exhaustively to this r-successor of x_a (which may add further concepts to $\mathcal{L}(x_0)$), and recursively apply the same procedure to x_0, i.e., exhaustively apply the augmenting rules, and then deal with the existential restrictions one at a time. As usual, the algorithm stops if a clash occurs; otherwise, when all of a new node's existential restrictions have been dealt with, we can delete it, including its label, and re-use the space. Using this technique, we can investigate the whole tree rooted at our old node x_a while only keeping a single branch in memory at any time. This branch is of length linear in $|\mathcal{A}|$, and can thus be stored with all its labels in size polynomial in $|\mathcal{A}|$. Continuing the investigation of all trees in the same manner, our algorithm only requires space polynomial in $|\mathcal{A}|$. This technique is called the *trace* technique since it only "traces" the tree-shaped part of a completion tree [149].

To show that we cannot do better, we will prove that consistency of $\mathcal{ALC}$ ABoxes is PSpace-hard, even for ABoxes that consist of a single assertion $\{a : C\}$. This proof is by a reduction of the validity problem for *quantified Boolean formulae*, which is known to be PSpace-hard [155]. A *quantified Boolean formula* (QBF for short) Φ is of the form

$$Q_1 p_1. Q_2 p_2. \ldots . Q_n p_n. \varphi$$

for $Q_i \in \{\forall, \exists\}$ and φ a Boolean formula over $p_1, \ldots, p_n$. The validity of QBFs is defined inductively:

$\exists p. \Phi$ is valid if $\Phi[p/t]$ or $\Phi[p/f]$ is valid
$\forall p. \Phi$ is valid if $\Phi[p/t]$ and $\Phi[p/f]$ are valid

For example, $\forall p. \exists q. (p \vee q)$ is valid, whereas $\forall p. \forall q. \exists r. ((p \vee r) \Rightarrow q)$ is not valid.

Since validity of QBFs is PSpace-hard, it remains to show that, for a given QBF Φ, we can construct in polynomial time an $\mathcal{ALC}$-concept C_Φ such that Φ is valid iff $\{a : C_\Phi\}$ is consistent. As an immediate consequence, consistency of $\mathcal{ALC}$ ABoxes and satisfiability of $\mathcal{ALC}$ concepts are PSpace-hard.

The idea underlying our reduction is to build, for a QBF as above, a concept C_Φ such that each instance x_0 of C_Φ is the root of a tree of depth n such that, for each $1 \leqslant i \leqslant n$, we have the following:

1. if $Q_i = \exists$, each $\underbrace{r \ldots r}_{i-1 \text{ times}}$ -successor of x_0 has one r-successor, which can be in p_i or in $\neg p_i$, and

2. if $Q_i = \forall$, each $\underbrace{r \ldots r}_{i-1 \text{ times}}$ -successor of x_0 has two r-successors one in p_i, one in $\neg p_i$.

To this end, for a QBF $\Phi = Q_1 p_1. Q_2 p_2. \ldots . Q_n p_n. \varphi$, we define C_Φ as follows, where $\hat{\varphi}$ is the DL counterpart of φ obtained by replacing $\wedge$ with $\sqcap$ and $\vee$ with $\sqcup$ in φ:

$$C_\Phi := L_1 \sqcap \forall r. (L_2 \sqcap \forall r. (L_3 \sqcap \cdots \sqcap \forall r. (L_n \sqcap \hat{\varphi})) \cdots), \quad \text{where}$$

$$L_i := D_i \sqcap \begin{cases} \exists r. \top & \text{if } Q_i = \exists, \\ \exists r. p_i \sqcap \exists r. \neg p_i & \text{if } Q_i = \forall, \end{cases}$$

$$D_i := \bigsqcap_{j<i} (p_j \Rightarrow \forall r. p_j) \sqcap (\neg p_j \Rightarrow \forall r. \neg p_j).$$

Through this definition we ensure that, if $x_0 \in C_\Phi^{\mathcal{I}}$ and there is a path $(x_0, x_1) \in r^{\mathcal{I}}$, $\ldots, (x_{i-1}, x_i) \in r^{\mathcal{I}}$, then $x_i \in L_i^{\mathcal{I}}$, and L_i is responsible for the branching pattern described above. The concepts D_i ensure that, if some x_j is (is not) an instance of p_j for $j < i$, then so is (neither is) x_{j+1}. These observations, together with the fact that x_n must be an instance of $\hat{\varphi}$, ensure that Φ is valid iff $\{a : C_\Phi\}$ is consistent.

Theorem 3.4. *Satisfiability and subsumption of $\mathcal{ALC}$ concepts and consistency of $\mathcal{ALC}$ ABoxes are PSpace-complete problems.*

3.5.2 Adding General TBoxes Results in ExpTime-Hardness

We will see in Section 3.6.1 that satisfiability of $\mathcal{ALC}$ concepts with respect to (general) TBoxes can be decided in exponential time, i.e., that this problem is in ExpTime. Again, one can show that we cannot do better, i.e., that this problem is also ExpTime-hard. Unfortunately, this proof goes beyond the scope of this chapter since, to the best of our knowledge, all proofs require the introduction of some "complexity theory machinery": one possible proof is by adapting the proof of ExpTime-hardness of propositional dynamic logic (PDL) in [71]. This proof uses a polynomial reduction of the word problem for *polynomially space-bounded, alternating Turing machines* to the satisfiability of PDL formulae. When translated into its DL counterpart, the reduction formula of this proof is of the form $C \sqcap \forall r^*.D$, where C and D are $\mathcal{ALC}$ concepts and r^* is the transitive-reflexive closure of r, i.e., this concept involves a constructor not available in $\mathcal{ALC}$. It is not hard to see, however, that $C \sqcap \forall r^*.D$ is satisfiable iff C is satisfiable with respect to the TBox $\{\top \sqsubseteq D\}$. This is the case since r is the only role name occurring in C and D. For more information on the relationship between TBoxes and PDL see, e.g., [144, 57] or Chapter 4 of [14].

It is worth noting that, for *definitorial* TBoxes and $\mathcal{ALC}$, this blow-up of the complexity from PSpace to ExpTime does not occur [114]. Yet, we will see in Section 3.6.2 that there are DLs where even the presence of definitorial TBoxes can lead to an increased complexity.

3.5.3 The Effect of other Constructors

In Section 3.2.3 we have seen various extensions of $\mathcal{ALC}$, and we will now briefly describe the influence they have on the computational complexity.

In general, number restrictions are "harmless": with only one exception, which we will come back to later, even qualified number restrictions can be added to a DL without increasing its complexity. For example, concept satisfiability in $\mathcal{ALCQ}$ is still in PSpace [159], and consistency of general $\mathcal{ALCQ}$ knowledge bases is still in ExpTime [56, 159].

Transitive roles are mostly harmless: all DLs between $\mathcal{ALC}$ and $\mathcal{ALCQIO}$ can be extended with transitive roles without increasing their computational complexity [142, 159]. One "dangerous" interaction we are aware of is with role hierarchies: concept satisfiability of $\mathcal{ALC}$ with transitive roles and role hierarchies is ExpTime-hard, whereas concept satisfiability in $\mathcal{ALC}$ with either transitive roles or role hierarchies is in PSpace [142]. The increase in complexity is due to the fact that transitive roles and role hierarchies can be used to internalize TBoxes [144]: given a TBox $\mathcal{T}$ and an $\mathcal{ALC}$ concept E that use role names $r_1, \ldots, r_n$, we have that E is satisfiable with respect to $\mathcal{T}$ if and only if the concept

$$\exists r.E \sqcap \forall r. \bigsqcap_{C \sqsubseteq D \in \mathcal{T}} (\neg C \sqcup D)$$

is satisfiable with respect to $\{r_1 \sqsubseteq r, \ldots, r_n \sqsubseteq r\}$, where r is a new, transitive role. The first conjunct ensures that the extension of E is indeed nonempty, and the second conjunct ensures that every element in a (connected) model satisfies each GCI in $\mathcal{T}$. Thus, in $\mathcal{ALC}$ with transitive roles and role hierarchies, we can polynomially reduce reasoning with respect to a TBox to pure concept reasoning, and hence pure concept reasoning is already ExpTime-hard. In the additional presence of number restrictions, we need to take special care not to use super-roles of transitive roles inside number restrictions since this leads to undecidability [92]. As a consequence, expressive DLs such as $\mathcal{SHIQ}$ allow only so-called *simple* roles to be used in number restrictions.

Nominals and inverse roles are also mostly harmless: concept satisfiability in $\mathcal{ALCQO}$ and $\mathcal{ALCI}$ with transitive roles is still in PSpace [92, 7], but concept satisfiability of $\mathcal{ALCIO}$ is ExpTime-hard [4]. This increase in complexity is again due to the fact that, with inverse roles and nominals, we can internalize TBoxes. Intuitively, we use a nominal as a "spy point", i.e., an individual that has all other elements of a (connected) model as t-successors, and we use inverse roles to ensure this spy-point behavior. More precisely, a concept E is satisfiable with respect to a TBox $\mathcal{T}$ if and only if the following concept is satisfiable, where o is a nominal, R is the set of roles r occurring in $\mathcal{T}$ or E and their inverses r^-, and t is a role that is not in R:

$$o \sqcap (\exists t.E) \sqcap \left(\forall t. \prod_{r \in R} \forall r.\exists t^-.o \right) \sqcap \forall t. \prod_{C \sqsubseteq D \in \mathcal{T}} (\neg C \sqcup D).$$

The third conjunct ensures that o indeed "sees" all elements in a connected model, i.e., if x_o is an instance of the above concept in a connected model $\mathcal{I}$ and there is an element $y \in \Delta^\mathcal{I}$, then $(x_o, y) \in t^\mathcal{I}$

Finally, we would like to point out that nominals, inverse roles, and number restrictions together have a dramatic influence on complexity: satisfiability of $\mathcal{ALCQIO}$ concepts is NExpTime-hard [159], even though satisfiability of $\mathcal{ALCQI}$, $\mathcal{ALCIO}$, and $\mathcal{ALCOQ}$ concepts with respect to TBoxes is in ExpTime [56, 143, 7].

3.6 Other Reasoning Techniques

Although the tableau based approach is currently the most widely used technique for reasoning in DLs, other approaches have been developed as well. In general, a reasoning algorithm can be used in an implementation, or to prove a decidability or computational complexity result. Certain approaches may (for a given logic) be better suited for the former task, whereas others may be better suited for the latter—and it is sometimes hard to find one that is well-suited for both. Examples of other approaches are the automata based approach, the structural subsumption approach, the resolution based approach, and translation based approaches. For certain logics and tasks, other approaches turn out to be superior to the tableau based approach. For example, it is not clear how the polynomiality result for subsumption in $\mathcal{EL}$ with GCIs [42, 6], which uses a structural subsumption algorithm, could be obtained with the help of a tableau based algorithm. Similarly, the automata based approach can be used to show that satisfiability and subsumption of $\mathcal{ALC}$ concepts with respect to TBoxes can be decided within exponential time [49, 117, 116, 159],[6] whereas this is very hard to prove using a tableau based approach [66]. Resolution based approaches [103, 5, 104, 107], which use the translation of DLs into first-order predicate logic, may have the advantage that they simultaneously yield a decision procedure for a certain decidable DL, and a semidecision procedure for a more expressive logic (such as OWL Full or first-order

---

[6]The cited papers actually use automata based approaches to show ExpTime results for *extensions* of $\mathcal{ALC}$.

predicate logic). Moreover, some of them are worst-case optimal [104], and others can be implemented through appropriate parameterization of existing first-order theorem provers [103]. Finally, the translation of very expressive DLs into propositional dynamic logic or the propositional mu-calculus [57, 58, 56, 59] allows one to transfer known decidability and complexity results for these logics to very expressive DLs. It is not clear how these results could be obtained with the help of the tableau based approach.

In this section, we restrict our attention to the automata based approach for $\mathcal{ALC}$ with GCIs, and to structural subsumption algorithms for the sub-Boolean DLs[7] $\mathcal{EL}$ and $\mathcal{FL}_0$.

3.6.1   The Automata Based Approach

In this subsection, we restrict our attention to concept satisfiability, possibly with respect to (general) TBoxes. This is not a severe restriction since most of the other interesting inference problem can be reduced to satisfiability.[8] There are various instances of the automata based approach, which differ not only with respect to the DL under consideration, but also with respect to the employed automaton model. However, in principle all these instances have the following general ideas in common:

- First, one shows that the DL in question has the *tree model property*.

- Second, one devises a translation from pairs $C, \mathcal{T}$, where C is a concept and $\mathcal{T}$ is a TBox, into an appropriate *tree automata* $\mathcal{A}_{C,\mathcal{T}}$ such that $\mathcal{A}_{C,\mathcal{T}}$ accepts exactly the tree models of C with respect to $\mathcal{T}$.

- Third, one applies the *emptiness test* for the employed automaton model to $\mathcal{A}_{C,\mathcal{T}}$ to test whether C has a (tree) model with respect to $\mathcal{T}$.

The complexity of the satisfiability algorithm obtained this way depends on the complexity of the translation and the complexity of the emptiness tests. The latter complexity in turn depends on which automaton model is employed.

Below, we will use a simple form of non-deterministic automata working on infinite trees of fixed arity, so-called *looping automata* [162]. In this case, the translation is exponential, but the emptiness test is polynomial (in the size of the already exponentially large automaton obtained through the translation). Thus, the whole algorithm runs in deterministic exponential time. Alternatively, one could use alternating tree automata [125], where a polynomial translation is possible, but the emptiness test is exponential.

Instead of considering automata working on trees of fixed arity, one could also consider so-called amorphous tree automata [31, 105], which can deal with arbitrary branching. This simplifies defining the translation, but uses a slightly more complicated automaton model. For some very expressive description logics (e.g., ones that allow for transitive closure of roles [8]), the simple looping automata introduced below are not sufficient since one needs additional acceptance conditions such as the Büchi

---

[7]Sub-Boolean DLs are DLs that are not equipped with all Boolean operators.

[8]Using the so-called pre-completion technique [88], this is also the case for inference problems involving ABoxes.

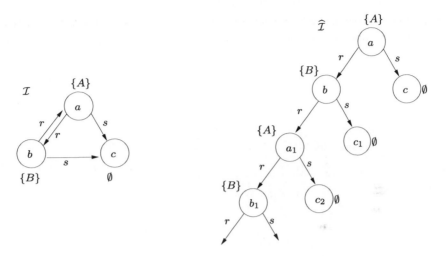

Figure 3.2: Unraveling of a model into a tree-shaped model.

condition [158] (which requires the occurrence of infinitely many final states in every path).

The tree model property

The first step towards showing that satisfiability in $\mathcal{ALC}$ with respect to general TBoxes can be decided with the automata based approach is to establish the tree model property, i.e., to show that any $\mathcal{ALC}$-concept C satisfiable with respect to an $\mathcal{ALC}$-TBox $\mathcal{T}$ has a tree-shaped model. Note that this model may, in general, be infinite. One way of seeing this is to consider the tableau algorithm introduced in Section 3.4.1, applied to the knowledge base $(\mathcal{T}, \{a : C\})$, and just dispose of blocking. Possibly infinite runs of the algorithm then generate tree-shaped models. However, one can also show the tree model property of $\mathcal{ALC}$ by using the well-known unraveling technique [32], in which an arbitrary model of C with respect to $\mathcal{T}$ is unraveled into a bisimilar tree-shaped interpretation. Invariance of $\mathcal{ALC}$ under bisimulation [110] (which it inherits from its syntactic variant multimodal $\mathbf{K_{(m)}}$) then implies that the tree shaped interpretation obtained by unraveling is also a model of C with respect to $\mathcal{T}$.

Instead of defining unraveling in detail, we just give an example in Fig. 3.2, and refer the reader to [32] for formal definitions and proofs. The graph on the left-hand side of Fig. 3.2 describes an interpretation $\mathcal{I}$: the nodes of the graph are the elements of $\Delta^{\mathcal{I}}$, the node labels express to which concept names the corresponding element belongs, and the labelled edges of the graph express the role relationships. For example, $a \in \Delta^{\mathcal{I}}$ belongs to $A^{\mathcal{I}}$, but not to $B^{\mathcal{I}}$, and it has r-successor b and s-successor c. It is easy to check that $\mathcal{I}$ is a model of the concept A with respect to the TBox

$$\mathcal{T} := \{A \sqsubseteq \exists r.B,\ B \sqsubseteq \exists r.A,\ A \sqcup B \sqsubseteq \exists s.\top\}.$$

The graph on the right-hand side of Fig. 3.2 describes (a finite part of) the corresponding unraveled model, where a was used as the start node for the unraveling. Basically, one considers all paths starting with a in the original model, but whenever one would

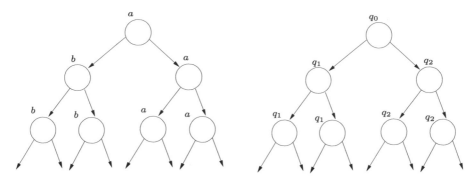

Figure 3.3: A tree and a run on it.

re-enter a node one makes a copy of it. Like $\mathcal{I}$, the corresponding unraveled interpretation $\widehat{\mathcal{I}}$ is a model of $\mathcal{T}$ and it satisfies $a \in A^{\widehat{\mathcal{I}}}$.

Looping tree automata

As mentioned above, we consider automata working on *infinite trees* of some fixed arity k. To be more precise, the nodes of the trees are labelled by elements from some finite alphabet Σ, whereas the edges are unlabeled, but ordered, i.e., there is a first, second, to kth successor for each node. Such trees, which we call k-ary Σ-trees, can formally be represented as mappings $T : \{0, \ldots, k-1\}^* \to \Sigma$. Thus, nodes are represented as words over $\{0, \ldots, k-1\}$, the root is the word ε, and a node u has exactly k successor nodes $u0, \ldots, u(k-1)$, and its label is $T(u)$. For example, the binary tree that has root label a, whose left subtree contains only nodes labelled by b, and whose right subtree has only nodes labelled by a (see the left-hand side of Fig. 3.3) is formally represented as the mapping

$$T : \{0, 1\}^* \to \{a, b\} \quad \text{with}$$
$$T(u) = \begin{cases} b & \text{if } u \text{ starts with } 0, \\ a & \text{otherwise.} \end{cases}$$

A *looping automaton* working on k-ary Σ-trees is of the form $\mathcal{A} = (Q, \Sigma, I, \Delta)$, where

- Q is a finite set of states and $I \subseteq Q$ is the set of initial states;

- Σ is a finite alphabet;

- $\Delta \subseteq Q \times \Sigma \times Q^k$ is the transition relation.

We will usually write tuples $(q, a, q_1, \ldots, q_k) \in \Delta$ in the form $(q, a) \to (q_1, \ldots, q_k)$.

A *run* of $\mathcal{A} = (Q, \Sigma, I, \Delta)$ on the tree $T : \{0, \ldots, k-1\}^* \to \Sigma$ is a k-ary Q-tree $R : \{0, \ldots, k-1\}^* \to Q$ such that $(R(u), T(u)) \to (R(u0), \ldots, R(u(k-1))) \in \Delta$ for all $u \in \{0, \ldots, k-1\}^*$. This run is called *accepting* if $R(\varepsilon) \in I$.

For example, consider the automaton $\mathcal{A} = (Q, \Sigma, I, \Delta)$, where

- $Q = \{q_0, q_1, q_2\}$ and $I = \{q_0\}$;

- $\Sigma = \{a, b\}$;

- Δ consists of the transitions

$$(q_0, a) \to (q_1, q_2), \quad (q_0, a) \to (q_2, q_1),$$
$$(q_1, b) \to (q_1, q_1), \quad (q_2, a) \to (q_2, q_2).$$

The k-ary Q-tree R from the right-hand side of Fig. 3.3 maps ε to q_0, nodes starting with 0 to q_1, and nodes starting with 1 to q_2. This tree R is an accepting run of $\mathcal{A}$ on the tree T on the left-hand side of Fig. 3.3.

The *tree language accepted* by a given looping automaton $\mathcal{A} = (Q, \Sigma, I, \Delta)$ is

$$L(\mathcal{A}) := \big\{ T : \{0, \ldots, k-1\}^* \to \Sigma \mid \text{there is an accepting run of } \mathcal{A} \text{ on } T \big\}.$$

In our example, the language accepted by the automaton consists of two trees, the tree T defined above and the symmetric tree where the left subtree contains only nodes labelled with a and the right subtree contains only nodes labelled with b.

The emptiness test

Given a looping tree automaton $\mathcal{A}$, the emptiness test decides whether $L(\mathcal{A}) = \emptyset$ or not. Based on the definition of the accepted language, one might be tempted to try to solve the problem in a *top–down* manner, by first choosing an initial state to label the root, then choose a transition starting with this state to label its successors, etc. However, the algorithm obtained this way is non-deterministic since one may have several initial states, and also several possible transitions for each state.

To obtain a *deterministic polynomial time emptiness test*, it helps to work *bottom-up*. The main idea is that one wants to compute the set of *bad states*, i.e., states that do not occur in any run of the automaton. Obviously, any state q that does not occur on the left-hand side of a transition $(q, \cdot) \to (\cdots)$ is bad. Starting with this set, one can then extend the set of states known to be bad using the fact that a state q is bad if all transitions $(q, \cdot) \to (q_1, \ldots, q_k)$ starting with q contain a bad state q_j in their right-hand side. Obviously, this process of extending the set of known bad states terminates after a linear number of additions of states to the set of known bad states, and it is easy to show that the final set obtained this way is indeed the set of all bad states. The accepted language is then empty iff all initial states are bad. By using appropriate data structures, one can ensure that the overall complexity of the algorithm is linear in the size of the automaton. A more detailed description of this emptiness test for looping tree automata can be found in [26].

The reduction

Recall that we want to reduce the satisfiability problem for $\mathcal{ALC}$-concepts with respect to general TBoxes to the emptiness problem for looping tree automata by constructing, for a given input $C, \mathcal{T}$, an automaton $\mathcal{A}_{C,\mathcal{T}}$ that accepts exactly the tree-shaped models of C with respect to $\mathcal{T}$.

Before this is possible, however, we need to overcome the *mismatch between the underlying kinds of trees*. The tree-shaped models of C with respect to $\mathcal{T}$ are trees with labelled edges, but without a fixed arity. In order to express such trees as k-ary Σ-trees for an appropriate k, where Σ consists of all sets of concept names, we consider all the existential restrictions occurring in C and $\mathcal{T}$. The number of these restrictions determines k. Using the bisimulation invariance of $\mathcal{ALC}$ [110], it is easy to show that the existence of a tree-shaped model of C with respect to $\mathcal{T}$ also implies the existence of a tree-shaped model where every node has at most k successor nodes. To get exactly k successors, we can do some padding with dummy nodes if needed. The edge label is simply pushed into the label of the successor node, i.e., each node label contains, in addition to concept names, exactly one role name, which expresses with which role the node is reached from its unique predecessor. For the root, an arbitrary role can be chosen.

The states of $\mathcal{A}_{C,\mathcal{T}}$ are sets of subexpressions of the concepts occurring in C and $\mathcal{T}$. Intuitively, a run of the automaton on a tree-shaped model of C with respect to $\mathcal{T}$ labels a node not only with the concept names to which this element of the model belongs, but also with all the subexpressions to which it belongs. For technical reasons, we need to normalize the input concept and TBox before we build these subexpressions. First, we ensure that all GCIs in $\mathcal{T}$ are of the form $\top \sqsubseteq D$ by using the fact that the GCIs $C_1 \sqsubseteq C_2$ and $\top \sqsubseteq \neg C_1 \sqcup C_2$ are equivalent. Second, we transform the input concept C and every concept D in a GCI $\top \sqsubseteq D$ into negation normal form as described in Section 3.4.1. In our example, the normalized TBox consists of the GCIs

$$\top \sqsubseteq \neg A \sqcup \exists r.B, \quad \top \sqsubseteq \neg B \sqcup \exists r.A, \quad \top \sqsubseteq (\neg A \sqcap \neg B) \sqcup \exists s.\top,$$

whose subexpressions are $\top, \neg A \sqcup \exists r.B, \neg A, A, \exists r.B, B, \neg B \sqcup \exists r.A, \neg B, \exists r.A, (\neg A \sqcap \neg B) \sqcup \exists s.\top, \neg A \sqcap \neg B, \exists s.\top$. Of these, the node a in the tree-shaped model depicted on the right-hand side of Fig. 3.2 belongs to $\top, \neg A \sqcup \exists r.B, A, \exists r.B, \neg B \sqcup \exists r.A, \neg B, (\neg A \sqcap \neg B) \sqcup \exists s.\top, \exists s.\top$.

We are now ready to give a *formal definition of the automaton* $\mathcal{A}_{C,\mathcal{T}} = (Q, \Sigma, I, \Delta)$. Let $S_{C,\mathcal{T}}$ denote the set of all subexpressions of C and $\mathcal{T}$, $R_{C,\mathcal{T}}$ denote the set of all role names occurring in C and $\mathcal{T}$, and k the number of existential restrictions contained in $S_{C,\mathcal{T}}$. The *alphabet* Σ basically consists of all subsets of the set of concept names occurring in C and $\mathcal{T}$. As mentioned above, in order to encode the edge labels (i.e., express for which role r the node is a successor node), each "letter" contains, additionally, exactly one role name. Finally, the alphabet contains the empty set (not even containing a role name), which is used to label nodes that are introduced for padding purposes.

The set of *states* Q of $\mathcal{A}_{C,\mathcal{T}}$ consists of the *Hintikka sets* for $C, \mathcal{T}$, i.e., subsets q of $S_{C,\mathcal{T}} \cup R_{C,\mathcal{T}}$ such that $q = \emptyset$ or

- q contains exactly one role name;

- if $\top \sqsubseteq D \in \mathcal{T}$ then $D \in q$;

- if $C_1 \sqcap C_2 \in q$ then $\{C_1, C_2\} \subseteq q$;

- if $C_1 \sqcup C_2 \in q$ then $\{C_1, C_2\} \cap q \neq \emptyset$; and

- $\{A, \neg A\} \not\subseteq q$ for all concept names A.

The set of *initial states* I consists of those states containing C.

Finally, the *transition relation* Δ consists of those transitions $(q, \sigma) \to (q_1, \ldots, q_k)$ satisfying the following properties:

- q and σ coincide with respect to the concept and role names contained in them;

- if $q = \emptyset$, then $q_1 = \cdots = q_k = \emptyset$;

- if $\exists r.D \in q$, then there is an i such that $\{D, r\} \subseteq q_i$; and

- if $\forall r.D \in q$ and $r \in q_i$, then $D \in q_i$.

It is not hard to show that the construction of $\mathcal{A}_{C,\mathcal{T}}$ indeed yields a polynomial reduction of satisfiability with respect to general TBoxes in $\mathcal{ALC}$ to the emptiness problem for looping tree automata.

Proposition 3.5. *An $\mathcal{ALC}$-concept C is satisfiable with respect to a general $\mathcal{ALC}$-TBox $\mathcal{T}$ iff $L(\mathcal{A}_{C,\mathcal{T}}) \neq \emptyset$.*

Obviously, the number of states of $\mathcal{A}_{C,\mathcal{T}}$ is exponential in the size of C and $\mathcal{T}$. Since the emptiness problem for looping tree automata can be decided in polynomial time, we obtain a deterministic exponential upper-bound for the time complexity of the satisfiability problem. Together with the EXPTIME-hardness result sketched in Section 3.5 we thus know the exact worst-case complexity of the problem.

Theorem 3.6. *Satisfiability in $\mathcal{ALC}$ with respect to general TBoxes is* EXPTIME-*complete.*

3.6.2 Structural Approaches

As mentioned in the introduction, early DL systems were based on so-called structural subsumption algorithms, which first normalize the concepts to be tested for subsumption, and then compare the syntactic structure of the normalized concepts. The claim was that these algorithms can decide subsumption in polynomial time. However, the first complexity results for DLs, also mentioned in the introduction, showed that these algorithms were neither polynomial nor decision procedures for subsumption. For example, all early systems used unfolding of concept definitions, which can cause an exponential blow-up of the size of concepts. Nebel's coNP-hardness result [127] for subsumption with respect to definitorial TBoxes showed that this blow-up cannot be avoided whenever the constructors conjunction and value restriction are available. In addition, the early structural subsumption algorithms were not complete, i.e., they were not able to detect all valid subsumption relationships. These negative results for structural subsumption algorithms together with the advent of tableau based algorithms for expressive DLs, which behaved well in practice, was probably the main reason why structural approaches—and with them the quest for DLs with a polynomial subsumption problem—were largely abandoned during the 1990s. More recent results [11, 42, 6] on the complexity of reasoning in DLs with existential restrictions, rather than value restrictions, have led to a partial rehabilitation of structural approaches.

When trying to find a DL with a polynomial subsumption problem, it is clear that one cannot allow for all Boolean operations, since then one would inherit NP-hardness from propositional logic. It should also be clear that conjunction cannot be dispensed with since one must be able to state that more than one property should hold when defining a concept. Finally, if one wants to call the logic a DL, one needs a constructor using roles. This leads to the following two minimal candidate DLs:

- the DL $\mathcal{FL}_0$, which offers the concept constructors conjunction, value restriction ($\forall r.C$), and the top concept;

- the DL $\mathcal{EL}$, which offers the concept constructors conjunction, existential restriction ($\exists r.C$), and the top concept.

In the following, we will look at the subsumption problem[9] in these two DLs in some detail. Whereas subsumption without a TBox turns out to be polynomial in both cases, we will also see that $\mathcal{EL}$ exhibits a more robust behavior with respect to the complexity of the subsumption problem in the presence of TBoxes.

Subsumption in $\mathcal{FL}_0$

First, we consider the case of subsumption of $\mathcal{FL}_0$-concepts without a TBox. There are basically two approaches for obtaining a structural subsumption algorithm in this case, which are based on two different normal forms. One can either use the equivalence $\forall r.(C \sqcap D) \equiv \forall r.C \sqcap \forall r.D$ as a rewrite rule from left-to-right or from right-to-left. Here we will consider the approach based on the left-to-right direction, whereas all of the early structural subsumption algorithms were based on a normal form obtained by rewriting in the other direction.[10]

By using the rewrite rule $\forall r.(C \sqcap D) \rightarrow \forall r.C \sqcap \forall r.D$ together with associativity, commutativity and idempotence[11] of $\sqcap$, any $\mathcal{FL}_0$-concept can be transformed into an equivalent one that is a conjunction of concepts of the form $\forall r_1. \cdots \forall r_m.A$ for $m \geqslant 0$ (not necessarily distinct) role names $r_1, \ldots, r_m$ and a concept name A. We abbreviate $\forall r_1. \cdots \forall r_m.A$ by $\forall r_1 \ldots r_m.A$, where $r_1 \ldots r_m$ is viewed as a word over the alphabet of all role names. In addition, instead of $\forall w_1.A \sqcap \cdots \sqcap \forall w_\ell.A$ we write $\forall L.A$ where $L := \{w_1, \ldots, w_\ell\}$ is a finite set of words over Σ. The term $\forall \emptyset.A$ is considered to be equivalent to the top concept $\top$, which means that it can be added to a conjunction without changing the meaning of the concept. Using these abbreviations, any pair of $\mathcal{FL}_0$-concepts C, D containing the concept names $A_1, \ldots, A_k$ can be rewritten as

$$C \equiv \forall U_1.A_1 \sqcap \cdots \sqcap \forall U_k.A_k \quad \text{and} \quad D \equiv \forall V_1.A_1 \sqcap \cdots \sqcap \forall V_k.A_k,$$

where U_i, V_i are finite sets of words over the alphabet of all role names. This normal form provides us with the following *characterization of subsumption* of $\mathcal{FL}_0$-concepts [24]:

$$C \sqsubseteq D \quad \text{iff} \quad U_i \supseteq V_i \text{ for all } i, 1 \leqslant i \leqslant k.$$

Since the size of the normal forms is polynomial in the size of the original concepts, and since the inclusion tests $U_i \supseteq V_i$ can also be realized in polynomial time, this yields a polynomial-time decision procedure for subsumption in $\mathcal{FL}_0$.

This characterization of subsumption via inclusion of finite sets of words can be extended to definitorial TBoxes as follows. A given TBox $\mathcal{T}$ can be translated into a

---

[9]Note that the satisfiability problem is trivial in $\mathcal{FL}_0$ and $\mathcal{EL}$, since any concept expressed in these languages is satisfiable. The reduction of subsumption to satisfiability is not possible due to the absence of negation.

[10]A comparison between the two approaches can be found in [21].

[11]I.e., $(A \sqcap B) \sqcap C \equiv A \sqcap (B \sqcap C)$, $A \sqcap B \equiv B \sqcap A$, and $A \sqcap A \equiv A$.

$$A \equiv C \sqcap \forall r.B \sqcap \forall s.\forall r.P$$
$$B \equiv \forall s.C$$
$$C \equiv \forall r.P$$

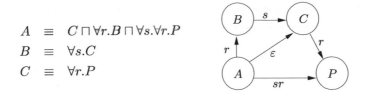

Figure 3.4: A definitorial $\mathcal{FL}_0$-TBox and the corresponding acyclic automaton.

finite (word) automaton[12] $\mathcal{A}_\mathcal{T}$, whose states are the concept names occurring in $\mathcal{T}$, and whose transitions are induced by the value restrictions occurring in $\mathcal{T}$ (see Fig. 3.4 for an example). A formal definition of this translation can be found in [9], where the more general case of cyclic TBoxes is treated. In the case of definitorial TBoxes, which are by definition acyclic, the resulting automata are also acyclic.

Let us call a concept name a *defined concept* in a definitorial TBox if it occurs on the left-hand side of a concept definition, and a *primitive concept* otherwise. For a defined concept A and a primitive concept P in $\mathcal{T}$, the language $L_{\mathcal{A}_\mathcal{T}}(A, P)$ is the set of all words labeling paths in $\mathcal{A}_\mathcal{T}$ from A to P. The languages $L_{\mathcal{A}_\mathcal{T}}(A, P)$ represent all the value restrictions that must be satisfied by instances of the concept A. With this intuition in mind, it should not be surprising that subsumption with respect to definitorial $\mathcal{FL}_0$-TBoxes can be characterized in terms of inclusion of languages accepted by acyclic automata. Indeed, the following is a *characterization of subsumption* in $\mathcal{FL}_0$ with respect to definitorial TBoxes:

$$A \sqsubseteq_\mathcal{T} B \quad \text{iff} \quad L_{\mathcal{A}_\mathcal{T}}(A, P) \supseteq L_\mathcal{T}(B, P) \text{ for all primitive concepts } P.$$

In the example of Fig. 3.4, we have $L_{\mathcal{A}_\mathcal{T}}(A, P) = \{r, sr, rsr\} \supset \{sr\} = L_{\mathcal{A}_\mathcal{T}}(B, P)$, and thus $A \sqsubseteq_\mathcal{T} B$, but $B \not\sqsubseteq_\mathcal{T} A$.

Since the inclusion problem for languages accepted by acyclic finite automata is coNP-complete [73], this reduction shows that the subsumption problem in $\mathcal{FL}_0$ with respect to definitorial TBoxes is in coNP. As shown by Nebel [127], the reduction also works in the opposite direction, which yields the matching lower bound. In the presence of general TBoxes, the subsumption problem in $\mathcal{FL}_0$ actually becomes as hard as for $\mathcal{ALC}$, namely ExpTime-hard [6, 87].

Theorem 3.7. *Subsumption in $\mathcal{FL}_0$ is polynomial without TBox, coNP-complete with respect to definitorial TBoxes, and* EXPTIME-*complete with respect to general TBoxes.*

Subsumption in $\mathcal{EL}$

In contrast to the negative complexity results for subsumption with respect to TBoxes in $\mathcal{FL}_0$, subsumption in $\mathcal{EL}$ remains polynomial even in the presence of general TBoxes [42]. The polynomial-time subsumption algorithm for $\mathcal{EL}$ that will be sketched below actually classifies a given TBox $\mathcal{T}$, i.e., it simultaneously computes all

---

[12]Strictly speaking, we obtain a finite automaton with word transitions, i.e., transitions that may be labelled with a word over Σ rather than a letter of Σ.

subsumption relationships between the concept names occurring in $\mathcal{T}$. This algorithm proceeds in four steps:

1. Normalize the TBox.

2. Translate the normalized TBox into a graph.

3. Complete the graph using completion rules.

4. Read off the subsumption relationships from the normalized graph.

A general $\mathcal{EL}$-TBox is *normalized* if it only contains GCIs of the following form:

$$A_1 \sqcap A_2 \sqsubseteq B, \qquad A \sqsubseteq \exists r.B, \quad \text{or} \quad \exists r.A \sqsubseteq B,$$

where A, A_1, A_2, B are concept names or the top-concept $\top$. One can transform a given TBox into a normalized one by applying normalization rules. Instead of describing these rules in the general case, we just illustrate them by an example, where we underline GCIs that need further rewriting:

$$\exists r.A \sqcap \exists r.\exists s.A \sqsubseteq A \sqcap B \quad \rightsquigarrow \quad \underline{\exists r.A \sqsubseteq B_1}, \ \underline{B_1 \sqcap \exists r.\exists s.A \sqsubseteq A \sqcap B},$$

$$B_1 \sqcap \exists r.\exists s.A \sqsubseteq A \sqcap B \quad \rightsquigarrow \quad \underline{\exists r.\exists s.A \sqsubseteq B_2}, \ \underline{B_1 \sqcap B_2 \sqsubseteq A \sqcap B},$$

$$\exists r.\exists s.A \sqsubseteq B_2 \quad \rightsquigarrow \quad \underline{\exists s.A \sqsubseteq B_3}, \ \exists r.B_3 \sqsubseteq B_2,$$

$$B_1 \sqcap B_2 \sqsubseteq A \sqcap B \quad \rightsquigarrow \quad B_1 \sqcap B_2 \sqsubseteq A, \ B_1 \sqcap B_2 \sqsubseteq B.$$

For example, in the first normalization step we introduce the abbreviation B_1 for the description $\exists r.A$. One might think that one must make B_1 equivalent to $\exists r.A$, i.e., also add the GCI $B_1 \sqsubseteq \exists r.A$. However, it can be shown that adding just $\exists r.A \sqsubseteq B_1$ is sufficient to obtain a *subsumption-equivalent* TBox, i.e., a TBox that induces the same subsumption relationships between the concept names occurring in the original TBox. All normalization rules preserve equivalence in this sense, and if one uses an appropriate strategy (which basically defers the applications of the rule applied in the last step of our example to the end), then the normal form can be computed in linear time.

In the next step, we build the *classification graph* $G_{\mathcal{T}} = (V, V \times V, S, R)$ where

- V is the set of concept names (including $\top$) occurring in the normalized TBox $\mathcal{T}$;

- S labels nodes with sets of concept names (again including $\top$);

- R labels edges with sets of role names.

It can be shown that the label sets satisfy the following *invariants*:

- $B \in S(A)$ implies $A \sqsubseteq_{\mathcal{T}} B$, i.e., $S(A)$ contains only subsumers of A with respect to $\mathcal{T}$.

- $r \in R(A, B)$ implies $A \sqsubseteq_{\mathcal{T}} \exists r.B$, i.e., $R(A, B)$ contains only roles r such that $\exists r.B$ subsumes A with respect to $\mathcal{T}$.

Initially, we set $S(A) := \{A, \top\}$ for all nodes $A \in V$, and $R(A, B) := \emptyset$ for all edges $(A, B) \in V \times V$. Obviously, the above invariants are satisfied by these initial label sets.

(R1)	$A_1 \sqcap A_2 \sqsubseteq B \in \mathcal{T}$	and	$A_1, A_2 \in S(A)$	then add B to $S(A)$
(R2)	$A_1 \sqsubseteq \exists r.B \in \mathcal{T}$	and	$A_1 \in S(A)$	then add r to $R(A, B)$
(R3)	$\exists r.B_1 \sqsubseteq A_1 \in \mathcal{T}$	and	$B_1 \in S(B), r \in R(A, B)$	then add A_1 to $S(A)$

Figure 3.5: The completion rules for subsumption in $\mathcal{EL}$ with respect to general TBoxes.

The labels of nodes and edges are then extended by applying the rules of Fig. 3.5, where we assume that a rule is only applied if it really extends a label set. It is easy to see that these rules preserve the above invariants. For example, consider the (most complicated) rule (R3). Obviously, $\exists r.B_1 \sqsubseteq A_1 \in \mathcal{T}$ implies $\exists r.B_1 \sqsubseteq_{\mathcal{T}} A_1$, and the assumption that the invariants are satisfied before applying the rule yields $B \sqsubseteq_{\mathcal{T}} B_1$ and $A \sqsubseteq_{\mathcal{T}} \exists r.B$. The subsumption relationship $B \sqsubseteq_{\mathcal{T}} B_1$ obviously implies $\exists r.B \sqsubseteq_{\mathcal{T}} \exists r.B_1$. By applying transitivity of the subsumption relation $\sqsubseteq_{\mathcal{T}}$, we thus obtain $A \sqsubseteq_{\mathcal{T}} A_1$.

The fact that subsumption in $\mathcal{EL}$ with respect to general TBoxes can be decided in polynomial time is an immediate consequence of the following statements:

1. Rule application terminates after a polynomial number of steps.

2. If no more rules are applicable, then $A \sqsubseteq_{\mathcal{T}} B$ iff $B \in S(A)$.

Regarding the first statement, note that the number of nodes is linear and the number of edges is quadratic in the size of $\mathcal{T}$. In addition, the size of the label sets is bounded by the number of concept names and role names, and each rule application extends at least one label. Regarding the equivalence in the second statement, the "if" direction follows from the fact that the above invariants are preserved under rule application. To show the "only-if" direction, assume that $B \notin S(A)$. Then the following interpretation $\mathcal{I}$ is a model of $\mathcal{T}$ in which $A \in A^{\mathcal{I}}$, but $A \notin B^{\mathcal{I}}$:

- $\Delta^{\mathcal{I}} := V$;

- $r^{\mathcal{I}} := \{(A', B') \mid r \in R(A', B')\}$ for all role names r;

- $B'^{\mathcal{I}} := \{A' \mid B' \in S(A')\}$ for all concept names A'.

More details can be found in [42, 6].

Theorem 3.8. *Subsumption in $\mathcal{EL}$ is polynomial with respect to general TBoxes.*

In [6] this result is extended to the DL $\mathcal{EL}^{++}$, which extends $\mathcal{EL}$ with the bottom concept, nominals, a restricted form of concrete domains, and a restricted form of so-called role-value maps. In addition, it is shown in [6] that basically all other additions of typical DL constructors to $\mathcal{EL}$ make subsumption with respect to general TBoxes EXPTIME-complete.

It should be noted that these results are not only of theoretical interest. In fact, large bio-medical ontologies such as the Gene Ontology [55] and SNOMED [153] can be expressed in $\mathcal{EL}$, and a first implementation of the subsumption algorithm for $\mathcal{EL}$ sketched above behaves very well on these very large knowledge bases [23].

3.7   DLs in Ontology Language Applications

Description Logics are (or have been) used in a wide range of applications, including configuration (e.g., of telecommunications equipment) [120], and software information and documentation systems [61]. DLs have also been extensively applied in the area of databases [34], where they have been used to support schema design [54, 30], schema and data integration [51, 52], and query answering [47, 48, 91].

Perhaps the most prominent application of DLs is, however, as the basis for ontology languages such as OIL, DAML + OIL and OWL [99]. In the following section we will briefly examine the motivation for and realization of a DL based ontology language, with particular reference to OWL; in Section 3.7.2 we will mention some ontology tools and applications that exploit DL reasoning.

3.7.1   The OWL Ontology Language

OWL is a semantic web ontology language, developed by the W3C Web-Ontology working group, whose semantics can be defined via a translation into an expressive DL.[13] This is not a coincidence—it was a design goal. The mapping allows OWL to exploit results from DL research (e.g., regarding the decidability and complexity of key inference problems), and to use implemented DL reasoners (e.g., FaCT [94] and RACER [81]) in order to provide reasoning services for OWL applications.

An OWL (Lite or DL) ontology can be seen to correspond to a DL TBox together with a role hierarchy, describing the domain in terms of *classes* (corresponding to concepts) and *properties* (corresponding to roles). An ontology consists of a set of *axioms* that assert, e.g., subsumption relationships between classes or properties.

As in a standard DL, OWL classes may be names or expressions built up from simpler classes and properties using a variety of constructors. The set of constructors supported by OWL, along with the equivalent DL syntax, is summarized in Fig. 3.6.[14] The full XML serialization of the RDF syntax is not shown as it is rather verbose, e.g., Human ⊓ Male would be written as

```
<owl:Class>
  <owl:intersectionOf rdf:parseType="Collection">
    <owl:Class rdf:about="#Human"/>
    <owl:Class rdf:about="#Male"/>
  </owl:intersectionOf>
</owl:Class>
```

while ($\geqslant$ 2 hasChild.Thing) would be written as

```
<owl:Restriction>
  <owl:onProperty rdf:resource="#hasChild"/>
  <owl:minCardinality
    rdf:datatype="&xsd;NonNegativeInteger">2
  </owl:minCardinality>
</owl:Restriction>
```

---

[13]In fact there are 3 "species" of OWL: OWL Lite, OWL DL and OWL full, only the first two of which have DL based semantics. The semantics of OWL full is given by an extension of the RDF model theory [83].

[14]In fact, there are a few additional constructors provided as "syntactic sugar", but all are trivially reducible to the ones described in Fig. 3.6.

Constructor	DL syntax	Example
intersectionOf	$C_1 \sqcap \cdots \sqcap C_n$	Human $\sqcap$ Male
unionOf	$C_1 \sqcup \cdots \sqcup C_n$	Doctor $\sqcup$ Lawyer
complementOf	$\neg C$	$\neg$Male
oneOf	$\{x_1 \ldots x_n\}$	{john, mary}
allValuesFrom	$\forall P.C$	$\forall$hasChild.Doctor
someValuesFrom	$\exists r.C$	$\exists$hasChild.Lawyer
hasValue	$\exists r.\{x\}$	$\exists$citizenOf.{USA}
minCardinality	$(\geqslant nr)$	$(\geqslant 2$ hasChild)
maxCardinality	$(\leqslant nr)$	$(\leqslant 1$ hasChild)
inverseOf	r^-	hasChild$^-$

Figure 3.6: OWL constructors.

Prefixes such as `owl:` and `&xsd;` specify XML namespaces for resources, while `rdf:parseType="Collection"` is an extension to RDF that provides a "short-hand" notation for lisp style lists defined using triples with the properties first and rest (it can be eliminated, but with a consequent increase in verbosity). E.g., the first example above consists of the triples $\langle r_1, \text{owl} : \text{intersectionOf}, r_2 \rangle$, $\langle r_2, \text{owl} : \text{first}, \text{Human} \rangle$, $\langle r_2, \text{rdfs} : \text{type}, \text{Class} \rangle$, $\langle r_2, \text{owl} : \text{rest}, r_3 \rangle$, etc., where r_i is an anonymous resource, Human stands for a URI naming the resource "Human", and owl : intersectionOf, owl : first, owl : rest and rdfs : type stand for URIs naming the properties in question.

An important feature of OWL is that, besides "abstract" classes defined by the ontology, one can also use XML Schema *datatypes* (e.g., string, decimal and float) in `someValuesFrom`, `allValuesFrom`, and `hasValue` restrictions. This can be seen as a restricted version of *concrete domains* as mentioned in Section 3.2.3. The kinds of datatype that can be used in OWL are, however, very limited (see [134]), essentially being limited to built-in XML datatypes, and so only allowing for concepts such as $\exists$age.xsd : nonNegativeInteger; this could, e.g., be used in an axiom Person $\sqcap$ $\exists$age.xsd : nonNegativeInteger to assert that all persons have an age that is a non-negative integer.

As already mentioned, an OWL ontology consists of a set of axioms. Fig. 3.7 summarizes the axioms supported by OWL. These axioms make it possible to assert subsumption or equivalence with respect to classes or properties, the disjointness of classes, and the equivalence or non-equivalence of individuals (resources). Moreover, OWL also allows properties of properties (i.e., DL roles) to be asserted. In particular, it is possible to assert that a property is transitive, functional, inverse functional or symmetric.

It is easy to see that, except for individuals and datatypes, the constructors and axioms of OWL can be translated into $\mathcal{SHIQ}$; in fact, OWL Lite is equivalent to $\mathcal{SHIN}(\mathbf{D})$ and OWL DL is equivalent to $\mathcal{SHOIN}(\mathbf{D})$ (see Section 3.2.3).

3.7.2 OWL Tools and Applications

As mentioned in Section 3.7.1, the ability to use DL reasoners to provide reasoning services for OWL applications was one of the motivations for basing the design of OWL on a DL. Several ontology design tools, both "academic" and commercial,

Axiom	DL syntax	Example
subClassOf	$C_1 \sqsubseteq C_2$	Human $\sqsubseteq$ Animal $\sqcap$ Biped
equivalentClass	$C_1 \equiv C_2$	Man $\equiv$ Human $\sqcap$ Male
subPropertyOf	$P_1 \sqsubseteq P_2$	hasDaughter $\sqsubseteq$ hasChild
equivalentProperty	$P_1 \equiv P_2$	cost $\equiv$ price
disjointWith	$C_1 \sqsubseteq \neg C_2$	Male $\sqsubseteq \neg$Female
sameAs	$\{x_1\} \equiv \{x_2\}$	{Pres_Bush} $\equiv$ {G_W_Bush}
differentFrom	$\{x_1\} \sqsubseteq \neg\{x_2\}$	{john} $\sqsubseteq \neg${peter}
TransitiveProperty	P transitive role	hasAncestor is a transitive role
FunctionalProperty	$\top \sqsubseteq (\leqslant 1\ P)$	$\top \sqsubseteq (\leqslant 1$ hasMother)
InverseFunctionalProperty	$\top \sqsubseteq (\leqslant 1\ P^-)$	$\top \sqsubseteq (\leqslant 1$ isMotherOf$^-$)
SymmetricProperty	$P \equiv P^-$	isSiblingOf $\equiv$ isSiblingOf$^-$

Figure 3.7: OWL axioms.

now exploit the correspondence between OWL and $\mathcal{SHOIN}(\mathbf{D})$ in order to support ontology design and maintenance by, for example, highlighting inconsistent classes and implicit subsumption relationships. Examples of such tools include Protégé [109], Swoop [106], OilEd [28] and TopBraid Composer.[15] Reasoning support for such tools is typically provided by a DL reasoner such as FaCT++ [160], RACER [81] or Pellet [151].

The availability of such tools has contributed to the increasingly widespread use of OWL, not only in the Semantic Web per se, but as a popular language for ontology development in fields as diverse as biology [150], medicine [74], geography [76], geology [156], astronomy [60], agriculture [152] and defence [112]. Applications of OWL are particularly prevalent in the life sciences where it has been used by the developers of several large biomedical ontologies, including the Biological Pathways Exchange (BioPAX) ontology [141], the GALEN ontology [139], the Foundational Model of Anatomy (FMA) [74], and the National Cancer Institute thesaurus [82].

The importance of reasoning support in such applications was highlighted in [108], which describes a project in which the Medical Entities Dictionary (MED), a large ontology (100,210 classes and 261 properties) that is used at the Columbia Presbyterian Medical Center, was converted into OWL, and checked using an OWL reasoner. This check revealed "systematic modeling errors", and a significant number of missed subClass relationships which, if not corrected, "could have cost the hospital many missing results in various decision support and infection control systems that routinely use MED to screen patients".

3.8 Further Reading

As mentioned in Section 3.1, we have endeavored to cover the most important areas of DL research, but the subject is a very large one, and many interesting topics have not been covered. We will briefly list a few of these here, and provide pointers into the literature.

---

[15] http://www.topbraidcomposer.com/.

Besides the ones discussed in Section 3.2, a great many other operators and extensions have been investigated. These include feature chain agreements, role value maps, fixpoint constructors, n-ary predicates, various role constructors (including intersection, union, complement, composition, (reflexive-)transitive closure and identity), probabilistic extensions and defaults. Details of all of these (and more) can be found in [14].

There is currently a great deal of interest in the idea of combining DLs with other KR formalisms such as rules and Answer Set Programming (ASP). With an appropriate integration, the advantages of the different paradigms might be combined, e.g., by extending the powerful schema language provided by DLs with the ability to describe more complex relationships between named individuals, or by adding support for non-monotonic features such as negation as failure. Important contributions in this area include work on rule support in the Classic system [40], the integration of Datalog with DLs in $\mathcal{AL}$-log and CARIN [65, 113], the integration of answer set programming with DLs [68], and the extension of DLs with so-called DL-safe rules [124, 140].

As well as studying the formal properties of DLs, considerable energy has been devoted to investigating the implementation and optimization of DL systems. Modern systems include CEL [6], FaCT++ [160], KAON2 [123], Pellet [136] and Racer [81]; for information on older systems, and on optimization techniques, the reader is referred to [14]. A number of tools are now available that use the above mentioned reasoners to support, e.g., ontology design or schema integration. These include Swoop [106], Protégé [109], OilEd [28], and ICom [72].

Finally, in Section 3.2 we focused on standard reasoning problems such as satisfiability and subsumption testing. These are not, however, the only reasoning problems that might be of interest in applications, and several other "non-standard" inference problems have also been investigated. These include matching [20, 19], least common subsumer (lcs) [111], approximation and difference [43], axiom pinpointing [147, 132, 121], and conjunctive query answering [47, 157].

Bibliography

[1] A. Acciarri, D. Calvanese, G. De Giacomo, D. Lembo, M. Lenzerini, M. Palmieri, and R. Rosati. Quonto: Querying ontologies. In M.M. Veloso and S. Kambhampati, editors. *Proc. of the 20th Nat. Conf. on Artificial Intelligence (AAAI-05)*, pages 1670–1671. AAAI Press/The MIT Press, 2005.

[2] H. Andréka, J. van Benthem, and I. Németi. Modal languages and bounded fragments of predicate logic. Technical Report ML-96-03, ILLC, University of Amsterdam, 1996.

[3] C. Areces. Logic engineering. The case of description and hybrid logics. PhD thesis, ILLC, University of Amsterdam, 2000. ILLC Dissertation Series 2000-5.

[4] C. Areces, P. Blackburn, and M. Marx. A road-map on complexity for hybrid logics. In *Proc. of the Annual Conf. of the Eur. Assoc. for Computer Science Logic (CSL'99), Lecture Notes in Computer Science*, vol. 1683, pages 307–321. Springer, 1999.

[5] C. Areces, M. de Rijke, and H. de Nivelle. Resolution in modal, description and hybrid logic. *J. of Logic and Computation*, 11(5):717–736, 2001.

[6] F. Baader, S. Brandt, and C. Lutz. Pushing the $\mathcal{EL}$ envelope. In *Proc. of the 19th Int. Joint Conf. on Artificial Intelligence (IJCAI 2005)*, pages 364–369, 2005.

[7] F. Baader, C. Lutz, M. Milicic, U. Sattler, and F. Wolter. Integrating description logics and action formalisms: First results. In *Proc. of the 20th National Conference on Artificial Intelligence (AAAI-05)*. AAAI Press/The MIT Press, pages 572–577, 2005.

[8] F. Baader. Augmenting concept languages by transitive closure of roles: An alternative to terminological cycles. In *Proc. of the 12th Int. Joint Conf. on Artificial Intelligence (IJCAI'91)*, pages 446–451, 1991.

[9] F. Baader. Using automata theory for characterizing the semantics of terminological cycles. *Annals of Mathematics and Artificial Intelligence*, 18:175–219, 1996.

[10] F. Baader. Description logic terminology. In [14], pages 485–495, 2003.

[11] F. Baader. Terminological cycles in a description logic with existential restrictions. In G. Gottlob and T. Walsh, editors, *Proc. of the 18th Int. Joint Conf. on Artificial Intelligence (IJCAI 2003)*, pages 325–330, Los Altos, Acapulco, Mexico, 2003. Morgan Kaufmann.

[12] F. Baader, M. Buchheit, and B. Hollunder. Cardinality restrictions on concepts. *Artificial Intelligence*, 88(1–2):195–213, 1996.

[13] F. Baader, H.-J. Bürckert, B. Hollunder, W. Nutt, and J.H. Siekmann. Concept logics. In J.W. Lloyd, editor. *Computational Logics, Symposium Proceedings*, pages 177–201. Springer, 1990.

[14] F. Baader, D. Calvanese, D. McGuinness, D. Nardi, and P.F. Patel-Schneider, editors. *The Description Logic Handbook: Theory, Implementation and Applications*. Cambridge University Press, 2003.

[15] F. Baader, E. Franconi, B. Hollunder, B. Nebel, and H.-J. Profitlich. An empirical analysis of optimization techniques for terminological representation systems or: Making KRIS get a move on. *Applied Artificial Intelligence*, 4:109–132, 1994 (Special Issue on Knowledge Base Management).

[16] F. Baader and P. Hanschke. A schema for integrating concrete domains into concept languages. In *Proc. of the 12th Int. Joint Conf. on Artificial Intelligence (IJCAI'91)*, pages 452–457, 1991.

[17] F. Baader and P. Hanschke. Extensions of concept languages for a mechanical engineering application. In *Proc. of the 16th German Workshop on Artificial Intelligence (GWAI'92)*, *Lecture Notes in Computer Science*, vol. 671, pages 132–143. Springer, 1992.

[18] F. Baader and B. Hollunder. A terminological knowledge representation system with complete inference algorithms. In *Proc. of the Workshop on Processing Declarative Knowledge (PDK'91)*, *Lecture Notes in Artificial Intelligence*, vol. 567, pages 67–86. Springer, 1991.

[19] F. Baader and R. Küsters. Matching in description logics with existential restrictions. In *Proc. of the 7th Int. Conf. on Principles of Knowledge Representation and Reasoning (KR 2000)*, pages 261–272, 2000.

[20] F. Baader, R. Küsters, A. Borgida, and D.L. McGuinness. Matching in description logics. *J. of Logic and Computation*, 9(3):411–447, 1999.

[21] F. Baader, R. Küsters, and R. Molitor. Structural subsumption considered from an automata theoretic point of view. In *Proc. of the 1998 Description Logic*

Workshop (DL'98), volume 11 of *CEUR Electronic Workshop Proceedings*, 1998.

[22] F. Baader, R. Küsters, and F. Wolter. Extensions to description logics. In [14], pages 219–261, 2003.

[23] F. Baader, C. Lutz, and B. Suntisrivaraporn. CEL—a polynomial-time reasoner for life science ontologies. In U. Furbach and N. Shankar, editors. *Proc. of the Int. Joint Conf. on Automated Reasoning (IJCAR 2006), Lecture Notes in Artificial Intelligence*, vol. 4130, pages 287–291. Springer-Verlag, 2006.

[24] F. Baader and P. Narendran. Unification of concepts terms in description logics. *J. of Symbolic Computation*, 31(3):277–305, 2001.

[25] F. Baader and U. Sattler. An overview of tableau algorithms for description logics. *Studia Logica*, 69(1):5–40, October 2001.

[26] F. Baader and S. Tobies. The inverse method implements the automata approach for modal satisfiability. In *Proc. of the Int. Joint Conf. on Automated Reasoning (IJCAR 2001), Lecture Notes in Artificial Intelligence*, vol. 2083, pages 92–106. Springer, 2001.

[27] A.B. Baker. Intelligent backtracking on constraint satisfaction problems: experimental and theoretical results. PhD thesis, University of Oregon, 1995.

[28] S. Bechhofer, I. Horrocks, C. Goble, and R. Stevens. OilEd: A reasonable ontology editor for the semantic web. In *Proc. of the Joint German/Austrian Conf. on Artificial Intelligence (KI 2001), Lecture Notes in Artificial Intelligence*, vol. 2174, pages 396–408. Springer, 2001.

[29] M. Ben-Ari, J.Y. Halpern, and A. Pnueli. Deterministic propositional dynamic logic: Finite models, complexity, and completeness. *J. of Computer and System Sciences*, 25:402–417, 1982.

[30] D. Berardi, D. Calvanese, and G. De Giacomo. Reasoning on UML class diagrams using description logic based systems. In *Proc. of the KI'2001 Workshop on Applications of Description Logics*, volume 44 of *CEUR Electronic Workshop Proceedings*, 2001.

[31] O. Bernholtz and O. Grumberg. Branching time temporal logic and amorphous tree automata. In E. Best, editor. *Proc. of the Int. Conf. on Concurrency Theory (CONCUR'93), Lecture Notes in Computer Science*, vol. 715, pages 262–277. Springer, 1993.

[32] P. Blackburn, M. de Rijke, and Y. Venema. *Modal Logic. Cambridge Tracts in Theoretical Computer Science*, vol. 53. Cambridge University Press, 2001.

[33] A. Borgida. On the relative expressiveness of description logics and predicate logics. *Artificial Intelligence*, 82(1–2):353–367, 1996.

[34] A. Borgida, M. Lenzerini, and R. Rosati. Description logics for data bases. In [14] (Chapter 16).

[35] R.J. Brachman. What's in a concept: Structural foundations for semantic networks. *Int. Journal of Man-Machine Studies*, 9(2):127–152, 1977.

[36] R.J. Brachman. Structured inheritance networks. In W.A. Woods and R.J. Brachman, editors, *Research in Natural Language Understanding*, Quarterly Progress Report No. 1, BBN Report No. 3742, pages 36–78. Bolt, Beranek and Newman Inc., Cambridge, MA, 1978.

[37] R.J. Brachman. "Reducing" CLASSIC to practice: Knowledge representation meets reality. In *Proc. of the 3rd Int. Conf. on the Principles of Knowledge Rep-

resentation and Reasoning (KR'92), pages 247–258. Morgan Kaufmann, Los Altos, CA, 1992.

[38] R.J. Brachman, R.E. Fikes, and H.J. Levesque. KRYPTON: A functional approach to knowledge representation. *IEEE Computer*:67–73, October 1983.

[39] R.J. Brachman and H.J. Levesque, editors. *Readings in Knowledge Representation*. Morgan Kaufmann, Los Altos, CA, 1985.

[40] R.J. Brachman, D.L. McGuinness, P.F. Patel-Schneider, L.A. Resnick, and A. Borgida. Living with CLASSIC: When and how to use a KL-ONE-like language. In J.F. Sowa, editor. *Principles of Semantic Networks*, pages 401–456. Morgan Kaufmann, Los Altos, CA, 1991.

[41] R.J. Brachman and J.G. Schmolze. An overview of the KL-ONE knowledge representation system. *Cognitive Science*, 9(2):171–216, 1985.

[42] S. Brandt. Polynomial time reasoning in a description logic with existential restrictions, GCI axioms, and—what else? In R. López de Mántaras and L. Saitta, editors, *Proc. of the 16th Eur. Conf. on Artificial Intelligence (ECAI 2004)*, pages 298–302, 2004.

[43] S. Brandt, R. Küsters, and A.-Y. Turhan. Approximation and difference in description logics. In *Proc. of the 8th Int. Conf. on Principles of Knowledge Representation and Reasoning (KR 2002)*, pages 203–214, 2002.

[44] P. Bresciani, E. Franconi, and S. Tessaris. Implementing and testing expressive description logics: Preliminary report. In *Proc. of the 1995 Description Logic Workshop (DL'95)*, pages 131–139, 1995.

[45] M. Buchheit, F.M. Donini, W. Nutt, and A. Schaerf. A refined architecture for terminological systems: Terminology = schema + views. *Artificial Intelligence*, 99(2):209–260, 1998.

[46] M. Buchheit, F.M. Donini, and A. Schaerf. Decidable reasoning in terminological knowledge representation systems. *J. of Artificial Intelligence Research*, 1:109–138, 1993.

[47] D. Calvanese, G. De Giacomo, and M. Lenzerini. On the decidability of query containment under constraints. In *Proc. of the 17th ACM SIGACT SIGMOD SIGART Symp. on Principles of Database Systems (PODS'98)*, pages 149–158, 1998.

[48] D. Calvanese, G. De Giacomo, and M. Lenzerini. Modeling and querying semistructured data. *Network and Information Systems*, 2(2), 1999.

[49] D. Calvanese, G. De Giacomo, and M. Lenzerini. Reasoning in expressive description logics with fixpoints based on automata on infinite trees. In *Proc. of the 16th Int. Joint Conf. on Artificial Intelligence (IJCAI'99)*, pages 84–89, 1999.

[50] D. Calvanese, G. De Giacomo, M. Lenzerini, and D. Nardi. Reasoning in expressive description logics. In A. Robinson and A. Voronkov, editors. *Handbook of Automated Reasoning*, pages 1581–1634. Elsevier Science Publishers (North-Holland), Amsterdam, 2001 (Chapter 23).

[51] D. Calvanese, G. De Giacomo, M. Lenzerini, D. Nardi, and R. Rosati. Description logic framework for information integration. In *Proc. of the 6th Int. Conf. on Principles of Knowledge Representation and Reasoning (KR'98)*, pages 2–13, 1998.

[52] D. Calvanese, G. De Giacomo, and R. Rosati. Data integration and reconciliation in data warehousing: Conceptual modeling and reasoning support. *Network and Information Systems*, 2(4):413–432, 1999.

[53] D. Calvanese, G. De Giacomo, D. Lembo, M. Lenzerini, and R. Rosati. DL-Lite: Tractable description logics for ontologies. In M.M. Veloso and S. Kambhampati, editors. *Proc. of the 20th Nat. Conf. on Artificial Intelligence (AAAI-05)*, pages 602–607. AAAI Press/The MIT Press, 2005.

[54] D. Calvanese, M. Lenzerini, and D. Nardi. Description logics for conceptual data modeling. In J. Chomicki and G. Saake, editors. *Logics for Databases and Information Systems*, pages 229–264. Kluwer Academic Publisher, 1998.

[55] The Gene ontology Consortium. Gene ontology: Tool for the unification of biology. *Nature Genetics*, 25:25–29, 2000.

[56] G. De Giacomo. Decidability of class-based knowledge representation formalisms. PhD thesis, Dipartimento di Informatica e Sistemistica, Università di Roma "La Sapienza", 1995.

[57] G. De Giacomo and M. Lenzerini. Boosting the correspondence between description logics and propositional dynamic logics. In *Proc. of the 12th Nat. Conf. on Artificial Intelligence (AAAI'94)*, pages 205–212, 1994.

[58] G. De Giacomo and M. Lenzerini. Concept language with number restrictions and fixpoints, and its relationship with μ-calculus. In *Proc. of the 11th Eur. Conf. on Artificial Intelligence (ECAI'94)*, pages 411–415, 1994.

[59] G. De Giacomo and M. Lenzerini. TBox and ABox reasoning in expressive description logics. In *Proc. of the 5th Int. Conf. on the Principles of Knowledge Representation and Reasoning (KR'96)*, pages 316–327, 1996.

[60] S. Derriere, A. Richard, and A. Preite-Martinez. An ontology of astronomical object types for the virtual observatory. In *Proc. of Special Session 3 of the 26th meeting of the IAU: Virtual Observatory in Action: New Science, New Technology, and Next Generation Facilities*, 2006.

[61] P. Devambu, R.J. Brachman, P.J. Selfridge, and B.W. Ballard. LASSIE: A knowledge-based software information system. *Communications of the ACM*, 34(5):36–49, 1991.

[62] F.M. Donini, B. Hollunder, M. Lenzerini, A.M. Spaccamela, D. Nardi, and W. Nutt. The complexity of existential quantification in concept languages. *Artificial Intelligence*, 2–3:309–327, 1992.

[63] F.M. Donini, M. Lenzerini, D. Nardi, and W. Nutt. The complexity of concept languages. In *Proc. of the 2nd Int. Conf. on the Principles of Knowledge Representation and Reasoning (KR'91)*, pages 151–162, 1991.

[64] F.M. Donini, M. Lenzerini, D. Nardi, and W. Nutt. Tractable concept languages. In *Proc. of the 12th Int. Joint Conf. on Artificial Intelligence (IJCAI'91)*, pages 458–463, 1991.

[65] F.M. Donini, M. Lenzerini, D. Nardi, and A. Schaerf. $\mathcal{AL}$-log: Integrating Datalog and description logics. *J. of Intelligent Information Systems*, 10(3):227–252, 1998.

[66] F.M. Donini and F. Massacci. EXPTIME tableaux for $\mathcal{ALC}$. *Artificial Intelligence*, 124(1):87–138, 2000.

[67] J. Doyle and R.S. Patil. Two theses of knowledge representation: Language restrictions, taxonomic classification, and the utility of representation services. *Artificial Intelligence*, 48:261–297, 1991.

[68] T. Eiter, T. Lukasiewicz, R. Schindlauer, and H. Tompits. Combining answer set programming with description logics for the semantic web. In *Proc. of the*

9th Int. Conf. on Principles of Knowledge Representation and Reasoning (KR 2004), pages 141–151. Morgan Kaufmann, Los Altos, CA, 2004.

[69] D. Fensel, F. van Harmelen, I. Horrocks, D. McGuinness, and P.F. Patel-Schneider. OIL: An ontology infrastructure for the semantic web. *IEEE Intelligent Systems*, 16(2):38–45, 2001.

[70] K. Fine. In so many possible worlds. *Notre Dame J. of Formal Logic*, 13(4):516–520, 1972.

[71] M.J. Fischer and R.E. Ladner. Propositional dynamic logic of regular programs. *J. of Computer and System Sciences*, 18:194–211, 1979.

[72] E. Franconi and G. Ng. The i.com tool for intelligent conceptual modeling. In *Proc. of the 7th Int. Workshop on Knowledge Representation meets Databases (KRDB 2000)*, volume 29 of *CEUR Electronic Workshop Proceedings*, 2000.

[73] M.R. Garey and D.S. Johnson. *Computers and Intractability—A Guide to NP-Completeness*. W.H. Freeman and Company, San Francisco, CA, USA, 1979.

[74] C. Golbreich, S. Zhang, and O. Bodenreider. The foundational model of anatomy in OWL: Experience and perspectives. *J. of Web Semantics*, 4(3), 2006.

[75] E. Gonçalvès and E. Grädel. Decidability issues for action guarded logics. In *Proc. of the 2000 Description Logic Workshop (DL 2000)*, volume 33 of *CEUR Electronic Workshop Proceedings*, 2000.

[76] J. Goodwin. Experiences of using OWL at the ordnance survey. In *Proc. of the First OWL Experiences and Directions Workshop*, volume 188 of *CEUR Electronic Workshop Proceedings*, 2005.

[77] E. Grädel. Guarded fragments of first-order logic: A perspective for new description logics? In *Proc. of the 1998 Description Logic Workshop (DL'98)*, volume 11 of *CEUR Electronic Workshop Proceedings*, 1998.

[78] E. Grädel. On the restraining power of guards. *J. of Symbolic Logic*, 64:1719–1742, 1999.

[79] E. Grädel, P.G. Kolaitis, and M.Y. Vardi. On the decision problem for two-variable first-order logic. *Bulletin of Symbolic Logic*, 3(1):53–69, 1997.

[80] V. Haarslev and R. Möller. RACE system description. In *Proc. of the 1999 Description Logic Workshop (DL'99)*, volume 22 of *CEUR Electronic Workshop Proceedings*, 1999.

[81] V. Haarslev and R. Möller. RACER system description. In *Proc. of the Int. Joint Conf. on Automated Reasoning (IJCAR 2001)*, *Lecture Notes in Artificial Intelligence*, vol. 2083, pages 701–705. Springer, 2001.

[82] F.W. Hartel, S. de Coronado, R. Dionne, G. Fragoso, and J. Golbeck. Modeling a description logic vocabulary for cancer research. *Journal of Biomedical Informatics*, 38(2):114–129, 2005.

[83] P. Hayes. RDF model theory. W3C Recommendation, 10 February 2004. Available at http://www.w3.org/TR/rdf-mt/.

[84] P.J. Hayes. In defense of logic. In *Proc. of the 5th Int. Joint Conf. on Artificial Intelligence (IJCAI'77)*, pages 559–565, 1977. A longer version appeared in *The Psychology of Computer Vision* (1975). Republished in [39].

[85] P.J. Hayes. The logic of frames. In D. Metzing, editor. *Frame Conceptions and Text Understanding*, pages 46–61. Walter de Gruyter and Co., 1979. Republished in [39].

[86] J. Heinsohn, D. Kudenko, B. Nebel, and H.-J. Profitlich. An empirical analysis of terminological representation systems. *Artificial Intelligence*, 68:367–397, 1994.

[87] M. Hofmann. Proof-theoretic approach to description-logic. In P. Panangaden, editor. *Proc. of the 20th Annual IEEE Symp. on Logic in Computer Science, LICS 2005*, pages 229–237. IEEE Computer Society Press, June 2005.

[88] B. Hollunder. Consistency checking reduced to satisfiability of concepts in terminological systems. *Ann. of Mathematics and Artificial Intelligence*, 18(2–4):133–157, 1996.

[89] B. Hollunder, W. Nutt, and M. Schmidt-Schauß. Subsumption algorithms for concept description languages. In *Proc. of the 9th Eur. Conf. on Artificial Intelligence (ECAI'90)*, pages 348–353, London (United Kingdom), 1990. Pitman.

[90] I. Horrocks and P.F. Patel-Schneider. Optimising propositional modal satisfiability for description logic subsumption. In *Proc. of the 4th Int. Conf. on Artificial Intelligence and Symbolic Computation (AISC'98)*, LNAI, vol. 1476, pages 234–246. Springer-Verlag, 1998.

[91] I. Horrocks, U. Sattler, S. Tessaris, and S. Tobies. How to decide query containment under constraints using a description logic. In *Proc. of the 7th Int. Conf. on Logic for Programming and Automated Reasoning (LPAR 2000), Lecture Notes in Artificial Intelligence*. Springer-Verlag, 2000.

[92] I. Horrocks, U. Sattler, and S. Tobies. Practical reasoning for expressive description logics. In H. Ganzinger, D. McAllester, and A. Voronkov, editors. *Proc. of the 6th Int. Conf. on Logic for Programming and Automated Reasoning (LPAR'99), Lecture Notes in Artificial Intelligence*, vol. 1705, pages 161–180. Springer, 1999.

[93] I. Horrocks and S. Tobies. Reasoning with axioms: Theory and practice. In *Proc. of the 7th Int. Conf. on Principles of Knowledge Representation and Reasoning (KR 2000)*, pages 285–296, 2000.

[94] I. Horrocks. The FaCT system. In H. de Swart, editor. *Proc. of the 2nd Int. Conf. on Analytic Tableaux and Related Methods (TABLEAUX'98), Lecture Notes in Artificial Intelligence*, vol. 1397, pages 307–312. Springer, 1998.

[95] I. Horrocks. Using an expressive description logic: FaCT or fiction? In *Proc. of the 6th Int. Conf. on Principles of Knowledge Representation and Reasoning (KR'98)*, pages 636–647, 1998.

[96] I. Horrocks and P.F. Patel-Schneider. Optimizing description logic subsumption. *J. of Logic and Computation*, 9(3):267–293, 1999.

[97] I. Horrocks and P.F. Patel-Schneider. The generation of DAML + OIL. In *Proc. of the 2001 Description Logic Workshop (DL 2001)*, volume 49 of *CEUR Electronic Workshop Proceedings*, 2001.

[98] I. Horrocks, P.F. Patel-Schneider, and F. van Harmelen. Reviewing the design of DAML + OIL: An ontology language for the semantic web. In *Proc. of the 18th Nat. Conf. on Artificial Intelligence (AAAI 2002)*, pages 792–797. AAAI Press, 2002.

[99] I. Horrocks, P.F. Patel-Schneider, and F. van Harmelen. From $\mathcal{SHIQ}$ and RDF to OWL: The making of a web ontology language. *J. of Web Semantics*, 1(1):7–26, 2003.

[100] I. Horrocks and U. Sattler. A description logic with transitive and inverse roles and role hierarchies. *J. of Logic and Computation*, 9(3):385–410, 1999.

[101] I. Horrocks and U. Sattler. Ontology reasoning in the $\mathcal{SHOQ}$(D) description logic. In *Proc. of the 17th Int. Joint Conf. on Artificial Intelligence (IJCAI 2001)*, pages 199–204. Morgan Kaufmann, Los Altos, CA, 2001.

[102] U. Hustadt and R.A. Schmidt. Using resolution for testing modal satisfiability and building models. In I.P. Gent, H. van Maaren, and T. Walsh, editors. *SAT 2000: Highlights of Satisfiability Research in the Year 2000, Frontiers in Artificial Intelligence and Applications*, vol. 63. IOS Press, Amsterdam, 2000. Also to appear in a special issue of *Journal of Automated Reasoning*.

[103] U. Hustadt, R.A. Schmidt, and C. Weidenbach. MSPASS: Subsumption testing with SPASS. In *Proc. of the 1999 Description Logic Workshop (DL'99)*, pages 136–137. Linköping University, 1999.

[104] U. Hustadt, B. Motik, and U. Sattler. Reducing SHIQ-description logic to disjunctive Datalog programs. In *Proc. of the 9th Int. Conf. on Principles of Knowledge Representation and Reasoning (KR 2004)*, pages 152–162, 2004.

[105] D. Janin and I. Walukiewicz. Automata for the modal mu-calculus and related results. In J. Wiedermann and P. Hájek, editors. *Int. Symp. on the Mathematical Foundation of Computer Science, Lecture Notes in Computer Science*, vol. 969, pages 552–562. Springer, 1995.

[106] A. Kalyanpur, B. Parsia, and J. Hendler. A tool for working with web ontologies. *International Journal on Semantic Web and Information Systems*, 1(1):36–49, 2005.

[107] Y. Kazakov and B. Motik. A resolution-based decision procedure for $\mathcal{SHOIQ}$. In U. Furbach and N. Shankar, editors. *Proc. of the Int. Joint Conf. on Automated Reasoning (IJCAR 2006), Lecture Notes in Computer Science*, vol. 4130, pages 662–677. Springer, 2006.

[108] A. Kershenbaum, A. Fokoue, C. Patel, C. Welty E. Schonberg, J. Cimino, L. Ma, K. Srinivas, R. Schloss, and J.W. Murdock. A view of OWL from the field: Use cases and experiences. In *Proc. of the Second OWL Experiences and Directions Workshop*, volume 216 of *CEUR Electronic Workshop Proceedings*, 2006.

[109] H. Knublauch, R. Fergerson, N. Noy, and M. Musen. The Protégé OWL Plugin: An open development environment for semantic web applications. In S.A. McIlraith, D. Plexousakis, and F. van Harmelen, editors. *Proc. of the 2004 International Semantic Web Conference (ISWC 2004), Lecture Notes in Computer Science*, vol. 3298, pages 229–243. Springer, 2004.

[110] N. Kurtonina and M. de Rijke. Classifying description logics. In *Proc. of the 1997 Description Logic Workshop (DL'97)*, pages 49–53, 1997.

[111] R. Küsters and R. Molitor. Computing least common subsumers in $\mathcal{ALEN}$. In *Proc. of the 17th Int. Joint Conf. on Artificial Intelligence (IJCAI 2001)*, pages 219–224, 2001.

[112] L. Lacy, G. Aviles, K. Fraser, W. Gerber, A. Mulvehill, and R. Gaskill. Experiences using OWL in military applications. In *Proc. of the First OWL Experiences and Directions Workshop*, volume 188 of *CEUR Electronic Workshop Proceedings*, 2005.

[113] A.Y. Levy and M.C. Rousset. Combining Horn rules and description logics in CARIN. *Artificial Intelligence*, 104(1–2):165–209, 1998.

[114] C. Lutz. Complexity of terminological reasoning revisited. In *Proc. of the 6th Int. Conf. on Logic for Programming and Automated Reasoning (LPAR'99)*,

Lecture Notes in Artificial Intelligence, vol. 1705, pages 181–200. Springer, 1999.

[115] C. Lutz. The complexity of reasoning with concrete domains. PhD thesis, Teaching and Research Area for Theoretical Computer Science, RWTH Aachen, 2001.

[116] C. Lutz. Interval-based temporal reasoning with general TBoxes. In *Proc. of the 17th Int. Joint Conf. on Artificial Intelligence (IJCAI 2001)*, pages 89–94, 2001.

[117] C. Lutz and U. Sattler. Mary likes all cats. In *Proc. of the 2000 Description Logic Workshop (DL 2000)*, volume 33 of *CEUR Electronic Workshop Proceedings*, 2000.

[118] R. MacGregor. The evolving technology of classification-based knowledge representation systems. In J.F. Sowa, editor. *Principles of Semantic Networks*, pages 385–400. Morgan Kaufmann, Los Altos, CA, 1991.

[119] E. Mays, R. Dionne, and R. Weida. K-Rep system overview. *SIGART Bull.*, 2(3):93–97, 1991.

[120] D.L. McGuinness and J. Wright. Conceptual modeling for configuration: A description logic-based approach. *Artificial Intelligence for Engineering Design, Analysis, and Manufacturing*, 12(4):333–344, 1998 (Special issue on Configuration).

[121] T. Meyer, K. Lee, R. Booth, and J.Z. Pan. Finding maximally satisfiable terminologies for the description logic $\mathcal{ALC}$. In *Proc. of the 21st Nat. Conf. on Artificial Intelligence (AAAI 2006)*. AAAI Press/The MIT Press, 2006.

[122] M. Minsky. A framework for representing knowledge. In J. Haugeland, editor. *Mind Design*. MIT Press, 1981. A longer version appeared in *The Psychology of Computer Vision* (1975). Republished in [39].

[123] B. Motik and U. Sattler. A comparison of reasoning techniques for querying large description logic aboxes. In *Proc. of the 13th International Conference on Logic for Programming, Artificial Intelligence (LPAR06)*, LNCS. Springer-Verlag, 2006.

[124] B. Motik, U. Sattler, and R. Studer. Query answering for OWL-DL with rules. *J. of Web Semantics*, 3(1):41–60, 2005.

[125] D.E. Muller and P.E. Schupp. Alternating automata on infinite trees. *Theoretical Computer Science*, 54:267–276, 1987.

[126] B. Nebel. *Reasoning and Revision in Hybrid Representation Systems. Lecture Notes in Artificial Intelligence*, vol. 422. Springer, 1990.

[127] B. Nebel. Terminological reasoning is inherently intractable. *Artificial Intelligence*, 43(2):235–249, 1990.

[128] F. Oppacher and E. Suen. HARP: A tableau-based theorem prover. *J. of Automated Reasoning*, 4:69–100, 1988.

[129] L. Pacholski, W. Szwast, and L. Tendera. Complexity of two-variable logic with counting. In *Proc. of the 12th IEEE Symp. on Logic in Computer Science (LICS'97)*, pages 318–327. IEEE Computer Society Press, 1997.

[130] L. Pacholski, W. Szwast, and L. Tendera. Complexity results for first-order two-variable logic with counting. *SIAM J. on Computing*, 29(4):1083–1117, 2000.

[131] C.H. Papadimitriou. *Computational Complexity*. Addison-Wesley Publ. Co., Reading, MA, 1994.

[132] B. Parsia, E. Sirin, and A. Kalyanpur. Debugging OWL ontologies. In A. Ellis and T. Hagino, editors. *Proc. of the 14th International Conference on World Wide Web (WWW'05)*, pages 633–640. ACM, 2005.

[133] P.F. Patel-Schneider. DLP. In *Proc. of the 1999 Description Logic Workshop (DL'99)*, volume 22 of *CEUR Electronic Workshop Proceedings*, 1999.

[134] P.F. Patel-Schneider, P. Hayes, and I. Horrocks. OWL Web Ontology Language semantics and abstract syntax. W3C Recommendation, 10 February 2004. Available at http://www.w3.org/TR/owl-semantics/.

[135] P.F. Patel-Schneider, D.L. McGuinness, R.J. Brachman, L.A. Resnick, and A. Borgida. The CLASSIC knowledge representation system: Guiding principles and implementation rational. *SIGART Bull.*, 2(3):108–113, 1991.

[136] Pellet OWL reasoner. Maryland Information and Network Dynamics Lab, 2003. http://www.mindswap.org/2003/pellet/index.shtml.

[137] C. Peltason. The BACK system—an overview. *SIGART Bull.*, 2(3):114–119, 1991.

[138] M.R. Quillian. Word concepts: A theory and simulation of some basic capabilities. *Behavioral Science*, 12:410–430, 1967. Republished in [39].

[139] A. Rector and J. Rogers. Ontological and practical issues in using a description logic to represent medical concept systems: Experience from GALEN. In *Reasoning Web, Second International Summer School, Tutorial Lectures, Lecture Notes in Computer Science*, vol. 4126, pages 197–231. Springer-Verlag, 2006.

[140] R. Rosati. On the decidability and complexity of integrating ontologies and rules. *J. of Web Semantics*, 3(1):61–73, 2005.

[141] A. Ruttenberg, J. Rees, and J. Luciano. Experience using OWL DL for the exchange of biological pathway information. In *Proc. of the First OWL Experiences and Directions Workshop*, volume 188 of *CEUR Electronic Workshop Proceedings*, 2005.

[142] U. Sattler. A concept language extended with different kinds of transitive roles. In G. Görz and S. Hölldobler, editors. *20. Deutsche Jahrestagung für Künstliche Intelligenz, Lecture Notes in Artificial Intelligence*, vol. 1137. Springer-Verlag, 1996.

[143] U. Sattler and M.Y. Vardi. The hybrid mu-calculus. In R. Goré, A. Leitsch, and T. Nipkow, editors. *Proc. of the International Joint Conference on Automated Reasoning (IJCAR-01), Lecture Notes in Artificial Intelligence*, vol. 2083. Springer-Verlag, 2001.

[144] K. Schild. A correspondence theory for terminological logics: Preliminary report. In *Proc. of the 12th Int. Joint Conf. on Artificial Intelligence (IJCAI'91)*, pages 466–471, 1991.

[145] K. Schild. Terminological cycles and the propositional μ-calculus. In *Proc. of the 4th Int. Conf. on the Principles of Knowledge Representation and Reasoning (KR'94)*, pages 509–520, 1994.

[146] K. Schild. Querying knowledge and data bases by a universal description logic with recursion. PhD thesis, Universität des Saarlandes, Germany, 1995.

[147] S. Schlobach and R. Cornet. Non-standard reasoning services for the debugging of description logic terminologies. In G. Gottlob and T. Walsh, editors. *Proc. of the 18th Int. Joint Conf. on Artificial Intelligence (IJCAI 2003)*, pages 355–362. Morgan Kaufmann, Los Altos, CA, 2003.

[148] M. Schmidt-Schauß. Subsumption in KL-ONE is undecidable. In R.J. Brachman, H.J. Levesque, and R. Reiter, editors. *Proc. of the 1st Int. Conf. on the Principles of Knowledge Representation and Reasoning (KR'89)*, pages 421–431. Morgan Kaufmann, Los Altos, CA, 1989.

[149] M. Schmidt-Schauß and G. Smolka. Attributive concept descriptions with complements. *Artificial Intelligence*, 48(1):1–26, 1991.

[150] A. Sidhu, T. Dillon, E. Chang, and B.S. Sidhu. Protein ontology development using OWL. In *Proc. of the First OWL Experiences and Directions Workshop*, volume 188 of *CEUR Electronic Workshop Proceedings*, 2005.

[151] E. Sirin, B. Parsia, B. Cuenca Grau, A. Kalyanpur, and Y. Katz. Pellet: A practical OWL-DL reasoner. *Journal of Web Semantics*, 5(2):51–53, 2007.

[152] D. Soergel, B. Lauser, A. Liang, F. Fisseha, J. Keizer, and S. Katz. Reengineering thesauri for new applications: The AGROVOC example. *J. of Digital Information*, 4(4), 2004.

[153] K.A. Spackman, K.E. Campbell, and R.A. Cote. SNOMED RT: A reference terminology for health care. *J. of the American Medical Informatics Association*:640–644, 1997 (Fall Symposium Supplement).

[154] P.-H. Speel, F. van Raalte, P.E. van der Vet, and N.J.I. Mars. Runtime and memory usage performance of description logics. In G. Ellis, R. A. Levinson, A. Fall, and V. Dahl, editors, *Knowledge Retrieval, Use and Storage for Efficiency: Proc. of the 1st Int. KRUSE Symposium*, pages 13–27, 1995.

[155] L. Stockmeyer and A. Meyer. Word problems requiring exponential time (preliminary report). In *Proc. of the 5th Annual ACM Symposium on Theory of Computing (STOC'73)*, pages 1–9. ACM Press, 1973.

[156] Semantic web for earth and environmental terminology (SWEET). Jet Propulsion Laboratory, California Institute of Technology, 2006. http://sweet.jpl.nasa.gov/.

[157] S. Tessaris. Questions and answers: reasoning and querying in description logic. PhD thesis, University of Manchester, Department of Computer Science, April 2001.

[158] W. Thomas. Automata on infinite objects. In J. van Leeuwen, editor. *Handbook of Theoretical Computer Science,* vol. B, pages 133–192. Elsevier Science Publishers (North-Holland), Amsterdam, 1990 (Chapter 4).

[159] S. Tobies. Complexity results and practical algorithms for logics in knowledge representation. PhD thesis, LuFG Theoretical Computer Science, RWTH-Aachen, Germany, 2001.

[160] D. Tsarkov and I. Horrocks. FaCT++ description logic reasoner: System description. In *Proc. of the Int. Joint Conf. on Automated Reasoning (IJCAR 2006)*, *Lecture Notes in Artificial Intelligence*, vol. 4130, pages 292–297. Springer, 2006.

[161] M.Y. Vardi and P. Wolper. Automata-theoretic techniques for modal logics of programs. *J. of Computer and System Sciences*, 32:183–221, 1986.

[162] M.Y. Vardi and P. Wolper. Reasoning about infinite computations. *Information and Computation*, 115(1):1–37, 1994.

[163] W.A. Woods. What's in a link: Foundations for semantic networks. In D.G. Bobrow and A.M. Collins, editors. *Representation and Understanding: Studies in Cognitive Science*, pages 35–82. Academic Press, 1975. Republished in [39].

Handbook of Knowledge Representation
Edited by F. van Harmelen, V. Lifschitz and B. Porter
© 2008 Elsevier B.V. All rights reserved
DOI: 10.1016/S1574-6526(07)03004-0

Chapter 4

Constraint Programming

Francesca Rossi, Peter van Beek, Toby Walsh

4.1 Introduction

Constraint programming is a powerful paradigm for solving combinatorial search problems that draws on a wide range of techniques from artificial intelligence, operations research, algorithms, graph theory and elsewhere. The basic idea in constraint programming is that the user states the constraints and a general purpose constraint solver is used to solve them. Constraints are just relations, and a constraint satisfaction problem (CSP) states which relations should hold among the given decision variables. More formally, a constraint satisfaction problem consists of a set of variables, each with some domain of values, and a set of relations on subsets of these variables. For example, in scheduling exams at an university, the decision variables might be the times and locations of the different exams, and the constraints might be on the capacity of each examination room (e.g., we cannot schedule more students to sit exams in a given room at any one time than the room's capacity) and on the exams scheduled at the same time (e.g., we cannot schedule two exams at the same time if they share students in common). Constraint solvers take a real-world problem like this represented in terms of decision variables and constraints, and find an assignment to all the variables that satisfies the constraints. Extensions of this framework may involve, for example, finding optimal solutions according to one or more optimization criterion (e.g., minimizing the number of days over which exams need to be scheduled), finding all solutions, replacing (some or all) constraints with preferences, and considering a distributed setting where constraints are distributed among several agents.

Constraint solvers search the solution space systematically, as with backtracking or branch and bound algorithms, or use forms of local search which may be incomplete. Systematic method often interleave search (see Section 4.3) and inference, where inference consists of propagating the information contained in one constraint to the neighboring constraints (see Section 4.2). Such inference reduces the parts of the search space that need to be visited. Special propagation procedures can be devised to suit specific constraints (called global constraints), which occur often in real life. Such global constraints are an important component in the success of constraint programming. They provide common patterns to help users model real-world problems. They also help make search for a solution more efficient and more effective.

While constraint problems are in general NP-complete, there are important classes which can be solved polynomially (see Section 4.4). They are identified by the connectivity structure among the variables sharing constraints, or by the language to define the constraints. For example, constraint problems where the connectivity graph has the form of a tree are polynomial to solve.

While defining a set of constraints may seem a simple way to model a real-world problem, finding a good model that works well with a chosen solver is not easy. A poorly chosen model may be very hard to solve. Moreover, solvers can be designed to take advantage of the features of the model such as symmetry to save time in finding a solution (see Section 4.5). Another problem with modeling real-world problems is that many are over-constrained. We may need to specify preferences rather than constraints. Soft constraints (see Section 4.6) provide a formalism to do this, as well as techniques to find an optimal solution according to the specified preferences. Many of the constraint solving methods like constraint propagation can be adapted to be used with soft constraints.

A constraint solver can be implemented in any language. However, there are languages especially designed to represent constraint relations and the chosen search strategy. These languages are logic-based, imperative, object-oriented, or rule-based. Languages based on logic programming (see Section 4.7) are well suited for a tight integration between the language and constraints since they are based on similar notions: relations and (backtracking) search.

Constraint solvers can also be extended to deal with relations over more than just finite (or enumerated) domains. For example, relations over the reals are useful to model many real-world problems (see Section 4.8). Another extension is to multi-agent systems. We may have several agents, each of which has their own constraints. Since agents may want to keep their knowledge private, or their knowledge is so large and dynamic that it does not make sense to collect it in a centralized site, distributed constraint programming has been developed (see Section 4.9).

This chapter necessarily covers some of the issues that are central to constraint programming somewhat superficially. A deeper treatment of these and many other issues can be found in the various books on constraint programming that have been written [5, 35, 53, 98, 70, 135–137].

4.2 Constraint Propagation

One of the most important concepts in the theory and practice of constraint programming is that of local consistency. A *local inconsistency* is an instantiation of some of the variables that satisfies the relevant constraints but cannot be extended to one or more additional variables and so cannot be part of any solution. If we are using a backtracking search to find a solution, such an inconsistency can be the reason for many deadends in the search and cause much futile search effort. This insight has led to: (a) the definition of conditions that characterize the level of local consistency of a CSP (e.g., [49, 95, 104]), (b) the development of constraint propagation algorithms—algorithms which enforce these levels of local consistency by removing inconsistencies from a CSP (e.g., [95, 104]), and (c) effective backtracking algorithms for finding solutions to CSPs that maintain a level of local consistency during the search (e.g., [30, 54, 68]). In this section, we survey definitions of local consistency and constraint propagation algorithms. Backtracking algorithms integrated with constraint propagation are the topic of a subsequent section.

4.2.1 Local Consistency

Currently, arc consistency [95, 96] is the most important local consistency in practice and has received the most attention. Given a constraint, a value for a variable in the constraint is said to have a *support* if there exists values for the other variables in the constraint such that the constraint is satisfied. A constraint is *arc consistent* or if every value in the domains of the variables of the constraint has a support. A constraint can be made arc consistent by repeatedly removing unsupported values from the domains of its variables. Removing unsupported values is often referred to as *pruning* the domains. For constraints involving more than two variables, arc consistency is often referred to as *hyper arc consistency* or *generalized arc consistency*. For example, let the domains of variables x and y be $\{0, 1, 2\}$ and consider the constraint $x + y = 1$. Enforcing arc consistency on this constraint would prune the domains of both variables to just $\{0, 1\}$. The values pruned from the domains of the variables are locally inconsistent—they do not belong to any set of assignments that satisfies the constraint—and so cannot be part of any solution to the entire CSP. Enforcing arc consistency on a CSP requires us to iterate over the domain value removal step until we reach a fixed point. Algorithms for enforcing arc consistency have been extensively studied and refined (see, e.g., [95, 11] and references therein). An optimal algorithm for an arbitrary constraint has $O(rd^r)$ worst case time complexity, where r is the arity of the constraint and d is the size of the domains of the variables [103].

In general, there is a trade-off between the cost of the constraint propagation performed at each node in the search tree, and the amount of pruning. One way to reduce the cost of constraint propagation, is to consider more restricted local consistencies. One important example is bounds consistency. Suppose that the domains of the variables are large and ordered and that the domains of the variables are represented by intervals (the minimum and the maximum value in the domain). With bounds consistency, instead of asking that each value in the domain has a support in the constraint, we only ask that the minimum value and the maximum value each have a support in the constraint. Although bounds consistency is weaker than arc consistency, it has been shown to be useful for arithmetic constraints and global constraints as it can sometimes be enforced more efficiently (see below).

For some types of problems, like temporal constraints, it may be worth enforcing even stronger levels of local consistency than path consistency [95]. A problem involving binary constraints (that is, relations over just two variables) is *path consistent* if every consistent pair of values for two variables can be extended to any third variables. To make a problem path consistent, we may have to add additional binary constraints to rule out consistent pairs of values which cannot be extended.

4.2.2 Global Constraints

Although global constraints are an important aspect of constraint programming, there is no clear definition of what is and is not a global constraint. A global constraint is a constraint over some sequence of variables. Global constraints also usually come with a constraint propagation algorithm that does more pruning or performs pruning cheaper than if we try to express the global constraint using smaller relations. The canonical example of a global constraint is the `all-different` constraint. An `all-different` constraint over a set of variables states that the variables must be pairwise different. The `all-different` constraint is widely used in practice and because of its importance is offered as a built-in constraint in most, if not all, major commercial and research-based constraint programming systems. Starting with the first global constraints in the CHIP constraint programming system [2], hundreds of global constraints have been proposed and implemented (see, e.g., [7]).

The power of global constraints is two-fold. First, global constraints ease the task of modeling an application as a CSP. Second, special purpose constraint propagation algorithms can be designed which take advantage of the semantics of the constraint and are therefore much more efficient. As an example, recall that enforcing arc consistency on an arbitrary has $O(rd^r)$ worst case time complexity, where r is the arity of the constraint and d is the size of the domains of the variables. In contrast, the `all-different` constraint can be made arc consistent in $O(r^2 d)$ time in the worst case [116], and can be made bounds consistent in $O(r)$ time [100].

Other examples of widely applicable global constraints are the global cardinality constraint (`gcc`) [117] and the `cumulative` constraint [2]. A `gcc` over a set of variables and values states that the number of variables instantiating to a value must be between a given upper and lower bound, where the bounds can be different for each value. A `cumulative` constraint over a set of variables representing the time where different tasks are performed ensures that the tasks are ordered such that the capacity of some resource used at any one time is not exceeded. Both of these types of constraint commonly occur in rostering, timetabling, sequencing, and scheduling applications.

4.3 Search

The main algorithmic technique for solving constraint satisfaction problems is search. A search algorithm for solving a CSP can be either complete or incomplete. Complete, or systematic algorithms, come with a guarantee that a solution will be found if one exists, and can be used to show that a CSP does not have a solution and to find a provably optimal solution. Incomplete, or non-systematic algorithms, cannot be used to show a CSP does not have a solution or to find a provably optimal solution. However, such algorithms are often effective at finding a solution if one exists and can be used to find an approximation to an optimal solution. In this section, we survey backtracking and local search algorithms for solving CSPs, as well as hybrid methods that draw upon ideas from both artificial intelligence (AI) and operations research (OR). Backtracking search algorithms are, in general, examples of systematic complete algorithms. Local search algorithms are examples of incomplete algorithms.

4.3.1 Backtracking Search

A backtracking search for a solution to a CSP can be seen as performing a depth-first traversal of a search tree. This search tree is generated as the search progresses. At a node in the search tree, an uninstantiated variable is selected and the node is extended where the branches out of the node represent alternative choices that may have to be examined in order to find a solution. The method of extending a node in the search tree is often called a branching strategy. Let x be the variable selected at a node. The two most common branching strategies are to instantiate x in turn to each value in its domain or to generate two branches, $x = a$ and $x \neq a$, for some value a in the domain of x. The constraints are used to check whether a node may possibly lead to a solution of the CSP and to prune subtrees containing no solutions.

Since the first uses of backtracking algorithms in computing [29, 65], many techniques for improving the efficiency of a backtracking search algorithm have been suggested and evaluated. Some of the most important techniques include constraint propagation, nogood recording, backjumping, heuristics for variable and value ordering, and randomization and restart strategies. The best combinations of these techniques result in robust backtracking algorithms that can now routinely solve large, and combinatorially challenging instances that are of practical importance.

Constraint propagation during search

An important technique for improving efficiency is to maintain a level of local consistency during the backtracking search by performing constraint propagation at each node in the search tree. This has two important benefits. First, removing inconsistencies during search can dramatically prune the search tree by removing many dead ends and by simplifying the remaining subproblem. In some cases, a variable will have an empty domain after constraint propagation; i.e., no value satisfies the unary constraints over that variable. In this case, backtracking can be initiated as there is no solution along this branch of the search tree. In other cases, the variables will have their domains reduced. If a domain is reduced to a single value, the value of the variable is forced and it does not need to be branched on in the future. Thus, it can be much easier to find a solution to a CSP after constraint propagation or to show that the CSP does not have a solution. Second, some of the most important variable ordering heuristics make use of the information gathered by constraint propagation to make effective variable ordering decisions. As a result of these benefits, it is now standard for a backtracking algorithm to incorporate some form of constraint propagation.

The idea of incorporating some form of constraint propagation into a backtracking algorithm arose from several directions. Davis and Putnam [30] propose unit propagation, a form of constraint propagation specialized to SAT. McGregor [99] and Haralick and Elliott proposed the *forward checking* backtracking algorithm [68] which makes the constraints involving the most recently instantiated variable arc consistent. Gaschnig [54] suggests *maintaining arc consistency* on all constraints during backtracking search and gives the first explicit algorithm containing this idea. Mackworth [95] generalizes Gaschnig's proposal to backtracking algorithms that interleave case-analysis with constraint propagation.

Nogood recording

One of the most effective techniques known for improving the performance of backtracking search on a CSP is to add implied constraints or nogoods. A constraint is *implied* if the set of solutions to the CSP is the same with and without the constraint.

A *nogood* is a special type of implied constraint, a set of assignments for some subset of variables which do not lead to a solution. Adding the "right" implied constraints to a CSP can mean that many deadends are removed from the search tree and other dead-ends are discovered after much less search effort. Three main techniques for adding implied constraints have been investigated. One technique is to add implied constraints by hand during the modeling phase. A second technique is to automatically add implied constraints by applying a constraint propagation algorithm. Both of the above techniques rule out local inconsistencies or deadends *before* they are encountered during the search. A third technique is to automatically add implied constraints *after* a local inconsistency or deadend is encountered in the search. The basis of this technique is the concept of a nogood—a set of assignments that is not consistent with any solution.

Once a nogood for a deadend is discovered, it can be ruled out by adding a constraint. The technique, first informally described by Stallman and Sussman [130], is often referred to as nogood or constraint recording. The hope is that the added constraints will prune the search space in the future. Dechter [31] provides the first formal account of discovering and recording nogoods. Ginsberg's [61] dynamic backtracking algorithm performs nogood recording coupled with a strategy for deleting nogoods in order to use only a polynomial amount of space. Schiex and Verfaillie [125] provide the first formal account of nogood recording within an algorithm that performs constraint propagation.

Backjumping

Upon discovering a deadend in the search, a backtracking algorithm must uninstantiate some previously instantiated variable. In the standard form of backtracking—called chronological backtracking—the most recently instantiated variable becomes uninstantiated. However, backtracking chronologically may not address the reason for the deadend. In backjumping, the algorithm backtracks to and retracts the decision which bears some responsibility for the deadend. The idea is to (sometimes implicitly) record nogoods or explanations for failures in the search. The algorithms then reason about these nogoods to determine the highest point in the search tree that can safely be jumped to without missing any solutions. Stallman and Sussman [130] were the first to informally propose a non-chronological backtracking algorithm—called dependency-directed backtracking—that discovered and maintained nogoods in order to backjump. The first explicit backjumping algorithm was given by Gaschnig [55]. Subsequent generalizations of Gaschnig's algorithm include Dechter's [32] graph-based backjumping algorithm and Prosser's [113] conflict-directed backjumping algorithm.

Variable and value ordering heuristics

When solving a CSP using backtracking search, a sequence of decisions must be made as to which variable to branch on or instantiate next and which value to give to the variable. These decisions are referred to as the variable and the value ordering. It has been shown that for many problems, the choice of variable and value ordering can be crucial to effectively solving the problem (e.g., [58, 62, 68]). When solving a CSP using backtracking search interleaved with constraint propagation, the domains of the unassigned variables are pruned using the constraints and the current set of branching constraints. Many of the most important variable ordering heuristics are based on choosing the variable with the smallest number of values remaining in its domain (e.g., [65, 15, 10]). The principle being followed in the design of many value ordering heuristics is to choose next the value that is most likely to succeed or be a part of a solution (e.g., [37, 56]).

Randomization and restart strategies

It has been widely observed that backtracking algorithms can be brittle on some instances. Seemingly small changes to a variable or value ordering heuristic, such as a change in the ordering of tie-breaking schemes, can lead to great differences in running time. An explanation for this phenomenon is that ordering heuristics make mistakes. Depending on the number of mistakes and how early in the search the mistakes are made (and therefore how costly they may be to correct), there can be a large variability in performance between different heuristics. A technique called randomization and restarts has been proposed for taking advantage of this variability (see, e.g., [69, 66, 144]). A restart strategy $S = (t_1, t_2, t_3, \ldots)$ is an infinite sequence where each t_i is either a positive integer or infinity. The idea is that a randomized backtracking algorithm is run for t_1 steps. If no solution is found within that cutoff, the algorithm is restarted and run for t_2 steps, and so on until a solution is found.

4.3.2 Local Search

In backtracking search, the nodes in the search tree represent partial sets of assignments to the variables in the CSP. In contrast, a local search for a solution to a CSP can be seen as performing a walk in a directed graph where the nodes represent complete assignments; i.e., every variable has been assigned a value from its domain. Each node is labeled with a cost value given by a cost function and the edges out of a node are given by a neighborhood function. The search graph is generated as the search progresses. At a node in the search graph, a neighbor or adjacent node is selected and the algorithm "moves" to that node, searching for a node of lowest cost. The basic framework applies to both satisfaction and optimization problems and can handle both hard (must be satisfied) and soft (desirable if satisfied) constraints (see, e.g., [73]). For satisfaction problems, a standard cost function is the number of constraints that are not satisfied. For optimization problems, the cost function is the measure of solution quality given by the problem. For example, in the Traveling Salesperson Problem (TSP), the cost of a node is the cost of the tour given by the set of assignments associated with the node.

Four important choices must be made when designing an effective local search algorithm. First is the choice of how to start search by selecting a starting node in the graph. One can randomly pick a complete set of assignments or attempt to construct a "good" starting point. Second is the choice of neighborhood. Example neighborhoods include picking a single variable/value assignment and assigning the variable a new value from its domain and picking a pair of variables/value assignments and swapping the values of the variables. The former neighborhood has been shown to work well in SAT and n-queens problems and the latter in TSP problems. Third is the choice of "move" or selection of adjacent node. In the popular min-conflicts heuristic [102], a variable x is chosen that appears in a constraint that is not satisfied. A new value is then chosen for x that minimizes the number of constraints that are not satisfied. In the successful GSAT algorithm for SAT problems [127], a best-improvement move is performed. A variable x is chosen and its value is flipped (true to false or vice versa) that leads to the largest reduction in the cost function—the number of clauses that are not satisfied. Fourth is the choice of stopping criteria for the algorithm. The stopping criteria is usually some combination of an upper bound on the maximum number of moves or iterations, a test whether a solution of low enough cost has been found, and a test whether the number of iterations since the last (big enough) improvement is too large.

The simplest local search algorithms continually make moves in the graph until all moves to neighbors would result in an increase in the cost function. The final node then represents the solution to the CSP. However, note that the solution may only be a local minima (relative to its neighbors) but not globally optimal. As well, if we are solving a satisfaction problem, the final node may not actually satisfy all of the constraints. Several techniques have been developed for improving the efficiency and the quality of the solutions found by local search. The most important of these include: multi-starts where the algorithm is restarted with different starting solutions and the best solution found from all runs is reported and threshold accepting algorithms that sometimes move to worse cost neighbors to escape local minima such as simulated annealing [83] and tabu search [63]. In simulated annealing, worse cost neighbors are moved to with a probability that is gradually decreased over time. In tabu search, a move is made to a neighbor with the best cost, even if it is worse than the cost of the current node. However, to prevent cycling, a history of the recently visited nodes called a tabu list is kept and a move to a node is blocked if it appears on the tabu list.

4.3.3 Hybrid Methods

Hybrid methods combine together two or more solution techniques. Whilst there exist interesting hybrids of systematic and local search methods, some of the most promising hybrid methods combine together AI and OR techniques like backtracking and linear programming. Linear programming (LP) is one of the most powerful techniques to have emerged out of OR. In fact, if a problem can be modeled by linear inequalities over continuous variables, then LP is almost certainly a better method to solve it than CP.

One of the most popular approaches to bring linear programming into CP is to create a *relaxation* of (some parts of) the CP problem that is linear. Relaxation may be both dropping the integrality requirement on some of the decision variables or on the tightness of the constraints. Linear relaxations have been proposed for a number of global constraints including the `all different`, `circuit` and `cumulative` constraints [72]. Such relaxations can then be given to a LP solver. The LP solution can be used in a number of ways to prune domains and guide search. For example, it can tighten bounds on a variable (e.g., the variable representing the optimization cost). We may also be able to prune domains by using reduced costs or Lagrange multipliers. In addition, the continuous LP solution may by chance be integral (and thus be a solution to the original CP model). Even if the LP solution is not integral, we can use it to guide search (e.g., branching on the most non-integral variable). One of the advantages of using a linear relaxation is that the LP solver takes a more global view than a CP solver which just makes "local" inferences.

Two other well-known OR techniques that have been combined with CP are branch and price and Bender's decomposition. With branch and price, CP can be used to perform the column generation, identifying variables to add dynamically to the search. With Bender's decomposition, CP can be used to perform the row generation, generating new constraints (nogoods) to add to the model. Hybrid methods like these have permitted us to solve problems beyond the reach of either CP or OR alone. For example, a CP based branch and price hybrid was the first to solve the 8-team traveling tournament problem to optimality [43].

4.4 Tractability

Constraint satisfaction is NP-complete and thus intractable in general. It is easy to see how to reduce a problem like graph 3-coloring or propositional satisfiability to a CSP. Considerable effort has therefore been invested in identifying restricted classes of constraint satisfaction problems which are tractable. For Boolean problems where the decision variables have just one of two possible values, Schaefer's dichotomy theorem gives an elegant characterization of the six tractable classes of relations [121]: those that are satisfied by only true assignments; those that are satisfied by only false assignments; Horn clauses; co-Horn clauses (i.e., at most one negated variable); 2-CNF clauses; and affine relations. It appears considerably more difficult to characterize tractable classes for non-Booleans domains. Research has typically broken the problem into two parts: tractable languages (where the relations are fixed but they can be combined in any way), and tractable constraint graphs (where the constraint graph is restricted but any sort of relation can be used).

4.4.1 Tractable Constraint Languages

We first restrict ourselves to instances of constraint satisfaction problems which can be built using some limited language of constraint relations. For example, we might consider the class of constraint satisfaction problems built from just the not-equals relation. For k-valued variables, this gives k-coloring problems. Hence, the problem class is tractable iff $k \leqslant 2$.

Some examples

We consider some examples of tractable constraint languages. Zero/one/all (or ZOA) constraints are binary constraints in which each value is supported by zero, one or all values [25]. Such constraints are useful in scene labeling and other problems. ZOA constraints are tractable [25] and can, in fact, be solved in $O(e(d + n))$ where e is the number of constraints, d is the domain size and n is the number of variables [149]. This results generalizes the result that 2-SAT is linear since every binary relation on a Boolean domain is a ZOA constraint. Similarly, this result generalizes the result that functional binary constraints are tractable. The ZOA constraint language is maximal in the sense that, if we add any relation to the language which is not ZOA, the language becomes NP-complete [25].

Another tractable constraint language is that of connected row-convex constraints [105]. A binary constraint C over the ordered domain D can be represented by a 0/1 matrix M_{ij} where $M_{ij} = 1$ iff $C(i, j)$ holds. Such a matrix is row-convex iff the non-zero entries in each row are consecutive, and connected row-convex iff it is row-convex and, after removing empty rows, it is connected (non-zero entries in consecutive rows are adjacent). Finally a constraint is connected row-convex iff the associated 0/1 matrix and its transpose are connected row-convex. Connected row-convex constraints include monotone relations. They can be solved without backtracking using a path-consistency algorithm. If a constraint problem is path-consistent and only contains row-convex constraints (not just connected row-convex constraints), then it can be solved in polynomial time [133]. Row-convexity is not enough on its own to guarantee tractability as enforcing path-consistency may destroy row-convexity.

A third example is the language of max-closed constraints. Specialized solvers have been developed for such constraints in a number of industrial scheduling tools. A constraint is max-closed iff for all pairs of satisfying assignments, if we take the maximum of each assignment, we obtain a satisfying assignment. Similarly a constraint is min-closed iff for all pairs of satisfying assignments, if we take the minimum of each assignment, we obtain a satisfying assignment. All unary constraints are max-closed and min-closed. Arithmetic constraints like $aX = bY + c$, and $\sum_i a_i X_i \geqslant b$ are also max-closed and min-closed. Max-closed constraints can be solved in quadratic time using a pairwise-consistency algorithm [82].

Constraint tightness

Some of the simplest possible tractability results come from looking at the constraint tightness. For example, Dechter shows that for a problem with domains of size d and constraints of arity at most k, enforcing strong $(d(r-1) + 1)$-consistency guarantees global consistency [33]. We can then construct a solution without backtracking by repeatedly assigning a variable and making the resulting subproblem globally consistent. Dechter's result is tight since certain types of constraints (e.g., binary inequality constraints in graph coloring) require exactly this level of local consistency.

Stronger results can be obtained by looking more closely at the constraints. For example, a k-ary constraint is m-tight iff given any assignment for $k - 1$ of the variables, there are at most m consistent values for the remaining variable. Dechter and van Beek prove that if all relations are m-tight and the network is strongly relational $(m + 1)$-consistent, then it is globally consistent [134]. A complementary result holds for constraint looseness. If constraints are sufficiently loose, we can guarantee that the network must have a certain level of local consistency.

Algebraic results

Jeavons et al. have given a powerful algebraic treatment of tractability of constraint languages using relational clones, and polymorphisms on these cones [79–81]. For example, they show how to construct a so-called "indicator" problem that determines whether a constraint language over finite domains is NP-complete or tractable. They are also able to show that the search problem (where we want to find a solution) is no harder than the corresponding decision problem (where we want to just determine if a solution exists or not).

Dichotomy results

As we explained, for Boolean domains, Schaefer's result completely characterizes the tractable constraint languages. For three valued variables, Bulatov has provided a more complex but nevertheless complete dichotomy result [16]. Bulatov also has given a cubic time algorithm for identifying these tractable cases. It remains an open question if a similar dichotomy result holds for constraint languages over any finite domain.

Infinite domains

Many (but not all) of the tractability results continue to hold if variable domains are infinite. For example, Allen's interval algebra introduces binary relations and compositions of such relations over time intervals [3]. This can be viewed as a binary constraint problem over intervals on the real line. Linear Horn is an important tractable class for temporal reasoning. It properly includes the point algebra, and ORD-Horn constraints. A constraint over an infinite ordered set is *linear Horn* when it is equivalent to a finite disjunction of linear disequalities and at most one weak linear inequality. For example, $(X - Y \leqslant Z) \vee (X + Y + Z \neq 0)$ is linear Horn [88, 84].

4.4.2 Tractable Constraint Graphs

We now consider tractability results where we permit any sort of relation but restrict the constraint graph in some way. Most of these results concern tree or tree-like structures. We need to distinguish between three types of constraint graph: the *primal* constraint graph has a node for each variable and edges between variables in the same constraint, the *dual* constraint graph has a node for each constraint and edges between constraints sharing variables, and the constraint *hypergraph* has a node for each variable and a hyperedge between all the variables in each constraint.

Mackworth gave one of the first tractability results for constraint satisfaction problems: a binary constraint networks whose primal graph is a tree can be solved in linear time [97]. More generally, a constraint problem can be solved in a time that is exponential in the induced width of the primal graph for a given variable ordering using a join-tree clustering or (for space efficiency) a variable elimination algorithm. The induced width is the maximum number of parents to any node in the induced graph (in which we add edges between any two parents that are both connected to the same child). For non-binary constraints, we tend to obtain tighter results by considering the constraint hypergraph [67]. For example, an acyclic non-binary constraint problem will have high tree-width, even though it can be solved in quadratic time. Indeed, results based on hypertree width have been proven to strongly dominate those based on cycle cutset width, biconnected width, and hinge width [67].

4.5 Modeling

Constraint programming is, in some respects, one of the purest realizations of the dream of declarative programming: you state the constraints and the computer solves them using one of a handful of standard methods like the maintaining arc consistency backtracking search procedure. In reality, constraint programming falls short of this dream. There are usually many logically equivalent ways to model a problem. The model we use is often critical as to whether or not the problem can be solved. Whilst modeling a problem so it can be successfully solved using constraint programming is an art, a number of key lessons have started to be identified.

4.5.1 CP $\vee \neg$ CP

We must first decide if constraint programming is a suitable technology in which to model our problem, or whether we should consider some other approach like mathematical programming or simulation. It is often hard to answer this question as the problem we are trying to solve is often not well defined. The constraints of the problem may not have been explicitly identified. We may therefore have to extract the problem constraints from the user in order to build a model. To compound matters, for economic and other reasons, problems are nearly always over-constrained. We must therefore also identify the often conflicting objectives (price, speed, weight, ...) that need to be considered. We must then decide which constraints to consider as hard, which constraints to compile into the search strategy and heuristics, and which constraints to ignore.

Real world combinatorial search problems are typically much too large to solve exactly. Problem decomposition is therefore a vital aspect of modeling. We have to decide how to divide the problem up and where to make simplifying approximations. For example, in a production planning problem, we might ignore how the availability of operators but focus first on scheduling the machines. Having decided on a production schedule for the machines, we can then attempt to minimize the labor costs.

Another key concern in modeling a problem is stability. How much variability is there between instances of the problem? How stable is the solution method to small changes? Is the problem very dynamic? What happens if (a small amount of) the data changes? Do solutions need to be robust to small changes? Many such questions need to be answered before we can be sure that constraint programming is indeed a suitable technology.

4.5.2 Viewpoints

Having decided to use constraint programming, we then need to decide the variables, their possible domains and the constraints that apply to these variables. The concept of viewpoint [57, 19] is often useful at this point. There are typically several different viewpoints that we can have of a problem. For example, if we are scheduling the next World Cup, are we assigning games to time slots, or time slots to games? Different models can be built corresponding to each of these viewpoints. We might have variables representing the games with their values being time slots, or we might have variables representing the time slots with their values being games.

A good rule of thumb is to choose the viewpoint which permits the constraints to be expressed easily. The hope is that the constraint solver will then be able to reason with the constraints effectively. In some cases, it is best to use multiple viewpoints and to maintain consistency between them with *channeling* constraints [19]. One common viewpoint is a *matrix model* in which the decision variables form a matrix or array [48, 47]. For example, we might need to decide which factory processes which order. This can be modeled with an 0/1 matrix O_{ij} which is 1 iff order i is processed in factory j.

The constraint that every order is processed then becomes the constraint that every row sums to 1.

To help specify the constraints, we might introduce auxiliary variables. For example, in the Golomb ruler problem (prob006 in CSPLib.org), we wish to mark ticks on an integer ruler so that all the distances between ticks are unique. The problem has applications in radio-astronomy and elsewhere. One viewpoint is to have a variable for each tick, whose value is the position on the ruler. To specify the constraint that all the distances between ticks are unique, we can an introduce auxiliary variable D_{ij} for the distance between the ith and jth tick [128]. We can then post a global all-different constraint on these auxiliary variables. It may be helpful to permit the constraint solver to branch on the auxiliary variables. It can also be useful to add implied (or redundant) constraints to help the constraint solver prune the search space. For example, in the Golomb ruler problem, we can add the implied constraint that $D_{ij} < D_{ik}$ for $j < k$ [128]. This will help reduce search.

4.5.3 Symmetry

A vital aspect of modeling is dealing with symmetry. Symmetry occurs naturally in many problems (e.g., if we have two identical machines to schedule, or two identical jobs to process). Symmetry can also be introduced when we model a problem (e.g., if we name the elements in a set, we introduce the possibility of permuting their order). We must deal with symmetry or we will waste much time visiting symmetric solutions, as well as parts of the search tree which are symmetric to already visited parts. One simple but highly effective mechanism to deal with symmetry is to add constraints which eliminate symmetric solutions [27]. Alternatively, we can modify the search procedure to avoid visiting symmetric states [44, 59, 118, 126].

Two common types of symmetry are variable symmetries (which act just on variables), and value symmetries (which act just on values) [21]. With variable symmetries, there are a number of well understood symmetry breaking methods. For example, many problems can be naturally modeled using a matrix model in which the rows and columns of the matrix are symmetric and can be freely permuted. We can break such symmetry by lexicographically ordering the rows and columns [47]. Efficient constraint propagation algorithms have therefore been developed for such ordering constraints [51, 17]. Similarly, with value symmetries, there are a number of well understood symmetry breaking methods. For example, if all values are interchangeable, we can break symmetry by posting some simple precedence constraints [92]. Alternatively, we can turn value symmetry into variable symmetry [47, 93, 114] and then use one of the standard methods for breaking variable symmetry.

4.6 Soft Constraints and Optimization

It is often the case that, after having listed the desired constraints among the decision variables, there is no way to satisfy them all. That is, the problem is *over-constrained*. Even when all the constraints can be satisfied, and there are several solutions, such solutions appear equally good, and there is no way to discriminate among them. These scenarios often occur when constraints are used to formalize desired properties rather than requirements that cannot be violated. Such desired properties should rather be considered as *preferences*, whose violation should be avoided as far as possible. *Soft constraints* provide one way to model such preferences.

4.6.1 Modeling Soft Constraints

There are many classes of soft constraints. The first one that was introduced concerns the so-called *fuzzy constraints* and it is based on fuzzy set theory [42, 41]. A fuzzy constraint is not a set (of allowed tuples of values to variables), but rather a *fuzzy set* [42], where each element has a graded degree of membership. For each assignment of values to its variables, we do not have to say whether it belongs to the set or not, but how much it does so. This allows us to represent the fact that a combination of values for the variables of the constraint is partially permitted. We can also say that the membership degree of an assignment gives us the *preference* for that assignment. In fuzzy constraints, preferences are between 0 and 1, with 1 being complete acceptance and 0 being total rejection. The preference of a solution is then computed by taking the minimal preference over the constraints. This may seem awkward in some scenarios, but it is instead very natural, for example, when we are reasoning about critical applications, such as space or medical applications, where we want to be as cautious as possible. *Possibilistic constraints* [122] are very similar to fuzzy constraints and they have the same expressive power: priorities are associated to constraints and the aim is to find an assignment which minimizes the priority of the most important violated constraint.

Lack of discrimination among solutions with the same minimal preferences is one of the main drawbacks of fuzzy constraints (the so-called *drowning effect*). To avoid this, one can use *fuzzy lexicographic constraints* [45]. The idea is to consider not just the least preference value, but all the preference values when evaluating a complete assignment, and to sort such values in increasing order. When two complete assignments are compared, the two sorted preference lists are then compared lexicographically.

There are situations where we are more interested in the damages we get by not satisfying a constraint rather than in the advantages we obtain when we satisfy it. A natural way to extend the classical constraint formalism to deal with these situations consists of associating a certain penalty or cost to each constraint, to be paid when the constraint is violated. A *weighted constraint* is thus just a classical constraint plus a weight. The cost of an assignment is the sum of all weights of those constraints which are violated. An optimal solution is a complete assignment with minimal cost. In the particular case when all penalties are equal to 1, this is called the MAX-CSP problem [50]. In fact, in this case the task consists of finding an assignment where the number of violated constraints is minimal, which is equivalent to say that the number of satisfied constraints is maximal.

Weighted constraints are among the most expressive soft constraint frameworks, in the sense that the task of finding an optimal solution for fuzzy, possibilistic, or lexicographic constraint problems can be efficiently reduced to the task of finding an optimal solution for a weighted constraint problem [124].

The literature contains also at least two general formalisms to model soft constraints, of which all the classes above are instances: *semiring-based constraints* [13, 14] and *valued constraints* [124]. Semiring-based constraints rely on a simple algebraic structure which is very similar to a semiring, and it is used to formalize the notion of preferences (or satisfaction degrees), the way preferences are ordered, and how to combine them. The minimum preference is used to capture the notion of absolute non-satisfaction, which is typical of hard constraints. Similarly for the maximal preference, which can model complete satisfaction. Valued constraints depend on a different algebraic structure, a positive totally ordered commutative monoid, and use a different syntax than semiring-based constraints. However, they have the same expressive power, if we assume preferences to be totally ordered [12]. Partially ordered preferences can be useful, for example, when we need to reason with more than one optimization criterion, since in this case there could be situations which are naturally not comparable.

Soft constraint problems are as expressive, and as difficult to solve, as constraint optimization problems, which are just constraint problems plus an objective function. In fact, given any soft constraint problem, we can always build a constraint optimization problem with the same solution ordering, and vice versa.

4.6.2 Searching for the Best Solution

The most natural way to solve a soft constraint problem, or a constraint optimization problem, is to use Branch and Bound. *Depth First Branch and bound* (DFBB) performs a depth-first traversal of the search tree. At each node, it keeps a lower bound *lb* and an upper bound *ub*. The *lower bound* is an underestimation of the violation degree of any complete assignment below the current node. The *upper bound ub* is the maximum violation degree that we are willing to accept. When $ub \leqslant lb(t)$, the subtree can be pruned because it contains no solution with violation degree lower than *ub*. The time complexity of DFBB is exponential, while its space complexity is linear. The efficiency of DFBB depends largely on its pruning capacity, that relies on the quality of its bounds: the higher *lb* and the lower *ub*, the better DFBB performs, since it does more pruning, exploring a smaller part of the search tree. Thus many efforts have been made to improve (that is, to increase) the lower bound.

While the simplest lower bound computation takes into account just the past variables (that is, those already assigned), more sophisticated lower bounds include contributions of other constraints or variables. For example, a lower bound which considers constraints among past and future variables has been implemented in the *Partial Forward Checking* (PFC) algorithm [50]. Another lower bound, which includes contributions from constraints among future variables, was first implemented in [143] and then used also in [89, 90], where the algorithm PFC-MRDAC has been shown to give a substantial improvement in performance with respect to previous approaches. An alternative lower bound is presented within the *Russian doll search* algorithm [140] and in the *specialized* RDS approach [101].

4.6.3 Inference in Soft Constraints

Inference in classical constraint problems consists of computing and adding implied constraints, producing a problem which is more explicit and hopefully easier to solve. If this process is always capable of solving the problem, then inference is said to be complete. Otherwise, inference is incomplete and it has to be complemented with search. For classical constraints, adaptive consistency enforcing is complete while local consistency (such as arc or path consistency) enforcing is in general incomplete.

Inference in soft constraints keeps the same basic idea: adding constraints that will make the problem more explicit without changing the set of solutions nor their preference. However, with soft constraints, the addition of a new constraint could change the semantics of the constraint problem. There are cases though where an arbitrary implied constraint can be added to an existing soft constraint problem while getting an equivalent problem: when preference combination is idempotent.

Bucket elimination

Bucket elimination (BE) [34, 35] is a complete inference algorithm which is able to compute all optimal solutions of a soft constraint problem (as opposed to one optimal solution, as usually done by search strategies). It is basically the extension of the *adaptive consistency* algorithm [37] to the soft case. BE has both a time and a space complexity which are exponential in the induced width of the constraint graph, which essentially measures the graph cyclicity. The high memory cost, that comes from the high arity of intermediate constraints that have to be stored as tables in memory, is the main drawback of BE to be used in practice. When the arity of these constraints remains reasonable, BE can perform very well [91]. It is always possible to limit the arity of intermediate constraints, at the cost of losing optimality with respect to the returned level and the solution found. This approach is called *mini-bucket elimination* and it is an approximation scheme for BE.

Soft constraint propagation

Because complete inference can be extremely time and space intensive, it is often interesting to have simpler processes which are capable of producing just a lower bound on the violation degree of an optimal solution. Such a lower bound can be immediately useful in Branch and Bound algorithms. This is what soft constraint propagation does.

Constraint propagation is an essential component of any constraint solver. A *local consistency* property is identified (such as arc or path consistency), and an associated enforcing algorithm (usually polynomial) is developed to transform a constraint problem into a unique and equivalent network which satisfies the local consistency property. If this equivalent network has no solution, then the initial network is obviously inconsistent too. This allows one to detect some inconsistencies very efficiently. A similar motivation exists for trying to adapt this approach to soft constraints: the hope that an equivalent locally consistent problem may provide a better lower bound during the search for an optimal solution. The first results in the area were obtained on fuzzy networks [129, 122]. Then, [13, 14] generalized them to semiring-based constraints with idempotent combination.

If we take the usual notions of local consistency like arc or path consistency and replace constraint conjunction by preference combination, and tuple elimination by preference lowering, we immediately obtain a soft constraint propagation algorithm. If preference combination is idempotent, then this algorithm terminates and yields a unique equivalent arc consistent soft constraints problem. Idempotency is only sufficient, and can be slightly relaxed, for termination. It is however possible to show that it is a necessary condition to guarantee equivalence.

However, many real problems do not rely on idempotent operators because such operators provide insufficient discrimination, and rather rely on frameworks such as weighted or lexicographic constraints, which are not idempotent. For these classes of soft constraints, equivalence can still be maintained, compensating the addition of new constraints by the "subtraction" of others. This can be done in all *fair* classes of soft constraints [24], where it is possible to define the notion of "subtraction". In this way, arc consistency has been extended to fair valued structures in [123, 26]. While equivalence and termination in polynomial time can be achieved, constraint propagation on non-idempotent classes of soft constraints does not assure the uniqueness of the resulting problem.

Several global constraints and their associated algorithms have been extended to handle soft constraints. All these proposals have been made using the approach of [111] where a soft constraint is represented as a hard constraint with an extra variable representing the cost of the assignment of the other variables. Examples of global constraints that have been defined for soft constraints are the soft `all-different` and soft `gcc` [112, 138, 139].

4.7 Constraint Logic Programming

Constraints can, and have been, embedded in many programming environments, but some are more suitable than others. The fact that constraints can be seen as relations or predicates, that their conjunction can be seen as a *logical and*, and that backtracking search is a basic methodology to solve them, makes them very compatible with logic programming [94], which is based on predicates, logical conjunctions, and depth-first search. The addition of constraints to logic programming has given the *constraint logic programming* paradigm [77, 98].

4.7.1 Logic Programs

Logic programming (LP) [94] is based on a unique declarative programming idea where programs are not made of statements (like in imperative programming) nor of functions (as in functional programming), but of logical implications between collections of predicates. A logic program is thus seen as a logical theory and has the form of a set of rules (called *clauses*) which relate the truth value of a literal (the *head* of the clause) to that of a collection of other literals (the *body* of the clause).

Executing a logic program means asking for the truth value of a certain statement, called the *goal*. Operationally, this is done by repeatedly transforming the goal via a sequence of *resolution steps*, until we either end up with the empty goal (in this case the proof is successful), or we cannot continue and we do not have the empty goal (and in this case we have a failure), or we continue forever (and in this case we have an infinite computation). Each resolution step involves the unification between a literal which is part of a goal and the head of a clause.

Finite domain CSPs can always be modeled in LP by using one clause for the definition of the problem graph and many facts to define the constraints. However, this modeling is not convenient, since LP's execution engine corresponds to depth-first search with chronological backtracking and this may not be the most efficient way to solve the CSP. Also, it ignores the power of constraint propagation in solving a CSP.

Constraint logic programming languages extend LP by providing many tools to improve the solution efficiency using constraint processing techniques. They also extend

CSPs by accommodating constraints defined via formulas over a specific language of constraints (like arithmetic equations and disequations over the reals, or term equations, or linear disequations over finite domains).

4.7.2   Constraint Logic Programs

Syntactically, constraints are added to logic programming by just considering a specific constraint type (for example, linear equations over the reals) and then allowing constraints of this type in the body of the clauses. Besides the usual resolution engine of logic programming, one has a (complete or incomplete) constraint solving system, which is able to check the consistency of constraints of the considered type. This simple change provides many improvements over logic programming. First, the concept of unification is generalized to constraint solving: the relationship between a goal and a clause (to be used in a resolution step) can be described not just via term equations but via more general statements, that is, constraints. This allows for a more general and flexible way to control the flow of the computation. Second, expressing constraints by some language (for example, linear equations and disequations) gives more compactness and structure. Finally, the presence of an underlying constraint solver, usually based on incomplete constraint propagation of some sort, allows for the combination of backtracking search and constraint propagation, which can give more efficient complete solvers.

To execute a CLP program, at each step we must find a most general unifier between the selected subgoal and the head. Moreover, we have to check the consistency of the current set of constraints with the constraints in the body of the clause. Thus two solvers are involved: unification, and the specific constraint solver for the constraints in use. The constraint consistency check can use some form of constraint propagation, thus applying the principle of combining depth-first backtracking search with constraint propagation, as usual in complete constraint solvers for CSPs.

Exceptional to CLP (and LP) is the existence of three different but equivalent semantics for such programs: declarative, fixpoint, and operational [98]. This means that a CLP program has a declarative meaning in terms of set of first-order formulas but can also be executed operationally on a machine.

CLP is not a single programming language, but a programming *paradigm*, which is parametric with respect to the class of constraints used in the language. Working with a particular CLP language means choosing a specific class of constraints (for example, finite domains, linear, or arithmetic) and a suitable constraint solver for that class. For example, CLP over finite domain constraints uses a constraint solver which is able to perform consistency checks and projection over this kind of constraints. Usually, the consistency check is based on constraint propagation similar to, but weaker than, arc consistency (called *bounds consistency*).

4.7.3   LP and CLP Languages

The concept of logic programming [94, 132] was first developed in the 1970s, while the first constraint logic programming language was Prolog II [23], which was designed by Colmerauer in the early 1980s. Prolog II could treat term equations like Prolog, but in addition could also handle term disequations. After this, Jaffar and Lassez observed that both term equations and disequations were just a special form of constraints, and developed the concept of a constraint logic programming scheme in 1987 [76]. From then on, several instances of the CLP scheme were developed: Prolog III [22], with constraints over terms, strings, booleans, and real linear arithmetic; CLP(R) [75], with constraints over terms and real arithmetics; and CHIP [39], with constraints over terms, finite domains, and finite ranges of integers.

Constraint logic programming over finite domains was first implemented in the late 1980s by Pascal Van Hentenryck [70] within the language CHIP [39]. Since then, newer constraint propagation algorithms have been developed and added to more recent CLP(FD) languages, like GNU Prolog [38] and ECLiPSe [142].

4.7.4 Other Programming Paradigms

Whilst constraints have been provided in declarative languages like CLP, constraint-based tools have also been provided for imperative languages in the form of libraries. The typical programming languages used to develop such solvers are C++ and Java. ILOG [1] is one the most successful companies to produce such constraint-based libraries and tools. ILOG has C++ and Java based constraint libraries, which uses many of the techniques described in this chapter, as well as a constraint-based configurator, scheduler and vehicle routing libraries.

Constraints have also been successfully embedded within concurrent constraint programming [120], where concurrent agents interact by posting and reading constraints in a shared store. Languages which follow this approach to programming are AKL [78] and Oz [71]. Finally, high level modeling languages exist for modeling constraint problems and specifying search strategies. For example, OPL [135] is a modeling language similar to AMPL in which constraint problems can be naturally modeled and the desired search strategy easily specified, while COMET is an OO programming language for constraint-based local search [136]. CHR (Constraint Handling Rules) is instead a rule-based language related to CLP where constraint solvers can be easily modeled [52].

4.8 Beyond Finite Domains

Real-world problems often take us beyond finite domain variables. For example, to reason about power consumption, we might want a decision variable to range over the reals. Constraint programming has therefore been extended to deal with more than just finite (or enumerated) domains of values. In this section, we consider three of the most important extensions.

4.8.1 Intervals

The constraint programming approach to deal with continuous decision variables is typically via intervals [20, 28, 74, 107]. We represent the domain of a continuous variable by a set of disjoint intervals. In practice, the bounds on an interval are represented by machine representable numbers such as floats. We usually solve a continuous problem by finding a covering of the solution space by means of a finite set of multi-dimensional interval boxes with some required precision. Such a covering can be found by means of a branch-and-reduce algorithm which branches (by splitting an interval box in some way into several interval boxes) and reduces (which applies some generalization of local consistency like box or hull consistency to narrow the size of the interval boxes [8]). If we also have an optimization criteria, a bounding procedure can compute bounds on the objective within the interval boxes. Such bounds can be used to eliminate interval boxes which cannot contain the optimal objective value. Alternatively, direct methods for solving a continuous constraint problem involve replacing the classical algebraic operators in the constraints by interval operators and using techniques like Newton's methods to narrow the intervals [137].

4.8.2 Temporal Problems

A special class of continuous constraint problems for which they are specialized and often more efficient solving methods are temporal constraint problems. Time may be represented by points (e.g., the point algebra) or by interval of time points (e.g., the interval algebra). Time points are typically represented by the integers, rationals or reals (or, in practice, by machine representations of these). For the interval algebra (IA), Allen introduced [3] an influential formalism in which constraints on time intervals are expressed in terms of 13 mutually exclusive and exhaustive binary relations (e.g., this interval is before this other interval, or this interval is during this other interval). Deciding the consistency of a set of such interval constraints is NP-complete. In fact, there are 18 maximal tractable (polynomial) subclasses of the interval algebra (e.g., the ORD-Horn subclass introduced by Nebel and Bürckert) [106]. The point algebra (PA) introduced by Vilain and Kautz [141] is more tractable. In this algebra, time points can be constrained by ordering, equality, or a disjunctive combination of ordering and equality constraints. Koubarakis proved that enforcing strong 5-consistency is a necessary and sufficient condition for achieving global consistency on the point algebra. Van Beek gave an $O(n^2)$ algorithm for consistency checking and finding a solution. Identical results hold for the pointisable subclass of the IA (PIA) [141]. This algebra consists of those elements of the IA that can be expressed as a conjunction of binary constraints using only elements of PA. A number of richer representations of temporal information have also been considered including disjunctive binary difference constraints [36] (i.e., $\bigvee_i a_i \leqslant x_j - x_k \leqslant b_i$), and simple disjunctive problems [131] (i.e., $\bigvee_i a_i \leqslant x_i - y_i \leqslant b_i$). Naturally, such richer representations tend to be more intractable.

4.8.3 Sets and other Datatypes

Many combinatorial search problems (e.g., bin packing, set covering, and network design) can be naturally represented in the language of sets, multisets, strings, graphs and other structured objects. Constraint programming has therefore been extended to deal with variables which range over such datatypes. For example, we can represent a decision variable which ranges over sets of integers by means of an upper and lower bound on the possible and necessary elements in the set (e.g., [60]). This is more compact both to represent and reason with than the exponential number of possible sets between these two bounds. Such a representation necessarily throws away some information. We cannot, for example, represent a decision variable which takes one of the two element sets: $\{1, 2\}$ or $\{3, 4\}$. To represent this, we need an empty lower bound and an upper bound of $\{1, 2, 3, 4\}$. Two element sets like $\{2, 3\}$ and $\{1, 4\}$ also lie within these bounds. Local consistency techniques have been extended to deal with such set variables. For instance, a set variable is bound consistent iff all the elements in its lower bound occur in every solution, and all the elements in its upper bound occur in at least one solution. Global constraints have also been defined for such set variables [119, 9, 115] (e.g., a sequence of set variables should be pairwise disjoint). Variables have also been defined over other richer datatypes like multisets (or bags) [87, 145], graphs [40], strings [64] and lattices [46].

4.9 Distributed Constraint Programming

Constraints are often generated by several different agents. Typical examples are scheduling meetings, where each person has his own constraints and all have to be satisfied to find a common time to meet. It is natural in such problems to have a decentralized solving algorithm. Of course, even when constraints are produced by several agents, one could always collect them all in one place and solve them by using a standard centralized algorithm. This certainly saves the time to exchange messages among agents during the execution of a distributed algorithm, which could make the execution slow. However, this is often not desirable, since agents may want to keep some constraints as private. Moreover, a centralized solver makes the whole system less robust.

Formally, a distributed CSP is just a CSP plus one agent for each variable. The agent controls the variable and all its constraints (see, e.g., [147]). Backtracking search, which is the basic form of systematic search for constraint solving, can be easily extended to the distributed case by passing a partial instantiation from an agent to another one, which will add the instantiation for a new variable, or will report the need to backtrack. Forward checking, backjumping, constraint propagation, and variable and value ordering heuristics can also be adapted to this form of distributed *synchronous backtracking*, by sending appropriate messages. However, in synchronous backtracking one agent is active at any given time, so the only advantage with respect to a centralized approach is that agents keep their constraints private.

On the contrary, in asynchronous distributed search, all agents are active at the same time, and they coordinate only to make sure that what they do on their variable is consistent with what other agents do on theirs. Asynchronous backtracking [148] is the main algorithm which follows this approach. Branch and bound can also be adapted to work in a distributed asynchronous setting.

Various improvements to these algorithms can be made. For example, variables can be instantiated with a dynamic rather than a fixed order, and agents can control constraints rather than variables. The Asynchronous Weak Commitment search algorithm [146] adopts a dynamic reordering. However, this is achieved via the use of much more space (to store the nogoods), otherwise completeness is lost.

Other search algorithms can be adapted to a distributed environment. For example, the DPOP algorithm [109] performs distributed dynamic programming. Also local search is very well suited for a distributed setting. In fact, local search works by making incremental modifications to a complete assignment, which are usually local to one or a small number of variables.

Open constraint problems are a different kind of distributed problems, where variable domains are incomplete and can be generated by several distributed agents.

Domains are therefore incrementally discovered, and the aim is to solve the problem even if domains are not completely known. Both solutions and optimal solutions for such problems can be obtained in a distributed way without the need to know the entire domains. This approach can be used within several algorithms, such as the DPOP algorithm for distributed dynamic programming [110].

4.10 Application Areas

Constraint programming has proven useful in important applications from industry, business, manufacturing, and science. In this section, we survey three general application areas—vehicle routine, scheduling, and configuration—with an emphasis on why constraint programming has been successful and why constraint programming is now often the method of choice for solving problems in these domains.

Vehicle Routing is the task of constructing routes for vehicles to visit customers at minimum cost. A vehicle has a maximum capacity which cannot be exceeded and the customers may specify time windows in which deliveries are permitted. Much work on constraint programming approaches to vehicle routing has focused on alternative constraint models and additional implied constraints to increase the amount of pruning performed by constraint propagation. Constraint programming is well-suited for vehicle routing because of its ability to handle real-world (or side) constraints. Vehicle routing problems that arise in practice often have unique constraints that are particular to a business entity. In non-constraint programming approaches, such side constraints often have to be handled in an ad hoc manner. In constraint programming a wide variety of side constraints can be handled simply by adding them to the core model (see, e.g., [86, 108]).

Scheduling is the task of assigning resources to a set of activities to minimize a cost function. Scheduling arises in diverse settings including in the allocation of gates to incoming planes at an airport, crews to an assembly line, and processes to a CPU. Constraint programming approaches to scheduling have aimed at generality, with the ability to seamlessly handle side constraints. As well, much effort has gone into improved implied constraints such as global constraints, edge-finding constraints and timetabling constraints, which lead to powerful constraint propagation. Additional advantages of a constraint propagation approach to scheduling include the ability to form hybrids of backtracking search and local search and the ease with which scheduling or domain specific heuristics can be incorporated within the search routines (see, e.g., [6, 18]).

Configuration is the task of assembling or configuring a customized system from a catalog of components. Configuration arises in diverse settings including in the assembly of home entertainment systems, cars and trucks, and travel packages. Constraint programming is well-suited to configuration because of (i) its flexibility in modeling and the declarativeness of the constraint model, (ii) the ability to explain a failure to find a customized system when the configuration task is over-constrained and to subsequently relax the user's constraints, (iii) the ability to perform interactive configuration where the user makes a sequence of choices and after each choice constraint propagation is used to restrict future possible choices, and (iv) the ability to incorporate reasoning about the user's preferences (see, e.g., [4, 85]).

4.11   Conclusions

Constraint programming is now a relatively mature technology for solving a wide range of difficult combinatorial search problems. The basic ideas behind constraint programming are simple: a declarative representation of the problem constraints, combined with generic solving methods like chronological backtracking or local search. Constraint programming has a number of strengths including: rich modeling languages in which to represent complex and dynamic real-world problems; fast and general purpose inference methods, like enforcing arc consistency, for pruning parts of the search space; fast and special purpose inference methods associated with global constraints; hybrid methods that combine the strengths of constraint programming and operations research; local search methods that quickly find near-optimal solutions; a wide range of extensions like soft constraint solving and distributed constraint solving in which we can represent more closely problems met in practice. As a result, constraint programming is now used in a wide range of businesses and industries including manufacturing, transportation, health care, advertising, telecommunications, financial services, energy and utilities, as well as marketing and sales. Companies like American Express, BMW, Coors, Danone, eBay, France Telecom, General Electric, HP, JB Hunt, LL Bean, Mitsubishi Chemical, Nippon Steel, Orange, Porsche, QAD, Royal Bank of Scotland, Shell, Travelocity, US Postal Service, Visa, Wal-Mart, Xerox, Yves Rocher, and Zurich Insurance all use constraint programming to optimize their business processes. Despite this success, constraint programming is not (and may never be) a push-button technology that works "out of the box". It requires sophisticated users who master a constraint programming system, know how to model problems and how to customize search methods to these models. Future research needs to find ways to lower this barrier to using this powerful technology.

Bibliography

[1] Ilog Solver 4.4. Reference Manual. ILOG SA, Gentilly, France, 1998.

[2] A. Aggoun and N. Beldiceanu. Extending CHIP in order to solve complex scheduling and placement problems. *Math. Comput. Modelling*, 17:57–73, 1993.

[3] J. Allen. Maintaining knowledge about temporal intervals. *Journal ACM*, 26(11):832–843, 1983.

[4] J. Amilhastre, H. Fargier, and P. Marquis. Consistency restoration and explanations in dynamic CSPs: Application to configuration. *Artificial Intelligence*, 135(1–2):199–234, 2002.

[5] K.R. Apt. *Principles of Constraint Programming*. Cambridge University Press, 2003.

[6] P. Baptiste, C. Le Pape, and W. Nuijten. *Constraint-Based Scheduling: Applying Constraint Programming to Scheduling Problems*. Kluwer, 2001.

[7] N. Beldiceanu. Global constraints as graph properties on structured network of elementary constraints of the same type. Technical Report T2000/01, SICS, 2000.

[8] F. Benhamou, D. McAllester, and P. Van Hentenryck. CLP(intervals). In M. Bruynooghe, editor. *Proceedings of International Symposium on Logic Programming*, pages 124–138. MIT Press, 1994.

[9] C. Bessiere, E. Hebrard, B. Hnich, and T. Walsh. Disjoint, partition and intersection constraints for set and multiset variables. In *10th International Conference on Principles and Practices of Constraint Programming (CP-2004)*. Springer-Verlag, 2004.

[10] C. Bessière and J.-C. Régin. MAC and combined heuristics: Two reasons to forsake FC (and CBJ?) on hard problems. In *Proceedings of the Second International Conference on Principles and Practice of Constraint Programming*, pages 61–75, Cambridge, MA, 1996.

[11] C. Bessière, J.-C. Régin, R.H.C. Yap, and Y. Zhang. An optimal coarse-grained arc consistency algorithm. *Artificial Intelligence*, 165:165–185, 2005.

[12] S. Bistarelli, H. Fargier, U. Montanari, F. Rossi, T. Schiex, and G. Verfaillie. Semiring-based CSPs and valued CSPs: Frameworks, properties and comparison. *Constraints*, 4:199–240, 1999.

[13] S. Bistarelli, U. Montanari, and F. Rossi. Constraint solving over semirings. In *Proc. IJCAI 1995*, 1995.

[14] S. Bistarelli, U. Montanari, and F. Rossi. Semiring based constraint solving and optimization. *Journal of the ACM*, 44(2):201–236, 1997.

[15] D. Brélaz. New methods to color the vertices of a graph. *Comm. ACM*, 22:251–256, 1979.

[16] A.A. Bulatov. A dichotomy theorem for constraints on a three-element set. In *Proceedings of 43rd IEEE Symposium on Foundations of Computer Science (FOCS'02)*, pages 649–658, 2002.

[17] M. Carlsson and N. Beldiceanu. Arc-consistency for a chain of lexicographic ordering constraints. Technical report T2002-18 Swedish Institute of Computer Science. ftp://ftp.sics.se/pub/SICS-reports/Reports/SICS-T–2002-18–SE.ps.Z, 2002.

[18] Y. Caseau and F. Laburthe. Improved CLP scheduling with task intervals. In *Proceedings of the Eleventh International Conference on Logic Programming*, pages 369–383, Santa Margherita Ligure, Italy, 1994.

[19] B.M.W. Cheng, K.M.F. Choi, J.H.M. Lee, and J.C.K. Wu. Increasing constraint propagation by redundant modeling: an experience report. *Constraints*, 4:167–192, 1999.

[20] J.G. Cleary. Logical arithmetic. *Future Computing Systems*, 2(2):125–149, 1987.

[21] D.A. Cohen, P. Jeavons, C. Jefferson, K.E. Petrie, and B.M. Smith. Symmetry definitions for constraint satisfaction problems. In P. van Beek, editor. *Proceedings of Eleventh International Conference on Principles and Practice of Constraint Programming (CP2005)*, pages 17–31. Springer, 2005.

[22] A. Colmerauer. An introduction to Prolog-III. *Comm. ACM*, 1990.

[23] A. Colmerauer. Prolog II reference manual and theoretical model. Technical report, Groupe Intelligence Artificielle, Université Aix-Marseille II, October 1982.

[24] M. Cooper. High-order consistency in valued constraint satisfaction. *Constraints*, 10:283–305, 2005.

[25] M. Cooper, D. Cohen, and P. Jeavons. Characterizing tractable constraints. *Artificial Intelligence*, 65:347–361, 1994.

[26] M. Cooper and T. Schiex. Arc consistency for soft constraints. *Artificial Intelligence*, 154(1–2):199–227, April 2004. See arXiv.org/abs/cs.AI/0111038.

[27] J. Crawford, G. Luks, M. Ginsberg, and A. Roy. Symmetry breaking predicates for search problems. In *Proceedings of the 5th International Conference on Knowledge Representation and Reasoning, (KR '96)*, pages 148–159, 1996.

[28] E. Davis. Constraint propagation with interval labels. *Artificial Intelligence*, 32:281–331, 1987.

[29] M. Davis, G. Logemann, and D. Loveland. A machine program for theorem-proving. *Comm. ACM*, 5:394–397, 1962.

[30] M. Davis and H. Putnam. A computing procedure for quantification theory. *J. ACM*, 7:201–215, 1960.

[31] R. Dechter. Learning while searching in constraint satisfaction problems. In *Proceedings of the Fifth National Conference on Artificial Intelligence*, pages 178–183, Philadelphia, 1986.

[32] R. Dechter. Enhancement schemes for constraint processing: Backjumping, learning, and cutset decomposition. *Artificial Intelligence*, 41:273–312, 1990.

[33] R. Dechter. From local to global consistency. *Artificial Intelligence*, 55:87–107, 1992.

[34] R. Dechter. Bucket elimination: A unifying framework for reasoning. *Artificial Intelligence*, 113(1–2):41–85, 1999.

[35] R. Dechter. *Constraint Processing*. Morgan Kaufmann, 2003.

[36] R. Dechter, I. Meiri, and J. Pearl. Temporal constraint networks. *Artificial Intelligence*, 49(1–3):61–95, 1991.

[37] R. Dechter and J. Pearl. Network-based heuristics for constraint-satisfaction problems. *Artificial Intelligence*, 34:1–38, 1988.

[38] D. Diaz. The GNU Prolog web site. http://pauillac.inria.fr/~diaz/gnu-prolog/.

[39] M. Dincbas, P. van Hentenryck, H. Simonis, A. Aggoun, T. Graf, and F. Berthier. The constraint logic programming language CHIP. In *Proc. International Conference on Fifth Generation Computer Systems*, Tokyo, Japan, 1988.

[40] G. Dooms, Y. Deville, and P. Dupont. CP(Graph): Introducing a graph computation domain in constraint programming. In *10th International Conference on Principles and Practices of Constraint Programming (CP-2004)*. Springer-Verlag, 2004.

[41] D. Dubois, H. Fargier, and H. Prade. Using fuzzy constraints in job-shop scheduling. In *Proc. of IJCAI-93/SIGMAN Workshop on Knowledge-based Production Planning, Scheduling and Control Chambery*, France, August 1993.

[42] D. Dubois and H. Prade. *Fuzzy Sets and Systems: Theory and Applications*. Academic Press, 1980.

[43] K. Easton, G. Nemhauser, and M. Trick. Solving the traveling tournament problem: a combined integer programming and constraint programming approach. In *Proceedings of the International Conference on the Practice and Theory of Automated Timetabling (PATAT 2002)*, 2002.

[44] T. Fahle, S. Schamberger, and M. Sellmann. Symmetry breaking. In T. Walsh, editor. *Proceedings of 7th International Conference on Principles and Practice of Constraint Programming (CP2001)*, pages 93–107. Springer, 2001.

[45] H. Fargier, J. Lang, and T. Schiex. Selecting preferred solutions in fuzzy constraint satisfaction problems. In *Proc. of the 1st European Congress on Fuzzy and Intelligent Technologies*, 1993.

[46] A.J. Fernandez and P.M. Hill. An interval constraint system for lattice domains. *ACM Transactions on Programming Languages and Systems (TOPLAS-2004)*, 26(1), 2004.

[47] P. Flener, A. Frisch, B. Hnich, Z. Kiziltan, I. Miguel, J. Pearson, and T. Walsh. Breaking row and column symmetry in matrix models. In *8th International Conference on Principles and Practices of Constraint Programming (CP-2002)*. Springer, 2002.

[48] P. Flener, A. Frisch, B. Hnich, Z. Kiziltan, I. Miguel, and T. Walsh. Matrix modelling. Technical Report APES-36-2001, APES group. Available from http://www.dcs.st-and.ac.uk/~apes/reports/apes-36-2001.ps.gz, 2001. Presented at FORMUL'01 Workshop on Modelling and Problem Formulation, CP2001 post-conference workshop.

[49] E.C. Freuder. Synthesizing constraint expressions. *Comm. ACM*, 21:958–966, 1978.

[50] E.C. Freuder and R.J. Wallace. Partial constraint satisfaction. *Artificial Intelligence*, 58:21–70, 1992.

[51] A. Frisch, B. Hnich, Z. Kiziltan, I. Miguel, and T. Walsh. Global constraints for lexicographic orderings. In *8th International Conference on Principles and Practices of Constraint Programming (CP-2002)*. Springer, 2002.

[52] T. Frühwirth. Theory and practice of constraint handling rules. *Journal of Logic Programming*, 37:95–138, 1998.

[53] T. Frühwirth and S. Abdennadher. *Essentials of Constraint Programming*. Springer, 2003.

[54] J. Gaschnig. A constraint satisfaction method for inference making. In *Proceedings Twelfth Annual Allerton Conference on Circuit and System Theory*, pages 866–874, Monticello, IL, 1974.

[55] J. Gaschnig. Experimental case studies of backtrack vs. Waltz-type vs. new algorithms for satisfying assignment problems. In *Proceedings of the Second Canadian Conference on Artificial Intelligence*, pages 268–277, Toronto, 1978.

[56] P.A. Geelen. Dual viewpoint heuristics for binary constraint satisfaction problems. In *Proceedings of the 10th European Conference on Artificial Intelligence*, pages 31–35, Vienna, 1992.

[57] P.A. Geelen. Dual viewpoint heuristics for binary constraint satisfaction problems. In *Proceedings of the 10th ECAI*, pages 31–35, European Conference on Artificial Intelligence, 1992.

[58] I.P. Gent, E. MacIntyre, P. Prosser, B.M. Smith, and T. Walsh. An empirical study of dynamic variable ordering heuristics for the constraint satisfaction problem. In *Proceedings of the Second International Conference on Principles and Practice of Constraint Programming*, pages 179–193, Cambridge, MA, 1996.

[59] I.P. Gent and B.M. Smith. Symmetry breaking in constraint programming. In W. Horn, editor. *Proceedings of ECAI-2000*, pages 599–603. IOS Press, 2000.

[60] C. Gervet. Interval propagation to reason about sets: definition and implementation of a practical language. *Constraints*, 1(3):191–244, 1997.

[61] M.L. Ginsberg. Dynamic backtracking. *J. Artificial Intelligence Res.*, 1:25–46, 1993.

[62] M.L. Ginsberg, M. Frank, M.P. Halpin, and M.C. Torrance. Search lessons learned from crossword puzzles. In *Proceedings of the Eighth National Conference on Artificial Intelligence*, pages 210–215, Boston, MA, 1990.

[63] F. Glover and M. Laguna. *Tabu Search*. Kluwer, 1997.

[64] K. Golden and W. Pang. Constraint reasoning over strings. In F. Rossi, editor. *Proceedings of Ninth International Conference on Principles and Practice of Constraint Programming (CP2003)*, pages 377–391. Springer, 2003.

[65] S. Golomb and L. Baumert. Backtrack programming. *J. ACM*, 12:516–524, 1965.

[66] C. Gomes, B. Selman, N. Crato, and H. Kautz. Heavy-tailed phenomena in satisfiability and constraint satisfaction problems. *J. Automated Reasoning*, 24:67–100, 2000.

[67] G. Gottlob, N. Leone, and F. Scarcello. A comparison of structural CSP decomposition methods. *Artificial Intelligence*, 124(2):243–282, 2000.

[68] R.M. Haralick and G.L. Elliott. Increasing tree search efficiency for constraint satisfaction problems. *Artificial Intelligence*, 14:263–313, 1980.

[69] W.D. Harvey. Nonsystematic backtracking search. PhD thesis, Stanford University, 1995.

[70] P. Van Hentenryck. *Constraint Satisfaction in Logic Programming*. MIT Press, 1989.

[71] M. Henz, G. Smolka, and J. Wurtz. Oz—a programming language for multi-agent systems. In *Proc. 13th IJCAI*, 1995.

[72] J. Hooker. *Logic-Based Methods for Optimization: Combining Optimization and Constraint Satisfaction*. Wiley, New York, 2000.

[73] H.H. Hoos and T. Stützle. *Stochastic Local Search: Foundations and Applications*. Morgan Kaufmann, 2004.

[74] E. Hyvönen. Constraint reasoning based on interval arithmetic. *Artificial Intelligence*, 58:71–112, 1992.

[75] J. Jaffar, et al. The CLP(R) language and system *ACM Transactions on Programming Languages and Systems*, 1992.

[76] J. Jaffar and J.L. Lassez. Constraint logic programming. In *Proc. POPL*. ACM, 1987.

[77] J. Jaffar and M.J. Maher. Constraint logic programming: A survey. *Journal of Logic Programming*, 19–20, 1994.

[78] S. Janson. AKL—A multiparadigm programming language, PhD thesis, Uppsala Theses in Computer Science 19, ISSN 0283-359X, ISBN 91-506-1046-5, Uppsala University, and SICS Dissertation Series 14, ISSN 1101-1335, ISRN SICS/D-14-SE, 1994.

[79] P. Jeavons, D.A. Cohen, and M. Cooper. Constraints, consistency and closure. *Artificial Intelligence*, 101(1–2):251–265, 1998.

[80] P. Jeavons, D.A. Cohen, and M. Gyssens. Closure properties of constraints. *J. ACM*, 44:527–548, 1997.

[81] P. Jeavons, D.A. Cohen, and M. Gyssens. How to determine the expressive power of constraints. *Constraints*, 4:113–131, 1999.

[82] P. Jeavons and M. Cooper. Tractable constraints on ordered domains. *Artificial Intelligence*, 79:327–339, 1995.

[83] D.S. Johnson, C.R. Aragon, L.A. McGeoch, and C. Schevon. Optimization by simulated annealing: An experimental evaluation: Part II. Graph coloring and number partitioning. *Operations Research*, 39(3):378–406, 1991.

[84] P. Jonsson and C. Backstrom. A unifying approach to temporal constraint reasoning. *Artificial Intelligence*, 102:143–155, 1998.

[85] U. Junker and D. Mailharro. Preference programming: Advanced problem solving for configuration. *Artificial Intelligence for Engineering Design, Analysis and Manufacturing*, 17(1):13–29, 2003.

[86] P. Kilby, P. Prosser, and P. Shaw. A comparison of traditional and constraint-based heuristic methods on vehicle routing problems with side constraints. *Constraints*, 5(4):389–414, 2000.

[87] Z. Kiziltan and T. Walsh. Constraint programming with multisets. In *Proceedings of the 2nd International Workshop on Symmetry in Constraint Satisfaction Problems (SymCon-02)*, 2002. Held alongside CP-02.

[88] M. Koubarakis. Tractable disjunctions of linear constraints. In E.C. Freuder, editor. *Proceedings of Second International Conference on Principles and Practice of Constraint Programming (CP96)*, pages 297–307. Springer, 1996.

[89] J. Larrosa and P. Meseguer. Exploiting the use of DAC in Max-CSP. In *Proc. of CP'96*, pages 308–322, Boston (MA), 1996.

[90] J. Larrosa and P. Meseguer. Partition-based lower bound for Max-CSP. In *Proc. of the 5th International Conference on Principles and Practice of Constraint Programming (CP-99)*, pages 303–315, 1999.

[91] J. Larrosa, E. Morancho, and D. Niso. On the practical applicability of bucket elimination: Still-life as a case study. *Journal of Artificial Intelligence Research*, 23:421–440, 2005.

[92] Y.C. Law and J.H.M. Lee. Global constraints for integer and set value precedence. In *Proceedings of 10th International Conference on Principles and Practice of Constraint Programming (CP2004)*, pages 362–376. Springer, 2004.

[93] Y.C. Law and J.H.M. Lee. Breaking value symmetries in matrix models using channeling constraints. In *Proceedings of the 20th Annual ACM Symposium on Applied Computing (SAC-2005)*, pages 375–380, 2005.

[94] J.W. Lloyd. *Foundations of Logic Programming*. Springer-Verlag, 1993.

[95] A.K. Mackworth. Consistency in networks of relations. *Artificial Intelligence*, 8:99–118, 1977.

[96] A.K. Mackworth. On reading sketch maps. In *Proceedings of the Fifth International Joint Conference on Artificial Intelligence*, pages 598–606, Cambridge, MA, 1977.

[97] A.K. Mackworth. Consistency in networks of relations. *Artificial Intelligence*, 8:99–118, 1977.

[98] K. Marriott and P.J. Stuckey. *Programming with Constraints: An Introduction*. MIT Press, 1998.

[99] J.J. McGregor. Relational consistency algorithms and their application in finding subgraph and graph isomorphisms. *Inform. Sci.*, 19:229–250, 1979.

[100] K. Mehlhorn and S. Thiel. Faster algorithms for bound-consistency of the sortedness and alldifferent constraint. In *Proceedings of the Sixth International Conference on Principles and Practice of Constraint Programming*, pages 306–319, Singapore, 2000.

[101] P. Meseguer and M. Sanchez. Specializing Russian doll search. In *Principles and Practice of Constraint Programming — CP 2001, LNCS*, vol. 2239, Paphos, Cyprus, November 2001, pages 464–478. Springer-Verlag, 2001.

[102] S. Minton, M.D. Johnston, A.B. Philips, and P. Laird. Minimizing conflicts: A heuristic repair method for constraint satisfaction and scheduling problems. *Artificial Intelligence*, 58:161–206, 1992.

[103] R. Mohr and G. Masini. Good old discrete relaxation. In *Proceedings of the 8th European Conference on Artificial Intelligence*, pages 651–656, Munchen, Germany, 1988.

[104] U. Montanari. Networks of constraints: Fundamental properties and applications to picture processing. *Inform. Sci.*, 7:95–132, 1974.

[105] U. Montanari. Networks of constraints: Fundamental properties and applications to picture processing. *Inform. Sci.*, 7:95–132, 1974.

[106] B. Nebel and H.-J. Burckert. Reasoning about temporal relations: A maximal tractable subclass of Allen's interval algebra. *J. ACM*, 42(1):43–66, 1995.

[107] W.J. Older and A. Vellino. Extending Prolog with constraint arithmetic on real intervals. In *Proceedings of IEEE Canadian Conference on Electrical and Computer Engineering*. IEEE Computer Society Press, 1990.

[108] G. Pesant, M. Gendreau, J. Potvin, and J. Rousseau. An exact constraint logic programming algorithm for the traveling salesman problem with time windows. *Transportation Science*, 32(1):12–29, 1998.

[109] A. Petcu and B. Faltings. A scalable method for multiagent constraint optimization. In *Proceedings of the 19th IJCAI*, pages 266–271, 2005.

[110] A. Petcu and B. Faltings. ODPOP: An algorithm for open distributed constraint optimization. In *AAMAS 06 Workshop on Distributed Constraint Reasoning*, 2006.

[111] T. Petit, J.-C. Régin, and C. Bessière. Meta-constraints on violations for over constrained problems. In *IEEE–ICTAI'2000 International Conference*, pages 358–365, Vancouver, Canada, November 2000.

[112] T. Petit, J.-C. Régin, and C. Bessière. Specific filtering algorithms for over-constrained problems. In *Principles and Practice of Constraint Programming— CP 2001, LNCS*, vol. 2239, Paphos, Cyprus, November 2001, pages 451–463. Springer-Verlag, 2001.

[113] P. Prosser. Hybrid algorithms for the constraint satisfaction problem. *Computational Intelligence*, 9:268–299, 1993.

[114] J.-F. Puget. Breaking all value symmetries in surjection problems. In P. van Beek, editor. *Proceedings of Eleventh International Conference on Principles and Practice of Constraint Programming (CP2005)*. Springer, 2005.

[115] C.-G. Quimper and T. Walsh. Beyond finite domains: The all different and global cardinality constraints. In *11th International Conference on Principles and Practices of Constraint Programming (CP-2005)*. Springer-Verlag, 2005.

[116] J.-C. Régin. A filtering algorithm for constraints of difference in CSPs. In *Proceedings of the Twelfth National Conference on Artificial Intelligence*, pages 362–367, Seattle, 1994.

[117] J.-C. Régin. Generalized arc consistency for global cardinality constraint. In *Proceedings of the Thirteenth National Conference on Artificial Intelligence*, pages 209–215, Portland, OR, 1996.

[118] C. Roney-Dougal, I. Gent, T. Kelsey, and S. Linton. Tractable symmetry breaking using restricted search trees. In *Proceedings of ECAI-2004*. IOS Press, 2004.

[119] A. Sadler and C. Gervet. Global reasoning on sets. In *Proceedings of Workshop
on Modelling and Problem Formulation (FORMUL'01)*, 2001. Held alongside
CP-01.

[120] V. Saraswat. *Concurrent Constraint Programming*. MIT Press, 1993.

[121] T. Schaefer. The complexity of satisfiability problems. In *Proceedings of 10th
ACM Symposium on Theory of Computation*, pages 216–226, 1978.

[122] T. Schiex. Possibilistic constraint satisfaction problems or "How to handle soft
constraints? In *Proc. of the 8th Int. Conf. on Uncertainty in Artificial Intelligence*, Stanford, CA, July 1992.

[123] T. Schiex. Arc consistency for soft constraints. In *Principles and Practice of
Constraint Programming—CP 2000, LNCS*, vol. 1894, Singapore, September
2000, pages 411–424. Springer, 2000.

[124] T. Schiex, H. Fargier, and G. Verfaillie. Valued constraint satisfaction problems:
hard and easy problems. In *Proc. IJCAI 1995*, pages 631–637, 1995.

[125] T. Schiex and G. Verfaillie. Nogood recording for static and dynamic constraint
satisfaction problems. *International Journal on Artificial Intelligence Tools*,
3:1–15, 1994.

[126] M. Sellmann and P. Van Hentenryck. Structural symmetry breaking. In *Proceedings of the 19th IJCAI, International Joint Conference on Artificial Intelligence*,
2005.

[127] B. Selman, H. Levesque, and D.G. Mitchell. A new method for solving hard
satisfiability problems. In *Proceedings of the Tenth National Conference on Artificial Intelligence*, pages 440–446, San Jose, CA, 1992.

[128] B. Smith, K. Stergiou, and T. Walsh. Using auxiliary variables and implied constraints to model non-binary problems. In *Proceedings of the 16th National
Conference on AI*, pages 182–187. American Association for Artificial Intelligence, 2000.

[129] P. Snow and E.C. Freuder. Improved relaxation and search methods for approximate constraint satisfaction with a maximin criterion. In *Proc. of the 8th Biennal
Conf. of the Canadian Society for Comput. Studies of Intelligence*, pages 227–
230, May 1990.

[130] R.M. Stallman and G.J. Sussman. Forward reasoning and dependency-directed
backtracking in a system for computer-aided circuit analysis. *Artificial Intelligence*, 9:135–196, 1977.

[131] K. Stergiou and M. Koubarakis. Backtracking algorithms for disjunctions of
temporal constraints. *Artificial Intelligence*, 120(1):81–117, 2000.

[132] L. Sterling and E. Shapiro. *The Art of Prolog*. MIT Press, 1994.

[133] P. van Beek. On the minimality and decomposability of constraint networks. In
Proceedings of 10th National Conference on Artificial Intelligence, pages 447–
452. AAAI Press/The MIT Press, 1992.

[134] P. van Beek and R. Dechter. Constraint tightness and looseness versus local and
global consistency. *J. ACM*, 44:549–566, 1997.

[135] P. van Hentenryck. *The OPL Optimization Programming Language*. MIT Press,
1999.

[136] P. van Hentenryck and L. Michel. *Constraint-Based Local Search*. MIT Press,
2005.

[137] P. van Hentenryck, L. Michel, and Y. Deville. *Numerica: A Modeling Language for Global Optimization*. MIT Press, 1997.

[138] W.J. van Hoeve. A hyper-arc consistency algorithm for the soft alldifferent constraint. In *Proc. of the Tenth International Conference on Principles and Practice of Constraint Programming (CP 2004), LNCS*, vol. 3258. Springer, 2004.

[139] W.J. van Hoeve, G. Pesant, and L.-M. Rousseau. On global warming (softening global constraints). In *Proc. of the 6th International Workshop on Preferences and Soft Constraints*, Toronto, Canada, 2004.

[140] G. Verfaillie, M. Lemaître, and T. Schiex. Russian doll search. In *Proc. AAAI 1996*, pages 181–187, Portland, OR, 1996.

[141] M. Vilain and H. Kautz. Constraint propagation algorithms for temporal reasoning. In *Proceedings of 5th National Conference on Artificial Intelligence*, pages 377–382. Morgan Kaufmann, 1986.

[142] M. Wallace, S. Novello, and J. Schimpf. ECLiPSe: A platform for constraint logic programming. *ICL Systems Journal*, 12(1):159–200, 1997. Available via http://eclipse.crosscoreop.com/eclipse/reports/index.html.

[143] R.J. Wallace. Directed arc consistency preprocessing. In M. Meyer, editor. *Selected Papers from the ECAI-94 Workshop on Constraint Processing, LNCS*, vol. 923, pages 121–137. Springer, Berlin, 1995.

[144] T. Walsh. Search in a small world. In *Proceedings of the Sixteenth International Joint Conference on Artificial Intelligence*, pages 1172–1177, Stockholm, 1999.

[145] T. Walsh. Consistency and propagation with multiset constraints: A formal viewpoint. In F. Rossi, editor. *9th International Conference on Principles and Practices of Constraint Programming (CP-2003)*. Springer, 2003.

[146] M. Yokoo. Weak-commitment search for solving constraint satisfaction problems. In *Proceedings of the 12th AAAI*, pages 313–318, 1994.

[147] M. Yokoo. *Distributed Constraint Satisfaction: Foundation of Cooperation in Multi-Agent Systems*. Springer, 2001.

[148] M. Yokoo, E.H. Durfee, T. Ishida, and K. Kuwabara. Distributed constraint satisfaction for formalizing distributed problem solving. In *Proceedings of the 12th ICDCS*, pages 614–621, 1992.

[149] Y. Zhang, R. Yap, and J. Jaffar. Functional eliminations and 0/1/all constraints. In *Proceedings of 16th National Conference on Artificial Intelligence*, pages 281–290. AAAI Press/The MIT Press, 1999.

Handbook of Knowledge Representation
Edited by F. van Harmelen, V. Lifschitz and B. Porter
© 2008 Elsevier B.V. All rights reserved
DOI: 10.1016/S1574-6526(07)03005-2

Chapter 5

Conceptual Graphs

John F. Sowa

Abstract
A conceptual graph (CG) is a graph representation for logic based on the semantic networks of artificial intelligence and the existential graphs of Charles Sanders Peirce. Several versions of CGs have been designed and implemented over the past thirty years. The simplest are the typeless *core* CGs, which correspond to Peirce's original existential graphs. More common are the *extended* CGs, which are a typed superset of the core. The *research* CGs have explored novel techniques for reasoning, knowledge representation, and natural language semantics. The semantics of the core and extended CGs is defined by a formal mapping to and from the ISO standard for Common Logic, but the research CGs are defined by a variety of formal and informal extensions. This article surveys the notation, applications, and reasoning methods used with CGs and their mapping to and from other versions of logic.

5.1 From Existential Graphs to Conceptual Graphs

During the 1960s, graph-based semantic representations were popular in both theoretical and computational linguistics. At one of the most impressive conferences of the decade, Margaret Masterman [21] introduced a graph-based notation, called a *semantic network*, which included a lattice of concept types; Silvio Ceccato [1] presented *correlational nets*, which were based on 56 different relations, including subtype, instance, part-whole, case relations, kinship relations, and various kinds of attributes; and David Hays [15] presented *dependency graphs*, which formalized the notation developed by the linguist Lucien Tesnière [40]. The early graph notations represented the relational structures underlying natural language semantics, but none of them could express full first-order logic. Woods [42] and McDermott [22] wrote scathing critiques of their logical weaknesses.

In the late 1970s, many graph notations were designed to represent first-order logic or a formally-defined subset [7]. Sowa [32] developed a version of *conceptual graphs* (CGs) as an intermediate language for mapping natural language questions and assertions to a relational database. Fig. 5.1 shows a CG for the sentence *John is going to*

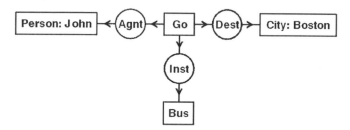

Figure 5.1: CG display form for *John is going to Boston by bus.*

Boston by bus. The rectangles are called *concepts*, and the circles are called *conceptual relations.* An arc pointing toward a circle marks the first *argument* of the relation, and an arc pointing away from a circle marks the last argument. If a relation has only one argument, the arrowhead is omitted. If a relation has more than two arguments, the arrowheads are replaced by integers $1, \ldots, n$.

The conceptual graph in Fig. 5.1 represents a typed or sorted version of logic. Each of the four concepts has a *type label*, which represents the type of entity the concept refers to: Person, Go, Boston, or Bus. Two of the concepts have *names*, which identify the referent: John or Boston. Each of the three conceptual relations has a type label that represents the type of relation: agent (Agnt), destination (Dest), or instrument (Inst). The CG as a whole indicates that the person John is the agent of some instance of going, the city Boston is the destination, and a bus is the instrument. Fig. 5.1 can be translated to the following formula:

$$(\exists x)(\exists y)(\text{Go}(x) \wedge \text{Person(John)} \wedge \text{City(Boston)} \wedge \text{Bus}(y) \wedge$$

$$\text{Agnt}(x, \text{John}) \wedge \text{Dest}(x, \text{Boston}) \wedge \text{Inst}(x, y)).$$

As this translation shows, the only logical operators used in Fig. 5.1 are conjunction and the existential quantifier. Those two operators are the most common in translations from natural languages, and many of the early semantic networks could not represent any others.

For his pioneering *Begriffsschrift* (concept writing), Frege [8] adopted a tree notation for representing full first-order logic, using only four operators: assertion (the "turnstile" operator $\vdash$), negation (a short vertical line), implication (a hook), and the universal quantifier (a cup containing the bound variable). Fig. 5.2 shows the Begriffsschrift equivalent of Fig. 5.1, and following is its translation to predicate calculus:

$$\sim(\forall x)(\forall y)(\text{Go}(x) \supset (\text{Person(John)} \supset (\text{City(Boston)} \supset$$

$$(\text{Bus}(y) \supset (\text{Agnt}(x, \text{John}) \supset (\text{Dest}(x, \text{Boston}) \supset \sim \text{Inst}(x, y)))))))$$

Frege's choice of operators simplified his rules of inference, but they lead to awkward paraphrases: *It is false that for every x and y, if x is an instance of going then if John is a person then if Boston is a city then if y is a bus then if the agent of x is John then if the destination of x is Boston then the instrument of x is not y.*

Unlike Frege, who rejected Boolean algebra, Peirce developed the algebraic notation for first-order logic as a generalization of the Boolean operators. Since Boole treated disjunction as logical addition and conjunction as logical multiplication,

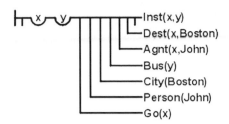

Figure 5.2: Frege's Begriffsschrift for *John is going to Boston by bus.*

Peirce [24] represented the existential quantifier by Σ for repeated disjunction and the universal quantifier by Π for repeated conjunction. In the notation of Peirce [25], Fig. 5.1 could be represented

$$\Sigma_x \Sigma_y (\text{Go}(x) \bullet \text{Person}(\text{John}) \bullet \text{City}(\text{Boston}) \bullet \text{Bus}(y) \bullet$$

$$\text{Agnt}(x, \text{John}) \bullet \text{Dest}(x, \text{Boston}) \bullet \text{Inst}(x, y)).$$

Peano adopted Peirce's notation, but he invented new symbols because he wanted to mix mathematical and logical symbols in the same formulas. Meanwhile, Peirce began to experiment with *relational graphs* for representing logic, as in Fig. 5.3. In that graph, an existential quantifier is represented by *a line of identity*, and conjunction is the default Boolean operator. Since Peirce's graphs did not distinguish proper names, the monadic predicates isJohn and isBoston may be used to represent names. Following is the algebraic notation for Fig. 5.3:

$$\Sigma_x \Sigma_y \Sigma_z \Sigma_w (\text{Go}(x) \bullet \text{Person}(y) \bullet \text{isJohn}(y) \bullet \text{City}(z) \bullet \text{isBoston}(z) \bullet$$

$$\text{Bus}(w) \bullet \text{Agnt}(x, y) \bullet \text{Dest}(x, z) \bullet \text{Inst}(x, w)).$$

Peirce experimented with various graphic methods for representing the other operators of his algebraic notation, but like the AI researchers of the 1960s, he could not find a good way of expressing the scope of quantifiers and negation. In 1897, however, he discovered a simple, but brilliant innovation for his new version of *existential graphs* (EGs): an oval enclosure for showing scope [27]. The default operator for an oval with no other marking is negation, but any metalevel relation can be linked to the oval. Sowa [33] adopted Peirce's convention for CGs, but with rectangles instead of ovals: rectangles nest better than ovals; and more importantly, each context box can be interpreted as a concept box that contains a nested CG. A nest of two negations

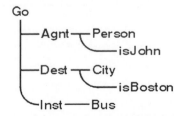

Figure 5.3: Peirce's relational graph for *John is going to Boston by bus.*

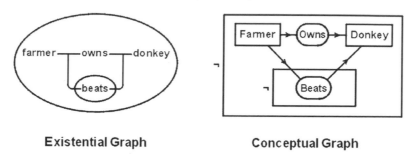

Existential Graph   **Conceptual Graph**

Figure 5.4: EG and CG for *If a farmer owns a donkey, then he beats it.*

indicates an implication, as in Fig. 5.4, which shows an EG and a CG for the sentence *If a farmer owns a donkey, then he beats it.*

As Fig. 5.4 illustrates, the primary difference between EGs and CGs is the interpretation of the links: in EGs, each line of identity represents an existentially quantified variable, which is attached to the relations; in CGs, the concept boxes represent existential quantifiers, and the arcs merely link relation nodes to their arguments. Another difference is that the CG type labels become monadic relations in EGs. Unlike EGs, in which an unmarked oval represents negation, the symbol ~ marks a negated CG context. Both the EG and the CG could be represented by the following formula:

$$\sim(\exists x)(\exists y)(\text{Farmer}(x) \wedge \text{Donkey}(y) \wedge \text{Owns}(x, y) \wedge \sim\text{Beats}(x, y)).$$

In order to preserve the correct scope of quantifiers, the implication operator ⊃ cannot be used to represent the English *if–then* construction unless the existential quantifiers are moved to the front and converted to universals:

$$(\forall x)(\forall y)((\text{Farmer}(x) \wedge \text{Donkey}(y) \wedge \text{Owns}(x, y)) \supset \text{Beats}(x, y)).$$

In English, this formula could be read *For every x and y, if x is a farmer who owns a donkey y, then x beats y.* The unusual nature of this paraphrase led Kamp [18] to develop *discourse representation structures* (DRSs) whose logical structure is isomorphic to Peirce's existential graphs (Fig. 5.5).

Kamp's primitives are the same as Peirce's: the default quantifier is the existential, and the default Boolean operator is conjunction; negation is represented by a context box, and implication is represented by two contexts. As Fig. 5.5 illustrates, the nesting

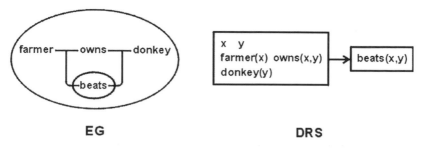

EG   **DRS**

Figure 5.5: EG and DRS for *If a farmer owns a donkey, then he beats it.*

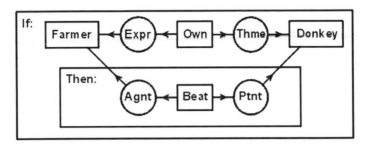

Figure 5.6: CG with case relations shown explicitly.

of Peirce's contexts allows the quantifiers in the antecedent of an implication to include the consequent within their scope. Although Kamp connected his boxes with an arrow, he made exactly the same assumption about the scope of quantifiers. Kamp and Reyle [19] went much further than Peirce in analyzing discourse and formulating the rules for interpreting anaphoric references, but any rule stated in terms of the DRS notation can also be applied to the EG or CG notation.

The CG in Fig. 5.4 represents the verbs *owns* and *beats* as dyadic relations. That was the choice of relations selected by Kamp, and it can also be used with the EG or CG notation. Peirce, however, noted that the event or state expressed by a verb is also an entity that could be referenced by a quantified variable. That point was independently rediscovered by linguists, computational linguists, and philosophers such as Davidson [6]. The CG in Fig. 5.6 shows a representation that treats events and states as entities linked to their participants by *case relations* or *thematic roles*.

The type labels If and Then in Fig. 5.6 are defined as synonyms for negated contexts. The state of owning is linked to its participants by the relations experiencer (Expr) and theme (Thme), and the act of beating by the relations agent (Agnt) and patient (Ptnt). Following is the equivalent in typed predicate calculus:

$$\sim(\exists x{:}\text{Farmer})(\exists y{:}\text{Own})(\exists z{:}\text{Donkey})(\text{Expr}(y, x) \wedge (\text{Thme}(y, z) \wedge$$

$$\sim(\exists w{:}\text{Beat})(\text{Agnt}(w, x) \wedge \text{Ptnt}(w, z))).$$

The model-theoretic semantics for the EGs and CGs shown in this section is specified in the ISO standard for Common Logic (CL) [17]. Section 5.2 of this article briefly describes the CL project, the CL model theory, and the mapping of the CL abstract syntax to and from the Conceptual Graph Interchange Format (CGIF), a linear notation that represents every semantic feature of the graphs. Section 5.3 presents the *canonical formation rules* for CGs and their use with Peirce's rules of inference for full FOL. Section 5.4 presents the use of CGs for representing propositions, situations, and metalevel reasoning. Section 5.5 discusses research issues that have inspired a variety of formal and informal extensions to the conceptual graph theory and notation.

5.2 Common Logic

Common Logic (CL) evolved from two projects to develop parallel ANSI standards for conceptual graphs and the Knowledge Interchange Format [9]. Eventually, those two projects were merged into a single ISO project to develop a common abstract syntax and model-theoretic foundation for a family of logic-based notations [17]. Hayes and Menzel [13] defined a very general model theory for CL, which Hayes and McBride [12] used to define the semantics for the languages RDF(S) and OWL. In addition to the abstract syntax and model theory, the CL standard specifies three concrete dialects that are capable of expressing the full CL semantics: the Common Logic Interchange Format (CLIF), the Conceptual Graph Interchange Format (CGIF), and the XML-based notation for CL (XCL). RDF and OWL can also be considered dialects that express subsets of the CL semantics: any statement in RDF or OWL can be translated to CLIF, CGIF, or XCL, but only a subset can be translated back to RDF or OWL.

The CL syntax allows quantifiers to range over functions and relations, but CL retains a first-order style of model theory and proof theory. To support a higher-order syntax, but without the computational complexity of higher-order semantics, the CL model theory uses a single domain D that includes individuals, functions, and relations. The option of limiting the domain of quantification to a single set was suggested by Quine [29] and used in various theorem provers that allow quantifiers to range over relations [3].

Conceptual graphs had been a typed version of logic since the first publication in 1976, but Peirce's untyped existential graphs are sufficiently general to express the full CL semantics. Therefore, two versions of the Conceptual Graph Interchange Format are defined in the ISO standard:

1. **Core CGIF**. A typeless version of logic that expresses the full CL semantics. This dialect corresponds to Peirce's existential graphs: its only primitives are conjunction, negation, and the existential quantifier. It does permit quantifiers to range over relations, but Peirce also experimented with that option for EGs.

2. **Extended CGIF**. An upward compatible extension of the core, which adds a universal quantifier; type labels for restricting the range of quantifiers; Boolean contexts with type labels If, Then, Either, Or, Equivalence, and Iff; and the option of importing external text into any CGIF text.

Although extended CGIF is a typed language, it is not *strongly typed*, because type labels are used only to restrict the range of quantifiers. Instead of causing a syntax error, as in the strongly typed logic Z [16], a type mismatch in CGIF just causes the subexpression in which the mismatch occurs to be false. If a typed sentence in Z is translated to CGIF, it will have the same truth value in both languages, but a type mismatch, such as the following, is handled differently in each:

```
~[ [Elephant: 23] ]
```

This CGIF sentence, which is syntactically correct and semantically true, says that 23 is not an elephant. If translated to Z, however, the type mismatch would cause a syntax error. The more lenient method of handling types is necessary for representing sentences derived from other languages, both natural and artificial. RDF and OWL, for example, can be translated to CGIF and CLIF, but not to Z.

The conceptual graph in Fig. 5.1, which represents the sentence *John is going to Boston by bus*, can be written in the following form in extended CGIF:

```
[Go *x] [Person: John] [City: Boston] [Bus *y]
(Agnt ?x John) (Dest ?x Boston) (Inst ?x ?y)
```

In CGIF, concepts are marked by square brackets, and conceptual relations are marked by parentheses. A character string prefixed with an asterisk, such as *x, marks a *defining node*, which may be referenced by the same string prefixed with a question mark, ?x. These strings, which are called *name sequences* in Common Logic, represent *coreference labels* in CGIF and variables in other versions of logic. Following is the equivalent in CLIF:

```
(exists ((x Go) (y Bus))
    (and (Person John) (city Boston)
        (Agnt x John) (Dest x Boston) (Inst x y) ))
```

In the CL standard, extended CGIF is defined by a translation to core CGIF, which is defined by a translation to the CL abstract syntax. Following is the untyped core CGIF and the corresponding CLIF for the above examples:

```
[*x] [*y]
(Go ?x) (Person John) (City Boston) (Bus ?y)
(Agnt ?x John) (Dest ?x Boston) (Inst ?x ?y)

(exists (x y)
    (and (Go x) (Person John) (city Boston) (Bus y)
        (Agnt x John) (Dest x Boston) (Inst x y) ))
```

In core CGIF, the most common use for concept nodes is to represent existential quantifiers. A node such as [*x] corresponds to an EG line of identity, such as the one attached to the relation Go in Fig. 5.3. It is permissible to write names in a concept node such as [: John], but in most cases, such nodes are unnecessary because names can also be written in relation nodes. A concept node may contain more than one name or coreference label, such as [: John ?z]. In EGs, that node corresponds to a *ligature* that links two lines of identity; in CLIF, it corresponds to an equality: (= John z).

Although CGIF and CLIF look similar, there are several fundamental differences:

1. Since CGIF is a serialized representation of a graph, labels such as x or y represent connections between nodes in CGIF, but variables in CLIF or predicate calculus.

2. Since the nodes of a graph have no inherent ordering, a CGIF sentence is an unordered list of nodes. Unless grouped by context brackets, the list may be permuted without affecting the semantics.

3. The CLIF operator and does not occur in CGIF because the conjunction of nodes within any context is implicit. Omitting the conjunction operator in CGIF tends to reduce the number of parentheses.

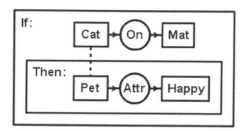

Figure 5.7: CG display form for *If a cat is on a mat, then it is a happy pet.*

4. Since CGIF labels show connections of nodes, they may be omitted when they are not needed. One way to reduce the number of labels is to move concept nodes inside the parentheses of relation nodes:

```
[Go *x]
   (Agnt ?x [Person: John])
   (Dest ?x [City: Boston])
   (Inst ?x [Bus])
```

When written in this way, CGIF looks like a frame notation. It is, however, much more general than frames, since it can represent the full semantics of CL.

As another example, Fig. 5.7 shows a CG for the sentence *If a cat is on a mat, then it is a happy pet.* The dotted line that connects the concept [Cat] to the concept [Pet], which is called a *coreference link*, indicates that they both refer to the same entity. The Attr relation indicates that the cat, also called a pet, has an attribute, which is an instance of happiness.

The coreference link in Fig. 5.7 is shown in CGIF by the defining label *x in the concept [Cat: *x] and the bound label ?x in the concept [Pet: ?x]. Following is the extended CGIF and its translation to core CGIF:

```
[If: [Cat *x] [Mat *y] (On ?x ?y)
   [Then: [Pet ?x] [Happy *z] (Attr ?x ?z) ]]

~[ [*x] [*y] (Cat ?x) (Mat ?y) (On ?x ?y)
   ~[ (Pet ?x) [*z] (Happy ?z) (Attr ?x ?z) ]]
```

In CGs, functions are represented by conceptual relations called *actors*. Fig. 5.8 is the CG display form for the following equation written in ordinary algebraic notation:

```
y = (x + 7)/sqrt(7)
```

The three functions in this equation would be represented by three actors, which are shown in Fig. 5.8 as diamond-shaped nodes with the type labels Add, Sqrt, and Divide. The concept nodes contain the input and output values of the actors. The two empty concept nodes contain the output values of Add and Sqrt.

In CGIF, actors are represented as relations with two kinds of arcs: a sequence of *input arcs* and a sequence of *output arcs*, which are separated by a vertical bar:

```
[Number: *x] [Number: *y] [Number: 7]
(Add ?x 7 | [*u]) (Sqrt 7 | [*v]) (Divide ?u ?v | ?y)
```

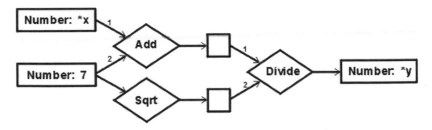

Figure 5.8: CL functions represented by actor nodes.

In the display form, the input arcs of `Add` and `Divide` are numbered 1 and 2 to indicate the order in which the arcs are written in CGIF. Following is the corresponding CLIF:

```
(exists ((x Number) (y Number))
    (and (Number 7) (= y (Divide (Add x 7) (Sqrt 7)))))
```

No CLIF variables are needed to represent the coreference labels `*u` and `*v` since the functional notation used in CLIF shows the connections directly.

CLIF only permits functions to have a single output, but extended CGIF allows actors to have multiple outputs. The following actor of type `IntegerDivide` has two inputs: an integer x and an integer 7. It also has two outputs: a quotient u and a remainder v.

```
(IntegerDivide [Integer: *x] [Integer: 7] | [*u] [*v])
```

When this actor is translated to core CGIF or CLIF, the vertical bar is removed, and the actor becomes an ordinary relation with four arguments; the distinction between inputs and outputs is lost. In order to assert the constraint that the last two arguments are functionally dependent on the first two arguments, the following CGIF sentence asserts that there exist two functions, identified by the coreference labels `Quotient` and `Remainder`, which for every combination of input and output values are logically equivalent to an actor of type `IntegerDivide` with the same input and output values:

```
[Function: *Quotient] [Function: *Remainder]
[[@every*x1] [@every*x2] [@every*x3] [@every*x4]
[Equiv: [Iff: (IntegerDivide ?x1 ?x2 | ?x3 ?x4)]
        [Iff: (#?Quotient ?x1 ?x2 | ?x3)
              (#?Remainder ?x1 ?x2 | ?x4)]]]
```

Each line of this example illustrates one or more features of CGIF. The first line represents existential quantifiers for two entities of type `Function`. On the second line, the context bracket [encloses the concept nodes with universal quantifiers, marked by `@every`, to show that the existential quantifiers for `Quotient` and `Remainder` include the universals within their scope. The equivalence on the last three lines shows that an actor of type `IntegerDivide` is logically equivalent to a conjunction of the quotient and remainder functions. Finally, the symbol # on the last two lines shows that the coreference labels ?Quotient and ?Remainder are being used as type labels. Following is the corresponding CLIF:

```
(exists ((Quotient Function) (Remainder Function))
 (forall (x1 x2 x3 x4)
  (iff (IntegerDivide x1 x2 x3 x4)
   (and (= x3 (Quotient x1 x2)) (= x4 (Remainder x1 x2))))))
```

As another example of the use of quantification over relations, someone might say "Bob and Sue are related", but not say exactly how they are related. The following sentences in CGIF and CLIF state that there exists some familial relation *r* that relates Bob and Sue:

```
[Relation: *r] (Familial ?r) (#?r Bob Sue)

(exists ((r Relation)) (and (Familial r) (r Bob Sue)))
```

The concept [Relation: *r] states that there exists a relation *r*. The next two relations state that *r* is familial and *r* relates Bob and Sue.

This brief survey has illustrated nearly every major feature of CGIF and CLIF. One important feature that has not been mentioned is the use of *sequence variables* to support relations with a variable number of arguments. Another is the use of comments, which can be placed before, after, or inside any concept or relation node in CGIF. The specifications in the CL standard guarantee that any sentence expressed in any of the three fully conformant dialects—CLIF, CGIF, or XCL—can be translated to any of the others in a logically equivalent form. Although the translation will preserve the semantics, it is not guaranteed to preserve all syntactic details: a sentence translated from one dialect to another and then back to the first will be logically equivalent to the original, but some subexpressions might be reordered or replaced by semantic equivalents.

In general, Common Logic is a superset of many different logic-based languages and notations, including the traditional predicate-calculus notation for first-order logic. But since various languages have been designed and implemented at widely separated times and places, that generalization must be qualified with different caveats for each case:

1. **Semantic Web Languages**. The draft CL standard supports the URIs defined by the W3C as valid CL name sequences, and it allows text stored on the web to be imported into CLIF, CGIF, or XCL documents. The tools that import the text could, if necessary, translate one dialect to another at import time. Since the semantics for RDF(S) and OWL was designed as a subset of the CL model theory, those languages can be translated to any fully conformant CL dialect [11].

2. **Z Specification Notation**. The Z model theory is a subset of the CL model theory, but the syntax of Z enforces strong type checking, and it does not permit quantifiers to range over functions and relations. Therefore, Z statements can be translated to CL, but only those statements that originally came from Z are guaranteed to be translatable back to Z.

3. **Unified Modeling Language (UML)**. Although the UML diagrams and notations are loosely based on logic, they have no formal specification in any version of logic. The best hope for providing a reliable foundation for UML would be to implement tools that translate UML to CL. If done properly, such tools could define a *de facto* standard for UML semantics.

4. **Logic-Programming Languages**. Well-behaved languages that support classical negation can be translated to CL while preserving the semantics. Languages based on negation as failure, such as Prolog, could be translated to CL, but with the usual caveats about ways of working around the discrepancies.

5. **SQL Database Language**. The WHERE clause in SQL queries and constraints can state an arbitrary FOL expression, but problems arise with the treatment of null values in the database and with differences between the open-world and closed-world assumptions. To avoid the nonlogical features of SQL, CL can be mapped to and from the Datalog language, which supports the Horn-clause subset of FOL and has a direct mapping to the SQL operations.

Most people have strong attachments to their favorite syntactic features. The goal of the Common Logic project is to provide a very general semantics that enables interoperability at the semantic level despite the inevitable syntactic differences. CL has demonstrated that such seemingly diverse notations as conceptual graphs, predicate calculus, and the languages of the Semantic Web can be treated as dialects with a common semantic foundation. An extension of CL called IKL, which is discussed in Section 5.5, can support an even wider range of logics.

5.3 Reasoning with Graphs

Graphs have some advantages over linear notations in both human factors and computational efficiency. As Figs. 5.1–5.8 illustrate, graphs show relationships at a glance that are harder to see in linear notations, including CGIF and CLIF. Graphs also have a highly regular structure that can simplify many algorithms for reasoning, searching, indexing, and pattern matching. Yet AI research has largely ignored the structural properties of graphs, and some of the most advanced research on representing, indexing, and manipulating graphs has been done in organic chemistry. With his BS degree in chemistry, Peirce was the first to recognize the similarity between chemical graphs and logical graphs. He wanted to represent the "atoms and molecules of logic" in his existential graphs, and he used the word *valence* for the number of arguments of a relation. By applying algorithms for chemical graphs to conceptual graphs, Levinson and Ellis [20] implemented the first type hierarchy that could support retrieval and classification in logarithmic time. More recent research on chemical graphs has been used in algorithms for computing semantic distance between CGs. Those techniques have enabled analogy finding in logarithmic time, instead of the polynomial-time computations of the older methods [37].

The six *canonical formation rules* [34] are examples of graph-based operators that focus on the semantics. Combinations of these rules, called *projection* and *maximal join*, perform larger semantic operations, such as answering a question or comparing

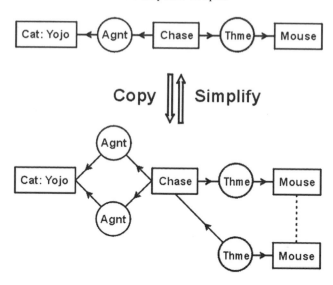

Figure 5.9: Copy and simplify rules.

the relevance of different alternatives. Each rule has one of three possible effects on the logical relationship between a starting graph u and the resulting graph v:

1. **Equivalence**. *Copy* and *simplify* are equivalence rules, which generate a graph v that is logically equivalent to the original: $u \supset v$ and $v \supset u$. Equivalent graphs are true in exactly the same models.

2. **Specialization**. *Join* and *restrict* are specialization rules, which generate a graph v that implies the original: $v \supset u$. Specialization rules monotonically decrease the set of models in which the result is true.

3. **Generalization**. *Detach* and *unrestrict* are generalization rules, which generate a graph v that is implied by the original: $u \supset v$. Generalization rules monotonically increase the set of models in which the result is true.

Each rule has an inverse rule that undoes any change caused by the other. The inverse of copy is simplify, the inverse of restrict is unrestrict, and the inverse of join is detach. These rules are fundamentally graphical: they are easier to show than to describe. Figures 5.9 to 5.11 illustrate these rules with *simple graphs*, which use only conjunction and existential quantifiers. When rules for handling negation are added, they form a complete proof procedure for first-order logic with equality.

The CG at the top of Fig. 5.9 represents the sentence *The cat Yojo is chasing a mouse*. The down arrow represents two applications of the copy rule. One application copies the Agnt relation, and a second copies the subgraph → (Thme) → [Mouse]. The coreference link connecting the two [Mouse] concepts indicates that both concepts refer to the same individual. The up arrow represents two applications of the simplify rule, which performs the inverse operations of erasing redundant copies. Following are the CGIF sentences for both graphs:

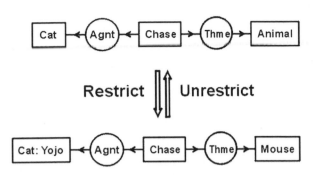

Figure 5.10: Restrict and unrestrict rules.

```
[Cat: Yojo] [Chase: *x] [Mouse: *y]
(Agent ?x Yojo) (Thme ?x ?y)

[Cat: Yojo] [Chase: *x] [Mouse: *y] [Mouse: ?y]
(Agent ?x Yojo) (Agent ?x Yojo) (Thme ?x ?y) (Thme ?x ?y)
```

As the CGIF illustrates, the copy rule makes redundant copies, which are erased by the simplify rule. In effect, the copy rule is $p \supset (p \wedge p)$, and the simplify rule is $(p \wedge p) \supset p$.

The CG at the top of Fig. 5.10 represents the sentence *A cat is chasing an animal*. By two applications of the restrict rule, it is transformed to the CG for *The cat Yojo is chasing a mouse*. In the first step, the concept [Cat], which says that there exists some cat, is *restricted by referent* to the more specific concept [Cat: Yojo], which says that there exists a cat named Yojo. In the second step, the concept [Animal], which says that there exists an animal, is *restricted by type* to a concept of a subtype [Mouse]. The more specialized graph implies the more general one: if the cat Yojo is chasing a mouse, then a cat is chasing an animal.

To show that the bottom graph v of Fig. 5.10 implies the top graph u, let c be a concept of u that is being restricted to a more specialized concept d, and let u be $c \wedge w$, where w is the remaining information in u. By hypothesis, $d \supset c$. Therefore, $(d \wedge w) \supset (c \wedge w)$. Hence, $v \supset u$.

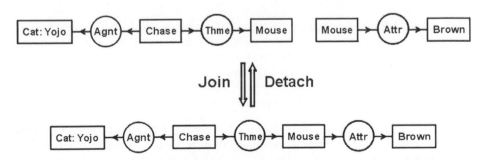

Figure 5.11: Join and detach rules.

At the top of Fig. 5.11 are two CGs for the sentences *Yojo is chasing a mouse* and *A mouse is brown*. The join rule overlays the two identical copies of the concept [Mouse] to form a single CG for the sentence *Yojo is chasing a brown mouse*. The detach rule undoes the join to restore the top graphs. Following are the CGIF sentences that represent the top and bottom graphs of Fig. 5.11:

```
[Cat: Yojo] [Chase: *x] [Mouse: *y] (Agent ?x Yojo)
(Thme ?x ?y) [Mouse: *z] [Brown: *w] (Attr ?z ?w)

[Cat: Yojo] [Chase: *x] [Mouse: *y] (Agent ?x Yojo)
(Thme ?x ?y) [Brown: *w] (Attr ?y ?w)
```

As the CGIF illustrates, the bottom graph consists of substituting y for every occurrence of z in the top graph and erasing redundant copies. In general, every join assumes an equality of the form $y = z$ and simplifies the result. If q is the equality and u is original pair of graphs at the top, then the bottom graph is equivalent to $q \wedge u$, which implies u. Therefore, the result of join implies the original graphs.

Together, the generalization and equivalence rules are sufficient for a complete proof procedure for the subset of logic whose only operators are conjunction and the existential quantifier. The specialization and equivalence rules can be used in a refutation procedure for a proof by contradiction. To handle full first-order logic, rules for negations must be added. Peirce defined a complete proof procedure for FOL whose rules depend on whether a context is positive (nested in an even number of negations, possibly zero) or negative (nested in an odd number of negations). Those rules are grouped in three pairs, one of which (i) inserts a graph and the other (e) erases a graph. The only axiom is a blank sheet of paper (an empty graph with no nodes); in effect, the blank is a generalization of all other graphs. Following is a restatement of Peirce's rules in terms of specialization and generalization. These same rules apply to both propositional logic and full first-order logic. In FOL, the operation of inserting or erasing a connection between two nodes has the effect of identifying two nodes (i.e., a substitution of a value for a variable) or treating them as possibly distinct.

1. (i) In a negative context, any graph or subgraph (including the blank) may be replaced by any specialization.
   (e) In a positive context, any graph or subgraph may be replaced by any generalization (including the blank).

2. (i) Any graph or subgraph in any context c may be copied in the same context c or into any context nested in c. (The only exception is that no graph may be copied directly into itself; however, it is permissible to copy a graph g in the context c and then to copy the copy into the original g.)
   (e) Any graph or subgraph that could have been derived by rule 2(i) may be erased. (Whether or not the graph was in fact derived by 2(i) is irrelevant.)

3. (i) A double negation (nest of two negations with nothing between the inner and outer) may be drawn around any graph, subgraph, or set of graphs in any context.
   (e) Any double negation in any context may be erased.

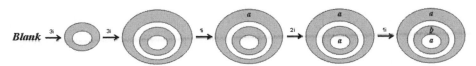

Figure 5.12: Proof of Frege's first axiom by Peirce's rules.

This version of the rules was adapted from a tutorial on existential graphs by Peirce [28]. He originally formulated these rules in 1897 and finally published them in 1906, but they are a simplification and generalization of the rules of *natural deduction* by Gentzen [10]. When these rules are applied to CGIF, some adjustments may be needed to rename coreference labels or to convert a bound label to a defining label or vice versa. For example, if a defining node is erased, a bound label may become the new defining label. Such adjustments are not needed in the pure graph notation.

All the axioms and rules of inference for classical FOL, including the rules of the *Principia Mathematica*, natural deduction, and resolution, can be proved in terms of Peirce's rules. As an example, Frege's first axiom, written in Peirce–Peano notation, is $a \supset (b \supset a)$. Fig. 5.12 shows a proof by Peirce's rules. (To improve contrast, positive areas are shown in white, and negative areas are shaded.)

In core CGIF, the propositions *a* and *b* could be represented as relations with zero arguments. Following are the five steps of Fig. 5.12 written in core CGIF:

1. By rule 3(i), Insert a double negation around the blank: `~[ ~[ ] ]`.

2. By 3(i), insert a double negation around the previous one:
   `~[ ~[ ~[ ~[ ] ] ] ]`.

3. By 1(i), insert `(a)`: `~[ (a) ~[ ~[ ~[ ] ] ] ]`.

4. By 2(i), copy `(a)`: `~[ (a) ~[ ~[ ~[ (a) ] ] ] ]`.

5. By 1(i), insert `(b)`: `~[ (a) ~[ ~[ (b) ~[ (a) ] ] ] ]`.

The theorem to be proved contains five symbols, and each step of the proof inserts one symbol into its proper place in the final result. Frege had a total of eight axioms, and the *Principia* had five. All of them could be derived by similarly short proofs.

Frege's two rules of inference, which Whitehead and Russell adopted, were *modus ponens* and *universal instantiation*. Fig. 5.13 is a proof of *modus ponens*, which derives *q* from a statement *p* and an implication $p \supset q$:

Following are the four steps of Fig. 5.13 written in core CGIF:

1. Starting graphs: `(p) ~[ (p) ~[ (q) ] ]`.

2. By 2(e), erase the nested copy of `(p)`: `(p) ~[ ~[ (q) ] ]`.

Figure 5.13: Proof of modus ponens.

Figure 5.14: Proof of universal instantiation.

3. By 1(e), erase `(p):~[ ~[ (q) ]]`.

4. By 3(e), erase the double negation: `(q)`.

Frege's other rule of inference is *universal instantiation*, which allows any term *t* to be substituted for a universally quantified variable in a statement of the form $(\forall x)P(x)$. In EGs, the term *t* would be represented by a graph of the form—*t*, which states that something satisfying the condition *t* exists, and the universal quantifier corresponds to a negated existential: a line whose outermost part (the existential quantifier) occurs in a negative area. Since a graph has no variables, there is no notion of substitution. Instead, the proof in Fig. 5.14 performs the equivalent operation by connecting the two lines.

The absence of labels on the EG lines simplifies the proofs by eliminating the need to relabel variables in CLIF or coreference links in CGIF. In core CGIF, the first step is the linear version of Fig. 5.14:

1. Starting graphs: `[*x] (t ?x) ~[ [*y] ~[ (P ?y) ]]`.

2. By 2(i), copy `[*x]` and change the defining label `*x` to a bound label `?x` in the copy: `[*x] (t ?x) ~[ [?x] [*y] ~[ (P ?y) ]]`.

3. By 1(i), insert a connection between the two lines. In CGIF, that corresponds to relabeling `*y` and `?y` to `?x` and erasing redundant copies of `[?x]`: `[*x] (t ?x) ~[ ~[ (P ?x) ]]`.

4. By 3(e), erase the double negation: `[*x] (t ?x) (P ?x)`.

With the universal quantifier in extended CGIF, the starting graphs of Fig. 5.14 could be written

    `[*x] (t ?x) [(P [@every*y])]`.

The extra brackets around the last node ensure that the existential quantifier `[*x]` includes the universal `@every*y` within its scope. Then universal instantiation could be used as a one-step derived rule to generate line 4. After `@every` has been erased, the brackets around the last node are not needed and may be erased.

In the *Principia Mathematica*, Whitehead and Russell proved the following theorem, which Leibniz called the *Praeclarum Theorema* (Splendid Theorem). It is one of the last and most complex theorems in propositional logic in the *Principia*, and it required a total of 43 steps, starting from five nonobvious axiom schemata

$$((p \supset r) \wedge (q \supset s)) \supset ((p \wedge q) \supset (r \wedge s)).$$

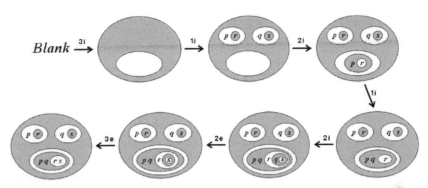

Figure 5.15: Proof in 7 steps instead of 43 in the *Principia*.

With Peirce's rules, this theorem can be proved in just seven steps starting with a blank sheet of paper (Fig. 5.15). Each step of the proof inserts or erases one graph, and the final graph is the statement of the theorem.

After only four steps, the graph looks almost like the desired conclusion, except for a missing copy of *s* inside the innermost area. Since that area is positive, it is not permissible to insert *s* directly. Instead, Rule 2(i) copies the graph that represents $q \supset s$. By Rule 2(e), the next step erases an unwanted copy of *q*. Finally, Rule 3(e) erases a double negation to derive the conclusion.

Unlike Gentzen's version of natural deduction, which uses a method of making and discharging assumptions, Peirce's proofs proceed in a straight line from a blank sheet to the conclusion: every step inserts or erases one subgraph in the immediately preceding graph. As Fig. 5.15 illustrates, the first two steps of any proof that starts with a blank must draw a double negation around the blank and insert a graph into the negative area. That graph is usually the entire hypothesis of the theorem to be proved. The remainder of the proof develops the conclusion in the doubly nested blank area. Those two steps are the equivalent of Gentzen's method of making and discharging an assumption, but in Gentzen's approach, the two steps may be separated by arbitrarily many intervening steps, and a system of bookkeeping is necessary to keep track of the assumptions. With Peirce's rules, the second step follows immediately after the first, and no bookkeeping is required.

Most common proofs take about the same number of steps with Peirce's rules as with Gentzen's version of natural deduction or his *sequent calculus*. For some kinds of proofs, however, Peirce's rules can be much faster because of a property that is not shared by any other common proof procedure: the rules depend only on whether an area is positive or negative; the depth of nesting is irrelevant. That property implies the "cut-and-paste theorem" [34], which is proved in terms of Peirce's rules, but it can be used in any notation for first-order logic:

1. **Theorem.** If a proof $p \vdash q$ is possible on a blank sheet, then in any positive area of a graph or formula where *p* occurs, *q* may be substituted for *p*.

2. **Proof.** Since the area in which *p* occurs is positive, every step of the proof of *q* can be carried out in that area. Therefore, it is permissible to "cut out" and "paste in" the steps of the proof from *p* to *q* in that area. After *q* has been

derived, Rule 1(e) can be applied to erase the original p and any remaining steps of the proof other than q.

Dau [4] showed that certain proofs that take advantage of this theorem or the features of Peirce's rules that support it can be orders of magnitude shorter than proofs based on other rules of inference. Conventional rules, for example, can only be applied to the outermost operator. If a graph or formula happens to contain a deeply nested sub-formula p, those rules cannot replace it with q. Instead, many steps may be needed to bring p to the surface of some formula to which conventional rules can be applied. An example is the *cut-free* version of Gentzen's sequent calculus, in which proofs can sometimes be exponentially longer than proofs in the usual version. With Peirce's rules, the corresponding cut-free proofs are only longer by a polynomial factor.

The canonical formation rules have been implemented in nearly all CG systems, and they have been used in formal logic-based methods, informal case-based reasoning, and various computational methods. A multistep combination, called a *maximal join*, is used to determine the extent of the unifiable overlap between two CGs. In natural language processing, maximal joins can help resolve ambiguities and determine the most likely connections of new information to background knowledge and the previous context of a discourse. Stewart [38] implemented Peirce's rules of inference in a first-order theorem prover for EGs and showed that its performance is comparable to resolution theorem provers. In all reasoning methods, formal and informal, a major part of the time is spent in searching for relevant rules, axioms, or background information. Ongoing research on efficient methods of indexing graphs and selecting the most relevant information has shown great improvement in many cases, but more work is needed to incorporate such indexing into conventional reasoning systems.

5.4 Propositions, Situations, and Metalanguage

Natural languages are highly expressive systems that can state anything that has ever been stated in any formal language or logic. They can even express metalevel statements about themselves, their relationships to other languages, and the truth of any such statements. Such enormous expressive power can easily generate contradictions and paradoxes, such as the statement *This sentence is false.* Most formal languages avoid such paradoxes by imposing restrictions on the expressive power. Common Logic, for example, can represent any sentence in any CL dialect as a quoted string, and it can even specify the syntactic structure of such strings. But CL has no mechanism for treating such strings as CL sentences and relating substrings in them to the corresponding CL names.

Although the paradoxes of logic are expressible in natural language, the most common use of language about language is to talk about the beliefs, desires, and intentions of the speaker and other people. Many versions of logic and knowledge representation languages, including conceptual graphs, have been used to express such language. As an example, the sentence *Tom believes that Mary wants to marry a sailor*, contains three clauses, whose nesting may be marked by brackets:

```
Tom believes that [Mary wants [to marry a sailor]].
```

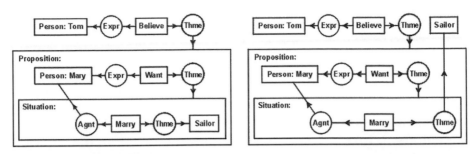

Figure 5.16: Two interpretations of *Tom believes that Mary wants to marry a sailor.*

The outer clause asserts that Tom has a belief, which is expressed by the object of the verb *believe*. Tom's belief is that Mary wants a situation described by the nested infinitive, whose subject is the same person who wants the situation. Each clause makes a comment about the clause or clauses nested in it. References to the individuals mentioned in those clauses may cross context boundaries in various ways, as in the following two interpretations of the original English sentence:

```
Tom believes that
[there is a sailor whom Mary wants [to marry]].

There is a sailor whom Tom believes that
[Mary wants [to marry]].
```

The two conceptual graphs in Fig. 5.16 represent the first and third interpretations. In the CG on the left, the existential quantifier for the concept [Sailor] is nested inside the situation that Mary wants. Whether such a sailor actually exists and whether Tom or Mary knows his identity are undetermined. The CG on the right explicitly states that such a sailor exists; the connections of contexts and relations imply that Tom knows him and that Tom believes that Mary also knows him. Another option (not shown) would place the concept [Sailor] inside the context of type Proposition; it would leave the sailor's existence undetermined, but it would imply that Tom believes he exists and that Tom believes Mary knows him.

The context boxes illustrated in Figs. 5.4 and 5.6 express negations or operators such as If and Then, which are defined in terms of negations. However, the contexts of the types Proposition and Situation in Fig. 5.16 raise new issues of logic and ontology. The CL semantics can represent entities of any type, including propositions and situations, but it has no provision for relating such entities to the internal structure of CL sentences. A more expressive language, called IKL [14], was defined as an upward compatible extension of CL. The IKL semantics introduces entities called *propositions* and a special operator, spelled that, which relates IKL sentences to the propositions they express. IKL semantics does not have a built-in type for situations, but it is possible in IKL to make statements that state the existence of entities of type Situation and relate them to propositions.

The first step toward translating the CGs in Fig. 5.16 to IKL is to write them in an extended version of CGIF, which allows CGs to be nested inside concept nodes of type Proposition or Situation. Following is the CGIF for the CG on the left:

```
[Person: Tom] [Believe: *x1] (Expr ?x1 Tom)
(Thme ?x1 [Proposition:
   [Person: Mary] [Want: *x2] (Expr ?x2 Mary)
   (Thme ?x2 [Situation:
      [Marry: *x3] [Sailor: *x4] (Agnt ?x3 Mary)
                                 (Thme ?x3 ?x4)])])
```

This statement uses the option to move the concept nodes for the types Propo-sition and Situation inside the relation nodes of type Thme. That option has no semantic significance, but it makes the order of writing the CGIF closer to English word order. A much more important semantic question is the relation between situations and propositions. In the ontology commonly used with CGs, that relation is spelled Dscr and called the *description relation*. The last two lines of the CGIF statement above could be rewritten in the following form:

```
(Thme ?x2 [Situation: *s] (Dscr ?s [Proposition:
   [Marry: *x3] [Sailor: *x4] (Agnt ?x3 Mary)
                              (Thme ?x3 ?x4)]))
```

The last line is unchanged, but the line before it states that the theme of x2 is the situation s and the description of s is the proposition stated on the last line. In effect, every concept of type Situation that contains a nested CG is an abbreviation for a situation that is described by a concept of type Proposition that has the same nested CG. This expanded CGIF statement can then be translated to IKL (which is based on CLIF syntax with the addition of the operator that).

```
(exists ((x1 Believe)) (and (Person Tom) (Expr x1 Tom)
(Thme x1 (that
   (exists ((x2 Want) (s Situation))
        (and (Person Mary) (Expr x2 Mary)
             (Thme x2 s) (Dscr s (that
             (exists ((x3 Marry) (x4 Sailor))
                  (and (Agnt x3 Mary)
                       (Thme x3 x4) )))))))))))
```

Each line of the IKL statement expresses the equivalent of the corresponding line in CGIF. Note that every occurrence of Proposition in CGIF corresponds to that in IKL. The syntax of CLIF or IKL requires more parentheses than CGIF because every occurrence of (exists or (and requires an extra closing parenthesis at the end.

As these examples illustrate, the operator that adds an enormous amount of ex-pressive power, but IKL still has a first-order style of semantics. The proposition nodes in CGs or the that operator in IKL introduce abstract entities of type Proposi-tion, but propositions are treated as zero-argument relations, which are supported by the semantics of Common Logic. Although language about propositions is a kind of metalanguage, it does not, by itself, go beyond first-order logic. Tarski [39], for example, demonstrated how a stratified series of metalevels, each of which is purely first order, can be used without creating paradoxes or going beyond the semantics of FOL. In effect, Tarski avoided paradoxes by declaring that certain kinds of sentences (those that violate the stratification) do not express propositions in his models. The

IKL model theory has a similar way of avoiding paradoxes: it does not require every model to include a proposition for every possible sentence. For example, the following English sentence, which sounds paradoxical, could be expressed in either IKL or CGIF syntax:

There exists a proposition p, p is true,
and p is the proposition that p is false.

Since IKL does not require every sentence to express a proposition in every model, there are permissible IKL models in which this sentence is false simply because no such proposition exists. Therefore, the paradox vanishes because the sentence has a stable, but false, truth value.

5.5 Research Extensions

Over the years, the term *conceptual graph* has been used in a broad sense as any notation that has a large overlap with the notation used in the book by Sowa [33]. That usage has led to a large number of dialects with varying degrees of compatibility. The purpose of a standard is to stabilize a design at a stage where it can provide a fixed, reliable platform for the development of products and applications. A fixed design, however, is an obstacle to innovation in the platform itself, although it is valuable for promoting innovation in applications that use the platform. In order to support fundamental research while providing a stable platform for applications, it is important to distinguish ISO standard CGs, IKL CGs, and research CGs. The first two provide rich and stable platforms for application development, while the third allows research projects to add extensions and modifications, which may be needed for a particular application and which may someday be added to the standard.

Most of the features of the research CGs are required to support natural language semantics. Some of them, such as modal operators, are as old as Aristotle, but they are not in the CL standard because their semantics involves open research issues. Following are the most common research extensions that have been proposed or implemented in various forms over the years:

1. **Contexts.** Peirce's first use for the oval was to negate the graphs nested inside, and that is the only use that is recognized by the CL standard. But Peirce [26] generalized the ovals to context enclosures, which allow relations other than negation to be linked to a context. Most of those features could be defined in terms of the IKL extensions described in Section 5.4, but there is no consensus on any definitions that could be considered for a standard.

2. **Metalanguage.** The basic use of a context enclosure is to quote the nested graphs. That metalevel syntax allows any semantic approach to be defined by axioms that specify how the nested graphs are interpreted. Sowa [35, 36] adapted that approach to a family of *nested graph models* (NGMs), which could be used to formalize the semantics of many kinds of modal and intensional logics. A hierarchy of metalevels with the NGM semantics can express the equivalent of a wide range of modal, temporal, and intentional logics. The most useful NGMs can be represented with the IKL semantics, but the many

variations and their application to natural languages have not yet been fully explored.

3. **Generalized quantifiers.** In addition to the usual quantifiers of *every* and *some*, natural languages support an open-ended number of quantificational expressions, such as *exactly one, at least seven,* or *considerably more.* Some of these quantifiers, such as *exactly one cat,* could be represented as [Cat: @1] and defined in terms of the CL standard. Others, such as *at least seven cats,* could be represented [Cat: @≤7] and defined with a version of set theory added to the base logic. But quantifiers such as *considerably more* would require some method of approximate reasoning, such as fuzzy sets or rough sets.

4. **Indexicals.** Peirce observed that every statement in logic requires at least one indexical to fix the referents of its symbols. The basic indexical, which corresponds to the definite article *the,* is represented by the symbol # inside a concept node: [Dog: #] would represent the phrase *the dog.* The pronouns *I, you,* and *she* would be represented [Person: #I], [Person: #you], and [Person: #she]. To process indexicals, some linguists propose versions of *dynamic semantics,* in which the model is updated during the discourse. A simpler method is to treat the # symbol as a syntactic marker that indicates a incomplete interpretation of the original sentence. With this approach, the truth value of a CG that contains any occurrences of # is not determined until those markers are replaced by names or coreference labels. This approach supports indexicals in an intermediate representation, but uses a conventional model theory to evaluate the final resolution.

5. **Plural nouns.** Plurals have been represented in CGs by set expressions inside the concept boxes. The concept [Cat: {*}@3] would represent *three cats,* and [Dog: {Lucky, Macula}] would represent *the dogs Lucky and Macula.* Various methods have been proposed for representing distributed and collective plurals and translating them to versions of set theory and mereology. But the representation of plurals is still a research area in linguistics, and it is premature to adopt a standard syntax or semantics.

6. **Procedural attachments.** The CL standard defines actors as purely functional relations, but various implementations have allowed more informal versions, in which the actors represent arbitrary procedures. Some versions have implemented *token passing* algorithms with the symbol ? for a backward-chaining request used in a *query graph,* and with the symbol ! for a forward-chaining trigger that asserts a new value. As examples, the concept [Employee: ?] would ask *which employee,* and the concept [Employee: John!] would assert *the employee John.*

As an example of applied research, one of the largest commercial CG systems is Sonetto [30], which uses extended versions of the earlier algorithms by Levinson and Ellis [20]. A key innovation of Sonetto is its semi-automated methods for extracting ontologies and business rules from unstructured documents. The users who assist Sonetto in the knowledge extraction process are familiar with the subject matter, but they have no training in programming or knowledge engineering. CGIF is the knowledge representation language for ontologies, rules, and queries. It is also used to manage the schemas of documents and other objects in the system and to represent the rules that translate CGIF to XML and other formats. For the early CG research, see the collections edited by Nagle et al. [23], Way [41], and Chein [2]. More recent research on CGs has been published in the annual proceedings of the International Conferences on Conceptual Structures [5, 31].

Bibliography

[1] S. Ceccato. *Linguistic Analysis and Programming for Mechanical Translation.* Gordon and Breach, New York, 1961.

[2] M. Chein, editor, *Revue d'intelligence artificielle*, 10(1), 1996 (Numéro Spécial Graphes Conceptuels).

[3] W. Chen, M. Kifer, and D.S. Warren. Hilog: A foundation for higher-order logic programming. *Journal of Logic Programming*, 15(3):187–230, 1993.

[4] F. Dau. Some notes on proofs with Alpha graphs. In [31], pages 172–188, 2006.

[5] F. Dau, M.-L. Mugnier, and G. Stumme, editors. *Conceptual Structures: Common Semantics for Sharing Knowledge, LNAI*, vol. 3596. Springer, Berlin, 2005.

[6] D. Davidson. The logical form of action sentences. Reprinted in D. Davidson. *Essays on Actions and Events*. Clarendon Press, Oxford, pages 105–148, 1980.

[7] N.V. Findler, editor, *Associative Networks: Representation and Use of Knowledge by Computers*. Academic Press, New York, 1979.

[8] G. Frege, *Begriffsschrift*. 1879; English translation in J. van Heijenoort, editor. *From Frege to Gödel*, pages 1–82. Harvard University Press, Cambridge, MA, 1967.

[9] M.R. Genesereth and R. Fikes, editors. *Knowledge Interchange Format, Version 3.0 Reference Manual, TR Logic-92-1*. Computer Science Department, Stanford University, 1992.

[10] G. Gentzen. Untersuchungen über das logische Schließen. In *The Collected Papers of Gerhard Gentzen* (Investigations into logical deduction), pages 68–131. North-Holland Publishing Co., Amsterdam, 1969 (edited and translated by M.E. Szabo).

[11] P. Hayes. Translating semantic web languages into Common Logic. http://www.ihmc.us/users/phayes/CL/SW2SCL.html, 2005.

[12] P. Hayes and B. McBride. RDF semantics, W3C Technical Report. http://www.w3.org/TR/rdf-mt/, 2003.

[13] P. Hayes and C. Menzel. A semantics for the knowledge interchange format. In *Proc. IJCAI 2001 Workshop on the IEEE Standard Upper Ontology*, Seattle, 2001.

[14] P. Hayes and C. Menzel. IKL Specification Document. http://www.ihmc.us/users/phayes/IKL/SPEC/SPEC.html, 2006.

[15] D.G. Hays. Dependency theory: a formalism and some observations. *Language*, 40(4):511–525, 1964.

[16] ISO/IEC, *Z Formal Specification Notation—Syntax, Type System, and Semantics*, IS 13568, International Organisation for Standardisation, 2002.

[17] ISO/IEC 24707, Information Technology, Common Logic (CL)—A Framework for a family of Logic-Based Languages, International Organisation for Standardisation, Geneva, 2007.

[18] H. Kamp. A theory of truth and semantic representation. In J.A.G. Groenendijk, T.M.V. Janssen, and M.B.J. Stokhof, editors. *Formal Methods in the Study of Language*, pages 277–322. Mathematical Centre Tracts, Amsterdam, 1981.

[19] H. Kamp and U. Reyle. *From Discourse to Logic*. Kluwer, Dordrecht, 1993.

[20] R.A. Levinson and G. Ellis. Multilevel hierarchical retrieval. *Knowledge Based Systems*, 5(3):233–244, 1992.

[21] M. Masterman. Semantic message detection for machine translation, using an interlingua. In *Proc. 1961 International Conf. on Machine Translation*, pages 438–475, 1961.

[22] D.V. McDermott. Artificial intelligence meets natural stupidity. *SIGART Newsletter*, 57, April 1976.

[23] T.E. Nagle, J.A. Nagle, L.L. Gerholz, and P.W. Eklund, editors. *Conceptual Structures: Current Research and Practice*. Ellis Horwood, New York, 1992.

[24] C.S. Peirce. On the algebra of logic. *American Journal of Mathematics*, 3:15–57, 1880.

[25] C.S. Peirce. On the algebra of logic. *American Journal of Mathematics*, 7:180–202, 1885.

[26] C.S. Peirce. Reasoning and the Logic of Things. In K.L. Ketner, editor. *The Cambridge Conferences Lectures of 1898*. Harvard University Press, Cambridge, MA, 1992.

[27] C.S. Peirce. Manuscripts on existential graphs. In *Collected Papers of Charles Sanders Peirce*, vol. 4, pages 320–410. Harvard University Press, Cambridge, MA, 1906.

[28] C.S. Peirce. Manuscript 514, with commentary by J.F. Sowa, http://www.jfsowa. com/peirce/ms514.htm, 1909.

[29] W.V. Orman Quine. Reduction to a dyadic predicate. *J. Symbolic Logic*, 19, 1954. Reprinted In W.V. Quine, editor. *Selected Logic Papers*, enlarged edition, pages 224–226. Harvard University Press, Cambridge, MA, 1995.

[30] Q. Sarraf and G. Ellis. Business rules in retail: The Tesco.com story. *Business Rules Journal*, 7(6), 2006, http://www.brcommunity.com/a2006/n014.html.

[31] H. Schärfe, P. Hitzler, and P. Øhrstrom, editors. *Conceptual Structures: Inspiration and Application, LNAI*, vol. 4068. Springer, Berlin, 2006.

[32] J.F. Sowa. Conceptual graphs for a database interface. *IBM Journal of Research and Development*, 20(4):336–357, 1976.

[33] J.F. Sowa. *Conceptual Structures: Information Processing in Mind and Machine*. Addison-Wesley, Reading, MA, 1984.

[34] J.F. Sowa. *Knowledge Representation: Logical, Philosophical, and Computational Foundations*. Brooks/Cole Publishing Co., Pacific Grove, CA, 2000.

[35] J.F. Sowa. Laws, facts, and contexts: Foundations for multimodal reasoning. In V.F. Hendricks, K.F. Jørgensen, and S.A. Pedersen, editors. *Knowledge Contributors*, pages 145–184. Kluwer Academic Publishers, Dordrecht, 2003.

[36] J.F. Sowa. Worlds, models, and descriptions. *Studia Logica, Ways of Worlds II*, 84(2):323–360, 2006 (Special Issue).

[37] J.F. Sowa and A.K. Majumdar. Analogical reasoning. In A. de Moor, W. Lex, and B. Ganter, editors. *Conceptual Structures for Knowledge Creation and Communication, LNAI*, vol. 2746, pages 16–36. Springer-Verlag, Berlin, 2003.

[38] J. Stewart. Theorem proving using existential graphs. MS thesis, Computer and Information Science, University of California at Santa Cruz, 1996.

[39] A. Tarski. The concept of truth in formalized languages. In A. Tarski, editor. *Logic, Semantics, Metamathematics*, 2nd edition, pages 152–278. Hackett Publishing Co., Indianapolis, 1933.

[40] L. Tesnière. *Éléments de Syntaxe structurale*, 2nd edition. Librairie C. Klincksieck, Paris, 1965.

[41] E.C. Way, editor, *Journal of Experimental and Theoretical Artificial Intelligence (JETAI)*, 4(2), 1992 (Special Issue on Conceptual Graphs).

[42] W.A. Woods. What's in a link: foundations for semantic networks. In D.G. Bobrow and A. Collins, editors. *Representation and Understanding*, pages 35–82. Academic Press, New York, 1975.

Handbook of Knowledge Representation
Edited by F. van Harmelen, V. Lifschitz and B. Porter
© 2008 Elsevier B.V. All rights reserved
DOI: 10.1016/S1574-6526(07)03006-4

Chapter 6

Nonmonotonic Reasoning

Gerhard Brewka, Ilkka Niemelä, Mirosław Truszczyński

6.1 Introduction

Classical logic is *monotonic* in the following sense: whenever a sentence A is a logical consequence of a set of sentences T, then A is also a consequence of an arbitrary superset of T. In other words, adding information never invalidates any conclusions.

Commonsense reasoning is different. We often draw plausible conclusions based on the assumption that the world in which we function and about which we reason is *normal* and *as expected*. This is far from being irrational. To the contrary, it is the best we can do in situations in which we have only incomplete information. However, as unexpected as it may be, it can happen that our normality assumptions turn out to be wrong. New information can show that the situation actually is abnormal in some respect. In this case we may have to revise our conclusions.

For example, let us assume that Professor Jones likes to have a good espresso after lunch in a campus cafe. You need to talk to her about a grant proposal. It is about 1:00 pm and, under normal circumstances, Professor Jones sticks to her daily routine. Thus, you draw a plausible conclusion that she is presently enjoying her favorite drink. You decide to go to the cafe and meet her there. As you get near the student center, where the cafe is located, you see people streaming out of the building. One of them tells you about the fire alarm that just went off. The new piece of information invalidates the normality assumption and so the conclusion about the present location of Professor Jones, too.

Such reasoning, where additional information may invalidate conclusions, is called *nonmonotonic*. It has been a focus of extensive studies by the knowledge representation community since the early eighties of the last century. This interest was fueled by several fundamental challenges facing knowledge representation such as modeling and reasoning about rules with exceptions or *defaults*, and solving the *frame* problem.

Rules with exceptions

Most rules we use in commonsense reasoning—like *university professors teach*, *birds fly*, *kids like ice-cream*, *Japanese cars are reliable*—have exceptions. The rules describe what is normally the case, but they do not necessarily hold without exception. This is obviously in contrast with universally quantified formulas in first order logic. The sentence

$$\forall x \left(prof(x) \supset teaches(x) \right)$$

simply excludes the possibility of non-teaching university professors and thus cannot be used to represent rules with exceptions. Of course, we can refine the sentence to

$$\forall x \left((prof(x) \land \neg abnormal(x)) \supset teaches(x) \right).$$

However, to apply this rule, say to Professor Jones, we need to know whether Professor Jones is exceptional (for instance, professors who are department Chairs do not teach). Even if we assume that the unary predicate *abnormal*(.) can be defined precisely, which is rarely the case in practice as the list of possible exceptions is hard—if not impossible—to complete, we will most often lack information to derive that Professor Jones is not exceptional. We want to apply the rule even if all we know about Dr. Jones is that she is a professor at a university. If we later learn she is a department Chair—well, then we have to retract our former conclusion about her teaching classes. Such scenarios can only be handled with a nonmonotonic reasoning formalism.

The frame problem

To express effects of actions and reason about changes in the world they incur, one has to indicate under what circumstances a proposition whose truth value may vary, a *fluent*, holds. One of the most elegant formalisms to represent change in logic, *situation calculus* [89, 88, 112], uses situations corresponding to sequences of actions to achieve this. For instance, the fact that Fred is in the kitchen after walking there, starting in initial situation S_0, is represented as

$$holds\left(in(Fred, Kitchen), do\left(walk(Fred, Kitchen), S_0 \right) \right).$$

The predicate *holds* allows us to state that a fluent, here *in(Fred, Kitchen)*, holds in a particular situation. The expression *walk(Fred, Kitchen)* is an action, and the expression *do(walk(Fred, Kitchen), S_0)* is the situation after Fred walked to the kitchen, while in situation S_0.

In situation calculus, effects of actions can easily be described. It is more problematic, however, to describe what does *not* change when an event occurs. For instance, the color of the kitchen, the position of chairs, and many other things remain unaffected by Fred walking to the kitchen. The frame problem asks how to represent the large amount of non-changes when reasoning about action.

One possibility is to use a persistence rule such as: *what holds in a situation typically holds in the situation after an action was performed, unless it contradicts the description of the effects of the action.* This rule is obviously nonmonotonic. Just adding such a persistence rule to an action theory is not nearly enough to solve problems arising in reasoning about action (see Chapters 16–19 in this volume). However, it is an important component of a solution, and so the frame problem has provided a major impetus to research of nonmonotonic reasoning.

About this chapter

Handling rules with exceptions and representing the frame problem are by no means the only applications that have been driving research in nonmonotonic reasoning. Belief revision, abstract nonmonotonic inference relations, reasoning with conditionals, semantics of logic programs with negation, and applications of nonmonotonic formalisms as database query languages and specification languages for search problems all provided motivation and new directions for research in nonmonotonic reasoning.

One of the first papers explicitly dealing with the issue of nonmonotonic reasoning was a paper by Erik Sandewall [115] written in 1972 at a time when it was sometimes argued that logic is irrelevant for AI since it is not capable of representing nonmonotonicity in the consequence relation. Sandewall argued that it is indeed possible, with a moderate modification of conventional (first order) logic, to accommodate this requirement. The basic idea in the 1972 paper is to allow rules of the form

$$A \text{ and Unless } B \Rightarrow C$$

where, informally, C can be inferred if A was inferred and B cannot be inferred. The 1972 paper discusses consequences of the proposed approach, and in particular it identifies that it leads to the possibility of multiple extensions. At about the same time Hewitt published his work on Planner [55], where he proposed using the *thnot* operator for referring to failed inference.

In this chapter we give a short introduction to the field. Given its present scope, we do not aim at a comprehensive survey. Instead, we will describe three of the major formalisms in more detail: default logic in Section 6.2, autoepistemic logic in Section 6.3, and circumscription in Section 6.4. We will then discuss connections between these formalisms. It is encouraging and esthetically satisfying that despite different origins and motivations, one can find common themes.

We chose default logic, autoepistemic logic, and circumscription for the more detailed presentation since they are prominent and typical representatives of two orthogonal approaches: fixed point logics and model preference logics. The former are based on a *fixed point operator* that is used to generate—possibly multiple—sets of acceptable beliefs (called extensions or expansions), taking into account certain consistency conditions. Nonmonotonicity in these approaches is achieved since what is consistent changes when new information is added. Model preference logics, on the other hand, are concerned with nonmonotonic inference relations rather than formation of belief sets. They select some *preferred* or *normal* models out of the set of all models and define nonmonotonic inference with respect to these preferred (normal) models only. Here nonmonotonicity arises since adding new information changes the set of preferred models: models that were not preferred before may become preferred once we learn new facts.

Preference logics and their generalizations are important not only as a broad framework for circumscription. They are also fundamental for studies of abstract nonmonotonic inference relations. In Section 6.5, we discuss this line of research in more detail and cover such related topics as reasoning about conditionals, rational closure, and system Z.

In the last section of the chapter, we discuss the relationship between the major approaches, and present an overview of some other research directions in nonmonotonic reasoning. By necessity we will be brief. For a more extensive treatment of non-monotonic reasoning we refer the reader to the books (in order of appearance) [43, 11, 78, 85, 25, 2, 16, 17, 80].

6.2 Default Logic

Default reasoning is common. It appears when we apply the Closed-World Assumption to derive negative information, when we use inference rules that admit exceptions (rules that hold under the *normality* assumption), and when we use frame axioms to reason about effects of actions. Ray Reiter, who provided one of the most robust formalizations of default reasoning, argued that understanding default reasoning is of foremost importance for knowledge representation and reasoning. According to Reiter defaults are meta-rules of the form "in the absence of any information to the contrary, assume ..." and default reasoning consists of applying them [111].

Usual inference rules sanction the derivation of a formula whenever some other formulas are derived. In contrast, Reiter's defaults require an additional consistency condition to hold. For instance, a default rule *normally, a university professor teaches* is represented in Reiter's default notation as

$$\frac{prof(x) : teaches(x)}{teaches(x)}.$$

It states that if $prof(J)$ is given or derived for a particular ground term J (which may represent Prof. Jones, for instance) and $teaches(J)$ is consistent (there is no information that $\neg teaches(J)$ holds), then $teaches(J)$ can be derived "by default". The key question of course is: consistent with what? Intuitively, $teaches(J)$ has to be consistent with the whole set of formulas which one can "reasonably" accept based on the available information. Reiter's far-reaching contribution is that he made this intuition formal. In his approach, depending on the choice of applied defaults, different sets of formulas may be taken as providing context for deciding consistency. Reiter calls these different sets *extensions*.

One can use extensions to define a *skeptical* inference relation (a formula is skeptically entailed by a default theory if it belongs to *all* of its extensions), or a *credulous* inference relation (a formula is credulously entailed by a default theory if it belongs to *at least one* of its extensions). In many applications such as diagnosis, planning and, more generally in all the situations where defaults model constraints, the extensions themselves are of interest as they represent different solutions to a problem (see Chapter 7 on Answer Sets in this volume).

6.2.1 Basic Definitions and Properties

In default logic, what we are certain about is represented by means of sentences of first-order logic (formulas without free variables). Defeasible inference rules which specify patterns of reasoning that normally hold are represented as defaults. Formally, a default d is an expression

$$\frac{A : B_1, \ldots, B_n}{C}, \tag{6.1}$$

where A, B_i, and C are formulas in first order logic. In this notation, A is the *prerequisite*, $B_1, \ldots, B_n$ are *consistency conditions* or *justifications*, and C is the *consequent*. We denote A, $\{B_1, \ldots, B_n\}$ and C by $\text{pre}(d)$, $\text{just}(d)$, and $\text{cons}(d)$, respectively. To save space, we will also write a default (6.1) as $A : B_1, \ldots, B_n / C$.

Definition 6.1. *A default theory is a pair* (D, W), *where W is a set of sentences in first order logic and D is a set of defaults.*

A default is *closed* if its prerequisite, justifications, and consequent are sentences. Otherwise, it is *open*. A default theory is *closed* if all its defaults are closed; otherwise, it is *open*. A default theory determines its Herbrand universe. We will interpret open defaults as schemata representing all of their ground instances. Therefore, open default theories are just a shorthand notation for their closed counterparts and so, in this chapter, the term *default theory* always stands for a *closed* default theory.[1]

Before we define extensions of a default theory (D, W) formally, let us discuss properties we expect an extension E of (D, W) to satisfy.

1. Since W represents certain knowledge, we want W to be contained in E, that is, we require that $W \subseteq E$.

2. We want E to be deductively closed in the sense of classical logic, that is, we want $\text{Cn}(E) = E$ to hold, where $\models$ is the classical logical consequence relation and $\text{Cn}(E) = \{A \mid E \models A\}$ denotes the set of logical consequences of a set of formulas E.

3. We use defaults to expand our knowledge. Thus, E should be *closed* under defaults in D: whenever the prerequisite of a default $d \in D$ is in E and all its justifications are consistent with E, the consequent of the default must be in E.

These three requirements do not yet specify the right concept of an extension. We still need some condition of *groundedness* of extensions: each formula in an extension needs sufficient reason to be included in the extension. Minimality with respect to the requirements (1)–(3) does not do the job. Let $W = \emptyset$ and $D = \{\top : a/b\}$. Then $\text{Cn}(\{\neg a\})$ is a minimal set satisfying the three properties, but the theory (D, W) gives no support for $\neg a$. Indeed $W = \emptyset$ and the only default in the theory cannot be used to derive anything else but b.

The problem is how to capture the inference-rule interpretation we ascribe to defaults. It is not a simple matter to adjust this as defaults have premises of two different types and this has to be taken into account. Reiter's proposal rests on an observation that given a set S of formulas to use when testing consistency of justifications, there is a *unique* least theory, say $\Gamma(S)$, containing W, closed under classical provability and also (in a certain sense determined by S) under defaults. Reiter argued that for a theory S to be grounded in (D, W), S must be precisely what (D, W) implies, given that S is used for testing the consistency of justifications, and used this property to define extensions [111].

---

[1] We note, however, that Reiter treats open defaults differently and uses a more complicated method to define extensions for them. A theory of open default theories was developed by [73]. Some problems with the existing treatments of open defaults are discussed in [5].

Definition 6.2 (Default logic extension). *Let (D, W) be a default theory. The operator Γ assigns to every set S of formulas the smallest set U of formulas such that:*

1. $W \subseteq U$,

2. $\text{Cn}(U) = U$,

3. *if $A : B_1, \dots, B_n / C \in D, U \models A, S \not\models \neg B_i, 1 \leqslant i \leqslant n$, then $C \in U$.*

A set E of formulas is an extension of (D, W) if and only if $E = \Gamma(E)$, that is, E is a fixed point of Γ.

One can show that such a least set U exists so the operator Γ is well defined. It is also not difficult to see that extensions defined as fixed points of Γ satisfy the requirements (1)–(3).

In addition, the way the operator Γ is defined also guarantees that extensions are grounded in (D, W). Indeed, $\Gamma(S)$ can be characterized as the set of all formulas that can be derived from W by means of classical derivability and by using those defaults whose justifications are each consistent with S as additional *standard* inference rules (once every justification in a default d turns out to be consistent with S, the default d starts to function as the inference rule $\text{pre}(d) / \text{cons}(d)$, other defaults are ignored). This observation is behind a quasi-inductive characterization of extensions, also due to Reiter [111].

Theorem 6.1. *Let (D, W) be a default theory and S a set of formulas. Let*

$$E_0 = W, \quad \text{and for } i \geqslant 0$$
$$E_{i+1} = \text{Cn}(E_i) \cup$$
$$\{C \mid A : B_1, \dots, B_n / C \in D, E_i \models A, S \not\models \neg B_i, 1 \leqslant i \leqslant n\}.$$

Then $\Gamma(S) = \bigcup_{i=0}^{\infty} E_i$. Moreover, a set E of formulas is an extension of (D, W) if and only if $E = \bigcup_{i=0}^{\infty} E_i$.

The appearance of E in the definition of E_{i+1} is what renders this alternative definition of extensions non-constructive. It is, however, quite useful. Reiter [111] used Theorem 6.1 to show that every extension of a default theory (D, W) can be represented as the logical closure of W and the consequents of a subset of defaults from D.

Let E be a set of formulas. A default d is *generating* for E if $E \models \text{pre}(d)$ and, for every $B \in \text{just}(d)$, $E \not\models \neg B$. If D is a set of defaults, we write $GD(D, E)$ for the set of defaults in D that are generating for E.

Theorem 6.2 (Generating defaults). *Let E be an extension of a default theory (D, W). Then $E = \text{Cn}(W \cup \{\text{cons}(d) \mid d \in GD(D, E)\})$.*

This result is fundamental for algorithms to compute extensions. We will come back to this issue later. For now, we will restrict ourselves to a few examples. Let

$$D_1 = \{prof(x) : teaches(x) / teaches(x)\},$$

$$W_1 = \{prof(J)\}.$$

We recall that we interpret an open default as the set of its ground instantiations. Since there is only one constant (J) in the theory, the corresponding *closed* default theory is

$$D'_1 = \{prof(J) : teaches(J)/teaches(J)\},$$
$$W_1 = \{prof(J)\}.$$

By Theorem 6.2 an extension is the deductive closure of W and some of the available default consequents. Hence, there are only two candidates for an extension here, namely $S_1 = Cn(\{prof(J)\})$ and $S_2 = Cn(\{prof(J), teaches(J)\})$. We can now use Theorem 6.1 to compute $\Gamma(S_1)$. Clearly, $E_0 = Cn(W_1)$. Since $teaches(J)$ is consistent with S_1 and $E_0 \models prof(J)$, $E_1 = Cn(\{prof(J), teaches(J)\})$. Moreover, for every $i > 2$, $E_i = E_1$. Thus, $\Gamma(S_1) = Cn(\{prof(J), teaches(J)\})$. Since $teaches(J) \notin S_1$, $S_1 \neq \Gamma(S_1)$ and so, S_1 is not an extension of (D_1, W_1) (nor of (D'_1, W_1)). On the other hand, the same argument shows that $\Gamma(S_2) = Cn(\{prof(J), teaches(J)\})$. Thus, $S_2 = \Gamma(S_2)$, that is, S_2 is an extension of (D_1, W_1) (and also (D'_1, W_1)).

Now let us consider a situation when Professor J is not a typical professor.

$$D_2 = D_1,$$
$$W_2 = \{prof(J), chair(J), \forall x.(chair(x) \supset \neg teaches(x))\}.$$

As before, there are two candidates for extensions, namely $S_1 = Cn(W_2)$ and $S_2 = Cn(W_2 \cup \{teaches(J)\})$. This time S_2 is inconsistent and one can compute, using Theorem 6.1, that $\Gamma(S_2) = Cn(W_2)$. Thus, S_2 is not a fixed point of Γ and so not an extension. On the other hand, $\Gamma(S_1) = Cn(W_2)$ and so S_1 is an extension of (D_2, W_2). Consequently, this default theory supports the inference that Professor J does not teach (as it should).

Finally, we will consider what happens if the universally quantified formula from W_2 is replaced by a corresponding default rule:

$$D_3 = \{prof(x) : teaches(x)/teaches(x), chair(x) : \neg teaches(x)/\neg teaches(x)\},$$
$$W_3 = \{prof(J), chair(J)\}.$$

The corresponding closed default theory has two defaults: $prof(J) : teaches(J)/teaches(J)$ and $chair(J) : \neg teaches(J)/\neg teaches(J)$. Thus, there are now four candidates for extensions:

$$Cn(\{prof(J), chair(J)\}),$$
$$Cn(\{prof(J), chair(J), teaches(J)\}),$$
$$Cn(\{prof(J), chair(J), \neg teaches(J)\}),$$
$$Cn(\{prof(J), chair(J), teaches(J), \neg teaches(J)\}).$$

In each case, one can compute the value of the operator Γ and check the condition for an extension. In this example, the second and third theories happen to be extensions. Since the theory offers no information whether Professor J is a typical professor or a typical chair (she cannot be both as this would lead to a contradiction), we get two extensions. In one of them Professor J is a typical professor and so teaches, in the other one she is a typical chair and so, does not teach.

Default theories can have an arbitrary number of extensions, including having no extensions at all. We have seen examples of default theories with one and two extensions above. A simple default theory without an extension is

$$(\{\top : \neg a/a\}, \emptyset).$$

If a deductively closed set of formulas S does not contain a, then S is not an extension since the default has not been applied even though $\neg a$ is consistent with S. In other words, $\Gamma(S)$ will contain a and thus $\Gamma(S) \neq S$. On the other hand, if S contains a, then $\Gamma(S)$ produces a set not containing a (more precisely: the set of all tautologies) since the default is inapplicable with respect to S. Again S is not an extension.

Theorem 6.2 has some immediate consequences.

Corollary 6.3. *Let (D, W) be a default theory.*

1. *If W is inconsistent, then (D, W) has a single extension, which consists of all formulas in the language.*

2. *If W is consistent and every default in D has at least one justification, then every extension of (D, W) is consistent.*

We noted that the minimality with respect to the requirements (1)–(3) we discussed prior to the formal definition of extensions does not guarantee groundedness. It turns out that the type of groundedness satisfied by extensions ensures their minimality and, consequently, implies that they form an antichain [111].

Theorem 6.4. *Let (D, W) be a default theory. If E is an extension of (D, W) and E' is a theory closed under classical consequence relation and defaults in D such that $E' \subseteq E$, then $E' = E$. In particular, if E and E' are extensions of (D, W) and $E \subseteq E'$, then $E = E'$.*

6.2.2 Computational Properties

The key reasoning problems for default logic are deciding *sceptical and credulous inference* and finding extensions. For first-order default logic these problems are not even semi-decidable [111]. This is different from classical first order logic which is semi-decidable. Hence, automated reasoning systems for first order default logic cannot provide a similar level of completeness as classical theorem provers: a formula can be a (nonmonotonic) consequence of a default theory but no algorithm is able to establish this. This can be compared to first order theorem proving where it can be guaranteed that for each valid formula a proof is eventually found.

Even in the propositional case extensions of a default theory are infinite sets of formulas. In order to handle them computationally we need characterizations in terms of formulas that appear in (D, W). We will now present two such characterizations which play an important role in clarifying computational properties of default logic and in developing algorithms for default reasoning.

We will write Mon(D) for the set of standard inference rules obtained by dropping justifications from defaults in D:

$$\text{Mon}(D) = \left\{ \frac{\text{pre}(d)}{\text{cons}(d)} \,\middle|\, d \in D \right\}.$$

We define $\text{Cn}_{\text{Mon}(D)}(.)$ to be the consequence operator induced by the classical consequence relation and the rules in Mon(D). That is, if W is a set of sentences, $\text{Cn}_{\text{Mon}(D)}(W)$ is the closure of W with respect to classical logical consequence and the rules Mon(D) (the least set of formulas containing W and closed under the classical consequence relation and the rules in Mon(D)).

The first characterization of extensions is based on the observation that extensions can be described in terms of their generating defaults (Theorem 6.2). The details can be found in [85, 114, 5]. We will only state the main result. The idea is to project the requirements we impose on an extension to a set of its generating defaults. Thus, a set of generating defaults should be grounded in W, which means that for every default in this set the prerequisite should be derivable (in a certain specific sense) from W. Second, the set of generating defaults should contain *all* defaults that apply.

Theorem 6.5 (Extensions in terms of generating defaults). *A set E of formulas is an extension of a default theory (D, W) if and only if there is a set $D' \subseteq D$ such that $E = \text{Cn}(W \cup \{\text{cons}(d) \mid d \in D'\})$ and*

1. *for every $d \in D'$, $\text{pre}(d) \in \text{Cn}_{\text{Mon}(D')}(W)$,*

2. *for all $d \in D$: $d \in D'$ if and only if $\text{pre}(d) \in \text{Cn}(W \cup \{\text{cons}(d) \mid d \in D'\})$ and for all $B \in \text{just}(d)$, $\neg B \notin \text{Cn}(W \cup \{\text{cons}(d) \mid d \in D'\})$.*

The second characterization was introduced in [98] and is focused on justifications. The idea is that default rules are inference rules guarded with consistency conditions given by the justifications. Hence, it is the set of justifications that determines the extension and the rest is just a monotonic derivation.

We denote by just(D) the set of all justifications in the set of defaults D. For a set S of formulas we define

$$\text{Mon}(D, S) = \big\{ \text{pre}(d)/\text{cons}(d) \mid d \in D, \ \text{just}(d) \subseteq S \big\}$$

as the set of monotonic inference rules enabled by S. A set of justifications is called *full* with respect to the default theory if it consists of the justifications which are consistent with the consequences of the monotonic inference rules enabled by the set.

Definition 6.3 (Full sets). *For a default theory (D, W), a set of justifications $S \subseteq \text{just}(D)$ is (D, W)-full if the following condition holds: for every $B \in \text{just}(D)$, $B \in S$ if and only if $\neg B \notin \text{Cn}_{\text{Mon}(D,S)}(W)$.*

For each full set there is a corresponding extension and for each extension a full set that induces it.

Theorem 6.6 (Extensions in terms of full sets). *Let (D, W) a default theory.*

1. *If $S \subseteq \mathrm{just}(D)$ is (D, W)-full, then $\mathrm{Cn}_{\mathrm{Mon}(D,S)}(W)$ is an extension of (D, W).*

2. *If E is an extension of (D, W), then $S = \{B \in \mathrm{just}(D) \mid \neg B \notin E\}$ is (D, W)-full and $E = \mathrm{Cn}_{\mathrm{Mon}(D,S)}(W)$.*

Example 6.1. Consider the default theory (D_3, W_3), where

$$D_3 = \{prof(J) : teaches(J)/teaches(J),$$
$$chair(J) : \neg teaches(J)/\neg teaches(J)\},$$
$$W_3 = \{prof(J), chair(J)\}.$$

The possible (D_3, W_3)-full sets are the four subsets of $\{teaches(J), \neg teaches(J)\}$. It is easy to verify that from these only $\{teaches(J)\}$ and $\{\neg teaches(J)\}$ satisfy the fullness condition given in Definition 6.3. For instance, for $S = \{\neg teaches(J)\}$

$$\mathrm{Mon}(D_3, S) = \left\{ \frac{chair(J)}{\neg teaches(J)} \right\}$$

and $\mathrm{Cn}_{\mathrm{Mon}(D_3,S)}(W_3) = \mathrm{Cn}(\{prof(J), chair(J), \neg teaches(J)\})$. As required we have $\neg\neg teaches(J) \notin \mathrm{Cn}_{\mathrm{Mon}(D_3,S)}(W_3)$ and $\neg teaches(J) \in \mathrm{Cn}_{\mathrm{Mon}(D_3,S)}(W_3)$.

The finitary characterization of extensions in Theorems 6.5 and 6.6 reveal important computational properties of default logic. A direct consequence is that propositional default reasoning is *decidable* and can be implemented in *polynomial space*. This is because the characterizations are based on classical reasoning which is decidable in polynomial space in the propositional case.

In order to contrast default logic more sharply to classical logic we consider a (hypothetical) setting where we have a highly efficient theorem prover for propositional logic and, hence, are able to decide classical consequences of a set of formulas W and inference rules R, that is $\mathrm{Cn}_R(W)$, efficiently. Theorems 6.5 and 6.6 suggest that even in this setting constructing an extension of a propositional default theory involves a non-trivial search problem of finding a set of generating defaults or a full set. However, the characterizations imply an upper bound on the computational complexity of propositional default reasoning showing that it is on the second level of the polynomial hierarchy.[2] It turns out this is a tight upper bound as deciding extension existence and credulous inference are actually Σ_2^P-complete problems and sceptical inference is Π_2^P-complete [51, 127].

The completeness results imply that (propositional) default reasoning is strictly harder than classical (propositional) reasoning unless the polynomial hierarchy collapses which is regarded unlikely. This means that there are two orthogonal sources of complexity in default reasoning. One source originates from classical logic on top of which default logic is built. The other source is related to nonmonotonicity of default rules. These sources are independent of each other because even if we assume

---

[2]For an introduction to computational complexity theory and for basic definitions and results on polynomial hierarchy, see, for example, [46, 103].

that we are able to decide classical consequence in one computation step, deciding a propositional default reasoning problem remains on the difficulty level of an NP/co-NP-complete problem and no polynomial time algorithms are known even under this assumption. Hence, it is highly unlikely that general default logic can be implemented on top of a classical theorem prover with only a polynomial overhead.

In order to achieve tractable reasoning it is not enough to limit the syntactic form of allowed formulas because this affects only one source of complexity but also the way default rules interact needs to be restricted. This is nicely demonstrated by complexity results on restricted subclasses of default theories [60, 126, 8, 100]. An interesting question is to find suitable trade-offs between expressive power and computational complexity. For example, while general default logic has higher computational complexity, it enables very compact representation of knowledge which is exponentially more succinct than when using classical logic [50].

A number of decision methods for general (propositional) default reasoning have been developed. Methods based on the characterization of extensions in terms of generating defaults (Theorem 6.2) can be found, for example, in [85, 5, 114, 30], and in terms of full sets (Theorem 6.6) in [98]. There are approaches where default reasoning is reduced into another problem like a truth maintenance problem [59] or a constraint satisfaction problem [8]. An interesting approach to provide proof theory for default reasoning based on sequent calculus was proposed in [18, 19]. More details on automating default reasoning can be found also in [36].

Notice that for general default reasoning it seems infeasible to develop a fully goal-directed procedure, that is, a procedure which would examine only those parts of the default theory which are somehow syntactically relevant to a given query. This is because extensions are defined with a global condition on the whole theory requiring that each applicable default rule should be applied. There are theories with no extensions and in the worst case it is necessary to examine every default rule in order to guarantee the existence of an extension. For achieving a goal-directed decision method, one can consider a weaker notion of extensions or syntactically restricted subclasses of default theories such as normal defaults (see below) [117, 118].

6.2.3 Normal Default Theories

By restricting the form of defaults one obtains special classes of default theories. One of the most important of them is the class of *normal* default theories, where all defaults are of the form

$$\frac{A : B}{B}.$$

The distinguishing feature of normal default theories is that they are guaranteed to have extensions and extensions are determined by enumerations of the set of defaults. Let (D, W) be a normal default theory (as always, assumed to be closed) and let $D = \{d_1, d_2, \ldots\}$.

1. We define $E_0 = \text{Cn}(W)$;

2. Let us assume E_i has been defined. We select the first default $d = A : B/B$ in the enumeration such that $E_i \models A$, $E_i \not\models B$ and $E_i \not\models \neg B$ and define $E_{i+1} = \text{Cn}(E_i \cup \{B\})$. If no such default exists, we set $E_{i+1} = E_i$.

Theorem 6.7. *Let (D, W) be a normal default theory. Then, for every enumeration $D = \{d_1, d_2, \ldots\}$, $E = \bigcup_{i=1}^{\infty} E_i$ is an extension of (D, W) (where E_i are sets constructed above). Furthermore, for every extension E of (D, W) there is an enumeration, which yields sets E_i such that $E = \bigcup_{i=1}^{\infty} E_i$.*

Theorem 6.7 not only establishes the existence of extensions of normal default theories but it also allows us to derive several properties of extensions. We gather them in the following theorem.

Theorem 6.8. *Let (D, W) be a normal default theory. Then,*

1. *if $W \cup \{\mathrm{cons}(d) \mid d \in D\}$ is consistent, then $\mathrm{Cn}(W \cup \{\mathrm{cons}(d) \mid d \in D\})$ is a unique extension of (D, W);*

2. *if E_1 and E_2 are extensions of (D, W) and $E_1 \neq E_2$, then $E_1 \cup E_2$ is inconsistent;*

3. *if E is an extension of (D, W), then for every set D' of normal defaults, the normal default theory $(D \cup D', W)$ has an extension E' such that $E \subseteq E'$.*

The last property is often called the *semi-monotonicity* of normal default logic. It asserts that adding normal defaults to a normal default theory does not destroy existing extensions but only possibly augments them.

A default rule of the form

$$\frac{\top : B_1, \ldots, B_n}{C}$$

is called *prerequisite-free*. Default theories possessing only prerequisite-free normal defaults are called *supernormal*. They are closely related to a formalism for non-monotonic reasoning proposed by Poole [107] and so, are sometimes called *Poole defaults*. We will not discuss Poole's formalism here but only point out that the connection is provided by the following property of supernormal default theories.

Theorem 6.9. *Let (D, W) be a supernormal default theory such that W is consistent. Then, E is an extension of (D, W) if and only if $E = \mathrm{Cn}(W \cup \{\mathrm{cons}(d) \mid d \in C\})$, where C is a maximal subset of D such that $W \cup \{\mathrm{cons}(d) \mid d \in C\}$ is consistent. In particular, if E is an extension of (D, W), then for every $d \in D$, $\mathrm{cons}(d) \in E$ or $\neg\mathrm{cons}(d) \in E$.*

Normal defaults are sufficient for many applications (cf. our discussion of CWA below). However, to represent more complex default reasoning involving interactions among defaults, non-normal defaults are necessary.

6.2.4 Closed-World Assumption and Normal Defaults

The *Closed-World Assumption* (or *CWA*, for short) was introduced by Reiter in [110] in an effort to formalize ways databases handle negative information. It is a defeasible inference rule based on the assumption that a set W of sentences designed to represent an application domain determines *all* ground atomic facts that hold in it (*closed-world assumption*). Taking this assumption literally, the CWA rule infers the *negation* of every ground atom not implied by W. Formally, for a set W of sentences we define

$$CWA(W) = W \cup \{\neg a \mid a \text{ is a ground atom and } W \not\models a\}.$$

To illustrate the idea, we will consider a simple example. Let GA be the set of all ground atoms in the language and let $W \subseteq GA$. It is easy to see that

$$CWA(W) = W \cup \{\neg a \mid a \in GA \setminus W\}.$$

In other words, CWA derives the negation of every ground atom not in W. This is precisely what happens when databases are queried. If a fact is not in the database (for instance, there is no information about a direct flight from Chicago to Dallas at 5:00 pm on Delta), the database infers that this fact is false and responds correspondingly (there is *no* direct flight from Chicago to Dallas at 5:00 pm on Delta).

We note that the database may contain errors (there may in fact be a flight from Chicago to Dallas at 5:00 pm on Delta). Once the database is fixed (a new ground atom is included that asserts the existence of the flight), the derivation sanctioned previously by the CWA rule, will not longer be made. It is a classic example of defeasible reasoning!

In the example above, CWA worked precisely as it should, and resulted in a consistent theory. In many cases, however, the CWA rule is too strong. It derives too many facts and yields an inconsistent theory. For instance, if $W = \{a \vee b\}$, where a, b are two ground atoms, then

$$W \not\models a \quad \text{and} \quad W \not\models b.$$

Thus, $CWA(W) = \{a \vee b, \neg a, \neg b\}$ is inconsistent. The question whether $CWA(W)$ is consistent is an important one. We note a necessary and sufficient condition given in [85].

Theorem 6.10. *Let W be a set of sentences. Then $CWA(W)$ is consistent if and only if W has a least Herbrand model.*

If W is a set of ground atoms (the case discussed above) or, more generally, a consistent Horn theory, then W has a least Herbrand model. Thus, we obtain the following corollary due to Reiter [110].

Corollary 6.11. *If W is a consistent Horn theory, then $CWA(W)$ is consistent.*

The main result of this section shows that CWA can be expressed by means of *supernormal* defaults under the semantics of extensions. For a ground atom a we define a supernormal default

$$cwa(a) = \frac{\top : \neg a}{\neg a}$$

and we set

$$D_{CWA} = \{cwa(a) \mid a \in GA\}.$$

We have the following result [85].

Theorem 6.12. *Let W be a set of sentences.*

1. *If CWA(W) is consistent, then* Cn(CWA(W)) *is the unique extension of the default theory* (D_{CWA}, W).

2. *If* (D_{CWA}, W) *has a unique consistent extension, then CWA(W) is consistent and* Cn(CWA(W)) *is this unique extension of* (D_{CWA}, W).

6.2.5   Variants of Default Logic

A number of modifications of Reiter's default logic have been proposed in the literature which handle several examples differently. We present some of them briefly here.

To guarantee existence of extensions, Lukaszewicz [77] has defined a default logic based on a two-place fixed point operator. The first argument contains the believed formulas, the second is used to keep track of justifications of applied defaults. A default is only applied if its consequent does not contradict the justification of any other applied default. Then, E is an extension if and only if there is a set S_E such that (E, S_E) is a fixed point. Lukaszewicz showed that, in his logic, both existence of extensions and semi-monotony are satisfied.

In [22], a cumulative version of default logic is presented. The basic elements of this logic are so-called *assertions* of the form (p, Q), in which p is a formula, and Q the set of consistency conditions needed to derive p. A default can only be applied in an extension if its justifications are jointly consistent with the extension and with all justifications of other applied defaults. The logic is called cumulative as the inference relation it determines satisfies the property of *Cumulativity* [79], now more commonly called *Cautious Monotony* (cf. Section 6.5).

Joint consistency is also enforced in variants of default logic called *constrained default logics*, which have been proposed independently by [116] and [31] (see also [32]). The major difference between cumulative default logic and these two variants is that the latter work with standard formulas and construct an additional single set containing all consistency conditions of applied defaults, whereas cumulative default logic keeps track of this information in the assertions.

A number of researchers have investigated default theories with preferences among the defaults, e.g., [85, 6, 23, 113, 26]. For a comparison of some of these approaches the reader is referred to [119]. Finally, [23] contains an approach in which reasoning not only with, but also about priorities is possible. In this approach, the preference information is represented in the logical language and can thus be derived and reasoned upon dynamically. This makes it possible to describe conflict resolution strategies declaratively and has interesting applications, for instance, in legal reasoning.

6.3   Autoepistemic Logic

In this section, we discuss autoepistemic logic, one of the most studied and influential nonmonotonic logics. It was proposed by Moore in [92, 93] in a reaction to an earlier modal nonmonotonic logic of McDermott and Doyle [91]. Historically, autoepistemic logic played a major role in the development of nonmonotonic logics of belief. Moreover, intuitions underlying autoepistemic logic and studied in [47] motivated the concept of a stable model of a logic program [49][3] as discussed in detail in the next chapter of the Handbook.

6.3.1   Preliminaries, Intuitions and Basic Results

Autoepistemic logic was introduced to provide a formal account of a way in which an *ideally rational* agent forms *belief* sets given some initial assumptions. It is a formalism in a modal language. In our discussion we assume implicitly a fixed set *At* of propositional variables. We denote by $\mathcal{L}_K$ the modal language generated from *At* by means of boolean connectives and a (unary) modal operator K. The role of the modal operator K is to mark formulas as "believed". That is, intuitively, formulas KA stand for "*A* is believed". We refer to subsets of $\mathcal{L}_K$ as *modal theories*. We call formulas in $\mathcal{L}_K$ that do not contain occurrences of K *modal-free* or *propositional*. We denote the language consisting of all modal-free formulas by $\mathcal{L}$.

Let us consider a situation in which we have a rule that Professor Jones, being a university professor, normally teaches. To capture this rule in modal logic, we might say that if we do not believe that Dr. Jones does not teach (that is, if it is possible that she does), then Dr. Jones does teach. We might represent this rule by a modal formula.[4]

$$K\,prof_J \wedge \neg K \neg teaches_J \supset teaches_J. \tag{6.2}$$

Knowing only *prof$_J$* (Dr. Jones is a professor) a rational agent should build a belief set containing *teaches$_J$*. The problem is to define the semantics of autoepistemic logic so that indeed it is so.

We see here a similarity with default logic, where the same rule is formalized by a default

$$prof(J) : teaches(J)/teaches(J) \tag{6.3}$$

(cf. Section 6.2.1). In default logic, given $W = \{prof(J)\}$, the conclusion $teaches(J)$ is supported as $(\{prof(J) : teaches(J)/teaches(J)\}, W)$ has exactly one extension and it does contain $teaches(J)$.

The correspondence between the formula (6.2) and the default (6.3) is intuitive and compelling. The key question is whether formally the autoepistemic logic interpretation of (6.2) is the same as the default logic interpretation of (6.3). We will return to this question later.

Before we proceed to present the semantics of autoepistemic logic, we will make a few comments on (classical) modal logics—formal systems of reasoning with modal formulas. This is a rich area and any overview that would do it justice is beyond the

---

[3] We note however, that default logic also played a role in the development of the stable-model semantics [13] and, in fact, the default-logic connection of stable models ultimately turned out to be more direct [82, 15, 14].

[4] To avoid problems with the treatment of quantifiers, we restrict our attention to the propositional case. Consequently, we have to list "normality" rules explicitly for each object in the domain rather than use schemata (formulas with variables) to represent concisely families of propositional rules, as it is possible in default logic. The "normality" rule in our example concerns Professor Jones only. If there were more professors in our domain, we would need rules of this type for each of them.

scope of this chapter. For a good introduction, we refer to [28, 57]. Here we only mention that many important modal logics are defined by a selection of modal axioms such K, T, D, 4, 5, etc. For instance, the axioms K, T, 4 and 5 yield the well-known modal logic S5. The consequence operator for a modal logic $\mathcal{S}$, say $\mathrm{Cn}_{\mathcal{S}}$, is defined syntactically in terms of the corresponding provability relation.[5]

For the reader familiar with *Kripke models* [28, 57], we note that the consequence operator $\mathrm{Cn}_{\mathcal{S}}$ can often be described in terms of a class of *Kripke models*, say $\mathcal{C}$: $A \in \mathrm{Cn}_{\mathcal{S}}(E)$ if and only if for every Kripke model $M \in \mathcal{C}$ such that $M \models_K E$, $M \models_K A$, where $\models_K$ stands for the relation of satisfiability of a formula or a set of formulas in a Kripke model. For instance, the consequence operator in the modal logic S5 is characterized by *universal* Kripke models. This characterization played a fundamental role in the development of autoepistemic logic. To make our chapter self-contained, rather than introducing Kripke models formally, we will use a different but equivalent characterization of the consequence operator in S5 in terms of *possible-world structures*, which we introduce formally later in the text.

After this brief digression we now come back to autoepistemic logic. What is an *ideally rational agent* or, more precisely, which modal theories could be taken as belief sets of such agents? Stalnaker [125] argued that to be a belief set of an ideally rational agent a modal theory $E \subseteq \mathcal{L}_K$ must satisfy three closure properties.

First, E must be closed under the propositional consequence operator. We will denote this operator by Cn.[6] Thus, the first property postulated by Stalnaker can be stated concisely as follows:

   (B1) $\mathrm{Cn}(E) \subseteq E$.

We note that modal logics offer consequence operators which are stronger than the operator Cn. One might argue that closure under one of these operators might be a more appropriate for the condition (B1). We will return to this issue in a moment.

Next, Stalnaker postulated that theories modeling belief sets of ideally rational agents must be closed under *positive introspection*: if an agent believes in A, then the agent believes she believes A. Formally, we will require that a belief set E satisfies:

   (B2) if $A \in E$, then $KA \in E$.

Finally, Stalnaker postulated that theories modeling belief sets of ideally rational agents must also be closed under *negative introspection*: if an agent does not believe A, then the agent believes she does not believe A. This property is formally captured by the condition:

   (B3) if $A \notin E$, then $\neg KA \in E$.

Stalnaker's postulates have become commonly accepted as the defining properties of belief sets of an ideally rational agent. Thus, we refer to modal theories satisfying conditions (B1)–(B3) simply as *belief sets*. The original term used by Stalnaker was a *stable* theory. We choose a different notation since in nonmonotonic reasoning the term

---

[5]Proofs in a modal logic use as premises given assumptions (if any), instances of propositional tautologies in the language $\mathcal{L}_K$, and instances of modal axioms of the logic. As inference rules, they use modus ponens and the *necessitation rule*, which allows one to conclude KA once A has been derived.

[6]When applying the propositional consequence operator to *modal* theories, as we do here, we treat formulas KA as propositional variables.

stable is now most commonly associated with a class of models of logic programs, and there are fundamental differences between the two notions.

Belief sets have a rich theory [85]. We cite here only two results that we use later in the chapter. The first result shows that in the context of the conditions (B2) and (B3) the choice of the consequence operator for the condition (B1) becomes essentially immaterial. Namely, it implies that no matter what consequence relation we choose for (B1), as long as it contains the propositional consequence relation and is contained in the consequence relation for S5, we obtain the same notion of a belief set.

Proposition 6.13. *If $E \subseteq \mathcal{L}_K$ is a belief set, then E is closed under the consequence relation in the modal logic S5.*

The second result shows that belief sets are determined by their modal-free formulas. This property leads to a representation result for belief sets.

Proposition 6.14. *Let $T \subseteq \mathcal{L}$ be closed under propositional consequence. Then $E = \text{Cn}_{S5}(T \cup \{\neg KA \mid A \in \mathcal{L} \setminus T\})$ is a belief set and $E \cap \mathcal{L} = T$. Moreover, if E is a belief set then $T = E \cap \mathcal{L}$ is closed under propositional consequence and $E = \text{Cn}_{S5}(T \cup \{\neg KA \mid A \in \mathcal{L} \setminus T\})$.*

Modal nonmonotonic logics are meant to provide formal means to study mechanisms by which an agent forms belief sets starting with a set T of initial assumptions. These belief sets must contain T but may also satisfy some additional properties. A precise mapping assigning to a set of modal formulas a family of belief sets is what determines a modal nonmonotonic logic.

An obvious possibility is to associate with a set $T \subseteq \mathcal{L}_K$ *all* belief sets E such that $T \subseteq E$. This choice, however, results in a formalism which is *monotone*. Namely, if $T \subseteq T'$, then every belief set for T' is a belief set for T. Consequently, the set of "safe" beliefs—beliefs that belong to every belief set associated with T—grows monotonically as T gets larger. In fact, this set of safe beliefs based on T coincides with the set of consequences of T in the logic S5. As we aim to capture nonmonotonic reasoning, this choice is not of interest to us here.

Another possibility is to employ a minimization principle. Minimizing entire belief sets is of little interest as belief sets are incomparable with respect to inclusion and so, each of them is inclusion-minimal. Thus, this form of minimization does not eliminate any of the belief sets containing T, and so, it is equivalent to the approach discussed above.

A more interesting direction is to apply the minimization principle to modal-free fragments of belief sets (cf. Proposition 6.14, which implies that there is a one-to-one correspondence between belief sets and sets of modal-free formulas closed under propositional consequence). The resulting logic is in fact nonmonotonic and it received some attention [54].

The principle put forth by Moore when defining the autoepistemic logic can be viewed as yet another form of minimization. The conditions (B1)–(B3) imply that every belief set E containing T satisfies the inclusion

$$\text{Cn}\big(T \cup \{KA \mid A \in E\} \cup \{\neg KA \mid A \notin E\}\big) \subseteq E.$$

Belief sets, for which the inclusion is proper, contain beliefs that do not follow from initial assumptions and from the results of "introspection" and so, are undesirable. Hence, Moore [93] proposed to associate with T only those belief sets E, which satisfy the *equality*:

$$\mathrm{Cn}\big(T \cup \{KA \mid A \in E\} \cup \{\neg KA \mid A \notin E\}\big) = E. \tag{6.4}$$

In fact, when a theory satisfies (6.4), we no longer need to assume that it is a belief set—(6.4) implies that it is.

Proposition 6.15. *For every* $T \subseteq \mathcal{L}_K$, *if* $E \subseteq \mathcal{L}_K$ *satisfies* (6.4), *then* E *satisfies* (B1)–(B3), *that is, it is a belief set.*

Moore called belief sets defined by (6.4) *stable expansions* of T. We will refer to them simply as *expansions* of T, dropping the term *stable* due to the same reason as before. We formalize our discussion in the following definition.

Definition 6.4. *Let* T *be a modal theory. A modal theory* E *is an expansion of* T *if* E *satisfies the identity* (6.4).

Belief sets have an elegant semantic characterization in terms of possible-world structures. Let $\mathcal{I}$ be the set of all 2-valued interpretations (truth assignments) of *At*. *Possible-world structures* are subsets of $\mathcal{I}$. Intuitively, a possible-world structure collects all interpretations that *might* be describing the actual world and leaves out those that definitely do not.

A possible-world structure is essentially a Kripke model with a total accessibility relation [28, 57]. The difference is that the universe of a Kripke model is required to be nonempty, which guarantees that the *theory* of the model (the set of all formulas true in the model) is consistent. Some modal theories consistent with respect to the propositional consequence relation determine inconsistent sets of beliefs. Allowing possible-world structures to be empty is a way to capture such situations and differentiate them from those situations, in which a modal theory determines no belief sets at all.

Possible-world structures interpret modal formulas, that is, assign to them truth values.

Definition 6.5. *Let* $Q \subseteq \mathcal{I}$ *be a possible-world structure and* $I \in \mathcal{I}$ *a two-valued interpretation. We define the truth function* $\mathcal{H}_{Q,I}$ *inductively as follows*:

1. $\mathcal{H}_{Q,I}(p) = I(p)$, *if* p *is an atom.*

2. $\mathcal{H}_{Q,I}(A_1 \wedge A_2) =$ **true** *if* $\mathcal{H}_{Q,I}(A_1) =$ **true** *and* $\mathcal{H}_{Q,I}(A_2) =$ **true**. *Otherwise,* $\mathcal{H}_{Q,I}(A_1 \wedge A_2) =$ **false**.

3. *Other boolean connectives are treated similarly.*

4. $\mathcal{H}_{Q,I}(KA) =$ **true**, *if for every interpretation* $J \in Q$, $\mathcal{H}_{Q,J}(A) =$ **true**. *Otherwise,* $\mathcal{H}_{Q,I}(KA) =$ **false**.

It follows directly from the definition that for every formula $A \in \mathcal{L}_K$, the truth value $\mathcal{H}_{Q,I}(KA)$ does not depend on I. It is fully determined by the possible-world structure Q and we will denote it by $\mathcal{H}_Q(KA)$, dropping I from the notation. Since Q determines the truth value of every modal atom, every modal formula A is either *believed* ($\mathcal{H}_Q(KA) = $ **true**) or *not believed* in Q ($\mathcal{H}_Q(KA) = $ **false**). In other words, the *epistemic* status of every modal formula is well defined in every possible-world structure.

The *theory* of a possible-world structure Q is the set of all modal formulas that are *believed* in Q. We denote it by $Th(Q)$. Thus, formally,

$$Th(Q) = \{A \mid \mathcal{H}_Q(KA) = \mathbf{true}\}.$$

We now present a characterization of belief sets in terms of possible-world structures, which we promised earlier.

Theorem 6.16. *A set of modal formulas $E \subseteq \mathcal{L}_K$ is a belief set if and only if there is a possible-world structure $Q \subseteq \mathcal{I}$ such that $E = Th(Q)$.*

Expansions of a modal theory can also be characterized in terms of possible-world structures. The underlying intuitions arise from considering a way to revise possible-world structures, given a set T of initial assumptions. The characterization is also due to Moore. Namely, for every modal theory T, Moore [92] defined an operator D_T on $\mathcal{P}(\mathcal{I})$ (the space of all possible-world structures) by setting

$$D_T(Q) = \{I \mid \mathcal{H}_{Q,I}(A) = \mathbf{true}, \text{ for every } A \in T\}.$$

The operator D_T specifies a process to revise belief sets encoded by the corresponding possible-world structures. Given a modal theory $T \subseteq \mathcal{L}_K$, the operator D_T revises a possible-world structure Q with a possible-world structure $D_T(Q)$. This revised structure consists of all interpretations that are *acceptable* given the current structure Q and the constraints on belief sets encoded by T. Specifically, the revision consists precisely of those interpretations that make all formulas in T true with respect to Q.

Fixed points of the operator D_T are of particular interest. They represent "stable" possible-world structures (and so, belief sets)—they cannot be revised any further. This property is behind the role they play in the autoepistemic logic.

Theorem 6.17. *Let $T \subseteq \mathcal{L}_K$. A set of modal formulas $E \subseteq \mathcal{L}_K$ is an expansion of T if and only if there is a possible-world structure $Q \subseteq \mathcal{I}$ such that $Q = D_T(Q)$ and $E = Th(Q)$.*

This theorem implies a systematic procedure for constructing expansions of *finite* modal theories (or, to be more precise, possible-world structures that determine expansions). Let us continue our "Professor Jones" example and let us look at a theory

$$T = \{prof_J, Kprof_J \wedge \neg K \neg teaches_J \supset teaches_J\}.$$

There are two propositional variables in our language and, consequently, four propositional interpretations:

$I_1 = \emptyset$ (neither $prof_J$ nor $teaches_J$ is true),

$I_2 = \{prof_J\}$,

$I_3 = \{teaches_J\}$,

$I_4 = \{prof_J, teaches_J\}$.

There are 16 possible-world structures one can build of these four interpretations. Only one of them, though, $Q = \{prof_J, teaches_J\}$, satisfies $D_T(Q) = Q$ and so, generates an expansion of T. We skip the details of verifying it, as the process is long and tedious, and we present a more efficient method in the next section. We note however, that for the basic "Professor Jones" example autoepistemic logic gives the same conclusions as default logic.

We close this section by noting that autoepistemic logic can also be obtained as a special case of a general fixed point schema to define modal nonmonotonic logics proposed by McDermott [90]. In this schema, we assume that an agent uses some modal logic S (extending propositional logic) to capture her basic means of inference. We then say that a modal theory $E \subseteq \mathcal{L}_K$ is an *S-expansion* of a modal theory T if

$$E = \mathrm{Cn}_S\big(T \cup \{\neg KA \mid A \notin E\}\big). \tag{6.5}$$

In this equation, Cn_S represents the consequence relation in the modal logic S. If E satisfies (6.5), then E is closed under the propositional consequence relation. Moreover, E is closed under the necessitation rule and so, E is closed under positive introspection. Finally, since $\{\neg KA \mid A \notin E\} \subseteq E$, E is closed under negative introspection. It follows that solutions to (6.5) are belief sets containing T. They can be taken as models of belief sets of agents reasoning by means of modal logic S and justifying what they believe on the basis of initial assumptions in T and *assumptions* about what *not* to believe (negative introspection). By choosing different monotone logics S, we obtain from this schema different classes of S-expansions of T.

If we disregard inconsistent expansions, autoepistemic logic can be viewed as a special instance of this schema, with $S = \mathrm{KD45}$, the modal logic determined by the axioms K, D, 4 and 5 [57, 85]. Namely, we have the following result.

Theorem 6.18. *Let* $T \subseteq \mathcal{L}_K$. *If* $E \subseteq \mathcal{L}_K$ *is consistent, then* E *is an expansion of* T *if and only if* E *is a* KD45*-expansion of* T, *that is,*

$$E = \mathrm{Cn}_{\mathrm{KD45}}\big(T \cup \{\neg KA \mid A \notin E\}\big).$$

6.3.2 Computational Properties

The key reasoning problems for autoepistemic logic are deciding *skeptical inference* (whether a formula is in all expansions), *credulous inference* (whether a formula is in some expansion), and finding expansions. Like default logic, first order autoepistemic logic is not semi-decidable even when quantifying into the scope of the modal operator is not allowed [94]. If quantifying-in is allowed, the reasoning problems are highly undecidable [63].

In order to clarify the computational properties of propositional autoepistemic logic we present a finitary characterization of expansions based on *full sets* [94, 95]. A full set is constructed from the KA and $\neg KA$ subformulas of the premises and it serves as the characterizing kernel of an expansion. An overview of other approaches to characterizing expansions can be found in [95].

The characterization is based on the set of all subformulas of the form KA in a set of premises T. We denote this set by $\mathrm{Sf}_K(T)$. We stress that in the characterization only the classical consequence relation (Cn) is used where KA formulas are treated as propositional variables and no modal consequence relation is needed. To simplify the notation, for a set T of formulas we will write $\neg T$ as a shorthand for $\{\neg F \mid F \in T\}$.

Definition 6.6 (Full sets). *For a set of formulas T, a set $S \subseteq \mathrm{Sf}_K(T) \cup \neg\,\mathrm{Sf}_K(T)$ is T-full if and only if the following two conditions hold for every $KA \in \mathrm{Sf}_K(T)$:*

- *$A \in \mathrm{Cn}(T \cup S)$ if and only if $KA \in S$.*

- *$A \notin \mathrm{Cn}(T \cup S)$ if and only if $\neg KA \in S$.*

In fact, for a T-full set S, the classical consequences of $T \cup S$ provide the modal-free part of an expansion. As explained in Proposition 6.14 this uniquely determines the expansion. Here we give an alternative way of constructing an expansion from a full set presented in [95] which is more suitable for automation. For this we employ a restricted notion of subformulas: $\mathrm{Sf}_K^p(F)$ is the set of *primary* subformulas of F, i.e., all subformulas of the form KA of F which are not in the scope of another K operator in F. For example, if p and q are atomic, $\mathrm{Sf}_K^p(K(\neg Kp \rightarrow q) \wedge K\neg q) = \{K(\neg Kp \rightarrow q), K\neg q\}$. The construction uses a simple consequence relation $\models_K$ which is given recursively on top of the classical consequence relation Cn. It turns out that this consequence relation corresponds exactly to membership in an expansion when given its characterizing full set.

Definition 6.7 (K-consequence). *Given a set of formulas T and a formula F,*

$$T \models_K F \quad \text{if and only if} \quad F \in \mathrm{Cn}(T \cup \mathrm{SB}_T(F))$$

where $\mathrm{SB}_T(F) = \{KA \in \mathrm{Sf}_K^p(F) \mid T \models_K A\} \cup \{\neg KA \in \neg\,\mathrm{Sf}_K^p(F) \mid T \not\models_K A\}$.

For an expansion E of T, there is a corresponding T-full set

$$\{KF \in E \mid KF \in \mathrm{Sf}_K(T)\} \cup \{\neg KF \in E \mid KF \in \mathrm{Sf}_K(T)\}$$

and for a T-full set S,

$$\{F \mid T \cup S \models_K F\}$$

is an expansion of T. In fact it can be shown [95] that there is a one-to-one correspondence between full sets and expansions.

Theorem 6.19 (Expansions in terms of full sets). *Let T be a set of autoepistemic formulas. Then a function SE_T defined as*

$$SE_T(S) = \{F \mid T \cup S \models_K F\}$$

gives a bijective mapping from the set of T-full sets to the set of expansions of T and for a T-full set S, $SE_T(S)$ is the unique expansion E of T such that $S \subseteq \{KF \mid F \in E\} \cup \{\neg KF \mid F \notin E\}$.

Example 6.2. Consider our "Professor Jones" example and a set of formulas

$$T = \{prof_J, Kprof_J \wedge \neg K \neg teaches_J \supset teaches_J\}.$$

Now $\mathrm{Sf}_K(T) = \{Kprof_J, K \neg teaches_J\}$ and there are four possible full sets:

$$\{\neg Kprof_J, \neg K \neg teaches_J\}, \quad \{Kprof_J, \neg K \neg teaches_J\},$$

$$\{\neg Kprof_J, K \neg teaches_J\}, \quad \{Kprof_J, K \neg teaches_J\}.$$

It is easy to verify that only $S_1 = \{Kprof_J, \neg K \neg teaches_J\}$ satisfies the conditions in Definition 6.6, that is, $prof \in \mathrm{Cn}(T \cup S_1)$ and $\neg teaches_J \notin \mathrm{Cn}(T \cup S_1)$. Hence, T has exactly one expansion $SE_T(S_1)$ which contains, for instance, $KKprof_J$ and $\neg K \neg K teaches_J$ as $T \cup S_1 \models_K KKprof_J$ and $T \cup S_1 \models_K \neg K \neg K teaches_J$ hold.

Example 6.3. Consider a set of formulas

$$T' = \{Kp \supset p\}.$$

Now $\mathrm{Sf}_K(T') = \{Kp\}$ and there are two possible full sets: $\{\neg Kp\}$ and $\{Kp\}$ which are both full. For instance, $p \in \mathrm{Cn}(T' \cup \{Kp\})$. Hence, T' has exactly two expansions $SE_{T'}(\{\neg Kp\})$ and $SE_{T'}(\{Kp\})$.

The finitary characterization of expansions in Theorem 6.19 implies that propositional autoepistemic reasoning is *decidable* and can be implemented in *polynomial space*. This is because the conditions on a full set and on membership of an arbitrary autoepistemic formula in an expansion induced by a full set are based on the classical propositional consequence relation which is decidable in polynomial space.

Similar to default logic, deciding whether an expansion exists and credulous inference are Σ_2^P-complete problems and sceptical inference is Π_2^P-complete for autoepistemic logic as well as for many other modal nonmonotonic logics [51, 94, 95, 121]. This implies that modal nonmonotonic reasoning is strictly harder than classical reasoning (unless the polynomial hierarchy collapses) and achieving tractability requires substantial restrictions on how modal operators can interact [83, 84]. For more information on automating autoepistemic reasoning, see for instance [97, 36].

6.4 Circumscription

6.4.1 Motivation

Circumscription was introduced by John McCarthy [86, 87]. Many of its formal aspects were worked out by Vladimir Lifschitz who also wrote an excellent overview [74]. We follow here the notation and terminology used in this overview article.

The idea underlying circumscription can be explained using the teaching professors example discussed in the introduction. There we considered using the following first order formula to express *professors normally teach*:

$$\forall x \big(prof(x) \wedge \neg abnormal(x) \supset teaches(x) \big).$$

The problem with this formula is the following: in order to apply it to Professor Jones, we need to prove that Jones is not abnormal. In many cases we simply do not have enough information to do this. Intuitively, we do not expect objects to be abnormal—unless we have explicit information that tells us they indeed are abnormal. Let us assume there is no reason to believe Jones is abnormal. We implicitly assume—in McCarthy's words: jump to the conclusion—$\neg abnormal(Jones)$ and use it to conclude *teaches(Jones)*.

What we would like to have is a mechanism which models this form of jumping to conclusions. Note that what is at work here is a minimization of the extent of the predicate *abnormal*: we want as few objects as possible—given the available information—to satisfy this predicate. How can this be achieved?

The answer provided by circumscription has a syntactical and a corresponding semantical side. From the syntactical point of view, circumscription is a transformation (more precisely, a family of transformations) of logical formulas. Given a sentence A representing the given information, circumscription produces a logically stronger sentence A^*. The formulas which follow from A using circumscription are simply the formulas classically entailed by A^*. In our example, A contains the given information about professors, their teaching duties, and Jones. In addition to this information, A^* also expresses that the extent of *abnormal* is minimal. Note that in order to express minimality of a predicate one has to quantify over predicates. For this reason A^* will be a second order formula.

Semantically, circumscription gives up the classical point of view that all models of a sentence A have to be regarded as equal possibilities. In our example, different models of A may have different extents for the predicate *abnormal* (the set of objects belonging to the interpretation of *abnormal*) even if the domain of the models is the same. It is natural to consider models with fewer abnormal objects—in the sense of set inclusion—as more plausible than those with more abnormal objects. This induces a preference relation on the set of all models. The idea now is to restrict the definition of entailment to the most preferred models only: a formula f is preferentially entailed by A if and only if f is true in all maximally preferred models of A.

We will see that this elegant model theoretic construction captures exactly the syntactic transformation described above.

6.4.2 Defining Circumscription

For the definition of circumscription some abbreviations are useful. Let P and Q be two predicate symbols of the same arity n:

$$P = Q \quad \text{abbreviates} \quad \forall x_1 \cdots x_n ((P(x_1, \ldots, x_n) \equiv Q(x_1, \ldots, x_n))),$$
$$P \leqslant Q \quad \text{abbreviates} \quad \forall x_1 \cdots x_n ((P(x_1, \ldots, x_n) \supset Q(x_1, \ldots, x_n))),$$
$$P < Q \quad \text{abbreviates} \quad (P \leqslant Q) \wedge \neg (P = Q).$$

The formulas express: P and Q have the same extent, the extent of P is a subset of the extent of Q, and the extent of P is a proper subset of the extent of Q, respectively.

Definition 6.8. *Let $A(P)$ be a sentence containing a predicate symbol P. Let p be a predicate variable of the same arity as P. The circumscription of P in $A(P)$, which will be denoted by $CIRC[A(P); P]$, is the second order sentence*

$$A(P) \wedge \neg \exists p [A(p) \wedge p < P].$$

Table 6.1. Examples of circumscribing P

$A(P)$	$CIRC[A(P); P]$
$P(a)$	$\forall x(P(x) \equiv x = a)$
$P(a) \wedge P(b)$	$\forall x(P(x) \equiv (x = a \vee x = b))$
$P(a) \vee P(b)$	$\forall x(P(x) \equiv (x = a)) \vee \forall x(P(x) \equiv (x = b))$
$\neg P(a)$	$\forall x \neg P(x)$
$\forall x(Q(x) \supset P(x))$	$\forall x(Q(x) \equiv P(x))$

By $A(p)$ we denote here the result of uniformly substituting predicate constant P in $A(P)$ by variable p. Intuitively, the second order formula $\neg \exists p[A(p) \wedge p < P]$ says: it is not possible to find a predicate p such that

1. p satisfies what is said in $A(P)$ about P, and

2. the extent of p is a proper subset of the extent of P.

In other words: the extent of P is minimal subject to the condition $A(P)$.

Table 6.1 presents some simple formulas $A(P)$ together with the result of circumscribing P in $A(P)$. The examples are taken from [74].

Although it gives desired results in simple cases, this form of circumscription is not yet powerful enough for most applications. It allows us to minimize the extent of a predicate, but only if this does not change the interpretation of any other symbol in the language. In the Professor Jones example, for instance, minimizing the predicate *abnormal* alone is not sufficient to conclude *teaches(Jones)*. To obtain this conclusion, we have to make sure that the extent of *teaches* is allowed to change during the minimization of *abnormal*. This can be achieved with the following more general definition:

Definition 6.9. *Let $A(P, Z_1, \ldots, Z_m)$ be a sentence containing the predicate constant P and predicate/function constants Z_i. Let $p, z_1, \ldots, z_m$ be predicate/function variables of the same type and arity as $P, Z_1, \ldots, Z_m$. The circumscription of P in $A(P, Z_1, \ldots, Z_m)$ with varied $Z_1, \ldots, Z_m$, denoted $CIRC[A(P, Z_1, \ldots, Z_m); P; Z_1, \ldots, Z_m]$, is the second order sentence*

$$A(P, Z_1, \ldots, Z_m) \wedge \neg \exists p z_1 \ldots z_m [A(p, z_1, \ldots, z_m) \wedge p < P].$$

A further generalization where several predicates can be minimized in parallel is also very useful. Whenever we want to represent several default rules, we need different abnormality predicates ab_1, ab_2 etc., since being abnormal with respect to one default is not necessarily related to being abnormal with respect to another default.

We first need to generalize the abbreviations $P = Q$, $P \leqslant Q$ and $P < Q$ to the case where P and Q are sequences of predicate symbols. Let $P = P_1, \ldots, P_n$ and $Q = Q_1, \ldots, Q_n$, respectively:

$$P = Q \quad \text{abbreviates} \quad P_1 = Q_1 \wedge \cdots \wedge P_n = Q_n,$$

$$P \leqslant Q \quad \text{abbreviates} \quad P_1 \leqslant Q_1 \wedge \cdots \wedge P_n \leqslant Q_n,$$

$$P < Q \quad \text{abbreviates} \quad P \leqslant Q \wedge \neg(P = Q).$$

Here is the generalized definition:

Definition 6.10. *Let $P = P_1, \ldots, P_k$ be a sequence of predicate constants, $Z = Z_1, \ldots, Z_m$ a sequence of predicate/function constants. Furthermore, let $A(P, Z)$ be a sentence containing the predicate constants P_i and predicate/function constants Z_j. Let $p = p_1, \ldots, p_k$ and $z = z_1, \ldots, z_m$ be predicate/function variables of the same type and arity as $P_1, \ldots, P_k$, respectively, $Z_1, \ldots, Z_m$. The (parallel) circumscription of P in $A(P, Z)$ with varied Z, denoted $CIRC[A(P, Z); P; Z]$, is the second order sentence*

$$A(P, Z) \wedge \neg \exists pz \big[A(p, z) \wedge p < P \big].$$

Predicate and function constants which are neither minimized nor varied, i.e., neither in P nor in Z, are called fixed.

6.4.3 Semantics

Circumscription allows us to minimize the extent of predicates. This can be elegantly described in terms of a preference relation on the models of the circumscribed sentence A. Intuitively, we prefer a model M_1 over a model M_2 whenever the extent of the minimized predicate(s) P is smaller in M_1 than in M_2. Of course, M_1 can only be preferred over M_2 if the two models are comparable: they must have the same universe, and they have to agree on the fixed constants.

In the following, for a structure M we use $|M|$ to denote the universe of M and $M[\![C]\!]$ to denote the interpretation of the (individual/function/predicate) constant C in M.

Definition 6.11. *Let M_1 and M_2 be structures, P a sequence of predicate constants, Z a sequence of predicate/function constants. M_1 is at least as $P; Z$-preferred as M_2, denoted $M_1 \leqslant^{P;Z} M_2$, whenever the following conditions hold:*

1. $|M_1| = |M_2|$,

2. $M_1[\![C]\!] = M_2[\![C]\!]$ *for every constant C which is neither in P nor in Z,*

3. $M_1[\![P_i]\!] \subseteq M_2[\![P_i]\!]$ *for every predicate constant P_i in P.*

The relation $\leqslant^{P;Z}$ is obviously transitive and reflexive. We say a structure M is $\leqslant^{P;Z}$-minimal within a set of structures $\mathcal{M}$ whenever there is no structure $M' \in \mathcal{M}$ such that $M' <^{P;Z} M$. Here $<^{P;Z}$ is the strict order induced by $\leqslant^{P;Z}$: $M' <^{P;Z} M$ if and only if $M' \leqslant^{P;Z} M$ and not $M \leqslant^{P;Z} M'$.

The following proposition shows that the $P; Z$-minimal models of A capture exactly the circumscription of P in A with varied Z:

Proposition 6.20. *M is a model of $CIRC[A; P; Z]$ if and only if M is $\leqslant^{P;Z}$-minimal among the models of A.*

It should be pointed out that circumscription may lead to inconsistency, even if the circumscribed sentence A is consistent. This happens whenever we can find a better model for each model, implying that there is an infinite chain of more and more preferred models. A discussion of conditions under which consistency of circumscription is guaranteed can be found in [74]. For instance, it is known that $CIRC[A; P; Z]$ is consistent whenever A is universal (of the form $\forall x A$ where x is a tuple of object variables and A is quantifier-free) and Z does not contain function symbols.

6.4.4 Computational Properties

In circumscription the key computational problem is that of sceptical inference, i.e., determining whether a formula is true in all minimal models. However, general first order circumscription is highly uncomputable [120]. This is not surprising as circumscription transforms a first order sentence into a second order formula and it is well known that second order logic is not even semi-decidable. This means that in order to compute circumscription we cannot just use our favorite second order prover—such a prover simply cannot exist. We can only hope to find computational methods for certain special cases of first order formulas.

We first discuss techniques for computing circumscriptive inference in the first order case and then present a finitary characterization of minimal models which illustrates computational properties of circumscription.

Methods for computing circumscription can be roughly categorized as follows:

- *guess and verify*: the idea is to guess right instances of second order variables to prove conjectures about circumscription. Of course, this is a method requiring adequate user interaction, not a full mechanization,

- *translation to first order logic*: this method is based on results depending on syntactic restrictions and transformation rules,

- *specialized proof procedures*: these can be modified first order proof procedures or procedures for restricted second order theories.

As an illustration of the guess and verify method consider the Jones example again. Abbreviating *abnormal* with *ab* we have

$$A(ab, teaches) = prof(J) \wedge \forall x(prof(x) \wedge \neg ab(x) \supset teaches(x)).$$

We are interested in $CIRC[A(ab, teaches); ab; teaches]$ which is

$$A(ab, teaches) \wedge \neg \exists pz\big[A(p, z) \wedge p < ab\big].$$

By simple equivalence transformations and by spelling out the abbreviation $p < ab$ we obtain

$$A(ab, teaches) \wedge \forall pz\big[A(p, z) \wedge \forall x(p(x) \supset ab(x)) \supset \forall x(ab(x) \supset p(x))\big].$$

If we substitute the right predicate expressions for the now universally quantified predicate variables p and z, we can indeed prove $teaches(J)$. By a predicate expression we mean an expression of the form $\lambda x_1, \ldots, x_n.F$ where F is a first order formula. Applying this predicate expression to n terms $t_1, \ldots, t_n$ yields the formula obtained by substituting all variables x_i in F uniformly by t_i.

In our example we guess that no object is *ab*, that is we substitute for p the expression $\lambda x.false$. Similarly, we guess that professors are the teaching objects, i.e., we substitute for z the expression $\lambda x.prof(x)$. The resulting first order formula (after simple equivalence transformations) is

$A(ab, teaches) \wedge$

$\quad \big[prof(J) \wedge \forall x(prof(x) \supset prof(x)) \wedge$

$\quad \forall x(false \supset ab(x)) \supset \forall x(ab(x) \supset false)\big].$

It is easy to verify that the first order formula obtained with these substitutions indeed implies *teaches*(J). In cases where derivations are more difficult one can, of course, use a standard first order theorem prover to verify conjectures after substituting predicate expressions.

For the second method, the translation of circumscription to first order logic, a number of helpful results are known. We cannot go into much detail here and refer the reader to [74] for an excellent overview. As an example of the kind of results used we present two useful propositions.

Let $A(P)$ be a formula and P a predicate symbol occurring in A. A formula A, without any occurrence of $\supset$ and $\equiv$, is *positive/negative* in P if all occurrences of P in $A(P)$ are positive/negative. (We recall that the occurrence of a predicate symbol P in a formula $A(P)$ without occurrences of $\supset$ and $\equiv$ is positive if the number of its occurrences in the range of the negation operator is positive. Otherwise, it is negative.)

Proposition 6.21. *Let $B(P)$ be a formula without any occurrences of $\supset$ and $\equiv$. If $B(P)$ is negative in P, then $CIRC[A(P) \wedge B(P); P]$ is equivalent to $CIRC[A(P); P] \wedge B(P)$.*

Proposition 6.22. *Let $A(P, Z)$ be a formula without any occurrences of $\supset$ and $\equiv$. If $A(P, Z)$ is positive in P, then $CIRC[A(P, Z); P; Z]$ is equivalent to*

$$A(P, Z) \wedge \neg \exists xz\big[P(x) \wedge A(\lambda y.(P(y) \wedge x \neq y), z)\big].$$

Here x and y stand for n-tuples of distinct object variables, where n is the arity of predicate symbol P. As a corollary of these propositions we obtain that $CIRC[A(P) \wedge B(P); P]$ is equivalent to a first order formula whenever $A(P)$ is positive and $B(P)$ negative in P (assuming $A(P)$ and $B(P)$ do not contain $\supset$ and $\equiv$).

Apart from translations to first order logic, translations to logic programming have also been investigated [48].

Several specialized theorem proving methods and systems have been developed for restricted classes of formulas. Among these we want to mention Przymusinski's MILO-resolution [109], Baker and Ginsberg's argument based circumscriptive prover [7], the tableaux based method developed by Niemelä [99], and two algorithms based on second order quantifier elimination: the SCAN algorithm [45, 102] and the DLS algorithm [37].

We now turn to the question how minimal models, the key notion in circumscription, can be characterized in order to shed light on computational properties of circumscription and its relationship to classical logic. We present a characterization of minimal models where the minimality of a model can be determined independently of other models using a test for classical consequence. We consider here parallel predicate circumscription in the clausal case and with respect to Herbrand interpretations and a characterization proposed in [99]. A similar characterization but for the propositional case has been used in [41] in the study of the computational complexity of propositional circumscription.

Definition 6.12 (Grounded models). *Let T be a set of clauses and let P and R be sets of predicates. A Herbrand interpretation M is said to be* grounded in $\langle T, P, R \rangle$ *if and only if for all ground atoms $p(\vec{t})$ such that $p \in P$, $M \models p(\vec{t})$ implies $p(\vec{t}) \in \mathrm{Cn}(T \cup \mathrm{N}^{\langle P, R \rangle}(M))$ where*

$$\mathrm{N}^{\langle P, R \rangle}(M) = \big\{\neg q(\vec{t}) \mid q(\vec{t}) \text{ is a ground atom}, q \in P \cup R, M \not\models q(\vec{t})\big\} \cup$$

$$\big\{q(\vec{t}) \mid q(\vec{t}) \text{ is a ground atom}, q \in R, M \models q(\vec{t})\big\}.$$

Theorem 6.23 (Minimal models). *Let T be a set of clauses and let P and Z be the sets of minimized and varied predicates, respectively. A Herbrand interpretation M is a $\leqslant^{P;Z}$-minimal model of T if and only if M is a model of T and grounded in $\langle T, P, R \rangle$ where R is the set of predicates in T that are in neither P nor Z.*

Example 6.4. Let $T = \{p(x) \vee \neg q(x)\}$ and let the underlying language have only one ground term a. Then the Herbrand base is $\{p(a), q(a)\}$. Consider the sets of minimized predicates $P = \{p\}$ and varied predicates $Z = \emptyset$. Then the set of fixed predicates $R = \{q\}$. Now the Herbrand interpretation $M = \{p(a), q(a)\}$, which is a model of T, is grounded in $\langle T, P, R \rangle$ because $\mathrm{N}^{\langle P, R \rangle}(M) = \{q(a)\}$ and $p(a) \in \mathrm{Cn}(T \cup \mathrm{N}^{\langle P, R \rangle}(M))$ holds. Hence, M is a minimal model of T. If $Z = \{q\}$, then $R = \emptyset$ and M is not grounded in $\langle T, P, R \rangle$ because $\mathrm{N}^{\langle P, R \rangle}(M) = \emptyset$ and $p(a) \notin \mathrm{Cn}(T \cup \mathrm{N}^{\langle P, R \rangle}(M))$. Thus, if p is minimized but q is varied, M is not a minimal model of T.

Theorem 6.23 implies that circumscriptive inference is decidable in polynomial space in the propositional case. Like for default logic, it is strictly harder than classical propositional reasoning unless the polynomial hierarchy collapses as it is Π_2^{P}-complete [40, 41]. For tractability considerable restrictions are needed [27].

6.4.5 Variants

Several variants of circumscription formalizing different kinds of minimization have been developed. For instance, pointwise circumscription [71] allows us to minimize the value of a predicate for each argument tuple separately, rather than minimizing the extension of the predicate. This makes it possible to specify very flexible minimization policies. Autocircumscription [105] combines minimization with introspection.

We will focus here on prioritized circumscription [70]. In many applications some defaults are more important than others. In inheritance hierarchies, for instance, a default representing more specific information is intuitively expected to "win" over a conflicting default: if birds normally fly, penguins normally do not, then one would expect to conclude that a penguin does not fly, although it is a bird. This can be modeled by minimizing some abnormality predicates with higher priority than others.

Prioritized circumscription splits the sequence P of minimized predicates into disjoint segments $P^1, \ldots, P^k$. Predicates in P^1 are minimized with highest priority, followed by those in P^2, etc. Semantically, this amounts to a lexicographic comparison of models. We first compare two models M_1 and M_2 with respect to $\leqslant^{P^1, Z}$, where Z are the varied symbols. If the models are incomparable, or if one of the models is strictly preferred ($<^{P^1, Z}$ holds), then the relationship between the models is established and we are done. If $M_1 =^{P^1, Z} M_2$, we go on with $\leqslant^{P^2, Z}$, etc.

The prioritized circumscription of $P^1, \ldots, P^k$ in A with varied Z is denoted

$$CIRC[A; P^1 > \cdots > P^k; Z].$$

We omit its original definition and rather present a characterization based on a result in [70] which shows that prioritized circumscription can be reduced to a sequence of parallel circumscriptions:

Proposition 6.24. $CIRC[A; P^1 > \cdots > P^k; Z]$ *is equivalent to the conjunction of circumscriptions*

$$\bigwedge_{i=1}^{k} CIRC[A; P^i; P^{i+1}, \ldots, P^k, Z].$$

6.5   Nonmonotonic Inference Relations

Having discussed three specific nonmonotonic formalisms in considerable detail, we will now move on to an orthogonal theme in nonmonotonic reasoning research: an abstract study of inference relations associated with nonmonotonic (defeasible) reasoning. Circumscription fits in this theme quite well—it can be viewed as an example of a preferential model approach, yielding a preferential inference relation. However, as we mention again at the end of this chapter, it is not so for default and autoepistemic logics. In fact, casting these two and other fixed point logics in terms of the semantic approach to nonmonotonic inference we are about to present is one of major problems of nonmonotonic reasoning research.

Given what we know about the world, when could a formula B reasonably be concluded from a formula A? One "safe" answer is provided by the classical concept of entailment. Let T be a set of first order logic sentences (an agent's knowledge about the world). The agent *classically* infers a formula B if B holds in *every* model of T in which A holds.

However, the agent's knowledge of the world is typically incomplete, and so, inference relations based on formalisms of defeasible reasoning are of significant interest, too. Under circumscription, the agent might infer B from A if B holds in every *minimal* model of T, in which A holds, $A \vdash_{T,circ} B$. In default logic, assuming the knowledge of the world is given in terms of a set D of defaults, the agent might infer B from A, $A \vdash_D B$, if B is in *every* extension of the default theory $(D, \{A\})$.

These examples suggest that inference can be modeled as a binary relation on $\mathcal{L}$. The question we deal with in this section is: which binary relations on $\mathcal{L}$ are inference relations and what are their properties?

In what follows, we restrict ourselves to the case when $\mathcal{L}$ consists of formulas of propositional logic. We use the infix notation for binary relations and write $A \mathrel{|\!\sim} B$ to denote that B follows from A, under a concept of inference modeled by a binary relation $\mathrel{|\!\sim}$ on $\mathcal{L}$.

6.5.1 Semantic Specification of Inference Relations

Every propositional theory T determines a set of its *models*, $Mod(T)$, consisting of propositional interpretations satisfying T. These interpretations can be regarded as complete specifications of worlds consistent with T or, in other words, possible given T.

An agent whose knowledge is described by T might reside in any of these worlds. Such an agent may decide to infer $B \in \mathcal{L}$ from $A \in \mathcal{L}$, written $A \vdash_T B$, if in *every* world in which A holds, B holds, as well. This approach sanctions only the most conservative inferences. They will hold no matter what additional information about the world an agent may acquire. Inference relations of the form $\vdash_T$ are important. They underlie classical propositional logic and are directly related to the logical entailment relation $\models$. Indeed, we have that $A \vdash_T B$ if and only if $T, A \models B$.

The class of inference relations of the form $\vdash_T$ has a characterization in terms of abstract properties of binary relations on $\mathcal{L}$. The list gives some examples of properties of binary relations relevant for the notion of inference.

Monotony	if $A \supset B$ is a tautology and $B \mathrel{|\!\sim} C$, then $A \mathrel{|\!\sim} C$,
Right Weakening	if $A \supset B$ is a tautology and $C \mathrel{|\!\sim} A$, then $C \mathrel{|\!\sim} B$,
Reflexivity	$A \mathrel{|\!\sim} A$,
And	if $A \mathrel{|\!\sim} B$ and $A \mathrel{|\!\sim} C$, then $A \mathrel{|\!\sim} B \wedge C$,
Or	if $A \mathrel{|\!\sim} C$ and $B \mathrel{|\!\sim} C$, then $A \vee B \mathrel{|\!\sim} C$.

It turns out that these properties provide an alternative (albeit non-constructive) specification of the class of relations of the form $\vdash_T$. Namely, we have the following theorem [64].

Theorem 6.25. *A binary relation on $\mathcal{L}$ is of the form $\vdash_T$ if and only if it satisfies the five properties given above.*

Due to the property of *Monotony*, inference relations $\vdash_T$ do not give rise to defeasible arguments. To model defeasible arguments we need less conservative inference relations. To this end, one may relax the requirement that B must hold in *every* world in which A holds. In commonsense reasoning, humans often differentiate between possible worlds, regarding some of them as more typical or normal than others. When making inferences they often consider only those worlds that are most typical given the knowledge they have. Thus, they might infer B from A if B holds in every most typical world in which A holds (and not in each such world).

Preferential models [64] provide a framework for this general approach. The key idea is to use a *strict* partial order,[7] called a *preference relation*, to compare worlds

---

[7] A binary relation that is irreflexive and transitive.

with respect to their "typicality", with more typical worlds preferred to less typical ones. Given a strict partial order $\prec$ on a set W, an element $w \in W$ is $\prec$-minimal if there is no element $w' \in W$ such that $w' \prec w$.

In the following definition, we use again the term a *possible-world structure*. This time, however, we use it to denote a slightly broader class of objects than sets of interpretations.

Definition 6.13. *A general possible-world structure is a tuple* $\langle W, v \rangle$, *where* W *is a set of worlds and* v *is a function mapping worlds to interpretations.*[8] *If A is a formula, we define*

$$W(A) = \{w \in W \mid v(w) \models A\}.$$

A preferential model is a tuple $\mathcal{W} = \langle W, v, \prec \rangle$, *where* $\langle W, v \rangle$ *is a general possible-world structure and* $\prec$ *is a strict partial order on* W *satisfying the following smoothness condition: for every sentence A and for every* $w \in W(A)$, w *is* $\prec$-*minimal in* $W(A)$ *or there is* $w' \in W(A)$ *such that* $w' \prec w$ *and* w' *is a* $\prec$-*minimal element of* $W(A)$.

The set $W(A)$ gathers worlds in which A holds. Minimal elements in $W(A)$ can be viewed as most typical states where A holds. The smoothness condition guarantees that for every world $w \in W(A)$ which is not most typical itself, there is a most typical state in $W(A)$ that is preferred to w.

Preferential models formalize the intuition of reasoning on the basis of most preferred (typical) models only and allow us to specify the corresponding concept of inference.

Definition 6.14. *If* $\mathcal{W}$ *is a preferential model (with the ordering* $\prec$), *then the inference relation determined by* $\mathcal{W}$, $\vdash_{\mathcal{W}}$, *is defined as follows: for* $A, B \in \mathcal{L}$, $A \vdash_{\mathcal{W}} B$ *if B holds in every* $\prec$-*minimal world in* $W(A)$.

We call inference relations of the form $\vdash_{\mathcal{W}}$, where $\mathcal{W}$ is a preferential model, *preferential*. In general, they do not satisfy the property of *Monotony*.

Propositional circumscription is an example of this general method of defining inference relations. Let $\mathcal{I}$ stand for the set of all interpretations of $\mathcal{L}$. Furthermore, let P and Z be two disjoint sets of propositional variables in the language. We note that the relation $<^{P;Z}$ satisfies the smoothness condition. Thus, $\langle \mathcal{I}, v, <^{P;Z} \rangle$, where v is the identity function, is a preferential model. Moreover, it defines the same inference relation as does circumscription.

Shoham's preference logic [123] is another specialization of the preferential model approach. As in circumscription, the set of worlds consists of all interpretations of $\mathcal{L}$ but an arbitrary strict partial order satisfying the smoothness condition[9] can be used.

Preference logics are very close to preferential models. However, allowing multiple worlds with the same interpretation (in other words, using general possible-world

---

[8]Typically, W is assumed to be nonempty. This assumption is not necessary for our considerations here and so we do not adopt it.

[9]In the original paper by Shoham, a stronger condition of well-foundedness was used.

structures rather than possible-world structures) is essential. The resulting class of inference relations is larger (we refer to [25] for an example).

Can preferential relations be characterized by means of meta properties? The answer is yes but we need two more properties of binary relations $\sim$ on $\mathcal{L}$:

Left Logical Equivalence if A and B are logically equivalent and $A \sim C$,
           then $B \sim C$

Cautious Monotony if $A \sim B$ and $A \sim C$, then $A \wedge B \sim C$

We have the following theorem [64].

Theorem 6.26. *A binary relation $\sim$ on $\mathcal{L}$ is a preferential inference relation if and only if it satisfies Left Logical Equivalence, Right Weakening, Reflexivity, And, Or and Cautious Monotony.*

We note that many other properties of binary relations were considered in an effort to formalize the concept of nonmonotonic inference. Gabbay [44] asked about the weakest set of conditions a binary relation should satisfy in order to be a nonmonotonic inference relation. The result of his studies as well as of Makinson [79] was the notion of a cumulative inference relation. A semantic characterization of cumulative relations exists but there are disputes whether cumulative relations are indeed the right ones. Thus, we do not discuss cumulative inference relations here.

Narrowing the class of orders in preferential models yields subclasses of preferential relations. One of these subclasses is especially important for nonmonotonic reasoning. A strict partial order $\prec$ on a set P is *ranked* if there is a function l from P to ordinals such that for every $x, y \in P$, $x \prec y$ if and only if $l(x) < l(y)$.

Definition 6.15. *A preferential model $\langle \mathcal{W}, v, \prec \rangle$ is ranked if $\prec$ is ranked.*

We will call inference relations defined by ranked models *rational*. It is easy to verify that rational inference relations satisfy the property of *Rational Monotony*:

Rational Monotony if $A \wedge B \not\sim C$ and $A \not\sim \neg B$, then $A \not\sim C$.

The converse is true, as well. We have the following theorem [68].

Theorem 6.27. *An inference relation is rational if and only if it is preferential and satisfies Rational Monotony.*

6.5.2 Default Conditionals

Default conditionals are meant to model defeasible statements such as *university professors normally give lectures*. Formally, a *default conditional* is a syntactic expression $A \sim B$, with an intuitive reading "if A then *normally* B". We denote the operator constructing default conditionals with the same symbol $\sim$ we used earlier for inference relations. While it might be confusing, there are good reasons to do so and they will become apparent as we proceed. It is important, however, to keep in mind that in one case, $\sim$ stands for a constructor of syntactic (language) expressions, and in the other it stands for a binary (inference) relation.

Given a set K of default conditionals, when is a default conditional $A \vDash B$ a consequence of K? When is a formula A a consequence of K? Somewhat disappointingly no single commonly accepted answer has emerged. We will now review one of the approaches proposed that received significant attention. It is based on the notion of a *rational closure* developed in [67, 68] and closely related to the system Z [104].

Let K be a set of default conditionals. The set of all default conditionals implied by K should be closed under some rules of inference for conditionals. For instance, we might require that if A and B are logically equivalent and $A \vDash C$ belongs to a closure of K, $B \vDash C$ belongs to the closure of K, as well. This rule is nothing else but *Left Logical Equivalence*, except that now we view expressions $A \vDash B$ as default conditionals and not as elements of an inference relation. In fact, modulo this correspondence (a conditional $A \vDash B$ versus an element $A \vDash B$ of an binary relation), several other rules we discussed in the previous section could be argued as possible candidates to use when defining a closure of K.

Based on this observation, we postulate that a closure of K should be a set of conditionals that corresponds to an inference relation. The question is, which inference relation extending K should one adopt as *the* closure of K. If one is given a preferential model whose inference relation extends K, this inference relation might be considered as the closure of K. This is not a satisfactory solution as, typically, all we have is K and we would like to determine the closure on the basis of K only. Another answer might be the intersection of all preferential relations extending K. The resulting relation does not in general satisfy *Rational monotony*, a property that arguably all *bona fide* nonmonotonic inference relations should satisfy. Ranked models determine inference relations that are preferential and, moreover, satisfy *Rational Monotony*. However, the intersection of all rational extensions of K coincides with the intersection of all preferential extensions and so, this approach collapses to the previous one.

If the closure of K is not the intersection of all rational extensions, perhaps it is a specific rational extension, if there is a natural way to define one. We will focus on this possibility now. Lehmann and Magidor [68] introduce a partial ordering on rational extensions of a set of conditional closures of K. In the case when this order has a least element, they call this element the *rational closure* of K. They say that $A \vDash B$ is a rational consequence of K if $A \vDash B$ belongs to the rational closure of K. They say that A is a rational consequence of K if the conditional **true** $\vDash A$ is in the rational closure of K.

There are sets of conditionals that do not have the rational closure. However, [68] show that in many cases, including the case when K is finite, the rational closure exists. Rather than discuss the ordering of rational extensions that underlies the definition of a rational closure, we will now discuss an approach which characterizes it in many cases when it exists.

A formula A is exceptional for K, if **true** $\vDash \neg A$ belongs to the preferential extension of K, that is, if $\neg A$ is true in every minimal world of every preferential model of K. A default conditional is exceptional for K, if its antecedent is exceptional for K. By $E(K)$ we denote the set of all default conditionals in K that are exceptional for K.

Given K, we define a sequence of subsets of K as follows: $C_0 = K$. If $\tau = \eta + 1$ is a successor ordinal, we define $C_\tau = E(C_\eta)$. If τ is a limit ordinal, we define $C_\tau = \bigcup_{\eta < \tau} C_\eta$.

The rank $r(A)$ of a formula A is the least ordinal τ such that A is not exceptional for C_τ. If for every ordinal τ, A is exceptional for C_τ, A has no rank.

A formula A is *inconsistent* with K if for every preferential model of K and every world w in the model, $w \models \neg A$.

A set of conditionals K is *admissible* if all formulas that have no rank are inconsistent for K. Admissible sets of default conditionals include all finite sets.

Theorem 6.28. *If K is admissible, then its rational closure $\bar{K}$ exists. A default conditional $A \mathrel{\v!\sim} B \in \bar{K}$ if and only if $A \wedge \neg B$ has no rank, or if A and $A \wedge \neg B$ have ranks and $r(A) < r(A \wedge \neg B)$.*

6.5.3 Discussion

Properties of inference relations can reveal differences between nonmonotonic formalisms. Earlier in this section, we showed how circumscription or default logic can be used to specify inference relations. The relation determined by circumscription is a special case of a preferential inference relation and so, satisfies all properties of preferential relations. The situation is different for the inference relation defined by a set of defaults. Let us recall that B can be inferred from A with respect to a set D of defaults, $A \mathrel{\v!\sim}_D B$, if B is in every extension of the default theory $(D, \{A\})$.

The inference relation $\mathrel{\v!\sim}_D$, where D consists of normal defaults, in general does not satisfy the properties *Or* and *Cautious Monotony*. For instance, let $D = \{A : C/C, B : C/C\}$. Then we have $A \mathrel{\v!\sim}_D C$ and $B \mathrel{\v!\sim}_D C$, but not $A \vee B \vdash_D C$. The reason, intuitively, is that none of the defaults can be applied if only the disjunction of prerequisites is given.

An example for the violation of cumulativity due to Makinson [79] is given by $D = \{\top : A/A, A \vee B : \neg A/\neg A\}$. We have $\top \mathrel{\v!\sim}_D A$ and thus $\top \mathrel{\v!\sim}_D A \vee B$, but not $A \vee B \vdash_D A$. The reason is that the default theory $(D, \{A \vee B\})$ has a second extension containing $\neg A$.

Contrary to normal defaults, supernormal defaults satisfy both *Cautious Monotony* and *Or* [35], as they happen to be preferential.

Finally, we conclude this section with a major unresolved problem of nonmonotonic reasoning. Nonmonotonicity can be achieved through fixed point constructions and this approach leads to such formalisms as default and autoepistemic logics. On the other hand, interesting nonmonotonic inference relations can be defined in terms of preferential models. What is missing is a clear link between the two approaches. An open question is: can nonmonotonic inference relations defined by default logic (or other fixed point system) be characterized in semantic terms along the lines of preferential models?

6.6 Further Issues and Conclusion

In this section we discuss the relationship between the major approaches we presented earlier. We first relate default logic and autoepistemic logic (Section 6.6.1), then default logic and circumscription (Section 6.6.2). Finally, we give pointers to some other approaches which we could not present in more detail in this chapter (Section 6.6.3).

6.6.1   Relating Default and Autoepistemic Logics

A basic pattern of nonmonotonic reasoning is: "*in the absence of any information contradicting B, infer B*". Normal defaults are designed specifically with this reasoning pattern in mind: it is modeled by the normal default $\frac{:B}{B}$. McDermott and Doyle [91] suggested that in modal nonmonotonic systems this reasoning pattern should be represented by the modal formula $\neg K\neg B \supset B$ (or using a common abbreviation M for $\neg K\neg$, which can be read as "consistent" or "possible": $MB \supset B$). Even though the modal nonmonotonic logic of [91] was found to have counterintuitive properties and was abandoned as a knowledge representation formalism, the connection between a default $\frac{:B}{B}$ and a modal formula $MB \supset B$ was an intriguing one and prompted extensive investigations. Since autoepistemic logic emerged in the mid 1980s as the modal nonmonotonic logic of choice, these investigations focused on relating default and autoepistemic logics.

Building on the suggestion of McDermott and Doyle, Konolige [61] proposed to encode an arbitrary default

$$d = \frac{A : B_1, \ldots, B_k}{C}$$

with a modal formula

$$T(d) = KA \wedge \neg K\neg B_1 \wedge \cdots \wedge \neg K\neg B_k \supset C,$$

and to translate a default theory $\Delta = (D, W)$ into a modal theory $T(\Delta) = W \cup \{T(d) \mid d \in D\}$.

The translation seems to capture correctly the intuitive reading of a default: if A is known and all B_i are possible (none is contradicted or inconsistent) then infer C. There is a problem, though. Let us consider a default theory $\Delta = (\{d\}, \emptyset)$, where

$$d = \frac{A : B}{A}.$$

Konolige's translation represents Δ as a modal theory

$$T(\Delta) = \{KA \wedge \neg K\neg B \supset A\}.$$

Using methods we presented earlier in this chapter one can verify that Δ has exactly one extension, $Cn(\emptyset)$, while $T(\Delta)$ has *two* expansions, $Cn_{S5}(\emptyset)$ and $Cn_{S5}(\{A\})$. It follows that Konolige's translation does not yield a connection between the two logics that would establish a one-to-one correspondence between extensions and expansions. Still several interesting properties hold.

First, as shown in [81], for prerequisite-free default theories, Konolige's translation does work! We have the following result.

Theorem 6.29. *Let Δ be a default theory such that each of its defaults is prerequisite-free. Then, a propositional theory E is an extension of Δ if and only if the belief set determined by E (cf. Proposition 6.14) is an expansion of $T(\Delta)$. Conversely, a modal theory E' is an expansion of $T(\Delta)$ if and only if the modal-free part of E', $E' \cap \mathcal{L}$, is an extension of Δ.*

Second, under Konolige's translation, extensions are mapped to expansions (although, as our example above shows—the converse fails in general).

Theorem 6.30. *Let* Δ *be a default theory. If a propositional theory* E *is an extension of* Δ, *then* $\mathrm{Cn}_{S5}(E)$ *is an expansion of* $T(\Delta)$.

Despite providing evidence that the two logics are related, ultimately, Konolige's translation does not properly match extensions with expansions. The reason boils down to a fundamental difference between extensions and expansions. Both extensions and expansions consist only of formulas that are justified ("grounded") in default and modal theories, respectively. However, expansions allow for self-justifications while extensions do not. The difference is well illustrated by the example we used before. The belief set determined by $\{A\}$ (cf. Proposition 6.14) is an expansion of the theory $\{KA \wedge \neg K\neg B \supset A\}$. In this expansion, A is justified through the formula $KA \wedge \neg K\neg B \supset A$ by means of a *circular* argument relying on believing in A (since there is no information contradicting B, the second premise needed for the argument, $\neg K \neg B$, holds). Such self-justifications are not sanctioned by extensions: in order to apply the default $\frac{A:B}{A}$ we must first *independently* derive A. Indeed, one can verify that the theory $\mathrm{Cn}(\{A\})$ is not an extension of $(\{\frac{A:B}{A}\}, \emptyset)$.

This discussion implies that extensions and expansions capture different types of nonmonotonic reasoning. As some research suggests default logic is about the modality of "knowing" (no self-supporting arguments) and autoepistemic logic is about the modality of "believing" (self-supporting arguments allowed) [75, 122].

Two natural questions arise. Is there a default logic counterpart of expansions, and is there an autoepistemic logic counterpart of extensions? The answer in each case is positive. Denecker et al. [34] developed a uniform treatment of default and autoepistemic logics exploiting some basic operators on possible-world structures that can be associated with default and modal theories. This algebraic approach (developed earlier in more abstract terms in [33]) endows each logic with both expansions and extensions in such a way that they are perfectly aligned under Konolige's translation. Moreover, extensions of default theories and expansions of modal theories defined by the algebraic approach of [34] coincide with the original notions defined by Reiter and Moore, respectively, while expansions of default theories and extensions of modal theories defined in [34] fill in the gaps to complete the picture.

A full discussion of the relation between default and autoepistemic logic is beyond the scope of this chapter and we refer to [34] for details. Similarly, we only briefly note other work attempting to explain the relationship between the two logics. Most efforts took as the starting point the observation that to capture a default logic within a modal system, a different modal nonmonotonic logic or a different translation must be used. Konolige related default logic to a *version* of autoepistemic logic based on the notion of a *strongly grounded expansion* [61]. Marek and Truszczyński [82] proposed an alternative translation and represented extensions as expansions in a certain modal nonmonotonic logic constructed following McDermott [90]. Truszczyński [128] found that the Gödel translation of intuitionistic logic to modal logic S4 could be used to translate the default logic into a nonmonotonic modal logic S4 (in fact, he showed that several modal nonmonotonic logics could be used in place of nonmonotonic S4).

Gottlob [52] returned to the original problem of relating default and autoepistemic logics with their original semantics. He described a mapping translating default theories into modal ones so that extensions correspond precisely to expansions. This translation is not modular. The autoepistemic representation of a default theory depends on the whole theory and cannot be obtained as the union of independent translations of individual defaults. Thus, the approach of Gottlob does not provide an autoepistemic reading of an individual default. In fact, in the same paper Gottlob proved that a modular translation from default logic with the semantics of extensions to autoepistemic logic with the semantics of expansions does not exist. In conclusion, there is *no* modal interpretation of a default under which *extensions* would correspond to *expansions*.

6.6.2 Relating Default Logic and Circumscription

The relationships between default logic and circumscription as well as between autoepistemic logic and circumscription have been investigated by a number of researchers [42, 43, 58, 72, 62]. Imielinski [58] points out that even normal default rules with prerequisites cannot be translated modularly into circumscription. This argument applies also to autoepistemic logic and thus circumscription cannot modularly capture autoepistemic reasoning [96].

On the other hand, circumscription is closely related to prerequisite-free normal defaults. For example, it is possible to capture minimal models of a set of formulas using such rules. The idea is easy to explain in the propositional case. Consider a set of formulas T and sets P and Z of minimized and varied atoms (0-ary predicates), respectively, and let R be the set of fixed atoms (those not in P or Z). Now $\leqslant^{P;Z}$-minimal models of T can be captured by the default theory $(\mathrm{MIN}(P) \cup \mathrm{FIX}(R), T)$ where the set of defaults consists of

$$\mathrm{MIN}(P) = \left\{ \frac{\top : \neg A}{\neg A} \,\middle|\, A \in P \right\},$$

$$\mathrm{FIX}(R) = \left\{ \frac{\top : \neg A}{\neg A} \,\middle|\, A \in R \right\} \cup \left\{ \frac{\top : A}{A} \,\middle|\, A \in R \right\}.$$

Now a formula F is true in every $\leqslant^{P;Z}$-minimal model of T if and only if F is in every extension of the default theory $(\mathrm{MIN}(P) \cup \mathrm{FIX}(R), T)$. The idea here is that defaults $\mathrm{MIN}(P)$ minimize atoms in P and defaults $\mathrm{FIX}(R)$ fix atoms in R by minimizing each atom and its complement.

The same approach can be used for autoepistemic logic as prerequisite-free default theories can be translated to autoepistemic logic as explained in Section 6.6.1. However, capturing first order circumscription is non-trivial and the results depend on the treatment of open defaults (or quantification into the scope of K operators in the case of autoepistemic logic). For example, Etherington [42] reports results on capturing circumscription using default logic in the first order case but without any fixed predicates and with a finite, fixed domain. Konolige [62] shows how to encode circumscription in the case of non-finite domains using a variant of autoepistemic logic which allows quantification into the scope of K operators.

6.6.3 Further Approaches

Several other formalizations of nonmonotonic reasoning have been proposed in the literature. Here we give a few references to those we consider most relevant but could not handle in more detail.

- Possibilistic logics [38] assign degrees of necessity and possibility to sentences. These degrees express the extent to which these sentences are believed to be necessarily or possibly true, respectively. One of the main advantages of this approach is that it leads to a notion of graded inconsistency which allows non-trivial deductions to be performed from inconsistent possibilistic knowledge bases. The resulting consequence relation is nonmonotonic and default rules can be conveniently represented in this approach [10].

- Defeasible logic, as proposed by Nute [101] and further developed by Antoniou and colleagues [4, 3], is an approach to nonmonotonic reasoning based on strict and defeasible rules as well as defeaters. The latter specify exceptions to defeasible rules. A preference relation among defeasible rules is used to break ties whenever possible. An advantage of defeasible logic is its low complexity: inferences can be computed very efficiently. On the other hand, some arguably intuitive conclusions are not captured. The relationship between defeasible logic and prioritized logic programs under well-founded semantics is discussed in [24].

- Inheritance networks are directed graphs whose nodes represent propositions and a directed (possibly negated) link between two nodes A and B stands for "*As are normally (not) B*s" (some types of networks also distinguish between strict and defeasible links). The main goal of approaches in this area is to capture the idea that more specific information should win in case of a conflict. Several notions of specificity have been formalized, and corresponding notions of inference were developed. Reasoning based on inheritance networks is nonmonotonic since new, possibly more specific links can lead to the retraction of former conclusions. [56] gives a good overview.

- Several authors have proposed approaches based on ranked knowledge bases, that is, sets of classical formulas together with a total preorder on the formulas [21, 9]. The preorder represents preferences reflecting the willingness to stick to a formula in case of conflict: if two formulas A and B lead to inconsistency, then the strictly less preferred formula is given up. If they are equally preferred, then different preferred maximal consistent subsets (preferred subtheories in the terminology of [21]) of the formulas will be generated. There are different ways to define the preferred subtheories. Brewka [21] uses a criterion based on set inclusion, Benferhat and colleagues [9] investigate a cardinality based approach.

- When considering knowledge-based agents it is natural to assume that the agent's beliefs are exactly those beliefs which follow from the assumption that the knowledge base is *all* that is believed. Levesque was the first to capture this notion in his logic of *only-knowing* [69]. The main advantage of this approach is that beliefs can be analyzed in terms of a modal logic without requiring additional meta-logical notions like fixpoints and the like. The logic uses two modal operators, *K* for belief and *O* for only knowing. Levesque showed that his logic captures autoepistemic logic. In [65] the approach was generalized to capture default logic as well. [66] presents a sound and complete axiomatization for the propositional case. Multi-agent only knowing is explored in [53].

- Formal argument systems (see, for instance, [76, 124, 106, 39, 20, 129, 1, 130, 12]) model the way agents reason on the basis of arguments. In some approaches arguments have internal structure, in others they remain abstract entities whose structure is not analyzed further. In each case a defeat relation among arguments plays a central role in determining acceptable arguments and acceptable beliefs. The approaches are too numerous to be discussed here in more detail. We refer the reader to the excellent overview articles [29] and [108].

With the above references to further work we conclude this overview chapter on formalizations of general nonmonotonic reasoning. As we said in the introduction, our aim was not to give a comprehensive overview of all the work that has been done in the area. We decided to focus on the most influential approaches, thus providing the necessary background for several of the other chapters of this Handbook. Indeed, the reader will notice that the topic of this chapter pops up again at various places in this book—with a different, more specialized focus. Examples are the chapters on Answer Sets (Chapter 7), Model-based Problem Solving (Chapter 10), and the various approaches to reasoning about action and causality (Chapters 16–19).

Acknowledgements

We would like to thank Vladimir Lifschitz and Hudson Turner for helpful comments and suggestions.

Bibliography

[1] L. Amgoud and C. Cayrol. A reasoning model based on the production of acceptable arguments. *Ann. Math. Artif. Intell.*, 34(1–3):197–215, 2002.
[2] G. Antoniou. *Nonmonotonic Reasoning*. 1st edition. MIT Press, Cambridge, 1997.
[3] G. Antoniou, D. Billington, G. Governatori, and M.J. Maher. Representation results for defeasible logic. *ACM Trans. Comput. Log.*, 2(2):255–287, 2001.
[4] G. Antoniou, D. Billington, G. Governatori, M.J. Maher, and A. Rock. A family of defeasible reasoning logics and its implementation. In W. Horn, editor. *ECAI*, pages 459–463. IOS Press, 2000.
[5] F. Baader and B. Hollunder. Embedding defaults into terminological knowledge representation formalisms. *J. Automat. Reason.*, 14:149–180, 1995.
[6] F. Baader and B. Hollunder. Priorities on defaults with prerequisites, and their application in treating specificity in terminological default logic. *J. Automat. Reason.*, 15(1):41–68, 1995.
[7] A.B. Baker and M.L. Ginsberg. A theorem prover for prioritized circumscription. In N.S. Sridharan, editor. *Proceedings of the Eleventh International Joint Conference on Artificial Intelligence*, pages 463–467. Morgan Kaufmann, San Mateo, CA, 1989.

[8] R. Ben-Eliyahu and R. Dechter. Default logic, propositional logic and constraints. In *Proceedings of the 9th National Conference on Artificial Intelligence*, pages 370–385. MIT Press, July 1991.

[9] S. Benferhat, C. Cayrol, D. Dubois, J. Lang, and H. Prade. Inconsistency management and prioritized syntax-based entailment. In *IJCAI*, pages 640–647, 1993.

[10] S. Benferhat, D. Dubois, and H. Prade. Representing default rules in possibilistic logic. In B. Nebel, C. Rich, and W. Swartout, editors. *KR'92. Principles of Knowledge Representation and Reasoning: Proceedings of the Third International Conference*, pages 673–684. Morgan Kaufmann, San Mateo, CA, 1992.

[11] P. Besnard. *An Introduction to Default Logic*. Springer-Verlag, New York, 1989.

[12] P. Besnard and A. Hunter. Practical first-order argumentation. In *Proceedings Twentieth National Conference on Artificial Intelligence, AAAI*, pages 590–595, 2005.

[13] N. Bidoit and C. Froidevaux. Minimalism subsumes default logic and circumscription. In *Proceedings of IEEE Symposium on Logic in Computer Science, LICS-87*, pages 89–97. IEEE Press, 1987.

[14] N. Bidoit and C. Froidevaux. General logical databases and programs: default logic semantics and stratification. *Inform. and Comput.*, 91(1):15–54, 1991.

[15] N. Bidoit and C. Froidevaux. Negation by default and unstratifiable logic programs. *Theoret. Comput. Sci. (Part B)*, 78(1):85–112, 1991.

[16] A. Bochman. *A Logical Theory of Nonmonotonic Inference and Belief Change*. 1st edition. Springer, Berlin, 2001.

[17] A. Bochman. *Explanatory Nonmonotonic Reasoning*. 1st edition. *Advances in Logic*, vol. 4. World Scientific, 2005.

[18] P.A. Bonatti. Sequent calculi for default and autoepistemic logics. In *Proceedings of the Fifth Workshop on Theorem Proving with Analytic Tableaux and Related Methods*, Terrasini, Italy, May 1996. *Lecture Notes in Artificial Intelligence*, vol. 1071, pages 127–142. Springer-Verlag, 1996.

[19] P.A. Bonatti and N. Olivetti. A sequent calculus for skeptical default logic. In *Proceedings of the International Conference on Automated Reasoning with Analytic Tableaux and Related Methods*, Pont-à-Mousson, France, May 1997. *Lecture Notes in Artificial Intelligence*, vol. 1227, pages 107–121. Springer-Verlag, 1997.

[20] A. Bondarenko, P.M. Dung, R.A. Kowalski, and F. Toni. An abstract, argumentation-theoretic approach to default reasoning. *Artificial Intelligence*, 93:63–101, 1997.

[21] G. Brewka. Preferred subtheories: An extended logical framework for default reasoning. In *IJCAI* pages 1043–1048, 1989.

[22] G. Brewka. Cumulative default logic: In defense of nonmonotonic inference rules. *Artificial Intelligence*, 50(2):183–205, 1991.

[23] G. Brewka. Reasoning about priorities in default logic. In *AAAI*, pages 940–945, 1994.

[24] G. Brewka. On the relationship between defeasible logic and well-founded semantics. *Lecture Notes in Computer Science*, 2173:121–132, 2001.

[25] G. Brewka, J. Dix, and K. Konolige. *Nonmonotonic Reasoning: An Overview*. 1st edition. CSLI Publications, Stanford, 1997.

[26] G. Brewka and T. Eiter. Preferred answer sets for extended logic programs. *Artificial Intelligence*, 109(1–2):297–356, 1999.

[27] M. Cadoli and M. Lenzerini. The complexity of propositional closed world reasoning and circumscription. *J. Comput. System Sci.*, 48(2):255–310, 1994.

[28] B.F. Chellas. *Modal Logic. An Introduction.* Cambridge University Press, Cambridge–New York, 1980.

[29] C.I. Chesñevar, A.G. Maguitman, and R.P. Loui. Logical models of argument. *ACM Comput. Surv.*, 32(4):337–383, 2000.

[30] P. Cholewiński, V.W. Marek, A. Mikitiuk, and M. Truszczyński. Computing with default logic. *Artificial Intelligence*, 112:105–146, 1999.

[31] J.P. Delgrande and W.K. Jackson. Default logic revisited. In *KR*, pages 118–127, 1991.

[32] J.P. Delgrande, T. Schaub, and W.K. Jackson. Alternative approaches to default logic. *Artificial Intelligence*, 70(1–2):167–237, 1994.

[33] M. Denecker, V.W. Marek, and M. Truszczyński. Approximations, stable operators, well-founded fixpoints and applications in nonmonotonic reasoning. In J. Minker, editor. *Logic-Based Artificial Intelligence*, pages 127–144. Kluwer Academic Publishers, 2000.

[34] M. Denecker, V.W. Marek, and M. Truszczyński. Uniform semantic treatment of default and autoepistemic logics. *Artificial Intelligence*, 143:79–122, 2003.

[35] J. Dix. Default theories of Poole-type and a method for constructing cumulative versions of default logic. In *ECAI*, pages 289–293, 1992.

[36] J. Dix, U. Furbach, and I. Niemelä. Nonmonotonic reasoning: Towards efficient calculi and implementations. In A. Voronkov and A. Robinson, editors. *Handbook of Automated Reasoning*, vol. II, pages 1241–1354. Elsevier Science, Amsterdam, 2001 (Chapter 19).

[37] P. Doherty, W. Lukaszewicz, and A. Szalas. Computing circumscription revisited: A reduction algorithm. *J. Automat. Reason.*, 18(3):297–336, 1997.

[38] D. Dubois, J. Lang, and H. Prade. Possibilistic logic. In D. Gabbay, C.J. Hogger, and J.A. Robinson, editors. *Nonmonotonic Reasoning and Uncertain Reasoning, Handbook of Logic in Artificial Intelligence and Logic Programming*, vol. 3, pages 439–513. Oxford University Press, Oxford, 1994.

[39] P.M. Dung. On the acceptability of arguments and its fundamental role in nonmonotonic reasoning, logic programming and n-person games. *Artificial Intelligence*, 77(2):321–358, 1995.

[40] T. Eiter and G. Gottlob. Propositional circumscription and extended closed world reasoning are Π_2^P-complete. *Theoret. Comput. Sci.*, 144(2):231–245, 1993; Addendum: *Theoret. Comput. Sci.*, 118:315, 1993.

[41] T. Eiter and G. Gottlob. On the computational cost of disjunctive logic programming: Propositional case. *Ann. Math. Artificial Intelligence*, 15(3–4):289–323, 1995.

[42] D.W. Etherington. Relating default logic and circumscription. In *Proceedings of the 10th International Joint Conference on Artificial Intelligence*, Milan, Italy, August 1987, pages 489–494. Morgan Kaufmann Publishers, 1987.

[43] D.W. Etherington. *Reasoning with Incomplete Information.* Pitman, London, 1988.

[44] D.M. Gabbay. Theoretical foundations for non-monotonic reasoning in expert systems. In *Proceedings of the NATO Advanced Study Institute on Logics and Models of Concurrent Systems*, pages 439–457. Springer, 1989.

[45] D.M. Gabbay and H.J. Ohlbach. Quantifier elimination in second-order predicate logic. In B. Nebel, C. Rich, and W. Swartout, editors. *Principles of Knowledge Representation and Reasoning (KR92)*, pages 425–435. Morgan Kaufmann, 1992.

[46] M.R. Garey and D.S. Johnson. *Computers and Intractability*. W.H. Freeman and Company, San Francisco, 1979.

[47] M. Gelfond. On stratified autoepistemic theories. In *Proceedings of AAAI-87*, pages 207–211. Morgan Kaufmann, 1987.

[48] M. Gelfond and V. Lifschitz. Compiling circumscriptive theories into logic programs. In *Proceedings of the 7th National Conference on Artificial Intelligence, AAAI-88*, pages 455–449, 1988.

[49] M. Gelfond and V. Lifschitz. The stable semantics for logic programs. In *Proceedings of the 5th International Conference on Logic Programming*, pages 1070–1080. MIT Press, 1988.

[50] G. Gogic, C. Papadimitriou, B. Selman, and H. Kautz. The comparative linguistics of knowledge representation. In *Proceedings of the 14th International Joint Conference on Artificial Intelligence*, Montreal, Canada, August 1995, pages 862–869. Morgan Kaufmann Publishers, 1995.

[51] G. Gottlob. Complexity results for nonmonotonic logics. *J. Logic Comput.*, 2(3):397–425, 1992.

[52] G. Gottlob. Translating default logic into standard autoepistemic logic. *J. ACM*, 42(4):711–740, 1995.

[53] J.Y. Halpern and G. Lakemeyer. Multi-agent only knowing. *J. Logic Comput.*, 11(1):41–70, 2001.

[54] J.Y. Halpern and Y. Moses. Towards a theory of knowledge and ignorance (preliminary report). In K. Apt, editor. *Logics and Models of Concurrent Systems (La Colle-sur-Loup, 1984), NATO ASI Series F: Computer and Systems Sciences*, vol. 13, pages 459–476. Springer, 1985.

[55] C. Hewitt. Description and theoretical analysis (using schemata) of planner: A language for proving theorems and manipulating models in a robot. PhD thesis, MIT, 1971.

[56] J.F. Horty. Some direct theories of nonmonotonic inheritance. In D. Gabbay, C.J. Hogger, and J.A. Robinson, editors. *Nonmonotonic Reasoning and Uncertain Reasoning, Handbook of Logic in Artificial Intelligence and Logic Programming*, vol. 3, pages 111–187. Oxford University Press, Oxford, 1994.

[57] G.E. Hughes and M.J. Cresswell. *A Companion to Modal Logic*. Methuen and Co., Ltd., London, 1984.

[58] T. Imielinski. Results on translating defaults to circumscription. *Artificial Intelligence*, 32:131–146, 1987.

[59] U. Junker and K. Konolige. Computing the extensions of autoepistemic and default logics with a truth maintenance system. In *Proceedings of the 8th National Conference on Artificial Intelligence*, Boston, MA, USA, July 1990, pages 278–283. MIT Press, 1990.

[60] H. Kautz and B. Selman. Hard problems for simple default logics. *Artificial Intelligence*, 49:243–279, 1991.

[61] K. Konolige. On the relation between default and autoepistemic logic. *Artificial Intelligence*, 35(3):343–382, 1988.

[62] K. Konolige. On the relation between autoepistemic logic and circumscription. In *Proceedings of the 11th International Joint Conference on Artificial Intelligence*, Detroit, MI, USA, August 1989, pages 1213–1218. Morgan Kaufmann Publishers, 1989.

[63] K. Konolige. Quantification in autoepistemic logic. Technical Note 510, SRI International, Menlo Park, CA, USA, September 1991.

[64] S. Kraus, D. Lehmann, and M. Magidor. Nonmonotonic reasoning, preferential models and cumulative logics. *Artificial Intelligence*, 44:167–207, 1990.

[65] G. Lakemeyer and H.J. Levesque. Only-knowing: Taking it beyond autoepistemic reasoning. In *Proceedings Twentieth National Conference on Artificial Intelligence, AAAI*, pages 633–638, 2005.

[66] G. Lakemeyer and H.J. Levesque. Towards an axiom system for default logic. In *Proc. AAAI-06*. AAAI Press, 2006.

[67] D. Lehmann. What does a conditional knowledge base entail? In *Proceedings of the 1st International Conference on Principles of Knowledge Representation and Reasoning, KR-89*, pages 212–222. Morgan Kaufmann, 1989.

[68] D. Lehmann and M. Magidor. What does a conditional knowledge base entail? *Artificial Intelligence*, 55:1–60, 1992.

[69] H.J. Levesque. All I know: A study in autoepistemic logic. *Artificial Intelligence*, 42(2–3):263–309, 1990.

[70] V. Lifschitz. Computing circumscription. In *IJCAI*, pages 121–127, 1985.

[71] V. Lifschitz. Pointwise circumscription: Preliminary report. In *AAAI*, pages 406–410, 1986.

[72] V. Lifschitz. Between circumscription and autoepistemic logic. In *Proceedings of the 1st International Conference on Principles of Knowledge Representation and Reasoning*, pages 235–244. Morgan Kaufmann Publishers, Toronto, Canada, May 1989.

[73] V. Lifschitz. On open defaults. In J. Lloyd, editor. *Proceedings of the Symposium on Computational Logic*, pages 80–95. Springer-Verlag, Berlin, 1990.

[74] V. Lifschitz. Circumscription. In D. Gabbay, C.J. Hogger, and J.A. Robinson, editors. *Nonmonotonic Reasoning and Uncertain Reasoning, Handbook of Logic in Artificial Intelligence and Logic Programming*, vol. 3, pages 298–352. Oxford University Press, 1994.

[75] V. Lifschitz. Minimal belief and negation as failure. *Artificial Intelligence*, 70(1–2):53–72, 1994.

[76] F. Lin and Y. Shoham. Argument systems: A uniform basis for nonmonotonic reasoning. In *KR*, pages 245–255, 1989.

[77] W. Lukaszewicz. Chronological minimization of abnormality: Simple theories of action. In *ECAI*, pages 574–576, 1988.

[78] W. Lukaszewicz. *Non-Monotonic Reasoning: Formalization of Commonsense Reasoning, Ellis Horwood Series in Artificial Intelligence*. Chichester, England, 1990.

[79] D. Makinson. General theory of cumulative inference. In *Proceedings of the 2nd International Workshop on Non-Monotonic Reasoning, NMR-88, Lecture Notes in Computer Science*, vol. 346, pages 1–18. Springer, 1989.

[80] D. Makinson. *Bridges from Classical to Nonmonotonic Logic. King's College Publications: Texts in Computing*, London, 2005.

[81] V.W. Marek and M. Truszczyński. Relating autoepistemic and default logics. In *Proceedings of the 1st International Conference on Principles of Knowledge Representation and Reasoning*, Toronto, ON, 1989, pages 276–288. Morgan Kaufmann, San Mateo, CA, 1989.

[82] V.W. Marek and M. Truszczyński. Stable semantics for logic programs and default theories. In E. Lusk and R. Overbeek, editors. *Proceedings of the North American Conference on Logic Programming*, pages 243–256. MIT Press, 1989.

[83] V.W. Marek and M. Truszczyński. Autoepistemic logic. *J. ACM*, 38:588–619, 1991.

[84] V.W. Marek and M. Truszczyński. Computing intersection of autoepistemic expansions. In *Proceedings of the 1st International Workshop on Logic Programming and Non-monotonic Reasoning*, pages 37–50, MIT Press, Washington, DC, USA, July 1991.

[85] V.W. Marek and M. Truszczyński. *Nonmonotonic Logics: Context-Dependent Reasoning*. 1st edition. Springer, Berlin, 1993.

[86] J. McCarthy. Circumscription—a form of non-monotonic reasoning. *Artificial Intelligence*, 13(1–2):27–39, 1980.

[87] J. McCarthy. Applications of circumscription to formalizing common-sense knowledge. *Artificial Intelligence*, 28(1):89–116, 1986.

[88] J. McCarthy. *Formalization of Common Sense*. Papers by John McCarthy edited by V. Lifschitz. Ablex, 1990.

[89] J. McCarthy and P.J. Hayes. Some philosophical problems from the standpoint of artificial intelligence. In B. Meltzer and D. Michie, editors. *Machine Intelligence 4*, pages 463–502. Edinburgh University Press, 1969 (reprinted in [88]).

[90] D. McDermott. Nonmonotonic logic II: Nonmonotonic modal theories. *J. ACM*, 29(1):33–57, 1982.

[91] D. McDermott and J. Doyle. Nonmonotonic logic I. *Artificial Intelligence*, 13(1–2):41–72, 1980.

[92] R.C. Moore. Possible-world semantics for autoepistemic logic. In *Proceedings of the Workshop on Non-Monotonic Reasoning*, pages 344–354, 1984. Reprinted in: M. Ginsberg, editor, *Readings on Nonmonotonic Reasoning*, pages 137–142. Morgan Kaufmann, 1990.

[93] R.C. Moore. Semantical considerations on nonmonotonic logic. *Artificial Intelligence*, 25(1):75–94, 1985.

[94] I. Niemelä. Towards automatic autoepistemic reasoning. In *Proceedings of the European Workshop on Logics in Artificial Intelligence—JELIA'90*, pages 428–443, Amsterdam, The Netherlands, September 1990. Springer-Verlag.

[95] I. Niemelä. On the decidability and complexity of autoepistemic reasoning. *Fundamenta Informaticae*, 17(1,2):117–155, 1992.

[96] I. Niemelä. Autoepistemic logic as a unified basis for nonmonotonic reasoning. Doctoral dissertation. Research report A24, Helsinki University of Technology, Digital Systems Laboratory, Espoo, Finland, August 1993.

[97] I. Niemelä. A decision method for nonmonotonic reasoning based on autoepistemic reasoning. *J. Automat. Reason.*, 14:3–42, 1995.

[98] I. Niemelä. Towards efficient default reasoning. In *Proceedings of the 14th International Joint Conference on Artificial Intelligence*, pages 312–318, Montreal, Canada, August 1995. Morgan Kaufmann Publishers.

[99] I. Niemelä. Implementing circumscription using a tableau method. In W. Wahlster, editor, *Proceedings of the European Conference on Artificial Intelligence*, pages 80–84, Budapest, Hungary, August 1996. J. Wiley.

[100] I. Niemelä and J. Rintanen. On the impact of stratification on the complexity of nonmonotonic reasoning. *Journal of Applied Non-Classical Logics*, 4(2):141–179, 1994.

[101] D. Nute. Defeasible logic. In D. Gabbay, C.J. Hogger, and J.A. Robinson, editors. *Nonmonotonic Reasoning and Uncertain Reasoning, Handbook of Logic in Artificial Intelligence and Logic Programming*, vol. 3, pages 353–395. Oxford University Press, Oxford, 1994.

[102] H.J. Ohlbach. SCAN—elimination of predicate quantifiers. In M.A. McRobbie and J.K. Slaney, editors. *Automated Deduction: CADE-13, Notes in Artificial Intelligence Lecture*, vol. 1104, pages 161–165. Springer, 1996.

[103] C. Papadimitriou. *Computational Complexity*. Addison-Wesley, 1994.

[104] J. Pearl. System Z: A natural ordering of defaults with tractable applications to nonmonotonic reasoning. In *Proceedings of the 3rd Conference on Theoretical Aspects of Reasoning about Knowledge, TARK-90*, pages 121–135. Morgan Kaufmann, 1990.

[105] D. Perlis. Autocircumscription. *Artificial Intelligence*, 36(2):223–236, 1988.

[106] J.L. Pollock. Justification and defeat. *Artificial Intelligence*, 67(2):377–407, 1994.

[107] D. Poole. A logical framework for default reasoning. *Artificial Intelligence*, 36:27–47, 1988.

[108] H. Prakken and G. Vreeswijk. Logical systems for defeasible argumentation. In D. Gabbay and F. Guenthner, editors. *Handbook of Philosophical Logic*, vol. 4, 2nd edition, pages 219–318. Kluwer Academic Publishers, Dordrecht, 2002.

[109] T.C. Przymusinski. An algorithm to compute circumscription. *Artificial Intelligence*, 38(1):49–73, 1989.

[110] R. Reiter. On closed world data bases. In H. Gallaire and J. Minker, editors. *Logic and Data Bases*, pages 55–76. Plenum Press, 1978.

[111] R. Reiter. A logic for default reasoning. *Artificial Intelligence*, 13:81–132, 1980.

[112] R. Reiter. *Knowledge in Action: Logical Foundations for Specifying and Implementing Dynamical Systems*. 1st edition. MIT Press, Cambridge, 2001.

[113] J. Rintanen. On specificity in default logic. In *IJCAI*, pages 1474–1479, 1995.

[114] V. Risch and C. Schwind. Tableau-based characterization and theorem proving for default logic. *J. Automat. Reason.*, 13:223–242, 1994.

[115] E. Sandewall. An approach to the frame problem, and its implementation. In B. Meltzer and D. Michie, editors. *Machine Intelligence*, vol. 7, pages 195–204. Edinburgh University Press, 1972.

[116] T. Schaub. On commitment and cumulativity in default logics. In *Proceedings of the European Conference on Symbolic and Quantitative Approaches to Reasoning and Uncertainty, ECSQARU-91, Lecture Notes in Computer Science*, vol. 548, pages 305–309. Springer, 1991.

[117] T. Schaub. A new methodology for query-answering in default logics via structure-oriented theorem proving. *J. Automat. Reason.*, 15(1):95–165, 1995.

[118] T. Schaub and S. Brüning. Prolog technology for default reasoning. In *Proceedings of the European Conference on Artificial Intelligence*, pages 105–109, Budapest, Hungary, August 1996. J. Wiley.

[119] T. Schaub and K. Wang. A comparative study of logic programs with preference. In *Proceedings of the 17th International Joint Conference on Artificial Intelligence, IJCAI-01*, pages 597–602, 2001.

[120] J.S. Schlipf. How uncomputable is general circumscription? In *Proceedings of the Symposium on Logic in Computer Science*, pages 92–95, Cambridge, USA, June 1986. IEEE Computer Society Press.

[121] G.F. Schwarz and M. Truszczyński. Nonmonotonic reasoning is sometimes simpler. In *Proceedings of the 3rd K. Gödel Colloquium on Computational Logic and Proof Theory*, pages 313–324, Brno, Czech Republic, August 1993. Springer.

[122] G.F. Schwarz and M. Truszczyński. Minimal knowledge problem: a new approach. *Artificial Intelligence*, 67(1):113–141, 1994.

[123] Y. Shoham. A semantical approach to nonmonotic logics. In *Proceedings of the Symposium on Logic in Computer Science, LICS-87*, pages 275–279. IEEE Computer Society, 1987.

[124] G.R. Simari and R.P. Loui. A mathematical treatment of defeasible reasoning and its implementation. *Artificial Intelligence*, 53(2–3):125–157, 1992.

[125] R. Stalnaker. A note on nonmonotonic modal logic. *Artificial Intelligence*, 64(2):183–196, 1993.

[126] J. Stillman. It's not my default: The complexity of membership problems in restricted propositional default logics. In *Proceedings of the 9th National Conference on Artificial Intelligence*, pages 571–578, Boston, MA, USA, July 1990. MIT Press.

[127] J. Stillman. The complexity of propositional default logics. In *Proceedings of the 10th National Conference on Artificial Intelligence*, pages 794–800, San Jose, CA, USA, July 1992. MIT Press.

[128] M. Truszczyński. Modal interpretations of default logic. In *Proceedings of IJCAI-91*, pages 393–398. Morgan Kaufmann, 1991.

[129] G. Vreeswijk. Abstract argumentation systems. *Artificial Intelligence*, 90˙1–2:225–279, 1997.

[130] M. Wooldridge, P. McBurney, and S. Parsons. On the meta-logic of arguments. In F. Dignum, V. Dignum, S. Koenig, S. Kraus, M.P. Singh, and M. Wooldridge, editors. *AAMAS*, pages 560–567. ACM, 2005.

Handbook of Knowledge Representation
Edited by F. van Harmelen, V. Lifschitz and B. Porter
© 2008 Elsevier B.V. All rights reserved
DOI: 10.1016/S1574-6526(07)03007-6

Chapter 7

Answer Sets

Michael Gelfond

7.1 Introduction

This chapter is an introduction to Answer Set Prolog—a language for knowledge representation and reasoning based on the *answer set/stable model* semantics of logic programs [44, 45]. The language has roots in declarative programing [52, 65], the syntax and semantics of standard Prolog [24, 23], disjunctive databases [66, 67] and nonmonotonic logic [79, 68, 61]. Unlike "standard" Prolog it allows us to express disjunction and "classical" or "strong" negation. It differs from many other knowledge representation languages by its ability to represent *defaults*, i.e., statements of the form *"Elements of a class C normally satisfy property P"*. A person may learn early in life that parents normally love their children. So knowing that Mary is John's mother he may conclude that Mary loves John and act accordingly. Later he may learn that Mary is an exception to the above default, conclude that Mary does not really like John, and use this new knowledge to change his behavior. One can argue that a substantial part of our education consists in learning various defaults, exceptions to these defaults, and the ways of using this information to draw reasonable conclusions about the world and the consequences of our actions. Answer Set Prolog provides a powerful logical model of this process. Its syntax allows for the simple representation of defaults and their exceptions, its consequence relation characterizes the corresponding set of valid conclusions, and its inference mechanisms often allow a program to find these conclusions in a reasonable amount of time.

There are other important types of statements which can be nicely expressed in Answer Set Prolog. This includes the causal effects of actions ("statement F becomes true as a result of performing an action a"), statements expressing a lack of information ("it is not known if statement P is true or false"), various completeness assumptions "statements not entailed by the knowledge base are false", etc.

There is by now a comparatively large number of inference engines associated with Answer Set Prolog. SLDNF-resolution based goal-oriented methods of "classical" Prolog and its variants [22] are sound with respect to the answer set semantics of their programs. The same is true for fix-point computations of deductive databases [93]. These systems can be used for answering various queries to a subset of

Answer Set Prolog which does not allow disjunction, "classical" negation, and rules with empty heads. In the last decade we have witnessed the coming of age of inference engines aimed at computing the answer sets of Answer Set Prolog programs [71, 72, 54, 29, 39, 47]. These engines are often referred to as *answer set solvers*. Normally they start with grounding the program, i.e., instantiating its variables by ground terms. The resulting program has the same answer sets as the original but is essentially propositional. The grounding techniques implemented by answer set solvers are rather sophisticated. Among other things they utilize algorithms from deductive databases, and require a good understanding of the relationship between various semantics of logic programming. The answer sets of the grounded program are often computed using substantially modified and expanded satisfiability checking algorithms. Another approach reduces the computation of answer sets to (possibly multiple) calls to satisfiability solvers [3, 47, 58].

The method of solving various combinatorial problems by reducing them to finding the answer sets of Answer Set Prolog programs which declaratively describe the problems is often called the *answer set programming paradigm* (*ASP*) [70, 62]. It has been used for finding solutions to a variety of programming tasks, ranging from building decision support systems for the Space Shuttle [74] and program configuration [87], to solving problems arising in bio-informatics [9], zoology and linguistics [20]. On the negative side, Answer Set Prolog in its current form is not adequate for reasoning with complex logical formulas—the things that classical logic is good at—and for reasoning with real numbers.

There is a substantial number of natural and mathematically elegant extensions of the original Answer Set Prolog. A long standing problem of expanding answer set programming by aggregates—functions on sets—is approaching its final solution in [33, 32, 88, 76, 35]. The rules of the language are generalized [38] to allow nested logical connectives and various means to express preferences between answer sets [18, 25, 82]. Weak constraints and consistency restoring rules are introduced to deal with possible inconsistencies [21, 7]. The logical reasoning of Answer Set Prolog is combined with probabilistic reasoning in [14] and with qualitative optimization in [19]. All of these languages have at least experimental implementations and an emerging theory and methodology of use.

7.2   Syntax and Semantics of Answer Set Prolog

We start with a description of syntax and semantics of Answer Set Prolog—a logic programming language based on the answer sets semantics of [45]. In what follows we use a standard notion of a sorted signature from classical logic. We will assume that our signatures contain sort N of non-negative integers and the standard functions and relations of arithmetic. (Nothing prevents us from allowing other numerical types but doing that will lengthen some of our definitions. So N will be the only numerical sort discussed in this paper.) Terms and atoms are defined as usual. An atom $p(\bar{t})$ and its negation $\neg p(\bar{t})$ will be referred to as *literals*. Literals of the form $p(\bar{t})$ and $\neg p(\bar{t})$ are called *contrary*. A rule of Answer Set Prolog is an expression of the form

$$l_0 \; or \; \ldots \; or \; l_k \; \leftarrow l_{k+1}, \ldots, l_m, not \; l_{m+1}, \ldots, not \; l_n, \tag{7.1}$$

where l_i's are literals. Connectives *not* and *or* are called *negation as failure* or *default negation*, and *epistemic disjunction*, respectively. Literals possibly preceded by default negation are called *extended literals*.

A rule of Answer Set Prolog which has a nonempty head and contains no occurrences of $\neg$ and no occurrences of *or* is called an *nlp* rule. Programs consisting of such rules will be referred to as *nlp* (*normal logic program*).

If r is a rule of type (7.1) then $head(r) = \{l_0, \ldots, l_k\}$, $pos(r) = \{l_{k+1}, \ldots, l_m\}$, $neg(r) = \{l_{m+1}, \ldots, l_n\}$, and $body(r) = \{l_{k+1}, \ldots, l_m, not\ l_{m+1}, \ldots, not\ l_n\}$. If $head(r) = \emptyset$ rule r is called a *constraint* and is written as

$$\leftarrow l_{k+1}, \ldots, l_m, not\ l_{m+1}, \ldots, not\ l_n. \tag{7.2}$$

If $k = 0$ then we write

$$l_0 \leftarrow l_1, \ldots, l_m, not\ l_{m+1}, \ldots, not\ l_n. \tag{7.3}$$

A rule r such that $body(r) = \emptyset$ is called a *fact* and is written as

$$l_0\ or\ \ldots\ or\ l_k. \tag{7.4}$$

Rules of Answer Set Prolog will often be referred to as *logic programming rules*.

Definition 7.2.1. *A program of Answer Set Prolog is a pair $\{\sigma, \Pi\}$ where σ is a signature and Π is a collection of logic programming rules over σ.*

In what follows we adhere to the convention used by all the inference engines of Answer Set Prolog and end every rule by a ".".

Consider for instance a signature σ with two sorts, $\tau_1 = \{a, b\}$ and $\tau_2 = N$. Suppose that σ contains predicate symbols $p(\tau_1)$, $q(\tau_1, \tau_2)$, $r(\tau_1)$, and the standard relation $<$ on N. The signature, together with rules

$$\Pi_0 \begin{cases} q(a, 1). \\ q(b, 2). \\ p(X) \leftarrow K + 1 < 2, \\ \qquad q(X, K). \\ r(X) \leftarrow not\ p(X). \end{cases}$$

constitute a program of Answer Set Prolog. Capital letters X and K denote variables of the appropriate types.

In this paper we will often refer to programs of Answer Set Prolog as *logic programs* and denote them by their second element Π. The corresponding signature will be denoted by $\sigma(\Pi)$. If $\sigma(\Pi)$ is not given explicitly, we assume that it consists of symbols occurring in the program.

To give the semantics of Answer Set Prolog we will need the following terminology. Terms, literals, and rules of program Π with signature σ are called *ground* if they contain no variables and no symbols for arithmetic functions. A program is called *ground* if all its rules are ground. A rule r' is called a *ground instance* of a rule r of Π if it is obtained from r by:

1. replacing r's non-integer variables by properly typed ground terms of $\sigma(\Pi)$;

2. replacing r's variables for non-negative integers by numbers from N;

3. replacing the remaining occurrences of numerical terms by their values.

A program $gr(\Pi)$ consisting of all ground instances of all rules of Π is called the *ground instantiation* of Π. Obviously $gr(\Pi)$ is a ground program.

Below is the ground instantiation of program Π_0

$$gr(\Pi_0) \begin{cases} q(a,1). \\ q(b,2). \\ p(a) \quad \leftarrow 1 < 2, \\ \qquad\quad q(a,0). \\ p(a) \quad \leftarrow 2 < 2, \\ \qquad\quad q(a,1). \\ \quad \cdots \\ r(a) \quad \leftarrow not\ p(a). \\ r(b) \quad \leftarrow not\ p(b). \end{cases}$$

Consistent sets of ground literals over σ, containing all arithmetic literals which are true under the standard interpretation of their symbols, are called *partial interpretations* of σ. Let l be a ground literal. By $\bar{l}$ we denote the literal contrary to l. We say that l is *true* in a partial interpretation S if $l \in S$; l is *false* in S if $\bar{l} \in S$; otherwise l is *unknown* in S. An extended literal *not l* is *true* in S if $l \notin S$; otherwise it is *false* in S. A set U of extended literals is understood as conjunction, and sometimes will be written with symbol $\wedge$. U is *true* in S if all elements of U are true in S; U is *false* in S if at least one element of U is false in S; otherwise U is *unknown*. Disjunction D of literals is *true* in S if at least one of its members is true in S; D is *false* in S if all members of D are false in S; otherwise D is *unknown*. Let e be an extended literal, a set of extended literals, or a disjunction of literals. We refer to such expressions as *formulas* of σ. For simplicity we identify expressions $\neg(l_1\ or\ \dots\ or\ l_n)$ and $\neg(l_1, \dots, l_n)$ with the conjunction $\bar{l}_1 \wedge \cdots \wedge \bar{l}_n$. and disjunction $\bar{l}_1\ or\ \dots\ or\ \bar{l}_n$, respectively. We say that S *satisfies e* if e is true in S. S *satisfies a logic programming rule r* if S satisfies r's head or does not satisfy its body.

Our definition of semantics of Answer Set Prolog will be given for ground programs. Rules with variables will be used only as a shorthand for the sets of their ground instances. This approach is justified for the so called closed domains, i.e. domains satisfying the *domain closure assumption* [78] which asserts that *all objects in the domain of discourse have names in the signature of Π*. Even though the assumption is undoubtedly useful for a broad range of applications, there are cases when it does not properly reflect the properties of the domain of discourse. Semantics of Answer Set Prolog for open domains can be found in [11, 84, 49].

The answer set semantics of a logic program Π assigns to Π a collection of *answer sets*—partial interpretations of $\sigma(\Pi)$ corresponding to possible sets of beliefs which can be built by a rational reasoner on the basis of rules of Π. In the construction of such a set, S, the reasoner is assumed to be guided by the following informal principles:

- *S* must satisfy the rules of Π;

- the reasoner should adhere to the *rationality principle* which says that *one shall not believe anything one is not forced to believe*.

The precise definition of answer sets will be first given for programs whose rules do not contain default negation. Let Π be such a program and let S be a partial interpretation of $\sigma(\Pi)$.

Definition 7.2.2 (Answer set—part one). *A partial interpretation S of $\sigma(\Pi)$ is an answer set for Π if S is minimal (in the sense of set-theoretic inclusion) among the partial interpretations satisfying the rules of Π.*

The rationality principle is captured in this definition by the minimality requirement.

Example 7.2.1 (Answer sets). A program

$$\Pi_1 \begin{cases} q(a). \\ p(a). \\ r(a) \leftarrow p(a), \\ \qquad\qquad q(a). \\ r(b) \leftarrow q(b). \end{cases}$$

has one answer set, $\{q(a), p(a), r(a)\}$.
  A program

$$\Pi_2 = \{q(a) \text{ or } q(b).\}$$

has two answer sets, $\{q(a)\}$ and $\{q(b)\}$, while a program

$$\Pi_3 \begin{cases} q(a) \text{ or } q(b). \\ \neg q(a). \end{cases}$$

has one answer set $\{\neg q(a), q(b)\}$.

We use the symbol *or* instead of classical $\vee$ to stress the difference between the two connectives. A formula $A \vee B$ of classical logic says that "A is *true* or B is *true*" while a rule, A *or* B, may be interpreted epistemically and means that every possible set of reasoner's beliefs must satisfy A or satisfy B. To better understand this intuition consider the following examples.

Example 7.2.2 (More answer sets). It is easy to see that program

$$\Pi_4 \begin{cases} p(a) \leftarrow q(a). \\ p(a) \leftarrow \neg q(a). \end{cases}$$

has unique answer set $A = \emptyset$, while program

$$\Pi_5 \begin{cases} p(a) \leftarrow q(a). \\ p(a) \leftarrow \neg q(a). \\ q(a) \text{ or } \neg q(a). \end{cases}$$

has two answer sets, $A_1 = \{q(a), p(a)\}$ and $A_2 = \{\neg q(a), p(a)\}$. The answer sets reflect the epistemic interpretation of *or*. The statement $q(a)$ *or* $\neg q(a)$ is not a tautology. The reasoner associated with program Π_4 has no reason to believe either $q(a)$ nor $\neg q(a)$. Hence he believes neither which leads to the answer set of Π_4 being empty. The last rule of program Π_5 forces the reasoner to only consider sets of beliefs which contain either $q(a)$ or $\neg q(a)$ which leads to two answer sets of Π_5.

Note also that it would be wrong to view epistemic disjunction *or* as exclusive. It is true that, due to the minimality condition in the definition of answer set, program

$$\Pi_2 = \{q(a) \ or \ q(b).\}$$

has two answer sets, $A_1 = \{q(a)\}$ and $A_2 = \{q(b)\}$. But consider a query $Q = q(a) \wedge q(b)$. Since neither Q nor $\neg Q$ are satisfied by answer sets A_1 and A_2 the Π_5's answer to query Q will be *unknown*. The exclusive interpretation of *or* requires the definite negative answer. It is instructive to contrast Π_5 with a program

$$\Pi_6 = \Pi_2 \cup \{\neg q(a) \ or \ \neg q(b)\}$$

which has answer sets $A_1 = \{q(a), \neg q(b)\}$ and $A_2 = \{q(b), \neg q(a)\}$ and clearly contains $\neg Q$ among its consequences.

The next two programs show that the connective $\leftarrow$ should not be confused with classical implication. Consider a program

$$\Pi_7 \begin{cases} \neg p(a) \leftarrow q(a). \\ q(a). \end{cases}$$

Obviously it has unique answer set $\{q(a), \neg p(a)\}$. But the program

$$\Pi_8 \begin{cases} \neg q(a) \leftarrow p(a). \\ q(a). \end{cases}$$

obtained from Π_7 by replacing its first rule by the rule's "contrapositive" has a different answer set, $\{q(a)\}$.

To extend the definition of answer sets to arbitrary programs, take any program Π, and let S be a partial interpretation of $\sigma(\Pi)$. The *reduct*, Π^S, of Π relative to S is the set of rules

$$l_0 \ or \ \ldots \ or \ l_k \leftarrow l_{k+1}, \ldots, l_m$$

for all rules (7.1) in Π such that $\{l_{m+1}, \ldots, l_n\} \cap S = \emptyset$. Thus Π^S is a program without default negation.

Definition 7.2.3 (Answer set—part two). *A partial interpretation S of $\sigma(\Pi)$ is an answer set for Π if S is an answer set for Π^S.*

The relationship between this fix-point definition and the informal principles which form the basis for the notion of answer set is given by the following proposition.

Proposition 7.2.1. (*See Baral and Gelfond [11].*) *Let S be an answer set of logic program Π.*

(a) *S is closed under the rules of the ground instantiation of Π.*

(b) *If literal $l \in S$ then there is a rule r from the ground instantiation of Π such that the body of r is satisfied by S and l is the only literal in the head of r satisfied by S.*

Rule r from (b) "forces" the reasoner to believe l.

Definition 7.2.4 (Entailment). *A program Π entails a ground literal l ($\Pi \models l$) if l is satisfied by every answer set of Π.*

(Sometimes the above entailment is referred to as *cautious*.) Program Π representing knowledge about some domain can be queried by a user with a query q. For simplicity we assume that q is a ground formula of $\sigma(\Pi)$.

Definition 7.2.5 (Answer to a query). *We say that the program Π's answer to a query q is yes if $\Pi \models q$, no if $\Pi \models \neg q$, and unknown otherwise.*

Example 7.2.3. Consider for instance a logic program

$$\Pi_9 \begin{cases} p(a) \leftarrow not\ q(a). \\ p(b) \leftarrow not\ q(b). \\ q(a). \end{cases}$$

Let us first use the informal principles stated above to find an answer set, A, of Π_9. Since A must be closed under the rules of Π, it must contain $q(a)$. There is no rule forcing the reasoner to believe $q(b)$. This implies that $q(b) \notin A$. Finally, the second rule forces the reasoner to believe $p(b)$. The first rule is already satisfied and hence the construction is completed.

Using the definition of answer sets one can easily show that $A = \{q(a), p(b)\}$ is an answer set of this program. In the next section we will introduce simple techniques which will allow us to show that it is the only answer set of Π_9. Thus $\Pi_9 \models q(a)$, $\Pi_9 \not\models q(b)$, $\Pi_9 \not\models \neg q(b)$ and Π_9's answers to queries $q(a)$ and $q(b)$ will be *yes* and *unknown*, respectively. If we expand Π_0 by a rule

$$\neg q(X) \leftarrow not\ q(X) \tag{7.5}$$

the resulting program

$$\Pi_{10} = \Pi_9 \cup (7.5)$$

would have the answer set $S = \{q(a), \neg q(b), p(b)\}$ and hence the answer to query $q(b)$ will become *no*.

The notion of answer set is an extension of an earlier notion of stable model defined in [44] for normal logic programs. But, even though stable models of an *nlp* Π are identical to its answer sets, the meaning of Π under the stable model semantics is different from that under answer set semantics. The difference is caused by the closed world assumption (*CWA*), [78] 'hard-wired' in the definition of stable entailment $\models_s$:

an *nlp* $\Pi \models_s \neg p(a)$ iff for every stable model S of Π, $p(a) \notin S$. In other words the absence of a reason for believing in $p(a)$ is sufficient to conclude its falsity. To match stable model semantics of Π in terms of answer sets, we need to expand Π by an explicit closed world assumption,

$$CWA(\Pi) = \Pi \cup \{\neg p(X_1, \ldots, X_n) \leftarrow not\ p(X_1, \ldots, X_n)\}$$

for every predicate symbol p of Π. Now it can be shown that for any ground literal l, $\Pi \models_s l$ iff $\Pi \models l$. Of course the closed world assumption does not have to be used for all of the relations of the program. If complete information is available about a particular relation p we call such relation *closed* and write $\neg p(X_1, \ldots, X_n) \leftarrow not\ p(X_1, \ldots, X_n)$. Relations which are not closed are referred to as *open*. Examples of open and closed relations will be given in Section 7.4.

7.3 Properties of Logic Programs

There is a large body of knowledge about mathematical properties of logic programs under the answer set semantics. The results presented in this section are aimed at providing a reader with a small sample of this knowledge. Due to the space limitations the presentation will be a mix of precise statements and informal explanations. For a much more complete coverage one may look at [8, 37].

7.3.1 Consistency of Logic Programs

Programs of Answer Set Prolog may have one, many, or zero answer sets. One can use the definition of answer sets to show that programs

$$\Pi_{11} = \{p(a) \leftarrow not\ p(a).\},$$
$$\Pi_{12} = \{p(a). \quad \neg p(a).\},$$

and

$$\Pi_{13} = \{p(a). \quad \leftarrow p(a).\}$$

have no answer sets while program

$$\Pi_{14} \begin{cases} e(0). \\ e(X+2) \leftarrow not\ e(X). \\ p(X+1) \leftarrow e(X), not\ p(X). \\ p(X) \quad \leftarrow e(X), not\ p(X+1). \end{cases}$$

has an infinite collection of them. Each answer set of Π_{14} consists of atoms $\{e(0), e(3), e(4), e(7), e(8), \ldots\}$ and a choice of $p(n)$ or $p(n+1)$ for each integer n satisfying e.

Definition 7.3.1. *A logic program is called* consistent *if it has an answer set.*

Inconsistency of a program can reflect an absence of a solution to the problem it models. It can also be caused by the improper use of the connective $\neg$ and/or constraints as in programs Π_{12} and Π_{13} or by the more subtly incorrect use of default negation as in Π_{11}. The simple transformation described below [42, 11] reduces programs of Answer Set Prolog to programs without $\neg$.

For any predicate symbol p occurring in Π, let p' be a new predicate symbol of the same arity. The atom $p'(\bar{t})$ will be called the *positive form* of the negative literal $\neg p(\bar{t})$. Every positive literal is, by definition, its own positive form. The positive form of a literal l will be denoted by l^+. Program Π^+, called *positive form* of Π, is obtained from Π by replacing each rule (7.1) by

$$\{l_0^+, \ldots, l_k^+\} \leftarrow l_{k+1}^+, \ldots, l_m^+, not\ l_{m+1}^+, \ldots, not\ l_n^+$$

and adding the rules

$$\leftarrow p(\bar{t}), p'(\bar{t})$$

for every atom $p(\bar{t})$ of $\sigma(\Pi)$. For any set S of literals, S^+ stands for the set of the positive forms of the elements of S.

Proposition 7.3.1. *A set S of literals of $\sigma(\Pi)$ is an answer set of Π if and only if S^+ is an answer set of Π^+.*

This leaves the responsibility for inconsistency to the use of constraints and default negation. It is of course important to be able to check consistency of a logic program. Unfortunately in general this problem is undecidable Of course consistency can be decided for programs with finite Herbrand universes but the problem is complex. Checking consistency of such a program is Σ_2^P [27]. For programs without epistemic disjunction and default negation checking consistency belongs to class P; if no epistemic disjunction is allowed the problem is in NP [85]. It is therefore important to find conditions guaranteeing consistency of logic programs. In what follows we will give an example of such a condition.

Definition 7.3.2 (Level mapping). *Functions $\|\ \|$ from ground atoms of $\sigma(\Pi)$ to natural numbers[1] are called* level mappings *of Π.*

The level $\|D\|$ where D is a disjunction or a conjunction of literals is defined as the *minimum level of atoms occurring in literals from D'*. (Note that this implies that $\|l\| = \|\neg l\|$.)

Definition 7.3.3 (Stratification). *A logic program Π is called* locally stratified *if $gr(\Pi)$ does not contain occurrences of $\neg$ and there is a level mapping $\|\ \|$ of Π such that for every rule r of $gr(\Pi)$*

1. *For any $l \in pos(r)$, $\|l\| \leqslant \|head(r)\|$;*

2. *For any $l \in neg(r)$, $\|l\| < \|head(r)\|$.*

If, in addition, for any predicate symbol p, $\|p(\bar{t}_1)\| = \|p(\bar{t}_2)\|$ for any $\bar{t}_1$ and $\bar{t}_2$ the program is called stratified *[1, 77].*

---

[1] For simplicity we consider a special case of the more general original definition which allows arbitrary countable ordinals.

It is easy to see that among programs Π_0–Π_{14} only programs Π_0, Π_1, Π_2, and Π_9 are (locally) stratified.

Theorem 7.3.1 (Properties of locally stratified programs).

- *A locally stratified program is consistent.*

- *A locally stratified program without disjunction has exactly one answer set.*

- *The above conditions hold for a union of a locally stratified program and a collection of closed world assumptions, i.e., rules of the form*

$$\neg p(X) \leftarrow not\ p(X)$$

  for some predicate symbols p.

The theorem immediately implies existence of answer sets of programs Π_9 and Π_{10} from the previous section.

We now use the notion of level mapping to define another syntactic condition on programs known as *order-consistency* [83].

Definition 7.3.4. *For any nlp Π and ground atom a, Π_a^+ and Π_a^- are the smallest sets of ground atoms such that $a \in \Pi_a^+$ and, for every rule $r \in gr(\Pi)$,*

- *if $head(r) \in \Pi_a^+$ then $pos(r) \subseteq \Pi_a^+$ and $neg(r) \subseteq \Pi_a^-$,*

- *if $head(r) \in \Pi_a^-$ then $pos(r) \subseteq \Pi_a^-$ and $neg(r) \subseteq \Pi_a^+$.*

Intuitively, Π_a^+ is the set of atoms on which atom a depends positively in Π, and Π_a^- is the set of atoms on which atom a depends negatively on Π. A program Π is *order-consistent* if there is a level mapping $\|\ \|$ such that $\|b\| < \|a\|$ whenever $b \in \Pi_a^+ \cap \Pi_a^-$. That is, if a depends both positively and negatively on b, then b is mapped to a lower stratum.

Obviously, every locally stratified *nlp* is order-consistent. The program

$$\Pi_{14} \begin{cases} p(X) \leftarrow not\ q(X). \\ q(X) \leftarrow not\ p(X). \\ r(X) \leftarrow p(X). \\ r(X) \leftarrow q(X). \end{cases}$$

with signature containing two object constants, c_1 and c_2 is order-consistent but not stratified, while the program

$$\Pi_{15} \begin{cases} a \leftarrow not\ b. \\ b \leftarrow c, \\ \qquad not\ a. \\ c \leftarrow a. \end{cases}$$

is not order-consistent.

Theorem 7.3.2 (First Fages' Theorem, [34]). *Order-consistent programs are consistent.*

7.3.2 Reasoning Methods for Answer Set Prolog

There are different algorithms which can be used for reasoning with programs of Answer Set Prolog. The choice of the algorithm normally depends on the form of the program and the type of queries one wants to be answered. Let us start with a simple example.

Definition 7.3.5 (Acyclic programs). *An nlp Π is called* acyclic *[2] if there is a level mapping $\| \ \|$ of Π such that for every rule r of $gr(\Pi)$ and every literal l which occurs in $pos(r)$ or $neg(r)$, $\|l\| < \|head(r)\|$.*

Obviously an acyclic logic program Π is stratified and therefore has a unique answer set. It can be shown that queries to an acyclic program Π can be answered by the SLDNF resolution based interpreter of Prolog. To justify this statement we will introduce the notion of Clark's completion [23]. The notion provided the original declarative semantics of *negation as finite failure* of the programming language Prolog. (Recall that in our terminology programs of Prolog are referred to as *nlp*.)

Let us consider the following three step transformation of a *nlp* Π into a collection of first-order formulae.

Step 1: Let $r \in \Pi$, $head(r) = p(t_1, \ldots, t_k)$, and $Y_1, \ldots, Y_s$ be the list of variables appearing in r. By $\alpha_1(r)$ we denote a formula:

$$\exists Y_1 \ldots Y_s : X_1 = t_1 \wedge \cdots \wedge X_k = t_k \wedge l_1 \wedge \cdots \wedge l_m \wedge \neg l_{m+1} \wedge \cdots \wedge \neg l_n$$
$$\supset p(X_1, \ldots, X_k),$$

where $X_1 \ldots X_k$ are variables not appearing in r.

$$\alpha_1(\Pi) = \{\alpha_1(r) \colon r \in \Pi\}.$$

Step 2: For each predicate symbol p if

$$E_1 \supset p(X_1, \ldots, X_k)$$
$$\vdots$$
$$E_j \supset p(X_1, \ldots, X_k)$$

are all the implications in $\alpha_1(\Pi)$ with p in their conclusions then replace these formulas by

$$\forall X_1 \ldots X_k \colon p(X_1, \ldots, X_k) \equiv E_1 \vee \cdots \vee E_j$$

if $j \geqslant 1$ and by

$$\forall X_1 \ldots X_k \colon \neg p(X_1, \ldots, X_k)$$

if $j = 0$.

Step 3: Expand the resulting set of formulas by *free equality axioms*:

$$f(X_1, \ldots, X_n) = f(Y_1, \ldots, Y_n) \supset X_1 = Y_1 \wedge \cdots \wedge X_n = Y_n,$$
$$f(X_1, \ldots, X_n) = g(Y_1, \ldots, Y_n) \quad \text{for all } f \text{ and } g \text{ such that } f \neq g,$$

X ≠ t for each variable X and term t such that X is different from t and X
occurs in t.

All the variables in free equality axioms are universally quantified; binary relation =
does not appear in Π; it is interpreted as identity in all models.

Definition 7.3.6 (Clark's completion, [23]). *The resulting first-order theory is called*
Clark's completion *of Π and is denoted by Comp(Π).*

Consider a program

$$\Pi_{16} \begin{cases} p(X) \leftarrow not\ q(X), \\ \qquad\qquad not\ r(X). \\ p(a). \\ q(b). \end{cases}$$

with the signature containing two object constants, a and b. It is easy to see that, after
some simplification, $Comp(\Pi_{16})$ will be equivalent to the theory consisting of axioms

$$\forall X:\ p(X) \equiv (\neg q(X) \vee X = a),$$
$$\forall X:\ q(X) \equiv X = b,$$
$$\forall X:\ \neg r(X)$$

and the free equality axioms. One may also notice that the answer set $\{p(a), p(b),$
$q(b)\}$ of Π_{16} coincides with the unique Herbrand model of $Comp(\Pi_{16})$.

The following theorem [1] generalizes this observation.

Theorem 7.3.3. *If Π is acyclic then the unique answer set of Π is the unique Her-*
brand model of Clark's completion of Π.

The theorem is important since it allows us to use a large number of results about
soundness and completeness of SLDNF resolution of Prolog with respect to Clark's
semantics to guarantee these properties for acyclic programs with respect to the answer
set semantics. Together with some results on termination this often guarantees that the
SLDNF resolution based interpreter of Prolog will always terminate on atomic queries
and produce the intended answers. Similar approximation of the Answer Set Prolog
entailment for larger classes of programs with unique answer sets can be obtained by
the system called *XSB* [22] implementing the well-founded semantics of [40].

In many cases, instead of checking if l is a consequence of *nlp* Π, we will be
interested in finding answer sets of Π. This of course can be done only if Π has a
finite Herbrand universe. There are various bottom up algorithms which can do such
a computation rather efficiently for acyclic and stratified programs. As Theorem 7.3.3
shows, the answer set of an acyclic program can be also found by computing a classical
model of propositional theory, $Comp(\Pi)$. The following generalization of the notion
of acyclicity ensures one-to-one correspondence between the answer sets of an *nlp*
Π and the models of its Clark's completion, and hence allows the use of efficient
propositional solvers for computing answer sets of Π.

Definition 7.3.7 (Tight programs). *A nlp Π is called* tight *if there is a level mapping*
$\| \ \|$ *of Π such that for every rule r of $gr(\Pi)$ and every $l \in pos(r)$, $\|head(r)\| > \|l\|$.*

It is easy to check that a program

$$\Pi_{17} \begin{cases} a \leftarrow b, \\ \quad\quad not\ a. \\ b. \end{cases}$$

is tight while program

$$a \leftarrow a$$

is not.

Theorem 7.3.4 (Second Fages' Theorem). *If nlp Π is tight then S is a model of Comp(Π) iff S is an answer set of Π.*

The above theorem is due to F. Fages [34]. In the last ten years a substantial amount of work was done to expand second Fages' theorem. One of the most important results in this direction is due to Fangzhen Lin and Yuting Zhao [58]. If program Π is tight then the corresponding propositional formula is simply the Clark's completion of Π; otherwise the corresponding formula is the conjunction of the completion of Π with the additional formulas that Lin and Zhao called the *loop formulas* of Π. The number of loop formulas is exponential in the size of Π in the worst case, and there are reasons for this in complexity theory [56]. But in many cases the Lin–Zhao translation of Π into propositional logic is not much bigger than Π. The reduction of the problem of computing answer sets to the satisfiability problem for propositional formulas given by the Lin–Zhao theorem has led to the development of answer set solvers such as ASET [58], CMODELS [3], etc. which are based on (possibly multiple) calls to propositional solvers.

Earlier solvers such as SMODELS and DLV compute answer sets of a program using substantially modified versions of Davis–Putnam algorithm, adopted for logic programs [55, 73, 72, 54]. All of these approaches are based on sophisticated methods for grounding logic programs. Even though the solvers are capable of working with hundreds of thousands and even millions of ground rules, the size of the grounding remains a major bottleneck of answer set solvers. There are new promising approaches to computing answer sets which combine Davis–Putnam like procedure with constraint satisfaction algorithms and resolution and only require partial grounding [31, 15]. We hope that this work will lead to substantial improvements in the efficiency of answer set solvers.

7.3.3 Properties of Entailment

Let us consider a program Π_{15} from Section 7.3. Its answer set is $\{a, c\}$ and hence both, a and c, are the consequences of Π_{15}. When augmented with the fact c the program gains a second answer set $\{b, c\}$, and loses consequence a. The example demonstrates that the answer set entailment relation does not satisfy the following condition

$$\frac{\Pi \models a, \quad \Pi \models b}{\Pi \cup \{a\} \models b} \tag{7.6}$$

called *cautious monotonicity*. The absence of cautious monotonicity is an unpleasant property of the answer set entailment. Among other things it prohibits the development of general inference algorithms for Answer Set Prolog in which already proven lemmas are simply added to the program. There are, however, large classes of programs for which this problem does not exist.

Definition 7.3.8 (Cautious monotonicity). *We will say that a class of programs is* cautiously monotonic *if programs from this class satisfy condition* (7.6).

The following important theorem is due to H. Turner [92]

Theorem 7.3.5 (First Turner's Theorem). *If Π is an order-consistent program and atom a belongs to every answer set of Π, then every answer set of $\Pi \cup \{a\}$ is an answer set of Π.*

This immediately implies condition (7.6) for order-consistent programs.

A much simpler observation guarantees that all *nlp*'s under the answer set semantics have the so-called *cut* property: If an atom a belongs to an answer set X of Π, then X is an answer set of $\Pi \cup \{a\}$.

Both results used together imply another nice property, called *cumulativity*: augmenting a program with one of its consequences does not alter its consequences. More precisely,

Theorem 7.3.6 (Second Turner's Theorem). *If an atom a belongs to every answer set of an order-consistent program Π, then Π and $\Pi \cup \{a\}$ have the same answer sets.*

Semantic properties such as cumulativity, cut, and cautious monotonicity were originally formulated for analysis of nonmonotonic consequence relations. Makinson's [59] handbook article includes a survey of such properties for nonmonotonic logics used in AI.

7.3.4   Relations between Programs

In this section we discuss several important relations between logic programs. We start with the notion of equivalence.

Definition 7.3.9 (Equivalence). *Logic programs are called equivalent if they have the same answer sets.*

It is easy to see, for instance, that programs

$$\Pi_{18} = \{p(a) \ or \ p(b)\},$$

$$\Pi_{19} = \{p(a) \leftarrow not \ p(b). \quad p(b) \leftarrow not \ p(a).\}$$

have the same answer sets, $\{p(a)\}$ and $\{p(b)\}$, and therefore are equivalent. Now consider programs Π_{20} and Π_{21} obtained by adding rules

$$p(a) \leftarrow p(b).$$

$$p(b) \leftarrow p(a).$$

to each of the programs Π_{18} and Π_{19}. It is easy to see that Π_{20} has one answer set, $\{p(a), p(b)\}$ while Π_{21} has no answer sets. The programs Π_{20} and Π_{21} are not equivalent. It is not of course surprising that, in general, epistemic disjunction cannot be eliminated from logic programs. As was mentioned before programs with and without *or* have different expressive powers. It can be shown, however, that for a large class of logic programs, called cycle-free [16], the disjunction can be eliminated by the generalization of the method applied above to Π_{18}. Program Π_{20} which does not belong to this class has a cycle (a mutual dependency) between elements $p(a)$ and $p(b)$ in the head of its rule. The above example suggests another important question: under what conditions can we be sure that replacing a part Π_1 of a knowledge base K by Π_2 will not change the answer sets of K? Obviously simple equivalence of Π_1 and Π_2 is not enough for this purpose. We need a stronger notion of equivalence [57].

Definition 7.3.10 (Strong equivalence). *Logic programs Π_1 and Π_1 with signature σ are called* strongly equivalent *if for every program Π with signature σ programs $\Pi \cup \Pi_1$ and $\Pi \cup \Pi_2$ have the same answer sets.*

The programs Π_{18} and

$$\Pi_{22} = \Pi_{18} \cup \{p(a) \leftarrow not\ p(b)\}$$

are strongly equivalent, while programs Π_{18} and Π_{19} are not. The notion of strong equivalence has deep and non-trivial connections with intuitionistic logics. One can show that if two programs in which *not*, *or*, and $\leftarrow$ are understood as intuitionistic negation, implication and disjunction, respectively, are intuitionistically equivalent, then they are also strongly equivalent. Furthermore in this statement intuitionistic logic can be replaced with a stronger subsystem of classical logic, called "the logic of here-and-there". Its role in logic programming was first recognized in [75], where it was used to define a nonmonotonic "equilibrium logic" which syntactically extends an original notion of a logic program. As shown in [57] two programs are equivalent iff they are equivalent in the logic of here-and-there.

There are other important forms of equivalence which were extensively studied in the last decade. Some of them weaken the notion of strong equivalence by limiting the class of equivalence preserving updates. For instance, programs Π_1 and Π_2 over signature σ are called *uniformly equivalent* if for any set of ground facts, F, of σ programs $\Pi_1 \cup F$ and $\Pi_2 \cup F$ have the same answer sets. Here the equivalence preserving updates are those which consist of collections of ground facts. It can be checked that programs Π_{18} and Π_{19}, while not strongly equivalent, are uniformly equivalent. Another way to weaken the original definition is to limit the signature of the updates. Programs Π_1 and Π_2 over signature σ are called *strongly equivalent relative to a given set A of ground atoms of σ* if for any program Π in the language of A, programs $\Pi_1 \cup \Pi$ and $\Pi_2 \cup \Pi$ have the same answer sets. Definition of the uniform equivalence can be relativized in a similar way. There is a substantial literature on the subject. As an illustration let us mention a few results established in [30]. We already mentioned that for head-cycle-free programs eliminating disjunction by shifting atoms from rule heads to the respective rule bodies preserves regular equivalence. In this paper the authors show that this transformation also preserves (relativized) uniform equivalence while it affects (relativized) strong equivalence. The systems for testing various forms of equivalence are described in [51].

7.4 A Simple Knowledge Base

To illustrate the basic methodology of representing knowledge in Answer Set Prolog, let us first consider a simple example from [43].

Example 7.4.1. Let *cs* be a small computer science department located in the college of science, *cos*, of university, *u*. The department, described by the list of its members and the catalog of its courses, is in the last stages of creating its summer teaching schedule. In this example we outline a construction of a simple Answer Set Prolog knowledge base $\mathcal{K}$ containing information about the department. For simplicity we assume an open-ended signature containing names, courses, departments, etc.

The list and the catalog naturally correspond to collections of atoms, say:

$$member(sam, cs). \quad member(bob, cs). \quad member(tom, cs).$$
$$course(java, cs). \quad course(c, cs). \tag{7.7}$$
$$course(ai, cs). \quad course(logic, cs).$$

together with the closed world assumptions expressed by the rules:

$$\neg member(P, cs) \leftarrow not\ member(P, cs).$$
$$\neg course(C, cs) \ \leftarrow not\ course(C, cs). \tag{7.8}$$

The assumptions are justified by completeness of the corresponding information. The preliminary schedule can be described by the list, say:

$$teaches(sam, java). \quad teaches(bob, ai). \tag{7.9}$$

Since the schedule is incomplete, the relation *teaches* is open and the use of *CWA* for this relation is not appropriate. The corresponding program correctly answers *no* to query '*member(mary, cs)*?' and *unknown* to query '*teaches(mary, c)*?'.

Let us now expand our knowledge base, $\mathcal{K}$, by the statement: "Normally, computer science courses are taught only by computer science professors. The logic course is an exception to this rule. It may be taught by faculty from the math department." This is a typical *default* with a *weak exception*[2] which can be represented in Answer Set Prolog by the rules:

$$\neg teaches(P, C) \ \leftarrow \neg member(P, cs),$$
$$\qquad\qquad\qquad course(C, cs),$$
$$\qquad\qquad\qquad not\ ab(d_1(P, C)), \tag{7.10}$$
$$\qquad\qquad\qquad not\ teaches(P, C).$$
$$ab(d_1(P, logic)) \leftarrow not\ \neg member(P, math).$$

---

[2] An exception to a default is called *weak* if it stops application of the default without defeating its conclusion.

Here $d_1(P, C)$ is the name of the default rule and $ab(d_1(P, C))$ says that default $d_1(P, C)$ is not applicable to the pair $\langle P, C \rangle$. The second rule above stops the application of the default to any P who *may be* a math professor. Assuming that

$$member(mary, math). \tag{7.11}$$

is in $\mathcal{K}$ we have that $\mathcal{K}$'s answer to query '*teaches(mary, c)*?' will become *no* while the answer to query '*teaches(mary, logic)*?' will remain *unknown*. It may be worth noting that, since our information about persons membership in departments is complete, the second rule of (7.10) can be replaced by a simpler rule

$$ab(d_1(P, logic)) \leftarrow member(P, math). \tag{7.12}$$

It is not difficult to show that the resulting programs have the same answer sets. To complete our definition of relation "*teaches*" let us expand $\mathcal{K}$ by the rule which says that "Normally a class is taught by one person". This can be easily done by the rule:

$$\begin{aligned}
\neg teaches(P_1, C) \leftarrow{}& teaches(P_2, C), \\
& P_1 \neq P_2, \\
& not\ ab(d_2(P_1, C)), \\
& not\ teaches(P_1, C).
\end{aligned} \tag{7.13}$$

Now if we learn that *logic* is taught by Bob we will be able to conclude that it is not taught by Mary.

The knowledge base $\mathcal{K}$ we constructed so far is elaboration tolerant with respect to simple updates. We can easily modify the departments membership lists and course catalogs. Our representation also allows *strong exceptions* to defaults, e.g., statements like

$$teaches(john, ai). \tag{7.14}$$

which defeats the corresponding conclusion of default (7.10). As expected, strong exceptions can be inserted in $\mathcal{K}$ without causing a contradiction.

Let us now switch our attention to defining the place of the department in the university. This can be done by expanding $\mathcal{K}$ by the rules

$$\begin{aligned}
& part(cs, cos). \\
& part(cos, u). \\
& part(E1, E2) \quad \leftarrow part(E1, E), \\
& \qquad\qquad\qquad\ \ part(E, E2). \\
& \neg part(E1, E2) \leftarrow not\ part(E1, E2).
\end{aligned} \tag{7.15}$$

$$\begin{aligned}
member(P, E1) \leftarrow{}& part(E2, E1), \\
& member(P, E2).
\end{aligned} \tag{7.16}$$

The first two facts form a part of the hierarchy from the university organizational chart. The next rule expresses the transitivity of the *part* relation. The last rule of (7.15) is the closed world assumption for *part*; it is justified only if $\mathcal{K}$ contains a complete organizational chart of the university. If this is the case then the closed world assumption for *member* can be also expanded by, say, the rule:

$$\neg member(P, Y) \leftarrow not\ member(P, Y). \tag{7.17}$$

The answer set of $\mathcal{K}$ can be computed by the DLV system directly; some minor modifications are needed to run $\mathcal{K}$ on Smodels to enforce "domain restrictedness" (see [72]).

To check that *sam* is a member of the university we form a query

$$member(sam, u)?$$ (7.18)

Asking DLV to answer *member(sam, u)*? on program $\mathcal{K}$ we get precisely the response to our query under cautious entailment.[3] The answer set solvers also provide simple means of displaying all the terms satisfying relations defined by a program and so we can use it to list, say, all members of the CS faculty, etc.

Let us now expand $\mathcal{K}$ by a new relation, *offered(C, D)*, defined by the following, self-explanatory, rules:

$$
\begin{aligned}
offered(C, D) &\leftarrow course(C, D), \\
&\quad teaches(P, C). \\
\neg offered(C, D) &\leftarrow course(C, D), \\
&\quad not\ offered(C, D).
\end{aligned}
$$ (7.19)

Suppose also that either Tom or Bob are scheduled to teach the class in logic. A natural representation of this fact requires disjunction and can be expressed as

$$teaches(tom, logic)\ or\ teaches(bob, logic).$$ (7.20)

It is easy to see that the resulting program has two answer sets and that each answer set contains *offered(logic, cs)*. The example shows that Answer Set Prolog with disjunction allows a natural form of reasoning by cases—a mode of reasoning not easily modeled by Reiter's default logic. The answer sets of the new program can be computed by DLV and SMODELS based disjunctive answer set solver GnT [50]. It is worth noting that this program is head-cycle free and therefore, the disjunctive rule (7.20) can be replaced by two non-disjunctive rules,

$$
\begin{aligned}
teaches(tom, logic) &\leftarrow not\ teaches(bob, logic). \\
teaches(bob, logic) &\leftarrow not\ teaches(tom, logic).
\end{aligned}
$$ (7.21)

and the resulting program will be equivalent to the original one. Now both, Smodels and DLV can be used to reason about the resulting knowledge base.

7.5   Reasoning in Dynamic Domains

In this section we discuss the Answer Set Prolog representation of knowledge about *dynamic domains*. We assume that such a domain is modeled by a *transition diagram* with nodes corresponding to possible states of the domain, and arcs labeled by actions. An arc (σ_1, a, σ_2) indicates that execution of an action a in state σ_1 may result in the domain moving to the state σ_2. If for every state σ_1 and action a the diagram contains at most one arc (σ_1, a, σ_2) then the domain is called *deterministic*. The transition diagram contains all possible trajectories of the domain. Its particular history is given by a

---

[3] In practice, this is done by adding *member(sam, u)*? to the file containing the program $\mathcal{K}$, and running it on DLV with option $-FC$ to specify that cautious entailment is required.

record of observations and actions. Due to the size of the diagram, the problem of finding its concise specification is not trivial and has been a subject of research for a comparatively long time. Its solution requires a good understanding of the nature of causal effects of actions in the presence of complex interrelations between fluents—propositions whose truth value may depend on the state of the domain. An additional level of complexity is added by the need to specify what is not changed by actions. The latter, known as the *frame problem* [48], is often reduced to the problem of finding a concise and accurate representation of the *inertia axiom*—a default which says that *things normally stay as they are*. The search for such a representation substantially influenced AI research during the last twenty years. An interesting account of history of this research together with some possible solutions can be found in [86].

To better understand the Answer Set Prolog way of specifying dynamic domains one may first look at a specification of such domains in the formalism of *action languages* (see, for instance, [46]). In this paper we limit our attention to an action description language *AL* from [12]. A *theory* of *AL* consists of a signature, Σ, and a collection of causal laws and executability conditions. The signature contains two disjoint, nonempty sets of symbols: the set F of fluents and the set A of *elementary actions*. A set $\{a_1, \ldots, a_n\}$ of elementary actions is called a *compound* action. It is interpreted as a collection of elementary actions performed simultaneously. By *actions* we mean both elementary and compound actions. By *fluent literals* we mean fluents and their negations. By $\bar{l}$ we denote the fluent literal complementary to l. A set S of fluent literals is called *complete* if, for any $f \in F$, $f \in S$ or $\neg f \in S$. *AL* contains the following causal laws and executability conditions of the form

1. a_e *causes* l *if* p;

2. l *if* p;

3. *impossible* a *if* p

where a_e and a are elementary and arbitrary actions, respectively, and p is a collection of fluent literals from Σ, often referred to as the *precondition* of the corresponding law. If p is empty the *if* part of the propositions will be omitted. The first proposition, called *dynamic causal laws*, says that, if the elementary action a_e were to be executed in a state which satisfies p, the system will move to a state satisfying l. The second proposition, called a *static causal law*, says that every state satisfying p must satisfy l. The last proposition says that action a cannot happen in a state satisfying p. Notice that here a can be compound; *impossible* $(\{a_1, a_2\})$ means that elementary actions a_1 and a_2 cannot occur concurrently.

Let $\mathcal{A}$ be an action description of *AL* over signature Σ. To define the transition diagram, $T_{\mathcal{A}}$, described by $\mathcal{A}$ we need the following terminology and notation. Let S be a set of fluent literals of Σ. The set $Cn_{\mathcal{A}}(S)$ is the smallest set of fluent literals of Σ that contains S and satisfies static causal laws of $\mathcal{A}$. $E(a_e, \sigma)$ stands for the set of all fluent literals l for which there is a dynamic causal law "a_e *causes* l *if* p" in $\mathcal{A}$ such that $p \subseteq \sigma$. $E(a, \sigma) = \bigcup_{a_e \in a} E(a_e, \sigma)$. The transition system $T = \langle S, \mathcal{R} \rangle$ *described* by an action description $\mathcal{A}$ is defined as follows:

1. S is the collection of all complete and consistent sets of fluent literals of Σ which satisfy static causal laws of $\mathcal{A}$;

2. $\mathcal{R}$ is the set of all triples (σ, a, σ') such that $\mathcal{A}$ does not contain a proposition of the form "*impossible a if p*" such that $p \subseteq \sigma$ and

$$\sigma' = Cn_{\mathcal{A}}(E(a, \sigma) \cup (\sigma \cap \sigma')). \tag{7.22}$$

The argument of $Cn_{\mathcal{A}}$ in (7.22) is the union of the set $E(a, \sigma)$ of the "direct effects" of action a with the set $\sigma \cap \sigma'$ of facts that are "preserved by inertia". The application of $Cn_{\mathcal{A}}$ adds the "indirect effects" to this union.

The above definition is from [63] and is the product of a long investigation of the nature of causality. (An action language based on this definition appeared in [91].) Theorem 7.5.1 [6] (a version of the result from [91]) shows the remarkable relationship between causality expressible in *AL* and beliefs of rational agents as captured by the notion of answer sets of logic programs.

To formulate the theorem we will need some terminology. We start by describing an encoding τ of causal laws of *AL* into a program of Answer Set Prolog suitable for execution by answer set solvers:

1. $\tau(a_e$ *causes* l_0 *if* $l_1 \ldots l_n)$ is the collection of atoms
   $dynamic\_law(d), head(d, l_0), action(d, a_e)$,
   $prec(d, i, l_i)$ for $1 \leqslant i \leqslant n$,
   $prec(d, n + 1, nil)$.
   Here d is a new term used to name the corresponding law, and *nil* is a special fluent constant. The last statement, $prec(d, n + 1, nil)$, is used to specify the end of the list of preconditions. (This arrangement simplifies the definition of relation $prec\_h(D, T)$ which holds when all the preconditions of default D hold at time step T.)

2. $\tau(l_0$ *if* $l_1 \ldots l_n)$ is the collection of atoms
   $static\_law(d), head(d, l_0)$,
   $prec(d, i, l_i)$ for $1 \leqslant i \leqslant n$,
   $prec(d, n + 1, nil)$.

3. $\tau(impossible \{a_1, \ldots, a_k\}$ *if* $l_1 \ldots l_n)$ is a constraint

$$\leftarrow h(l_1, T), \ldots, h(l_n, T), occurs(a_1, T), \ldots, occurs(a_k, T).$$

Here T ranges over non-negative integers, $occurs(a, t)$ says that action a occurred at moment t, and $h(l, t)$ means that fluent literal l holds at t. (More precisely, $h(p(\bar{t}), T)$ stands for $holds(p(\bar{t}), T)$, while $h(\neg p(\bar{t}), T)$ is a shorthand for $\neg holds(p(\bar{t}), T)$. If σ is a collection of literals then $h(\sigma, T) = \{h(l, T): l \in \sigma\}$. Finally, for any action description $\mathcal{A}$

$$\tau(\mathcal{A}) = \{\tau(law): law \in \mathcal{A}\}, \tag{7.23}$$

$$\phi(\mathcal{A}) = \tau(\mathcal{A}) \cup \Pi(1), \tag{7.24}$$

$$\phi_n(\mathcal{A}) = \tau(\mathcal{A}) \cup \Pi(n), \tag{7.25}$$

where $\Pi(1)$ is an instance of the following program

$$\Pi(n) \begin{cases} 1.\ h(L, T') & \leftarrow dynamic\_law(D), \\ & \qquad head(D, L), \\ & \qquad action(D, A), \\ & \qquad occurs(A, T), \\ & \qquad prec\_h(D, T). \\ 2.\ h(L, T) & \leftarrow static\_law(D), \\ & \qquad head(D, L), \\ & \qquad prec\_h(D, T). \\ 3.\ all\_h(D, K, T) \leftarrow prec(D, K, nil). \\ 4.\ all\_h(D, K, T) \leftarrow prec(D, K, P), \\ & \qquad h(P, T), \\ & \qquad all\_h(D, K', T). \\ 5.\ prec\_h(D, T) & \leftarrow all\_h(D, 1, T). \\ 6.\ h(L, T') & \leftarrow h(L, T), \\ & \qquad not\ h(\overline{L}, T'). \end{cases}$$

Here D, A, L are variables for the names of laws, actions, and fluent literals, respectively, T, T' are consecutive time points from interval $[0, n]$ and K, K' stand for consecutive integers used to enumerate preconditions of causal laws of $\mathcal{A}$. The first two rules describe the meaning of dynamic and static causal laws, rules (3), (4), (5) define what it means for all the preconditions of law D to succeed, and rule (6) represents the inertia axiom.

Theorem 7.5.1. *For any action description $\mathcal{A}$ of AL the transition diagram $T_{\mathcal{A}}$ contains a link (σ, a, σ') iff there is an answer set S of logic program*

$$\phi(\mathcal{A}) \cup h(\sigma, 0) \cup \{occurs(a_i, 0): a_i \in a\}$$

such that, $\sigma' = \{l: h(l, 1) \in S\}$.

The theorem establishes a close relationship between the notion of causality and the notion of rational beliefs of an agent.

This and similar results are used as a basis for the answer set planning, diagnostics, learning, etc. Consider for instance an action description $\mathcal{A}$ which contains a collection of elementary actions $e_0, \ldots, e_n$ which can be performed by an intelligent agent associated with the domain. Let us assume that the transition system $T_{\mathcal{A}}$ is deterministic, i.e., any state σ and action a have at most one successor state. The agent, who is currently in a state σ, needs to find a sequential plan of length k to achieve a goal $g = \{l_1, \ldots, l_m\}$. In other words the agent is looking for a trajectory $\langle \sigma, e_0, \ldots, e_{k_1}, \sigma' \rangle$ of $T_{\mathcal{A}}$ where $g \subseteq \sigma'$. Using Theorem 7.5.1 it is not difficult to show that there is one to one correspondence between such trajectories and answer sets of the program

$$pl(\mathcal{A}, k) = \phi(n) \cup h(\sigma, 0) \cup P_M,$$

where

$$P_M \begin{cases} occurs(e, T) \; or \; \neg occurs(e, T) \leftarrow T < k. \\ \neg occurs(e_2, T) \leftarrow occurs(e_1, T), e_1 \neq e_2. \\ goal \leftarrow h(g, k). \\ \leftarrow not \; goal. \end{cases}$$

The first two rules guarantee the occurrence of exactly one agent's action at each time step of the trajectory. The next two ensure that every answer set of the program satisfies the goal at step k. The correspondence allows to reduce the problem of classical planning to the problem of finding answer sets of logic programs. A simple loop calls an answer set solver with the program $pl(\mathcal{A}, i)$ as an input for i ranging from 0 to k. A plan is easily extracted from the first answer set returned by the solver. If no answer set is found then the planning problem has no solution of the length less than or equal to k. The method, first suggested in [90, 26], has a number of practical applications [74] and in some cases may be preferable to other approaches. Typical classical planners for instance do not allow the input language with static causal laws, which can be essential for modeling some domains, as well as for efficiency of planning. Moreover such planners may require special languages describing properties of the plans, etc. To illustrate this point let us consider a complex hydraulic module from the reaction control system of the space shuttle. In a very simplified view the system can be viewed as a graph whose nodes are labeled by tanks containing propellant, jets, junctions of pipes, etc. Arcs of the graph are labeled by valves which can be open or closed by a collection of switches. The goal is to open or close valves to deliver propellant from tanks to a proper combination of jets. The graph can be described by a collection of atoms of the form $connected(n_1, v, n_2)$—valve v labels the ark from n_1 to n_2—and $controls(s, v)$—switch s controls the valve v. The description of the system may also contain a collection of faults, e.g., $stuck(V)$, which indicates that valve V is stuck. We assume that our information about malfunctioning of valves is complete, i.e.,

$$\neg stuck(V) \leftarrow not \; stuck(V).$$

The domain contains actions $flip(S)$. The dynamic causal laws for this action are given by the rules

$$\begin{aligned} h(state(S, open), T + 1) \;\; &\leftarrow occurs(flip(S), T), \\ & \quad h(state(S, closed), T). \\ h(state(S, closed), T + 1) &\leftarrow occurs(flip(S), T), \\ & \quad h(state(S, open), T). \end{aligned}$$

The next rule is a static causal law describing the connections between positions of switches and valves.

$$\begin{aligned} h(state(V, P), T) \leftarrow & controls(S, V), \\ & h(state(S, P), T), \\ & \neg stuck(V). \end{aligned}$$

The next static causal law describes the relationship between the values of fluent $pressurized(N)$ for neighboring nodes.

$$\begin{aligned} h(pressurized(N_2), T) \leftarrow & connected(N_1, V, N_2), \\ & h(pressurized(N_1), T), \\ & h(state(V, open), T). \end{aligned}$$

We also assume that tanks are always pressurized which will be encoded by the rule

$$h(pressurized(N), T) \leftarrow tank(N).$$

The laws describe a comparatively complex effect of a simple *flip* operation which propagates the pressure through the system. It seems that without static causal laws the substantially longer description will be needed to achieve this goal. Suppose now that some of the valves may be leaking. It is natural to look for plans which do not open leaking valves. This can be achieved by expanding the standard planning module by the rule

$$\neg occurs(flip(S), T) \leftarrow controls(S, V),$$
$$h(state(S, closed), T),$$
$$is\_leaking(V).$$

Adding the rule

$$\neg occurs(flip(S), T) \leftarrow controls(S, V),$$
$$stuck(V).$$

will help to avoid generation of unnecessary actions, etc. These and similar rules can be used to improve quality of plans and efficiency of the planner. It is also worth noticing that simple modification of the planner will allow search for parallel plans, that similar techniques can be used to search for conformant and conditional plans [10, 89], for diagnostics [6] and even for learning [5, 81].

7.6 Extensions of Answer Set Prolog

In this section we briefly discuss extensions of Answer Set Prolog by aggregates [32] and by consistency restoring rules [7]. To see the need for the first extension let us consider the following example.

Example 7.6.1. Suppose that we are given a complete collection of records

$registered(john, cs1).$ $registered(mary, cs2).$
$registered(bob, cs1).$ $registered(sam, cs2).$
$registered(mike, cs1).$

and that our goal is to define the notion of a large class—a class with at least three registered students. In the language DLP^A from [32] this can be done by the rule

$$large\_class(C) \leftarrow \#count(\{S : registered(S, C)\}) \geqslant 3.$$

Here $\#count(X)$ is the cardinality of the set X. Clearly $\#count(\{S: registered(S, cs1)\}) = 3$ and hence $cs1$ is a large class.

The syntax of DLP^A [4] allows *aggregate atoms* of the form $f(\{X : p(X)\})$ rel n where *rel* is a standard arithmetic relation and n is a number. The occurrence of variable X in the above aggregate atom is called *bound*. Such occurrences remain

---

[4]For simplicity we omit several less important features of the language.

untouched by the grounding process. Rules of DLP^A are of the form

$$a_1 \text{ or } \ldots \text{ or } a_n \leftarrow b_1, \ldots, b_k, not\ b_{k+1}, \ldots, not\ b_m,$$

where a's are standard (non-aggregate) atoms and b's are atoms. The program, P_0, from Example 7.6.1 is a ground program of DLP^A.

Let S be a set of standard ground atoms from the signature of a DLP^A program P.

Definition 7.6.1 (Answer sets of DLP^A). *An aggregate atom $f(\{X : p(X)\})$ rel n is true in S if $f(\{X : p(X) \in S\})$ rel n; it is false otherwise. The DLV^A reduct, $P^{[S]}$ of P with respect to S is obtained from $gr(P)$ by removing all rules whose bodies contain extended literals which are false in S. S is an* answer set *of P if it is a minimal set closed under the rules of $P^{[S]}$.*

For programs not containing aggregate atoms the definition is equivalent to the original definition of answer sets. It is easy to check that program P_0 from Example 7.6.1 has unique answer set consisting of the facts of the program and the atom *large_class*(cs1). The next two programs illustrate the DLV^A treatment of recursion through aggregates. Such a recursion caused various difficulties for a number of other approaches to expending logic programs with aggregates. Let

$$\Pi_1 = \{p(a) \leftarrow \#count(\{X : p(X)\}) > 0.\}$$

and

$$\Pi_2 = \{p(a) \leftarrow \#count(\{X : p(X)\}) < 1.\}$$

and consider sets $S_1 = \{p(a)\}$ and $S_2 = \emptyset$. Since $\Pi_1^{[S_1]} = \Pi_1$ and $\emptyset$ is closed under Π_1, S_1 is not an answer set of Π_1. But $\Pi_1^{[S_2]} = \emptyset$ and hence S_2 is the only answer set of Π_1. Since $\Pi_2^{[S_1]} = \emptyset$ and $\Pi_2^{[S_2]} = \Pi_2$ program Π_2 has no answer sets.

Now we give a brief description of CR-Prolog—an extension of Answer Set Prolog capable of encoding rare events. We start with a description of syntax and semantics of the language. For simplicity we omit the CR-Prolog treatment of preferences.

A program of CR-Prolog is a pair consisting of signature and a collection of regular rules of Answer Set Prolog and rules of the form

$$l_0 +- l_1, \ldots, l_k, not\ l_{k+1}, \ldots, not\ l_n \tag{7.26}$$

where l's are literals. Rules of type (7.26) are called *consistency restoring* rules (cr-rules). Intuitively the rule says that if the reasoner associated with the program believes the body of the rule then it "may possibly" believe one element of the head. This possibility however may be used only if there is no way to obtain a consistent set of beliefs by using only regular rules of the program.

The set of regular rules of a CR-Prolog-program Π will be denoted by Π^r; the set of cr-rules of Π will be denoted by Π^{cr}. By $\alpha(r)$ we denote a regular rule obtained from a consistency restoring rule r by replacing $+-$ by $\leftarrow$; α is expended in a standard way to a set R of cr-rules. As usual, the semantics of CR-Prolog will be given for ground programs, and a rule with variables will be viewed as a shorthand for schema of ground rules.

Definition 7.6.2 (Answer sets of CR-Prolog). *A minimal (with respect to set theoretic inclusion) collection R of cr-rules of Π such that Π^r ∪ α(R) is consistent (i.e. has an answer set) is called an* abductive support *of Π*.

A set A is called an answer set *of Π if it is an answer set of a regular program Π^r ∪ α(R) for some abductive support R of Π*.

Example 7.6.2. Consider a program, T, of CR-Prolog consisting of rules

$p(X)$ ← *not ab(X)*.
$ab(e1)$.
$ab(e2)$.
$q(e)$.
$r(X)$ ← $p(X), q(X)$.
$ab(X)$ +−.

The program includes a default with two exceptions, a partial definition of r in terms of p and q, and consistency restoring rule which acknowledges the possibility of existence of unknown exceptions to the default. Since normally such a possibility is ignored the answer set of the program consists of its facts and atoms $p(e), r(e)$.

Suppose now that the program is expanded by a new atom, ¬$r(e)$. The regular part of the new program has no answer set. The cr-rule solves the problem by assuming that e is a previously unknown exception to the default. The resulting answer set consists of the program facts and the atom $ab(e)$.

The possibility to encode rare events which may serve as unknown exceptions to defaults proved to be very useful for various knowledge representation tasks, including planning, diagnostics, and reasoning about the agents intentions [4, 13].

7.7 Conclusion

We hope that the material is this chapter is sufficient to introduce the reader to Answer Set Prolog, its mathematical theory, and its applications. We will conclude by briefly outlining the relationship between this formalism and other areas of Knowledge Representation presented in this book. The semantics of the language has its roots in nonmonotonic logics discussed in Chapter 6. The original intuition of stable model semantics comes from the mapping of logic programming rules into formulas of Moore's autoepistemic logic [68]. The mapping, first presented in [41], interprets default negation, *not p*, of Prolog as ¬Lp where L is the belief operator of Autoepistemic Logic. This interpretation is responsible for the epistemic character of the stable model semantics. In [17, 60, 45] logic programs with classical negation (but without disjunction) were mapped into Reiter's Default Theory [79]. Very close relationship between Answer Set Prolog and Circumscription [64] was recently established in [36]. There is also a close relationship between Answer Set Prolog and Causal Logic discussed in Chapter 19. As was discussed in Section 7.3.2 computational methods of ASP are closely related to topics discussed in chapters on satisfiability and constraint programming. The designers of ASP solvers commonly use ideas from these areas. The additional power of ASP, its ability to represent transitive closure, aggregates, and other features not immediately available in satisfiability solvers, together with sophisticated grounding methods can undoubtedly be useful for the SAT community. Planning and diagnostic algorithms based on ASP can nicely complement more traditional planning methods discussed in Chapter 22. These methods are especially useful when successful planning requires a large body of knowledge and when the agent needs to solve both, planning and diagnostic, problems. It is our hope that the ongoing work on combining the traditional ASP methods with constraint programming algorithms will help to overcome the limitations caused by grounding, and lead to the development of efficient planning and scheduling systems. The methodology of modeling dynamic systems in Answer Set Prolog discussed in Section 7.5 has much in common with other model-based problem solving methods of Chapter 10. It will be interesting to investigate the range of applicability and advantages and disadvantages of various styles of description of states and possible trajectories of the domain, and of reasoning methods used in model-based problem solving. There is also a substantial cross-fertilization between answer set based reasoning about actions and change and other similar formalisms including Situation Calculus [48, 80], Event Calculus [53, 69], and various temporal logics. There are, for instance, logic programming based counterparts of Situation Calculus, which allow elegant solutions to the frame and ramification problem. Original versions of Event Calculus were directly expressed in the language of logic programming. The ability of temporal logic to reason about properties of paths is modeled by logic programming based specification of goals in [8]. Chapter 20 gives an example of the use of Answer Set Prolog and its reasoning methods for representing and reasoning about commonsense and linguistic knowledge needed for intelligent question answering from natural language texts. There are several interesting efforts of combining Answer Sets with Bayesian net based probabilistic reasoning, which substantially increases expressive power of both knowledge representation languages and promises to lead to efficient algorithms for answering some forms of probabilistic queries. Finally, new results establishing some relationship between Description Logic and Answer Sets (see, for instance, [28]) may open the way for interesting applications of Answer Sets to Semantic Web.

Acknowledgements

This work was partially supported by ARDA grant ASU06-C-0143 and NASA grant NASA-NNG05GP48G. The author wish to thank Gerhard Brewka, Vladimir Lifschitz, and Hudson Turner for many useful comments.

Bibliography

[1] K. Apt, H. Blair, and A. Walker. Towards a theory of declarative knowledge. In *Foundations of Deductive Databases and Logic Programming*, pages 89–148. Morgan Kaufmann, 1988.

[2] K. Apt and D. Pedreschi. Proving termination in general Prolog programs. In *Proc. of the Internat. Conf. on Theoretical Aspects of Computer Software, LNCS*, vol. 526, pages 265–289. Springer-Verlag, 1991.

[3] Y. Babovich and M. Maratea. Cmodels-2: SAT-based answer set solver enhanced to non-tight programs. In *International Conference on Logic Programming and Nonmonotonic Reasoning, LPNMR-05*, Jan. 2004.

[4] M. Balduccini. USA-Smart: Improving the quality of plans in answer set planning. In *PADL'04, Lecture Notes in Artificial Intelligence (LNCS)*. Springer, June 2004.

[5] M. Balduccini. Answer set based design of highly autonomous, rational agents. PhD thesis, Texas Tech University, Dec. 2005.

[6] M. Balduccini and M. Gelfond. Diagnostic reasoning with A-Prolog. *Journal of Theory and Practice of Logic Programming (TPLP)*, 3(4–5):425–461, July 2003.

[7] M. Balduccini and M. Gelfond. Logic programs with consistency-restoring rules. In P. Doherty, J. McCarthy, and M.-A. Williams, editors, *International Symposium on Logical Formalization of Commonsense Reasoning, AAAI 2003 Spring Symposium Series*, pages 9–18, March 2003.

[8] C. Baral. *Knowledge Representation, Reasoning and Declarative Problem Solving with Answer Sets*. Cambridge University Press, 2003.

[9] C. Baral, K. Chancellor, N. Tran, A. Joy, and M. Berens. A knowledge based approach for representing and reasoning about cell signalling networks. In *Proceedings of European Conference on Computational Biology, Supplement on Bioinformatics*, pages 15–22, 2004.

[10] C. Baral, T. Eiter, and Y. Zhao. Using SAT and logic programming to design polynomial-time algorithms for planning in non-deterministic domains. In *Proceedings of AAAI-05*, pages 575–583, 2005.

[11] C. Baral and M. Gelfond. Logic programming and knowledge representation. *Journal of Logic Programming*, 19(20):73–148, 1994.

[12] C. Baral and M. Gelfond. Reasoning agents in dynamic domains. In *Workshop on Logic-Based Artificial Intelligence*. Kluwer Academic Publishers, June 2000.

[13] C. Baral and M. Gelfond. Reasoning about intended actions. In *Proceedings of AAAI05*, pages 689–694, 2005.

[14] C. Baral, M. Gelfond, and N. Rushton. Probabilistic reasoning with answer sets. In *Proceedings of LPNMR-7*, January 2004.

[15] S. Baselice, P.A. Bonatti, and M. Gelfond. Towards an integration of answer set and constraint solving. In *Proceedings of ICLP-05*, pages 52–66, 2005.

[16] R. Ben-Eliyahu and R. Dechter. Propositional semantics for disjunctive logic programs. *Annals of Mathematics and Artificial Intelligence*, 12:53–87, 1994.

[17] N. Bidoit and C. Froidevaux. Negation by default and unstratifiable logic programs. *Theoretical Computer Science*, 79(1):86–112, 1991.

[18] G. Brewka. Logic programming with ordered disjunction. In *Proceedings of AAAI-02*, pages 100–105, 2002.

[19] G. Brewka. Answer sets: From constraint programming towards qualitative optimization. In *Proc. of 7th International Conference on Logic Programming and Non Monotonic Reasoning (LPNMR-04)*, pages 34–46. Springer-Verlag, Berlin, 2004.

[20] D.R. Brooks, E. Erdem, J.W. Minett, and D. Ringe. Character-based cladistics and answer set programming. In *Proceedings of International Symposium on Practical Aspects of Declarative Languages*, pages 37–51, 2005.

[21] F. Buccafurri, N. Leone, and P. Rullo. Adding weak constraints to disjunctive datalog. In *Proceedings of the 1997 Joint Conference on Declarative Programming APPIA-GULP-PRODE'97*, 1997.

[22] W. Chen, T. Swift, and D.S. Warren. Efficient top–down computation of queries under the well-founded semantics. *Journal of Logic Programming*, 24(3):161–201, 1995.

[23] K. Clark. Negation as failure. In *Logic and Data Bases*, pages 293–322. Plenum Press, 1978.

[24] A. Colmerauer, H. Kanoui, R. Pasero, and P. Roussel. Un système de communication homme–machine en français. Technical report, Groupe de Intelligence Artificielle Université de Aix-Marseille, 1973.

[25] J.P. Delgrande, T. Schaub, H. Tompits, and K. Wang. A classification and survey of preference handling approaches in nonmonotonic reasoning. *Computational Intelligence*, 20(2):308–334, 2004.

[26] Y. Dimopoulos, J. Koehler, and B. Nebel. Encoding planning problems in non-monotonic logic programs. In *Proceedings of the 4th European Conference on Planning, Lecture Notes in Artificial Intelligence (LNCS)*, vol. 1348, pages 169–181. Springer, 1997.

[27] T. Eiter, G. Gottlob, and H. Mannila. Disjunctive Datalog. *ACM Transactions on Database Systems*, 22(3):364–418, 1997.

[28] T. Eiter, G. Ianni, T. Lukasiewicz, R. Schindlauer, and H. Tompits. Combining answer set programming with description logics for the semantic web. Technical Report INFSYS RR-1843-07-04, Institut für Informationssysteme, Technische Universität Wien, A-1040 Vienna, Austria, January 2007. Preliminary version appeared in *Proc. KR 2004*, pages 141–151.

[29] T. Eiter, N. Leone, C. Mateis, G. Pfeifer, and F. Scarcello. A deductive system for nonmonotonic reasoning. In *International Conference on Logic Programming and Nonmonotonic Reasoning, LPNMR97, LNAI*, vol. 1265, pages 363–374. Springer-Verlag, Berlin, 1997.

[30] T. Eiter, S. Woltran, and M. Fink. Semantical characterizations and complexity of equivalences in answer set programming. *ACM Transactions on Computational Logic*, 2006.

[31] I. Elkabani, E. Pontelli, and T.C. Son. Smodels with CLP and its applications: A simple and effective approach to aggregates in asp. In *Proceedings of ICLP-04*, pages 73–89, 2004.

[32] W. Faber. Unfounded sets for disjunctive logic programs with arbitrary aggregates. In *In Proc. of 8th International Conference on Logic Programming and Non Monotonic Reasoning (LPNMR 2005), LNAI*, vol. 3662, pages 40–52. Springer-Verlag, Berlin, 2005.

[33] W. Faber, N. Leone, and G. Pfeifer. Recursive aggregates in disjunctive logic programs: Semantics and complexity. In *Proceedings of the 8th European Conference on Artificial Intelligence (JELIA 2004)*, pages 200–212, 2004.

[34] F. Fages. Consistency of Clark's completion and existence of stable models. *Journal of Methods of Logic in Computer Science*, 1(1):51–60, 1994.

[35] P. Ferraris. Answer sets for propositional theories. In *Proceedings of International Conference on Logic Programming and Nonmonotonic Reasoning (LPNMR)*, pages 119–131, 2005.

[36] P. Ferraris, J. Lee, and V. Lifschitz. A new perspective on stable models. In *Proceedings of International Joint Conference on Artificial Intelligence (IJCAI)*, pages 372–379, 2007.

[37] P. Ferraris and V. Lifschitz. Mathematical foundations of answer set programming. In *We Will Show Them, Essays in Honour of Dov Gabbay*, vol. 1, pages 615–654. College Publications.

[38] P. Ferraris and V. Lifschitz. Weight constraints as nested expressions. *Theory and Practice of Logic Programming*, 5:45–74, 2005.

[39] M. Gebser, B. Kaufman, A. Neumann, and T. Schaub. Conflict-deriven answer set enumeration. In C. Baral, G. Brewka, and J. Schlipf, editors. *Proceedings of the 9th International Conference on Logic Programming and Nonmonotonic Reasoning (LPNMR'07)*, *LNAI*, vol. 3662, pages 136–148. Springer, 2007.

[40] A.V. Gelder, K.A. Ross, and J.S. Schlipf. The well-founded semantics for general logic programs. *Journal of ACM*, 38(3):620–650, 1991.

[41] M. Gelfond. On stratified autoepistemic theories. In *Proceedings of Sixth National Conference on Artificial Intelligence*, pages 207–212, 1987.

[42] M. Gelfond. Epistemic approach to formalization of commonsense reasoning. Technical Report TR-91-2, University of Texas at El Paso, 1991.

[43] M. Gelfond and N. Leone. Knowledge representation and logic programming. *Artificial Intelligence*, 138(1–2), 2002.

[44] M. Gelfond and V. Lifschitz. The stable model semantics for logic programming. In *Proceedings of ICLP-88*, pages 1070–1080, 1988.

[45] M. Gelfond and V. Lifschitz. Classical negation in logic programs and disjunctive databases. *New Generation Computing*, 9(3–4):365–386, 1991.

[46] M. Gelfond and V. Lifschitz. Action languages. *Electronic Transactions on AI*, 3(16):193–210, 1998.

[47] E. Giunchiglia, Y. Lierler, and M. Maratea. Answer set programming based on propositional satisfiability. *Journal of Automated Reasoning*, 36:345–377, 2006.

[48] P.J. Hayes and J. McCarthy. Some philosophical problems from the standpoint of artificial intelligence. In B. Meltzer and D. Michie, editors. *Machine Intelligence 4*, pages 463–502. Edinburgh University Press, 1969.

[49] S. Heymans, D.V. Nieuwenborgh, and D. Vermeir. Guarded open answer set programming. In *Proc. of 8th International Conference on Logic Programming and Non Monotonic Reasoning (LPNMR 2005)*, *LNAI*, vol. 3662, pages 92–104. Springer-Verlag, Berlin, 2005.

[50] T. Janhunen, I. Niemela, P. Simons, and J. You. Partiality and disjunction in stable model semantics. In *Proceedings of the 2000 KR Conference*, pages 411–419, 2000.

[51] T. Janhunen and E. Oikarinen. LPEQ and DLPEQ—translators for automated equivalence testing of logic programs. In *Proc. of 8th International Conference on Logic Programming and Non Monotonic Reasoning (LPNMR 2004)*, *LNAI*, vol. 2923, pages 336–340. Springer-Verlag, Berlin, 2004.

[52] R. Kowalski. *Logic for Problem Solving*. North-Holland, 1979.

[53] R.A. Kowalski and M. Sergot. A logic-based calculus of events. *New Generation Computing*, 4(4):319–340, 1986.

[54] N. Leone, G. Pfeifer, W. Faber, T. Eiter, G. Gottlob, S. Perri, and F. Scarcello. The DLV system for knowledge representation and reasoning. *ACM Transactions on Computational Logic*, 7:499–562, 2006.

[55] N. Leone, P. Rullo, and F. Scarcello. Disjunctive stable models: Unfounded sets, fixpoint semantics and computation. *Information and Computation*, 135:69–112, 1997.

[56] V. Lifschitz and A. Razborov. Why are there so many loop formulas? *ACM Transactions on Computational Logic*, 7(2):261–268, 2006.

[57] V. Lifschitz, D. Pearce, and A. Valverde. Strongly equivalent logic programs. *ACM Transactions on Computational Logic*, 2:526–541, 2001.

[58] F. Lin and Y. Zhao. ASSAT: Computing answer sets of a logic program by SAT solvers. *Artificial Intelligence*, 157(1–2):115–137, 2004.

[59] D. Makinson. General patterns in nonmonotonic reasoning. In *The Handbook on Logic in AI and Logic Programming*, vol. 3, pages 35–110. Oxford University Press, 1993.

[60] V.W. Marek and M. Truszczynski. Stable semantics for logic programs and default reasoning. In *Proc. of the North American Conf. on Logic Programming*, pages 243–257, 1989.

[61] V.W. Marek and M. Truszczynski. *Nonmonotonic Logics; Context Dependent Reasoning*. Springer-Verlag, Berlin, 1993.

[62] V.W. Marek and M. Truszczynski. Stable models and an alternative logic programming paradigm. In *The Logic Programming Paradigm: a 25-Year Perspective*, pages 375–398. Springer-Verlag, Berlin, 1999.

[63] N. McCain and H. Turner. A causal theory of ramifications and qualifications. In *Proceedings of IJCAI-95*, pages 1978–1984, 1995.

[64] J. McCarthy. Circumscription—a form of non-monotonic reasoning. *Artificial Intelligence*, 13:27–39, 1980.

[65] J. McCarthy. In V. Lifschitz, editor. *Formalization of Common Sense*. Ablex, 1990.

[66] J. Minker. On indefinite data bases and the closed world assumption. In *Proceedings of CADE-82*, pages 292–308, 1982.

[67] J. Minker. Logic and databases: a 20 year retrospective. In H. Levesque and F. Pirri, editors. *Logical Foundations for Cognitive Agents: Contributions in Honor of Ray Reiter*, pages 234–299. Springer, 1999.

[68] R.C. Moore. Semantical considerations on nonmonotonic logic. In *Proceedings of the 8th International Joint Conference on Artificial Intelligence*, pages 272–279. Morgan Kaufmann, August 1983.

[69] E.T. Mueller. *Commonsense Reasoning*. Morgan Kaufmann, 2006.

[70] I. Niemela. Logic programs with stable model semantics as a constraint programming paradigm. *Annals of Mathematics and Artificial Intelligence*, 25(3–4):241–247, 1999.

[71] I. Niemela and P. Simons. Smodels—an implementation of the stable model and well-founded semantics for normal logic programs. In *Proceedings of the 4th International Conference on Logic Programming and Non-Monotonic Reasoning (LPNMR'97), Lecture Notes in Artificial Intelligence (LNCS)*, vol. 1265, pages 420–429. Springer, 1997.

[72] I. Niemela, P. Simons, and T. Soininen. Extending and implementing the stable model semantics. *Artificial Intelligence*, 138(1–2):181–234, June 2002.

[73] I. Niemela and P. Simons. Smodels—an implementation of the stable model and well-founded semantics for normal logic programs. In *Proceedings of the*

4th International Conference on Logic Programming and Non-Monotonic Reasoning (LPNMR'97), Lecture Notes in Artificial Intelligence (LNCS), vol. 1265, pages 420–429. Springer, 1997.

[74] M. Nogueira, M. Balduccini, M. Gelfond, R. Watson, and M. Barry. An A-Prolog decision support system for the Space Shuttle. In *PADL 2001*, pages 169–183, 2001.

[75] D. Pearce. A new logical characterization of stable models and answer sets. In *Non-Monotonic Extension of Logic Programming, Lecture Notes in Artificial Intelligence (LNCS)*, vol. 1216, pages 57–70. Springer-Verlag, 1997.

[76] N. Pelov, M. Denecker, and M. Bruynooghe. Well-founded and stable semantics of logic programs with aggregates. *Theory and Practice of Logic Programming*, 7:355–375, 2007.

[77] T. Przymusinski. On the declarative semantics of deductive databases and logic programs. In J. Minker, editor. *Foundations of Deductive Databases and Logic Programming*, pages 193–216. Morgan Kaufmann, 1988.

[78] R. Reiter. On closed world data bases. In *Logic and Data Bases*, pages 119–140. Plenum Press, 1978.

[79] R. Reiter. A logic for default reasoning. *Artificial Intelligence*, 13(1–2):81–132, 1980.

[80] R. Reiter. *Knowledge in Action—Logical Foundations for Specifying and Implementing Dynamical Systems*. MIT Press, September 2001.

[81] C. Sakama. Induction from answer sets in nonmonotonic logic programs. *ACM Transactions on Computational Logic*, 6(2):203–231, April 2005.

[82] C. Sakama and K. Inoue. Prioritized logic programming and its application to commonsense reasoning. *Artificial Intelligence*, 123:185–222, 2000.

[83] T. Sato. Completed logic programs and their consistency. *Journal of Logic Programming*, 9:33–44, 1990.

[84] J. Schlipf. Some remarks on computability and open domain semantics. In *Proceedings of the Workshop on Structural Complexity and Recursion-Theoretic Methods in Logic Programming of the International Logic Programming Symposium*, 1993.

[85] J. Schlipf. The expressive powers of logic programming semantics. *Journal of Computer and System Sciences*, 51(1):64–86, 1995.

[86] M. Shanahan. *Solving the Frame Problem: A Mathematical Investigation of the Commonsense Law of Inertia*. MIT Press, 1997.

[87] T. Soininen and I. Niemela. Developing a declarative rule language for applications in product configuration. In *Proceedings of International Symposium on Practical Aspects of Declarative Languages*, pages 305–319, 1998.

[88] T.C. Son and E. Pontelli. A constructive semantic characterization of aggregates in answer set programming. *Theory and Practice of Logic Programming*, 7:355–375, 2007.

[89] T.C. Son, P.H. Tu, M. Gelfond, and A.R. Morales. An approximation of action theories of and its application to conformant planning. In *Proc. of 8th International Conference on Logic Programming and Non Monotonic Reasoning (LPNMR 2005), LNAI*, vol. 3662, pages 172–184. Springer-Verlag, Berlin, 2005.

[90] V.S. Subrahmanian and C. Zaniolo. Relating stable models and AI planning domains. In *Proceedings of ICLP-95*, pages 233–247, 1995.

[91] H. Turner. Representing actions in logic programs and default theories: A situation calculus approach. *Journal of Logic Programming*, 31(1–3):245–298, June 1997.

[92] H. Turner. Order-consistent programs are cautiously monotonic. *Journal of Theory and Practice of Logic Programming (TPLP)*, 1(4):487–495, 2001.

[93] J. Vaghani, K. Ramamohanarao, D.B. Kemp, Z. Somogyi, P.J. Stuckey, T.S. Leask, and J. Harland. The Aditi deductive database system. *The VLDB Journal*, 3(2):245–288, 1994.

Handbook of Knowledge Representation
Edited by F. van Harmelen, V. Lifschitz and B. Porter
© 2008 Elsevier B.V. All rights reserved
DOI: 10.1016/S1574-6526(07)03008-8

Chapter 8

Belief Revision

Pavlos Peppas

8.1 Introduction

Philippa, a Greek nineteen year old student at Patras University, has just discovered that Nikos and Angela are not her true parents; she was adopted when she was six months old from an orphanage in Sao Paulo. The news really shook Philippa. Much of what she used to believe all her life about herself and her family was wrong. After recovering from the initial shock she started putting her thoughts back in order: so that means that Alexandros is not really her cousin, and she did not take her brown eyes from (who she used to believe was) her grandmother, and she no longer needs to worry about developing high blood pressure because of the bad family history from both Nikos' and Angela's side. Moreover, she probably has siblings somewhere in Brazil, and if she really looked into it, she might be entitled to a Brazilian citizenship which could come in handy for that long trip she always wanted to make to Latin America.

This is a typical (although rather dramatic) instance of a belief revision scenario: a rational agent receives new information that makes her change her beliefs. In the principal case where the new information contradicts her initial belief state, the agent needs to withdraw some of the old beliefs before she can accommodate the new information; she also needs to accept the consequences that might result from the interaction of the new information with the (remaining) old beliefs.

The study of the process of belief revision, which gave rise to an exciting research area with the same name,[1] can be traced back to the early 1980s. The article that is widely considered to mark the birth of the field is the seminal work of Alchourron, Gardenfors, and Makinson reported in [1]. As a matter of fact, the framework that evolved from [1]—now known as the *AGM paradigm* (or simply *AGM*) after the initials of its three founders—is to this date the dominant framework in Belief Revision.

Of course much has happened since 1985. The formal apparatus developed in [1] has been enhanced and thoroughly studied, new research directions have emerged from

---

[1] We shall use the capitalized term "Belief Revision" to refer to the *research area*; the same term in lower case letters will be used for the *process* of belief change.

it, connections with neighboring fields have been established, and a lot more is currently under way. This article will journey through the main developments in Belief Revision, pretty much in a historical order, starting with the classical AGM paradigm and following the trail till the present day.

8.2   Preliminaries

Let us first fix some notation and terminology. Alchourron, Gardenfors, and Makinson build their framework working with a formal language L governed by a logic which is identified by its consequence relation $\vdash$. Very little is assumed about L and $\vdash$, making the AGM paradigm quite general. In particular, L is taken to be closed under all Boolean connectives, and $\vdash$ has to satisfy the following properties:

(i) $\vdash \varphi$ for all truth-functional tautologies A (superclassicality).

(ii) If $\vdash (\varphi \to \psi)$ and $\vdash \varphi$, then $\vdash \psi$ (modus ponens).

(iii) $\vdash$ is consistent, i.e. $\nvdash L$.

(iv) $\vdash$ satisfies the deduction theorem, that is, $\{\varphi_1, \varphi_2, \ldots, \varphi_n\} \vdash \psi$ iff $\vdash \varphi_1 \wedge \varphi_2 \wedge \cdots \wedge \varphi_n \to \psi$.

(v) $\vdash$ is compact.

For a set of sentences Γ of L, we denote by $Cn(\Gamma)$ the set of all logical consequences of Γ, i.e. $Cn(\Gamma) = \{\varphi \in L: \Gamma \vdash \varphi\}$. A theory K of L is any set of sentences of L closed under $\vdash$, i.e. $K = Cn(K)$. We shall denote the set of all theories of L by $\mathbb{K}_L$. A theory K of L is complete iff for all sentences $\varphi \in L$, $\varphi \in K$ or $\neg\varphi \in K$. We shall denote the set of all consistent complete theories of L by $\mathbb{M}_L$. For a set of sentences Γ of L, $[\Gamma]$ denotes the set of all consistent complete theories of L that contain Γ. Often we shall use the notation $[\varphi]$ for a sentence $\varphi \in L$, as an abbreviation of $[\{\varphi\}]$. For a theory K and a set of sentences Γ of L, we shall denote by $K + \Gamma$ the closure under $\vdash$ of $K \cup \Gamma$, i.e. $K + \Gamma = Cn(K \cup \Gamma)$. For a sentence $\varphi \in L$ we shall often write $K + \varphi$ as an abbreviation of $K + \{\varphi\}$. Finally, the symbols $\top$ and $\bot$ will be used to denote an arbitrary (but fixed) tautology and contradiction of L, respectively.

8.3   The AGM Paradigm

In AGM, beliefs are represented as sentences of L and belief sets as theories of L.[2] The process of belief revision is modeled as a function $*$ mapping a theory K and a sentence φ to a new theory $K * \varphi$. Of course certain constraints need to be imposed on $*$ in order for it to capture the notion of *rational belief revision* correctly. A guiding intuition in formulating these constraints has been the *principle of minimal change* according to which a rational agent ought to change her beliefs *as little as possible* in order to (consistently) accommodate the new information. Of course, at first glance it

---

[2]It should be noted that representing a belief set as a theory, presupposes that agents are *logically omniscient*. In this sense the AGM paradigm is tailored for *ideal reasoners*.

is not clear how one should measure change between belief sets, or even if the notion of minimal change is at all expressible within a purely logical framework.

8.3.1   The AGM Postulates for Belief Revision

Despite the apparent difficulties, Gardenfors [29] succeeded in formulating a set of eight postulates, known as the *AGM postulates for belief revision*,[3] which are now widely regarded to have captured much of what is the essence of rational belief revision:

$(K * 1)$ $K * \varphi$ is a theory of L.

$(K * 2)$ $\varphi \in K * \varphi$.

$(K * 3)$ $K * \varphi \subseteq K + \varphi$.

$(K * 4)$ If $\neg\varphi \notin K$ then $K + \varphi \subseteq K * \varphi$.

$(K * 5)$ If φ is consistent then $K * \varphi$ is also consistent.

$(K * 6)$ If $\vdash \varphi \leftrightarrow \psi$ then $K * \varphi = K * \psi$.

$(K * 7)$ $K * (\varphi \wedge \psi) \subseteq (K * \varphi) + \psi$.

$(K * 8)$ If $\neg\psi \notin K * \varphi$ then $(K * \varphi) + \psi \subseteq K * (\varphi \wedge \psi)$.

Any function $* : \mathbb{K}_L \times L \mapsto \mathbb{K}_L$ satisfying the AGM postulates for revision $(K * 1)$–$(K * 8)$ is called an *AGM revision function*. The first six postulates $(K * 1)$–$(K * 6)$ are known as the *basic* AGM postulates (for revision), while $(K * 7)$–$(K * 8)$ are called the *supplementary* AGM postulates.

Postulate $(K * 1)$ says that the agent, being an ideal reasoner, remains logically omniscient after she revises her beliefs. Postulate $(K * 2)$ says that the new information φ should *always* be included in the new belief set. $(K * 2)$ places enormous faith on the reliability of φ. The new information is perceived to be so reliable that it prevails over all previous conflicting beliefs, no matter what these beliefs might be.[4] Later in this chapter (Section 8.7) we shall consider ways of relaxing $(K * 2)$. Postulates $(K * 3)$ and $(K * 4)$ viewed together state that whenever the new information φ does not contradict the initial belief set K, there is no reason to remove any of the original beliefs at all; the new belief state $K * \varphi$ will contain the whole of K, the new information φ, and whatever follows from the logical closure of K and φ (and nothing more). Essentially $(K * 3)$ and $(K * 4)$ express the notion of minimal change in the limiting case where the new information is consistent with the initial beliefs. $(K * 5)$ says that the agent should aim for consistency at any cost; the *only* case where it is "acceptable" for the agent to fail is when the new information in itself is inconsistent (in which case, because of $(K * 2)$, the agent cannot do anything about it). $(K * 6)$ is known as

---

[3] Although these postulate where first proposed by Gardenfors alone, they were extensively studied in collaboration with Alchourron and Makinson in [2]; thus their name.

[4] The high priority of φ over previous beliefs may not always be related to its reliability. For example, in the context of the *Ramsey Test* for conditionals, φ is incorporated into a theory K as part of the process of evaluating the acceptability of a counterfactual conditional $\varphi > \psi$ (see [30]).

the *irrelevance of syntax postulate*. It says that the syntax of the new information has no effect on the revision process; all that matters is its content (i.e. the proposition it represents). Hence, logically equivalent sentences φ and ψ change a theory K in the same way.

Finally, postulates $(K * 7)$ and $(K * 8)$ are best understood taken together. They say that for any two sentences φ and ψ, if in revising the initial belief set K by φ one is lucky enough to reach a belief set $K * \varphi$ that is consistent with ψ, then to produce $K * (\varphi \wedge \psi)$ all that one needs to do is to expand $K * \varphi$ with ψ; in symbols $K * (\varphi \wedge \psi) = (K * \varphi) + \psi$. The motivation for $(K * 7)$ and $(K * 8)$ comes again from the principle of minimal change. The rationale is (loosely speaking) as follows: $K * \varphi$ is a minimal change of K to include φ and therefore there is no way to arrive at $K * (\varphi \wedge \psi)$ from K with "less change". In fact, because $K * (\varphi \wedge \psi)$ also includes ψ one might have to make further changes apart from those needed to include φ. If however ψ is consistent with $K * \varphi$, these further changes can be limited to simply adding ψ to $K * \varphi$ and closing under logical implications—no further withdrawals are necessary.

The postulates $(K * 1)$–$(K * 8)$ are certainly very reasonable. They are simple, elegant, jointly consistent, and they follow quite naturally from the notion of minimal change. Moreover, according to Alchourron, Gardenfors, and Makinson, these postulates are not only sound but, given the limited expressiveness of a purely logical framework, there are also (in some sense) *complete*. Now this is a strong statement, especially since one can show that $(K * 1)$–$(K * 8)$ do not suffice to uniquely determine the belief set $K * \varphi$ resulting from revising K by φ, given K and φ alone. In other words, there is more than one function $*$ that satisfies $(K * 1)$–$(K * 8)$. Yet the plurality of AGM revision functions should not be seen as a weakness of the postulates but rather as expressing the fact that different people may change their mind in different ways. Hence the AGM postulates simply circumscribe the territory of all different rational ways of revising belief sets.

Nevertheless, one may still be skeptical about whether the territory staked out by $(K * 1)$–$(K * 8)$ contains nothing more but just rational belief revision functions. Further evidence is needed to support such a strong claim. Such evidence was indeed provided mainly in the form of formal results known as *representation results* connecting the AGM postulates with other models of belief revision. Some of the most important representation results will be discussed later in this chapter.

8.3.2   The AGM Postulates for Belief Contraction

Apart from belief revision, Alchourron, Gardenfors, and Makinson studied another type of belief change called *belief contraction* (or simply *contraction*), which can be described as the process of *rationally* removing from a belief set K a certain belief φ. Contraction typically occurs when an agent loses faith in φ and decides to give it up.[5] Simply taking out φ from K however will not suffice since other sentences that are present in K may reproduce φ through logical closure. Consider, for example, the theory $K = Cn(\{p \rightarrow q, p, q\})$ and assume that we want to contract K by q. Then,

---

[5] Another interesting instance of contraction is during argumentation. Consider two agents A and B that argue about a certain issue for which they have opposite views. It is quite likely that *for the sake of argument* the two agents will (temporarily) contract their beliefs to reach some common ground from which they will then starting building their case.

not only do we have to remove q from K, but we also need to give up (at least) one of $p \rightarrow q$ or p, for otherwise q will resurface via logical closure.

Like belief revision, belief contraction is formally defined as a function $\dot{-}$ mapping a theory K and a sentence φ to a new theory $K \dot{-} \varphi$. Once again a set of eight postulates was proposed, motivated by the principle of minimal change,[6] to constraint $\dot{-}$ in a way that captures the essence of *rational* belief contraction. These postulates, known as the *AGM postulates for belief contraction*, are the following:

$(K \dot{-} 1)$ $K \dot{-} \varphi$ is a theory.

$(K \dot{-} 2)$ $K \dot{-} \varphi \subseteq K$.

$(K \dot{-} 3)$ If $\varphi \notin K$ then $K \dot{-} \varphi = K$.

$(K \dot{-} 4)$ If $\nvdash \varphi$ then $\varphi \notin K \dot{-} \varphi$.

$(K \dot{-} 5)$ If $\varphi \in K$, then $K \subseteq (K \dot{-} \varphi) + \varphi$.

$(K \dot{-} 6)$ If $\vdash \varphi \leftrightarrow \psi$ then $K \dot{-} \varphi = K \dot{-} \psi$.

$(K \dot{-} 7)$ $(K \dot{-} \varphi) \cap (K \dot{-} \psi) \subseteq K \dot{-} (\varphi \wedge \psi)$.

$(K \dot{-} 8)$ If $\varphi \notin K \dot{-} (\varphi \wedge \psi)$ then $K \dot{-} (\varphi \wedge \psi) \subseteq K \dot{-} \varphi$.

Any function $\dot{-} : \mathbb{K}_L \times L \mapsto \mathbb{K}_L$ that satisfies $(K \dot{-} 1)$–$(K \dot{-} 8)$ is called an *AGM contraction function*. Like the postulates for revision, $(K \dot{-} 1)$–$(K \dot{-} 8)$ split into two groups: the first six postulates $(K \dot{-} 1)$–$(K \dot{-} 6)$ are known as the *basic* AGM postulates for contraction, while $(K \dot{-} 7)$–$(K \dot{-} 8)$ are called the *supplementary* AGM postulates for contraction.

Given the agent's logical omniscience, postulate $(K \dot{-} 1)$ is self-evident. Also self-evident is $(K \dot{-} 2)$ since by its very nature, contraction produces a belief set smaller than the original. Postulate $(K \dot{-} 3)$ says that if φ is not in the initial belief set K to start with, then there is no reason to change anything at all. $(K \dot{-} 4)$ tells us that the only sentences that are "immutable" are tautologies; all other sentences φ can in principle be removed from the initial beliefs K, and contraction will perform this removal no matter what the cost in epistemic value might be.[7] Postulate $(K \dot{-} 5)$, known as the *recovery postulate* says that contracting and then expanding by φ will give us back (at least) the initial theory K; in fact, because of $(K \dot{-} 2)$, we get back precisely K. The motivation behind $(K \dot{-} 5)$ is again the notion of minimal change: when contracting K by φ we should cut off only the part of K that is "related" to φ and *nothing else*. Hence adding φ back should restore our initial belief set.[8]

Postulate $(K \dot{-} 6)$, like its belief revision counterpart $(K * 6)$, tells us that contraction is not syntax-sensitive: contraction by logically equivalent sentences produces the same result. The last two postulates relate the individual contractions by two sentences φ and ψ, to the contraction by their conjunction $\varphi \wedge \psi$. Firstly notice that to contract

---

[6]In this context the principle of minimal change runs as follows: during contraction as little as possible should be given up from the initial belief set K in order to remove φ.

[7]The remarks for postulate $(K * 2)$ are also relevant here.

[8]It should be noted though that, despite its intuitive appeal, the recovery postulate is among the most controversial AGM postulates—see [60] for a detailed discussion.

K by $\varphi \wedge \psi$ we need to give up either φ or ψ or both. Consider now a belief $\chi \in K$ that survives the contraction by φ, as well as the contraction by ψ (i.e. $\chi \in K \dot{-} \varphi$ and $\chi \in K \dot{-} \psi$). This in a sense means that, within the context of K, χ is not related to neither φ nor ψ and therefore it is also not related to their conjunction $\varphi \wedge \psi$; hence, says $(K \dot{-} 7)$, by the principle of minimal change χ should not be affected by the contraction of K by $\varphi \wedge \psi$. Finally, for $(K \dot{-} 8)$ assume that $\varphi \notin K \dot{-} (\varphi \wedge \psi)$. Since $K \dot{-} \varphi$ is the minimal change of K to remove φ, it follows that $K \dot{-} (\varphi \wedge \psi)$ cannot be larger than $K \dot{-} \varphi$. Postulate $(K \dot{-} 8)$ in fact makes it smaller or equal to it; in symbols $K \dot{-} (\varphi \wedge \psi) \subseteq K \dot{-} \varphi$.

The AGM postulates for contraction are subject to the same criticism as their counterparts for revision: if completeness is to be claimed, one would need more than just informal arguments about their intuitive appeal. Some hard evidence is necessary.[9]

A first piece of such evidence comes from the relation between AGM revision and contraction functions. That such a connection between the two types of belief change should exist was suggested by Isaac Levi before Alchourron, Gardenfors, and Makinson formulated their postulates. More precisely, Levi argued that one should in principle be able to define revision in terms of contraction as follows: to revise K by φ, first contract K by $\neg\varphi$ (thus removing anything that may contradict the new information) and then expand the resulting theory with φ. This is now known as the *Levi Identity*:

$$K * \varphi = (K \dot{-} \neg\varphi) + \varphi \quad \text{(Levi Identity)}.$$

Alchourron, Gardenfors, and Makinson proved that the functions induced from their postulates do indeed satisfy the Levi Identity:

Theorem 8.1 (See Alchourron, Gardenfors, and Makinson [1]). *Let $\dot{-}$ be any function from $\mathbb{K}_L \times L$ to $\mathbb{K}_L$ that satisfies the postulates $(K \dot{-} 1)$–$(K \dot{-} 8)$. Then the function $*$ produced from $\dot{-}$ by means of the Levi Identity, satisfies the postulates $(K * 1)$–$(K * 8)$.*[10]

As a matter of fact it turns out that Levi's method of producing revision functions is powerful enough to cover the *entire territory* of AGM revision functions; i.e. for *every* AGM revision function $*$ there is an AGM contraction function $\dot{-}$ that produces $*$ by means of the Levi Identity.

The fact that AGM revision and contraction functions are related so nicely in the way predicted by Levi, is the first piece of formal evidence to provide mutual support for the AGM postulates for contraction and revision.

A process that defines contraction in terms of revision is also available. This is known as the *Harper Identity*:

$$K \dot{-} \varphi = (K * \neg\varphi) \cap K \quad \text{(Harper Identity)}.$$

Like the Levi Identity, the Harper Identity is a sound and complete method for constructing contraction functions; i.e. the function $\dot{-}$ generated from an AGM revision

---

[9]Incidentally, like with the AGM postulates for belief revision, one can show that there exists more than one function $\dot{-}$ satisfying $(K \dot{-} 1)$–$(K \dot{-} 8)$.

[10]The result still holds even if $\dot{-}$ does not satisfy $(K \dot{-} 5)$ (i.e. the *recovery postulate*).

function by means of the Harper Identity satisfies $(K \mathbin{\dot{-}} 1)$–$(K \mathbin{\dot{-}} 8)$ and conversely, every AGM contraction function can be generated from a revision function by means of the Harper Identity. In fact, by combining the Levi and the Harper Identity one makes a full circle: if we start with an AGM contraction function $\dot{-}$ and use the Levi Identity to produce a revision function $*$, which in turn is then used to produce a contraction function via the Harper Identity, we end up with the same contraction function $\dot{-}$ we started with.

8.3.3 Selection Functions

Having identified the class of rational revision and contraction functions axiomatically, the next item on the agenda is to develop *constructive models* for these functions. It should be noted that, because of the Levi Identity, any constructive model for contraction functions can immediately be turned into a constructive model for revision functions; the converse is also true thanks to the Harper Identity. In this and the following two sections we shall review the most popular constructions for revision and contraction, starting with *partial meet contractions*—a construction for contraction functions.

Consider a theory K, and let φ be some non-tautological sentence in K that we would like to remove from K. Given that we need to adhere to the principle of minimal change, perhaps the first thing that comes to mind is to identify a maximal subset of K that fails to entail φ and define that to be the contraction of K by φ. Unfortunately, there is, in general, more than one such subset, and it is not at all obvious how to choose between them.[11] Nevertheless, these subsets are a very good starting point. We shall therefore give them a name: any maximal subset of K that fails to entail φ is called a *φ-remainder*.[12] The set of all φ remainders is denoted by $K \perp\!\!\!\perp \varphi$.[13]

As already mentioned, it is not clear how to choose between φ-remainders, since they are all equally good from a purely logical point of view. *Extra-logical factors* need to be taken into consideration to separate the *most plausible* φ-remainders from the rest. In the AGM paradigm, this is accomplished through *selection functions*. Formally, a selection function for a theory K is any function γ that maps a non-empty collection X of subsets of K to a non-empty subset $\gamma(X)$ of X; i.e. $\emptyset \neq \gamma(X) \subseteq X$. Intuitively, a selection function is used to pick up the "best" φ-remainders; i.e. the elements of $\gamma(K \perp\!\!\!\perp \varphi)$ are the most "valuable" (in an epistemological sense) among all φ-remainders.

Clearly, for a fixed theory K, there are many different selection functions, each one with a different set of "best" remainders. Only one of them though corresponds to the extra-logical factors that determine the agent's behavior. Once this function is given, it is possible to uniquely determine the contraction of K by any sentence φ by means of the following condition:

(M-) $K \mathbin{\dot{-}} \varphi = \bigcap \gamma(K \perp\!\!\!\perp \varphi)$.

---

[11] Consider, for example, the theory $K = Cn(\{p, q\})$, where p and q are propositional variables, and suppose that we want to contract by $p \wedge q$. There are more that one maximal subsets of K failing to entail $p \wedge q$, one of which contains p but not q, while another contains q but not p.

[12] In other words, a φ-remainder is a subset K' of K such that (i) $K' \nvdash \varphi$, and (ii) for any $K'' \subseteq K$, if $K' \subset K''$ then $K'' \vdash \varphi$.

[13] In the limiting case where φ is a tautology, $K \perp\!\!\!\perp \varphi$ is defined to be $\{K\}$.

Condition (M-) tells us that in contracting K by φ we should keep only the sentences of K that belong to all maximally plausible φ-remainders. This is a neat and intuitive construction, and it turns out that the functions $\dot{-}$ so produced satisfy many (but not all) of the AGM postulates for contraction.[14] To achieve an exact match between the functions produced from (M-) and the AGM contraction functions, we need to confine the selection functions γ fed to (M-) to those that are *transitively relational*.

A selection function γ is *transitively relational* iff it can be produced from a transitive binary relation $\ll$ in 2^K by means of the following condition:

(TR) $\gamma(K \perp\!\!\!\perp \varphi) = \{K' \in K \perp\!\!\!\perp \varphi: \text{for all } K'' \in K \perp\!\!\!\perp \varphi, \ K'' \ll K'\}$.

Intuitively, $\ll$ is to be understood as an ordering on subsets of K representing comparative epistemological value; i.e. $K'' \ll K'$ iff K' is at least as valuable as K''. Hence, (TR) tells us that a selection function γ is transitively relational if it makes its choices based on an underlying ordering $\ll$; i.e. the "best" remainders picked up by γ are the ones that are most valuable according to $\ll$.

Since this is the first time we encounter an ordering $\ll$ as part of a constructive model for belief change, it is worth noting that such orderings are central to the study of Belief Revision and we shall encounter many of them in the sequel. They come with different names (epistemic entrenchment, system of spheres, ensconcement, etc.), they apply at different objects (remainders, sentences, possible worlds, etc.) and they may have different intended meanings. In all cases though they are used (either directly or indirectly) to capture the extra-logical factors that come into play during the process of belief revision/contraction.

Any function $\dot{-}$ constructed from a transitive relational selection function by means of (M-), is called a *transitive relational partial meet contraction function*. The following theorem is one of the first major results of the AGM paradigm, and the second piece of formal evidence reported herein in support of the postulates $(K \dot{-} 1)$–$(K \dot{-} 8)$ for contraction (and via the Levi Identity, of the postulates $(K * 1)$–$(K * 8)$ for revision):

Theorem 8.2 (See Alchourron, Gardenfors, and Makinson [1]). *Let K be a theory of L and $\dot{-}$ a function from $\mathbb{K}_L \times L$ to $\mathbb{K}_L$. Then $\dot{-}$ is a transitive relational partial meet contraction function iff it satisfies the postulates $(K \dot{-} 1)$–$(K \dot{-} 8)$.*

In other words, when (M-) is fed transitively relational selection functions γ it generates functions $\dot{-}$ that satisfy *all* the AGM postulates for contraction; conversely, *any* AGM contraction function $\dot{-}$ can be constructed from a transitively relational selection function γ by means of (M-).

We conclude this section by considering two special cases of selection functions lying at opposite ends of the selection-functions-spectrum. The first, which we shall denote by γ_F, always selects *all* elements of its argument; i.e. for any X, $\gamma_F(X) = X$. Hence for a fixed theory K the function γ_F for K, picks up *all* φ-remainders for any φ. The contraction function produced from γ_F by means of (M-) is called a *full meet contraction function*. Notice that in the construction of a full meet contraction

---

[14]In particular, they satisfy the *basic* postulates $(K \dot{-} 1)$–$(K \dot{-} 6)$ but fail to satisfy the *supplementary* postulates $(K \dot{-} 7)$ and $(K \dot{-} 8)$.

function $\dot{-}$, γ_F is superfluous since $\dot{-}$ can be produced by means of the following condition:

(F-) $K \dot{-} \varphi = \bigcap K \perp\!\!\!\perp \varphi.$

The distinctive feature of a full meet contraction function is that, among all contraction functions, it always produces the *smallest* theory. In particular, any function $\dot{-} : \mathbb{K}_L \times L \mapsto \mathbb{K}_L$ that satisfies $(K \dot{-} 1)$–$(K \dot{-} 3)$ and $(K \dot{-} 5)$, is such that $K \dot{-} \varphi$ always includes $\bigcap K \perp\!\!\!\perp \varphi$ for any $\varphi \in L$. As an indication of how severe full meet contraction is, we note that the revision function $*$ produced from it (via the Levi Identity) is such that $K * \varphi = Cn(\varphi)$ for all φ contradicting K; in other words, for any $\neg\varphi \in K$, the (full-meet-produced) revision of K by φ removes *all* previous beliefs (other than the consequences of φ).

At the opposite end of the spectrum are *maxichoice* contraction functions. These are the functions constructed from selection functions γ_M that always pick up only *one* element of their arguments; i.e., for any X, $\gamma_M(X)$ is a *singleton*. Hence, for any sentence φ, when γ_M is applied to the set $K \perp\!\!\!\perp \varphi$ of all φ-remainders, it selects only one of them as the "best" φ-remainder. It should be noted that such selection functions γ_M are *not* in general transitively relational, and maxichoice contraction functions do not satisfy all the AGM postulates for contraction. A peculiar feature of maxichoice contractions $\dot{-}$ is that they produce (via the Levi Identity) highly "opinionated" revision functions $*$; i.e., whenever the new information φ contradicts the initial belief set K, such functions $*$ always return a *complete* theory $K * \varphi$.

8.3.4 Epistemic Entrenchment

As mentioned earlier, selection functions are essentially a formal way of encoding the extra-logical factors that determine the beliefs that a sentence φ should take away with it when it is rooted out of a theory K.

These extra-logical factors relate to the *epistemic value* that the agent perceives her individual beliefs to have within the context of K. For example, a law-like belief ψ such as "all swans are white", is likely to be more important to the agent than the belief χ that "Lucy is a swan". Consequently, if a case arises where the agent needs to choose between giving up ψ or giving up χ (e.g., when contracting with the belief "Lucy is white") the agent will surrender the latter.

Considerations like these led Gardenfors and Makinson [32] to introduce the notion of *epistemic entrenchment* as another means of encoding the extra-logical factors that are relevant to belief contraction. Intuitively, the epistemic entrenchment of a belief ψ is the degree of resistance that ψ exhibits to change: the more entrenched ψ is, the less likely it is to be swept away during contraction by some other belief φ.

Formally, epistemic entrenchment is defined as a preorder $\leq$ on L encoding the relative "retractibility" of individual beliefs; i.e. $\chi \leq \psi$ iff the agent is at least as (or more) reluctant to give up ψ than she is to give up χ. Once again, certain constraints need to be imposed on $\leq$ for it to capture its intended meaning:

(EE1)   If $\varphi \leq \psi$ and $\psi \leq \chi$ then $\varphi \leq \chi$.

(EE2)   If $\varphi \vdash \psi$ then $\varphi \leq \psi$.

(EE3) $\varphi \leq \varphi \wedge \psi$ or $\psi \leq \varphi \wedge \psi$.

(EE4)   When K is consistent, $\varphi \notin K$ iff $\varphi \leqslant \psi$ for all $\psi \in L$.

(EE5)   If $\psi \leqslant \varphi$ for all $\psi \in L$, then $\vdash \varphi$.

Axiom (EE1) states that $\leqslant$ is transitive. (EE2) says that the stronger a belief is logically, the less entrenched it is. At first this may seem counter-intuitive. A closer look however will convince us otherwise. Consider two beliefs φ and ψ both of them members of a belief set K, and such that $\varphi \vdash \psi$. Then clearly, if one decides to give up ψ one will also have to remove φ (for otherwise logical closure will bring ψ back). On the other hand, it is possible to give up φ and retain ψ. Hence giving up φ produces less epistemic loss than giving up ψ and therefore the former should be preferred whenever a choice exists between the two. Thus axiom (EE2). For axiom (EE3) notice that, again because of logical closure, one cannot give up $\varphi \wedge \psi$ without removing at least one of the sentences φ or ψ. Hence either φ or ψ (or even both) are at least as vulnerable as $\varphi \wedge \psi$ during contraction. We note that from (EE1)–(EE3) it follows that $\leqslant$ is *total*; i.e., for any two sentences $\varphi, \psi \in L$, $\varphi \leqslant \psi$ or $\psi \leqslant \varphi$.

The final two axioms deal with the two ends of this total preorder $\leqslant$, i.e., with its minimal and its maximal elements. In particular, axiom (EE4) says that in the principal case where K is consistent, all non-beliefs (i.e., all the sentences that are not in K) are minimally entrenched. At the other end of the entrenchment spectrum we have all tautologies, which according to (EE5) are the only maximal elements of $\leqslant$ and therefore the hardest to remove (in fact, in the AGM paradigm it is impossible to remove them).

Perhaps not surprisingly it turns out that for a fixed belief set K there is more than one preorder $\leqslant$ that satisfies the axioms (EE1)–(EE5). Once again this is explained by the subjective nature of epistemic entrenchment (different agents may perceive the epistemic importance of a sentence φ differently). However, once the epistemic entrenchment $\leqslant$ chosen by an agent is given, it should be possible to determine uniquely the result of contracting her belief set K by *any* sentence φ. This is indeed the case; condition (C-) below defines contraction in terms of epistemic entrenchment[15]:

(C-) $\psi \in K \dot- \varphi$ iff $\psi \in K$ and either $\varphi < \varphi \vee \psi$ or $\vdash \varphi$.

Gardenfors and Makinson proved the following representation result which essentially shows that for the purpose of belief contraction, an epistemic entrenchment $\leqslant$ is all the information ones needs to know about extra-logical factors:

Theorem 8.3 (See Gardenfors and Makinson [32]). *Let K be a theory of L. If $\leqslant$ is a preorder in L that satisfies the axioms* (EE1)–(EE5) *then the function defined by* (C-) *is an AGM contraction function. Conversely, if $\dot-$ is an AGM contraction function, then there is preorder $\leqslant$ in L that satisfies the axioms* (EE1)–(EE5) *as well as condition* (C-).

Theorem 8.3 is the third piece of formal evidence in support of the postulates $(K \dot- 1)$–$(K \dot- 8)$ for contraction.

---

[15]At first glance, condition (C-) may seem unnatural. Indeed there is an equivalent and much more intuitive way to relate epistemic entrenchments with contraction functions (see condition (C$\leqslant$) in [31]). However, condition (C-) is more useful as a construction mechanism for contraction functions.

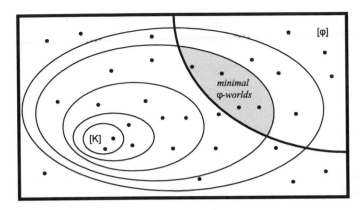

Figure 8.1: A system of spheres.

It should be noted that, thanks to the Levi Identity, (C-) can be reformulated in a way that defines directly a revision function $*$ from an epistemic entrenchment $\leqslant$:

(E*) $\psi \in K * \varphi$ iff either $(\varphi \to \neg\psi) < (\varphi \to \psi)$ or $\vdash \neg\varphi$.

An analog to Theorem 8.3, connecting epistemic entrenchments with AGM revision functions via (E*), is easily established [83, 75].

8.3.5   System of Spheres

Epistemic entrenchment together with condition (C-) is a *constructive approach* to modeling belief contraction, as opposed to the AGM postulates $(K \dot{-} 1)$–$(K \dot{-} 8)$ which model contraction axiomatically. Another constructive approach, this time for belief revision, has been proposed by Grove in [38]. Building on earlier work by Lewis [56], Grove uses a structure called a *system of spheres* to construct revision functions. Like an epistemic entrenchment, a system of sphere is essentially a preorder. However the objects being ordered are no longer sentences but consistent complete theories.

Given an initial belief set K a *system of spheres centered on* $[K]$ is formally defined as a collection S of subsets of $\mathbb{M}_L$, called *spheres*, satisfying the following conditions (see Fig. 8.1)[16]

(S1) S is totally ordered with respect to set inclusion; that is, if $V, U \in S$ then $V \subseteq U$ or $U \subseteq V$.

(S2)   The smallest sphere in S is $[K]$; that is, $[K] \in S$, and if $V \in S$ then $[K] \subseteq V$.

(S3) $\mathbb{M}_L \in S$ (and therefore $\mathbb{M}_L$ is the largest sphere in S).

(S4)   For every $\varphi \in L$, if there is any sphere in S intersecting $[\varphi]$ then there is also a smallest sphere in S intersecting $[\varphi]$.

Intuitively a system of spheres S centered on $[K]$ represents the *relative plausibility* of consistent complete theories, which in this context play the role of possible

---

[16]Recall that $\mathbb{M}_L$ is the set of all consistent complete theories of L, and for a theory K of L, $[K]$ is the set of all consistent complete theories that contain K.

worlds: the closer a consistent complete theory is to the center of S, the more plausible it is. Conditions (S1)–(S4) are then read as follows. (S1) says that any two worlds in S are always comparable in terms of plausibility. Condition (S2) tells us that the most plausible worlds are those compatible with the agent's initial belief set K. Condition (S3) says that all worlds appear somewhere in the plausibility spectrum. Finally, condition (S4), also known as the *Limit Assumption*, is of a more technical nature. It guarantees that for any consistent sentence φ, if one starts at the outermost sphere $\mathbb{M}_L$ (which clearly contains a φ-world) and gradually progresses towards the center of S, one will eventually meet the *smallest* sphere containing φ-worlds. In other words, the spheres in S containing φ-worlds do not form an infinitely decreasing chain; they always converge to a *limit* which is also *in S*. The smallest sphere in S intersecting $[\varphi]$ is denoted $c(\varphi)$. In the limiting case where φ is inconsistent, $c(\varphi)$ is defined to be equal to $\mathbb{M}_L$.

Suppose now that we want to revise K by a sentence φ. Intuitively, the rational thing to do is to select the most plausible φ-worlds and define through them the new belief set $K * \varphi$:

$$(S^*) \quad K * \varphi = \begin{cases} \bigcap(c(\varphi) \cap [\varphi]) & \text{if } \varphi \text{ is consistent,} \\ L & \text{otherwise.} \end{cases}$$

Condition (S*) is precisely what Grove proposed as a means of constructing a revision function $*$ from a system of spheres S. Moreover Grove proved that his construction is sound and complete with respect to the AGM postulates for revision:

Theorem 8.4 (See Grove [38]). *Let K be a theory and S a system of spheres centered on $[K]$. Then the revision function $*$ defined via (S*) satisfies the AGM postulates $(K * 1)$–$(K * 8)$. Conversely, for any theory K and AGM revision function $*$, there exists a system of spheres S centered on $[K]$ that satisfies (S*).*

Theorem 8.4 is the fourth and final piece of formal evidence in support of the AGM postulates for revision (and contraction). In a sense, it also marks the end of the "classical era" in Belief Revision.[17] Therefore this is a good point to take a step back and quickly review what has been discussed so far.

Two types of belief change were examined: belief revision and belief contraction. For each of them a set of postulates was proposed to capture the notion of rationality in each case. In formulating the postulates, Alchourron, Gardenfors, and Makinson relied on the principle of minimal change for guidance. Although the two sets of postulates were motivated independently, the connection between revision and contraction predicted by Levi was shown to hold within the AGM paradigm. This result provided the first formal evidence in support of the appropriateness of the AGM postulates.

The second piece of evidence came with the first constructive model proposed by Alchourron, Gardenfors, and Makinson based on selection functions, together with the corresponding representation result matching partial meet contraction functions with the postulates $(K \overset{.}{-} 1)$–$(K \overset{.}{-} 8)$.

---

[17]With one notable exception: Spohn's work [93] on iterated revision which will be discussed in Section 8.6.

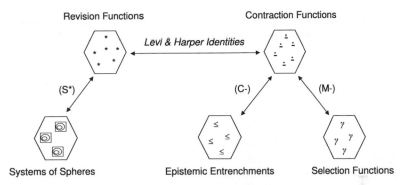

Figure 8.2: The AGM paradigm in the late 1980's.

Later, a second constructive model for contraction functions was introduced by Gardenfors and Makinson, based on the notion of epistemic entrenchment. Formally an epistemic entrenchment is a special preorder on sentences representing the relative resistance of beliefs to change. Gardenfors and Makinson proved that the class of contraction functions produced by epistemic entrenchments coincides precisely with those satisfying the AGM postulates for contraction—yet another piece of strong evidence in support of the AGM postulates.

Grove completed the picture by providing what essentially amounts to a possible world semantics for the AGM postulates $(K * 1)$–$(K * 8)$ for revision. His semantics is based on a special preorder on possible worlds called a system of spheres, which is intended to represent the relative plausibility of possible worlds, given the agent's initial belief set. Based on systems of spheres, Grove provided a very natural definition of belief revision. The fact that Grove's intuitive semantics were proven to be sound and complete with respect to the AGM postulates for revision, is perhaps the most compelling formal evidence for the appropriateness of the AGM postulates. Fig. 8.2 summaries the first main results of the AGM paradigm.

8.4 Belief Base Change

The models and results of the AGM paradigm depicted in Fig. 8.2 are so neat, that one almost feels reluctant to change anything at all. Yet these elegant results rest on assumptions that, in a more realistic context, are disputable; moreover some important issues on Belief Revision were left unanswered by the (original) AGM paradigm. Hence researchers in the area took on the task of extending the AGM paradigm while at the same time preserving its elegance and intuitive appeal that has made it so popular and powerful. Considerable efforts have been made to maintain the connections depicted in Fig. 8.2 in a more generalized or more pragmatic framework.

Among AGM's founding assumptions, one of the most controversial is the modeling of an agent's beliefs as a *theory*. This is unrealistic for a number of reasons. Firstly, theories are *infinite* objects and as such cannot be incorporated directly into a computational framework. Therefore any attempt to use AGM's revision functions in an artificial intelligence application will have to be based on *finite representations* for theories, called *theory bases*. Ideally, a theory base would not only represent (in a finite manner) the sentences of the theory, but also the extra-logical information needed for belief revision.

Computational considerations however are not the only reason that one may choose to move from theories to theory bases. Many authors [27, 85, 39, 65] make a distinction between the *explicit beliefs* of an agent, i.e., beliefs that the agent accepts in their own right, and beliefs that follow from logical closure. This distinction, goes the argument, plays a crucial role in belief revision since derived beliefs should not be retained if their support in explicit beliefs is gone. To take a concrete example, suppose that Philippa believes that "Picasso was Polish"; call this sentence φ. Due to logical closure, Philippa also holds the derived belief $\varphi \vee \psi$, where ψ can be any sentence expressible in the language, like "Picasso was Australian" or even "There is life on Mars". If later Philippa drops φ, it seems unreasonable to retain $\varphi \vee \psi$, since the latter has no independent standing but owes its presence solely to φ.[18]

Most of the work on belief base revision starts with a theory base B and a preference ordering $<$ on the sentences in B, and provides methods of revising B in accordance with $<$. The belief base B is a set of sentences of L, which in principle (but not necessarily) is not closed under logical implication and for all practical purposes it is in fact *finite*. Nebel [69] distinguishes between approaches that aim to take into account the difference between explicit and derived beliefs on one hand, and approaches that aim to provide a computational model for theory revision on the other. The former give rise to *belief base revision operations*, whereas the latter define *belief base revision schemes*. The main difference between the two is that the output of a belief base revision operation is again a belief base, whereas the output of a belief base revision scheme is a *theory*. This difference is due to the different aims and assumptions of the two groups. Belief base revision operations assume that the primary objects of change are belief bases, not theories.[19] Of course a revision on belief bases can be "lifted" to a revision on theories via logical closure. However this theory revision is simply an epiphenomenon; revision operators act only on the set of explicit beliefs. If one adopts this view, it is clear why the result of a belief base revision operation is again a belief base.

Belief base revision schemes on the other hand have been developed with a different goal in mind: to provide a concise representation of *theory* revision. We have seen that AGM revision functions need the entire theory K and an epistemic entrenchment $\leqslant$ associated with it to produce the new theory $K * \varphi$ (for any φ). However both K and $\leqslant$ are infinite objects. Moreover even when K is finite modulo logical equivalence, the amount of information necessary for $\leqslant$ is (in the worst case) exponential in the size of the finite axiomatization of K. By operating on a belief base B and an associated preference ordering $<$, belief base revision schemes provide a method of producing $K * \varphi$ from succinct representations. In that sense, as noted in [69], belief base revision schemes can be viewed as just another construction model for belief revision alongside epistemic entrenchments, systems of spheres, and selection functions.

In the following we shall review some of the most important belief base revision operations and belief base revision schemes. Our presentation follows the notation and terminology of [69].

---

[18]This is often called the *foundational approach* to belief revision.

[19]Apart from the degenerate case where the two are identical.

8.4.1 Belief Base Change Operations

An obvious approach to define belief base operations is to follow the lead of the partial meet construction in Section 8.3.3.

In particular, let B be a belief base and φ a sentence in L. The definition of a φ-remainder can be applied to B without any changes despite the fact that B is (in principle) not closed under logical implication. The same is true for selection functions over subsets of B. Hence condition (M-) can be used verbatim for constructing belief base contraction functions. We repeat (M-) below for convenience, this time with a B subscript to indicate that it is no longer restricted to theories (for the same reason K is replaced by B):

(M-)$_B$ $\qquad B \overset{.}{-} \varphi = \bigcap \gamma(B \perp\!\!\!\perp \varphi)$.

Any function $\overset{.}{-}$ constructed from a selection function γ by means of (M-)$_B$ is called a *partial meet belief base contraction function*. Hansson [41] characterized partial meet belief base contraction in terms of the following postulates[20]:

$(B \overset{.}{-} 1)$ $\quad$ If $\nvdash \varphi$ then $\varphi \notin Cn(B \overset{.}{-} \varphi)$.

$(B \overset{.}{-} 2)$ $\quad B \overset{.}{-} \varphi \subseteq B$.

$(B \overset{.}{-} 3)$ $\quad$ If it holds for all subsets B' of B that $\varphi \in B'$ iff $\psi \in B'$, then $B \overset{.}{-} \varphi = B \overset{.}{-} \psi$.

$(B \overset{.}{-} 4)$ $\quad$ If $\psi \in B$ and $\psi \notin B \overset{.}{-} \varphi$, then there is a set B' such that $B \overset{.}{-} \varphi \subseteq B' \subseteq B$ and that $\varphi \notin Cn(B')$ but $\varphi \in Cn(B' \cup \{\psi\})$.

Theorem 8.5 (See Hansson [41]). *A function $\overset{.}{-}$ from $2^L \times L$ to 2^L is a partial meet belief base contraction function iff it satisfies $(B \overset{.}{-} 1)$–$(B \overset{.}{-} 4)$.*

Some remarks are due regarding partial meet belief base contractions and their associated representation result. Firstly, the extra-logical information needed to produce $\overset{.}{-}$ is not encoded as an ordering on the sentences of B (as it is typically the case with belief base revision schemes), but by a selection function γ on the subsets of B. Secondly, γ is not necessarily *relational*; i.e., γ is not necessarily defined in terms of a binary relation $\ll$. If such an assumption is made, further properties of the produced belief base contraction function $\overset{.}{-}$ can be derived (see [41]). Finally, although this construction generates belief base contractions, it can also be used to produce belief base revisions by means of the following variant of the Levi Identity:

(BL) $\qquad B * \varphi = (B \overset{.}{-} \neg\varphi) \cup \{\varphi\}$.

An alternative to partial meet belief base contraction is *kernel contraction* introduced by Hansson in [39] and originating from the work of Alchourron and Makinson on *safe contraction* [2].

Let B be a belief base and φ a sentence of L. A φ-*kernel* of B is a minimal subset of B that entails φ; i.e., B' is a φ-kernel of B iff $B' \subseteq B$, $B' \vdash \varphi$, and no proper subset

---

[20]Earlier publications by Hansson also report on similar results. However [41] gives a more detailed and uniform presentation of his work on belief base contraction.

of B' entails φ. We shall denote the set of all φ-kernels by $B \parallel \varphi$. An *incision function* σ for B is a function that maps a set X of subsets of B to a subset of $\bigcup X$ such that for all $T \in X$, $\sigma(X) \cap T \neq \emptyset$; i.e., σ picks up a subset of $\bigcup X$ that cuts across all elements of X.

Given an incision function σ for a belief base B, one can construct a contraction function $\dot{-}$ as follows:

$(B\dot{-})$ $B \dot{-} \varphi = B - \sigma(B \parallel \varphi)$.

A function $\dot{-}$ constructed from an incision function σ by means of $(K\dot{-})$ is called a *kernel contraction function*. Once again Hansson [39, 41] has provided an axiomatic characterization of kernel contractions. To this end, consider the postulate $(B \dot{-} 5)$ below:

$(B \dot{-} 5)$ If $\psi \in B$ and $\psi \notin B \dot{-} \varphi$, then there is a set B' such that $B' \subseteq B$ and that $\varphi \notin Cn(B')$ but $\varphi \in Cn(B' \cup \{\psi\})$.

Clearly $(B \dot{-} 5)$ is a weaker version of $(B \dot{-} 4)$. It turns out that this weakening of $(B \dot{-} 4)$ is all that is needed for a precise characterization of kernel contractions:

Theorem 8.6 (See Hansson [39, 41]). *A function $\dot{-}$ from $2^L \times L$ to 2^L is a kernel contraction function iff it satisfies $(B \dot{-} 1)$–$(B \dot{-} 3)$ and $(B \dot{-} 5)$.*

It follows immediately from Theorems 8.5 and 8.6, that every partial meet belief base contraction is also a kernel contraction. The converse is not true. It is however possible to devise restrictions on incision functions such that the induced subclass of kernel contractions, called *smooth* kernel contractions, coincides with the family of partial meet belief base contraction (see [39]).

Once again, the belief base variant of the Levi Identity (BL) can be used to produce belief base revisions from kernel contractions.

8.4.2   Belief Base Change Schemes

Turning to belief base revision schemes, we need to keep in mind that, while these schemes operate on (prioritized) belief bases, their outcome are theories.

Perhaps the simplest such scheme is the analog of full meet contractions for belief bases shown below. As usual in condition $(F\text{-})_B$ below B denotes a belief base and φ a sentence of L.

$(F\text{-})_B$ $B \dot{-} \varphi = \bigcap_{B' \in (B \perp\!\!\!\perp \varphi)} Cn(B' \cup \{\varphi \to \psi : \psi \in B\})$.

Let us call the functions produced from $(F\text{-})_B$ *base-generated full meet contraction functions*. In a sense $(F\text{-})_B$ can be viewed as a special case of $(M\text{-})_B$; namely the case where the selection function γ picks up *all* φ-remainders. There are however two important differences between the two conditions. Firstly a new term, $\{\varphi \to \psi : \psi \in B\}$, has been added to $(F\text{-})_B$ whose purpose is to secure the validity of the recovery postulate $(K \dot{-} 6)$ (see Theorems 8.7, 8.8 below). Secondly, in $(F\text{-})_B$ the φ-remainders (together with the new term) are first *closed under logical implication* before intersected. Hence $B \dot{-} \varphi$, as defined by $(F\text{-})_B$, is always a *theory*, which, furthermore, is not necessarily expressible as the logical closure of some subset of the initial belief base B.

As mentioned earlier, (F-)$_B$ can be viewed as the construction of a contraction function $\dot{-}$ mapping $Cn(B)$ and φ to the theory $B \dot{-} \varphi$. As such, one can assess base-generated full meet contraction functions against the AGM postulates. To this end, consider the following two new postulates from [85]:

($\dot{-}$8r) $K \dot{-} (\varphi \wedge \psi) \subseteq Cn(K \dot{-} \varphi \cup K \dot{-} \psi)$.

($\dot{-}$8c)   If $\psi \in K \dot{-} (\varphi \wedge \psi)$ then $K \dot{-} (\varphi \wedge \psi) \subseteq K \dot{-} \varphi$.

It turns out that in the presence of $(K \dot{-} 1)$–$(K \dot{-} 7)$, the above two postulates follow from $(K \dot{-} 8)$. Rott and del Val independently proved the following characterization of base-generated full meet contraction functions:

Theorem 8.7 (See Rott [85], del Val [15]). *A function $\dot{-}$ from $\mathbb{K}_L \times L$ to $\mathbb{K}_L$ is a base-generated full meet contraction function iff it satisfies $(K \dot{-} 1)$–$(K \dot{-} 7)$, ($\dot{-}$8r) and ($\dot{-}$8c).*

Notice that, by selecting all φ-remainders, condition (F-)$_B$ treats all sentences in the belief base B as equal. If however the belief base B is *prioritized*, a refined version of (F-)$_B$ is needed; one which among all φ-remainders selects only those whose sentences have the highest priority. In particular, assume that the belief base B is partitioned into n priority classes $B_1, B_2, \ldots, B_n$, listed in increasing order of importance (i.e., for $i < j$, the sentences in B_i are less important than the sentences in B_j). Given such a prioritization of B one can define an ordering on subsets of B as follows:

(B$\ll$)   For any $T, E \subseteq B, T \ll E$ iff there is an $1 \leqslant i \leqslant n$ such that $T \cap B_i \subset E \cap B_i$ and for all $i < j \leqslant n, T \cap B_j = E \cap B_j$.

We can now refine (F-)$_B$ to select only the best φ-remainders with respect to $\ll$. In particular, let $\max(B \perp\!\!\!\perp \varphi)$ denote the set of maximal φ-remainders with respect to $\ll$; i.e. $\max(B \perp\!\!\!\perp \varphi) = \{B' \in (B \perp\!\!\!\perp \varphi)$: for all $E \subseteq B$, if $B' \ll E$ then $E \vdash \varphi\}$. The prioritized version of (F-)$_B$ is condition (P-)$_B$ below:

(P-)$_B$ $B \dot{-} \varphi = \bigcap_{B' \in \max(B \perp\!\!\!\perp \varphi)} Cn(B' \cup \{\varphi \to \psi : \psi \in B\})$.

All functions induced from (P-)$_B$ are called *base-generated partial meet contraction functions*. Clearly, all base-generated full meet contraction functions are also partial meet (simply set the partition of B to be a singleton; i.e., only containing B itself). Perhaps surprisingly, the converse is also true:

Theorem 8.8 (See Rott [85], del Val [15]). *A function $\dot{-}$ from $\mathbb{K}_L \times L$ to $\mathbb{K}_L$ is a base-generated partial meet contraction function iff it satisfies $(K \dot{-} 1)$–$(K \dot{-} 7)$, ($\dot{-}$8r) and ($\dot{-}$8c).*

It is important not to misread the equivalence between full meet and partial meet base-generated contraction functions implied by Theorem 8.8. In particular, Theorem 8.8 *does not* imply that for a given prioritized belief base B the function induced by (P-)$_B$ is the same as the function induced by (F-)$_B$. What Theorem 8.8 does entail is that for any prioritized belief base B there exists a non-prioritized belief base B', which is logically equivalent to B (i.e., $Cn(B) = Cn(B')$), and such that the contraction function produced from B and (P-)$_B$ is the same as the contraction function produced from B' and (F-)$_B$.

Clearly partial meet base-generated contraction functions can be used to construct revision functions via the Levi Identity; predictably, these functions are called *partial meet base-generated revision functions*. Among them, Nebel [68, 69] identified a special class, called *linear belief base revision functions*, with some interesting properties. Formally a linear belief base revision function is defined as a partial meet base-generated revision function that is produced from a *totally ordered* prioritized belief base; that is, the priority classes $B_1, B_2, \ldots, B_n$ of the initial belief base B are all *singletons*. It turns out that linear belief base revision functions coincide precisely with the original AGM revision functions:

Theorem 8.9 (See Nebel [68], del Val [15]). *A function $*$ from $\mathbb{K}_L \times L$ to $\mathbb{K}_L$ is a linear belief base revision function iff it satisfies $(K * 1)$–$(K * 8)$.*

The last belief base change scheme that we shall consider in this section is based on the notion of *ensconcement* [97, 99, 98]. Intuitively, an ensconcement is an ordering $\preccurlyeq$ on a belief base B that can be "blown up" to a full epistemic entrenchment $\leqslant$ related to $Cn(B)$. We can also think of it in another way. Consider a theory K and an epistemic entrenchment $\leqslant$ related to K that defines (via (E*)) a revision function $*$.[21] If we want to generate $*$ from a belief base B of K, we also need some sort of "base" for $\leqslant$. That is precisely what an ensconcement is: a (typically) concise representation of an epistemic entrenchment.

Formally, an ensconcement ordering $\preccurlyeq$ on a belief base B is a total preorder on B satisfying the following conditions:

($\preccurlyeq 1$)   For all non-tautological sentences φ in B, $\{\psi \in B : \varphi \prec \psi\} \nvdash \varphi$.

($\preccurlyeq 2$)   For all $\varphi \in B$, φ is a tautology iff $\psi \preccurlyeq \varphi$ for all $\psi \in B$.

Clearly an ensconcement ordering $\preccurlyeq$ satisfies the following *priority consistency condition* [84]:

(PCC)   For all $\varphi \in B$, if B' is a nonempty subset of B that entails φ then there is a $\psi \in B'$ such that $\psi \preccurlyeq \varphi$.

Rott, [84], has shown that (PCC) is a *necessary and sufficient* condition for the extension of any total preorder $\preccurlyeq$ to an epistemic entrenchment $\leqslant$ related to $Cn(B)$. Hence ensconcement orderings are always extensible to epistemic entrenchments; Williams in [99, 98], provided an explicit construction of such an extension.

In particular, Williams starts by defining the notion of a *cut* of an ensconcement ordering $\preccurlyeq$ with respect to a sentence φ as follows:

(Cut) $cut(\varphi) = \begin{cases} \{\psi \in B : \{\chi \in B : \psi \preccurlyeq \chi\} \nvdash \varphi\} & \text{if } \nvdash \varphi, \\ \emptyset & \text{otherwise.} \end{cases}$

Using the notion of a cut, Williams then proceeds to generate a binary relation $\leqslant$ over the entire language from a given ensconcement ordering $\preccurlyeq$, by means of the following condition:

---

[21]To be more precise, $\leqslant$ gives only a *partial* definition of $*$; namely only its restriction to K. For a complete specification of $*$ we would need a whole family of epistemic entrenchments, one for every theory of L. This abuse in terminology occurs quite frequently in this chapter.

(EN1)   For any $\varphi, \psi \in L$, $\varphi \leqslant \psi$ iff $cut(\psi) \subseteq cut(\varphi)$.

It turns out that the binary relation $\leqslant$ so defined is indeed an epistemic entrenchment:

Theorem 8.10 (See Williams [97–99]). *Let B be a belief base and $\preccurlyeq$ an ensconcement ordering on B. The binary relation $\leqslant$ generated from $\preccurlyeq$ by means of* (EN1) *is an epistemic entrenchment related to Cn(B) (i.e., it satisfies the axioms* (EE1)–(EE5)).

From Theorem 8.10 and (E*) (Section 8.3.4) it follows immediately that the function * defined by condition (EN2) below is an AGM revision function (i.e., it satisfies the postulates $(K * 1)$–$(K * 8)$).

(EN2) $\psi \in Cn(B) * \varphi$ iff $cut(\varphi \to \psi) \subset cut(\varphi \to \neg\psi)$ or $\vdash \neg\varphi$.

In fact, it turns out that the converse is also true; i.e., any AGM revision function can be constructed from some ensconcement ordering by means of (EN2). Hence the belief base change scheme produced from ensconcement orderings and (EN2) is as expressive as any of the constructive models discussed in Section 8.3, with the additional bonus of being generated from finite structures (in principle). This however is not the only virtue of ensconcement orderings; combined with condition (EN3) below, they produce a very attractive belief base change operator ⊛:

(EN3) $B \circledast \varphi = cut(\neg\varphi) \cup \{\varphi\}$.

Notice that, as expected from belief base change operators, the outcome of ⊛ is (typically) not a theory but rather a *theory base*. What makes ⊛ such an attractive belief base change operator is that, when lifted to the theory level via logical closure, it generates AGM revision functions.

More precisely, let B be a belief base, $\preccurlyeq$ an ensconcement ordering on B, and ⊛ the belief base change operator produced from B and $\preccurlyeq$ via (EN3). The function * defined as $Cn(B) * \varphi = Cn(B \circledast \varphi)$ is called an *ensconcement-generated revision function*.[22]

Theorem 8.11 (See Williams [98, 99]). *The class of ensconcement-generated revision functions coincides with the class of AGM revision functions.*

We conclude this section by noting that, in principle, the computational complexity of (propositional) belief revision is NP-hard (typically at the second level of the polynomial hierarchy). For an excellent survey on computational complexity results for belief revision, see [69].

8.5   Multiple Belief Change

From belief base revision we will now move to the other end of the spectrum and examine the body of work in *multiple* belief change. Here, not only is the initial belief

---

[22]It turns out that this ensconcement-generated revision function * has yet another interesting property. It can be constructed from $\preccurlyeq$ following another route: $\preccurlyeq$ gives rise to an epistemic entrenchment $\leqslant$ by means of (EN1), which in turn produces a revision function by means of (E*), which turns out to be identical with *.

set K infinite (since it is closed under logical implication), but it can also be revised by an *infinite* set of sentences. The process of rationally revising K by a (possibly infinite) set of sentences Γ is called *multiple revision*. Similarly, rationally contracting K by a (possibly infinite) Γ is called *multiple contraction*.

Extending the AGM paradigm to include multiple revision and contraction is not as straightforward as it may first appear. Subtleties introduced by infinity need to be treated with care if the connections within the AGM paradigm between postulates and constructive models are to be preserved.

8.5.1   Multiple Revision

As it might be expected, multiple revision is modeled as a function $\oplus$ mapping a theory K and a (possibly infinite) set of sentences Γ, to a new theory $K \oplus \Gamma$. To contrast multiple revision functions with the revision functions discussed so far (whose input are sentences), we shall often call the latter *sentence* revision functions.

Lindstrom [58] proposed the following generalization of the AGM postulates for multiple revision[23]:

($K \oplus 1$) $K \oplus \Gamma$ is a theory of L.

($K \oplus 2$) $\Gamma \subseteq K \oplus \Gamma$.

($K \oplus 3$) $K \oplus \Gamma \subseteq K + \Gamma$.

($K \oplus 4$)   If $K \cup \Gamma$ is consistent then $K + \Gamma \subseteq K \oplus \Gamma$.

($K \oplus 5$)   If Γ is consistent then $K \oplus \Gamma$ is also consistent.

($K \oplus 6$)   If $Cn(\Gamma) = Cn(\Delta)$ then $K \oplus \Gamma = K \oplus \Delta$.

($K \oplus 7$) $K \oplus (\Gamma \cup \Delta) \subseteq (K \oplus \Gamma) + \Delta$.

($K \oplus 8$)   If $(K \oplus \Gamma) \cup \Delta$ is consistent then $(K \oplus \Gamma) + \Delta \subseteq K \oplus (\Gamma \cup \Delta)$.

It is not hard to verify that ($K \oplus 1$)–($K \oplus 8$) are indeed generalizations of ($K * 1$)–($K * 8$), in the sense that multiple revision collapses to sentence revision whenever the input set Γ is a singleton. To put it more formally, if $\oplus$ satisfies ($K \oplus 1$)–($K \oplus 8$) then the function $* : \mathbb{K}_L \times L \mapsto \mathbb{K}_L$ defined as $K * \varphi = K \oplus \{\varphi\}$, satisfies the AGM postulates ($K * 1$)–($K * 8$).

In [76, 79] it was also shown that multiple revision can be constructed from systems of spheres, pretty much in the same way that its sentence counterpart is constructed. More precisely, let K be a theory and S a system of spheres centered on $[K]$. From S a multiple revision function $\oplus$ can be produced as follows:

(S$\oplus$) $K \oplus \Gamma = \begin{cases} \bigcap(c(\Gamma) \cap [\Gamma]) & \text{if } [\Gamma] \neq \emptyset, \\ L & \text{otherwise.} \end{cases}$

Condition (S$\oplus$) is a straightforward generalization of (S*) and has the same intuitive interpretation: to revise a theory K by a (consistent) set of sentences Γ, pick the

---

[23]There are in fact some subtle differences between the definition of $\oplus$ presented herein and the one given by Lindstrom in [58], which however are only superficial; the essence remains the same.

most plausible Γ-worlds and define $K \oplus \Gamma$ to be the theory corresponding to those worlds.

Yet, not every system of spheres is good enough to produce a multiple revision function. Two additional constraints, named (SM) and (SD), are needed that are presented below. First however one more definition: we shall say that a set V of consistent complete theories is *elementary* iff $V = [\bigcap V]$.[24]

(SM)   For every nonempty consistent set of sentences Γ, there exists a smallest sphere in S intersecting $[\Gamma]$.

(SD)   For every nonempty $\Gamma \subseteq L$, if there is a smallest sphere $c(\Gamma)$ in S intersecting $[\Gamma]$, then $c(\Gamma) \cap [\Gamma]$ is *elementary*.

A system of spheres S which on top of (S1)–(S4) satisfies (SM) and (SD) is called *well-ranked*.

The motivation for condition (SM) should be clear. Like (S4) (to which (SM) is a generalization) condition (SM) guarantees the existence of minimal Γ-worlds (for any consistent Γ), through which the revised theory $K \oplus \Gamma$ is produced.

What may not be clear is the need for condition (SD). It can be shown that conditions (S1)–(S4) do not suffice to guarantee that all spheres in an arbitrary system of spheres are elementary.[25] Condition (SD) requires that at the very least, whenever a non-elementary sphere V *minimally* intersects $[\Gamma]$, the set $V \cap [\Gamma]$ is elementary.

Condition (SD) is a technical one necessitated by the possibility of an infinite input Γ (see [79] for details). Fortunately however (SD) and (SM) are the only additional conditions necessary to elevate the connection between revision functions and systems of spheres to the infinite case:

Theorem 8.12 (See Peppas [76, 79]). *Let K be a theory of L. If S is a well ranked system of spheres centered on $[K]$ then the function $\oplus$ induced from S by means of (S$\oplus$) satisfies the postulates $(K \oplus 1)$–$(K \oplus 8)$. Conversely, for any function $\oplus : \mathbb{K}_L \times 2^L \mapsto \mathbb{K}_L$ that satisfies the postulates $(K \oplus 1)$–$(K \oplus 8)$, there exists a well ranked system of spheres S centered on $[K]$ such that (S$\oplus$) holds for all $\Gamma \subseteq L$.*

Apart from the above systems-of-spheres construction for multiple revision, Zhang and Foo [107] also lifted the epistemic-entrenchment-based construction to the infinite case.

More precisely, Zhang and Foo start by introducing a variant of an epistemic entrenchment called a *nicely ordered partition*. Loosely speaking, a nicely ordered partition is equivalent to an *inductive epistemic entrenchment*; i.e., an epistemic entrenchment $\leqslant$ which (in addition to satisfying (EE1)–(EE5)) is such that every nonempty set of sentences Γ has a minimal element with respect to $\leqslant$.[26] From a nicely ordered par-

---

[24] In classical Model Theory, the term "elementary" refers to a class of *models* rather than a set of consistent complete theories (see [11]). Yet, since in this context consistent complete theories play the role of possible worlds, this slight abuse of terminology can be tolerated.

[25] If that was the case, (SD) would had been vacuous since the intersection of any two elementary sets of consistent complete theories is also elementary.

[26] A sentence φ is minimal in Γ with respect to $\leqslant$ iff $\varphi \in \Gamma$ and for all $\psi \in \Gamma$, if $\psi \leqslant \varphi$ then $\varphi \leqslant \psi$. Notice that inductiveness is weaker than the better known property of *well-orderedness*; the latter requires the minimal element in each nonempty set Γ to be *unique*.

tition one can construct a multiple revision function, pretty much in the same way that a sentence revision function is produced from an epistemic entrenchment.[27] Zhang and Foo prove that the family of multiple revision functions so constructed is *almost* the same as the class of functions satisfying the postulates $(K \oplus 1)$–$(K \oplus 8)$; for an *exact* match between the two an extra postulate is needed (see [107] for details).

We conclude this section with a result about the possibility of reducing multiple revision to sentence revision.

We have already seen that when Γ is a singleton, the multiple revision of K by Γ is the same as the sentence revision of K by the sentence in Γ. Similarly, one can easily show that when Γ is finite, $K \oplus \Gamma = K * \bigwedge \Gamma$, where $\bigwedge \Gamma$ is defined as the conjunction of all sentences in Γ. But what happens when Γ is infinite? Is there still some way of reducing multiple revision to sentence revision? Consider the following condition:

$(K \oplus F)$ $K \oplus \Gamma = \bigcap \{((K * \bigwedge \Delta) + \Gamma): \Delta \text{ is a finite subset of } \Gamma\}.$

According to condition $(K \oplus F)$, to reduce multiple revision to sentence revisions when the input Γ is infinite, one should proceed as follows: firstly, the initial theory K is revised by every finite conjunction $\bigwedge \Delta$ of sentences in Γ, then each such revised theory $K * \bigwedge \Delta$ is expanded by Γ, and finally all expanded theories $(K * \bigwedge \Delta) + \Gamma$ are intersected.

Let us call a multiple revision function $\oplus$ that can be reduced to sentence revision by means of $(K \oplus F)$ *sentence-reducible* at K. In [79], a precise characterization of sentence reducible functions was given in terms of the systems of spheres that correspond to them. More precisely, consider the condition (SF) below regarding a system of sphere S centered on $[K]$:

(SF)   For every $H \subseteq S$, $\bigcup H$ is elementary.

According to (SF), for any collection H of spheres in S, the set resulting from the union of the spheres in H is elementary.[28] The theorem below shows that the multiple revision functions produced by well-ranked systems of spheres satisfying (SF), are precisely those that are sentence reducible at K:

Theorem 8.13 (See Peppas [79]). *Let K be a theory of L and $\oplus$ a multiple revision function. The function $\oplus$ is sentence-reducible at K iff there exists a well-ranked system of spheres S centered on $[K]$ that induces $\oplus$ by means of $(S\oplus)$ and that satisfies* (SF).

8.5.2 Multiple Contraction

Unlike multiple revision where the AGM postulates have an obvious generalization, in multiple contraction things are not as clear. The reason is that there are (at least) three different ways of interpreting multiple contraction, giving rise to three different

---

[27] A synonym for multiple revision is *infinitary* revision. In fact this is the term used by Zhang and Foo in [107].

[28] It is not hard to see that (SF) entails (SD). Simply notice that from (SF) it follows that all spheres in S are elementary, and consequently, the intersection of $[\Gamma]$ (for any set of sentences Γ) with *any* sphere of S is also elementary.

operators called *package contraction, choice contraction,* and *set contraction.* The first two are due to Fuhrmann and Hansson [28] while the third has been introduced and analyzed by Zhang and Foo [105, 107].

Given a theory K and a (possibly infinite) set of sentences Γ, package contraction removes all (non-tautological) sentences in Γ from K. Choice contraction on the other hand is more liberal; it only requires that *some* (but not necessarily all) of the sentences in Γ are removed from K. Fuhrmann and Hansson [28] have proposed natural generalizations of the AGM postulates for both package contraction and choice contraction. They also obtained preliminary representation results relating their postulates with constructive methods for package and choice contraction. These results however are limited to generalizations of the *basic* AGM postulates; they do not include (generalizations of) the supplementary ones. A few years later, Zhang and Foo [105, 107] obtained such fully-fledged representation results for set contraction.

Set contraction is slightly different in spirit from both package and choice contraction. Given a theory K and a set of sentences Γ, the goal with set contraction is not to remove part or the whole of Γ from K, but rather *to make K consistent with Γ*. At first sight this may seem like an entirely new game, but in fact it is not. For example, it can be shown that for any consistent sentence φ, the set contraction of K by $\{\varphi\}$ is the same as the sentence contraction of K by $\neg\varphi$.[29]

Zhang and Foo define set contraction as a function $\ominus$ mapping a theory K and a set of sentences Γ to the theory $K \ominus \Gamma$, that satisfies the following postulates:

$(K \ominus 1)$ $K \ominus \Gamma$ is a theory of L.

$(K \ominus 2)$ $K \ominus \Gamma \subseteq K$.

$(K \ominus 3)$ If $K \cup \Gamma$ is consistent then $K \ominus \Gamma = K$.

$(K \ominus 4)$ If Γ is consistent then $\Gamma \cup (K \ominus \Gamma)$ is consistent.

$(K \ominus 5)$ If $\varphi \in K$ and $\Gamma \vdash \neg\varphi$ then $K \subseteq (K \ominus \Gamma) + \varphi$.

$(K \ominus 6)$ If $Cn(\Gamma) = Cn(\Delta)$ then $K \ominus \Gamma = K \ominus \Delta$.

$(K \ominus 7)$ If $\Gamma \subseteq \Delta$ then $K \ominus \Delta \subseteq (K \ominus \Gamma) + \Delta$.

$(K \ominus 8)$ If $\Gamma \subseteq \Delta$ and $\Delta \cup (K \ominus \Gamma)$ is consistent, then $K \ominus \Gamma \subseteq K \ominus \Delta$.

Given the different aims of sentence and set contraction, it should not be surprising that $(K \ominus 1)$–$(K \ominus 8)$ are not a straightforward generalization of $(K \dot{-} 1)$–$(K \dot{-} 8)$. For the same reason the generalized version of Levi and Harper Identities presented below [107] are slightly different from what might be expected:

$$K \oplus \Gamma = (K \ominus \Gamma) + \Gamma \quad \text{(Generalized Levi Identity)}$$

$$K \ominus \Gamma = (K \oplus \Gamma) \cap K \quad \text{(Generalized Harper Identity)}.$$

Zhang provides support for the set contraction postulates by lifting the validity of the Harper and Levi Identities to the infinite case:

---

[29] Similarly to sentence revision, in this section we shall use the term *sentence contraction* to refer to the original contraction functions whose inputs are sentences rather than sets of sentences.

Theorem 8.14 (See Zhang [105]). *Let $\ominus$ be a set contraction function satisfying the postulates $(K \ominus 1)$–$(K \ominus 8)$. Then the function $\oplus$ produced from $\ominus$ by means of the Generalized Levi Identity, satisfies the postulates $(K \oplus 1)$–$(K \oplus 8)$.*

Theorem 8.15 (See Zhang [105]). *Let $\oplus$ be a multiple revision function that satisfies the postulates $(K \oplus 1)$–$(K \oplus 8)$. Then the function $\ominus$ produced from $\oplus$ by means of the Generalized Harper Identity, satisfies the postulates $(K \ominus 1)$–$(K \ominus 8)$.*

Apart from the above results, Zhang and Foo reproduced for set contraction Gardenfors' and Makinson's epistemic-entrenchment construction. More precisely, Zhang and Foo presented a construction for set contractions based on nicely ordered partitions, and proved that the family of set contractions so defined is *almost* the same (in fact is a proper subset of) the family of functions satisfying the postulates $(K \ominus 1)$–$(K \ominus 8)$; once again an exact match can be obtained if an extra postulate is added to $(K \ominus 1)$–$(K \ominus 8)$.

8.6   Iterated Revision

We shall now turn to one of the main shortcomings of the early AGM paradigm: its lack of any guidelines for *iterated revision*.

Consider a theory K coupled with a structure encoding extra-logical information relevant to belief change, say a system of spheres S centered on $[K]$. Suppose that we now receive new information φ, such that $\varphi \notin K$, thus leading us to the new theory $K * \varphi$. Notice that $K * \varphi$ is *fully determined* by K, φ, and S, and moreover, as Grove has shown, the transition from the old to the new belief set satisfies the AGM postulates. But what if at this point we receive further evidence ψ, which, to make the case interesting, is inconsistent with $K * \varphi$ (but not self-contradictory; i.e., $\nvdash \neg\psi$). Can we produce $K * \varphi * \psi$ from what we already know (i.e., K, S, φ, and ψ)? The answer, perhaps surprisingly, is *no*. The reason is that at $K * \varphi$ we no longer have the additional structure necessary for belief revision; i.e., we do not know what the "appropriate" system of spheres for $K * \varphi$ is, and without that there is very little we can infer about $K * \varphi * \psi$.[30] But why not simply keep the original system of spheres S? For one thing, this would violate condition (S2) which requires that the minimal worlds (i.e., the worlds in the smallest sphere) are $(K * \varphi)$-worlds (and not K-worlds as they are in S). We need a new system of spheres S' centered on $[K * \varphi]$ that is in some sense the *rational* offspring of S and φ. Unfortunately the AGM postulates give us no clue about how to produce S'. The AGM paradigm focuses only on one-step belief change; iterated belief change was left unattended.

8.6.1   Iterated Revision with Enriched Epistemic Input

Spohn [93] was one of the first to address the problem of iterated belief revision, and the elegance of his solution has influenced most of the proposals that followed. This elegance however comes with a price; to produce the new preference structure from the old one, Spohn requires as input not only the new information φ, but also the *degree of*

---

[30]In fact, all we can deduce is that $K * \varphi * \psi$ is a theory containing ψ.

firmness by which the agent accepts the new information. Let us take a closer look at Spohn's solution (to simplify discussion, in this section we shall consider only revision by *consistent* sentences on *consistent* theories).

To start with, Spohn uses a richer structure than a system of spheres to represent the preference information related to a belief set K. He calls this structure an *ordinal conditional function* (OCF). Formally, an OCF κ is a function from the set $\mathbb{M}_L$ of possible worlds to the class of ordinals such that at least one world is assigned the ordinal 0. Intuitively, κ assigns a plausibility grading to possible worlds: the larger $\kappa(r)$ is for some world r, the less plausible r is.[31] This plausibility grading can easily be extended to sentences: for any consistent sentence φ, we define $\kappa(\varphi)$ to be the κ-value of the most plausible φ-world; in symbols, $\kappa(\varphi) = \min(\{\kappa(r): r \in [\varphi]\})$.

Clearly, the most plausible worlds of all are those whose κ-value is zero. These worlds define the belief set that κ is related to. In particular, we shall say that the belief set K is related to the OCF κ iff $K = \bigcap\{r \in \mathbb{M}_L: \kappa(r) = 0\}$. Given a theory K and an OCF κ related to it, Spohn can produce the revision of K by any sentence φ, *as well as* the new ordinal conditional function related to $K * \varphi$. The catch is, as mentioned earlier, that apart from φ, its degree of firmness d is also needed as input. The new OCF produced from κ and the pair $\langle \varphi, d \rangle$ is denoted $\kappa * \langle \varphi, d \rangle$ and it is defined as follows[32]:

$$(\text{CON}) \quad \kappa * \langle \varphi, d \rangle(r) = \begin{cases} \kappa(r) - \kappa(\varphi) & \text{if } r \in [\varphi], \\ \kappa(r) - \kappa(\neg\varphi) + d & \text{otherwise.} \end{cases}$$

Essentially condition (CON) works as follows. Starting with κ, all φ-worlds are shifted "downwards" against all $\neg\varphi$-worlds until the most plausible of them hit the bottom of the rank; moreover, all $\neg\varphi$-worlds are shifted "upwards" until the most plausible of them are at distance d from the bottom (see Fig. 8.3). Spohn calls this process *conditionalization* (more precisely, the $\langle \varphi, d \rangle$-*conditionalization* of κ) and argues that is the right process for revising OCFs.

Conditionalization is indeed intuitively appealing and has many nice formal properties, including compliance with the AGM postulates[33] (see [93, 31, 100]). Moreover notice that the restriction of κ to $[\varphi]$ and to $[\neg\varphi]$ remains unchanged during conditionalization, hence in this sense the principle of minimal change is observed not only for transitions between belief sets, but also for their associated OCFs.

There are however other ways of interpreting minimal change in the context of iterated revision. Williams in [100] proposes the process of *adjustment* as an alternative to conditionalization. Given an OCF κ, Williams defines the $\langle \varphi, d \rangle$-*adjustment* of κ, which we denote by $\kappa \circ \langle \varphi, d \rangle$, as follows:

$$(\text{ADJ}) \quad \kappa \circ \langle \varphi, d \rangle(r) = \begin{cases} 0 & \text{if } r \in [\varphi], \ d > 0, \text{ and } \kappa(r) = \kappa(\varphi), \\ d & \text{if } r \in [\neg\varphi], \text{ and } \kappa(r) = \kappa(\neg\varphi) \text{ or } \kappa(r) \leqslant d, \\ \kappa(r) & \text{otherwise.} \end{cases}$$

---

[31] In this sense an ordinal conditional function κ is quite similar to a system of spheres S: both are formal devices for ranking possible worlds in terms of plausibility. However κ not only tells us which of any two worlds is more plausible; it also tells us by *how much* is one world more plausible than the other.

[32] The left subtraction of two ordinals α, β such that $\alpha \geqslant \beta$, is defined as the unique ordinal γ such that $\alpha = \beta + \gamma$.

[33] That is, given an OCF κ and any $d > 0$, the function $*$ defined as $K * \varphi = \bigcap\{r \in \mathbb{M}_L: \kappa * \langle \varphi, d \rangle(r) = 0\}$ satisfies the AGM postulates $(K * 1)$–$(K * 8)$.

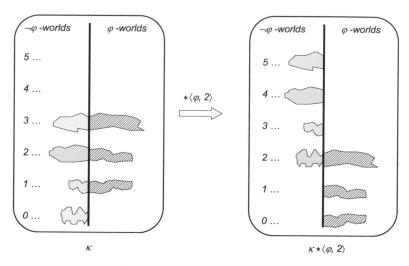

Figure 8.3: Spohn's conditionalization.

Adjustment minimizes changes to the grades of possible worlds in *absolute* terms. To see this, notice that in the principal case where $\kappa(\varphi) > 0$ and $d > 0$,[34] the only φ-worlds that change grades are the most plausible ones (with respect to κ), whose grade becomes zero. Moreover, the only $\neg\varphi$-worlds that change grades are those with grades smaller that d, or, if no such world exists, the minimal $\neg\varphi$-worlds whose grade becomes d. Like conditionalization, adjustment satisfies all AGM postulates for revision.

The entire apparatus of OCFs and their dynamics (conditionalization or adjustment) can be reproduced using sentences rather than possible worlds as building blocks. To this end, Williams [100] defined the notion of *ordinal epistemic entrenchments functions* (OEF) as a special mapping from sentences to ordinals, intended to encode the resistance of sentences to change: the higher the ordinal assigned to sentence, the higher the resistance of the sentence. As the name suggests, an OEF is an enriched version of an epistemic entrenchment (in the same way that an OCF is an enriched version of a system of spheres). Williams formulated the counterparts of conditionalization and adjustment for OEF and proved their equivalence with the corresponding operation on OCFs.

In [66], Nayak took this line of work one step further. Using the original epistemic entrenchment model to encode sentences resistance to change, he considers the general problem of epistemic entrenchment dynamics. The novelty in Nayak's approach is that the epistemic input is no longer a simple sentence as in AGM, or even a sentence coupled with a degree of firmness as in OCF dynamics, but rather another epistemic entrenchment; i.e., an initial epistemic entrenchment $\leqslant$ is revised by another epistemic entrenchment $\leqslant'$, producing a new epistemic entrenchment $\leqslant * \leqslant'$. Notice that because of (EE4) (see Section 8.3.4), an epistemic entrenchment uniquely determines

---

[34]This is the case where the new information φ contradicts the original belief set (since $\kappa(\neg\varphi) > 0$, the agent originally believes $\neg\varphi$).

the belief set it relates to; we shall call this set the *content* of an epistemic entrenchment. Hence epistemic entrenchment revision should be interpreted as follows. The initial epistemic entrenchment $\leqslant$ represents both the original belief set K (defined as its content) as well as the preference structure related to K. The input $\leqslant'$ represents prioritized evidence: the content K' of $\leqslant'$ describes the new information, while the ordering on K' is related (but not identical) to the relative strength of acceptance of the sentences in K'. Finally, $\leqslant \ast \leqslant'$ encodes both the posterior belief set as well as the preference structure associated with it.

Nayak proposes a particular construction for epistemic entrenchment dynamics and shows that the induced operator satisfies (a generalized version of) the AGM postulates for revision. Compared to Williams' OEFs dynamics, Nayak's work is closer to the AGM tradition (both use epistemic entrenchments to represent belief states and plausibility is represented in relative rather than absolute terms). On the other hand however, when it comes to the modeling the epistemic input, Nayak departs even further than Williams from the AGM paradigm; an epistemic entrenchment (used by Nayak) is a much more complex structure than a weighted sentence (used by Williams), which in turn is richer than a simple sentence (used in the original AGM paradigm).

8.6.2 Iterated Revision with Simple Epistemic Input

This raises the question of whether a solution to iterated revision can be produced using only the apparatus of the original AGM framework; that is, using epistemic entrenchments (or systems of spheres or selection functions) to model belief states, and simple sentences to model epistemic input.

One of the most influential proposals to this end is the work of Darwiche and Pearl ("DP" for short) [14]. The first important feature of this work is that, contrary to the original approach of Alchourron, Gardenfors and Makinson (but similarly to Spohn [93], Williams [100], and Nayak [66]), revision functions operate on *belief states*, not on *belief sets*. In the present context a belief state (also referred to as an *epistemic state*) is defined as a belief set coupled with a structure that encodes relative plausibility (e.g., an epistemic entrenchment, a system of spheres, etc.). Clearly a belief state is a richer model that a belief set. Hence it could well be the case that two belief states agree on their belief content (i.e., their belief sets), but behave differently under revision because of differences in their preference structures. For ease of presentation, and although this is not required by Darwiche and Pearl, in the rest of this section we shall identify belief states with systems of spheres; note that given a system of spheres S we can easily retrieve its belief content—simply notice that $c(\top)$ is the smallest sphere of S and therefore $\bigcap c(\top)$ is the belief set associated with S.[35] We shall often abuse notation and write for a sentence φ that $\varphi \in S$ instead of $\varphi \in \bigcap c(\top)$.

With these conventions, $\ast$ becomes a function that maps a system of spheres S and a sentence φ, to a new system of spheres $S \ast \varphi$. Darwiche and Pearl reformulated the AGM postulates accordingly to reflect the shift from belief sets to belief states. They also proposed the following four additional postulates to regulate iterated revisions[36]:

---

[35]Recall that for any sentence ψ, $c(\psi)$ denotes the smallest sphere in S intersecting $[\psi]$.

[36]The postulates are expressed in terms of the Katsuno and Mendelzon formalism [49]; herein however we have rephrased them in the AGM terminology.

(DP1)   If $\varphi \vdash \chi$ then $(S * \chi) * \varphi = S * \varphi$.

(DP2)   If $\varphi \vdash \neg\chi$ then $(S * \chi) * \varphi = S * \varphi$.

(DP3)   If $\chi \in S * \varphi$ then $\chi \in (S * \chi) * \varphi$.

(DP4)   If $\neg\chi \notin S * \varphi$ then $\neg\chi \notin (S * \chi) * \varphi$.

Postulate (DP1) says that if the subsequent evidence φ is logically stronger than the initial evidence χ then φ overrides whatever changes χ may have made. (DP2) says that if two contradictory pieces of evidence arrive sequentially one after the other, it is the later that will prevail. (DP3) says that if revising S by φ causes χ to be accepted in the new belief state, then revising first by χ and then by φ cannot possibly block the acceptance of χ. Finally, (DP4) captures the intuition that "no evidence can contribute to its own demise" [14]; if the revision of S by φ does not cause the acceptance of $\neg\chi$, then surely this should still be the case if S is first revised by χ before revised by φ.

Apart from their simplicity and intuitive appeal, postulates (DP1)–(DP4) also have a nice characterization in terms of systems-of-spheres dynamics. First however some more notation. Let S be a system of spheres and r, r' any two possible worlds. We shall write $r \sqsubseteq_S r'$ iff every sphere in S that contains r' also contains r (i.e., r is at least as plausible as r' in S); we shall write $r \sqsubset_S r'$ iff there is a sphere in S that contains r but not r' (i.e., r is strictly more plausible than r' with respect to S). It is not hard to verify that $\sqsubseteq_S$ is a total preorder in $\mathbb{M}_L$ with the center of S as its minimal elements, while $\sqsubset_S$ is the strict part of $\sqsubseteq_S$. Darwiche and Pearl proved that there is a one-to-one correspondence between (DP1)–(DP4) and the following constraints on system-of-spheres dynamics:

(DPS1)   If $r, r' \in [\varphi]$ then $r \sqsubseteq_{S*\phi} r'$ iff $r \sqsubseteq_S r'$.

(DPS2)   If $r, r' \in [\neg\varphi]$ then $r \sqsubseteq_{S*\phi} r'$ iff $r \sqsubseteq_S r'$.

(DPS3)   If $r \in [\varphi]$ and $r' \in [\neg\varphi]$ then $r \sqsubset_S r'$ entails $r \sqsubset_{S*\phi} r'$.

(DPS4)   If $r \in [\varphi]$ and $r' \in [\neg\varphi]$ then $r \sqsubseteq_S r'$ entails $r \sqsubseteq_{S*\phi} r'$.

Theorem 8.16 (See Darwiche and Pearl [14]). *Let S be a belief state and $*$ a revision function satisfying the (DP-modified) AGM postulates. Then $*$ satisfies* (DP1)–(DP4) *iff it satisfies* (DPS1)–(DPS4), *respectively.*

In a way, Darwiche and Pearl were forced to make the shift from belief sets to belief states, for otherwise (DP2) would have conflicted with the AGM postulates (see [25, 67]).[37] Nayak, Pagnucco, and Peppas [67] proposed another way to reconcile (DP2) with the AGM postulates that does not require moving away from belief sets. It does however require two other changes to the original formulation of belief revision. Firstly, $*$ is defined as a *unary* rather than a binary function, mapping sentences to theories. That is, each theory K is assigned its own revision function which for any

---

[37] Although it should be noted that Darwiche and Pearl argue that this shift is not necessitated by technical reasons alone; conceptual considerations also point the same way.

sentence φ produces the revision of K by φ. We shall denote the unary revision function assigned to K by $*_K$ and the result of revising K by φ as $*_K(\varphi)$. This change in notation will serve as a reminder of the unary nature of revision functions adopted in [67]. Notice that this reformulation of revision functions does not require any modification to the AGM postulates, since all of them refer only to a single theory K.

The second modification to revision functions proposed in [67] is that they are *dynamic*; i.e., they could change as new evidence arrives. The implications of this modification are best illustrated in the following scenario. Consider an agent whose belief set at time t_0 is K_0, and who receives a sequence of new evidence $\varphi_1, \varphi_2, \ldots, \varphi_n$ and performs the corresponding n revisions that take him at time t_n to the belief set K_n. Suppose now that it so happens that $K_n = K_0$; i.e., after incorporating all the new evidence, the agent ended up with the theory she started with. Because of the dynamic nature of revision functions in [67], it is possible that the revision function assigned to K_0 at time t_0 is different from the one assigned to it at time t_n. Hence although the evidence $\varphi_1, \varphi_2, \ldots, \varphi_n$ did not change the agent's beliefs, they did alter her attitude towards new epistemic input.

These two modifications to revision functions take care of the inconsistency between (DP2) and the AGM postulates when applied to belief sets. There is however another problem with (DP1)–(DP4) identified in [67]. Nayak et al. argue that (DP1)–(DP4) are also too permissive; i.e., there are revision functions that comply with both the AGM and DP postulates and nevertheless lead to counter-intuitive results. Moreover, an earlier proposal by Boutilier [7, 9] which strengthens (DP1)–(DP4) still fails to block the unintended revision functions (and introduces some problems of its own—see [14]). Hence Nayak et al. proposed the following addition to (DP1)–(DP4) instead, called the *Conjunction Postulate*:

(CNJ)   If $\chi \wedge \varphi \nvdash \bot$, then $*^{\chi}_{*_K(\chi)}(\varphi) = *_K(\chi \wedge \varphi)$.

Some comments on the notation in (CNJ) are in order. As usual, K denotes the initial belief set, and $*_K$ the unary revision function associated with it. When K is revised by a sentence χ, a new theory $*_K(\chi)$ is produced. This however is not the only outcome of the revision of K by χ; a new revision function associated with $*_K(\chi)$ is also produced. This new revision function is denoted in (CNJ) by $*^{\chi}_{*_K(\chi)}$. The need for the superscript χ is due to the dynamic nature of $*$ (as discussed earlier, along a sequence of revisions, the same belief set may appear more than once, each time with a different revision function associated to it, depending on the input sequence).

Postulate (CNJ) essentially says that if two pieces of evidence χ and φ are consistent with each other, then it makes no difference whether they arrive sequentially or simultaneously; in both cases the revision of the initial belief set K produces the same theory.

Nayak et al. show that (CNJ) is consistent with both AGM and DP postulates, and it blocks the counterexamples known at the time. In fact (CNJ) is strong enough to *uniquely* determine (together with $(K * 1)$–$(K * 8)$ and (DP1)–(DP4)) the new revision function $*^{\chi}_{*_K(\chi)}$. A construction of this new revision function from $*_K$ and χ is given is [67].

Yet, some authors have argued [108, 47] that while (DP1)–(DP4) are too permissive, the addition of (CNJ) is too radical (at least in some cases). Accordingly, Jin and

Thielscher proposed a weakening of (CNJ), which they call the *Independence postulate* [47]. The Independence postulate is formulated within the DP framework; that is, it assumes that belief states rather than belief sets are the primary objects of change:

(Ind)   If $\neg\chi \notin S * \varphi$ then $\chi \in (S * \chi) * \varphi$.

The Independence postulate, apart from performing well in indicative examples (see [47]), also has a nice characterization in terms of system of spheres dynamics:

(IndR)   If $r \in [\varphi]$ and $r' \in [\neg\varphi]$ then $r \sqsubseteq_S r'$ entails $r \sqsubseteq_{S*\phi} r'$.

Theorem 8.17 (See Jin and Thielscher [47]). *Let S be a belief state and $*$ a revision function satisfying the (DP-modified) AGM postulates. Then $*$ satisfies* (Ind) *iff it satisfies* (IndR).

The Independence postulate can be shown to be weaker than (CNJ) and in view of Theorems 8.16, 8.17, it is clearly stronger than (DP3) and (DP4). Jin and Thielscher show that (Ind) is consistent with the AGM and DP postulates combined.

Other important works on iterated revision are [6] which proposes a different strengthening of the DP approach, [45] that considers the interaction between iterated revisions and updates (see Section 8.8), [90] that defines belief revision in terms of distances between possible worlds and derives interesting properties for iterated revision, as well as [17, 19, 50, 55, 101].

8.7   Non-Prioritized Revision

A fundamental assumption in our discussion on belief revision so far has been that the new information the agent receives comes from a reliable source and therefore it should be accepted without second thoughts, no matter how implausible it may seem given the agent's initial beliefs.

This assumption is of course a rather strong one and a number of researchers have proposed alterations to the AGM paradigm in order to lift it. The resulting new type of belief change is called *non-prioritized belief revision*. Depending on a number of parameters, a non-prioritized belief revision operator may fully accept, partially accept, or even totally reject the new information.

One of the earliest proposals for non-prioritized belief revision is Makinson's *screened revision* [62]. The basic idea here is that the fate of the new information depends on its disposition towards a set of *core* beliefs. More precisely, a set of beliefs A is given *a priori* that is considered to be immune to contraction. This set A together with the agent's initial belief set K determine the set of core beliefs defined as $A \cap K$. If the new information φ is inconsistent with $A \cap K$ then it is rejected as implausible; otherwise φ is accepted and K is revised accordingly. In the latter case however, the revision of K by φ should be such that none of the core beliefs are removed. Makinson denotes by $*_A$ an AGM revision function that satisfies the following condition:

(CR)   If φ is consistent with $A \cap K$ then $A \cap K \subseteq K *_A \varphi$.

With the aid of $*_A$ Makinson defines a screened revision operator, denoted by $\#_A$, as follows:

(SC) $K \#_A \varphi = \begin{cases} K *_A \varphi & \text{if } \varphi \text{ is consistent with } A \cap K, \\ K & \text{otherwise.} \end{cases}$

Makinson then proceeds to introduce a more flexible variant of screened revision which he calls *relationally screened revision*. The main new feature of this variant is that the core beliefs are not fixed but they depend on the new information φ. In particular, instead of A, a binary relation $<$ is given *a priori* representing comparative credibility; i.e., if $\chi < \psi$ then χ is less credible than ψ. Then for input φ the set of core beliefs is defined as $\{\chi: \varphi < \chi\} \cap K$. Accordingly, the condition that defines a relationally screened revision, denoted $\#_<$, is the following:

(RSC) $K \#_< \varphi = \begin{cases} K *_{\{\chi: \varphi < \chi\}} \varphi & \text{if } \varphi \text{ is consistent with } \{\chi: \varphi < \chi\} \cap K, \\ K & \text{otherwise.} \end{cases}$

It is not hard to verify that screened revision is a special case of relationally screened revision. Simply set, for a given A, the binary relation $<$ to be $L \times A$.[38]

Hansson et al. [43] proposed a different approach to non-prioritized revision called *credibility-limited revision*. According to this approach, a set $\mathbb{C}$ of *credible sentences* is given *a priori* and any new information φ is accepted only if it belongs to $\mathbb{C}$:

(CL) $K \odot \varphi = \begin{cases} K * \varphi & \text{if } \varphi \in \mathbb{C}, \\ K & \text{otherwise.} \end{cases}$

In the above condition $\odot$ is the new credibility-limited revision operator and $*$ is an AGM revision function.[39]

Depending on the constraints that one places on $\mathbb{C}$ and $*$, a number of interesting results can be obtained for the induced operator $\odot$. In particular, assume that $\mathbb{C}$ can be generated from a subset A of the initial belief set K by means of the following condition:

(CCL) $\varphi \in \mathbb{C}$ iff $A \nvdash \neg\varphi$.

The credibility-limited revision operator induced from such a $\mathbb{C}$ is called a *core belief revision* operator and can be characterized both axiomatically and constructively (see [43]). Below we briefly review a constructive model of core belief revision based on system of spheres.[40]

Let S be a system of spheres centered on $[K]$ and assume that S contains $[A]$ as one of its spheres. Consider the following construction of $\odot$ (recall that for any consistent sentence φ, $c(\varphi)$ denotes the smallest sphere in S intersecting $[\varphi]$):

(S$\odot$) $K \odot \varphi = \begin{cases} \bigcap(c(\varphi) \cap [\varphi]) & \text{if } c(\varphi) \subseteq [A], \\ K & \text{otherwise.} \end{cases}$

Intuitively the sphere $[A]$ circumscribes the set of "entertainable" worlds; any world outside $[A]$ is so implausible that it should never be accepted as a possible

---

[38]If $<$ is required to be a strict order (i.e., transitive and antisymmetric), then things are not as simple but it is still possible (in principle) to reduce screened revision to relationally screened revision.

[39]To be precise, in [43] the function $*$ does not have to satisfy the AGM postulates; when it does, the induced operator $\odot$ is called a *credibility-limited AGM revision*. Herein we focus only on such operators and therefore, for the sake of readability, we have dropped the AGM advert from the title of $\odot$.

[40]This constructive model is slightly different from the one discussed in [43] but it is nevertheless equivalent to it.

state of affairs. Consequently, says condition (S⊙), any sentence φ that takes us to the "forbidden land" of non-entertainable worlds (i.e., any sentence φ for which all φ-world are outside $[A]$) should be rejected; otherwise it is business as usual and the next belief set is determined by the minimal φ-worlds. Hansson et al. in [43] show that the operators constructed through (S⊙) coincide with the family of core belief revision operators.

Both screened revision and credibility-limited revision work in two stages: firstly they check whether the new information φ should be accepted (each with its own decision mechanism) and then, if φ is credible, they revise the initial belief set K by φ. As a result, φ is either accepted in its entirety or not at all; there is no middle ground (such as accepting part of φ). Hansson in [40] proposed non-prioritized belief revision operators that escape this black-and-white attitude towards φ.

The basic idea is the following: add the new information φ to the initial beliefs without checking its credibility and then remove all inconsistencies that may result. Of course in the process of restoring consistency, one may also lose φ. Even so, it may still be possible to keep some *parts* of φ; i.e., non-tautological sentences ψ that follow logically from φ and which were not among the initial beliefs. Hansson calls this operation *semi-revision* and it is clearly more flexible in its treatment of φ than any of the operators discussed so far. It should be noted that semi-revision is defined over *belief bases* rather than belief sets. The extra structure of a belief base is used to guide the restoration of consistency after the addition of φ. Formally the semi-revision of a belief base B by a sentence φ, which we denote by $B \oplus \varphi$, is defined as follows:

(SR) $B \oplus \varphi = (B \cup \{\varphi\}) \overset{.}{-} \perp.$

In the condition above, $\overset{.}{-}$ is a belief base contraction operator, and depending on the constraints one places on $\overset{.}{-}$, different types of semi-revision functions are produced. Of particular interest are the class of semi-revision operators induced from kernel contractions, and the class generated from partial meet belief base contractions; both these classes have been characterized axiomatically in [43].

A totally different approach to non-prioritized belief revision was proposed by Schlechta in [91]. Schlechta's proposal is based on a notion of distance between possible worlds. In this context, the distance between two worlds r' and r'' does not have some numerical value, but it is defined in reference to a third world r. In particular, a ternary relation between worlds is introduced such that whenever it holds between the worlds r, r', and r'', it means that r' is closer to r than is r''. Based on this ternary relation, Schlechta defines the non-prioritized belief revision of K by φ to be the belief set determined by the set of K-worlds and φ-worlds that have minimal distance between them among all pairs of K-worlds and φ-worlds.

Yet another important approach to non-prioritized belief revision can be found in [12, 34], while the process of *extraction* reported in [103] can also be used to this end. See also Hansson's survey on this subject [42].

We shall conclude this section with a quick look at *Belief Merging* which started with a similar agenda to non-prioritized belief revision [81, 57] but quickly developed into a fully-fledged research area of its own addressing much more general and diverse issues.[41]

---

[41] Nevertheless, many would still classify Belief Merging as a sub-area of Belief Revision.

In Belief Merging one starts with a set of belief bases $B = \{B_1, B_2, \ldots, B_n\}$ (possibly with weights assigned to each B_i or with some other structure expressing relative importance) and has to produce an aggregate belief base $\Delta(B)$ that is in some sense the result of rationally merging all B_i's. What makes the problem non-trivial is that in principle $\bigcup B_i$ is inconsistent, whereas the aggregate belief base $\Delta(B)$ is required to be consistent. Moreover, a set of *integrity constraints IC* is typically given together with B, to which $\Delta(B)$ needs to adhere to.

Most work in Belief Merging can be classified either as *model-based* [81, 57, 51] or *syntax-based* [3, 50, 5]. In the first case $\Delta(B)$ is defined in terms of the *most preferred* models of *IC*. Preference in turn is defined according to some criterion that depends on B—usually a notion of distance between possible worlds and B with the worlds closest to B being the most preferred.

Syntax-based approaches on the other hand typically select consistent subsets of $\bigcup B$ taking into account the syntax of the belief bases B_i and any additional preference information that might be given.

Recently, S. Konieczny, J. Lang and P. Marquis [52] developed a unifying framework that can encompass many of the existing merging operators both from the model-based and the syntax-based families.

8.8 Belief Update

In this final section we shall examine a type of belief change that was initially mistaken to be identical with belief revision, but it turns out to be different from it.

Consider the following scenario. Philippa is looking through an open door at a room with a table, a magazine, and a book. One of the two items is on the table and the other on the floor, but because of poor lighting Philippa cannot distinguish which is which. Let us represent by b the proposition that "the book is on the table", and by m the proposition that "the magazine is on the table". Philippa's belief set is then represented by $K = Cn((b \wedge \neg m) \vee (\neg b \wedge m))$. Suppose now that Philippa instructs a robot standing beside her to enter the room and make sure that the book is placed on the floor. The robot will approach the table and if the book is on the table the robot will place it on the floor; otherwise it will do nothing. In either case the robot will go back to Philippa and report "mission accomplished!".

What would be Philippa's belief set K' after the robot reports back to her that the book is on the floor? Presumably it will be the initial belief set K modified by $\neg b$. Suppose now that we use an AGM revision function to perform the modification. Notice that $\neg b$ is consistent with K, and therefore by $(K * 3)$–$(K * 4)$, $K * \neg b = K + \neg b = Cn(\neg b \wedge m)$. So according to the AGM paradigm, if the book was initially on the table, putting it on the floor somehow makes the magazine jump onto the table!

This counter-intuitive behavior of AGM revision functions was first observed by Katsuno and Mendelzon in [48] who also proposed a solution to the problem. Their solution does not dismiss (or even alter) the AGM paradigm; it simply carefully defines its range of applicability.

According to Katsuno and Mendelzon, the reason that the AGM postulates fail to produce the right results in the book/magazine example is because they were never meant to deal with these situations in the first place. Belief revision should *only* be used to modify an incomplete or incorrect belief set K in the light of new information

φ that was previously inaccessible to the agent. It *should not* be used in cases where an agent needs to bring her belief set K up-to-date with changes in the world that brought about φ; in the latter case a new type of belief change takes place called *belief update*. In a nutshell, the difference between belief revision and belief update is that the former is used when new information φ is received about a static world, and the latter is used when the agent is informed that a change in the world has occurred that brought about φ; in the first case the initial belief set K needs to be modified because it is incorrect or incomplete, whereas in the latter case K is modified because it is out-of-date (it was initially correct but in the meantime changes have occurred in the world).

Following the AGM tradition, Katsuno and Mendelzon characterized the process of belief update (or simply update) in terms of a set of postulates, now known as the KM postulates. Like the AGM postulates, the KM postulates are also motivated by the principle of minimal change. However in this context the notion of minimal change applies to world states, *not* to belief sets; when an agent updates her beliefs in response to a minimal change in the world, her new belief set does not necessarily differ minimally from the original. This is a subtle point that has been the source of some confusion before Winslett (see [104]) and finally Katsuno and Mendelzon set things straight.

For ease of comparison we have rephrased the KM postulates in the tradition of the AGM paradigm:

$(K \diamond 1)$ $K \diamond \varphi$ is a theory of L.

$(K \diamond 2)$ $\varphi \in K \diamond \varphi$.

$(K \diamond 3)$ If $\varphi \in K$ then $K \diamond \varphi = K$.

$(K \diamond 4)$ If K and φ are individually consistent then $K \diamond \varphi$ is consistent.

$(K \diamond 5)$ If $\vdash \varphi \leftrightarrow \psi$ then $K \diamond \varphi = K \diamond \psi$.

$(K \diamond 6)$ $K \diamond (\varphi \wedge \psi) \subseteq (K \diamond \varphi) + \psi$.

$(K \diamond 7)$ If $\psi \in K \diamond \varphi$ and $\varphi \in K \diamond \psi$ then $K \diamond \varphi = K \diamond \psi$.

$(K \diamond 8)$ If K is complete then $K \diamond (\varphi \vee \psi) \subseteq Cn((K \diamond \varphi) \cup (K \diamond \psi))$.

$(K \diamond 9)$ $K \diamond \varphi = \bigcap_{r \in [K]} r \diamond \varphi$.

Postulates $(K \diamond 1)$, $(K \diamond 2)$, $(K \diamond 5)$, and $(K \diamond 6)$ are identical with $(K * 1)$, $(K * 2)$, $(K * 6)$ and $(K * 7)$, respectively, and need no further explanation. Postulate $(K \diamond 3)$ is a restricted version of the postulates $(K * 3)$ and $(K * 4)$ combined; it says that if the new proposition φ is already in the initial belief set K then updating K by φ changes nothing. Notice however that $(K \diamond 3)$ puts no constraints on updates when φ is *consistent* with, but not a member of K. This liberty of $(K \diamond 3)$ is the first main difference between revision and update (recall that for such cases $(K * 3)$ and $(K * 4)$ uniquely determine the result of revision to be $K + \varphi$). The book/magazine example mentioned above falls into this category.

Postulate $(K \diamond 4)$ is the update analog of $(K * 5)$ highlighting the importance of reaching consistency after update. Once again however $(K \diamond 4)$ is more liberal than

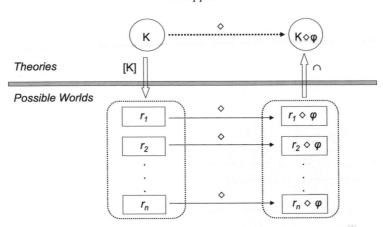

Figure 8.4: Updating a theory via possible worlds.

$(K * 5)$ since it does not apply when the initial belief set K is inconsistent; $(K \diamond 4)$ only *preserves* consistency, it doesn't *generate* it. Postulate $(K \diamond 7)$ essentially says that there is only one way to *minimally* change the world to bring about φ. To see this, consider two sentences φ and ψ for which the precondition of $(K \diamond 7)$ holds. Because $\psi \in K \diamond \varphi$, updating by ψ does not produce more change than updating by φ; conversely, since $\varphi \in K \diamond \psi$, updating by φ is not more "expensive" (in terms of induced change) than updating by ψ. Consequently, says $(K \diamond 7)$, since the two sentences induce the same degree of change, they actually produce exactly the *same* change.

For the last two postulates, recall that an update at K is triggered by the occurrence of an action in the world. Hence $(K \diamond 8)$ relates the agent's belief set $K \diamond (\varphi \vee \psi)$ after the occurrence of a non-deterministic action with possible effects φ or ψ, with the belief sets $K \diamond \varphi$ and $K \diamond \psi$ resulting from deterministic actions with direct effect φ and ψ respectively. $(K \diamond 8)$ states that the former cannot be larger than the union of the latter two belief sets, with the provision that the original belief set K is complete.

The last postulate $(K \diamond 9)$ reduces the update of any belief set K to the update of all K-worlds. To see the motivation behind this postulate, suppose that $r_1, r_2, \ldots, r_n$ are all the consistent complete theories in L that are compatible with the agent's initial belief set K; i.e., $[K] = \{r_1, r_2, \ldots, r_n\}$. Then, as far as the agent knows, any of $r_1, r_2, \ldots, r_n$ could be the initial state of the world. Consequently, after the occurrence of an action with direct effect φ, the world can be at any of the state $r_1 \diamond \varphi, r_2 \diamond \varphi, \ldots, r_n \diamond \varphi$. Thus the agent's new belief set is $K \diamond \varphi = \bigcap_{r \in [K]} r \diamond \varphi$ (see Fig. 8.4).

Apart from their postulates, Katsuno and Mendelzon also introduced semantics for update which, like Grove's semantics for revision, are based on preorders on possible worlds. More precisely, consider a theory K of L, and let $\leqslant$ be a function that assigns to every world r compatible with K (i.e., $r \in [K]$), a preorder on $\mathbb{M}_L$ denoted $\leqslant_r$. The function $\leqslant$ is called a *faithful assignment* iff for every $r \in [K]$ it satisfies the following two conditions: (i) r is the minimum element of $\mathbb{M}_L$ with respect to $\leqslant_r$ (i.e., for all $r' \in \mathbb{M}_L$, if $r \neq r'$ then $r <_r r'$), [42] and, (ii) for any consistent sentence φ, the set $[\varphi]$ has a minimal element with respect to $\leqslant_r$.[43] Intuitively, $\leqslant_r$ represents the comparative similarity of possible worlds with respect to r; the further away a world is from r the less similar it is to r.

Based on a faithful assignment $\leqslant$ for a theory K, Katsuno and Mendelzon define constructively the update of K by a sentence φ as follows:

(KM) $K \diamond \varphi = \begin{cases} \bigcap(\bigcup_{r \in [K]} \min([\varphi], \leqslant_r)) & \text{if } [K] \neq 0 \text{ and } [\varphi] \neq 0 \\ L & \text{otherwise.} \end{cases}$

In the above definition, $\min([\varphi], \leqslant_r)$ represents the set of minimal elements in $[\varphi]$ with respect to $\leqslant_r$; i.e., $\min([\varphi], \leqslant_r) = \{z \in [\varphi]:$ there is no $z' \in [\varphi]$ such that $z' <_r z\}$.

Let us take a closer look at the above construction of belief updates. Katsuno and Mendelzon tell us that to update K by φ, we first need to consider every possible world r compatible with K *individually* and identify the minimal φ-worlds with respect to $\leqslant_r$ (i.e., $\min([\varphi], \leqslant_r)$). The principle of minimal change tells us that these minimal φ-worlds are the states that can result from the occurrence of an action bringing about φ at r. But the agent is not certain that r is the initial state of the world; as far as the agent knows, initially the world can be at any state in $[K]$. Consequently, after the occurrence of φ the world can be at any of the minimal φ-worlds with respect to some $r \in [K]$ (i.e., at any state in $\bigcup_{r \in [K]} \min([\varphi], \leqslant_r)$).

Katsuno and Mendelzon proved the following representation result showing that their semantics is sound and complete with respect to their postulates for update:

Theorem 8.18 (See Katsuno and Mendelzon [48]). *Let K be a theory of L. If $\leqslant$ is a faithful assignment for K then the function $\diamond$ induced from $\leqslant$ by means of* (KM) *satisfies the KM postulates $(K \diamond 1)$–$(K \diamond 9)$. Conversely, for any function $\diamond : \mathbb{K}_L \times L \mapsto \mathbb{K}_L$ that satisfies the KM postulates $(K \diamond 1)$–$(K \diamond 9)$ there exists a faithful assignment $\leqslant$ for K such that* (KM) *is satisfied.*

As mentioned already, the Katsuno and Mendelzon semantics for update is quite similar to Grove's system-of-sphere semantics for revision. There are however two major differences between the two: firstly, to a fixed theory K, Katsuno and Mendelzon assign a whole *family* of preorders on possible worlds (one for each world compatible with K) as opposed to a *single* preorder—alias system of spheres—assigned by Grove; secondly, Grove's preorders are always *total* whereas the preorders used by Katsuno and Mendelzon are (in general) partial. For more details on the relationship between belief revision and update, see [74, 75, 77].

8.9   Conclusion

Clearly it is not possible to provide a detailed account of all the work in Belief Revision in a few pages; an entire book would be needed for that. Instead our aim in this chapter was to expose the reader to some of the main ideas and results of the field.

---

[42] As usual, $<_r$ denotes the strict part of $\leqslant_r$.

[43] Once again, the definition of a faithful assignment presented herein is slightly different, in its phrasing but not in essence, from the original one in [48].

Nevertheless, a few of the missing topics need to be mentioned, even if only in passing.

A large amount of work exists on variations of the AGM postulates and appropriate adjustments to the corresponding constructive models [18, 23, 24, 64, 70, 71, 78, 80, 86, 87, 95]. Moreover, specific belief change operators have been proposed in [13, 89, 96], and their computational complexity has been studied in a seminal article by Eiter and Gottlob [22]. Interesting applications of Belief Revision can be found in [110, 102, 53, 54, 94].

Finally, there is an important body of work on the relationship between Belief Revision and other research areas in Knowledge Representation. Numerous results have been established that reveal profound connections between Belief Revision and areas like *Nonmonotonic Reasoning* [10, 33, 61, 63, 106], *Reasoning about Action* [8, 16, 36, 44, 46, 72–74, 77, 92, 109], *Conditionals* [26, 30, 35, 37, 59, 88, 82] and *Possibility Theory* [20, 21, 4].

Acknowledgements

I am grateful to Mary-Anne Williams, Jim Delgrande, Michael Thielscher, and Tommie Meyer for their valuable comments on this chapter, and to the editors of this book, Frank van Harmelen, Vladimir Lifschitz, and Bruce Porter, for their excellent work in coordinating our joint efforts.

Bibliography

[1] C. Alchourron, P. Gardenfors, and D. Makinson. On the logic of theory change: Partial meet functions for contraction and revision. *Journal of Symbolic Logic*, 50:510–530, 1985.

[2] C. Alchourron and D. Makinson. On the logic of theory change: Safe contractions. *Studia Logica*, 44:405–422, 1985.

[3] C. Baral, S. Kraus, and J. Minker. Combining multiple knowledge bases. *IEEE Transactions on Knowledge and Data Engineering*, 3(2):208–220, 1991.

[4] S. Benferhat, D. Dubois, H. Prade, and M.-A. Williams. A practical approach to revising prioritized knowledge bases. *Studia Logica*, 70:105–130, 2002.

[5] S. Benferhat, S. Kaci, D. Le Berre, and M.-A. Williams. Weakening conflicting information for iterated revision and knowledge integration. *Artificial Intelligence*, 153(1–2):339–371, 2004.

[6] R. Booth and T. Meyer. Admissible and restrained revision. *Journal of Artificial Intelligence Research*, 26:127–151, 2006.

[7] C. Boutilier. Revision sequences and nested conditionals. In *Proceedings of the 13th International Joint Conference in Artificial Intelligence*, pages 519–525, 1993.

[8] C. Boutilier. Generalised update: Belief change in dynamic settings. In *Proceedings of the 14th International Joint Conference in Artificial Intelligence*, pages 1550–1556, Montreal, 1995.

[9] C. Boutilier. Iterated revision and minimal change of conditional beliefs. *Journal of Philosophical Logic*, 25(3), 1996.

[10] G. Brewka. Belief revision in a framework of default reasoning. In *The Logic of Theory Change, LNCS*, vol. 465. Springer-Verlag, 1991.

[11] C. Chang and H. Keisler. *Model Theory. Studies in Logic and the Foundation of Mathematics*, vol. 73. Elsevier Science Publications, 1991.

[12] S. Chopra, A. Ghose, and T. Meyer. Non-prioritized ranked belief change. *Journal of Philosophical Logic*, 32(4):417–443, 2003.

[13] M. Dalal. Investigations into a theory of knowledge base revision: preliminary report. In *Proceedings of the 7th National (USA) Conference on Artificial Intelligence (AAAI'88)*, pages 475–479, 1988.

[14] A. Darwiche and J. Pearl. On the logic of iterated belief revision. *Artificial Intelligence*, 89:1–29, 1997.

[15] A. del Val. On the relation between the coherence and foundations theories of belief revision. In *Proceedings of the 12th National (USA) Conference on Artificial Intelligence (AAAI'94)*, pages 909–914. MIT Press, July 1994.

[16] A. del Val and Y. Shoham. Deriving properties of belief update from theories of action. *Journal Logic, Language and Information*, 3(2):81–119, 1994.

[17] J. Delgrande and T. Schaub. A consistency-based approach for belief change. *Artificial Intelligence*, 151:1–41, 2003.

[18] J. Delgrande, A. Nayak, and M. Pagnucco. Gricean belief change. *Studia Logica*, 79(1), 2005.

[19] J. Delgrande, D. Dubois, and J. Lang. Iterated revision as prioritized merging. In *Proceedings of the 10th International Conference on Principles of Knowledge Representation and Reasoning*, pages 210–220. Morgan Kauffman, 2006.

[20] D. Dubois and H. Prade. Epistemic entrenchment and possibilistic logic. *Artificial Intelligence*, 50:223–239, 1991.

[21] D. Dubois and H. Prade. Belief change and possibility theory. In P. Gardenfors, editor. *Belief Revision*, pages 142–182. Cambridge University Press, 1992.

[22] T. Eiter and G. Gottlob. On the complexity of propositional knowledge base revision updates and counterfactuals. *Artificial Intelligence*, 57:227–270, 1992.

[23] E. Ferme and H. Rott. Revision by comparison. *Artificial Intelligence*, 157, 2004.

[24] G. Flouris, D. Plexousakis, and G. Antoniou. On generalizing the AGM postulates. In *Proceedings of the 3rd European Starting AI Researcher Symposium*. IOS Press, Riva del Garda, 2006.

[25] M. Freund and D. Lehmann. Belief revision and rational inference. Technical Report 94-16, Leibniz Center for Research in Computer Science, Institute of Computer Science, Hebrew University, 1994.

[26] N. Friedman and J. Halpern. Conditional logics of belief change. In *Proceedings of the 12th National (USA) Conference on Artificial Intelligence (AAAI'94)*, Seattle, 1994.

[27] A. Fuhrmann. Theory contraction through base contraction. *Journal of Philosophical Logic*, 20:175–203, 1991.

[28] A. Fuhrmann and S. Hansson. A survey on multiple contraction. *Journal of Logic, Language, and Information*, 3:39–76, 1994.

[29] P. Gardenfors. Epistemic importance and minimal changes of belief. *Australasian Journal of Philosophy*, 62:136–157, 1984.

[30] P. Gardenfors. Belief revision and the Ramsey test for conditionals. *The Philosophical Review*, 95:81–93, 1986.

[31] P. Gardenfors. *Knowledge in Flux*. MIT Press, 1988.

[32] P. Gardenfors and D. Makinson. Revisions of knowledge systems using epistemic entrenchment. In *Proceedings of Theoretical Aspects of Reasoning about Knowledge*, pages 83–95. Morgan Kaufmann, 1988.

[33] P. Gardenfors and D. Makinson. Nonmonotonic inference based on expectations. *Artificial Intelligence*, 65:197–245, 1994.

[34] A. Ghose and G. Goebel. Belief states as default theories: Studies in nonprioritized belief change. In *Proceedings of the 13th European Conference on Artificial Intelligence (ECAI'98)*, pages 8–12, 1998.

[35] L. Giordano, V. Gliozzi, and N. Olivetti. Weak AGM postulates and strong Ramsey test: A logical formalization. *Artificial Intelligence*, 168:1–37, 2005.

[36] M. Goldszmidt and J. Pearl. Rank-based systems: A simple approach to belief revision, belief update and reasoning about evidence and actions. In *Proceedings 3rd International Conference on Principles of Knowledge Representation and Reasoning (KR'92)*, pages 661–672, Cambridge, MA, 1992.

[37] G. Grahne. Updates and counterfactuals. In *Proceedings of the 2nd International Conference on the Principles of Knowledge Representation and Reasoning (KR'91)*, pages 269–276, Cambridge, MA, 1991.

[38] A. Grove. Two modellings for theory change. *Journal of Philosophical Logic*, 17:157–170, 1988.

[39] S.-O. Hansson. Kernel contraction. *Journal of Symbolic Logic*, 59, 1994.

[40] S.-O. Hansson. Semi-revision. *JANCL*, 7:151–175, 1997.

[41] S.-O. Hansson. *A Textbook of Belief Dynamics. Theory Change and Database Updating*. Kluwer Academic Publishers, 1999.

[42] S.-O. Hansson. A survey of non-prioritized belief revision. *Erkenntnis*, 50:413–427, 1998.

[43] S.-O. Hansson, E.L. Ferme, J. Cantwell, and M.A. Falappa. Credibility limited revision. *Journal of Symbolic Logic*, 66(4):1581–1596, 2001.

[44] A. Herzig. The PMA revisited. In *Proceedings of the International Conference on the Principles of Knowledge Representation and Reasoning*, Cambridge, MA, 1996.

[45] A. Hunter and J. Delgrande. Iterated belief change: A transition system approach. In *Proceedings of the 19th International Joint Conference in Artificial Intelligence*, pages 460–465, Edinburgh, 2005.

[46] A. Hunter and J. Delgrande. An action description language for iterated belief change. In *Proceedings of the 20th International Joint Conference in Artificial Intelligence*, pages 2498–2503, Hyderabad, 2007.

[47] Y. Jin and M. Thielscher. Iterated revision, revised. In *Proceedings of the 19th International Joint Conference in Artificial Intelligence*, pages 478–483, Edinburgh, 2005.

[48] H. Katsuno and A. Mendelzon. On the difference between updating a knowledge base and revising it. In *Proceedings of the 2nd International Conference on Principles of Knowledge Representation and Reasoning*. Morgan Kauffman, 1991.

[49] H. Katsuno and A. Mendelzon. Propositional knowledge base revision and minimal change. *Artificial Intelligence*, 52:263–294, 1991.

[50] S. Konieczny and R.P. Perez. A framework for iterated revision. *Journal of Applied Non-Classical Logics*, 10(3–4), 2000.

[51] S. Konieczny and R. Perez. Merging with integrity constraints. In *Proceedings of the 5th European Conference on Symbolic and Quantitative Approaches to Reasoning with Uncertainty (ECSQARU99), Lecture Notes in Artificial Intelligence*, vol. 1638, pages 233–244. Springer, Berlin, 1999.

[52] S. Konieczny, J. Lang, and P. Marquis. DA^2 merging operators. *Artificial Intelligence*, 157:49–79, 2004.

[53] R.Y.K. Lau. Belief revision for adaptive recommender agents in E-commerce. In *Proceedings of the 4th International Conference on Intelligent Data Engineering and Automated Learning (IDEAL'2003)*, Hong Kong, 2003.

[54] R.Y.K. Lau. Context-sensitive text mining and belief revision for intelligent information retrieval on the web. *Journal of Web Intelligence and Agent Systems*, 1(3–4):151–172, 2003.

[55] D. Lehmann. Belief revision, revised. In *Proceedings of the 14th International Joint Conference on Artificial Intelligence*, pages 1534–1540, Montreal, 1995.

[56] D. Lewis. *Counterfactuals*. Harvard University Press, Cambridge, MA, 1973.

[57] P. Liberatore and M. Schaerf. Arbitration (or how to merge knowledge bases). *IEEE Transactions on Knowledge and Data Engineering*, 10(1):76–90, 1998.

[58] S. Lindstrom. A semantic approach to nonmonotonic reasoning: Inference operations and choice. Technical report, Dept. of Philosophy, Uppsala University, 1991.

[59] S. Lindstrom and W. Rabinowicz. The Ramsey test revisited. In G. Crocco, L. Fariñas del Cerro, and A. Herzig, editors. *Conditionals from Philosophy to Computer Science*. Oxford University Press, Oxford, 1995.

[60] D. Makinson. On the status of the postulate of recovery in the logic of theory change. *Journal of Philosophical Logic*, 16:383–394, 1987.

[61] D. Makinson. Five faces of minimality. *Studia Logica*, 52:339–379, 1993.

[62] D. Makinson. Screened revision. *Theoria*, 63:14–23, 1997.

[63] D. Makinson. *Bridges from Classical to Nonmonotonic Logic. Texts in Computing*. King's College Publications, 2005.

[64] T. Meyer, J. Heidema, W. Labuschagne, and L. Leenen. Systematic withdrawal. *Journal of Philosophical Logic*, 31(5):415–443, 2002.

[65] A. Nayak. Foundational belief change. *Journal of Philosophical Logic*, 23:495–533, 1994.

[66] A. Nayak. Iterated belief change based on epistemic entrenchment. *Erkenntnis*, 41:353–390, 1994.

[67] A. Nayak, M. Pagnucco, and P. Peppas. Dynamic belief revision operators. *Artificial Intelligence*, 146:193–228, 2003.

[68] B. Nebel. Base revision operations and schemes: Semantics, representation, and complexity. In *Proceedings of the 11th European Conference on Artificial Intelligence*, pages 341–345. Wiley, August 1994.

[69] B. Nebel. How hard is it to revise a belief base? In D. Dubois and H. Prade, editors. *Belief Change, Handbook of Defeasible Reasoning and Uncertainty Management Systems*, vol. 3, pages 77–145. Kluwer Academic, 1998.

[70] M. Pagnucco. The role of abductive reasoning within the process of belief revision. PhD thesis, Department of Computer Science, University of Sydney, February 1996.

[71] R. Parikh. Beliefs, belief revision, and splitting languages. In J.L. Moss and M. de Rijke, editors, *Logic, Language, and Computation, CSLI Lecture Notes 96*, vol. 2, pages 266–268. CSLI Publications, 1999.

[72] P. Peppas, N. Foo, and W. Wobcke. Events as theory operators. In *Proceedings of the 1st World Conference on the Fundamentals of Artificial Intelligence*, pages 413–426, Angkor, Paris, 1991.

[73] P. Peppas and W. Wobcke. On the use of epistemic entrenchment in reasoning about action. In *Proceedings of the 10th European Conference on Artificial Intelligence (ECAI'92)*, pages 403–407. Wiley & Sons, Vienna, 1992.

[74] P. Peppas. Belief change and reasoning about action. PhD thesis, Basser Dept. of Computer Science, University of Sydney, 1994.

[75] P. Peppas and M. Williams. Constructive modelings for theory change. *Notre Dame Journal of Formal Logic*, 36(1):120–133, 1995.

[76] P. Peppas. Well behaved and multiple belief revision. In *Proceedings of the 12th European Conference on Artificial Intelligence (ECAI'96)*, pages 90–94, Budapest, 1996.

[77] P. Peppas, A. Nayak, M. Pagnucco, N. Foo, R. Kwok, and M. Prokopenko. Revision vs. update: Taking a closer look. In *Proceedings of the 12th European Conference on Artificial Intelligence (ECAI'96)*, pages 95–99. Wiley & Sons, Budapest, 1996.

[78] P. Peppas, N. Foo, and A. Nayak. Measuring similarity in belief revision. *Journal of Logic and Computation*, 10(4), 2000.

[79] P. Peppas. The limit assumption and multiple revision. *Journal of Logic and Computation*, 14(3):355–371, 2004.

[80] P. Peppas, S. Chopra, and N. Foo. Distance semantics for relevance-sensitive belief revision. In *Proceedings of the 9th International Conference on the Principles of Knowledge Representation and Reasoning (KR2004)*, Whistler, Canada, June 2004.

[81] P.Z. Revesz. On the semantics of theory change: Arbitration between old and new information. In *Proceedings of the 12th ACM SIGACT SIGMOD SIGART Symposium on Principles of Database Systems (PODS-93)*, pages 71–82, 1993.

[82] H. Rott. Conditionals and theory change: Revisions, expansions, and additions. *Synthese*, 81:91–113, 1989.

[83] H. Rott. Two methods of constructing contractions and revisions of knowledge systems. *Journal of Philosophical Logic*, 20:149–173, 1991.

[84] H. Rott. *A Nonmonotonic Conditional Logic for Belief Revision, The Logic of Theory Change. Lecture Notes in Artificial Intelligence*, vol. 465. Springer-Verlag, 1991.

[85] H. Rott. Belief contraction in the context of the general theory of rational choice. *Journal of Symbolic Logic*, 58, 1993.

[86] H. Rott and M. Pagnucco. Severe withdrawal (and recovery). *Journal of Philosophical Logic*, 28(5), 1999.

[87] H. Rott. *Change, Choice and Inference*. Oxford University Press, 2001.

[88] M. Ryan and P. Schobbens. Intertranslating counterfactuals and updates. *Journal of Logic, Language and Information*, 6(2):123–146, 1997.

[89] K. Satoh. Nonmonotonic reasoning by minimal belief revision. In *Proceedings of the International Conference on 5th Generation Computer Systems*. Springer, 1988.

[90] K. Schlechta, D. Lehmann, and M. Magidor. Distance semantics for belief revision. In *Proceedings of: Theoretical Aspects of Rationality and Knowledge (TARK VI)*, pages 137–145. Morgan Kaufmann, San Francisco, 1996.

[91] K. Schlechta. Non-prioritized belief revision based on distances between models. *Theoria*, 63:34–53, 1997.

[92] S. Shapiro, M. Pagnucco, Y. Lesperance, and H. Levesque. Iterated belief change in the situation calculus. In *Proceedings of the 10th International Conference on Principles of Knowledge Representation and Reasoning (KR'00)*. Morgan Kaufmann, 2000.

[93] W. Spohn. Ordinal conditional functions: A dynamic theory of epistemic states. In *Causation in Decision, Belief Change and Statistics*, vol. 2, pages 105–134. Kluwer Academic Publishers, 1988.

[94] D. Stavrinoudis, M. Xenos, P. Peppas, and D. Christodoulakis. Early estimation of user's perception of software quality. *Software Quality Journal*, 13(2):155–175, 2005.

[95] R. Wassermann. Resource bounded belief revision. *Erkenntnis*, 50, 1999.

[96] A. Weber. Updating propositional formulas. In *Expert Database Systems—Proceedings from the 1st International Conference*. Benjamin/Cummings, 1986.

[97] M.-A. Williams. Two operators for theory bases. In *Proceedings of the Australian Joint Conference on Artificial Intelligence*, pages 325–332. World Scientific, 1992.

[98] M.-A. Williams. Transmutations of knowledge systems. PhD thesis, University of Sydney, Australia, 1993.

[99] M.-A. Williams. On the logic of theory base change. In C. MacNish, D. Pearce, and L. Pereira, editors. *Logics in Artificial Intelligence—European Workshop JELIA'94*, pages 86–105. Springer-Verlag, 1994.

[100] M.-A. Williams. Transmutations of knowledge systems. In *Proceedings of the 4th International Conference on Principles of Knowledge Representation and Reasoning*, pages 619–629. Morgan Kaufmann, 1994.

[101] M.-A. Williams. Iterated theory base change: A computational model. In *Proceedings of the 14th International Joint Conference in Artificial Intelligence*, pages 1541–1547, 1995.

[102] M.-A. Williams. *Applications of Belief Revision. Lecture Notes in Computer Science*, vol. 1472. Springer, 1998.

[103] M.-A. Williams and A. Sims. SATEN: An object-oriented web-based revision and extraction engine. CoRR cs.AI/0003059, 2000.

[104] M. Winslett. Reasoning about action using a possible models approach. In *Proceedings of the 7th National (USA) Conference on Artificial Intelligence (AAAI'88)*, pages 89–93, 1988.

[105] D. Zhang. Belief revision by sets of sentences. *Journal of Computer Science and Technology*, 11(2):108–125, 1996.

[106] D. Zhang, S. Chen, W. Zhu, and H. Li. Nonmonotonic reasoning and multiple belief revision. In *Proceedings of the 15th International Joint Conference in Artificial Intelligence*, 1997.

[107] D. Zhang and N. Foo. Infinitary belief revision. *Journal of Philosophical Logic*, 30(6):525–570, 2001.

[108] D. Zhang. Properties of iterated multiple belief revision. In *Proceedings of the 7th International Conference on Logic Programming and Nonmonotonic Reasoning (LPNMR)*, pages 314–325. Springer, 2004.

[109] Y. Zhang and N.Y. Foo. Update with disjunctive information: From syntactical and semantical perspective. *Journal of Computational Intelligence*, 16(1), 2000.

[110] D. Zowghi, A. Ghose, and P. Peppas. A framework for reasoning about requirements evolution. In *Proceedings of the 4th Pacific Rim International Conference on Artificial Intelligence*. Springer-Verlag, Cairns, 1996.

Handbook of Knowledge Representation
Edited by F. van Harmelen, V. Lifschitz and B. Porter
© 2008 Elsevier B.V. All rights reserved
DOI: 10.1016/S1574-6526(07)03009-X

Chapter 9

Qualitative Modeling

Kenneth D. Forbus

9.1 Introduction

Qualitative modeling concerns representation and reasoning about continuous aspects of entities and systems in a symbolic, human-like manner. People who have never heard of differential equations successfully reason about the common sense world of quantities, motion, space, and time. They do so often in circumstances offering little information, using the ability to characterize broad categories of outcomes to ascertain what might happen. For many tasks this is enough: Knowing that a valuable fragile object might be pushed off a table is sufficient reason to rearrange things so that it cannot happen. For other tasks, knowing the possible outcomes suggests further analyses, perhaps involving more detailed models. For example, an engineer designing a tea warmer must keep the tea at a drinkable temperature, while not allowing it to boil. Reasoning directly with qualitative models can capture important behavior patterns, automatically producing descriptions that are closer to the level of what people call insights about system behavior, making them useful for science, engineering, education and decision-support. Capturing the representational and reasoning capabilities that enable robust reasoning about continuous systems is the goal of qualitative modeling.

Qualitative modeling is today most commonly referred to in the literature as qualitative reasoning, but we use qualitative modeling here to emphasize that the representational work in this area shared equal importance with work on reasoning techniques per se. (As will be seen below, the tradeoffs in them are deeply intertwined.) Qualitative physics has often been used for research in this area as well, since understanding physical systems has been a central focus of much of the work in the area. However, this term has become less popular as the applicability of these ideas to areas such as finance, ecology, and natural language semantics have been explored.

We start by outlining some of the key principles of qualitative modeling, and sketch the kinds of reasoning that is involved. This sketch provides the terminology and basis for the summaries of the key ideas that constitute the bulk of this chapter. Specifically, we summarize the key ideas in qualitative mathematics, ontologies for organizing qualitative knowledge, causality, compositional modeling, states and simulation, and qualitative spatial reasoning. We close with a few examples of applications of qualitative modeling, to illustrate how these ideas play out in real examples.

9.1.1 Key Principles

There are three key principles that govern qualitative modeling.

Discretization

Qualitative representations quantize continuous properties. Discretization provides two functions. First, it turns a continuous media into entities, things which can be represented and reasoned about symbolically. Second, it provides a means of abstraction: Instead of a continuous parameter taking on an infinity of possible values, for example, one might represent its value via its sign (i.e., is it positive, negative, or zero?), or via comparison with important other values. Abstraction is crucial because qualitative modeling needs to work in situation where few if any details are known. If a rubber ball is dropped onto a hard wood floor, we know that it will bounce, without knowing the specific coefficient of restitution for the particular rubber used in the ball nor knowing the details of the stiffness of the wood in the floor. Qualitative models are focused on inferring as much as possible from minimal information.

Relevance

The discretizations chosen for qualitative representations are imposed via constraints from both the nature of the system and the reasoning to be done about it. That is, qualitative values are constructed to be relevant for some class of tasks. In reasoning about the thermal properties of a fluid, for example, the freezing point and boiling point of that substance are natural comparisons to make, defining three ranges[1] for the value of temperature for that fluid. Similarly, the regions within which a vehicle of a given type might move represent a useful qualitative distinction for reasoning about an off-road driving situation. Within a specific region constituting a qualitative value, the behavior of the system is the same, with respect to some task-specific criteria. For example, if one is only concerned with knowing whether or not a fluid is solid, liquid, or gas, every specific numerical value of temperature between the freezing point and the boiling point are equivalent. But if one also wants the fluid to be drinkable, there are further subdivisions imposed by that task upon temperature.

Ambiguity

Working a high level of abstraction has a cost: There often is not enough information to ascertain which of several possible behaviors will occur. That is, the predictions made by qualitative models are often ambiguous. This makes qualitative models an ideal complement to traditional mathematical and numerical techniques. Traditional techniques require someone to first frame the problem, by identifying what phenomena are relevant and what categories of behaviors are conceivable. Mathematical models for the relevant phenomena can then be used to ascertain exactly what behaviors will

---

[1] Ignoring high pressure situations at which both the freezing point and the boiling point are the same, known as the triple point in thermodynamics.

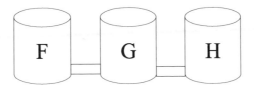

Figure 9.1: Three containers.

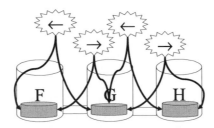

Figure 9.2: Model formulation leads to new conceptual entities, including processes.

occur, up to the resolution and accuracy of the models used. Qualitative models formalize this framing process, via automatic modeling algorithms to identify relevant phenomena and identify conceivable kinds of behaviors.

9.1.2 Overview of Basic Qualitative Reasoning

To ground our subsequent discussion, we outline how fundamental steps in qualitative reasoning fit together to construct a description of possible behaviors. We use the three containers example, shown in Fig. 9.1, as an illustration.

Model formulation

The first step in reasoning is to construct a model of the system or situation. The input description is typically called the *scenario*. The knowledge of the kinds of entities and phenomena that can occur are represented as *model fragments*, typically stored in a library called the *domain theory*. A model for the scenario is assembled from relevant model fragments via a reasoning process called *model formulation*. Model formulation uses both the contents of the scenario and constraints imposed by the task for which the model is being constructed.

In our example, the domain theory might include model fragments for describing the properties of pieces of liquid within a container, and the possibilities of flows between them, if the pipes are open. We depict instances of these entities graphically in Fig. 9.2, using pieces of water for the contained liquids and starbursts for the possible flows that might, depending on circumstances, occur.

Elaborating a qualitative state

The scenario model consists of a set of model fragments, representing properties and relationships that may or may not hold at any given time. The set of entities that are

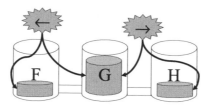

Figure 9.3: Active processes given assumed initial levels.

held to exist by the model and what parameters they have are defined by the set of active model fragments. The qualitative values of the parameters are typically only partially constrained by the set of active model fragments. A *qualitative state* is defined by the set of active model fragments plus the qualitative values for all of the parameters of the system.

If the scenario describes some specific initial condition, then once a scenario model has been constructed one or more qualitative states describing that scenario can be derived. Notice that there can be more than one qualitative state describing the scenario because the initial scenario description might be incomplete. This is often the first step in understanding a complex system, for monitoring or diagnosis. The causality imposed by qualitative models can be important, since achieving desired states and avoiding undesirable states requires tracing back through the antecedents for the state to manipulable aspects of the system. For example, it is the low level of fuel in the tank that causes a warning light in a car to come on; to extinguish the warning light requires adding fuel to the tank.

Returning to our running example, suppose the level of water is higher in G than it is in either F or H. Then, assuming the pipes are open, there will be two instances of water flows, representing water leaving G, as shown in Fig. 9.3. While this example looks simple, it involves some surprising subtleties. For example, our inference that water is flowing out of G rests on the heights of the bottoms of the containers all being the same: if H were much higher, its pressure would be higher and flow would go in the reverse direction in that path. If we modeled gasses in the containers and they were closed, then we would have to take their contribution to the pressure into account. The ability to reason about different modeling assumptions is discussed below.

Qualitative simulation

Some qualitative states can last forever, but most do not. Qualitative simulation identifies what states can happen next. This process can be applied recursively, to derive all of the states that can follow from a given initial qualitative state. Generating all possible categories of behaviors is called *envisioning*. For very simple systems envisioning can be polynomial in the complexity of the qualitative spatial model used, but in general it is exponential in the number of constituents of the qualitative state. When landmark introduction is used, the number of qualitative states can be infinite even for simple systems. This means that the choice of qualitative representations and what is needed in terms of predictions must be considered carefully when designing reasoning systems for a specific task.

Returning one last time to our three containers: Fig. 9.4 summarizes the envisionment for the situation in Fig. 9.3. Small arrows indicate liquid flows inside a state

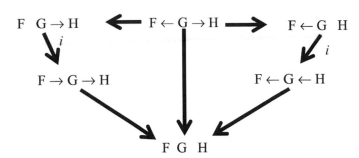

Figure 9.4: An envisionment for the three containers situation, starting from the qualitative state of Fig. 9.3.

between two containers, big arrows indicate transitions. The state in the middle represents the qualitative state depicted in Fig. 9.3.

Notice that we actually do not know which of the two flows might stop first. Although the pipes have been drawn the same size, we do not know if one of them is partially clogged, for example. So there are three possible next states. Transitions marked with an "i" occur in an instant, whereas all others require an interval of time to occur. Thus we can see that, if either flow stops before the other, it will then reverse, stopping only when the entire system reaches equilibrium (the bottom state). From the fact that there are transitions into this state and no transitions out, we can conclude that this state will last forever, unless something else disturbs the system.

9.2 Qualitative Mathematics

Qualitative mathematics formalizes notions of quantity and relationships at a more abstract level of detail than mathematics as traditionally used in science and engineering. While causality is intimately linked with qualitative mathematics in some systems of qualitative modeling, this is not universal and so causality is discussed later.

9.2.1 Quantities

Qualitative notions of value

There is a surprising range of qualitative representations for continuous one-dimensional parameters. Any account of qualitative value must address three issues:

1. What is the set of values used? For most traditional models, parameters take on real values (i.e., elements of $\Re$) or floating point approximations thereof. Most qualitative value systems identify a finite set of values. In some systems the set of values is described statically, while in others the set of values varies dynamically, providing variable precision.

2. How can they be reasoned with? Traditional values can be plugged into equations and used to derive new values. Most qualitative systems support some form of propagation of value information through qualitative relationships, enabling information about one part of a system to be used to infer information about other parts. Some qualitative systems support more equation-like

algebraic manipulations, although the set of allowable manipulations is more restricted due to the nature of qualitative values [110].

3. How can they be generated from other sources of information? Often scenario descriptions are automatically derived from sensor data or other noisy, limited-accuracy numerical information. Techniques used for this include simple range calculations, fuzzy logic [22, 6], and trendline analyses [30].

The status abstraction   The simplest notion of qualitative value is simply describing a parameter as normal/abnormal, the *status abstraction* developed by Abbott [1] to support diagnosis of aircraft engine failures and subsequently used in photocopier modeling [5]. Reasoning with such values is via propagation through a qualitative model of the system, and the values themselves are computed via tables that describe ranges of values for particular sensors that are considered nominal.

Signs   Almost as simple is the sign algebra developed by de Kleer and Brown [26], where parameters are characterized as positive (+), negative, (−), or zero (0). The sign algebra is the simplest system that enables continuity constraints to be applied: A qualitative value cannot jump directly from + to −, or from − to +, without first going through 0. When applied to derivatives, it provides a natural formal expression for the intuitive idea of a parameter either being increasing, decreasing, or remaining constant. By judicious introduction of quantities during model formulation, a surprisingly wide range of systems can be modeled with this algebra. For example, if freezing can be ignored the temperature of a fluid could be modeled by the difference of its temperature with the boiling temperature, so that − corresponded to liquid and + corresponded to gas.

Signs also make concrete the central role of ambiguity in qualitative models. Consider the equation

$$[x] + [y] = [z],$$

where $[a]$ means "the qualitative value of a". (This is an example of a *confluence* [25].) If we know that x and y are +, then we know that z must be + as well. However, if we know that $[x]$ is + and $[y]$ is −, then we can say nothing about $[z]$—whether it is +, −, or 0 depends on the relative magnitude of x and y. This ambiguity has been handled in two different ways in qualitative sign algebras. One way is to introduce a new value, often labeled ?, to explicitly represent ambiguity. This provides a compact representation of the ambiguity which can then be propagated through the rest of the system. The other way is to introduce branching, characterizing the ambiguity either by creating alternate models corresponding to combinations of different values, or carrying through the model complex labels representing the possibilities, in an ATMS-like fashion [27].

Finite symbolic value systems   Early efforts to characterize numerical values in AI often focused on describing parameters in terms of a small number of terms, such as `high`, `medium`, or `low`, but without much consideration about how to reason with such systems or how to construct them from numerical parameters. Defining consistent algebras for combining such values can be tricky: `high` + `high` clearly equals high, but does medium + low equal medium or high? Whatever system of combination is chosen must be consistent with how the qualitative values are computed from underlying information, which can be tricky. Nevertheless, such systems have important uses. For example, Guerrin [56] observes that ecology researchers gathering data have particular discretizations of this form that they find natural, and described how to create algebras that map between different resolution finite symbolic value systems. Similarly, a number of researchers have found adapting the fuzzy logic notion of overlapping values in qualitative representations to be valuable (cf. [101, 10]).

Expressiveness is one side of a tradeoff for the choice of qualitative value representation. The other side is tractability. When constructing qualitative states using parameters whose values are represented as signs, each parameter introduces three (or four, if there is an explicit ambiguity value) potential choices. If there are N parameters and M possible qualitative values for a parameter, then there are M^N possible states that are distinguished by parameter values. There are typically additional choices involved in defining states, including status of model fragments and the truth of external statements, as discussed below. Moreover, the laws governing system behavior typically rule out the vast majority of these possible states. But the point remains true: The more expressive the qualitative value representation, the less tractable qualitative simulation tends to become.

Quantity spaces, limit points, and landmarks

One limitation of the schemes outlined so far is that they have particular fixed levels of resolution. Sometimes the set of distinctions to be drawn needs to change dynamically, during the course of reasoning. Typically this happens due to some comparison between two values becoming relevant that could not have been predicted before reasoning began. Returning to fluid temperature, one might be able to determine that for a specific task, either the boiling point, the freezing point, or both might be relevant for that task, and define ranges accordingly. However, if the fluid is in contact with multiple objects (directly or indirectly), there are possible heat flows to be considered. Heat flows are conditioned on temperature differences between the entities involved. The relevant temperatures to compare against are therefore determined also by the heat flows that the fluid can potentially participate in. Consider, for example, planning the cooking of a complex meal. Many dishes will be brought to various temperatures by a variety of means, and solids and fluids placed in different locations and combined in a variety of ways. It is hard to see how a fixed vocabulary symbolic algebra could be constructed for this situation that would be small enough to be tractable. This is why many qualitative modeling systems use dynamic resolution value representations.

The *quantity space* representation for a quantity Q defines the value of Q in terms of ordinal relationships with a set of other quantities, the *limit points* for that quantity space [43]. The set of limit points is determined by what comparisons are relevant for the current task. In some qualitative modeling systems (e.g., QSIM [74, 75], GARP [13], the set of limit points is determined by the modeler. In others (e.g., qualitative process theory [43]), limit points are derived automatically on the basis of the model fragments that have been created and reasoning about the interactions in the model. For example, zero is always a limit point in the quantity space for derivatives, since the relationship of the derivative to this value determines the important property of whether a value is increasing, decreasing, or constant (*D*s values, in QP theory).

Quantity spaces can be partially ordered, which is useful for explicitly representing partial states of knowledge. One might know when cooking, for example, that both the sautéed onions and the sauce are hotter than room temperature, but may not know their relative temperatures when combining them. A *value space* is a totally ordered quantity space. Imposing a total order can be useful for qualitative simulation algorithms, since it reduces one source of ambiguity (and hence possible branching) and allows graph-like depictions of parameter values to be created for visualization. A value space with N limit points is essentially a $2N + 1$ finite symbolic algebra, with the symbols being the specific limit points and the regions above, below, and between them.

Another source of potential comparisons are *landmark values*, or *landmarks*. A landmark is a fixed (although typically unknown) numerical value. Some qualitative modeling systems (notably QSIM) introduce landmark values dynamically. For example, when a partially elastic ball bounces, energy is lost with each collision, and the maximum height it reaches on each successive bounce decreases each time. Each such maximum height can be represented as a landmark value, and the fact that the system is losing energy can be inferred from the fact that each subsequent landmark value is smaller than the previous one. It is important to note that all landmark values are limit points, but not all limit points are landmark values. All landmark values are limit points because the newly introduced distinction is used to carve up future states: Otherwise, it would not be useful to introduce them. But limit points need not be defined in terms of specific fixed values, as the temperatures in the cooking example illustrates. One can, for example, infer that two temperatures can become equal without introducing a new entity to represent what that equilibrium temperature is.

The tradeoff with landmark introduction is, again, expressiveness versus tractability. With landmark introduction, whether a system is oscillating steadily, decaying, or growing via positive feedback can be "read off" directly by comparing subsequent landmarks, in a correct qualitative simulation. However, the number of possible states grows from finite to infinite, since between two landmarks one can always introduce another one.[2] Moreover, formulating the laws governing a system so that the landmarks produced are always correct can be problematic, as discussed below.

Interval arithmetic and tolerances

A more quantitative method of providing dynamic resolution is to put numerical constraints on values. In interval arithmetic, values are represented as closed intervals whose end points are specified numerically. In tolerances, values are described as a numerical value plus a numerical tolerance, essentially a small interval around the given value within which the real value can be found. There are well-known problems with interval arithmetic, e.g., given $Z = X/Y$, with $X = [1, 2]$ and $Y = [-1, 1]$, then $Z = \{[-\infty, -1], [1, \infty]\}$. However, progress in this area (cf. [61]) may change how practical it is.

Order of magnitude representations

Sometimes effects can be ignored because they are negligible compared to others. For example, the level of water lost through evaporation can safely be ignored when com-

---

[2]It might even be possible to construct the reals over an interval using landmark introduction, via a method analogous to Dedekind cuts.

puting how fast the level of water is rising during a flood in a city. Such intuitions can be formalized through *order of magnitude* representations. Two distinct strategies have been used for formalizing order of magnitude knowledge. *Absolute* order of magnitude representations partition the reals into distinct equivalence classes. For example, the effect of evaporation on the water level in New Orleans would be represented in a Q-Algebra [105] as Negative Small, while the water pouring in through the levee would be represented as Positive Large. The relationships between these values would enable a reasoner to determine that the net effect will be an increase of water, all else being equal. *Relative* order of magnitude representations use a set of relationships to impose partitions dynamically. For example, in Raiman's [93] FOG, one would state that the rate of evaporation ≪ rate of inflow from levee, where ≪ is read "is negligible compared to", which would license ignoring the effect of evaporation while flooding is occurring. As with other kinds of value-based versus relation-based representation schemes, there are circumstances where each is more natural, and translations between them exist [106].

9.2.2 Functions and Relationships

Relationships between quantities express constraints imposed by the world, and describe the dynamics of a system. Just as qualitative values can be viewed as levels of abstraction over the underlying reals, qualitative mathematical relationships can be viewed as abstractions over the relationships of traditional mathematics. As before, the art is in selecting a level of representation that is appropriate for a given task, both in terms of the information available and in terms of the reasoning required.

In traditional mathematics, there is a standard distinction between algebraic relationships and integral or differential relationships. The former suffice for static situations, the latter are required for describing systems that change over time. Every modeling system that handles continuous dynamical systems always has both types of relationships, although the particular methods for handling them vary. We discuss each in turn, after focusing on compositionality.

Importance of compositionality

A hallmark of qualitative reasoning is that it handles partial information about mathematical relationships. This provides a form of *elaboration tolerance* [82]. The main tool for compositionality is defining relational primitives that express partial information about an underlying relationship, such as the use of influences in QP theory. This is the same technique used in traditional mathematics when, for instance, one uses addition to combine effects. New terms representing additional factors to include can be added when the set of models considered to be relevant changes, or correction terms can be added when models are found to be inadequate. Qualitative representations take these practices further, providing more levels of partial information, and formalizing the reasoning involved. Notice that this requires *non-monotonic reasoning*, since adding information about a relationship can change previous conclusions drawn using it.

For example, consider again reasoning about a flood. The rate of water flowing in through a breached levee will depend on a number of factors, in complex ways. There is the level of water behind the levee, the size and shape of the holes and/or gaps, and the level of water already in the city to be considered, for instance, among others. Common sense tells us some relationships already: The higher the level of water behind the levee, the faster the rate of inflow. Similarly, water will flow faster through a larger gap than a smaller one. Both of these everyday statements are constraints on the rate of water flow, which, together with the other factors, can be used to construct a function that will allow us to reason about how changes in these parameters will affect the rate of water flowing into the city. In circumstances like these, quantities are not irrelevant—if the levees had held, evacuation would not have been necessary—but it is simply not possible to create a detailed model of the situation that would allow an accurate, detailed quantitative prediction of what will happen over time. Knowing that there could be a problem, and understanding what data should be gathered to figure out how bad it is, is an essential service that qualitative models provide, formalizing what is now done intuitively and informally.

Algebraic relationships

Monotonic functional relationships play a special role in qualitative reasoning because they are the weakest relationship that enables the propagation of signs of derivatives. For example, the *qualitative proportionality* of QP theory is defined as

$$A \propto_{Q^+} B \equiv \exists f | A = f(\ldots, B, \ldots) \wedge f \text{ is increasing monotonic in } B$$

$\propto_{Q^-}$ is the same, except that f in that case is decreasing monotonic in B. (There is also a causal interpretation which is part of the definition, described in the section on causality below.) If we know that B is increasing, then, all else being equal, we know that A must be increasing. The "all else being equal" requires a closed-world assumption over the set of possible qualitative proportionalities constraining A. Such closed-world assumptions are useful for two reasons. First, they enable us to proceed with partial information. Second, if our conclusions turn out to be wrong, closed-world assumptions can be re-examined for backtracking. The function M^+, defined in [74], is similar, except that it is presumed that its arguments are the only inputs.

There is no weaker description of the relationship between two parameters that licenses the inference that "if B goes up, then A must go up". Thus monotonic functions provide an abstraction that covers a wide range of more concrete mathematical expressions, assuming that their range of validity is appropriately scoped. Such scoping is carried out in qualitative modeling systems via *model fragments* that provide explicit conditions of applicability, as discussed below.

There are times when one needs more details in combining parameters. In keeping with the goal of compositionality, the *compositional modeling language* (CML; [9]) defines compositional operators C^+, C^-, C^*, and $C/$, all of which are compositional in the same way that qualitative proportionalities are, e.g., one might state a one-dimensional form of Newton's Second Law as

$$C^*(F, M) \wedge C/(F, A)$$

Integral/differential relationships

To describe changes over time requires expressing relationships involving derivatives. This can be done via an explicit relationship involving derivatives. For example, the confluence [26]

$$\partial W + \partial F - \partial D = 0$$

describes how the changes in the amount of flood water in the city (W), water flooding in (F), and water flowing out through storm drains (D) might be related in a model of flooding. The confluence derivative relationship (∂) is defined as

$$\partial Q \equiv [dQ/dt], \text{ i.e., the qualitative value of the time-derivative of } Q$$

If, for example, the water flooding in (F) increases while the outflow (D) remains constant, then the water level in the city must be increasing. QP theory uses more compositional primitives to achieve the same end, through the I^+ and I^- relationships:

$$I^+(A, B) \equiv dA/dt = \cdots + B + \cdots$$

for I^-, B is a negative term in the sum. This is similar to the definition of qualitative proportionality, but differs in two important ways. First, what is constrained is the time derivative of A, not A itself. Second, the combinator is addition, rather than being unspecified. This is important because it enables knowledge of relative rates to determine the existence of dynamic equilibria. For example,

$$I^+(W, F) \wedge I^-(W, D)$$

enables us to deduce that, if D were large enough, then the city would never flood.

Tradeoffs in qualitative mathematics systems

The relative sparseness of relationship modeling choices compared to modeling choices for quantities may seem surprising. Fundamentally, the reason is that the set of analytic functions in mathematics is huge: Almost all of the useful abstractions, except for the very weakest relationships, may have already been explored by traditional mathematics.

An important question to ask is, how complete are qualitative representations relative to ordinary differential equations? By appropriate scoping, so that (mathematically) non-monotonic functions are decomposed into monotonic segments, one can create a qualitative differential equation (QDE) for any ordinary differential equation, as discussed in [75].

9.3 Ontology

Modeling systems based on traditional mathematics tend to be informal about ontological issues. Informal decisions, based on experience with the world as well as professional expertise, are used to decide what entities should be included in a situation, what phenomena are relevant, and what simplifications are sensible. One goal of qualitative modeling is to make such tacit knowledge explicit, providing formalisms that can be used for automating (either fully or partially, depending on task) the modeling process itself. For some applications, automated modeling is not necessary, and systems of qualitative mathematical equations can be constructed to do useful work, as long as the task and situations they are used in are carefully circumscribed. However, both scientifically and as a practical matter, automated modeling is of great interest. For example, in educational applications, learners typically do not have the expertise to formulate models themselves, so careful model formulation (or selection) can be essential.

There are three ontologies commonly used in qualitative modeling: *components*, *processes*, and *fields*. We discuss each in turn.

9.3.1   Component Ontologies

The component ontology is a generalization of the idea of analog electronic circuits [26]. That is, a system is considered to be a network of components. Each type of component has a defined set of terminals that can be used to connect it to others, and the only possible interactions are through such connections. Consider, for example, the circuit shown in Fig. 9.5. When the input voltage Vin rises, it causes more current to flow between the base and emitter of the transistor. This small increase of current flow causes a much larger flow between the collector and the emitter, which produces a larger voltage swing at the output Vout (which is why transistors are used as amplifiers). Note that this explanation was created by tracing through the laws associated with components, and propagating effects through their connections. In the physical world, under some conditions other kinds of interactions matter: at high frequencies shapes and distances in physical layouts matter, and at high power thermal effects must be taken into account. But for many kinds of analyses, networks of components provide an excellent way of organizing models.

While analog electronics is the paradigmatic domain for the component ontology, component models have been used in other domains, such as VLSI and chemical engineering [14]. Sometimes mixed ontologies, combining processes with components, is required (e.g., engineering thermodynamics, see [52]). In general, component models work best when the kinds of interactions there can be between entities remain relatively fixed. Modeling motion in a three-dimensional world, for example, would be an unnatural domain to use a component ontology for, since the "network" changes frequently. Component models are also poor choices when the set of entities that exists can change frequently, e.g., agent-level modeling of an ecosystem.

Bond graphs are an important category of component ontology. Structurally, bond graphs were developed as a generalization of the idea of chemical bonds, where the "molecules" become instances of components, drawn from a small library of possible types. Bond graphs have been used in a wide variety of engineering domains, and are

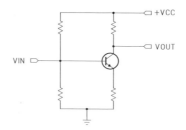

Figure 9.5: A simple electronic circuit.

attractive because of its well-worked out methodology for constructing models, most if not all aspects of which appear as applicable to qualitative modeling as to traditional modeling, although this is still being explored (cf. [83]).

9.3.2 Process Ontologies

In process ontologies (cf. [43]), processes are treated as a distinct category of entity from the other kinds of objects in the world. Processes arise from the relationships and properties of those objects, e.g., an instance of liquid flow can occur when two contained liquids are connected by an open path and the pressure of one of them is higher than the other. Note that the process is not the same as the pattern of its effects, since multiple processes can affect the same parameters. Consider a house that is losing heat to the snow outside while also being heated by its furnace inside. Whether the house is getting hotter, colder, or remains steady, as long as it is warmer than its surroundings, the heat flow out of it will continue. Thus the need to reason about multiple effects requires distinguishing a process from the outcomes it can cause.

Here is an example of a heat flow process:

```
(defmodelfragment heat-flow
  :subclass-of (physical-process)
  :participants ((the-src :type thermal-physob)
                 (the-dst :type thermal-physob)
                 (the-path :type heat-path
                    :constraints ((heat-connection
                                       the-path the-src the-dst))))
  :conditions ((heat-aligned the-path)
               (> (temperature the-src) (temperature the-dst)))
  :quantities ((heat-flow-rate :type heat-flow-rate))
  :consequences ((q= heat-flow-rate
                      (- (temperature the-src)
                         (temperature the-dst)))
                 (i- (heat the-src) heat-flow-rate)
                 (i+ (heat the-dst) heat-flow-rate)))
```

The participants represent the formal parameters of this type of process, with the type information and constraints providing sufficient conditions for deriving the existence of an instance of this type of process. Existence is not the same as acting: One can have a window that is no longer leaking heat, for example, because one has temporarily sealed it with plastic (thus making heat-aligned false). Reasoning about existence provides a useful intermediate stage in constructing explanations: Process instances that exist become candidates for actually doing something. An instance of a process is *active* when its conditions hold, in this case, that the temperature of the source (the-src) is higher than that of the destination (the-dst). The consequences hold only when it is active, here, that a heat flow rate, which depends on the temperature differential, acts to increase the heat of the destination and decrease the heat of the source. One can model a home heating system, for example, in terms of processes such as heat flow, liquid or gas flow, pumping, etc. (depending on the type of heating system).

Process ontologies are a natural fit to most everyday physical phenomena. Indeed, there is evidence suggesting that the notions of flow and transformations that are often encoded into natural language seem to be reasonably well described using processes [77]. However, they also have disadvantages: They require reasoning about the relationship between objects to automatically derive the existence of processes, and the dynamic nature of existence supported by the process ontology creates additional complexities in the reasoning it requires.

9.3.3 Field Ontologies

Both component and process ontologies are forms of what are called *lumped parameter* models. Many important phenomena, however, such as weather patterns and phase portraits, are spatially distributed, and cannot be understood without reasoning about that spatial structure. Field ontologies represent that structure by dividing space into regions where some parameter of interest takes on qualitatively equivalent values. This space can be physical space, e.g., for reasoning about heat transfer or meteorology, or phase space, e.g., for reasoning about dynamics, or configuration space, e.g., for reasoning about mechanical systems. For example, Yip [111] showed that qualitative reasoning about regions in phase space could lead to the automatic generation of publication-quality research results in a branch of fluid dynamics, and Bradley [12] showed that such representations could be used in designing control systems that exploit chaos to gain efficiency.

Qualitative reasoning in this ontology typically uses representations and algorithms drawn from computer vision and computational geometry to construct symbolic representations of numerical data. The most general framework, the *Spatial Aggregation Language* [3], describes the process of moving from visual representations to symbolic representations in a recursive manner. This enables lower-level symbolic constructions that still contain numerical properties (e.g., constructing iso-bar segments in weather data, see [63]) to give rise to higher-level patterns in subsequent analyses (e.g., automatically identifying pressure troughs by reasoning over the iso-bar segments).

While the state of the art in qualitative analysis using field ontologies is quite advanced, relatively little work has been done to determine the properties of qualitative simulation within this ontology. The only work to date is that of Lundell [79], who developed a spatially distributed notion of process and formulated spatial constraints for governing the process of deriving changes in regions over time. This is an area that could greatly repay further investigation.

9.4 Causality

Causality tends to be important in qualitative models because they are often formulated for tasks that involve figuring out how to change the world, such as design, monitoring, and diagnosis. The central role of causality in human explanations means that effective qualitative models for explanatory and educational purposes must be compatible with human notions of causality. The exploration of causality in complex technical domains has led to the development of more sophisticated accounts of causality in continuous systems than found in other areas of cognitive science. For example, a surprising number of models still maintain as a core constraint (inherited from classical philosophy) that a cause must always precede an effect. Empirically, people are quite happy to use causality to describe relationships that are algebraic in form (i.e., the increase in heat causes an increase in temperature, which in turn causes an increase in pressure), and do not find the simultaneity between cause and effect alarming.

There are two basic kinds of causal accounts used in qualitative modeling, *structural* and *dynamical*. We discuss each in turn.

Structural accounts of causality endow particular representational primitives with causal powers. For example, in QP theory, the *sole mechanism assumption* is that physical processes are ultimately the only source of causal changes in purely dynamical systems. These causal effects are propagated through direct influences, and then through qualitative proportionalities (which are sometimes called *indirect influences* for this reason). For example, a heat flow process directly influences the internal energy of the source and destination. If nothing else is occurring, then, since the temperatures of the source and destination are qualitatively proportional to the internal energy (aka heat, in everyday parlance) in any reasonable model, this causes the temperature of the destination to rise and the temperature of the source to fall.

In structural accounts, the relationships in qualitative mathematics are given specific causal interpretations. For example, in QP theory,

$I^{+}(A, B)$: B being non-zero causes A to increase, all else being equal.

$A \propto_{Q+} B$: B increasing causes A to increase, all else being equal.

This simplifies explanation generation, since describing causality within a state can be done by identifying which processes are active, describing how they cause changes to the directly influenced parameters, and then how those changes cause in turn changes in the rest of the system.

The alternative to a structural causality account is to dynamically derive casual structure. This requires choosing a place to start, identifying the beginning of the causal chain. In confluences, this is done by providing an input to the system, and viewing all changes as being caused by the effects of that input [26]. In *causal ordering*, exogenous variables are viewed as the start of causal chains, and a set of causal relationships is found by analyzing the set of (qualitative or quantitative) algebraic equations governing the system [65].

Both accounts of causal reasoning are compatible with different aspects of human causal reasoning. In many domains, causal relationships are strongly directional. Acceleration causes changes in velocity, and changes in internal energy always cause changes in temperature, and never the other way around, for example. By contrast, in an input-driven scheme, the order chosen for propagation of change can influence the direction of causality about different instances of the same component. For example, in one part of a causal explanation of the effects of a change on an analog electronic circuit, an increase in voltage across a resistor might cause the current through it to increase, whereas in another part of the same circuit, an increase in current through a resistor could cause an increase in voltage across it. Empirically, it seems most human mental models involve strongly directed causality, with analog electronics being an exceptional case. How many other domains involve reversible causality is an open question at this writing. It is important to note that strongly directed causality does not necessitate a structural account. For example, if the set of exogenous parameters governing a system being modeled through causal ordering is the same as the union of the directly influenced and uninfluenced parameters in a QP model of a system, the causal stories produced by the systems are likely to be very similar, assuming equivalent domain theories.

So far we have focused on within-state causal explanations. Across-state causal explanations describe why transitions between states occur. For example, "the increasing temperature of the water in the kettle reached its boiling point, causing it to boil." As noted above, changes in a quantity's relationships with its limit points often corresponds to a change in whether or not some model fragment is active, and hence a change in qualitative state. Thus the within-state changes that lead to the signs of derivatives involved in the comparison that changed, plus the change in the comparison itself, are viewed as the cause of the state change. (In general, there can be more than one comparison changing at once.) As always with causal reasoning, there is an implicit set of conditions that could negate it—for example, some other change might have occurred first if rates were different. Philosophically, making a distinction between these two kinds of conditions has proven difficult, but the computational grounds provided by this account provide, at least for this category of example, a clear distinction between foreground and background information that seems to match human causal explanations well.

It should be noted that this notion of causality is similar in some respects to that used by minimal-model change action frameworks (cf. [16]), in that they both provide ontological reasons for distinguishing some aspects of a situation as being more causally primitive than others, and use minimal-change heuristics (e.g., continuity in qualitative modeling) to derive potential next states. They are significantly different than probability-based accounts (cf. [91]), which are attempting to formalize conditions for inferring causal relations based on statistical information.

9.5   Compositional Modeling

Modeling is typically considered an art. One goal of qualitative modeling is to turn it into more of a science, by formalizing the process of constructing models, called *model formulation*. This involves reasoning about the entities and relationships between them in the system being modeled, the properties of the task for which the model is being constructed, and the knowledge available for modeling.

The primary methodology developed for this is *compositional modeling* [37]. The basic idea is that the knowledge available for modeling, the *domain theory*, includes a collection of *model fragments*. A model fragment is a piece of knowledge about how to model a particular entity or relationships. For example, suppose we are constructing a model of the flooding of New Orleans. One important event was a breach in the levees, which created a fluid path from the rising floodwaters to the city. The rate of flow through this path depends on a variety of factors, one of which can be considered as the fluid conductance of the path. The dependence on fluid conductance on geometry might be described as follows:

```
(defmodelfragment fluid-path-geometric-properties
 :participants ((path :type fluid-path))
 :conditions ((unblocked path))
 :consequences ((qprop (fluid-conductance path) (size path))
                (qprop- (fluid-conductance path) (length path))))
```

That is, the bigger the breach, the more fluid can potentially flow. But how should size be modeled? Perhaps that is something which can directly be ascertained from available data. But if not, it must be calculated in terms of other properties. Which properties should be used will depend on the particulars of the situation:

```
(defmodelfragment 2D-size-rectangular-estimate
  :participants ((entity :type 2D-surface))
  :conditions ((approximately-rectangular-2D-projection entity))
  :consequences ((= (size entity) (* (width entity)
                                     (height entity))))))
```

Notice that both qualitative and quantitative information can be specified in model fragments. The compositional nature of qualitative mathematics means that models appropriate for particular purposes can be assembled out of a number of such fragments, by model formulation algorithms, as described below.

One of the key problems in modeling is knowing what to include and what not to include. Quantum mechanics, for instance, is not terribly useful when considering whether or not a city might be flooded. What level of detail is relevant depends on the particular question being asked: Knowing that levees might be breached depends on estimates of how much water will build up and their state of repair, knowing when that might happen depends on estimating how quickly water is building up, and knowing where that might happen depends on knowing the detailed spatial configurations involved. Most systems can be modeled at multiple levels of detail, and from different perspectives. The information needed to make such choices is represented by explicit *modeling assumptions* and relationships among them. An important kind of relationship are *assumption classes*. An assumption class is a mutually exclusive, collectively exhaustive set of modeling alternatives for something. A model is coherent only if it includes a choice from every valid assumption class. For example,

```
(defAssumptionClass (fluid-path ?obj)
  ((consider (abstract-fluid-path ?obj))
   (consider (geometric-fluid-path ?obj))))
```

That is, for any fluid path, one should either consider its geometry or not. Choosing to consider its geometry, in turn, can lead to new assumption classes being relevant, e.g.,

```
(defAssumptionClass (geometric-fluid-path ?obj)
  ((consider (approximately-rectangular-2D-projection ?obj))
   (consider (approximately-circular-2D-projection ?obj))
   (consider (irregular-shaped-2D-projection ?obj)))
```

Notice that one of the modeling assumptions in this assumption class is the condition for the rectangular size estimation model fragment introduced above. In addition to such explicit dependencies, some compositional modeling languages define the semantics of model fragments in terms of an implicit negation, i.e., given a potential instance of a model fragment MF, it can only be instantiated if one can derive (consider MF) and/or not derive a fact of the form (ignore MF).

9.5.1   Model Formulation Algorithms

Model formulation algorithms can be characterized as follows. Given

- A domain theory DT, consisting of a set of model fragments, assumption classes, and other axioms,

- A structural description SD, consisting of a set of entities and statements about them describing the structure of the system to be modeled,

- A query Q, which is a question about some aspect of the system

The output is a coherent model M such that some reasoning engine operating over M can derive a sufficiently accurate answer to Q. By coherent, we mean that the modeling choices throughout M are consistent with each other. For example, in thinking about a home heating system, one might choose to ignore properties of the system's working fluid in a question about overall thermal capacity, but then it would not make sense to include in M the relief valve used in the boiler. Any such model is called an *adequate* model. Typically there can be more than one adequate model, but in general, the more complex a model is, the more costly it is to compute with it. (Contrast, for instance, a back of the envelope calculation of a home heating system's efficiency with a computational fluid dynamics simulation of its operation over an entire winter.) Thus there is great interest in finding the *simplest* adequate model.

The original algorithm of Falkenhainer and Forbus [37] worked in two passes. First, it instantiated all of the relevant constraints by instantiating every potentially relevant model fragment from DT on SD. By using an assumption-based truth maintenance system, all sets of assumptions which would provide a model constraining the terms in Q were found. Coherence was enforced by axioms relating modeling constraints, e.g.,

```
(forAll ?sys
   (implies (and (system ?sys) (consider (black-box ?sys)))
            (forAll ?sub (implies (subsystem ?sub ?sys)
                                  (not (consider ?sub))))))
```

That is, if one is treating a system as a black box, none of its subsystems should be included in M. It was assumed that the smallest set of assumptions yielded the simplest model. The initial set of propositions were then thrown away, and only the relevant subset reinstantiated to produce M. While simple to implement, the exponential nature of the ATMS computations made it quite inefficient for large systems.

The most efficient model formulation algorithm was developed by Nayak [87], which operates in polynomial time. This algorithm is based on three assumptions:

1. Choices made in one assumption class cannot depend on choices made in others.

2. Choices in an assumption class can be partially ordered with regard to simplicity.

3. The optimality condition can be weakened from finding the simplest model to finding a simplest model.

Search for a model proceeds by walking up each assumption class implies by SD, starting with a simplest choice from each, and moving upwards until an adequate model is reached. Since the choices are independent, there is no need for backtracking due to found inconsistencies. The weaker optimality constraint means that the set of simplest satisfactory models is a surface partitioning the adequate from inadequate models, and any point on this surface is satisfactory by assumption, hence eliminating the need to optimize simplicity.

An important property of complex systems is that they typically incorporate phenomena that operate at multiple time-scales. For most of the lifetime of a building, for example, most of the interesting changes that happen to a building are best described in terms of months, years, and decades, rather than microseconds or millennia. For a particular query Q, phenomena that operate at faster time-scales can be replaced by functional relationships and phenomena that operate at slower time-scales can essentially be ignored. Rickel and Porter [95, 96] demonstrate how to use this insight in model formulation. Since the form of Q they focus on is explaining changes in a parameter (an important task for intelligent tutoring systems and explanation more generally), their adequacy criterion consists of finding at least one directly influenced parameter in the causal account constructed. They use an elegant backchaining algorithm that incrementally instantiates possible influence graphs based on the model fragments of DT, starting with the fastest time-scale, and moving to slower time-scales when an adequate model cannot be found.

9.6 Qualitative States and Qualitative Simulation

A traditional way to think about the behaviors of a complex system D consisting of a set of N continuous parameters is to define the *state space* $S(D)$ as a subset of $\Re^N$. We can define qualitative states as partitions on $S(D)$, carving it up into regions in which some set of relevant distinctions remains constant. The set of relevant distinctions includes what model fragment instances are active and the qualitative values of D's parameters. The status of model fragment instances is necessary for distinguishing qualitative states because they determine the causal constraints (including in some models quantitative equations) that govern the system. The qualitative values of parameters are important because they help determine what state transitions may occur. The difference between flood waters rising and falling, for example, is quite significant.

Since there can be multiple adequate models M of D, there can of course be multiple qualitative representations of $S(D)$. Let $QS(M)$ be the set of qualitative states implied by a model. $QS(M)$ will be finite under two conditions: (1) The set of model fragment instances must be finite and (2) the set of qualitative values for all parameters must be finite. The first condition is satisfied when the structural description of D is finite and the model fragments in DT can only create finite numbers of new individuals for any finite structural description. The second condition is satisfied if landmark introduction is not used—as noted above, landmark introduction can introduce an infinite number of qualitative distinctions.

Finite does not necessarily imply small, of course. The earliest qualitative models, which focused on modeling various kinds of motion (i.e., [24, 42]) used a small vocabulary of types of actions and qualitative decompositions of state to describe space, leading to $QS(M)$s that were polynomial in the spatial complexity of D. Suppose one has an N parameter model and uses the sign representation for qualitative values, and there are M model fragment instances, each of which can be either active or inactive. In the worst case, $|QS(M)| = 3^N * 2^M$. For large-scale engineered systems, N can be in the thousands and M can be in the hundreds. However, this worst-case estimate assumes that every parameter and model fragment are independent, whereas in reasonable domain theories, there is a strong network of constraints among them. As described below, there are applications where it is worthwhile to generate $QS(M)$ entirely, but more often, subsets of $QS(M)$ are generated incrementally on an as-needed basis.

Qualitative simulation is generating a set of qualitative states from some given initial state, constituting predictions about possible future behaviors of the system. A qualitative state can have transitions to more than one possible next state, due to the abstractness of qualitative representations. Generating all behaviors of some class is called *envisioning*. The set of all states that are possible from some initial state S is the *attainable envisionment* of S, which is a subset of the *total envisionment* of a model (i.e., $QS(M)$ itself). Typically tightly bounded subsets of $QS(M)$ are generated, but some applications (cf. [92]) require total envisionments.

An essential step in any qualitative simulation algorithm is finding transitions between states. Transitions between qualitative states occur when some condition of a model fragment changes or when a qualitative value changes. Changes in the condition of a model fragment typically reduce to changes in qualitative values (e.g., pressure equilibrates, ending a flow), and otherwise is due to an action taken to change a proposition in the model, which we will ignore for now, and focus only on value changes.

Suppose a quantity Q has limit point L in its quantity space, and in a qualitative state S, $Q < L$. For Q to reach L, it must be the case that $D(Q) > D(L)$. Transition-finding requires finding such hypothetical changes (called *limit hypotheses* in QP theory) and determining what, if any, transitions follow from them. Not all limit hypotheses lead to state transitions, because, in the absence of discontinuous changes, transitions between states must respect continuity. That is, if in state S1 $Q < L$, then there cannot be a transition directly to a state S2 where $Q > L$, since there must be some time during which $Q = L$ before. (There are ways of modeling discontinuous changes, cf. [71, 83, 84].) Transition-finding can be viewed as a constraint satisfaction problem, finding the minimal-change model from the current qualitative state in which the changes represented by a specific limit hypothesis hold, where continuity constraints are not violated, and aspects of the situation that are not causally connected to the changes are held constant. See [26, 44] and [75] for examples of algorithms.

Good qualitative simulation algorithms are complete, in that they generate the entire space of possible behaviors, but unsound, because they can include predicted futures which are not actually possible. (Kuipers [75] prefers a less intuitive formulation of these terms for qualitative simulation which enables it to be considered as sound but incomplete.) Consider a spring-block oscillator, subject to static and dynamic friction. Without friction, the envisionment of such an oscillator consists of eight states. Considering dynamic friction adds an additional state, corresponding to the block coming to rest where the spring is relaxed. Considering static friction adds two additional states, one where the block is stopped and the spring is slightly compressed, the other where the block is stopped and the spring is slightly stretched. Suppose one allows landmark introduction in reasoning about this system. Each maximal excursion of the block from the resting position of the spring then becomes a new landmark. In the physically correct qualitative simulation of this system, each subsequent landmark is closer to the resting position than the previous one. However, in the simplest spring-block oscillator formulation, there is nothing to prevent subsequent landmarks from being larger, smaller, or the same. In other words, there are paths through the set of qualitative states that do not correspond to any behavior of a real physical spring-block system, even though locally every state transition is correct.

With enough additional constraints, typically in the form of energy constraints (cf. [75]), the possible behaviors can be trimmed appropriately, for at least some systems. However, it is an open question as to how much information it takes to ensure soundness of predictions from qualitative simulation in the general case. If we take detailed numerical simulations as stand-ins for physical behavior, then there is a clear lower bound on abstractness—floating point numbers. But whether a more abstract level of representation exists that is always sufficient remains unknown. Given the ways that qualitative simulations are used, this question has proven less than urgent. Qualitative simulations are typically used to frame analyses by proposing behaviors, which are then examined as needed by more detailed models or confirmed/ruled out by data. Some spurious behaviors are, empirically, a small price to pay for the value these models provide.

9.7 Qualitative Spatial Reasoning

The ability of qualitative representations to provide a bridge between the perceptual and conceptual, by imposing discrete, symbolic frameworks on the continuous world, is perhaps most strongly evident in qualitative spatial reasoning. We start with purely qualitative representations, and then describe diagrammatic representations. The interested reader should also see the Spatial Reasoning chapter in this Handbook.

9.7.1 Topological Representations

The most fundamental qualitative representations of space are centered around topology, that is, how things are connected. Connectivity is important because it is a factor in determining whether, and how, a set of entities might interact. The best-known representation is *RCC8*, the Region Connection Calculus with 8 relationships [19]. RCC8 defines eight mutually exclusive and jointly exhaustive relationships between 2D regions: equal (=), non-tangential proper part (NTTP), tangential proper part (TTP), partially overlapping (PO), edge coupled (EC), disjoint (DC), plus the inverses NTTPi and TTPi. Intuitively, NTTP means that one thing is completely inside the other, while TTP means that the inside thing shares a surface with the outside thing, but otherwise is completely inside it. The sequence of relationships NTTP, TTP, PO, EC, DC captures the changes in connectivity as something moves from inside something to outside it, whereas the reverse sequence captures what happens when something is absorbed or ingested. A transitivity table defines what can be inferred about the relationship between regions R1 and R3, given a third region R2 and knowledge about the relationships between R1 and R2 and R2 and R3.

A variety of more complex schemes have been developed, to handle different degrees and/or dimensions of overlap, multiple piece regions, holes, and other topological phenomena (cf. [32, 17]). See [20] for an excellent survey.

9.7.2 Shape, Location, and Orientation Representations

For entities with spatial extent, their shape is one of their most fundamental properties. Qualitative shape representations focus on carving up complex objects into parts, for purposes of recognition or for ascertaining functional properties, e.g., could something serve as a handle? Hoffman and Richards [62] suggest that the human visual system uses the sign of boundary curvature as one partitioning constraint. Museros and Escrig [85] show how additional information, including relative lengths of sides and qualitative descriptions of angles, can be used with curvature decomposition to match tiles in mosaics. Nielsen [89] showed that, for reasoning about motion, shape decompositions also need to take into account mechanical constraints, such as centers of rotation.

Purely qualitative notions of orientation have been developed for a variety of purposes. For example, Kim [70] shows how representing angles in terms of quadrants and relative inclination to define a qualitative vector algebra powerful enough to reason about the motion of four-bar linkages. One of the most important uses of orientation is in creating purely qualitative descriptions of location. Freksa [54] uses orientation to introduce conceptual neighborhoods for defining locations. Clementini et al. [18] use Hernandez' [60] representation of orientation to define qualitative representations of position and distance. An alternate approach is that of Bittner and Smith [8], which defines location relative to a set of regions that partitions space (e.g., the provinces of a country), thus reducing position to qualitative topology.

9.7.3 Diagrammatic Reasoning

Qualitative spatial reasoning suffices for some tasks, but not for all. Metric information is simply necessary for some tasks: Predicting whether or not a pair of gears will bind, for instance, requires high-precision shape representations. Between these two extremes, it is often more efficient or more convenient to use metric information. Such approaches are often called *diagrammatic reasoning*, since they rely on representations that serve functional roles similar to that of diagrams or sketches in human spatial reasoning.

Metric diagram/place vocabulary model

The *metric diagram/place vocabulary* model [45] characterizes the relationship between diagrammatic and qualitative reasoning as follows. Conceptually, a metric diagram provides the same services for a reasoning system as vision does for humans: It identifies what entities are available, and provides a number of spatial operations on them that can be treated as predicates by the reasoner, although they typically are implemented by schemes that rely on, for example, computational geometry. This general-purpose input description is used to compute qualitative representations (place vocabularies) for specific tasks. In reasoning about motion through space, for example, the place vocabulary consists of regions of free space, including areas like wells where something can be trapped, depending on how much energy it has. In reasoning about kinematic mechanisms (e.g., [38, 50, 68]), the place vocabulary consists of regions of *configuration space*, i.e., the joint angles of the parts of the mechanism. For reasoning about trafficability [29], a GIS serves as the metric diagram, with the place vocabulary being the no-go/slow-go/go regions a vehicle can travel in that a terrain analyst would compute.

The Spatial Aggregation Language, described above, exploits the important insight that for many problems, there is a hierarchical set of place vocabularies, each of which rests on lower-level vocabularies.

Sketch understanding and cognitive vision

Qualitative representations provide a robust intermediate representation for handling messy perceptual inputs. Given the naturalness of hand-drawn sketches, a growing number of researchers have started to apply qualitative techniques to sketch understanding. Egenhofer [33] uses qualitative spatial topology to help formulate GIS queries from hand-drawn sketches. Hammond and Davis [57] use a qualitative vocabulary of relationships to describe representations for sketch recognition. Qualitative spatial representations have been used to reason about sketch maps [51] and for solving everyday physical reasoning problems by using analogies over sketches to formulate qualitative models [73]. Second order analogies over qualitative representations computed from sketches suffice to perform the original Evans [35] analogy task [104].

Research in cognitive vision uses qualitative representations to interpret visual data. Understanding moving objects, such as traffic patterns, is aided by imposing spatio-temporal continuity constraints via qualitative topology [21, 41]. A particularly impressive example is the learning of a table-top game from audio-visual inputs [88].

9.8 Qualitative Modeling Applications

Much of the research in qualitative modeling has been driven by applications such as those below. These are only a sample of the available papers, see the Qualitative Reasoning Workshop proceedings (available on-line at several mirror sites) and journals/conference proceedings in the relevant application areas for more details.

For simplicity, we divide up the applications and application-oriented research into three areas: Automating or assisting professional reasoning, education, and cognitive modeling. We discuss each in turn.

9.8.1 Automating or Assisting Professional Reasoning

Professional reasoning typically involves combining qualitative models with either more detailed quantitative models (e.g., early stages of design and analysis) or numerical data (e.g., late stages of design and analysis, monitoring).

Engineering problem solving

The earliest known fielded QR applications were in process control [78] and in designing photocopiers [102]. While the majority of the application efforts using qualitative modeling involve engineering domains, these are surveyed in the Model-Based Reasoning chapter of this Handbook. Consequently, we focus on areas that are more distant from the model-based reasoning community here.

Creating systems that can understanding and design mechanical systems has been one of the successes of qualitative modeling. Systems have been built that can understand mechanisms such as clocks from scanned descriptions of the parts [50], simulate mechanical designs with behavior discontinuities [98], generate designs from sketches [103], and generate innovative designs via case-based adaptation [39]. These systems use place vocabularies consisting of regions in configuration space, constructed from quantitative representations (CAD data structures, sketches) which serve as metric diagrams.

The Spatial Aggregation Language described above has been used in a variety of applications, including synthesizing thermal control strategies by deriving placements for heat sources [2], data mining in spatial data sets [94], and interpreting spatial data [64].

Economics and decision support

Informal qualitative reasoning has had a long history in economics [40], making formalized qualitative modeling a natural fit. For example, the utility of using qualitative representations to structure quantitative data is illustrated by [97], who describe how to use an order of magnitude representation to improve supervised learning for credit risk prediction. The ability to explicitly characterize categories of outcomes makes qualitative representations potentially valuable for supporting decision-making. For example, [31] illustrates how ecosystem management strategies and their outcomes can be modeled. Improving social science theories more generally, by providing formal tools for working through the consequences of theories, is another promising application. For example, [69] illustrate how to use qualitative modeling to work out consequences of a particular theory of organizational ecology.

Ecology and bioinformatics

In ecology, data can be difficult to obtain, fragmentary, and/or non-existent, making quantitative modeling often a highly speculative proposition. By capturing whole classes of behaviors, qualitative models can be produced without making as many ancillary assumptions. This has lead to an increasing interest in qualitative modeling of ecology (cf. [59, 100]), including papers by ecologists (cf. [90, 108]).

By contrast, the problem in bioinformatics is that of too much data. Here, the ability of qualitative models to characterize abstract hypotheses provides a search space of models that is more tractable for system identification from data. For example, [72] describes how to learn models of glycolysis by inductive logic programming over qualitative models. *In silico* experiments often use a variety of simulation paradigms; Trelease and Park [107] show how qualitative models of immune functions can be used to set up agent-based cellular automata simulations. de Jong and his collaborators have developed the Genetic Network Analyzer (GNA) which has been used to study genetic regulatory networks in a variety of organisms [23].

9.8.2 Education

Education is a natural application for qualitative modeling, since the closeness of qualitative models to human mental models can simplify the production of understandable explanations. In early science education, for example, most curriculum content is qualitative: What parameters and phenomena are relevant in different types of situations, and causal models interrelating them. In later science education, such concerns remain relevant, but with the additional complexity of incorporating quantitative mathematics. Formalisms for qualitative models have thus seen widespread adoption at many levels of education.

Modeling environments for education

Modeling environments can be divided into two types: Those where the primary type of modeling is qualitative, and those where qualitative models are used as one component in the modeling system. We start with the purely qualitative systems.

Concept maps are often used in education, but in a very free-form, open way. This has the advantage that it is easy to get students as young as fourth grade to generate them, but the disadvantage that it is not clear what they mean, even to the students themselves. Qualitative modeling formalisms provide a crisp but natural semantics that can be used in concept mapping tools that are both usable by students and whose models can be reasoned with, to provide coaching. For example, in the Teachable Agents project [7], a system was developed to help middle-school students create models of stream ecosystems. Students would debug their explanations by thinking of themselves as building "Betty's Brain", and would quiz the system, repairing their models until "Betty" gave the right answers. The VModel system [46] is a general-purpose concept mapping system that uses QP theory. It was designed for middle-school students to learn science by model-building, and has been used by teachers in the Chicago Public School system.

Both Betty's Brain and VModel focus on single-state reasoning, since that is sufficient for most middle-school science instruction. (For many middle-school students, mastering the idea of parameter as used in science proves quite difficult.) However, multi-state qualitative simulation is crucial for understanding more advanced phenomena. VisiGarp [11] provides an environment for students to explore multi-state qualitative simulations, filtering them according to imposed constraints and asking questions about them. Homer [80] provides tools for students to create models, which can then be explored via VisiGarp. Both of these systems, and their descendants, are being used in projects for public education, to build an understanding of sustainable development and inform policy makers as to possible consequences of different resource management decisions [99]. The challenge with such tools is that student mistakes can often lead to massive simulations, and digging through the results to figure out what went wrong can be difficult. Making the modeling environments smarter still, to characterize where the critical ambiguities are and make suggestions about what to do about them, is an important research question.

The majority of modeling environments that use qualitative models use them in combination with some variety of quantitative simulation or analysis tools. For example, Model-It [66] provides an environment for students to do systems dynamics modeling, using qualitative mathematics in the interface to provide a friendly front-end to quantitative models that are then used with a traditional numerical simulator. The Qualitative Analysis and Qualitative Simulation Laboratory [86] uses a combination of qualitative reasoning and numerical constraint reasoning to help students learn inorganic chemistry. LSDM [81] uses qualitative reasoning combined with simple numerical models to help buyers learn about different financing options. CyclePad [52] uses qualitative representations with numerical analysis and evidential reasoning to help detect inconsistent designs and recognize intended teleology in students' designs of thermodynamic cycles [36]. These systems illustrate different ways that qualitative modeling can be used to organize analyses and/or provide understandable results from quantitative data.

Self-explanatory simulators and virtual reality

Simulations can be powerful tools for education, but interpreting their results is often hard for students. Self-explanatory simulators integrate qualitative models with numerical simulations to provide causal explanations of the simulated behavior. Self-explanatory simulators for specific systems can be constructed automatically from domain theories that incorporate both qualitative and quantitative model fragments. For example, the SIMGEN compiler [47] produces a simulator runtime that looks and operates much like a traditional numerical simulator, but incorporates a compact encoding of a qualitative model that the compiler generated during the process of writing the numerical code. The simulator produces qualitative histories in addition to numerical values, for a small additional runtime cost of transition-finding (so that qualitative transitions are detected, ensuring the coherence of the qualitative and quantitative explanations) and storage for the history. Self-explanatory simulators have been used in several curricula in the Chicago Public Schools.

Virtual reality systems, either using CAVE-style immersive environments or desktop game-technology environments, have traditionally been hard to author. By mapping model fragments onto an object-oriented runtime and doing real-time reasoning about paths of interaction, qualitative models can be "assembled" as a side-effect of actions taken in a VR environment [34]. Such techniques can be used to create training systems (cf. [15]) and environments for virtual prototyping and artists (cf. [58]).

Conceptual tutoring

The potential for using qualitative modeling for coaching has only begun to be tapped. For example, [28] showed that the dependency structures created during qualitative reasoning could be manipulated to form a structure that could diagnose student errors via standard model-based reasoning, where the "components" being debugged were the ability to do particular operations or remember certain facts. In the Why2-Atlas tutoring system [67], qualitative models are being used with natural language processing to attempt to understand student explanations well enough to identify misconceptions and provide corrective feedback. These are exciting first steps at what could lead to a revolutionary technology for education.

9.8.3 Cognitive Modeling

One of the inspirations for qualitative modeling was observations of human reasoning, both about the everyday physical world and in the professional contexts of science and engineering. Unfortunately, relatively little effort has gone into using qualitative modeling to better understand human cognition, compared to more application-driven research. This is a frontier that could lead to important results on how minds work.

Mental models reasoning

Qualitative modeling has been used by a number of cognitive science efforts exploring *mental models* [55], the representations that people use in their everyday lives to understand the world around them. Kuipers and Kassirer [76] argued that some medical reasoning appears to be governed by qualitative models, based on an analysis of protocol data. Forbus and Gentner [48] used protocol evidence to argue that people use multiple models of causation in everyday reasoning. White and Frederickson [109] argue that a sequence of causal models is needed to help learners master a domain.

While existing studies of human reasoning suggest that the representations developed by the QR community may be psychologically plausible, there are reasons to doubt the psychological plausibility of purely first-principles qualitative simulation algorithms [49].

Natural language semantics

If qualitative models are part of the representational catalog used in human cognition, then one would expect to see evidence of it in many relevant aspects of human cognition. In particular, the semantics of natural language seems to be a natural place to look for such connections, given that there are similarities in the event structure representations commonly used in natural language semantics and in qualitative reasoning. It is possible to map qualitative process theory onto FrameNet [4] style conventions, and create natural language understanding systems that can construct formal qualitative representations from controlled language text [77]. This is one of the areas where a multidisciplinary approach will be needed to gain the deepest insights.

9.9 Frontiers and Resources

Qualitative modeling at this writing has a stable core of techniques, and a rapidly expanding set of applications. These applications in turn will no doubt lead to the expansion of the library of techniques over time, as new problems are discovered and addressed. While traditional application areas, such as engineering and education, remain active, part of the excitement is due to the growth of new application areas (e.g., robotics (cf. [53]), biology, cognitive modeling). The interested reader should also examine the chapter on Physical Reasoning in this Handbook, which examines logical formalizations of common sense problems.

There are a number of resources available for learning more about qualitative modeling. Most of the literature is available on-line; for example, the proceedings of the International Qualitative Reasoning workshops, which started in 1987, are available for free on-line at several mirror sites. Reference implementations of systems, including Kuipers' QSIM, Bredeweg's GARP3, Northwestern's VModel, CyclePad, and self-explanatory simulators, are available as free downloads.

Bibliography

[1] K. Abbott, P. Schutte, M. Palmer, and W. Ricks. Faultfinder: a diagnostic expert system with graceful degradation for onboard aircraft application. In *14th Int. Symp. Aircraft Integrated Monitoring Syst.*, 1987.

[2] C. Bailley-Kellogg and F. Zhao. Spatial aggregation: Modeling and controlling physical fields. In *Proceedings of QR97*, 1997.

[3] C. Bailley-Kellogg and F. Zhao. Qualitative spatial reasoning: Extracting and reasoning with spatial aggregates. *AI Magazine*, 24:47–60, 2004.

[4] C. Baker, C. Fillmore, and J. Lowe. The Berkeley FrameNet Project. In *Proceedings of COLING-ACL-98*, 1998.

[5] D. Bell, D. Bobrow, B. Falkenhainer, M. Fromherz, V. Saraswat, and V. Shirley. RAPPER: The copier modeling project. In *Proceedings of QR94*, 1994.

[6] R. Bellazzi, R. Guglielmann, and L. Ironi. A qualitative-fuzzy framework for nonlinear black-box system identification. In *Proceedings of QR95*, 1995.

[7] G. Biswas, D. Schwartz, J. Bransford, and The Teachable Agents Group at Vanderbilt. Technology support for complex problem solving: From SAD environments to AI. In K. Forbus and P. Feltovich, editors. *Smart Machines in Education*. AAAI Press/MIT Press, Menlo Park, CA, USA, 2001.

[8] T. Bittner and B. Smith. Vagueness and granular partitions. In *Proceedings of FOIS2001*. ACM Press, 2001.

[9] D. Bobrow, B. Falkenhainer, A. Farquhar, R. Fikes, K. Forbus, T. Gruber, Y. Iwasaki, and K. Kuipers. A compositional modeling language. In *Proceedings of QR96*, 1996.

[10] A. Bonarini and G. Bontempi. A qualitative simulation approach for fuzzy dynamical models. *Modeling and Computer Simulation*, 4(4):285–313, 1994.

[11] A. Bouwer and B. Bredeweg. VisiGarp: Graphical representation of qualitative simulation models. In *Proceedings of QR01*, 2001.

[12] E. Bradley. Autonomous exploration and control of chaotic systems. *Cybernetics and Systems*, 26:299–319, 1995.

[13] B. Bredeweg. Expertise in qualitative prediction of behavior. PhD thesis, University of Amsterdam, The Netherlands, 1992.

[14] C. Catino and L. Ungar. Model-based approach to automated hazard identification of chemical plants. *AIChE Journal*, 41(1):97–109, 1994.

[15] M. Cavazza and A. Simo. Qualitative physiology: From qualitative processes to virtual patients. In *Proceedings of QR03*, 2003.

[16] T. Chou and M. Winslette. A model-based belief revision system. *Journal of Automated Reasoning*, 12(2):157–208, 1994.

[17] D. Clementini, P. Di Felice, and P. Oosterom. A small set of formal topological relationships suitable for end-user interaction. In D. Abel and B. Ooi, editors. *Advances in Spatial Databases: Proc. 3rd Int. Symposium on Spatial Databases (SSD'93), LNCS*, vol. 692, pages 277–295. Springer-Verlag, 1993.

[18] E. Clementini, P. Di Felice, and D. Hernandez. Qualitative representation of positional information. *Artificial Intelligence*, 95(2):317–356, 1997.

[19] A. Cohn, B. Bennett, J. Gooday, and N. Gotts. Qualitative spatial representation and reasoning with the region connection calculus. *Geoinformatica*, 1:1–44, 1997.

[20] A.G. Cohn and S.M. Hazarika. Qualitative spatial representation and reasoning: An overview. *Fundamenta Informaticae*, 46(1–2):1–29, 2001.

[21] A. Cohn, D. Magee, A. Galata, D. Hogg, and S. Hazarika. Towards an architecture for cognitive vision using qualitative spatio-temporal representations and abduction. In C. Freksa, C. Habel, and K. Wender, editors. *Spatial Cognition III, LNCS*, pages 232–248. Springer, 2002.

[22] D. de Coste. Dynamic across-time measurement interpretation. *Artificial Intelligence*, 51:273–341, 1991.

[23] H. de Jong, J. Geiselmann, G. Batt, C. Hernandez, and M. Page. Qualitative simulation of the initiation of sporulation in *Bacillus subtillis*. *Bulletin of Mathematical Biology*, 66(2):216–300, 2004.

[24] J. de Kleer. Multiple representations of knowledge in a mechanics problem solver. In *Proc. IJCAI-77*, pages 299–304, 1977.

[25] J. de Kleer. How circuits work. *Artificial Intelligence*, 24:205–280, 1984.

[26] J. de Kleer and J.S. Brown. A qualitative physics based on confluences. *Artificial Intelligence*, 24:7–83, 1984.

[27] J. de Kleer. An assumption-based truth maintenance system. *Artificial Intelligence*, 28:127–162, 1986.

[28] K. de Koning, B. Bredeweg, J. Breuker, and B. Wielinga. Model-based reasoning about learner behaviour. *Artificial Intelligence*, 117(2):173–229, 2000.

[29] J. Donlon and K. Forbus. Using a geographic information system for qualitative spatial reasoning about trafficability. In *Proceedings of QR99*, 1999.

[30] R. Doyle. Determining the loci of anomalies using minimal causal models. In *Proc. IJCAI-95*, pages 1821–1827, 1995.

[31] K. Eisenack. Qualitative viability analysis of a bio-socio-economic system. In *Proceedings of QR03*, 2003.

[32] M. Egenhofer. Deriving the composition of binary topological relations. *Journal of Visual Languages and Computing*, 5(2):133–149, 1994.

[33] M. Egenhofer. Query processing in spatial query-by-sketch. *Journal of Visual Languages and Computing*, 8(4):403–424, 1997.

[34] C. Erignac. Interactive semi-qualitative simulation. In *Proceedings of QR00*, 2000.

[35] T. Evans. A program for the solution of a class of geometric-analogy intelligence test questions. In M. Minsky, editor. *Semantic Information Processing*. MIT Press, 1968.

[36] J. Everett. Topological inference of teleology: Deriving function from structure via evidential reasoning. *Artificial Intelligence*, 113(1–2):149–202, 1999.

[37] B. Falkenhainer and K. Forbus. Compositional modeling: finding the right model for the job. *Artificial Intelligence*, 51:95–143, 1991.

[38] B. Faltings. Qualitative kinematics in mechanisms. *Artificial Intelligence*, 44(1):89–119, 1990.

[39] B. Faltings and K. Sun. FAMING: Supporting innovative mechanism shape design. *Computer-Aided Design*, 28:207–216, 1996.

[40] A. Farley and K. Lin. Qualitative reasoning in economics. *Journal of Economic Dynamics and Control*, 14:465–490, 1990.

[41] J. Fernyhough, A.G. Cohn, and D. Hogg. Constructing qualitative event models automatically from video input. *Image and Vision Computing*, 18:81–103, 2000.

[42] K. Forbus. Spatial and qualitative aspects of reasoning about motion. In *Proceedings of AAAI-80*, 1980.

[43] K. Forbus. Qualitative process theory. *Artificial Intelligence*, 24:85–168, 1984.

[44] K. Forbus. QPE: A study in assumption-based truth maintenance. *International Journal of Artificial Intelligence in Engineering*, 1989.

[45] K. Forbus. Qualitative spatial reasoning: Framework and frontiers. In J. Glasgow, H. Narayanan, and B. Chandrasekaran, editors. *Diagrammatic Reasoning: Computational and Cognitive Perspectives*. AAAI Press, 1994.

[46] K. Forbus, K. Carney, B. Sherin, and L. Ureel. VModel: A visual qualitative modeling environment for middle-school students. In *Proceedings of the 16th Innovative Applications of Artificial Intelligence Conference*, San Jose, July, 2004.

[47] K. Forbus and B. Falkenhainer. Scaling up self-explanatory simulators: Polynomial-time compilation. In *Proceedings of IJCAI-95*, 1995.

[48] K. Forbus and D. Gentner. Causal reasoning about quantities. In *Proceedings of the Eighth Annual Conference of the Cognitive Science Society*, Amherst, MA, August, 1986.

[49] K. Forbus and D. Gentner. Qualitative mental models: Simulations or memories? In *Proceedings of the Eleventh International Workshop on Qualitative Reasoning*, Cortona, Italy, 1997.

[50] K. Forbus, P. Nielsen, and B. Faltings. Qualitative spatial reasoning: the CLOCK project. *Artificial Intelligence*, 51:417–471, 1991.

[51] K. Forbus, J. Usher, and V. Chapman. Sketching for military courses of action diagrams. In *Proceedings of IUI'03*, Miami, FL, January, 2003.

[52] K. Forbus, P. Whalley, J. Everett, L. Ureel, M. Brokowski, J. Baher, and S. Kuehne. CyclePad: An articulate virtual laboratory for engineering thermodynamics. *Artificial Intelligence*, 114:297–347, 1991.

[53] G. Fraser, G. Steinbauer, and F. Wotawa. Application of qualitative reasoning to robotic soccer. In *Proceedings of QR04*, 2004.

[54] C. Freksa. Using orientation information for qualitative spatial reasoning. In A. Frank, I. Campari, and U. Formentini, editors. *Theories and Methods of Spatio-Temporal Reasoning in Geographic Space*, *LNCS*, vol. 639. Springer-Verlag, Berlin, 1992.

[55] D. Gentner and A. Stevens, editors. *Mental Models*. Erldaum, Hillsdale, NJ, 1983.

[56] F. Guerrin. Qualitative reasoning about an ecological process: Interpretation in hydroecology. *Ecological Modeling*, 59:165–201, 1991.

[57] T. Hammond and R. Davis. LADDER: A language to describe drawing, display, and editing in sketch recognition. In *Proceedings of IJCAI 2003*, 2003.

[58] S. Hartley, M. Cavazza, J. Lugrin, and M. Le Bras. Visualization of qualitative processes. In *Proceedings of QR04*, 2004.

[59] U. Heller and P. Struss. Transformation of qualitative dynamic models—application in hydro-ecology. In *Proceedings of QR96*, 1996.

[60] D. Hernandez. *Qualitative Representation of Spatial Knowledge. Lecture Notes in Artificial Intelligence*, vol. 804. Springer, Berlin, 1994.

[61] T. Hickey, Q. Ju, and M.H. Van Emden. Interval arithmetic: From principles to implementation. *Journal of the ACM*, 48(5):1038–1068, 2001.

[62] D. Hoffman and W. Richards. Parts of recognition. *Cognition*, 18:65–96, 1984.

[63] X. Huang and F. Zhao. Relation based aggregation: Finding objects in large spatial datasets. *Intelligent Data Analysis*, 4:129–147, 2000.

[64] L. Ironi and S. Tentoni. In *Electrocardiographic Imaging: Towards Automated Interpretation of Activation Maps, Lecture Notes in Artificial Intelligence*, vol. 3581, pages 323–332. Springer, 2005.

[65] Y. Iwasaki and H. Simon. Theories of causal observing: reply to de Kleer and Brown. *Artificial Intelligence*, 29(1):63–68, 1986.

[66] S. Jackson, S. Stratford, J. Krajcik, and E. Soloway. Making system dynamics modeling accessible to pre-college science students. *Interactive Learning Environments*, 4(3):233–257, 1996.

[67] P. Jordan, M. Makatchev, U. Pappuswamy, K. VanLehn, and P. Albacete. A natural language tutorial dialogue system for physics. In *Proceedings of the 19th International FLAIRS Conference*, 2006.

[68] L. Joskowicz and E. Sacks. Automated modeling and kinematic simulation of mechanisms. *Computer Aided Design*, 25(2), 1993.

[69] J. Kamps and G. Peli. Qualitative reasoning beyond the physics domain: The density dependence theory of organizational ecology. In *Proceedings of QR95*, 1995.

[70] H. Kim. Qualitative kinematics of linkages. In B. Faltings and P. Struss, editors. *Recent Advances in Qualitative Physics*. MIT Press, Cambridge, MA, 1992.

[71] H. Kim. Qualitative reasoning about fluids and mechanics. PhD thesis and ILS Technical Report, 1993.

[72] R. King, S. Garrett, and G. Coghill. On the use of qualitative reasoning to simulate and identify metabolic pathways. *Bioinformatics*, 21:2017–2026, 2005.

[73] M. Klenk, K. Forbus, E. Tomai, H. Kim, and B. Kyckelhahn. Solving everyday physical reasoning problems by analogy using sketches. In *Proceedings of AAAI-05*, 2005.

[74] B. Kuipers. Qualitative simulation. *Artificial Intelligence*, 29:289–338, 1986.

[75] B. Kuipers. *Qualitative Reasoning: Modeling and Simulation with Incomplete Knowledge*. MIT Press, Cambridge, MA, 1994.

[76] B. Kuipers and J. Kassirer. Causal reasoning in medicine: Analysis of a protocol. *Cognitive Science*, 8:363–385, 1984.

[77] S. Kuehne and K. Forbus. Capturing QP-relevant information from natural language text. In *Proceedings of QR04*, 2004.

[78] S. Le Clair, F. Abrams, and R. Matejka. Qualitative process automation: self directed manufacture of composite materials. *Artif. Intell. Eng. Design Manuf.*, 3(2):125–136, 1989.

[79] M. Lundell. A qualitative model of physical fields. In *Proceedings of AAAI-96*, 1996.

[80] B. Machado and B. Bredeweg. Building qualitative models with HOMER: A study in usability and support. In *Proceedings of QR-03*, 2003.

[81] T. Matsuo, T. Shintani, and T. Ito. An economic education support system based on qualitative/quantitative simulations. In *Proceedings of QR04*, 2004.

[82] J. McCarthy. Elaboration tolerance. In CommonSense '98 and http://www-formal.stanford.edu/jmc/elaboration.html, 1998.

[83] P. Mosterman and G. Biswas. Modeling discontinuous behavior with hybrid bond graphs. In *Proceedings of QR95*, pages 139–147, Amsterdam, May, 1995.

[84] P. Mosterman and G. Biswas. Deriving discontinuous changes for reduced order systems and the effect on compositionality. In *Proceedings of QR99*, 1999.

[85] L. Museros and M. Escrig. A qualitative theory for shape representation and matching. In *Proceedings of QR04*, 2004.

[86] S. Mustapha, P. Jen-Sen, and S. Zain. Application qualitative process theory to qualitative simulation and analysis of inorganic chemical reaction. In *Proceedings of QR02.*

[87] P. Nayak. Causal approximations. *Artificial Intelligence*, 70:277–334, 1994.

[88] C. Needham, P. Santos, D. Magee, V. Devin, D. Hogg, and A. Cohn. Protocols from perceptual observations. *Artificial Intelligence*, 167:103–136, 2005.

[89] P. Nielsen. A qualitative approach to mechanical constraint. In *Proc. AAAI-88*, 1988.

[90] T. Nuttle, B. Bredeweg, and P. Salles. Qualitative reasoning about food webs: Exploring alternate representations. In *Proceedings of QR04*, 2004.

[91] J. Pearl. *Causality: Models, Reasoning, and Inference.* Cambridge University Press, 2000.

[92] C.J. Price. AutoSteve: Automated electrical design analysis. In *Proceedings ECAI-2000*, pages 721–725, August 2000.

[93] O. Raiman. Order of magnitude reasoning. *Artificial Intelligence*, 1991.

[94] N. Ramakrishnan, C. Bailey-Kellogg, S. Tadepalli, and V. Pandey. Gaussian processes for active data mining of spatial aggregates. In *Proceedings of QR04*, 2004.

[95] J. Rickel and B. Porter. Automated modeling for answering prediction questions: selecting the time scale and system boundary. In *Proc. AAAI-94*, pages 1191–1198, 1994.

[96] J. Rickel and B. Porter. Automated modeling of complex systems to answer prediction questions. *Artificial Intelligence*, 93:201–260, 1997.

[97] X. Rovira, N. Agell, M. Sanchez, F. Prats, and X. Parra. An approach to qualitative radial basis function networks over orders of magnitude. In *Proceedings of QR04*, 2004.

[98] E. Sacks and L. Joskowicz. Automated modeling and kinematic simulation of mechanisms. *Computer-Aided Design*, 25(2):107–118, 1993.

[99] P. Salles and B. Bredeweg. Constructing progressive learning routes through qualitative simulation models in ecology. In *Proceedings of the Fifteenth International Workshop on Qualitative Reasoning*, San Antonio, TX, USA, 2001.

[100] P. Salles, B. Bredeweg, and S. Araujo. *Ecological Modelling*, 194:80–89, 2006.

[101] Q. Shen and R. Leitch. Fuzzy qualitative simulation. *IEEE Transactions on Systems, Man, and Cybernetics*, 23(4):1038–1061, 1993.

[102] Y. Shimomura, S. Tanigawa, Y. Umeda, and T. Tomiyama. Development of self maintenance photocopiers. In *Proc. IAAI-95*, pages 171–180, 1995.

[103] T.F. Stahovich, R. Davis, and H. Shrobe. Generating multiple new designs from a sketch. *Artificial Intelligence*, 104:211–264, 1998.

[104] E. Tomai, A. Lovett, and K. Forbus. A structure-mapping model for solving geometric analogy problems. In *Proceedings of the 27th Annual Conference of the Cognitive Science Society*, pages 2190–2195, 2005.

[105] L. Trave-Massuyes and N. Piera. The orders of magnitude models as qualitative algebras. In *Proceedings of IJCAI-89*, Detroit, USA, 1989.

[106] L. Trave-Massuyes, F. Prats, M. Sanchez, and N. Agell. Consistent relative and absolute order-of-magnitude models. In *Proceedings of QR-2002*, Sitges, Spain, 2002.

[107] R. Trelease and J. Park. Qualitative process modeling of cell–cell-pathogen interactions in the immune system. *Computer Methods and Programs in Biomedicine*, 51:171–181, 1996.

[108] D. Tullos, M. Neumann, and J. Sanchez. Development of a qualitative model for investigating benthic community response to anthropogenic activities. In *Proceedings of QR04*, 2004.

[109] B. White and J. Fredrickson. Causal model progressions as a foundation for intelligent learning environments. *Artificial Intelligence*, 42(1):99–157, 1990.

[110] B. Williams. A theory of interactions: unifying qualitative and quantitative algebraic reasoning. *Artificial Intelligence*, 51(1–3):39–94, 1991.

[111] K. Yip. *KAM: A System for Intelligently Guiding Numerical Experimentation by Computer*. MIT Press, Cambridge, MA, 1991.

Handbook of Knowledge Representation
Edited by F. van Harmelen, V. Lifschitz and B. Porter
© 2008 Elsevier B.V. All rights reserved
DOI: 10.1016/S1574-6526(07)03010-6

Chapter 10

Model-based Problem Solving

Peter Struss

10.1 Introduction

The development of the concept of model-based systems was an answer to the limitations of rule-based "expert systems", which base problem solving (e.g., diagnosis) on a representation of experiential knowledge in a domain. These limitations are not due to the syntactic form of representing knowledge (rules), but result from the nature of the represented knowledge: termed "empirical associations" in the pioneering paper [11] or "shallow knowledge" in others. This has to be contrasted with "1st principles" knowledge (or "deep knowledge"), such as the representation of the understanding of the physical behavior of the components of a system.

To illustrate this distinction and its implications by an example, consider the simplified electrical subsystem of a vehicle comprising the starter, the rear lights, and the head lights with their power supply (Fig. 10.1(a)). Some simple diagnostic rules for such a system, gained from experience or some analysis of the system, might be

> IF Engine_Does_Not_Start
>   THEN Possible_Cause_Battery_Flat
> IF Engine_Does_Not_Start
>   THEN Possible_Cause_Starter_Defect
> . . .
> IF Rlights_On OR Hlights_On
>   THEN NOT(Possible_Cause_Battery_Flat)

which would allow to suspect the starter, but not the battery, if the engine does not start and the lights are on. However, they lead to wrong consequences, when we face a system with two batteries, as indicated in Fig. 10.1(b).

Experience is obtained in a specific context. In our example, the specific structure of the system is compiled into the rules, it is implicit, and this is why the applicability of the last rule is limited to systems sharing the same structure or, rather, the same structural properties that underlie the rule. A rule may be reusable for the modified system (such as the first one), but the conditions for its reuse remain hidden. Furthermore, there is the question whether the empirical basis has the required coverage.

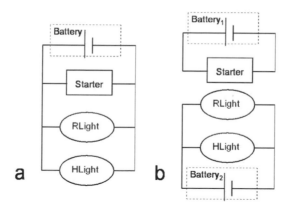

Figure 10.1: Two variants of electrical systems in a vehicle.

Even for moderately complex systems, we cannot expect that all possible faults have already been encountered in practice, let alone all combinations of independent faults.

More fundamentally, there may be no empirical data at all available for a particular kind of system. If we buy the latest model of a car, we would not accept the recommendation of a workshop mechanic that we should return with our problem next year to give them some time to gain experience. For certain systems and failures, we would not want to collect the empirical associations—think of airplanes or nuclear power plants.

It is a constitutive feature of human intelligence to extract principled knowledge from experience that can be used in a different context and for other purposes, and reproducing this capability is a major challenge to AI.

Taking a second look at the example, we notice that the rules do not only have a particular context in terms of the system structure compiled into them, they also represent the application of some principled knowledge to a **specific task**, namely diagnosis. However, the same fragment of knowledge, such as "A flat battery does not provide voltage and, hence, may cause the starter not to work", can also be used to solve a different task, such as failure-modes-and-effects analysis (FMEA), which aims at predicting the effect component failures have on the system function, the generation of a test that can reveal the presence of this fault, etc. In reflection of these challenges, model-based systems aim at

- representing the knowledge about a class of real-world systems as a **library of models** with a maximum of versatility and re-use to different system instances and for different tasks,

- providing model-based **problem solving engines** that support or automate the exploitation of such models to solve certain tasks.

These objectives meet urgent needs in industry, where complexity and variability of products demand computer support to capturing and applying the corporate knowledge. Also society benefits from powerful model-based systems, e.g., in improving the understanding, monitoring, and influencing of ecological, environmental, and climate systems.

These objectives strongly suggest the architectural principle of knowledge-based systems, namely a clear separation and independence of

- the **domain-specific knowledge** as a model-library, a declarative, decompositional representation of the behavior of elementary constituents of systems in the domain,

- the **task-specific knowledge**, in terms of problem solving engines that perform inferences based on a model library.

Independence of these two constituents of model-based systems is not to be understood at a low technical level (data structures), but at a conceptual level: the models should be stated in a way that is not committed to one particular task; and the problem solving engine should avoid encoding specificities of a particular domain and, hence, be able to operate on different model libraries. This is the basis for high reusability of both types of modules.

Of course, in practice (in research as well as in application-oriented work) the space of answers to the challenge has many dimensions. Perhaps more than in other areas of knowledge representation, the diversity of real-world problems induces a tremendous diversity in the proposed solutions. In this field, we are (or should be) facing systems in the real world, and there are many different kinds: electrical circuits, thermodynamic systems, water treatment plants, interacting species of flora and fauna, software, ... We would like to solve tasks like system design, diagnosis, testing, repair, automated recovery, ...

The Cartesian product *systems* × *tasks* is further expanded when researchers and developers choose formalisms (ordinary differential equations, finite state machines, predicate calculus, Bond graphs, Petri-nets, ...) and apply their favorite inference scheme (qualitative simulation, finite constraint satisfaction, theorem proving, optimization, model checking, PROLOG, ...). Although some modeling approaches seem to be more appropriate for certain classes of systems than others, the mapping *systems* ↔ *models* is $m : n$, and so is the mapping *tasks* ↔ *inference engines*.

As a result, any attempt of a comprehensive survey is prohibitive, even when confined to the solution ideas, let alone implementation. However, we will try to show that, at a certain level of abstraction, several tasks can be formalized using a small set of inferences (which can be realized in different ways). This will be done in the following section.

And we will choose a very general notion of "model" (which can be represented in many specific ways) and discuss required or advantageous properties (Section 10.3).

The remainder of the chapter will then be structured along different tasks. Diagnostic theories and systems (Section 10.4) will take the largest share for two reasons: diagnosis is the task with the most advanced theories and applications. On the other hand, some of the theories and implementation principles carry over to other problems as motivated in Section 10.2. We first present the foundations for a large class of diagnostic systems, consistency-based diagnosis based on component-oriented models, but will also identify its underlying assumptions and limitations and characterize alternative approaches.

Then we discuss test generation and diagnosability analysis (Section 10.5), generation of remedies (Section 10.6), and some other tasks (Section 10.7), and, finally, try to identify some major challenges in the field.

As stated before, due to the diversity of the solutions and the purpose and restriction of this chapter, our goal cannot be a comprehensive presentation of all proposed approaches and systems (and not even a comprehensive list of references), but, rather, conveying the key ideas of selected solutions with some formalization and, perhaps, some hints on a possible implementation. In the selection, we give preference to solutions that address the important requirements of the application context in a principled and general way over approaches that are heavily influenced by specific features of a particular application domain or that fail to reflect essential conditions of the real-world task.

10.2   Tasks

In this section, we characterize the essence of different tasks we would like to address based on some model. For this purpose, we are not very specific about the content of the model and the special form it is represented in. Requirements on the model, part of which follow from this analysis, will be discussed in the next section. Here, a model is a description of the possible ways a certain system can behave. This can be a real physical system or a hypothetical one (e.g., in design), a system that is in order or faulted (e.g., in diagnosis). In this section, we assume for the sake of a formal presentation that such a model, whatever the chosen representation is, can be equivalently stated as a set of logical formulas. Of course, in practice, representations will be chosen that are more suited for the description of physical systems. In this case, it has to be analyzed how the logical concepts and inferences carry over to the different formalism.

As it turns out, all we expect from a model is that it can be decided whether or not a certain behavior description contradicts the model (i.e. the notion of **consistency**) and whether it follows from the model (**entailment**).

10.2.1   Situation Assessment/Diagnosis

Diagnosis is about finding out that and why something does not behave the way it should. We have a model $MODEL_{OK}$ of the correctly working system, a set OBS of observations of the actual behavior of the system, and a set $GOALS$ specifying its intended behavior. Then, **fault detection**, the first step in diagnosis, means to check whether the joined theory is consistent

$$MODEL_{OK} \cup OBS \cup GOALS \nvDash \bot$$

or, stronger, to ask whether the $GOALS$ are entailed:

$$MODEL_{OK} \cup OBS \vDash GOALS$$

We may assume that the system is well-designed, i.e., if nothing is broken, the specified behavior is guaranteed to be achieved,

$$MODEL_{OK} \vDash GOALS$$

In this case, the check is reduced to

$$MODEL_{OK} \cup OBS \nvDash \bot$$

If this check reveals an inconsistency, we can conclude that $MODEL_{OK}$ does not describe the system under its current physical conditions; there must be a fault. In order to fix the problem, we need to know where the fault lies (**fault localization**) and/or what kind of fault is present (**fault identification**). In model-based diagnosis, this can be stated as the task of deriving a model $MODEL_F$ (or several alternative ones) that is, at least, consistent with the observations (*consistency-based diagnosis*)

$$MODEL_F \cup OBS \nvDash \bot$$

or even entails them (*abductive diagnosis*, see Section 10.4.3).

In diagnosis, the space of models that are candidates for $MODEL_F$, is not arbitrary. Usually, the system performed well before and is now suffering from some particular malfunctions or disturbances. For instance, unless a major accident has happened, there will usually be one or two broken components in our car. This is why we can expect some restricted space of models that contains the solutions we are looking for, although it will often be too large to allow for an exhaustive consistency check of all candidates, and, hence, require search. In this search, we can exploit an ordering on the candidate models that is induced by the degree of deviations from $MODEL_{OK}$, e.g., indicated by the number of faulty components. This provides the basis for a hypothesize-and-test cycle where the new hypotheses are obtained by some elementary revision of the failing candidates, e.g., by assuming a different fault, an additional faulty component, etc. What we need in order to realize such a search-based approach is a module that checks the consistency of the model with the given observations and a component that produces new model hypotheses by revision of inconsistent ones based on some description of the possible disturbances in the model library (Fig. 10.2(a)). In Section 10.4, we present more details about such solutions.

10.2.2 Test Generation, Measurement Proposal, Diagnosability Analysis

If diagnosis does not provide a sufficiently focused answer, more observations are required to help discriminating between the remaining fault hypotheses. This means, we are looking for some stimulus INP to the system such that its observed response reveals the differences between the various hypotheses. In our model-based context, this means: given two behavior models $MODEL_1$ and $MODEL_2$, the target situation is

$$INP \cup MODEL_1 \vDash OBS_1$$
$$INP \cup MODEL_2 \vDash OBS_2$$
$$OBS_1 \cup OBS_2 \vDash \bot$$

Test generation is the task of determining inputs INP with this property and the appropriate observables, in case they can vary. In testing for diagnosis, this needs to be done for all pairs of models that represent relevant diagnoses. In end-of-line testing, $MODEL_{OK}$ needs to be discriminated from the models of relevant faults. **Measurement proposal** can be seen as a special case, where INP is fixed by the current situation, and the task is focused on determining where to probe for discrimination.

Also in the design phase of a system, this analysis can be relevant. **Detectability analysis** has to determine whether, under a given set of observables (e.g., by the sen-

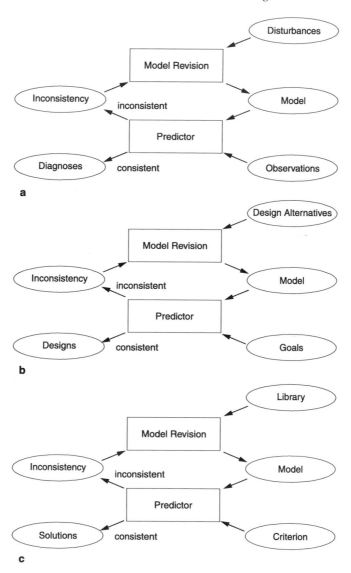

Figure 10.2: Consistency check and model revision in searching for diagnostic hypotheses (a), design solutions (b), and remedies (c).

sors built in), they reveal the distinction between a fault and the normal behavior, and, perhaps, under which conditions (represented by *INP*) this is the case, while **discriminability analysis** asks for distinguishing between two faults, which can be important to trigger some appropriate automatic response to the fault (e.g., in on-board recovery actions on vehicles). This analysis is relevant to sensor placement and also part of failure-modes-and effects analysis.

10.2.3 Design and Failure-Modes-and-Effects Analysis

The **design** of a system that has to generate a specified behavior demands strongly for a model-based approach, if a trial-and-error process by building physical prototypes should be avoided or limited. Unfortunately, in the general case, it is more challenging than diagnosis. If *GOALS* represents the behavior specification, then the design task can be solved by finding a model that entails this behavior:

$$MODEL \models GOALS$$

A necessary precondition for such a solution is that it is consistent with the specified behavior, which may be exploited at least in a first step to reduce the space of candidate models:

$$MODEL \cup GOALS \not\models \bot$$

We would usually not be satisfied by a product design that **may**, but is not guaranteed to, serve its purpose. However, the consistency check may be the only possible one in early phases of the design process, which may leave open the choice of specific components or parameters or even some structural properties, and it is helpful because it can refute certain design alternatives. Furthermore, the design process is rarely a single jump to a solution, but approaching one by modifying previously refuted design hypotheses in a way that inconsistencies with the specification are removed. Again, we can organize this process as a search in a space of candidate models (Fig. 10.2(b)). They need to be checked for consistency with the goals and, in case of inconsistency with the goals, revised by changing design decisions. What makes the task harder is, first of all, the nature and size of the space of possible alternatives. Usually, this space is much less restricted than, say, in diagnosis, where the structure of the system may be fixed and the possible component failures limited. In design, the structure may be what needs to be developed and modified.

Obviously, the revision-based search can only work if there is an initial hypothesis that can lead to a solution after a limited number of modifications. In fact, the vast majority in industrial design is not completely innovative, but emerges from a modification of a predecessor product. And often, the structure is more or less fixed, which turns design into the more tractable task of selecting appropriate components from a given set (**configuration**) or only determining parameters of fixed component classes (**parametric design**).

As a special task during design, **failure-modes-and-effects analysis**, has gained importance (and is mandatory, for instance, in the aeronautics and automotive industries). It is concerned with the task of making sure that, for a given design, even under the occurrence of a fault (usually a single fault) the resulting behavior of the system would not be critical or even catastrophic. The analysis has to find out for a set of given scenarios (e.g., the landing phase of an aircraft) and a set of relevant component failures whether one of the specified effects, i.e. violations of the functionality (e.g., "landing gear not extended"), can occur. The result of this analysis may be requested changes of the design.

Given a model of the system behavior under the presence of a possible failure, $MODEL_F$, it has to be determined whether it entails some *EFFECT* in a scenario specified by *INP*:

$$INP \cup MODEL_F \models EFFECT$$

or does not exclude (is consistent with) the effect:

$$INP \cup MODEL_F \cup EFFECT \not\models \perp$$

10.2.4   Proposal of Remedial Actions (Repair, Reconfiguration, Recovery, Therapy)

Diagnosis is only a step towards the real goal, which is restoring the functionality of a disturbed system, as far as it is possible. This is a trivial step, at least at the level of inferences, if it amounts to the **replacement** of broken components, in which case fault localization provides the direct answer. In other cases, built-in structural redundancy can be exploited for **reconfiguration** of a system in a way that (a part of) the objectives can be achieved despite a fault. For instance, breakers in a power network are opened and closed to provide continued power supply before the actual cause of a disturbance has been removed. This means to determine a target state, *STATE*, such that

$$STATE \cup MODEL_F \models GOALS$$

or, in the consistency-based form,

$$STATE \cup MODEL_F \cup GOALS \not\models \perp$$

Reconfiguration leaves the designed structure of the system unchanged and has a well-specified, though potentially large, search space: the space of states of the switching elements. The search can be guided by the number or cost of the required state changes with respect to the actual states.

In the more general case, which we may call **therapy**, remedial actions may have to modify the real system in order to bring it back to a healthy state. This often holds, for instance, for natural systems or plants that involve chemical or biological processes. Adding substances may trigger new processes and, hence, lead to a new system model:

$$ACTIONS \cup MODEL_F \models GOALS'$$

or, in the consistency-based form,

$$ACTIONS \cup MODEL_F \cup GOALS' \not\models \perp$$

GOALS' will usually be some intermediate goals, which represent the direction towards the ultimate *GOALS*. Increased irrigation of the almost destroyed Everglades will only after some time lead to a healthy state of the flora and fauna, if at all.

We derive the same pattern again (Fig. 10.2(c)), and the feasibility will heavily depend on the size and structure of the space of revisions, which in this case correspond to the available remedial actions.

10.2.5   Ingredients of Model-based Problem Solving

This attempt to analyze and formalize the core of various real-world tasks and the exploitation of behavior models at a very abstract level reveals some of the fundamental technical tasks that have to be addressed by any model-based solution that aims at automating the respective problem solving. It also shows that they are shared across the various tasks, which opens the chance to reuse even algorithms, although the specific nature of the models and the structure of the model space will influence the details and appropriate heuristics.

This analysis, despite its abstract nature, also leads to some fairly important requirements on the modeling formalism which will be discussed in the next section.

10.3   Requirements on Modeling

In the previous section, we formalized the considered tasks using notions of consistency and entailment. This has sometimes led to the misconception that the system model has to be formulated as a logical theory (and has turned away some researchers, engineers, and users from this approach). While logic is one formalism with a precise semantics of entailment and consistency, it is not the only one, and, in fact, it is not an appropriate modeling language for most applications of model-based reasoning. Many applications lie in the engineering domain, others in social, ecological, biological, etc. domains and are difficult or impossible to model in first-order logic. Fortunately, this is not necessary. Although some widely used modeling formalisms can be translated into first-order logic, such as component-oriented modeling with finite domain constraints, even this is not a prerequisite for applying the problem solving engines we will discuss in the subsequent sections. This is possible thanks to the architectural principle of model-based systems, namely the separation of the model from the problem solving reasoning. The latter is often described in terms of logical inferences (although some of the most important and successful systems are not) which allows to analyze and prove properties of algorithms used in solutions, whereas the model is almost never stated in logic.

Of course, the modeling formalism has to fulfill certain theoretical and technical requirements in order to support the kind of problem solving described in the previous section, and we will now discuss these general requirements, rather than listing and describing candidates for modeling formalisms (algebraic and differential equations, qualitative differential equations, constraints, difference equations, causal graphs, rules, logic, finite state machines, Petri nets, discrete event models, Bond graphs, ...). This may seem to be a drawback, but it should be considered as an advantage, because this perspective allows for the exploitation of ideas, methods, and algorithms in combination with different types of models and for the choice of the models best suited for a particular domain and problem.

There are some fundamental requirements that originate from the application context and imply some of the technical ones.

- **Domain-oriented models**: this includes the **expressiveness** of models and the **efficiency** of model-based inferences, and, often, a trade-off between these two aspects. In contrast to a resistive circuit, a copier needs some representation of duration (of processing and transportation). A diagnosis system on-board a vehicle needs real-time performance. Model-based failure-modes-and effects analysis demands for qualitative models, since it aims at determining effects of classes of faults with unspecified parameters.

    In most areas, model-based reasoning meets a set of developed and established modeling formalisms and tools used in current practice. On the one hand, they promise to capture some of the essential features and, hence, cannot and should not be ignored by model-based systems. On the other hand, they often fail to provide some of the required capabilities that can be provided by AI techniques. Integration is often difficult, but important in order to obtain acceptance of the domain experts and users. If AI researcher ignore these aspects, this renders their work ineffective.

- **Libraries of reusable models**: model-based reasoning techniques rarely refer to a task that is not already performed by humans, and, often, performed quite well without an explicit representation of models. Model-based systems are only interesting if they offer some improvement in this performance, in terms of the quality of the result, or in terms of the cost needed to obtain the result. In any case, if the construction of the required model consumes more time than the traditional way of solving the problem, a model-based solution is not a solution. The fact that model-based reasoning aims at capturing the basic domain knowledge, which can be applied to different tasks and/or systems sets the challenge to represent this knowledge as a set of re-usable model fragments. This forms the basis for producing system models by composition of such model fragments, thus reducing the modeling efforts and time. Again, approaches that ignore this requirement, in treating a system model as a hand manufactured unstructured system model, fail to provide a suitable basis for solutions.

Together with these requirements, the formalized tasks presented in Section 10.2 translate into a set of relevant theoretical and technical properties and requirements of modeling.

10.3.1   Behavior Prediction and Consistency Check

Whatever the preferred modeling formalism is, in order to be useful for consistency-based problem solving, it has to have at least some sort of concept of consistency and, for abductive solutions, of entailment. Given some (fraction of) a model of a system's behavior, it must be possible to tell whether or not it contradicts given observations, goals etc. (and to draw conclusions about unobserved features, e.g., related to goals). This is a basic requirement and one that should be met by most modeling formalisms, because they are designed for prediction, and one can compare the predicted behavior to the observed or intended features. Nevertheless, in designing a model-based reasoner, it is important to precisely define the notion of inconsistency specific to a particular model-based predictor. If it can decide that a model is inconsistent (and, perhaps, which part of the model caused the inconsistency), this suffices to enable the problem solver to perform its task.

There may be cases where there is a continuum of compliance and contradiction, rather than a binary decision (e.g., when predictions underlie some probability distribution). But, usually, there are natural thresholds that express tolerable deviations (from normal behavior, the design specification, etc.).

To be effective in the framework of consistency-based problem solving, completeness matters, i.e. its ability to detect all existing (or relevant) inconsistencies. Besides the fact that this can be expensive, model-based predictors can be inherently incomplete. A numerical simulation model (say, in Matlab) may appear as an appropriate solution in some cases (and even be readily available from engineering practice), but its fixed computational directionality may prevent the detection of all inconsistencies.

10.3.2 Validity of Behavior Modeling

The condition discussed above ensures that an inconsistency between the **model** and a description of some (real or hypothetical) situation is detectable. However, in order to draw safe conclusions about the **actual system**, the model has to represent its behavior in a valid way. While this seems pretty obvious, we can, and need to be, more specific. For consistency-based problem solving, it is essential that an inconsistency between a **model** and some criterion really indicates that the modeled **system** contradicts the criterion. In order to avoid spurious inconsistencies, we must postulate that **a model is guaranteed to be consistent with all situations the modeled real system can experience in reality**. As a consequence of this requirement, appropriate models tend to be conservative, for instance, by using the most generous tolerances of parameters. Of course, it can never be satisfied in an ideal way. The application context determines the scope of such really occurring situations, and, e.g., in circuit diagnosis, there is usually no need to include super conductivity at low temperatures in the model. However, the model must cover situations beyond the intended use of the component, e.g., a higher voltage caused by some defective transformer.

Again, this may appear obvious, but is sometimes hard to achieve and actually not fulfilled by many models in engineering, which are developed to work in a particular context and under certain environmental conditions.

10.3.3 Conceptual Modeling

Behavior prediction and consistency check refers to the **behavior** description, i.e. some mathematical, logical or other formalism that characterizes the state of the system. However, problem solvers refer to **concepts** of the real systems: components and their faults, design decisions, unwanted effects, unexpected substances and processes, etc. The solution space of models is spanned by these concepts, rather than by the mathematical, etc. expressions constraining the respective behavior, and the search and reasoning of the problem solver is performed in this space. Hence, these concepts and their relations have to be explicitly represented in model-based reasoning systems. Actually, this is lacking in most formalisms used in mathematical and engineering modeling, and this is where AI can make an essential contribution. This distinguishes, for instance, model-based diagnosis in AI from diagnosis systems in control engineering that perform a search in a space of mathematical models in order to find one that matches the observations (e.g., by means of parameter identification) without any representation of the physical structure of the device, its component faults, etc.

The decomposition of a real system into its entities (components, objects, relevant processes, ...) has to be made explicit and induces a structure of the behavior model. If this link between the relevant entities of the system and the behavior model is weak, then the conclusions that a model-based problem solver can draw at the conceptual level from a behavioral inconsistency are limited. If an equation solver only delivers the information that the entire system model is over-determined without any reference to a subset of component models that cause this, there is not much to be gained for localizing the fault.

It is clear that this feature is important for the efficient construction and maintenance of a model library.

10.3.4   (Automated) Model Composition

Having argued for the **decomposition** of a system model into fragments that correspond to the relevant constituents, we also need the opposite: the **composition** of model fragments in order to obtain a model of the overall system or subsystems. More precisely, what we need are algorithms for **automatically** composing system models. This is mandatory if the problem solver follows a generate-and-test strategy. If it generates a new hypothesis to be checked for consistency (say, a new combination of faults) then the generation of the respective model based on the model library must not involve the agent that usually composes models: a human modeler. Although the principle of modular and compositional modeling is not an invention of model-based reasoning, it is not straightforward and not supported in many modeling environments used in practice. For instance, although Matlab/Simulink provides means to organize a system model in a hierarchical manner as interlinked subsystem models, the lower level models cannot be arbitrarily combined because of the fixed computational directionality. Even if we model the same system, but start the computation from a different set of observed variables, the models of the subsystems are different and cannot be reused. In contrast, constraint systems ([13, 63] and Modelica [76]) are undirected and support compositionality.

10.3.5   Genericity

Compositionality of models is not only a matter of computational or structural aspects, such as directionality and compatible variable domains. The behavior models of the system constituents have to be stated in a context-independent manner in order to be usable in different contexts. Otherwise, the composed model will not cover the entire system behavior and violate validity as discussed in Section 10.3.2. For instance, if the scope of a task includes the occurrence of fault situations (as in diagnosis or FMEA), then a component model has to cover the response of the component to this faulty environment, which is one reason why many models developed for control purposes are not suited for model-based diagnosis. For instance, if a pipe is connected to a check valve, its model must nevertheless also cover a reversed flow in order to avoid wrong predictions and inconsistencies in case the check valve is broken. This principle has been termed "no function in structure" in [17]. For systems and variable-based models that treat some variables as exogenous, the requirement implies that the model must consider the entire Cartesian product of the respective variable domains. If it would not include the response of the component to some input, it would generate a spurious inconsistency if the respective situation appears.

Such sets of exogenous variables need not be unique for a single component. In a valve model, we can treat pressure at both sides as such a set and determine the flow from it. However, if the flow on one side is restricted to zero by a neighboring component (say, a clogged pipe), then it becomes an exogenous variable. Often, approaches to using causal models (e.g., causal graphs or Bayes' nets) suffer from a similar deficiency, because the overall structure, the behavior of neighboring components, or certain assumptions are compiled into them. Also, the causal structure may change, even under normal behavior: the electric motor of a tram way can intentionally be turned into a generator and, hence, function as a brake. Even more frequently, faults modify the causal structure. Even if it is possible to capture all these variations in a causal graph, the model will hardly be compositional, and the effort of building complete causal models of large systems is prohibitive. Only ontologies that are based on local, independent causal interactions, such as qualitative process theory [34, 35] promise to provide a basis for model-based problem solving along these lines.

Limited genericity of the model fragments results in limited reusability and, as discussed earlier, reduces the application benefit.

10.3.6 Appropriate Granularity

Granularity refers to the degree of "resolution" of both the **structure** and the **behavior**. The structural granularity has to allow the reference to the concepts required by the task, e.g., the fault modes of the relevant components. For a compositional model, it is determined by the granularity of model fragments in the library, which may be more fine-grained than required. For instance, in on-board diagnosis, the set of observables is usually fixed, and all that matters for computation of diagnostics is the relation between these observables and the fault modes, while the model includes many unobservable internal and intermediate variables. In order to achieve a compact representation and efficient computation, as required by on-board diagnosis, it can make sense to transform the composite model appropriately [26].

The granularity of behavior descriptions, expressed, e.g., by the domains of variables, is determined by the purpose, namely to detect inconsistencies. For instance, if all values of a certain observable in one interval are consistent with the same set of models, it is not necessary to distinguish between them in the model. Because a fault can be characterized by causing a **significant deviation** from some intended behavior, tasks related to diagnosis and fault analysis even of continuous systems can often be based on qualitative models [81, 35, 4]. Since the required distinctions may depend on the task and the structure and intended function of the system and, hence, cannot be anticipated by the model fragments in the library, a composite model may have inappropriate domains. If they are too fine-grained, it may pay off to transform the composed model to a more abstract level [67].

There is a tension between the requirement of having compositional, generic, and reusable model fragments in a library and the necessity to achieve a compact representation of a model that is yet powerful enough for consistency checking and efficient computation. Violating one of them may eliminate the feasibility or at least the benefit of model-based systems in industrial applications. This is why research on multiple modeling and automated model transformation and compilation [69, 52, 21, 10] can make an important contribution.

10.4 Diagnosis

There is a huge variety of diagnostic tasks, and they may impose quite different requirements on modeling, model-based prediction and consistency check, the search algorithm, etc. The type of system and the practical context may emphasize different problems. On-board diagnosis on a vehicle has to be based on a fixed, and usually small, set of sensor values, while a fault in a power network generates an overwhelming burst of messages. Also, on-board diagnosis has to discriminate between different classes of faults according to their safety relevance and the resulting recovery actions, while diagnosis in the workshop only needs to identify the broken part in order to re-place it. The latter case usually involves a number of testing activities, while a huge gas turbine in a plant does not allow interruptions for carrying out experiments. Most of the time, we are confronted with "post-mortem" diagnosis, but often, it is desir-able to perform prognostic diagnosis in order to schedule maintenance before a failure occurs. And so forth.

Rather than outlining all specific answers to such specific requirements, we fo-cus on the presentation of some principled and sufficiently general and influential approaches. We will identify the underlying assumptions that confine the scope of applicability. Even for some fundamental work, they were often left implicit, and sometimes, the authors even seem to be unaware of them.

We first describe consistency-based diagnosis with component-oriented models, whose idea has been the basis for the analysis in Section 10.2 and contains important principles and techniques, which partly carry over to other tasks. It represents probably the largest class of implemented systems and provides a systematic framework to the community for discussing variants and alternatives of the techniques.

Section 10.4.2 discusses the problem of performing diagnosis over time. We then outline an alternative concept, abductive diagnosis (Section 10.4.3) and consistency-based diagnosis using an alternative type of models, process-oriented diagnosis (Sec-tion 10.4.4).

10.4.1   Consistency-based Diagnosis with Component-oriented Models

The classical theory [62, 19] and realization of consistency-based diagnosis [20, 22, 24, 64] consider systems that contain a **fixed set of components**, *COMPS*, that interact in a **fixed structure**. Furthermore, it is assumed that a **disturbance** of the entire system is caused by a **malfunctioning** of one or more of these **components**. This includes the assumption that the entire system performs as intended if all components perform properly, i.e. the **well-designed system** assumption.

Diagnosis is then seen as the task to decide whether there are components that are not exhibiting their intended behavior (*fault detection*) and to determine which components work in a fault mode (*fault localization*) and in which fault mode they operate (*fault identification*).

Hence, each component C_i has a set of possible associated **behavior modes** $modes(C_i)$ (usually determined by the component type), and assigning one mode to each component provides an answer to a diagnosis problem.

Definition 10.1 (Mode assignment). *Let COMPS' $\subseteq$ COMPS.*

$$\bigwedge_{C_i \in COMPS'} m_{j_i}(C_i), \quad where\ m_{j_i} \in modes(C_i)$$

is a mode assignment. It is called complete if COMPS' = COMPS.

$ok(C_i)$ always has to be an element of $modes(C_i)$ and characterizes uniquely the intended, normal behavior of the component. Modes are mutually exclusive,

$$m_{ji}(C_i) \wedge m_{ki}(C_i) \ \Rightarrow \ j = k$$

which also means that all modes different from $ok(C_i)$ represent some sort of faulty behavior:

$$\forall m_{ji}(C_i) \in modes(C_i) \setminus \{ok(C_i)\}, \quad m_{ji}(C_i) \Rightarrow \neg ok(C_i).$$

The model library *LIB* associates a behavior model with each mode:

$$m_{ji}(C_i) \Rightarrow model_{ji}(C_i).$$

If the models are stated in terms of variables, then *LIB* must also contain *domain axioms* for the variables, i.e., the (exclusive) disjunction of their possible values.

Then each mode assignment

$$MA = \bigwedge_{C_i \in COMPS} m_{ji}(C_i)$$

together with the structural description *STRUCTURE*, which specifies the connections between components in terms of variables shared by the components, and the library *LIB* implies a behavior model *MODEL(MA)* of the entire system for the mode assignment *MA*:

$$LIB \cup STRUCTURE \cup \{MA\} \Rightarrow MODEL(MA)$$

Some papers use the term *system description* (*SD*) to refer to knowledge about the system without further specification. If we assume that there are no general restrictions on the possible mode assignments, we consider

$$SD = LIB \cup STRUCTURE$$

which has the disadvantage of obscuring the different nature of these elements: *LIB* usually contains domain-specific knowledge about the behavior of components, while *STRUCTURE* is system-specific.

In the following, we will always assume that modeling has led to a proper result, i.e., *SD* is consistent. If the modes of the components are assumed to be independent of each other, then also *MODEL(MA)* is consistent for every mode assignment *MA*. This requires valid models, as discussed in Section 10.3.2.

In this approach, model-based diagnosis is regarded as generation of system models that are consistent with the observations and amounts to generating hypotheses about the actually present behavior modes of the components. Therefore, we define

Definition 10.2 (Consistency-based diagnosis). *A complete mode assignment MA is a consistency-based diagnosis for a system description SD and a set of observations OBS if*

$$SD \cup \{MA\} \cup OBS \nvDash \bot.$$

Fault detection

In particular, the assignment of *ok* to all components

$$MA_{OK} = \bigwedge_{C \in COMPS} ok(C)$$

specifies the normal behavior of the overall system:

$$LIB \cup STRUCTURE \cup \{MA_{OK}\} \Rightarrow MODEL_{OK}.$$

The well-designed-system assumption,

$$MODEL_{OK} \Rightarrow GOALS$$

turns the question whether the system behaves as intended into checking whether

$$SD \cup \{MA_{OK}\} \cup OBS \models \bot$$

which is realized by checking whether the resulting model is consistent with the observations:

$$MODEL_{OK} \cup OBS \models \bot.$$

Fault localization

If diagnosis is seen as fault localization, as, for instance, in [62, 20, 19], then this is related to another hidden assumption, namely that this information suffices to repair the broken system, which is true if **replacement of components** is the means for re-establishing the functionality of the system. (Sometimes, fault localization may be performed not in order to repair the system, but to identify flaws in manufacturing process.)

Fault localization is only interested in differentiating the broken components from the correctly working ones and, hence, aims at the special case of

$$modes(C) = \{ok(C), \neg ok(C)\}.$$

As stated above, if there are more specific fault modes, then they imply $\neg ok(C)$. A fault localization has to hypothesize the set of broken components consistently with the observations:

Definition 10.3 (Fault localization). *FAULTY $\subset$ COMPS is a fault localization for SD and OBS, if the mode assignment MA_{FAULTY}*

$$\bigwedge_{C \in FAULTY} \neg ok(C) \wedge \bigwedge_{C \in OK} ok(C)$$

with OK = COMPS \ FAULTY is a diagnosis for SD and OBS. It is called minimal, if no proper subset of FAULTY is also a fault localization.

This corresponds to the definitions in [20, 62, 19] (where fault localizations are called diagnoses and also *candidates*, because they might be refuted when additional observations are available) and is the basis for the *General Diagnosis Engine* (*GDE*) [20]. Minimal fault localizations are of practical interest because if a certain set of defective components suffices to explain the symptoms, why would we assume additional components also to be broken?

Computing (minimal) fault localization requires checking the consistency of the respective system models with the observations. If only the correct behavior is modeled, $\neg ok(C)$ has no model associated (which is equivalent to associating a model that does not impose any restrictions on the values of local variables). In this case, a search could be performed by eliminating the OK models of components from the entire model and checking the consistency of the remaining models. This approach which in practice might work in an exhaustive manner only for single or small sets of faults has actually been proposed in [12] as *constraint suspension*. However, there is a possibility for a more focused generation of fault localizations which has an intuitive basis: if the windshield wipers in our car do not work, we will focus our analysis on s small subset of components, such as their motor, the connecting cables, etc., but not consider, say, parts of the engine or of the braking system, because they do not influence the observed behavior of the car. Carried over to model-based diagnosis, this means that the observations may not simply be inconsistent with the complete system model, but with a model obtained from some partial mode assignment, which we call a *conflict*.

Definition 10.4 (Conflict). *Let COMPS' $\subset$ COMPS and*

$$MA = \bigwedge_{C_i \in COMPS'} m_{j_i}(C_i)$$

be a mode assignment such that

$$SD \cup \{MA\} \cup OBS \vDash \bot.$$

The negation of MA,

$$\bigvee_{C_i \in COMPS'} \neg m_{j_i}(C_i)$$

is called a conflict. *It is called minimal, if it is not implied by a different conflict. It is called* basic *if*

$$\forall C_i \in COMPS', \quad m_{j_i}(C_i) = ok(C_i) \vee m_{j_i}(C_i) = \neg ok(C_i)$$

and positive, *if*

$$\forall C_i \in COMPS', \quad m_{j_i}(C_i) = ok(C_i).$$

Since [19] considers only the two basic modes, a basic conflict corresponds to their definition of a conflict. Minimal conflicts are the most focused restrictions on the possible combinations of modes, and non-minimal conflicts do not provide additional information. Obviously, positive conflicts are important to fault localization, because they state that at least one of the mentioned components is broken. Even stronger, the following theorems [19] states that conflicts capture exactly the available information for fault localization, can replace $SD \cup OBS$ and be used to logically characterize the solutions.

Theorem 10.1. *Let MB-CONFLICTS be the set of all minimal basic conflicts for SD $\cup$ OBS. FAULTY $\subset$ COMPS is a fault localization for SD $\cup$ OBS iff the respective mode assignment is consistent with the minimal basic conflicts:*

$$MB\text{-}CONFLICTS \cup \{MA_{FAULTY}\} \nvDash \bot.$$

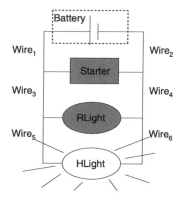

Figure 10.3: A simple diagnostic problem: the head lights are lit, while the rear lights are not, and the starter does not work.

Theorem 10.2. *FAULTY $\subset$ COMPS is a minimal fault localization iff the mode assignment*

$$\bigwedge_{C \in FAULTY} \neg ok(C)$$

is a prime implicant of the positive minimal conflicts.

A prime implicant of a set of formulas is a minimal conjunctive clause of literals (in our case representing $ok(C)$, $\neg ok(C)$) that entails each formula in the set. This captures the intuition that (minimal) fault localizations have to satisfy exactly each (minimal) disjunction of suspect components. One way to obtain them is to compute minimal hitting sets of the components contained in the minimal positive conflicts [62, 38]. A hitting set of a set of sets $\{A_i\}$ is defined by having a nonempty intersection with each A_i. As an illustrative example, we reconsider a slightly modified example from [64]: the starter of a car and its rear lights and front lights supplied by a battery in parallel (Fig. 10.3). However, we observe that the rear lights are dark and the starter does not work, while the head lights are lit. We assume that the library contains (only) models of the correct behavior of the involved components: a battery supplies voltage, wires act as electrical connectors, and, if supplied with a voltage drop, light bulbs are lit and the starter acts. Such models for the battery, the starter and Wire_1, Wire_2 will predict all together that the starter is active, contradictory to the observation:

$ok(\text{Battery}) \wedge ok(\text{Wire}_1) \wedge ok(\text{Wire}_2) \wedge ok(\text{Starter}) \Rightarrow active(\text{Starter})$,

$OBS \Rightarrow \neg active(\text{Starter})$.

This yields a conflict

$\text{Conflict}_1 \equiv \neg ok(\text{Battery}) \vee \neg ok(\text{Wire}_1) \vee \neg ok(\text{Wire}_2) \vee \neg ok(\text{Starter})$

which is positive and minimal. Similarly we obtain

$\text{Conflict}_2 \equiv \neg ok(\text{Battery}) \vee \neg ok(\text{Wire}_1)$
$\vee \neg ok(\text{Wire}_2) \vee \neg ok(\text{Wire}_3) \vee \neg ok(\text{Wire}_4) \vee \neg ok(\text{RLight})$.

Furthermore, the lit head lights imply the existence of a voltage drop which should also cause the rear lights to be lit, leading to

$$\text{Conflict}_3 \equiv \neg ok(\text{HLight}) \vee \neg ok(\text{Wire}_5) \vee \neg ok(\text{Wire}_6) \vee \neg ok(\text{RLight}).$$

Analogously, we find

$$\text{Conflict}_4 \equiv \neg ok(\text{HLight}) \vee \neg ok(\text{Wire}_5) \vee \neg ok(\text{Wire}_6)$$
$$\vee \neg ok(\text{Wire}_3) \vee \neg ok(\text{Wire}_4) \vee \neg ok(\text{Starter}).$$

In fact, these are all minimal and positive conflicts. As a side-remark, the last two conflicts are only derived if the predictor is complete enough to reason not only in the causal direction, but also draw conclusions from the effect, namely the lit head lights. The mode assignment

$$\neg ok(\text{RLight}) \wedge \neg ok(\text{Starter})$$

implies all conflicts and is minimal, hence a prime implicant of all positive minimal conflicts. Thus,

$$\{\text{RLight, Starter}\}$$

is a fault localization, in accordance with our expectation.

At this point, we emphasize, that the described approach allows for

- fault localization with models of correct component behavior only, i.e. without any restriction on the possible faulty behaviors,

- localizing multiple faults.

This is an advantage over systems based on empirical symptom-fault associations, which require explicitly known faults and face natural limitations on known symptoms of multiple faults.

If the library does not contain fault models, there is no way to refute $\neg ok(C_i)$, all basic conflicts are positive ones, and extending a fault localization by additional components also yields a fault localization. In general, we have [19]:

Theorem 10.3. *For each fault localization FAULTY $\in$ COMPS every superset FAULTY$'$ $\supset$ FAULTY is also a fault localization iff all basic conflicts of SD $\cup$ OBS are positive.*

In this case, the minimal fault localizations are a compact representation of all fault localizations, namely as a lower bound in the subset lattice of *COMPS*.

Fault localization with fault models

When taking a second look at the example, we notice that, while we are satisfied with the fault localization {RLight, Starter}, we would not consider, for instance, its superset {RLight, Starter, Battery} as a reasonable fault localization, despite Theorem 10.3. Furthermore, we notice that there are many more prime implicants of the four conflicts, namely 21, and among them are, for instance,

$$\neg ok(\text{Wire}_1) \wedge \neg ok(\text{Wire}_5)$$

and

$$\neg ok(\text{Battery}) \land \neg ok(\text{HLight})$$

which we may not want to accept as a plausible fault localization! The reason why we find them implausible lies in the fact that the observations contradict the expected faulty behavior of the suspected components: the head lights would not be lit if they were broken. While **not requiring** models of faulty behavior, fault localization may become more focused and realistic when exploiting fault models.

One way to do this has been introduced in GDE$^+$ [64] by associating models with fault modes and *physical negation* axioms

$$\neg ok(C_i) \;\Rightarrow\; \bigvee_j fault_{ji}(C_i)$$

in order to express that the negation of the ok behavior in physical systems does not lead to totally unrestricted behavior, but to a certain set of unintended behaviors that can still be described. If the fault modes of some component C_i can be refuted by the observations in conjunction with a mode assignment to other components, *MA*, or directly, i.e. ($MA = \emptyset$), i.e. for all i

$$SD \cup \{MA \land fault_{ji}(C_i)\} \cup OBS \models \bot$$

then C can be exonerated in this context:

$$SD \cup \{MA\} \cup OBS \models ok(C_i)$$

by means of the physical negation axiom. By adding meaningful fault models for the components in our example (expressing "broken lights are never lit", etc.) and the physical negation rule, the only remaining fault localization will the plausible one. However, if some exotic faults are ignored in our model, the proper fault localization may be missed. For instance, if Wire$_1$ were open, while Wire$_5$ is open, but shorted to source at the end towards the head lights, the fault localization {Wire$_1$, Wire$_5$} would make sense. We may try to account for such unforeseen faults by introducing a fault mode with unspecified behavior. But this could not be refuted and the exoneration not be concluded, which means that fault localization would also be not affected by the use of the other fault models. We need some additional concepts which will be discussed in the following subsection.

As an alternative, Friedrich et al. [31] propose to represent situations that are physically impossible (under all modes) instead of the various faults (e.g., that head lights without voltage are never lit).

With the introduction of fault models and, hence, the possibility of conflicts that are not positive, the minimal fault localizations are no longer the generators of all fault localizations. Intuitively, this is because a minimal fault localization may become inconsistent if a fault mode of another component is added. In our example, the fault localization {RLight, Starter, HLight} is a superset of {RLight, Starter}, but inconsistent (because a fault in HLight directly contradicts the observations).

To obtain a generating set for the case of fault models, the concept of *kernel diagnosis* was introduced [19].

Definition 10.5 (Kernel diagnosis). *A kernel diagnosis is a minimal partial mode assignment MA_k with the property that every mode assignment that extends it is consistent with $SD \cup OBS$, i.e.*

for all consistent MA holds
if MA entails MA_k
then MA is a diagnosis of $SD \cup OBS$.

In other words, the modes of the components not mentioned in MA_k do not matter. Obviously, all fault localizations are obtained from an extension of some kernel diagnoses. Also, the kernel diagnoses can be characterized as prime implicants of all minimal conflicts.

Fault identification

Besides helping to refine fault localization, fault models provide the basis for identifying which particular component faults may be responsible for the disturbed system behavior. If the list of behavior modes contains specific faults of a component (type), then the diagnoses according to the definition given above are the answer to the task of fault identification.

However, the inclusion of explicit fault models in *SD* is a qualitative jump from a single system model (of the ok behavior) to a large space of models, corresponding to all possible mode assignments. This is important from both a technical and an application point of view.

Technically, it implies that many system models may have to be checked for consistency with observations, and for conflict-driven approaches, it means that the space of minimal conflicts grows. Fortunately, the application perspective implies that most of the mode assignments are not interesting and many conflicts need not be discovered. To most diagnosis applications, it is not interesting to **characterize** the space of **all** diagnoses, but to **compute** the most **relevant** ones. This is because its purpose is to provide information just enough to restore the functionality. Therefore, of course, what makes a diagnosis relevant depends on the type of system and its application context. But to be of practical interest, diagnostic theories and systems should provide generic means to express some ranking of the expected diagnoses and algorithms to effectively and efficiently compute the best ones under such a ranking. Unfortunately, there have not been as many theoretical contributions to this important area as to the logical characterization and approaches assuming exhaustive computation.

The applied principle of Occam's razor, namely not to assume more components to be broken than necessary, is usually a fundamental criterion we would like to preserve for fault identification, as well.

Definition 10.6 (Minimal diagnosis). *A diagnosis MA for $SD \cup OBS$ is a minimal diagnosis, iff the corresponding fault localization*

$$FAULTY := \{C_i \in COMPS \mid ok(C_i) \notin MA\}$$

is minimal.

This set of minimal diagnoses may still be large and ignore additional ranking criteria. Both a broken (open) light bulb and its pin being shorted to ground may explain why the bulb is not lit, but the shorted fault may be much more unlikely and, hence, only considered if the other one has been ruled out. We can define such a general preference on the modes of a component.

Definition 10.7 (Preference on modes and mode assignments). *A mode preference for C_i is a partial order "$\geqslant$" on modes(C_i):*

$$\geqslant \; \subseteq modes(C_i) \times modes(C_i),$$

where $ok(C_i)$ is the maximal element and an unknown fault mode unknown(C_i), if present, is the minimal element:

$$\forall m_j(C_i) \in modes(C_i) \setminus \{ok(C_i)\}: ok(C_i) > m_j(C_i),$$
$$\forall m_j(C_i) \in modes(C_i) \setminus \{unknown(C_i)\}: m_j(C_i) > unknown(C_i).$$

"$>$" is defined as

$$x > y \quad :\Leftrightarrow \quad x \geqslant y \wedge \neg(y \geqslant x).$$

This induces a preference on mode assignments: for

$$MA = \{m_{j_i}(C_i)\},$$
$$MA' = \{m'_{j_i}(C_i)\},$$

we define

$$MA \geqslant MA' \quad :\Leftrightarrow \quad \forall i \; m_{j_i}(C_i) \geqslant m'_{j_i}(C_i).$$

Definition 10.8 (Preferred diagnosis). *A diagnosis MA is a preferred diagnosis, if there is no diagnosis MA' that is strictly preferred over MA*

$$\forall MA' \; MA' \geqslant MA \quad \Rightarrow \quad MA' = MA.$$

Intuitively, the definition expresses, that a certain fault mode $m_j(C_i)$ should appear in a preferred diagnosis *MA* if

1. all mode assignments that are obtained by *MA* replacing $m_j(C_i)$ in *MA* by a strictly preferred mode $m'_j(C_i) > m_j(C_i)$ are not a diagnosis, and, of course,

2. *MA* is a diagnosis.

In order to characterize preferred diagnoses, [24] uses default logic [61, 5]. A (normal) default is an inference rule of the form

$$a : b/b$$

which expresses, intuitively, "If a is true, and it is consistent to assume b is true, then b holds". A default theory is a pair (D, P), where P is a set of classical formulas and D a set of defaults. Since defaults may exclude each other mutually, there are different (maximal) sets of defaults applicable, which leads to different sets of conclusions, called *extensions*.

For instance, assuming a certain mode of a component, we cannot associate another mode of the same component that might also be consistent. Indeed, we can encode the rule that $m_j(C_i)$ should be assumed only if all its strictly preferred predecessors

$$pre_j(C_i) := \{m_k(C_i) \mid m_k(C_i) > m_j(C_i)\}$$

have been refuted, and if $m_j(C_i)$ can be consistently assumed as a default

$$def_{ij} \equiv \bigwedge_{m_k(C_i) \in pre_j(C_i)} \neg m_k(C_i) : m_j(C_i)/m_j(C_i).$$

Especially, the ok behavior will be assumed first:

$$: ok(C_i)/ok(C_i)$$

The following theorem [24] captures the intuition that these preference defaults determine the preferred diagnoses:

Theorem 10.4. *Let* $DEF = \{def_{ij}\}$ *be the set of all preference defaults. MA is a preferred diagnosis if*

$$Cn(SD \cup OBS \cup MA)$$

is an extension of the default theory $(DEF, SD \cup OBS)$. *Here,* $Cn(.)$ *denotes the deductive hull:*

$$Cn(P) := \{p \mid P \models p\}.$$

The theorem provides the logical characterization of (preferred) diagnoses for fault identification and contains as a special case, namely $modes(C_i) = \{ok(C_i), \neg ok(C_i)\}$, the characterization for fault localizations given in [62]. The theory was implemented as the *Default-based Diagnosis Engine (DDE)* [25] which generates the successor mode assignments for the refuted diagnosis hypotheses according to the preference relation and checks their consistency only if all strictly preferred diagnoses have been refuted. This means, in particular, if an unknown fault is included, it will only be considered if no other fault mode survives the consistency check, but its existence prevents exoneration as performed in GDE^+.

DDE's preferences are local to each component and only an ordering. It does not use preferences among modes of different components and, hence, does, for instance, not order single faults involving different components. A refinement can be obtained by exploiting a global scale for ranking of modes, such as failure probabilities. In *SHERLOCK* [22], mode assignments are checked for consistency in the order of their probability which is obtained from the probabilities of modes (assuming their independence). Starting with a-priori probabilities, *SHERLOCK* recomputes probabilities when new conflicts have been detected. Unknown faults can be included, usually with low probability, and termination criteria specified, e.g., as a function of the probabilities of the diagnoses obtained so far. Although there is no formal characterization, it should be clear that *SHERLOCK* generates a subset of the preferred diagnoses if the preference is the order induced by mode probabilities. The core of this technique is fairly general and has been introduced as *conflict-directed A* search* [86].

10.4.2   Computation of Diagnoses

Since diagnosis is formalized as finding a model that is consistent with the observations, one might (and some authors do) suggest using any (efficient) generic algorithm that generates a solution for

$$SD \cup \{MA\} \cup OBS$$

such as constraint satisfaction algorithms [13, 63] and SAT-solvers. However, while many such algorithms produce **some single** solution quite efficiently, their naive use may ignore requirements and context of the real task. The same holds for the, usually infeasible, attempt to compute the set of **all** diagnoses. Diagnosis in the real world is not interested in a single arbitrary solution, but in **finding a set of diagnoses that fulfill some criteria dictated by the practical context of the task**. Such criteria vary and can be quite complex. Minimality (with respect to cardinality or set inclusion) of diagnoses is only one example, which is independent of domain and task. In reality, the relevance criteria for diagnoses are mainly determined by the ultimate objective, namely re-establishing the proper system behavior at minimal cost and risk, and, hence, may vary with the means and restrictions for reaching the objective (see the discussion in Section 10.6). Focusing on the most likely or "preferred" faults as done in *SHERLOCK* [22] and GDE^+ [24], respectively, reduces the risk of fixing the wrong component and, thus, the average cost. In some applications, certain highly critical faults may have to be explicitly ruled out (e.g., to select appropriate recovery actions based on on-board diagnosis of vehicles).

Another important requirement in many applications is due to the fact that computing diagnoses from observations is not a one-shot activity, but happens multiple times in a process of gathering information through testing and observation (see Section 10.5). This has to be reflected by the requirement for algorithms that support an efficient **incremental** computation of diagnoses when the set of observations is extended.

The design of a diagnosis algorithm has to reflect a number of choices imposed by the respective application:

- The task: fault **localization** vs. fault **identification**.

- The models: existence or non-existence of **fault models**.

- Fault models: existence or non-existence of an **unknown fault** (with unrestricted behavior).

- The result: criteria for the **relevance of diagnoses** to be produced (rarely all).

In the theories presented above, the concept of conflicts played an important role in characterizing the solution space. We discuss some aspects of exploiting conflicts in some more detail.

Computing fault localizations/diagnoses from conflicts

Theorem 10.2 suggests a two-step computation: first compute all minimal (positive) conflicts, then compute their prime implicants to obtain fault localizations. This is feasible and useful, if only the *OK* behavior is modeled. *GDE* [20] is the archetype of this solution. The presence of fault models modifies the set of minimal positive conflicts, if the *physical negation* rule is applied (i.e. the set of fault models is considered complete and does not contain an unknown fault as in GDE^+ [64]). For instance, in our example:

$$Conflict_3 \equiv \neg ok(HLight) \lor \neg ok(Wire_5) \lor \neg ok(Wire_6) \lor \neg ok(RLight)$$

is reduced to

$$Conflict_3 \equiv \neg ok(Wire_5) \lor \neg ok(Wire_6) \lor \neg ok(RLight)$$

by the non-positive conflict

$$\neg broken(HLight)$$

(which is obtained from the observation that HLight is lit) and the physical negation rule:

$$\neg ok(HLight) \Rightarrow broken(HLight).$$

The introduction of fault models implies the step from a single system model (the *OK* model) to a large set of models (for all mode assignments). This is a qualitative leap, which usually makes a complete check of all mode assignments infeasible.

Computing kernel diagnoses

The concept of kernel diagnoses, introduced in Section 10.4.1, is attractive from a theoretical point of view, because it provides a generator for the set of all diagnoses in case of the existence of fault models. However, it does not offer the basis for any practical solution, because it requires an unrestricted consistency check of mode assignments. Also, many of the kernel diagnoses may be completely irrelevant to any practical consideration. We illustrate this by the following example. Consider, say, 17 "Equal components" $Equal_i$ in series which have the modes

$$ok(\text{Equal}_i) : in_i = out_i,$$
$$neg(\text{Equal}_i) : in_i - 1 = out_i,$$
$$pos(\text{Equal}_i) : in_i + 1 = out_i$$

and the observations

$$in_1 = 0,$$
$$out_{17} = 1.$$

Then there exist 17 singleton fault localizations, namely $\{pos(\text{Equal}_i)\}$, which are the interesting ones to focus on under practical considerations. The space of all fault localizations is given by all subsets of *COMPS* with odd cardinality. As a consequence, the set of kernel diagnoses is identical to the set of all fault localizations, which means, in particular, all of them are complete mode assignments. From a computational point of view, the example also illustrates that the set of non-positive conflicts is large namely the set of all subsets of *COMPS* with even cardinality and the empty set, and that determining them requires checking all complete mode assignments (but then, you have the fault localizations directly).

In summary, an exhaustive computation of conflicts rarely lends itself to a computational solution (except for fault localization with *OK* models only). However, there is no interest in computing all diagnoses, anyway.

Search for diagnoses and the exploitation of conflicts

The response to this insight is to organize the generation of relevant diagnoses as search, instantiating and checking mode assignments only after checking those with higher relevance. Given a criterion for (potentially dynamically) ordering mode assignments according to their importance, one could perform some best-first search in the space of mode assignments in a hypothesize-and-test cycle in a straightforward manner. However, (minimal) conflicts provide a powerful means to improve the efficiency of the search. This is due to the fact that a model of a mode assignment that does not satisfy all existing (minimal) conflicts does not need to be instantiated and checked for consistency with the observations. Stated differently, after each detection of a new (minimal) conflict, the search space can be pruned by eliminating all mode assignments that imply the respective inconsistent partial mode assignment (i.e. the negation of this conflict).

In GDE^+ [24], the preference defaults serve two purposes: on the one hand, they encode the ordering of the modes and ensure that a mode of a component is only considered for consistency checking in a context if all more preferred modes have been refuted. On the other hand, it will not be checked, if it is already known to be inconsistent because it is subsumed by some previously detected inconsistency. *SHERLOCK* [22], which checks mode assignments according to their probabilities, also exploits conflicts to prune the space of mode assignments. This principle has been generalized to *Conflict-directed A^** [86] for cost functions satisfying certain criteria.

Determining (minimal) conflicts

Exploiting conflicts for computing fault localizations and pruning the search space requires that the consistency check delivers more than a Yes/No answer for a complete mode assignment. It has to identify partial mode assignments that generate the inconsistency, and the smaller they are, the stronger is the impact on the accuracy of the computed fault localization and on search space pruning. The "classical" way of finding conflicts (as in *GDE*, GDE^+, and *SHERLOCK*) is by means of a **propagation-based predictor** interfaced to some dependency-recording mechanism (e.g., exploiting an *Assumption-based Truth-Maintenance System, ATMS* [14]). Whenever a contradiction (two conflicting values of a variable) is detected, the underlying behavior modes that derived it together can be determined. Incompleteness of the predictor may lead to missing (minimal) conflicts and, hence, suboptimal fault localization (although the proper one will never be falsely refuted). However, while this works for some systems, such as combinatorial circuits, there is a vast space of system models for which propagation is highly incomplete or does not derive anything (resistive electrical circuits, hydraulic systems, . . .). In this case, other more complete algorithms for consistency checking are needed, and if generic efficient ones are used (CSP, SAT, . . .), then their utility depends on whether and to what extent they can deliver (minimal) conflicts.

Pre-compilation of models

If one does not use dependency recording or some equivalent technique, the alternative is to check partial mode assignments for consistency in order to find conflicts. But this is a large space, and one would want to anticipate which assignments can possibly lead to the detection of a conflict. This means to decompose the system into chunks in a way that checking these respective partial mode assignments can possibly lead to a conflict. The analysis needed for such an approach, which may be called **conflict-oriented model decomposition** [56], has to reflect the structure of the system **and** the set of observable variables. Intuitively, the task is to find sets of observations that partition the system model into subsystems that can become over-determined, which often requires to make certain assumptions about the model (e.g., linear functions). There are a number of caveats. Firstly, the approach is obviously only suited for applications where the set of possible observables is fixed (and not too large), an assumption that can be valid for online-diagnosis of monitored or controlled systems. Secondly, the potential conflicts can comprise quite different subsets of components for different mode assignments, and even for different states and inputs of the system. Performing the analysis exhaustively for all cases, particularly under the presence of fault models seems prohibitive. Hence, thirdly, if we use purely structurally oriented algorithms, we may fail to find the minimal potential conflicts.

There are other proposals to compile system descriptions in order to achieve better performance at diagnosis runtime. Ultimately, only the interdependencies between observable variables and the mode assignments matter, whereas the overall system model may contain many more intermediate and unobservable variables, especially due to the fact that the model is a compositional one. A straightforward step is, therefore, to eliminate all unobservable variables from the model. This works best if the set of observable variables is fixed (and small), as, for instance, in on-board diagnosis and monitoring systems, where the set of observables is determined by the existing sensors [26]. This has enabled the generation of a model-based on-board diagnostic system, that runs on an actual control unit of a passenger vehicle [74]. Darwiche [10] proposes to compile a system description into a special form (negation normal form) in order to achieve better performance for diagnosis tasks.

Obviously, for all such solutions holds that the complexity of the task is shifted into the compilation step which even may become intractable.

Hierarchical models

Another option is to represent the system to be diagnosed by a hierarchical model and apply the described techniques at each level to those subsystems that have been determined as suspects at the higher level. This keeps the number of components and, hence, the size of mode assignments and conflicts small. (See, e.g., [48].) While a solution along these lines is theoretically straightforward, in practice it comes at considerable cost and raises some problems. Obviously, we need models of subsystems above the level of elementary components. There are two ways to obtain them: automatically or "by hand". The latter option, though feasible in some cases, increases the modeling effort. The bad part is that only the models of the very bottom layers can be expected to be reusable, the rest is likely to be system-specific. Therefore, in most applications, the effort of creating models of higher-level components (which are hardly re-usable) manually will probably kill the economic benefit of a model-based solution. An automated solution is needed.

The reductionist approach implies that we can obtain the behavior models of the subsystems in a bottom-up fashion as the composition of the models of its components, which means we face the task of automated model compilation (e.g., by transforming a constraint network to a single constraint relating state and interface variables of the aggregate and covering all observable variables). If we would like to exploit fault models not only at the lowest level to improve fault localization, we have a complexity problem, because we have to generate not only the ok model of the aggregate, but also its fault models, which would mean compiling models of all or a selected set of mode assignments. An option is to focus on single faults (or the most probable ones) and capture the rest by an unknown fault mode of the aggregate. Still the result can be many fault modes for the aggregate. Often, they can be conveniently summarized by a smaller set of fault modes in a more abstract representation, but generating such abstractions automatically is a serious challenge to automated modeling—or we are back at manual modeling.

10.4.3   Solution Scope and Limitations of Component-Oriented Diagnosis

Although what has been surveyed so far in this section has often been considered as theories and solutions to **the** task of diagnosis based on first principles, it turns out to be a very specific one. We need to be aware that there are a number of underlying assumptions and limitations that confine the scope of applicability from a practical perspective.

- **Fixed, well-specified set of components**: many systems in process industries (e.g., in chemical plants) and, even more so, natural systems cannot be modeled conveniently as a set of components.

- **Known, fixed structure**: For the types of systems just mentioned, this is also not satisfied. And in some devices, we might have to consider the processed objects as components, such as sheets in a copier.

- **Well-designed system**: This assumes the intended functionality (*"GOALS"*) is implied by the system with correct components. This is even not given for many carefully designed artifacts: often, the parameter tolerances of components in a circuit may well allow an unintended behavior, which is just not happening due to the statistical distribution of parameter deviations. And ecological systems are not designed anyway and, hence, always require an explicit representation and consideration of *GOALS* [41].

- **Component faults only**: Disturbances of the system behavior are always caused by a fault of one of the known components. However, often, the cause of a malfunction is due to some additional, unexpected object, substance, or agent intruding the system.

- **No structural faults**: Even if the structure of the correct device is well-specified, the fault may lie in a violation of this structure (e.g., a bridge fault) [16].

- **"Crisp" faults**: although the models of different faults may overlap, there is the assumption that the presence of a fault is a yes/no decision. In order to incorporate degradation and "soft" faults, one would have to introduce thresholds that, perhaps artificially, distinguish a tolerable degradation from a real fault.

But there are some **non-assumptions**, contrary to what is sometimes believed:

- Sometimes, it is believed that consistency-based diagnosis can only work with **specific modeling formalisms**, e.g., models that are expressed in, or can be transformed into, logical formulas, such as finite constraints. Engineering models do not come as logical formulas. However, the principles underlying consistency-based diagnosis are general. As discussed in Section 10.3, any modeling formalism that is suited to capture the diagnosis-relevant behavior aspects of component modes and that has some notion of and mechanisms for checking the consistency of a model with observations can be used. This includes numerical models and simulators, provided there is a way to avoid the creation of spurious inconsistencies due to noise, model inaccuracy, measurement imprecision, etc. Also, if computation is fixed to one direction (from "input" to "output"), they have to reflect the available observations what makes the system models specific and reduces their reusability, and they may suffer from incompleteness regarding the detection of all conflicts (because this may require inferences starting from outputs).

- In particular, it is often assumed that only **static system** behavior can be diagnosed. This is not true, since neither the theory nor the technical principles prevent the use of models that describe the dynamic behavior and of observations that capture the system evolution over time. Still, the temporal dimension introduces some additional problems and specific answers, which will be the subject of the next section.

Furthermore, it should be pointed out that there is a useful generalization of the theory and the techniques if we replace "behavior modes" by "states", where a state is the assignment of a value to a state variable of a component (in analogy to assigning a particular mode to a component). This way, hypotheses not only about the occurrence of faults, but also about the internal states of a system can be generated [84]. However, there is no general preference criterion (like minimality for sets of faulty components) for states, although, perhaps, for state changes.

10.4.4 Diagnosis across Time

If observations are available not just for one snapshot of system behavior, but for a whole observation period, this may strengthen the basis for diagnosis, but also triggers some special problems to solve. Extending the basic definitions appropriately is not too difficult. First, we have a **history** or sequence of observations

$$OBSH = \{OBS_i\} = \{\{obs_{ij}(t_i)\}\}$$

related to a finite set of time points t_i in some time interval of interest, $t_i \in I_\omega$. Secondly, not only the behavior of the system to be diagnosed may evolve over time, but also the behavior **modes** of components may change over time, i.e. faults may occur and also disappear. Therefore, in the general case, a diagnostic hypothesis is no longer **one** mode assignment, but a **history** of mode assignments

$$MH = \{(MA_k, I_k)\}, \quad \bigcup_k I_k = I_\omega, \quad MA_k \neq MA_{k+1},$$

where MA_k is a mode assignment that holds for all time points in some interval $I_k = (t_k, t_{k+1}) \subset I_\omega$, that is consistent with the observation history (see, e.g., [33]).

Definition 10.9 (Consistency-based temporal diagnosis). *A history of complete mode assignments*

$$MH = \{(MA_k, I_k)\}$$

in I_ω is a consistency-based temporal diagnosis for a system description SD and an observation history

$$OBSH = \{\{obs_{ij}(t_i)\}\}$$

in I_ω if

$$SD \cup MH \cup OBSH \not\models \bot.$$

This concept of a temporal diagnosis subsumes the static version in the sense that for each observation point, the mode assignment must be a diagnosis according to Definition 10.2.

Definition 10.10 (State-based diagnosis). *A mode history*

$$MH = \{(MA_k, I_k)\}$$

is a state-based diagnosis for

$$OBSH = \{\{obs_{ij}(t_i)\}\}$$

if

> *for all t_i holds*
> *if $t_i \in I_k$*
> *then MA_k is a diagnosis for SD and OBS_i.*

Lemma 10.1. *If $MH = \{(MA_k, I_k)\}$ is a temporal diagnosis of SD and*
> $OBSH = \{\{obs_{ij}(t_i)\}\}$,
> *then*
> *MH is a state-based diagnosis for SD and $OBSH$.*

In other words, being a state-based diagnosis is a **necessary** condition for obtaining a temporal diagnosis. Amazingly enough, it is also a sufficient condition for an interesting and large class of systems and tasks, as discussed in the following.

Whether this holds strictly, depends also on the available observations, because some *sequence-constraints*, i.e. restrictions on the possible transitions between states, may compensate for limited observability. Let us illustrate this by a trivial example. Assume we parked our car in a street in San Francisco with considerable and applied the park brake. When we return 10 minutes later, we find the car is no longer at the place where we left it, but 50 m down the street in front of a wall (with some dents). We certainly suspect that the park brake did not do its job, despite the fact that the car was at stand-still when we left, but also the car in front of the wall is perfectly consistent with a well-functioning park brake. However, we can conclude that, since the positions are different, there must have been an unobserved state in between, where the speed of the car was non-zero which contradicts the *OK* mode of the park brake. This case shows that the *sequence-constraints* can compensate for gaps in observations in two ways: gaps in time (by conclusions for unobserved states) and regarding observable variables (esp. derivatives, here: the speed).

Computation of temporal diagnoses

The example does not only illustrate that the *sequence-constraints* can be essential to diagnosis, it also sheds a light on the implication for computational considerations; We did not have to simulate the vehicle's behavior under *OK* mode and the broken-park-brake mode to obtain a conclusion.

Instead, we inferred the existence of a state with *speed* > 0, which directly contradicts the *OK* model, while being consistent with the fault model. This illustrates: even if we cannot drop the temporal aspects from the consistency check of different mode assignments MA_j

$$SD \cup \{MA_j\} \cup OBSH,$$

which means

$$\textit{state-constraints}_{ji} \cup \textit{sequence-constraints} \cup OBSH,$$

without loss, this still does not force us to simulate the model of every candidate mode assignment MA_j, which is likely to be impossible anyway (e.g., in our example, we do not know when the car started to move and how). Instead, we can apply *sequence-constraints* first, to complement the observed history by indirect observations

$$OBSH \cup \textit{sequence-constraints} \models OBSH_{ext}$$

and then perform consistency checks of

$$\textit{state-constraints}_{ji} \cup OBSH_{ext}.$$

The computational advantage of the second solution is tremendous, since we avoid simulation of many fault hypotheses, apply *sequence-constraints* only once and perform cheaper consistency checks on states only. The most common application and exploitation of this approach is the computation of derivatives from observations to avoid simulation and obtain equivalent results (as analyzed and confirmed in [6] for numerical models). In essence, the good message is: **diagnosis of dynamic systems does not require simulation.**

If we perform state-based diagnosis of persistent faults as described above, then the mode assignment in the temporal diagnosis has to be a prime implicant of the union of all sets of conflicts detected at the various time points (or, rather, the minimal elements of this union). Hence, diagnoses can be computed incrementally by adding newly detected (minimal) conflicts for each observed snapshot. For systems that perform a best-first search, such as *SHERLOCK* and *DDE*, the set of diagnoses obtained from one snapshot (e.g., the most probable or the preferred diagnoses) forms the set of mode assignments to be checked against the observations for the next snapshot. Whenever, based on these checks, some diagnoses are refuted and new ones are generated, these also ought to be checked against all previous snapshots.

State-based vs. simulation-based diagnosis

When confronted with the necessity to diagnose a system whose behavior is observed and changes over time, the immediate consequence seems to be that one has to simulate the behavior under different mode assignments and check for consistency with the actual tracked behavior ([15] is an examples of such a solution). Triggered by the observation that in applications of consistency-based diagnosis conflicts always were generated from observations stemming from one snapshot [23], the analysis revealed that the underlying reasons are quite fundamental and lead to a fairly general characterization of preconditions for being able to refrain from simulation without affecting the quality of the resulting diagnoses [71].

The key consideration is that many computational modeling formalisms decompose a description of the temporal evolution of a system into a set of restrictions that hold for the state at each time point and a part that restricts the set of possible sequences of such states:

$$model = state\text{-}constraints \cup sequence\text{-}constraints$$

For instance, in a numerical simulation system, the former one is an ordinary differential equation, while the latter is incorporated in the integration algorithm. In this case, the specificity of *model* of a particular mode (assignment) is captured by the first part only, while the second part represents general laws that apply to all models, namely the laws of continuity, derivatives, and integration, and is shared by all possible behaviors an their models. As a consequence, any observed behavior of a particular mode assignment will be consistent with the model, if and only if it is consistent with its *state-constraints*. This provides an intuition for why checking the individual observation snapshots for consistency with the *state-constraints* suffices for diagnosis, and applying *sequence-constraints* and simulation can be avoided. However, if the observations have gaps, i.e., miss a state of the actual behavior, or the set of observable variables is too small to reveal an inconsistency, then exploiting *sequence-constraints* in simulation might compensate for it, because they could infer information about an intermediate state or additional information about a partially observed state (e.g., about derivates). This consideration can be turned into a rigorous argument [71] and a foundation for solutions of high importance to industrial applications, especially if faults are persistent. Faults are persistent if they do not vanish without repair (such as leakages or broken bulbs).

Definition 10.11 (Persistence of modes). *A (fault) mode $m_{ji}(C_i)$ is called persistent if for all temporal diagnoses $\{(MA_k, I_k)\}$*

$$\exists k' \, m_{ji}(C_i) \in MA_{k'} \quad \Rightarrow \quad \forall k > k' \, m_{ji}(C_i) \in MA_k$$

must hold.
 It is called persistent in I_ω if

$$\forall k \, m_{ji}(C_i) \in MA_k.$$

We prefer this definition over the one proposed by [60] who calls a behavior persistent if the output of a component is a function of its inputs (and not of time), for two fundamental reasons: Firstly, persistence is a property of a **mode**, rather than of **model** as in [60]. Continuous models that reflect noise and uncertainty often cannot be stated in terms of functions, and a qualitative model that is obtained by abstracting a real-valued function is usually no longer a function. Secondly, there are only few kinds of systems that can be modeled in a directional way.

In contrast, the condition concerning the commonality of *sequence-constraints* is a property of the model.

Definition 10.12 (Homogeneity). *A model library LIB is called homogeneous, if there exists a set* sequence-constraints *that links states of the system at different time points and is shared by all models, i.e. for all modes* m_{ji},

$$model_{ji} = state\text{-}constraints_{ji} \cup sequence\text{-}constraints,$$

and state-constraints$_{ji}$ contains only restrictions for each single time point.

If the above properties hold, then for persistent faults, being a state-based diagnosis can be not only a necessary condition for a temporal diagnosis (Lemma 10.1) but also a sufficient one [71], i.e. *MH* is a temporal diagnosis for *SD* and *OBSH* if and only if

$$MH = \{(MA, I_{\omega})\}$$

and *MA* is a state-based diagnosis for *SD* and *OBSH*. Since the *sequence-constraints* do not contribute to a consistency check at a single time point, *MA* is obtained as a diagnosis for *SD sequence-constraints* and all *OBS$_i$*.

The above considerations apply, in particular, if all modeled behaviors are continuous. However, if the model contains discrete states and transitions between them, then homogeneity is usually violated, because the possible transitions are specific to a particular behavior mode. For instance, transitions between states *OPEN* and *CLOSED* do occur in the *OK* model, but not for a *STUCK* mode.

Even more fundamentally, the homogeneity property becomes obsolete, if the persistence assumption is dropped. So far, we considered only models that describe the component (system) **behavior** under each **mode** (assignment). In temporal diagnosis, we may want or need to model also, in which ways **mode changes** occur. Most attempts to do so make the assumption that this happens as a discrete change. Thus, the evolution of system behavior may be described by state changes within a mode and mode changes:

$$sequence\text{-}constraints = states\text{-}sequence\text{-}constraints$$

$$\cup\, modes\text{-}sequence\text{-}constraints,$$

although many formalisms represent them in the same way, namely as discrete transitions.

If we make a Markov assumption, then *sequence-constraints* become *transition-constraints*, which restrict pairs of adjacent states.

Transition-based diagnosis

There are a number of approaches to incorporating transitions to fault modes in the model, covering the spectrum from discrete-event models to models of continuous behavior. As basing such models on the concepts of states and transitions is natural, most of them are some variant of finite state machines or similar formalisms. There are many approaches, reflecting different types of systems, tasks, observations, temporal information, etc. Here, we can only provide a preliminary formal account for the common underlying ideas and refer to some specific instances. We represent a model of the possible evolution of the behavior a component, C_i, as a tuple

$$model(C_i) = (S_i, s_{i,0}, E_i, E_{i,obs}, T_i, T_{i,F})$$

with

- a finite set of **states**, S_i, which can represent operating modes under normal behavior (e.g., a proper valve in its closed state) or faulty behavior (the valve stuck closed),

- an **initial state**, $s_{i,0}$,

- a finite set of **events**, E_i, which may be exogenous influences, control commands (external or internal ones), the occurrence of faults, alarms or other observables, etc.,

- the **observable events**, $E_{i,obs} \subset E_i$, which exclude, at least, the events that trigger fault transitions (otherwise, there is no diagnostic problem),

- a finite set of **transitions**, T_i, shifting the system from one state to the next (deterministically or non-deterministically), based on the triggering event and possibly generating an event:

$$T_i \subset S_i \times E_i \times S_i \times E_i.$$

  A transition $t \in T_i$ may represent switches between operating modes, shifts to a fault mode, but possibly also the return to a correct behavior in case of an intermittent fault or due to some repair or reset action,

- the set of **fault transitions**, $T_{i,F} \subset T_i$, which correspond to the occurrence of faults.

Such a model uses only the simplest representation of time, namely a (partial) ordering of states. A formal specification of the semantics can be based on some temporal logic containing a *next* operator [32]. Sometimes, metric temporal information (numerical or qualitative) may be necessary and/or available.

Such component models fulfill the important requirement to be **compositional**. We obtain a model of a system comprising a set of concurrently active components $COMPS = \{C_i\}$

$$MODEL = (S, s_0, E, E_{obs}, T, T_F)$$

as a product of the component models, where

$$S = S_1 \times \cdots \times S_n,$$

$$s_0 = (s_{1,0}, \ldots, s_{n,0}),$$

$$E = P\left(\bigcup E_i\right),$$

$$E_{obs} = P\left(\bigcup E_{i,obs}\right)$$

(which means, only part of the composite event may be observable). The way transitions are specified may depend on different assumptions, especially about synchronization of the local transitions.

A diagnosis is then, intuitively, some explanation of a sequence of observed events in terms of a path through the finite state machine which generates this observable trace and can be defined as follows.

Definition 10.13 (Transition-based diagnosis). *Let*

$$MODEL = (S, s_0, E, E_{obs}, T, T_F)$$

be the model of a system and

$$OBS = (OBS_1, \ldots, OBS_n) \in E_{obs}^n$$

be a sequence of observations.
A sequence of events

$$e = (e_1, \ldots, e_m) \in E^m$$

is an extension *of OBS, iff it contains OBS in the proper order, i.e.*

(i) $\forall k \, \exists j(k) \, e_{j(k)} \cap \bigcup_i E_{i,obs} = OBS_k,$

(ii) $k_1 < k_2 \implies j(k_1) < j(k_2);$

e is a transition-based diagnosis *of (MODEL, OBS) iff*

(i) *e is an extension of OBS,*

(ii) $\exists (s_1, \ldots, s_m) \in S^m \, \forall 1 < j < m \, (s_{j-1}, e_j, s_j, e_{j+1}) \in T.$

Fault detection is performed, if every diagnosis contains some fault transition. Fault identification corresponds to the subsequence of fault transitions in a diagnosis, and fault localization is done by looking for the components where these fault transitions occur. Like for the snapshot case, we can apply some minimality criteria for ranking diagnoses and fault localizations. One could also recast the definition in terms of fault events or fault states (in the latter case with a modified minimality criterion). There are many directions for variations, specializations, and extensions of this perspective on diagnosis across time.

Diagnosis with discrete-event models

[65] uses a deterministic finite state machine without emitted events and approaches the diagnostic problem by compiling the original finite state machine into one that contains only observable transitions and produces the same language in terms of observations, called *diagnoser*. Its states represent the respective sets of nodes in the original model that can be reached via paths that contain also unobservable transitions,

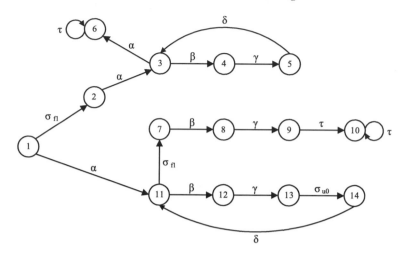

THE SYSTEM G

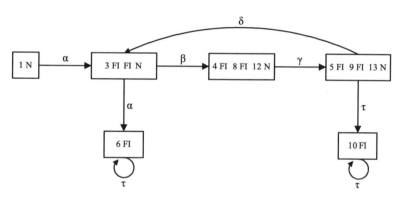

THE DIAGNOSER G_d

Figure 10.4: The system model (top) with observable transitions α, β, γ, δ, τ and the fault transition σ_{FI}. The nodes of the diagnoser contain the potentially reached original states together with the faults on the path ("FI") or "N" (i.e. no fault). From [65].

labeled with the fault transitions on these paths. This means that, after a sequence of observations, the diagnoses can be read off of these labels (together with a prediction of the possible current states of the system). Fig. 10.4 gives a simple example of a finite state machine and its diagnoser.

Related work is described in [46] and [47]. [77] discusses links between this approach and diagnosability based on continuous models. When a system comprises many components that operate concurrently, the explosion of the Cartesian product of the states is an obvious problem and motivates a decentralized approach as in [54] applied to telecommunication networks.

Diagnosis with hybrid models

The view on a system's behavior as a sequence of state transitions lends itself to modeling various kinds of systems including combinations of software and physical components. In this case, the (continuous) behavior during a state may have to be modeled, as well, because it can be the cause of discrete changes. In *Livingstone* [84], components are also modeled as a graph of transitions between states of the component, which represent normal operating modes and fault modes. A component's behavior is characterized by a set of variables (physical quantities, commands, etc.). States are characterized by constraints on these variables, actually the assignment of a single value to some of the variables. As for the models of many of the consistency-based diagnosis systems discussed earlier in this section, qualitative modeling [81, 35, 4] turns the representation of the continuous behavior into a finite one (e.g., in terms of finite constraints or propositional logic).

A *Livingstone* model can be interpreted in the general framework outlined above in the following way. A component C_i has an associated vector of variables $\underline{v}_i$ with the finite domain $\mathrm{DOM}(\underline{v}_i)$. The behaviors under the different states $s_{ij} \in S_i$ are specified by constraints:

$$s_{ij} \Rightarrow C_{ij} \quad \text{with } C_{ij} \subset \mathrm{DOM}(\underline{v}_i).$$

Events E_{ij} are also specified in terms of constraints on the variables:

$$E_{ij} \subset \mathrm{DOM}(\underline{v}_i)$$

and transitions move from states that fulfill the triggering conditions to states that satisfy the resulting condition. In each state, besides a nominal transition, also a number of fault transitions can occur non-deterministically. Again, the entire model can be understood as split into a set of *state-constraints* and *transition-constraints*, with some non-determinism concerning the latter.

In order to form a system model, the composition of such component models happens at two levels. On the one hand, as usual, the interaction of components along the system structure is represented by shared variables between component models. They may correspond to physical quantities, such as pressure and flow, commands of a controller, etc. On the other hand, states, events, and transitions are aggregated (in a synchronous way).

Because events are specified as restrictions on variables, the observable ones correspond directly to the snapshot observations (e.g., measurement of a set of variables) discussed earlier. In contrast to the compilation of the transition system into the diagnoser, *Livingstone* generates diagnoses incrementally from snapshot to snapshot. Because of the combinatorics of multiple transitions from each local state, complete generation of all potential successor states is prohibitive for interesting applications. Like *SHERLOCK*, *Livingstone* focuses on tracking the most likely paths, exploiting the a posteriori probabilities of the transitions given the observations about the resulting state. The system and its predecessors were applied prototypically to spacecraft self-diagnosis as a basis for self-reconfiguration [84].

10.4.5 Abductive Diagnosis

The concept of diagnosis, so far, is based on finding system models that do not contradict the given observations. This may seem quite weak. In fact, if the system shows

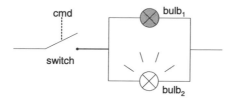

Figure 10.5: A fragment of a circuit with two parallel light bulbs.

some symptoms, we may want a diagnosis that provides a **causal account** for them. This idea leads to a new logical definition of a diagnosis, which requires that a model logically **entails** the given observations, rather than simply being consistent with them:

$$MODEL \models OBS$$

[57]. However, we have to be cautious when using this definition of *abductive diagnosis*. For instance, if the observations include a command "CLOSE" to the switch in the fragment of a circuit shown in Fig. 10.5, but bulb$_1$ remains dark while bulb$_2$ is lit, then the single fault in bulb$_1$ explains the observations of the bulbs, but we do not expect it could provide a reason for *switch.cmd* $=$ *CLOSE*. Intuitively, we want the system response (the "output" variables) to be entailed, but not the exogenous features (the "input" or independent variables). The most general definition reflecting this intention is the following.

Definition 10.14 (Abductive diagnosis). *Let MODEL$_F$ be a model of a fault and* $OBS = OBS_C \cup OBS_A$ *be a set of observations. MODEL$_F$ is an abductive diagnosis iff it is consistent with OBS$_C$ and entails OBS$_A$:*

$$MODEL_F \cup OBS_C \not\models \bot,$$

$$MODEL_F \cup OBS_C \models OBS_A.$$

A complete mode assignment MA is a component-oriented abductive diagnosis for a system description SD and a set of observations OBS iff

$$SD \cup \{MA\} \cup OBS_C \not\models \bot,$$

$$SD \cup \{MA\} \cup OBS_C \models OBS_A.$$

Please, note that if OBS_C refers to exogenous variables, the first condition is satisfied by any valid model (as discussed in Section 10.3). Console and Torasso [9] discuss the consequences of different possibilities to specify OBS_C and OBS_A. In our example, we would choose

$$OBS_C = \{switch.cmd = CLOSE\},$$

$$OBS_A = \{bulb_1.light = OFF, bulb_2.light = ON\}.$$

Unfortunately, a single fault in bulb$_1$ does not entail OBS_A based on OBS_C, because there is no information about the voltage supply and is not found as an abductive diagnosis, unless also the voltage supply is abduced.

Poole [57] raises the issue of how to represent the observations. Rather than treating them as a conjunction of inputs and outputs, we could try to find an explanation for observations stating that the input implies the output. This means in our example, we use

$$OBS = \{\text{switch.cmd} = \text{CLOSE} \Rightarrow (\text{bulb}_1.\text{light} = \text{OFF} \land \text{bulb}_2.\text{light} = \text{ON})\}$$

which would have to be entailed by an abductive diagnosis (which is again not the case). Note that we (humans) can even obtain a diagnosis solely based on observation of the outputs:

$$OBS = \{\text{bulb}_1.\text{light} = \text{OFF}, \text{bulb}_2.\text{light} = \text{ON}\}$$

and that consistency-based diagnosis with fault models produces the proper result.

Abductive diagnosis is attractive, because it provides a stronger notion of diagnosis which seems to reflect the aspect of causality in our human conception of diagnosis. However, apart from the fact that logical entailment is generally unrelated to causality, this stronger notion of diagnosis imposes stronger requirements on the model and the possible inferences, as illustrated by the above example. When compared to consistency-based diagnosis, the results are more sensitive to the particular representation and strength of the model and the observations. If an observation states that, say, a flow at some point is positive, while a model can only predict a disjunction *flow = zero* ∨ *flow = positive* (e.g., based on the model of a check valve), it would not be an abductive diagnosis. If the domain of flow (both in the model and the observation) would contain only the values *negative* and *non-negative*, then this would yield an abductive diagnosis. However, this coarser domain may then be too weak to derive some other predictions.

Of course, consistency-based diagnosis depends on the strength of the model, as well, and, in particular, on the granularity of the domains. This is because this can render the model unable to detect some of the existing conflicts. However, it is still guaranteed that the correct diagnosis (as a mode assignment) is never excluded. Such a guarantee cannot be obtained for abductive diagnosis.

Depending on the available observations, an abductive diagnosis may include not only the modes, but also the current state of the system and even numerical parameters (as suggested by [57]) which makes the abduction task even harder for systems of an interesting kind and size.

Abductive diagnosis seems to become feasible and provide some basis for meeting our intuition behind an explanation, if the model has causal notion embedded (as opposed to purely constraint- or equation-based behavior descriptions). In fact, many of the examples used for explaining abductive techniques come as causal networks that explicitly link faults to effects. As already discussed in Section 10.3, this kind of system-specific diagnosis task compiled into a system model is a non-solution to diagnostic applications (although in engineering practice, something similar is done in constructing fault trees for safety analysis), because it violates genericity, compositionality, and reusability of the model. What is required is a modeling ontology that captures causality and is compositional. As stated earlier, process-oriented modeling [34, 35, 41] is a candidate. This also paves a way to overcome some of the restrictive assumptions and limitations of component-oriented diagnosis discussed in Section 10.4.1.

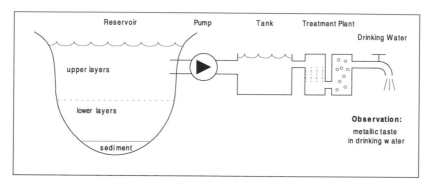

Figure 10.6: The drinking water has a high iron concentration, because solid iron in the sediment was re-dissolved into the water and transported to the tap.

10.4.6   Process-Oriented Diagnosis

In a simplified (though real) scenario of drinking water treatment (Fig. 10.6) [41], a high concentration of dissolved iron is detected in the drinking water. Since it exceeds the legally allowed level, and there is no source of iron the operators are aware of, this is a challenge for diagnosis. Human analysis yields to the following result: there is solid iron in the sediment of the reservoir, which was not known before. When the pH of the lower water layer, which is usually neutral, became acidic (most likely caused by some algal bloom phenomenon), this started a chemical process of redissolving of iron into the water body. The dissolved iron ascended to the surface layers, was captured with the raw water intake, and the treatment process did not reduce the unexpectedly high concentrations of iron as required. While we would claim that the case is clearly a diagnostic task, let us revisit the assumptions underlying component-oriented diagnosis as discussed in Section 10.4.1.

- **Fixed, well-specified set of components**: although there are components, such as pumps, containers, etc., the relevant diagnostic reasoning refers to biological, chemical, and physical processes; it would not be convenient to consider algae, water layers, etc. as components, and even if we do, solid iron was not a known "component" of the system.

- **Known, fixed structure**: the system and its model does not have a static structure; rather, there is a dynamically changing pattern of active processes and objects, substances, etc. appearing and disappearing.

- **Well-designed system**: although the treatment plant itself could be considered as such, the notion makes no sense for the reservoir and the processes involved. The *GOALS* are external to the model, and without making them explicit, there is no inconsistency.

- **Component faults only**: obviously, algae are not a fault, even if their biomass grows exponentially in an algal bloom period, nor is redissolving of iron under acidic conditions a fault mode of something; it is simply natural. But it is unwanted from the perspective of the violated *GOALS*.

- **No structural faults**: the nature of the disturbance **is** a structural change in the system, triggering unforeseen processes.

- **"Crisp" faults**: even more than with respect to artifacts, healthiness of ecological and biological systems, but also process plants is often expressed in terms of a spectrum of degradation, rather than a qualitative behavior change. Of course, in our example, the legal restrictions make it crisp.

Obviously, addressing such a diagnosis task in theory and implementation requires a different formalization of modeling and the diagnosis task. However, what we stick with is the idea that the answer to the diagnosis task is given by a model that is "compliant" with the observations of system behavior.

The example suggests the use of *process-oriented modeling*. Collins [7] develops the *Process Diagnosis Engine (PDE)* as abductive diagnosis on such a model. Heller and Struss [41] present a theory of process-oriented consistency-based diagnosis, realized as the *Generalized Diagnosis Engine (G+DE)*.

In a nutshell (see [34, 35, 41] for details), a process is considered as some elementary phenomenon, which can be modeled independently of others and is, therefore, suited to compositional modeling. This has two consequences: one is that a process model has to state explicitly all preconditions for the process to occur by listing the (typed) objects that interact in a particular configuration (*structural-conditions*) and constraints on involved quantities (*quantity-conditions*). A process can create new objects and relations between them (*structural-effects*) and affects quantities of the participating objects (*quantity-effects*). The second consequence of the required compositionality is that *quantity-effects* cannot all be simply stated as constraints on the quantities. This is because each (type of) process can only state a *partial* contribution to some overall effect. For instance, the model of the iron-redissolving process can only state that it adds to the concentration of dissolved iron in the water layer, but it cannot claim that this concentration effectively increases, because in a particular scenario, there may be other, counteracting, processes active that override the effect (e.g., oxidation of iron). In response to this, process-oriented modeling involves the concept of *influences* that goes beyond mathematical modeling based on (differential) equations, constraints, or first order logic. If some variable x influences a variable y, say, positively, written $I^+(x, y)$, this means basically that the derivative of y is a monotonic function of x:

$$I^+(x, y) \quad \Leftrightarrow \quad \exists f \; \frac{dy}{dt} = f(\ldots, x, \ldots) \wedge \frac{df}{dx} > 0.$$

The actual value of $\frac{dy}{dt}$ can only be determined after **all existing influences** can be (e.g., linearly) combined. But this requires a *closed-world assumption*, which provides an important hook for model revision during the search for a consistent model.

Thus, a process implies the effects, if the conditions are true:

    structural-conditions ∧ *quantity-conditions*
      ⇒ *structural-effects* ∧ *quantity-effects*

How can we state the diagnosis problem, which we call *situation assessment*, because there is not necessarily "something wrong"? We start with a partial description of a scenario in terms of objects, object relations, and variable values. This may include real observations, *OBS* (e.g., measurements, such as "iron concentration above threshold") and assumptions, *ASSM* (e.g., assertions that usually hold, such as "pH neutral"). The target is to construct process models that, based on propositions about structure (objects and object relations) and quantities, are consistent with *OBS* and, if possible, with *ASSM*. Again, we apply Occam's razor and prefer models that satisfy some minimality criteria. There are two orthogonal dimensions:

- do not drop more assumptions than required to obtain a consistent model,

- do not introduce more unanticipated objects than necessary in order to derive an explanation (why assume both solid iron in the sediment **and** iron in an affluent to the reservoir?): the structural basis should not be larger than necessary.

We should be more precise about the latter criterion: what we would like to minimize is the set of objects in the model that are not generated by some process, but are introduced without further justification by the model. In our example, the dissolved iron is an effect of the redissolving process, whereas the solid iron in the sediment does not have an explanation in the model. Hence, the issue relates to the question of the model boundaries: where should we stop to ask for reasons, because they are beyond what is captured by the model library? In our case, iron in the tank requires a causal explanation, whereas the existence of solid iron or algae does not. We characterize those types of object that sit "on the boundary" of the model as *introducible*. Obviously, they comprise those that never occur as a structural effect of a process in the library. But we may want to regards additional ones as introducible for certain problems or scenarios.

Based on this, we can give an informal definition of a process-oriented diagnosis (a formal account using default logic is described in [40]).

Definition 10.15 (Situation assessment). *Let LIB be a process library, OBJ-INTRO the set of introducible objects, OBJ-OBS and OBJ-ASSM the objects mentioned in OBS and ASSM, respectively. A situation assessment for (LIB, OBS, ASSM) is a triple (STRUCTURE, QUANT, ASSM-RETR); where STRUCTURE is a set of objects, and relations, QUANT is a set of value assignments to quantities, and ASSM-RETR ⊂ ASSM a set of assumptions such that the resulting model is consistent with the observations and a subset of the assumptions*:

(i) $STRUCTURE \cup QUANT \cup LIB \cup OBS \cup (ASSM \setminus ASSM\text{-}RETR) \nvDash \bot$

The structure contains the observed objects and a subset of the assumed ones:

(ii) *OBJ-OBS ⊂ STRUCTURE, OBJ-ASSM \ ASSM-RETR ⊂ STRUCTURE,*

(iii) *the model contains exactly the objects that are entailed by the introducible objects, i.e. the introducibles themselves and the ones created by processes,*

(iv) *(STRUCTURE ∩ OBJ-INTRO) ∪ ASSM-RETR is a (with respect to set inclusion) minimal set that satisfies (i) through (iii).*

Different applications may require modifications to this definition which minimizes the set of newly introduced objects and retracted assumptions, while introduced

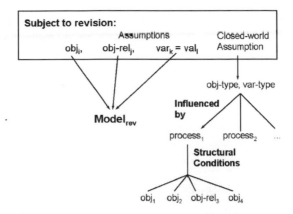

Figure 10.7: The options for model revisions.

relations do not count. Also, the likelihood of the occurrence of objects may further constrain the focus.

Regarding the implementation of a process-oriented diagnosis system, condition (i) suggests that algorithms from component-oriented consistency-based diagnosis can be applied: conflicts can be generated that contain user assumptions from *ASSM* and the closed world assumptions underlying the influence resolution for quantities. We point out that the latter introduce an element of abductive diagnosis: influence resolution implies that the derivative of a variable is zero if there is no influence acting on this variable. Therefore, if a change in a variable is observed (or postulated), any model that contains no process influencing this variable will be inconsistent, and the closed-world assumption for this variable occurs in a conflict. The same happens, of course, if the known influences contradict the (direction of) change in a variable. A similar technique can be used, if the *deviation* of some variable from an expected value is observed and the model captures how such deviations can emerge and propagate through a system. Resolving such conflicts and revising the model in a search process starts from the retraction of these closed-world assumptions. While in component-oriented diagnosis retraction of a mode assumption means switching to a different mode, retraction of the closed-world assumption requires to find (additional) potential influences on this variable. The search space for this revision is given by the process library: it contains a finite set of processes that can possibly influence a variable of the respective type associated with an object of the respective type. Extending the model by such a process may lead to a new inconsistency, if its quantity conditions are not satisfied. Also, the structural conditions need to be satisfied, and if they contain objects that are not yet included in the model, then condition (iii) requires that they either be introducible or explained by the structural effect of yet another process to be included. Also for this revision, the processes in the library can be searched for the appropriate candidates. Fig. 10.7 illustrates the search process. Compared to the component-oriented best-first search algorithms, the minimality criterion is less effective in this case, because it relates to the **ultimate** cause (the introducible objects), and a one-step look-ahead will not help.

The existing approaches along these lines (*PDE* [7], G^+DE [41]) are performing diagnosis in **one snapshot**. This is a serious limitation for many relevant diagnosis problems, since the origin of some disturbance may already have ceased to exist, while the effects persist. For instance, if we expect to detect a cause for the deviation in the pH (e.g., algal bloom), the actual observation may state that there is none and render such an explanation inconsistent.

Including the temporal dimension adds to the complexity issues of this approach and, together with the demand for good search heuristics makes it a real challenge to model-based diagnosis research. Any progress would contribute to a significant extension of the application scope of model-based diagnosis.

10.4.7   Model-based Diagnosis in Control Engineering

There exists another research area also called "model-based fault diagnosis and isolation". It has emerged in control engineering, and, while sharing some basic commonalities with model-based diagnosis in Artificial Intelligence, involves quite different techniques. The common idea is to start diagnosis from the deviation of an observed behavior from a model of correct behavior and to view a diagnostic hypothesis as a model revision that removes this deviation. However, the techniques are purely mathematical, and the models used are usually numerical, non-compositional black-box models with a fixed (mathematical) structure, lacking an explicit conceptual layer of modeling and, hence, any symbolic reasoning and inferences. Partly, this reflects the application domain of process control and the kind of models used for this purpose. As a consequence, the kinds of faults that can be handled are limited to those that can be expressed as a variation of the mathematical OK-model (e.g., parameter deviations). Faults that modify the causal structure of the system and/or its mathematical structure constitute a problem, as opposed to the model-based methods described in this chapter. There are several attempts to compare, relate, and combine the different types of model-based diagnosis [18, 42, 1, 53].

10.5   Test and Measurement Proposal, Diagnosability Analysis

Usually, a diagnosis based on some initial set of observations does not yield a unique diagnosis result, even under certain preference criteria, such as minimality or likelihood. If the model has been fully applied and cannot provide more diagnostic information, the only source for further discrimination between the remaining diagnostic hypotheses is additional observations of the system behavior. This means observing additional variables and/or performing observations of the system in a different state or with different input. Therefore, the test generation task can be stated as determining which influences on the system and which observables promise information that refutes some of the current (diagnostic) hypotheses. A variant of this task is end-of-line testing, i.e. performing tests of a manufactured product that are suited to confirm that the product is not faulted. This may seem to be a different task, but it can only be achieved by tests that are designed to refute all possible faults (since this is not feasible in reality a set of plausible faults has to be selected, e.g., single faults, or the most probable ones). There is no way to confirm the presence of a particular behavior other than refuting all competing behavior hypotheses.

10.5.1 Test Generation

The core problem is to determine tests for discriminating between two possible behaviors of a system, i.e. two models. A test has to specify

- how to stimulate the system and

- what to observe of the system's response to this stimulus

in order to gain discriminating information. This requires fixing the possibilities of influencing the system, called *test inputs* or *stimuli* in the following, and the potential observations, *OBS*.

In the most general way, testing aims at finding out which model hypothesis out of a set *Hyp* is correct (if any) by stimulating a system such that the available observations of the system responses to the stimuli refute all but one hypotheses (or even all of them). This is captured by the following definition.

Definition 10.16 (Discriminating test input). *Let*

$TI = \{ti\}$ *be the set of possible test inputs (stimuli),*

$OBS = \{obs\}$ *the set of possible observations (system responses), and*

$Hyp = \{model_i\}$ *a set of hypotheses.*

*$ti \in TI$ is called a **definitely discriminating** test input for Hyp if*

(i) $\forall model_i \in Hyp \; \exists obs \in OBS, \; ti \wedge model_i \wedge obs \nvDash \perp$

and

(ii) $\forall model_i \in Hyp \quad \forall obs \in OBS$
  if $ti \wedge model_i \wedge obs \nvDash \perp$
  then $\forall model_j \neq model_i, \; ti \wedge model_j \wedge obs \vDash \perp$.

*ti is a **possibly discriminating** test input if*

(ii') $\forall model_i \in Hyp \; \exists obs \in OBS$ such that
  $ti \wedge model_i \wedge obs \nvDash \perp$
  and $\forall model_j \neq model_i, \; ti \wedge model_j \wedge obs \vDash \perp$.

*ti is a **not discriminating** otherwise.*

In this definition, condition (i) expresses that there exists an observable system response for each hypothesis under the test input. It also implies that test inputs are consistent with all hypotheses, i.e., we are able to apply the stimulus, because it is causally independent of the hypotheses. Regarding the model, this corresponds to the requirement that it captures the behavior under each tuple in the Cartesian product of the domains of exogenous variables, as discussed in Section 10.3. Condition (ii) formulates the requirement that the resulting observation guarantees that at most one hypothesis will not be refuted, while (ii') states that each hypothesis **may** generate an observation that refutes all others.

Usually, one stimulus is not enough to perform the discrimination task which motivates the following definition.

Definition 10.17 (Discriminating test input set). $\{ti_k\} = TI' \subset TI$ *is called a discriminating test input set for* $Hyp = \{model_i\}$
if $\forall model_i, model_j$ *with* $model_i \neq model_j$
$\exists ti_k \in TI'$
such that ti_k *is a* (definitely or possibly) *discriminating test input*
for $\{model_i, model_j\}$.
It is called **definitely discriminating** *if all* ti_k *have this property, and* **possibly discriminating** *otherwise. It is called* **minimal** *if it has no proper subset* $TI'' \subset TI'$ *which is discriminating.*

This defines what we would like to obtain. Actually computing solutions faces a different dimension of complexity compared to diagnosis. In diagnosis, **one observation** of the system behavior in **one situation** (or a sequence of such situations) is **given** and needs to be checked for consistency with various models. For test generation, the space of **all situations and observations** has to be searched in order to find some that are inconsistent with at least one of the models. Intuitively, one would like to identify the differences in the space of all possible behaviors under two or more models. In contrast to consistency-based diagnostic reasoning which happens at the conceptual level (e.g., component behavior modes in component-oriented diagnosis), test generation has to analyze the behavior model itself, unless we apply an algorithm that generates test inputs and then tests them for consistency with the models.

Test generation with relational models

In the following, we outline a fairly general approach that assumes that models are represented as relations over a set of variables, but whose underlying ideas might be adapted to other modeling formalisms. The approach covers models that are given by equations and implemented by constraints. It is assumed that test inputs and observations can be described as value assignments to system variables. If the system is modeled as an aggregate of components, the hypotheses to be tested are given by (usually single) faults of components. If $\underline{v}_{Ci}$ is the vector of variables local to a component C_i with a domain $\mathrm{DOM}(\underline{v}_{Ci})$, each possible behavior mode $mode_{ij}$ of C_i has an associated relation

$$R_{ij} \subseteq \mathrm{DOM}(\underline{v}_{Ci})$$

as a behavior model. A fault hypothesis in testing is then given by the join of the relations that correspond to a particular assignment of modes, MA, to the components:

$$R(MA) = \underset{mode_{ij} \in MA}{\bowtie} R_{ij}.$$

Once this relation is constructed, the component structure is no longer relevant. Hence, we can choose a more general relational representation which covers testing of arbitrary hypotheses that can be stated in terms of a set of interrelated variables. This includes tests that aim at identifying a state variable which is not directly observable, testing applied to systems that are modeled in a process-oriented formalism, and the design of experiments for checking different modeling hypotheses. Thus, the system behavior is assumed to be characterized by a vector

$$\underline{v}_S = (v_1, v_2, v_3, \ldots, v_n)$$

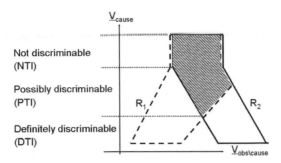

Figure 10.8: Discriminating inputs.

of system variables with domains

$$\mathrm{DOM}(\underline{v}_S) = \mathrm{DOM}(v_1) \times \mathrm{DOM}(v_2) \times \mathrm{DOM}(v_3) \times \cdots \times \mathrm{DOM}(v_n).$$

Then a hypothesis *model$_i$* $\in$ *Hyp* is given as a relation

$$R_i \subseteq \mathrm{DOM}(\underline{v}_S).$$

Observations are value assignments to a subvector of the variables, $\underline{v}_{obs}$, and also the stimuli are described by assigning values to a vector $\underline{v}_{cause}$ of susceptible ("causal" or input) variables. We make the, not very restrictive, assumption that we always know the applied stimulus which means the causal variables are a subvector of the observable ones:

$$\underline{v}_{cause} \subseteq \underline{v}_{obs} \subseteq \{v_i\}.$$

The basic idea underlying test generation [70] is then that the construction of test inputs is done by computing them from the observable differences of the relations that represent the various hypotheses. Fig. 10.8 illustrates this. Firstly, for testing, only the observables matter. Accordingly, Fig. 10.8 depicts only the projections, $p_{obs}(R_1)$, $p_{obs}(R_2)$, of two relations, R_1 and R_2, (which are defined over a larger set of variables) to the observable variables. The vertical axis represents the causal variables, whereas the horizontal axis shows the other observable variables (which represent the observable response of the system). To construct a (definitely) discriminating test input, we have to avoid stimuli that can lead to the same observable system response for both relations, i.e. stimuli that may lead to an observation in the intersection

$$(p_{obs}(R_i) \cap p_{obs}(R_j))$$

shaded in Fig. 10.8. These test inputs we find by projecting the intersection to the causal variables:

$$p_{cause}(p_{obs}(R_i) \cap p_{obs}(R_j)).$$

The complement of this is the complete set of all test inputs that are guaranteed to produce different system responses under the two hypotheses:

$$DTI_{ij} = \mathrm{DOM}(\underline{v}_{cause}) \setminus p_{cause}(p_{obs}(R_i) \cap p_{obs}(R_j)).$$

Lemma 10.2. *If $model_i = R_i$, $model_j = R_j$, $TI = \text{DOM}(\underline{v}_{cause})$, and $OBS = \text{DOM}(\underline{v}_{obs})$, then DTI_{ij} is the set of all definitely discriminating test inputs for $\{model_i, model_j\}$.*

Please, note that we assume that the projections of R_i and R_j cover the entire domain of the causal variables which corresponds to condition (i) in the definition of the test input.

We only mention the fact, that, when applying tests in practice, one may have to avoid certain stimuli because they carry the risk of damaging or destroying the system or to create catastrophic effects as long as certain faults have not been ruled out. In this case, the admissible test inputs are given by some set $R_{adm} \subseteq \text{DOM}(\underline{v}_{cause})$, and we obtain

$$DTI_{adm,ij} = R_{adm} \setminus p_{cause}(p_{obs}(R_i) \cap p_{obs}(R_j)).$$

In a similar way as DTI_{ij}, we can compute the set of test inputs that are guaranteed to create indistinguishable observable responses under both hypotheses, i.e. they cannot produce observations in the difference of the relations:

$$(p_{obs}(R_i) \setminus p_{obs}(R_j)) \cup (p_{obs}(R_i) \setminus p_{obs}(R_i)).$$

Then the non-discriminating test inputs are

$$NTI_{ij} = \text{DOM}(\underline{v}_{cause}) \setminus p_{cause}((p_{obs}(R_j) \setminus p_{obs}(R_i))$$
$$\cup (p_{obs}(R_i) \setminus p_{obs}(R_j)))$$

All other test inputs may or may not lead to discrimination.

Lemma 10.3. *The set of all possibly discriminating test inputs for a pair of hypotheses $\{model_i, model_j\}$ is given by*

$$PTI_{ij} = \text{DOM}(\underline{v}_{cause}) \setminus (NTI_{ij} \cup DTI_{ij}).$$

The $\frac{1}{2} * (n^2 - n)$ sets DTI_{ij} for all pairs $\{model_i, model_j\}$, $i < j$, provide the space for constructing (minimal) discriminating test input sets.

Lemma 10.4. *The (minimal) hitting sets of the set $\{DTI_{ij}\}$ are the (minimal) definitely discriminating test input sets.*

Note that Lemma 10.4 has only the purpose to characterize all discriminating test input sets. Since we need **only one** test input to perform the test, which can be computed in linear time, we are not bothered by the complexity of computing all hitting sets.

This way, the number of tests constructed can be less than $\frac{1}{2} * (n^2 - n)$. If the tests have a fixed cost associated, then the cheapest test set can be found among the minimal sets. However, it is worth noting that the test input sets are the minimal ones that **guarantee** the discrimination among the hypotheses in *Hyp*. In practice, only a subset of the tests may have to be executed, because some of them refute more hypotheses than guaranteed (because they are a *possibly discriminating* test for some other pair of hypotheses) and render other tests unnecessary.

Note that the required operations on the relations are applied to the **observable variables** only (including the causal variables). The projection of the entire relation R_i to this space is a step of compiling the composite model to one that directly relates the stimuli and the observable response. In some relevant applications, this space is predefined and small. For instance, when testing of car subsystems exploits the on-board actuators and sensors only, this may involve some 10–20 variables or so. The entire workshop diagnosis task has more potential probing points, but still involves only a small subset of the variables in the entire behavior relation R_i. Also note that this compiled model can be re-used for diagnosis purposes. Such a compact model may actually make the computation of the set $\{DTI_{ij}\}$ feasible if, for instance, finite relations representing qualitative models are used. [26] perform the computation on an ordered multiple decision diagrams OMDD representation. However, the compilation step can become expensive and practically infeasible. In cases where the complete computation of $\{DTI_{ij}\}$ is not possible, test generation can be done by search, and Lemmata 10.2 and 10.4 describe the search space.

[49] assumes a model stated in first order logic, which leads to a characterization of tests as prime implicants. In [80], sets of behaviors generated by qualitative simulation of competing models are used to search for discriminating experiments.

Although the **set** of discriminating test inputs given by Lemma 10.4 is minimal, the individual **test inputs** are not necessarily minimal in the sense that they are always specified by the entire given set of observables, despite the fact that only a subset of the stimuli and/or a subset of the other observables may suffice to produce the same discrimination effect. This is important for applications, since both the production of a stimulus and the performance of an observation are actions that determine the cost of testing, and justifies spending computation time on the reduction of test inputs. In [73], this is done by analysis and operations of the entire relations DTI_{ij}. Tests as prime implicants in the work of [49] already include this minimization step, but finding them is also exponential. But, again, under economic considerations, spending even days of computation time pays off, if it saves only seconds for an individual test that is carried out many times or if it allows workshop mechanics to avoid some expensive experiments in diagnosis.

If hypotheses are given as models of mode assignments, the set of definitely discriminating test inputs as defined above may be empty for two models, although discrimination may be possible through **several** tests. This may occur when there are internal states that cannot be observed or unambiguously inferred. As stated above, the approach can be used for state identification, as well, and the solution to the problem is to make hypotheses about the (relevant) states explicit as a set Hyp_{state} and include their determination in the testing. Since the new set of hypotheses becomes the Cartesian product

$$Hyp' = Hyp \times Hyp_{state}$$

this step increases the complexity of the task like the consideration of multiple faults does. Obviously, the solution is based on an assumption of persistence of states during testing.

Intrusive testing and probing

The solutions outlined above ignore or, a least, do not explicitly treat, an important feature of the real task in a practical context: unless we are using only pre-established sensors that are reflected in the system model, performing a test involves often much more than manipulating the input and/or state of the systems and some passive observation of its response. It may, temporarily or permanently, modify the structure of the system and, hence, the model. Even simply opening an electrical circuit and attaching a measurement device creates a new circuit. Other tests (e.g., in the medical domain) may even modify the system structure in an irreversible way. Hence, we do not only have to consider preparatory actions like removing a cover or lifting a vehicle, but modifications that affect the behavior of the system and, hence, have to be reflected by a change in the structure of its model. We will return to this issue in a broader context in Section 10.6.

10.5.2 Entropy-based Test Selection

Achieving optimality with respect to the cost during repeated use of a set of tests also requires to take into account the likelihood of different model hypotheses. This can be reflected in the sequence of tests or by dynamically choosing a new test based on the result of the previous one. If we assume that each hypothesis $model_i \in Hyp$ has a probability $p(model_i)$, then

$$H = - \sum_{model_i \in HYP} \left(p(model_i) \cdot \log\left(p(model_i) \right) \right)$$

is the entropy, a measure for the uncertainty in the information at this stage. In our context, it can be understood as an estimation of the number of tests to be performed in order to identify the true model. In the component-oriented case, the initial probabilities could be computed as the product of the a priori probabilities of the respective modes (under the condition that they are independent). When choosing the next test input, $ti \in TI$, we would like to maximize the expected information gain

$$H - H_e(ti),$$

where the entropy after applying ti has to be estimated over all observations that can possibly result from ti under the different hypotheses:

$$H_e(ti) = - \sum_{obs \in OBS(ti)} \left(p(obs) \cdot \sum_{model_i \in HYP} \left(p(model_i \mid obs, ti) \right. \right.$$
$$\left. \left. \cdot \log\left(p(model_i \mid obs, ti) \right) \right) \right).$$

If a hypothesis $model_i$ is specified by a relation R_i, then

$$OBS(ti) = \bigcup_i p_{obs}(ti \bowtie R_i).$$

Finally, we include the possibility that the observation after a applying a test input under a hypothesis is not unique, but, instead, there is a probability distribution:

$$p(obs \mid model_i, ti).$$

After applying Bayes' rule and some transformations [70], we derive the following

Probabilistic test selection strategy

In order to discriminate among hypotheses $model_i \in Hyp$, choose a test input ti and a vector of observable variables $\underline{v}_{obs}$, such that

$$- \sum_{obs \in OBS(ti)} \left(p(obs \mid ti) \cdot \log\big(p(obs \mid ti)\big) \right)$$

$$+ \sum_{model_i \in HYP} \left(p(model_i) \cdot \sum_{obs \in OBS(ti)} \big(p(obs \mid model_i, ti) \right.$$

$$\left. \cdot \log\big(p(obs \mid model_i, ti)\big) \big) \right)$$

is maximal, where $obs \in \mathrm{DOM}(\underline{v}_{obs})$ and the probabilities of observations are determined from hypothesis-specific distributions:

$$p(obs \mid ti) = \sum_{model_i \in HYP} \big(p(obs \mid model_i, ti) \cdot p(model_i) \big).$$

There is an intuitive interpretation of the criterion used in the strategy: the first term is the entropy of the observations given the test input, which is maximal if they are equally distributed. The second term will be minimal if each model predicts unique values. Together, this meets our intuition that says a test is most informative if it leads to distinct values for the various hypotheses.

10.5.3 Probe Selection

The above strategy allows varying both, the input ti and the observable variables $\underline{v}_{obs}$. On the one hand, this includes the situation where the set of observables is fixed (e.g., by the existing on-board sensors of a space craft). On the other hand, applying stimuli to the system in order to gain diagnostically relevant information may not always be possible (e.g., in plants under continuous operation or in natural systems), but information may be obtained by measuring additional variables in the given situation. This task which appears as probe selection, measurement proposal, and sensor placement can be handled as a specialization of the above strategy, where the stimulus is fixed and an informative set of observable variables has to be determined.

It can be seen as a generalization of the probe selection strategy in *GDE* [20], which determines the best individual variable v_{obs} to be measured, based on the assumption that each hypothesis either implies a unique prediction of a value $obs_i \in \mathrm{DOM}(v_{obs})$ (defining the subsets HYP_i) or no prediction at all (the subset HYP_u), which is reasonable for the implementation based on value propagation and dependency recording. Furthermore, Kleer and Williams [20] use an equal distribution of values for the hypotheses in HYP_u, and, hence, estimates the probability of a measurement $obs_i \in \mathrm{DOM}(v_{obs})$ for v_{obs} as

$$p(obs_i) = p(HYP_i) + \frac{1}{m} \cdot p(HYP_u) \quad \text{where } m = \big|\mathrm{DOM}(v_{obs})\big|.$$

This transforms the criterion in the strategy to the expression

$$\sum_{obs_i \in \text{DOM}(v_{obs})} \left(p(obs_i) \log\left(p(obs_i)\right) \right) + p(H_u) \cdot \log m$$

which should be minimized to obtain the best next measurement. One should note that even if no fault models are used, fault hypotheses do predict values based on the models of the non-faulty components. If, as in *GDE*, an *ATMS* is used for recording the dependency of predicted values on mode assignments this delivers the basis for determining the sets HYP_i and only the entropy computation has to be realized.

While probing helps, if the initial observations are not sufficiently discriminating, the probe selection strategy can also be beneficial in the opposite case, namely when there is an overwhelming amount of observations. [2] exploits it as a filter to extract relevant information from a message burst caused by a disturbance in a power distribution network.

10.5.4 Diagnosability Analysis

The question whether and how faults can be detected or discriminated from each other is relevant already during the design phase. If design for diagnosability and, in particular, placement of sensors for diagnostic purposes is a concern, variants of the techniques described above can be applied. Also failure-modes-and-effects analysis (FMEA) includes an analysis of the detectability of a fault. In this kind of analysis, the consideration is usually not on actively influencing the system. Rather, we expect **discriminability analysis** to answer the question *"For a particular design and a chosen set of sensors, determine whether and under which circumstances the considered (classes of) faults considered can be distinguished from each other (based on the sensor readings)"*. Fault detectability can be seen as a special case, namely the discrimination of faulty behaviors from the OK behavior.

Discriminability may depend on certain external conditions and internal states of the system. For instance, a certain fault of a particular sensor may only show up in a special temperature range, and a problem in the gear box may only affect driving in 2nd gear. If we replace the test inputs in the above definitions and algorithms by the set of such possible conditions, the techniques for test generation can be re-used. In [26], this is done using the relational behavior presentation. Detectability analysis has also been treated for discrete-event models, by analyzing whether a fault transition results in a visible trace different from OK behavior (within a certain number of transitions) (see [65, 77]).

10.6 Remedy Proposal

So far, all the tasks considered were focused on obtaining and using information in order to assess the behavior mode or state of systems, especially of systems whose behavior deviates from the normal and intended one. However, this is never a goal in itself, but only interesting as an input to some decision and action that requires this information. Diagnosis is only relevant if it supports a decision (whether and) how to re-establish the functionality of the misbehaving system, at least to a possible degree.

Actually, this purpose, which varies according to the type of system and the practical context of the task, ought to influence the nature of the expected diagnostic result and also the diagnostic process itself. For instance, on-board diagnostics for a vehicle subsystem should aim at the discrimination between classes of faults that, due to their nature and criticality, require different immediate recovery and safety actions, whereas off-board diagnosis of the same subsystem is focusing on discrimination between different suspect components in order to find the ones that need to be replaced. Usually, there is no need for continued discrimination if this does not influence the choice of the remedial action. Although this issue is both obvious and fundamental to diagnosis, it has been mainly ignored in theoretical work, and there are (too) few contributions to treating this means-end relationship in a general and systematic way [58].

In fact, in the context of real diagnosis work processes, the interdependency often becomes even tighter, bidirectional and more complex, because the respective activities become intermingled: (partial) repair actions may be carried out to support the overall diagnosis process. As pointed out earlier, the focus on fault localization in early work on diagnosis can be explained by an (implicit) focus on replacement of components as the remedial action. However, component replacement is but one special instance of actions for moving a system back to a healthy state and, in fact, impossible in some applications (e.g., space craft outside an orbit).

The diagnostic and testing theories and systems presented above are attempts to automate **reasoning** tasks, namely to infer diagnoses from observations and to propose informative observations based on the previous results. However, in particular in an industrial environment, in general, it is not these reasoning activities that are expensive, but efforts spent on **acting**, such as de-assembling a device, installing measurement equipment, and repairing the device. Compared to this, the time and cost spent on thinking is often negligible, and the result of this thinking matters only if it contributes to optimizing the overall workflow. The chance for diagnostic solutions to be really employed in practice is heavily reduced if they are not designed and developed under this perspective. It should be noted, though, that the above considerations apply only in a restricted way to on-board diagnostics, because they do not trigger directly expensive human activities.

These considerations motivate work aiming at model-based generation of proposals for remedies, at an integrated perspective on diagnosis, testing, and applying remedies, and at the integration of planning with model-based problem solving. Remedies can involve a whole range of different actions that need to be reflected in model-based systems in different:

- **replacement of components** that are suspect of failing usually leaves the structure of the device (and, hence, of the model) unchanged and simply changes the behavior mode (if successful); however, sometimes, a component may be replaced by one with different parameters or of a different type,

- **reconfiguration** exploits the structural redundancy of a device, which might achieve the specified purpose in different ways and even under fault conditions. Aircraft and space craft are equipped with redundant subsystems for critical functions, and power networks are huge networks of switches that enable the generation of different topologies with different paths between voltage sources and sinks; since the components that modify the topology (switches, valves, etc.)

are also components, the structure of the system (and of the model) remains unchanged, only the states of these components are affected,

- **modification of operating regions** is based on a system property that allows achieving certain goals with different settings of parameters and inputs; if one out of three heating elements in a room is not working, you may compensate for this by increasing the set point of the other two elements [79]; again, the structure of the device and the model remains the same,

- **modification of control** affects a special component, software; this step may correspond to implementing the previous two remedies, but it may also mean switching to a different control regime (e.g., from closed-loop to open-loop control in the case a sensor is suspect, or a control unit on a vehicle may replace an implausible value of one wheel speed sensor by some approximation gained from the other three sensors),

- **structural modifications** cover a wide range, from inserting new components (e.g., an electrical heating element) and establishing new connections (e.g., to bridge a series of electrical connectors, one of which is open, by a cable) to introducing ozone in a water treatment plant in order to trigger a process of oxidation of dissolved metals in the water; all this clearly results in a model that might be quite different from the designed or previous one. As stated above, also measurement actions may affect the structure of the system.

Some of these actions require continuing the analysis after their performance with a **new model**. But even those that do not, raise the question how they affect the state of the system, i.e., about the persistence of what has been observed or inferred before. What remains true after replacing a capacitor in a circuit? Some of the measured values may, others may not, and redoing all measurements may be a waste of efforts. (Immediately) after adding ozone to the water, the iron concentration is still the same, but its derivative is modified due to the oxidation process. This can be seen as an instance of problems connected to reasoning about actions (see, e.g., [45]), but the specific context (and the existence of a model) can offer special solutions.

10.6.1   Integration of Diagnosis and Remedy Actions

The discussion above shows that, rather than considering diagnosis in isolation (as in Section 10.4), we need to model a process that

- integrates actions of testing and therapy and the inference of diagnostic hypotheses based on the results of such actions,

- may change the system model dynamically,

- is guided by the goal of re-establishing the original or some weakened functionality of the system.

Thus, we have a task similar to diagnosis across time in the sense that a history of possible diagnoses has to be maintained and updated over time. The difference is that transitions may be due to actions, that they may affect the system structure, and that the intended function of the system has to be modeled and reasoned about. Producing a complete representation of all possible transitions, e.g., in terms of a finite state machine, appears feasible only if there are no significant structural changes included in the remedy actions, for instance, if only state changes, reset, or replacement actions are available.

[30] proposed a general formalization of such an integrated process for component-oriented diagnosis and repair, which also takes into account that actions may fail. Slightly modifying and simplifying their proposal (assuming actions are instantaneous and cannot fail), we obtain an extension of our Definition 10.8 (Temporal diagnosis). We introduce an *action history*

$$AH = \{(ACT_l, t_l)\}, \quad t_l \in I_\omega$$

and a *goal history*

$$GOALH = \{(GOAL_m, I_m)\}, \quad I_m \in I_\omega,$$

which allows us to express both ultimate and intermediate goals. For instance, during the reconfiguration of a power transportation network, one has to avoid overload of certain lines, and may also have to make sure that certain critical consumers are never temporarily cut off from power supply. For replacement and reconfiguration, actions modify the modes and states of components, and in the latter case, change the system topology within the limits determined by the redundancy in the original structure. While this leaves

$$SD = LIB \cup STRUCTURE$$

unmodified and stable as in component-oriented diagnosis, the structure may also be subject to modification by remedial (and also measurement) actions. In this case, an extended system description $\overline{SD}$ has to comprise constraints on admissible structures.

The task is then to find a sequence of actions that is consistent with or achieves *GOAL* or a set thereof.

Definition 10.18 (Remedy). *An action history AH is a consistency-based remedy for $\overline{SD}$, OBSH, GOALSH and a mode history, MH if*

$$\overline{SD} \cup MH \cup AH \cup OBSH \cup GOALSH \nvdash \bot$$

and an abductive remedy if

$$\overline{SD} \cup MH \cup AH \cup OBSH \vDash GOALSH.$$

It is called a consistency-based (abductive) remedy of mode histories, $\{MH_i\}$ if it is a remedy for each MH_i.

The second part of the definition reflects the fact that one may want a remedy that is known to work even though there is no unique diagnosis.

Unless there is a pre-specified set of repair plans to choose from, a planner is needed to generate such plans, and probabilities and cost have to be considered when selecting some optimized plan. While [75] present a cost function for a process including measurement and replacement, [30] propose an estimation of costs of plans for their approach that also takes into account down time of the system, which is a major issue in several applications (e.g., power transportation systems).

10.6.2   Component-oriented Reconfiguration

The idea of consistency-based diagnosis can be extended in a natural way to address the reconfiguration problem (see, e.g., [8]). In diagnosis, we are searching for a (minimal) revision, MA, of the mode assignment MA_{OK} that is consistent with observations:

$$SD \cup \{MA\} \cup OBS \nvDash \bot,$$

where $MA \setminus MA_{OK}$ is minimal.

In analogy, we can consider the reconfiguration problem as a search for a (minimal) revision of the actual states of the reconfigurable components that is consistent with the behavior specification of the system, $GOALS$. More precisely, we assume that there exists a subset $COMPS_R \subseteq COMPS$ of components that enable the modification of the system topology (i.e. the interaction paths among the components) through manipulation of their states. Typical examples of such components are electrical switches (e.g., breakers in a power network) and valves (e.g., in the propulsion system of a space craft). In addition, there may be other components that can be (de-)activated, such as power generators, pumps, etc.

To support reconfiguration, the diagnosis step has to produce not only consistent mode assignments, MA, but also information about the states of the reconfigurable components.

Definition 10.19 (State assignment). *Let $COMPS'_R \subseteq COMPS_R \subseteq COMPS$ be a subset of the reconfigurable components. Then*

$$\bigwedge_{C_i \in COMPS'_R} s_{i_j}(C_i), \quad \text{where } s_{i_j} \in states(C_i)$$

is a state assignment. It is called complete if $COMPS'_R = COMPS_R$.

A diagnosis, MA, and a consistent (actual) state assignment SA_A, i.e.

$$SD \cup \{MA\} \cup \{SA_A\} \cup OBS \nvDash \bot$$

require reconfiguration if they are inconsistent with $GOALS$:

$$SD \cup \{MA\} \cup \{SA_A\} \cup OBS \cup GOALS \vDash \bot.$$

If a replacement, self-healing, or reset of the broken components is not possible (i.e. MA is fixed), reconfiguration looks for a different state assignment that removes the inconsistency. The attempt to capture this intuition in a rigorous way, is not as straightforward as it appears at a first glance. The reason for this lies in the fact that modifying the state assignment will also modify the values of variables (actually, that is the purpose) and render observed variables obsolete in the goal situation. Some observed values will persist, and their information may be essential for the achievement of the goal. For instance, modifying switch positions in the power network affects voltages and current on the connected lines, but not the output of the generators in the network, and the observation of the latter can be essential for determining an appropriate reconfiguration; after all, you do not want to connect a consumer to an inactive generator.

The problem is an instance of the frame problem that occurs in reasoning about action and time. A general solution would have to be based on inferences that implement the idea that "only those observations persist that are not forced to change by the reconfiguration". There may be domain-specific solutions that are based on an a-priori classification of persistent and non-persistent types of observations, as indicated for the power network example. They could also be ontology-specific, as discussed in Section 10.6.3. The following definition assumes that the set of persistent observations, OBS_P, can be determined in some way.

Definition 10.20 (Consistency-based reconfiguration). *Let MA be a diagnosis of SD and OBS, $OBS_P \subset OBS$ its persistent subset, and SA_A be the actual state assignment such that*

$$SD \cup MA \cup SA_A \cup OBS \nvDash \perp.$$

A state assignment SA_G that is consistent with SD, MA, OBS_P and GOALS,

$$SD \cup MA \cup SA_G \cup OBS_P \cup GOALS \nvDash \perp$$

is called a (consistency-based) reconfiguration for MA.
  It is called minimal with respect to SA_A, if

$$SA_G \setminus SA_A$$

is minimal with respect to set inclusion.
  Let $\{MA_i\}$ be a set of diagnoses, and for each i_0, SA_{M,i_0} the maximal entailed (partial) state assignment:

$$SD \cup \{MA_{i_0}\} \cup OBS \vDash SA_{M,i_0}.$$

SA_G is called a reconfiguration for $\{MA_i\}$, if it is a reconfiguration for each MA_i.
  It is called minimal, if

$$SA_G \setminus \bigcap_i SA_{M,i}$$

is minimal.

There is no guarantee that, for a given diagnosis *MA*, a reconfiguration actually exists. But it does exist if and only if

$$SD \cup \{MA\} \cup GOALS \nvDash \perp$$

(provided *SD* contains the domain axioms for the states).
  As already stated earlier in a more general way, what is really wanted is a **guarantee** that the reconfiguration achieves the goals,

$$SD \cup \{MA_i\} \cup \{SA_G\} \vDash GOALS$$

rather than being merely **consistent** with them. With both definitions, we may encounter problems in case of insufficient observations, an incomplete predictor and consistency check, and a weak model. The latter case may occur, for example, due to the lack of expressiveness regarding causality. For instance, in a relational behavior model, without further constructs, the **observation** of voltage being present may not be distinguishable from stating the **goal** that voltage be present. The local model of an open power line or breaker does not restrict the voltage on either side and may, hence, be consistent with the goal of a voltage request of a consumer, if the causal aspect is not represented that there has to be a source connected to produce it.

Incomplete information

The second part (on sets of diagnoses) of Definition 10.18 reflects one important motivation for the integration of diagnosis and repair, namely to avoid spending more efforts on the diagnosis step (i.e. the identification of modes and states) than necessary to determine appropriate remedies. There may be competing possible diagnoses and limited information about the actual states of components, but a reconfiguration might exist that can be shown to achieve the (or some) functionality again. For instance, the messages transmitted to the operator of a power network will often not enable him to localize the shorted component unambiguously, but nevertheless allow him to re-establish power supply by a topology that does not rely on any of the suspect components and, actually, he has to, within a minute or so. Later, of course, before sending off the repair staff, one better determines the fault location as accurately as possible, which may require more detailed (numerical) data and analysis.

These considerations mainly apply in case obtaining more discriminative observations requires costly actions. In on-board diagnosis, the set of available observations is usually fixed and basically comes for free. As pointed out earlier, it may be case, though, that the amount of data is overwhelming (but highly redundant) and require computation for selecting the most informative bulk of data. In this case, which occurs, for instance, in the power network application, the techniques for probe selection (Section 10.5.3) can be exploited as a filter (see [2]).

Minimality and cost

The definition of a minimal reconfiguration captures the idea that a maximal number of reconfigurable components should maintain their actual states. There can be many reasons why this may not suffice to reflect practical requirements appropriately. First of all, to select the best reconfiguration, costs of (types of) reconfiguration actions have to be considered which may differ (e.g., changing a switch position vs. turning on a new generator). Also one might prefer reversible actions over irreversible ones (such as firing a pyro valve). Under the assumption that the cost of reconfiguration grows monotonically with the set of actions, the set of minimal reconfigurations contains the cheapest one(s).

Secondly, our definition does not exclude the reconfiguration of components with an unknown state which could be problematic in specific cases. Thirdly, usually broken components are not candidates for reconfiguration, unless they can be reset, and one may want to ignore them.

Computation

The analogy between consistency-based reconfiguration and diagnosis expressed by Definition 10.20 suggests how solutions to the characterization and computation of diagnoses may carry over to reconfiguration. If, for a given (set of) mode assignment(s) and observations, a state assignment is inconsistent with *GOALS*, in any reconfiguration at least one of the assigned states has to be modified. For instance, the set of open switches that together isolate a consumer from the generators produce an inconsistency with the goal of supplying this customer, and at least one of them must be closed. Reconfigurations can be calculated from such (minimal) "state conflicts".

The computation of consistent mode and state assignments could be done jointly. However, the minimality (or preference) of assignments will only apply to modes, since, usually, there is no distinction between states that is analogous to "OK vs. faulty" for modes.

Since the effect of a proposed state change has to be checked for consistency explicitly (changing the position of a switch may connect one consumer, but disconnect another one, which causes an inconsistency regarding another goal), the problem is equivalent to fault identification. Search heuristics and (cost-based) preferences are important, and the problem has triggered the generalization of the algorithm used in *SHERLOCK* (see Section 10.4.1) to *"conflict-directed A* search"* [86].

Reconfiguration planning

What we have defined as a reconfiguration, is, stated more precisely, the goal state of the reconfiguration. In most cases, achieving this goal is not a straightforward task, such as simply changing switch positions in an arbitrary order. The individual state changes may require a sequence of low level actions. Often, there are constraints on the order of the reconfiguration actions (e.g., first activate a generator, then change the topology). Also, (temporary) state changes that are not directly implied by the goal reconfiguration may be required. This may result from intermediate goals, safety criteria and restrictions. For instance, reconfiguration of a power network has to avoid states that cause an overload to individual lines. It can be the case that a perfect goal state cannot be achieved by a plan that respects all intermediate restrictions. As a result, planning is needed to turn a computed reconfiguration into a sequence of executable actions [3, 44].

10.6.3 Process-oriented Therapy Proposal

In contrast to component-oriented reconfiguration, which generates remedies exploiting the given system structure, a process-oriented model supports a more general class of therapies, which may include structural modifications of the system (model) [41, 72].

An appropriate treatment of the problem of an increased concentration of iron in drinking water is to add some oxidizer, such as ozone or chlorine, in the plant. This corresponds to an extension of the model: an object (substance) is added, triggering an oxidation process, which in turn produces a (potentially) new structural element, iron oxide, etc. Again, the search aims at a model that is consistent with therapy goals. In contrast to diagnosis (situation assessment), the introducibles for the possible model revisions are not origins of disturbances, but due to human intervention. The library has to contain interventions. They can be modeled as processes with conditions that simply correspond to the decision to perform the respective intervention. These "action triggers" can syntactically be introduced as objects and are the introducibles for the therapy search. The task of finding a therapy for a given situation assessment is then formalized as a search for a (minimal) set of "action triggers" that modify the model such that it becomes consistent with (or entails) the therapy goals, $GOALS_T$. Again, the question arises which part of the information about the current situation persists and which one becomes obsolete due to the intervention. Process-oriented modeling suggests a solution in which the stimulation of additional processes can only cause continuous changes of quantities, i.e., the absolute values of quantities persists (and so do the existing objects), but their derivatives may change. In the water treatment scenario, the oxidizing process does not cause a discontinuous jump of the iron concentration below the threshold, but turns its derivative negative. In fact, this appears to be a natural formulation of therapy goals in this context: if a quantity has an undesired deviation, a goal is forcing its derivative to an opposite sign. For the assumptions $ASSM'$ in a situation assessment, their persistent part $ASSM'_p$ needs to be determined.

Definition 10.21 (Process-oriented therapy). *Let*

$$SIT_P = (STRUCTURE, QUANT_P, ASSM'_P) \cup OBS$$

be the persistent part of a situation assessment and the observations.

A set of action triggers DEC is called a consistency-based therapy for SIT_P and a set of therapy goals $GOALS_T$, if it is consistent with SIT_P and $GOALS_T$:

$$DEC \cup SIT_P \cup LIB \cup GOALS_T \nvDash \bot.$$

DEC is called a minimal therapy, if it is minimal with respect to set inclusion among the set of therapies.

Specifying the therapy goals may not be as straightforward as it appears. On the one hand, there are therapy goals related to the violated ones in the current situation ("reduce the concentration of dissolved iron"). On the other hand, a therapy should not sacrifice other goals, which are maintained in the current situation (for instance, achieving a reduction of the iron concentration by stopping the pumps that transport water into the plant is definitely in conflict with the maintenance of a certain amount of supply to the city). Secondly, it may be impossible to achieve all therapy goals in a single step, and, hence, one has to find a therapy that achieves a subset of them, a maximal one, the most critical ones, etc. In this case, a trade-off needs to be found between minimizing DEC and optimizing the set of satisfied goals.

Note that decisions need to specify a location for the respective intervention. For instance, one needs to distinguish the (probably preferred) decision of adding an oxidizer in the tank from the decision to do so in the reservoir. This can be achieved by exploiting the spatial relations needed for located objects in general.

Finally, it has to be pointed out that the solution outlined here takes a static perspective on therapy (analogously to situation assessment) and does not address the task of planning a sequence of interventions needed to ultimately achieve a set of goals.

10.7 Other Tasks

10.7.1 Configuration and Design

In the previous sections, we mainly looked at tasks that are concerned with some faulty or unwanted behavior of a system. As we stated before, this reflects a major focus of the field and also the fact that the existing solutions are the most advanced ones. At a first glance, it may sound counterintuitive that handling the many ways in which systems might fail should be easier to solve than, for instance, a design task, in which commonly only the OK behavior is regarded. After all, in Section 10.2, we pointed out the general common denominator of diagnosis and design: searching for a model that is consistent with the observations or the goal specification, respectively. It is useful to analyze the preconditions that make diagnosis manageable, in order to understand what can make design hard in general or feasible in special cases. The main reasons are probably the following: In component-oriented diagnosis

1. the **structure** of the system is usually **fixed**. The search space defined by the considered fault modes of components and finite, although potentially huge. (If the structure is subject to variation, e.g., due to unforeseen component interactions or in process-oriented diagnosis, the task becomes more difficult to solve),

2. there exists a **good initial hypothesis** (namely the OK mode assignment), and the proper diagnosis is only a few revision steps away, due to a plausible minimality criterion,

3. **observations** can effectively **reduce the search space**.

In contrast, design in the most general sense includes **finding** an appropriate structure, which turns the search space infinite in principle. This might be overcome when there exists a good initial design hypothesis not too far from an existing solution. This could even exist in innovative design, for instance, provided by analogy to a solution in some other domain (based on the correspondence of mechanical, electrical, hydraulic laws) [82, 83]. However, most real design tasks in industry are more routine and often provide restrictions that allow for the exploitation of the diagnostic techniques. In many situations, the structure of a solution is given as the one of a similar device or a basic structure plus a limited set of possible modifications (variant design). Or the structure is fixed, and the task is to refine it by specialization of the component types and connections and/or choice of parameters (configuration and parametric design). However, systems supporting such tasks are usually not based on explicit behavior models of the available component types. Instead, the requirements for achieving a certain functionality are directly expressed as interdependencies among component types, parameters of components, restrictions on viable structures, etc. A typical example, the configuration of telephone switching systems, is described in [28]. A configuration *CONF* can be understood as a specification of the structure and parameters of a system,

$$CONF = STRUCTURE \cup PARS$$

(in the same sense as for diagnosis) that respects all general constraints in the respective configuration domain, the domain description *DD*, and is consistent with a specification of the configuration goals, *CONFGOALS* [29].

Definition 10.22 (Configuration). *CONF is a configuration for a domain description, DD, and configuration goals, CONFGOALS, if*

$$DD \cup CONF \cup CONFGOALS \not\models \bot.$$

This suggests the analogy to diagnosis and the general design task, but emphasizes also that *DD* may not fully specify the structure (contrary to *SD* in diagnosis), which becomes part of the solution to be generated.

Diagnostic techniques may be of help to generating designs in identifying the design decisions underlying the inconsistency of some intermediate design result with the *GOALS* (in analogy to conflicts in diagnosis). This may support the human designer in identifying decisions that need to be revised in order to approach a solution.

An example is work on the debugging of hardware designs in [37], which uses a *VHDL* (*Very High Speed Integrated Circuit Hardware Description Language*) to describe the design *GOALS* to be checked against the simulation of a layer in this hierarchical description.

10.7.2   Failure-Modes-and-Effects Analysis

A subtask in the design process that can be supported by model-based systems is failure-model-and-effects analysis (FMEA). The core of this task, which is widespread and standardized to some extent in military, aeronautics, and automotive industries, is to determine the impact each possible component fault may have on the functionality and then to assess the severity and detectability, which, together with the fault probability, determines its criticality and the demand for potential design changes.

Model-based support is feasible, since the design is given and usually, the analysis considers only single faults (or double faults if a single fault can be masked). As another input to the analysis, the user can specify the relevant functions or directly the unwanted violations of the functions, the effects, *EFFECTS*, as well as possibly a set of different scenarios to which the analysis should be applied.

Given a library with fault models, a fault *F* causes the effect, *EFFECT*, in a scenario, *SCEN*, if

$$SD \cup \{MA_F\} \cup SCEN \models EFFECT,$$

and may cause it if

$$SD \cup \{MA_F\} \cup SCEN \cup EFFECT \not\models \bot$$

(see [55]).

Alternatively, the model-based system can compute the behavior for the OK case and derive effects as any deviation of the fault model with respect to some functionally relevant variable [59].

10.7.3   Debugging and Testing of Software

At a first glance, it seems to be straightforward to apply the (component-oriented) diagnosis techniques to a special class of artifacts, namely software, and, thus, provide model-based tools for the debugging of programs. However, a proper analysis of the task reveals that there are substantial differences compared to diagnosis of physical devices. While there are straightforward and justified ways to consider a program to be structured into components (modules, functions, procedures, lines of code, ...), a number of assumptions underlying most consistency-based diagnosis theories and techniques (as discussed in Section 10.4.1) are violated in principle:

- **Component faults only:** A wrong behavior of a program often cannot be blamed to any of the existing "components", but may be caused by some **missing** step or computation.

- **No structural faults:** This is violated because of the fact stated above, but possibly even for a more fundamental bug in the overall structuring of the program.

- **Well-designed system:** This does not hold for principled reasons: after all, debugging of a program becomes necessary **because** it is **not** well-designed!

While the physical device is assumed to have worked properly before some component(s) broke, the program has never performed correctly (and never will).

Stated systematically, software debugging is not a special case of diagnosis, but an instance of the task of identifying flaws in a **design**. This implies, in particular, that the behavior specification contradicts the assumption that all system components are *OK*, instead of being implied by it. As a consequence, the intended behavior, *GOALS*, has to be made explicit and checked against the results produced by the program:

$$MODEL \cup GOALS \vDash \bot.$$

The usual ways for capturing *GOALS* are by an explicit specification (as an abstract representation of the intended behavior of the program) or, in a more fragmentary way, by a set of tests (which define an input to the system and the expected output or a classification of the actual output as correct or incorrect). Any inconsistencies detected can then be exploited by consistency-based techniques as for fault localization in physical systems, but under caveats that stem from the potentially violated preconditions of these techniques. It is not obvious that fault localization in this style delivers useful results in case structural bugs are present in the program.

Performing fault localization requires an appropriate representation of the structure of the program. While the "components" in this structure could be directly given by the code (lines of code, functions, ...), the interaction among these components (the "connections") have to be generated exploiting the syntax and semantics of the respective programming language. Further structuring (e.g., additional entities in a hierarchy) may be gained from the specification or by abstraction from the code.

Fault models, which enabled fault identification and often tighter fault localization in case of physical devices, are hard to obtain for software and can hardly be expected to be exhaustive, except at a very abstract level of modeling. While in the physical world, the behavior of a faulty (elementary) component is often fairly constrained and predictable, the space of possible bugs in a program is spanned by the creativity of programmers and, hence, practically infinite.

Despite and within these limitations, research on model-based debugging aids has produced encouraging results if only for small programs [43, 50, 51, 85], and also work on fault-model-based software testing is carried out [27].

A related task is debugging of knowledge bases. In [29], consistency-based techniques are applied to localize faults in a knowledge base for a configuration system. Here, the *GOALS* are represented as a set of (positive and negative) examples.

10.8   State and Challenges

The field of model-based systems started off by **building systems** that exploited reasoning from first principles instead of purely experiential knowledge. In contrast to work on diagnosis in engineering, which tends to be very domain or even device-specific, it aimed at generic solutions and focused for a while on developing a rigorous theoretical foundation [62, 19, 69, 24]. Basically, the main part of this work was completed more than ten years ago and is still quite well represented in [39].

While some work at the purely theoretical level has been continued until today, also considerable attempts were made to apply theory and technology to serious real-life and industrial problems during the last ten years or so (see [42, 78, 53, 59, 68, 74, 66, 84]. Most of them resulted in feasibility studies and (often quite advanced) prototypes, but few solutions could be commercialized and used in every-day practice so far. The industrial potential of model-based systems technology has been recognized and is considered plausible. It offers

- a systematic way to generate and adapt solutions based on model libraries;

- model libraries as an important corporate knowledge repository whose elements can be exploited and re-used during the entire life-cycle of a product;

- a reduction of manual work and a guaranteed coverage of a model-based solution;

- the enablement of system autonomy through self-diagnosis and self-reconfiguration.

The existing theory and technology of model-based systems now needs to improve the basis for a transfer into industrial applications. Some of the important issues are

- **distributed/cooperative diagnosis** if local diagnostic capabilities exist and need to be designed, interfaced and exploited (highly relevant, for instance, in the automotive industries);

- diagnosis of **structural faults** if unanticipated interactions occur (e.g., bridge faults in circuits);

- diagnosis of **non-component-oriented systems** (for instance, for applications in process industries or environmental/ecological applications);

- **scaling up** algorithms to handle large systems, for instance, by precompilation steps.

However, the most essential current challenges appear to be the following.

Creation of a theory, methodology, and powerful tools to build libraries of (diagnostic) models

Model-building is a distinctive feature of the technology. All projects that solved a problem relevant to industrial practice had to build component models. However, to our knowledge, none of them developed a serious library of behavior models that could be easily reused in another project. Only few attempts have been made to develop a theory of building diagnostic models (e.g., [69, 67]). Especially, a well-founded theory and methodology for developing **reusable** model libraries is needed. For industrial applications, the creation of such libraries is crucial. If generating a system model cannot be done easily based on a library, the model-based diagnostic algorithms may be rendered useless, because encoding diagnostics by hand may be cheaper.

What is the problem? Usually, the models used for successful projects have some specificities of the diagnostic task, domain, or even device compiled into them. While this is justified and can even be essential for obtaining an efficient solution, it prevents the reuse of the models even in similar applications where some of the modeling assumptions do not hold. Including the most general descriptions, which cover all potentially relevant features of a component's behavior in the library can lead to overloaded models and useless predictions in each single application. For instance, a model of a pipe in the air intake of a vehicle engine may need to include the oxygen concentration, whereas a pipe model in the exhaust system has to propagate emissions. The model of a pipe that supplies a control valve with pressure, however, should do just this, rather than involving the oxygen and CO_2 concentration. Especially the field of qualitative modeling is challenged to produce solutions that are of help for **effectively and efficiently** producing libraries of reusable model fragments and generating tailored system models using their fragments for **industrial practice**. Such solutions also have to include a methodology and tools for the **distributed** production and maintenance of such libraries.

Furthermore, the challenge includes the problem of incorporating numerical distinctions and models. On the one hand, many diagnostic tasks require distinctions between different modes based on numerical thresholds. This enforces numerical distinctions in model fragments that are not determined locally, but by a specific context, the necessary distinctions in other component models, the structure, the precision of observations, to name a few important factors. The second reason is that numerical models of systems and components often do exist in industrial practice that can and must be exploited and placed in a well-defined relation to the more abstract diagnostic models.

Involving numerical models and modeling environments in model-based systems solutions is important because they reflect current engineering practice and education, which leads to the second major prerequisite for a systematic exploitation of model-based technology in industry.

Creation of models of the problem solving tasks as work processes that enable the integration of model-based systems into current practice and tool chains

The tasks addressed by model-based systems are not novel. Diagnosis, FMEA, testing, etc. are existing activities of human experts, mainly engineers, often carried out in teams or collaboration and supported by a variety of (software) tools, such as CAD tools, workshop testers, FMEA-editors. A model-based system is no solution, if it is not a solution to effectively supporting these work processes in real practice. Hardly any product offered by model-based technologies can claim to aim at the complete automation of some task. And even if it does, it depends on appropriate input, a model library being the minimum, and it has to deliver results in a way that supports interaction with its environment, a physical system, human agents, or an organization. Offering real support requires, among other issues,

- that the user concepts and perspectives on the system and the task are properly reflected in the model-based system,

- that the required input to the system can (easily) be made available in practice and the results are of a kind and form that can be further processed by other tools and/or people,

- that the system actually addresses the **difficult or costly** steps in the workflow.

The last issue is crucial to the application of a technology. The model-based problem solvers of today are mostly concerned with the formalization and automation of **reasoning** tasks (such as diagnosis in the above sense, test generation, etc.), but these tasks are sometimes not too difficult or cheap. However, the **actions** involved in finding and removing faults essentially determine the costs (and downtime). An automated system for workshop diagnosis will only pay off, if it helps to generate good plans for the required activities, which reduce the costs.

What is required is a scientific analysis and formalization of the tasks and the concepts and activities of human organizations to master them. The field now needs to move forward from developing abstract problem solving algorithms to developing **models of work processes** the algorithms and problem solvers have to be embedded in and to studying the practical context of developing model-based solutions and, in particular model libraries.

Acknowledgements

I would like to thank for various kinds of support, especially Gautam Biswas, Johan de Kleer, Oskar Dressler, Michael Esser, Alessandro Fraracci, Gerhard Friedrich, Michael Gelfond, Dominik Goby, Lukas Kuhn, Markus Stumptner, Christian Unger, Brian Williams, and Franz Wotawa. Special thanks to the editors of this handbook for their efforts and their patience.

Bibliography

[1] G. Biswas, M.O. Cordier, J. Lunze, M. Staroswiecki, and L. Trave-Massuyes. *IEEE SMC Transactions, Part B*, 34, 2005 (Special Volume on Diagnosis of Complex Systems: Bridging the Methodologies of the FDI and DX Communities).

[2] A. Beschta, O. Dressler, H. Freitag, M. Montag, and P. Struss. A model-based approach to fault localization in power transmission networks. *Intelligent Systems Engineering*, 2, 1993.

[3] M. Balduccini and M. Gelfond. Diagnostic reasoning with a-Prolog. *Theory and Practice of Logic Programming*, 3, 2003.

[4] B. Bredeweg and P. Struss (guest eds.). Qualitative reasoning. *AI Magazine*, 2004.

[5] G. Brewka, I. Niemela, and M. Truszczynski. Nonmonotonic reasoning. In V. Lifschitz, B. Porter, and F. van Harmelen, editors. *Handbook of Knowledge Representation*. Elsevier, 2007.

[6] M. Chantler, S. Daus, T. Vikatos, and G. Coghill. The use of quantitative dynamic models and dependency recording engines. In *7th International Workshop on Principles of Diagnosis (DX-96)*, 1996.

[7] J.W. Collins. Process-based diagnosis: An approach to understanding novel failures. PhD thesis, Institute for the Learning Sciences, Northwestern University, 1993.

[8] J. Crow and J. Rushby. Model-based reconfiguration: Toward an integration with diagnosis. In *Proceedings of AAAI-91*, 1991.

[9] L. Console and P. Torasso. A spectrum of logical definitions of model-based diagnosis. *Computational Intelligence*, 7(3), 1991. Also in [39].

[10] A. Darwiche. Compiling devices: A structure-based approach. In *Principles of Knowledge Representation and Reasoning (KR 98)*, 1998.

[11] R. Davis. Expert systems: Where are we? and where do we go from here? *Artificial Intelligence*, 3(2), 1982.

[12] R. Davis. Diagnostic reasoning based on structure and behavior. *Artificial Intelligence*, 1984. Also in [39].

[13] R. Dechter. *Constraint Processing*. Morgan Kaufmann, 2003.

[14] J. de Kleer. An assumption-based TMS. *Artificial Intelligence*, 28, 1986.

[15] D. Dvorak and B.J. Kuipers. Model-based monitoring of dynamic systems. In *International Joint Conference on Artificial Intelligence*, 1989.

[16] J. de Kleer. Modeling when connections are the problem. In *Twentieth International Joint Conference on Artificial Intelligence*, 2007.

[17] J.D. de Kleer and J.S. Brown. A qualitative physics based on confluences. *Artificial Intelligence*, 24, 1984. Also in [81].

[18] J. de Kleer and J. Kurien. Fundamentals of model-based diagnosis. In *Proceedings of SafeProcess03*, 2003.

[19] J. de Kleer, A. Mackworth, and R. Reiter. Characterizing diagnoses and systems. *Artificial Intelligence*, 56, 1992.

[20] J.D. de Kleer and B.C. Williams. Diagnosing multiple faults. *Artificial Intelligence*, 31(1), 1987. Also in [39].

[21] J. de Kleer and B.C. Williams. Compiling devices: Locality in a TMS. In B. Faltings and P. Struss, editors. *Recent Advances in Qualitative Physics*. MIT Press, 1992.

[22] J. de Kleer and B.C. Williams. Diagnosis with behavioral modes. In *Proceedings of the 11th International Joint Conference on Artificial Intelligence*, 1993. Also in [39].

[23] O. Dressler. On-line diagnosis and monitoring of dynamic systems based on qualitative models and dependency-based diagnostic engines. In *Proceedings of the European Conference on Artificial Intelligence*, 1996.

[24] O. Dressler and P. Struss. Back to defaults: Characterizing and computing diagnoses as coherent assumption sets. In *Proceedings of the European Conference on Artificial Intelligence (ECAI-92)*, 1992.

[25] O. Dressler and P. Struss. Model-based diagnosis with the default-based diagnostic engine: Effective control strategies that work in practise. In *11th European Conference on Artificial Intelligence*, 1994.

[26] O. Dressler and P. Struss. A toolbox integrating model-based diagnosability analysis and automated generation of diagnostics. In *Proceedings of the 14th International Workshop on Principles of Diagnosis*, June 2003.

[27] M. Esser and P. Struss. Fault-model-based test generation for embedded software. In *International Joint Conference on Artificial Intelligence*, 2007.

[28] G. Fleischanderl, G. Friedrich, A. Haselboeck, H. Schreiner, and M. Stumptner. Configuring large systems using generative constraint satisfaction. *Intelligent Systems Archive*, 13(4), 1998.

[29] A. Felfernig, G. Friedrich, D. Jannach, and M. Stumptner. Consistency-based diagnosis of configuration knowledge bases. *Artificial Intelligence*, 152, 2004.

[30] G. Friedrich, G. Gottlob, and W. Nejdl. Formalizing the repair process. In *Proceedings of the 10th European conference on Artificial intelligence*, 1992.

[31] G. Friedrich, G. Gottlob, and W. Nejdl. Physical impossibility instead of fault models. In [39], 1992.

[32] M. Fisher. Temporal representation and reasoning. In V. Lifschitz, B. Porter, and F. van Harmelen, editors. *Handbook of Knowledge Representation*. Elsevier, 2007.

[33] G. Friedrich and F. Lackinger. Diagnosing temporal misbehavior. In *IJCAI-91*, 1991.

[34] K. Forbus. Qualitative process theory. *Artificial Intelligence*, 24, 1984. Also in [81].

[35] K. Forbus. Qualitative reasoning. In *Handbook of Knowledge Representation*. Elsevier, 2008.

[36] B. Faltings and P. Struss. *Recent Advances in Qualitative Physics*. MIT Press, 1992.

[37] G. Friedrich, M. Stumptner, and F. Wotawa. Model-based diagnosis of hardware designs. *Artificial Intelligence*, 3, 1999.

[38] R. Greiner, B.A. Smith, and R.W. Wilkerson. A correction to the algorithm in Reiters theory of diagnosis. *Artificial Intelligence*, 41, 1989.

[39] W. Hamscher, J. de Kleer, and L. Console, editors. *Readings in Model-based Diagnosis: Diagnosis of Designed Artifacts Based on Descriptions of their Structure and Function*. Morgan Kaufmann, 1992.

[40] U. Heller. Process-oriented consistency-based diagnosis-theory, implementation and applications. PhD thesis, Akademische V.-G., 2001.

[41] U. Heller and P. Struss. Consistency-based problem solving for environmental decision support. *Computer-Aided Civil and Infrastructure Engineering*, 17, 2002.

[42] G. Karsai, G. Biswas, S. Narasimhan, T. Szemethy, G. Peceli, G. Simon, and T. Kovacshazy. Towards fault-adaptive control of complex dynamic systems. In T. Samad and G. Balas, editors. *Software-Enabled Control: Information Technologies for Dynamical Systems*. Wiley–IEEE Press, 2003.

[43] D. Koeb and F. Wotawa. Fundamentals of debugging using a resolution calculus. In *International Conference on Fundamental Approaches to Software Engineering (FASE), LNCS*, vol. 3922. Springer, 2006.

[44] P. Kim, B. Williams, and M. Abramson. Executing reactive, model-based programs through graph-based temporal planning. In *Proceedings of the International Joint Conference on Artificial Intelligence*, 2001.

[45] F. Lin. Situation calculus. In V. Lifschitz, B. Porter, and F. van Harmelen, editors. *Handbook of Knowledge Representation*. Elsevier, 2007.

[46] G. Lamperti and M. Zanella. *Diagnosis of Active Systems—Principles and Techniques*. Kluwer Academic Publisher, 2003.

[47] P. Mosterman and G. Biswas. A comprehensive methodology for building hybrid models of physical systems. *Artificial Intelligence*, 121, 2000.

[48] I. Mozetic. Hierarchical model-based diagnosis. *Int. J. of Man-Machine Studies*, 35, 1991.

[49] S. McIlraith and R. Reiter. On tests for hypothetical reasoning. In [39], 1992.

[50] W. Mayer and M. Stumptner. Extending diagnosis to debug programs with exception. In *IEEE Automated Software Engineering Conference*, 2003.

[51] W. Mayer and M. Stumptner. Abstract interpretation of programs for model-based debugging. In *International Joint Conference on Artificial Intelligence (IJCAI)*, 2007.

[52] P. Nayak. *Automated Modeling of Physical Systems*. Springer, 1995.

[53] S. Narasimhan and G. Biswas. Model-based diagnosis of hybrid systems. *IEEE Trans. on Systems, Man, and Cybernetics, Part A*, 37(3), 2007.

[54] Y. Pencole and M.-O. Cordier. A formal framework for the decentralised diagnosis of large scale discrete event systems and its application to telecommunication networks. *Artificial Intelligence*, 164, 2005.

[55] C. Picardi, L. Console, F. Berger, J. Breeman, T. Kanakis, J. Moelands, S. Collas, E. Arbaretier, N. De Domenico, E. Girardelli, O. Dressler, P. Struss, and B. Zilbermann. AUTAS: a tool for supporting FMECA generation in aeronautic systems. In *Proceeding of the 16th European Conference on Artificial Intelligence*, 2004.

[56] B. Pulido and C.A. Gonzalez. Possible conflicts: a compilation technique for consistency-based diagnosis. *IEEE Transactions on Systems, Man and Cybernetics, Part B*, 34(5), 2004.

[57] D. Poole. Normality and faults in logic-based diagnosis. In *11th International Joint Conference on Artificial Intelligence*, 1989. Also in [39].

[58] G. Provan and D. Pool. The utility of consistency-based diagnostic techniques. In *Proc. Second International Conference on Principles of Knowledge Representation and Reasoning*, 1991.

[59] C. Price. Autosteve: Automated electrical design analysis. In *Proceedings ECAI-2000*, 2000.

[60] O. Raiman, J. de Kleer, V. Saraswat, and M. Shirley. Characterizing non-intermittent faults. In *Proceedings of AAAI-91*, 1991. Also in [39].

[61] R. Reiter. A logic for default reasoning. *Artificial Intelligence*, 13, 1980.

[62] R. Reiter. A theory of diagnosis from first principles. *Artificial Intelligence*, 32(1), 1987. Also in [39].

[63] F. Rossi, P. van Beek, and T. Walsh. Constraint programming. In *Handbook of Knowledge Representation*. Elsevier, 2008.

[64] P. Struss and O. Dressler. Physical negation—integrating fault models into the general diagnostic engine. In *Proceedings of the International Joint Conference on Artificial Intelligence (IJCAI-89)*, 1989.

[65] M. Sampath, S. Lafortune, and D. Teneketzis. Active diagnosis of discrete-event system. *IEEE Transactions on Automatic Control*, 43(7), 1998.

[66] P. Struss and C. Price. Model-based systems in the automotive industry. *AI Magazine*, 24, 2004.

[67] M. Sachenbacher and P. Struss. Task-dependent qualitative domain abstraction. *Artificial Intelligence*, 162, 2005.

[68] M. Sachenbacher, P. Struss, and R. Weber. Advances in design and implementation of OBD functions for diesel injection systems based on a qualitative approach to diagnosis. In *SAE 2000 World Congress*, Detroit, USA, 2000.

[69] P. Struss. What's in SD? Towards a theory of modeling for diagnosis. In [39], 1992.

[70] P. Struss. Testing for discrimination of diagnoses. In *5th International Workshop on Principles of Diagnosis*, 1994.

[71] P. Struss. Fundamentals of model-based diagnosis of dynamic systems. In *15th International Joint Conference on Artificial Intelligence*, 1997.

[72] P. Struss. Artificial intelligence methods for environmental decision support. In *e-Environment: Progress and Challenge*, 2004.

[73] P. Struss. Automated test reduction. In *19th Int. Workshop on Qualitative Reasoning. 16th International Workshop on Principles of Diagnosis*, 2005.

[74] P. Struss. A model-based methodology for the integration of diagnosis and fault analysis during the entire life cycle. In *Proceedings Volume from the 6th IFAC Symposium on Fault Detection, Supervision and Safety of Technical Processes (Safeprocess06)*, 2006.

[75] Y. Sun and D. Weld. A framework for model-based repair. In *Proceedings of AAAI-93*, 1993.

[76] M. Tiller. Introduction to Physical Modeling with MODELICA. *The Springer International Series in Engineering and Computer Science*, vol. 615. Springer, 2001.

[77] L. Trave-Massuyes, M.O. Cordier, and X. Pucel. Comparing diagnosability in CS and DES. In *Proceedings Volume from the 6th IFAC Symposium on Fault Detection, Supervision and Safety of Technical Processes (Safeprocess06)*, 2006.

[78] L. Trave-Massuyes and R. Milne. TIGER™—gas turbine condition monitoring using qualitative model-based diagnosis. *IEEE Expert*, 12(3), 1997.

[79] Y. Umeda, T. Tomiyama, H. Yoshikawa, and Y. Shimomura. A design methodology for self-maintenance machines. *IEEE Expert: Intelligent Systems and their Applications Archive*, 9(3), 1994.

[80] I. Vatcheva, O. Bernhard, H. de Jong, and N.J.I. Mars. Experiment selection for the discrimination of semi-quantitative models of dynamical systems. *Artificial Intelligence*, 170, 2006.

[81] D. Weld and J. de Kleer. *Readings in Qualitative Reasoning about Physical Systems*. Morgan Kaufmann, 1990.

[82] B. Williams. Interaction-based invention: Designing novel devices from first principles. In *Proceedings of the National Conference on Artificial Intelligence*, 1990.

[83] B. Williams. Interaction-based invention: Designing novel devices from first principles. In [36], 1992.

[84] B. Williams and P. Nayak. A model-based approach to reactive self-configuring systems. In *Proceedings of AAAI-96*, 1996.

[85] F. Wotawa. On the relationship between model-based debugging and program slicing. *Artificial Intelligence*, 135, 2002.

[86] B. Williams and R. Ragno. Conflict-directed A* and its role in model-based embedded systems. *Journal of Discrete Applied Math.*, 2003.

Edited by F. van Harmelen, V. Lifschitz and B. Porter
© 2008 Elsevier B.V. All rights reserved
DOI: 10.1016/S1574-6526(07)03011-8

Chapter 11

Bayesian Networks

A. Darwiche

11.1 Introduction

A Bayesian network is a tool for modeling and reasoning with uncertain beliefs. A Bayesian network consists of two parts: a qualitative component in the form of a directed acyclic graph (DAG), and a quantitative component in the form conditional probabilities; see Fig. 11.1. Intuitively, the DAG of a Bayesian network explicates variables of interest (DAG nodes) and the direct influences among them (DAG edges). The conditional probabilities of a Bayesian network quantify the dependencies between variables and their parents in the DAG. Formally though, a Bayesian network is interpreted as specifying a unique probability distribution over its variables. Hence, the network can be viewed as a factored (compact) representation of an exponentially-sized probability distribution. The formal syntax and semantics of Bayesian networks will be discussed in Section 11.2.

The power of Bayesian networks as a representational tool stems both from this ability to represent large probability distributions compactly, and the availability of inference algorithms that can answer queries about these distributions without necessarily constructing them explicitly. Exact inference algorithms will be discussed in Section 11.3 and approximate inference algorithms will be discussed in Section 11.4.

Bayesian networks can be constructed in a variety of ways, depending on the application at hand and the available information. In particular, one can construct Bayesian networks using traditional knowledge engineering sessions with domain experts, by automatically synthesizing them from high level specifications, or by learning them from data. The construction of Bayesian networks will be discussed in Section 11.5.

There are two interpretations of a Bayesian network structure, a standard interpretation in terms of probabilistic independence and a stronger interpretation in terms of causality. According to the stronger interpretation, the Bayesian network specifies a family of probability distributions, each resulting from applying an intervention to the situation of interest. These causal Bayesian networks lead to additional types of queries, and require more specialized algorithms for computing them. Causal Bayesian networks will be discussed in Section 11.6.

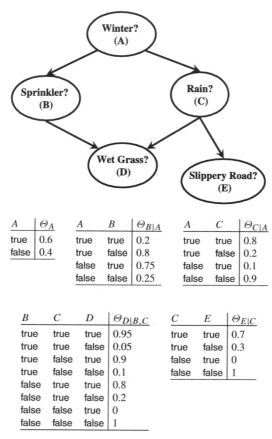

A	Θ_A
true	0.6
false	0.4

A	B	$\Theta_{B|A}$
true	true	0.2
true	false	0.8
false	true	0.75
false	false	0.25

A	C	$\Theta_{C|A}$
true	true	0.8
true	false	0.2
false	true	0.1
false	false	0.9

B	C	D	$\Theta_{D|B,C}$
true	true	true	0.95
true	true	false	0.05
true	false	true	0.9
true	false	false	0.1
false	true	true	0.8
false	true	false	0.2
false	false	true	0
false	false	false	1

C	E	$\Theta_{E|C}$
true	true	0.7
true	false	0.3
false	true	0
false	false	1

Figure 11.1: A Bayesian network over five propositional variables. A table is associated with each node in the network, containing conditional probabilities of that node given its parents.

11.2   Syntax and Semantics of Bayesian Networks

We will discuss the syntax and semantics of Bayesian networks in this section, starting with some notational conventions.

11.2.1   Notational Conventions

We will denote variables by upper-case letters (A) and their values by lower-case letters (a). Sets of variables will be denoted by bold-face upper-case letters (**A**) and their instantiations by bold-face lower-case letters (**a**). For variable A and value a, we will often write a instead of $A = a$ and, hence, $\Pr(a)$ instead of $\Pr(A = a)$ for the probability of $A = a$. For a variable A with values true and false, we may use A or a to denote $A =$ true and $\neg A$ or $\bar{a}$ to denote $A =$ false. Therefore, $\Pr(A)$, $\Pr(A =$ true$)$ and $\Pr(a)$ all represent the same probability in this case. Similarly, $\Pr(\neg A)$, $\Pr(A =$ false$)$ and $\Pr(\bar{a})$ all represent the same probability.

Table 11.1. A probability distribution Pr(.) and the result of conditioning it on evidence Alarm, Pr(.|Alarm)

World	Earthquake	Burglary	Alarm	Pr(.)	Pr(.|Alarm)
ω_1	true	true	true	0.0190	0.0190/0.2442
ω_2	true	true	false	0.0010	0
ω_3	true	false	true	0.0560	0.0560/0.2442
ω_4	true	false	false	0.0240	0
ω_5	false	true	true	0.1620	0.1620/0.2442
ω_6	false	true	false	0.0180	0
ω_7	false	false	true	0.0072	0.0072/0.2442
ω_8	false	false	false	0.7128	0

11.2.2 Probabilistic Beliefs

The semantics of Bayesian networks is given in terms of probability distributions and is founded on the notion of probabilistic independence. We review both of these notions in this section.

Let $X_1, \ldots, X_n$ be a set of variables, where each variable X_i has a finite number of values x_i. Every instantiation $x_1, \ldots, x_n$ of these variables will be called a *possible world*, denoted by ω, with the set of all possible worlds denoted by Ω. A *probability distribution* Pr over variables $X_1, \ldots, X_n$ is a mapping from the set of worlds Ω induced by variables $X_1, \ldots, X_n$ into the interval [0, 1], such that $\sum_\omega \Pr(\omega) = 1$; see Table 11.1. An *event* η is a set of worlds. A probability distribution Pr assigns a probability in [0, 1] to each event η as follows: $\Pr(\eta) = \sum_{\omega \in \eta} \Pr(\omega)$.

Events are typically denoted by *propositional sentences*, which are defined inductively as follows: A sentence is either primitive, having the form $X = x$, or complex, having the form $\neg\alpha$, $\alpha \vee \beta$, $\alpha \wedge \beta$, where α and β are sentences. A propositional sentence α denotes the event $Mods(\alpha)$, defined as follows: $Mods(X = x)$ is the set of worlds in which X is set to x, $Mods(\neg\alpha) = \Omega \setminus Mods(\alpha)$, $Mods(\alpha \vee \beta) = Mods(\alpha) \cup Mods(\beta)$, and $Mods(\alpha \wedge \beta) = Mods(\alpha) \cap Mods(\beta)$. In Table 11.1, the event $\{\omega_1, \omega_2, \omega_3, \omega_4, \omega_5, \omega_6\}$ can be denoted by the sentence Burglary $\vee$ Earthquake and has a probability of 0.28.

If some event β is observed and does not have a probability of 0 according to the current distribution Pr, the distribution is updated to a new distribution, denoted Pr(.|β), using *Bayes conditioning*:

$$\Pr(\alpha|\beta) = \frac{\Pr(\alpha \wedge \beta)}{\Pr(\beta)}. \tag{11.1}$$

Bayes conditioning follows from two commitments: worlds that contradict evidence β must have zero probabilities, and worlds that are consistent with β must maintain their relative probabilities.[1] Table 11.1 depicts the result of conditioning the given distribution on evidence Alarm = true, which initially has a probability of 0.2442.

When evidence β is accommodated, the belief is some event α may remain the same. We say in this case that α is independent of β. More generally, event α is inde-

---

[1] This is known as the principle of probability kinematics [88].

pendent of event β given event γ iff

$$\Pr(\alpha|\beta \wedge \gamma) = \Pr(\alpha|\gamma) \quad \text{or} \quad \Pr(\beta \wedge \gamma) = 0. \tag{11.2}$$

We can also generalize the definition of independence to variables. In particular, we will say that variables $\mathbf{X}$ are independent of variables $\mathbf{Y}$ given variables $\mathbf{Z}$, written $I(\mathbf{X}, \mathbf{Z}, \mathbf{Y})$, iff

$$\Pr(\mathbf{x}|\mathbf{y}, \mathbf{z}) = \Pr(\mathbf{x}|\mathbf{z}) \quad \text{or} \quad \Pr(\mathbf{y}, \mathbf{z}) = 0$$

for all instantiations $\mathbf{x}, \mathbf{y}, \mathbf{z}$ of variables $\mathbf{X}, \mathbf{Y}$ and $\mathbf{Z}$. Hence, the statement $I(\mathbf{X}, \mathbf{Z}, \mathbf{Y})$ is a compact representation of an exponential number of independence statements of the form given in (11.2).

Probabilistic independence satisfies some interesting properties known as the graphoid axioms [130], which can be summarized as follows:

$$I(\mathbf{X}, \mathbf{Z}, \mathbf{Y}) \quad \text{iff} \quad I(\mathbf{Y}, \mathbf{Z}, \mathbf{X})$$
$$I(\mathbf{X}, \mathbf{Z}, \mathbf{Y}) \,\&\, I(\mathbf{X}, \mathbf{ZW}, \mathbf{Y}) \quad \text{iff} \quad I(\mathbf{X}, \mathbf{Z}, \mathbf{YW}).$$

The first axiom is called Symmetry, and the second axiom is usually broken down into three axioms called decomposition, contraction and weak union; see [130] for details.

We will discuss the syntax and semantics of Bayesian networks next, showing the key role that independence plays in the representational power of these networks.

11.2.3 Bayesian Networks

A *Bayesian network* over variables $\mathbf{X}$ is a pair (G, Θ), where

- G is a directed acyclic graph over variables $\mathbf{X}$;

- Θ is a set of conditional probability tables (CPTs), one CPT $\Theta_{X|\mathbf{U}}$ for each variable X and its parents $\mathbf{U}$ in G. The CPT $\Theta_{X|\mathbf{U}}$ maps each instantiation $x\mathbf{u}$ to a probability $\theta_{x|\mathbf{u}}$ such that $\sum_x \theta_{x|\mathbf{u}} = 1$.

We will refer to the probability $\theta_{x|\mathbf{u}}$ as a *parameter* of the Bayesian network, and to the set of CPTs Θ as a *parametrization* of the DAG G.

A Bayesian network over variables $\mathbf{X}$ specifies a unique probability distributions over its variables, defined as follows [130]:

$$\Pr(\mathbf{x}) \overset{\text{def}}{=} \prod_{\theta_{x|\mathbf{u}}: x\mathbf{u} \sim \mathbf{x}} \theta_{x|\mathbf{u}}, \tag{11.3}$$

where $\sim$ represents the compatibility relationship among variable instantiations; hence, $x\mathbf{u} \sim \mathbf{x}$ means that instantiations $x\mathbf{u}$ and $\mathbf{x}$ agree on the values of their common variables. In the Bayesian network of Fig. 11.1, Eq. (11.3) gives:

$$\Pr(a, b, c, d, e) = \theta_{e|c}\theta_{d|b,c}\theta_{c|a}\theta_{b|a}\theta_a,$$

where a, b, c, d, e are values of variables A, B, C, D, E, respectively.

The distribution given by Eq. (11.3) follows from a particular interpretation of the structure and parameters of a Bayesian network (G, Θ). In particular:

- *Parameters:* Each parameter $\theta_{x|\mathbf{u}}$ is interpreted as the conditional probability of x given $\mathbf{u}$, $\Pr(x|\mathbf{u})$.

- *Structure:* Each variable X is assumed to be independent of its nondescendants $\mathbf{Z}$ given its parents $\mathbf{U}$: $I(X, \mathbf{U}, \mathbf{Z})$.[2]

The above interpretation is satisfied by a unique probability distribution, the one given in Eq. (11.3).

11.2.4 Structured Representations of CPTs

The size of a CPT $\Theta_{X|\mathbf{U}}$ in a Bayesian network is exponential in the number of parents $\mathbf{U}$. In general, if every variable can take up to d values, and has at most k parents, the size of any CPT is bounded by $O(d^{k+1})$. Moreover, if we have n network variables, the total number of Bayesian network parameters is bounded by $O(nd^{k+1})$. This number is usually quite reasonable as long as the number of parents per variable is relatively small. If number of parents $\mathbf{U}$ for variable X is large, the Bayesian network representation looses its main advantage as a compact representation of probability distributions, unless one employs a more structured representation for network parameters than CPTs.

The solutions to the problem of large CPTs fall in one of two categories. First, we may assume that the parents $\mathbf{U}$ interact with their child X according to a specific model, which allows us to specify the CPT $\Theta_{X|\mathbf{U}}$ using a smaller number of parameters (than exponential in the number of parents $\mathbf{U}$). One of the most popular examples of this approach is the *noisy-or model* of interaction and its generalizations [130, 77, 161, 51]. In its simplest form, this model assumes that variables have binary values true/false, that each parent $U \in \mathbf{U}$ being true is sufficient to make X true, except if some exception α_U materializes. By assuming that exceptions α_U are independent, one can induce the CPT $\Theta_{X|\mathbf{U}}$ using only the probabilities of these exceptions. Hence, the CPT for X can be specified using a number of parameters which is linear in the number of parents $\mathbf{U}$, instead of being exponential in the number of these parents.

The second approach for dealing with large CPTs is to appeal to nontabular representations of network parameters that exploit the *local structure* in network CPTs. In broad terms, local structure refers to the existence of nonsystematic redundancy in the probabilities appearing in a CPT. Local structure typically occurs in the form of *determinism*, where the CPT parameters take extreme values (0, 1). Another form of local structure is *context-specific independence* (*CSI*) [15], where the distribution for X can sometimes be determined by only a subset of its parents $\mathbf{U}$. Rules [136, 134] and decision trees (and graphs) [61, 80] are among the more common structured representations of CPTs.

11.2.5 Reasoning about Independence

We have seen earlier how the structure of a Bayesian network is interpreted as declaring a number of independence statements. We have also seen how probabilistic independence satisfies the graphoid axioms. When applying these axioms to the independencies declared by a Bayesian network structure, one can derive new independencies.

---

[2]A variable Z is a nondescendant of X if $Z \notin X\mathbf{U}$ and there is no directed path from X to Z.

In fact, any independence statement derived this way can be read off the Bayesian network structure using a graphical criterion known as *d-separation* [166, 35, 64]. In particular, we say that variables $\mathbf{X}$ are d-separated from variables $\mathbf{Y}$ by variables $\mathbf{Z}$ if every (undirected) path from a node in $\mathbf{X}$ to a node in $\mathbf{Y}$ is blocked by $\mathbf{Z}$. A path is blocked by $\mathbf{Z}$ if it has a *sequential* or *divergent* node in $\mathbf{Z}$, or if it has a *convergent* node that is not in $\mathbf{Z}$ nor any of its descendants are in $\mathbf{Z}$. Whether a node $Z \in \mathbf{Z}$ is sequential, divergent, or convergent depends on the way it appears on the path: $\rightarrow Z \rightarrow$ is sequential, $\leftarrow Z \rightarrow$ is divergent, and $\rightarrow Z \leftarrow$ is convergent. There are a number of important facts about the d-separation test. First, it can be implemented in polynomial time. Second, it is sound and complete with respect to the graphoid axioms. That is, $\mathbf{X}$ and $\mathbf{Y}$ are d-separated by $\mathbf{Z}$ in DAG G if and only if the graphoid axioms can be used to show that $\mathbf{X}$ and $\mathbf{Y}$ are independent given $\mathbf{Z}$.

There are secondary structures that one can build from a Bayesian network which can also be used to derive independence statements that hold in the distribution induced by the network. In particular, the *moral graph* G_m of a Bayesian network is an undirected graph obtained by adding an undirected edge between any two nodes that share a common child in DAG G, and then dropping the directionality of edges. If variables $\mathbf{X}$ and $\mathbf{Y}$ are separated by variables $\mathbf{Z}$ in moral graph G_m, we also have that $\mathbf{X}$ and $\mathbf{Y}$ are independent given $\mathbf{Z}$ in any distribution induced by the corresponding Bayesian network.

Another secondary structure that can be used to derive independence statements for a Bayesian network is the jointree [109]. This is a tree of clusters, where each cluster is a set of variables in the Bayesian network, with two conditions. First, every family (a node and its parents) in the Bayesian network must appear in some cluster. Second, if a variable appears in two clusters, it must also appear in every cluster on the path between them; see Fig. 11.4. Given a jointree for a Bayesian network (G, Θ), any two clusters are independent given any cluster on the path connecting them [130]. One can usually build multiple jointrees for a given Bayesian network, each revealing different types of independence information. In general, the smaller the clusters of a jointree, the more independence information it reveals. Jointrees play an important role in exact inference algorithms as we shall discuss later.

11.2.6 Dynamic Bayesian Networks

The *dynamic Bayesian network* (*DBN*) is a Bayesian network with a particular structure that deserves special attention [44, 119]. In particular, in a DBN, nodes are partitioned into *slices*, $0, 1, \ldots, t$, corresponding to different time points. Each slice has the same set of nodes and the same set of inter-slice edges, except possibly for the first slice which may have different edges. Moreover, intra-slice edges can only cross from nodes in slice t to nodes in a following slice $t + 1$. Because of their recurrent structure, DBNs are usually specified using two slices only for t and $t + 1$; see Fig. 11.2.

By restricting the structure of a DBN further at each time slice, one obtains more specialized types of networks, some of which are common enough to be studied outside the framework of Bayesian networks. Fig. 11.3 depicts one such restriction, known as a *Hidden Markov Model* [160]. Here, variables S_i typically represent unobservable states of a dynamic system, and variables O_i represent observable sensors

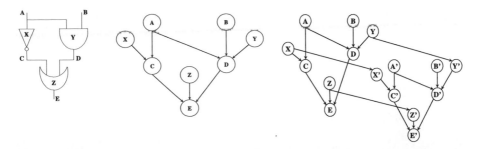

Figure 11.2: Two Bayesian network structures for a digital circuit. The one on the right is a DBN, representing the state of the circuit at two times steps. Here, variables $A, \ldots, E$ represent the state of wires in the circuit, while variables X, Y, Z represent the health of corresponding gates.

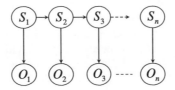

Figure 11.3: A Bayesian network structure corresponding to a Hidden Markov Model.

that may provide information on the corresponding system state. HMMs are usually studied as a special purpose model, and are equipped with three algorithms, known as the *forward–backward*, *Viterbi* and *Baum–Welch* algorithms (see [138] for a description of these algorithms and example applications of HMMs). These are all special cases of Bayesian network algorithms that we discuss in later sections.

Given the recurrent and potentially unbounded structure of DBNs (their size grows with time), they present particular challenges and also special opportunities for inference algorithms. They also admit a more refined class of queries than general Bayesian networks. Hence, it is not uncommon to use specialized inference algorithms for DBNs, instead of applying general purpose algorithms that one may use for arbitrary Bayesian networks. We will see examples of such algorithms in the following sections.

11.3   Exact Inference

Given a Bayesian (G, Θ) over variables $\mathbf{X}$, which induces a probability distribution Pr, one can pose a number of fundamental queries with respect to the distribution Pr:

- *Most Probable Explanation* (*MPE*): What's the most likely instantiation of network variables $\mathbf{X}$, given some evidence $\mathbf{e}$?

$$MPE(\mathbf{e}) = \underset{\mathbf{x}}{\arg\max} \Pr(\mathbf{x}, \mathbf{e}).$$

- *Probability of Evidence* (*PR*): What's the probability of evidence **e**, Pr(**e**)? Related to this query is *Posterior Marginals*: What's the conditional probability Pr(X|**e**) for every variable X in the network[3]?

- *Maximum a Posteriori Hypothesis* (*MAP*): What's the most likely instantiation of some network variables **M**, given some evidence **e**?

$$MAP(\mathbf{e}, \mathbf{M}) = \underset{\mathbf{m}}{\mathrm{argmax}}\, \Pr(\mathbf{m}, \mathbf{e}).$$

These problems are all difficult. In particular, the decision version of MPE, PR, and MAP, are known to be NP-complete, PP-complete and NP^{PP}-complete, respectively [32, 158, 145, 123]. We will discuss exact algorithms for answering these queries in this section, and then discuss approximate algorithms in Section 11.4. We start in Section 11.3.1 with a class of algorithms known as *structure-based* as their complexity is only a function of the network topology. We then discuss in Section 11.3.2 refinements of these algorithms that can exploit local structure in network parameters, leading to a complexity which is both a function of network topology and parameters. Section 11.3.3 discusses a class of algorithms based on search, specialized for MAP and MPE problems. Section 11.3.4 discusses an orthogonal class of methods for *compiling* Bayesian networks, and Section 11.3.5 discusses the technique of reducing exact probabilistic reasoning to logical inference.

It should noted here that by *evidence*, we mean a variable instantiation **e** of some network variables **E**. In general, one can define evidence as an arbitrary event α, yet most of the algorithms we shall discuss assume the more specific interpretation of evidence. These algorithms can be extended to handle more general notions of evidence as discussed in Section 11.3.6, which discusses a variety of additional extensions to inference algorithms.

11.3.1 Structure-Based Algorithms

When discussing inference algorithms, it is quite helpful to view the distribution induced by a Bayesian network as a product of *factors*, where a factor $f(\mathbf{X})$ is simply a mapping from instantiations **x** of variables **X** to real numbers. Hence, each CPT $\Theta_{X|\mathbf{U}}$ of a Bayesian network is a factor over variables $X\mathbf{U}$; see Fig. 11.1. The product of two factors $f(\mathbf{X})$ and $f(\mathbf{Y})$ is another factor over variables $\mathbf{Z} = \mathbf{X} \cup \mathbf{Y}$: $f(\mathbf{z}) = f(\mathbf{x})f(\mathbf{y})$ where $\mathbf{z} \sim \mathbf{x}$ and $\mathbf{z} \sim \mathbf{y}$.[4] The distribution induced by a Bayesian network (G, Θ) can then be expressed as a product of its CPTs (factors) and the inference problem in Bayesian networks can then be formulated as follows. We are given a function $f(\mathbf{X})$ (i.e., probability distribution) expressed as a product of factors $f_1(\mathbf{X}_1), \ldots, f_n(\mathbf{X}_n)$ and our goal is to answer questions about the function $f(\mathbf{X})$ without necessarily computing the explicit product of these factors.

We will next describe three computational paradigms for exact inference in Bayesian networks, which share the same computational guarantees. In particular, all methods can solve the PR and MPE problems in time and space which is exponential

---

[3]From a complexity viewpoint, all posterior marginals can be computed using a number of PR queries that is linear in the number of network variables.

[4]Recall, that $\sim$ represents the compatibility relation among variable instantiations.

only in the network *treewidth* [8, 144]. Moreover, all can solve the MAP problem exponential only in the network *constrained treewidth* [123]. Treewidth (and constrained treewidth) are functions of the network topology, measuring the extent to which a network resembles a tree. A more formal definition will be given later.

Inference by variable elimination

The first inference paradigm we shall discuss is based on the influential concept of variable elimination [153, 181, 45]. Given a function $f(\mathbf{X})$ in factored form, $\prod_{i=1}^{n} f_i(\mathbf{X}_i)$, and some corresponding query, the method will eliminate a variable X from this function to produce another function $f'(\mathbf{X} - X)$, while ensuring that the new function is as good as the old function as far as answering the query of interest. The idea is then to keep eliminating variables one at a time, until we can extract the answer we want from the result. The key insight here is that when eliminating a variable, we will only need to multiply factors that mention the eliminated variable. The order in which variables are eliminated is therefore important as far as complexity is concerned, as it dictates the extent to which the function can be kept in factored form.

The specific method for eliminating a variable depends on the query at hand. In particular, if the goal is to solve PR, then we eliminate variables by *summing* them out. If we are solving the MPE problem, we eliminate variables by *maxing* them out. If we are solving MAP, we will have to perform both types of elimination. To sum out a variable X from factor $f(\mathbf{X})$ is to produce another factor over variables $\mathbf{Y} = \mathbf{X} - X$, denoted $\sum_X f$, where $(\sum_X f)(\mathbf{y}) = \sum_x f(\mathbf{y}, x)$. To max out variable X is similar: $(\max_X f)(\mathbf{y}) = \max_x f(\mathbf{y}, x)$. Note that summing out variables is commutative and so is maxing out variables. However, summing out and maxing out do not commute. For a Bayesian network (G, Θ) over variables $\mathbf{X}$, map variables $\mathbf{M}$, and some evidence $\mathbf{e}$, inference by variable elimination is then a process of evaluating the following expressions:

- *MPE*: $\max_{\mathbf{X}} \prod_X \Theta_{X|\mathbf{U}} \lambda_X$.

- *PR*: $\sum_{\mathbf{X}} \prod_X \Theta_{X|\mathbf{U}} \lambda_X$.

- *MAP*: $\max_{\mathbf{M}} \sum_{\mathbf{X}-\mathbf{M}} \prod_X \Theta_{X|\mathbf{U}} \lambda_X$.

Here, λ_X is a factor over variable X, called an *evidence indicator*, used to capture evidence $\mathbf{e}$: $\lambda_X(x) = 1$ if x is consistent with evidence $\mathbf{e}$ and $\lambda_X(x) = 0$ otherwise. Evaluating the above expressions leads to computing the probability of MPE, the probability of evidence, and the probability of MAP, respectively. Some extra bookkeeping allows one to recover the identity of MPE and MAP [130, 45].

As mentioned earlier, the order in which variables are eliminated is critical for the complexity of variable elimination algorithms. In fact, one can define the width of an elimination order as one smaller than the size of the largest factor constructed during the elimination process, where the size of a factor is the number of variables over which it is defined. One can then show that variable elimination has a complexity which is exponential only in the width of used elimination order. In fact, the treewidth of a Bayesian network can be defined as the width of its best elimination order. Hence, the time and space complexity of variable elimination is bounded by $O(n \exp(w))$, where n is the number of network variables (also number of initial factors), and w is

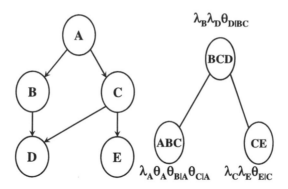

Figure 11.4: A Bayesian network (left) and a corresponding jointree (right), with the network factors and evidence indicators assigned to jointree clusters.

the width of used elimination order [45]. Note that w is lower bounded by the network treewidth. Moreover, computing an optimal elimination order and network treewidth are both known to be NP-hard [9].

Since summing out and maxing out do not commute, we must max out variables **M** last when computing MAP. This means that not all variable orders are legitimate; only those in which variables **M** come last are. The **M**-constrained treewidth of a Bayesian network can then be defined as the width of its best elimination order having variables **M** last in the order. Solving MAP using variable elimination is then exponential in the constrained treewidth [123].

Inference by tree clustering

Tree clustering is another algorithm for exact inference, which is also known as the jointree algorithm [89, 105, 157]. There are different ways for deriving the jointree algorithm, one of which treats the algorithm as a refined way of applying variable elimination.

The idea is to organize the given set of factors into a tree structure, using a jointree for the given Bayesian network. Fig. 11.4 depicts a Bayesian network, a corresponding jointree, and assignment of the factors to the jointree clusters. We can then use the join-tree structure to control the process of variable elimination as follows. We pick a leaf cluster $\mathbf{C}_i$ (having a single neighbor $\mathbf{C}_j$) in the jointree and then eliminate variables that appear in that cluster but in no other jointree cluster. Given the jointree properties, these variables are nothing but $\mathbf{C}_i \setminus \mathbf{C}_j$. Moreover, eliminating these variables requires that we compute the product of all factors assigned to cluster $\mathbf{C}_i$ and then eliminate $\mathbf{C}_i \setminus \mathbf{C}_j$ from the resulting factor. The result of this elimination is usually viewed as a message sent from cluster $\mathbf{C}_i$ to cluster $\mathbf{C}_j$. By the time we eliminate every cluster but one, we would have projected the factored function on the variables of that cluster (called the root). The basic insight of the jointree algorithm is that by choosing different roots, we can project the factored function on every cluster in the jointree. Moreover, some of the work we do in performing the elimination process towards one root (saved as messages) can be reused when eliminating towards another root. In fact, the amount of work that can be reused is such that we can project the function f on all clusters in the jointree with time and space bounded by $O(n \exp(w))$, where n is the number of jointree clusters and w is the width of given jointree (size of its largest cluster minus 1). This is indeed the main advantage of the jointree algorithm over the basic variable elimination algorithm, which would need $O(n^2 \exp(w))$ time and space to obtain the same result. Interesting enough, if a network has treewidth w, then it must have a jointree whose largest cluster has size $w + 1$. In fact, every jointree for the network must have some cluster of size $\geqslant w + 1$. Hence, another definition for the treewidth of a Bayesian network is as the width of its best jointree (the one with the smallest maximum cluster).[5]

The classical description of a jointree algorithm is as follows (e.g., [83]). We first construct a jointree for the given Bayesian network; assign each network CPT $\Theta_{X|U}$ to a cluster that contains $X\mathbf{U}$; and then assign each evidence indicator λ_X to a cluster that contains X. Fig. 11.4 provides an example of this process. Given evidence $\mathbf{e}$, a jointree algorithm starts by setting evidence indicators according to given evidence. A cluster is then selected as the root and message propagation proceeds in two phases, inward and outward. In the *inward phase*, messages are passed toward the root. In the *outward phase*, messages are passed away from the root. The inward phase is also known as the *collect* or *pull* phase, and the outward phase is known as the *distribute* or *push* phase. Cluster i sends a message to cluster j only when it has received messages from all its other neighbors k. A message from cluster i to cluster j is a factor M_{ij} defined as follows:

$$M_{i,j} = \sum_{\mathbf{C}_i \backslash \mathbf{C}_j} \Phi_i \prod_{k \neq j} M_{k,i},$$

where Φ_i is the product of factors and evidence indicators assigned to cluster i. Once message propagation is finished, we have the following for each cluster i in the jointree:

$$\Pr(\mathbf{C}_i, \mathbf{e}) = \Phi_i \prod_k M_{k,i}.$$

Hence, we can compute the joint marginal for any subset of variables that is included in a cluster.

The above description corresponds to a version of the jointree algorithm known as the Shenoy–Shafer architecture [157]. Another popular version of the algorithm is the Hugin architecture [89]. The two versions differ in their space and time complexity on arbitrary jointrees [106]. The jointree algorithm is quite versatile allowing even more architectures (e.g., [122]), more complex types of queries (e.g., [91, 143, 34]), including MAP and MPE, and a framework for time space tradeoffs [47].

Inference by conditioning

A third class of exact inference algorithms is based on the concept of *conditioning* [129, 130, 39, 81, 162, 152, 37, 52]. The key concept here is that if we know the value of a variable X in a Bayesian network, then we can remove edges outgoing from X, modify the CPTs for children of X, and then perform inference equivalently on the simplified network. If the value of variable X is not known, we can still exploit this idea by doing a case analysis on variable X, hence, instead of computing

---

[5]Jointrees correspond to tree-decompositions [144] in the graph theoretic literature.

$\Pr(\mathbf{e})$, we compute $\sum_x \Pr(\mathbf{e}, x)$. This idea of conditioning can be exploited in different ways. The first exploitation of this idea was in the context of loop-cutset conditioning [129, 130, 11]. A loop-cutset for a Bayesian network is a set of variables $\mathbf{C}$ such that removing edges outgoing from $\mathbf{C}$ will render the network a polytree: one in which we have a single (undirected) path between any two nodes. Inference on polytree networks can indeed be performed in time and space linear in their size [129]. Hence, by using the concept of conditioning, performing case analysis on a loop-cutset $\mathbf{C}$, one can reduce the query $\Pr(\mathbf{e})$ into a set of queries $\sum_{\mathbf{c}} \Pr(\mathbf{e}, \mathbf{c})$, each of which can be answered in linear time and space using the polytree algorithm.

This algorithm has linear space complexity as one needs to only save modest information across the different cases. This is a very attractive feature compared to algorithms based on elimination. The bottleneck for loop-cutset conditioning, however, is the size of cutset $\mathbf{C}$ since the time complexity of the algorithm is exponential in this set. One can indeed construct networks which have a bounded treewidth, leading to linear time complexity by elimination algorithms, yet an unbounded loop-cutset. A number of improvements have been proposed on loop-cutset conditioning (e.g., [39, 81, 162, 152, 37, 52]), yet only *recursive conditioning* [39] and its variants [10, 46] have a treewidth-based complexity similar to elimination algorithms.

The basic idea behind recursive conditioning is to identify a cutset $\mathbf{C}$ that is not necessarily a loop-cutset, but that can decompose a network $\mathcal{N}$ in two (or more) subnetworks, say, $\mathcal{N}_{\mathbf{c}}^l$ and $\mathcal{N}_{\mathbf{c}}^r$ with corresponding distributions $\Pr_{\mathbf{c}}^l$ and $\Pr_{\mathbf{c}}^r$ for each instantiation $\mathbf{c}$ of cutset $\mathbf{C}$. In this case, we can write

$$\Pr(\mathbf{e}) = \sum_{\mathbf{c}} \Pr(\mathbf{e}, \mathbf{c}) = \sum_{\mathbf{c}} \Pr_{\mathbf{c}}^l(\mathbf{e}^l, \mathbf{c}^l) \Pr_{\mathbf{c}}^r(\mathbf{e}^r, \mathbf{c}^r),$$

where $\mathbf{e}^l/\mathbf{c}^l$ and $\mathbf{e}^r/\mathbf{c}^r$ are parts of evidence/cutset pertaining to networks $\mathcal{N}^l$ and $\mathcal{N}^r$, respectively. The subqueries $\Pr_{\mathbf{c}}^l(\mathbf{e}^l, \mathbf{c}^l)$ and $\Pr_{\mathbf{c}}^r(\mathbf{e}^r, \mathbf{c}^r)$ can then be solved using the same technique, recursively, by finding cutsets for the corresponding subnetworks $\mathcal{N}_{\mathbf{c}}^l$ and $\mathcal{N}_{\mathbf{c}}^r$. This algorithm is typically driven by a structure known as a *dtree*, which is a binary tree with its leaves corresponding to the network CPTs. Each dtree provides a complete recursive decomposition over the corresponding network, with a cutset for each level of the decomposition [39].

Given a dtree where each internal node T has children T^l and T^r, and each leaf node has a CPT associated with it, recursive conditioning can then compute the probability of evidence $\mathbf{e}$ as follows:

$$rc(T, \mathbf{e}) = \begin{cases} \sum_{\mathbf{c}} rc(T^l, \mathbf{ec}) rc(T^r, \mathbf{ec}), & T \text{ is an internal node with cutset } \mathbf{C}; \\ \sum_{\mathbf{u}x \sim \mathbf{e}} \theta_{x|\mathbf{u}}, & T \text{ is a leaf node with CPT } \Theta_{X|\mathbf{U}}. \end{cases}$$

Note that similar to loop-cutset conditioning, the above algorithm also has a linear space complexity which is better than the space complexity of elimination algorithms. Moreover, if the Bayesian network has treewidth w, there is then a dtree which is both balanced and has cutsets whose sizes are bounded by $w + 1$. This means that the above algorithm can run in $O(n \exp(w \log n))$ time and $O(n)$ space. This is worse than the time complexity of elimination algorithms, due to the $\log n$ factor, where n is the number of network nodes.

A careful analysis of the above algorithm, however, reveals that it may make identical recursive calls in different parts of the recursion tree. By caching the value of a recursive call $rc(T, .)$, one can avoid evaluating the same recursive call multiple times. In fact, if a network has a treewidth w, one can always construct a dtree on which caching will reduce the running time from $O(n \exp(w \log n))$ to $O(n \exp(w))$, while bounding the space complexity by $O(n \exp(w))$, which is identical to the complexity of elimination algorithms. In principle, one can cache as many results as available memory would allow, leading to a framework for trading off time and space [3], where space complexity ranges from $O(n)$ to $O(n \exp(w))$, and time complexity ranges from $O(n \exp(w \log n))$ to $O(n \exp(w))$. Recursive conditioning can also be used to compute multiple marginals [4], in addition to MAP and MPE queries [38], within the same complexity discussed above.

We note here that the quality of a variable elimination order, a jointree and a dtree can all be measured in terms of the notion of *width*, which is lower bounded by the network treewidth. Moreover, the complexity of algorithms based on these structures are all exponential only in the width of used structure. Polynomial time algorithms exists for converting between any of these structures, while preserving the corresponding width, showing the equivalence of these methods with regards to their computational complexity in terms of treewidth [42].

11.3.2 Inference with Local (Parametric) Structure

The computational complexity bounds given for elimination, clustering and conditioning algorithms are based on the network topology, as captured by the notions of treewidth and constrained treewidth. There are two interesting aspects of these complexity bounds. First, they are independent of the particular parameters used to quantify Bayesian networks. Second, they are both best-case and worst-case bounds for the specific statements given for elimination and conditioning algorithms.

Given these results, only networks with reasonable treewidth are accessible to these structure-based algorithms. One can provide refinements of both elimination/clustering and conditioning algorithms, however, that exploit the parametric structure of a Bayesian network, allowing them to solve some networks whose treewidth can be quite large.

For elimination algorithms, the key is to adopt nontabular representations of factors as initially suggested by [182] and developed further by other works (e.g., [134, 50, 80, 120]). Recall that a factor $f(\mathbf{X})$ over variables $\mathbf{X}$ is a mapping from instantiations $\mathbf{x}$ of variables $\mathbf{X}$ to real numbers. The standard statements of elimination algorithms assume that a factor $f(\mathbf{X})$ is represented by a table that has one row of each instantiation $\mathbf{x}$. Hence, the size of factor $f(\mathbf{X})$ is always exponential in the number of variables in $\mathbf{X}$. This also dictates the complexity of factor operations, including multiplication, summation and maximization. In the presence of parametric structure, one can afford to use more structured representations of factors that need not be exponential in the variables over which they are defined. In fact, one can use any factor representation as long as they provide corresponding implementations of the factor operations of multiplication, summing out, and maxing out, which are used in the context of elimination algorithms. One of the more effective structured representations of factors is the *algebraic decision diagram (ADD)* [139, 80], which provides efficient implementations of these operations.

In the context of conditioning algorithms, local structure can be exploited at multiple levels. First, when considering the cases $\mathbf{c}$ of a cutset $\mathbf{C}$, one can skip a case $\mathbf{c}$ if it is logically inconsistent with the logical constraints implied by the network parameters. This inconsistency can be detected by some efficient logic propagation techniques that run in the background of conditioning algorithms [2]. Second, one does not always need to instantiate all cutset variables before a network is disconnected or converted into a polytree, as some partial cutset instantiations may have the same effect if we have context-specific independence [15, 25]. Third, local structure in the form of equal network parameters within the same CPT will reduce the number of distinct subproblems that need to be solved by recursive conditioning, allowing caching to be much more effective [25]. Considering various experimental results reported in recent years, it appears that conditioning algorithms have been more effective in exploiting local structure, especially determinism, as compared to algorithms based on variable eliminating (and, hence, clustering).

Network preprocessing can also be quite effective in the presence of local structure, especially determinism, and is orthogonal to the algorithms used afterwards. For example, preprocessing has proven quite effective and critical for networks corresponding to genetic linkage analysis, allowing exact inference on networks with very high treewidth [2, 54, 55, 49]. A fundamental form of preprocessing is CPT decomposition, in which one decomposes a CPT with local structure (e.g., [73]) into a series of CPTs by introducing auxiliary variables [53, 167]. This decomposition can reduce the treewidth of given network, allowing inference to be performed much more efficiently. The problem of finding an optimal CPT decomposition corresponds to the problem of determining tensor rank [150], which is NP-hard [82]. Closed form solutions are known, however, for CPTs with a particular local structure [150].

11.3.3 Solving MAP and MPE by Search

MAP and MPE queries are conceptually different from PR queries as they correspond to optimization problems whose outcome is a variable instantiation instead of a probability. These queries admit a very effective class of algorithms based on branch and bound search. For MPE, the search tree includes a leaf for each instantiation $\mathbf{x}$ of nonevidence variables $\mathbf{X}$, whose probability can be computed quite efficiently given Eq. (11.3). Hence, the key to the success of these search algorithms is the use of evaluation functions that can be applied to internal nodes in the search tree, which correspond to partial variable instantiations $\mathbf{i}$, to upper bound the probability of any completion $\mathbf{x}$ of instantiation $\mathbf{i}$. Using such an evaluation function, one can possibly prune part of the search space, therefore, solving MPE without necessarily examining the space of all variable instantiations. The most successful evaluation functions are based on relaxations of the variable elimination algorithm, allowing one to eliminate a variable without necessarily multiplying all factors that include the variable [95, 110]. These relaxations lead to a spectrum of evaluation functions, that can trade accuracy with efficiency.

A similar idea can be applied to solving MAP, with a notable distinction. In MAP, the search tree will be over the space of instantiations of a subset $\mathbf{M}$ of network variables. Moreover, each leaf node in the search tree will correspond to an instantiation $\mathbf{m}$ in this case. Computing the probability of a partial instantiation $\mathbf{m}$ requires a PR query

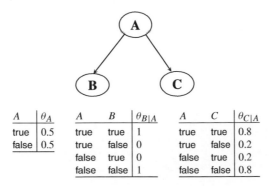

A	θ_A		A	B	$\theta_{B\mid A}$		A	C	$\theta_{C\mid A}$
true	0.5		true	true	1		true	true	0.8
false	0.5		true	false	0		true	false	0.2
			false	true	0		false	true	0.2
			false	false	1		false	false	0.8

Figure 11.5: A Bayesian network.

though, which itself can be exponential in the network treewidth. Therefore, the success of search-based algorithms for MAP depends on both the efficient evaluation of leaf nodes in the search tree, and on evaluation functions for computing upper bounds on the completion of partial variable instantiations [123, 121]. The most successful evaluation function for MAP is based on a relaxation of the variable elimination algorithm for computing MAP, allowing one to use any variable order instead of insisting on a constrained variable order [121].

11.3.4 Compiling Bayesian Networks

The probability distribution induced by a Bayesian network can be compiled into an *arithmetic circuit*, allowing various probabilistic queries to be answered in time linear in the compiled circuit size [41]. The compilation time can be amortized over many online queries, which can lead to extremely efficient online inference [25, 27]. Compiling Bayesian networks is especially effective in the presence of local structure, as the exploitation of local structure tends to incur some overhead that may not be justifiable in the context of standard algorithms when the local structure is not excessive. In the context of compilation, this overhead is incurred only once in the offline compilation phase.

To expose the semantics of this compilation process, we first observe that the probability distribution induced by a Bayesian network, as given by Eq. (11.3), can be expressed in a more general form:

$$f = \sum_{\mathbf{x}} \prod_{\lambda_x : x \sim \mathbf{x}} \lambda_x \prod_{\theta_{x\mid\mathbf{u}} : x\mathbf{u} \sim \mathbf{x}} \theta_{x\mid\mathbf{u}}, \tag{11.4}$$

where λ_x is called an evidence indicator variable (we have one indicator λ_x for each variable X and value x). This form is known as the *network polynomial* and represents the distribution as follows. Given any evidence $\mathbf{e}$, let $f(\mathbf{e})$ denotes the value of polynomial f with each indicator variable λ_x set to 1 if x is consistent with evidence $\mathbf{e}$ and set to 0 otherwise. It then follows that $f(\mathbf{e})$ is the probability of evidence $\mathbf{e}$. Following is the polynomial for the network in Fig. 11.5:

$$f = \lambda_a \lambda_b \lambda_c \theta_a \theta_{b\mid a} \theta_{c\mid a} + \lambda_a \lambda_b \lambda_{\bar{c}} \theta_a \theta_{b\mid a} \theta_{\bar{c}\mid a} + \cdots \lambda_{\bar{a}} \lambda_{\bar{b}} \lambda_{\bar{c}} \theta_{\bar{a}} \theta_{\bar{b}\mid\bar{a}} \theta_{\bar{c}\mid\bar{a}}.$$

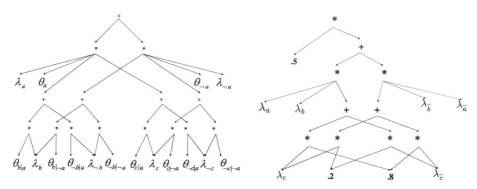

Figure 11.6: Two circuits for the Bayesian network in Fig. 11.5.

The network polynomial has an exponential number of terms, but can be factored and represented more compactly using an arithmetic circuit, which is a rooted, directed acyclic graph whose leaf nodes are labeled with evidence indicators and network parameters, and internal nodes are labeled with multiplication and addition operations. The size of an arithmetic circuit is measured by the number of edges that it contains. Fig. 11.6 depicts an arithmetic circuit for the above network polynomial. This arithmetic circuit is therefore a compilation of corresponding Bayesian network as it can be used to compute the probability of any evidence **e** by evaluating the circuit while setting the indicators to $1/0$ depending on their consistency with evidence **e**. In fact, the partial derivatives of this circuit with respect to indicators λ_x and parameters $\theta_{x|\mathbf{u}}$ can all be computed in a single second pass on the circuit. Moreover, the values of these derivatives can be used to immediately answer various probabilistic queries, including the marginals over networks variables and families [41]. Hence, for a given evidence, one can compute the probability of evidence and posterior marginals on all network variables and families in two passes on the arithmetic circuit.

One can compile a Bayesian network using exact algorithms based on elimination [26] or conditioning [25], by replacing their addition and multiplication operations by corresponding operations for building the circuit. In fact, for jointree algorithms, the arithmetic circuit can be generated directly from the jointree structure [124]. One can also generate these compilations by reducing the problem to logical inference as discussed in the following section. If structure-based versions of elimination and conditioning algorithms are used to compile Bayesian networks, the size of compiled arithmetic circuits will be exponential in the network treewidth in the best case. If one uses versions that exploit parametric structure, the resulting compilation may not be lower bounded by treewidth [25, 27]. Fig. 11.6 depicts two arithmetic circuits for the same network, the one on the right taking advantage of network parameters and is therefore smaller than the one on the left, which is valid for any value of network parameters.

11.3.5   Inference by Reduction to Logic

One of the more effective approaches for exact probabilistic inference in the presence of local structure, especially determinism, is based on reducing the problem to one of

A	Θ_A
a_1	0.1
a_2	0.9

A	B	$\Theta_{B\mid A}$
a_1	b_1	0.1
a_1	b_2	0.9
a_2	b_1	0.2
a_2	b_2	0.8

A	C	$\Theta_{C\mid A}$
a_1	c_1	0.1
a_1	c_2	0.9
a_2	c_1	0.2
a_2	c_2	0.8

Figure 11.7: The CPTs of Bayesian network with two edges $A \to B$ and $A \to C$.

logical inference. The key technique is to encode the Bayesian network as a propositional theory in conjunctive normal form (CNF) and then apply algorithms for model counting [147] or knowledge compilation to the resulting CNF [40]. The encoding can be done in multiple ways [40, 147], yet we focus on one particular encoding [40] in this section to illustrate the reduction technique.

We will now discuss the CNF encoding for the Bayesian network in Fig. 11.7. We first define the CNF variables which are in one-to-one correspondence with evidence indicators and network parameters as defined in Section 11.3.4, but treated as propositional variables in this case. The CNF Δ is then obtained by processing network variables and CPTs, writing corresponding clauses as follows:

Variable A:	$\lambda_{a_1} \vee \lambda_{a_2}$	$\neg\lambda_{a_1} \vee \neg\lambda_{a_2}$
Variable B:	$\lambda_{b_1} \vee \lambda_{b_2}$	$\neg\lambda_{b_1} \vee \neg\lambda_{b_2}$
Variable C:	$\lambda_{c_1} \vee \lambda_{c_2}$	$\neg\lambda_{c_1} \vee \neg\lambda_{c_2}$
CPT for A:	$\lambda_{a_1} \Leftrightarrow \theta_{a_1}$	
CPT for B:	$\lambda_{a_1} \wedge \lambda_{b_1} \Leftrightarrow \theta_{b_1\mid a_1}$	$\lambda_{a_1} \wedge \lambda_{b_2} \Leftrightarrow \theta_{b_2\mid a_1}$
	$\lambda_{a_2} \wedge \lambda_{b_1} \Leftrightarrow \theta_{b_1\mid a_2}$	$\lambda_{a_2} \wedge \lambda_{b_2} \Leftrightarrow \theta_{b_2\mid a_2}$
CPT for C:	$\lambda_{a_1} \wedge \lambda_{c_1} \Leftrightarrow \theta_{c_1\mid a_1}$	$\lambda_{a_1} \wedge \lambda_{c_2} \Leftrightarrow \theta_{c_2\mid a_1}$
	$\lambda_{a_2} \wedge \lambda_{c_1} \Leftrightarrow \theta_{c_1\mid a_2}$	$\lambda_{a_2} \wedge \lambda_{c_2} \Leftrightarrow \theta_{c_2\mid a_2}$

The clauses for variables are simply asserting that exactly one evidence indicator must be true. The clauses for CPTs are establishing an equivalence between each network parameter and its corresponding indicators. This resulting CNF has two important properties. First, its size is linear in the network size. Second, its models are in one-to-one correspondence with the instantiations of network variables. Table 11.2 illustrates the variable instantiations and corresponding CNF models for the previous example.

We can now either apply a model counter to the CNF queries [147], or compile the CNF to obtain an arithmetic circuit for the Bayesian network [40]. If we want to apply a model counter to the CNF, we must first assign weights to the CNF variables (hence, we will be performing weighted model counting). All literals of the form λ_x, $\neg\lambda_x$ and $\neg\theta_{x\mid\mathbf{u}}$ get weight 1, while literals of the form $\theta_{x\mid\mathbf{u}}$ get a weight equal to the value of parameter $\theta_{x\mid\mathbf{u}}$ as defined by the Bayesian network; see Table 11.2. To compute the probability of any event α, all we need to do then is computed the weighted model count of $\Delta \wedge \alpha$.

This reduction of probabilistic inference to logical inference is currently the most effective technique for exploiting certain types of parametric structure, including determinism and parameter equality. It also provides a very effective framework for exploiting evidence computationally and for accommodating general types evidence [25, 24, 147, 27].

Table 11.2. Illustrating the models and corresponding weights of a CNF encoding a Bayesian network

Network instantiation	CNF model	ω_i sets these CNF vars to true and all others to false	Model weight
$a_1 b_1 c_1$	ω_0	$\lambda_{a_1} \lambda_{b_1} \lambda_{c_1} \theta_{a_1} \theta_{b_1\mid a_1} \theta_{c_1\mid a_1}$	$0.1 \cdot 0.1 \cdot 0.1 = 0.001$
$a_1 b_1 c_2$	ω_1	$\lambda_{a_1} \lambda_{b_1} \lambda_{c_2} \theta_{a_1} \theta_{b_1\mid a_1} \theta_{c_2\mid a_1}$	$0.1 \cdot 0.1 \cdot 0.9 = 0.009$
$a_1 b_2 c_1$	ω_2	$\lambda_{a_1} \lambda_{b_2} \lambda_{c_1} \theta_{a_1} \theta_{b_2\mid a_1} \theta_{c_1\mid a_1}$	$0.1 \cdot 0.9 \cdot 0.1 = 0.009$
$a_1 b_2 c_2$	ω_3	$\lambda_{a_1} \lambda_{b_2} \lambda_{c_2} \theta_{a_1} \theta_{b_2\mid a_1} \theta_{c_2\mid a_1}$	$0.1 \cdot 0.9 \cdot 0.9 = 0.081$
$a_2 b_1 c_1$	ω_4	$\lambda_{a_2} \lambda_{b_1} \lambda_{c_1} \theta_{a_2} \theta_{b_1\mid a_1} \theta_{c_1\mid a_2}$	$0.9 \cdot 0.2 \cdot 0.2 = 0.036$
$a_2 b_1 c_2$	ω_5	$\lambda_{a_2} \lambda_{b_1} \lambda_{c_2} \theta_{a_2} \theta_{b_1\mid a_1} \theta_{c_2\mid a_2}$	$0.9 \cdot 0.2 \cdot 0.8 = 0.144$
$a_2 b_2 c_1$	ω_6	$\lambda_{a_2} \lambda_{b_2} \lambda_{c_1} \theta_{a_2} \theta_{b_2\mid a_1} \theta_{c_1\mid a_2}$	$0.9 \cdot 0.8 \cdot 0.2 = 0.144$
$a_2 b_2 c_2$	ω_7	$\lambda_{a_2} \lambda_{b_2} \lambda_{c_2} \theta_{a_2} \theta_{b_2\mid a_1} \theta_{c_2\mid a_2}$	$0.9 \cdot 0.8 \cdot 0.8 = 0.576$

11.3.6 Additional Inference Techniques

We discuss in this section some additional inference techniques which can be crucial in certain circumstances.

First, all of the methods discussed earlier are immediately applicable to DBNs. However, the specific, recurrent structure of these networks calls for some special attention. For example, PR queries can be further refined depending on the location of evidence and query variables within the network structure, leading to specialized queries, such as *monitoring*. Here, the evidence is restricted to network slices $t = 0$, $\ldots, t = i$ and the query variables are restricted to slice $t = i$. In such a case, and by using restricted elimination orders, one can perform inference in space which is better than linear in the network size [13, 97, 12]. This is important for DBNs as a linear space complexity can be unpractical if we have too many slices.

Second, depending on the given evidence and query variables, a network can potentially be pruned before inference is performed. In particular, one can always remove edges outgoing from evidence variables [156]. One can also remove leaf nodes in the network as long as they do not correspond to evidence or query variables [155]. This process of node removal can be repeated, possibly simplifying the network structure considerably. More sophisticated pruning techniques are also possible [107].

Third, we have so far considered only simple evidence corresponding to the instantiation **e** of some variables **E**. If evidence corresponds to a general event α, we can add an auxiliary node X_α to the network, making it a child of all variables **U** appearing in α, setting the CPT $\Theta_{X_\alpha\mid U}$ based on α, and asserting evidence on X_α [130]. A more effective solution to this problem can be achieved in the context of approaches that reduce the problem to logical inference. Here, we can simply add the event α to the encoded CNF before we apply logical inference [147, 24]. Another type of evidence we did not consider is *soft evidence*. This can be specified in two forms. We can declare that the evidence changes the probability of some variable X from $\Pr(X)$ to $\Pr'(X)$. Or we can assert that the new evidence on X changes its odds by a given factor k, known as the Bayes factor: $O'(X)/O(X) = k$. Both types of evidence can be handled by adding an auxiliary child $X_\mathbf{e}$ for node X, setting its CPT $\Theta_{X_\mathbf{e}\mid X}$ depending on the strength of soft evidence, and finally simulating the soft evidence by hard evidence on $X_\mathbf{e}$ [130, 22].

11.4   Approximate Inference

All exact inference algorithms we have discussed for PR have a complexity which is exponential in the network treewidth. Approximate inference algorithms are generally not sensitive to treewidth, however, and can be quite efficient regardless of the network topology. The issue with these methods is related to the quality of answers the compute, which for some algorithms is quite related to the amount of time budgeted by the algorithm. We discuss two major classes of approximate inference algorithms in this section. The first and more classical class is based on sampling. The second and more recent class of methods can be understood in terms of a reduction to optimization problems. We note, however, that none of these algorithms offer general guarantees on the quality of approximations they produce, which is not surprising since the problem of approximating inference to any desired precision is known to be NP-hard [36].

11.4.1   Inference by Stochastic Sampling

Sampling from a probability distribution $Pr(\mathbf{X})$ is a process of generating complete instantiations $\mathbf{x}_1, \ldots, \mathbf{x}_n$ of variables $\mathbf{X}$. A key property of a sampling process is its *consistency:* generating samples $\mathbf{x}$ with a frequency that converges to their probability $Pr(\mathbf{x})$ as the number of samples approaches infinity. By generating such consistent samples, one can approximate the probability of some event α, $Pr(\alpha)$, in terms of the fractions of samples that satisfy α, $\widehat{Pr}(\alpha)$. This approximated probability will then converge to the true probability as the number of samples reaches infinity. Hence, the precision of sampling methods will generally increase with the number of samples, where the complexity of generating a sample is linear in the size of the network, and is usually only weakly dependent on its topology.

Indeed, one can easily generate consistent samples from a distribution Pr that is induced by a Bayesian network (G, Θ), using time that is linear in the network size to generate each sample. This can be done by visiting the network nodes in topological order, parents before children, choosing a value for each node X by sampling from the distribution $Pr(X|\mathbf{u}) = \Theta_{X|\mathbf{u}}$, where $\mathbf{u}$ is the chosen values for X's parents $\mathbf{U}$. The key question with sampling methods is therefore related to the speed of convergence (as opposed to the speed of generating samples), which is usually affected by two major factors: the query at hand (whether it has a low probability) and the specific network parameters (whether they are extreme).

Consider, for example, approximating the query $Pr(\alpha|\mathbf{e})$ by approximating $Pr(\alpha, \mathbf{e})$ and $Pr(\mathbf{e})$ and then computing $\widehat{Pr}(\alpha|\mathbf{e}) = \widehat{Pr}(\alpha, \mathbf{e})/\widehat{Pr}(\mathbf{e})$ according to the above sampling method, known as *logic sampling* [76]. If the evidence $\mathbf{e}$ has a low probability, the fraction of samples that satisfy $\mathbf{e}$ (and $\alpha, \mathbf{e}$ for that matter) will be small, decreasing exponentially in the number of variables instantiated by evidence $\mathbf{e}$, and correspondingly increasing the convergence time. The fundamental problem here is that we are generating samples based on the original distribution $Pr(\mathbf{X})$, where we ideally want to generate samples based on the posterior distribution $Pr(\mathbf{X}|\mathbf{e})$, which can be shown to be the optimal choice in a precise sense [28]. The problem, however, is that $Pr(\mathbf{X}|\mathbf{e})$ is not readily available to sample from. Hence, more sophisticated approaches for sampling attempt to sample from distributions that are meant to be close to $Pr(\mathbf{X}|\mathbf{e})$, possibly changing the sampling distribution (also known as an importance function) as the sampling process proceeds and more information is gained. This includes the methods of *likelihood weighting* [154, 63], *self-importance sampling* [154], *heuristic importance* [154], *adaptive importance sampling* [28], and *evidence pre-propagation importance sampling* (EPIS-BN) algorithm [179]. Likelihood weighing is perhaps the simplest of these methods. It works by generating samples that are guaranteed to be consistent with evidence **e**, by avoiding to sample values for variables **E**, always setting them to **e** instead. It also assigns a weight of $\prod_{\theta_{e|\mathbf{u}}:e\mathbf{u}\sim\mathbf{x}} \theta_{e|\mathbf{u}}$ to each sample **x**. Likelihood weighing will then use these weighted samples for approximating the probabilities of events. The current state of the art for sampling in Bayesian networks is probably the EPIS-BN algorithm, which estimates the optimal importance function using belief propagation (see Section 11.4.2) and then proceeds with sampling.

Another class of sampling methods is based on *Markov Chain Monte Carlo* (*MCMC*) simulation [23, 128]. Procedurally, samples in MCMC are generated by first starting with a random sample $\mathbf{x}_0$ that is consistent with evidence **e**. A sample $\mathbf{x}_i$ is then generated based on sample $\mathbf{x}_{i-1}$ by choosing a new value of some nonevidence variable X by sampling from the distribution $\Pr(X|\mathbf{x}_i - X)$. This means that samples $\mathbf{x}_i$ and $\mathbf{x}_{i+1}$ will disagree on at most one variable. It also means that the sampling distribution is potentially changed after each sample is generated. MCMC approximations will converge to the true probabilities if the network parameters are strictly positive, yet the algorithm is known to suffer from convergence problems in case the network parameters are extreme. Moreover, the sampling distribution of MCMC will convergence to the optimal one if the network parameters satisfy some (ergodic) properties [178].

One specialized class of sampling methods, known as *particle filtering*, deserves particular attention at it applies to DBNs [93]. In this class, one generates *particles* instead of *samples*, where a particle is an instantiation of the variables at a given time slice t. One starts by a set of n particles for the initial time slice $t = 0$, and then moves forward generating particles $\mathbf{x}^t$ for time t based on the particles $\mathbf{x}^{t-1}$ generated for time $t - 1$. In particular, for each particle $\mathbf{x}^{t-1}$, we sample a particle $\mathbf{x}^t$ based on the distributions $\Pr(X^t|\mathbf{x}^{t-1})$, in a fashion similar to logic sampling. The particles for time t can then be used to approximate the probabilities of events corresponding to that slice. As with other sampling algorithms, particle filtering needs to deal with the problem of unlikely evidence, a problem that is more exaggerated in the context of DBNs as the evidence pertaining to slices $t > i$ is generally not available when we generate particles for times $t \leqslant i$. One simple approach for addressing this problem is to *resample* the particles for time t based on the extent to which they are compatible with the evidence $\mathbf{e}^t$ at time t. In particular, we regenerate n particles for time t from the original set based on the weight $\Pr(\mathbf{e}^t|\mathbf{x}^t)$ assigned to each particle $\mathbf{x}^t$. The family of particle filtering algorithms include other proposals for addressing this problem.

11.4.2 Inference as Optimization

The second class of approximate inference algorithms for PR can be understood in terms of reducing the problem of inference to one of optimization. This class includes *belief propagation* (e.g., [130, 117, 56, 176]) and *variational* methods (e.g., [92, 85]).

Given a Bayesian network which induces a distribution Pr, variational methods work by formulating approximate inference as an optimization problem. For example, say we are interested in searching for an approximate distribution $\widehat{\Pr}$ which is more well behaved computationally than Pr. In particular, if Pr is induced by a Bayesian network $\mathcal{N}$ which has a high treewidth, then $\widehat{Pr}$ could possibly be induced by another network $\widehat{\mathcal{N}}$ which has a manageable treewidth. Typically, one starts by choosing the structure of network $\widehat{\mathcal{N}}$ to meet certain computational constraints and then search for a parametrization of $\widehat{\mathcal{N}}$ that minimizes the KL-divergence between the original distribution Pr and the approximate one $\widehat{Pr}$ [100]:

$$KL\big(\widehat{Pr}(.|\mathbf{e}), Pr(.|\mathbf{e})\big) = \sum_{w} \widehat{Pr}(w|\mathbf{e}) \log \frac{\widehat{Pr}(w|\mathbf{e})}{Pr(w|\mathbf{e})}.$$

Ideally, we want parameters of network $\widehat{\mathcal{N}}$ that minimize this KL-divergence, while possibly satisfying additional constraints. Often, we can simply set to zero the partial derivatives of $KL(\widehat{Pr}(.|\mathbf{e}), Pr(.|\mathbf{e}))$ with respect to the parameters, and perform an iterative search for parameters that solve the resulting system of equations. Note that the KL-divergence is not symmetric. In fact, one would probably want to minimize $KL(Pr(.|\mathbf{e}), \widehat{Pr}(.|\mathbf{e}))$ instead, but this is not typically done due to computational considerations (see [57, 114] for approaches using this divergence, based on local optimizations).

One of the simplest variational approaches is to choose a completely disconnected network $\widehat{\mathcal{N}}$, leading to what is known as a *mean-field* approximation [72]. Other variational approaches typically assume a particular structure of the approximate model, such as chains [67], trees [57, 114], disconnected subnetworks [149, 72, 175], or just tractable substructures in general [173, 65]. These methods are typically phrased in the more general setting of graphical models (which includes other representational schemes, such as Markov Networks), but can typically be adapted to Bayesian networks as well. We should note here that the choice of approximate network $\widehat{\mathcal{N}}$ should at least permit one to evaluate the KL-divergence between $\widehat{\mathcal{N}}$ and the original network $\mathcal{N}$ efficiently. As mentioned earlier, such approaches seek minima of the KL-divergence, but typically search for parameters where the partial derivatives of the KL-divergence are zero, i.e., parameters that are stationary points of the KL-divergence. In this sense, variational approaches can reduce the problem of inference to one of optimization. Note that methods identifying stationary points, while convenient, only approximate the optimization problem since stationary points do not necessarily represent minima of the KL-divergence, and even when they do, they do not necessarily represent global minima.

Methods based on belief propagation [130, 117, 56] are similar in the sense that they also can be understood as solving an optimization problem. However, this understanding is more recent and comes as an after fact of having discovered the first belief propagation algorithm, known as loopy belief propagation or iterative belief propagation (IBP). In IBP, the approximate distribution $\widehat{Pr}$ is assumed to have a particular factored form:

$$\widehat{Pr}(\mathbf{X}|\mathbf{e}) = \prod_{X \in \mathbf{X}} \frac{\widehat{Pr}(X\mathbf{U}|\mathbf{e})}{\prod_{U \in \mathbf{U}} \widehat{Pr}(U|\mathbf{e})}, \tag{11.5}$$

where $U \in \mathbf{U}$ are parents of the node X in the original Bayesian network $\mathcal{N}$. This form allows one to decompose the KL-divergence between the original and approximate distributions as follows:

$$KL\big(\widehat{\Pr}(.|\mathbf{e}), \Pr(.|\mathbf{e})\big)$$

$$= \sum_{x\mathbf{u}} \widehat{\Pr}(x\mathbf{u}|\mathbf{e}) \log \frac{\widehat{\Pr}(x\mathbf{u}|\mathbf{e})}{\prod_{u\sim\mathbf{u}} \widehat{\Pr}(u|\mathbf{e})} - \sum_{x\mathbf{u}} \widehat{\Pr}(x\mathbf{u}|\mathbf{e}) \log \theta_{x|\mathbf{u}} + \log \Pr(\mathbf{e}).$$

This decomposition of the KL-divergence has important properties. First, the term $\Pr(\mathbf{e})$ does not depend on the approximate distribution and can be ignored in the optimization process. Second, all other terms are expressed as a function of the approximate marginals $\widehat{\Pr}(x\mathbf{u}|\mathbf{e})$ and $\widehat{\Pr}(u|\mathbf{e})$, in addition to the original network parameters $\theta_{x|\mathbf{u}}$. In fact, IBP can be interpreted as searching for values of these approximate marginals that correspond to stationary points of the KL-divergence: ones that set to zero the partial derivatives of the divergence with respect to these marginals (under certain constraints). There is a key difference between the variational approaches based on searching for parameters of approximate networks and those based on searching for approximate marginals: The computed marginals may not actually correspond to any particular distribution as the optimization problem solved does not include enough constraints to ensure the global coherence of these marginals (only node marginals are consistent, e.g., $\widehat{\Pr}(x|\mathbf{e}) = \sum_{\mathbf{u}} \widehat{\Pr}(x\mathbf{u}|\mathbf{e})$).

The quality of approximations found by IBP depends on the extent to which the original distribution can indeed be expressed as given in (11.5). If the original network $\mathcal{N}$ has a polytree structure, the original distribution can be expressed as given in (11.5) and the stationary point obtained by IBP corresponds to exact marginals. In fact, the form given in (11.5) is not the only one that allows one to set up an optimization problem as given above. In particular, any factored form that has the structure:

$$\widehat{\Pr}(.|\mathbf{e}) = \frac{\prod_{\mathbf{C}} \widehat{\Pr}(\mathbf{C}|\mathbf{e})}{\prod_{\mathbf{S}} \widehat{\Pr}(\mathbf{S}|\mathbf{e})}, \tag{11.6}$$

where $\mathbf{C}$ and $\mathbf{S}$ are sets of variables, will permit a similar decomposition of the KL-divergence in terms of marginals $\widehat{\Pr}(\mathbf{C}|\mathbf{e})$ and $\widehat{\Pr}(\mathbf{S}|\mathbf{e})$. This leads to a more general framework for approximate inference, known as *generalized belief propagation* [176]. Note, however, that this more general optimization problem is exponential in the sizes of sets $\mathbf{C}$ and $\mathbf{S}$. In fact, any distribution induced by a Bayesian network $\mathcal{N}$ can be expressed in the above form, if the sets $\mathbf{C}$ and $\mathbf{S}$ correspond to the clusters and separators of a jointree for network $\mathcal{N}$ [130]. In that case, the stationary point of the optimization problem will correspond to exact marginals, yet the size of the optimization problem will be at least exponential in the network treewidth. The form in (11.6) can therefore be viewed as allowing one to trade the complexity of approximate inference with the quality of computed approximations, with IBP and jointree factorizations being two extreme cases on this spectrum. Methods for exploring this spectrum include joingraphs (which generalize jointrees) [1, 48], region graphs [176, 169, 170], and partially ordered sets (or posets) [111], which are structured methods for generating factorizations with interesting properties.

The above optimization perspective on belief propagation algorithms is only meant to expose the semantics behind these methods. In general, belief propagation algorithms do not set up an explicit optimization problem as discussed above. Instead, they operate by passing messages in a Bayesian network (as is done by IBP), a jo-ingraph, or some other structure such as a region graph. For example, in a Bayesian network, the message sent from a node X to its neighbor Y is based on the messages that node X receives from its other neighbors $Z \neq Y$. Messages are typically initial-ized according to some fixed strategy, and then propagated according to some message passing schedule. For example, one may update messages in parallel or sequentially [168, 164]. Additional techniques are used to fine tune the propagation method, in-cluding message dampening [117, 78]. When message propagation converges (if it does), the computed marginals are known to correspond to stationary points of the KL-divergence as discussed above [176, 79]. There are methods that seek to optimize the divergence directly, but they may be slow to converge [180, 171, 94, 174].

Statistical physics happens to be the source of inspiration for many of these meth-ods and perspectives. In particular, we can reformulate the optimization of the KL-divergence in terms of optimizing a *variational free energy* that approximates a free energy (e.g., in thermodynamics). The free energy approximation corresponding to IBP and Eq. (11.5) is often referred to as the *Bethe free energy* [176]. Other free en-ergy approximations in physics that improve on, or generalize, the Bethe free energy have indeed lent themselves to generalizing belief propagation. Among them is the *Kikuchi free energy* [177], which led to *region-based free energy* approximations for generalized belief propagation algorithms [176].

11.5   Constructing Bayesian Networks

Bayesian networks can be constructed in a variety of methods. Traditionally, Bayesian networks have been constructed by knowledge engineers in collaboration with do-main experts, mostly in the domain of medical diagnosis. In more recent applications, Bayesian networks are typically synthesized from high level specifications, or learned from data. We will review each of these approaches in the following sections.

11.5.1   Knowledge Engineering

The construction of Bayesian networks using traditional knowledge engineering tech-niques has been most prevalent in medical reasoning, which also constitute some of the first significant applications of Bayesian networks to real-world problems. Some of the notable examples in this regard include: The Quick Medical Reference (QMR) model [113] which was later reformulated as a Bayesian network model [159] that covers more than 600 diseases and 4000 symptoms; the CPCS-PM network [137, 125], which simulates patient scenarios in the medical field of hepatobiliary disease; and the MUNIN model for diagnosing neuromuscular disorders from data acquired by elec-tromyographic (EMG) examinations [7, 5, 6], which covers 8 nerves and 6 muscles.

The construction of Bayesian networks using traditional knowledge engineering techniques has been recently made more effective through progress on the subject of *sensitivity analysis*: a form of analysis which focuses on understanding the relationship between local network parameters and global conclusions drawn from the network [102, 18, 90, 98, 19–21]. These results have lead to the creation of efficient sensitivity analysis tools which allow experts to assess the significance of network parameters, and to easily isolate problematic parameters when obtaining counterintuitive results to posed queries.

11.5.2   High-Level Specifications

The manual construction of large Bayesian networks can be laborious and error-prone. In many domains, however, these networks tend to exhibit regular and repetitive structures, with the regularities manifesting themselves both at the level of individual CPTs and at the level of network structure. We have already seen in Section 11.2.4 how regularities in a CPT can reduce the specification of a large CPT to the specification of a few parameters. A similar situation can arise in the specification of a whole Bayesian network, allowing one to synthesize a large Bayesian network automatically from a compact, high-level specification that encodes probabilistic dependencies among network nodes, in addition to network parameters.

This general *knowledge-based model construction* paradigm [172] has given rise to many concrete high-level specification frameworks, with a variety of representation styles. All of these frameworks afford a certain degree of modularity, thus facilitating the adaptation of existing specifications to changing domains. A further benefit of high-level specifications lies in the fact that the smaller number of parameters they contain can often be learned from empirical data with higher accuracy than the larger number of parameters found in the full Bayesian network [59, 96]. We next describe some fundamental paradigms for high-level representation languages, where we distinguish between two main paradigms: template-based and programming-based. It must be acknowledged, however, that this simple distinction is hardly adequate to account for the whole variety of existing representation languages.

Template-based representations

The prototypical example of template-based representations is the dynamic Bayesian network described in Section 11.2.6. In this case, one specifies a DBN having an arbitrary number of slices using only two templates: one for the initial time slice, and one for all subsequent slices. By further specifying the number of required slices t, a Bayesian network of arbitrary size can be compiled from the given templates and temporal horizon t.

One can similarly specify other types of large Bayesian networks that are composed of identical, recurring segments. In general, the template-based approach requires two components for specifying a Bayesian network: a set of network templates whose instantiation leads to network segments, and a specification of which segments to generate and how to connect them together. Fig. 11.8 depicts three templates from the domain of genetics, involving two classes of variables: genotypes (gt) and phenotypes (pt). Each template contains nodes of two kinds: nodes representing random variables that are created by instantiating the template (solid circles, annotated with CPTs), and nodes for input variables (dashed circles). Given these templates, together with a pedigree which enumerates particular individuals with their parental relationships, one can then generate a concrete Bayesian network by instantiating one genotype template and one phenotype template for each individual, and then connecting the resulting segments depending on the pedigree structure. The particular genotype template instantiated for an individual will depend on whether the individual is a founder (has no parents) in the pedigree.

The most basic type of template-based representations, such as the one in Fig. 11.8, is quite rigid as all generated segments will have exactly the same structure. More

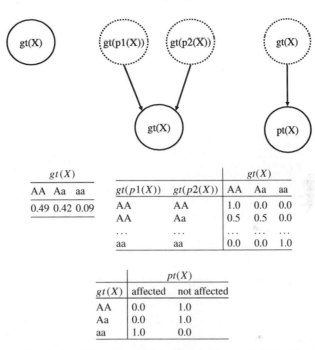

	gt(X)		
AA	Aa	aa	
0.49	0.42	0.09	

		gt(X)		
gt(p1(X))	*gt(p2(X))*	AA	Aa	aa
AA	AA	1.0	0.0	0.0
AA	Aa	0.5	0.5	0.0
...	...	...	...	...
aa	aa	0.0	0.0	1.0

	pt(X)	
gt(X)	affected	not affected
AA	0.0	1.0
Aa	0.0	1.0
aa	1.0	0.0

Figure 11.8: Templates for specifying a Bayesian network in the domain of genetics. The templates assume three possible genotypes (AA, Aa, aa) and two possible phenotypes (affected, not affected).

sophisticated template-based representations add flexibility to the specification in various ways. *Network fragments* [103] allow nodes in a template to have an unspecified number of parents. The CPT for such nodes must then be specified by generic rules. *Object oriented Bayesian networks* [99] introduce abstract classes of network templates that are defined by their interface with other templates. *Probabilistic relational models* enhance the template approach with elements of relational database concepts [59, 66], by allowing one to define probabilities conditional on aggregates of the values of an unspecified number of parents. For example, one might include nodes *life_expectancy*(X) and *age_at_death*(X) into a template for individuals X, and condition the distribution of *life_expectancy*(X) on the average value of the nodes *age_at_death*(Y) for all ancestors Y of X.

Programming-based representations

Frameworks in this group contain some of the earliest high-level representation languages. They use procedural or declarative specifications, which are not as directly connected to graphical representations as template-based representations. Many are based on logic programming languages [17, 132, 71, 118, 96]; others resemble functional programming [86] or deductive database [69] languages. Compared to template-based approaches, programming-based representations can sometimes allow more modular and intuitive representations of high-level probabilistic knowledge. On the other hand, the compilation of the Bayesian network from the high-level specification

Table 11.3. A probabilistic Horn clause specification

alarm(*X*)	←	*burglary*(*X*): 0.95
alarm(*X*)	←	*quake*(*Y*), *lives_in*(*X*, *Y*): 0.8
call(*X*, *Z*)	←	*alarm*(*X*), *neighbor*(*X*, *Z*): 0.7
call(*X*, *Z*)	←	*prankster*(*Z*), *neighbor*(*X*, *Z*): 0.1
comb(*alarm*): noisy-or		
comb(*call*): noisy-or		

Table 11.4. CPT for ground atom *alarm*(Holmes)

burglary(Holmes)	*quake*(LA)	*lives_in*(Holmes, LA)	*quake*(SF)	*lives_in*(Holmes, SF)	*alarm*(Holmes)
t	*t*	*t*	*t*	*t*	0.998
t	*t*	*t*	*t*	*f*	0.99
f	*t*	*t*	*f*	*f*	0.8
t	*f*	*f*	*f*	*f*	0.95
...	...	...	...	...	...

is usually not as straightforward, and part of the semantics of the specification can be hidden in the details of the compilation process.

Table 11.3 shows a basic version of a representation based on probabilistic Horn clauses [71]. The logical atoms *alarm*(*X*), *burglary*(*X*), ... represent generic random variables. Ground instances of these atoms, e.g., *alarm*(Holmes), *alarm*(Watson), become the actual nodes in the constructed Bayesian network. Each clause in the probabilistic rule base is a partial specification of the CPT for (ground instances of) the atom in the head of the clause. The second clause in Table 11.3, for example, stipulates that *alarm*(*X*) depends on variables *quake*(*Y*) and *lives_in*(*X*, *Y*). The parameters associated with the clauses, together with the *combination rules* associated with each relation determine how a full CPT is to be constructed for a ground atom. Table 11.4 depicts part of the CPT constructed for *alarm*(Holmes) when Table 11.3 is instantiated over a domain containing an individual Holmes and two cities LA and SF. The basic probabilistic Horn clause paradigm illustrated in Table 11.3 can be extended and modified in many ways; see for example *Context-sensitive probabilistic knowledge bases* [118] and *Relational Bayesian networks* [86].

Specifications such as the one in Table 11.3 need not necessarily be seen as high-level specifications of Bayesian networks. Provided the representation language is equipped with a well-defined probabilistic semantics that is not defined procedurally in terms of the compilation process, such high-level specifications are also stand-alone probabilistic knowledge representation languages. It is not surprising, therefore, that some closely related representation languages have been developed which were not intended as high-level Bayesian network specifications [148, 116, 135, 140].

Inference

Inference on Bayesian networks generated from high-level specifications can be performed using standard inference algorithms discussed earlier. Note, however, that the

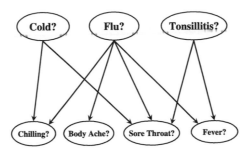

Figure 11.9: A Bayesian network structure for medical diagnosis.

Table 11.5. A data set for learning the structure in Fig. 11.9

Case	Cold?	Flu?	Tonsillitis?	Chilling?	Body ache?	Sore throat?	Fever?
1	true	false	?	true	false	false	false
2	false	true	false	true	true	false	true
3	?	?	true	false	?	true	false
⋮	⋮	⋮	⋮	⋮	⋮	⋮	⋮

generated networks can be very large and very connected (large treewidth), and therefore often pose particular challenges to inference algorithms. As an example, observe that the size of the CPT for *alarm*(Holmes) in Table 11.4 grows exponentially in the number of cities in the domain. Approximate inference techniques, as described in Section 11.4, are therefore particularly important for Bayesian networks generated from high-level specifications. One can also optimize some of these algorithms, such as sampling methods, for Bayesian networks compiled from these specifications [126]. It should also be noted that such Bayesian networks can sometimes be rich with local structure, allowing exact inference even when the network treewidth is quite high [27].

Exact inference algorithms that operate directly on high-level specifications have also been investigated. Theoretical complexity results show that in the worst case one cannot hope to obtain more efficient algorithms than standard exact inference on the compiled network [87]. This does not, however, preclude the possibility that high-level inference methods can be developed that are more efficient for particular applications and particular queries [133, 43].

11.5.3 Learning Bayesian Networks

A Bayesian network over variables $X_1, \ldots, X_n$ can be learned from a data set over these variables, which is a table with each row representing a partial instantiation of variables $X_1, \ldots, X_n$. Table 11.5 depicts an example data set for the network in Fig. 11.9.

Each row in the above table represents a medical case of a particular patient, where ? indicates the unavailability of corresponding data for that patient. It is typically assumed that when variables have missing values, one cannot conclude anything from that fact that the values are missing (e.g., a patient did not take an X-ray because the X-ray happened to be unavailable that day) [108].

There are two orthogonal dimensions that define the process of learning a Bayesian network from data: the task for which the Bayesian network will be used, and the amount of information available to the learning process. The first dimension decides the criteria by which we judge the quality of a learned network, that is, it decides the objective function that the learning process will need to optimize. This dimension calls for distinguishing between learning *generative* versus *discriminative* Bayesian networks. To make this distinction more concrete, consider again the data set shown in Table 11.5. A good *generative* Bayesian network is one that correctly models all of the correlations among the variables. This model could be used to accurately answer any query, such as the correlations between *Chilling?* and *BodyAche?*, as well as whether a patient has *Tonsilitis* given any other (partial) description of that patient. On the other hand, a discriminative Bayesian network is one that is intended to be used only as a classifier: determining the value of one particular variable, called the *class variable*, given the values of some other variables, called the *attributes* or *features*. When learning a discriminative network, we will therefore optimize the classification power of the learned network, without necessarily insisting on the global quality of the distribution it induces. Hence, the answers that the network may generate for other types of queries may not be meaningful. This section will focus on generative learning of networks; for information on discriminative learning of networks, see [84, 70].

The second dimension calls for distinguishing between four cases:

1. *Known network structure, complete data.* Here, the goal is only to learn the parameters Θ of a Bayesian network as the structure G is given as input to the learning process. Moreover, the given data is complete in the sense that each row in the data set provides a value for each network variable.

2. *Known network structure, incomplete data.* This is similar to the above case, but some of the rows may not have values for some of the network variables; see Table 11.5.

3. *Unknown network structure, complete data.* The goal here is to learn both the network structure and parameters, from complete data.

4. *Unknown network structure, incomplete data.* This is similar to Case 3 above, but where the data is incomplete.

In the following discussion, we will only consider the learning of Bayesian networks in which CPTs have tabular representations, but see [60] for results on learning networks with structured CPT representations.

Learning network parameters

We will now consider the task of learning Bayesian networks whose structure is already known and then discuss the case of unknown structure. Suppose that we have a complete data set $\mathcal{D}$ over variables $\mathbf{X} = X_1, \ldots, X_n$. The first observation here is to view this data set as defining a probability distribution $\widehat{\Pr}$ over these variables, where $\widehat{\Pr}(\mathbf{x}) = count(\mathbf{x}, \mathcal{D})/|\mathcal{D}|$ is simply the percentage of rows in $\mathcal{D}$ that contain the instantiation $\mathbf{x}$. Suppose now that we have a Bayesian network structure G and our goal is to learn the parameters Θ of this network given the data set $\mathcal{D}$. This is done by choosing parameters Θ so that the network (G, Θ) will induce a distribution Pr_Θ that is as close to $\widehat{\mathrm{Pr}}$ as possible, according to the KL-divergence. That is, the goal is to minimize:

$$KL(\widehat{\mathrm{Pr}}, \mathrm{Pr}_\Theta) = \sum_{\mathbf{x}} \widehat{\mathrm{Pr}}(\mathbf{x}) \log \frac{\widehat{\mathrm{Pr}}(\mathbf{x})}{\mathrm{Pr}_\Theta(\mathbf{x})}$$

$$= \sum_{\mathbf{x}} \widehat{\mathrm{Pr}}(\mathbf{x}) \log \widehat{\mathrm{Pr}}(\mathbf{x}) - \sum_{\mathbf{x}} \widehat{\mathrm{Pr}}(\mathbf{x}) \log \mathrm{Pr}_\Theta(\mathbf{x}).$$

Since the term $\sum_{\mathbf{x}} \widehat{\mathrm{Pr}}(\mathbf{x}) \log \widehat{\mathrm{Pr}}(\mathbf{x})$ does not depend on the choice of parameters Θ, this corresponds to maximizing $\sum_{\mathbf{x}} \widehat{\mathrm{Pr}}(\mathbf{x}) \log \mathrm{Pr}_\Theta(\mathbf{x})$, which can be shown to equal[6]:

$$g(\Theta) = \sum_{\mathbf{x}} \widehat{\mathrm{Pr}}(\mathbf{x}) \log \mathrm{Pr}_\Theta(\mathbf{x}) = \frac{1}{|\mathcal{D}|} \log \prod_{d \in \mathcal{D}} \mathrm{Pr}_\Theta(d). \tag{11.7}$$

Note that parameters which maximize the above quantity will also maximize the probability of data, $\prod_{d \in \mathcal{D}} \mathrm{Pr}_\Theta(d)$ and are known as *maximum likelihood parameters*. A number of observations are in order about this method of learning. First, there is a unique set of parameters $\Theta = \{\theta_{x|\mathbf{u}}\}$ that satisfy the above property, defined as follows: $\theta_{x|\mathbf{u}} = count(x\mathbf{u}, \mathcal{D})/count(\mathbf{u}, \mathcal{D})$ (e.g., see [115]). Second, this method may have problems when the data set does not contain enough cases, leading possibly to $count(\mathbf{u}, \mathcal{D}) = 0$ and a division by zero. This is usually handled by using (something like) a Laplacian correction; using, say

$$\theta_{x|\mathbf{u}} = \frac{1 + count(x, \mathbf{u}, \mathcal{D})}{|X| + count(\mathbf{u}, \mathcal{D})}, \tag{11.8}$$

where $|X|$ is the number of values for variable X. We will refer to these parameters as $\widehat{\Theta}(G, \mathcal{D})$ from now on.

When the data is incomplete, the situation is not as simple for a number of reasons. First, we may have multiple sets of maximum likelihood parameters. Second, the two most commonly used methods that search for such parameters are not optimal, and both can be computationally intensive. Both methods are based on observing, from Eq. (11.7), that we are trying to optimize a function $g(\Theta)$ of the network parameters. The first method tries to optimize this function using standard gradient ascent techniques [146]. That is, we first compute the gradient which happens to have the following form:

$$\frac{\partial g}{\partial \theta_{x|\mathbf{u}}}(\Theta) = \sum_{d \in \mathcal{D}} \frac{\mathrm{Pr}_\Theta(x\mathbf{u}|d)}{\theta_{x|\mathbf{u}}}, \tag{11.9}$$

and then use it to drive a gradient ascent procedure that attempts to find a local maxima of the function g. This method will start with some initial parameter Θ^0, leading to an initial Bayesian network (G, Θ^0) with distribution Pr_Θ^0. It will then use Eq. (11.9) to compute the gradient $\partial g/\partial \theta_{x|\mathbf{u}}(\Theta^0)$, which is then used to find the next set of parameters Θ^1, with corresponding network (G, Θ^1) and distribution Pr^1. The process

---

[6]We are treating a data set as a multi-set, which can include repeated elements.

continues, computing a new set of parameters Θ^i based on the previous set Θ^{i-1}, until some convergence criteria is satisfied. Standard techniques of gradient ascent all are applicable in this case, including conjugate gradient, line search and random restarts [14].

A more commonly used method in this case is the *expectation maximization (EM)* algorithm [104, 112], which works as follows. The method starts with some initial parameters Θ^0, leading to an initial distribution $\Pr_\Theta^0$. It then uses the distribution to complete the data set $\mathcal{D}$ as follows. If d is a row in $\mathcal{D}$ for which some variable values are missing, the algorithm will (conceptually) consider every completion d' of this row and assign it a weight of $\Pr_\Theta^0(d'|d)$. The algorithm will then pretend as if it had a complete (but weighted) data set, and use the method for complete data to compute a new set of parameters Θ^1, leading to a new distribution $\Pr_\Theta^1$. This process continues, computing a new set of parameters Θ^i based on the previous set Θ^{i-1}, until some convergence criteria is satisfied. This method has a number of interesting properties. First, the value of parameters at iteration i have the following closed from:

$$\theta^i_{x|\mathbf{u}} = \frac{\sum_{d\in\mathcal{D}} \Pr_\Theta^{i-1}(x\mathbf{u}|d)}{\sum_{d\in\mathcal{D}} \Pr_\Theta^{i-1}(\mathbf{u}|d)},$$

which has the same complexity as the gradient ascent method (see Eq. (11.9)). Second, the probability of the data set is guaranteed to never decrease after each iteration of the method. There are many techniques to make this algorithm even more efficient; see [112].

Learning network structure

We now turn to the problem of learning a network *structure* (as well as the associated parameters), given complete data. As this task is NP-hard in general [30], the main algorithms are iterative, starting with a single structure (perhaps the empty graph), and incrementally modifying this structure, until reaching some termination condition. There are two main classes of algorithms, score-based and independence-based.

As the name suggests, the algorithms based on independence will basically run a set of independence tests, between perhaps every pair of currently-unconnected nodes in the current graph, to see if the data set supports the claim that they are independent given the rest of the graph structure; see [68, 127].

Score-based algorithms will typically employ local search, although systematic search has been used in some cases too (e.g., [165]). Local search algorithms will evaluate the current structure, as well as every structure formed by some simple modification—such as adding one addition arc, or deleting one existing arc, or changing the direction of one arc [29]—and climb to the new structure with the highest score. One plausible score is based on favoring structures that lead to higher probability of the data:

$$g_\mathcal{D}(G) = \max_\Theta \log \prod_{d\in\mathcal{D}} \Pr_{G,\Theta}(d). \tag{11.10}$$

Unfortunately, this does not always work. To understand why, consider the simpler problem of fitting a polynomial to some pairs of real numbers. If we do not fix the degree of the polynomial, we would probably end up fitting the data perfectly by

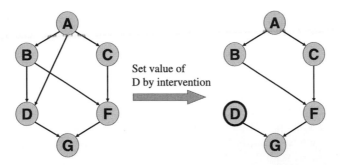

Figure 11.10: Modeling intervention on causal networks.

selecting a high degree polynomial. Even though this may lead to a perfect fit over the given data points, the learned polynomial may not generalize the data well, and so do poorly at labeling other novel data points. The same phenomena, called *overfitting* [141], shows up in learning Bayesian networks, as it means we would favor a fully connected network, as clearly this complete graph would maximize the probability of data due to its large set of parameters (maximal degrees of freedom). To deal with this overfitting problem, other scoring functions are used, many explicitly including a penalty term for complex structure. This includes the Minimum Description Length (MDL) score [142, 62, 101, 163], the Akaike Information Criterion (AIC) score [16], and the "Bayesian Dirichlet, equal" (BDe) [33, 75, 74]. For example, the MDL score is given by:

$$MDL_{\mathcal{D}}(G) = g_{\mathcal{D}}(G) - \frac{\log m}{2}k(G),$$

where m is the size of data set $\mathcal{D}$ and $k(G)$ is the number of independent network parameters (this also corresponds to the Bayesian Information Criterion (BIC) [151]). Each of these scores is asymptotically correct in that it will identify the correct structures in the limit as the data increases.

The above discussion has focused on learning arbitrary network structures. There are also efficient algorithms for computing the optimal structures, for some restricted class of structures, including trees [31] and polytrees [131].

If the data is incomplete, learning structures becomes much more complicated as we have two nested optimization problems: one for choosing the structure, which can again be accomplished by either greedy or optimal search, and one for choosing the parameters for a given structure, which can be accomplished using methods like EM [75]. One can improve the double search problem by using techniques such as *structural EM* [58], which uses particular data structures that allow computational results to be used across the different iterations of the algorithm.

11.6 Causality and Intervention

The directed nature of Bayesian networks can be used to provide causal semantics for these networks, based on the notion of *intervention* [127], leading to models that not only represent probability distributions, but also permit one to induce new probability distributions that result from intervention. In particular, a *causal network*, intuitively speaking, is a Bayesian network with the added property that the parents of each node are its direct causes. For example, *Cold* → *HeadAche* is a causal network whereas *HeadAche* → *Cold* is not, even though both networks are equally capable of representing any joint distribution on the two variables. Causal networks can be used to compute the result of intervention as illustrated in Fig. 11.10. In this example, we want to compute the probability distribution that results from having set the value of variable *D* by *intervention*, as opposed to having observed the value of *D*. This can be done by deactivating the current causal mechanism for *D*—by disconnecting *D* from its direct causes *A* and *B*—and then conditioning the modified causal model on the set value of *D*. Note how different this process is from the classical operation of *Bayes conditioning* (Eq. (11.1)), which is appropriate for modeling observations but not immediately for intervention. For example, intervening on variable *D* in Fig. 11.10 would have no effect on the probability associated with *F*, while measurements taken on variable *D* would affect the probability associated with *F*.[7] Causal networks are more properly defined, then, as Bayesian networks in which each parents–child family represents a stable causal mechanism. These mechanisms may be reconfigured locally by interventions, but remain invariant to other observations and manipulations.

Causal networks and their semantics based on intervention can then be used to answer additional types of queries that are beyond the scope of general Bayesian networks. This includes determining the truth of counterfactual sentences of the form $\alpha \rightarrow \beta \mid \gamma$, which read: "Given that we have observed γ, if α were true, then β would have been true". The counterfactual antecedent α consists of a conjunction of value assignments to variables that are forced to hold true by external intervention. Typically, to justify being called "counterfactual", α conflicts with γ. The truth (or probability) of a counterfactual conditional $\alpha \rightarrow \beta \mid \gamma$ requires a causal model. For example, the probability that "the patient would be alive had he not taken the drug" cannot be computed from the information provided in a Bayesian network, but requires a functional causal networks, where each variable is functionally determined by its parents (plus noise factors). This more refined specification allows one to assign unique probabilities to all counterfactual statements. Other types of queries that have been formulated with respect to functional causal networks include ones for distinguishing between direct and indirect causes and for determining the sufficiency and necessity aspects of causation [127].

Acknowledgements

Marek Druzdzel contributed to Section 11.4.1, Arthur Choi contributed to Section 11.4.2, Manfred Jaeger contributed to Section 11.5.2, Russ Greiner contributed to Section 11.5.3, and Judea Pearl contributed to Section 11.6. Mark Chavira, Arthur Choi, Rina Dechter, and David Poole provided valuable comments on different versions of this chapter.

---

[7]For a simple distinction between observing and intervening, note that observing *D* leads us to increase our belief in its direct causes, *A* and *B*. Yet, our beliefs will not undergo this increase when intervening to set *D*.

Bibliography

[1] S.M. Aji and R.J. McEliece. The generalized distributive law and free energy minimization. In *Proceedings of the 39th Allerton Conference on Communication, Control and Computing*, pages 672–681, 2001.

[2] D. Allen and A. Darwiche. New advances in inference by recursive conditioning. In *Proceedings of the Conference on Uncertainty in Artificial Intelligence*, pages 2–10, 2003.

[3] D. Allen and A. Darwiche. Optimal time–space tradeoff in probabilistic inference. In *Proc. International Joint Conference on Artificial Intelligence (IJCAI)*, pages 969–975, 2003.

[4] D. Allen and A. Darwiche. Advances in Bayesian networks. In *Studies in Fuzziness and Soft Computing*, vol. 146, pages 39–55. Springer-Verlag, New York, 2004 (chapter *Optimal Time–Space Tradeoff in Probabilistic Inference*).

[5] S. Andreassen, F.V. Jensen, S.K. Andersen, B. Falck, U. Kjærulff, M. Woldbye, A.R. Sorensen, A. Rosenfalck, and F. Jensen. MUNIN—an expert EMG assistant. In J.E. Desmedt, editor. *Computer-Aided Electromyography and Expert Systems*. Elsevier Science Publishers, Amsterdam, 1989 (Chapter 21).

[6] S. Andreassen, M. Suojanen, B. Falck, and K.G. Olesen. Improving the diagnostic performance of MUNIN by remodelling of the diseases. In *Proceedings of the 8th Conference on AI in Medicine in Europe*, pages 167–176. Springer-Verlag, 2001.

[7] S. Andreassen, M. Woldbye, B. Falck, and S.K. Andersen. Munin—a causal probabilistic network for interpretation of electromyographic findings. In J. McDermott, editor. *Proceedings of the 10th International Joint Conference on Artificial Intelligence (IJCAI-87)*, pages 366–372. Morgan Kaufmann Publishers, 1987.

[8] S.A. Arnborg. Efficient algorithms for combinatorial problems on graphs with bounded decomposability—a survey. *BIT*, 25:2–23, 1985.

[9] S. Arnborg, D.G. Corneil, and A. Proskurowski. Complexity of finding embeddings in a *k*-tree. *SIAM J. Algebraic and Discrete Methods*, 8:277–284, 1987.

[10] F. Bacchus, S. Dalmao, and T. Pitassi. Value elimination: Bayesian inference via backtracking search. In *Proceedings of the 19th Annual Conference on Uncertainty in Artificial Intelligence (UAI-03)*, pages 20–28. Morgan Kaufmann Publishers, San Francisco, CA, 2003.

[11] A. Becker, R. Bar-Yehuda, and D. Geiger. Random algorithms for the loop cutset problem. In *Proceedings of the 15th Conference on Uncertainty in Artificial Intelligence (UAI)*, 1999.

[12] J. Bilmes and C. Bartels. Triangulating dynamic graphical models. In *Uncertainty in Artificial Intelligence: Proceedings of the Nineteenth Conference*, pages 47–56, 2003.

[13] J. Binder, K. Murphy, and S. Russell. Space-efficient inference in dynamic probabilistic networks. In *Proc. International Joint Conference on Artificial Intelligence (IJCAI)*, 1997.

[14] C. Bishop. Neural Networks for Pattern Recognition. Oxford University Press, Oxford, 1998.

[15] C. Boutilier, N. Friedman, M. Goldszmidt, and D. Koller. Context-specific independence in Bayesian networks. In *Proceedings of the 12th Conference on Uncertainty in Artificial Intelligence (UAI)*, pages 115–123, 1996.

[16] H. Bozdogan. Model selection and Akaike's Information Criterion (AIC): the general theory and its analytical extensions. *Psychometrica*, 52:345–370, 1987.

[17] J.S. Breese. Construction of belief and decision networks. *Computational Intelligence*, 8(4):624–647, 1992.

[18] E. Castillo, J.M. Gutiérrez, and A.S. Hadi. Sensitivity analysis in discrete Bayesian networks. *IEEE Transactions on Systems, Man, and Cybernetics*, 27:412–423, 1997.

[19] H. Chan and A. Darwiche. When do numbers really matter? *Journal of Artificial Intelligence Research*, 17:265–287, 2002.

[20] H. Chan and A. Darwiche. Sensitivity analysis in Bayesian networks: From single to multiple parameters. In *Proceedings of the Twentieth Conference on Uncertainty in Artificial Intelligence (UAI)*, pages 67–75. AUAI Press, Arlington, VA, 2004.

[21] H. Chan and A. Darwiche. A distance measure for bounding probabilistic belief change. *International Journal of Approximate Reasoning*, 38:149–174, 2005.

[22] H. Chan and A. Darwiche. On the revision of probabilistic beliefs using uncertain evidence. *Artificial Intelligence*, 163:67–90, 2005.

[23] M.R. Chavez and G.F. Cooper. A randomized approximation algorithm for probabilistic inference on Bayesian belief networks. *Networks*, 20(5):661–685, 1990.

[24] M. Chavira, D. Allen, and A. Darwiche. Exploiting evidence in probabilistic inference. In *Proceedings of the 21st Conference on Uncertainty in Artificial Intelligence (UAI)*, pages 112–119, 2005.

[25] M. Chavira and A. Darwiche. Compiling Bayesian networks with local structure. In *Proceedings of the 19th International Joint Conference on Artificial Intelligence (IJCAI)*, pages 1306–1312, 2005.

[26] M. Chavira and A. Darwiche. Compiling Bayesian networks using variable elimination. In *Proceedings of the 20th International Joint Conference on Artificial Intelligence (IJCAI)*, pages 2443–2449, 2007.

[27] M. Chavira, A. Darwiche, and M. Jaeger. Compiling relational Bayesian networks for exact inference. *International Journal of Approximate Reasoning*, 42(1–2):4–20, May 2006.

[28] J. Cheng and M.J. Druzdzel. BN-AIS: An adaptive importance sampling algorithm for evidential reasoning in large Bayesian networks. *Journal of Artificial Intelligence Research*, 13:155–188, 2000.

[29] D.M. Chickering. Optimal structure identification with greedy search. *JMLR*, 2002.

[30] D.M. Chickering and D. Heckerman. Large-sample learning of Bayesian networks is NP-hard. *JMLR*, 2004.

[31] C.K. Chow and C.N. Lui. Approximating discrete probability distributions with dependence trees. *IEEE Transactions on Information Theory*, 14(3):462–467, 1968.

[32] F.G. Cooper. The computational complexity of probabilistic inference using Bayesian belief networks. *Artificial Intelligence*, 42(2–3):393–405, 1990.

[33] G. Cooper and E. Herskovits. A Bayesian method for the induction of probabilistic networks from data. *MLJ*, 9:309–347, 1992.

[34] R. Cowell, A. Dawid, S. Lauritzen, and D. Spiegelhalter. *Probabilistic Networks and Expert Systems*. Springer, 1999.

[35] T. Verma, D. Geiger, and J. Pearl. d-separation: from theorems to algorithms. In *Proceedings of the Sixth Conference on Uncertainty in Artificial Intelligence (UAI)*, pages 139–148, 1990.

[36] P. Dagum and M. Luby. Approximating probabilistic inference in Bayesian belief networks is NP-hard. *Artificial Intelligence*, 60(1):141–153, 1993.

[37] A. Darwiche. Conditioning algorithms for exact and approximate inference in causal networks. In *Proceedings of the 11th Conference on Uncertainty in Artificial Intelligence (UAI)*, pages 99–107, 1995.

[38] A. Darwiche. Any-space probabilistic inference. In *Proceedings of the 16th Conference on Uncertainty in Artificial Intelligence (UAI)*, pages 133–142, 2000.

[39] A. Darwiche. Recursive conditioning. *Artificial Intelligence*, 126(1–2):5–41, 2001.

[40] A. Darwiche. A logical approach to factoring belief networks. In *Proceedings of KR*, pages 409–420, 2002.

[41] A. Darwiche. A differential approach to inference in Bayesian networks. *Journal of the ACM*, 50(3):280–305, 2003.

[42] A. Darwiche and M. Hopkins. Using recursive decomposition to construct elimination orders, jointrees and dtrees. In *Trends in Artificial Intelligence, Lecture Notes in Artificial Intelligence*, vol. 2143, pages 180–191. Springer-Verlag, 2001.

[43] R. de Salvo Braz, E. Amir, and D. Roth. Lifted first-order probabilistic inference. In *Proceedings of the Nineteenth Int. Joint Conf. on Artificial Intelligence (IJCAI-05)*, pages 1319–1325, 2005.

[44] T. Dean and K. Kanazawa. A model for reasoning about persistence and causation. *Computational Intelligence*, 5(3):142–150, 1989.

[45] R. Dechter. Bucket elimination: A unifying framework for reasoning. *Artificial Intelligence*, 113:41–85, 1999.

[46] R. Dechter and R. Mateescu. Mixtures of deterministic-probabilistic networks and their and/or search space. In *Proceedings of the Twentieth Conference on Uncertainty in Artificial Intelligence (UAI'04)*, pages 120–129, 2004.

[47] R. Dechter and Y. El Fattah. Topological parameters for time-space tradeoff. *Artificial Intelligence*, 125(1–2):93–118, 2001.

[48] R. Dechter, K. Kask, and R. Mateescu. Iterative join-graph propagation. In *Proceedings of the Conference on Uncertainty in Artificial Intelligence*, pages 128–136, 2002.

[49] R. Dechter and D. Larkin. Hybrid processing of beliefs and constraints. In *Uncertainty in Artificial Intelligence: Proceedings of the Seventeenth Conference (UAI-2001)*, pages 112–119. Morgan Kaufmann Publishers, San Francisco, CA, 2001.

[50] R. Dechter and D. Larkin. Bayesian inference in the presence of determinism. In C.M. Bishop and B.J. Frey, editors, In *Proceedings of the Ninth International Workshop on Artificial Intelligence and Statistics*, Key West, FL, 2003.

[51] F.J. Díez. Parameter adjustment in Bayesian networks: the generalized noisy-or gate. In *Proceedings of the Ninth Conference on Uncertainty in Artificial Intelligence (UAI)*, 1993.

[52] F.J. Díez. Local conditioning in Bayesian networks. *Artificial Intelligence*, 87(1):1–20, 1996.

[53] F.J. Díez and S.F. Galán. An efficient factorization for the noisy MAX. *International Journal of Intelligent Systems*, 18:165–177, 2003.

[54] M. Fishelson and D. Geiger. Exact genetic linkage computations for general pedigrees. *Bioinformatics*, 18(1):189–198, 2002.

[55] M. Fishelson and D. Geiger. Optimizing exact genetic linkage computations. In *RECOMB'03*, 2003.

[56] B.J. Frey and D.J.C. MacKay. A revolution: Belief propagation in graphs with cycles. In *NIPS*, pages 479–485, 1997.

[57] B.J. Frey, R. Patrascu, T. Jaakkola, and J. Moran. Sequentially fitting "inclusive" trees for inference in noisy-or networks. In *NIPS*, pages 493–499, 2000.

[58] N. Friedman. The Bayesian structural EM algorithm. In *Proceedings of the 14th Conference on Uncertainty in Artificial Intelligence (UAI)*, 1998.

[59] N. Friedman, L. Getoor, D. Koller, and A. Pfeffer. Learning probabilistic relational models. In *Proceedings of the 16th International Joint Conference on Artificial Intelligence (IJCAI-99)*, 1999.

[60] N. Friedman and M. Goldszmidt. Learning Bayesian networks with local structure. In *Proceedings of the 12th Conference on Uncertainty in Artificial Intelligence (UAI)*, 1996.

[61] N. Friedman and M. Goldszmidt. Learning Bayesian networks with local structure. In *Proceedings of the 12th Conference on Uncertainty in Artificial Intelligence (UAI)*, pages 252–262, 1996.

[62] N. Friedman and Z. Yakhini. On the sample complexity of learning Bayesian networks. In *Proceedings of the 12th Conference on Uncertainty in Artificial Intelligence (UAI)*, 1996.

[63] R. Fung and K.-C. Chang. Weighing and integrating evidence for stochastic simulation in Bayesian networks. In M. Henrion, R.D. Shachter, L.N. Kanal, and J.F. Lemmer, editors. *Uncertainty in Artificial Intelligence*, vol. 5, pages 209–219. Elsevier Science Publishing Company, Inc., New York, NY, 1989.

[64] D. Geiger, T. Verma, and J. Pearl. Identifying independence in Bayesian networks. *Networks*:507–534, 1990.

[65] D. Geiger and C. Meek. Structured variational inference procedures and their realizations. In *Proceedings of Tenth International Workshop on Artificial Intelligence and Statistics*. The Society for Artificial Intelligence and Statistics, The Barbados, January 2005.

[66] L. Getoor, N. Friedman, D. Koller, and B. Taskar. Learning probabilistic models of relational structure. In *Proceedings of the 18th International Conference on Machine Learning*, pages 170–177, 2001.

[67] Z. Ghahramani and M.I. Jordan. Factorial hidden Markov models. *Machine Learning*, 29(2–3):245–273, 1997.

[68] C. Glymour, R. Scheines, P. Spirtes, and K. Kelly. *Discovering Causal Structure*. Academic Press, Inc., London, 1987.

[69] R.P. Goldman and E. Charniak. Dynamic construction of belief networks. In P.P. Bonissone, M. Henrion, L.N. Kanal, and J.F. Lemmer, editors, *Uncertainty in Artificial Intelligence*, vol. 6, pages 171–184, Elsevier Science, 1991.

[70] Y. Guo and R. Greiner. Discriminative model selection for belief net structures. In *Twentieth National Conference on Artificial Intelligence (AAAI-05)*, pages 770–776, Pittsburgh, July 2005.

[71] P. Haddawy. Generating Bayesian networks from probability logic knowledge bases. In *Proceedings of the Tenth Conference on Uncertainty in Artificial Intelligence (UAI-94)*, pages 262–269, 1994.

[72] M. Haft, R. Hofmann, and V. Tresp. Model-independent mean-field theory as a local method for approximate propagation of information. *Network: Computation in Neural Systems*, 10:93–105, 1999.

[73] D. Heckerman. Causal independence for knowledge acquisition and inference. In D. Heckerman and A. Mamdani, editors, *Proc. of the Ninth Conf. on Uncertainty in AI*, pages 122–127, 1993.

[74] D. Heckerman, D. Geiger, and D. Chickering. Learning Bayesian networks: The combination of knowledge and statistical data. *Machine Learning*, 20:197–243, 1995.

[75] D.E. Heckerman. A tutorial on learning with Bayesian networks. In M.I. Jordan, editor. *Learning in Graphical Models*. MIT Press, 1998.

[76] M. Henrion. Propagating uncertainty in Bayesian networks by probabilistic logic sampling. In *Uncertainty in Artificial Intelligence*, vol. 2, pages 149–163. Elsevier Science Publishing Company, Inc., New York, NY, 1988.

[77] M. Henrion. Some practical issues in constructing belief networks. In L.N. Kanal, T.S. Levitt, and J.F. Lemmer, editors. *Uncertainty in Artificial Intelligence*, vol. 3, pages 161–173. Elsevier Science Publishers B.V., North-Holland, 1989.

[78] T. Heskes. Stable fixed points of loopy belief propagation are local minima of the Bethe free energy. In *NIPS*, pages 343–350, 2002.

[79] T. Heskes. On the uniqueness of loopy belief propagation fixed points. *Neural Computation*, 16(11):2379–2413, 2004.

[80] J. Hoey, R. St-Aubin, A. Hu, and G. Boutilier. SPUDD: Stochastic planning using decision diagrams. In *Proceedings of the 15th Conference on Uncertainty in Artificial Intelligence (UAI)*, pages 279–288, 1999.

[81] E.J. Horvitz, H.J. Suermondt, and G.F. Cooper. Bounded conditioning: Flexible inference for decisions under scarce resources. In *Proceedings of Conference on Uncertainty in Artificial Intelligence, Windsor, ON*, pages 182–193. Association for Uncertainty in Artificial Intelligence, Mountain View, CA, August 1989.

[82] J. Hastad. Tensor rank is NP-complete. *Journal of Algorithms*, 11:644–654, 1990.

[83] C. Huang and A. Darwiche. Inference in belief networks: A procedural guide. *International Journal of Approximate Reasoning*, 15(3):225–263, 1996.

[84] I. Inza, P. Larranaga, J. Lozano, and J. Pena. *Machine Learning Journal*, 59, June 2005 (Special Issue: Probabilistic Graphical Models for Classification).

[85] T. Jaakkola. *Advanced Mean Field Methods—Theory and Practice*. MIT Press, 2000 (chapter *Tutorial on Variational Approximation Methods*).

[86] M. Jaeger. Relational Bayesian networks. In D. Geiger and P.P. Shenoy, editors. *Proceedings of the 13th Conference of Uncertainty in Artificial Intelligence (UAI-13)*, pages 266–273. Morgan Kaufmann, Providence, USA, 1997.

[87] M. Jaeger. On the complexity of inference about probabilistic relational models. *Artificial Intelligence*, 117:297–308, 2000.

[88] R. Jeffrey. *The Logic of Decision*. McGraw-Hill, New York, 1965.

[89] F.V. Jensen, S.L. Lauritzen, and K.G. Olesen. Bayesian updating in recursive graphical models by local computation. *Computational Statistics Quarterly*, 4:269–282, 1990.

[90] F.V. Jensen. Gradient descent training of Bayesian networks. In *Proceedings of the Fifth European Conference on Symbolic and Quantitative Approaches to Reasoning with Uncertainty (ECSQARU)*, pages 5–9, 1999.

[91] F.V. Jensen. *Bayesian Networks and Decision Graphs*. Springer-Verlag, 2001.

[92] M.I. Jordan, Z. Ghahramani, T. Jaakkola, and L.K. Saul. An introduction to variational methods for graphical models. *Machine Learning*, 37(2):183–233, 1999.

[93] K. Kanazawa, D. Koller, and S.J. Russell. Stochastic simulation algorithms for dynamic probabilistic networks. In *Uncertainty in Artificial Intelligence: Proceedings of the Eleventh Conference*, pages 346–351, 1995.

[94] H.J. Kappen and W. Wiegerinck. Novel iteration schemes for the cluster variation method. In *NIPS*, pages 415–422, 2001.

[95] K. Kask and R. Dechter. A general scheme for automatic generation of search heuristics from specification dependencies. *Artificial Intelligence*, 129:91–131, 2001.

[96] K. Kersting and L. De Raedt. Towards combining inductive logic programming and Bayesian networks. In *Proceedings of the Eleventh International Conference on Inductive Logic Programming (ILP-2001), Springer Lecture Notes in AI*, vol. 2157. Springer, 2001.

[97] U. Kjaerulff. A computational scheme for reasoning in dynamic probabilistic networks. In *Uncertainty in Artificial Intelligence: Proceedings of the Eight Conference*, pages 121–129, 1992.

[98] U. Kjaerulff and L.C. van der Gaag. Making sensitivity analysis computationally efficient. In *Proceedings of the 16th Conference on Uncertainty in Artificial Intelligence (UAI)*, 2000.

[99] D. Koller and A. Pfeffer. Object-oriented Bayesian networks. In *Proceedings of the Thirteenth Annual Conference on Uncertainty in Artificial Intelligence (UAI–97)*, pages 302–313. Morgan Kaufmann Publishers, San Francisco, CA, 1997.

[100] S. Kullback and R.A. Leibler. On information and sufficiency. *Annals of Mathematical Statistics*, 22:79–86, 1951.

[101] W. Lam and F. Bacchus. Learning Bayesian belief networks: An approach based on the MDL principle. *Computation Intelligence*, 10(4):269–293, 1994.

[102] K.B. Laskey. Sensitivity analysis for probability assessments in Bayesian networks. *IEEE Transactions on Systems, Man, and Cybernetics*, 25:901–909, 1995.

[103] K.B. Laskey and S.M. Mahoney. Network fragments: Representing knowledge for constructing probabilistic models. In *Proceedings of the Thirteenth Annual*

Conference on Uncertainty in Artificial Intelligence (UAI–97), pages 334–341. San Morgan Kaufmann Publishers, Francisco, CA, 1997.

[104] S.L. Lauritzen. The EM algorithm for graphical association models with missing data. *Computational Statistics and Data Analysis*, 19:191–201, 1995.

[105] S.L. Lauritzen and D.J. Spiegelhalter. Local computations with probabilities on graphical structures and their application to expert systems. *Journal of Royal Statistics Society, Series B*, 50(2):157–224, 1988.

[106] V. Lepar and P.P. Shenoy. A comparison of Lauritzen–Spiegelhalter, Hugin, and Shenoy–Shafer architectures for computing marginals of probability distributions. In *Proceedings of the Fourteenth Annual Conference on Uncertainty in Artificial Intelligence (UAI-98)*, pages 328–337. Morgan Kaufmann Publishers, San Francisco, CA, 1998.

[107] Y. Lin and M. Druzdzel. Computational advantages of relevance reasoning in Bayesian belief networks. In *Proceedings of the 13th Annual Conference on Uncertainty in Artificial Intelligence (UAI-97)*, pages 342–350, 1997.

[108] J.A. Little and D.B. Rubin. *Statistical Analysis with Missing Data*. Wiley, New York, 1987.

[109] D. Maier. *The Theory of Relational Databases*. Computer Science Press, Rockville, MD, 1983.

[110] R. Marinescu and R. Dechter. And/or branch-and-bound for graphical models. In *Proceedings of International Joint Conference on Artificial Intelligence (IJCAI)*, 2005.

[111] R.J. McEliece and M. Yildirim. Belief propagation on partially ordered sets. In J. Rosenthal and D.S. Gilliam, editors, *Mathematical Systems Theory in Biology, Communications, Computation and Finance*.

[112] G.J. McLachlan and T. Krishnan. *The EM Algorithm and Extensions. Wiley Series in Probability and Statistics. Applied Probability and Statistics*. Wiley, New York, 1997.

[113] R.A. Miller, F.E. Fasarie, and J.D. Myers. Quick medical reference (QMR) for diagnostic assistance. *Medical Computing*, 3:34–48, 1986.

[114] T.P. Minka and Y.(A.) Qi. Tree-structured approximations by expectation propagation. In *Proceedings of the Annual Conference on Neural Information Processing Systems*, 2003.

[115] T.M. Mitchell. *Machine Learning*. McGraw-Hill, 1997.

[116] S. Muggleton. Stochastic logic programs. In L. de Raedt, editor. *Advances in Inductive Logic Programming*, pages 254–264. IOS Press, 1996.

[117] K.P. Murphy, Y. Weiss, and M.I. Jordan. Loopy belief propagation for approximate inference: An empirical study. In *Proceedings of the Conference on Uncertainty in Artificial Intelligence*, pages 467–475, 1999.

[118] L. Ngo and P. Haddawy. Answering queries from context-sensitive probabilistic knowledge bases. *Theoretical Computer Science*, 171:147–177, 1997.

[119] A. Nicholson and J.M. Brady. The data association problem when monitoring robot vehicles using dynamic belief networks. In *10th European Conference on Artificial Intelligence Proceedings*, pages 689–693, 1992.

[120] T. Nielsen, P. Wuillemin, F. Jensen, and U. Kjaerulff. Using ROBDDs for inference in Bayesian networks with troubleshooting as an example. In *Proceedings of the 16th Conference on Uncertainty in Artificial Intelligence (UAI)*, pages 426–435, 2000.

[121] J.D. Park and A. Darwiche. Solving MAP exactly using systematic search. In *Proceedings of the 19th Conference on Uncertainty in Artificial Intelligence (UAI–03)*, pages 459–468. Morgan Kaufmann Publishers, San Francisco, CA, 2003.

[122] J. Park and A. Darwiche. Morphing the Hugin and Shenoy–Shafer architectures. In *Trends in Artificial Intelligence, Lecture Notes in AI*, vol. 2711, pages 149–160. Springer-Verlag, 2003.

[123] J. Park and A. Darwiche. Complexity results and approximation strategies for map explanations. *Journal of Artificial Intelligence Research*, 21:101–133, 2004.

[124] J. Park and A. Darwiche. A differential semantics for jointree algorithms. *Artificial Intelligence*, 156:197–216, 2004.

[125] R.C. Parker and R.A. Miller. Using causal knowledge to create simulated patient cases: The CPCS project as an extension of Internist-1. In *Proceedings of the Eleventh Annual Symposium on Computer Applications in Medical Care*, pages 473–480. IEEE Comp. Soc. Press, 1987.

[126] H. Pasula and S. Russell. Approximate inference for first-order probabilistic languages. In *Proceedings of IJCAI-01*, pages 741–748, 2001.

[127] J. Pearl. *Causality: Models, Reasoning, and Inference*. Cambridge University Press, New York, 2000.

[128] J. Pearl. Evidential reasoning using stochastic simulation of causal models. *Artificial Intelligence*, 32(2):245–257, 1987.

[129] J. Pearl. Fusion, propagation and structuring in belief networks. *Artificial Intelligence*, 29(3):241–288, 1986.

[130] J. Pearl. *Probabilistic Reasoning in Intelligent Systems: Networks of Plausible Inference*. Morgan Kaufmann Publishers, Inc., San Mateo, CA, 1988.

[131] J. Pearl. *Probabilistic Reasoning in Intelligent Systems: Networks of Plausible Inference*. Morgan Kaufmann, San Mateo, CA, 1988.

[132] D. Poole. Probabilistic horn abduction and Bayesian networks. *Artificial Intelligence*, 64:81–129, 1993.

[133] D. Poole. First-order probabilistic inference. In *Proceedings of International Joint Conference on Artificial Intelligence (IJCAI)*, 2003.

[134] D. Poole and N.L. Zhang. Exploiting contextual independence in probabilistic inference. *Journal of Artificial Intelligence*, 18:263–313, 2003.

[135] D. Poole. The independent choice logic for modelling multiple agents under uncertainty. *Artificial Intelligence*, 94(1–2):7–56, 1997.

[136] D. Poole. Context-specific approximation in probabilistic inference. In *Proceedings of the 14th Conference on Uncertainty in Artificial Intelligence (UAI)*, pages 447–454, 1998.

[137] M. Pradhan, G. Provan, B. Middleton, and M. Henrion. Knowledge engineering for large belief networks. In *Uncertainty in Artificial Intelligence: Proceedings of the Tenth Conference (UAI-94)*, pages 484–490. Morgan Kaufmann Publishers, San Francisco, CA, 1994.

[138] A. Krogh, R. Durbin, S. Eddy, and G. Mitchison. *Biological Sequence Analysis: Probabilistic Models of Proteins and Nucleic Acids*. Cambridge University Press, 1998.

[139] R.I. Bahar, E.A. Frohm, C.M. Gaona, G.D. Hachtel, E. Macii, A. Pardo, and F. Somenzi. Algebraic decision diagrams and their applications. In *IEEE/ACM International Conference on CAD*, pages 188–191. IEEE Computer Society Press, Santa Clara, CA, 1993.

[140] M. Richardson and P. Domingos. Markov logic networks. *Machine Learning*, 62(1–2):107–136, 2006.

[141] B. Ripley. *Pattern Recognition and Neural Networks*. Cambridge University Press, Cambridge, UK, 1996.

[142] J. Rissanen. *Stochastic Complexity in Statistical Inquiry*. World Scientific, 1989.

[143] S.L. Lauritzen, D.J. Spiegelhalter, R.G. Cowell, and A.P. Dawid. *Probabilistic Networks and Expert Systems*. Springer, 1999.

[144] N. Robertson and P.D. Seymour. Graph minors II: Algorithmic aspects of treewidth. *J. Algorithms*, 7:309–322, 1986.

[145] D. Roth. On the hardness of approximate reasoning. *Artificial Intelligence*, 82(1–2):273–302, April 1996.

[146] S. Russell, J. Binder, D. Koller, and K. Kanazawa. Local learning in probabilistic networks with hidden variables. In *Proceedings of the 11th Conference on Uncertainty in Artificial Intelligence (UAI)*, pages 1146–1152, 1995.

[147] T. Sang, P. Beame, and H. Kautz. Solving Bayesian networks by weighted model counting. In *Proceedings of the Twentieth National Conference on Artificial Intelligence (AAAI-05)*, vol. 1, pages 475–482. AAAI Press, 2005.

[148] T. Sato. A statistical learning method for logic programs with distribution semantics. In *Proceedings of the 12th International Conference on Logic Programming (ICLP'95)*, pages 715–729, 1995.

[149] L.K. Saul and M.I. Jordan. Exploiting tractable substructures in intractable networks. In *NIPS*, pages 486–492, 1995.

[150] P. Savicky and J. Vomlel. Tensor rank-one decomposition of probability tables. In *Proceedings of the Eleventh Conference on Information Processing and Management of Uncertainty in Knowledge-based Systems (IPMU)*, pages 2292–2299, 2006.

[151] G. Schwartz. Estimating the dimension of a model. *Annals of Statistics*, 6:461–464, 1978.

[152] R. Shachter, S.K. Andersen, and P. Szolovits. Global Conditioning for Probabilistic Inference in Belief Networks. In *Proc. Tenth Conference on Uncertainty in AI*, pages 514–522, Seattle WA, 1994.

[153] R. Shachter, B.D. D'Ambrosio, and B. del Favero. Symbolic probabilistic inference in belief networks. In *Proc. Conf. on Uncertainty in AI*, pages 126–131, 1990.

[154] R.D. Shachter and M.A. Peot. Simulation approaches to general probabilistic inference on belief networks. In M. Henrion, R.D. Shachter, L.N. Kanal, and J.F. Lemmer, editors. *Uncertainty in Artificial Intelligence*, vol. 5, pages 221–231. Elsevier Science Publishing Company, Inc., New York, NY, 1989.

[155] R. Shachter. Evaluating influence diagrams. *Operations Research*, 34(6):871–882, 1986.

[156] R. Shachter. Evidence absorption and propagation through evidence reversals. In M. Henrion, R.D. Shachter, L.N. Kanal, and J.F. Lemmer, editors, *Uncertainty in Artificial Intelligence*, vol. 5, pages 173–189, Elsvier Science, 1990.

[157] P.P. Shenoy and G. Shafer. Propagating belief functions with local computations. *IEEE Expert*, 1(3):43–52, 1986.

[158] S.E. Shimony. Finding MAPs for belief networks is NP-hard. *Artificial Intelligence*, 68:399–410, 1994.

[159] M. Shwe, B. Middleton, D. Heckerman, M. Henrion, E. Horvitz, H. Lehmann, and G. Cooper. Probabilistic diagnosis using a reformulation of the INTERNIST-1/QMR knowledge base I. The probabilistic model and inference algorithms. *Methods of Information in Medicine*, 30:241–255, 1991.

[160] P. Smyth, D. Heckerman, and M.I. Jordan. Probabilistic independence networks for hidden Markov probability models. *Neural Computation*, 9(2):227–269, 1997.

[161] S. Srinivas. A generalization of the noisy-or model. In *Proceedings of the Ninth Conference on Uncertainty in Artificial Intelligence (UAI)*, 1993.

[162] H.J. Suermondt, G.F. Cooper, and D.E. Heckerman. A combination of cutset conditioning with clique-tree propagation in the Pathfinder system. In *Proceedings of the 6th Annual Conference on Uncertainty in Artificial Intelligence (UAI-91)*, pages 245–253. Elsvier Science, New York, NY, 1991.

[163] J. Suzuki. Learning Bayesian belief networks based on the MDL principle: An efficient algorithm using the branch and bound technique. *Annals of Statistics*, 6, 1978.

[164] M.F. Tappen and W.T. Freeman. Comparison of graph cuts with belief propagation for stereo, using identical MRF parameters. In *ICCV*, pages 900–907, 2003.

[165] J. Tian. A branch-and-bound algorithm for MDL learning Bayesian networks. In C. Boutilier and M. Goldszmidt, editors, *Proceedings of the Sixteenth Conference on Uncertainty in Artificial Intelligence*, Stanford, CA, pages 580–588, 2000.

[166] T. Verma and J. Pearl. Causal networks: Semantics and expressiveness. In *Proceedings of the 4th Workshop on Uncertainty in AI*, pages 352–359, Minneapolis, MN, 1988.

[167] J. Vomlel. Exploiting functional dependence in Bayesian network inference. In *Proceedings of the Eighteenth Conference on Uncertainty in Artificial Intelligence (UAI)*, pages 528–535. Morgan Kaufmann Publishers, 2002.

[168] M.J. Wainwright, T. Jaakkola, and A.S. Willsky. Tree-based reparameterization for approximate inference on loopy graphs. In *Proceedings of the Annual Conference on Neural Information Processing Systems*, pages 1001–1008, 2001.

[169] M. Welling. On the choice of regions for generalized belief propagation. In *Proceedings of the Conference on Uncertainty in Artificial Intelligence*, page 585. AUAI Press, Arlington, VA, 2004.

[170] M. Welling, T.P. Minka, and Y.W. Teh. Structured region graphs: morphing EP into GBP. In *Proceedings of the Conference on Uncertainty in Artificial Intelligence*, 2005.

[171] M. Welling and Y.W. Teh. Belief optimization for binary networks: A stable alternative to loopy belief propagation. In *Proceedings of the Conference on Uncertainty in Artificial Intelligence*, pages 554–561, 2001.

[172] M.P. Wellman, J.S. Breese, and R.P. Goldman. From knowledge bases to decision models. *The Knowledge Engineering Review*, 7(1):35–53, 1992.

[173] W. Wiegerinck. Variational approximations between mean field theory and the junction tree algorithm. In *UAI*, pages 626–633, 2000.

[174] W. Wiegerinck and T. Heskes. Fractional belief propagation. In *NIPS*, pages 438–445, 2002.

[175] E.P. Xing, M.I. Jordan, and S.J. Russell. A generalized mean field algorithm for variational inference in exponential families. In *UAI*, pages 583–591, 2003.

[176] J. Yedidia, W. Freeman, and Y. Weiss. Constructing free-energy approximations and generalized belief propagation algorithms. *IEEE Transactions on Information Theory*, 51(7):2282–2312, 2005.

[177] J.S. Yedidia, W.T. Freeman, and Y. Weiss. Understanding belief propagation and its generalizations. Technical Report TR-2001-022, MERL, 2001. Available online at http://www.merl.com/publications/TR2001-022/.

[178] J. York. Use of the Gibbs sampler in expert systems. *Artificial Intelligence*, 56(1):115–130, 1992, http://dx.doi.org/10.1016/0004-3702(92)90066-7.

[179] C. Yuan and M.J. Druzdzel. An importance sampling algorithm based on evidence pre-propagation. In *Proceedings of the 19th Conference on Uncertainty in Artificial Intelligence (UAI-03)*, pages 624–631. Morgan Kaufmann Publishers, San Francisco, CA, 2003.

[180] A.L. Yuille. Cccp algorithms to minimize the Bethe and Kikuchi free energies: Convergent alternatives to belief propagation. *Neural Computation*, 14(7):1691–1722, 2002.

[181] N.L. Zhang and D. Poole. A simple approach to Bayesian network computations. In *Proceedings of the Tenth Conference on Uncertainty in Artificial Intelligence (UAI)*, pages 171–178, 1994.

[182] N.L. Zhang and D. Poole. Exploiting causal independence in Bayesian network inference. *Journal of Artificial Intelligence Research*, 5:301–328, 1996.

Part II

Classes of Knowledge and Specialized Representations

DOI: 10.1016/S1574-6526(07)03012-X

Chapter 12

Temporal Representation and Reasoning

Michael Fisher

This book is about representing *knowledge* in all its various forms. Yet, whatever phenomenon we aim to represent, be it natural, computational, or abstract, it is unlikely
to be static. The natural world is always decaying or evolving. Thus, computational
processes, by their nature, are dynamic, and most abstract notions, if they are to be
useful, are likely to incorporate change. Consequently, the notion of representations
changing through time is vital. And so, we need a clear way of representing both our
temporal basis, and the way in which entities change over time. This is exactly what
this chapter is about.

We aim to provide the reader with an overview of many of the ways temporal
phenomena can be *modelled*, *described*, *reasoned about*, and *applied*. In this, we will
often overlap with other chapters in this collection. Some of these topics we will refer
to very little, as they will be covered directly by other chapters, for example, *temporal
action logic* [84], *situation calculus* [185], *event calculus* [209], *spatio-temporal reasoning* [74], *temporal constraint satisfaction* [291], *temporal planning* [84, 271], and
qualitative temporal reasoning [102]. Other topics will be described in this chapter,
but overlap with descriptions in other chapters, in particular:

- *automated reasoning*, in Section 12.3.2 and in [290];

- *description logics*, in Section 12.4.6 and in [154]; and

- *natural language*, in Section 12.4.1 and in [250].

The topics in several other chapters, such as *reasoning about knowledge and belief* [203], *query answering* [34] and *multi-agent systems* [277], will only be referred
to very briefly.

Although this chapter is not intended to be a comprehensive survey of *all* approaches to temporal representation and reasoning, it does outline many of the most
prominent ones, though necessarily at a high-level. If more detail is required, many
references are provided. Indeed, the first volume of the *Foundations of Artificial Intel-*

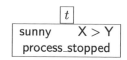

Figure 12.1: State at time *t*.

ligence series, in which this collection appears, contains much more detail on the use of temporal reasoning in Artificial Intelligence [100] while [112, 56, 129, 114, 148] all provide an alternative logic-based view of temporal logics. In addition, there are many, more detailed, survey papers which we refer to throughout.

The structure of this chapter is as follows. We begin, in Section 12.1, by considering structures for modelling different aspects of time, aiming at providing an overview of many alternatives. In Section 12.2, we discuss languages for talking about such temporal representations and their properties. Typically, these languages are forms of *temporal logic*. Section 12.3 addresses the problem of reasoning about descriptions given in these temporal languages and highlights a number of significant techniques. In order to provide further context for this discussion, Section 12.4 outlines a selection of application areas for temporal representation and reasoning. Finally, in Section 12.5, concluding remarks are provided.

12.1 Temporal Structures

While we will not enter into a philosophical discussion about the nature of time itself (see, for example, [287, 119]), we will examine a variety of different structures that underlie representations of time. Where possible, we will provide mathematical descriptions in order to make the discussions more formal.

We are only able to describe temporal concepts if we are able to refer to a particular time and so relate different times to this. Without prejudicing later decisions, we will describe such times as *states* and will refer to each one via an unique index. Thus, at a particular time, say *t*, we can describe facts such as "it is sunny", "the process is stopped", and "X is bigger than Y". For example, in Fig. 12.1 we have one such state, *t*.

Now, as soon as we go beyond this simple view, we face a number of choices, all of which can significantly affect the complexity and applicability of the temporal representation.

12.1.1 Instants and Durations

It may seem as though the index *t* described above naturally represents an instant in time. Indeed, by describing *t* as a *state*, we have already implied this. While this is a popular view, it is not the only one. Another approach is to consider *t* as ranging over a set of temporal *intervals*. An interval is a sequence of time with duration. Thus, if *t* now refers to an interval, for example, an hour, then Fig. 12.1 represents properties true during that hour: "it is sunny throughout that hour", "the process is stopped in that hour", and "X is bigger than Y for an hour". It is important to note that the language we use to describe properties is vital. Thus, we have just used "throughout", "in", and

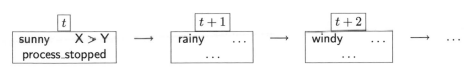

Figure 12.2: Organising states as $\mathbb{N}$.

"for" in describing properties holding over intervals. The differences that such choices make will be considered in more detail in Section 12.2.5. We have also referred to *explicit* times, such as one hour; again, the possibility of talking directly about real values of time will be explored in Section 12.2.6.

Related to the question of whether points or intervals should be used as the basis for temporal representation is the question of whether temporal elements should be *discrete*. If we consider points as the basis for a temporal representation, then it is important to describe the relationship *between* points. An obvious approach is to have each point representing a discrete moment in time, i.e., distinguishably separate from other points. This corresponds to our intuition of 'ticks' of a clock and is so appealing that the most popular propositional temporal logic is based upon this view. This logic, called *Propositional Temporal Logic* (PTL) [113, 223], views time as being isomorphic to the Natural Numbers, with:

- an identifiable start point, characterised by '0';

- discrete time points, characterised by '0', '1', '2', etc.;

- an infinite future; and

- a simple operation for moving from one point ('i') to the *next* (characterised by '$i + 1$').

There are a number of variations of the above properties that we will discuss soon, but let us consider a model for PTL as simply $\langle \mathbb{N}, \pi \rangle$ with π being a function mapping each element of the Natural Numbers, $\mathbb{N}$, to the set of propositions *true* at that moment. We will see later that this is used for the semantics of PTL. We can visualise this as in Fig. 12.2, where π captures the elements inside each temporal element (i.e. all the *true* propositions; those not mentioned are, by default, *false*).

12.1.2 From Discreteness to Density

We next consider some variations on the basic type of model given above. In Section 12.1.4, we re-examine the above assumptions of having an identifiable start state and linearity. For the moment, however, we only review the decision to have a set of *discrete* time points between which we can move via a simple function. Although this corresponds to the Natural Numbers (or Integers), what if we take the Rational Numbers as a basis? Or the Real Numbers? Or, indeed, what if we take a structure that has no analogue in Number Theory?

In general, the model for point-based temporal logic is $\langle S, R, \pi \rangle$, where S is the set of time points, π again maps each point to those propositions true at that point, and R is an earlier–later relation between points in S. In the case of discrete temporal logics, we can replace the general accessibility relation, R, by a relation between adjacent points, N. This *next-time* relation applies over the set of all discrete moments in time (S). Thus, for all s_1 and s_2 in S, $N(s_1, s_2)$ is true if s_2 is the *next* discrete moment after s_1.

If we go further and use a standard arithmetical structure, we can replace the combination of N and S (or R and S) by the structure itself, e.g., $\mathbb{N}$ with the associated ordering.

Now, if we consider non-discrete structures, such as $\mathbb{R}$, there is no clear notion of the *next* point in time. $\mathbb{R}$ is *dense*, and so if a temporal relation, R, is based on this domain, then if two time points are related, there is always another point that occurs *between* them:

$$\forall i \in S. \, \forall k \in S. \, R(i, k) \quad \Rightarrow \quad [\exists j \in S. \, R(i, j) \wedge R(j, k)].$$

Consequently, the concept of a *next* point in time makes little sense in this context and so logics based on dense models typically use specific operators relating to intervals over the underlying domain; see Section 12.2.4. And so we have almost come full circle: dense temporal logics, such as those based on $\mathbb{R}$, require interval-like operators in their language. (By *interval-like*, we mean operators that refer to particular subsequences of points.)

There is a further aspect that we want to mention and that will become important later once we consider representing point-based temporal logics within classical first-order logic (see Section 12.3.2). As we have seen, some constraints on the accessibility relation (for example, density, above) can be defined using a first-order language over such relations. However, there are some restrictions (for example, finiteness) that cannot be defined in this way [161, 274, 112].

There is much more work in this area, covering a wide variety of base domains for temporal logics. However, we will just mention one further aspect of underlying models of time, namely *granularity*, before moving on to more general organisation within the temporal structure (in Section 12.1.4).

12.1.3   Granularity Hierarchies

The models of time we have seen so far are relatively simple. In mentioning the possibility of an underlying dense domain above we can begin to see some of the complexity; between any two time points there are an infinite number of other time points. Thus, time can be described at arbitrary *granularities*. However, it is often the case that a description is needed at a particular granularity, and only later do we need to consider finer time distinctions. A simple example from practical reasoning concerns a discussion between participants who agree to organise a meeting *every month*. They must agree to either a date, e.g., the 25th, or to a particular day, e.g., the last Tuesday in the month. Later, they will consider times within that day. Then they might possibly consider more detailed times within the meeting itself, and so on. In the first case, the participants wish to represent the possibilities without having to deal with minutes, or even hours. Later, hours, minutes and seconds may be needed. In practical terms such requirements have led to systems such as *calendar logic* [213]. More generally, significant work has been carried out on hierarchies of differing granularities, for example, in [202, 105, 59, 232], with a comprehensive descriptions being given in [93, 46]. Finally, the work on interval temporal logics described later has also led to alternative views of granularity and projection [206, 130, 58, 131].

12.1.4   Temporal Organisation

In general, the accessibility relation between temporal points is an arbitrary relation. However, as we have seen above, many domains provide additional constraints on this. Typically, the accessibility relation is *irreflexive* and *transitive*. In addition, the use of arithmetical domains, such as $\mathbb{N}$, $\mathbb{Q}$, and $\mathbb{R}$, ensures that the temporal structure is both linear and infinite in the future. While a linear model of time is adopted within the most popular approaches [223], there is significant use of the branching (in to the future) model [91, 281], particularly in model checking (see Section 12.4.4). Yet there are many other ways of organising the flow[1] of time, including a *circular* view [239], a *partial-order*, or trace-based, view [163, 218, 139, 268], or an *alternating* view [68, 17]. These last two varieties have been found to be very useful in specific applications, particularly partial-order temporal logics for partial/trace-based requirements specifications, such as Message Sequence Charts or concurrent systems, and alternating-time temporal logics for both the logic of games and the verification of multi-process (and multi-agent, see [277]) systems [18, 14, 200].

All these considerations are closely related to finite automata over infinite strings (ω-automata). There has been a considerable amount of research developing the link between forms of ω-automata (such as Büchi automata) and both temporal and modal logics [254, 279, 280]. It is beyond the scope of this article to delve much into this, yet it is important to recognise that much of the development of (point-based) temporal representation and reasoning is closely related to automata-theoretic counterparts.

12.1.5   Moving in Real Time

So far we have considered the *relative* movement through time, where time is represented by abstract entities organised in structures such as trees or sequences. Even in discrete temporal models, the idea of the *next* moment in time is an abstract one. Each step does not directly correspond to explicit elements of time, such as seconds, days or years. In this section, we will outline the addition of such *real-time* aspects. These allow us to compare times, not just in terms of before/after or earlier/later relations, but also in *quantitative* terms.

Since there are many useful articles on structures for representing real-time temporal properties, such as the influential [12, 13], together with overviews of the work (particularly on timed automata) [15, 19, 44], we will simply give an outline of the *timed automata* approach on discrete, linear models. (Note that a collection of early, but influential, papers can be found in [79].)

Recall that discrete, linear models of time correspond to sequences of 'moments'. These, in turn, can be recognised as infinite words in specific finite automata over infinite strings called Büchi automata. The only relationship between such moments is that each subsequent one is considered as the *next* moment in time. In order to develop a *real-time* version of this approach, we can consider such sequences, but with timing

---

[1] However, describing time as *flowing* might even be an assumption too far! Several authors have considered time with *gaps* in it [112, 28].

Figure 12.3: Model with timing constraints.

statements referring to particular clocks (in the case in Fig. 12.3, the clock is t) added between each consecutive moment. See Fig. 12.3 for an example of a timed model (here $t < 1$ is a constraint stating that the time, t, is less than 1 on this transition, while the time t is at least 8 on the $t \geq 8$ transition).

Where only a finite number of different states exist, Büchi automata can also be extended to recognise these *timed sequences* [12, 13]. In practical applications of such models (see Section 12.4.4) various automata-theoretic operations, such as emptiness checking, are used. These tend to be complex [19], but vary greatly depending on the type of clocks and constraints used.

As well as being developed further, for example, with *clocked transition systems* [165], and extended into *hybrid automata* [11], timed automata have led to many useful and practical verification tools, particularly UPPAAL (see Section 12.4.4).

12.1.6 Intervals

As mentioned above, an *interval* captures some duration of time over which certain properties hold. As in the case of point-based approaches described earlier, there are many different possibilities concerning how intervals are defined. Given a linear model of time, then questions such as whether the 'moments' within this linear order are represented as points or not, whether the order is infinite in either (or both) future or past, etc., must still be decided upon. Additionally, we now have the notion of an interval. Simply, this represents the period of time between two 'moments'. But, of course, there are *many* possibilities here [275]. Does the interval include the end points? Can we have intervals where the start point and end point are the same? Can we have zero length intervals? And so on.

Assuming we have decided on the basic structure of intervals, then the key questions concerned with reasoning in such models are those relating points to intervals, and relating intervals to other intervals. For example, imagine that we have the simple model of time based on $\mathbb{N}$, as described above. Then, let us denote the interval between two time points a and b by $[a, b]$. Now, we might ask:

- does a particular time point c occur within the interval $[a, b]$?

- is a particular time point d adjacent to (i.e., immediately before or immediately after) the interval $[a, b]$ (and what interval do we get if we add d to $[a, b]$)?

- does another interval, $[e, f]$, overlap $[a, b]$?

- is the interval $[h, i]$ a strict *sub-interval* of $[a, b]$?

- what interval represents the overlap of the intervals $[j, k]$ and $[a, b]$?

And so on. As we can see, there are *many* questions that can be formulated. Indeed, we have not even addressed the question of whether intervals are *open* or *closed*. This question really becomes relevant we consider underlying sets such as the Rational or Real Numbers. Informally, an element x in the temporal domain are within the *open* interval (a, b) if $a < x$ and $x < b$, and is within the *closed* interval $[a, b]$ if $a \leqslant x$ and $x \leqslant b$.

Yet, that is not all. In the temporal models described earlier, we defined temporal properties. Such properties, usually represented by propositions, were satisfied at particular times. Thus, with intervals, we not only have these aspects, but can also ask questions such as:

- does the proposition φ hold *throughout* the interval $[a, b]$?

- does the proposition φ hold anywhere *within* the interval $[a, b]$?

- does the proposition φ hold by the *end* of interval $[a, b]$?

- does the proposition φ hold immediately *before* the interval $[a, b]$?

And so on. Various connectives allow us to express even more:

- given an interval $[a, b]$ where φ holds, is there another interval, $[l, m]$, occurring in the future (i.e., strictly *after* $[a, b]$), on which φ also holds?

- can we split up an interval $[a, b]$ into two sub-intervals, $[a, c_1]$ and $[c_2, b]$ such that φ holds continuously throughout $[a, c_1]$ but not at c_2 (and where joining $[a, c_1]$ and $[c_2, b]$ back together gives $[a, b]$)?

In general, there are *many* questions that can be asked, even when only considering the underlying interval representations. As we will see in Section 12.2.5, once we add specific languages to reason about intervals, then the variation in linguistic constructs brings an even greater set of possibilities.

In a historical context, although work in Philosophy, Linguistics and Logic had earlier considered time periods, for example, [65], interval temporal representations came to prominence in Computer Science and Artificial Intelligence via two important routes:

1. the development, in the early 1980s, of interval temporal logics for the description of computer systems, typically hardware and protocols [135, 204, 208, 252]; and

2. the development, by Allen, of interval representations within Artificial Intelligence, primarily for use in planning systems [6, 9, 7].

We will consider the languages used to describe such phenomena in Section 12.2.5 and will outline some to the applications of interval representations later.

Finally, in this section, we note that there are a number of excellent articles covering much more than we can here: introductory articles, such as [287, 190]; surveys of interval problems in Artificial Intelligence, such as [85, 121]; and the comprehensive survey of interval and duration calculi by Goranko, Montanari, and Sciavicco [127].

12.2 Temporal Language

Just as there are many models for representing temporal situations, there is an abundance of languages for describing temporal properties. Again, many of these languages have evolved from earlier work on modal [181, 61] or tense logics [107, 66]. Yet, with each new type of phenomenon, a different logical approach is often introduced. Thus, there are so many different temporal logics, that we are only able to introduce a few of the more common ones in the following.

12.2.1 Modal Temporal Logic

We will begin with a common language for describing temporal properties, often termed *modal temporal logic* due to its obvious links with modal and tense logics [229, 238, 53, 37]. This is the type of language originally applied by Pnueli [222] and is now widely used in Computer Science. Based on modal notions of *necessity* and *possibility*, the basic (modal) temporal operators are

$\Box \varphi$ — "φ is *always* true in the future"

$\Diamond \varphi$ — "φ is true at *some time* in the future"

These *always* and *sometime* operators form the basis for many logics operating over linear models of time. Yet there are temporal aspects that are impossible to represent simply using '$\Diamond$' and '$\Box$' [161, 292, 53]. Thus, the *until* operator ('$\mathcal{U}$') together with its counterpart, the *unless* operator ('$\mathcal{W}$'), are often imported from tense logic [161, 64]:

$\varphi \mathcal{U} \psi$ — "there exists a moment when ψ holds and φ will continuously hold from now *until* this moment"

$\varphi \mathcal{W} \psi$ — "φ will continuously hold from now on unless ψ occurs, in which case φ will cease"

(Note that there are several variations on the semantics of these operators, for example, differing on whether φ must be satisfied at the current moment.) The similarities between the above connectives means that the *unless* operator is often termed *weak until*. This is generally enough to handle common situations, as both *sometime* and *always* can be defined using *until*. However, in the case of a discrete model of time, it is often convenient to add the *next time* operator, '$\bigcirc$':

$\bigcirc \varphi$ — "φ is true at the *next* moment in time"

The formal semantics for such temporal operators can be given, in the discrete case, using the *next-time* relation introduced earlier. Over models $M = \langle S, N, \pi \rangle$, example semantics can be given as follows.

$$\langle M, s \rangle \models \bigcirc \varphi \quad \text{if, and only if,} \quad \forall t \in S. \text{ if } N(s, t) \text{ then } \langle M, t \rangle \models \varphi$$

Note that, depending on the semantics of the '$\mathcal{U}$' operator, the '$\bigcirc$' operator may be able to be defined directly using '$\mathcal{U}$' [87].

12.2.2 Back to the Future

Work on tense logics typically incorporated a notion of *past-time* connectives, such as *since* [161, 64]. Though such past-time connectives were omitted from the early temporal logics used in Computer Science, researchers have found it convenient to re-introduce past-time into temporal logics [38, 182].

Thus, temporal logics can contain operators that are the past-time counterparts of $\Box$, $\Diamond$, etc. Discrete temporal logics also incorporate the *previous* operator, '$\bullet$', which is the past-time dual of the "next" operator.

$\bullet\varphi$ — "φ is true at the *previous* moment in time"

In order to indicate some of the interesting interactions between these two operators, we provide more general definitions that depend only on the discreteness of the underlying model, not on its linearity. For this purpose, we again the *next-time* relation introduced earlier and define the semantics for $\bullet$ (over models $M = \langle S, N, \pi \rangle$) as follows.

$$\langle M, s \rangle \models \bigcirc\varphi \quad \text{if, and only if,} \quad \forall t \in S. \text{ if } N(s, t) \text{ then } \langle M, t \rangle \models \varphi,$$
$$\langle M, t \rangle \models \bullet\varphi \quad \text{if, and only if,} \quad \forall s \in S. \text{ if } N(s, t) \text{ then } \langle M, s \rangle \models \varphi.$$

It is important to note the duality between the semantics of '$\bullet$' and '$\bigcirc$' given earlier. This duality allows us to describe some interesting properties. First of all, note that $\bullet$**false** (or $\bigcirc$**false**) is only satisfiable at the first (or last) moments in the temporal model. Examining the definition above, the only way that $\bullet$**false** can be satisfied is if there are *no* previous moments in time. If there were any previous ones, then **false** would have had to be satisfied at them! Similarly, $\bigcirc$**false** corresponds closely to the ITL operator $\mathtt{fin}$ describing the end of finite intervals (see Section 12.2.5).

An interesting aspect of the past/future combination is given by the possible interactions between the previous and next operators. For example, the axiom $\varphi \Leftrightarrow \bullet\bigcirc\varphi$ implies that, in models such as that described below, either the state s is disallowed, or if it is allowed, it is indistinguishable from the "now" state by any temporal formula.

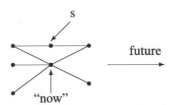

As we can see, there is much scope for interesting combinations even with just the *next* and *previous* operators. A large range of interactions can be explored with the *sometime in the future* and the *sometime in the past* operators, or with *until* and *since* [240, 112, 267]. In addition, questions of whether both past and future operators are needed can also been considered [179].

12.2.3 Temporal Arguments and Reified Temporal Logics

While variations of modal temporal logics are widely used in Computer Science, there are alternative approaches that have been developed within Artificial Intelligence. An obvious alternative to the modal-temporal approach is to essentially use first-order logic statements, treating one of the arguments to each predicate as a reference to time. To see this, let us give the semantics of PTL in classical logic by representing temporal propositions as classical predicates parameterised by the moment in time being considered. Below we look at several temporal formulae and, assuming they are to be evaluated at the moment i, show how these formulae can be represented in classical logic.

$$p \wedge \bigcirc q \quad \rightarrow \quad p(i) \wedge q(i+1).$$

$$\Diamond r \quad \rightarrow \quad \exists j. \, (j \geqslant i) \wedge r(j).$$

$$\Box s \quad \rightarrow \quad \forall k. \, (k \geqslant i) \Rightarrow s(k).$$

This is often termed the *temporal arguments* approach, because the temporal propositions are defined as predicates taking times as arguments.

A further approach that became popular in Artificial Intelligence research is the *reification* approach. Here, the idea is to have predicates such as *holds* and *occurs* applied to properties (often called *fluents*) and times (points or intervals) over which the properties hold (or occur).

Since Allen's Interval Algebra, considered in Section 12.2.5, is of this form, we will not mention these possibilities further. However, there are a great many publications in this area, beginning with initial work on reified approaches, such as McDermott's logic of plans [197], Allen's Interval Algebra [7] (and Section 12.2.5), Situation Calculus [237, 185] and the Event Calculus [169]. In addition, there are numerous surveys and overviews concerning these approaches, including [117, 189, 236, 35].

12.2.4 Operators over Non-discrete Models

As we outlined in Section 12.2.2, various temporal operators have been devised, beginning with *until* and *since* or, alternatively with *sometime in the future* and *sometime in the past*. Indeed, these operators are useful for general linear orders, not just discrete ones [161]. Consequently, if we move away from discrete temporal models towards dense (and, generally, non-discrete) models, these temporal operators form the basis of languages used to describe temporal properties.

Sometime in the future and *sometime in the past* (often referred to as F and P) have been used to analyse a variety of non-discrete logics, for example, those based on $\mathbb{R}$ [111, 112, 114]. Past and future operators, such as *until* and *since* have been productively used in transforming arbitrary formulae into more useful normal forms, for example, separating past-time from future-time [108, 36, 97, 147].

Finally, it is informative to consider the approach taken in *TLR* [39, 164]. Here, the temporal model is based on $\mathbb{R}$ and *until* is taken as the basic temporal operator (only the future time fragment is considered). However, the difficulty of dealing with properties over $\mathbb{R}$ meant that the authors introduced an additional constraint, termed *finite variability*. Here, any property may only change value a *finite* number of times between any two points in time. This avoids the problem of a temporal property, say p, varying between **true** and **false** infinitely over a finite period of time, for example, between 1 and 2 on the Real Number line. (This aspect has also been explored in [77, 118].)

12.2.5 Intervals

As mentioned earlier, the two strong influences for the use of interval temporal representations were from Allen, in Artificial Intelligence, and Moszkowski et al., in Computer Science. We will give a brief flavour of the two different approaches, before mentioning some more recent work.

Allen's interval algebra

Allen was concerned with developing an appropriate formal representation for temporal aspects which could be used in a variety of systems, particularly planning systems. He developed a formal model of intervals, or time periods, and provided syntax to describe the relationships between such intervals [6, 7]. Thus, I_1 *overlaps* I_2 is true if the intervals I_1 and I_2 overlap, I_3 *during* I_4 is true if the interval I_3 is completely contained within I_4, while I_5 *before* I_6 is true if I_5 occurs before I_6. This led on to 13 such binary relations between intervals, giving the Allen Interval Algebra.

Further work on the formalisation and checking of Allen's interval relations can be found in [8, 175, 183, 136, 184, 176] with the algebraic aspects being explored further in [144, 145]. In addition, the basic interval algebra has been extended and improved in many different ways; see [121] for some of these aspects and [85] for a thorough analysis of the computational problems associated with such interval reasoning. These last two references also bring in the work on representing such problems as temporal constraint networks [80, 251] and solving them via constraint satisfaction techniques [291].

Moszkowski's ITL

The interval logic developed by Moszkowski et al. in the early 1980s was much closer in spirit to the propositional (discrete) temporal logics being developed at that time [113]. Moszkowski's logic is called ITL and was originally developed in order to model digital circuits [135, 204]. Although the basic temporal model is similar to that of PTL given earlier, ITL formulae are interpreted in a sub-sequence (defined by $\sigma_b, \ldots, \sigma_e$) of, rather than at a point within, the model σ. Thus, basic propositions (such as P) are evaluated at the *start* of an interval:

$$\langle \sigma_b, \ldots, \sigma_e \rangle \models P \quad \text{if, and only if,} \quad P \in \sigma_b.$$

Now, the semantics of two common PTL operators can be given as follows.

$$\langle \sigma_b, \ldots, \sigma_e \rangle \models \Box\varphi \quad \text{if, and only if,} \quad \text{for all } i, \text{ if } b \leqslant i \leqslant e$$
$$\text{then } \langle \sigma_i, \ldots, \sigma_e \rangle \models \varphi,$$

$$\langle \sigma_b, \ldots, \sigma_e \rangle \models \bigcirc\varphi \quad \text{if, and only if,} \quad e > b \text{ and } \langle \sigma_{b+1}, \ldots, \sigma_e \rangle \models \varphi.$$

A key aspect of ITL is that it contains the basic temporal operators of PTL, together with the *chop* operator, ';', which is used to fuse intervals together (see also [245, 283]). Thus:

$$\langle \sigma_b, \ldots, \sigma_e \rangle \models \varphi; \psi \quad \text{if, and only if,} \quad \text{there exists } i \text{ such that } b \leqslant i \leqslant e$$
$$\text{and both } \langle \sigma_b, \ldots, \sigma_i \rangle \models \varphi \text{ and } \langle \sigma_i, \ldots, \sigma_e \rangle \models \psi.$$

This powerful operator is both useful and problematic (in that the operator ensures a high complexity logic). Useful in that it allows intervals to be split based on their properties; for example, '◊' can be derived in terms of ';', i.e.

$$\Diamond \varphi \equiv \mathbf{true}; \varphi$$

meaning that there is some (finite) sub-interval in which **true** is satisfied that is followed (immediately) by a sub-interval in which φ is satisfied.

To explain further, simple examples of formulae in ITL are given below, together with English explanations.

- p persists through the current interval: $\Box p$

- The following defines steps within an interval:

  $$up \wedge \bigcirc down \wedge \bigcirc\bigcirc up \wedge \bigcirc\bigcirc\bigcirc down.$$

- The following allows sequences of intervals to be constructed:

  $$\Box january; \ \bigcirc\Box february; \ \bigcirc\Box march; \ldots.$$

- p enjoys a period of being **false** followed by a period of being **true**, i.e., it becomes positive:

  $$\Box\neg p; \bigcirc\Box p.$$

As mentioned earlier, there has also been work on granularity within ITL, particularly via the *temporal projection* operation [206, 130, 58, 131].

In [136], Halpern and Shoham provide a powerful logic (HS) over intervals (not just of linear orders). This logic has been very influential as it subsumes Allen's algebra. Indeed, the HS language with unary modal operators captures entirely Allen's algebra; binary operators are needed to capture the '*chop*' operator within ITL [127], reflecting its additional complexity.

Finally, we note that, there are natural extensions of the above interval approaches. One is to consider intervals, not just over linear orders, but also over arbitrary relations. This moves towards spatial and spatio-temporal logics, see [115] or [74]. Another extension is to bring real-time aspects into interval temporal logics. This has been developed within the work on *duration calculi* [296, 69]. Pointers to such applications of interval temporal logics are provided in Section 12.4. Finally, an interesting extension to interval temporal logic is to add operators that allow endpoints to be moved, thus giving *compass logic* [193].

12.2.6 Real-Time and Hybrid Temporal Languages

In describing real-time aspects, a number of languages can be developed [15]. For instance, standard modal-temporal logic can be extended with annotations expressing real-time constraints [170]. Thus, "I will finish reading this section within 8 time units" might be represented by:

$$\Diamond_{\leq 8} finish.$$

Another approach is to use *freeze quantification*. This is similar to the approach taken with hybrid logics (see Section 12.2.8) where a moment in time can be recorded by a variable and then referred to (and used in calculations) later. In addition, there is the possibility of explicitly relating to clocks (and clock variables) within a temporal logic [216]. Consequently, there are a great many different real-time temporal logics (and axiomatisations [249]). There are several excellent surveys of work in this area, including those by Alur and Henzinger [15, 16], Ostroff [217], and Henzinger [140].

In a different direction, the *duration calculus* [78, 69] was introduced in [296], and can be seen as a combination of an interval temporal representation with real-time aspects. It has been applied to many applications in real-time systems, with behaviours mapping on to the dense underlying temporal model.

In developing temporal logics for real-time systems, it became clear that many (hard) practical problems, for example, in complex control systems, required even more expressive power. And so *hybrid systems* were analysed and formalisms for these developed. Hybrid systems combine the standard discrete steps from the automata approach with more complex mathematical techniques related to continuous systems (e.g., differential equations). While we will not delve into this complex area further, we direct the interested reader to the HyTech system [141, 157], the RED system [235] and to work on *hybrid automata* [11].

12.2.7 Quantification

So far we have examined essentially *propositional* languages, most often over discrete, linear models of time. In this section, we will consider the addition of various forms of quantification.[2] Again, we will not provide a comprehensive survey, but will examine a variety of different linguistic extensions that allow us to describe more interesting temporal properties.

Quantification over paths

Although quantification in classical first-order logic is typically used to quantify over a particular data domain, the additional aspect of an underlying temporal structure provides a further possibility in temporal logics, namely the ability to quantify over some aspects of the structure. As we have seen, temporal operators such as '□' typically quantify over moments of time. Yet, there are other possibilities for quantification, the most common of which is to quantify over possible *paths*. If we consider a linear sequence of time points as a path, then many temporal structures (most obviously, trees) comprise multiple paths [248, 246]. Temporal logics over such branching time structures allow for the possibility of *quantifying* over the paths within the branching structure.

Although branching structures in tense logic were previously studied by Prior (see also [132]), we will exemplify the branching approach by considering two popular temporal logics over branching structures from Computer Science. Computation Tree Logic (CTL) was introduced in [88, 89] and basically used Pnueli's modal temporal logic for describing properties along paths (sequences). However, to deal with the

---

[2] As one might expect, quantification in temporal logics is related quite closely to quantification in modal logics, though quantified modal logics are not without difficulties [120, 195].

possibility of multiple paths through a tree-like temporal structure, two new logical *path operators* were introduced:

A—'on all future paths starting here'

E—'on some future path starting here'

The CTL approach, however, is to restrict the combinations of temporal/path operators that can occur. Thus, each temporal operator *must* be prefixed by a path operator.

The CTL logic has been popular in specifying properties of reactive systems, for example,

> **A**□ *safe*   **E**○ *active*   **A**◊ *terminate*

Here, '**A**□' effectively considers all future moments, while '**E**○' must find at least one path such that the required property is true at the next moment in the path, while '**A**◊' is useful for describing the fact that, whichever future path is considered, the property will hold at some point on that path.

Although restricted in its syntax, CTL has found important uses in verification through *model checking* (see Section 12.4.4) since the complexity of this technique for CTL is relatively low [72].

Just as CTL puts a restriction on the combination of temporal and path quantifiers, the need for more complex temporal formulae, such as '□◊', over paths in branching structures led to various other branching logics [86, 92, 91, 72], most notably *Full Computation Tree Logic* (CTL*). With CTL* there is no restriction on the combinations of path and temporal operators allowed. Thus, formulae such as

> **A**□◊**EA** *p*

can be given. However, there is a price to pay for this increased expressiveness [201], as the decision problem for CTL* is quite complex [92], and so this logic is less often used in practical verification tools.

A further significant development of logics over branching structures was the introduction of *alternating-time temporal logics*. To quote from the abstract of [17]:

> "Temporal logic comes in two varieties: linear-time temporal logic assumes implicit universal quantification over all paths that are generated by the execution of a system; branching-time temporal logic allows explicit existential and universal quantification over all paths. We introduce a third, more general variety of temporal logic: alternating-time temporal logic offers selective quantification over those paths that are possible outcomes of games, such as the game in which the system and the environment alternate moves. While linear-time and branching-time logics are natural specification languages for closed systems, alternating-time logics are natural specification languages for open systems. For example, by preceding the temporal operator 'eventually' with a selective path quantifier, we can specify that in the game between the system and the environment, the system has a strategy to reach a certain state. The problems of receptiveness, realisability, and controllability can be formulated as model-checking problems for alternating-time formulae. Depending on whether or not we admit arbitrary nesting of selective path quantifiers and temporal operators, we obtain the two alternating-time temporal logics ATL and ATL*."

Given a set (a *coalition*) of agents, *A*, ATL allows operators such as $\langle\langle A \rangle\rangle \varphi$, meaning that the set of agents have a collective strategy that will achieve φ. This approach has been very influential, not only on the specification and verification of open, distributed systems, but also on the modelling of the behaviour of groups of intelligent agents [277, 276].

Finally, we note that the development of the *modal μ-calculus* [171] provided a language that subsumed CTL, CTL*, and many other branching (and linear) logics [76], and there are even timed μ-calculi [142].

Quantification over propositions

In extending from a propositional temporal logic, a small (but significant) step to take is to allow *quantification* over propositions. Thus, the usual first-order quantifier symbols, '∀' and '∃', can be used, but only over Boolean valued variables, namely propositions of the language. Thus, using such a logic, called *quantified propositional temporal logic* (QPTL) [254], it is possible to write formulae such as

$$\exists p.\ p \wedge \bigcirc\bigcirc p \wedge \Diamond\Box\neg p.$$

It is important to note that the particular form of quantification provided here, termed the *substitutional interpretation* [133], can be defined as:

$\langle M, s \rangle \models \exists p.\ \varphi$ if, and only if,   there exists a model M' such that
$\langle M', s \rangle \models \varphi$ and M' differs from M
in at most the valuation given to p.

This style of quantification is used in QPTL and in other extensions of PTL we mention below, such as fixpoint extensions. Note that Haack [133] engages in a thorough discussion of the philosophical arguments between the proponents of the above and the, more standard in classical logic, *objectual interpretation* of quantification:

$\langle M, s \rangle \models \exists p.\ \varphi$ if, and only if,   there exists a proposition $q \in \text{PROP}$
such that $\langle M, s \rangle \models \varphi(p/q)$

where $\varphi(p/q)$ is the formula φ with p replaced by q throughout

QPTL gives an extension of PTL (though still representable using Büchi automata) that allows regular properties to be defined. It was inspired by Wolper's work on extending PTL with grammar operators (termed ETL) [292]. Another approach that followed on from Wolper's work was the development of *fixpoint* extensions [55] of PTL [32, 33, 278, 109], extending PTL with least ('μ') and greatest ('ν') fixpoint operators. In such fixpoint languages, one could write more complex expressions. For a simple example, though, consider:

$$\Box\varphi \equiv \nu\xi.\ \varphi \wedge \bigcirc\xi.$$

Here, $\Box\varphi$ is defined as the maximal (with respect to implication) fixpoint (ξ) of the formula $\xi \Rightarrow (\varphi \wedge \bigcirc\xi)$. Thus, the maximal fixpoint above defines $\Box\varphi$ as the 'infinite' formula

$$\varphi \wedge \bigcirc \varphi \wedge \bigcirc\bigcirc \varphi \wedge \bigcirc\bigcirc\bigcirc \varphi \wedge \cdots.$$

Finally, it is important to note that all these extensions QPTL, ETL, and fixpoint extensions can be shown to be expressively equivalent under certain circumstances [292, 32, 254, 282].

First-order TL

Adding standard first-order (and, in the sense above, objectual) quantification to temporal logic, for example, PTL, is appealing yet fraught with danger. Such a logic is very convenient for describing many scenarios, but is so powerful that we can write down formulae that capture a form of arithmetical induction, from which it is but a short step to being able to represent full arithmetic [262, 263, 1]. Consequently, full first-order temporal logic is incomplete; in other words the set of valid formulae is *not* recursively enumerable (or finitely axiomatisable) when considered over models such as the Natural Numbers.

While some work was carried out on methods for handling, where possible, such specifications [191], first-order temporal logic was generally avoided. Even "small" fragments of first-order temporal logic, such as the *two-variable monadic* fragment, are not recursively enumerable [199, 149].

However, a breakthrough by Hodkinson et al. [149] showed that *monodic* fragments of first-order temporal logics could have complete axiomatisations and even be decidable. A monodic temporal formula is one whose temporal subformulae have, at most, one free variable. Thus, $\forall x.\ p(x)\ \Rightarrow\ \bigcirc q(x)$ is monodic, while $\forall x.\forall y.$ $p(x, y) \Rightarrow \bigcirc q(x, y)$ is not. Wolter and Zakharyaschev showed that any set of valid *monodic* formulae is finitely axiomatisable [295] over a temporal model based on the Natural Numbers. Intuitively, the monodic fragment restricts the amount of information transferred between temporal states so that, effectively, only individual elements of information are passed between temporal states. This avoids the possibility of describing the evolution through time of more complex items, such as relations, and so retains desirable properties of the logic. In spite of this, the addition of equality or function symbols can again lead to the loss of recursive enumerability from these monodic fragments [295, 82], though recovery of this property is sometimes possible [146].

12.2.8   Hybrid Temporal Logic and the Concept of "now"

The term *hybrid logic* is here used to refer to logical systems comprising a hybrid of modal/temporal and classical aspects [156]. Basically, hybrid modal logics provide a language for referring to specific points in a model. This approach is widely used in *description logics*, with nominals typically referring to individuals [27]. In the case of temporal logics, such a possibility was suggested by Prior [229] in tense logics, but did not become popular until the 1990s, for example, with [52, 54].

The ability to refer to specific time points, for example *now*, has been found to be very useful in a number of applications. Consequently, operators such as '↓' are used to bind a variable to the current point [125]. This allows the specifier to describe a temporal situation, record the point at which it occurs, then use a reference to this point in later formulae. This usefulness, has led to work on both reasoning techniques and complexity for such logics [83, 20].

12.3   Temporal Reasoning

Having considered the underlying temporal representations, together with languages that are used to describe such situations, we now take a brief look at a few of the *reasoning methods* developed for these languages.

12.3.1 Proof Systems

There are a wide variety of axiom systems for temporal logics and, consequently, proof methods based upon them. For PTL, the most popular modal-temporal logic, an axiomatisation was provided in [113], and revisited in [243]:

$$\vdash \neg \bigcirc \varphi \Leftrightarrow \bigcirc \neg \varphi$$

$$\vdash \bigcirc(\varphi \Rightarrow \psi) \Rightarrow (\bigcirc \varphi \Rightarrow \bigcirc \psi)$$

$$\vdash \Box(\varphi \Rightarrow \psi) \Rightarrow (\Box \varphi \Rightarrow \Box \psi)$$

$$\vdash \Box \varphi \Rightarrow (\varphi \wedge \bigcirc \Box \varphi)$$

$$\vdash \Box(\varphi \Rightarrow \bigcirc \varphi) \Rightarrow (\varphi \Rightarrow \Box \varphi)$$

$$\vdash (\varphi \mathcal{U} \psi) \Rightarrow \Diamond \psi$$

$$\vdash (\varphi \mathcal{U} \psi) \Leftrightarrow (\psi \vee (\varphi \wedge \bigcirc(\varphi \mathcal{U} \psi)))$$

In addition, all propositional tautologies are theorems and the inference rules used are *modus ponens* together with *temporal generalisation*:

$$\frac{\vdash \varphi}{\vdash \Box \varphi}.$$

However, several other proof systems, even for this logic have been given [172, 191, 87, 260]. Many proof systems for temporal logics are based on their tense logic predecessors, such as those systems developed by van Benthem [275] and Goldblatt [123].

As to other varieties of temporal logic, perhaps the most widely studied are variants of branching-time logics. Thus, there are proof systems for CTL [225] and, recently, CTL* [241, 242].

Concerning quantifier extensions, proof systems have been developed for QPTL [106, 166]. For full first-order temporal logics, an arithmetical axiomatisation has been given in [262]. Recently, complete (*monodic*) fragments of both linear and branching temporal logics have been provided [295, 150] while proof systems have been developed for alternative fragments of first-order temporal logics [221].

12.3.2 Automated Deduction

Given the utility of temporal formalisms, it is not surprising that many computational tools for establishing the truth of temporal statements have been developed. In some approaches, such as model checking (see Section 12.4.4), temporal conditions are often replaced by finite automata over infinite words. The close link between temporal logics and such finite automata [254, 279, 280] means that decisions about the truth of temporal statements can often be reduced to automata-theoretic questions. Rather than discussing this further, we will consider more traditional automated approaches, such as *tableau* and *resolution* systems. However, before doing this, we note that the *temporal arguments* view of temporal representations given earlier points to an obvious way to automate temporal reasoning, namely to translate statements in temporal logic to corresponding statements in classical logic, adding an extra argument. Thus the implication

$$(p \wedge \bigcirc q) \Rightarrow \Box r$$

might become, if we consider the simple Natural Number basis for temporal logic, the following formula

$$\forall t. \, (p(t) \wedge q(t + 1)) \quad \Rightarrow \quad (\forall u. \, (u \geqslant t) \Rightarrow r(u)).$$

This is an appealing approach, and has been successfully applied to the translation of modal logics [212]. However, the translation approach has been used relatively little [210], possibly because the fragment of logic translated to often has high complexity; see [143, 124].

Probably the most popular approach to deciding the truth of temporal formulae is the *tableau* method. The basis of the tableau approach is to recursively take the formula apart, until atomic formulae are dealt with, then assess the truth of the formula in light of the truth constraints imposed by these atomic literals [75]. In classical logic, this typically generates a *tree* of subformulae. However, in temporal logics, as in many modal logics [101], either an infinite tree or, more commonly, a graph structure is generated. The main work in this area was carried out by Wolper [292, 293], who developed a tableau system for discrete, propositional, linear temporal logic. Several other tableau approaches have been reported, both for the above logic [128, 253], and for other varieties of temporal logic [90, 194, 126, 220, 168]. However, the structures built using the tableau method are very close to the ω-automata representing the formulae. Thus, particularly in the case of logics such as CTL*, automata theoretic approaches are often used [92].

In recent years, *resolution* based approaches [244, 30] have been developed. These have consisted of both *non-clausal* resolution, where the formulae in question do not have to be translated to a specific clausal form [3, 5], and *clausal* resolution, where such a form is required [67, 284, 95, 99]. Again, resolution techniques have been extended beyond the basic propositional, discrete, linear temporal logics [57, 81, 167], leading to some practical systems (see Section 12.4.3). For further details on such approaches, particularly for discrete temporal logics, the article [243] is recommended.

Automated deduction for interval temporal logics has often been subsumed by work on temporal planning or temporal constraint satisfaction (see Section 12.4.3), though some work has been carried out on SAT-like procedures for interval temporal problems [269] and tableau methods for interval logics [126, 58].

12.4 Applications

In this section we will provide an outline of some of the ways in which the concepts described in the previous sections can be used to describe and reason about different temporal phenomena. This is not intended to be a comprehensive survey and, again, there are a number of excellent publications covering these topics in detail. However, we aim, through the descriptions below, to provide a sense of the breadth of representational capabilities of temporal logics.

12.4.1 Natural Language

The representation of elements of natural language, particularly *tense*, is not only an intuitively appealing use of temporal logic but provides the starting point for much of the work on temporal logics described in this chapter. The main reason for this is the work of Prior [138] on the formal representation of tense [229]. The sentence:

"I am *writing* this section, will *write* the next section later, and eventually will have *written* the whole chapter"

naturally contains the verb "to write" under different tenses. The tenses used depend upon the moment in time referred to, relative to the person describing it. Prior carried out a logical analysis of such uses of tense, developing *tense logic*, and captured a variety of temporal connectives that have subsequently been used in many temporal logics, for example, *until, since, before, after,* and *during.*

Subsequent work by Kamp [161] related tense operators, such as *since* and *until,* to first-order languages of linear order. This work has been very influential, leading to deeper analysis of tense logic [107, 64, 65], and then to work on temporal logics. An excellent summary of such work on tense logic is given in [66].

The representation of natural language using various temporal representations has also moved on, for example, through the work of van Benthem [275], Galton [116], Kamp and Reyle [162], Steedman [257, 258], ter Meulen [265] and Pratt-Hartmann [228]. A more detailed overview of temporal representation in natural language can be found in [266].

Finally, work in this area naturally impacts upon practical applications, such as the use of temporal representation in *legal reasoning* [288].

12.4.2 Reactive System Specification

It is in the description of complex (interacting, concurrent or distributed) systems that temporal representations have been so widely used. While it is clearly impossible to give a thorough survey of all the ways that temporal notations have been used, particularly as formal specifications, we will give some initial pointers to this area below.

Probably the best known style of temporal specification, which has been used in the specification and verification of programs, is that instigated by Pnueli [222, 113, 223] and continued by Manna and Pnueli through a series of books [191, 192] and papers. In such an approach, the expressive power of modal temporal languages is used in order to specify properties such as *safety*:

$$\Box(temperature < 500)$$

ensuring, in this case, that in any current or future situation, the temperature must be less than 500, *liveness*:

$$\Diamond(terminate \wedge successful)$$

where, for example, some process is guaranteed to eventually terminate successfully, and *fairness*:

$$\Box\Diamond request \Rightarrow \Diamond respond$$

guaranteeing that if a request is made often enough ('$\Box\Diamond$' implies "infinitely often") then, eventually, a response will be given.

In parallel with the Manna/Pnueli line of work, Lamport developed a *Temporal Logic of Actions* (TLA) [177]. This has also been successful, leading to a large body of work on temporal specifications of a variety of systems [178]. Finally, it should be noted that descriptions of many real-world applications have been given using other varieties of temporal language, such as real-time temporal logics (see Section 12.2.6), interval temporal logics (see Section 12.2.5), partial-order temporal logics [268], etc.

Once a system has been specified, for example, using the logical approach above, a number of techniques may be used. These include: *refinement*, in order to develop a modified specification [2]; *execution*, where the specification is treated like a program and executed directly [205, 36, 98]; *deductive verification*, whereby the relationship between two logical specifications is proved (see Sections 12.3.2 and 12.4.3); *algorithmic verification*, where the match between the specification and a finite-state description (for example, a program) is established (see Section 12.4.4); and *synthesis*, whereby such a finite-state description (program) is generated (semi-) automatically from the specification [226].

12.4.3 Theorem-Proving

Several of the reasoning techniques described in Section 12.3 have been developed into powerful proving tools. In the case of modal-temporal logic, the best known is the *Stanford Temporal Prover* (*STeP*) developed over a number of years by Manna and colleagues [259, 51, 50]. STeP supports the "the computer-aided formal verification of reactive, real-time and hybrid systems based on their temporal specification". It incorporates both model checking and proof procedures and is therefore able to tackle more complex, even infinite state, verification problems.

For modal-temporal logics, several other systems have been developed, notably TeMP [155], based on the clausal temporal resolution approach [167], TLPVS [270, 224], built on top of PVS [233], and the Logics Workbench [188, 253].

In terms of interval temporal logics, many of the reasoning techniques and uses of interval algebras have been incorporated in temporal planning [104, 271] and temporal constraint satisfaction systems [85, 291]. These topics are covered in depth elsewhere, but we here just cite some of the relevant work on temporal planning, notably that by Bacchus and Kabanza on using temporal logics to control the planning process [29], by Fox and Long on describing complex temporal domains [103], by Geffner and Vidal on constraint-based temporal planning [286], by Mayer et al. on planning using first-order temporal logics [196], by Gerevini et al. on developing the LPG planning system [187], and by Doherty on planning in temporal action logic [84].

There has been less development and implementation of Moszkowski's ITL, but see [159] for several tools based on this approach. However, the direct execution of ITL statements is the basis for the *Tempura* programming language [205, 134] which is important in the development of compositional reasoning [207]. Just as Tempura is based on forward-chaining execution of ITL statements, the METATEM approach forward-chains through PTL formulae, though in a specific normal form [36, 98]. Alternative approaches to the execution of temporal statements are based on the extension of logic programming to modal temporal logic, giving Templog [4, 40] or Chronolog [215, 186] or the addition of interval constructs to logic programming, giving the temporal event calculus [169, 35, 209, 34]. For introductions to the ideas behind executable temporal logic, see [214, 96].

12.4.4 Model Checking

Undoubtedly the most practical use of temporal logic is in *model checking*. This is simply based on the idea of satisfiability checking. Thus, given a model, M, and a property, φ, is it the case that φ is true throughout M? If M represents all the possible paths through a hardware design, or all the possible executions of a program, then answering this question corresponds to checking whether all the executions/paths satisfy the property. Consequently, this is used extensively in the formal verification of hardware descriptions, network protocols and complex software [151, 73].

That model checking has become so popular is due mainly to improvements in the *engineering* of model checking algorithms and model checkers. Simply enumerating all the paths through the model M and checking whether φ is satisfied on that path can clearly be slow. However, an automata-theoretic view of the approach helped suggest improvements [254]. Here, the idea is that a Büchi automaton, A_M, can be developed to represent all the paths through M, while another Büchi automaton, $A_{\neg\varphi}$, can be developed to capture all paths that *do not* satisfy φ. Thus, $A_{\neg\varphi}$ represents all the *bad* paths. Now, once we have these two automata, we simply take the product, $A_M \times A_{\neg\varphi}$, which produces a new automaton whose paths are those that satisfy *both* automata. Thus, a path through $A_M \times A_{\neg\varphi}$ would be a path through A_M that also *did not* satisfy φ. Now, the question of whether "all paths through M satisfy φ" can be reduced to the question of whether "the automaton $A_M \times A_{\neg\varphi}$ has *no* accepting runs". This automata theoretic view was very appealing and led to significant theoretical advances [279]. However, a key practical problem is that the space (and time) needed to construct the product of the two automata can be prohibitively large. Thus, mechanisms for reducing this were required before model checking could be widely used.

Two approaches have been developed that have led to widespread use of model checking in system verification. The first is the idea of *on-the-fly model checking* [122, 152]. Here, the product automaton is only constructed as needed (i.e., it is built *on the fly*), avoiding expensive product construction in many cases. This approach has been particularly successful in the `Spin` model checker [153, 256], which checks specifications written in linear temporal logic against systems represented in the `Promela` modelling language [153].

The second approach is to still carry out automata composition, but to find a much better (and more efficient) representation for the structures involved. This is termed *symbolic model checking* [63] and uses Binary Decision Diagrams (BDDs) [60] to represent both the system and property. BDDs are a notation in which Boolean formulae can be represented as a graph structure on which certain logical operations can be very quick. This is dependent on finding a good ordering for the Boolean predicates within the graph structure. The use of varieties of BDDs has led to a significant increase in the size of system that can be verified using model checking, and is particularly successful in the SMV [198, 62] and nu_smv [71, 211] model checkers, which check branching temporal formulae (in CTL) over finite automata.

Model checking has also been applied to real-time systems [10, 47, 272, 219, 173, 234, 285], most successfully via the UPPAAL system. This has been used to model and verify networks of timed automata, and uses model checking as a key component [180, 42].

Although model checking has been relatively successful, much work still remains. Current work on abstraction techniques (i.e., reducing complex systems to simpler ones amenable to model checking), SAT based and bounded model checking [48, 49, 26, 227], probabilistic model checking [174, 230], and model checking for high-level languages such as C [31, 255] and Java [289, 160] promise even greater advances in the future.

12.4.5 PSL/Sugar

The success of model checking, particularly in the realm of *hardware* design, has led to the use of temporal techniques in a number of industrial areas. Standards for specifying the functional properties of hardware logic designs are now based upon temporal logics. For example, there is a large consortium developing and applying PSL/Sugar [41, 231]. This, and other approaches such as ForSpec [21] and SystemVerilog Assertions [261], extend temporal logic adding regular expressions and clocks and even allowing more complex combinations of automata and regular expressions [43].

12.4.6 Temporal Description Logics

It is often desirable to combine temporal logic with description logic, to give a *temporal description logic*. While there have been some attempts to consider the general problem of combining such non-classical logics [45], it is only in specific areas that a systematic examination of detailed combinations has been carried out. Temporal description logics are just such an area.

The motivation for studying temporal description logics primarily arose from work on temporal databases [94, 24] and dynamic knowledge/plan representation [247, 22, 23]. A thorough survey of the varieties of combination, and their properties, is provided by Artale and Franconi in [25]. Different logical combinations can be produced, depending on what type of temporal logic is used (e.g., point-based or interval) and how the temporal dimension is incorporated. A simple temporal description logic can be obtained by combining a basic description logic with a standard point-based temporal logic, such as PTL. This combination can be carried out in a number of ways, two of which are termed *external* and *internal* in [25]:

- using an *external* approach, the temporal dimension is used to relate different (static) 'snapshots' of the system, each of which is described by a description logic formula;

- using an *internal* approach, the temporal dimension is effectively embedded within the description logic.

For simplicity, we consider the first view; for example,

> parentof(Michael, Christopher)
>
> $\Rightarrow \bigcirc$ parentof(Michael, James)

Here parentof(Michael, Christopher) is true at present, and within the current description logic theory, while parentof(Michael, James) will be true at the next moment in time. This, relatively simple, approach allows us to add a dynamic element to description logics. Yet, it is also important to be able to carry information between temporal states, for example,

$$\forall x. \text{parentof}(\text{Michael}, x) \Rightarrow \bigcirc \text{parentof}(\text{Michael}, x) \qquad (12.1)$$

However, just as in first-order temporal logics [263, 1] (see Section 12.2.7), the amount of information transferred between temporal states can drastically affect the properties of the logic. Thus, varieties including (12.1) above, where only individual elements of information are passed between temporal states, correspond to the class of *monodic* first-order temporal logics [149] in which decidability can be retained. Correspondingly, temporal description logics where concepts can evolve over time, but where the temporal evolution of roles is limited, can retain recursive enumerability and, often, decidability [294, 25].

12.5 Concluding Remarks

In this chapter we have provided an overview of a variety of aspects concerning temporal representation and reasoning. Even though this is not meant to be exhaustive, it is clear that not only are there many subtle aspects within the general area of temporal representation, but there is also a vast number of other areas and applications within which temporal approaches are relevant.

Although we have described many aspects of temporal representation and reasoning, others that we have omitted include:

- *temporal data mining*—the extraction of temporal patterns either from large datasets or streams of data [264, 46];

- *temporal databases*—the incorporation in (relational) databases and query languages of various temporal constraints [46, 273, 70]; and

- *probabilistic temporal logics*—the extension of temporal representations with probabilities and uncertainty [137], together with various applications such as probabilistic model checking [230].

As is clear in these areas, as well as in the topics examined within this chapter, research on temporal representation and reasoning continues to expand and progress. New formalisms, techniques and tools are being developed, and all of this points to the increasing relevance of temporal representation and reasoning to knowledge representation, and to Computer Science and Artificial Intelligence in general.

Acknowledgements

The author would like to thank a number of experts in the area who have reviewed this chapter and provided valuable insights and corrections, in particular: Anthony Galton; Valentin Goranko; Ian Hodkinson; Jixin Ma; Angelo Montanari; Ben Moszkowski; Wojciech Penczek; Ian Pratt-Hartmann; Mark Reynolds; Pierre-Yves Schobbens; and Mike Wooldridge.

Bibliography

[1] M. Abadi. The power of temporal proofs. *Theoretical Computer Science*, 65(1):35–83, 1989.

[2] M. Abadi and L. Lamport. The existence of refinement mappings. *Theoretical Computer Science*, 82(2):253–284, 1991.

[3] M. Abadi and Z. Manna. Non-clausal temporal deduction. In *Proc. Workshop on Logics of Programs, Lecture Notes in Computer Science*, vol. 193, pages 1–15. Springer, June 1985.

[4] M. Abadi and Z. Manna. Temporal logic programming. *Journal of Symbolic Computation*, 8(3):277–295, 1989.

[5] M. Abadi and Z. Manna. Nonclausal deduction in first-order temporal logic. *ACM Journal*, 37(2):279–317, April 1990.

[6] J.F. Allen. Maintaining knowledge about temporal intervals. *ACM Communications*, 26(11):832–843, November 1983.

[7] J.F. Allen. Towards a general theory of action and time. *Artificial Intelligence*, 23:123–154, 1984.

[8] J.F. Allen and P.J. Hayes. A common sense theory of time. In *Proc. 9th International Joint Conference on Artificial Intelligence (IJCAI)*, pages 528–531, August 1985.

[9] J.F. Allen and J.A. Koomen. Planning using a temporal world model. In *Proc. 8th International Joint Conference on Artificial Intelligence (IJCAI)*, pages 741–747, August 1983.

[10] R. Alur, C. Courcoubetis, and D.L. Dill. Model-checking in dense real-time. *Information and Computation*, 104(1):2–34, May 1993.

[11] R. Alur, C. Courcoubetis, N. Halbwachs, T.A. Henzinger, P.-H. Ho, X. Nicollin, A. Olivero, J. Sifakis, and S. Yovine. The algorithmic analysis of hybrid systems. *Theoretical Computer Science*, 138(1):3–34, 1995.

[12] R. Alur and D.L. Dill. The theory of timed automata. In de Bakker et al. [79], pages 45–73.

[13] R. Alur and D.L. Dill. A theory of timed automata. *Theoretical Computer Science*, 126(1):183–235, 1994.

[14] R. Alur, K. Etessami, and M. Yannakakis. Realizability and verification of MSC graphs. *Theoretical Computer Science*, 331(1):97–114, 2005.

[15] R. Alur and T.A. Henzinger. Logics and models of real time: A survey. In de Bakker et al. [79], pages 74–106.

[16] R. Alur and T.A. Henzinger. Real-time logics: complexity and expressiveness. *Information and Computation*, 104(1):35–77, 1993.

[17] R. Alur, T.A. Henzinger, and O. Kupferman. Alternating-time temporal logic. *ACM Journal*, 49(5):672–713, 2002.

[18] R. Alur, T.A. Henzinger, F.Y.C. Mang, S. Qadeer, S.K. Rajamani, and S. Tasiran. MOCHA: Modularity in model checking. In *Proc. 10th International Conference on Computer Aided Verification (CAV), Lecture Notes in Computer Science*, vol. 1427, pages 521–525. Springer, 1998.

[19] R. Alur and P. Madhusudan. Decision problems for timed automata: a survey. In *Formal Methods for the Design of Real-Time Systems (International School on Formal Methods for the Design of Computer, Communication and Software Systems), Lecture Notes in Computer Science*, vol. 3185, pages 1–24. Springer, 2004.

[20] C. Areces, P. Blackburn, and M. Marx. The computational complexity of hybrid temporal logics. *The Logic Journal of the IGPL*, 8(5):653–679, 1999.

[21] R. Armoni, L. Fix, A. Flaisher, R. Gerth, B. Ginsburg, T. Kanza, A. Landver, S. Mador-Haim, E. Singerman, A. Tiemeyer, M.Y. Vardi, and Y. Zbar. The For-Spec temporal logic: a new temporal property-specification language. In *Proc. 8th International Conference on Tools and Algorithms for the Construction and Analysis of Systems (TACAS), Lecture Notes in Computer Science*, vol. 2280, pages 296–311. Springer, 2002.

[22] A. Artale and E. Franconi. A temporal description logic for reasoning about actions and plans. *Journal of Artificial Intelligence Research (JAIR)*, 9:463–506, 1998.

[23] A. Artale and E. Franconi. Representing a robotic domain using temporal description logics. *Journal of Artificial Intelligence for Engineering Design, Analysis and Manufacturing (AIEDAM)*, 13(2):105–117, April 1999.

[24] A. Artale and E. Franconi. Temporal entity-relationship modeling with description logics. In *Proc. International Conference on Conceptual Modelling (ER)*. Springer-Verlag, November 1999.

[25] A. Artale and E. Franconi. Temporal description logics. In Fisher et al. [100], pages 375–388.

[26] G. Audemard, A. Cimatti, A. Kornilowicz, and R. Sebastiani. Bounded model checking for timed systems. In *Proc. 22nd IFIP WG 6.1 International Conference on Formal Techniques for Networked and Distributed Systems (FORTE), Lecture Notes in Computer Science*, vol. 2529, pages 243–259. Springer, 2002.

[27] F. Baader, D. Calvanese, D.L. McGuinness, D. Nardi, and P.F. Patel-Schneider, editors. *The Description Logic Handbook: Theory, Implementation, and Applications*. Cambridge University Press, 2003.

[28] M. Baaz, A. Leitsch, and R. Zach. Completeness of a first-order temporal logic with time-gaps. *Theoretical Computer Science*, 160(1–2):241–270, 1996.

[29] F. Bacchus and F. Kabanza. Using temporal logics to express search control knowledge for planning. *Artificial Intelligence*, 116(1–2):123–191, 2000.

[30] L. Bachmair and H. Ganzinger. Resolution theorem proving. In A. Robinson and A. Voronkov, editors. *Handbook of Automated Reasoning*, vol. I, pages 19–99. Elsevier Science, 2001 (Chapter 2).

[31] T. Ball and S.K. Rajamani. The SLAM toolkit. In *Proc. 13th International Conference on Computer Aided Verification (CAV), Lecture Notes in Computer Science*, vol. 2102, pages 260–264. Springer, 2001.

[32] B. Banieqbal and H. Barringer. A study of an extended temporal language and a temporal fixed point calculus. Technical Report UMCS-86-10-2, Department of Computer Science, University of Manchester, November 1986.

[33] B. Banieqbal and H. Barringer. Temporal logic with fixed points. In *Proc. Temporal Logic in Specification, Lecture Notes in Computer Science*, vol. 398, pages 62–74. Springer, 1987.

[34] C. Baral. Query Answering, 2007. (*In this volume*).

[35] C. Baral and M. Gelfond. Logic programming and reasoning about actions. In Fisher et al. [100], pages 389–428.

[36] H. Barringer, M. Fisher, D. Gabbay, R. Owens, and M. Reynolds, editors. *The Imperative Future: Principles of Executable Temporal Logics*. Research Studies Press, Chichester, United Kingdom, 1996.

[37] H. Barringer and D. Gabbay. Modal varieties of temporal logic. In Fisher et al. [100], pages 119–166.

[38] H. Barringer, R. Kuiper, and A. Pnueli. A compositional temporal approach to a CSP-like language. In *Proc. IFIP Working Conference "The Role of Abstract Models in Information Processing"*, Vienna, 1985.

[39] H. Barringer, R. Kuiper, and A. Pnueli. A really abstract concurrent model and its temporal logic. In *Proc. 13th ACM Symposium on the Principles of Programming Languages (POPL)*, January 1986.

[40] M. Baudinet. On the expressiveness of temporal logic programming. *Information and Computation*, 117(2):157–180, 1995.

[41] I. Beer, S. Ben-David, C. Eisner, D. Fisman, A. Gringauze, and Y. Rodeh. The temporal logic sugar. In *Proc. 13th International Conference on Computer Aided Verification (CAV), Lecture Notes in Computer Science*, vol. 2102, pages 363–367. Springer, 2001.

[42] G. Behrmann, A. David, K.G. Larsen, O. Möller, P. Pettersson, and W. Yi. UP-PAAL—present and future. In *Proc. 40th IEEE Conference on Decision and Control (CDC)*. IEEE Computer Society Press, 2001.

[43] S. Ben-David, D. Fisman, and S. Ruah. Embedding finite automata within regular expressions. In *Proc. 1st International Symposium on Leveraging Applications of Formal Methods (ISoLA)*. Springer, 2004.

[44] J. Bengtsson and W. Yi. Timed automata: semantics, algorithms and tools. In *Lecture Notes on Concurrency and Petri Nets, Lecture Notes in Computer Science*, vol. 3098. Springer-Verlag, 2004.

[45] B. Bennett, C. Dixon, M. Fisher, E. Franconi, I. Horrocks, and M. de Rijke. Combinations of modal logics. *AI Review*, 17(1):1–20, 2002.

[46] C. Bettini, S. Jajodia, and S. Wang. *Time Granularities in Databases, Data Mining and Temporal Reasoning*. Springer-Verlag, New York, USA, 2000.

[47] D. Beyer, C. Lewerentz, and A. Noack. Rabbit: A tool for BDD-based verification of real-time systems. In *Proc. 15th International Conference on Computer Aided Verification, (CAV), Lecture Notes in Computer Science*, vol. 2725, pages 122–125. Springer, 2003.

[48] A. Biere, A. Cimatti, E.M. Clarke, M. Fujita, and Y. Zhu. Symbolic model checking using SAT procedures instead of BDDs. In *Proc. Design Automation Conference (DAC)*, pages 317–320, 1999.

[49] A. Biere, A. Cimatti, E.M. Clarke, and Y. Zhu. Symbolic model checking without BDDs. In *Proc. 5th International Conference on Tools and Algorithms for Construction and Analysis of Systems (TACAS), Lecture Notes in Computer Science*, vol. 1579, pages 193–207. Springer, 1999.

[50] N. Bjørner, A. Browne, M. Colón, B. Finkbeiner, Z. Manna, H. Sipma, and T. Uribe. Verifying temporal properties of reactive systems: A STeP tutorial. *Formal Methods in System Design*, 16(3):227–270, 2000.

[51] N. Bjørner, Z. Manna, H. Sipma, and T. Uribe. Deductive verification of real-time systems using STeP. *Theoretical Computer Science*, 253(1):27–60, 2001.

[52] P. Blackburn. Nominal tense logic. *Notre Dame Journal of Formal Logic*, 34(1):56–83, 1993.

[53] P. Blackburn, M. de Rijke, and Y. Venema. *Modal Logic. Cambridge Tracts in Theoretical Computer Science*. Cambridge University Press, 2001.

[54] P. Blackburn and M. Tzakova. Hybrid languages and temporal logic. *Logic Journal of the IGPL*, 7(1):27–54, 1999.

[55] A. Blass and Y. Gurevich. Existential fixed-point logic. In *Computation Theory and Logic, Lecture Notes in Computer Science*, vol. 270, pages 20–36. Springer, 1987.

[56] L. Bolc and A. Szalas, editors. *Time and Logic: A Computational Approach.* Univ. College London Press, 1995.

[57] A. Bolotov and M. Fisher. A clausal resolution method for CTL branching-time temporal logic. *Journal of Experimental and Theoretical Artificial Intelligence*, 11:77–93, 1999.

[58] H. Bowman and S. Thompson. A decision procedure and complete axiomatization of finite interval temporal logic with projection. *Journal of Logic and Computation*, 13(2):195–239, 2003.

[59] D. Bresolin, A. Montanari, and G. Puppis. Time granularities and ultimately periodic automata. In *Proc. 9th European Conference on Logics in Artificial Intelligence (JELIA), Lecture Notes in Computer Science*, vol. 3229, pages 513–525. Springer, 2004.

[60] R.E. Bryant. Graph-based algorithms for boolean function manipulation. *IEEE Transactions on Computers*, C-35(8):677–691, August 1986.

[61] R.A. Bull and K. Segerberg. Basic modal logic. In Gabbay and Guenthner [110], Chapter II.1, pages 1–88.

[62] J.R. Burch, E.M. Clarke, D.E. Long, K.L. McMillan, and D.L. Dill. Symbolic model checking for sequential circuit verification. *IEEE Transactions on Computer-Aided Design of Integrated Circuits and Systems*, 13(4):401–424, 1994.

[63] J.R. Burch, E.M. Clarke, K.L. McMillan, D.L. Dill, and L.J. Hwang. Symbolic model checking: 10^{20} states and beyond. In *Proc. 5th IEEE Symposium on Logic in Computer Science (LICS)*, pages 428–439. IEEE Computer Society Press, 1990.

[64] J.P. Burgess. Axioms for tense logic; 1—'Since' and 'until'. *Notre Dame Journal of Formal Logic*, 23(4):367–374, October 1982.

[65] J.P. Burgess. Axioms for tense logic; 2—Time periods. *Notre Dame Journal of Formal Logic*, 23(4):375–383, October 1982.

[66] J.P. Burgess. Basic tense logic. In Gabbay and Guenthner [110], Chapter II.2, pages 89–134.

[67] A. Cavali and L. Fariñas del Cerro. A decision method for linear temporal logic. In *Proc. 7th International Conference on Automated Deduction (CADE), Lecture Notes in Computer Science*, vol. 170, pages 113–127. Springer, 1984.

[68] A.K. Chandra, D.C. Kozen, and L.J. Stockmeyer. Alternation. *ACM Journal*, 28(1):114–133, January 1981.

[69] Z. Chaochen and M.R. Hansen. *Duration Calculus—A Formal Approach to Real-Time Systems. EATCS Monographs in Theoretical Computer Science.* Springer, 2004.

[70] J. Chomicki and D. Toman. Temporal databases. In Fisher et al. [100], pages 429–468.

[71] A. Cimatti, E.M. Clarke, F. Giunchiglia, and M. Roveri. NUSMV: A new symbolic model verifier. In *Proc. 11th International Conference on Computer Aided Verification (CAV), Lecture Notes in Computer Science*, vol. 1633, pages 495–499. Springer, 1999.

[72] E.M. Clarke, E.A. Emerson, and A.P. Sistla. Automatic verification of finite-state concurrent systems using temporal logic specifications. *ACM Transactions on Programming Languages and Systems*, 8(2):244–263, 1986.

[73] E.M. Clarke, O. Grumberg, and D. Peled. *Model Checking*. MIT Press, December 1999.

[74] A. Cohn. Spatial Reasoning, 2007. (*In this volume*).

[75] M. D'Agostino, D. Gabbay, R. Hähnle, and J. Posegga, editors. *Handbook of Tableau Methods*. Kluwer Academic Press, 1999.

[76] M. Dam. CTL* and ECTL* as fragments of the modal mu-calculus. *Theoretical Computer Science*, 126(1):77–96, 1994.

[77] E. Davis. Infinite loops in finite time: Some observations. In *Proc. International Conference on Knowledge Representation and Reasoning (KR)*, pages 47–58, 1992.

[78] Duration calculus. http://www.iist.unu.edu/dc.

[79] J.W. de Bakker, C. Huizing, W.P. de Roever, and G. Rozenberg, editors. *Proc. REX Workshop on Real-Time: Theory in Practice, Lecture Notes in Computer Science*, vol. 600. Springer, 1991.

[80] R. Dechter, I. Meiri, and J. Pearl. Temporal constraint networks. *Artificial Intelligence*, 49(1–3):61–95, 1991.

[81] A. Degtyarev, M. Fisher, and B. Konev. Monodic temporal resolution. *ACM Transactions on Computational Logic*, 7(1):108–150, January 2006.

[82] A. Degtyarev, M. Fisher, and A. Lisitsa. Equality and monodic first-order temporal logic. *Studia Logica*, 72(2):147–156, 2002.

[83] S. Demri and R. Goré. Cut-free display calculi for nominal tense logics. In *Proc. Conference on Tableaux Calculi and Related Methods (TABLEAUX), Lecture Notes in Artificial Intelligence*, vol. 1617, pages 155–170. Springer-Verlag, 1999.

[84] P. Doherty. Temporal Action Logic, 2007. (*In this volume*).

[85] T. Drakengren and P. Jonsson. Computational complexity of temporal constraint problems. In Fisher et al. [100], pages 197–218.

[86] E.A. Emerson. Alternative semantics for temporal logics. *Theoretical Computer Science*, 26:121–130, 1983.

[87] E.A. Emerson. In *Handbook of Theoretical Computer Science*, pages 997–1071. Elsevier Science Publishers B.V., 1990 (chapter *Temporal Modal Logic*).

[88] E.A. Emerson and E.M. Clarke. Characterizing correctness properties of parallel programs using fixpoints. In *Proc. 7th International Colloquium on Automata, Languages and Programming (ICALP), Lecture Notes in Computer Science*, vol. 85, pages 169–181. Springer, 1980.

[89] E.A. Emerson and E.M. Clarke. Using branching time temporal logic to synthesize synchronization skeletons. *Science of Computer Programming*, 2(3):241–266, 1982.

[90] E.A. Emerson and J.Y. Halpern. Decision procedures and expressiveness in the temporal logic of branching time. *Journal of Computer and System Sciences*, 30:1–24, 1985.

[91] E.A. Emerson and J.Y. Halpern. "Sometimes" and "Not never" revisited: on branching versus linear time temporal logic. *ACM Journal*, 33(1):151–178, January 1986.

[92] E.A. Emerson and A.P. Sistla. Deciding full branching time logic. *Information and Control*, 61:175–201, 1984.

[93] J. Euzenat and A. Montanari. Time granularity. In Fisher et al. [100], pages 59–118.

[94] M. Finger and D. Gabbay. Adding a temporal dimension to a logic system. *Journal of Logic, Language, and Information*, 1:203–234, 1992.

[95] M. Fisher. A resolution method for temporal logic. In *Proc. 12th International Joint Conference on Artificial Intelligence (IJCAI)*, Sydney, Australia, 1991. Morgan Kaufman.

[96] M. Fisher. An introduction to executable temporal logics. *Knowledge Engineering Review*, 11(1):43–56, March 1996.

[97] M. Fisher. A normal form for temporal logic and its application in theorem-proving and execution. *Journal of Logic and Computation*, 7(4), July 1997.

[98] M. Fisher. METATEM: the story so far. In *Proc. 3rd International Workshop on Programming Multiagent Systems (ProMAS), Lecture Notes in Artificial Intelligence*, vol. 3862. Springer-Verlag, 2006.

[99] M. Fisher, C. Dixon, and M. Peim. Clausal temporal resolution. *ACM Transactions on Computational Logic*, 2(1):12–56, January 2001.

[100] M. Fisher, D. Gabbay, and L. Vila, editors. *Handbook of Temporal Reasoning in Artificial Intelligence, Foundations of Artificial Intelligence*, vol. 1. Elsevier Press, 2005.

[101] M. Fitting. Tableau methods of proof for modal logics. *Notre Dame Journal of Formal Logic*, 13(2):237–247, April 1972.

[102] K. Forbus. Qualitative Reasoning, 2007. (*In this volume*).

[103] M. Fox and D. Long. PDDL2.1: an extension to PDDL for expressing temporal planning domains. *Journal of Artificial Intelligence Research (JAIR)*, 20:61–124, 2003.

[104] M. Fox and D. Long. Time in planning. In Fisher et al. [100], pages 497–536.

[105] M. Franceschet. Dividing and conquering the layered land. PhD thesis, Department of Mathematics and Computer Science, University of Udine, Italy, 2001.

[106] T. French and M. Reynolds. A sound and complete proof system for QPTL. In *Proc. International Conference on Advances in Modal Logic (AiML)*, 2002.

[107] D. Gabbay. Model theory for tense logics and decidability results for non-classical logics. *Annals of Mathematical Logic*, 8:185–295, 1975.

[108] D. Gabbay. Expressive functional completeness in tense logic (preliminary report). In U. Monnich, editor. *Aspects of Philosophical Logic*, pages 91–117. Reidel, Dordrecht, 1981.

[109] D. Gabbay. Declarative past and imperative future: executable temporal logic for interactive systems. In *Proc. International Colloquium on Temporal Logic in Specification, Lecture Notes in Computer Science*, vol. 398, pages 67–89. Springer-Verlag, 1989.

[110] D. Gabbay and F. Guenthner, editors. *Handbook of Philosophical Logic (II), Synthese Library*, vol. 165. Reidel, 1984.

[111] D. Gabbay and I. Hodkinson. An axiomitization of the temporal logic with until and since over the real numbers. *Journal of Logic and Computation*, 1(2):229–259, 1990.

[112] D. Gabbay, I. Hodkinson, and M. Reynolds. *Temporal Logic: Mathematical Foundations and Computational Aspects*, vol. 1. Clarendon Press, Oxford, 1994.

[113] D. Gabbay, A. Pnueli, S. Shelah, and J. Stavi. The temporal analysis of fairness. In *Proc. 7th ACM Symposium on the Principles of Programming Languages (POPL)*, pages 163–173, Las Vegas, Nevada, January 1980.

[114] D. Gabbay, M. Reynolds, and M. Finger. *Temporal Logic: Mathematical Foundations and Computational Aspects*, vol. 2. Clarendon Press, Oxford, 2000.

[115] D. Gabelaia, R. Kontchakov, A. Kurucz, F. Wolter, and M. Zakharyaschev. Combining spatial and temporal logics: expressiveness vs. complexity. *Journal of Artificial Intelligence Research (JAIR)*, 23:167–243, 2005.

[116] A.P. Galton. *The Logic of Aspect*. Clarendon Press, Oxford, 1984.

[117] A.P. Galton. A critical examination of Allen's theory of action and time. *Artificial Intelligence*, 42:159–188, 1990.

[118] A.P. Galton. An investigation of 'Non-intermingling' principles in temporal logic. *Journal of Logic and Computation*, 6(2):271–294, 1996.

[119] A.P. Galton. Eventualities. In Fisher et al. [100], pages 25–58.

[120] J. Garson. Quantification in modal logic. In Gabbay and Guenthner [110], Chapter II.6, pages 249–307.

[121] A. Gerevini. Processing qualitative temporal constraints. In Fisher et al. [100], pages 247–278.

[122] R. Gerth, D. Peled, M.Y. Vardi, and P. Wolper. Simple on-the-fly automatic verification of linear temporal logic. In *Proc. 15th IFIP WG6.1 International Symposium on Protocol Specification, Testing and Verification (PSTV)*, IFIP Conference Proceedings, vol. 38, pages 3–18. Chapman & Hall, 1996.

[123] R. Goldblatt. *Logics of Time and Computation*. CSLI Lecture Notes Stanford, CA, 1987.

[124] R. Gómez and H. Bowman. PITL2MONA: implementing a decision procedure for propositional interval temporal logic. *Journal of Applied Non-Classical Logics*, 14(1–2):105–148, 2004.

[125] V. Goranko. Temporal logic with reference pointers. In ICTL'94 [158], pages 133–148.

[126] V. Goranko, A. Montanari, and G. Sciavicco. A general tableau method for propositional interval temporal logics. In *Proc. International Conference on Automated Reasoning with Analytic Tableaux and Related Methods (TABLEAUX)*, Lecture Notes in Computer Science, vol. 2796, pages 102–116. Springer, 2003.

[127] V. Goranko, A. Montanari, and G. Sciavicco. A road map of interval temporal logics and duration calculi. *Journal of Applied Non-Classical Logics*, 14(1–2):9–54, 2004.

[128] G.D. Gough. Decision procedures for temporal logic. Master's thesis, Department of Computer Science, University of Manchester, UK, October 1984.

[129] P. Gribomont and P. Wolper. In *From Modal Logic to Deductive Databases: Introducing a Logic Based Approach to Artificial Intelligence*, pages 165–234. Wiley, 1989 (chapter *Temporal Logic*).

[130] D. Guelev. A complete proof system for first-order interval temporal logic with projection. *Journal of Logic and Computation*, 14(2):215–249, 2004.

[131] D. Guelev and D. van Hung. A relatively complete axiomatisation of projection onto state in the duration Calculus. *Journal of Applied Non-Classical Logics*, 14(1–2):149–180, 2004.

[132] Y. Gurevich and S. Shelah. The decision problem for branching time logic. *Journal of Symbolic Logic*, 50(3):668–681, 1985.

[133] S. Haack. *Philosophy of Logics*. Cambridge University Press, 1978.

[134] R. Hale and B. Moszkowski. Parallel programming in temporal logic. In *Proc. Parallel Architectures and Languages Europe (PARLE), Lecture Notes in Computer Science*, vol. 259, pages 277–296. Springer, 1987.

[135] J. Halpern, Z. Manna, and B. Moszkowski. A hardware semantics based on temporal intervals. In *Proc. International Colloquium on Automata Languages and Programming (ICALP), Lecture Notes in Computer Science*, vol. 154, pages 278–291. Springer-Verlag, 1983.

[136] J. Halpern and Y. Shoham. A propositional modal logic of time intervals. *ACM Journal*, 38(4):935–962, 1991.

[137] S. Hanks and D. Madigan. Probabilistic temporal reasoning. In Fisher et al. [100], pages 315–342.

[138] P. Hasle and P. Øhrstrøm. Foundations of temporal logic—The WWW-site for prior-studies. http://www.kommunikation.aau.dk/prior.

[139] J.G. Henriksen and P.S. Thiagarajan. Dynamic linear time temporal logic. *Annals of Pure and Applied Logic*, 96(1–3):187–207, 1999.

[140] T. Henzinger. It's about time: real-time logics reviewed. In *Proc. 9th International Conference on Concurrency Theory (CONCUR), Lecture Notes in Computer Science*, vol. 1466, pages 439–454. Springer, 1998.

[141] T. Henzinger, P.-H. Ho, and H. Wong-Toi. HYTECH: A model checker for hybrid systems. *International Journal on Software Tools for Technology Transfer*, 1(1–2):110–122, 1997.

[142] T.A. Henzinger, X. Nicollin, J. Sifakis, and S. Yovine. Symbolic model checking for real-time systems. *Information and Computation*, 111(2):193–244, 1994.

[143] B. Hirsch and U. Hustadt. Translating PLTL into WS1S: Application description. In *Proc. Methods for Modalities (M4M) II*, Amsterdam, Netherlands, 2001.

[144] R. Hirsch. From points to intervals. *Journal of Applied Non-Classical Logics*, 4(1):7–27, 1994.

[145] R. Hirsch. Relation algebras of intervals. *Artificial Intelligence*, 83:1–29, 1996.

[146] I. Hodkinson. Monodic packed fragment with equality is decidable. *Studia Logica*, 72:185–197, 2002.

[147] I. Hodkinson and M. Reynolds. Separation—past, present, and future. In *We Will Show Them! Essays in Honour of Dov Gabbay*, vol. 2, pages 117–142. College Publications, 2005.

[148] I. Hodkinson and M. Reynolds. Temporal logic. In P. Blackburn, J. van Benthem, and F. Wolter, editors. *Handbook of Modal Logic*. Elsevier, 2006 (Chapter 11).

[149] I. Hodkinson, F. Wolter, and M. Zakharyaschev. Decidable fragments of first-order temporal logics. *Annals of Pure and Applied Logic*, 106:85–134, 2000.

[150] I. Hodkinson, F. Wolter, and M. Zakharyaschev. Decidable and undecidable fragments of first-order branching temporal logics. In *Proc. 17th IEEE Symposium on Logic in Computer Science (LICS)*, pages 393–402. IEEE Computer Society, 2002.

[151] G.J. Holzmann. *Design and Validation of Computer Protocols*. Prentice-Hall, Englewood Cliffs, NJ, 1991.

[152] G.J. Holzmann. The model checker spin. *IEEE Transactions on Software Engineering*, 23(5):279–295, May 1997 (Special issue on Formal Methods in Software Practice).

[153] G.J. Holzmann. *The Spin Model Checker: Primer and Reference Manual.* Addison-Wesley, November 2003.

[154] I. Horrocks. Description Logics, 2007. (*In this volume*).

[155] U. Hustadt, B. Konev, A. Riazanov, and A. Voronkov. TeMP: A temporal monodic prover. In *Proc. 2nd International Joint Conference on Automated Reasoning (IJCAR), Lecture Notes in Artificial Intelligence*, vol. 3097, pages 326–330. Springer, 2004.

[156] Hybrid logics web page. http://hylo.loria.fr.

[157] HyTech: The HYbrid TECHnology tool. http://embedded.eecs.berkeley.edu/research/hytech.

[158] D. Gabbay and H.-J. Ohlbach, editors. In *Proc. First International Conference on Temporal Logic (ICTL). Lecture Notes in Computer Science*, vol. 827. Springer, 1994.

[159] Interval temporal logic. http://www.cse.dmu.ac.uk/STRL/ITL//itlhomepage.html.

[160] Java PathFinder. http://javapathfinder.sourceforge.net.

[161] J. Kamp. Tense logic and the theory of linear order. PhD thesis, University of California, Los Angeles, May 1968.

[162] J. Kamp and U. Reyle. *From Discourse to Logic*. Kluwer, Dordrecht, 1993.

[163] S. Katz and D. Peled. Interleaving set temporal logic. *Theoretical Computer Science*, 75(3):263–287, 1990.

[164] Y. Kesten, Z. Manna, and A. Pnueli. Temporal verification of simulation and refinement. In *A Decade of Concurrency, Reflections and Perspectives, REX School/Symposium, Lecture Notes in Computer Science*, vol. 803. Springer, 1994.

[165] Y. Kesten, Z. Manna, and A. Pnueli. Verification of clocked and hybrid systems. *Acta Informatica*, 36(11):837–912, 2000.

[166] Y. Kesten and A. Pnueli. Complete proof system for QPTL. *Journal of Logic and Computation*, 12(5):701–745, 2002.

[167] B. Konev, A. Degtyarev, C. Dixon, M. Fisher, and U. Hustadt. Mechanising first-order temporal resolution. *Information and Computation*, 199(1–2):55–86, 2005.

[168] R. Kontchakov, C. Lutz, F. Wolter, and M. Zakharyaschev. Temporalizing tableaux. *Studia Logica*, 76(1):91–134, 2004.

[169] R. Kowalski and M. Sergot. A logic-based calculus of events. *New Generation Computing*, 1(4):67–95, 1986.

[170] R. Koymans. Specifying message passing systems requires extending temporal logic. In *Proc. Temporal Logic in Specification, Lecture Notes in Computer Science*, vol. 398, pages 213–223. Springer, 1987.

[171] D. Kozen. Results on the propositional mu-calculus. *Theoretical Computer Science*, 27:333–354, 1983.

[172] F. Kröger. *Temporal Logic of Programs. EATCS Monographs on Theoretical Computer Science*, vol. 8. Springer-Verlag, Berlin, 1987.

[173] Kronos tool. http://www-verimag.imag.fr/TEMPORISE/kronos/.

[174] M.Z. Kwiatkowska, G. Norman, and D. Parker. Probabilistic symbolic model checking with PRISM: a hybrid approach. In *Proc. 8th International Conference on Tools and Algorithms for the Construction and Analysis of Systems (TACAS), Lecture Notes in Computer Science*, vol. 2280, pages 52–66. Springer, 2002.

[175] P. Ladkin. The completeness of a natural system for reasoning with time intervals. In *Proc. 10th International Joint Conference on Artificial Intelligence (IJCAI)*, pages 462–467, August 1987.

[176] P. Ladkin and R. Maddux. On binary constraint problems. *ACM Journal*, 41:435–469, 1994.

[177] L. Lamport. The temporal logic of actions. *ACM Transactions on Programming Languages and Systems*, 16(3):872–923, May 1994.

[178] L. Lamport. *Specifying Systems, The TLA+ Language and Tools for Hardware and Software Engineers*. Addison-Wesley, 2002.

[179] F. Laroussinie, N. Markey, and Ph. Schnoebelen. Temporal logic with forgettable past. In *Proc. 17th IEEE Symposium on Logic in Computer Science (LICS)*, pages 383–392. IEEE Computer Society, 2002.

[180] K.G. Larsen, P. Pettersson, and W. Yi. Model-checking for real-time systems. In *Proc. Conference on Fundamentals of Computation Theory, Lecture Notes in Computer Science*, vol. 965, pages 62–88. August 1995.

[181] E.J. Lemmon and D. Scott. *An Introduction to Modal Logic. American Philosophical Quarterly, Monograph Series*, vol. 11. 1977. (Originally written in 1963 as a draft for a book.).

[182] O. Lichtenstein, A. Pnueli, and L. Zuck. The glory of the past. In *Proc. Workshop on Logics of Programs, Lecture Notes in Computer Science*, vol. 193, pages 196–218. Springer, 1985.

[183] G. Ligozat. Weak representation of interval algebras. In *Proc. 8th American National Conference on Artificial Intelligence (AAAI)*, pages 715–720, 1990.

[184] G. Ligozat. Tractable relations in temporal reasoning: pre-convex relations. In *Proc. ECAI Workshop on Spatial and Temporal Reasoning*, August 1994.

[185] F. Lin. Situation Calculus, 2007. (*In this volume*).

[186] C. Liu and M. Orgun. Dealing with multiple granularity of time in temporal logic programming. *Journal of Symbolic Computation*, 22(5–6):699–720, 1996.

[187] LPG: A fully-automated domain-independent planner for PDDL2.2 domains. http://zeus.ing.unibs.it/lpg.

[188] The logics workbench. http://www.lwb.unibe.ch.

[189] J. Ma and B. Knight. Reified temporal logics: an overview. *Artificial Intelligence Review*, 15(3):189–217, 2001.

[190] J. Ma, B. Knight, and T. Peng. Temporal reasoning about action and change. In K. Anjaneyulu, M. Sasikumar, and S. Ramani, editors. *Knowledge Based Computer Systems—Research and Applications*, pages 193–204. Narosa Publishing House, 1996.

[191] Z. Manna and A. Pnueli. *The Temporal Logic of Reactive and Concurrent Systems: Specification*. Springer-Verlag, 1992.

[192] Z. Manna and A. Pnueli. *The Temporal Verification of Reactive Systems: Safety*. Springer-Verlag, New York, 1995.

[193] M. Marx and M. Reynolds. Undecidability of compass logic. *Journal of Logic and Computation*, 9:897–914, 1999.

[194] W. May and P.H. Schmitt. A tableau calculus for first-order branching time logic. In *Proc. International Conference on Formal and Applied Practical Reasoning (FAPR), Lecture Notes in Computer Science*, vol. 1085, pages 399–413. Springer, 1996.

[195] M.C. Mayer and S. Cerrito. Variants of first-order modal logics. In *Proc. International Conference on Automated Reasoning with Analytic Tableaux and Related Methods (TABLEAUX), Lecture Notes in Computer Science*, vol. 1847, pages 175–189. Springer, 2000.

[196] M.C. Mayer, A. Orlandini, G. Balestreri, and C. Limongelli. A planner fully based on linear time logic. In *Proc. AI Planning Systems*, pages 347–354, 2000.

[197] D. McDermott. A temporal logic for reasoning about processes and plans. *Cognitive Science*, 6:101–155, 1982.

[198] K.L. McMillan. *Symbolic Model Checking*. Kluwer Academic Publishers, 1993.

[199] S. Merz. Decidability and incompleteness results for first-order temporal logic of linear time. *Journal of Applied Non-Classical Logics*, 2:139–156, 1992.

[200] Mocha: Exploiting modularity in model checking. http://www.cis.upenn.edu/~mocha.

[201] F. Moller and A. Rabinovich. Counting on CTL*: on the expressive power of monadic path logic. *Information and Computation*, 184(1):147–159, 2003.

[202] A. Montanari. Metric and layered temporal logic for time granularity. PhD thesis, University of Amsterdam, Amsterdam, Netherlands, September 1996. ILLC Dissertation Series 1996-02.

[203] Y. Moses. Reasoning about Knowledge and Belief, 2007. (*In this volume*).

[204] B. Moszkowski. Reasoning about digital circuits. PhD thesis, Computer Science Department, Stanford University, 1983.

[205] B. Moszkowski. *Executing Temporal Logic Programs*. Cambridge University Press, Cambridge, UK, 1986.

[206] B. Moszkowski. Compositional reasoning about projected and infinite time. In *Proc. 1st IEEE International Conference on Engineering of Complex Computer Systems (ICECCS)*, pages 238–245. IEEE Computer Society Press, 1995.

[207] B. Moszkowski. Compositional reasoning using interval temporal logic and tempura. In *Compositionality: The Significant Difference, Lecture Notes in Computer Science*, vol. 1536, pages 439–464. Springer, 1998.

[208] B. Moszkowski and Z. Manna. Reasoning in interval temporal logic. In *Proc. AMC/NSF/ONR Workshop on Logics of Programs, Lecture Notes in Computer Science*, vol. 164, pages 371–383. Springer-Verlag, 1984.

[209] E. Mueller. Event Calculus, 2007. (*In this volume*).

[210] A. Nonnengart. Resolution-based calculi for modal and temporal logics. In *Proc. 13th International Conference on Automated Deduction (CADE), Lecture Notes in Artificial Intelligence*, vol. 1104, pages 598–612. Springer, 1996.

[211] NuSMV: A new symbolic model checker. http://nusmv.irst.itc.it.

[212] H.-J. Ohlbach. Translation methods for non-classical logics—an overview. *Bulletin of the Interest Group in Propositional and Predicate Logics (IGPL)*, 1(1):69–90, 1993.

[213] H.-J. Ohlbach and D. Gabbay. Calendar logic. *Journal of Applied Non-Classical Logics*, 8(4):291–324, 1998.

[214] M. Orgun and W. Ma. An overview of temporal and modal logic programming, In ICTL'94 [158], pages 445–479.

[215] M. Orgun and W. Wadge. Theory and practice of temporal logic programming. In L. Fariñas del Cerro and M. Penttonen, editors. *Intensional Logics for Programming*. Oxford University Press, 1992.

[216] J. Ostroff. *Temporal Logic of Real-Time Systems*. Research Studies Press, 1990.

[217] J. Ostroff. Formal methods for the specification and design of real-time safety critical systems. *Journal of Systems and Software*, 18(1):33–60, 1992.

[218] W. Penczek. Axiomatizations of temporal logics on trace systems. *Fundamenta Informaticae*, 25(2):183–200, 1996.

[219] W. Penczek and A. Polrola. *Advances in Verification of Time Petri Nets and Timed Automata: A Temporal Logic Approach. Studies in Computational Intelligence*, vol. 20. Springer, 2006.

[220] R. Pliuskevicius. The saturated tableaux for linear miniscoped Horn-like temporal logic. *Journal of Automated Reasoning*, 13:391–407, 1994.

[221] R. Pliuskevicius. On an *omega*-decidable deductive procedure for non-Horn sequents of a restricted FTL. In *Proc. 1st International Conference on Computational Logic, Lecture Notes in Computer Science*, vol. 1861, pages 523–537. Springer, 2000.

[222] A. Pnueli. The temporal logic of programs. In *Proc. 18th Symposium on the Foundations of Computer Science (FOCS)*, Providence, USA, November 1977.

[223] A. Pnueli. The temporal semantics of concurrent programs. *Theoretical Computer Science*, 13:45–60, 1981.

[224] A. Pnueli and T. Arons. TLPVS: A PVS-based LTL verification system. In *Verification: Theory and Practice, Lecture Notes in Computer Science*, vol. 2772, pages 598–625. Springer, 2003.

[225] A. Pnueli and Y. Kesten. A deductive proof system for CTL. In *Proc. 13th International Conference on Concurrency Theory (CONCUR), Lecture Notes in Computer Science*, vol. 2421, pages 24–40. Springer, 2002.

[226] A. Pnueli and R. Rosner. On the synthesis of a reactive module. In *Proc. 16th ACM Symposium on Principles of Programming Languages (POPL)*, pages 179–190, New York, 1989.

[227] M.R. Prasad, A. Biere, and A. Gupta. A survey of recent advances in SAT-based formal verification. *International Journal on Software Tools for Technology Transfer (STTT)*, 7(2):156–173, 2005.

[228] I. Pratt-Hartmann. Temporal prepositions and their logic. *Artificial Intelligence*, 166(1–2):1–36, 2005.

[229] A. Prior. *Past, Present and Future*. Clarendon Press, Oxford, UK, 1967.

[230] PRISM: Probabilistic symbolic model checker. http://www.cs.bham.ac.uk/~dxp/prism.

[231] PSL/Sugar Consortium Web Page. http://www.pslsugar.org.

[232] G. Puppis. Automata for branching and layered temporal structures. PhD thesis, Department of Mathematics and Computer Science, University of Udine, Italy, 2006.

[233] The PVS specification and verification system. http://pvs.csl.sri.com.

[234] Rabbit timed automata. http://www-sst.informatik.tu-cottbus.de/~db/Rabbit.

[235] The RED (Region Encoding Diagram) system. http://cc.ee.ntu.edu.tw/~farn/red.

[236] H. Reichgelt and L. Vila. Temporal qualification in artificial intelligence. In Fisher et al. [100], pages 167–196.

[237] R. Reiter. *Knowledge in Action*. MIT Press, 2001.

[238] N. Rescher and A. Urquart. *Temporal Logic*. Springer-Verlag, 1971.

[239] M. Reynolds. Axiomatisation and decidability of F and P in cyclical time. *Journal of Philosophical Logic*, 23:197–224, 1994.

[240] M. Reynolds. More past glories. In *Proc. IEEE Symposium on Logic in Computer Science (LICS)*. IEEE Press, 2000.

[241] M. Reynolds. An axiomatization of full computation tree logic. *Journal of Symbolic Logic*, 66(3):1011–1057, 2001.

[242] M. Reynolds. An axiomatization of PCTL*. *Information and Computation*, 201(1):72–119, 2005.

[243] M. Reynolds and C. Dixon. Theorem-proving for discrete temporal logic. In Fisher et al. [100], pages 279–314.

[244] J.A. Robinson. A machine based logic based on the resolution principle. *ACM Journal*, 12(1):23–41, January 1965.

[245] R. Rosner and A. Pnueli. A choppy logic. In *Proc. IEEE Symposium on Logic in Computer Science (LICS)*, pages 306–313. IEEE Computer Society, 1986.

[246] M. Sabbadin and A. Zanardo. Topological aspects of branching-time semantics. *Studia Logica*, 75(3):271–286, 2003.

[247] K.D. Schild. Combining terminological logics with tense logic. In *Progress in Artificial Intelligence—Proc. 6th Portuguese Conference on Artificial Intelligence (EPIA)*, *Lecture Notes in Computer Science*, vol. 727, pages 105–120. Springer, 1993.

[248] B.-H. Schlingloff. Expressive completeness of temporal logic of trees. *Journal of Applied Non-Classical Logics*, 2(2), 1992.

[249] P.-Y. Schobbens, J.-F. Raskin, and T. Henzinger. Axioms for real-time logics. *Theoretical Computer Science*, 274(1–2):151–182, 2002.

[250] L. Schubert. Natural Language Processing, 2007. (*In this volume*).

[251] E. Schwalb and L. Vila. Temporal constraints: a survey. *Constraints*, 3(2–3):129–149, 1998.

[252] R.L. Schwartz, P.M. Melliar-Smith, and F.H. Vogt. An interval-based temporal logic. In *Proc. AMC/NSF/ONR Workshop on Logics of Programs*, *Lecture Notes in Computer Science*, vol. 164, pages 443–457. Springer, June 1984.

[253] S. Schwendimann. A new one-pass tableau calculus for PLTL. In *Proc. Workshop on Automated Reasoning with Analytic Tableaux and Related Methods (TABLEAUX)*, *Lectures Notes in Computer Science*, vol. 1397, pages 277–291. Springer-Verlag, 1998.

[254] A.P. Sistla, M.Y. Vardi, and P. Wolper. The complementation problem for Büchi automata with applications to temporal logic. *Theoretical Computer Science*, 49:217–237, 1987.

[255] The SLAM Project: Debugging system software via static analysis. http://research.microsoft.com/slam.

[256] On-the-fly, LTL model checking with SPIN. http://spinroot.com/spin/whatispin.html.

[257] M. Steedman. Dynamic semantics for tense and aspect. In *Proc. 14th International Joint Conference on Artificial Intelligence (IJCAI)*, pages 1292–1298, 1995.

[258] M. Steedman. Temporality. In J.F.A.K. van Benthem and A. Ter Meulen, editors. *Handbook of Logic and Language*. MIT Press, 1997.

[259] The Stanford Temporal Prover. http://www-step.stanford.edu.

[260] C. Stirling. Modal and temporal logics. In S. Abramsky, D. Gabbay, and T. Maibaum, editors. *Handbook of Logic in Computer Science*. Oxford University Press, 1992.

[261] SystemVerilog assertions. http://www.eda-stds.org/sv-ac.
[262] A. Szalas. Arithmetical axiomatisation of first-order temporal logic. *Information Processing Letters*, 26:111–116, November 1987.
[263] A. Szalas and L. Holenderski. Incompleteness of first-order temporal logic with until. *Theoretical Computer Science*, 57:317–325, 1988.
[264] Temporal data mining website. http://www.temporaldatamining.com.
[265] A. ter Meulen. *Representing Time in Natural Language: The Dynamic Interpretation of Tense and Aspect*. The MIT Press, Cambridge, MA, 1995.
[266] A. ter Meulen. Temporal reasoning in natural language. In Fisher et al. [100], pages 559–586.
[267] D. Thérien and T. Wilke. Nesting until and since in linear temporal logic. *Theory of Computing Systems*, 37(1):111–131, 2004.
[268] P.S. Thiagarajan and I. Walukiewicz. An expressively complete linear time temporal logic for Mazurkiewicz traces. *Information and Computation*, 179(2):230–249, 2002.
[269] J. Thornton, M. Beaumont, A. Sattar, and M.J. Maher. Applying local search to temporal reasoning. In *Proc. International Symposium on Temporal Representation and Reasoning (TIME)*, pages 94–99, 2002.
[270] The TLPVS WWW page. http://www.wisdom.weizmann.ac.il/~verify/tlpvs/index.shtml.
[271] P. Traverso. Planning, 2007. (*In this volume*).
[272] S. Tripakis, S. Yovine, and A. Bouajjani. Checking timed Büchi automata emptiness efficiently. *Formal Methods in System Design*, 26(3):267–292, 2005.
[273] TSQL2 Temporal Query Language. http://www.cs.arizona.edu/~rts/tsql2.html.
[274] J.F.A.K. van Benthem. Correspondence theory. In Gabbay and Guenthner [110], Chapter II.4, pages 167–248.
[275] J.F.A.K. van Benthem. *The Logic of Time*. 2nd edition. Kluwer Academic Publishers, 1991.
[276] W. van der Hoek and M. Wooldridge. Cooperation, knowledge, and time: alternating-time temporal epistemic logic and its applications. *Studia Logica*, 75(1):125–157, 2003.
[277] W. van der Hoek and M. Wooldridge. Multi-Agent Systems, 2007. (*In this volume*).
[278] M.Y. Vardi. A temporal fixpoint calculus. In *Proc. 15th ACM Symposium on Principles of Programming Languages (POPL)*, pages 250–259, 1988.
[279] M.Y. Vardi. An automata-theoretic approach to linear temporal logic. In *Logics for Concurrency—Structure versus Automata (Proc. 8th Banff Higher Order Workshop)*, Lecture Notes in Computer Science, vol. 1043, pages 238–266. Springer, 1996.
[280] M.Y. Vardi. Alternating automata: unifying truth and validity checking for temporal logics. In *Proc. 14th International Conference on Automated Deduction (CADE)*, Lecture Notes in Computer Science, vol. 1249, pages 191–206. Springer, 1997.
[281] M.Y. Vardi. Branching vs. linear time: final showdown. In *Proc. 7th International Conference on Tools and Algorithms for the Construction and Analysis of Systems (TACAS)*, Lecture Notes in Computer Science, vol. 2031, pages 1–22. Springer-Verlag, 2001.

[282] M.Y. Vardi and P. Wolper. Reasoning about infinite computations. *Information and Computation*, 115(1):1–37, 1994.

[283] Y. Venema. A logic with the chop operator. *Journal of Logic and Computation*, 1:453–476, 1991.

[284] G. Venkatesh. A decision method for temporal logic based on resolution. In *Proc. Conference on Foundations of Software Technology and Theoretical Computer Science (FSTTCS), Lecture Notes in Computer Science*, vol. 206, pages 272–289. Springer-Verlag, Berlin–Heidelberg–New York, 1986.

[285] Verics system. http://www.ipipan.waw.pl/~penczek/abmpw/verics-ang.htm.

[286] V. Vidal and H. Geffner. Branching and pruning: an optimal temporal POCL planner based on constraint programming. *Artificial Intelligence*, 170(3):298–335, 2006.

[287] L. Vila. Formal theories of time and temporal incidence. In Fisher et al. [100], pages 1–24.

[288] L. Vila and H. Yoshino. Time in automated legal reasoning. In Fisher et al. [100], pages 537–558.

[289] W. Visser, K. Havelund, G. Brat, and S. Park. Model checking programs. In *Proc. International Conference on Automated Software Engineering (ASE)*, 2000.

[290] A. Voronkov. First-Order Reasoning, 2007. (*In this volume*).

[291] T. Walsh. Constraint Satisfaction, 2007. (*In this volume*).

[292] P. Wolper. Temporal logic can be more expressive. *Information and Control*, 56(1–2):72–99, 1983.

[293] P. Wolper. The tableau method for temporal logic: an overview. *Logique et Analyse*, 110–111:119–136, June–Sept. 1985.

[294] F. Wolter and M. Zakharyaschev. Temporalizing description logics. In *Proc. 2nd International Workshop on Frontiers of Combining Systems (FroCoS)*, Amsterdam, NL, 1998.

[295] F. Wolter and M. Zakharyaschev. Axiomatizing the monodic fragment of first-order temporal logic. *Annals of Pure and Applied Logic*, 118(1–2):133–145, 2002.

[296] C. Zhou, C.A.R. Hoare, and A.P. Ravn. A calculus of durations. *Information Processing Letters*, 40(5):269–276, 1991.

Handbook of Knowledge Representation
Edited by F. van Harmelen, V. Lifschitz and B. Porter
© 2008 Elsevier B.V. All rights reserved
DOI: 10.1016/S1574-6526(07)03013-1

Chapter 13

Qualitative Spatial Representation and Reasoning

Anthony G. Cohn and Jochen Renz

13.1 Introduction

The need for spatial representations and spatial reasoning is ubiquitous in AI—from robot planning and navigation, to interpreting visual inputs, to understanding natural language—in all these cases the need to represent and reason about spatial aspects of the world is of key importance. Related fields of research, such as geographic information science (GIScience) [70], have also driven the spatial representation and reasoning community to produce efficient, expressive and useful calculi.

Whereas there has been considerable research in spatial representations which are based on metric measurements, in particular within the vision (e.g., [62, 137]) and robotics communities (e.g., [198]), and also on raster and vector representations in GIScience (e.g., [214]), in this chapter we concentrate on symbolic, and in particular *qualitative* representations. Chapter 9 is devoted to qualitative reasoning (QR) more generally, whereas here we limit our attention specifically to qualitative spatial, and spatio-temporal reasoning (henceforth QSR).

13.1.1 What is Qualitative Spatial Reasoning?

Chapter 9 concentrates on linear quantities; in some cases this suffices to reason about space in a qualitative way, for example, when reasoning about the position of a sliding block, or the level of a tank. However, space is multidimensional, and is not in general adequately represented by a single scalar quantity. Consider using Allen's interval calculus, briefly mentioned in Chapter 12, which distinguishes 13 jointly exhaustive and pairwise disjoint relations that may hold between a pair of convex (one-piece) intervals, see Fig. 13.1(a). Now we consider using this representation to model two-dimensional regions, by projecting 2D space onto two separate linear dimensions; in

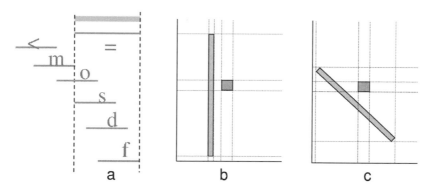

Figure 13.1: (a) The 13 jointly exhaustive and pairwise disjoint Allen interval relations between a pair of convex intervals (the top thick line and each of the thinner lines below)—only seven are displayed—the last six are asymmetric and have inverses. Projecting regions onto axes and using Allen's interval calculus can give misleading results: in (b) the small region is discrete from the larger along the x-axis, whilst in (c) it is contained in the larger region along both axes.

Fig. 13.1(b) this works well, but in Fig. 13.1(c) it is not so satisfactory—the smaller region appears to be contained in the larger.[1]

Early attempts at qualitative spatial reasoning within the QR community led to the 'poverty conjecture' [84]. Although purely qualitative representations were quite successful in reasoning about many physical systems [209], there was much less success in developing purely qualitative reasoners about spatial and kinematic mechanisms and the poverty conjecture is that this is in fact impossible—there is no purely qualitative spatial reasoning mechanism. Forbus et al. correctly identify transitivity of values as a key feature of qualitative quantity spaces but doubt that this can be exploited much in higher dimensions and conclude that the space of representations in higher dimensions is sparse and for spatial reasoning nothing weaker than numbers will do.

The challenge of QSR then is to provide calculi which allow a machine to represent and reason with spatial entities without resort to the traditional quantitative techniques prevalent in, for, e.g., the computer graphics or computer vision communities.

There has been an increasing amount of research in recent years which tends to refute, or at least weaken the 'poverty conjecture'. Qualitative spatial representations addressing many different aspects of space including topology, orientation, shape, size and distance have been put forward. There is a rich diversity of these representations and they exploit the 'transitivity' as demonstrated by the relatively sparse *composition tables* (cf. the well known table for Allen's interval temporal logic [209]) which have been built for these representations.

This chapter is an overview of some of the major qualitative spatial representation and reasoning techniques. We focus on the main ideas that have emerged from research in the area; there is not sufficient space here to be comprehensive and some

---

[1] In certain domains, containing rectangular objects which are uniformly aligned, this can still be a useful representation, see, for example, [208] where the layout of text blocks on envelopes is learned. A theoretical analysis into the n-dimensional generalisation of the Allen calculus can be found in [9].

interesting approaches have had to be omitted though we give some pointers to the wider literature.[2]

In Section 13.1.2 we will mention some possible applications of qualitative spatial reasoning. Thereafter, in Section 13.2 we survey the main aspects of the representation of qualitative spatial knowledge including ontological aspects, topology, distance, orientation and shape. Section 13.3 discusses qualitative spatial reasoning and Section 13.4 reasoning about spatial change. The chapter concludes with some remarks on cognitive validity in Section 13.5 and a glimpse at future work in Section 13.6. This chapter is based on a number of earlier papers, in particular [47].

13.1.2 Applications of Qualitative Spatial Reasoning

Research in QSR is motivated by a wide variety of possible application areas including Geographic Information System (GIS), robotic navigation, high level vision, spatial propositional semantics of natural languages, engineering design, common-sense reasoning about physical systems and specifying visual language syntax and semantics. There are numerous other application areas including qualitative document-structure recognition [208], biology (e.g., [191, 42]) and domains where space is used as a metaphor (e.g., [127, 160]).

Even though GIS are now a commonplace, the major problem is that of interaction. With gigabytes of information stored either in vector or raster format, present-day GISs do not sufficiently support intuitive or common-sense oriented human–computer interaction. Users may wish to abstract away from the mass of numerical data and specify a query in a way which is essentially, or at least largely, qualitative. Arguably, the next generation GIS will be built on concepts arising from *Naive Geography* [70], wherein QSR techniques are fundamental. Examples of research employing qualitative spatial techniques in geography include reasoning about shape in a qualitative way such as [32].

Although robotic navigation ultimately requires numerically specified directions to the robot to move or turn, hierarchical planning with detailed decisions (e.g., how or exactly where to move) being delayed until a high level plan have been achieved has been shown to be effective [196]. Further, the robot's model of its environment may be imperfect, leading to an inability to use standard robot navigation techniques. Under such circumstances, a qualitative model of space may facilitate planning. One such approach is the development of a robust qualitative method for robot exploration, mapping and navigation in large-scale spatial environments described in [125]; another is the work of Liu and Daneshmend [133] on spatial planning for robotic motion and path planning using qualitative spatial representation and reasoning. Another example of using QSR for robotic navigation is [207]. A qualitative solution to the well known 'piano mover's problem' is [78]. Some work in cognitive robotics has addressed the issue of building topological maps of the robot's environment (rather than metrical ones), e.g., [165, 123].

---

[2]Much relevant material is published in the proceedings of COSIT (the Conference on Spatial Information Theory), GIScience (the International Conference on Geographical Information Science), the journal Spatial Cognition and Computation, as well as regular AI outlets such as the AI journal, the Journal of Artificial Intelligence Research (JAIR) the International Journal of Geographical Information Science, and the proceedings of such conferences as KR, AAAI, IJCAI, PRICAI and ECAI.

QSR has been used in computer vision for visual object recognition at a higher level which includes the interpretation and integration of visual information. QSR techniques have been used to interpret the results of low-level computations as higher level descriptions of the scene or video input [80, 121]. The use of qualitative predicates helps to ensure that scenes which are semantically close have identical or at least very similar descriptions. Work in this area from a cognitive robotics viewpoint includes that of Santos [181, 180].

In natural language, the use and interpretation of spatial propositions tend to be ambiguous. There are multiple ways in which natural language spatial prepositions can be used (e.g., [114] cites many different meanings of "in"); this motivates the use of qualitative spatial representation for finding some formal way of describing these prepositions (e.g., [5, 178, 24]).

Engineering design, like robotic navigation, ultimately normally requires a fully metric description. However, at the early stages of the design process, a reasonable qualitative description would suffice. The field of qualitative kinematics (e.g., [77]) is largely concerned with supporting this type of activity.

Finally, visual languages, either visual programming languages or some kind of representation language, lack a formal specification of the kind that is normally expected of a textual programming or representation language. Although some of these languages make metric distinctions, the bulk of it is often predominantly qualitative in the sense that the exact shape, size, length, etc. of the various components of the diagram or picture is unimportant—rather, what is important is the topological relationship between these components [98, 107]. In a similar vein, research continues on the application of qualitative spatial reasoning for sketch interpretation, e.g., [83, 79, 66, 183, 107, 85].

13.2   Aspects of Qualitative Spatial Representation

Representing space has a rich history in the physical sciences—and serves to locate objects in a quantitative framework. At the other extreme, spatial expressions in natural languages tend to operate on a loose partitioning of the domain. Representation for this less precise description of space proliferated, more or less on an *ad hoc* basis until the emergence of qualitative spatial reasoning; thereafter the partitioning was done more systematically [142].

There are many different aspects to space and therefore to its representation. Not only do we have to decide on what kind of spatial entity we will admit (i.e., commit to a particular ontology of space), but also we can consider developing different kinds of ways of describing the relationship between these kinds of spatial entities; for example, we may consider just their topology, or their sizes or the distance between them, their relative orientation or their shape. In the following sections we will overview the principal techniques which have emerged to represent these different aspects of qualitative spatial knowledge.

13.2.1   Ontology

In this chapter we concentrate on what might be termed "pure space", i.e., purely spatial entities such as points, lines and regions, rather than entities which have spatial extensions, such as physical objects or geographic regions.

Traditionally, in mathematical theories of space, points are considered as the primary primitive spatial entities (or perhaps points and lines), and extended spatial entities such as regions are defined, if necessary, as sets of points. A minority tradition ('mereology' or 'calculus of individuals'—Section 13.2.3) regards this as a philosophical error.[3] Within the QSR community, there is a strong tendency to take regions of space as the primitive spatial entity—see [206]. Even though this ontological shift means building new theories for most spatial and geometrical concepts, there are strong reasons for taking regions as the ontological primitive. If one is interested in using the spatial theory for reasoning about physical objects, then one might argue that the spatial extension of any physical object must be region-like rather than a lower dimension entity. Further, one can always define points, if required, in terms of regions [18]. However, it needs to be admitted that at times it is advantageous to view a 3D physical entity as a 2D or even a 1D entity. Of course, once entities of various dimensions are permitted, a pertinent question would be whether mixed dimension entities are allowed. Further discussion of this issue can be found in [43, 44, 100] and also in [155, 157] who argues that in a first order 2D planar *mereotopology*,[4] a region based ontology is not as parsimonious as a point based one, from a model theoretic viewpoint. Whether points or regions are taken as primitive, it is clear that regions nevertheless are conceptually important in modelling physical and geographic objects.

However, even once one has committed to an ontology which includes regions as primitive spatial entities, there are still several choices facing the modeller. For example, in most mereotopologies, the null region is excluded (since no physical object can have the null region as its extension) though technically it may be simpler to include it [13, 193]. It is fairly standard to insist that regions are all *regular*, though this choice becomes harder to enforce once one allows regions of differing dimensionalities (e.g., 2D and 3D, or even 4D) since the sum of two regions of differing dimensions will not be regular. One can also distinguish between regular-open and regular-closed alternatives. Some calculi [21, 65] insist that regions are connected (i.e. one-piece). A yet stronger condition would be that they are *interior connected*—e.g., a 2D region which pinches to a point is not interior connected. In practice, a reasonable constraint to impose would be that regions are all rational polygons [156].

Another ontological question is what is the nature of the embedding space, i.e., the universal spatial entity? Conventionally, one might take this to be R^n for some n, but one can imagine applications where discrete (e.g., [71]), finite (e.g., [99]), or non-convex (e.g., non-connected) universes might be useful. There is a tension between the continuous-space models favoured by high-level approaches to handling spatial information and discrete, digital representations used at the lower level. An attempt to bridge this gap by developing a high-level qualitative spatial theory based on a discrete model of space is [91]. For another investigation into discrete vs continuous space, see [139].

Once one has decided on these ontological questions, there are further issues: in particular, what primitive "computations" should be allowed? In a logical theory, this amounts to deciding what primitive non-logical symbols one will admit without definition, only being constrained by some set of axioms. One could argue that this set of

---

[3] Simons [189] says: "No one has ever perceived a point, or ever will do so, whereas people have perceived individuals of finite extent".

[4] Mereotopology is defined and discussed in detail in Section 13.2.4 below.

primitives should be small, not only for mathematical elegance and to make it easier to assess the consistency of the theory, but also because this will simplify the interface of the symbolic system to a perceptual component because fewer primitives have to be implemented. The converse argument might be that the resulting symbolic inferences may be more complicated or that it is more natural to have a large and rich set of concepts which are given meaning by many axioms which connect them in many different ways [108]. As we shall see below, in a full first order theory one can define perhaps surprisingly many concepts from just a few primitives; however sometimes it is desirable to restrict the language used to a less expressive language for computational reasons—in this case one will typically need to increase the number of primitives. The next section considers the most common class of such primitives, relations between spatial entities.

13.2.2 Spatial Relations

It is one of the basic assumptions of qualitative representation and reasoning that situations are represented by specifying the relationships between the considered entities. Hence it is natural to represent qualitative information using relations, and in this chapter spatial relations. Formally, a *relation R* is a set of tuples $(d_1, \ldots, d_k)$ of the same arity k, where d_i is a member of a corresponding *domain* $\mathcal{D}_i$. In other words, a relation R of arity k is a subset of the cross-product of k domains, i.e., $R \subseteq \mathcal{D}_1 \times \cdots \times \mathcal{D}_k$.

Very often, *spatial relations* are *binary relations* and very often the considered domains are identical, namely, the set of all spatial entities of a particular space. In these cases spatial relations are of the form $R = \{(a, b) \mid a, b \in \mathcal{D}\}$. The considered domain is usually an infinite domain and the spatial relations contain infinitely many tuples.

Given a set of relations $\mathcal{R} = \{R_1, \ldots, R_n\}$ we can use algebraic operators such as union, intersection, complement, converse, or composition of relations and in this way obtain an *algebra of relations*.[5] Since the relations contain an infinite number of tuples, applying these operators might not be feasible. It is therefore a common assumption in qualitative representation and reasoning to select a (small) finite set of relations which are *jointly exhaustive and pairwise disjoint* (*JEPD*), i.e., each tuple $(a, b) \in \mathcal{D} \times \mathcal{D}$ is a member of exactly one relation. JEPD relations are also called *atomic, base,* or *basic relations*. Given a set of JEPD relations, the relationship between any two spatial entities of the considered domain must be exactly one of the JEPD relations. Indefinite information can be expressed by taking the union of those base relations that can possibly hold (representing the disjunction of the base relations). If no information is known and all possible base relations can hold, we use the *universal relation* which is the union of all base relations. The set of all possible relations is then the powerset of the set of base relations, i.e., all possible unions of the JEPD relations.

In the following sections we discuss various sets of spatial relations, and in particular some different sets of JEPD relations that have been studied in the literature. These are usually restricted to one particular aspect of space such as topology, orientation, shape, etc. How to reason about these relations and more about the consequences of having infinite domains is covered in Section 13.3, while more about general considerations of defining a qualitative calculus can be found in [132].

---

[5] See [59] for a review of the use of relation algebras in spatial and temporal reasoning.

13.2.3 Mereology

Mereology is concerned with the theory of *parthood*, deriving from the Greek $\mu\epsilon\rho o\varsigma$ (*part*), and forms a fundamental aspect of spatial representation, with practical applications in many fields, e.g., [187]. The books by Simons [189], and more recently by Casati and Varzi [27] are excellent reference works for mereology. Simons proposes a number of different mereological theories, depending on what properties one wishes to ascribe to. Perhaps the most widely used theory is his *minimal extensional mereology* [189, pp. 25–30]. The proper part relation is taken as primitive, symbolised PP.[6] The logical basis of the system is:

(SA0)   Any axiom set sufficient for first-order predicate calculus with identity.

(SA1) $\forall x, y[PP(x, y) \rightarrow \neg PP(y, x)]$.

(SA2) $\forall x, y, z[[(PP(x, y) \land PP(y, z)] \rightarrow PP(x, z)]$.

(SA1) and (SA2) simply assert that the system's basic relation is a strict partial ordering. Simons goes on to define part (symbolised 'P'). The next step is to require that an individual cannot have a *single* proper part. After defining overlapping ('O', having a common part), Simons gives the 3rd axiom:

(SA3) $\forall x, y[PP(x, y) \rightarrow \exists z[PP(z, y) \land \neg O(z, x)]]$.

This axiom he refers to as the *Weak Supplementation Principle* (WSP), asserting that any individual with a proper part has another that is disjoint with the first. The axiom set (SA0)–(SA3) still permits various models Simons regards as unsatisfactory, in which overlapping individuals do not have a unique product or intersection. Such models are ruled out by adding:

(SA6) $\forall x, y[O(x, y) \rightarrow \exists z \forall w[P(w, z) \equiv P(w, x) \land P(w, y)]]$,

which ensures the existence of such a unique product. This system of four axioms defines the system known as minimal extensional mereology. We do not have space here to present the many other variations of mereology, but refer the reader to the literature, in particular [189, 27].

13.2.4 Mereotopology

It is clear that topology must form a fundamental aspect of qualitative spatial reasoning since topology certainly can only make qualitative distinctions. Although topology has been studied extensively within the mathematical literature, much of it is too abstract to be of relevance to those attempting to formalise common-sense spatial reasoning. Although various qualitative spatial theories have been influenced by mathematical topology, there are number of reasons why such a wholesale importation seems undesirable in general [100], in particular, the absence of consideration of computational aspects, such as we consider below in Section 13.3. In fact mereotopology is the most studied aspect of QSR and for this reason we devote particular attention to it in this chapter.

---

[6]For the sake of uniformity, in a number of cases we have renamed predicate and other symbols in this chapter from the original formulation.

Although Whitehead tried to define topological notions within mereology [210], this is not possible, and requires some further primitive notions. Varzi [205, 204] presents a systematic account of the subtle relations between mereology and topology. He notes that whilst mereology is not sufficient by itself, there are theories in literature which have proposed integrating topology and mereology (henceforth, *mereotopology*). There are three main strategies of integrating the two:

- Generalise mereology by adding a topological primitive. Borgo et al. [21] add the topological primitive $SC(x)$, i.e., x is a self connected (one-piece) spatial entity to the mereological part relation. Alternatively a single primitive can be used as in [205]: "x and y are connected parts of z". The main advantage of separate theories of mereology and topology is that it allows collocation without sharing parts[7] which is not possible in the second two approaches below.

- Topology is primal and mereology is a subtheory. For example in the topological theories based on $C(x, y)$ (x is connected to y, discussed further below) one defines $P(x, y)$ from $C(x, y)$. This has the elegance of being a single unified theory, but collocation implies sharing of parts. These theories are normally boundary-less (i.e., without lower dimensional spatial entities) but this is not absolutely necessary [161, 4], as discussed further below.

- The final approach is that taken by [73], i.e., topology is introduced as a specialised domain specific subtheory of mereology. An additional primitive needs to be introduced. The idea is to use restricted quantification by introducing a sortal predicate, $Rg(x)$, to denote a region. $C(x, y)$ can then be defined thus: $C(x, y) =_{df} O(x, y) \land Rg(x) \land Rg(y)$.

In the remainder of this subsection, we concentrate on the first two approaches, which are largely based on approaches based on work to be found in the philosophical logic community in particular the work of Clarke [33, 34] which was in turn based on the theory of extensive connection outlined by Whitehead in Process and Reality [211]. Other work in this tradition is cited below and more extensively in [49], in each case building axiomatic theories of space which are predominantly topological in nature, and which take regions rather than points as primitive—indeed, this tradition has been termed as "pointless geometries" [96]. We concentrate here on overviewing the axiomatic approach to mereotopology; the reader is referred to [17] for a thorough treatment of the algebraic and axiomatic approaches to mereotopology and their relationship.

As has been pointed out [49], not all this work agrees in its basic terms; even where there is agreement on vocabulary, such as the use of a binary *connection* predicate, it is not always interpreted in the same way. A model-theoretic framework for investigating the logical space of mereotopological theories and comparing the main options in light of their intended models has been set out [49]. We now describe this framework further since it also provides an overview of the various approaches to mereotopology (for details see [49]).

All the theories are interpreted with respect to some topological space, T, on which a closure operator $c(x)$ is axiomatised in a standard way:

---

[7]For further discussion of this issue see [27, 58].

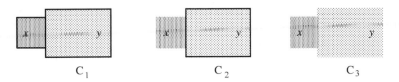

Figure 13.2: The three C relations (limit cases); a solid line indicates closure.

(A0) $\emptyset = c(\emptyset)$.

(A1) $x \subseteq c(x)$.

(A2) $c(c(x)) \subseteq c(x)$.

(A3) $c(x) \cup c(y) = c(x \cup y)$.

Three different notions of connection are then defined (which are illustrated in Fig. 13.2), the semantics which are given by:

$$C_1(x, y) \Leftrightarrow x \cap y \neq \emptyset,$$
$$C_2(x, y) \Leftrightarrow x \cap c(y) \neq \emptyset \text{ or } c(x) \cap y \neq \emptyset.$$
$$C_3(x, y) \Leftrightarrow c(x) \cap c(y) \neq \emptyset,$$

However, since some mereotopologies (e.g., see the first of the three strategies outlined above) have multiple primitives, two further primitives are made available:

$$P_n(x, y) =_{df} \forall z(C_n(z, x) \rightarrow C_n(z, y)) \quad (1 \leqslant n \leqslant 3)$$
$$\sigma_n x \phi =_{df} \iota z \forall y(C_n(y, z) \leftrightarrow \exists x(\phi \wedge C_n(y, x))) \quad (1 \leqslant n \leqslant 3)$$

Intuitively: x is part (P_n) of y iff whatever is connected (C_n) to x is also connected (C_n) to y, and the fusion (σ_n) of all ϕ-ers (where ϕ is some formula with x free) is that thing (if it exists at all) that connects$_n$ precisely to those things that ϕ (i.e., for which ϕ holds for that particular binding of x). Many theories define these notions in terms of the same connection relation that is assumed as a topological primitive, in which case the above reduce to ordinary definitions in the object language of the theory. However, this need not be the case, and in fact an important family of theories stem precisely from the intuition that parthood and connection cannot be defined in terms of each other. This effectively amounts to using two distinct primitives—two notions of connection (one of which is used in defining parthood), or a notion of connection and an independent notion of parthood. Accordingly, and more generally, the framework considers the entire space of mereotopological theories that result from the options determined by the above definitions when $1 \leqslant n \leqslant 3$. That is to say, in the object language all three connection predicates are available as primitives, and the framework models theories in which some such predicates are defined in term of others by adding suitable axioms in place of the corresponding definitions. The choice of which primitives are used will be indicated with a triple,[8] which is called a *type*, $\tau = \langle i, j, k \rangle$ (where $1 \leqslant i, j, k \leqslant 3$), the three components, respectively, indicating which C_i, P_j and σ_k relation is being

---

[8]In fact, in [49] a type is quadruple, but we ignore the final component here.

used in the corresponding τ-theory, thus:

$$C_{\langle i,j,k\rangle}(x, y) =_{df} C_i(x, y),$$

$$P_{\langle i,j,k\rangle}(x, y) =_{df} P_j(x, y),$$

$$\sigma_{\langle i,j,k\rangle}x\phi =_{df} \sigma_k x\phi.$$

There are a great many mereotopological relations which can be defined using these three primitives. We list some of the most common here:

$O_\tau(x, y) =_{df} \exists z(P_\tau(z, x) \wedge P_\tau(z, y))$	x τ-overlaps y
$A_\tau(x, y) =_{df} C_\tau(x, y) \wedge \neg O_\tau(x, y)$	x τ-abuts y
$E_\tau(x, y) =_{df} P_\tau(x, y) \wedge P_\tau(y, x)$	x τ-equals y
$PP_\tau(x, y) =_{df} P_\tau(x, y) \wedge \neg P_\tau(y, x)$	x is a proper τ-part of y
$TP_\tau(x, y) =_{df} P_\tau(x, y) \wedge \exists z(A_\tau(z, x) \wedge A_\tau(z, y))$	x is a tangential τ-part of y
$IP_\tau(x, y) =_{df} P_\tau(x, y) \wedge \neg TP_\tau(x, y)$	x is an interior τ-part of y
$BP_\tau(x, y) =_{df} \forall z(P_\tau(z, x) \rightarrow TP_\tau(z, y))$	x is a boundary τ-part of y
$PO_\tau(x, y) =_{df} O_\tau(x, y) \wedge \neg P_\tau(x, y) \wedge \neg P_\tau(y, x)$	x properly τ-overlaps y
$TO_\tau(x, y) =_{df} \exists z(TP_\tau(z, x) \wedge TP_\tau(z, y))$	x tangentially τ-overlaps y
$IO_\tau(x, y) =_{df} \exists z(IP_\tau(z, x) \wedge IP_\tau(z, y))$	x internally τ-overlaps y
$BO_\tau(x, y) =_{df} O_\tau(x, y) \wedge \neg IO_\tau(x, y)$	x boundary τ-overlaps y
$\pi_\tau x\phi =_{df} \sigma_\tau z \forall x(\phi \rightarrow P_\tau(z, x))$	τ-product of ϕ-ers
$x +_\tau y =_{df} \sigma_\tau z(P_\tau(z, x) \vee P_\tau(z, y))$	τ-sum of x and y
$x \times_\tau y =_{df} \sigma_\tau z(P_\tau(z, x) \wedge P_\tau(z, y))$	τ-product of x and y
$x -_\tau y =_{df} \sigma_\tau z(P_\tau(z, x) \wedge \neg O_\tau(z, y))$	τ-difference of x and y
$k_\tau(x) =_{df} \sigma_\tau z \neg O_\tau(z, x)$	τ-complement of x
$i_\tau(x) =_{df} \sigma_\tau z IP_\tau(z, x)$	τ-interior of x
$e_\tau(x) =_{df} i_\tau(k_\tau(x))$	τ-exterior of x
$c_\tau(x) =_{df} k_\tau(e_\tau(x))$	τ-closure of x
$b_\tau(x) =_{df} c_\tau(x) -_\tau i_\tau(x)$	τ-boundary of x
$U_\tau =_{df} \sigma_\tau z O_\tau(z, z)$	τ-universe
$Bd_\tau(x) =_{df} \exists y BP_\tau(x, y)$	x is a τ-boundary
$Rg_\tau(x) =_{df} \exists y IP_\tau(y, x)$	x is a τ-region
$Op_\tau(x) =_{df} E_\tau(x, i_\tau(x))$	x is τ-open
$Cl_\tau(x) =_{df} E_\tau(x, c_\tau(x))$	x is τ-closed
$Re_\tau(x) =_{df} E_\tau(i_\tau(x), i_\tau(c_\tau(x)))$	x is τ-regular
$Cn_\tau(x) =_{df} \forall y \forall z(E_\tau(x, y +_\tau z) \rightarrow C_\tau(y, z))$	x is τ-connected (i.e. in one piece)
$CP_\tau(x, y) =_{df} P_\tau(x, y) \wedge Cn_\tau(x)$	x is a τ-connected part of y

Depending on the structure of τ, the notions thus defined may receive different interpretations, hence the gloss on the right should not be taken too strictly. One intended interpretation of the binary relations relative to the Euclidean plane R^2—an interpretation that justifies the gloss—is illustrated in Figs. 2 and 3 in [49]. However, the exact semantic consequence of these definitions may change radically from one framework to another, depending on the type τ and on the constraints in the model theory.

It is easy to see that the following formulas are true in every canonical model for all types τ (i.e., C_τ is reflexive and symmetric), and indeed these formulae are normally included as axioms in any mereotopology based on a binary connection relation:

$(C1_\tau)$ $\quad C_\tau(x, x)$.

$(C2_\tau)$ $\quad C_\tau(x, y) \to C_\tau(y, x)$.

Similarly, the following are always logically true in view of the definition of P_τ (and are included as axioms if parthood is not defined in terms of connection, i.e., the first and second indices of the type are different):

$(P1_\tau)$ $\quad P_\tau(x, x)$.

$(P2_\tau)$ $\quad (P_\tau(x, y) \wedge P_\tau(y, z)) \to P_\tau(x, z)$.

Another important property that is often associated with parthood is antisymmetry. There are two formulations of this property, depending on whether we use τ-equality (E_τ) or plain equality $(=)$. The first formulation:

$(P3_\tau)$ $\quad (P_\tau(x, y) \wedge P_\tau(y, x)) \to E_\tau(x, y)$

is obviously true by definition. However, the second formulation:

$(P3_{\tau=})$ $\quad (P_\tau(x, y) \wedge P_\tau(y, x)) \to x = y$

is stronger and may fail in some models. Antisymmetry in the sense of $(P3_{\tau=})$ is logically equivalent to the requirement that parthood be extensional in the following sense:

$(P4_{\tau=})$ $\quad \forall z(P_\tau(z, x) \leftrightarrow P_\tau(z, y)) \to x = y$,

which in turn is equivalent to the requirement that connection is likewise extensional:

$(C3_{\tau=})$ $\quad \forall z(C_\tau(z, x) \leftrightarrow C_\tau(z, y)) \to x = y$.

These requirements are stronger than the corresponding versions for E_τ. These latter are logically true, but whether a model satisfies $(P4_{\tau=})$ and $(C3_{\tau=})$ depends crucially on the relevant closure operator c and on which sets are included in the universe U.

It can easily be shown that for any pair of types $\tau_1 = \langle i_1, j, k \rangle$ and $\tau_2 = \langle i_2, j, k \rangle$, the following holds whenever $i_1 \leqslant i_2$:

$(C4_{i_1 i_2})$ $\quad C_{\tau_1}(x, y) \to C_{\tau_2}(x, y)$.

The three parthood predicates are not, in general, related in a similar fashion. In fact, no instance of the following *inclusion* schema is generally true when $\tau_1 \neq \tau_2$:

$(P5_{i_1 i_2})$ $\quad P_{\tau_1}(x, y) \to P_{\tau_2}(x, y)$.

Some mereotopologies include boundaries (i.e., lower dimensional entities) in their domain of discourse; others do not; these cases are examined separately below.

Boundary-tolerant theories

It turns out that none of the cases where τ is uniform $(i = j = k)$ are viable:

(a) The option $i = 1$ yields implausible topologies in which the boundary of a region is never connected to the region's interior (since the boundary and the interior never share any points).

(b) The option $i = 2$ yields implausible mereologies in which every boundary is part of its own complement (since anything connected to the former is connected to the latter).

(c) The option $i = 3$ yields implausible mereotopologies in which the interior of a region is always connected to its exterior (so that boundaries make no difference) and in which the closure of a region is always part of the regions interior.

There is also a sense in which these theories trivialise all mereotopological distinctions in the presence of boundaries. For (a)–(c) imply that if τ is uniform, any model that includes the boundaries of its elements satisfies the conditional: $C_\tau(x, y) \rightarrow O_\tau(x, y)$.

Hence, in every such model the τ-abut predicate A_τ defines the empty relation, and so do the predicates of tangential and boundary parthood (TP_τ, BP_τ) and tangential and boundary overlap (TO_τ, BO_τ). Thus if boundaries are admitted in the domain, uniformly typed theories appear to be inadequate. In fact, this applies not only to uniform types, but to all types where $i = j$. (See [18, 96] for related material.)

Moving on to non-uniform types, we may note that some theories have been explicitly proposed in the literature, specifically for the case $\tau = \langle 2, 1, 1 \rangle$. An early example is to be found in [25], though the topological primitive there is Op_τ rather than C_τ. (One gets a definitionally equivalent characterisation of C_τ via the definitions above. A similar warning applies to some other theories discussed below.) Other examples are in [49]. Since parthood P_τ is not defined in terms of the connection primitive C_τ, these theories need at least two distinct primitives (corresponding to the parameters 1 and 2 in the type); but since fusion σ_τ is typically understood using the same primitive as parthood, a third primitive is not needed (whence the equality of the second and third coordinates in the type). These theories typically represent an attempt to reconstruct ordinary topological intuitions on top of a mereological basis. In fact, it is immediate from the definition that in this case C_τ corresponds to the notion of connection of ordinary point-set topology: two regions are connected if the closure of one intersects the other, or vice versa. Moreover, P_τ is typically assumed to satisfy the relevant extensionality and inclusion principles.

Thus, a minimal theory of this kind is typically axiomatised using $(C1_\tau)$, $(C2_\tau)$, $(P1_\tau)$, $(P2_\tau)$, $(P3_\tau)$, $(P5_{12})$. If a fusion principle is added, the result is a mereotopology subsuming what is known as classical extensional mereology [189, 27], in which P_τ defines a complete Boolean algebra with the null element deleted. Further adding:

$(A1')$ $\quad P_\tau(x, c_\tau(x))$.

$(A2')$ $\quad P_\tau(c_\tau(c_\tau(x)), c_\tau(x))$.

$(A3')$ $\quad E_\tau(c_\tau(x) +_\tau c_\tau(y), c_\tau(x +_\tau y))$

gives what may be called a full mereotopology, in which c_τ behaves like the standard Kuratowski closure operator. $((A0)$ has no analogue due to the lack of a null element.)

All of these theories, of course, must account in some way for the intuitive difficulties that arise out of the notion of a boundary, and correspondingly of the distinction between open and closed entities. For instance, Smith [57] considers various ways of supplementing a full mereotopology with a rendering of the intuition that boundaries are ontologically dependent entities [190], i.e., can only exist as boundaries of some open entity (contrary to the ordinary set-theoretic conception). In the notation here the simplest formulation of this intuition is given by the axiom:

$(B1)$ $\quad \mathsf{BP}_\tau(x, y) \rightarrow \exists z(\mathsf{Op}_\tau(z) \wedge \mathsf{BP}_\tau(x, \mathsf{c}_\tau(z)))$.

It is noteworthy that all theories of this sort have type $\langle 2, 1, 1 \rangle$. It is conjectured [49] that this is indeed the only viable option.

Boundary-free theories

Though the idea of a uniform type appears to founder in the case of boundary-tolerant theories, it has been taken very seriously in the context of boundary-free theories, i.e., theories that leave out boundaries from the universe of discourse in the intended models. Theories of this sort are rooted in [210, 56] and have recently become popular under the impact of Clarke's formulation [33, 34] (see also [96]). Clarke's own is a $\langle 1, 1, 1 \rangle$-theory, and some later authors followed this account (e.g., [4, 5, 161]). However, one also finds examples of theories of type $\langle 2, 2, 2 \rangle$ (e.g., in [105, 156]) as well as of type $\langle 3, 3, 3 \rangle$ (especially in the work of Cohn et al., [43, 48, 100, 163]) which has led to an extended body of results and applications in the area of spatial reasoning; see [81] for an independent example of a type $\langle 3, 3, 3 \rangle$ theory. Indeed, all boundary-free theories in the literature appear to be uniformly typed: this is remarkable but not surprising, since the main difficulties in reducing mereology to topology lies precisely in the presence of boundaries. Now, by definition, a boundary-free τ-theory admits of no boundary elements. In axiomatic terms, this is typically accomplished by adding a further postulate to the effect that everything is a region (i.e., has interior parts):

(R) $\quad \forall x \mathsf{Rg}_\tau(x)$

which implies the emptiness of the relations BP_τ and BO_τ, hence of Bd_τ. So $\mathsf{b}_\tau(x)$ is never defined in this case. It is worth noting that such theories typically afford some indirect way of modelling boundary talk, e.g., as talk about infinite series of extended regions (cf. [18, 34, 72]). In this sense, these theories do have room for boundary elements, albeit only as higher-order entities. Note also the discussion of points and regions above in Section 13.2.1.

Consider now the three main options mentioned in the previous section, where τ is a basic uniform type of the form $\langle i, i, i \rangle$. Unlike their boundary-tolerant counterparts, none of these options yields a collapse of the distinction between tangential and interior parthood (TP_τ, IP_τ) or between tangential and interior overlap (TO_τ, IO_τ). However, the three options diverge noticeably with regard to the distinction between open and closed regions (Op_τ, Cl_τ). The general picture is as follows.

(a) The case $i = 1$ allows for the open/closed distinction, yielding theories in which the relation of abutting (A_τ) is a prerogative of closed regions (open regions abut nothing). As a corollary, such theories determine non-standard mereologies that violate the supplementation principle given above in Section 13.2.3. This is a feature that some authors have found unpalatable: as Simons [189] put it, one can discriminate regions that differ by as little as a point, but one cannot discriminate the point. There are also some topological peculiarities that follow from the choice of C_1 as a connection relation. For instance, it follows immediately that no region is connected to its complement, hence that the universe is bound to be disconnected. This was noted in [4, 34], where the suggestion is made that self-connectedness should be redefined accordingly:

$$\mathsf{Cn}'_\tau(x) =_{df} \forall y \forall z (\mathsf{E}_\tau(x, y +_\tau z) \to \mathsf{C}_\tau(\mathsf{c}_\tau(y), \mathsf{c}_\tau(z))).$$

This, however, is just a way of saying that self-connectedness must be defined with reference to a different notion of connection (namely, the notion obtained by taking $i = 3$).

(b) The case $i = 2$ also allows for the open/closed distinction, but yields theories in which the relation of abutting may only hold between two regions one of which is open and the other closed in the relevant contact area. This results in a rather standard topological apparatus, modulo the absence of boundary elements. However, also in this case the mereology is bound to violate (WSP). (Again, just take y open and x equal to the closure of y.)

(c) The case $i = 3$ is the only one where the open/closed distinction dissolves: in this case every region turns out to be τ-equal to its interior as well as to its closure. This follows from (P3$_\tau$), i.e., equivalently, from (C3$_\tau$) or (P4$_\tau$). This means that τ-theories of this sort cannot be extensional—in fact, they yield highly non-standard mereologies. However, this is coherent with the fundamental idea of a boundary-free approach. For one of the main motivations for going boundary-free is precisely to avoid the many conundrums that seem to arise from the distinction between open and closed regions [100]. In addition, and for this very same reason, such theories can validate (SA3), thereby eschewing the problem mentioned in (a) and (b) above.

The best known case of (c), i.e., a mereotopology with type $\langle 3, 3, 3 \rangle$ was first presented in [163], and elaborated subsequently in a series of papers including [43, 48, 100, 44], which has been called the *Region Connection Calculus (RCC)*.[9]

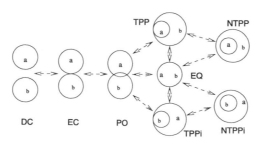

Figure 13.3: 2D illustrations of the relations of RCC-8 calculus and their continuous transitions (*conceptual neighbourhood*).

---

[9]Galton [92] coined this name.

In particular, a set of eight JEPD relations has been defined within the RCC mereotopology and this is now generally known as RCC-8, see Fig. 13.3.[10] The relation names used here differ from the relations defined above, but correspond thus (assuming the type is $\langle 3, 3, 3 \rangle$ in each case): DC: ¬C, EC: A, PO: PO, TPP: TP ∧ ¬E, NTPP: IP, EQ: E; TPPi and NTPPi are simply the inverses of TPP and NTPP. The definitions of RCC-8 symbols, in particular k(x), differ from that given above—see [163], and in particular the discussion in [13, Section 3.3.3].

Examples of non-uniformly typed boundary-free theories are much rarer. However, one may imagine that such theories could also alleviate some of the unpalatable properties of the uniformly typed mereotopologies mentioned in (a) and (b) above. For example, a type of the form $\langle 1, 3, k \rangle$ would correspond to a mereotopology in which a type-1 notion of connection is combined with a type-3 parthood relation that satisfies the supplementation principle (WSP). Similarly with a type of the form $\langle 2, 3, k \rangle$. An example of a theory with a type 3 connection relation interpreted in boundary free models and a separate parthood relation is [128]—influenced by [177] this generalises the RCC system and the discrete mereotopology of Galton [91] to allow for discrete models of RCC (not possible in the standard theory cited above).

Topology via "n-intersections"

An alternative approach to representing and reasoning about topological relations has been promulgated via a series of papers including [65, 64, 69]. Three sets of points are associated with every region—its interior, boundary and complement. The relationship between any two regions can be characterised by a 3×3 matrix[11] called the *9-intersection* model, in which every entry in the matrix takes one of two values, denoting whether the intersection of the two point sets is empty or not; for example, the matrix in which every entry takes the non-empty value corresponds to the PO relation above.[12] Although it would seem that there are $2^9 = 512$ possible matrices, after taking into account the physical reality of 2D space and some specific assumptions about the nature of regions, it turns out that the there are exactly 8 remaining matrices, which correspond to the RCC-8 relations. Note, however, that the 9-intersection model only considers one-piece regions without holes in two-dimensional space, while RCC-8 allows much more general domains. Therefore, even though the two sets of relations appear similar, their computational properties differ considerably and reasoning in RCC-8 is much simpler than reasoning in the 9-intersection model [166]. One can also use the 9-intersection calculus to reason about regions which have holes by classifying the relationship not only between each pair of regions, but also the relationship between each hole of each region and the other region and each of its holes [68].

---

[10]A simpler, purely mereological calculus (usually called RCC-5), in which the distinctions between TPP and NTPP, TPPi and NTPPi, and DC and EC are collapsed has also been defined and investigated [127, 117].

[11]Actually, a simpler 2×2 matrix [65] known as the 4-intersection featuring just the interior and the boundary is sufficient to describe the eight RCC relations. However the 3×3 matrix allows more expressive sets of relations to be defined as noted below since it takes into account the relationship between the regions and its embedding space.

[12]The RCC-8 relations have different names in the 9-intersection model, in fact English words such as "overlap" instead of PO.

Different calculi with more JEPD relations can be derived by changing the underlying assumptions about what a region is and by allowing the matrix to represent the codimension of intersection. For example, one may derive a calculus for representing and reasoning about regions in Z^2 rather than R^2 [71]. Alternatively, one can extend the representation in each matrix cell by the specifying dimension of the intersection rather than simply whether it exists or not [36]. This allows one to enumerate all the relations between areas, lines and points and is known as the "dimension extended method" (DEM). A very large number of possible relationships may be defined in this way and a way termed as the "calculus based method" (CBM) to generate all these from a set of five polymorphic binary relations between a pair of spatial entities x and y: disjoint, touch, in, overlap, cross has been proposed [41]. A complex relation between x and y may then be formed by conjoining atomic propositions formed by using one of the five relations above, whose arguments may be either x or y or a boundary or endpoint operator applied to x or y. For the most expressive calculus (either the CBM or the combination of the 9-intersection and the DEM) there are 9 JEPD area/area relations, 31 line/area relations, 3 point/area relations, 33 line/line relations, 3 point/line relations and 2 point/point relations giving a total of 81 JEPD relations [41].

13.2.5   Between Mereotopology and Fully Metric Spatial Representation

Mereology and mereotopology can be seen as perhaps the most abstract and most qualitative spatial representations. However, there are many situations where mereotopological information alone is insufficient. The following subsections explore the different ways in which other qualitative information may be represented. After this, in Section 13.2.6 we look at how easily a spatial representation with a coordinate system and thus the full power of a geometry can be defined from qualitative primitives.

Direction and orientation

Direction relations describe the direction of one object to another, and can be defined in terms of three basic concepts: the primary object, the reference object and the frame of reference. Thus, unlike the mereotopological relations on spatial entities described in the preceding sections, a binary relation is not sufficient; i.e., if we want to specify the orientation of a *primary object* with respect to a *reference object*, then we need to have some kind of a *frame of reference*. This characterisation manifests itself in the display of qualitative direction calculi to be found in the literature: certain calculi have an explicit triadic relation while others presuppose an extrinsic frame of reference (such as the cardinal directions of E, N, S, W) [86, 112], or assume that objects have an intrinsic front (so that we can talk, for example, of being to the left of a person or vehicle); in this case we normally speak of *orientation* calculi, being the special case of a direction calculus when the primary object has an intrinsic front.

Of those with explicit triadic relations, a common scheme is to define (assuming attention is restricted to a 2D plane—as is usually the case in the literature) three relations between triples of points, denoting, clockwise, anti-clockwise or collinear ordering [184, 186, 176]. Schlieder developed a calculus [185] for reasoning about the relative orientation of pairs of line segments. Another triadic calculus is [116] which first defines binary relations on directed line segments using left/right relations

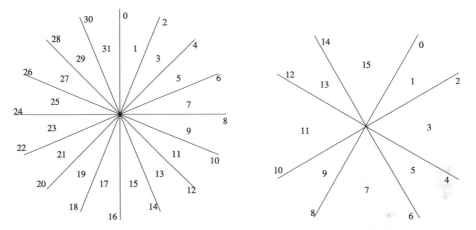

Figure 13.4: Different STAR calculi, the left one is defined using eight intersecting lines which result in 33 JEPD relations, the right one using four intersecting lines resulting in 17 JEPD relations. The STAR calculus allows any number and orientation of intersecting lines.

based on the intrinsic directedness of the line, and then defines ternary relations in terms of these, giving a 24 JEPD relation set, from which relations defining clockwise, anticlockwise and collinear can be recovered via disjunction.

For those calculi that use an extrinsic frame of reference, it is most common to use a given reference direction. This allows the orientation between two objects to be represented with respect to the reference direction using just binary relations. The first approaches described the directions of points in a 2D space. Frank [86] distinguished different ways of defining sectors for the different direction relations, cone-based and projection based (also called the cardinal direction algebra [130]), which both divide the plane into sectors relative to a point by using lines that intersect at the corresponding point. These calculi were later generalised for direction sectors generated by an arbitrary number of intersecting lines and form the STAR algebra [171] shown in Fig. 13.4. Interestingly, it turned out that once more than two intersecting lines are used for defining sectors, it is possible to generate a coordinate system and thus the distinction between qualitative and quantitative representation disappears. The solution to this dilemma is not to consider the lines as separate relations but to integrate them with sectors.

Most calculi for direction and orientation are based on points rather than regions, as calculi become rather coarse grained in the latter case. There are exceptions, for example, [101] or [135] in which directions *within* regions are considered (*London is in the south of England*). Directions for extended regions have mainly been developed for objects whose boundaries are parallel to the axes of the frame of reference, for example, the reference direction and the axis orthogonal to the reference direction, or by using a minimal bounding box which is parallel to the axes [8, 152]. A calculus which combines regions, mereotopology and a simple notion of unidimensional direction is the occlusion calculus of [164].

Distance and size

Spatial representations of distance can be divided into two main groups: those which measure on some "absolute" scale, and those which provide some kind of relative measurement. Of course, since traditional Qualitative Reasoning [209] is primarily concerned with dealing with linear quantity spaces, the qualitative algebras and the transitivity of such quantity spaces mentioned earlier can be used as a distance or size measuring representation, see Chapter 9.

Also of interest in this context are the order of magnitude calculi [140, 158] developed in the QR community. Most of these traditional QR formalisms are of the "absolute" kind of representations,[13] as in the delta calculus of [216]—which introduces a triadic relation: $x(>, d)y$ to note that x is larger/bigger than y by an amount d; terms such as $x(>, y)y$ mean that x is more than twice as big as y.

Of the "relative" representations specifically developed within the qualitative spatial reasoning community, perhaps the earliest is the triadic CanConnect(x, y, z) primitive [56]—which is true if body x can connect y and z by simple translation (i.e., without scaling, rotation or shape change). From this primitive it is easy to define notions such as equidistance, nearer than and farther than. This primitive allows a metric on the extent of regions to be defined: one region is larger than another if it can connect regions that the other cannot. Another method of determining the relative size of two objects relies on being able to translate regions (assumed to be shape and size invariant) and then exploit topological relationships—if a translation is possible so that one region becomes a proper part of another, then it must be smaller [143]; this idea is exploited in [51] to represent and reason about object location.

Of particular interest is the framework for representing distance [113] which has been extended to include orientation [40]. A distance system is composed of an ordered sequence of *distance relations* and a set of *structure relations* which give additional information about how the distance relations relate to each other. Each distance has an *acceptance area*; the distance between successive acceptance areas defines sequence of intervals: $\delta_1, \delta_2, \dots$. The structure relations define relationships between these δ_i. Typical structure relations might specify a monotonicity property (the δ_i are increasing), or that each δ_i is greater than the sum of all the preceding δ_i. The structure relationships can also be used to specify order of magnitude relationships, e.g., that $\delta_i + \delta_j \sim \delta_i$ for $j < i$. The structure relationships are important in refining the *composition tables*.[14] In a *homogeneous* distance system all distance relations have the same structure relations; however this need not be the case in a *heterogeneous* distance system. The proposed system also allows for the fact that the context may affect the distance relationships: this is handled by having different frames of reference, each with its own distance system and with inferences in different frames of reference being composed using *articulation rules* (cf. [115]).

One obvious effect of moving from one scale, or context to another, is that qualitative distance terms such as "close" will vary greatly; more subtly, distances can behave in various "non-mathematical" ways in some contexts or spaces: e.g., distances may

---

[13] Actually it is straightforward to specify relative measurements given an "absolute" calculus: to say that $x > y$, one may simply write $x - y = +$.

[14] Section 13.3.2 introduces composition tables.

not be symmetrical.[15] Another "mathematical aberration" is that in some domains the shortest distance between two points may not be a straight line (e.g., because a lake or a building might be in the way), or the "Manhattan Distance" found in typical North American cities laid out in a grid system.

Shape

Shape is perhaps one of the most important characteristics of an object, and particularly difficult to describe qualitatively. In a purely mereotopological theory, very limited statements can be made about the shape of a region: e.g., whether it has holes, or interior voids, or whether it is one piece or not. It has been observed [92] that one can (weakly) constrain the shape of rigid objects by topological constraints using RCC-8 relations.

However, if an application demands finer grained distinctions, then some kind of semi-metric information has to be introduced.[16] For an explicit qualitative shape description one needs to go beyond mereotopology, introducing some kind of shape primitives whilst still retaining a qualitative representation. Of course, as [39] note: the mathematical community have developed many different geometries which are less expressive than Euclidean geometry, for example, projective and affine geometries, but have not necessarily investigated reasoning techniques for them (though see [7, 10, 35]).

A dichotomy can be drawn between representations which primarily describe the shape via the boundary of an object compared to those which represent its interior. Approaches to qualitative boundary description have been investigated using a variety of sets of primitives. The work of Meathrel and Galton [141] generalises much of this work. The basic idea is to consider the tangent at each point on the boundary of a 2D shape—it is either defined (D) or undefined (U)—in this latter case the boundary is at a cusp or kink point. If it is defined, then the rate of change of the tangent at that point can be considered (assuming a fixed (anticlockwise) traversal of the boundary), as can all the higher order derivatives (until it becomes undefined). Each derivative takes one of the qualitative values $+, 0, -$, and at the level of the first derivative denotes whether the shape is locally convex, straight or concave. Depending on how many higher order derivatives are considered, the description becomes progressively more and more detailed, and a greater variety of different shapes can be distinguished. The values $+$ and $-$ can only hold over a boundary segment, whereas 0 and U can hold at a single boundary point. Thus the description of a boundary starts at a particular point, and then proceeds, anticlockwise, to label maximal boundary segments having a particular qualitative value, and isolated points that may separate these. There are constraints on what sequences of descriptions are possible, and the rules for construction a *Token Ordering Graph* (which is an instance of the continuity networks/conceptual neighbourhoods discussed in Section 13.4 below) have been formulated. For example, a $+$ segment cannot directly transition to a $-$ segment without passing through a $U/0$ point or a 0 segment.

---

[15]E.g., because distances are sometimes measured by time taken to travel, and an uphill journey may take longer than a return downhill journey [113].

[16]Of course, orientation and distance primitives as discussed above already add something to pure topology, but as already mentioned these are largely point based and thus not directly applicable to describing shape of a region.

Shape description by looking at global properties of the region rather than its boundary has been investigated too, for example, the work of [39] describes shape via properties such as compactness and elongation by using the minimum bounding rectangle of the shape and the order of magnitude calculus of [140]: elongation is computed via the ratio of the sides of the minimum bounding rectangle whilst compactness by comparing the area of the shape and its minimum bounding rectangle. The medial axis can also be used as a proxy for shape, and has been used extensively in the computer vision community, and within a KR setting in [179] for distinguishing lakes from rivers. The notion of a Voronoi hull has also been used (e.g., [63]).

Combinations of different aspects

Although we have attempted to present various aspects of spatial representation separately, in general they interact with each other. For example, knowing the relative size of two regions (smaller, larger, equal) can effect which mereotopological relationships are possible [95]. There is also a relationship between distance and the notion of orientation: e.g., distances cannot usually be summed unless they are in the same direction, and the distance between a point and a region may vary depending on the orientation. Thus it is perhaps not surprising that there have been a number of calculi which are based on a primitive which combines distance and orientation information. One straightforward idea [86] is to combine directions as represented by segments of the compass with a simple distance metric (*far, close*). A slightly more sophisticated idea is to introduce a primitive which defines the position of a third point with respect to a directed line segment between two other points [217] (generalised to the 3D case in [150]). Another approach that combines knowledge about distances and positions in a qualitative way—through a combination of the Delta-calculus [216] and orientation is presented in [215]. Liu [134] explicitly defines the semantics of qualitative distance and qualitative orientation angles and formulates a representation of qualitative trigonometry. A example of a combined distance and position calculus is [75]. A discussion of different ways to combine different aspects can be found in [174].

13.2.6   Mereogeometry

Just as mereotopology extends mereology with topological notions, so mereogeometry extends mereology with geometrical concepts. In principle one could add any of the notions of orientation or distance/size discussed above to mereology, but most of those are defined on points rather than regions which mereology presumes. In the style of [49] for mereotopology, Borgo and Masolo [22] compare and contrast a range of mereogeometries. The benchmark system is *Region Based Geometry* (RBG) [14, 16] which builds on the earlier work of Tarski [195]. This uses $P(x, y)$ and $S(x)$ (x is a sphere) as primitives, and captures full Euclidean geometry, in a region based setting. RBG is axiomatised in second order logic, and has been shown to be categorical [14]. Three other systems [21, 148, 56, 57] are shown to be equivalent, and all are termed *Full Mereogeometries*; these other systems have different sets of primitives, for example, the CanConnect primitive mentioned above in Section 13.2.5 or the primitive $CG(x, y)$ (x is congruent to y). A fifth system [200, 6], which uses the primitive Closer(x, y, z) (x is closer to y than to z) reported there to be slightly weaker, is in fact also a full mereogeometry, a result which follows as an immediate consequence of the results in [54]. It is conjectured in [22] that the theory obtained by adding a convex hull primitive to mereotopology (as in extensions of RCC [43]) is strictly weaker. In fact, in [54] it is shown that this is indeed the case since such a language is invariant under affine transformations, and thus unable to express properties such as $S(x)$ which is not invariant. This followed on from an earlier result, in which it was shown that in a constraint language [55] the primitives for adjacency, parthood and convexity are sufficient in combination to provide an affine geometry. A similar result is provided in [156] where it is demonstrated that the first order language with parthood and congruence of primitives also enables the distinction of any two regions not related by an affine transformation. Moreover, it is shown that a coordinate system can be defined in this language, thus raising the question of whether it deserves the label *qualitative*— and indeed this result and question also apply to any full mereogeometry. A similar observation has already been made above for the STAR calculus [171] described in Section 13.2.5, and also indeed for the affine mereogeometries based on convexity mentioned just above [54].

An application of a mereogeometry based on congruence and parthood to reasoning about the location of mobile rigid objects is [51]. A simple constraint language whose four primitives combine notions of congruence and mereology has been defined and investigated from a computational viewpoint [50]—the primitives are EQ, CGPP, CGPPi (congruent to a proper part, and the inverse relation), and CNO (where none of the other relations hold).

13.2.7 Spatial Vagueness

The problem of vagueness permeates almost every domain of knowledge representation. In the spatial domain, this is certainly true, for example, it is often hard to determine a region's boundaries (e.g., "southern England").

Vagueness of spatial concepts can be distinguished from that associated with spatially situated objects and the regions they occupy. An adequate treatment of vagueness in spatial information needs to account for vague regions as well as vague relationships [46]. Although there has been some philosophical debate concerning whether vague objects can exist [76], formal theories dealing with vagueness of extent are not well-established.

Existing techniques for representing and reasoning about vagueness such as supervaluation theory have been extended and applied in a spatial context [179] and [15], which also specifically addresses the issue of the preservation of object identity in the face of loss of 'small' parts.

There have also been extensions of existing spatial calculi specifically designed to address spatial indeterminacy. In particular there have been extensions of both the RCC calculus [45, 46] (called the "egg-yolk" calculus) and the 9-intersection [37]; the broad approach in each of these is essentially the same—to identify a core region which always belongs to the region in question (the *yolk* in the terminology of former), and an extended region which might or might not be part of it (together forming the *egg*). It turns out that if one generalises RCC-8 in this way [46] there are 252 JEPD relations between non-crisp regions which can be naturally clustered into 40 equivalence classes, and 46 JEPD relations, clustered into 13 equivalence classes in the case of the extension to the purely mereological RCC-5. The axiomatic presentation of the egg-yolk calculus in [46] extends the ontology of crisp regions with vague (non-crisp) ones and relies on an additional binary relation, 'x is crisper than region y'. An application of the egg-yolk calculus to reasoning about a non-spatial domain, class integration across databases, is [127].

It has been shown [38] that the extension of the 9-intersection model to model regions with broad boundaries can be used to reason not just about regions with indeterminate boundaries but also can be specialised to cover a number of other kinds of regions including convex hulls of regions, minimum bounding rectangles, buffer zones and rasters. (This last specialization generalises the application of the n-intersection model to rasters previously undertaken [71].)

Another notion of indefiniteness relates to locations. Bittner [19] deals with the notion of exact, part and rough location for spatial objects. The exact location is the region of space taken up by the object. The notion of part location (as introduced by [26]) relates parts of a spatial object to parts of spatial regions. The rough location of a spatial object is characterised by the part location of spatial objects with respect to a set of regions of space that form regional partitions. Consequently, the notion of rough location links parts of spatial objects to parts of partition regions.

Bittner [19] argues that the observations and measurements of location in physical reality yield knowledge about rough location: a vaguely defined object o is located within a regional partition consisting of the three concentric regions: 'core', 'wide boundary' and 'exterior'. In this context, the notion of rough location within a partition consisting of the three concentric regions coincides with the notion of vague regions introduced by [45].

It is worth noting the similarity of these ideas to rough sets [60], though the exact relationship has yet to be fully explored, though see, for example, [154, 20]. Other approaches to spatial uncertainty are to work with an indistinguishability relation which is not transitive and thus fails to generate equivalence classes [199, 118], and the development of nonmonotonic spatial logics [188, 3].

13.3   Spatial Reasoning

In the previous section we described some approaches to representing spatial information and gave different examples of spatial representations from the vast literature on this topic. For some purposes it is enough to have a representation for spatial knowledge, but what makes intelligent systems intelligent is their ability to reason about given knowledge. There are different reasoning tasks an intelligent system might have to perform. These include deriving new knowledge from the given information, checking consistency of given information, updating the given knowledge, or finding a minimal representation. Even though these reasoning problems are quite different, they can be transformed into each other, and algorithms developed for one reasoning problem can often easily be modified to solving other reasoning problems. Much of the research on spatial reasoning has therefore focused on one particular reasoning problem, the *consistency problem*, i.e., given some spatial information, is the given information consistent or inconsistent.

In principle, reasoning about spatial knowledge given in the form of a logical representation is not different from reasoning about other kinds of knowledge. However, much of the qualitative spatial knowledge we are dealing with is of a very particular form and can be represented as relations between spatial entities. We are usually considering binary and sometimes ternary relations which can be represented as constraints restricting the spatial properties of the entities we are describing. This constraint-based representation gives us the possibility to develop reasoning algorithms which are much more efficient than standard logical deduction, albeit less powerful.

A constraint-based representation of spatial knowledge takes the form of an existentially quantified first-order logical expression: $\exists x_1 \ldots \exists x_n \bigwedge_{i,j} \bigvee_{R \in \mathcal{A}} R(x_i, x_j)$, where $x_1, \ldots, x_n$ are variables over the domain of spatial entities, $\mathcal{A}$ is the set of available base relations, and $R(x_i, x_j)$ is a binary constraint which restricts the possible instantiations of x_i, x_j to the tuples of R. Solving this formula is basically a *constraint satisfaction problem* (*CSP*) as described in Chapter 4. One of the major differences of spatial relations and spatial constraints to those constraints described in Chapter 4 is that the domain of spatial entities is usually infinite, i.e., there is an infinite number of spatial entities that can be assigned to the variables $x_1, \ldots, x_n$ and which might have to be tested when deciding consistency of spatial information. While standard CSPs over finite domains are in general NP-complete, spatial CSPs over *infinite domains* are potentially undecidable.

Spatial reasoning with constraints and relations mainly relies on algebraic operators on the relations, the most important being the *composition* operator. Two relations R and S are composed according to the following definition: $R \circ S = \{(x, y) \mid \exists z: (x, z) \in R \text{ and } (z, y) \in S\}$. Composition has to be computed using the formal semantics of the relations. Due to the infinite domains, computing composition can be an undecidable problem. If the compositions of the base relations can be computed, they can be stored in a composition table and reasoning becomes a matter of table look-ups.

The main research topics in spatial reasoning in the past decade include the following:

- determining the complexity of reasoning over different spatial calculi,

- proving that a formalism is decidable and if so, possibly identifying tractable or even maximal tractable subsets of spatial calculi,

- finding representations of qualitative spatial knowledge which allow for more efficient reasoning,

- developing efficient algorithms for spatial reasoning as well as approximation methods and heuristics which lead to faster solutions in practice,

- developing methods for proving tractability,

- computing composition tables and verifying their correctness,

- determining whether a qualitative spatial description is *realisable*, i.e., whether a planar interpretation exists.

In this section we give an overview of some of the main achievements in this area. It is worth mentioning that some of these research questions originated in the area of temporal reasoning and most methods can be applied to both spatial and temporal reasoning (see Chapter 12).

13.3.1 Deduction

If the properties of the spatial relations and entities under consideration are represented axiomatically in a logical formalism, then of course a standard deduction mechanism for the formalism could be used for reasoning about the spatial knowledge so represented. As described in Section 13.2.4, the Region Connection Calculus was defined in first-order logic [163]. Even though reasoning in this first order representation of RCC (or indeed any first order mereotopology) is undecidable [104], first order theorem proving has been used to verify a number of theorems including those relating to the RCC-8 composition table [162] and its *conceptual neighbourhood* [110].

In order to create a decidable reasoning procedure, Bennett developed encodings of the RCC-8 relations first in propositional intuitionistic logic [11] and later an advanced encoding in propositional modal logic [12]. The encoding does not reflect the full expressive power of the first order RCC-8 theory, but does enable a decision procedure to be built. In the modal encoding, regions are represented as propositional atoms and a modal operator $\mathbf{I}$ is used to represent the interior of a region, i.e., if X represents a region, then $\mathbf{I}X$ represents the interior of X. The interior operator is an S4 modality and goes back to work by Tarski [194]. The usual propositional operators are used to represent intersection, union, or complement or regions. In addition, Bennett divides the propositional formulas into two types, *model constraints* which have to hold in all models of the encoding, and *entailment constraints* which are not allowed to hold in any model of the encoding. The model and entailment constraints are combined to a single formula using another modal operator $\square$ which Bennett calls a strong S5 modality.

When encoding spatial relations in different logics, it is important to not only encode the properties of the relations, but also the properties of the spatial entities that are being used. Bennett's initial encodings were missing the regularity property of regions which was later added to the encoding [172]. The extended modal encoding was shown to be equivalent to the intended interpretation of the RCC-8 relations [149].

The intuitionistic and modal encodings were not only useful for providing a decidable decision procedure for reasoning about spatial information represented using RCC-8 relations, but also formed the basis for the subsequent computational analysis of RCC-8. Nebel [145] used the intuitionistic encoding for showing that the RCC-8 consistency problem is tractable if only base relations are used.[17] Renz and Nebel [172] used Bennett's modal encoding and transformed it into a classical propositional encoding. As well as performing actual spatial reasoning on an RCC-8 representation, the propositional encoding has also been used for analysing the computational properties of RCC-8. Since modern SAT solvers are extremely efficient, it might be possible that deductive reasoning can be used for obtaining efficient solutions to spatial reasoning problems. A similar analysis has been done by Pham et al. [153] who compared reasoning over the interval algebra using constraint-based reasoning methods with deductive reasoning using modern SAT solvers. First results indicate that deductive reasoning can be more efficient in some cases than constraint based reasoning.

---

[17]Due to the missing regularity conditions in the intuitionistic encoding, Nebel's result turned out to be incomplete.

There have been several extensions of the modal encoding of RCC-8 to deal with more expressive spatial and also with spatio-temporal information. BRCC-8 generalises the RCC-8 modal encoding to also cover Boolean combinations of spatial regions [212]. $S4_u$ which is the propositional modal logic S4 extended with the universal modalities is the most general version and contains both BRCC and RCC-8 as fragments [213]. Several of these fragments have been combined with different temporal logics and compared with respect to their expressiveness and their complexity [89]. Modal logics are closely related to Description Logics, and in this context, we note that some research has been on spatial description logics [106].

Some work has also investigated constraint languages more expressive than mereotopology: it has been shown that the constraint language of $EC(x, y)$, $PP(x, y)$ and $conv(x)$ is intractable (it is at least as hard as determining whether a set of algebraic constraints over the reals is consistent) [55].

13.3.2 Composition

Given a domain of spatial entities $\mathcal{D}$, spatial relations are subsets of the cross-product of $\mathcal{D}$ and may contain an infinite number of tuples, i.e., $R \subseteq \{(a, b) \mid a, b \in \mathcal{D}\}$, since $\mathcal{D}$ may itself be infinite. Having a set of jointly exhaustive and pairwise disjoint base relations $\mathcal{A}$ and considering the powerset $2^{\mathcal{A}}$ of the base relations as the set of possible relations, the algebraic operations union, intersection, and complement of relations are straightforward to compute. If the set of base relations is chosen in a way such that the converse relations of all base relations are also base relations, then the converse operator is also easy to compute. The most important algebraic operator which is the basis for reasoning over spatial relations is the *composition* operator which is defined as $R \circ S = \{(x, y) \mid \exists z \colon (x, z) \in R \text{ and } (z, y) \in S\}$ for two relations R and S. If composition is known for all pairs of base relations, then composition of all relations can be computed as the union of the pairwise compositions of all base relations contained in the relation, i.e., $R \circ S = \{R_i \circ S_j \mid R_i, S_j \in \mathcal{A}, R_i \subseteq R, S_j \subseteq S\}$. Therefore, if the composition and the converse of all base relations are known and if they are all contained in $2^{\mathcal{A}}$, i.e., if $2^{\mathcal{A}}$ is closed under composition and converse, then it is possible to reason about spatial relations without having to consider the tuples contained in the relations. The relations can then be treated as symbols that can be manipulated using the algebraic operators. In the following section we describe how this can be done using constraint-based reasoning methods.

The question remains how the composition of base relations can be computed if the domains are infinite. While it is possible to compute composition in situations where the domains can be ordered or are otherwise well-structured (for example, domains based on linear orders such as the Directed Interval Algebra [168] or the rectangle algebra [8]), in many cases it is not possible to compute composition effectively. This includes RCC-8 where it is possible to find example scenarios which show that the given composition table is not correct. One example given by Düntsch [61] considers three regions A, B, C in two-dimensional space where A is a doughnut and B its hole. It is not possible to find a region C which is externally connected to A and B and therefore the tuple (A, B) which is contained in the relation EC is not contained in EC ∘ EC. So the composition of EC with EC does not contain EC even though this is specified in the RCC-8 composition table. In cases where it is not possible to compute composition or where a set of relations is not closed under composition, it is necessary to resort to a weaker form of composition in order to apply constraint-based reasoning mechanisms. Düntsch [61] proposed using *weak composition*. The weak composition of two relations $R, S \in 2^{\mathcal{A}}$ is the strongest relation of $2^{\mathcal{A}}$ which contains the actual composition, i.e., $R \circ_w S = \{B \mid B \in \mathcal{A}, B \cap (R \circ S) \neq \emptyset\}$. It is clear that any set $2^{\mathcal{A}}$ is always closed under weak-composition and therefore constraint-based reasoning methods can be applied to these relations. The RCC-8 composition table [162] is actually a weak composition table.

   If only weak composition can be used, some of the inferences made by composing relations are not correct and might lead to wrong results. It has been shown that correctness of the inferences does not depend on whether composition or only weak composition is used, but on a different property, namely, whether a set of relations is closed under constraints [170]. A set of relations $2^{\mathcal{A}}$ is *closed under constraints* if for none of its base relations $R \in \mathcal{A}$ there exists two sets Θ_1, Θ_2 of constraints over $2^{\mathcal{A}}$ which both contain the constraint $x R y$ such that the following property holds: Θ_1 and Θ_2 refine the constraint $x R y$ to the constraints $x R_1 y$ and $x R_2 y$, respectively, where $R_1, R_2 \subseteq R$ and $R_1 \cap R_2 = \emptyset$. That is none of the atomic relations can be refined to two non-overlapping sub-atomic relations by using arbitrary sets of constraints.

13.3.3   Constraint-based Spatial Reasoning

Using constraint-based methods for spatial reasoning gives the possibility to capture much of spatial reasoning within a unified framework. Even though qualitative spatial information is very diverse and covers different spatial aspects, it is usually expressed in terms of spatial relations between spatial entities which can be expressed using constraints. As mentioned in the introduction of this section, many different spatial reasoning tasks can be reduced to the *consistency problem*, on which we will focus on in this section.

Definition 1. *Let $\mathcal{A}$ be a finite set of JEPD binary relations and over a (possibly infinite) domain $\mathcal{D}$ and $\mathcal{S} \subseteq 2^{\mathcal{A}}$. The consistency problem* CSPSAT($\mathcal{S}$) *is defined as follows*:

   Instance: *A finite set V of variables over the domain $\mathcal{D}$ and a finite set Θ of binary constraints $x R y$, where $R \in \mathcal{S}$ and $x, y \in V$.*

   Question: *Is there an instantiation of all variables in Θ with values from $\mathcal{D}$ such that all constraints in Θ are satisfied?*

   Constraint-based reasoning uses constraint propagation in order to eliminate values from the domains which are not consistent with the constraints (see Chapter 4). Since the domains used in spatial and temporal reasoning are usually infinite, restricting the domains is not feasible. Instead, it is possible to restrict the domains indirectly by restricting the relations that can hold between the spatial entities. This can only be done if there is a finite number of relations and an effective way of propagating relations, which is the case if we have a set of relations $\mathcal{S} \subseteq 2^{\mathcal{A}}$ which is closed under intersection, converse and weak composition. These operators are the only means we have for propagating constraints. While it is possible to use composition of higher arity, usually only binary composition is used for propagating constraints.

The best known constraint propagation algorithm for spatial CSPs is the *path-consistency algorithm* [136] (see also Chapter 4 of this Handbook). It is a local consistency algorithm which makes all triples of variables of Θ consistent by successively refining all constraints using the following operation until either a fixed point is reached or one constraint is refined to the empty relation: $\forall x, y, z. x\{R\}y := x\{R\}y \cap (x\{S\}z \circ z\{T\}y)$. If the empty relation occurs, then Θ is inconsistent, otherwise the resulting set is called *path-consistent*. If $2^{\mathcal{A}}$ is closed under composition, intersection and converse, then the path-consistency algorithm terminates in cubic time.

Path-consistency is equivalent to 3-consistency [88] which holds if for every consistent instantiation of two variables is always possible to find an instantiation for any third variable such that the three variables together are consistent. 3-consistency can be generalised to *k-consistency* which holds if for any consistent instantiation of $k - 1$ variables there is always a consistent instantiation for any kth variable. In order to compute k-consistency, it is necessary to have $(k - 1)$-ary composition. In the following we restrict ourselves to 3-consistency and the associated path-consistency algorithm which uses binary composition.

In many cases, composition cannot be computed and only weak composition is available. In these cases, the path-consistency algorithm cannot be applied and a weaker algorithm, the *algebraic-closure algorithm* must be used [132]. Both algorithms are identical except that the path-consistency algorithm uses composition while the algebraic-closure algorithm uses weak composition. If the algebraic closure algorithm is applied to a set of constraints and a fixed point is reached, the resulting set is called *algebraically closed* or *a-closed*. It is clear that unless weak-composition is equivalent to composition, an a-closed set is usually not 3-consistent.

Local consistency algorithms such as path-consistency and algebraic-closure, and possible variants of these algorithms which make use of composition of higher arity, are the central methods that constraint-based reasoning offers to solving the consistency problem. It is highly desirable that for a given set of relations $2^{\mathcal{A}}$, the consistency problem for the base relations, i.e., CSPSAT($\mathcal{A}$), can be decided using a local consistency algorithm. It has been shown that algebraic-closure decides CSPSAT($\mathcal{A}$) if and only if $2^{\mathcal{A}}$ is closed under constraints [170]. While this is mainly useful for showing that algebraic closure does not decide CSPSAT($\mathcal{A}$), the other direction has to be manually proven for each set $\mathcal{A}$ and for each domain $\mathcal{D}$. If a decision procedure for CSPSAT($\mathcal{A}$) can be found, then the consistency problem for the full set of relations is also decidable and can be decided by backtracking over all sub-instances which contain only base relations.

The basic backtracking algorithm takes as input a set of constraints Θ over a set of relations $\mathcal{S} \subseteq 2^{\mathcal{A}}$, selects an unprocessed constraint $x\{R\}y$ of Θ, splits R into its base relations $B_1, \ldots, B_k$, replaces $x\{R\}y$ with $x\{B_i\}y$ and repeats this process recursively until all constraints are refined. If the resulting set of constraints is consistent, which can be shown using the local consistency algorithm, then Θ is consistent. Otherwise the algorithm backtracks and replaces the last constraint with the next possible base relation $x\{B_j\}y$. If all possible refinements of Θ are inconsistent, then Θ is inconsistent. The backtracking algorithm spans a search tree where each recursive call is a node and each leaf is a refinement of Θ which contains only base relations. If CSPSAT($\mathcal{A}$) can be decided in polynomial time, then CSPSAT($2^{\mathcal{A}}$) is in NP and the runtime of the backtracking algorithm is exponential in the worst case.

There are several ways of improving the performance of the backtracking algorithm. The easiest way is to apply the local consistency algorithm at every recursive step. This prunes the search tree by removing base relations that cannot lead to a solution. Nebel [147] has shown that the interleaved application of the path-consistency algorithm does not alter the outcome of the backtracking algorithm, but considerably speeds up its performance. The performance can also be improved by using heuristics for selecting the next unprocessed constraint and for selecting the next base relations. The first choice can reduce the size of the search tree while the second choice can help finding a consistent sub-instance earlier. While the basic backtracking algorithm refines a set Θ to sets containing only base relations, it is also possible to use any other set of relations $\mathcal{T}$ which contains all base relations and for which there is an algorithm which decides consistency for this set. If $\mathsf{CSPSAT}(\mathcal{T})$ can be decided in polynomial time, $\mathcal{T}$ is a *tractable subset* of $2^{\mathcal{A}}$. A tractable subset is a *maximal tractable subset*, if adding any other relation not contained in the tractable subset leads to an intractable subset. Tractable subsets can be used to improve backtracking by splitting each constraint $x\{R\}y \in \Theta$ into constraints $x\{T_1\}y, x\{T_2\}, \ldots, x\{T_s\}y$ such that $\bigcup_i T_i = R$ and all $T_i \in \mathcal{T}$, and by backtracking over these constraints. This considerably reduces the *branching factor* of the search tree. Instead of splitting each relation into all of its base relations, they can be split into sub-relations contained in $\mathcal{T}$ [126]. The average branching factor of the resulting search tree depends on how well $\mathcal{T}$ splits the relations of $2^{\mathcal{A}}$. The lower the average branching factor, the smaller the search tree.

It has been shown in detailed empirical analyses [173] that large tractable subsets combined with different heuristics can lead to very efficient solutions of the consistency problem. While it is not possible to determine in advance which choice of heuristics will be most successful for solving an instance of a spatial reasoning problem, it is clear that having large tractable subsets will always be an advantage. A lot of research effort has therefore been spent on identifying tractable subsets of spatial calculi.

The methods described above of using constraint propagation for determining local consistency and using backtracking for solving the general consistency problem can be applied to all kinds of spatial information if the spatial relations used are constructed from a set of base relations and the information is expressed in the form of constraints over these relations. This has the advantage that general methods and algorithms can be applied and that results for one set of spatial relations can be carried over to other sets. One problem with this approach is that spatial entities are treated as variables which have to be instantiated using values of an infinite domain. How to integrate this with settings where some spatial entities are known or can only be from a small domain is still unknown and is one of the main future challenges of constraint-based spatial reasoning.

13.3.4 Finding Efficient Reasoning Algorithms

As discussed in the previous section, large tractable subsets of spatial calculi are the most important part of efficient spatial reasoning. In order to find tractable subsets, or even maximal tractable subsets, several ingredients have to be provided:

1. One ingredient is a method for proving the complexity of a given subset, or slightly weaker, a sound method for proving that a given subset is tractable.

2. The second ingredient is a way of finding subsets that might be tractable subsets and for which the method described above can be used. A set of n base relations contains 2^n relations and $2^{(2^n)}$ different subsets. It is impossible to test all subsets for tractability, so the number of candidate sets should be made as small as possible.

3. In order to show that a tractable subset is a maximal tractable subset, it must be shown that any relation which is not contained in the tractable subset leads to an NP-hard subset when added to the tractable subset. For this it is necessary to have a method for proving NP-hardness of a given subset.

4. For a complete analysis of tractability, it must be shown that the identified tractable subsets are maximal tractable subsets and that no other subset which is not contained in one of the maximal tractable subsets is tractable.

In this section we are interested in finding tractable subsets of 2^A for efficiently solving the consistency problem CSPSAT(A). We are therefore only interested in finding tractable subsets which contain all base relations as only these subsets can be used as split-sets in our backtracking algorithm. There has been a series of papers on finding tractable subsets of the Interval Algebra (e.g., [122]) and also of RCC-5 [117] which do not contain all base relations and which are mainly interesting for a theoretical understanding of what properties lead to intractability.

The number of subsets which have to be considered for analysing complexity can be greatly reduced by applying the closure property [172]: the closure of a set $S \subseteq 2^A$ under composition, intersection and converse has the same complexity as S itself. For finding tractable subsets this means that only subsets which are closed under the operators have to be considered, as all subsets of a tractable set are also tractable. This can only be applied if a set is closed under composition. Since in many cases only weak composition is known, it is not obvious that the closure under weak composition has the same complexity. It has only recently been shown [170] that whenever algebraic-closure decides consistency of CSPSAT(A), i.e., for atomic CSPs, then the closure under weak composition preserves complexity.

There have been several methods for finding tractable subsets of NP-hard sets of relations. The most obvious way is to find a polynomial one-to-one transformation of CSPSAT to another NP-hard problem for which tractable subclasses are known. The most popular problem is certainly the propositional satisfiability problem SAT for which two tractable subclasses are known, HORNSAT where each clause contains at most one positive literal, and 2SAT where each clause contains at most two literals. If CSPSAT(2^A) can be reduced to SAT and it is possible to find relations of 2^A which lead to Horn clauses (HORNSAT) or Krom clauses (2SAT), respectively, then the set of all these relations is tractable. This method has first been applied by Nebel and Bürckert [146] for the Interval Algebra and later also by Nebel [145] and by Renz and Nebel [172] for RCC-8.

A different method has been proposed by Ligozat [129] who transformed the relations of the Interval Algebra to regions on a plane and to the lines that separate the regions. The dimension of a relation is the dimension to which a relation is transformed to, a two-dimensional region, a one-dimensional line, or a zero-dimensional point (the intersection of lines). Ligozat showed that the set of those relations that can be transformed to a convex set are tractable (the *convex relations*), and also those relations which do not yield a convex region but a region for which the convex closure adds only relations of lower dimension (the *preconvex relations*). This method has also been applied to other sets of relations, in particular those which are somehow derived from the interval algebra [131], but it seems that the preconvexity method cannot be generalised for every algebra.

These methods have in common that they can only be used for proving tractability of one or maybe two different particular subsets, but not for showing tractability for arbitrary subsets. Another method that has been proposed, the *refinement method* [167], is more general and can be applied to any subset. The refinement method takes as input a refinement strategy, which is a mapping of every relation of the to be tested subset S to a subset T for which it is known that algebraic closure decides consistency in polynomial time. The mapping must be a refinement, i.e., every relation $S \in S$ must be mapped to a relation $T \in T$ such that $T \subseteq S$. The refinement method then checks every a-closed triple of relations over S and tests whether making the refinements leads to an inconsistency. If none of the original refinements nor the new refinements obtained by applying the method result in an inconsistency, then algebraic closure also decides consistency for S and therefore S is a tractable subset. The refinement method relies upon finding a suitable refinement strategy. It has been shown that using the identity refinement strategy, i.e., removing all identity relations, was successful for all the tested subsets of RCC-8 and the interval algebra [167].

Even though the refinement method is very general, it does not help with finding candidate sets to which it can be applied. All candidates have in common that they must be closed under (weak) composition, converse and intersection and they must not contain any relation which is known to be an NP-hard relation. Therefore we also need methods for identifying NP-hard relations, i.e., relations that make the consistency problem NP-hard when combined with the base relations. In order to show NP-hardness of a set of relations $\mathcal{N} \subseteq 2^{\mathcal{A}}$, it is sufficient to find a known NP-hard problem which can be polynomially reduced to CSPSAT($\mathcal{N}$). This is a difficult problem and might require a different transformation from a different NP-hard problem for each different set $\mathcal{N}$. However, since CSPSAT has a common structure for all sets of relations, namely, a constraint graph where the labels on the edges are unions of base relations, it is possible to generate the transformations with computer assisted methods.

Renz and Nebel [172] proposed a scheme for transforming 3SAT variants to CSPSAT by translating variables, literals and clauses to a set of spatial constraints and to relations $R_t, R_f \in 2^{\mathcal{A}}$ which correspond to variables and literals being true (R_t) or false (R_f). For example, each variable p is transformed to the constraints $x_p^+ \{R_t, R_f\} y_p^+$ and $x_p^- \{R_t, R_f\} y_p^-$ where the first constraint is refined to the relation R_t if p is true and the second one to R_f if p is true. In order to ensure this, additional *polarity constraints* between the remaining pairs of x_p^+, x_p^-, y_p^+ and y_p^- are needed. *Clause constraints* which ensure that the requirements imposed by the clauses hold for the spatial variables are also needed. The relations R_t and R_f as well as the relations contained in the polarity and clause constraints can be found by exhaustive search over all possible relations. If an assignment of relations of $2^{\mathcal{A}}$ to this constraint schema can be found and if it can be shown that the transformation preserves consistency, then the set $\mathcal{N}$ of all relations used in this schema is NP-hard.

Based on this NP-hard subset $\mathcal{N}$, it is possible to identify other NP-hard subsets using the closure property and a computer assisted enumeration of different subsets. Every subset of $2^{\mathcal{A}}$ whose closure contains $\mathcal{N}$ is also an NP-hard subset. Easier to compute and more useful is the property that for a known tractable subset $\mathcal{T}$ and every relation $R \in 2^{\mathcal{A}}$ which is not contained in $\mathcal{T}$, $\mathcal{T} \cup \{R\}$ is NP-hard if its closure contains a known NP-hard set. This property can be used to compute whether a tractable subset is a maximal tractable subset, namely, if every extension of the set is NP-hard.

By combining the presented methods, the closure property, the refinement method, the transformation schema and computer assisted enumerations, a complete analysis of tractability can be made. This has been demonstrated for RCC-8 [167] where three maximal tractable subsets were identified. These subsets combined with different backtracking heuristics lead to very efficient solutions of the RCC-8 consistency problem and most of the hardest randomly generated instances were solved very efficiently [173].

In a recent paper, Renz [169] extended the refinement method and presented a procedure which automatically identifies large tractable subsets given only the base relations $\mathcal{A}$ and the corresponding weak composition table. The sets generated by Renz's procedure are guaranteed to be tractable if algebraic-closure decides CSPSAT($\mathcal{A}$). The procedure automatically identified all maximal tractable subsets of RCC-8 in less than 5 minutes and for the Interval Algebra in less than one hour.

13.3.5 Planar Realizability

Given a metric spatial description it is a simple matter to display it. But given a purely qualitative spatial configuration then finding a metric interpretation which satisfies it is not, in general, trivial. A particular problem of interest here is whether mereotopological descriptions have planar realizations, where all the regions are simply connected; clearly this is not possible in general, since it is easy to specify a 5-clique using a set of externally connected regions, and a 5-clique graph is not realisable in the plane. This problem has been studied, initially in [103][18] which considers an RCC-8 like calculus and two simpler calculi and determines which of a number of different problem instances of relational consistency and planar realizability are tractable and which are not—the latter is the harder problem. Planar realizability is of particular interest for the 9-intersection calculus since it is defined for planar regions. Until recently it was unknown if the consistency problem for the 9-intersection calculus is decidable at all and it has only recently been shown that the problem is NP-complete [182].

13.4 Reasoning about Spatial Change

So far we have concentrated purely on static spatial calculi (although we briefly mentioned the combination of modal spatial and temporal logics above in Section 13.3.1). However it is important to develop calculi which combine space and time in an in-

---

[18]Claim 24 in this paper is subsequently admitted not to hold [28]; further work on this problem, generally known as the "map graph" recognition problem can be found in [29, 30, 197, 31].

tegrated fashion. We do not have the space here to deal with this topic in any detail. Galton's book [93] is an extended treatment of this topic.

As discussed in Chapter 9, an important aspect of qualitative reasoning is the standard assumption that change is continuous. A simple consequence is that while changing, a quantity must pass through all the intermediate values. For example, in the frequently used quantity space $\{-, 0, +\}$, a variable cannot transition from '$-$' to '$+$' without going through the intermediate value 0. In the relational spatial calculi we have concentrated on in this chapter, this requirement manifests itself in knowing which relations are neighbours in the sense that if the predicate holds at a particular time, then there is some continuous change possible such that the next predicate to hold will be a neighbour. *Continuity networks* defining such neighbours are often called *conceptual neighbourhoods* in the literature following the use of the term [87] to describe the structure of Allen's 13 JEPD relations [2] according to their conceptual closeness[19] (e.g., *meets* is a neighbour of both *overlaps* and *before*). Most of the qualitative spatial calculi reported in this paper have had conceptual neighbourhoods constructed for them,[20] for example, Fig. 13.3 illustrates the case for RCC-8. Continuity networks have been used as the basis of qualitative spatial simulations and reasoning about motion [52, 159, 67, 201, 202]. Continuity networks are presented essentially as axioms in most calculi; however there has been some work on inferring these from first principles [53, 110, 93].

There are two main approaches to spatio-temporal representation; in one, *snapshots* of the world at different instants of time are considered; alternatively, a true spatio-temporal ontology, typically a 4D region based representation is used, with time being one of the dimensions. Grenon and Smith discuss this *snap-scan* ontology [102] in more detail. Examples of 4D approaches to spatio-temporal representation include [144, 110, 111, 109].

13.5   Cognitive Validity

An issue that has not been much addressed yet in the QSR literature is the issue of cognitive validity. Claims are often made that qualitative reasoning is akin to human reasoning, but with little or no empirical justification. One exception to this is the study made of a calculus for representing topological relations between regions and lines [138]. Another study is [120] that has investigated the preferred Allen relation (interpreted as a 1D spatial relation) in the case that the composition table entry is a disjunction. Perhaps the fact that humans seem to have a preferred model explains why they are able to reason efficiently in the presence of the kind of ambiguity engendered by qualitative representations. In [119, 175] they extend their evaluation to topological relations.

---

[19]Note that one can lift this notion of closeness from individual relations to entire scenes via the set of relations between the common objects and thus gain some measure of their conceptual similarity as suggested by [23].

[20]A closely related notion is that of "closest topological distance" [67]—two predicates are neighbours if their respective n-intersection matrices differ by fewer entries than any other predicates; however the resulting neighbourhood graph is not identical to the true conceptual neighbourhood or continuity graph—some links are missing.

13.6   Final Remarks

In this paper we have presented some of the key ideas and results in the QSR literature, but space has certainly not allowed an exhaustive survey. A handbook on spatial logics [1] will cover some of the topics briefly described here in much more detail. As in so many other fields of knowledge representation it is unlikely that a single universal spatial representation language will emerge—rather, the best we can hope for is that the field will develop a library of representational and reasoning devices and some criteria for their most successful application. What we have outlined here are the major axes of the space of qualitative spatial representation and reasoning systems, and in particular the dimensions of variability, such as the choice of representational formalism (e.g., first order logic, modal logic, relation algebra), the ontology of spatial entities (e.g., points, lines, regions), the primitive relations and operators (such as the various JEPD sets of relations discussed above), and the different kinds of reasoning techniques (such as constraint based spatial reasoning).

As in the case of non-spatial qualitative reasoning, quantitative knowledge and reasoning must not be ignored—qualitative and quantitative reasoning are complementary techniques and research is needed to ensure they can be integrated—for example, by developing reliable ways of translating between the two kinds of formalisms[21]—this problem naturally presents itself when spatial information is acquired from sensors, in particular image/video data—i.e. how qualitative symbolic spatial representations are grounded in sensory and sensorimotor experience. Of particular interest is how to automatically learn appropriate spatial abstractions and representations, for example see [124, 90]. Equally, interfacing symbolic QSR to the techniques being developed by the diagrammatic reasoning community [97] is an interesting and important challenge.

In many situations, a hierarchical representation of space is desirable, for example, in robotics. Kuipers has promulgated the "Spatial Semantic Hierarchy" [123] as one such hierarchical model which consists of a number of distinct levels. Simply put, the "control level" is composed of sensor values, from which local 2D geometry and control laws can be determined. The next level is the "causal level"—a partially determined network in which actions determine transitions between states identified at the previous control level. The "topological level" describes space as being composed of paths, regions and places with relations between them such as we have described in this chapter. Being at a place corresponds to a distinct state of the causal layer. Finally the "metrical level" augments the topological level with metric information such as distance and orientation. There has also been work on hierarchical spatial reasoning in the context of a particular kind of spatial information, such as direction relations [151].

Another important part of future work in this area is to find general ways of combining different spatial calculi and analysing combined calculi. Most applications require more than just one spatial aspect. Even though many calculi are using constraint-based reasoning methods, combining constraints over different relations is a difficult problem as the relations have infinite domains. That means their interactions must be taken care of on a semantic level. This might require defining new relations which can negatively or positively affect properties of the combined calculi [95, 94, 74].

---

[21] Some existing research on this problem includes [82, 80, 192].

Acknowledgements

The first author gratefully acknowledges the financial support of several EPSRC grants (most recently GR/M56807, EP/DO61334/1 and EP/C014707/1). This chapter contains material from [47] and the second author of that review (Shyamanta Hazarika) is thanked for his contributions, as is Achille Varzi for his collaboration on [49] discussed in Section 13.2.4. Ernie Davis and Ben Kuipers made useful comments on a draft of this chapter for which we thank them. We also thank the many people with whom we have discussed spatial representation and reasoning, particularly members of the Leeds QSR group and the former SPACENET network.

Bibliography

[1] M. Aiello, J. van Benthem, and I. Pratt-Hartmann. *Handbook of Spatial Logics*. Springer, 2007.

[2] J.F. Allen. Maintaining knowledge about temporal intervals. *Communications of the ACM*, 26(11):832–843, 1983.

[3] N. Asher and J. Lang. When nonmonotonicity comes from distance. In B. Nebel and L. Dreschler-Fischer, editors. *KI-94: Advances in Artificial Intelligence*, pages 308–318. Springer-Verlag, 1994.

[4] N. Asher and L. Vieu. Toward a geometry of common sense: A semantics and a complete axiomatization of mereotopology. In *Proceedings of the 14th International Joint Conference on Artificial Intelligence (IJCAI-95)*, Montreal, 1995.

[5] M. Aurnague and L. Vieu. A three-level approach to the semantics of space. In C. Zelinsky-Wibbelt, editor. *The Semantics of Prepositions—from Mental Processing to Natural Language Processing*. Mouton de Gruyter, Berlin, 1993.

[6] M. Aurnague, L. Vieu, and A. Borillo. La représentation formelle des concepts spatiaux dans la langue. In M. Denis, editor. *Langage et Cognition Spatiale*, pages 69–102. Mason, Paris, 1997.

[7] B. Balbiani, V. Dugat, L.F. del Cerro, and A. Lopez. *Eléments de géométrie mécanique*. Editions Hermes, 1994.

[8] P. Balbiani, J.-F. Condotta, and L.F. del Cerro. A new tractable subclass of the rectangle algebra. In *Proceedings of the Sixteenth International Joint Conference on Artificial Intelligence (IJCAI-99)*, pages 442–447, 1999.

[9] P. Balbiani, J.-F. Condotta, and L.F. del Cerro. Tractability results in the block algebra. *Journal of Logic and Computations*, 12(5):885–909, 2002.

[10] P. Balbiani, L.F. del Cerro, T. Tinchev, and D. Vakarelov. Modal logics for incidence geometries. *Journal of Logic and Computations*, 7(1):59–78, 1997.

[11] B. Bennett. Spatial reasoning with propositional logics. In J. Doyle, E. Sandewall, and P. Torasso, editors. *Principles of Knowledge Representation and Reasoning: Proceedings of the 4th International Conference (KR94)*. Morgan Kaufmann, San Francisco, CA, 1994.

[12] B. Bennett. Modal logics for qualitative spatial reasoning. *Bulletin of the Interest Group in Pure and Applied Logic (IGPL)*, 4(1):23–45, 1996.

[13] B. Bennett. Logical representations for automated reasoning about spatial relationships. PhD thesis, School of Computer Studies, The University of Leeds, 1997.

[14] B. Bennett. A categorical axiomatisation of region-based geometry. *Fundamenta Informaticae*, 46:145–158, 2001.

[15] B. Bennett. Physical objects, identity and vagueness. In D. Fensel, D. McGuinness, and M.-A. Williams, editors. *Principles of Knowledge Representation and Reasoning: Proceedings of the Eighth International Conference (KR2002)*. Morgan Kaufmann, San Francisco, CA, 2002.

[16] B. Bennett, A.G. Cohn, P. Torrini, and S.M. Hazarika. A foundation for region-based qualitative geometry. In W. Horn, editor, *Proceedings of the 14th European Conference on Artificial Intelligence (ECAI'00)*, pages 204–208, 2000.

[17] B. Bennett and I. Düntsch. Axioms, algebras and topology. In I. Pratt-Hartmann, M. Aiello, and J. van Benthem, editors. *Handbook of Spatial Logics*. Springer, 2007.

[18] L. Biacino and G. Gerla. Connection structures. *Notre Dame Journal of Formal Logic*, 32(2):242–247, 1991.

[19] T. Bittner. On ontology and epistemology of rough location. In C. Freksa and D.M. Mark, editors. *Spatial Information Theory—Cognitive and Computational Foundations of Geographic Information Science*, *Lecture Notes in Computer Science*, vol. 1661, pages 433–448. Springer, 1999.

[20] T. Bittner and J.G. Stell. Rough sets in qualitative spatial reasoning. In *Rough Sets and Current Trends in Computing, Banff, October 2000, Proceedings*, *Lecture Notes in Computer Science*, vol. 2005, pages 445–453. Springer, 2001.

[21] S. Borgo, N. Guarino, and C. Masolo. A pointless theory of space based on strong connection and congruence. In L.C. Aiello and J. Doyle, editors. *Principles of Knowledge Representation and Reasoning: Proceedings of the 5th International Conference (KR94)*. Morgan Kaufmann, 1996.

[22] S. Borgo and M. Masolo. Full mereogeometries. *Journal of Philosophical Logic*, submitted for publication.

[23] H.T. Bruns and M. Egenhofer. Similarity of spatial scenes. In *Proceedings of the 7th International Symposium on Spatial Data Handling, SDH'96*, pages 173–184. Francis Taylor, Delft, 1996.

[24] L. Carlson and E. van der Zee. *Representing Directions in Language and Space*. Oxford University Press, Oxford, 2003.

[25] R. Cartwright. Scattered objects. In K. Lehrer, editor. *Analysis and Metaphysics*, pages 153–171. Reidel, Dordrecht, 1975.

[26] R. Casati and A. Varzi. The structure of spatial localization. *Philosophical Studies*, 82:205–239, 1996.

[27] R. Casati and A. Varzi. *Parts and Places: The Structures of Spatial Representation*. MIT Press, Cambridge, MA and London, 1999.

[28] Z.-Z. Chen, M. Grigni, and C.H. Papadimitriou. Planar map graphs. In *Proceedings of the Thirtieth Annual ACM Symposium on the Theory of Computing (STOC 1998)*, pages 514–523, 1998.

[29] Z.-Z. Chen, M. Grigni, and C.H. Papadimitriou. Map graphs. *Journal of the ACM*, 49(2):127–138, 2002.

[30] Z.-Z. Chen, M. Grigni, and C.H. Papadimitriou. Recognizing hole-free 4-map graphs in cubic time. *Algorithmica*, 45(2):227–262, 2006.

[31] Z.-Z. Chen, Z.-Z. He, and M.-Y. Kao. Nonplanar topological inference and political-map graphs. In *Proceedings of the Tenth Annual ACM–SIAM Symposium on Discrete Algorithms (SODA 1999)*, pages 195–204, 1999.

[32] Y. Chevriaux, E. Saux, and C. Claramunt. A landform-based approach for the representation of terrain silhouettes. In *GIS '05: Proceedings of the 13th Annual ACM International Workshop on Geographic Information Systems*, pages 260–266. ACM Press, New York, NY, USA, 2005.

[33] B.L. Clarke. A calculus of individuals based on 'connection'. *Notre Dame Journal of Formal Logic*, 23(3):204–218, July 1981.

[34] B.L. Clarke. Individuals and points. *Notre Dame Journal of Formal Logic*, 26(1):61–75, 1985.

[35] E. Clementini and R. Billen. Modeling and computing ternary projective relations between regions. *IEEE Transactions on Knowledge and Data Engineering*, 18(6):799–814, 2006.

[36] E. Clementini and P. Di Felice. A comparison of methods for representing topological relationships. *Information Sciences*, 3:149–178, 1995.

[37] E. Clementini and P. Di Felice. An algebraic model for spatial objects with undetermined boundaries. In P. Burrough and A.M. Frank, editors. *Proceedings, GISDATA Specialist Meeting on Geographical Entities with Undetermined Boundaries*. Taylor Francis, 1996.

[38] E. Clementini and P. Di Felice. Approximate topological relations. *International Journal of Approximate Reasoning*, 16:173–204, 1997.

[39] E. Clementini and P. Di Felice. A global framework for qualitative shape description. *GeoInformatica*, 1(1), 1997.

[40] E. Clementini, P. Di Felice, and D. Hernández. Qualitative representation of positional information. *Artificial Intelligence*, 95(2):317–356, 1997.

[41] E. Clementini, P. Di Felice, and P. Oosterom. A small set of formal topological relationships suitable for end user interaction. In D. Abel and B.C. Ooi, editors. *Advances in Spatial Databases, Proceedings of the 3rd International Symposium on Spatial Databases (SSD'93), Singapore, Lecture Notes in Computer Science*, vol. 692, pages 277–295. Springer-Verlag, 1994.

[42] A.G. Cohn. Formalising bio-spatial knowledge. In C. Welty and B. Smith, editors. *Proc. 2nd International Conference on Formal Ontology in Information Systems (FOIS'01)*, pages 198–209. ACM, 2001.

[43] A.G. Cohn, B. Bennett, J. Gooday, and N. Gotts. RCC: a calculus for region based qualitative spatial reasoning. *GeoInformatica*, 1:275–316, 1997.

[44] A.G. Cohn, B. Bennett, J. Gooday, and N. Gotts. Representing and reasoning with qualitative spatial relations about regions. In O. Stock, editor. *Spatial and Temporal Reasoning*, pages 97–134. Kluwer, 1997.

[45] A.G. Cohn and N.M. Gotts. The 'egg-yolk' representation of regions with indeterminate boundaries. In P. Burrough and A.M. Frank, editors. *Proceedings, GISDATA Specialist Meeting on Geographical Objects with Undetermined Boundaries*, pages 171–187. Francis Taylor, 1996.

[46] A.G. Cohn and N.M. Gotts. A mereological approach to representing spatial vagueness. In L.C. Aiello, J. Doyle, and S. Shapiro, editors. *Principles of Knowledge Representation and Reasoning: Proceedings of the 5th International Conference (KR 1996)*, pages 230–241. Morgan Kaufmann, 1996.

[47] A.G. Cohn and S.M. Hazarika. Qualitative spatial representation and reasoning: An overview. *Fundamenta Informaticae*, 46(1–2):1–29, 2001.

[48] A.G. Cohn, D.A. Randell, and Z. Cui. Taxonomies of logically defined qualitative spatial relations. *Int. J. of Human-Computer Studies*, 43:831–846, 1995.

[49] A.G. Cohn and A. Varzi. Mereotopological connection. *Journal of Philosophical Logic*, 32:357–390, 2003.

[50] M. Cristani. The complexity of reasoning about spatial congruence. *Journal of Artificial Intelligence Research*, 11:361–390, 1999.

[51] M. Cristani, A. Cohn, and B. Bennett. Spatial locations via morpho-mereology. In A.G. Cohn, F. Giunchiglia, and B. Selman, editors. *Principles of Knowledge Representation and Reasoning: Proceedings of the 7th International Conference (KR 2000)*, pages 15–25. Morgan Kaufmann, 2000.

[52] Z. Cui, A.G. Cohn, and D.A. Randell. Qualitative simulation based on a logical formalism of space and time. In *Proceedings of the 10th National Conference on Artificial Intelligence (AAAI-92)*, pages 679–684. AAAI Press, Menlo Park, CA, 1992.

[53] E. Davis. Continuous shape transformation and metrics on regions. *Fundamenta Informaticae*, 46(1–2):31–54, 2001.

[54] E. Davis. The expressivity of quantifying over regions. *Journal of Logic and Computation*, 16(6):891–916, 2006.

[55] E. Davis, N.M. Gotts, and A.G. Cohn. Constraint networks of topological relations and convexity. *Constraints*, 4(3):241–280, 1999.

[56] T. de Laguna. Point, line and surface as sets of solids. *The Journal of Philosophy*, 19:449–461, 1922.

[57] M. Donnelly. An axiomatic theory of common-sense geometry. PhD thesis, University of Texas, 2001.

[58] M. Donnelly. A formal theory for reasoning about parthood, connection, and location. *Artificial Intelligence*, 160(1–2):145–172, 2004.

[59] I. Düntsch. Relation algebras and their application in temporal and spatial reasoning. *Artificial Intelligence Review*, 23:315–357, 2005.

[60] I. Düntsch and G. Gediga. Uncertainty measures of rough set predictions. *Artificial Intelligence*, 106:109–137, 1998.

[61] I. Düntsch, J. Wang, and S. McCloskey. A relation-algebraic approach to the region connection calculus. *Theoretical Computer Science*, 255(1–2):63–83, 2001.

[62] S. Edelman. *Representation and Recognition in Vision*. MIT Press, Cambridge, MA, 1999.

[63] G. Edwards. The Voronoi model and cultural space: Applications to the social sciences and humanities. In A.U. Frank and I. Campari, editors. *Spatial Information Theory: A Theoretical Basis for GIS, Lecture Notes in Computer Science*, vol. 716, pages 202–214. Berlin, Springer-Verlag, 1993.

[64] M. Egenhofer. Topological similarity. In *Proceedings of the FISI workshop on the Topological Foundations of Cognitive Science, Reports of the Doctoral Series in Cognitive Science*, vol. 37. University of Hamburg, 1994.

[65] M. Egenhofer and R. Franzosa. Point-set topological spatial relations. *International Journal of Geographical Information Systems*, 5(2):161–174, 1991.

[66] M.J. Egenhofer. Query processing in spatial-query-by-sketch. *Journal of Visual Languages and Computing*, 8(4):403–424, 1997.

[67] M.J. Egenhofer and K.K. Al-Taha. Reasoning about gradual changes of topological relationships. In A.U. Frank, I. Campari, and U. Formentini, editors.

Theories and Methods of Spatio-temporal Reasoning in Geographic Space, Lecture Notes in Computer Science, vol. 639, pages 196–219. Springer-Verlag, Berlin, 1992.

[68] M.J. Egenhofer, E. Clementini, and P. Di Felice. Topological relations between regions with holes. *Int. Journal of Geographical Information Systems*, 8(2):129–144, 1994.

[69] M.J. Egenhofer and R.D. Franzosa. On the equivalence of topological relations. *International Journal of Geographical Information Systems*, 9(2):133–152, 1995.

[70] M.J. Egenhofer and D. Mark. Naive geography. In A.U. Frank and W. Kuhn, editors. *Spatial Information Theory: A Theoretical Basis for GIS, Lecture Notes in Computer Science*, vol. 988, pages 1–16. Springer-Verlag, Berlin, 1995.

[71] M.J. Egenhofer and J. Sharma. Topological relations between regions in R^2 and Z^2. In A. David and B. Ooi, editors. *Proceedings of the 3rd International Symposium on Advances in Spatial Databases, SSD'93, Singapore, Lecture Notes in Computer Science*, vol. 692. Springer, June 1993.

[72] C. Eschenbach. A mereotopological definition of point. In C. Eschenbach, C. Habel, and B. Smith, editors, *Topological Foundations of Cognitive Science, Papers from the Workshop at the FISI-CS*, Buffalo, 1994.

[73] C. Eschenbach and W. Heydrich. Classical mereology and restricted domains. *International Journal of Human-Computer Studies*, 43:723–740, 1995.

[74] M.T. Escrig, L.M. Cabedo, J. Pacheco, and F. Toledo. Several models on qualitative motion as instances of the CSP. *Inteligencia Artificial, Revista Iberoamericana de Inteligencia Artificial*, 17:55–71, 2002.

[75] M.T. Escrig and F. Toledo. A framework based on CLP extended with CHRs for reasoning with qualitative orientation and positional information. *Journal of Visual Languages and Computing*, 9:81–101, 1998.

[76] M. Evans. Can there be vague objects? *Analysis*, 38:208, 1978; Reprinted in his *Collected Papers*. Clarendon Press, Oxford, 1985.

[77] B. Faltings. A symbolic approach to qualitative kinematics. *Artificial Intelligence*, 56(2), 1992.

[78] B. Faltings. Qualitative spatial reasoning using algebraic topology. In A.U. Frank and W. Kuhn, editors. *Spatial Information Theory: A Theoretical Basis for GIS, Lecture Notes in Computer Science*, vol. 988, pages 17–30. Springer-Verlag, Berlin, 1995.

[79] R.W. Ferguson, J.L. Bokor, R.L. Mappus IV, and A. Feldman. Maintaining spatial relations in an incremental diagrammatic reasoner. In W. Kuhn, M.F. Worboys, and S. Timpf, editors. *COSIT, Lecture Notes in Computer Science*, vol. 2825, pages 136–150. Springer, 2003.

[80] J. Fernyhough, A.G. Cohn, and D. Hogg. Constructing qualitative event models automatically from video input. *Image and Vision Computing*, 18:81–103, 2000.

[81] M.M. Fleck. The topology of boundaries. *Artificial Intelligence*, 80(1):1–27, 1996.

[82] K. Forbus, P. Nielsen, and B. Faltings. Qualitative kinematics: A framework. In *Proceedings of the 10th International Joint Conference on Artificial Intelligence (IJCAI-87)*, pages 430–436, 1987.

[83] K.D. Forbus, R.W. Ferguson, and J.M. Usher. Towards a computational model of sketching. In *Intelligent User Interfaces*, pages 77–83, 2001.

[84] K.D. Forbus, P. Nielsen, and B. Faltings. Qualitative spatial reasoning: The clock project. *Artificial Intelligence*, 51:417–471, 1991.

[85] K.D. Forbus, J. Usher, and V. Chapman. Qualitative spatial reasoning about sketch maps. *AI Magazine*, 25(3):61–72, 2004.

[86] A.U. Frank. Qualitative spatial reasoning about distance and directions in geographic space. *Journal of Visual Languages and Computing*, 3:343–373, 1992.

[87] C. Freksa. Temporal reasoning based on semi-intervals. *Artificial Intelligence*, 54:199–227, 1992.

[88] E.C. Freuder. Synthesizing constraint expressions. *Communications of the ACM*, 21:958–966, 1978.

[89] D. Gabelaia, R. Kontchakov, A. Kurucz, F. Wolter, and M. Zakharyaschev. Combining spatial and temporal logics: expressiveness vs. complexity. *Journal of Artificial Intelligence Research*, 23:167–243, 2005.

[90] A. Galata, A.G. Cohn, D.R. Magee, and D. Hogg. Modeling interaction using learnt qualitative spatio-temporal relations and variable length Markov models. In F. van Harmelen, editor, *Proceedings of the 15th European Conference on Artificial Intelligence (ECAI'02)*, pages 741–745, 2002.

[91] A. Galton. The mereotopology of discrete space. In *Spatial Information Theory—Cognitive and Computational Foundations of Geographic Information Science, Lecture Notes in Computer Science*, vol. 1661, pages 251–266. Springer, 1999.

[92] A.P. Galton. Towards an integrated logic of space time and motion. In *Proceedings of the 13th International Joint Conference on Artificial Intelligence (IJCAI-93)*, Chambery, France, September 1993.

[93] A.P. Galton. *Qualitative Spatial Change*. Oxford University Press, 2000.

[94] A. Gerevini and B. Nebel. Qualitative spatio-temporal reasoning with RCC-8 and Allen's interval calculus: Computational complexity. In F. van Harmelen, editor. *Proceedings of the 15th European Conference on Artificial Intelligence, ECAI'2002*, Lyon, France, July 2002, pages 312–316. IOS Press, 2002.

[95] A. Gerevini and J. Renz. Combining topological and size information for spatial reasoning. *Artificial Intelligence*, 137(1–2):1–42, 2002.

[96] G. Gerla. Pointless geometries. In F. Buekenhout, editor. *Handbook of Incidence Geometry*, pages 1015–1031. Elsevier Science B.V., 1995 (Chapter 18).

[97] J. Glasgow, N.H. Narayanan, and B. Chandrasekara. *Diagrammatic Reasoning*. MIT Press, 1995.

[98] J.M. Gooday and A.G. Cohn. Visual language syntax and semantics: A spatial logic approach. In K. Marriott and B. Meyer, editors. *Proc. Workshop on Theory of Visual Languages*, Gubbio, Italy, 1996.

[99] N.M. Gotts. Using the RCC formalism to describe the topology of spherical regions. Technical report, Report 96.24, School of Computer Studies, University of Leeds, 1996.

[100] N.M. Gotts, J.M. Gooday, and A.G. Cohn. A connection based approach to common-sense topological description and reasoning. *The Monist*, 79(1):51–75, 1996.

[101] R. Goyal and M. Egenhofer. Consistent queries over cardinal directions across different levels of detail. In *Proceedings of the 11th International Workshop on Database and Expert Systems Applications*, pages 876–880, 2000.

[102] P. Grenon and B. Smith. Snap and span: Towards dynamic spatial ontology. *Spatial Cognition and Computation*, 5(1):69–104, 2004.

[103] M. Grigni, D. Papadias, and C. Papadimitriou. Topological inference. In *Proceedings of the 14th International Joint Conference on Artificial Intelligence (IJCAI-95)*, pages 901–906. Morgan Kaufmann, 1995.

[104] A. Grzegorczyk. Undecidability of some topological theories. *Fundamenta Mathematicae*, 38:137–152, 1951.

[105] A. Grzegorczyk. Axiomatizability of geometry without points. *Synthese*, 12:228–235, 1960.

[106] V. Haarslev. Theory and practice of visual languages and description logics. Habilitationsschrift, Fachbereich Informatik, Universität Hamburg.

[107] V. Haarslev and M. Wessel. Querying GIS with animated spatial sketches. In *Proceedings 1997 IEEE Symposium on Visual Languages (VL-97)*, pages 201–208, 1997.

[108] P.J. Hayes. The naive physics manifesto. In D. Mitchie, editor. *Expert Systems in the Micro-Electronic Age*. Edinburgh University Press, 1979.

[109] P.J. Hayes. Naive physics I: Ontology for liquids. In J.R. Hobbs and B. Moore, editors. *Formal Theories of the Commonsense World*, pages 71–89. Ablex, 1985.

[110] S. Hazarika. Qualitative spatial change: space–time histories continuity. PhD thesis, School of Computing, 2005.

[111] S.M. Hazarika and A.G. Cohn. Abducing qualitative spatio-temporal histories from partial observations. In D. Fensel, F. Guinchiglia, D. McGuinness, and A. Williams, editors. *Proceedings of the Eighth Conference on Principles of Knowledge Representation and Reasoning (KR 2002)*, pages 14–25. Morgan Kaufmann, 2002.

[112] D. Hernández. *Qualitative Representation of Spatial Knowledge. Lecture Notes in Artificial Intelligence*, vol. 804. Springer-Verlag, 1994.

[113] D. Hernández, E. Clementini, and P. Di Felice. Qualitative distances. In A. Frank and W. Kuhn, editors. *Spatial Information Theory: A Theoretical Basis for GIS, Lecture Notes in Computer Science*, vol. 988, pages 45–58. Springer-Verlag, Berlin, 1995.

[114] A. Herskovits. *Language and Spatial Cognition. An Interdisciplinary Study of Prepositions in English*. Cambridge University Press, 1986.

[115] J. Hobbs. Granularity. In *Proceedings of the 9th International Joint Conference on Artificial Intelligence (IJCAI-85)*, pages 432–435, 1985.

[116] A. Isli and A. Cohn. A new approach to cyclic ordering of 2d orientations using ternary relation algebras. *Artificial Intelligence*, 122(1–2):137–187, 2000.

[117] P. Jonsson and T. Drakengren. A complete classification of tractability in RCC-5. *Journal of Artificial Intelligence Research (JAIR)*, 6:211–221, 1997.

[118] S. Kaufman. A formal theory of spatial reasoning. In *Proceedings of the 2nd International Conference on Principles of Knowledge Representation and Reasoning (KR'91)*, pages 347–356, 1991.

[119] M. Knauff, R. Rauh, and J. Renz. A cognitive assessment of topological spatial relations: Results from an empirical investigation. In *Spatial Information Theory: A Theoretical Basis for GIS, Lecture Notes in Computer Science*, vol. 1329, pages 193–206. Springer, 1997.

[120] M. Knauff, R. Rauh, and C. Schlieder. Preferred mental models in qualitative spatial reasoning: A cognitive assessment of Allen's calculus. In *Proc. 17th Annual Conf. of the Cognitive Science Society*, 1995.

[121] C. Köhler, A. Ottlik, H.-H. Nagel, and B. Nebel. Qualitative reasoning feeding back into quantitative model-based tracking. In R.L. de Mántaras and L. Saitta, editors. *Proceedings of the 16th European Conference on Artificial Intelligence (ECAI-04)*, pages 1041–1042. IOS Press, 2004.

[122] A.A. Krokhin, P. Jeavons, and P. Jonsson. Reasoning about temporal relations: The tractable subalgebras of Allen's interval algebra. *Journal of the ACM*, 50(5):591–640, 2003.

[123] B. Kuipers. An intellectual history of the spatial semantic hierarchy. In M. Jefferies and A.W.-K. Yeap, editors. *Robot and Cognitive Approaches to Spatial Mapping*. Springer-Verlag, 2006.

[124] B. Kuipers, P. Beeson, J. Modayil, and J. Provost. Bootstrap learning of foundational representations. *Connection Science*, 18(2):145–158, 2006.

[125] B.J. Kuipers and Y.-T. Byun. A robot exploration and mapping strategy based on a semantic hierarchy of spatial representations. *Journal of Robotics and Autonomous Systems*, 8:47–63, 1991.

[126] P.B. Ladkin and A. Reinefeld. Effective solution of qualitative interval constraint problems. *Artificial Intelligence*, 57(1):105–124, Sept. 1992.

[127] F. Lehmann and A.G. Cohn. The EGG/YOLK reliability hierarchy: Semantic data integration using sorts with prototypes. In *Proc. Conf. on Information Knowledge Management*, pages 272–279. ACM Press, 1994.

[128] S. Li and M. Ying. Generalized region connection calculus. *Artificial Intelligence*, 160(1–2):1–34, 2004.

[129] G. Ligozat. A new proof of tractability for ORD–Horn relations. In *Proceedings of the 13th National Conference on Artificial Intelligence (AAAI 96)*, pages 395–401, 1996.

[130] G. Ligozat. Reasoning about cardinal directions. *Journal of Visual Languages and Computing*, 9:23–44, 1998.

[131] G. Ligozat, D. Mitra, and J.-F. Condotta. Spatial and temporal reasoning: beyond Allen's calculus. *AI Communications*, 17(4):223–233, 2004.

[132] G. Ligozat and J. Renz. What is a qualitative calculus? a general framework. In *Proceedings of the 8th Pacific Rim International Conference on Artificial Intelligence*, pages 53–64, 2004.

[133] J. Liu and L.K. Daneshmend. *Spatial Reasoning and Planning: Geometry, Mechanism, and Motion*. Springer, 2004.

[134] J. Liu. A method of spatial reasoning based on qualitative trigonometry. *Artificial Intelligence*, 98:137–168, 1998.

[135] Y. Liu, X. Wang, X. Jin, and L. Wu. On internal cardinal direction relations. In *Spatial Information Theory: International Conference, COSIT 2005, Lecture Notes in Computer Science*, vol. 3693, pages 283–299. Springer, 2005.

[136] A.K. Mackworth. Consistency in networks of relations. *Artificial Intelligence*, 8:99–118, 1977.

[137] H.A. Mallot and J.S. Allen. *Computational Vision: Information Processing in Perception and Visual Behavior*. MIT Press, Cambridge, MA, 2000.

[138] D. Mark, D. Comas, M. Egenhofer, S. Freundschuh, J. Gould, and J. Nunes. Evaluating and refining computational models of spatial relations through cross-linguistic human-subjects testing. In A. Frank and W. Kuhn, editors. *Spatial Information Theory: A Theoretical Basis for GIS, Lecture Notes in Computer Science*, vol. 988, pages 553–568. Springer-Verlag, Berlin, 1995.

[139] C. Masolo and L. Vieu. Atomicity vs. infinite divisibility of space. In *Spatial Information Theory—Cognitive and Computational Foundations of Geographic Information Science, Lecture Notes in Computer Science*, vol. 1661, pages 235–250. Springer, 1999.

[140] M. Mavrovouniotis and G. Stephanopoulos. Formal order-of-magnitude reasoning in process engineering. *Computers and Chemical Engineering*, 12:867–881, 1988.

[141] R.C. Meathrel and A.P. Galton. A hierarchy of boundary-based shape descriptors. In *Proceedings of the 17th International Joint Conference on Artificial Intelligence (IJCAI-01)*, pages 1359–1364, 2001.

[142] A. Mukerjee. Neat vs. scruffy: A survey of computational models for spatial expressions. In P. Oliver and K.-P. Gapp, editors. *Representation and Processing of Spatial Expressions*. Kluwer, 1998.

[143] A. Mukerjee and G. Joe. A qualitative model for space. In *Proceedings of the 8th National Conference on Artificial Intelligence (AAAI-90)*, pages 721–727. Morgan Kaufmann, Los Altos, CA, 1990.

[144] P. Muller. Topological spatio-temporal reasoning and representation. *Computational Intelligence*, 18(3):420–450, 2002.

[145] B. Nebel. Computational properties of qualitative spatial reasoning: First results. In I. Wachsmuth, R. Rollinger, and W. Brauer, editors. *Proceedings of the 19th German AI Conference (KI-95), Lecture Notes in Computer Science*, vol. 981, pages 233–244. Springer-Verlag, 1995.

[146] B. Nebel. Reasoning about temporal relations: a maximal tractable subset of Allen's interval algebra. *Journal of the ACM*, 42(1):43–66, January 1995.

[147] B. Nebel. Solving hard qualitative temporal reasoning problems: Evaluating the efficiency of using the ORD-Horn class. *CONSTRAINTS*, 3(1):175–190, 1997.

[148] J. Nicod. Geometry in the sensible world. Doctoral thesis, Sorbonne, 1924; English translation in *Geometry and Induction*. Routledge and Kegan Paul, 1969.

[149] W. Nutt. On the translation of qualitative spatial reasoning problems into modal logics. In *Proceedings of KI-99, Lecture Notes in Artificial Intelligence*, vol. 1701, pages 113–124. Springer, 1999.

[150] J. Pacheco, M.T. Escrig, and F. Toledo. Representing and reasoning on three-dimensional qualitative orientation point objects. In P. Brazdil and A. Jorge, editors. *Progress in Artificial Intelligence, Knowledge Extraction, Multi-agent Systems, Logic Programming and Constraint Solving, 10th Portuguese Conference on Artificial Intelligence, Lecture Notes in Computer Science*, vol. 2258, pages 298–305. Springer, 2001.

[151] D. Papadias and M.J. Egenhofer. Algorithms for hierarchical spatial reasoning. *GeoInformatica*, 1(3):251–273, 1997.

[152] D. Papadias and Y. Theodoridis. Spatial relations, minimum bounding rectangles, and spatial data structures. *International Journal of Geographic Information Systems*, 11(2):111–138, 1997.

[153] D.N. Pham, J.R. Thornton, and A. Sattar. Modelling and solving temporal reasoning as propositional satisfiability. In *Proceeding of the 4th International Workshop on Modelling and Reformulating*, Sitges, Spain, 2005.

[154] L. Polkowski and A. Skowron. Rough mereology in information systems. A case study: qualitative spatial reasoning. In *Rough Set Methods and Applications: New Developments in Knowledge Discovery in Information Systems*, pages 89–135. Physica-Verlag GmbH, Heidelberg, Germany, 2000.

[155] I. Pratt and O. Lemon. Ontologies for plane, polygonal mereotopology. *Notre Dame Journal of Formal Logic*, 38(2):225–245, 1997.

[156] I. Pratt and D. Schoop. A complete axiom system for polygonal mereotopology of the real plane. *Journal of Philosophical Logic*, 27:621–658, 1998.

[157] I. Pratt-Hartmann. Empiricism and rationalism in region-based theories of space. *Fundamenta Informaticae*, 46(1–2):159–186, 2001.

[158] O. Raiman. Order of magnitude reasoning. In *Proceedings of the 5th National Conference on Artificial Intelligence (AAAI-86)*, pages 100–104, 1986.

[159] R. Rajagopalan. A model for integrated qualitative spatial and dynamic reasoning about physical systems. In *Proceedings of the 12th National Conference on Artificial Intelligence (AAAI-94)*, pages 1411–1417, 1994.

[160] C.G. Ralha. A framework for dynamic structuring of information. PhD thesis, University of Leeds, 1996.

[161] D. Randell and A. Cohn. Modelling topological and metrical properties of physical processes. In R. Brachman, H. Levesque, and R. Reiter, editors. *Proceedings 1st International Conference on the Principles of Knowledge Representation and Reasoning (KR-89)*, pages 55–66. Morgan Kaufmann, Los Altos, CA, 1989.

[162] D.A. Randell, A.G. Cohn, and Z. Cui. Computing transitivity tables: A challenge for automated theorem provers. In *Proceedings of the 11th International Conference on Automated Deduction (CADE-92)*. Springer-Verlag, Berlin, 1992.

[163] D.A. Randell, Z. Cui, and A.G. Cohn. A spatial logic based on regions and connection. In *Proc. 3rd Int. Conf. on Knowledge Representation and Reasoning*, pages 165–176. Morgan Kaufmann, San Mateo, CA, 1992.

[164] D.A. Randell, M. Witkowski, and M. Shanahan. From images to bodies: Modelling and exploiting spatial occlusion and motion parallax. In *Proceedings of the 17th International Joint Conference on Artificial Intelligence (IJCAI-01)*, pages 57–66. Morgan Kaufmann, 2001.

[165] E. Remolina and B. Kuipers. Towards a general theory of topological maps. *Artificial Intelligence*, 152(1):47–104, 2004.

[166] J. Renz. A canonical model of the region connection calculus. In A.G. Cohn, L.K. Schubert, and S. Shapiro, editors. *Principles of Knowledge Representation and Reasoning: Proceedings of the 6th International Conference (KR-98)*, pages 330–341. Morgan Kaufman, 1998.

[167] J. Renz. Maximal tractable fragments of the region connection calculus: A complete analysis. In *Proceedings of the Sixteenth International Joint Conference on Artificial Intelligence (IJCAI-99)*, pages 448–455, 1999.

[168] J. Renz. A spatial odyssey of the interval algebra: 1. Directed intervals. In B. Nebel, editor. *Proceedings of the 17th International Joint Conference on Artificial Intelligence (IJCAI-01)*, pages 51–56. Morgan Kaufmann, 2001.

[169] J. Renz. Qualitative spatial and temporal reasoning: Efficient algorithms for everyone. In M.M. Veloso, editor. *Proceedings of the 20th International Joint Conference on Artificial Intelligence (IJCAI-07)*, pages 526–531, 2007.

[170] J. Renz and G. Ligozat. Weak composition for qualitative spatial and temporal reasoning. In *Principles and Practice of Constraint Programming—CP 2005, 11th International Conference*, pages 534–548, 2005.

[171] J. Renz and D. Mitra. Qualitative direction calculi with arbitrary granularity. In *Proceedings of the 8th Pacific Rim International Conference on Artificial Intelligence*, pages 65–74, 2004.

[172] J. Renz and B. Nebel. On the complexity of qualitative spatial reasoning: A maximal tractable fragment of the region connection calculus. *Artificial Intelligence*, 108(1–2):69–123, 1999.

[173] J. Renz and B. Nebel. Efficient methods for qualitative spatial reasoning. *Journal of Artificial Intelligence Research*, 15:289–318, 2001.

[174] J. Renz and B. Nebel. Qualitative spatial reasoning using constraint calculi. In M. Aiello, I. Pratt-Hartmann, and J. van Benthem, editors. *Handbook of Spatial Logics*. Springer-Verlag, Berlin, 2007.

[175] J. Renz, R. Rauh, and M. Knauff. Towards cognitive adequacy of topological spatial relations. In C. Freksa, W. Brauer, C. Habel, and K.F. Wender, editors. *Spatial Cognition, Lecture Notes in Computer Science*, vol. 1849, pages 184–197. Springer, 2000.

[176] R. Röhrig. A theory for qualitative spatial reasoning based on order relations. In *Proceedings of the 12th National Conference on Artificial Intelligence (AAAI-94)*, vol. 2, pages 1418–1423, Seattle, 1994.

[177] A.J.O. Roy and J.G. Stell. A qualitative account of discrete space. In M.J. Egenhofer and D.M. Mark, editors. *Proceedings of GIScience 2002, Lecture Notes in Computer Science*, vol. 2478, pages 276–290. Springer, 2002.

[178] P. Sablayrolles. Spatio-temporal semantics in natural language: the case of motion. In *Semantics of Time, Space, Movement and Spatio-Temporal Reasoning*, pages 69–88, 1992. Working Papers of the 4th International Workshop.

[179] P. Santos, B. Bennett, and G. Sakellariou. Supervaluation semantics for an inland water feature ontology. In L.P. Kaelbling and A. Saffiotti, editors. *Proceedings of the 19th International Joint Conference on Artificial Intelligence (IJCAI-05)*, pages 564–569. Professional Book Center, Edinburgh, 2005.

[180] P. Santos and M. Shanahan. Hypothesising object relations from image transitions. In van Harmelen [203], pages 292–296.

[181] P. Santos and M. Shanahan. A logic-based algorithm for image sequence interpretation and anchoring. In G. Gottlob and T. Walsh, editors. *Proceedings of the 18th International Joint Conference on Artificial Intelligence (IJCAI-03)*, pages 1408–1410. Morgan Kaufmann, 2003.

[182] M. Schaefer, E. Sedgwick, and D. Stefankovic. Recognizing string graphs in NP. *Journal of Computer and System Sciences*, 67(2):365–380, 2003.

[183] I. Schlaisich and M.J. Egenhofer. Multimodal spatial querying: what people sketch and talk about. In C. Stephanidis, editor. *Proceedings of the 9th International Conference on Human-Computer Interaction (HCI-01)*, pages 732–736. Lawrence Erlbaum, 2001.

[184] C. Schlieder. Representing visible locations for qualitative navigation. In N.P. Carreté and M.G. Singh, editors. *Qualitative Reasoning and Decision Technologies*, pages 523–532. CIMNE, Barcelona, 1993.

[185] C. Schlieder. Reasoning about ordering. In A. Frank and W. Kuhn, editors. *Spatial Information Theory: A Theoretical Basis for GIS, Lecture Notes in Computer Science*, vol. 988, pages 341–349. Springer-Verlag, Berlin, 1995.

[186] C. Schlieder. Qualitative shape representation. In P. Burrough and A.M. Frank, editors. *Proceedings, GISDATA Specialist Meeting on Geographical Objects with Undetermined Boundaries*. Francis Taylor, 1996.

[187] S. Schulz, P. Daumke, B. Smith, and U. Hahn. How to distinguish parthood from location in bioontologies. In *Proc. AMIA Symposium 2005*, pages 669–673, Washington DC, 2005.

[188] M. Shanahan. Default reasoning about spatial occupancy. *Artificial Intelligence*, 1995.

[189] P. Simons. *Parts: A Study in Ontology*. Clarendon Press, Oxford, 1987.

[190] B. Smith. Mereotopology: a theory of parts and boundaries. *Data and Knowledge Engineering*, 20(3):287–303, 1996.

[191] B. Smith and A.C. Varzi. The nîche. *Noûs*, 33(2):198–222, 1999.

[192] T. Sogo, H. Ishiguro, and T. Ishida. Acquisition of qualitative spatial representation by visual observation. In *Proceedings of the 16th International Joint Conference on Artificial Intelligence (IJCAI-99)*, pages 1054–1060, Stockholm, Sweden, 1999.

[193] J.G. Stell. Boolean connection algebras: A new approach to the region connection calculus. *Artificial Intelligence*, 122:111–136, 2000.

[194] A. Tarski. Les fondaments de la géométrie des corps. *Ksiega Pamiatkowa Pierwszego Polskiego Zjazdu Matematycznego*, pages 29–33, 1929. A suplement to *Annales de la Société Polonaise de Mathématique*. English translation: Foundations of the geometry of solids. In A. Tarski. *Logic, Semantics, Metamathematics*. Oxford Clarendon Press, 1956.

[195] A. Tarski. A Decision Method for Elementary Algebra and Geometry. In J.C.C. McKinsey, editor. The RAND Corporation, Santa Monica, CA, 1948.

[196] A. Tate, J. Hendler, and M. Drummond. A review of AI planning techniques. In J. Allen, J. Hendler, and A. Tate, editors. *Readings in Planning*. Morgan Kaufman, San Mateo, CA, 1990.

[197] M. Thorup. Map graphs in polynomial time. In *39th Annual Symposium on Foundations of Computer Science (FOCS-98)*, pages 396–405, 1998.

[198] S. Thrun. Robotic mapping: A survey. In G. Lakemeyer and B. Nebel, editors. *Exploring Artificial Intelligence in the New Millennium*. Morgan Kaufmann, 2002.

[199] T. Topaloglou. First order theories of approximate space. In F. Anger et al., editors. *Working Notes of AAAI Workshop on Spatial and Temporal Reasoning*, pages 283–296, Seattle, 1994. American Association for Artificial Intelligence.

[200] J.F.A.K. Van Benthem. *The Logic of Time*. D. Reidel Publishing Company, Dordrecht, Holland, 1983.

[201] N. Van de Weghe, A.G. Cohn, P. De Maeyer, and F. Witlox. Representing moving objects in computer-based expert systems: The overtake event example. *Expert Systems with Applications*, 29(4):977–983, November 2005.

[202] N. Van de Weghe, A.G. Cohn, G. De Tre, and P. De Maeyer. A qualitative trajectory calculus as a basis for representing moving objects in geographical information systems. *Cybernetics and Control*, 35(1):97–119, 2006.

[203] F. van Harmelen, editor. *Proceedings of the 15th European Conference on Artificial Intelligence (ECAI'2002)*, Lyon, France, July 2002. IOS Press, 2002.

[204] A. Varzi. Parts, wholes and part-whole relations: the prospects of mereotopology. *Data and Knowledge Engineering*, 20(3):259–286, 1996.

[205] A.C. Varzi. On the boundary between mereology and topology. In R. Casati, B. Smith, and G. White, editors. *Philosophy and the Cognitive Sciences: Proceedings of the 16th Wittgenstein Symposium*. Hölder–Pichler–Tempsky, Vienna, 1994.

[206] L. Vieu. Spatial representation and reasoning in AI. In O. Stock, editor. *Spatial and Temporal Reasoning*, pages 3–40. Kluwer, 1997.

[207] T. Wagner and K. Hübner. An egocentric qualitative spatial knowledge representation based on ordering information for physical robot navigation. In D. Nardi, M. Riedmiller, C. Sammut, and J. Santos-Victor, editors. *RobuCup, Lecture Notes in Computer Science*, vol. 3276, pages 134–149. Springer, 2004.

[208] H. Walischewski. Learning regions of interest in postal automation. In *Proceedings of 5th International Conference on Document Analysis and Recognition (ICDAR'99)*, Bangalore, India, 1999.

[209] D.S. Weld and J. De Kleer, editors. *Readings in Qualitative Reasoning About Physical Systems*. Morgan Kaufman, San Mateo, CA, 1990.

[210] A.N. Whitehead. *Process and Reality*. The MacMillan Company, New York, 1929. Corrected edition published in 1978 by Macmillan.

[211] A.N. Whitehead. In D.R. Griffin and D.W. Sherburne, editors. *Process and Reality*, corrected edition. The Free Press, Macmillan Pub. Co., New York, 1978.

[212] F. Wolter and M. Zakharyaschev. Spatial reasoning in RCC-8 with Boolean region terms. In *Proceedings of the 14th European Conference on Artificial Intelligence*, pages 244–250, 2000.

[213] F. Wolter and M. Zakharyaschev. Spatio-temporal representation reasoning based on RCC-8. In *Principles of Knowledge Representation and Reasoning Proceedings of the Seventh International Conference (KR'2000)*, pages 3–14, 2000.

[214] M.F. Worboys and M. Duckham. *Geographic Information Systems: A Computing Perspective*. 2nd edition. CRC Press, Boca Raton, FL, 2004.

[215] K. Zimmermann. Enhancing qualitative spatial reasoning—combining orientation and distance. In A. Frank and I. Campari, editors. *Spatial Information Theory: A Theoretical Basis for GIS, Lecture Notes in Computer Science*, vol. 716, pages 69–76. Springer-Verlag, Berlin, 1993.

[216] K. Zimmermann. Measuring without distances: the delta calculus. In A. Frank and W. Kuhn, editors. *Spatial Information Theory: A Theoretical Basis for GIS, Lecture Notes in Computer Science*, vol. 988, pages 59–68. Springer-Verlag, Berlin, 1995.

[217] K. Zimmermann and C. Freksa. Enhancing spatial reasoning by the concept of motion. In A. Sloman, editor. *Prospects for Artificial Intelligence*, pages 140–147. IOS Press, 1993.

Handbook of Knowledge Representation
Edited by F. van Harmelen, V. Lifschitz and B. Porter
© 2008 Elsevier B.V. All rights reserved
DOI: 10.1016/S1574-6526(07)03014-3

Chapter 14

Physical Reasoning

Ernest Davis

An intelligent creature or automaton that is set in a complex uncontrolled world will be able to act more effectively and flexibly if it understands the physical laws that govern its surroundings and their relation to its own actions and the actions of other agents. In this chapter we discuss work by KR researchers that tries to represent commonsense knowledge and carry out commonsense reasoning over some basic physical domains.

There is, of course, a vast body of computer science and scientific computing which deals in one way or another with physical phenomena; almost all of this lies outside the scope of KR research and hence of this chapter. Even within AI, there are many types of physical reasoning that are excluded here. For instance, the automated visual recognition of a scene is, in a sense, a type of physical reasoning. Image formation is a physical process; the problem in vision is to infer plausible characteristics of a scene given an image of it. Why is this not considered a problem for KR physical reasoning? Mainly because the physics involved is too specialized. A single, quite complex, physical process, and a single type of inference about the process are at issue; and the computational techniques to be applied are highly tuned to that process and that inference and hardly generalize to any other kind of problem.[1]

At the other end of the spectrum, most of the physical theories that appear in the KR literature, such as the STRIPS representations of actions, are too crude and narrow in scope to be of any interest as a physical theory. For instance, the classic blocks world theory applies only to rectangular blocks piled in strict stacks and manipulators constrained to moving a single block from one top of a stack to another; moreover, it does not characterize the positions or motions of the block or manipulator while being moved. The theory is therefore not even a useful start toward a general realistic theory of blocks of general shape in general positions being moved by an actual manipulator.

The most important difference between KR physical reasoning and scientific computing is that, whereas scientific computing almost always aims at achieving a high

---

[1] In principle, high-level physical reasoning could enter into visual recognition, either by providing constraints or measures of likelihood for possible scenes [44] or by relating physical conditions of the image formation process to qualities of the image—e.g., if the lens cap is left on, the image will be black. In practice, the former has been rarely attempted in vision research, and the latter, as far as I know, has never been attempted.

degree of numerical accuracy, KR is almost always content to achieve just a qualitative description. In many cases, predicting qualitative behavior with a high degree of certainty depends on predicting numerical values with a high degree of accuracy— e.g., will the car fall off the cliff, or stop short? In such cases, qualitative reasoning necessarily gives ambiguous results; either the car will stop short and remain intact, or it will fall over the edge and will crash and possibly explode. The quest for numerical accuracy means that most scientific computations involve a fine-grained division of time or space or both (except in the special cases of problems that have an exact symbolic solution). By contrast, KR physical reasoning almost always divides space, time, or space–time into physically significant intervals/regions/histories bounded by significant events/boundaries.

KR also differs from scientific computing in that it often attempts to:

- Incorporate a theory of action.

- Use knowledge for inference in different directions.

- Generate explanations in addition to answers.

- Address everyday domains at the human scale, rather domains that are esoteric, highly specialized, very small or very large.

- Use theories that are psychological plausible but not necessarily scientifically correct.

- Use explicit theories of causality.

- Study explicitly the interaction between alternative theories at different levels of abstraction. Scientific computation uses many theories at different levels of abstraction, but the problem of choosing the theory appropriate to a situation or of integrating multiple theories in solving a problem is generally left to a human understander (or hard-wired into code).

As contrasted with the *ad hoc* physical theories used in most planning and temporal reasoning, KR work in physical reasoning is distinguished by:

- Generality. The attempt to deal with all or nearly all possible configurations within a given domain. E.g., dealing with arbitrary configurations of blocks of arbitrary shape rather than with stacks of rectangular blocks.

- Continuous time and continuous change over time.

- Geometry and continuous change over space.

Of course, the dividing lines between KR physical reasoning and *ad hoc* KR theories at one end and conventional scientific computing at the other is not a sharp one; indeed, a very important problem for KR is how to integrate all these together.

KR physical reasoning generally involves two important forms of nonmonotonic reasoning. The first is a closed-world assumption, that all the entities that will influence a physical system are known or easily determined. This assumption is made both at the level of theory, that the domain theory accounts for all relevant types of events, processes, and so on; and at the level of the specific problem, that the problem statement accounts for all the individual objects, actions, and so on. The second is an idealization assumption, that a particular idealization can be safely used. Again this can either be at the level of the choice of theory, such as assuming that the objects in a problem can be modeled as rigid, or at the level of problem description, such as taking a block to be strictly rectangular. Ultimately, it must be expected that KR physical reasoning will have to deal with combining degrees of certainty, and thus require probabilistic or some similar form of reasoning, but little or no such work has yet been done.

Research in KR physical reasoning—which, for the remainder of this chapter we will call simply "physical reasoning"—can largely be divided into four categories:

Qualitative calculus. The development of representations and inference techniques for numeric quantities and functions whose value and relations are specified qualitatively. These calculi are the subject of Chapter 9 of this Handbook and are therefore not further discussed here.

Architecture. The development of general frameworks which support the statement of physical theories and the description of specific problems and scenarios. Section 14.1 describes the component model and the process model. Again, these theories are presented in Chapter 9, so our description here is brief and focuses on the ontology used in these architectures.

Domain theories. The analysis of particular physical domains. Section 14.2 describes kinematic and dynamic theories of solid objects and the theory of liquids.

Multiple models and levels of abstraction. Any model of a physical situation used in a reasoning task will include some features of the situation and abstract away others. Thus, a single situation may have many different models, which vary in the features and the detail they include. For instance, depending on the reasoning task, it may be suitable to model a soccer ball as a point object, a perfect sphere, or an irregular sphere; a rigid object or an elastic object; an object of uniform material, a uniform closed rubber shell around an interior of air, or a rubber shell with an inflation hole around an interior of air. Moreover, a reasoner may use more than one of these models in the course of a single reasoning task. The issues of choosing an appropriate model and combining models are therefore critical aspects of physical reasoning. These issues are discussed in Section 14.3.

We conclude in Section 14.4 with a historical and bibliographical survey; here we will mention some further work in the area that falls outside the above categories.

Terminological comment: In this chapter a *fluent* is an entity whose value may change as a function of time. For instance, the fluent "Temperature(O1)" represents the temperature of object O1 as function of time; the fluent "Place(O1)" represents the region occupied by object O1 as a function of time; the Boolean fluent "On(OA, OB)" represents the function of time which is TRUE at times when object OA is on OB and FALSE at other times. A *parameter* is a fluent whose value is in a numeric-valued space, such as temperature. Standard mathematical numerical and geometric functions are extended to fluents in the obvious way; for instance, if f and g are parameters, then $f + g$ denotes the parameter whose value at any time t is the sum of the values of f and g at t.

14.1 Architectures

An *architecture* for physical reasoning is a representational schema; that is, it is a structure that defines a high-level ontology and a basic set of relations and that supports the representation of various general domains and of specific problems, and the carrying out of particular types of inferences over those representations. Thus, it is roughly analogous to the STRIPS or PDDL representation for planning. The best established and most extensively studied architectures for physical reasoning are the component model and the process model; since these have been already considered in Chapter 9, our treatment of them here is brief and focuses on their ontologies rather than on reasoning methods.

14.1.1 Component Analysis

Many complex systems are designed and can be analyzed as a fixed configuration of standard *components*.

A component is an atomic entity with a number of *ports*. Each port has associated with it a number of *parameters* with numerical values. The component imposes constraints on the values of the parameters over time. These constraint are generally either algebraic constraints over the values of the parameters at a given time, or differential equations, relating the derivatives of the parameters at a given time to their values. In the component model, these constraints comprise the entire physical characteristics of the component; aside from the constraints, the component is a black box.

For example, a resistor has two ports a and b. Each port p has two parameters: the inflowing current $\text{InCurrent}(p)$ and the voltage $\text{Voltage}(p)$. A resistor r is characterized by two equations:

$$\text{InCurrent}(a) = -\text{InCurrent}(b) \quad \text{and}$$

$$\text{Voltage}(b) - \text{Voltage}(a) = \text{resistance}(r) \cdot \text{InCurrent}(b).$$

A capacitor c has the same types of ports and parameters and is characterized by the equations

$$\text{InCurrent}(a) = -\text{InCurrent}(b) \quad \text{and}$$

$$\text{InCurrent}(b) = \text{Capacitance}(c) \cdot \text{Derivative}(\text{Voltage}(b) - \text{Voltage}(a)).$$

A *node* is a collection of ports connected together. The node imposes a constraint on the parameters of the ports determined by the domain theory. For instance, in the electronics domain, if ports $p_1 \ldots p_k$ are connected at a node, then that creates the constraints

$$\text{InCurrent}(p_1) + \cdots + \text{InCurrent}(p_k) = 0 \quad \text{and}$$

$$\text{Voltage}(p_1) = \text{Voltage}(p_2) = \cdots \text{Voltage}(p_k).$$

A *system* is defined by a collection of components, and a partition of their ports into nodes. The structure of connections and the component characteristics are fixed over time; what varies over time are the values of the parameters. The set of constraints generated by the components and by the nodes determines the behavior of the system over time.

Electronic systems are the archetypal and best example of a domain that can be analyzed using the component model. The model has also been applied to hydraulic devices, heat transfer systems, and mechanical systems of certain types.

Actions can be incorporated into the component architecture by modeling an agent as an exogenous signal. That is, an agent is modeled as a component for which the values of the parameters are not determined by the theory and the remainder of the system, but rather can be "chosen". For example, in the electronics domain, an agent could be a voltage source that can choose a waveform to output; the waveform it chooses is its action.

Typical reasoning tasks carried out over component models include:

- *Static evaluation.* If all the constraints are algebraic, then determine the state (or the set of possible states) of the system.

- *Initial value problem.* If the constraints include differential equations, then determine the progress of the system following some starting condition.

- *Signal response.* Determine the output of a system in response to a specified signal at some input.

- *Comparative static evaluation.* Determine the effect of changing some component characteristic on the static state of the system.

- *Comparative dynamic evaluation.* Determine the effect of changing some component characteristic on the dynamic progress of the system.

The best known program using the component model was the ENVISION program of de Kleer and Brown [17]. ENVISION used the sign calculus to solve qualitatively the initial value problem and the comparative static evaluation problem. ENVISION also proposed a model of causality, in which an change to some exogenous parameter in the system causes changes to other parameters by propagating through the network, in a manner that has a sequence, though no measurable time duration.

14.1.2 Process Model

In the process model [23], change is brought about by *processes*, *events*, *actions*, and *indirect influences* between parameters.

A *process* is active over a time interval. It is characterized by preconditions and effects. The preconditions must hold for the process to begin. and they must continue to hold throughout the interval in which the process is active. If the preconditions cease to hold, then the process stops. The effects of a process are *direct influences* on numeric fluents. A direct influence is a contribution to the derivative of the fluent; the derivative of the fluent is the sum of the influences of all the processes that act on it.

For example, consider the process of a tap *t* filling a bucket *b*. The preconditions are that the tap is open, the bucket is under the tap, and the bucket is not yet full.

The process directly influences the fluent "volume of water in the bucket"; that is, the derivative of the volume of water is a sum of terms, one of which is the flow-rate of the tap t. For example, if there are several taps filling b and also a leak from the bottom of b, then the derivative of the volume of water in b is the sum of the flow-rates of the taps minus the flow-rate of the leak.

An *action* takes place at an instant. It is characterized by preconditions, which must hold for the action to be feasible, and effects, which are discontinuous changes in the value of a discrete or numeric fluent. For example, turning on a tap is an action. The precondition is that the agent is next to the tap and that the tap is closed. The effect is that the tap is open. If the preconditions of an action are satisfied, then an agent has the choice of whether or not he wishes to perform the action.

An *event* is similar to an action except that it is not a matter of choice; it is a natural discontinuous change that must take place if the conditions are met. For instance, suppose that you have a weak bucket whose bottom will fall out when the bucket is half full. Then the event "Bottom of B falls out" has the precondition that the bucket is at least half full and has the effect that what was formerly a bucket is now a disconnected cylinder and a pan.

Finally, parameter p is an *indirect influence* on parameter q if there is a natural constraint relating their two values. For example, the volume of liquid in a bucket is an indirect influence on the height of liquid in the bucket. It is assumed that the system of influences on system parameters can be structured in such a way that (a) no parameter is both directly and indirectly influenced; (b) the relation "p indirectly influences q" is acyclic.

The QP program [23] uses a process model to carry out qualitative projection. Conditions are conjunctions of discrete values, such as "The tap is open" and inequalities, either between one parameter and another, or between a parameter and a constant "landmark" value, such as "The level of water in the bucket is less than the depth of the bucket." Influences are specified in terms of their sign; e.g., the process of a tap filling a bucket has a positive influence on the volume of water in the bucket, while the process of leaking has a negative influence. Using this information QP can generate an "envisionment graph", a transition graph between states of the system. Any possible behavior of the system corresponds to a path through the envisionment graph. (The converse does not in general hold; there are often paths through the envisionment graph that do not correspond to physically possible behaviors.)

Both the component model and qualitative process theory are discussed at much greater length in Chapter 9.

14.2   Domain Theories

The person on the street is familiar with hundreds, perhaps thousands, of physical categories, qualities, and phenomena; an expert (scientist or engineer) knows perhaps tens or hundreds of thousands; collective scientific knowledge must include many millions. It seems likely that the largest part of achieving general purpose physical reasoning, at either the commonsense or the expert level, will be the representation of all the different concepts involved. To date very few physical domains—certainly fewer than a dozen—has been studied in any depth in the KR literature. In this section, we will look at theories of rigid solid objects and theories of liquids.

14.2.1 Rigid Object Kinematics

Solid objects enter into almost all scenarios that physical reasoning in a terrestrial, human-scale environment deals with. More specifically, in a significant fraction of physical reasoning, only solid objects are significant, only the motions of the objects are significant, and the objects can be idealized as rigid (constant shape).[2]

The complete theory of rigid object dynamics is discussed in Section 14.2.2. First, however, we will discussed the *kinematic* theory of rigid solid objects. The kinematic theory is much less informative than the dynamic theory but is nonetheless sufficient in many important applications, and in fact has been applied much more extensively and successfully.

The kinematic theory asserts four rules governing the shape and motion of solid objects:

- The shape of an object is a closed, regular, connected region.[3]

- The shape of an object is constant over time.

- The position of an object is a continuous function of time.

- At any given time, the regions occupied by two distinct objects do not overlap.

In the kinematic theory, therefore, the only significant time-invariant characteristic of an object is its shape, and its only significant time-varying characteristic is its position. The shape can be characterized in terms of the spatial region occupied by the object in some standard position. The position of object o at time t can be characterized in terms of a rigid (orthonormal) mapping, characterizing its displacement from its standard position to its position at t (Fig. 14.1).[4] Thus the kinematic theory can be formulated in first-order logic using the functions Shape(o) which maps an object o to the region which is its shape; Position(o) which maps object o to the fluent of its position over time; Place(o) which maps object o to the fluent of the region it occupies over time; combined with suitable temporal and geometric primitives.

Given a set of objects $o_1 \ldots o_k$ and given the shapes of these objects, a *configuration* is a specification of the position of each object. A configuration is *feasible* if no two objects overlap. A configuration $c2$ is *attainable* from configuration $c1$ if it is possible to move the objects from $c1$ to $c2$ without causing two objects to overlap. Given a set of objects and an initial configuration $c1$ the *attainable configuration space* is the set of feasible configurations attainable from $c1$. Since the position of objects is a

---

[2]One reflection of the cognitive salience of this category is the persistent attempt in eighteenth- and nineteenth-century physics to reduce all physics to mechanical interactions of small solid objects; e.g., the kinetic theory of heat, or Maxwell's mechanical model of electrodynamics.

[3]A *closed* region is one that includes its boundary. The decision to use a closed rather than an open region is arbitrary, but it simplifies description to specify one or the other. A closed region is *regular* if it is equal to the closure of its interior, and thus is "thick" everywhere and does not have any one- or two-dimensional pieces.

[4]A displacement is a composition of a rotation around the origin and a translation. A translation in k dimensions is characterized by a vector $\vec{t}$; any point x is mapped into $x + \vec{t}$. A rotation in two dimensions (relative to a fixed origin) is characterized by an angle ϕ. A rotation in three dimensions is characterized by three angles; there are a number of different systems of angles that can be used for this purpose, such as the Euler angles. Alternatively, a k-dimensional rotation can be characterized by a $k \times k$ orthonormal matrix.

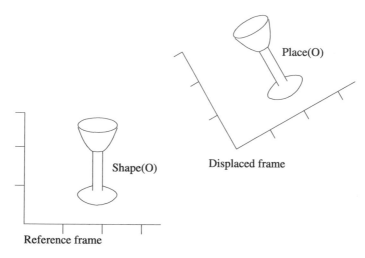

Figure 14.1: Shape, place, and relative position of a rigid object.

continuous function of time, a configuration $c2$ is attainable from $c1$ just if there is a path from $c1$ to $c2$ through the space of feasible configurations for the objects; thus, an attainable configuration space is a path-connected component of the space of feasible configurations. For initial-value problems, in which the shapes of the objects and the initial configuration are given, it suffices to consider only attainable configurations, since no other configurations can ever occur.

Indeed, initial value problems with complete shape specifications can be addressed as follows: One begins by computing the attainable configuration space for the system; that is, the connected component of the configuration space containing the initial configuration. Having done that, the entire content of the kinematic theory lies in the statement that the configuration moves continuously through that space. This technique is particularly effective if the configuration space is of low dimension; that is, the physical system has few degrees of freedom. Significantly, this is often the case with man-made mechanisms; indeed, for many mechanisms, such as gear trains, the configuration space is one-dimensional, or nearly so.[5] In such cases, it is easy to determine the consequences of the constraint that the configuration changes continuously. For example, if the configuration space is partitioned into regions, then the continuity constraint means that the configuration must move between adjacent regions in the space.

A number of methods for qualitative analysis for kinematic systems have been developed. The most common method [20, 48, 50] starts with exact shape descriptions, computes the configuration space exactly, divides the configuration space into significant regions, and then characterizes qualitative properties of the system from the connectivity of these regions. Kim [38] describes a system for qualitative reasoning about linkages, analyzing the relation between the directions between the ends

---

[5]Man-made mechanisms tend to rely on kinematic constraints when possible, because they are extremely robust. A large external force or impact is generally required to make solid objects significantly bend or break, and there is no way to cause two solid objects to spatially overlap.

of the arms (discretized into quadrants), the angles between the arms (likewise), and inequalities between the lengths of the arms.

A theory of action can be integrated into a kinematic theory by specifying that specified objects are *manipulable*, and that their motions are thus chosen by the agent. In this setting, a standard projection problem consists of a specification of the shapes and initial positions of all the objects and the motions of the manipulable objects. The kinematic theory asserts that the other objects will move through the configuration space along a path that accommodates the specified motions of the manipulable objects, if there is such a path; if there is not, then the specified motions are infeasible. The most difficult aspect of formulating this theory is asserting that an action is feasible unless it leads to an infeasible configuration.

In some cases, it is convenient to abstract a kinematic system using a simplified shape description together with a set of imposed constraints. For example, mechanical systems often contain parts such as gears that are pinned by a circular pin to a fixed frame so that they can rotate around the pin. It is common to abstract away both the frame and the pin, and to view the gear as subject to an abstract constraint that enforces the condition that the center of the gear remains fixed (Fig. 14.2) (e.g., Faltings [20] and Joskowicz [34] use this device for gears rotating on a frame, and Kim [38] uses the analogous device for linkages).

14.2.2 Rigid Object Dynamics

The kinematic theory of solid objects, though often very useful, is in general much too weakly constraining for commonsense reasoning. The *dynamic* theory of rigid solid objects describes the motions of solid objects in all circumstances in which they do not break or significantly bend. Thus, for example, the fact that a book remains on a bookshelf rather than floating off into the air, or that a chair will be stable when standing on four legs but not when standing on one leg lie beyond the scope of the kinematic theory; they require at least part of the dynamic theory.

It has been known since the early eighteenth century that the interaction of rigid solid objects is characterized by the following rules: the kinematic principles listed above; Newton's second and third laws; the existence of a normal force between objects at a contact point; static and sliding Coulomb friction between objects at a contact point; and a theory of instantaneous momentum transfer when objects collide. For terrestrial problems at the human scale, these must be supplemented by the existence of a uniform downward gravitational force; the existence of fixed objects (such as the ground) which never move; the existence of manipulators which can be subjected to an applied force at the will of an agent; and a closed world assumption that the only types of forces that act on objects are those enumerated in this theory.

Somewhat surprisingly, there is still no complete, accepted formulation of this theory in the scientific literature, particularly the theory of collisions. Even in the simple case of two objects colliding at a point, there is debate over the proper theory,[6] and

---

[6]The desiderata for such a theory are that it corresponds to experiment; that it satisfies global constraints, such as conservation of energy, momentum, and angular momentum; that it yields a solution for all well-posed initial-value problems; that numerical calculations converge; and that it can be justified in terms of a more detailed elastic model of solid objects.

Concrete: Gears pinned to a frame.

Abstraction: 2D Gears constrained to rotate
around a fixed center.

Figure 14.2: Gears and their abstraction.

there is no standard theory to use in either the case of two objects that collide along a surface or a curve, or the case of collisions involving multiple objects simultaneously. Stewart [56] reviews the state of the art in the current theory.

In any case, the scientific theory outlined above is not well-suited to the needs of reasoning in ordinary applications. It involves determining entities, such as forces, which are only occasionally of interest in commonsense reasoning, and it characterizes behavior over differential time, whereas the reasoner is generally concerned with behavior over extended time. For example, if you put a book on a shelf, you are not usually concerned with the forces between the book, the shelf, and the other books; you are only concerned to predict that the book will stay on the shelf. Similarly, if you carry a loose collection of objects in a closed box from one place to another, you are not usually concerned with the forces between the objects during the journey, or even with how the objects shift their relative positions inside the box. Generally, it suffices to determine that the objects remain inside the box throughout the journey.

Though a few AI programs have addressed the general problem of solid object dynamics by doing full numerical simulation (e.g., [29]) most AI program have dealt with restricted special cases:

- *Point objects.* The NEWTON program [16] performed qualitative prediction of the behavior of a point object on a track. The shape of the track was characterized in terms of the signs of its slope and its curvature. This was the first application of the sign calculus in AI physical reasoning. The FROB program [22] similarly performed qualitative predication of the behaviors of a collection of point objects moving in a world with fixed barriers, and one vertical and one horizontal dimension.

- *Statics.* An important category of physical prediction is to predict that an object will remain unchanged: a book will remain on a shelf, a building or bridge will continue to stand. (Note the contrast here with the usual attitude in KR that this can simply be assumed by default.) The equations of motion and their analysis are of course very much simplified if all that is required is to distinguish between situations that have a static solution and those that do not. Fahlman [21] implemented a static analysis of configurations in the blocks world.

- *Quasi-statics.* In a quasi-static problem, objects all move so slowly that their momentum is negligible as compared to the frictive forces acting on them. Hence objects only move while being pushed, directly or indirectly, by an exogenous force such as a manipulator. The standard scenario for quasi-static problems is a collection of flat objects on a horizontal surface being pushed around, though other scenarios are possible (e.g., a collection of three-dimensional objects in a highly viscous liquid). Exact quasi-static predictions were carried out by Mason [43] to carry out "sensorless manipulation"; i.e., finding ways to maneuver objects to a desired target position without any sensory feedback describing the positions of the objects. Qualitative quasi-static predictions were carried out by Forbus, Nielsen, and Faltings [24], and Stahovich, R. Davis, and Shrobe [55] using qualitative representation of configuration space and of the driving forces. If the motions of the objects are highly constrained, then the quasi-static theory is often equivalent to just the kinematic theory plus the default assumption that objects only move when necessary.

As mentioned above, a theory of action can be integrated into a dynamic theory of rigid objects by designating particular objects as manipulators which are subject to exogenous forces chosen by the agent. Thus, one conceptualizes the robot's hand as a rigid object which, at the robot's command, fires invisible rockets to exert specified forces on it. The advantage of this model is that it gives a well-formed boundary problem; a problem consisting of a specification of the initial state plus the forces on the manipulators always has a solution [56]. The disadvantage is that this is not usually a very natural way to think about a manipulator. The natural way to think about a manipulator, indeed, depends on the circumstance: often, it is just a geometric specification of the motion of the manipulator, but sometimes it is a force exerted by a stationary manipulator against an object, sometimes, it is the combination of a motion of the manipulator together with a force exerted on an external object, and sometimes, as in compliant motion, it is a control strategy where the force and motion of the manipulator depends on feedback. No general high-level language suitable for commonsense reasoning has been found for this.

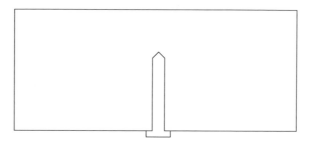

Figure 14.3: Nail in a board.

Another difficulty in the theory of the dynamic theory of solid objects is that the theory is sporadically underdetermined. In most cases, a specification of the initial positions and velocities of all the objects and their material characteristics is sufficient to determine their behavior, but there are exceptions, and these exceptions can be difficult to deal with. The most important category of exceptions is configuration in which an object is jammed. For instance, consider a nail in a hole in a board, pointing up (Fig. 14.3). Will the nail fall out of the hole? It depends on whether the nail was placed in the hole or whether it was driven into the hole. In the latter case, there are large, normal forces on the nail from the board and a corresponding large frictional force holding the nail in place. Thus, the boundary conditions in this problem include a specification of the forces, whereas in most cases forces generally determined by the positions and velocities. This makes it difficult to state what constitutes an adequate representation of a situation.

In some cases, considerations of mechanical energy give powerful constraints. For instance, de Kleer's NEWTON [16] uses an energy-based calculation to predict whether a roller-coaster on a track will go around a loop-the-loop, slide back, or fall off. Davis [9] shows how energy considerations can be used to construct an argument that a marble dropped inside a funnel will come out the bottom. (It cannot come out the top, because of conservation of energy; it cannot attain a stable resting position inside, because of the slope of the sides; it cannot remain inside forever moving around, because the kinetic energy will dissipate. Hence, the only possibility is that it will come out the bottom.)

KR work to date has barely scratched the surface of a commonsense understanding of this domain. Most commonsense inferences involving solid objects cannot even be represented in current KR theories, much less implemented.

14.2.3   Liquids

Liquids are in one way simpler than solid objects; they do not have a fixed shape that has to be represented and reasoned about. Thus, for example, it is often easier to determine whether a liquid will flow out of a tilted cup than whether an object will fall out of a tilted box. If you are tilting a cup of liquid, then the liquid will start to flow over the side of the cup just when, if there were no such flow, the volume of the inside of the cup below the opening would be less than the volume of the liquid. No such simple rule can be stated for tipping solid objects out of boxes.

On the whole, however, liquids are much more difficult to reason about than solids, because they are not individuated into objects. Rather, a system with liquids can be characterized in three complementary ways [33]. The first method is to define fluents Volume(l, r), the volume of liquid l in region r, and Flow(l, b), the flow out liquid l through directed surface b. (The regions involved need not be fixed regions in space; they can be fluents whose value at an instant is a region, such as "the inside of a pail", which moves if the pail moves.)

The second method is to define a fluent Place(c) which denotes the region occupied by a "chunk" c of liquid. Note that Place(c) may be a disconnected region. A variant on the second method is to fix a starting reference time T_0, to identify the region place(L, T_0) occupied by liquid L time T_0, and then to characterize the evolution of the liquid over time in terms of a fluent LiquidTrajectory(X, L). For any point $X \in$ place(L, T_0), liquid L, and time T, the value of LiquidTrajectory(X, L) at T is the location at T of the particle of L that was at X at T_0

A third approach is to treat the liquid as a collection of molecules or small particles [7, 30, 53, 18], whose positions and velocities can be tracked (if there are few enough) or characterized. The chief difficulty here is to characterization the interaction between particles in such a way as to give the characteristic liquid behavior.

If we exclude from consideration both mixtures of liquids and phase changes such as evaporation, and we assume that all liquids are incompressible, then we can state the following three kinematic properties:

1. A liquid moves continuously.

2. A liquid does not overlap with a solid, nor do two liquids overlap.

3. A quantity of liquid maintains a constant volume.

In a region-based representation. constraints (1) and (3) above are achieved by asserting the divergence theorem that Derivative(Volume(l, r)) = $-$Flow(l, Boundary(r)) and that the flow out through boundary b is the negative of the flow through b with the reversed orientation. In a chunk-based representation, these constraints are achieved by asserting that Place(c) is a continuous function of time for every chunk c and that Volume(Place(c)) is constant over time.

However, unlike the solid case, the kinematic theory of liquids is not by itself strong enough to analyze many interesting physical situations; a stronger dynamic theory must be used. The dynamic theory of liquids is much less well understood than the dynamic theory of solid objects, both in scientific and in commonsense theories. A few special cases are worth noting:

Statics, bulk liquid: If we ignore the phenomenon of a liquid wetting a solid surface, then we may state the following rule: If a body of liquid occupies a connected region R and is at rest, then the boundary of R must meet solid objects everywhere except at a collection of horizontal upper surfaces of the liquid. If at all such surfaces the liquid meets the open air, then all these surfaces are at the same height. Otherwise, if some of the surfaces meet bodies of gas that are themselves enclosed by solids, then the difference in heights among the surfaces is proportional to the difference in pressure in the bodies of gas involved (Fig. 14.4). (Note that in such cases, it is necessary to represent the gas explicitly, whereas this is not necessary if all bodies of gas are

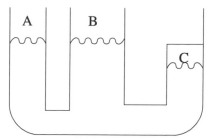

The heights in A and B are equal because both meet the open air.
The pressure of the gas at the top of C is greater than atmospheric pressure,
by an amount proportional to the difference in heights.

Figure 14.4: Liquid statics.

connected to the outside air.) In particular, if a volume V of liquid is poured into a open solid container, then it will reach a height h such that the volume of the interior of the container below h is equal to V.

Quasi-statics: If the solid objects that are in contact with the liquid, and with the contained gases that meet the liquid, are all moving slowly, then it is sometimes possible for the liquid to flow in such a way that the above static constraints are maintained. When this is possible, it generally happens. (It becomes impossible when the liquid is poured out from its container.) In such a case, the above static rules can be used to predict the trajectory of the regions occupied by the liquids and gas, and the flow of the liquid, given the motion of the solids.

Kim [38] describes a system that carries out qualitative predictions of the motions of liquids in response to the motions of pistons. She also includes in her model a special case of solids being acted on by liquids, namely the opening and closing of one-way valves.

Hayes [33] identified 15 disjoint and exhaustive physical states of liquids (Table 14.1). Any quantity of liquid at any time can be divided into parts, each of which is in one of these states. Any quantity of liquid, considered over an interval of time, can be divided into *histories*—that is, regions of space–time—each of which is in a single state. Hayes proposed that a qualitative physics of liquids could be developed in terms of axioms describing how different types of histories meet one another and meet histories of solid object trajectories, on both spatial and temporal faces; and he began work on such an axiomatization. For example, the bottom face of a "falling" history must have a downward flow through it. All but the top, horizontal face of a "pool" history must meet the outer face of solid objects. This axiomatic work was never completed (or even extended beyond Hayes' original article) for a number of reasons, chiefly because a useful theory would require a much stronger spatial language than Hayes originally envisioned.

Table 14.1. The possible states of liquid (from [33])

	Lazy still	Lazy moving	Energetic moving
Bulk on surface	Wet surface	Flowing down a surface, e.g., a sloping roof	Waves lapping a shore (?) jet hitting a surface (?)
Bulk in space	Contained in container	Flowing along a channel, e.g., river	Pumped along pipeline
Bulk unsupported		Falling column of liquid, e.g., pouring from a jug	Waterspout, fountain, jet from hose
Divided on surface	Dew, drops on a surface		
Divided in space	Mist filling a valley	Mist rolling down a valley	Steam or mist blown along a tube
Divided unsupported	Mist, cloud	Rain, shower	Spray, splash driving rain

14.3   Abstraction and Multiple Models

A characteristic of physical reasoning, at both the commonsense and the expert level, is the existence of many different theories for a given domain, and many different ways and levels of detail for describing a given situation, and many different abstraction techniques for simplifying problem statements and problem solving. A reasoner faced with a real-world problem must almost always choose among these in formulating his problem; frequently, he must apply different, mutually inconsistent, theories to different parts of the problem-solving process. Some interesting, but very preliminary, studies have been made of the ways in which appropriate theories/descriptions can be chosen and integrated in problem solving.

Some of the more important categories of abstraction include:

Alternative physical theories. Two physical theories $\mathcal{U}$ and $\mathcal{V}$ of the same physical domain may be related in that

- $\mathcal{U}$ adds additional constraints to $\mathcal{V}$; that is, $\mathcal{V}$ is logically a subtheory of $\mathcal{U}$. E.g., the relation between the dynamic and the kinematic theory of solid objects. $\mathcal{U}$ is called a "theorem increasing" [31] or "model decreasing" [47] extension of $\mathcal{V}$.

- $\mathcal{U}$ adds additional entities to $\mathcal{V}$. E.g., the relation between dynamic theories with and without friction.

- $\mathcal{U}$ is a limiting case of $\mathcal{V}$. E.g., the theory of rigid solid objects corresponds to the theory of elastic solid objects in the limit as the elasticity goes to zero. Classical mechanics corresponds to relativistic mechanics in the limit as the speed of light goes to infinity.

- $\mathcal{U}$ adds more mathematical precision to $\mathcal{V}$. E.g., the relation between a theory in which terrestrial gravitation is taken as constant and one in which it is taken as diminishing with elevation.

- $\mathcal{U}$ is a discretized form of $\mathcal{V}$ obtained by selecting key states of $\mathcal{V}$ and treating the transitions between these states as atomic actions or events. E.g., the relation between the representation of the blocks world in STRIPS and its representation in solid object dynamics.

- $\mathcal{U}$ is a smoothed form of $\mathcal{V}$ in which elements or events that are discrete in $\mathcal{V}$ are replaced by a continuous function governed by a differential equation. E.g., the relation between atomic and continuous models of matter; the use of continuous models of animal population.

- $\mathcal{U}$ and $\mathcal{V}$ conceptualize the domain in radically different ways. E.g., the relation between wave and particle theories.

It should not be taken for granted that simplifying the form of the theory will make it easier to solve the problem at hand. For instance, problems in statics, where objects are in a stable position and will stand still, are often easier than the same problem in kinematics, where one has to consider all possible motions of the objects that do not make them overlap. Similarly, a theory with friction is simpler to use than a theory without friction in the common case where the friction serves to hold the objects in a fixed position.

Ignoring small quantities. For instance, if a problem involving solid objects takes place over regions at different temperatures, it is often reasonable to ignore thermal expansion and contraction, though occasionally, of course, these are critical. Relativistic corrections are ignored in almost all problems that do not involve speeds comparable to the speed of light.

Dimension reduction. Dimensions that are irrelevant or along which there is little change may be projected out of a problem. For instance, a problem that involves little change over time may be treated as an atemporal problem. A problem involving moving objects on a surface may be treated as a two dimensional problem. A problem involving moving objects on a track may be treated as a one-dimensional problem. Alternatively, particular entities in the problem may be treated as possessing fewer dimensions than they actually do. For instance, a ball may be abstracted as a point object; a rod in a linkage may be abstracted as a line segment.

Finally, dimension reduction may be carried out in abstract spaces. Consider, for example, a train of n gears that do not mesh tightly. The coordinated motion of the gears, where they all rotate in sync, constitutes a path through configuration space. More precisely, there is one path through configuration space corresponding to the case where the gear train is moving in one direction, and the front edges of the teeth of the kth gear meet the back edge of the teeth of the $(k + 1)$st; and there is a slightly different path through configuration space corresponding to the case where the gear train is moving in the opposite direction, and the back edges of the teeth of the kth gear meet the front edge of the $(k + 1)$st. In between these two paths, there is a narrow k-dimensional tube of configurations, corresponding to the free play of the gears in the small angle range where their teeth do not meet. For many purposes, the radius of the tube can be ignored, and the system can be analyzed as if the configuration space contained only the central path [48].

An extensive survey by Joskowicz and Sacks [36] of the kinematics of 2500 mechanisms in a standard encyclopedia of mechanisms [1] found that some kind of dimensional reduction is possible for the analysis of most mechanisms; it is only a minority of mechanisms that require a full three-dimensional representation of the parts involved.

Object coalescence. A collection of objects whose internal relations are fixed can sometimes be treated as a single object. For instance, a table can be treated as a single solid object, rather than reasoning separately about the top, the legs, and the screws as separate interacting objects. (This abstraction breaks down exactly when the table itself breaks down.) A fabric can be treated as a single object made of cloth rather than as a large number of interacting threads.

Hierarchical analysis of devices. A complex mechanism can be analyzed as a hierarchy of components at different scales and levels of abstraction. An archetypal, though of course extremely difficult, example is the analysis of an organism as decomposed into organs, tissues, and cells, and sub-cells. This kind of analysis has been carried out with some success for electronic systems [57], but it is in general difficult, first, because it is hard to find a systematic language to characterize the functionality or behavior of high-level components, and second because in order to achieve efficiency, systems are often designed so that high-level modules share sub-parts. The same problems arise in the hierarchical analysis of plans.

Some types of abstraction are easy to carry out computationally but difficult to characterize logically. One such is the abstraction mentioned in Section 14.2.1 in which a kinematic joint is abstracted as a constraint in configuration space. Computationally, such constraints are easily incorporated into the routines that compute the configuration space; once the configuration space has been computed, all subsequent calculations are done purely on the basis of the configuration space and it no longer matters how the configuration space was computed. From a logical point of view, things are more complicated. Are these constraints reified as entities or stated as axioms? If they are reified, then the theory of kinematics must be rewritten to describe the properties of "constraints" and to state how "constraints" enter into the laws of motion. If they are axioms, then there is no longer a clean separation between the problem-specific description of the physical system and the problem-independent physical theory; rather, part of the description of the physical system consists of physical laws (the constraints) that are generated outside the theory itself. Moreover, there will have to be meta-logical rules stating what constraint axioms are reasonable; i.e., can actually be implemented in physical systems. Put it another way: The abstraction of the joints as constraints is simple only under a particular computational approach: The configuration space is computed from the system description and all further calculations are done from the configuration space, without referring back to the original geometry. But a logical representation does not mandate any particular computational technique, and specifically it cannot prohibit a reasoner from combining results derived from the configuration space with the original system description. This combination will be difficult if there are aspects of the configuration space that are not derived from the original system description.

14.4   Historical and Bibliographical

The history of research in AI physical reasoning is punctuated by three major landmarks: in decreasing order of impact, these are

- The publication of the three major qualitative reasoning programs—de Kleer and Brown's ENVISION [17], Forbus' QP [23] and Kuipers' QSIM [39]—in a special issue of *Artificial Intelligence* in 1984. (This was republished as a book a year later [4].) These were in many respects outgrowths of de Kleer's NEWTON program [16], and Forbus' FROB [22] which carried out qualitative reasoning for a roller coaster on a track and for balls bouncing among fixed obstacles, respectively. (In both of these programs the moving objects were modeled as point objects.) NEWTON was the first substantial study of commonsense physical reasoning in the AI literature.

- The publication of Pat Hayes' "Naive Physics Manifesto" [32] and "Ontology for Liquids" [33] in 1978–1979. (The latter circulated for years as a photocopied working paper, until finally being published in 1985.)

- The application of configuration space techniques to problems in solid object kinematics by Faltings [20] and Joskowicz [34] independently in 1987.

Most of the work in physical reasoning relates fairly directly to one of these three.

The very large body of research associated with the qualitative reasoning programs ENVISION, QP, and QSIM is surveyed in Chapter 9, and it would be redundant to repeat that here.

14.4.1   Logic-based Representations

In his 1978 paper, "The Naive Physics Manifesto", Pat Hayes [32] argues the following points. First, an effective strategy in automating commonsense reasoning is to study the logical structure of reasoning in various domains prior to, and largely independently of, considering issues of implementation or application. Second, physical reasoning will be a fruitful domain for this kind of research. Third, commonsense knowledge of physics divides naturally into "clusters" of concepts and axioms, and an effective research strategy will be to axiomatize the clusters separately and then combine the axiomatizations. Fourth, the concept of a "history", a region in space–time, will be a powerful tool in axiomatizing physical knowledge. Hayes then initiated his research program with "Ontology for Liquids" [33], described above in Section 14.2.3.

"The Naive Physics Manifesto" has inspired and encouraged two separate parts of the KR research community in two different ways. One group of researchers has embraced the endorsement of research into representations at the logical level, though without being particularly interested in physical reasoning. Another group of researchers has embraced the interest in physical reasoning, but with no enthusiasm about logic. Only a rather small body of work actually attempts to continue Hayes' programme of logical analysis of physical reasoning.

Schmolze [53] presents an axiomatization for a domain that includes actions, events, processes, liquids, solid containers, and faucets. A liquid is modeled as a collection of "granules".

Sandewall [52] developed a logical description of a microworld of points objects moving along surfaces. The chief focus of this work was integrating nonmonotonic logic with a continuous model of time.

Three parallel papers by Lifschitz, Morgenstern, and Shanahan [41, 45, 54] axiomatize various aspects of the process of cracking an egg into a bowl.

Bennett et al. [3] present an axiomatization of solid object kinematics built up from geometrical primitives.

Davis has developed a number of first-order axiomatizations for physical domains, and shown how they can be applied to commonsense inference An axiomatization of a small part of solid object dynamics, sufficient to support the inference that a marble dropped in a funnel will fall out the bottom is given in [9]. The most significant technical innovation here is the concept of a "pseudo-object", a geometric entity that "moves around" with a rigid object, such as the hole of a doughnut or the center of mass of an object. Chapter 7 of [10] gives preliminary axiomatizations for a number of physical domains, including liquids. An axiomatization of qualitative process theory is given in [11]. The main issue here is to formulate the closed world assumptions correctly.

An axiomatization of a kinematic model of one solid object cutting another is given in [12]. Two theories are presented. The "object" theory views the process of a blade cutting a target object as involving a continuous change in the shape of the target until it splits, when it becomes two objects. The "chunk" theory views the same process in terms of the chunks of solid material contained in the target. (Every separate region defines a separate chunk.) A chunk persists until it is penetrated by the blade, at which point it ceases to exist.

Davis' "Naive Physics Perplex" [15] reconsiders the methodology promoted in Hayes' "Naive Physics Manifesto", and advocates a methodology based around microworlds rather than clusters.

14.4.2 Solid Objects: Kinematics

The idea of configuration space was first developed in robotics to characterize the motions of a robot [42]. Faltings [20] analyzes in detail the kinematics of two-dimensional mechanisms composed of parts each with one degree of freedom, such as mechanical clocks. Joskowicz [34] studies the kinematics of a system that has few degrees of freedom by virtue of the interaction of its components. Forbus et al. [24] carry out a qualitative analysis of a kinematic system, based on the topology of configuration space. Gelsey [28] discusses the construction of kinematic models of varying degree of detail from the geometric specification of a physical system and the use of kinematic models in prediction. Joskowicz and Addanki [35] propose methods for designing the shape of a kinematic system given a specification of desired properties of the configuration space. Joskowicz and Sacks [36] survey the mechanisms enumerated in a standard encyclopedia of mechanisms and analyzed the complexity of the kinematic analysis required. The robustness of kinematic analysis if it is assumed that shape descriptions are only accurate to within a specified tolerance is discussed in [37] and [13].

14.4.3 Solid Object Dynamics

Simulators for the behavior of solid objects using a full dynamic theory have been developed in the contexts of computer-aided engineering [58] and of AI [29]. These carry out a exact simulation of behavior given exact geometric specifications of the objects involved. Sacks and Joskowicz [51] present an algorithm that efficiently carries out dynamic simulation for two-dimensional assemblies using configuration spaces to expedite the problem of collision detection. WHISPER [27] simulates dynamic behavior of two-dimensional systems of solid objects in a occupancy array representation.

The CLOCK program of Forbus, Nielsen, and Faltings [24] extends the qualitative kinematic analysis of [48] with a qualitative representation of forces and motions, thus producing a system for qualitative dynamic prediction. The system takes as input a scanned photograph of a mechanical system such as a mechanical clock with gears, computes the exact configuration space, simplifies and abstracts the configuration space to a qualitative representation, and uses the qualitative configuration space to construct qualitative predictions of behavior. The work of Stahovich, Davis, and Shrobe [55] is similar in spirit to [24]; it is more restricted in scope but more elegant and systematic. This program does qualitative simulation for planar systems of objects, each of which moves with one degree of freedom under the quasi-static assumption that the inertia of objects is negligible as compared to the driving forces and frictive (dissipative) forces, and that collisions are inelastic. The input to the program is a representation of the "qc-space", which gives, for each pair of interacting objects, a qualitative description of the configuration space of the feasible (non-overlapping) positions and the contact positions of the two objects. (The paper vaguely states that the qc-space can be computed from an informal sketch of the mechanism, but it is not at all clear how this is to be done.) The possible qualitative behaviors of the mechanism is then predicted in terms of trajectories through qc-space, using rules for balancing forces.

14.4.4 Abstraction and Multiple Models

The use of multiple models for physical reasoning is proposed in [2]. General studies of the use of abstraction in physical reasoning include [19, 46, 47, 59, 60, 8]. Studies of abstraction in solid object kinematics include [48, 14].

14.4.5 Other

Collins and Forbus [7] describe a program that reasons about liquids qualitatively as collections of small particles. The particles are large enough that they can be characterized by thermodynamic properties such as temperature, but small enough that they remain undivided. Gardin and Meltzer [30] simulate rigid objects, flexible objects, liquids, and strings in terms of interacting molecules. DeCuyper et al. [18] propose a hybrid architecture for reasoning about liquids, combining a qualitative theory similar to Hayes', a particle-based model similar to Gardin and Meltzer's, and a model based on tracking the motion of liquid through a fixed fine-grained decomposition of space.

Rajagopalan [49] uses a qualitative representation of shape and motion to predict magnetic flux and induced current.

Specialized expert systems for specific reasoning in the physical sciences date back to DENDRAL [6], which inferred molecular structure from mass spectroscopy data. But these are highly specific to a narrow domain and task, and hardly connected to more general physical reasoning, either in the knowledge or in the methods of inference used.

An ambitious long-term project, called Project Halo, is underway to encode scientific knowledge in a knowledge base, the Digital Aristotle [25, 26]. The first stage of this project encoded the knowledge in about a chapter's worth of an introductory college chemistry textbook [5]. The project was attempted by three competing knowledge-engineering teams and achieved a fair degree of success; the three systems achieved about the mean human score on questions in the area from the high school AP chemistry test. The subject matter in this first stage—balancing chemical equations and computing acidity of solutions—was chosen specifically to avoid the issues of spatial reasoning and of commonsense reasoning [25].

Great emphasis was placed in Project Halo on carrying out systematic evaluation. The measure is the success rate on answering questions from the relevant section of the advanced placement high school chemistry exam, both in finding the correct answer, and in explaining the answer. The three competing KR teams were presented with a training set of problems, and then their systems were tested on a separate, previously unseen, test set drawn from the same corpus. The grading of the answers was done by an independent set of domain experts. The translation of the English language AP questions into the input formalism was done by the system designers, but overseen by the administrators of Halo.

However, there has been very little analysis or description published of the actual knowledge or representation used. The knowledge bases are available on the Web; see [25]. The current author's examination of the knowledge base created by the Ontoprise group suggests that the representation was very highly geared toward the particular class of problems involved, and avoids even fundamental issues in the area if they do not appear in AP exam questions, as one would expect of a project done under extreme time pressure aiming toward a specified measure of success. For example, the representation does not seem to have any conception of *time*; its representation of an equation like $2H_2 + O_2 \rightarrow 2H_2O$ does not allow the inference that first the hydrogen and oxygen is present but not the water, and later the water is present but not the hydrogen and oxygen. Apparently this aspect of chemical equations is taken for granted by the designers of AP tests, and not tested.

14.4.6 Books

There are three major books in the area. *Qualitative Reasoning about Physical Systems* (D. Bobrow, ed., 1985) [4] is a reprint of the 1984 special issue of *Artificial Intelligence*; it includes the original papers on ENVISION, QP, and QSIM. *Readings in*

Qualitative Reasoning about Physical Systems (D. Weld and J. de Kleer, eds., 1989) [61] contains essentially all of the important papers in the area published before 1989; it is still the best source for the field. *Qualitative Reasoning: Modeling and Simulation with Incomplete Knowledge* (Kuipers, 1994) [40] presents the QSIM theory and its extensions.

Bibliography

[1] I. Artobolevsky. *Mechanisms in Modern Engineering Design*. MIR Publishers, Moscow, 1979.

[2] S. Addanki, R. Cremonini, and J.S. Penberthy. Reasoning about assumptions in graphs of models. In *Proc. IJCAI-89*, pages 1432–1438.

[3] B. Bennett, A.G. Cohn, P. Torrini, and S.M. Hazarika. Describing rigid body motions in a qualitative theory of spatial regions. In *AAAI-00*, pages 503–509.

[4] D. Bobrow, editor. *Qualitative Reasoning about Physical Systems*. MIT Press, Cambridge, MA, 1985.

[5] T.L. Brown, H.E. LeMay, and B. Bursten. *Chemistry: The Central Science*. Prentice-Hall, 2003.

[6] B.G. Buchanan, G.L. Sutherland, and E.A. Feigenbaum. Heuristic DENDRAL: A program for generating explanatory hypotheses in organic chemistry. In B. Meltzer, D. Michie, and M. Swann, editors. *Machine Intelligence*, vol. 4, pages 209–254. Edinburgh University Press, 1969.

[7] J. Collins and K. Forbus. Reasoning about fluids via molecular collections. In *AAAI-87*, pages 590–595.

[8] B. Choueiry, Y. Iwasaki, and S. McIlraith. Towards a practical theory of reformulation for reasoning about physical systems. *Artificial Intelligence*, 162:145–204, 2005.

[9] E. Davis. A logical framework for commonsense predictions of solid object behavior. *Int. Journal of AI in Engineering*, 3(3):125–140, 1988.

[10] E. Davis. *Representations of Commonsense Reasoning*. Morgan Kaufmann, 1990.

[11] E. Davis. Axiomatizing qualitative process theory. In *KR-92*, pages 177–188.

[12] E. Davis. The kinematics of cutting solid objects. *Annals of Mathematics and Artificial Intelligence*, 9:253–305, 1993.

[13] E. Davis. Approximations of shape and configuration space. NYU Computer Science Tech. Report #703, 1995.

[14] E. Davis. Approximation and abstraction in solid object kinematics. NYU Computer Science Tech. Report #706, 1995.

[15] E. Davis. The naive physics perplex. *AI Magazine*, 19(4):51–79, Winter 1998.

[16] J. de Kleer. Multiple representations of knowledge in a mechanics problem solver. In *IJCAI-77*, pages 299–304.

[17] J. de Kleer and J.S. Brown. A Qualitative physics based on confluences. In D. Bobrow, editor. *Qualitative Reasoning about Physical Systems*, pages 7–83. MIT Press, Cambridge, MA, 1985.

[18] J. DeCuyper, D. Keymeulen, and L. Steels. A hybrid architecture for modelling liquid behavior. In J. Glasgow, B. Chandrasekaran, and N.H. Narayanan, editors. *Diagrammatic Reasoning*, pages 731–751. MIT Press, 1995.

[19] B. Falkenhainer. Ideal physical systems. In *Proc. AAAI-93*, pages 600–605,

[20] B. Faltings. Qualitative kinematics in mechanisms. In *Proc. IJCAI-87*, pages 436–443.

[21] S. Fahlman. A planning system for robot construction tasks. *Artificial Intelligence*, 4:1–49, 1974.

[22] K. Forbus. Spatial and qualitative aspects of reasoning about motion. In *Proc. AAAI-80*, pages 170–173.

[23] K. Forbus. Qualitative process theory. In D. Bobrow, editor. *Qualitative Reasoning about Physical Systems*, pages 85–186. MIT Press, Cambridge, MA, 1985.

[24] K. Forbus, P. Nielsen, and B. Faltings. Qualitative spatial reasoning: The CLOCK project. *Artificial Intelligence*, 51:417–471, 1991.

[25] N. Friedland, et al. Toward a quantitative platform-independent quantitative analysis of knowledge systems. In *KR-2004*, pages 507–514.

[26] N. Friedland. Project halo: toward a digital Aristotle. *AI Magazine*, 25(4):29–47, Winter 2004.

[27] B. Funt. Problem-solving with diagrammatic representations. *Artificial Intelligence*, 13(3):201–230, 1980.

[28] A. Gelsey. Automated reasoning about machine geometry and kinematics. In D. Weld and J. de Kleer, editors. *Readings in Qualitative Reasoning about Physical Systems*, pages 580–591. Morgan Kaufmann, 1989.

[29] A. Gelsey. Automated reasoning about machines. *Artificial Intelligence*, 74:1–53, 1995.

[30] F. Gardin and B. Meltzer. Analogical representations of naive physics. In J. Glasgow, B. Chandrasekaran, and N.H. Narayanan, editors. *Diagrammatic Reasoning*, pages 669–689. MIT Press, 1995.

[31] F. Giunchiglia and T. Walsh. A theory of abstraction. *Artificial Intelligence*, 57:323–389, 1992.

[32] P. Hayes. The naive physics manifesto. In D. Michie, editor. *Expert Systems in the Microelectronic Age*. Edinburgh University Press, Edinburgh, 1979.

[33] P. Hayes. Naive physics 1: Ontology for liquids. In J. Hobbs and R. Moore, editors. *Formal Theories of the Commonsense World*. Ablex Pubs, Norwood, NJ, 1985.

[34] L. Joskowicz. Shape and function in mechanical devices. In *IJCAI-87*, pages 611–615.

[35] L. Joskowicz and S. Addanki. From kinematics to shape: an approach to innovative design. In *Proc. AAAI-88*, pages 347–352.

[36] L. Joskowicz and E. Sacks. Computational kinematics. *Artificial Intelligence*, 51:381–416, 1991.

[37] L. Joskowicz, E. Sacks, and V. Srinivasan. Kinematic tolerance analysis. *Computer-Aided Design*, 29(2):147–157, 1997.

[38] H. Kim. Qualitative reasoning about fluids and mechanics. PhD thesis, Institute of Learning Sciences, Northwestern University, 1993.

[39] B. Kuipers. Qualitative simulation. In D. Bobrow, editor. *Qualitative Reasoning about Physical Systems*, pages 169–203. MIT Press, Cambridge, MA, 1985.

[40] B. Kuipers, *Qualitative Reasoning: Modeling and Simulation with Incomplete Knowledge*. MIT Press, 1994.

[41] V. Lifschitz. Cracking an egg: An exercise in formalizing commonsense reasoning. In *Fourth Symposium on Logical Formalizations of Commonsense Reasoning*.

[42] T. Lozano-Perez. Spatial planning: A configuration-space approach. *IEEE Transactions on Computers*, C-32:108–120, 1983.

[43] M. Mason. On the scope of quasi-static pushing. In *Proc. 1985 Third Int. Symp. on Robotics Research*. MIT Press, 1985.

[44] M. Minsky. A framework for representing knowledge. In J. Haugeland, editor, *Mind Design: Philosophy, Psychology, Artificial Intelligence*, 1981, pages 95–128.

[45] L. Morgenstern. Mid-sized axiomatizations of commonsense problems: a case study in egg cracking. *Studia Logica*, 67:333–384, 2001.

[46] P. Nayak. Causal approximations. *Artificial Intelligence*, 70:277–334, 1994.

[47] P. Nayak and A. Levy. A semantic theory of abstractions. In *IJCAI-95*, pages 196–203, 1994.

[48] P. Nielsen. A qualitative approach to mechanical constraint. In *Proc. AAAI-88*, pages 270–274.

[49] R. Rajagopalan. A model for integrated qualitative spatial and dynamic reasoning about physical systems. In *Proc. AAAI-94*, pages 1411–1417.

[50] E. Sacks and L. Joskowicz. Automated modelling and kinematic simulation of mechanisms. *Computer-Aided Design*, 25(2):106–118, 1993.

[51] E. Sacks and L. Joskowicz. Dynamical simulation of planar assemblies with changing contacts using configuration spaces. *J. Mechanical Design*, 120, 1998.

[52] E. Sandewall. Combining logic and differential equations for describing real-world systems. In *KR-89*, pages 412–420.

[53] J. Schmolze. Physics for robots. In *AAAI-86*, pages 44–50.

[54] M. Shanahan. An attempt to formalise a non-trivial problem in common sense reasoning. *Artificial Intelligence*, 153:141–165, 2004.

[55] T. Stahovich, R. Davis, and H. Shrobe. Qualitative rigid-body mechanics. *Artificial Intelligence*, 119:19–60, 2000.

[56] D. Stewart. Rigid-body dynamics with friction and impact. *SIAM Review*, 41(1):3–39, 2000.

[57] G. Sussman and G.L. Steele. CONSTRAINTS—A language for expressing almost hierarchical descriptions. *Artificial Intelligence*, 14:1–40, 1980.

[58] R.A. Wehage and E.J. Haug. Dynamic analysis of mechanical systems with intermittent motion. *J. Mechanical Design*, 104:784–788, 1982.

[59] D. Weld. Approximation reformulations. In *Proc. AAAI-90*, pages 407–412, 1990.

[60] D. Weld. Reasoning about model accuracy. *Artificial Intelligence*, 56:255–300, 1992.

[61] D. Weld and J. de Kleer. *Readings in Qualitative Reasoning about Physical Systems*. Morgan Kaufmann, San Mateo, CA, 1989.

Handbook of Knowledge Representation
Edited by F. van Harmelen, V. Lifschitz and B. Porter
© 2008 Elsevier B.V. All rights reserved
DOI: 10.1016/S1574-6526(07)03015-5

Chapter 15

Reasoning about Knowledge and Belief

Yoram Moses

15.1 Introduction

An agent operating in a complex environment can benefit from adapting its behavior to the situation at hand. The agent's choice of actions at any point in time can, however, be based only on its local knowledge and beliefs. When many agents are present, the success of one's agent's actions will typically depend on the actions of the other agents. These, in turn, are based on the other agents' own knowledge and beliefs. It follows that to operate effectively in a setting containing other agents, an agent must, in addition to its knowledge about the physical features of the outside world, consider its knowledge about other agent's knowledge. This line of reasoning can be extended to justify the need for using deeper levels of knowledge, of course. Moreover, the task of obtaining relevant knowledge and that of affecting the knowledge of other agents, become important goals in many applications. This crucial connection between knowledge and action is what makes knowledge and belief two of the most frequently used notions in everyday discourse. It also suggests that rigorous frameworks for reasoning about knowledge and belief can be of value when analyzing scenarios involving multiple agents.

Philosophers have been concerned with *epistemology*, the study of knowledge, for thousands of years, going back to the great Chinese, Greek, and Indian thinkers. The focus of much of their analysis was on fundamental questions about the nature of knowledge: What can be known? When does someone know something? How does knowledge relate to truth and to belief? Rigorous logical treatment of knowledge and belief go back to the work of von Wright in the 1950's. It gained substantial grounding in Hintikka's seminal book *Knowledge and Belief* in 1962 [28], which based modal logics of knowledge on Kripke's possible-worlds semantic modeling of modal logics [30]. Hintikka's work was followed by a wave of research in the 1960's on logics for knowledge and belief and their proper axiomatizations, with a focus on the relationship between knowledge and belief [15, 31].

In the second half of the Twentieth century, researchers in different fields of science recognized the need to understand the role that knowledge and belief play in multi-agent systems and multi-agent interaction. In 1969, David K. Lewis published the book *Conventions*, which contained the first explicit definition of *common knowledge* among a set of agents (or individuals). Extensions of this work in the context of linguistics and the philosophy of language were made by Schiffer and by Clark and Marshall [9]. In game theory, Schelling [40] and Harsanyi [25–27] recognized the role that uncertainty plays in the analysis of games in the 1960's, and a model for knowledge and common knowledge in games was first presented by Aumann in 1976 [1]. In artificial intelligence, McCarthy argued for modeling agents' knowledge and beliefs as essential components of an agent in the mid-1970's. This ultimately gave rise to the BDI *Belief, Desire and Intentions* model of agent-hood [39] discussed in Chapter 24. The role of explicit, knowledge-based analyses of distributed protocols and distributed systems was initiated by Halpern and Moses in 1984 [17], while Goldwasser, Micali and Rackoff introduced tools for reasoning about cryptographical protocols that provide *zero knowledge* [16] in 1985. Since the 1980's, a large body of literature consisting of many books and hundreds if not thousands of conference and journal papers have been written continuing and extending these lines of research.

Surveying the state of the art is well beyond the scope of this chapter. Instead, this chapter aims at providing a somewhat biased introduction to the topic of reasoning about knowledge and belief, based in large part on the book *Reasoning about Knowledge* [12], where the reader is advised to seek further detail and additional references to the literature. Half of this chapter is devoted to introducing basic concepts, and the other half focuses on illustrating how the runs and systems framework can be set up to model multi-agent applications of interest. This involves properly matching the agents' behaviors or strategies, modeled by protocols, with a careful definition of the environment in which the agents operate, which is in turn modeled using the notion of a context.

15.2 The Possible Worlds Model

15.2.1 A Language for Knowledge and Belief

Before attempting to model knowledge and belief, we need to observe that these terms are used in many different senses in natural language. Thus, we may talk about knowing a language, knowing a profession, or knowing how to perform a particular task. We may *believe* in a higher power, or in a person. One may consider knowing what the time is, or knowing what sequence of numbers will open a safe. While all of these are perfectly reasonable uses of the terms in question and are worthy of investigation in their own right, we will focus on knowledge and belief in the truth of facts. Thus, we will be interested in expressing and modeling statements such as that "*agent i believes that it is midnight*", or that "*Alice knows that the key is hidden under the rug*". We will also be interested in statements such as "*Alice knows that Bob does not know that Alice knows that Bob spilled the beans*", of an agent's knowledge about other agents' knowledge, as well as issues having to do with what a group of agents knows.

Let Φ be a set of *primitive propositions*, standing for the basic facts that we wish to reason about in a given application of interest. The particulars of Φ typically depend on the application considered, and do not affect the general framework for reasoning about knowledge. We will therefore omit explicit mention of Φ if no confusion arises. Denote by $[n] = \{1, \ldots, n\}$ a set of agents. The language $\mathcal{L}_n^K = \mathcal{L}_n^K(\Phi)$ for knowledge among the agents in $[n]$ is defined to be the smallest set of formulas that contains Φ and is closed under the standard Boolean connectives $\wedge$ and $\neg$ (all other connectives of propositional logic can be expressed using $\wedge$ and $\neg$), and under modal operators K_i, for every $i \in [n]$.[1] Thus, every proposition $p \in \Phi$ is a formula of $\mathcal{L}_n^K$ and, inductively, if $i \in [n]$ while φ and ψ are formulas of $\mathcal{L}_n^K$, then $\neg\varphi$, $\varphi \wedge \psi$ and $K_i\varphi$ are formulas of $\mathcal{L}_n^K$. We also use standard abbreviations from propositional logic, such as $\varphi \vee \psi$ for $\neg(\neg\varphi \wedge \neg\psi)$, $\varphi \Rightarrow \psi$ for $\neg\varphi \vee \psi$, and $\varphi \Leftrightarrow \psi$ for $(\varphi \Rightarrow \psi) \wedge (\psi \Rightarrow \varphi)$. It is also convenient to use the notation **true** as shorthand for the tautologically true formula $p \vee \neg p$ and **false** as shorthand for $\neg$**true**. We read $K_i\varphi$ as "agent i knows φ". Thus, if p stands for "The lock on Bob's office door is broken", and we identify Alice with agent 1 and Bob with 2, then $K_1 p \wedge K_1 \neg K_2 p$ will state that Alice knows that the lock is broken, and that she also knows that Bob does not know this. By further nesting of knowledge and Boolean operators it is possible to express more complex statements involving agents' knowledge about other agents knowledge (or lack thereof), etc. in $\mathcal{L}_n^K$. Indeed, these can quite quickly express statements that appear to be fairly tricky. Consider the formula $K_1 K_2 K_1 p \wedge \neg K_2 K_1 \neg K_2 K_1 p$, stating that Alice knows that Bob knows that Alice knows p, and Bob does not know that Alice knows that Bob does not know that Alice knows p. Even such a short formula may require the listener to pause before its meaning is understood. We thus need a clear framework for interpreting such statements in a precise way.

Most rigorous approaches to modeling knowledge and belief capture these notions in terms of *possible-worlds semantics*. The idea here is that an agent in a given scenario is typically not omniscient regarding all aspects of the current state of the world. Rather, it considers many possibilities for the true state of the world. If, say, a given door is locked in all of the worlds that the agent considers possible, then the agent may be said to know (or believe) that the door is locked. More generally, agent i will know a fact φ if φ holds in all of the worlds that i considers possible. Conversely, φ is *not* known by i if i considers possible at least one world in which φ does not hold. Notice that knowledge is defined in terms of (a more primitive notion of) possibility. Clearly, the set of worlds an agent considers possible will generally be different in distinct states of the world. In particular, this set changes over time, as the state of the world changes, and as the agent learns new facts and perhaps forgets others. Following Hintikka, we model knowledge in terms of a Kripke structure $M = (S, \pi, \mathcal{K}_1, \ldots, \mathcal{K}_n)$, where S is a set of states of the world, $\pi : \Phi \to 2^S$ specifies for each primitive proposition the set of states at which the proposition holds, and $\mathcal{K}_i \subseteq S \times S$ is a binary relation on the states of the world where, intuitively, $(s, t) \in \mathcal{K}_i$ means that when the actual state of the world is s, agent i considers the world represented by t to be *possible*. Formulas of $\mathcal{L}_n^K$ are considered true or false at a world (M, s) consisting of a state s in a structure M. We denote by $(M, s) \models \varphi$ the fact that a formula φ is true, or *satisfied* at a world (M, s). The satisfaction relation $\models$ is formally defined by induction on the structure of φ.

---

[1] A similar language, $\mathcal{L}_n^B$, can be defined for reasoning about belief if we substitute the modal knowledge operators K_i by analogous belief operators B_i, for all $i \in [n]$. We will speak in terms of knowledge and make explicit mention of belief when this is warranted.

Primitive propositions $p \in \Phi$ form the base of the induction, and their truth is determined according to the assignment π:

$(M, s) \models p$ (for a primitive proposition $p \in \Phi$)   iff $s \in \pi(p)$.

Negations and conjunctions are handled in the standard way:

$(M, s) \models \neg\psi$ iff $(M, s) \not\models \psi$.

$(M, s) \models \psi \wedge \psi'$ iff   both $(M, s) \models \psi$ and $(M, s) \models \psi'$.

Finally, the crucial clause handles formulas of the form $\varphi = K_i\psi$. Here, the intuition that knowledge corresponds to truth in all possible worlds is captured by:

$(M, s) \models K_i\psi$ iff $(M, t) \models \psi$ for all t such that $(s, t) \in \mathcal{K}_i$.

A formula φ is said to be *valid in (the structure)* $M = (S, \ldots)$ if $(M, s) \models \varphi$ holds for all $s \in S$. Moreover, φ is called *valid* if it is valid in all structures M. We say that φ is *satisfiable* if $(M, s) \models \varphi$ holds for some M and s. It is not hard to verify that φ is satisfiable exactly if $\neg\varphi$ is not valid.

Observe that the set of $\mathcal{L}_n^K$ formulas that are true at a state s in a structure M depends on the $\mathcal{K}_i$ relations as well as on the assignment π. Two states can satisfy the same primitive propositions as determined by the assignment π, and yet differ considerably in the $\mathcal{L}_n^K$ formulas that they satisfy.

Example 15.1. To illustrate these definitions, let us consider a very simple example, involving two agents, named Alice and Bob. Initially, Alice has a coin and Bob is in the other room. Alice tosses the coin to the floor. (Nothing is known about the bias or fairness of the coin, except that it has two different faces.) Once Bob hears the coin hit the floor, he enters the room and observes whether the coin shows Heads or Tails. There are many ways to model this example using the possible-worlds framework we have discussed. We now present one particular choice. We model the scenario by way of a Kripke structure $M = (S, \pi, \mathcal{K}_A, \mathcal{K}_B)$. The set Φ of primitive propositions in M consists of three basic facts: $\Phi = \{\mathsf{Toss}, \mathsf{Heads}, \mathsf{Tails}\}$. Intuitively, Toss stands for the fact that the coin has been tossed, Heads holds if the coin toss resulted in the coin landing Heads, and Tails stands for the tossed coin having landed Tails. The model should allow us to reason about what is true (and what is known) at each of the three stages of this scenario: Initially, immediately after Alice tosses the coin, and finally after Bob enters the room. To this end, we consider the set of states $S = \{s_0, s_1, t_1, s_2, t_2\}$, where s_0 is the initial state, s_1 and t_1 are the intermediate states where the coin landed Heads and Tails, respectively, while s_2 and t_2 are the final states that occur following s_1 and t_1, respectively, once Bob has entered the room and he sees the tossed coin. The assignment π specifies what states the primitive propositions are true in, and is based on the above description. Consequently, $\pi(\mathsf{Toss}) = \{s_1, t_1, s_2, t_2\}$, $\pi(\mathsf{Heads}) = \{s_1, s_2\}$, and $\pi(\mathsf{Tails}) = \{t_1, t_2\}$. Finally, we need to define the possibility relations $\mathcal{K}_A$ and $\mathcal{K}_B$ over the states of S. Assuming that Alice can see the outcome of her coin toss immediately, and can see if Bob is in the room, in all states of this example she knows exactly what the actual state is. So $\mathcal{K}_A = \{(s, s) \mid s \in S\}$. Bob, in turn, knows the actual state at the first and third stages, and is unable to distinguish between the states at the second stage—after Alice tosses the coin but before he enters the room. Thus,

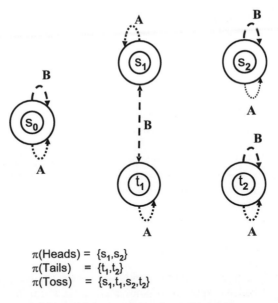

π(Heads) = {s$_1$,s$_2$}
π(Tails) = {t$_1$,t$_2$}
π(Toss)   = {s$_1$,t$_1$,s$_2$,t$_2$}

Figure 15.1: Knowledge via possible worlds.

$\mathcal{K}_B = \{(s,s) \mid s \in S\} \cup \{(s_1, t_1), (t_1, s_1)\}$. A visual illustration of the structure M is given in Fig. 15.1, where the binary relations $\mathcal{K}_A$ and $\mathcal{K}_B$ are represented by directed edges labeled by A and B, respectively.

With this model for the coin-toss scenario, we can now establish the truth of some nontrivial statements in this model. One is

$$(M, s_0) \models K_A \neg \text{Toss} \wedge K_B K_A K_B (\neg \text{Heads} \wedge \neg \text{Tails}),$$

capturing the fact that in the initial state s_0 Alice knows that the coin has not been tossed, and Bob knows that Alice knows that Bob knows the coin is currently showing neither Heads nor Tails; or

$$(M, s_1) \models \text{Heads} \wedge \neg K_B \text{Heads} \wedge \neg K_B \text{Tails} \wedge K_B (K_A \text{Heads} \vee K_A \text{Tails}),$$

which establishes that at s_1 the coin is showing Heads, Bob does not know this, but Bob knows that Alice knows whether the coin shows Heads or Tails.

This example illustrates that explicitly constructing a model of knowledge even for a scenario with a simple structure and very little uncertainty may be quite laborious. In more interesting situations, the state space and the possibility relations quickly become much more complex. Notice that a number of choices and simplifying assumptions are built into modeling the scenario as we have done. One has to do with the granularity of the modeling. Intuitively, the states chosen for S in the above example "sample" the world at three distinct stages. Moreover, given the choice of primitive propositions in this example, the language is restricted to expressing facts about the coin tossing and its outcome (and knowledge about these). Thus, for example, while in all possible worlds in this model, both Bob and Alice know whether or not they are in the same room, we cannot express this without extending the set Φ of primitive propositions defined in the example. Finally, having a very small number of states in S automatically implies that agents have strong knowledge about each other's knowledge. We shall return to this issue later on once we define common knowledge.

Observe that both possibility relations $\mathcal{K}_A$ and $\mathcal{K}_B$ in the above example are equivalence relations: Reflexive, symmetric and transitive. This is not a coincidence. In many applications, it is natural to consider the knowledge of agent i at a state s as being based of some concrete *view* $v_i(s)$ that the agent is assumed to have at s. Two states s and t are then indistinguishable, so that $(s, t) \in \mathcal{K}_i$, exactly if $v_i(s) = v_i(t)$. The view $v_i(s)$ in such applications is typically a function of the agent's observations so far. It may consist, for example, of her complete history, what she sees in front of her, the state of her memory or the set of formulas in the agent's database. Possibility relations that are obtained in this fashion are automatically equivalence relations.

15.3 Properties of Knowledge

The possible-worlds approach to modeling knowledge and belief is quite popular and attractive, and view-based definitions of knowledge are natural in many applications. They turn out, however, to model the cognitive state of an idealized agent, as we shall see by analyzing the properties of knowledge and belief under these definitions. We capture the properties of knowledge by considering the valid formulas of $\mathcal{L}_n^K$.

Even before considering the definition of $\models$ for the knowledge operators, our definition inherits valid formulas from its propositional component, from the fact that the Boolean operators $\neg$ and $\wedge$ are treated as they are in propositional logic. We thus obtain that

A0. All instances of propositional tautologies are valid,

which we think of as the *Propositional Axiom*, and the inference rule of *Modus Ponens*:

MP. If φ is valid and $\varphi \Rightarrow \psi$ is valid, then ψ is valid.

Intuitively, the pair **A0** and **MP** ensure that our logic is an extension of propositional logic.

One central property that follows from the definition that $K_i \varphi$ holds if φ holds at all worlds that i considers possible is that an agent knows all the logical consequences of his knowledge. If an agent knows both φ and that φ implies ψ, then both φ and $\varphi \Rightarrow \psi$ are true at all worlds he considers possible. Thus ψ must be true at all worlds that the agent considers possible, so he must also know ψ. It follows that the *Distribution Axiom*

A1. $(K_i \varphi \wedge K_i (\varphi \Rightarrow \psi)) \Rightarrow K_i \psi$,

which states that knowledge is closed under implication, is valid. This is clearly a nontrivial assumption, which does not always match our intuitions regarding knowledge in everyday life.

Further evidence that our definition of knowledge assumes rather powerful agents comes from the fact that agents know all tautologies. In fact, they are guaranteed to know all formulas that are valid in the structure. If φ is true at all the worlds of a structure M, then φ must, in particular, be true at all the worlds that agent i considers possible at every world (M, s). Thus, $K_i\varphi$ must also hold at all worlds of M. More formally, we have the following *Knowledge Generalization Rule*:

G. For all structures M, if $M \models \varphi$ then $M \models K_i\varphi$.

While this implies that if φ is valid then so is $K_i\varphi$, this does *not* mean that the formula $\varphi \Rightarrow K_i\varphi$ is valid. The formula φ is valid in M only if it holds at all worlds in M. Indeed, it is quite common for a formula φ to hold, without $K_i\varphi$ being true. In the example above, at state s_1 the coin has landed Heads, but Bob does not know this. Notice that the Generalization rule can be applied repeatedly, and yield, for example (if repeated twice), that if $M \models \varphi$ then $M \models K_i K_j K_i\varphi$.

The Distribution Axiom **A1** and Generalization Rule **G** are forced by the possible-worlds modeling. They are shared by every normal modal operator [29]. It turns out that, in a precise sense, the logic **K**, consisting of axioms **A0** and **A1** and the rules **MP** and **G** completely characterizes the set of valid formulas of $\mathcal{L}_n^K$.

Considering the valid $\mathcal{L}_n^K$ formulas does not present "epistemic" properties for the K_i operators beyond those implied by the logic **K**. Thus, for example, there is no necessary connection between what is known and the facts that are true. This changes once we restrict the class of structures in a useful way. Recall from our discussion after Example 15.1 that if knowledge is derived in a view-based manner, then the possibility relations $\mathcal{K}_i$ are equivalence relations. We now turn to consider the set of formulas that are valid in this case. For the remainder of this section, we study validity with respect to the class of structures with equivalence possibility relations.

When possibility is an equivalence relation, each relation $\mathcal{K}_i$ is, in particular, reflexive. This means that, at every world (M, s), the current world is always one of the possible worlds. (In other words, since $(s, s) \in \mathcal{K}_i$, the world (M, s) is considered "possible" at (M, s).) From the definition of when $(M, s) \models K_i\varphi$ holds it follows that if an agent knows a fact, then it is true. More formally, the so-called *Knowledge Axiom*:

A2. $K_i\varphi \Rightarrow \varphi$

is valid. The Knowledge Axiom **A2** is often considered to be the central property distinguishing knowledge from belief. The intuition behind this is that while it possible to have false beliefs, known facts are necessarily true.

Two additional properties of knowledge that hold in this class of structures state that an agent has strong abilities to introspect into his own knowledge. An agent knows precisely which are the facts that he knows and which facts he does not know. These are captured by the *Positive Introspection Axiom* **A3** and the *Negative Introspection Axiom* **A4** given by:

A3. $K_i\varphi \Rightarrow K_i K_i\varphi$, and

A4. $\neg K_i\varphi \Rightarrow K_i\neg K_i\varphi$.

The Positive Introspection Axiom states that, if i knows φ then i knows that he knows φ, while the Negative Introspection Axiom states the converse: When i does not know φ, he knows that he does not know φ. Thus, while an agent may have only partial knowledge about what is true in the world, these axioms guarantee that he has perfect knowledge about his own knowledge. In the philosophy literature, **A3** is considered more acceptable as a property of knowledge and belief than **A4**. Both are determined to hold in structures in which the possibility relations are equivalence relations.

The collection of properties that we have considered so far—the Distribution Axiom, the Knowledge Axiom, the Positive and Negative Introspection Axioms, and the Knowledge Generalization Rule—has been studied in some depth in the literature. They are often called the S5 properties.

The axioms and rules discussed above are often viewed as an axiom system, with **MP** and **G** interpreted as *rules of inference*. Axiom systems provide a means for proving formulas. Given a set Γ of axioms, $\Gamma \vdash \varphi$ (or just "$\vdash \varphi$" if Γ is clear from context) stands for "φ is provable (from Γ)". In this context, **MP** is interpreted as saying that if $\vdash \varphi$ and $\vdash \varphi \Rightarrow \psi$ (so that both φ and $\varphi \Rightarrow \psi$ are provable), then we can conclude $\vdash \psi$ (so ψ can be considered provable). The rule **G** then states that from $\vdash \varphi$ we can conclude $\vdash K_i \varphi$.

The axiom system consisting of axioms **A0** and **A1** and the rules **MP** and **G** is called the modal logic K, and it is satisfied by any normal modal operator [29]. The full suite of axioms and rules above: **A0–A4** together with the rules **MP** and **G**, constitute the logical system S5, while removing **A4** yields the logical system S4. From the validity properties cited above, it is possible to show that every formula of $\mathcal{L}_n^K$ provable in K is valid in every Kripke structure $M = (S, \pi, \mathcal{K}_1, \ldots, \mathcal{K}_n)$, while every formula provable in S5 is valid in every structure in which all of the possibility relations $\mathcal{K}_i$ are equivalence relations. That these axiom systems truly capture the set of valid formulas follows from the fact that the converse is also true: For either class of structures, every valid fact is provable from the corresponding axiom system.

In settings involving *belief*, rather than knowledge, the Knowledge Axiom **A2** is typically dropped, often replaced by the axiom:

A2′. $\neg K_i$ **false**.

If the possibility relations in a Kripke structure M are *serial*, meaning that for every $s \in S$ and $i \in [n]$ there exists a state $t \in S$ such that $(s, t) \in \mathcal{K}_i$, then axiom **A2′** is valid in M. If we replace **A2** by **A2′** in S5, we obtain the logic known as KD45.

15.4 The Knowledge of Groups

Formulas of $\mathcal{L}_n^K$ that contain several epistemic operators can often be thought of as describing states of knowledge of *groups* of agents. Thus, for example, $K_i p \wedge \neg K_j p$ describes a situation in which i and j have asymmetric knowledge about the truth of p. In the case of belief, the formula $B_i B_j p \wedge \neg B_j p$ describes a situation in which i has a misconception about j's beliefs. A state of knowledge that appears quite often in speech and in the analysis of multi-agent systems is captured by the $\mathcal{L}_n^K$ formula $K_1 \varphi \wedge \cdots \wedge K_n \varphi$. This corresponds to *everyone* knowing φ. It is convenient to abbreviate this $\mathcal{L}_n^K$ formula by $E\varphi$, as this allows us to compactly write facts such as $E\varphi \wedge \neg EE\varphi$ in which "everyone knowing" is nested. It is not hard to see that $E\varphi$ and $EE\varphi$ are not equivalent. As a counterexample consider a formula ψ stating that a given team has won the world cup finals. If each of the agents learns of the outcome independently, say by hearing about it on the radio or reading a newspaper, then $E\psi$ clearly holds, but $EE\psi$ need not. More generally, let us define $E^1\varphi = E\varphi$ and inductively define $E^{k+1}\varphi = E(E^k\varphi)$ for $k \geqslant 1$. It can be shown that $E^{k+1}\varphi$ and $E^k\varphi$ are not, in general, equivalent. For every level k there is a world (M, s) and formula φ such that $(M, s) \models E^k\varphi \wedge \neg E^{k+1}\varphi$ (see [17]).[2]

15.4.1 Common Knowledge

While $E\varphi$ is expressible in $\mathcal{L}_n^K$, there are other natural states of group knowledge that are not. Perhaps the most important of these is *common knowledge*, which corresponds to everyone knowing a fact, everyone knowing that everyone knows it, etc. Let us denote by $C\varphi$ the fact that φ is common knowledge. Intuitively, we think of $C\varphi$ as satisfying

$$C\varphi \equiv E\varphi \wedge E^2\varphi \wedge \cdots \wedge E^k\varphi \wedge \cdots.$$

The right-hand side of this equivalence is an infinite conjunction. It is not an $\mathcal{L}_n^K$ formula, because all $\mathcal{L}_n^K$ formulas are finite. Fortunately, there are various ways to define common knowledge formally. Practically all of them coincide when interpreted using Kripke structures. One is the following. Given a Kripke structure $M = (S, \pi, \mathcal{K}_1, \ldots, \mathcal{K}_n)$, define let $\mathcal{E} = \bigcup_{i\in[n]} \mathcal{K}_i$. Thus, $\mathcal{E}$ is a binary relation over S consisting of every pair (s, t) such that $(s, t) \in \mathcal{K}_i$ for *some i*. It is easy to verify that

$$(M, s) \models E\psi \quad \text{iff} \quad (M, t) \models \psi \text{ for all } t \text{ such that } (s, t) \in \mathcal{E}.$$

It is straightforward to verify that E satisfies

$$E\varphi \equiv \bigwedge_{i\in[n]} K_i\varphi.$$

Even when all of the $\mathcal{K}_i$ possibility relations are equivalence relations, their union $\mathcal{E} = \bigcup_{i\in[n]} \mathcal{K}_i$ is not. The E operator will not, in general satisfy analogues of the Introspection Axioms **A3** and **A4**.

We now define the binary relation $\mathcal{C}$, which will correspond to common knowledge, to be the transitive closure of $\mathcal{E}$. Thus, $(s, t) \in \mathcal{C}$ if there is a sequence $s = s_0, s_1, \ldots, s_k = t$ such that $(s_i, s_{i+1}) \in \mathcal{E}$ holds for all $0 \leqslant i \leqslant k - 1$. Notice that both $\mathcal{E}$ and $\mathcal{C}$ are completely determined by the $\mathcal{K}_i$ relations of a structure M. We extend $\mathcal{L}_n^K$ by closing off under the common knowledge operator C (so that in the inductive definition of formulas, if φ is a formula then so is $C\varphi$). Common knowledge is then formally defined by

$$(M, s) \models C\psi \quad \text{iff} \quad (M, t) \models \psi \text{ for all } t \text{ such that } (s, t) \in \mathcal{C}.$$

---

[2]It is often convenient to think of E as a state of knowledge of the group of all agents. Indeed, there are cases where a fact can be known to all members of a given set G of agents, but not to the rest. For example, we may be interested in whether all students of a given class know that the exam date has been changed. Within a larger framework, it might not be of interest to ensure that, say, everyone in the university knows this. When analyzing such scenarios, it is customary to use operators such as E_G, which stand for *everyone in G knows*. Similar restriction to groups of agents will be applicable to other states of knowledge that we discuss below.

This definition of common knowledge is essentially equivalent to the infinite conjunction of $E^k\varphi$ mentioned above. Indeed, if $(M, s) \models C\varphi$ holds then $(M, s) \models E^k\varphi$ holds for all $k \geqslant 1$. The converse is also true: If $(M, s) \models E^k\varphi$ holds for all $k \geqslant 1$, then $(M, s) \models C\varphi$. It is often convenient to think of common knowledge by viewing the Kripke structure as a graph (as is done in Fig. 15.1). The definition of C and $\mathcal{E}$ immediately implies that $(s, t) \in C$ exactly if there is a directed path (possibly consisting of edges from $\mathcal{K}_i$'s of different agents) from s to t. In the special but commonly occurring case in which the $\mathcal{K}_i$'s are equivalence relations, C is also an equivalence relation, and its equivalence classes are precisely the connected components of the graph of M. A fact φ is then common knowledge at s exactly if it holds at all states in the connected component of s in the graph defined by M.

The notion of common knowledge appears to have been discussed informally in the sociology literature on the nature of consensus as early as 1967 [41]. It was given a formal definition, using the term *shared awareness*, by Friedell [13]. The name *common knowledge* was coined by the Philosopher by David K. Lewis in 1969 [32], who identified it as an inherent property of conventions. Later work in Game Theory [1], Linguistics [9] and Computer Science [17] showed the relevance of common knowledge to central issues in each of these fields. McCarthy suggested having a logic of knowledge in which common knowledge is represented by an agent he termed the *Fool* and common knowledge is then taken to be what "*any fool*" knows. Given our definition above, the possibility relation corresponding to the Fool's knowledge would be C. We remark that if the $\mathcal{K}_i$ possibility relations in M are equivalence relations, then so is the relation C defined based on them. Thus, in settings in which knowledge satisfies the properties of S5, the common knowledge operator satisfies S5 as well. In particular, the Generalization Rule **G** now becomes

If $M \models \varphi$ then $M \models C\varphi$.

Let us return to our example concerning Alice and Bob and the precious coin, depicted in Fig. 15.1. Since the $\mathcal{K}_i$ relations in the example are equivalence relations, so is C. The equivalence classes of C in this simple example are given by:

$$C = \big\{\{s_0\}, \{s_1, t_1\}, \{s_2\}, \{t_2\}\big\}.$$

Thus, in the states s_0, s_2 and t_2, the actual state is the only possibility according to C, and hence, in the corresponding worlds (M, s_0), (M, s_2) and (M, t_2), all true formulas are common knowledge. In both states of the C-equivalence class $\{s_1, t_1\}$, Alice knows the outcome of the coin, and so $C(K_A\mathsf{Heads} \vee K_A\mathsf{Tails})$ holds at both. Similarly, since Bob does not know the outcome in either of the states, $C(\neg K_B\mathsf{Heads} \wedge \neg K_B\mathsf{Tails})$ holds at both states. Notice that the common knowledge about Alice knowing the outcome of the toss after the first stage in this example is built into the model. If the scenario were changed slightly to one in which Bob does not know that Alice has tossed the coin before he enters Alice's room in the second stage (states s_2 and t_2)—for example, suppose that Bob were to consider s_0 possible in both s_1 and t_1—then both agents would know the same about the propositional facts Toss, Heads and Tails at s_1 and t_1 as in the original example, but then there would be much weaker common knowledge regarding these facts at the two states. Since S is small in this example, and the connected components are even smaller, the amount of common knowledge here is considerable. Observe that in a given Kripke structure $M = (S, \ldots)$ only states in S can ever be reachable from (or in the same connected component as) a given state. Hence, it is common knowledge at all states of the model that no state outside of S is possible. E.g., if cars in all states of S cars are either Red or Green, it will be common knowledge that all cars are Red or Green (provided that Φ contains appropriate propositions that correspond to colors of cars). Moreover, Kripke structures with a small number of states typically model situations in which there is a great deal of common knowledge. It follows that modeling a situation in which agents have considerable uncertainty regarding each others' knowledge normally requires a fairly large set of states S to represent the agents' ignorance. In fact, even when there are only two agents and Φ consists of a single proposition, representing a sufficient degree of mutual ignorance (lack of knowledge about each other's knowledge) may require a Kripke structure of unbounded, even infinite, size.

Common knowledge is often thought to be such a strong state of knowledge, that people wonder whether it can be attained in practice. After all, achieving a small number of levels of knowledge about knowledge among more than one agent already seems quite complex. Intuitively, one might expect that to attain infinitely many levels of interactive knowledge would require an infinite interchange of messages, or a similar unreal feat. This intuition is, however, misguided. Under reasonable assumptions, common knowledge occurs quite frequently. A typical scenario in which common knowledge arises in a natural way is a setting in which some fact φ is "public", so that whenever φ holds, all agents know that it does. Such, for example, is the situation arising when two people shake hands. Inherent in the act of shaking hands is the fact that both parties know that they are shaking hands. In every world either agent considers possible, the handshake is taking place. It follows by induction that a handshake takes place in every world that is connected to the current one, and the agents thus have common knowledge of the handshake. A similar situation arises when someone makes a public announcement in a lecture hall, or when a couple shares a candlelight dinner. The intuition that "public" facts are common knowledge is formally captured by the *Induction Rule* for common knowledge, which is stated as:

Ind. If $M \models \varphi \Rightarrow E\varphi$ then $M \models \varphi \Rightarrow C\varphi$.

In practice, facts become common knowledge by becoming public in the sense of the induction rule. In many cases, in order to prove that ψ is common knowledge we find a stronger fact φ (so that $M \models \varphi \Rightarrow \psi$) to which the Induction Rule can be applied.

Another important property of common knowledge is captured by the *Fixedpoint Axiom* for common knowledge, which is in a way a converse of the Induction Rule, since it states that when a fact φ is common knowledge, then everyone knows φ and, moreover, everyone knows that φ is common knowledge:

CK. $C\varphi \Rightarrow E\varphi \wedge EC\varphi$.

The Fixedpoint Axiom captures an aspect of common knowledge that relates it to conventions and agreements: Whatever is common knowledge is automatically known by all to be common knowledge. At least at an intuitive level, this is a property we expect from conventions and agreements.

15.4.2   Distributed Knowledge

At the other end of the spectrum from common knowledge is *distributed knowledge*, which roughly corresponds to the knowledge that results from combining the knowledge of all agents, and considering them as one "super agent". If Alan knows the first six numbers in an eight-number sequence that won last week's lottery, and Beth knows the last three numbers in the sequence, then together Alan and Bet can be said to have distributed knowledge of the winning sequence. Despite the fact that neither Alan nor Beth knows the winning sequence by themselves.

We denote distributed knowledge by a modal operator D, and define

$$(M, s) \models D\psi \quad \text{iff} \quad (M, t) \models \psi \text{ for all } t \text{ such that } (s, t) \in \bigcap_i \mathcal{K}_i.$$

Intuitively, $\bigcap_i \mathcal{K}_i$ corresponds to combining the agents' knowledge because, for every state $s \in S$, each state that is known at s by at least one agent to be impossible, is also considered impossible according to the intersection. Thus, we can think of distributed knowledge as representing the knowledge that an agent with access to all agent's information would have.

The definition of satisfaction for Distributed knowledge has the same structure as that for K_i, but with respect to the possibility relation $\mathcal{D} = \bigcap_i \mathcal{K}_i$. It follows that D is a normal modal operator, so that it satisfies Axiom **A1** and the Generalization Rule **G**. Moreover, if all $\mathcal{K}_i$'s are equivalence relations, then their intersection is also an equivalence relation. In this case, distributed knowledge satisfies all of the properties of S5. An axiom connecting knowledge and distributed knowledge is:

Ad. $\models K_i\varphi \Rightarrow D\varphi$.

Using axioms **Ad** and **A1** we can show, for example, that $\models (K_i\varphi \wedge K_j\psi) \Rightarrow D(\varphi \wedge \psi)$. This is one property that we would expect the combined knowledge of the agents to satisfy. In particular, it can be used to establish that Alan and Beth know the winning sequence of lottery numbers in the example discussed above.

In actual applications, we are sometimes interested in states of knowledge of a subset of the agents. Thus, for example, if in our Alice and Bob example there was a third agent Chris that was in the second room with Bob and stayed there when Bob moved into Alice's room, then the outcome of the coin toss would be common knowledge to the subset consisting of Alice and Bob only. Depending on how we would modify the example in this case, the fact Toss that the coin has been tossed could be common knowledge among all three agents or just among Alice and Bob. In an analogous fashion, in particular, applications we may be interested in the knowledge distributed among a particular subset of the agents, and not only in the distributed knowledge for the set of all agents. To accommodate such finer distinctions concerning distributed knowledge and common knowledge, it is possible to subscript the C and D operators by a group $G \subseteq [n]$. The definitions for C_G and D_G are then modified by restricting attention to the possibility relations of the agents participating in G. The logical language obtained by closing $\mathcal{L}_n^K$ off with all operators C_G and D_G for common and distributed knowledge is denoted by $\mathcal{L}_n^{CD}$.

15.5 Runs and Systems

When reasoning about knowledge, one is often interested in modeling a dynamic situation, in which the world evolves, and with it the state of knowledge of the agents changes. In this section we consider a natural way to model these.

We think of every agent at any given instant as being in a well-defined *local state*. The precise structure and contents of this local state typically depends on the application. The local state in our setting captures all of the information that is available to the agent when it determines its next action. A *global state* corresponds to a snapshot of the state of the world frozen at an instant. Formally, it is modeled by an $(n + 1)$-tuple of the form $(s_e, s_1, \ldots, s_n)$, where s_i is i's local state, for $1 \leqslant i \leqslant n$. The additional state s_e is called the *local state of the environment*, and it accounts for all else that is relevant to the analysis, possibly keeping track of aspects of the world that are not part of any agent's local state. These may include, for example, messages in transit in a communication network, the state of entities that are not being modeled as agents in a given application (perhaps a traffic light), or even temporary properties of an agent that the agent might not be aware of. Intuitively, an agent's local state captures exactly what is visible to the agent at the current point. The agent is able to distinguish two points exactly if its local state in one is different from its local state in the other. Thus, we may think of a mailbox as belonging to (or even being part of) an agent in a given application. But if the agent accesses the contents of the mailbox only by performing an explicit *read* operation, then the contents of the mailbox at any given time are modeled as part of the environment state, and the local state may contain the result of actual reads the agent has performed. One final use of the environment state in many applications is for keeping track of various aspects of the history of the run. If different actions may lead to the same global states, or if an agent's state does not keep track of the actions the agent has performed, it is often convenient to add this information as part of the environment's state.

The evolution of a world over time produces a history, which in our terminology will be called a *run*. Formally, a run r is a function assigning every time instant t a global state $r(t)$. If $r(t) = (s_e, s_1, \ldots, s_n)$ then we denote by $r_i(t)$ the local state s_i, for $i = e, 1, \ldots, n$. It is often convenient to identify time with the natural numbers, in which case the run is identified with the sequence $r(0), r(1), \ldots$. We typically reason about knowledge in a setting in which many different histories are possible, at least at the outset. The structure that represents these possibilities is called a *system*, and it is identified with a set R of possible runs. A possible world is now represented by a *point* (r, m) consisting of a run r at a time m. Viewed appropriately, a system induces a Kripke structure, and we can consider formulas as being true or false at a point (r, m) with respect to a system R. Given a set Φ of primitive propositions, we add an interpretation π that determines the truth of the propositions at every point in R. It is convenient to define π to be a function $\pi : \mathcal{G} \times \Phi \to \{\textbf{true}, \textbf{false}\}$, where $\mathcal{G}$ contains the global states in R. Once π is added, we can define the truth of all propositional formulas at points of a system in the standard way. We next define a notion of indistinguishability among points that induces possibility relations $\mathcal{K}_i$ for every agent i. We say that (r, m) and (r', m') are *indistinguishable* to agent i, denoted $(r, m) \sim_i (r', m')$, if $r_i(m) = r'_i(m')$. In words, an agent cannot distinguish among points exactly if it has the same local state in both. Observe that $\sim_i$ is an equivalence relation. A pair $\mathcal{I} = (R, \pi)$, which we call an *interpreted* system, now induces a Kripke structure $M_{\mathcal{I}}$ whose possibility relations are equivalence classes. Consequently, we can write $(\mathcal{I}, r, m) \models \varphi$ and say that $\varphi \in \mathcal{L}_n^K(\Phi)$ holds at (r, m) in (interpreted) system $\mathcal{I} = (R, \pi)$, if φ holds at (r, m) in the induced Kripke structure $M_{\mathcal{I}}$.

We now consider how Alice and Bob's coin-tossing example would be modeled as a system. The local states of each agent can be described by three observable parameters: (i) The current time (0, 1, 2), (ii) the room (ρ_1 or ρ_2) that the agent is in, and (iii) if the agent is in the first room ρ_1, and the coin has been tossed, then what face of the coin is showing. Alice would have five local states $a^0 = (0, \rho_1), a^{1h} = (1, \rho_1, H)$, $a^{1t} = (1, \rho_1, T), a^{2h} = (2, \rho_1, H)$ and $a^{2t} = (2, \rho_1, T)$, while Bob would have four local states $b^0 = (0, \rho_2), b^1 = (1, \rho_2), b^{2h} = (2, \rho_1, H)$, and $b^{2t} = (2, \rho_1, T)$. The environment state can be chosen in different ways. Indeed, in this particular example all of the relevant information is already captured in the local states of the agents; it is therefore possible to consider the environment state as being identically λ. In order to fit an extension of this modeling in Section 15.7.1 we will instead choose the environment's state to record the current time at each state. If we consider Alice as agent 1 and Bob as agent 2, then each of the states in Fig. 15.1 corresponds to a global state. Specifically, $s_0 = (a^0, b^0, 0), s_1 = (a^{1h}, b^1, 1), t_1 = (a^{1t}, b^1, 1)$, $s_2 = (a^{2h}, b^{2h}, 2)$ and $t_2 = (a^{2t}, b^{2t}, 2)$. The set of global states in the example is thus $\mathcal{G} = \{s_0, s_1, t_1, s_2, t_2\}$. The interpretation π for $\Phi = \{\mathsf{Toss}, \mathsf{Heads}, \mathsf{Tails}\}$ is the one defined in the original example and depicted in Fig. 15.1.

The system consists of two runs $R = \{r, r'\}$, where $r(0) = s_0, r(1) = s_1$, and $r(2) = s_2$, while $r'(0) = s_0, r'(1) = t_1$, and $r'(2) = t_2$. With respect to the interpreted system $\mathcal{I} = (R, \pi)$ the truth of epistemic formulas is now well-defined and works as expected. It is instructive to observe that the state s_0 which served to specify a world in the original Kripke structure is represented in $\mathcal{I}$ by two *different* points: $(r, 0)$ and $(r', 0)$. It is straightforward to verify that the exact same formulas of $\mathcal{L}_n^K(\Phi)$ hold at $(\mathcal{I}, r, 0)$ and $(\mathcal{I}, r', 0)$. As expected, these are the same formulas that are satisfied at (M, s_0) in the original example. What distinguishes these two points is the fact that they appear in different runs (histories). Indeed, the coin lands Heads in the future of $(r, 0)$ and lands Tails in that of $(r', 0)$. In the next section we enrich the language with temporal operators. Once we do this, the sets of formulas satisfied at the two points no longer coincide.

The runs and systems modeling of knowledge allows considerable control over the manner in which knowledge evolves over time. By varying the way in which events change the agents' local states, we can obtain different flavors of knowledge. Thus, for example, suppose that local states consist of a sequence of all events that the agent has observed so far. In this case, agents would have *perfect recall* and would not forget their past knowledge. Conversely, if information is removed from an agent's local state, then the agent can "forget" facts that it knows. This reflects the natural property that the evolution of knowledge depends on memory and how it is utilized. There are cases in which, during the design of a solution to a problem in a distributed setting, it is convenient to start out assuming that agents have perfect recall. An analysis in terms of knowledge is often simpler to perform in such a setting. Once a basic solution is obtained, it is typically possible to try to optimize the solution by reducing the size and contents of the local states, while maintaining the correctness of the solution. Such a scheme can be found in [7, 24, 37, 38, 35].

15.6 Adding Time

In many applications, it is natural to model time as ranging over the natural numbers (or a prefix of the natural numbers). In this case, a run is a sequence of global states. As shown in Chapter 12 linear-time temporal operators can thus readily be added to the language, and the satisfaction relation $\models$ can be defined for temporal operators in the standard way. For example, suppose that we add the operators O (standing for *at the next time instant*), $\square$ (standing for *forever in the future*) and $\lozenge$ (standing for *eventually*) to the language. We denote the resulting language by $\mathcal{L}_n^{KT}$. Then we can define

$$(\mathcal{I}, r, m) \models O\varphi \quad \text{iff} \quad (\mathcal{I}, r, m+1) \models \varphi,$$

and

$$(\mathcal{I}, r, m) \models \square\varphi \quad \text{iff} \quad (\mathcal{I}, r, m') \models \varphi \quad \text{for all } m' \geqslant m.$$

The $\lozenge$ operator is treated as the dual of $\square$, so that $\lozenge\varphi$ is considered as shorthand for $\neg\square\neg\varphi$. Additional operators, such as Until and past operators can be added in a similar fashion.

In the Alice and Bob example we would now have, for example:

$$(\mathcal{I}, r, 0) \models O\text{Heads} \wedge K_B O(\text{Heads} \vee \text{Tails}) \wedge K_B \square(\text{Tails} \Rightarrow K_A \text{Tails}).$$

Once temporal operators are added to the logical language, we can express the fact that things will be known at times other than the present, and we can also express knowledge about temporal facts. Knowledge and time are complementary notions and, to a large extent, are orthogonal to each other. Indeed, temporal operators allow us to reason along the time axis within a run, while knowledge operators allow reasoning across runs (as well as, sometimes, within the run if local states repeat).

It is natural to seek an axiom system for the runs and systems model in terms of the temporal-epistemic language $\mathcal{L}_n^{KT}$. Clearly, knowledge satisfies S5, because it is determined based on possibility relations that are equivalence relations. Similarly, the temporal operators satisfy the axioms of standard linear-time temporal logic [34]. More interesting is the interaction between knowledge and time. For example, consider the formula

$$K_i\varphi \Rightarrow OK_i\varphi, \tag{15.1}$$

which states that if agent i currently knows φ, then i will still know φ at the next state. This property can not be expected to hold for arbitrary formulas. For example, consider the proposition time $= 3$ where $\pi(\text{time} = 3) = \{(r, m): m = 3\}$. If $K_i(\text{time} = 3)$ holds at a given point, it would fail to hold one time step later, since time $= 3$ would not hold at time 4. We say that a formula ψ is *stable* with respect to an interpreted system $\mathcal{I}$ if $\mathcal{I} \models \psi \Rightarrow \square\psi$. Stable formulas are ones that, once true, are guaranteed to remain true forever. The argument showing that property (15.1) is not valid made use of the nonstable formula time $= 3$. Is the property valid for stable formulas? Recall that an agent that does not have perfect recall may forget that it knew certain facts. It turns out that property (15.1) holds in systems in which the formula φ is stable, and agent i has perfect recall. We now make this claim more precise. Agent i's *local state sequence* at a point (r, m) is the sequence of local states obtained from $[r_i(0), r_i(1), \ldots, r_i(m)]$ once we remove immediate repetition of states. Intuitively, if the agent's state does not change from one time instant to the next, then the agent cannot observe that time has passed. Consequently, according to agent i's subjective point of view, at two points in which the agent has the same local state sequence, it has had the same local history. We say that i has perfect recall in the system R if at all points of R, whenever $r_i(m) = r_i'(m')$ the agent i has the same local state sequence at (r, m) and at (r', m'). It is not hard to prove that $K_i\varphi \Rightarrow \mathsf{O}K_i\varphi$ is valid for stable formulas φ in systems in which i has perfect recall.

Let us consider another natural property relating knowledge and time:

$$K_i\mathsf{O}\varphi \Rightarrow \mathsf{O}K_i\varphi. \tag{15.2}$$

This formula states that if agent i knows that tomorrow φ will hold, then tomorrow the agent will know φ. This reasonable property is not a valid axiom for the runs and systems model, however. There are two factors that can render this formula false. One is the fact, discussed in the previous section, that agents might be forgetful. Thus, i may know something today, and no longer be aware tomorrow that this knowledge existed. (This can, for example, result from the agent deleting some messages from its mail file.) In particular, the agent can forget knowledge about what will be true at the next time instant. The second factor that can foil this property involves the agent's awareness of the passage of time. The "next" operator O refers to a point in time that is one time step into the future. There are systems in which agents are fully aware of the passage of time, and ones in which agents need not have perfect knowledge of it. A system is said to be *synchronous* if agents can always distinguish points at different times. In such a system, if $m \neq m'$ then $r_i(m) \neq r_i'(m')$ holds for all runs r and r' and agents i. For the class of synchronous systems, in which agents have perfect recall, the formula in (15.2) is indeed a valid axiom.

As these examples illustrate, the interaction between knowledge and time is subtle, and it depends on the particular assumptions one makes about properties of the system at hand. There has been extensive work on characterizing complete axiom systems for classes of interpreted systems with various sets of properties (see, e.g., [23]).

15.6.1 Common Knowledge and Time

The fixedpoint axiom for common knowledge implies that $\models C\varphi \Rightarrow EC\varphi$, which intuitively means that common knowledge is inherently "public": Everyone knows what is common knowledge. Since knowledge satisfies the Knowledge Axiom, at any given moment either nobody knows $C\varphi$ or all agents do. An agent cannot come to know $C\varphi$ before $C\varphi$ holds, and all agents do. Thus, the transition from $\neg C\varphi$ to $C\varphi$ requires a *simultaneous* change in the local states of all (relevant) agents. It follows that in systems where it is not possible to coordinate simultaneous transitions (or at least to identify a simultaneous transition once it has occurred), it is impossible for facts that are not commonly known to become common knowledge. In particular, no common knowledge can arise in asynchronous systems or when communication is not reliable [17, 12, 5].

This raises a philosophical issue that has practical modeling implications. Recall that we typically think of common knowledge as arising naturally from public or shared events such as a handshake. But can we really say that the agents come to know that they are shaking hands simultaneously? Apparently not. Indeed, it may very well be the case that the tactile sensation of the handshake reaches one agent's brain two milliseconds before it reaches the second agent's brain. And even if the sensations arrive truly at the same instant, the agents cannot reasonably rule out the possibility that they arrived at slightly different times. In fact, if time is modeled at a sufficiently fine granularity then real systems do not allow for simultaneity, and hence also not for common knowledge. When we choose the model for a given problem, however, it often makes sense to keep the model as simple as possible to faithfully model the situation (but no simpler). In such a model, we may well find common knowledge arising. Thus, for example, in the synchronous models mentioned earlier, where $r_i(m) = r_i'(m')$ can hold only if $m = m'$, we immediately obtain that the current time is always common knowledge, provided Φ is expressive enough to talk about the current time (e.g., has propositions of the form time $= m$ for $m = 0, 1, \ldots$). Moreover, in synchronous systems in which messages are guaranteed to take exactly k time steps to be delivered, when Alice receives a message from Bob, they share common knowledge that she has received this message, provided that Bob remembers the message and its sending time for at least k time units. The common knowledge paradox comes from the fact that as the model becomes more detailed, transitions are no longer simultaneous, and common knowledge vanishes [17, 12].

15.7 Knowledge-based Behaviors

15.7.1 Contexts and Protocols

As we have seen, each systems and runs model directly induces a Kripke structure and consequently allows reasoning about knowledge and belief. But where do the systems come from? In many applications, we wish to reason about knowledge in a given setting in which the agents are following particular strategies, or programs. The system corresponding to such a scenario consists of all possible runs (histories) that can arise. Strategies, or programs, are not executed in a void. Rather, they are carried out within a particular context. This context determines how Nature, or the environment, evolves and interacts with the behavior of the agents. More formally, suppose that we fix sets of local states $L_e, L_1, \ldots, L_n$ and local actions $\mathsf{ACT}_e, \mathsf{ACT}_1, \ldots, \mathsf{ACT}_n$ for the agents and the environment. A *protocol* for $i = e, 1, \ldots, n$ is a function $P_i : L_i \to (2^{\mathsf{ACT}_i} \setminus \{\{\ \}\})$ determining, possibly in a nondeterministic fashion, what action i performs as a function of its local state. If $P_i(\ell_i) = A$, then A is a nonempty set A of actions, and the action performed by i when in state ℓ_i will be one of the members of A. If $P_i(\ell_i)$ is a singleton for all $\ell_i \in L_i$, then P_i reduces to a function from states to actions, and is thus a deterministic protocol.

Let $\mathcal{G} = L_e \times L_1 \times \cdots \times L_n$. In order to reason about knowledge and belief, we typically assume a fixed set Φ of primitive propositions, and an interpretation $\pi : \mathcal{G} \times \Phi \to \{\textbf{true}, \textbf{false}\}$. A *joint action* is a tuple $\vec{\mathsf{a}} = (a_e, a_1, \ldots, a_n)$ consisting of an action $a_i \in \mathsf{ACT}_i$ for $i = e, 1, \ldots, n$. We will assume that at every point each of the agents performs an action. The fact that in many applications we do not think of all agents as moving at all times can be handled by assuming that the environment actions can influence the scheduling of which agent actions are enabled and hence may in fact affect the global state.

A *context* is a tuple $\gamma = (\mathcal{G}_0, \tau, P_e)$, where $\mathcal{G}_0 \subset \mathcal{G}$ is a set of *initial* global states, τ is a *transition function*, mapping every global state g and joint action $\vec{a}$ to a global state g'. Intuitively, if $\tau(g, \vec{a}) = g'$ then the result of $\vec{a}$ being performed in g is that the global state becomes g'. Finally, P_e is a protocol (often nondeterministic) for the environment. In many applications in which the environment's protocol P_e is nondeterministic, it is often natural to assume that the context also ensures certain *fairness* of the actions performed by the environment over time. We shall soon discuss how a fourth component can be added to the context to handle such cases.

We now turn to consider how protocols for the agents give rise to runs and systems. Define a *joint protocol* to be a tuple $\vec{P} = (P_1, \ldots, P_n)$ associating a protocol with each one of the agents, but not with the environment. We say that a run r is a *run of $\vec{P}$ in the context γ* If $r(0) \in \mathcal{G}_0$, and at every point (r, m) there is a joint action $\vec{a}$ consisting of local actions $a_i \in P_i(r_i(m))$, for $i = e, 1, \ldots, n$, such that $\tau(r(m), \vec{a}) = r(m + 1)$. Intuitively, this means that the runs begins in a legal state according to γ, and it proceeds at every step in a legal fashion: there is a joint action that can be generated by P_e and $\vec{P}$ that can transform the global state into the successor, according to the transition function τ. We can thus define the system $R(\vec{P}, \gamma)$ generated by $\vec{P}$ in γ to consist of the set of all runs of $\vec{P}$ in γ. Moreover, assuming that we have a fixed Φ and interpretation π in mind for $\mathcal{G}$, the corresponding interpreted system is $\mathcal{I}(\vec{P}, \gamma) = (R(\vec{P}, \gamma), \pi)$. Observe that in our framework contexts and joint protocols play complementary roles. Taken together, they give rise to a single, well-defined, interpreted system. This framework allows us to consider running a given protocol in different contexts, and similarly allows us to compare different protocols being run in the same system.

Let us briefly outline how Alice and Bob's coin tossing example can be represented in the framework that we have just described. The local states and global states are as described in Section 15.5, and the set of initial states is $\mathcal{G}_0 = \{s_0\}$. Let $\mathsf{ACT}_e = \{\mathsf{skip}, \mathsf{land\_heads}, \mathsf{land\_tails}\}$, $\mathsf{ACT}_1 = \{\mathsf{skip}, \mathsf{flip}\}$, and $\mathsf{ACT}_2 = \{\mathsf{skip}, \mathsf{move}\}$. The transition function is such that skip is the null action for all three entities, move changes Bob's location from room ρ_2 to ρ_1, flip is a toss of the coin by Alice, and land_heads and land_tails are environment actions that determine what side the coin will land on, in case the coin is flipped. To complete the description of the context γ we need to determine the environment's protocol P_e. We take it to perform skip at times 1 and 2, while at time 0 it prescribes a nondeterministic choice from the set {land_heads, land_tails}. Notice that the current time is a component in the local states of the environment, as well as of those of Alice and Bob. Hence, protocols defined as a function of the time (or round number) are in particular functions of the local states, as required. The joint protocol $\vec{P} = (P_1, P_2)$, where Alice's protocol P_1 performs flip at time 0 and skip at times 1 and 2. Finally, Bob's protocol P_2 performs skip at times 0 and 2, while performing move at time 1. It is straightforward to check that the interpreted system $\mathcal{I}$ from Section 15.5 is precisely $\mathcal{I} = \mathcal{I}(\vec{P}, \gamma)$ for the protocol and context just described.

We mentioned above the occasional need to add a fourth component to the context. An example is a distributed computer system in which communication is reliable, but there is no bound on message delivery times. Thus, every message that is sent is guaranteed to reach its destination. The environment's protocol at any given instant may nondeterministically choose between delivering a message that is in transit or not delivering it yet. But our assumption about the context is that the message may not remain in transit until the end of time. When such issues need to be accounted for, we add a fourth component Ψ to the context, where Ψ is an *admissibility condition* specifying the set of "acceptable" runs. Now r is a run of $\vec{P}$ in $\gamma = (\mathcal{G}_0, \tau, P_e, \Psi)$ if r is a run of $\vec{P}$ in the larger context $\hat{\gamma} = (\mathcal{G}_0, \tau, P_e)$, **and** r satisfies Ψ. Thus, runs that do not comply with Ψ do not arise in γ.

The admissibility condition Ψ in a context $\gamma = (\mathcal{G}_0, \tau, P_e, \Psi)$ should be *non-exclusive*, which means that for every protocol $\vec{P}$ for the agents, every finite prefix of a run of $\vec{P}$ in $\hat{\gamma} = (\mathcal{G}_0, \tau, P_e)$ must be a prefix of a run of $\vec{P}$ in $\gamma = (\mathcal{G}_0, \tau, P_e, \Psi)$. Roughly speaking, this ensures that Ψ captures aspects of the environment's infinite behavior, and does not influence the possible finite executions of protocols in the context.

15.7.2 Knowledge-based Programs

The close connection between knowledge and action is a central motivation for reasoning about knowledge. In fact, there are many settings in which it is natural to think of particular choices of actions or strategies as being triggered by an agent's knowledge. Thus, for example, an agent called Noah may start to build and ark if he knows that a flood is soon to come; his neighbors, who may not be privy to such knowledge, may instead prefer to herd their sheep and dismiss the looming danger. The essential role that knowledge plays in determining the actions that agents perform often makes knowledge into a goal in its own right: Indeed, a central goal of communication among agents typically has to do with ensuring that particular agents obtain certain knowledge (or beliefs). Conversely, many personal, financial, and political activities are required to satisfy secrecy constraints, which in turn mean that certain agents do not obtain particular knowledge. In some of these cases, it is useful to reason about actions at the knowledge level. Suppose that Bob does not know that Alice knows where to meet him for Dinner. His goal is then be simply to ensure that she comes to know where to meet him for Dinner. Alice's decision on where to go for Dinner may depend on whether she knows where Bob reserved a table. In this particular example, it may not matter to Bob whether he informs Alice by phone, by way of a messenger, or indeed by other means. The mode of communication that he uses is merely one way of implementing his goal, which is best thought of at the knowledge level. Assuming that Bob will not rest until he is confident that Alice has obtained this piece of knowledge, Alice may also wish to notify Bob once she has received his message. Again, the essential property Alice would wish to ensure is conveniently stated as a formula of $\mathcal{L}_2^K$ —at the knowledge level. As this brief example illustrates, parts of everyday activity involves planning and acting to achieve goals that are best expressed at the knowledge level. One convenient tool for reasoning at the knowledge level is provided by *knowledge-*

based programs (kb programs, for short). We can think of a kb program for an agent i as having the form

> **if** κ_1 **then** a_1,
>
> **if** κ_2 **then** a_2,
>
> $\ldots$
>
> **if** κ_m **then** a_m,

where each knowledge test κ_j is a Boolean combination of formulas of the form $K_i\varphi$, where $\varphi \in \mathcal{L}_n^K$ may contain nested occurrences of K_j operators. We assume that the tests $\kappa_1, \kappa_2, \ldots, \kappa_m$ are mutually exclusive and exhaustive, so that exactly one will evaluate to true whenever i performs an action. Denote this particular program by Pg_i. Suppose that Alice and Bob typically dine at the restaurant R_2, but they had previously agreed that on this particular day Bob would try to make a reservation at *Chez Panis* (restaurant R_1). Once Bob manages to reserve a table, his program (which he performs repeatedly) may be:

> **if** $\neg K_B K_A$Reserved_at(R_1) **then** phone Alice and tell her

The program that Alice follows at 8 pm may then be

> **if** K_AReserved_at(R_1) **then** go to R_1,
>
> **if** $\neg K_A$Reserved_at(R_1) **then** go to R_2.

Knowledge-based programs are very similar in form to standard computer programs. The main difference is that actions in kb programs are determined based on the actor's knowledge, rather than on the values of her local variables or computer memory. If we fix an interpreted system $\mathcal{I}$ for evaluating the truth of knowledge tests, a kb program such as Pg_i induces a unique deterministic protocol for i. Indeed, for every knowledge test κ_j in Pg_i, there is a set $L_i^{\kappa_j}(\mathcal{I})$ for i such that $(\mathcal{I}, r, m) \models \kappa_j$ exactly if $r_i(m) \in L_i^{\kappa_j}(\mathcal{I})$. Denoting agent i's current local state by ℓ_i, once $\mathcal{I}$ is fixed, the kb program reduces to the following standard program $Pg_i^{\mathcal{I}}$:

> **if** $\ell_i \in L_i^{\kappa_1}(\mathcal{I})$ **then** a_1,
>
> **if** $\ell_i \in L_i^{\kappa_2}(\mathcal{I})$ **then** a_2,
>
> $\ldots$
>
> **if** $\ell_i \in L_i^{\kappa_m}(\mathcal{I})$ **then** a_m.

We identify $Pg^{\mathcal{I}}$ with the protocol it induces. The question of what we should choose as the system $\mathcal{I}$ here is somewhat delicate. As we have seen, it is natural to think of a protocol or program as generating a well-defined system in a given context γ. This system is the set of runs of the program. In the case of a kb program, however, we need the system in order to figure out what the program that generates the system is! We can avoid this vicious circularity by considering a kb program as a *specification* which may or may not be implemented by a given standard program. Fix a context γ. A given joint protocol $\vec{P}$ generates a unique interpreted system $\mathcal{I}^{\vec{P}} = \mathcal{I}(\vec{P}, \gamma)$ in this context. We can now say that $\vec{P}$ *implements* $Pg = (Pg_1, \ldots, Pg_n)$ in (γ) if $\vec{P}$ is equivalent to the program $\text{Pg}^{\mathcal{I}\vec{P}}$. Intuitively, if $\vec{P}$ implements Pg, then we are justified in viewing all agents in $\vec{P}$ as acting according to, or following, the knowledge-based program Pg.

Knowledge-based programs are indeed specifications, in the sense that some have a unique implementation, some have many different implementations, and some will have no implementation in a given context. We now consider an example in which a natural knowledge-based program has two different implementations.

15.7.3 A Subtle kb Program

Consider a mobile robot controlling a rail cart that travels on a track with discrete locations numbered $0, 1, 2, \ldots$. The cart starts out at location 0 and can move only in the positive direction. The cart's motion is determined by the environment, and the robot can only control whether to stop the cart. Moreover, the robot has no memory, and it has access only to an imperfect location sensor. For every location $q \geqslant 0$, it is guaranteed that whenever the robot is at location q, the sensor-reading σ will be one of $\{q - 1, q, q + 1\}$. The robot's goal is to stop the cart at one of the locations 4, 5, or 6. Stopping outside this region is not allowed. What should the robot's program be? Define a proposition goal that is true at all points at which the robot's location is $q \in \{4, 5, 6\}$. Intuitively, as long as the robot does not know that goal holds, it should not halt. On the other hand, once the robot does know that goal holds, it should be able to stop the cart in the goal region, as desired. Thus, $K_r$goal seems to be both a necessary and a sufficient condition for stopping in the goal region.

More formally, we assume that the environment's local state consists of the current location (q), while the robot's local state consists solely of the sensor reading (σ) (recall that the robot cannot recall the past—it is assumed to be memoryless). The environment actions are $\text{ACT}_e = \{\text{stay}, \text{move}\} \times \{-1, 0, 1\}$, where the first component determines whether or not the robot's cart will be moved one position to the right on the track, and the second component determines how the sensor reading σ is related to the actual position q. The robot's actions are $\text{ACT}_r = \{\text{skip}, \text{halt}\}$, where the action halt overrules the environment's action, the cart stops at the current location, and never moves again. The environment's protocol P_e is as follows. At all times m not of the form $m = k^{100}$, the protocol prescribes a nondeterministic choice among the actions of ACT_e. At the few times m of the form $m = k^{100}$, the choice is restricted to $\{\text{move}\} \times \{-1, 0, 1\}$—so that, if not halted, the robot moves one step to the right. It is straightforward to define the transition function τ that matches this description, thereby completing the definition of the context γ_r. We take $\Phi = \{\text{goal}\}$, and π assigns goal the value true at $r(m) = (q, \sigma)$ exactly if $q \in \{4, 5, 6\}$.

Consider the knowledge-based program Rob

> **if** $K_r(\text{goal})$ **then** halt.

Clearly, Rob guarantees that the robot will never halt the cart outside of the goal region. But does it also guarantee that the robot always succeeds in halting in the goal region? The answer is not clear cut.

The properties of the sensor in this context ensure that, for every protocol P executed in γ_r we have $\mathcal{I}(P, \gamma_r) \models (\sigma = 5) \Rightarrow K_r(\text{goal})$. This suggests that the following standard program, denoted Rob_s,

> **if** $\sigma = 5$ **then** halt,

should be an implementation of Rob in γ_r. It is not hard to check that this is indeed the case. Unfortunately, this implementation of Rob does not guarantee that the robot halts in the goal region. There are many runs of Rob_s in this context in which $\sigma \neq 5$ holds throughout the run, despite the fact that the robot crosses the goal region and exits it. It follows that, in spite of its "obviousness", the knowledge-based program Rob does not guarantee that the robot will succeed in γ_r. It may appear that this situation is unavoidable. However, there is a twist to the story. For consider now the program Rob'_s:

if $\sigma > 4$ **then** halt.

Following this program, the robot will never stop before reaching position $q = 4$, because $\sigma > 4$ is not satisfied when $q < 4$. Moreover, when following this program, the robot *is* guaranteed to stop the cart if it ever reaches the position $q = 6$, since at that point the sensor reading must satisfy $\sigma \in \{5, 6, 7\}$, so that the condition $\sigma > 4$ is true. Finally, the environment's protocol in γ_r guarantees that, if the robot has not halted the cart, then the cart will be at position 6 no later than time $6^{100} + 1$.

The protocol described by Rob'_s is a standard implementation of the kb-program Rob. Thus, Rob has two qualitatively different implementations, with one being guaranteed to reach the goal in every run, while the other is not. This justifies considering knowledge-based programs as specifications that can be satisfied in different ways. We remark that small changes in the assumptions of this example can change the outcome of the analysis. In particular, if we change γ_r so that the robot has perfect recall, then Rob_s is *no longer* an implementation of Rob, and the protocol described by Rob'_s is the only implementation, and a good one at that.

Admittedly, our assumption about the environment's protocol being forced to perform at least k move actions in every k^{100} steps was somewhat unnatural. It was intended to capture the idea that if the robot does not perform a halt action, then it will eventually move beyond any finite point. A somewhat cleaner, alternative way, to capture this would have been to add an admissibility condition Ψ to the context, which would admit only runs for which the following temporal formula holds at the initial state: $\varphi = (\Diamond \text{halt} \vee \Box \Diamond \text{move})$: A run is admissible if either the robot eventually halts, or it is moved infinitely often.

In summary, the robot example shows a fairly natural scenario in which a knowledge-based program can have more than one implementation. As we have mentioned, there are kb programs that have no implementations, ones that have a single implementation, and ones that have many implementations. Fortunately, there are many cases in which a knowledge-based program is guaranteed to have a unique implementation. This happens, for example, in a context in which the agents have a global clock and the knowledge tests in the program do not refer to the future (see [11]). Indeed in our robot example, if the robot's local state contains the round number in addition to the sensor reading, then the only implementation of the knowledge-based program Rob is the more efficient Rob'_s.

The definition of implementation for knowledge-based programs that we have presented is fairly strict, because the agent following such a program must be able to evaluate all knowledge tests at all times. This is good for certain types of analyses and may be overkill in certain applications. There are also variations on knowledge-based programs [8] that use a more liberal notion of implementation, in which the knowledge tests are replaced by *sound* standard tests which, when true, guarantee that the tested knowledge actually exist. A standard test "implementing" a knowledge test in this case is allowed to fail when the agent does have the tested knowledge.

15.8 Beyond Square One

So far we have discussed the basic possible-worlds setting, considered the basic properties of knowledge and belief, and considered how the runs and systems (protocols & contexts) framework can be used to capture the knowledge and belief aspects of an application. There are hundreds of contributions to the literature that deal with the analysis of properties of knowledge and belief, and the properties of their logics. Other contributions apply reasoning about knowledge to particular domains such as distributed computing systems, multi-agent planning, philosophical puzzles, or game theory. There are various approaches and formalisms for modeling knowledge, some similar to our description, and others quite distinct from it. For example, in game theory the accepted model for knowledge is influenced by the terminology of probability theory, with the possibility relations typically being defined by associating with each agent (or player) a partition on the states of the universe [1]. Cells of the partition are equivalence classes, and the outcome is essentially an instance of the familiar S5-knowledge.

A more recent formalism for reasoning about knowledge is based on marrying possible-worlds modeling for knowledge with Dynamic Logic [3, 2, 4]. Here the idea is to explicitly model the effect that action have on the state of knowledge of the agents. Thus, for example, a public announcement of φ by a trustworthy agent causes φ to become common knowledge; hence, the state immediately following such an announcement satisfies $C\varphi$.

The properties of knowledge as captured by the S5 axioms are not considered an acceptable characterization of human knowledge. Clearly, the Propositional Axiom **A0** which states that all tautologies are known to all agents assumes an idealized notion of agent. Perhaps equally objectionable is the property captured by the Distribution Axiom **A1**, which states that an agent's knowledge is essentially closed under logical deduction. These properties are generally termed *logical omniscience*. They are unreasonable not only for describing the knowledge of humans, but also when an agent's knowledge is meant to be accessible by some form of tractable computation. We remark that the success obtained by using the formalism introduced in this chapter so far in treating a variety of problems in different domains was possible mainly in cases where logical omniscience was not the main issue to contend with. For example, in a setting where Alice receives an acknowledgment from Bob that he has received a particular message sent to him, there is no conceptual problem with using the formal conclusion that she *knows* he has received the message.

There have been many attempts at defining weaker variants of knowledge that will not suffer from logical omniscience. Some of these are syntactic, in which what is known may be a list of formulas [22]. Others involve a syntactic element of *awareness*, which gives rise to a distinction between implicit and explicit knowledge. Traditional (possible-worlds based) knowledge is thought of as being implicit, and an agent that implicitly knows φ and is also *aware* of φ, is considered as having explicit knowledge of φ [10]. In other approaches, the limitations on knowledge are either based on explicit resource bounds of the agents [36, 19], or are based on agents having access to an explicit set of algorithms for computing knowledge [20]. In the latter case, $K_i\varphi$ would hold at a given point if applying one of the algorithms at its disposal at that point can establish that it does.

15.9   How to Reason about Knowledge and Belief

We have defined logics for the language $\mathcal{L}_n^K$ of knowledge, and discussed axioms for common knowledge, distributed knowledge, and time. All of these are modal logics, and one might hope to be able to use general-purpose methods to reason about them. In fact, however, there are many hurdles to doing so. First of all, even for the logics we have considered for the basic language $\mathcal{L}_n^K$, deciding the satisfiability of formulas is PSPACE-complete [18]. The complexity of logics of knowledge and time depends on our assumptions about perfect recall, synchrony, and the properties of communication. In [21] Halpern and Vardi consider ninety six logics. In all cases the complexity of the satisfiability problem ranges between the intractable exponential time and the undecidable Π_1^1. Second, the properties of knowledge and its interaction with related modal operators such as time are very sensitive to the features of the system in question, or to those of the underlying context. They can differ significantly from one application to another. We have seen how issues such as whether communication is synchronous or asynchronous, and whether agents have perfect recall can affect the axioms. Other structural properties of a given system can make a significant difference. For example, in a given application φ might be local to agent i—so that $\varphi \equiv K_i\varphi$ is valid in the system. In another, Eve might receive a copy of every message exchanged between Alice and Bob. This imposes specific but sometimes crucial structure on the way knowledge can evolve in the system. Because of the richness of systems and contexts, no single set of axioms completely characterizes the properties of knowledge is a wide variety of applications. Recall that in the standard runs and systems framework of Sections 15.5 and beyond knowledge satisfies the axioms of S5. Since in any given system additional properties may hold, it follows that S5 provides properties that are *sound* in all such systems, but it does not in general completely characterize knowledge in the system. It follows that decision procedures for modal logics of, say, knowledge and time are not likely to be helpful for reasoning about multi-agent systems in practice.

Much closer to the nature of reasoning we are interested in is the notion of *model-checking* [6], which has proven very successful for reasoning about temporal properties of finite-state systems and is widely used in the hardware industry. As shown in [22], the model-checking problem of model checking an $\mathcal{L}_n^K$ formula φ with m symbols at a point of a structure with K points is bounded above by mnK^2. This appears much more tractable than deciding satisfiability, but since K might be large, this could still be a considerable challenge. In fact, as model-checking techniques and optimizations improve, there is hope for variations on this theme. One of the best approaches for reasoning about knowledge in multi-agent systems appears to be the use of special-purpose model-checkers designed for the task such as [14]. Another approach that is gaining in popularity has to do with adapting existing theorem provers or model checkers such as PVS, SMV or MOCHA to the epistemic domain [33]. In most cases the classes of systems that can be treated is limited in some way—in the number of states involved, or in the diversity of actions that can be applied. The MCK tool has the unique feature that while the underlying context being modeled is finite state, the agents' local states can grow unbounded. The field of tools and case studies is growing rapidly and will most likely yield practical results in the coming years.

15.9.1 Concluding Remark

This chapter presented some of the basic notions having to do with knowledge and belief in multi-agent systems. Its main focus and use to the reader may be as a short introduction to the task of modeling knowledge and belief in systems. There is a huge body of work in the area that we did not have time to even hint at. We believe that knowledge-based analyses of multi-agent systems, and reasoning about knowledge and belief will find more and more applications in the coming years and decades, and will continue to develop rapidly. For additional material beyond the cited references, the reader may also consult [42, 43, 45–49].

Bibliography

[1] R.J. Aumann. Agreeing to disagree. *Annals of Statistics*, 4(6):1236–1239, 1976.

[2] A. Baltag and L.S. Moss. Logics for epistemic programs. *Synthese*, 139(2):165–224, 2004.

[3] J. van Benthem. Epistemic logic: from knowledge to cognition. In Y. Moses, editor. *Proceedings 4th Conf. on Theoretical Aspects of Reasoning about Knowledge*, pages 167–168. Morgan Kaufmann Publishers, 1992.

[4] J. van Benthem, J. van Eijck, and B. Kooi. Logics of communication and change. *Information and Computation*, 204(11):1620–1662, 2005.

[5] K.M. Chandy and J. Misra. How processes learn. *Distrib. Comput.*, 1(1):40–52, 1986.

[6] E.M. Clarke, O. Grumberg, and D. Peled. *Model Checking*. The MIT Press, 1980.

[7] C. Dwork and Y. Moses. Knowledge and common knowledge in a Byzantine environment: crash failures. *Information and Computation*, 88(2):156–186, 1990.

[8] K. Engelhardt, R. van der Meyden, and Y. Moses. Knowledge and the logic of local propositions. In I. Gilboa, editor. *Proceedings 7th. Conf. on Theoretical Aspects of Rationality and Knowledge*, pages 29–41. Morgan Kaufmann Publishers, 1998.

[9] H.H. Clark and C.R. Marshall. Definite reference and mutual knowledge. In A.K. Joshi, B.L. Webber, and I.A. Sag, editors. *Elements of Discourse Understanding*, pages 10–63. Cambridge University Press, Cambridge, 1981.

[10] R. Fagin and J.Y. Halpern. Belief, awareness and limited reasoning. *Artificial Intelligence*, 34(1):39–76, 1987.

[11] R. Fagin, J.Y. Halpern, Y. Moses, and M.Y. Vardi. Knowledge-based programs. *Distributed Computing*, 10(4):199–225, 1997.

[12] R. Fagin, J.Y. Halpern, Y. Moses, and M.Y. Vardi. *Reasoning about Knowledge*. The MIT Press, 2003.

[13] M.F. Friedell. On the structure of shared awareness. *Behavioral Science*, 14(1):28–39, 1969.

[14] P. Gammie and R. van der Meyden. MCK: Model checking the logic of knowledge. In *Proc. Computer Aided Verification, 16th International Conference (CAV)*, pages 479–483, 2004.

[15] E. Gettier. Is justified true belief knowledge? *Analysis*, 23(6):121–123, 1963.

[16] S. Goldwasser, S. Micali, and C. Rackoff. The knowledge complexity of interactive proof systems. *SIAM J. Comput.*, 18(1):186–208, 1989.

[17] J.Y. Halpern and Y. Moses. Knowledge and common knowledge in a distributed environment. *J. ACM*, 37(3):549–587, 1990. An early version in *Proc. 3rd ACM Conf. on Principles of Distributed Computing*, 1984, pages 50–61.

[18] J.Y. Halpern and Y. Moses. A guide to completeness and complexity for modal logics of knowledge and belief. *Artificial Intelligence*, 54(3):319–379, 1992.

[19] J.Y. Halpern, Y. Moses, and M.R. Tuttle. A knowledge-based analysis of zero knowledge. In *Proceedings 12th ACM Symp. on Theory of Comput. (STOC)*, pages 132–147, 1988.

[20] J.Y. Halpern, Y. Moses, and M.Y. Vardi. Algorithmic knowledge. In R. Fagin, editor. *Proceedings 5th. Conf. on Theoretical Aspects of Reasoning about Knowledge*, pages 255–266. Morgan Kaufmann Publishers, 1994.

[21] J.Y. Halpern and M.Y. Vardi. The complexity of reasoning about knowledge and time, I: Lower bounds. *Journal of Computer Systems Science*, 38(1):195–237, 1991.

[22] J.Y. Halpern and M.Y. Vardi. Model checking vs. theorem proving: A manifesto. In J. Allen, R.E. Fikes, and E. Sandewall, editors, *Proc. 2nd Int. Conf. on Principles of Knowledge Representation and Reasoning, KR'91*, pages 325–334, 1991.

[23] J.Y. Halpern, M.Y. Vardi, and R. van der Meyden. Complete axiomatizations for reasoning about knowledge and time. *SIAM Journal on Computing*, 33(3):674–703, 2004.

[24] J.Y. Halpern and L.D. Zuck. A little knowledge goes a long way: Knowledge-based derivations and correctness proofs for a family of protocols. *Journal of the ACM*, 39(3):449–478, 1992.

[25] J. Harsanyi. Games of incomplete information played by Bayesian players I. *Management Science*, 14:159–182, 1967.

[26] J. Harsanyi. Games of incomplete information played by Bayesian players II. *Management Science*, 14:320–334, 1967.

[27] J. Harsanyi. Games of incomplete information played by Bayesian players III. *Management Science*, 14:486–502, 1968.

[28] J. Hintikka. *Knowledge and Belief*. Cornell University Press, Ithaca, NY, 1962.

[29] G.E. Hughes and M.J. Cresswell. *A New Introduction to Modal Logic*. Routledge, 1996.

[30] S.A. Kripke. A completeness theorem in modal logic. *J. Symbolic Logic*, 24:1–14, 1959.

[31] W. Lenzen. Recent work in epistemic logic. *Acta Philosophica Fennica*, 30, 1978.

[32] D. Lewis. *Convention: A Philosophical Study*. Harvard University Press, Cambridge, 1969.

[33] A. Lomuscio and F. Raimondi. MCMAS: A model checker for multi-agent systems. In *Proc. 12th TACAS*, pages 450–454, 2006.

[34] Z. Manna and A. Pnueli. *The Temporal Logic of Reactive and Concurrent Systems: Specification*. Springer-Verlag, 1992.

[35] T. Mizrahi and Y. Moses. Continuous consensus via common knowledge. In *Proceedings 10th Conf. on Theoretical Aspects of Rationality and Knowledge*, pages 236–252, 2005. *Distributed Computing*, 2008, submitted for publication.

[36] Y. Moses. Resource-bounded knowledge. In M.Y. Vardi, editor. *Proceedings 2nd Conf. on Theoretical Aspects of Reasoning about Knowledge*, pages 261–275. Morgan Kaufmann Publishers, 1988.

[37] Y. Moses and M.R. Tuttle. Programming simultaneous actions using common knowledge. *Algorithmica*, 3(1):121–169, 1988.

[38] G. Neiger and M.R. Tuttle. Common knowledge and consistent simultaneous coordination. *Distributed Computing*, 6(3):181–192, 1993.

[39] S.J. Rosenschein and L.P. Kaelbling. The synthesis of digital machines with provable epistemic properties. In *Proc. 1st Conference on Theoretical Aspects of Reasoning about Knowledge*, pages 83–98. Morgan Kaufmann Publishers, 1986.

[40] T. Schelling. *The Strategy of Conflict*. Harvard University Press, 1960.

[41] T.J. Scheff. Towards a sociological theory of consensus. *American Sociological Review*, 37:32–46, 1967.

Further reading

[42] B.F. Chellas. *Modal Logic: An Introduction*. Cambridge University Press, 1980.

[43] R. Demolombe and M.P. Pozos Parra. A simple and tractable extension of situation calculus to epistemic logic. In *Proceedings of the Twelfth International Symposium on Methodologies for Intelligent Systems (ISMIS-2000)*, pages 515–524, 2000.

[44] S.A. Kripke. Semantical analysis of modal logic I: Normal modal propositional calculi. *Zeitschrift für Mathematische Logik und Grundlagen der Mathematik*, 9:67–96, 1963.

[45] J.-J.Ch. Meyer and W. van der Hoek. *Epistemic Logic for AI and Computer Science*. Cambridge University Press, 1995.

[46] R.C. Moore. A formal theory of knowledge and action. In J.R. Hobbs and R.C. Moore, editors. *Formal Theories of the Commonsense World*, pages 319–358. Ablex, Norwood, NJ, 1985.

[47] R. Parikh and R. Ramanujam. Distributed processes and the logic of knowledge. In *Logic of Programs*, pages 256–268, 1985.

[48] R. Petrick and H. Levesque. Knowledge equivalence in combined action theories. In *Proc. of KR-02*, 2002.

[49] R.B. Scherl and H.J. Levesque. Knowledge, action, and the frame problem. *Artificial Intelligence*, 144, 2003.

Handbook of Knowledge Representation
Edited by F. van Harmelen, V. Lifschitz and B. Porter
© 2008 Elsevier B.V. All rights reserved
DOI: 10.1016/S1574-6526(07)03016-7

Chapter 16

Situation Calculus

Fangzhen Lin

The situation calculus is a logical language for representing changes. It was first introduced by McCarthy in 1963,[1] and described in further details by McCarthy and Hayes [29] in 1969.

The basic concepts in the situation calculus are *situations*, *actions* and *fluents*. Briefly, actions are what make the dynamic world change from one situation to another when performed by agents. Fluents are situation-dependent functions used to describe the effects of actions. There are two kinds of them, *relational* fluents and *functional* fluents. The former have only two values: true or false, while the latter can take a range of values. For instance, one may have a relational fluent called *handempty* which is true in a situation if the robot's hand is not holding anything. We may need a relation like this in a robot domain. One may also have a functional fluent called *battery-level* whose value in a situation is an integer between 0 and 100 denoting the total battery power remaining on one's laptop computer.

According to McCarthy and Hayes [29], a situation is "the complete state of the universe at an instance of time". But for Reiter [34], a situation is the same as its history which is the finite sequence of actions that has been performed since the initial situation S_0. We shall discuss Reiter's foundational axioms that make this precise later. Whatever the interpretation, the unique feature of the situation calculus is that situations are first-order objects that can be quantified over. This is what makes the situation calculus a powerful formalism for representing change, and distinguishes it from other formalisms such as dynamic logic [11].

To describe a dynamic domain in the situation calculus, one has to decide on the set of actions available for the agents to perform, and the set of fluents needed to describe the changes these actions will have on the world. For example, consider the classic blocks world where some blocks of equal size can be arranged into a set of towers on a table. The set of actions in this domain depends on what the imaginary agent can do. If we imagine the agent to be a one-handed robot that can be directed to grasp any block that is on the top of a tower, and either add it to the top of another tower or put it down on the table to make a new tower, then we can have the following actions [30]:

---

[1] In a Stanford Technical Report that was later published as [25].

- *stack(x, y)*—put block *x* on block *y*, provided the robot is holding *x*, and *y* is clear, i.e. there is no other block on it;

- *unstack(x, y)*—pick up block *x* from block *y*, provided the robot's hand is empty, *x* is on *y*, and *x* is clear;

- *putdown(x)*—put block *x* down on the table, provided the robot is holding *x*;

- *pickup(x)*—pick up block *x* from the table, provided the robot's hand is empty, *x* is on the table and clear.

To describe the effects of these actions, we can use the following relational fluents:

- *handempty*—true in a situation if the robot's hand is empty;

- *holding(x)*—true in a situation if the robot's hand is holding block *x*;

- *on(x, y)*—true in a situation if block *x* is on block *y*;

- *ontable(x)*—true in a situation if block *x* is on the table;

- *clear(x)*—true in a situation if block *x* is the top block of a tower, i.e. the robot is not holding it, and there is no other block on it.

So, for example, we can say that for action *stack(x, y)* to be performed in a situation, *holding(x)* and *clear(y)* must be true, and that after *stack(x, y)* is performed, in the resulting new situation, *on(x, y)* and *handempty* will be true, and *holding(x)* and *clear(y)* will no longer be true.

If, however, the agent in this world can move a block from a clear position to another clear position, then we only need the following action:

- *move(x, y)*—move block *x* to position *y*, provided that block *x* is clear to move, where a position is either a block or the table.

To describe the effects of this action, it suffices to use two fluents *on(x, y)* and *clear(x)*: action *move(x, y)* can be performed in a situation if $x \neq table$, *clear(x)*, and *clear(y)* are true in the situation, and that after *move(x, y)* is performed, in the resulting new situation, *x* is no longer where it was but on *y* now.

To axiomatize dynamic domains like these in the situation calculus, we will need to be a bit more precise about the language.

16.1   Axiomatizations

We said that the situation calculus is a logical language for reasoning about change. More precisely, it is a first-order language, sometime enriched with some second-order features. It represents situations and actions as first-order objects that can be quantified over. Thus we can have a first-order sentence saying that among all actions, *putdown(x)* is the only one that can make *ontable(x)* true. We can also have a first-order sentence saying that in any situation, executing different actions will always yield different situations. As we mentioned, being able to quantify over situations makes the situation calculus a very expressive language, and distinguishes it from other formalisms for representing dynamic systems.

As we mentioned, fluents are functions on situations. Of special interest are relational fluents that are either true or false in a situation. Initially, McCarthy and Hayes represented relational fluents as predicates whose last argument is a situation term [29]. For instance, to say that block x is on the table in situation s, one would use a binary predicate like *ontable* and write *ontable*(x, s). This was also the approach taken by Reiter [33, 34]. Later, McCarthy [26, 28] proposed to reify relational fluents as first-order objects as well, and introduced a special binary predicate "*Holds*(p, s)" to express the truth value of a relational fluent p in situation s. Here we shall follow McCarthy's later work, and represent relational fluents as first-order objects as well. This allows us to quantify over fluents. But more importantly, it allows us to talk about other properties of fluents like causal relationships among them [15]. One could continue to write formulas like *ontable*(x, s), which will be taken as a shorthand for *Holds*$($*ontable*$(x), s)$.

To summarize, the situation calculus is a first-order language with the following special sorts: *situation*, *action*, and *fluent* (for relational fluents). There could be other sorts, some of them domain dependent like *block* for blocks in the blocks world or *loc* for locations in logistics domain, and others domain independent like *truth* for truth values. For now we assume the following special domain independent predicates and functions:

- *Holds*(p, s)—fluent p is true in situation s;

- *do*(a, s)—the situation that results from performing action a in situation s;

- *Poss*(a, s)—action a is executable in situation s.

Other special predicates and functions may be introduced. For instance, to specify Golog programs [12], one can use a ternary predicate called *Do*(P, s_1, s_2), meaning that s_2 is a terminating situation of performing program P in s_1. To specify causal relations among fluents, one can use another ternary predicate *Caused*(p, v, s), meaning that fluent p is caused to have truth value v in situation s.

Under these conventions, a relational fluent is represented by a function that does not have a situation argument, and a functional fluent is represented by a function whose last argument is of sort *situation*. For instance, *clear*(x) is a unary relational fluent. We often write *clear*(x, s) which as we mentioned earlier, is just a shorthand for *Holds*$($*clear*$(x), s)$. On the other hand, *color*(x, s) is a binary functional fluent, and we write axioms about it like

$$color(x, do(paint(x, c), s)) = c.$$

We can now axiomatize our first blocks world domain with the following first-order sentences (all free variables are assumed to be universally quantified):

$$Poss(stack(x, y), s) \equiv holding(x, s) \wedge clear(y, s), \tag{16.1}$$

$$Poss(unstack(x, y), s) \equiv on(x, y, s) \wedge clear(x, s) \wedge handempty(s), \tag{16.2}$$

$$Poss(pickup(x), s) \equiv ontable(x, s) \wedge clear(x, s) \wedge handempty(s), \tag{16.3}$$

$$Poss(putdown(x), s) \equiv holding(x, s), \tag{16.4}$$

$$holding(u, do(stack(x, y), s)) \equiv holding(u, s) \wedge u \neq x, \tag{16.5}$$

$$handempty(do(stack(x, y), s)),\tag{16.6}$$

$$on(u, v, do(stack(x, y), s)) \equiv (u = x \wedge v = y) \vee on(u, v, s),\tag{16.7}$$

$$clear(u, do(stack(x, y), s)) \equiv u = x \vee (clear(u, s) \wedge u \neq y),\tag{16.8}$$

$$ontable(u, do(stack(x, y), s)) \equiv ontable(u, s),\tag{16.9}$$

$$holding(u, do(unstack(x, y), s)) \equiv u = x,\tag{16.10}$$

$$\neg handempty(do(unstack(x, y), s)),\tag{16.11}$$

$$on(u, v, do(unstack(x, y), s)) \equiv on(u, v, s) \wedge \neg(x = u \wedge y = v),\tag{16.12}$$

$$clear(u, do(unstack(x, y), s)) \equiv u = y \vee (clear(u, s) \wedge u \neq x),\tag{16.13}$$

$$ontable(u, do(unstack(x, y), s)) \equiv ontable(u, s),\tag{16.14}$$

$$holding(u, do(pickup(x), s)) \equiv u = x,\tag{16.15}$$

$$\neg handempty(do(pickup(x), s)),\tag{16.16}$$

$$on(u, v, do(pickup(x), s)) \equiv on(u, v, s),\tag{16.17}$$

$$clear(u, do(pickup(x), s)) \equiv clear(u, s) \wedge u \neq x,\tag{16.18}$$

$$ontable(u, do(pickup(x), s)) \equiv ontable(u, s) \wedge x \neq u,\tag{16.19}$$

$$holding(u, do(putdown(x), s)) \equiv holding(u, s) \wedge u \neq x,\tag{16.20}$$

$$handempty(do(putdown(x), s)),\tag{16.21}$$

$$on(u, v, do(putdown(x), s)) \equiv on(u, v, s),\tag{16.22}$$

$$clear(u, do(putdown(x), s)) \equiv u = x \vee clear(u, s),\tag{16.23}$$

$$ontable(u, do(putdown(x), s)) \equiv u = x \vee ontable(u, s).\tag{16.24}$$

Similarly, we can write the following axioms for our second version of the blocks world domain.

$$Poss(move(x, y), s) \equiv x \neq table \wedge clear(x, s) \wedge clear(y, s)\tag{16.25}$$

$$clear(u, do(move(x, y), s)) \equiv$$
$$u = table \vee on(x, u, s) \vee (clear(u, s) \wedge u \neq y),\tag{16.26}$$

$$on(u, v, do(move(x, y), s)) \equiv$$
$$(x = u \wedge y = v) \vee (on(u, v, s) \wedge u \neq x).\tag{16.27}$$

16.2 The Frame, the Ramification and the Qualification Problems

The set of axioms (16.1)–(16.24) provides a complete logical characterization of the effects of actions for our first blocks world domain. For each action, it gives necessary and sufficient conditions for it to be executable in any situation, and fully specifies the effects of this action on every fluent. Similarly, the set of axioms (16.25)–(16.27) completely captures the effects of actions for our second blocks world domain.

However, there is something unsatisfying about these two sets of axioms. When we informally described the effects of actions, we did not describe it this way. For instance, we said that after *stack(x, y)* is performed, in the resulting new situation, *on(x, y)* and *handempty* will be true, and *holding(x)* and *clear(y)* will no longer be true. We did not have to say, for instance, that if *y* is initially on the table, it will still be on the table. Many researchers believe that when people remember the effects of an action, they do not explicitly store the facts that are not changed by the action, rather they just remember the changes that this action will bring about. Consequently, when we axiomatize an action, we should only need to specify the changes that will be made by the action. But if we specify in our theory only the changes that an action will make, there is then a problem of how to derive those that are not changed by the action. This problem was identified by McCarthy and Hayes [29] in 1969, and they called it *the frame problem*. For our blocks world example, we can view the frame problem as the problem of looking for an appropriate logic that when given, for example the following so-called "effect axioms" about *stack(x, y)*:

$$on(x, y, do(stack(x, y), s)),$$

$$clear(x, do(stack(x, y), s)),$$

$$\neg clear(y, do(stack(x, y), s)),$$

$$handempty(do(stack(x, y), s)),$$

$$\neg holding(x, do(stack(x, y), s)),$$

will derive a complete specification of the effects of action *stack(x, y)*, like what the set of axioms (16.5)–(16.9) does in first-order logic [21].

The frame problem is one of the most well-known AI problems, if not the most well-known one, and a lot of work has been done on solving it. It motivated much of the early work on nonmonotonic logic (see papers in [6] and Chapter 6). While the problem was identified in the situation calculus, it shows up in other formalisms like the event calculus (Chapter 17), temporal action logics (Chapter 18), and non-monotonic causal logic (Chapter 19). In fact, the general consensus is that any formalism for reasoning about change will have to deal with it.

McCarthy [27] initially proposed to solve the frame problem by the following generic frame axiom:

$$Holds(p, s) \wedge \neg abnormal(p, a, s) Holds(p, do(a, s)) \tag{16.28}$$

with the abnormality predicate *abnormal* circumscribed. Unfortunately, Hanks and McDermott [10] showed that this approach does not work using by now the infamous Yale Shooting Problem as a counterexample. This is a simple problem with three actions: *wait* (do nothing), *load* (load the gun), and *shoot* (fire the gun). Their effects can be axiomatrized by the following axioms:

$$loaded(do(load, s)), \tag{16.29}$$

$$loaded(s) \supset dead(do(shoot, s)). \tag{16.30}$$

Now suppose S_0 is a situation such that the following is true:

$$\neg loaded(S_0) \wedge \neg dead(S_0). \tag{16.31}$$

Hanks and McDermott showed that the circumscription of *abnormal* in the theory
{(16.28), (16.29), (16.30), (16.31)} with *Holds* allowed to vary has two models, one
in which

$$loaded(do(load, S_0)) \land loaded(do(wait, do(load, S_0))) \land$$

$$dead(do(shoot, do(wait, do(load, S_0))))$$

is true as desired, and the other in which

$$loaded(do(load, S_0)) \land \neg loaded(do(wait, do(load, S_0))) \land$$

$$\neg dead(do(shoot, do(wait, do(load, S_0))))$$

is true, which is counter-intuitive as the action *wait*, which is supposed to do nothing,
mysteriosly unloaded the gun.

For the next few years, the YSP motivated much of the work on the frame problem,
and the frame problem became the focus of the research on nonmonotonic reasoning.
In response to the problem, Shoham [37] proposed chronological minimization that
prefers changes at later times. Many other proposals were put forward (e.g. [13, 14, 2,
33, 21, 35, 15, 38, 24]).

The thrust of modern solutions to the frame problem is to separate the specification
of the effects of actions from the tasks of reasoning about these actions. For instance,
given the effect axioms (16.29) and (16.30), one can obtain the following complete
specification of the effects of the actions concerned:

$$loaded(do(load, s)),$$

$$dead(do(load, s)) \equiv dead(s),$$

$$loaded(do(shoot, s)) \equiv loaded(s),$$

$$dead(do(shoot, s)) \equiv loaded(s) \lor dead(s),$$

$$loaded(do(wait, s)) \equiv loaded(s),$$

$$dead(do(wait, s)) \equiv dead(s).$$

Now given the initial state axiom (16.31), one can easily infer that $dead(do(shoot, do(wait, do(load, S_0))))$ holds.

This separation between the specification of action theories and the tasks of reasoning under these theories can be done syntactically by distinguishing general effect
axioms like (16.29) from specific facts like (16.31) about some particular situations,
as in Reiter's solution [33] that we shall describe next. It can also be done by encoding
general effect axioms in a special language using predicates like *Caused*, as in Lin's
causal theories of action [15] for solving the ramification problem.

16.2.1 The Frame Problem—Reiter's Solution

Based on earlier work by Pednault [31], Haas [9] and Schubert [36], Reiter [33, 34]
proposed a simple syntactic manipulation much in the style of Clark's predicate completion [4] (see Chapter 7) that turns a set of effect axioms into a set of successor state
axioms that completely captures the true value of each fluent in any successor situation. It is best to illustrate Reiter's method by an example. Consider our first blocks
world domain, and let us write down all the effect axioms:

$$on(x, y, do(stack(x, y), s)),$$ (16.32)

$$clear(x, do(stack(x, y), s)),$$ (16.33)

$$\neg clear(y, do(stack(x, y), s)),$$ (16.34)

$$handempty(do(stack(x, y), s)),$$ (16.35)

$$\neg holding(x, do(stack(x, y), s)),$$ (16.36)

$$\neg on(x, y, do(unstack(x, y), s)),$$ (16.37)

$$\neg clear(x, do(unstack(x, y), s)),$$ (16.38)

$$clear(y, do(unstack(x, y), s)),$$ (16.39)

$$\neg handempty(do(unstack(x, y), s)),$$ (16.40)

$$holding(x, do(unstack(x, y), s)),$$ (16.41)

$$ontable(x, do(putdown(x), s)),$$ (16.42)

$$clear(x, do(putdown(x), s)),$$ (16.43)

$$handempty(do(putdown(x), s)),$$ (16.44)

$$\neg holding(x, do(putdown(x), s)),$$ (16.45)

$$\neg ontable(x, do(pickup(x), s)),$$ (16.46)

$$\neg clear(x, do(pickup(x), s)),$$ (16.47)

$$\neg handempty(do(pickup(x), s)),$$ (16.48)

$$holding(x, do(pickup(x), s)).$$ (16.49)

Now for each of these effect axioms, transform it into one of the following two forms:

$$\gamma(a, \vec{x}, s) \supset F(\vec{x}, do(a, s)),$$

$$\gamma(a, \vec{x}, s) \supset \neg F(\vec{x}, do(a, s)).$$

For instance, the effect axiom (16.32) can be transformed equivalently into the following axiom:

$$a = stack(x, y) \supset on(x, y, do(a, s)),$$

and the effect axiom (16.34) can be transformed equivalently into the following axiom:

$$(\exists y)a = stack(y, x) \supset \neg clear(x, do(a, s)).$$

Now for each fluent F, suppose the following is the list of all such axioms so obtained:

$$\gamma_1^+(a, \vec{x}, s) \supset F(\vec{x}, do(a, s)),$$

$$\ldots$$

$$\gamma_m^+(a, \vec{x}, s) \supset F(\vec{x}, do(a, s)),$$

$$\gamma_1^-(a, \vec{x}, s) \supset \neg F(\vec{x}, do(a, s)),$$

$$\ldots$$

$$\gamma_n^-(a, \vec{x}, s) \supset \neg F(\vec{x}, do(a, s)).$$

Then under what Reiter called *the causal completeness assumption*, which says that the above axioms characterize all the conditions under which action a causes F to become true or false in the successor situation, we conclude the following *successor state axiom* [33] for fluent F:

$$F(\vec{x}, do(a, s)) \equiv \gamma^+(a, \vec{x}, s) \vee (F(\vec{x}, s) \wedge \neg\gamma^-(a, \vec{x}, s)), \tag{16.50}$$

where $\gamma^+(a, \vec{x}, s)$ is $\gamma_1^+(a, \vec{x}, s) \vee \cdots \vee \gamma_m^+(a, \vec{x}, s)$, and $\gamma^-(a, \vec{x}, s)$ is $\gamma_1^-(a, \vec{x}, s) \vee \cdots \vee \gamma_n^-(a, \vec{x}, s)$.

For instance, for our first blocks world, we can transform the effect axioms about *clear*(x) into the following axioms:

$(\exists y.a = stack(x, y)) \supset clear(x, do(a, s))$,

$(\exists y.a = unstack(y, x)) \supset clear(x, do(a, s))$,

$a = putdon(x) \supset clear(x, do(a, s))$,

$(\exists y.a = stack(y, x)) \supset \neg clear(x, do(a, s))$,

$(\exists y.a = unstack(x, y)) \supset \neg clear(x, do(a, s))$,

$a = pickup(x) \supset \neg clear(x, do(a, s))$.

Thus we have the following successor state axiom for *clear*(x):

$clear(x, do(a, s)) \equiv$

$\quad \exists y.a = stack(x, y) \vee \exists y.a = unstack(y, x) \vee$

$\quad a = putdown(x) \vee clear(x, s) \wedge$

$\quad \neg[\exists y.a = stack(y, x) \vee \exists y.a = unstack(x, y) \vee a = pickup(x)]$.

Once we have a successor state axiom for each fluent in the domain, we will then have an action theory that is complete in the same way as the set of axioms (16.1)–(16.24) is.

This procedure can be given a semantics in nonmonotonic logics, in particular circumscription [27] (see Chapter 6). This in fact has been done by Lin and Reiter [19].

We should also mention that for this approach to work, when generating the successor state axiom (16.50) from effect axioms, one should also assume what Reiter called *the consistency assumption*: the background theory should entail that $\neg(\gamma^+ \wedge \gamma^-)$. Once we have a set of successor state axioms, to reason with them we need the unique names assumption about actions: for each n-ary action A:

$$A(x_1, \ldots, x_n) = A(y_1, \ldots, y_n) \supset x_1 = y_1 \wedge \cdots \wedge x_n = y_n,$$

and for each distinct actions A and A',

$$A(x_1, \ldots, x_n) \neq A'(y_1, \ldots, y_m).$$

For more details, see [33, 34].

16.2.2 The Ramification Problem and Lin's Solution

Recall that the frame problem is about how one can obtain a complete axiomatization of the effects of actions from a set of effect axioms that specifies the changes that the actions have on the world. Thus Reiter's solution to the frame problem makes the assumption that the given effect axioms characterize completely the conditions under which an action can cause a fluent to be true or false. However, in some action domains, providing such a complete list of effect axioms may not be feasible. This is because in these action domains, there are rich domain constraints that can entail new effect axioms. To see how domain constraints can entail new effect axioms, consider again the blocks world. We know that each block can be at only one location: either being held by the robot's hand, on another block, or on the table. Thus when action *stack*(x, y) causes x to be on y, it also makes *holding*(x) false. The *ramification problem*, first discussed by Finger [5] in 1986, is about how to encode constraints like this in an action domain, and how these constraints can be used to derive the effects of the actions in the domain.

In the situation calculus, for a long time the only way to represent domain constraints was by universal sentences of the form $\forall s.C(s)$. For example, the aforementioned constraint that a block can be (and must be) at only one location in the blocks world can be represented by the following sentences:

$$holding(x, s) \lor ontable(x, s) \lor \exists y.on(x, y),$$

$$holding(x, s) \supset \neg(ontable(x, s) \lor \exists y.on(x, y)),$$

$$ontable(x, s) \supset \neg(holding(x, s) \lor \exists y.on(x, y)),$$

$$(\exists y.on(x, y)) \supset \neg(holding(x, s) \lor ontable(x, s)).$$

So, for example, these axioms and the following effect axiom about *putdown*(x),

$$ontable(x, do(putdown(x), s))$$

will entail in first-order logic the following effect axiom:

$$\neg holding(x, do(putdown(x), s)).$$

However, domain constraints represented this way may not be strong enough for determining the effects of actions. Consider the suitcase problem from [15]. Imagine a suitcase with two locks and a spring loaded mechanism which will open the suitcase when both of the locks are in the up position. Apparently, because of the spring loaded mechanism, if an action changes the status of the locks, then this action may also cause, as an indirect effect, the suitcase to open.

As with the blocks world, we can represent the constraint that this spring loaded mechanism gives rise to as the following sentence:

$$up(L1, s) \land up(L2, s) \supset open(s). \tag{16.51}$$

Although summarizing concisely the relationship among the truth values of the three relevant propositions at any particular instance of time, this constraint is too weak to describe the indirect effects of actions. For instance, suppose that initially the suitcase is closed, the first lock in the down position, and the second lock in the up position.

Suppose an action is then performed to turn up the first lock. Then this constraint is ambiguous about what will happen next. According to it, either the suitcase may spring open or the second lock may get turned down. Although we have the intuition that the former is what will happen, this constraint is not strong enough to enforce that because there is a different mechanism that will yield a logically equivalent constraint. For instance, a mechanism that turns down the second lock when the suitcase is closed and the first lock is up will yield the following logically equivalent one:

$$up(L1, s) \land \neg open(s) \supset \neg up(L2, s).$$

So to faithfully represent the ramification of the spring loaded mechanism on the effects of actions, something stronger than the constraint (16.51) is needed. The proposed solution by Lin [15] is to represent this constraint as a causal constraint: (through the spring loaded mechanism) the fact that both of the locks are in the up position *causes* the suitcase to open. To axiomatize this, Lin introduced a ternary predicate $Caused(p, v, s)$, meaning that fluent p is caused to have truth value v in situation s. The following are some basic properties of $Caused$ [15]:

$$Caused(p, true, s) \supset Holds(p, s), \tag{16.52}$$

$$Caused(p, false, s) \supset \neg Holds(p, s), \tag{16.53}$$

$$true \neq false \land (\forall v)(v = true \lor v = false), \tag{16.54}$$

where v is a variable ranging over a new sort *truthValues*.

Let us illustrate how this approach works using the suitcase example. Suppose that $flip(x)$ is an action that flips the status of the lock x. Its direct effect can be described by the following axioms:

$$up(x, s) \supset Caused(up(x), false, do(flip(x), s)), \tag{16.55}$$

$$\neg up(x, s) \supset Caused(up(x), true, do(flip(x), s)). \tag{16.56}$$

Assume that $L1$ and $L2$ are the two locks on the suitcase, the spring loaded mechanism is now represented by the following causal rule:

$$up(L1, s) \land up(L2, s) \supset Caused(open, true, s). \tag{16.57}$$

Notice that this causal rule, together with the basic axiom (16.52) about causality, entails the state constraint (16.51). Notice also that the physical, spring loaded mechanism behind the causal rule has been abstracted away. For all we care, it may just as well be that the device is not made of spring, but of bombs that will blow open the suitcase each time the two locks are in the up position. It then seems natural to say that the fluent *open* is caused to be true by the fact that the two locks are both in the up position. This is an instance of what has been called *static* causal rules as it mentions only one situation. In comparison, causal statements like the effect axioms (16.55) and (16.56) are *dynamic* as they mention more than one situations.

The above axioms constitute the starting theory for the domain. To describe fully the effects of the actions, suitable frame axioms need to be added. Using predicate $Caused$, a generic frame axiom can be stated as follows [15]: Unless caused otherwise, a fluent's truth value will persist:

$$\neg(\exists v)Caused(p, v, do(a, s)) \supset [Holds(p, do(a, s)) \equiv Holds(p, s)]. \tag{16.58}$$

For this frame axiom to make sense, one needs to minimize the predicate *Caused*. Technically this is done by circumscribing *Caused* in the above set of axioms with all other predicates (*Poss* and *Holds*) fixed. However, given the form of the axioms, this circumscription coincides with Clark's completion of *Caused*, and it yields the following *causation axioms*:

$$Caused(open, v, s) \equiv$$
$$v = true \land up(L1, s) \land up(L2, s), \tag{16.59}$$

$$Caused(up(x), v, s) \equiv$$
$$v = true \land (\exists s')[s = do(flip(x), s') \land \neg up(x, s')] \lor$$
$$v = false \land (\exists s')[s = do(flip(x), s') \land up(x, s')]. \tag{16.60}$$

Notice that these axioms entail the two direct effect axioms (16.55), (16.56) and the causal rule (16.57).

Having computed the causal relation, the next step is to use the frame axiom (16.58) to compute the effects of actions. It is easy to see that from the frame axiom (16.58) and the two basic axioms (16.52), (16.53) about causality, one can infer the following pseudo successor state axiom:

$$Holds(p, do(a, s)) \equiv$$
$$Caused(p, true, do(a, s)) \lor$$
$$Holds(p, s) \land \neg Caused(p, false, do(a, s)). \tag{16.61}$$

From this axiom and the causation axiom (16.60) for the fluent *up*, one then obtains the following real successor state axiom for the fluent *up*:

$$up(x, do(a, s)) \equiv$$
$$(a = flip(x) \land \neg up(x, s)) \lor (up(x, s) \land a \neq flip(x)).$$

Similarly for the fluent *open*, we have

$$open(do(a, s)) \equiv$$
$$[up(L1, do(a, s)) \land up(L2, do(a, s))] \lor open(s).$$

Now from this axiom, first eliminating $up(L1, do(a, s))$ and $up(L2, do(a, s))$ using the successor state axiom for *up*, then using the unique names axioms for actions, and the constraint (16.51) which, as we pointed out earlier, is a consequence of our axioms, we can deduce the following successor state axiom for the fluent *open*:

$$open(do(a, s)) \equiv a = flip(L1) \land \neg up(L1, s) \land up(L2, s) \lor$$
$$a = flip(L2) \land \neg up(L2, s) \land up(L1, s) \lor$$
$$open(s).$$

Obtaining these successor state axioms solves the frame and the ramification problems for the suitcase example.

Lin [15] showed that this procedure can be applied to a general class of action theories, and Lin [18] described an implemented system that can compile these causal action theories into Reiter's successor state axioms and STRIPS-like systems, and demonstrated the effectiveness of the system by applying it to many benchmark AI planning domains.

16.2.3   The Qualification Problem

Finally, we notice that so far we have given the condition for an action a to be executable in a situation s, $Poss(a, s)$, directly. It can be argued that this is not a reasonable thing to do. In general, the executability of an action may depend on the circumstances where it is performed. For instance, we have defined $Poss(putdown(x), s) \equiv holding(x, s)$. But if the action is to be performed in a crowd, then we may want to add that for the action to be executable, the robot's hand must not be blocked by someone; and if the robot is running low on battery, then we may want to ensure that the robot is not running out of battery; etc. It is clear that no one can anticipate all these possible circumstances, thus no one can list all possible conditions for an action to be executable ahead of time. This problem of how best to specify the precondition of an action is called the *qualification problem* [26].

One possible solution to this problem is to assume that an action is always executable unless explicitly ruled out by the theory. This can be achieved by maximizing the predicate *Poss*, or in terms of circumscription, circumscribing ¬*Poss*. If the axioms about *Poss* all have the form

$$Poss(A, s) \supset \varphi(s),$$

that is, the user always provides explicit qualifications to an action, then one can compute *Poss* by a procedure like Clark's predicate completion by rewriting the above axiom as:

$$\neg\varphi(s) \supset \neg Poss(A, s).$$

The problem becomes more complex when some domain constraints-like axioms can influence *Poss*. This problem was first recognized by Ginsberg and Smith [7], and discussed in more detailed by Lin and Reiter [19]. For instance, we may want to add into the blocks world a constraint that says "only yellow blocks can be directly on the table". Now if the robot is holding a red block, should she put it down on the table? Probably she should not. This means that this constraint has two roles: it rules out initial states that do not satisfy it, and it forbids agents to perform any action that will result in a successor situation that violates it. What this constraint should not do is to cause additional effects of actions. For instance, it should not be the case that $putdown(x)$ would cause x to become yellow just to maintain this constraint in the successor situation.

Lin and Reiter [19] called those constraints that yield indirect effects of actions *ramification constraints*, and those that yield additional qualifications of actions *qualification constraints*. They are both represented as sentences of the form $\forall s.C(s)$, and it is up to the user to classify which category they belong to.

A uniform way of handling these two kinds of constraints is to use Lin's causal theories of actions as described above. Under this framework, only constraints represented as causal rules using *Caused* can derive new effects of actions, and ordinary situation calculus sentences of the form $\forall s.C(s)$ can only derive new qualifications on actions. However, for this to work, action effect axioms like (16.55) need to have *Poss* as a precondition:

$$Poss(flip(x), s) \supset [up(x, s) \supset Caused(up(x), false, do(flip(x), s))],$$

and the generic frame axiom (16.58) need to be modified similarly:

$$Poss(a, s) \supset \{\neg(\exists v)Caused(p, v, do(a, s)) \supset$$
$$[Holds(p, do(a, s)) \equiv Holds(p, s)]\}.$$

In fact, this was how action effect axioms and frame axioms are represented in [15]. An interesting observation made in [15] was that some causal rules may give rise to both new action effects and action qualifications. Our presentation of Lin's causal theories in the previous subsection has dropped *Poss* so that, in line with the presentation in [34], the final successor state axioms do not have *Poss* as a precondition.

16.3   Reiter's Foundational Axioms and Basic Action Theories

We have defined the situation calculus as a first-order language with special sorts for situations, actions, and fluents. There are no axioms to constrain these sorts, and all axioms are domain specific given by the user for axiomatizing a particular dynamic system. We have used a binary function $do(a, s)$ to denote the situation resulted from performing a in s, thus for a specific finite sequence of actions $a_1, \ldots, a_k$, we have a term denoting the situation resulted from performing the sequence of actions in s: $do(a_k, do(a_{k-1}, \ldots, do(a_1, s) \ldots))$. However, there is no way for us to say that one situation is the result of performing *some* finite sequence of actions in another situation. This is needed for many applications, such as planning where the achievability of a goal is defined to be the existence of an executable finite sequence of actions that will make the goal true once executed. We now introduce Reiter's foundational axioms that make this possible.

Briefly, under Reiter's foundational axioms, there is a unique initial situation, and all situations are the result of performing some finite sequences of actions in this initial situation. This initial situation will be denoted by S_0, which formally is a constant of sort *situation*.

It is worth mentioning here that while the constant S_0 has been used before to informally stand for a starting situation, it was not assumed to be *the* starting situation as under Reiter's situation calculus. It can be said that the difference between Reiter's version of the situation calculus and McCarthy's original version is that Reiter assumed the following foundational axioms that postulate the space of situations as a tree with S_0 as the root:

$$do(a, s) = do(a', s') \supset a = a' \wedge s = s', \tag{16.62}$$

$$\forall P.[P(S_0) \wedge \forall a, s.P(s) \supset P(do(a, s))] \supset \forall s P(s). \tag{16.63}$$

Axiom (16.63) is a second-order induction axiom that says that for any property P, to prove that $\forall s.P(s)$, it is sufficient to show that $P(S_0)$, and inductively, for any situation s, if $P(s)$ then for any action a, $P(do(a, s))$. In particular, we can conclude that

- S_0 is a situation;

- if s is a situation, and a an action, then $do(a, s)$ is a situation;

- nothing else is a situation.

Together with the unique names axiom (16.62), this means that we can view the domain of situations as a tree whose root is S_0, and for each action a, $do(a, s)$ is a child of s. Thus for each situation s there is a unique finite sequence α of actions such that $s = do(\alpha, S_0)$, where for any finite sequence α' of actions, and any situation s', $do(\alpha', s')$ is defined inductively as $do([], s') = s'$, and $do([a|\alpha'], s') = do(a, do(\alpha', s'))$, here we have written a sequence in Prolog notation. Thus there is a one-to-one correspondence between situations and finite sequences of actions under Reiter's foundational axioms, and because of this, Reiter identified situations with finite sequences of actions.

As we mentioned, there is a need to express assertions like "situation s_1 is the result of performing a sequence of actions in s_2". This is achieved by using a partial order relation $\sqsubset$ on situations: informally $s \sqsubset s'$ if s' is the result of performing a finite nonempty sequence of actions in s. Formally, it is defined by the following two axioms:

$$\neg s \sqsubset S_0, \tag{16.64}$$

$$s \sqsubset do(a, s') \equiv s \sqsubseteq s', \tag{16.65}$$

where $s \sqsubseteq s'$ is a shorthand for $s \sqsubset s' \vee s = s'$.

Notice that under the correspondence between situations and finite sequence of actions, the partial order $\sqsubset$ is really the sub-sequence relation: $s \sqsubset s'$ iff the action sequence of s is a sub-sequence of that of s'. Thus to say that a goal g is achievable in situation s, we write

$$\exists s'.s \sqsubseteq s' \wedge Holds(g, s') \wedge Executable(s, s'),$$

where $Executable(s, s')$ means that the sequence of actions that takes s to s' is executable in s, and is defined inductively as:

$$Executable(s, s),$$

$$Executable(s, do(a, s')) \equiv Poss(a, s') \wedge Executable(s, s').$$

Reiter's foundational axioms (16.62)–(16.65) make it possible to formally prove many interesting properties such as the achievability of a goal. They also lay the foundation for using the situation calculus to formalize strategic and control information (see, e.g., [16, 17]). They are particularly useful in conjunction with Reiter's successor state axioms, and are part of what Reiter called the *basic action theories* as we proceed to describe now.

To define Reiter's basic action theories, we first need to define the notion of *uniform formulas*. Intuitively, if σ is a situation term, then a formula is uniform in σ if the truth value of the formula depends only on σ. Formally, a situation calculus formula is uniform in σ if it satisfies the following conditions:

- it does not contain any quantification over situation;

- it does not mention any variables for relational fluents;

- it does not mention any situation term other than σ;

- it does not mention any predicate that has a situation argument other than *Holds*; and

- it does not mention any function that has a situation argument unless the function is a functional fluent.

Thus $clear(x, s)$ is uniform in s (recall that this is a shorthand for $Holds(clear(x), s)$), but $\forall s.clear(x, s)$ is not as it quantifies over situations. The formula $\forall p.Holds(p, s)$ is not uniform in s either as it contains p which is a variable for relational fluents. Notice that a uniform formula cannot mention domain-independent situation-dependent predicates like *Poss*, $\sqsubset$, and *Caused*. It cannot even contain equalities between situations such as $s = s$, but it can contain equalities between actions and between domain objects such as $x \neq y$, where x and y are variables of sort *block* in the blocks world.

Another way to view uniform formulas is by using a first-order language without the special *situation* sort. The predicates of this language are relational fluents and other situation independent predicates. The functions are functional fluents, actions, and other situation independent functions. A situation calculus formula Φ is uniform in σ iff there is a formula φ in this language such that Φ is the result of replacing every relational fluent atom $F(t_1, \ldots, t_k)$ in φ by $Holds(F(t_1, \ldots, t_k), \sigma)$ (or $F(t_1, \ldots, t_k, \sigma)$) and every functional fluent term $f(t_1, \ldots, t_k)$ by $f(t_1, \ldots, t_k, \sigma)$. In the following, and in Chapter 24 on Cognitive Robotics, this formula Φ is written as $\varphi[\sigma]$.

Uniform formulas are used in Reiter's action precondition axioms and successor state axioms. In Reiter's basic action theories, an action precondition axiom for an action $A(x_1, \ldots, x_n)$ is a sentence of the form:

$$Poss(A(x_1, \ldots, x_n), s) \equiv \Pi(x_1, \ldots, x_n, s),$$

where $\Pi(x_1, \ldots, x_n, s)$ is a formula uniform in s and whose free variables are among $x_1, \ldots, x_n, s$. Thus whether $A(x_1, \ldots, x_n)$ can be performed in a situation s depends entirely on s.

We have seen successor state axioms for relational fluents (16.50). In general, in Reiter's basic action theories, a successor state axiom for an n-ary relational fluent F is a sentence of the form

$$F(x_1, \ldots, x_n, do(a, s)) \equiv \Phi_F(x_1, \ldots, x_n, a, s), \tag{16.66}$$

where Φ_F is a formula uniform in s, and whose free variables are among $x_1, \ldots, x_n, a, s$.

Similarly, if f is an $(n + 1)$-ary functional fluent, then a successor state axiom for it is a sentence of the form

$$f(x_1, \ldots, x_n, do(a, s)) = v \equiv \varphi(x_1, \ldots, x_n, v, a, s), \tag{16.67}$$

where φ is a formula uniform in s, and whose free variables are among $x_1, \ldots, x_n, v, a, s$.

Notice that requiring the formulas Φ_F and φ in successor state axioms to be uniform amounts to making Markov assumption in systems and control theory: the effect of an action depends only on the current situation.

We can now define Reiter's basic action theories [34]. A basic action theory $\mathcal{D}$ is a set of axioms of the following form:

$$\Sigma \cup \mathcal{D}_{ss} \cup \mathcal{D}_{ap} \cup \mathcal{D}_{una} \cup \mathcal{D}_{S_0},$$

where

- Σ is the set of the four foundational axioms (16.62)–(16.65).

- $\mathcal{D}_{ss}$ is a set of successor state axioms. It must satisfy the following *functional fluent consistency property*: if (16.67) is in $\mathcal{D}_{ss}$, then

$$\mathcal{D}_{una} \cup \mathcal{D}_{S_0} \models \forall \vec{x}. \exists v \varphi(\vec{x}, v, a, s) \wedge$$
$$[\forall v, v'. \varphi(\vec{x}, v, a, s) \wedge \varphi(\vec{x}, v', a, s) \supset v = v'].$$

- $\mathcal{D}_{ap}$ is a set of action precondition axioms.

- $\mathcal{D}_{una}$ is the set of unique names axioms about actions.

- $\mathcal{D}_{S_0}$ is a set of sentences that are uniform in S_0. This is the knowledge base for the initial situation S_0.

The following theorem is proved by Pirri and Reiter [32].

Theorem 16.1 (Relative satisfiability). *A basic action theory $\mathcal{D}$ is satisfiable iff $\mathcal{D}_{una} \cup \mathcal{D}_{S_0}$ is.*

As we mentioned above, the basic action theories are the starting point to solve various problems in dynamic systems. Many of these problems can be solved using basic action theories by first-order deduction. But some of them require induction. Those that require induction are typically about proving general assertions of the form $\forall s. C(s)$, such as proving that a certain goal is not achievable. For instance, consider the basic action theory $\mathcal{D}$ where $\mathcal{D}_{ap} = \emptyset$, $\mathcal{D}_{ss} = \{\forall a, s. loaded(do(a, s)) \equiv loaded(s)\}$, and $\mathcal{D}_{S_0} = \{loaded(S_0)\}$. It is certainly true that $\mathcal{D} \models \forall s. loaded(s)$. But proving this formally requires induction.

The ones that can be done in first-order logic include checking whether a sequence of ground actions is executable in S_0 and the temporal projection problem, which asks whether a formula holds after a sequence of actions is performed in S_0. One very effective tool for solving these problems is *regression*,[2] which transforms a formula

$$\varphi(do([\alpha_1, \ldots, \alpha_n], S_0))$$

that is uniform in $do([\alpha_1, \ldots, \alpha_n], S_0)$ to a formula $\varphi'(S_0)$ that is uniform in S_0 such that

$$\mathcal{D} \models \varphi(do([\alpha_1, \ldots, \alpha_n], S_0)) \quad \text{iff} \quad \mathcal{D}_{una} \cup \mathcal{D}_{S_0} \models \varphi'(S_0).$$

If $\varphi(do([\alpha_1, \ldots, \alpha_n], S_0))$ does not have functional fluents, then the regression can be defined inductively as follows: the regression of $\varphi(S_0)$ is $\varphi(S_0)$, and inductively, if

---

[2]Reiter [34] defined regression for a more general class of formulas that can contain *Poss* atoms.

α is an action term, and σ a situation term, then the regression of $\varphi(do(\alpha, \sigma))$ is the regression of the formula obtained by replacing in $\varphi(do(\alpha, \sigma))$ each relational fluent atom $F(\vec{t}, do(\alpha, \sigma))$ by $\Phi_F(\vec{t}, \alpha, \sigma)$, where Φ_F is the formula in the right side of the successor state axiom (16.66) for F. When φ contains functional fluents, the definition of regression is more involved, see [34].

For instance, given the following successor state axioms:

$$F(do(a, s)) \equiv a = A \vee F(s),$$

$$G(do(a, s)) \equiv (a = B \wedge F(s)) \vee G(s),$$

the regression of $G(do(B, do(A, S_0)))$ is the regression of

$$(B = B \wedge F(do(A, S_0))) \vee G(do(A, S_0)),$$

which is the following sentence about S_0:

$$(B = B \wedge (A = A \vee F(S_0))) \vee (A = B \wedge F(S_0)) \vee G(S_0),$$

which is equivalent to *true*.

Using regression, we can check the executability of a sequence of actions in S_0, say $[stack(A, B), pickup(C), putdown(C)]$, as follows:

1. This sequence of actions is executable in S_0 iff the following formulas are entailed by $\mathcal{D}$:

   $Poss(stack(A, B), S_0)$,

   $Poss(pickup(C), do(stack(A, B), S_0))$,

   $Poss(putdown(C), do(pickup(C), do(stack(A, B), S_0)))$.

2. Use action precondition axioms to rewrite the above sentences into uniform sentences. For instance, the first two sentences can be rewritten into the following sentences:

   $clear(B, S_0) \wedge holding(A, S_0)$,

   $handempty(do(stack(A, B), S_0)) \wedge ontable(C, (do(stack(A, B), S_0))) \wedge$

   $clear(C, (do(stack(A, B), S_0)))$.

3. Regress the uniform sentences obtained in step 2, and check whether the regressed formulas are entailed by $\mathcal{D}_{una} \cup \mathcal{D}_{S_0}$.

16.4 Applications

The situation calculus provides a rich framework for solving problems in dynamic systems. Indeed, Reiter [34] showed that many such problems can be formulated in the situation calculus and solved using a formal situation calculus specification. He even had the slogan "No implementation without a SitCalc specification".

The first application of the situation calculus is in planning where an agent needs to figure out a course of actions that will achieve a given goal. Green [8] formulated this problem as a theorem proving task in the situation calculus:

$$T \models \exists s.G(s),$$

where T is the situation calculus theory for the planning problem, and G the goal. Green's idea was that if one can find a proof of the above theorem constructively, then a plan can be read off from the witness situation term in the proof. He actually implemented a planning system based on this idea using a first-order theorem prover. For various reasons, the system could solve only extremely simple problems. Some researchers believe that Green's idea is correct. What one needs is a good way to encode domain specific control knowledge as the situation calculus sentences to direct the theorem prover intelligently.

One reason that Green's system performed poorly was that the theory T that encodes the planning problem is not very effective. Assuming that the planning problem is specified by a basic action theory, Reiter implemented a planner in Prolog that can efficiently make use of domain-specific control information like that in [1]. It can even do open-world planning where the initial situation is not completely specified. For more details see [34].

The situation calculus has also been used to formalize and reason about computer programs. Burstall used it to formalize Algol-like programs [3]. Manna and Waldinger used it to formalize general assignments in Algol 68 [22], and later Lisp imperative programs [23].

More recently, Lin and Reiter used it to axiomatize logic programs with negation-as-failure [20]. The basic idea is as follows. A rule (clause) $P \leftarrow G$ means that whenever G is proved, we can use this rule to prove P. Thus we can name this rule by an action so that the consequence of the rule becomes the effect of the action, and the body of the rule becomes the context under which the action will have the effect.[3] Formally, for each rule

$$F(t_1, \ldots, t_n) \leftarrow Q_1, \ldots, Q_k, \text{not } Q_{k+1}, \ldots, \text{not } Q_m$$

Lin and Reiter introduced a corresponding n-ary action A, and axiomatized it with the following axioms:

$$Poss(A(\vec{x}), s),$$
$$[\exists \vec{y_1} Holds(Q_1, s) \wedge \cdots \wedge \exists \vec{y_k} Holds(Q_k, s) \wedge$$
$$\neg(\exists \vec{y_{k+1}}, s) Holds(Q_{k+1}, s) \wedge \cdots \wedge$$
$$\neg(\exists \vec{y_m}, s) Holds(Q_m, s)] \supset F(t_1, \ldots, t_n, do(A(\vec{x}), s)),$$

where $\vec{y_i}$ is the tuple of variables in Q_i but not in $F(t_1, \ldots, t_n)$.

Notice that $\neg(\exists \vec{y_i}, s) Holds(Q_i, s)$ means that the goal Q_i is not achievable (provable) no matter how one instantiate the variables that are in Q_i but not in the head of the rule. This is meant to capture the "negation-as-failure" feature of the operator "not" in logic programming.

Now for a logic program Π, which is a finite set of rules, one can apply Reiter's solution to the effect axioms obtained this way for all rules in Π, and obtain a set of

---

[3]Alternatively, one could also view the body of a rule as the precondition of the corresponding action.

successor state axioms, one for each predicate occurring in the program.[4] Thus for each program Π, we have a corresponding basic action theory[5] $\mathcal{D}$ for it with

$$\mathcal{D}_{S_0} = \{F(\vec{x}, S_0) \equiv false \mid F \text{ is a predicate in } \Pi\}.$$

In other words, in the initial situation, all fluents are false. Now query answering in a logic program becomes planning under the corresponding basic action theory.

As it turned out, this formalization of logic programs in the situation calculus yields a semantics that is equivalent to Gelfond and Lifschitz's stable model semantics. This situation calculus semantics can be used to formally study some interesting properties of logic programs. For instance, it can be proved that program unfolding preserves this semantics. More interestingly, under this semantics and Reiter's foundational axioms, derivations under a program are isomorphic to situations. Thus those operators that constrain derivations in logic programming can be axiomatized in the situations calculus by their corresponding constraints on situations. Based on this idea, Lin proposed a situation calculus semantics for the "cut" operator in logic programming [16].

The most significant application so far is the use of the situation calculus as a working language for Cognitive Robotics. For details about this application, the reader is referred to the chapter on Cognitive Robotics in this Handbook.

16.5   Concluding Remarks

What we have described so far is just the elemental of the situation calculus. The only thing that we care about an action so far is its logical effects on the physical environment. We have ignored many other aspects of actions, such as their durations and their effects on the agent's mental state. We have also assumed that actions are performed sequentially one at a time and that they are the only force that may change the state of the world. These and other issues in reasoning about action have been addressed in the situation calculus, primarily as a result of using the situation calculus as the working language for Cognitive Robotics. We refer the interested readers to Chapter 24 and [34].

Acknowledgements

I would like to thank Gerhard Lakemeyer, Hector Levesque, and Abhaya Nayak for their very useful comments on an earlier version of this article.

Bibliography

[1] F. Bacchus and F. Kabanza. Using temporal logics to express search control knowledge for planning. *Artificial Intelligence*, 16:123–191, 2000.

---

[4]If a predicate does not occur as the head of a rule, then add an axiom to say that this relation does not hold for any situation.

[5]Strictly speaking, it is not a basic action theory as the right side of a successor state axiom may contain $\exists s. Q(s)$ when there is a negation in front of Q in a rule, thus is not a uniform formula.

[2] A.B. Baker. Nonmonotonic reasoning in the framework of the situation calculus. *Artificial Intelligence*, 49:5–23, 1991.

[3] R.M. Burstall. Formal description of program structure and semantics in first-order logic. In B. Meltzer and D. Michie, editors. *Machine Intelligence*, vol. 5, pages 79–98. Edinburgh University Press, Edinburgh, 1969.

[4] K.L. Clark. Negation as failure. In H. Gallaire and J. Minker, editors. *Logics and Databases*, pages 293–322. Plenum Press, New York, 1978.

[5] J. Finger. Exploiting constraints in design synthesis. PhD thesis, Department of Computer Science, Stanford University Stanford, CA, 1986.

[6] M.L. Ginsberg. *Readings in Nonmonotonic Reasoning*. Morgan Kaufmann, San Mateo, CA, 1987.

[7] M.L. Ginsberg and D.E. Smith. Reasoning about action II: The qualification problem. *Artificial Intelligence*, 35:311–342, 1988.

[8] C.C. Green. Application of theorem proving to problem solving. In *Proceedings of the International Joint Conference on Artificial Intelligence (IJCAI-69)*, pages 219–239, 1969.

[9] A.R. Haas. The case for domain-specific frame axioms. In F.M. Brown, editor, *The Frame Problem in Artificial Intelligence. Proceedings of the 1987 Workshop on Reasoning about Action*, pages 343–348. Morgan Kaufmann Publishers, Inc, San Jose, CA, 1987.

[10] S. Hanks and D. McDermott. Nonmonotonic logic and temporal projection. *Artificial Intelligence*, 33:379–412, 1987.

[11] D. Harel. *First-Order Dynamic Logic. Lecture Notes in Computer Science*, vol. 68. Springer-Verlag, New York, 1979.

[12] H. Levesque, R. Reiter, Y. Lespérance, F. Lin, and R. Scherl. GOLOG: A logic programming language for dynamic domains. *Journal of Logic Programming*, 31:59–84, 1997 (Special issue on Reasoning about Action and Change).

[13] V. Lifschitz. Pointwise circumscription. In *Proceedings of the Fifth National Conference on Artificial Intelligence (AAAI-86)*, pages 406–410. Philadelphia, PA, 1986.

[14] V. Lifschitz. Formal theories of action. In *Proceedings of the Tenth International Joint Conference on Artificial Intelligence (IJCAI-87)*, pages 966–972, 1987.

[15] F. Lin. Embracing causality in specifying the indirect effects of actions. In *Proceedings of the Fourteenth International Joint Conference on Artificial Intelligence (IJCAI-95)*, pages 1985–1993. IJCAI Inc., Morgan Kaufmann, San Mateo, CA, 1995.

[16] F. Lin. Applications of the situation calculus to formalizing control and strategic information: The Prolog cut operator. *Artificial Intelligence*, 103:273–294, 1998.

[17] F. Lin. Search algorithms in the situation calculus. In H. Levesque and F. Pirri, editors. *Logical Foundations for Cognitive Agents: Contributions in Honor of Ray Reiter*, pages 213–233. Springer, Berlin, 1999.

[18] F. Lin. Compiling causal theories to successor state axioms and STRIPS-like systems. *Journal of Artificial Intelligence Research*, 19:279–314, 2003.

[19] F. Lin and R. Reiter. State constraints revisited. *Journal of Logic and Computation*, 4(5):655–678, 1994 (Special Issue on Actions and Processes).

[20] F. Lin and R. Reiter. Rules as actions: A situation calculus semantics for logic programs. *J. of Logic Programming*, 31(1–3):299–330, 1997.

[21] F. Lin and Y. Shoham. Provably correct theories of action. *Journal of the ACM*, 42(2):293–320, 1995.

[22] Z. Manna and R. Waldinger. Problematic features of programming languages: A situational-calculus approach. *Acta Informatica*, 16:371–426, 1981.

[23] Z. Manna and R. Waldinger. The deductive synthesis of imperative LISP programs. In *Proceedings of the Sixth National Conference on Artificial Intelligence (AAAI-87)*, pages 155–160, Seattle, WA, 1987.

[24] N. McCain and H. Turner. Causal theories of action and change. In *Proceedings of the 14th National Conference on Artificial Intelligence (AAAI-97)*, pages 460–465. Menlo Park, CA, 1997, AAAI Press.

[25] J. McCarthy. Situations, actions and causal laws. In M. Minsky, editor. *Semantic Information Processing*, pages 410–417. MIT Press, Cambridge, MA, 1968.

[26] J. McCarthy. Epistemological problems of Artificial Intelligence. In *IJCAI-77*, pages 1038–1044, Cambridge, MA, 1977.

[27] J. McCarthy. Applications of circumscription to formalizing commonsense knowledge. *Artificial Intelligence*, 28:89–118, 1986.

[28] J. McCarthy. Actions and other events in situation calculus. In *Proceedings of the Eighth International Conference on Principles of Knowledge Representation and Reasoning (KR2002)*, pages 615–628, 2002.

[29] J. McCarthy and P. Hayes. Some philosophical problems from the standpoint of artificial intelligence. In B. Meltzer and D. Michie, editors. *Machine Intelligence*, vol. 4, pages 463–502. Edinburgh University Press, Edinburgh, 1969.

[30] N.J. Nilsson. *Principles of Artificial Intelligence*. Morgan Kaufmann, Los Altos, CA, 1980.

[31] E.P. Pednault. ADL: Exploring the middle ground between STRIPS and the situation calculus. In *Proceedings of the First International Conference on Principles of Knowledge Representation and Reasoning (KR'89)*, pages 324–332. Morgan Kaufmann Publishers, Inc, 1989.

[32] F. Pirri and R. Reiter. Some contributions to the metatheory of the situation calculus. *J. ACM*, 46(3):325–361, 1999.

[33] R. Reiter. The frame problem in the situation calculus: a simple solution (sometimes) and a completeness result for goal regression. In V. Lifschitz, editor. *Artificial Intelligence and Mathematical Theory of Computation: Papers in Honor of John McCarthy*, pages 418–420. Academic Press, San Diego, CA, 1991.

[34] R. Reiter. *Knowledge in Action: Logical Foundations for Specifying and Implementing Dynamical Systems*. The MIT Press, 2001.

[35] E. Sandewall. *Features and Fluents. A Systematic Approach to the Representation of Knowledge about Dynamical Systems*, vol. I. Oxford University Press, 1994.

[36] L.K. Schubert. Monotonic solution to the frame problem in the situation calculus: an efficient method for worlds with fully specified actions. In H. Kyberg, R. Loui, and G. Carlson, editors. *Knowledge Representation and Defeasible Reasoning*, pages 23–67. Kluwer Academic Press, Boston, MA, 1990.

[37] Y. Shoham. Chronological ignorance: experiments in nonmonotonic temporal reasoning. *Artificial Intelligence*, 36:279–331, 1988.

[38] M. Thielscher. Ramification and causality. *Artificial Intelligence*, 89:317–364, 1997.

Handbook of Knowledge Representation
Edited by F. van Harmelen, V. Lifschitz and B. Porter
© 2008 Elsevier B.V. All rights reserved
DOI: 10.1016/S1574-6526(07)03017-9

Chapter 17

Event Calculus

Erik T. Mueller

17.1 Introduction

The event calculus [45, 66, 74, 98, 100] is a formalism for reasoning about action and change. Like the situation calculus, the event calculus has actions, which are called *events*, and time-varying properties or *fluents*. In the situation calculus, performing an action in a situation gives rise to a successor situation. Situation calculus actions are hypothetical, and time is tree-like. In the event calculus, there is a single time line on which actual events occur.

A *narrative* is a possibly incomplete specification of a set of actual event occurrences [63, 98]. The event calculus is narrative-based, unlike the standard situation calculus in which an exact sequence of hypothetical actions is represented.

Like the situation calculus, the event calculus supports context-sensitive effects of events, indirect effects, action preconditions, and the commonsense law of inertia. Certain phenomena are addressed more naturally in the event calculus, including concurrent events, continuous time, continuous change, events with duration, nondeterministic effects, partially ordered events, and triggered events.

We use a simple example to illustrate what the event calculus does. Suppose we wish to reason about turning on and off a light. We start by representing general knowledge about the effects of events:

> If a light's switch is flipped up, then the light will be on.
> If a light's switch is flipped down, then the light will be off.

We then represent a specific scenario:

> The light was off at time 0.
> Then the light's switch was flipped up at time 5.
> Then the light's switch was flipped down at time 8.

We use the event calculus to conclude the following:

> At time 3, the light was off.
> At time 7, the light was on.
> At time 10, the light was off.

Table 17.1. Original event calculus (OEC) predicates and functions (e, e_1, e_2 = event occurrences, f, f_1, f_2 = fluents, p = time period)

Predicate/function	Meaning
$Holds(p)$	p holds
$Start(p, e)$	e starts p
$End(p, e)$	e ends p
$Initiates(e, f)$	e initiates f
$Terminates(e, f)$	e terminates f
$e_1 < e_2$	e_1 precedes e_2
$Broken(e_1, f, e_2)$	f is broken between e_1 and e_2
$Incompatible(f_1, f_2)$	f_1 and f_2 are incompatible
$After(e, f)$	time period after e in which f holds
$Before(e, f)$	time period before e in which f holds

In this chapter, we discuss several versions of the event calculus, the use of circumscription in the event calculus, methods of knowledge representation using the event calculus, automated event calculus reasoning, and applications of the event calculus. We use languages of classical many-sorted predicate logic with equality.[1]

17.2   Versions of the Event Calculus

The event calculus has evolved considerably from its original version. In this section, we trace the development of the event calculus and present its important versions.

17.2.1   Original Event Calculus (OEC)

The original event calculus (OEC) was introduced in 1986 by Kowalski and Sergot [45]. OEC has sorts for event occurrences, fluents, and time periods. The predicates and functions of the original event calculus are shown in Table 17.1. The axioms of the original event calculus are as follows.

OEC1. $Initiates(e, f) \equiv Holds(After(e, f))$.[2]

OEC2. $Terminates(e, f) \equiv Holds(Before(e, f))$.

OEC3. $Start(After(e, f), e)$.

OEC4. $End(Before(e, f), e)$.

OEC5. $After(e_1, f) = Before(e_2, f) \supset Start(Before(e_2, f), e_1)$.

OEC6. $After(e_1, f) = Before(e_2, f) \supset End(After(e_1, f), e_2)$.

---

[1] We do not treat modal logic versions of the event calculus [9].

[2] Kowalski and Sergot [45] use implication ($\supset$) in OEC1 and OEC2. Sadri [87, p. 134] points out that bi-implication ($\equiv$) was intended by Kowalski and Sergot but not used in order to prevent looping when running the axioms in Prolog.

OEC7. $Holds(After(e_1, f)) \wedge Holds(Before(e_2, f)) \wedge e_1 < e_2 \wedge \neg Broken(e_1, f, e_2) \supset After(e_1, f) = Before(e_2, f)$.

OEC8. $Broken(e_1, f, e_2) \equiv \exists e, f_1 ((Holds(After(e, f_1)) \vee Holds(Before(e, f_1))) \wedge Incompatible(f, f_1) \wedge e_1 < e < e_2)$.

Let OEC be the conjunction of OEC1 through OEC8.

Example 17.1. Consider the example of turning on and off a light. We have an event occurrence E_1, which precedes event occurrence E_2:

$$E_1 < E_2 \tag{17.1}$$

E_1 turns on the light and E_2 turns it off:

$$Initiates(e, f) \equiv (e = E_1 \wedge f = On) \vee (e = E_2 \wedge f = Off) \tag{17.2}$$

$$Terminates(e, f) \equiv (e = E_1 \wedge f = Off) \vee (e = E_2 \wedge f = On) \tag{17.3}$$

The light cannot be both on and off:

$$Incompatible(f_1, f_2) \equiv (f_1 = On \wedge f_2 = Off) \vee (f_1 = Off \wedge f_2 = On) \tag{17.4}$$

We also assume the following:

$$E_1 \neq E_2 \tag{17.5}$$

$$On \neq Off \tag{17.6}$$

$$\neg(e < e) \tag{17.7}$$

We can then prove that the time period after E_1 in which the light is on equals the time period before E_2 in which the light is on. Let Σ be the conjunction of (17.1) through (17.7).

Proposition 17.1. $\Sigma \wedge OEC \models After(E_1, On) = Before(E_2, On)$.

Proof. From (17.2), (17.3), OEC1, and OEC2, we have

$$Holds(After(e, f)) \equiv (e = E_1 \wedge f = On) \vee (e = E_2 \wedge f = Off) \tag{17.8}$$

$$Holds(Before(e, f)) \equiv (e = E_1 \wedge f = Off) \vee (e = E_2 \wedge f = On) \tag{17.9}$$

From (17.8), (17.9), (17.4), (17.6), (17.7), and OEC8, we get $\neg Broken(E_1, On, E_2)$. From this, $Holds(After(E_1, On)$ (which follows from (17.8)), $Holds(Before(E_2, On)$ (which follows from (17.9)), (17.1), and OEC7, we have $After(E_1, On) = Before(E_2, On)$. $\square$

We can also prove that E_1 starts the time period before E_2 in which On holds and that E_2 ends the time period after E_1 in which On holds.

Proposition 17.2. $\Sigma \wedge OEC \models Start(Before(E_2, On), E_1) \wedge End(After(E_1, On), E_2)$.

Table 17.2. Simplified event calculus (SEC) predicates (e = event, f = fluent, t, t_1, t_2 = timepoints)

Predicate	Meaning
$Initially(f)$	f is true at timepoint 0
$HoldsAt(f, t)$	f is true at t
$Happens(e, t)$	e occurs at t
$Initiates(e, f, t)$	if e occurs at t, then f is true after t
$Terminates(e, f, t)$	if e occurs at t, then f is false after t
$StoppedIn(t_1, f, t_2)$	f is stopped between t_1 and t_2

Proof. This follows from Proposition 17.1, OEC5, and OEC6. □

Pinto and Reiter [82] argue that the *Holds* predicate of the original event calculus is problematic, because it represents that "time periods hold". They point out some undesirable consequences of axioms OEC3 and OEC4. In our light example, $Start(After(E_1, Off), E_1)$ follows from OEC3. But what is the time period $After(E_1, Off)$? Whatever it is, it does not hold. From (17.5), (17.6), and (17.8), we have $\neg Holds(After(E_1, Off))$. Similarly, from OEC3, we get $Start(After(E_2, On), E_2)$ and from OEC4, we get $End(Before(E_2, Off), E_2)$. Sadri and Kowalski [88] suggest modifying OEC3 to $Holds(After(e, f)) \supset Start(After(e, f), e)$ and OEC4 to $Holds(Before(e, f)) \supset End(Before(e, f), e)$.

17.2.2   Simplified Event Calculus (SEC)

The simplified event calculus (SEC) was proposed in 1986 by Kowalski [40, p. 25] (see also [41]) and developed by Sadri [87, pp. 137–139], Eshghi [17], and Shanahan [93, 94, 98]. It differs from the original event calculus in the following ways:

- It replaces time periods with timepoints, which are either nonnegative integers or nonnegative real numbers.

- It replaces event occurrences or tokens with event types. The predicate $Happens(e, t)$ represents that event (type) e occurs at timepoint t.

- It eliminates the notion of incompatible fluents.

- It adds a predicate $Initially(f)$, which represents that fluent f is initially true [95, p. 254] (see also [12] and [98, p. 253]).

The predicates of the simplified event calculus are shown in Table 17.2. The axioms of the simplified event calculus are as follows.

SEC1. $((Initially(f) \land \neg StoppedIn(0, f, t)) \lor \exists e, t_1 (Happens(e, t_1) \land Initiates(e, f, t_1) \land t_1 < t \land \neg StoppedIn(t_1, f, t))) \equiv HoldsAt(f, t)$[3].

SEC2. $StoppedIn(t_1, f, t_2) \equiv \exists e, t (Happens(e, t) \land t_1 < t < t_2 \land Terminates(e, f, t))$.

---

[3] Kowalski [40] uses implication, whereas Sadri [87] uses bi-implication.

Let SEC be the conjunction of SEC1 and SEC2.

SEC1 represents that (1) a fluent that is initially true remains true until it is terminated, and (2) a fluent that is initiated remains true until it is terminated. Thus fluents are subject to the *commonsense law of inertia* [48, 49, 98], which states that a fluent's truth value persists unless the fluent is affected by an event.

Example 17.2. Consider again the example of turning on and off a light. If a light is turned on, it will be on, and if a light is turned off, it will no longer be on:

$$Initiates(e, f, t) \equiv (e = TurnOn \wedge f = On) \tag{17.10}$$

$$Terminates(e, f, t) \equiv (e = TurnOff \wedge f = On) \tag{17.11}$$

Initially, the light is off:

$$\neg Initially(On) \tag{17.12}$$

The light is turned on at timepoint 2 and turned off at timepoint 4:

$$Happens(e, t) \equiv (e = TurnOn \wedge t = 2) \vee (e = TurnOff \wedge t = 4) \tag{17.13}$$

We further assume the following:

$$TurnOn \neq TurnOff \tag{17.14}$$

We can then show that the light will be off at timepoint 1, on at timepoint 3, and off again at timepoint 5. Let Σ be the conjunction of (17.10) through (17.14).

Proposition 17.3. $\Sigma \wedge SEC \models \neg HoldsAt(On, 1)$.

Proof. From (17.13), we have $\neg \exists e, t_1 (Happens(e, t_1) \wedge Initiates(e, On, t_1) \wedge t_1 < 1 \wedge \neg StoppedIn(t_1, On, 1))$. From this, (17.12), and SEC1, we have $\neg HoldsAt(On, 1)$. $\square$

Proposition 17.4. $\Sigma \wedge SEC \models HoldsAt(On, 3)$.

Proof. From (17.13) and SEC2, we have $\neg StoppedIn(2, On, 3)$. From this, $Happens(TurnOn, 2)$ (which follows from (17.13)), $Initiates(TurnOn, On, 2)$ (which follows from (17.10)), $2 < 3$, and SEC1, we have $HoldsAt(On, 3)$. $\square$

Proposition 17.5. $\Sigma \wedge SEC \models \neg HoldsAt(On, 5)$.

Proof. From $Happens(TurnOff, 4)$ (which follows from (17.13)), $2 < 4 < 5$, $Terminates(TurnOff, On, 4)$ (which follows from (17.11)), and SEC2, we have $StoppedIn(2, On, 5)$. From this, (17.13), and (17.10), we have $\neg \exists e, t_1 (Happens(e, t_1) \wedge Initiates(e, On, t_1) \wedge t_1 < 5 \wedge \neg StoppedIn(t_1, On, 5))$. From this, (17.12), and SEC1, we have $\neg HoldsAt(On, 5)$. $\square$

Table 17.3. Basic event calculus (BEC) predicates (e = event, f, f_1, f_2 = fluents, t, t_1, t_2 = timepoints)

Predicate	Meaning
$InitiallyN(f)$	f is false at timepoint 0
$InitiallyP(f)$	f is true at timepoint 0
$HoldsAt(f, t)$	f is true at t
$Happens(e, t)$	e occurs at t
$Initiates(e, f, t)$	if e occurs at t, then f is true and not released from the commonsense law of inertia after t
$Terminates(e, f, t)$	if e occurs at t, then f is false and not released from the commonsense law of inertia after t
$Releases(e, f, t)$	if e occurs at t, then f is released from the commonsense law of inertia after t
$StoppedIn(t_1, f, t_2)$	f is stopped between t_1 and t_2
$StartedIn(t_1, f, t_2)$	f is started between t_1 and t_2
$Trajectory(f_1, t_1, f_2, t_2)$	if f_1 is initiated by an event that occurs at t_1, then f_2 is true at $t_1 + t_2$

17.2.3 Basic Event Calculus (BEC)

Shanahan [94–96, 98] extended the simplified event calculus by allowing fluents to be released from the commonsense law of inertia via the *Releases* predicate, and adding the ability to represent continuous change via the *Trajectory* predicate. The *Initially* predicate is broken into two predicates *InitiallyP* and *InitiallyN*. We call this version of the event calculus the basic event calculus (BEC).

Releases(e, f, t) represents that, if event e occurs at timepoint t, then fluent f will be released from the commonsense law of inertia after t. In SEC, a fluent that is initiated remains true until it is terminated, and a fluent that is terminated remains false until it is initiated. In BEC, a fluent that is initiated remains true until it is terminated or released, and a fluent that is terminated remains false until it is initiated or released. After a fluent is released, its truth value is not determined by BEC and is permitted to vary. Thus there are models in which the fluent is true, and models in which the fluent is false.

This opens up several possibilities. First, releasing a fluent frees it up so that other axioms in the domain description can be used to determine its truth value. This allows us to represent continuous change using *Trajectory*, as discussed in Section 17.5.7, and indirect effects, as discussed in Section 17.5.9. Second, released fluents can be used to represent nondeterministic effects of events, as discussed in Section 17.5.8.

Trajectory(f_1, t_1, f_2, t_2) represents that, if fluent f_1 is initiated by an event that occurs at timepoint t_1, then fluent f_2 will be true at timepoint $t_1 + t_2$. This can be used to represent fluents that change as a function of time. The domain description is usually written so that the fluent f_2 is released by the events that initiate f_1.

The predicates of the basic event calculus are shown in Table 17.3. The axioms of the basic event calculus are as follows.

    BEC1. $StoppedIn(t_1, f, t_2) \equiv \exists e, t \ (Happens(e, t) \wedge t_1 < t < t_2 \wedge$
        $(Terminates(e, f, t) \vee Releases(e, f, t)))$.

BEC2. $StartedIn(t_1, f, t_2) \equiv \exists e, t\ (Happens(e, t) \wedge t_1 < t < t_2 \wedge (Initiates(e, f, t)$
$\vee Releases(e, f, t)))$.

BEC3. $Happens(e, t_1) \wedge Initiates(e, f_1, t_1) \wedge 0 < t_2 \wedge Trajectory(f_1, t_1, f_2, t_2) \wedge$
$\neg StoppedIn(t_1, f_1, t_1 + t_2) \supset HoldsAt(f_2, t_1 + t_2)$.

BEC4. $InitiallyP(f) \wedge \neg StoppedIn(0, f, t) \supset HoldsAt(f, t)$.

BEC5. $InitiallyN(f) \wedge \neg StartedIn(0, f, t) \supset \neg HoldsAt(f, t)$.

BEC6. $Happens(e, t_1) \wedge Initiates(e, f, t_1) \wedge t_1 < t_2 \wedge \neg StoppedIn(t_1, f, t_2) \supset$
$HoldsAt(f, t_2)$.

BEC7. $Happens(e, t_1) \wedge Terminates(e, f, t_1) \wedge t_1 < t_2 \wedge \neg StartedIn(t_1, f, t_2) \supset$
$\neg HoldsAt(f, t_2)$.

Let BEC be the conjunction of BEC1 through BEC7.

Example 17.3. Consider once again the example of turning on and off a light. We replace (17.12) with the following:

$$InitiallyN(On) \tag{17.15}$$

We add the following:

$$\neg Releases(e, f, t) \tag{17.16}$$

Let Σ be the conjunction of (17.10), (17.11), (17.13), (17.14), (17.15), and (17.16). We then have the same results as for SEC.

Proposition 17.6. $\Sigma \wedge BEC \models \neg HoldsAt(On, 1)$.

Proof. From (17.13) and BEC2, we have $\neg StartedIn(0, On, 1)$. From this, (17.15), and BEC5, we have $\neg HoldsAt(On, 1)$. $\square$

Proposition 17.7. $\Sigma \wedge BEC \models HoldsAt(On, 3)$.

Proof. From (17.13) and BEC1, we have $\neg StoppedIn(2, On, 3)$. From this, $Happens(TurnOn, 2)$ (which follows from (17.13)), $Initiates(TurnOn, On, 2)$ (which follows from (17.10)), $2 < 3$, and BEC6, we have $HoldsAt(On, 3)$. $\square$

Proposition 17.8. $\Sigma \wedge BEC \models \neg HoldsAt(On, 5)$.

Proof. From (17.13) and BEC2, we have $\neg StartedIn(4, On, 5)$. From this, $Happens(TurnOff, 4)$ (which follows from (17.13)), $Terminates(TurnOff, On, 4)$ (which follows from (17.11)), $4 < 5$, and BEC7, we have $\neg HoldsAt(On, 5)$. $\square$

Example 17.4. We can use *Releases* and *Trajectory* to represent a light that alternately emits red and green when it is turned on. If a light is turned on, it will be on:

$$Initiates(e, f, t) \equiv (e = TurnOn \wedge f = On) \tag{17.17}$$

If a light is turned on, whether it is red or green will be released from the commonsense law of inertia:

$$Releases(e, f, t) \equiv (e = TurnOn \land (f = Red \lor f = Green)) \qquad (17.18)$$

If a light is turned off, it will not be on, red, or green:

$$Terminates(e, f, t) \equiv (e = TurnOff \land (f = On \lor f = Red \lor f = Green)) \qquad (17.19)$$

After a light is turned on, it will alternately emit red for two seconds and green for two seconds:

$$(t_2 \bmod 4) < 2 \supset Trajectory(On, t_1, Red, t_2) \qquad (17.20)$$

$$(t_2 \bmod 4) \geqslant 2 \supset Trajectory(On, t_1, Green, t_2) \qquad (17.21)$$

The light is not simultaneously red and green:

$$\neg HoldsAt(Red, t) \lor \neg HoldsAt(Green, t) \qquad (17.22)$$

The light is turned on at timepoint 2:

$$Happens(e, t) \equiv (e = TurnOn \land t = 2) \qquad (17.23)$$

We also assume

$$TurnOn \neq TurnOff \qquad (17.24)$$

We can then show that the light will be red at timepoint 3, green at timepoint 5, red at timepoint 7, and so on. Let Σ be the conjunction of (17.17) through (17.24).

Proposition 17.9. $\Sigma \land \mathrm{BEC} \models HoldsAt(Red, 3)$.

Proof. From (17.20) by universal instantiation, we have

$$Trajectory(On, 2, Red, 1) \qquad (17.25)$$

From (17.23) and BEC1, we have $\neg StoppedIn(2, On, 3)$. From this, $Happens(TurnOn, 2)$ (which follows from (17.23)), $Initiates(TurnOn, On, 2)$ (which follows from (17.17)), $0 < 1$, (17.25), and BEC3, we have $HoldsAt(Red, 3)$. $\qquad \square$

Proposition 17.10. $\Sigma \land \mathrm{BEC} \models HoldsAt(Green, 5)$.

Proof. From (17.21) by universal instantiation, we have

$$Trajectory(On, 2, Green, 3) \qquad (17.26)$$

From (17.23) and BEC1, we have $\neg StoppedIn(2, On, 5)$. From this, $Happens(TurnOn, 2)$ (which follows from (17.23)), $Initiates(TurnOn, On, 2)$ (which follows from (17.17)), $0 < 3$, (17.26), and BEC3, we have $HoldsAt(Green, 5)$. $\qquad \square$

Proposition 17.11. $\Sigma \land \mathrm{BEC} \models HoldsAt(Red, 7)$.

Table 17.4. EC and DEC predicates (e = event, f, f_1, f_2 = fluents, t, t_1, t_2 = timepoints)

Predicate	Meaning
$HoldsAt(f, t)$	f is true at t
$Happens(e, t)$	e occurs at t
$ReleasedAt(f, t)$	f is released from the commonsense law of inertia at t
$Initiates(e, f, t)$	if e occurs at t, then f is true and not released from the commonsense law of inertia after t
$Terminates(e, f, t)$	if e occurs at t, then f is false and not released from the commonsense law of inertia after t
$Releases(e, f, t)$	if e occurs at t, then f is released from the commonsense law of inertia after t
$Trajectory(f_1, t_1, f_2, t_2)$	if f_1 is initiated by an event that occurs at t_1, then f_2 is true at $t_1 + t_2$
$AntiTrajectory(f_1, t_1, f_2, t_2)$	if f_1 is terminated by an event that occurs at t_1, then f_2 is true at $t_1 + t_2$

Proof. From (17.20) by universal instantiation, we have

$$Trajectory(On, 2, Red, 5) \tag{17.27}$$

From (17.23) and BEC1, we have $\neg StoppedIn(2, On, 7)$. From this, $Happens(TurnOn, 2)$ (which follows from (17.23)), $Initiates(TurnOn, On, 2)$ (which follows from (17.17)), $0 < 5$, (17.27), and BEC3, we have $HoldsAt(Red, 7)$. □

17.2.4 Event Calculus (EC)

Miller and Shanahan [65, 66] introduced several alternative formulations of the basic event calculus. A number of their axioms can be combined [70] to produce what we call EC, which differs from the basic event calculus in the following ways:

- It allows negative time. Timepoints are either integers or real numbers.

- It eliminates the *InitiallyN* and *InitiallyP* predicates.

- It explicitly represents that a fluent is released from the commonsense law of inertia using the *ReleasedAt* predicate.

- It adds *AntiTrajectory*.

- It treats *StoppedIn* and *StartedIn* as abbreviations rather than predicates, and introduces other abbreviations.

$ReleasedAt(f, t)$ represents that fluent f is released from the commonsense law of inertia at timepoint t. $AntiTrajectory(f_1, t_1, f_2, t_2)$ represents that, if fluent f_1 is terminated by an event that occurs at timepoint t_1, then fluent f_2 will be true at timepoint $t_1 + t_2$.

The predicates of EC are shown in Table 17.4. The axioms and definitions of EC are as follows.

EC1. *Clipped*$(t_1, f, t_2) \overset{\text{def}}{\equiv} \exists e, t$ *(Happens*$(e, t) \wedge t_1 \leqslant t < t_2 \wedge$
 Terminates$(e, f, t))$.

EC2. *Declipped*$(t_1, f, t_2) \overset{\text{def}}{\equiv} \exists e, t$ *(Happens*$(e, t) \wedge t_1 \leqslant t < t_2 \wedge$
 Initiates$(e, f, t))$.

EC3. *StoppedIn*$(t_1, f, t_2) \overset{\text{def}}{\equiv} \exists e, t$ *(Happens*$(e, t) \wedge t_1 < t < t_2 \wedge$
 Terminates$(e, f, t))$.

EC4. *StartedIn*$(t_1, f, t_2) \overset{\text{def}}{\equiv} \exists e, t$ *(Happens*$(e, t) \wedge t_1 < t < t_2 \wedge$
 Initiates$(e, f, t))$.

EC5. *Happens*$(e, t_1) \wedge$ *Initiates*$(e, f_1, t_1) \wedge 0 < t_2 \wedge$ *Trajectory*$(f_1, t_1, f_2, t_2) \wedge$
 $\neg$*StoppedIn*$(t_1, f_1, t_1 + t_2) \supset$ *HoldsAt*$(f_2, t_1 + t_2)$.

EC6. *Happens*$(e, t_1) \wedge$ *Terminates*$(e, f_1, t_1) \wedge 0 < t_2 \wedge$ *AntiTrajectory*$(f_1, t_1,$
 $f_2, t_2) \wedge \neg$*StartedIn*$(t_1, f_1, t_1 + t_2) \supset$ *HoldsAt*$(f_2, t_1 + t_2)$.

EC7. *PersistsBetween*$(t_1, f, t_2) \overset{\text{def}}{\equiv} \neg\exists t$ *(ReleasedAt*$(f, t) \wedge t_1 < t \leqslant t_2)$.

EC8. *ReleasedBetween*$(t_1, f, t_2) \overset{\text{def}}{\equiv} \exists e, t$ *(Happens*$(e, t) \wedge t_1 \leqslant t < t_2 \wedge$
 Releases$(e, f, t))$.

EC9. *HoldsAt*$(f, t_1) \wedge t_1 < t_2 \wedge$ *PersistsBetween*$(t_1, f, t_2) \wedge$
 $\neg$*Clipped*$(t_1, f, t_2) \supset$ *HoldsAt*(f, t_2).

EC10. $\neg$*HoldsAt*$(f, t_1) \wedge t_1 < t_2 \wedge$ *PersistsBetween*$(t_1, f, t_2) \wedge$
 $\neg$*Declipped*$(t_1, f, t_2) \supset \neg$*HoldsAt*$(f, t_2)$.

EC11. *ReleasedAt*$(f, t_1) \wedge t_1 < t_2 \wedge \neg$*Clipped*$(t_1, f, t_2) \wedge \neg$*Declipped*$(t_1, f, t_2) \supset$
 ReleasedAt(f, t_2).

EC12. $\neg$*ReleasedAt*$(f, t_1) \wedge t_1 < t_2 \wedge \neg$*ReleasedBetween*$(t_1, f, t_2) \supset$
 $\neg$*ReleasedAt*(f, t_2).

EC13. *ReleasedIn*$(t_1, f, t_2) \overset{\text{def}}{\equiv} \exists e, t$ *(Happens*$(e, t) \wedge t_1 < t < t_2 \wedge$
 Releases$(e, f, t))$.

EC14. *Happens*$(e, t_1) \wedge$ *Initiates*$(e, f, t_1) \wedge t_1 < t_2 \wedge \neg$*StoppedIn*$(t_1, f, t_2) \wedge$
 $\neg$*ReleasedIn*$(t_1, f, t_2) \supset$ *HoldsAt*(f, t_2).

EC15. *Happens*$(e, t_1) \wedge$ *Terminates*$(e, f, t_1) \wedge t_1 < t_2 \wedge \neg$*StartedIn*$(t_1, f, t_2) \wedge$
 $\neg$*ReleasedIn*$(t_1, f, t_2) \supset \neg$*HoldsAt*$(f, t_2)$.

EC16. *Happens*$(e, t_1) \wedge$ *Releases*$(e, f, t_1) \wedge t_1 < t_2 \wedge \neg$*StoppedIn*$(t_1, f, t_2) \wedge$
 $\neg$*StartedIn*$(t_1, f, t_2) \supset$ *ReleasedAt*(f, t_2).

EC17. *Happens*$(e, t_1) \wedge ($*Initiates*$(e, f, t_1) \vee$ *Terminates*$(e, f, t_1)) \wedge t_1 < t_2 \wedge$
 $\neg$*ReleasedIn*$(t_1, f, t_2) \supset \neg$*ReleasedAt*$(f, t_2)$.

Let EC be the formula generated by conjoining axioms EC5, EC6, EC9, EC10, EC11, EC12, EC14, EC15, EC16, and EC17 and then expanding the predicates *Clipped*, *Declipped*, *StoppedIn*, *StartedIn*, *PersistsBetween*, *ReleasedBetween*, and *ReleasedIn* using definitions EC1, EC2, EC3, EC4, EC7, EC8, and EC13.

Example 17.5. Consider again the light example. We replace (17.15) with the following:

$$\neg HoldsAt(On, 0) \tag{17.28}$$

We add the following:

$$\neg ReleasedAt(f, t) \tag{17.29}$$

Let Σ be the conjunction of (17.10), (17.11), (17.13), (17.14), (17.16), (17.28), and (17.29). Again, we get the same results.

Proposition 17.12. $\Sigma \wedge EC \models \neg HoldsAt(On, 1)$.

Proof. From (17.13) and EC2, we have $\neg Declipped(0, On, 1)$. From this, (17.28), $0 < 1$, $PersistsBetween(0, On, 1)$ (which follows from (17.29) and EC7), and EC10, we have $\neg HoldsAt(On, 1)$. $\square$

Proposition 17.13. $\Sigma \wedge EC \models HoldsAt(On, 3)$.

Proof. From (17.13) and EC3, we have $\neg StoppedIn(2, On, 3)$. From this, $Happens(TurnOn, 2)$ (which follows from (17.13)), $Initiates(TurnOn, On, 2)$ (which follows from (17.10)), $2 < 3$, $\neg ReleasedIn(2, On, 3)$ (which follows from (17.13) and EC13), and EC14, we have $HoldsAt(On, 3)$. $\square$

Proposition 17.14. $\Sigma \wedge EC \models \neg HoldsAt(On, 5)$.

Proof. From (17.13) and EC4, we have $\neg StartedIn(4, On, 5)$. From this, $Happens(TurnOff, 4)$ (which follows from (17.13)), $Terminates(TurnOff, On, 4)$ (which follows from (17.11)), $4 < 5$, $\neg ReleasedIn(4, On, 5)$ (which follows from (17.13) and EC13), and EC15, we have $\neg HoldsAt(On, 5)$. $\square$

17.2.5 Discrete Event Calculus (DEC)

Mueller [70, 74] developed the discrete event calculus (DEC) to improve the efficiency of automated reasoning in the event calculus. DEC improves efficiency by limiting time to the integers, and eliminating triply quantified time from many of the axioms.

The predicates of DEC are the same as those of EC, as shown in Table 17.4. The axioms and definitions of DEC are as follows.

DEC1. $StoppedIn(t_1, f, t_2) \stackrel{\text{def}}{=} \exists e, t (Happens(e, t) \wedge t_1 < t < t_2 \wedge Terminates(e, f, t))$.

DEC2. $StartedIn(t_1, f, t_2) \overset{\text{def}}{\equiv} \exists e, t \, (Happens(e, t) \wedge t_1 < t < t_2 \wedge Initiates(e, f, t))$.

DEC3. $Happens(e, t_1) \wedge Initiates(e, f_1, t_1) \wedge 0 < t_2 \wedge Trajectory(f_1, t_1, f_2, t_2) \wedge \neg StoppedIn(t_1, f_1, t_1 + t_2) \supset HoldsAt(f_2, t_1 + t_2)$.

DEC4. $Happens(e, t_1) \wedge Terminates(e, f_1, t_1) \wedge 0 < t_2 \wedge AntiTrajectory(f_1, t_1, f_2, t_2) \wedge \neg StartedIn(t_1, f_1, t_1 + t_2) \supset HoldsAt(f_2, t_1 + t_2)$.

DEC5. $HoldsAt(f, t) \wedge \neg ReleasedAt(f, t + 1) \wedge \neg \exists e \, (Happens(e, t) \wedge Terminates(e, f, t)) \supset HoldsAt(f, t + 1)$.

DEC6. $\neg HoldsAt(f, t) \wedge \neg ReleasedAt(f, t + 1) \wedge \neg \exists e \, (Happens(e, t) \wedge Initiates(e, f, t)) \supset \neg HoldsAt(f, t + 1)$.

DEC7. $ReleasedAt(f, t) \wedge \neg \exists e \, (Happens(e, t) \wedge (Initiates(e, f, t) \vee Terminates(e, f, t))) \supset ReleasedAt(f, t + 1)$.

DEC8. $\neg ReleasedAt(f, t) \wedge \neg \exists e \, (Happens(e, t) \wedge Releases(e, f, t)) \supset \neg ReleasedAt(f, t + 1)$.

DEC9. $Happens(e, t) \wedge Initiates(e, f, t) \supset HoldsAt(f, t + 1)$.

DEC10. $Happens(e, t) \wedge Terminates(e, f, t) \supset \neg HoldsAt(f, t + 1)$.

DEC11. $Happens(e, t) \wedge Releases(e, f, t) \supset ReleasedAt(f, t + 1)$.

DEC12. $Happens(e, t) \wedge (Initiates(e, f, t) \vee Terminates(e, f, t)) \supset \neg ReleasedAt(f, t + 1)$.

Let DEC be the formula generated by conjoining axioms DEC3 through DEC12 and then expanding the predicates *StoppedIn* and *StartedIn* using definitions DEC1 and DEC2.

The difference between EC and DEC is that EC operates over spans of timepoints, whereas DEC operates timepoint by timepoint. For example, EC14 states that a fluent that is initiated remains true until it is terminated or released. This corresponds to several DEC axioms. DEC9 states that a fluent that is initiated is true at the next timepoint. DEC5 states that a fluent that is true, not released from the commonsense law of inertia, and not terminated, is true at the next timepoint. The axioms dealing with *Trajectory* and *AntiTrajectory*, DEC3 and DEC4, are the same as EC5 and EC6. The definitions of *StoppedIn* and *StartedIn*, DEC1 and DEC2, are the same as EC3 and EC4.

Example 17.6. Consider again the light example. Let Σ be as for EC.

Proposition 17.15. $\Sigma \wedge \text{DEC} \models \neg HoldsAt(On, 1)$.

Proof. From (17.13), we have $\neg \exists e \, (Happens(e, 0) \wedge Initiates(e, On, 0))$. From this, (17.28), $\neg ReleasedAt(On, 1)$ (which follows from (17.29)), and DEC6, we have $\neg HoldsAt(On, 1)$.   □

Proposition 17.16. $\Sigma \wedge \mathrm{DEC} \models HoldsAt(On, 3)$.

Proof. From *Happens(TurnOn, 2)* (which follows from (17.13)), *Initiates(TurnOn, On, 2)* (which follows from (17.10)), and DEC9, we have *HoldsAt(On, 3)*. □

Proposition 17.17. $\Sigma \wedge \mathrm{DEC} \models \neg HoldsAt(On, 5)$.

Proof. From *Happens(TurnOff, 4)* (which follows from (17.13)), *Terminates(TurnOff, On, 4)* (which follows from (17.11)), and DEC10, we have ¬*HoldsAt(On, 5)*. □

17.2.6 Equivalence of DEC and EC

We have the following equivalence between DEC and EC.

Proposition 17.18. *If the domain of the timepoint sort is restricted to the integers, then DEC is logically equivalent to EC.*

Proof. (EC $\models$ DEC) By universal instantiation, substituting $t_1 + 1$ for t_2. For example, DEC9 is obtained from EC14 via the following chain of equivalences:

$$Happens(e, t_1) \wedge Initiates(e, f, t_1) \wedge t_1 < t_1 + 1 \wedge \neg StoppedIn(t_1, f, t_1 + 1) \wedge$$
$$\neg ReleasedIn(t_1, f, t_1 + 1) \supset HoldsAt(f, t_1 + 1)$$
$$\equiv$$
$$Happens(e, t_1) \wedge Initiates(e, f, t_1) \wedge$$
$$\neg \exists e, t \, (Happens(e, t) \wedge t_1 < t < t_1 + 1 \wedge Terminates(e, f, t)) \wedge$$
$$\neg \exists e, t \, (Happens(e, t) \wedge t_1 < t < t_1 + 1 \wedge Releases(e, f, t)) \supset$$
$$HoldsAt(f, t_1 + 1)$$
$$\equiv \ (for \ integer \ time)$$
$$Happens(e, t_1) \wedge Initiates(e, f, t_1) \supset HoldsAt(f, t_1 + 1)$$

(DEC $\models$ EC) By a series of lemmas showing that each EC axiom follows from DEC. See [70] or [74]. □

17.2.7 Other Versions

Other versions of the event calculus have been developed to support

- causal constraints for instantaneously interacting indirect effects [101].

- continuously changing parameters using differential equations [64, 66].

- events with duration[4] [66, 97, 100].

- hierarchical or compound events [97, 100].

---

[4]Events with duration may also be represented as fluents that are initiated and terminated by instantaneous events. For example, a moving event with duration can be represented using the axioms *Initiates(StartMoving, Moving, t)* and *Terminates(StopMoving, Moving, t)*. See also the discussion of continuous change in Section 17.5.7.

17.3   Relationship to other Formalisms

The event calculus is closely related to the situation calculus (see Chapter 16) and temporal action logics (see Chapter 18). The relation between the event calculus and the situation calculus is treated by Kowalski and Sadri [43, 44] and Van Belleghem, Denecker, and De Schreye [112]. The relation between the event calculus and temporal action logics is treated by Mueller [75]. Bennett and Galton [4] define a versatile event logic (VEL) and use it to describe versions of the situation calculus and the event calculus. A problem for future research is the relation of the event calculus and nonmonotonic causal logic.

17.4   Default Reasoning

An axiomatization is *elaboration tolerant* to the degree that it can be extended easily [61]. In the examples given so far, we have fully specified the effects of events and the event occurrences. That is, we have supplied bi-implications for the predicates *Initiates*, *Terminates*, *Releases*, and *Happens*. This is not very elaboration tolerant, because whenever we wish to add event effects and occurrences, we must modify these bi-implications.

Instead, we should be able to write individual axioms specifying what effects particular events have on particular fluents and what events occur. But then we have two problems:

1. how to derive what effects particular events do *not* have on particular fluents, or the *frame problem* [8, 62, 98, 105] (see also Section 16.2), and

2. how to derive what events do *not* occur.

These problems can be solved using any framework for default or nonmonotonic reasoning [5, 7] (see also Chapters 6 and 7). In this section, we discuss the use of circumscription [51, 56, 57, 59] (see Section 6.4) and negation as failure [11].

17.4.1   Circumscription

Consider the light example. Instead of writing the single axiom

$$Happens(e, t) \equiv (e = TurnOn \wedge t = 2) \vee (e = TurnOff \wedge t = 4) \qquad (17.30)$$

we write several axioms:

$$Happens(TurnOn, 2) \qquad (17.31)$$

$$Happens(TurnOff, 4) \qquad (17.32)$$

Then we circumscribe *Happens* in (17.31) $\wedge$ (17.32), which yields (17.30).

Circumscription allows us to assume by default that the events known to occur are the only events that occur. That is, there are no extraneous events. If we allowed extraneous events, then we could no longer prove, say, that the light is off at timepoint 6, because we could no longer prove the absence of events turning on the light between timepoints 4 and 6. If we later add the axiom

$$Happens(TurnOn, 5)$$

then we recompute the circumscription, which allows us to prove that in fact the light is on at timepoint 6.

Similarly, we write separate axioms for *Initiates*, *Terminates*, and *Releases*, and circumscribe these predicates, which allows us to assume by default that the known effects of events are the only effects of events. That is, there are no extraneous event effects. If we allowed extraneous event effects, then we could no longer prove that the light is off at timepoint 6 if some unrelated event occurred between timepoints 4 and 6, because we could no longer prove that the unrelated event does not turn on the light.

17.4.2 Computing Circumscription

It is difficult to compute circumscription in general [16]. The circumscription of a predicate in a formula, which is defined by a formula of second-order logic, does not always reduce to a formula of first-order logic [47]. In many cases, however, we can compute circumscription using the following two propositions. The first proposition asserts that certain circumscriptions reduce to predicate completion. (See Section 7.3.2.)

Proposition 17.19. *Let ρ be an n-ary predicate symbol and $\Delta(x_1, \ldots, x_n)$ be a formula whose only free variables are $x_1, \ldots, x_n$. If $\Delta(x_1, \ldots, x_n)$ does not contain ρ, then the circumscription $CIRC[\forall x_1, \ldots, x_n (\Delta(x_1, \ldots, x_n) \supset \rho(x_1, \ldots, x_n)]; \rho)$ is equivalent to $\forall x_1, \ldots, x_n (\Delta(x_1, \ldots, x_n) \equiv \rho(x_1, \ldots, x_n))$.*

Proof. See the proof of Proposition 2 of Lifschitz [51]. (See also [84].) $\square$

This gives us the following method for computing circumscription of ρ in a formula:

1. Rewrite the formula in the form $\forall x_1, \ldots, x_n (\Delta(x_1, \ldots, x_n) \supset \rho(x_1, \ldots, x_n))$, where $\Delta(x_1, \ldots, x_n)$ does not contain ρ.

2. Apply Proposition 17.19.

Example 17.7. Let $\Sigma = Initiates(E_1, F_1, t) \wedge Initiates(E_2, F_2, t)$. We compute $CIRC[\Sigma; Initiates]$ by rewriting Σ as

$$(e = E_1 \wedge f = F_1) \vee (e = E_2 \wedge f = F_2) \supset Initiates(e, f, t)$$

and then applying Proposition 17.19, which gives

$$Initiates(e, f, t) \equiv (e = E_1 \wedge f = F_1) \vee (e = E_2 \wedge f = F_2)$$

The second proposition allows us to compute the circumscription of several predicates, called parallel circumscription. We start with a definition.

Definition 17.1. *A formula Δ is positive relative to a predicate symbol ρ if and only if all occurrences of ρ in Δ are in the range of an even number of negations in an equivalent formula obtained by eliminating $\supset$ and $\equiv$ from Δ.*

Proposition 17.20. *Let* $\rho_1, \ldots, \rho_n$ *be predicate symbols and* Δ *be a formula. If* Δ *is positive relative to every* ρ_i, *then the parallel circumscription* $CIRC[\Delta; \rho_1, \ldots, \rho_n]$ *is equivalent to* $\bigwedge_{i=1}^{n} CIRC[\Delta; \rho_i]$.

Proof. See the proof of Proposition 14 of Lifschitz [51].   □

Further methods for computing circumscription are discussed in Section 6.4.4.

Example 17.8. Let Σ be the conjunction of the following axioms:

$Initiates(TurnOn, On, t)$

$Terminates(TurnOff, On, t)$

Let Δ be the conjunction of the following axioms:

$Happens(TurnOn, 2)$

$Happens(TurnOff, 4)$

Let Γ be the conjunction of (17.14), (17.28), and (17.29). We can use circumscription to prove that the light is on at timepoint 3.

Proposition 17.21.

$CIRC[\Sigma; Initiates, Terminates, Releases] \wedge CIRC[\Delta; Happens] \wedge \Gamma \wedge EC$
$\models HoldsAt(On, 3)$

Proof. From $CIRC[\Sigma; Initiates, Terminates, Releases]$, Propositions 17.20 and 17.19, we have

$(Initiates(e, f, t) \equiv (e = TurnOn \wedge f = On)) \wedge$

$(Terminates(e, f, t) \equiv (e = TurnOff \wedge f = On)) \wedge$

$\neg Releases(e, f, t)$ (17.33)

From $CIRC[\Delta; Happens]$ and Proposition 17.19, we have

$Happens(e, t) \equiv (e = TurnOn \wedge t = 2) \vee (e = TurnOff \wedge t = 4)$ (17.34)

From this and EC3, we have $\neg StoppedIn(2, On, 3)$. From this, $Happens(TurnOn, 2)$ (which follows from (17.34)), $Initiates(TurnOn, On, 2)$ (which follows from (17.33)), $2 < 3$, $\neg ReleasedIn(2, On, 3)$ (which follows from (17.34) and EC13), and EC14, we have $HoldsAt(On, 3)$.   □

17.4.3 Historical Note

Notice that we keep the event calculus axioms EC outside the scope of any circumscription. This technique, known as *filtering*, was introduced in the features and fluents framework [14, 15, 89, 90] (see also Chapter 18) and incorporated into the event calculus by Shanahan [96, 98]. The need for filtering became clear after Hanks and McDermott [32] introduced the Yale shooting scenario, which exposed problems with simply circumscribing the entire situation calculus axiomatization of the scenario, Shanahan [98] describes treatments of the Yale shooting scenario in the situation calculus and the event calculus; Shanahan [105] and Lifschitz [52] provide a modern perspective.

17.4.4 Negation as Failure

Instead of using circumscription for default reasoning in the event calculus, logic programming with the negation as failure operator **not** may be used [41, 45, 93, 94]. For example, we write rules such as the following:

$clipped(T1, F, T2) \leftarrow happens(E, T), T1 <= T, T < T2,$

  $terminates(E, F, T).$

$holds\_at(F, T2) \leftarrow holds\_at(F, T1), T1 < T2,$ **not** $clipped(T1, F, T2).$

These rules are similar to axioms EC1 and EC9. Then we add rules such as the following to our domain description:

$initiates(turn\_on, on, T).$

$terminates(turn\_off, on, T).$

$happens(turn\_on, 2).$

$happens(turn\_off, 4).$

Mueller [73] provides complete lists of event calculus rules for use with answer set solvers [3, 79] along with sample domain descriptions.

17.5 Event Calculus Knowledge Representation

This section describes methods for representing knowledge using the event calculus. These methods can be used with BEC, EC, and DEC. Those that do not involve trajectories or release from the commonsense law of inertia can also be used with SEC.

17.5.1 Parameters

We represent events and fluents with parameters as functions that return event and fluent terms. For example, we may represent the event of person p turning on light l using a function $TurnOn(p, l)$, and the property that light l is turned on using a function $On(l)$. We then require the following unique names axioms:

$$TurnOn(p_1, l_1) = TurnOn(p_2, l_2) \supset p_1 = p_2 \wedge l_1 = l_2 \tag{17.35}$$

$$On(l_1) = On(l_2) \supset l_1 = l_2 \tag{17.36}$$

If we have another event $TurnOff(p, l)$, then we also require the unique names axiom:

$$TurnOn(p_1, l_1) \neq TurnOff(p_2, l_2) \tag{17.37}$$

The U notation [48] is convenient for defining unique names axioms. If $\phi_1, \ldots, \phi_k$ are function symbols, then $U[\phi_1, \ldots, \phi_k]$ is an abbreviation for the conjunction of the formulas

$$\phi_i(x_1, \ldots, x_m) \neq \phi_j(y_1, \ldots, y_n)$$

where m is the arity of ϕ_i, n is the arity of ϕ_j, and $x_1, \ldots, x_m$ and $y_1, \ldots, y_n$ are distinct variables such that the sort of x_p is the sort of the pth argument position of ϕ_i and the sort of y_p is the sort of the pth argument position of ϕ_j, for each $1 \leqslant i < j \leqslant k$, and the conjunction of the formulas

$$\phi_i(x_1, \ldots, x_m) = \phi_i(y_1, \ldots, y_m) \supset x_1 = y_1 \land \cdots \land x_m = y_m$$

where m is the arity of ϕ_i and $x_1, \ldots, x_m$ and $y_1, \ldots, y_m$ are distinct variables such that the sort of x_p and y_p is the sort of the pth argument position of ϕ_i, for each $1 \leqslant i \leqslant k$.

We may then use this notation to replace (17.35), (17.36), and (17.37) with

$$U[TurnOn, TurnOff] \land U[On]$$

In the remainder of this section, we assume that appropriate unique names axioms are defined.

17.5.2   Event Effects

The effects of events are represented using *effect axioms*, which are of the form

$$\gamma \supset Initiates(\alpha, \beta, \tau), \quad \text{or}$$

$$\gamma \supset Terminates(\alpha, \beta, \tau)$$

where γ is a condition, α is an event, β is a fluent, and τ is a timepoint. A condition is a formula containing atoms of the form $HoldsAt(\beta, \tau)$ and $\neg HoldsAt(\beta, \tau)$, where β is a fluent and τ is a timepoint.

Example 17.9. Consider a counter that can be incremented and reset. The fluent $Value(c, v)$ represents that counter c has value v. The event $Increment(c)$ represents that counter c is incremented, and the event $Reset(c)$ represents that the counter c is reset. We use two effect axioms to represent that, if the value of a counter is v and the counter is incremented, its value will be $v + 1$ and will no longer be v:

$$HoldsAt(Value(c, v), t) \supset Initiates(Increment(c), Value(c, v + 1), t) \quad (17.38)$$

$$HoldsAt(Value(c, v), t) \supset Terminates(Increment(c), Value(c, v), t) \quad (17.39)$$

We use two more effect axioms to represent that, if the value of a counter is v and the counter is reset, its value will be 0 and will no longer be v:

$$Initiates(Reset(c), Value(c, 0), t) \quad (17.40)$$

$$HoldsAt(Value(c, v), t) \land c \neq 0 \supset Terminates(Reset(c), Value(c, v), t) \quad (17.41)$$

The effect of an event can depend on the context in which it occurs. The condition γ represents the context. In the example of the counter, the effect of incrementing the counter depends on its current value.

17.5.3 Preconditions

We might represent the effect of turning on a device as follows:

$$Initiates(TurnOn(p, d), On(d), t)$$

But there are many things that could prevent a device from going on. It could be unplugged or broken, its on-off switch could be broken, and so on. A *qualification* is a condition that prevents an event from having its intended effects. The *qualification problem* is the problem of representing and reasoning about qualifications.

A partial solution to the qualification problem is to use *preconditions*. The condition γ of effect axioms can be used to represent preconditions.

Example 17.10. If a person turns on a device, then, provided the device is not broken, the device will be on:

$$\neg HoldsAt(Broken(d), t) \supset Initiates(TurnOn(p, d), On(d), t) \tag{17.42}$$

But this is not elaboration tolerant, because whenever we wish to add qualifications, we must modify (17.42). Instead we can use default reasoning.

Example 17.11. Instead of writing (17.42), we write

$$\neg Ab_1(d, t) \supset Initiates(TurnOn(p, d), On(d), t) \tag{17.43}$$

$Ab_1(d, t)$ is an *abnormality predicate* [28, 58–60]. It represents that at timepoint t, device d is abnormal in some way that prevents it from being turned on. In general, we use a distinct abnormality predicate for each type of abnormality. We then add qualifications by writing *cancellation axioms* [23, 51, 59]:

$$HoldsAt(Broken(d), t) \supset Ab_1(d, t) \tag{17.44}$$

$$\neg HoldsAt(PluggedIn(d), t) \supset Ab_1(d, t) \tag{17.45}$$

We then circumscribe the abnormality predicate Ab_1 in the conjunction of cancellation axioms (17.44) and (17.45), which yields

$$Ab_1(d, t) \equiv HoldsAt(Broken(d), t) \vee \neg HoldsAt(PluggedIn(d), t) \tag{17.46}$$

We then reason using (17.43) and (17.46). Whenever we wish to add additional qualifications, we add cancellation axioms and recompute the circumscription of the abnormality predicates in the cancellation axioms.

17.5.4 State Constraints

Law-like relationships among properties are represented using *state constraint*, which are formulas containing atoms of the form $HoldsAt(\beta, \tau)$ and $\neg HoldsAt(\beta, \tau)$, where β is a fluent and τ is a timepoint.

For example, we may use two state constraints to represent that a counter has exactly one value at a time:

$$\exists v \, HoldsAt(Value(c, v), t) \tag{17.47}$$

$$HoldsAt(Value(c, v_1), t) \wedge HoldsAt(Value(c, v_2), t) \supset v_1 = v_2 \tag{17.48}$$

17.5.5 Concurrent Events

In the event calculus, events may occur concurrently. That is, we may have $Happens(e_1, t_1)$ and $Happens(e_2, t_2)$ where $e_1 \neq e_2$ and $t_1 = t_2$. We represent the effects of concurrent events using effect axioms whose conditions contain atoms of the form $Happens(\alpha, \tau)$ and $\neg Happens(\alpha, \tau)$, where α is an event and τ is a timepoint [66].

Example 17.12. Consider again the example of the counter. Suppose that the value of a counter C is 5 at timepoint 0:

$$HoldsAt(Value(C, 5), 0) \tag{17.49}$$

Further suppose that the counter is simultaneously incremented and reset at timepoint 1:

$$Happens(Increment(C), 1) \tag{17.50}$$
$$Happens(Reset(C), 1) \tag{17.51}$$

(17.50) leads us to conclude

$$HoldsAt(Value(C, 6), 2)$$

whereas (17.51) leads us to conclude

$$HoldsAt(Value(C, 0), 2)$$

These formulas contradict the state constraint (17.48).

In order to deal with this, we may specify exactly what happens when a counter is simultaneously incremented and reset. There are a number of possibilities.

One possibility is that nothing happens. We replace the effect axioms (17.38), (17.39), (17.40), and (17.41) with the following effect axioms:

$$\neg Happens(Reset(c), t) \wedge HoldsAt(Value(c, v), t) \supset$$
$$Initiates(Increment(c), Value(c, v + 1), t) \tag{17.52}$$

$$\neg Happens(Reset(c), t) \wedge HoldsAt(Value(c, v), t) \supset$$
$$Terminates(Increment(c), Value(c, v), t) \tag{17.53}$$

$$\neg Happens(Increment(c), t) \supset$$
$$Initiates(Reset(c), Value(c, 0), t) \tag{17.54}$$

$$\neg Happens(Increment(c), t) \wedge HoldsAt(Value(c, v), t) \wedge c \neq 0 \supset$$
$$Terminates(Reset(c), Value(c, v), t) \tag{17.55}$$

Another possibility is that the counter is neither incremented nor reset, but that the counter enters an error state. We use the effect axioms (17.52), (17.53), (17.54), and (17.55), and a further effect axiom that represents that, if a counter is simultaneously reset and incremented, it will be in an error state:

$Happens(Reset(c), t) \supset$

$Initiates(Increment(c), Error(c), t)$

We could also have written this as

$Happens(Increment(c), t) \supset$

$Initiates(Reset(c), Error(c), t)$

Another possibility is that, if a counter is simultaneously reset and incremented, the incrementing takes priority and the counter is incremented:

$HoldsAt(Value(c, v), t) \supset$

$Initiates(Increment(c), Value(c, v + 1), t)$

$HoldsAt(Value(c, v), t) \supset$

$Terminates(Increment(c), Value(c, v), t)$

$\neg Happens(Increment(c), t) \supset$

$Initiates(Reset(c), Value(c, 0), t)$

$\neg Happens(Increment(c), t) \wedge HoldsAt(Value(c, v), t) \wedge c \neq 0 \supset$

$Terminates(Reset(c), Value(c, v), t)$

Similarly, we could represent that, if a counter is simultaneously reset and incremented, the resetting takes priority and the counter is reset.

17.5.6 Triggered Events

Events that are triggered under certain circumstances are represented using *trigger axioms* [94, 96, 98], which are of the form

$\gamma \supset Happens(\alpha, \tau)$

where γ is a condition, α is an event, and τ is a timepoint.

Example 17.13. Consider a thermostat that turns on a heater when the temperature drops below A, and turns off the heater when the temperature rises above B. We represent this using two effect axioms and two trigger axioms:

$Initiates(TurnOn, On, t)$

$Terminates(TurnOff, On, t)$

$HoldsAt(Temperature(v), t) \wedge v < A \wedge \neg HoldsAt(On, t) \supset$

$\quad Happens(TurnOn, t)$

$HoldsAt(Temperature(v), t) \wedge v > B \wedge HoldsAt(On, t) \supset$

$\quad Happens(TurnOff, t)$

The conditions $\neg HoldsAt(On, t)$ and $HoldsAt(On, t)$ are required to prevent *TurnOn* and *TurnOff* from repeatedly triggering.

17.5.7 Continuous Change

Examples of continuous change include falling objects, expanding balloons, and containers being filled. Continuous change is represented using *trajectory axioms* [94, 95, 98], which are of the form

$$\gamma \supset Trajectory(\beta_1, \tau_1, \beta_2, \tau_2), \quad \text{or}$$

$$\gamma \supset AntiTrajectory(\beta_1, \tau_1, \beta_2, \tau_2)$$

where γ is a condition, β_1 and β_2 are fluents, and τ_1 and τ_2 are timepoints. *Trajectory* is used to determine the truth value of fluent β_2 after fluent β_1 is initiated, until β_1 is terminated. *AntiTrajectory* is used to determine the truth value of fluent β_2 after fluent β_1 is terminated, until β_1 is initiated.

Although DEC does not support continuous time, we may still use *Trajectory* and *AntiTrajectory* in DEC to represent gradual change. Gradual change is a discrete approximation to continuous change in which the value of a changing fluent is only represented for integer timepoints.

Example 17.14. Consider a falling object. We use effect axioms to represent that, if a person drops an object, then it will be falling, and if an object hits the ground, then it will no longer be falling:

$$Initiates(Drop(p, o), Falling(o), t) \tag{17.56}$$

$$Terminates(HitGround(o), Falling(o), t) \tag{17.57}$$

We represent that, if a person drops an object, then its height will be released from the commonsense law of inertia:

$$Releases(Drop(p, o), Height(o, h), t) \tag{17.58}$$

(For an object o, $Height(o, h)$ is released for all h.) We use a trajectory axiom to represent that the height of the object is given by an equation of free-fall motion, where G is the acceleration due to gravity (9.8 m/sec^2):

$$HoldsAt(Height(o, h), t_1) \supset$$

$$Trajectory(Falling(o), t_1, Height(o, h - \tfrac{1}{2}Gt_2^2), t_2) \tag{17.59}$$

We use a trigger axiom to represent that, when an object is falling and its height is 0, it hits the ground:

$$HoldsAt(Falling(o), t) \wedge HoldsAt(Height(o, 0), t) \supset$$

$$Happens(HitGround(o), t) \tag{17.60}$$

We specify that, if an object hits the ground and its height is h, then its height will be h and its height will no longer be released from the commonsense law of inertia:

$$HoldsAt(Height(o, h), t) \supset Initiates(HitGround(o), Height(o, h), t) \tag{17.61}$$

We specify that an object has a unique height:

$$HoldsAt(Height(o, h_1), t) \land HoldsAt(Height(o, h_2), t) \supset h_1 = h_2 \qquad (17.62)$$

At timepoint 0, Nathan drops an apple whose height is $G/2$:

$$\neg HoldsAt(Falling(Apple), 0) \qquad\qquad\qquad (17.63)$$

$$HoldsAt(Height(Apple, G/2), 0) \qquad\qquad\qquad (17.64)$$

$$Happens(Drop(Nathan, Apple), 0) \qquad\qquad\qquad (17.65)$$

We can then show that the apple will hit the ground at timepoint 1, and its height at timepoint 2 will be zero.

Proposition 17.22. *Let* $\Sigma = (17.56) \land (17.57) \land (17.58) \land (17.61)$, $\Delta = (17.60) \land$ (17.65), $\Omega = U[Drop, HitGround] \land U[Falling, Height]$, $\Gamma = (17.59) \land (17.62) \land$ $(17.63) \land (17.64)$. *Then we have*

$$CIRC[\Sigma; Initiates, Terminates, Releases] \land$$
$$\quad CIRC[\Delta; Happens] \land \Omega \land \Gamma \land EC$$
$$\quad \models HoldsAt(Height(Apple, 0), 1) \land$$
$$\quad Happens(HitGround(Apple), 1) \land$$
$$\quad HoldsAt(Height(Apple, 0), 2).$$

Proof. See the proofs of Propositions 7.2 and 7.3 of Mueller [74]. $\qquad\qquad\square$

17.5.8 Nondeterministic Effects

Nondeterministic effects of events can be represented in the event calculus using *determining fluents* [98], or fluents released from the commonsense law of inertia that are used within the conditions of effect axioms.

Example 17.15. Consider the example of rolling a die with six sides. We define a determining fluent $DieDF(d, s)$ which represents that die d will land on side s. This fluent is released from the commonsense law of inertia. In EC and DEC, we require the axiom

$$ReleasedAt(DieDF(d, s), t)$$

In BEC, a fluent that is never initiated or terminated and is neither *InitiallyN* nor *InitiallyP* is released from the commonsense law of inertia, so no further axioms are required to released *DieDF* from the commonsense law of inertia.

We use state constraints to represent that, at any timepoint, $DieDF(d, s)$ assigns one of the sides $\{1, \ldots, 6\}$ to a die:

$$\exists s\, HoldsAt(DieDF(d, s), t)$$

$$HoldsAt(DieDF(d, s_1), t) \land HoldsAt(DieDF(d, s_2), t) \supset s_1 = s_2$$

$$HoldsAt(DieDF(d, s), t) \supset s = 1 \lor s = 2 \lor s = 3 \lor s = 4 \lor s = 5 \lor s = 6$$

We use effect axioms to represent that, if a die is rolled at a timepoint, it will land on the side assigned to the die by *DieDF* at that timepoint:

$$HoldsAt(DieDF(d, s), t) \supset Initiates(Roll(d), Side(d, s), t)$$

$$HoldsAt(Side(d, s_1), t) \wedge HoldsAt(DieDF(d, s_2), t) \wedge s_1 \neq s_2 \supset$$
$$Terminates(Roll(d), Side(d, s_1), t)$$

Suppose a die *D* is rolled at timepoint 0:

$$Happens(Roll(D), 0)$$

What side of the die faces up at timepoint 1? Because *DieDF* is free to take on any of six values at timepoint 0, we get six classes of models: one in which $HoldsAt(DieDF(D, 1), 0)$ and therefore $HoldsAt(Side(D, 1), 1)$, one in which $HoldsAt(DieDF(D, 2), 0)$ and therefore $HoldsAt(Side(D, 2), 1)$, and so on.

17.5.9 Indirect Effects

Suppose that a person and a book are in the living room of a house. When the person walks out of the living room, the book will normally remain in the living room. But if the person is holding the book and walks out of the living room, then the book will no longer be in the living room. That is, an *indirect effect* or *ramification* of the person walking out of the living room is that the book the person is holding changes location. The *ramification problem* [19, 24, 101] is the problem of representing and reasoning about the indirect effects of events. Much research has been performed on the ramification problem [2, 19, 24, 29, 30, 35, 48, 50, 53–55, 85, 91, 101, 111]. Several methods can be used for solving this problem in the event calculus.

Example 17.16 (State constraints). Consider again the example of a light. We represent the direct effect of turning on a light using an effect axiom:

$$Initiates(TurnOn(l), On(l), t)$$

We may use a state constraint to represent the indirect effect of turning on the light, namely that the light is not off:

$$\neg HoldsAt(Off(l), t) \equiv HoldsAt(On(l), t)$$

The fluent *Off*(*l*) must be released from the commonsense law of inertia. In EC and DEC, we require the axiom

$$ReleasedAt(Off(l), t)$$

This method of representing indirect effects works if it is possible to divide fluents into primitive and derived fluents [39, 48, 50, 101]. Here *On* is primitive and *Off* is derived. The direct effects of events on primitive fluents are represented using effect axioms, whereas the indirect effects of events on derived fluents are represented using state constraints.

Example 17.17 (Release from inertia and state constraints). Suppose that we wish to represent the indirect effects of walking while holding an object, namely that the object moves along with the person holding it. We create a simple axiomatization of space. We start by representing the direct effects of walking. If a person walks from location l_1 to location l_2, then the person will be at l_2 and will no longer be at l_1:

$$Initiates(Walk(p, l_1, l_2), At(p, l_2), t)$$

$$l_1 \neq l_2 \supset Terminates(Walk(p, l_1, l_2), At(p, l_1), t)$$

We also represent the direct effects of picking up and setting down an object. If a person and an object are at the same location and the person picks up the object, then the person will be holding the object:

$$HoldsAt(At(p, l), t) \wedge HoldsAt(At(o, l), t) \supset$$
$$Initiates(PickUp(p, o), Holding(p, o), t)$$

If a person sets down an object, then the person will no longer be holding it:

$$Terminates(SetDown(p, o), Holding(p, o), t)$$

We then represent the indirect effects of walking with a *Releases* axiom, a state constraint, and an effect axiom. If a person and an object are at the same location and the person picks up the object, then the object's location will be released from the commonsense law of inertia:

$$HoldsAt(At(p, l), t) \wedge HoldsAt(At(o, l), t) \supset$$
$$Releases(PickUp(p, o), At(o, l'), t) \tag{17.66}$$

(For any given object o, $At(o, l')$ is released for all l'.) If a person who is holding an object is located at l, then the object is also located at l:

$$HoldsAt(Holding(p, o), t) \wedge HoldsAt(At(p, l), t) \supset HoldsAt(At(o, l), t) \tag{17.67}$$

If a person is holding an object, the person is located at l, and the person sets down the object, then the object will be located at l and the object's location will no longer be released from the commonsense law of inertia:

$$HoldsAt(Holding(p, o), t) \wedge HoldsAt(At(p, l), t) \supset$$
$$Initiates(SetDown(p, o), At(o, l), t) \tag{17.68}$$

Example 17.18 *(Effect axioms).* Another way of representing indirect effects is simply to add more effect axioms. We replace (17.66), (17.67), and (17.68) with effect axioms that state that, if a person who is holding an object walks from location l_1 to location l_2, then the object will be at location l_2 and will no longer be at l_1:

$$HoldsAt(Holding(p, o), t) \supset Initiates(Walk(p, l_1, l_2), At(o, l_2), t)$$

$$HoldsAt(Holding(p, o), t) \wedge l_1 \neq l_2 \supset$$
$$Terminates(Walk(p, l_1, l_2), At(o, l_1), t)$$

Example 17.19 (Effect constraints). Another way of representing indirect effects is to use *effect constraints* [98, 101], which are of the form

$$\gamma \wedge \pi_1(\alpha, \beta_1, \tau) \supset \pi_2(\alpha, \beta_2, \tau)$$

where γ is a condition, π_1 and π_2 are *Initiates* or *Terminates*, α is an event variable, β_1 and β_2 are fluents, and τ is a timepoint. We use effect constraints to represent that an object moves along with the person holding it:

$$HoldsAt(Holding(p, o), t) \wedge Initiates(e, At(p, l), t) \supset Initiates(e, At(o, l), t)$$

$$HoldsAt(Holding(p, o), t) \wedge Terminates(e, At(p, l), t) \supset$$

$$Terminates(e, At(o, l), t)$$

The event calculus can also be extended to deal with instantaneously interacting indirect effects [101].

The aforementioned methods for dealing with ramifications have various advantages and disadvantages. The method of state constraints is simple, but it requires a clear separation of fluents into those directly affected by events (primitive fluents) and those indirectly affected by events (derived fluents).

The method of releasing a fluent from the commonsense law of inertia allows a fluent to be primitive at some timepoints and derived at other timepoints. But then more bookkeeping is required. We must release the fluent from the commonsense law of inertia, and later make the fluent again subject to this law.

The method of using effect axioms is also simple, but it is less elaboration tolerant. In our example, if we add another way for a person to change location, such as running, we must also add axioms for the indirect effects of running:

$$HoldsAt(Holding(p, o), t) \supset Initiates(Run(p, l_1, l_2), At(o, l_2), t)$$

$$HoldsAt(Holding(p, o), t) \wedge l_1 \neq l_2 \supset Terminates(Run(p, l_1, l_2), At(o, l_1), t)$$

The method of using effect constraints is the most elaboration tolerant. But we cannot apply Proposition 17.19 in order to compute the circumscription of *Initiates* and *Terminates* in effect constraints.

17.5.10 Partially Ordered Events

We may represent partially ordered events using inequalities involving timepoints. For example, we may represent that John picked up a pen and a pad in some unspecified order, and then walked from the office to the living room as follows:

$$Happens(PickUp(John, Pen), T_1)$$

$$Happens(PickUp(John, Pad), T_2)$$

$$Happens(Walk(John, Office, LivingRoom), T_3)$$

$$T_1 < T_3$$

$$T_2 < T_3$$

Using the simple axiomatization of space of Example 17.17 in Section 17.5.9, we can conclude that John was holding both the pen and the pad at T_3, and that the pen and the pad are both in the living room after T_3. But we cannot conclude that John was holding the pad when he picked up the pen, or that John was holding the pen when he picked up the pad. There are three classes of models:

1. those in which John picks up the pen and then the pad ($T_1 < T_2$),

2. those in which John picks up the pad and then the pen ($T_2 < T_1$), and

3. those in which John picks up the pen and pad simultaneously ($T_1 = T_2$).

17.6   Action Language $\mathcal{E}$

Instead of using classical logic for reasoning about action and change, specialized action languages [22, 25, 26, 81] can be used. The $\mathcal{E}$ action language introduced by Antonis C. Kakas and Rob Miller [35, 36] is closely related to the event calculus.

A language of $\mathcal{E}$ is specified by a set of fluents, a set of events, a set of timepoints, and a partial order on the set of timepoints. An $\mathcal{E}$ domain description consists of a set of statements, which are defined as follows.

Definition 17.2. *If β is a fluent, then β and $\neg\beta$ are fluent literals.*

Definition 17.3. *If γ is a fluent literal and τ is a timepoint, then*

γ **holds-at** τ

is a statement.

Definition 17.4. *If α is an event and τ is a timepoint, then*

α **happens-at** τ

is a statement.

Definition 17.5. *If α is an event, β is a fluent, and Γ is a set of fluent literals, then*

α **initiates** β **when** Γ

and

α **terminates** β **when** Γ

are statements.

The notation α **initiates** β is an abbreviation for α **initiates** β **when** $\emptyset$, and the notation α **terminates** β is an abbreviation for α **terminates** β **when** $\emptyset$.

Example 17.20. We represent the example of turning on and off a light using the following $\mathcal{E}$ domain description:

> *TurnOn* **initiates** *On*
>
> *TurnOff* **terminates** *On*
>
> $\neg On$ **holds-at** 0
>
> *TurnOn* **happens-at** 2
>
> *TurnOff* **happens-at** 4

This domain description entails the following:

> $\neg On$ **holds-at** 1
>
> *On* **holds-at** 3
>
> $\neg On$ **holds-at** 5

Kakas and Miller [35, 36] specify the semantics of $\mathcal{E}$ using simple definitions of structures and models. Miller and Shanahan [66] show that $\mathcal{E}$ corresponds to the EC of Section 17.2.4 without the predicates *ReleasedAt*, *Releases*, *Trajectory*, and *AntiTrajectory*. They define conditions under which an $\mathcal{E}$ domain description matches an EC domain description and prove that, if an $\mathcal{E}$ domain description matches an EC domain description, the domain descriptions entail the same fluent truth values. Dimopoulos, Kakas, and Michael [13] give a translation of $\mathcal{E}$ domain descriptions into answer set programs [3, 20, 21] (see also Chapter 7).

An $\mathcal{E}$ domain description can be translated into an EC or DEC domain description as follows. We assume that the timepoints are the integers and the partial order is $\leqslant$. We divide the $\mathcal{E}$ domain description into sets of **holds-at**, **happens-at**, **initiates**, and **terminates** statements. We translate each **holds-at** statement

> $[\neg]\beta$ **holds-at** τ

into the formula

> $[\neg]HoldsAt(\beta, \tau)$

We translate the set of **happens-at** statements

> α_1 **happens-at** τ_1
>
> $\vdots$
>
> α_n **happens-at** τ_n

into the formula

> $Happens(e, t) \equiv (e = \alpha_1 \wedge t = \tau_1) \vee \cdots \vee (e = \alpha_n \wedge t = \tau_n)$

We translate the set of **initiates/terminates** statements

> α_1 **initiates/terminates** β_1 **when** $[\neg]\gamma_{1,1}, \ldots, [\neg]\gamma_{1,p}$
>
> $\vdots$
>
> α_n **initiates/terminates** β_n **when** $[\neg]\gamma_{n,1}, \ldots, [\neg]\gamma_{n,q}$

Table 17.5. Online resources for automated event calculus reasoning

Event calculus planner [103, 104]
http://www.iis.ee.ic.ac.uk/~mpsha/planners.html

Event calculus answer set programming [73]
http://www.signiform.com/csr/ecas/ (event calculus rules)
http://www.tcs.hut.fi/Software/smodels/ (solver)

Discrete Event Calculus Reasoner [70, 71]
http://decreasoner.sourceforge.net

TPTP problem library [110]
http://www.cs.miami.edu/~tptp/ (see CSR problem domain)

$\mathcal{E}$-RES [37, 38]
http://www2.cs.ucy.ac.cy/~pslogic/

into the formula

$$Initiates/Terminates(e, f, t) \equiv$$
$$(e = \alpha_1 \wedge f = \beta_1 \wedge [\neg]HoldsAt(\gamma_{1,1}, t) \wedge \cdots \wedge [\neg]HoldsAt(\gamma_{1,p}, t)) \vee \cdots \vee$$
$$(e = \alpha_n \wedge f = \beta_n \wedge [\neg]HoldsAt(\gamma_{n,1}, t) \wedge \cdots \wedge [\neg]HoldsAt(\gamma_{n,q}, t))$$

An extension to $\mathcal{E}$ [35] provides support for indirect effects. The statement

γ **whenever** Γ

where γ is a fluent literal and Γ is a set of fluent literals represents that (1) γ holds at every timepoint at which Γ holds, and (2) every event occurrence that brings about Γ also brings about γ. The language $\mathcal{E}$ has been further developed into the language $\mathcal{M}odular\text{-}\mathcal{E}$ [34], which addresses the ramification and qualification problems along with the issues of elaboration tolerance and modularity.

17.7 Automated Event Calculus Reasoning

A number of techniques can be used to perform automated reasoning in the event calculus, including logic programming in Prolog, answer set programming, satisfiability solving, and first-order logic automated theorem proving. Table 17.5 provides pointers to online resources for event calculus reasoning.

17.7.1 Prolog

The original event calculus was formulated as a logic program, and logic programming in Prolog can be used to perform event calculus reasoning. If Prolog is used, however, special care must be taken to avoid infinite loops [10, 45, 87, 93, 94, 98, 103]. Event calculus reasoning can be performed through abductive logic programming [6, 12, 17, 103].

17.7.2   Answer Set Programming

Answer set solvers [3] such as smodels [79] can be used to solve event calculus deduction problems [73]. Answer set solvers can also be used for reasoning in the $\mathcal{E}$ language [13].

17.7.3   Satisfiability (SAT) Solving

As a result of the growth in the capabilities of propositional satisfiability (SAT) solvers [92], several event calculus reasoning programs have been built that exploit off-the-shelf SAT solvers. The program of Shanahan and Witkowski [109] solves planning problems using SAT solvers. The Discrete Event Calculus Reasoner [70, 71] uses SAT solvers to perform various types of event calculus reasoning including deduction, abduction, postdiction, and model finding. The $\mathcal{E}$-RES program [37, 38] for solving $\mathcal{E}$ reasoning problems uses SAT solvers to generate classical models of state constraints.

The Discrete Event Calculus Reasoner uses several techniques to reduce the size of the SAT encoding of event calculus problems [70]:

1. The domains of arguments to predicates are restricted by using many-sorted logic.

2. Atom definitions are expanded [80, p. 361] in order to eliminate a large number of *Initiates*, *Terminates*, *Releases*, *Trajectory*, and *AntiTrajectory* ground atoms.

3. Triply quantified time is eliminated from most event calculus axioms by using DEC [70].

4. A compact conjunctive normal form is computed using the technique of renaming subformulas [27, 80, 83].

The Discrete Event Calculus Reasoner distribution includes a library of 99 event calculus reasoning problems that can be solved using the program.

17.7.4   First-Order Logic Automated Theorem Proving

Although first-order logic entailment is undecidable, first-order logic automated theorem proving (ATP) systems [86] have been applied successfully to event calculus deduction problems [77, 78]. But in some cases, the systems require human guidance in the form of lemmas. Event calculus problems are included in the TPTP problem library [110] along with the results of running ATP systems on them.

17.8   Applications of the Event Calculus

An important area of application of the event calculus is commonsense reasoning [74]. Event calculus formalizations have been developed for a number of commonsense domains, including beliefs [46], egg cracking [68, 99, 106], emotions [74], goals and plans [74], object identity [74], space [68, 96], and the zoo world [1, 33, 71]. The event calculus has also been used to model electronic circuits [101] and water tanks [64].

The event calculus can be applied to problems in high-level cognition including natural language understanding and vision. It has been used to build models of story events and states in space and time [69, 72, 76], represent the semantics of natural language tense and aspect [113], and represent event occurrences in stories [31]. The event calculus has been used to implement the higher-level vision component of an upper-torso humanoid robot [102, 107, 108].

Another application area of the event calculus is business systems. The event calculus has been used to track the state of contracts for performance monitoring [18], to model workflows [10, 114], and to improve the flexibility of applications that use electronic payment systems [115]. Other applications of the event calculus include database updates [41], planning [12, 17, 67, 97, 103, 109], and representing legislation [42].

Bibliography

[1] V. Akman, S.T. Erdogan, J. Lee, V. Lifschitz, and H. Turner. Representing the zoo world and the traffic world in the language of the causal calculator. *Artificial Intelligence*, 153:105–140, 2004.

[2] A.B. Baker. Nonmonotonic reasoning in the framework of situation calculus. *Artificial Intelligence*, 49(1–3):5–23, 1991.

[3] C. Baral. *Knowledge Representation, Reasoning and Declarative Problem Solving*. Cambridge University Press, Cambridge, 2003.

[4] B. Bennett and A.P. Galton. A unifying semantics for time and events. *Artificial Intelligence*, 153(1–2):13–48, 2004.

[5] D.G. Bobrow. Editor's preface. *Artificial Intelligence*, 13(1–2), 1980 (Special issue on Non-monotonic Reasoning).

[6] A. Bracciali and A.C. Kakas. Frame consistency: Computing with causal explanations. In J.P. Delgrande and T. Schaub, editors, *Proceedings of the Tenth International Workshop on Non-Monotonic Reasoning*, pages 79–87. Whistler, Canada, 2004.

[7] G. Brewka, J. Dix, and K. Konolige. *Nonmonotonic Reasoning: An Overview*. CSLI, Stanford, CA, 1997.

[8] F.M. Brown, editor. *The Frame Problem in Artificial Intelligence: Proceedings of the 1987 Workshop*, Los Altos, CA, 1987. Morgan Kaufmann.

[9] I. Cervesato, M. Franceschet, and A. Montanari. A guided tour through some extensions of the event calculus. *Computational Intelligence*, 16(2):307–347, 2000.

[10] N.K. Cicekli and Y. Yildirim. Formalizing workflows using the event calculus. In M.T. Ibrahim, J. Küng, and N. Revell, editors. *Database and Expert Systems Applications, Lecture Notes in Computer Science*, vol. 1873, pages 222–231. Springer, Berlin, 2000.

[11] K.L. Clark. Negation as failure. In H. Gallaire and J. Minker, editors. *Logic and Data Bases*, pages 293–322. Plenum, New York, 1978.

[12] M. Denecker, L. Missiaen, and M. Bruynooghe. Temporal reasoning with abductive event calculus. In B. Neumann, editor, *Proceedings of the Tenth European Conference on Artificial Intelligence*, pages 384–388, Chichester, UK, 1992. John Wiley.

[13] Y. Dimopoulos, A.C. Kakas, and L. Michael. Reasoning about actions and change in answer set programming. In V. Lifschitz and I. Niemelä, editors.

Proceedings of the Seventh International Conference on Logic Programming and Nonmonotonic Reasoning, Lecture Notes in Computer Science, vol. 2923, pages 61–73. Springer, Berlin, 2004.

[14] P. Doherty. Reasoning about action and change using occlusion. In A.G. Cohn, editor, *Proceedings of the Eleventh European Conference on Artificial Intelligence*, pages 401–405, Chichester, UK, 1994. John Wiley.

[15] P. Doherty and W. Łukaszewicz. Circumscribing features and fluents. In D.M. Gabbay and H.J. Ohlbach, editors. *Temporal Logic*, Lecture Notes in Computer Science, vol. 827, pages 82–100. Springer, Berlin, 1994.

[16] P. Doherty, W. Łukaszewicz, and A. Szałas. Computing circumscription revisited: A reduction algorithm. *Journal of Automated Reasoning*, 18(3):297–336, 1997.

[17] K. Eshghi. Abductive planning with event calculus. In R.A. Kowalski and K.A. Bowen, editors. *Logic Programming*: *Proceedings of the Fifth International Conference and Symposium*, vol. 1, pages 562–579. MIT Press, Cambridge, MA, 1988.

[18] A.D.H. Farrell, M.J. Sergot, M. Sallé, and C. Bartolini. Using the event calculus for tracking the normative state of contracts. *International Journal of Cooperative Information Systems*, 14(2–3):99–129, 2005.

[19] J.J. Finger. Exploiting constraints in design synthesis. PhD thesis, Department of Computer Science, Stanford University, Stanford, CA, 1987.

[20] M. Gelfond and V. Lifschitz. The stable model semantics for logic programming. In R.A. Kowalski and K.A. Bowen, editors. *Logic Programming: Proceedings of the Fifth International Conference and Symposium*, vol. 2, pages 1070–1080. MIT Press, Cambridge, MA, 1988.

[21] M. Gelfond and V. Lifschitz. Classical negation in logic programs and disjunctive databases. *New Generation Computing*, 9(3–4):365–386, 1991.

[22] M. Gelfond and V. Lifschitz. Representing action and change by logic programs. *Journal of Logic Programming*, 17(2–4):301–321, 1993.

[23] M.R. Genesereth and N.J. Nilsson. *Logical Foundations of Artificial Intelligence*. Morgan Kaufmann, Palo Alto, CA, 1987.

[24] M.L. Ginsberg and D.E. Smith. Reasoning about action I: A possible worlds approach. *Artificial Intelligence*, 35(2):165–195, 1988.

[25] E. Giunchiglia, J. Lee, V. Lifschitz, N.C. McCain, and H. Turner. Nonmonotonic causal theories. *Artificial Intelligence*, 153:49–104, 2004.

[26] E. Giunchiglia and V. Lifschitz. An action language based on causal explanation: Preliminary report. In *Proceedings of the Fifteenth National Conference on Artificial Intelligence and Tenth Conference on Innovative Applications of Artificial Intelligence*, pages 623–630, Menlo Park, CA, 1998. AAAI Press.

[27] E. Giunchiglia and R. Sebastiani. Applying the Davis–Putnam procedure to non-clausal formulas. In *Proceedings of the Sixth Congress of the Italian Association for Artificial Intelligence*, Bologna, 1999.

[28] B. Grosof. Default reasoning as circumscription: A translation of default logic into circumscription or maximizing defaults is minimizing predicates. In *Proceedings of the Non-Monotonic Reasoning Workshop*, pages 115–124, Menlo Park, CA, 1984. AAAI Press.

[29] J. Gustafsson and P. Doherty. Embracing occlusion in specifying the indirect effects of actions. In L.C. Aiello, J. Doyle, and S.C. Shapiro, editors, *Proceedings of the Fifth International Conference on Principles of Knowledge Representation and Reasoning*, pages 87–98, San Francisco, 1996. Morgan Kaufmann.

[30] A.R. Haas. The case for domain-specific frame axioms. In F.M. Brown, editor, *The Frame Problem in Artificial Intelligence: Proceedings of the 1987 Workshop*, pages 343–348, Los Altos, CA, 1987. Morgan Kaufmann.

[31] H. Halpin, J.D. Moore, and J. Robertson. Automatic analysis of plot for story rewriting. In D. Lin and D. Wu, editors, *Proceedings of the 2004 Conference on Empirical Methods in Natural Language Processing*, pages 127–133, Barcelona, Spain, 2004.

[32] S. Hanks and D.V. McDermott. Nonmonotonic logic and temporal projection. *Artificial Intelligence*, 33(3):379–412, 1987.

[33] A.C. Kakas and L. Michael. Modeling complex domains of actions and change. In S. Benferhat and E. Giunchiglia, editors, *Proceedings of the Ninth International Workshop on Non-Monotonic Reasoning*, pages 380–390, Toulouse, France, 2002.

[34] A.C. Kakas, L. Michael, and R. Miller. Modular-E: an elaboration tolerant approach to the ramification and qualification problems. In S. McIlraith, P. Peppas, and M. Thielscher, editors, *Seventh International Symposium on Logical Formalizations of Commonsense Reasoning*, Corfu, Greece, 2005.

[35] A.C. Kakas and R. Miller. Reasoning about actions, narratives and ramifications. *Linköping Electronic Articles in Computer and Information Science*, 2(012), 1997.

[36] A.C. Kakas and R. Miller. A simple declarative language for describing narratives with actions. *Journal of Logic Programming*, 31(1–3):157–200, 1997.

[37] A.C. Kakas, R. Miller, and F. Toni. An argumentation framework for reasoning about actions and change. In M. Gelfond, N. Leone, and G. Pfeifer, editors. *Proceedings of the Fifth International Conference on Logic Programming and Nonmonotonic Reasoning*, Lecture Notes in Computer Science, vol. 1730, pages 78–91. Springer, Berlin, 1999.

[38] A.C. Kakas, R. Miller, and F. Toni. E-RES—A system for reasoning about actions, events and observations. In C. Baral and M. Truszczynski, editors, *Proceedings of the Eighth International Workshop on Non-Monotonic Reasoning*, Breckenridge, CO, 2000.

[39] R.A. Kowalski. *Logic for Problem Solving*. North-Holland, New York, 1979.

[40] R.A. Kowalski. Database updates in the event calculus. Technical Report DOC 86/12, London: Imperial College of Science, Technology, and Medicine, 1986.

[41] R.A. Kowalski. Database updates in the event calculus. *Journal of Logic Programming*, 12:121–146, 1992.

[42] R.A. Kowalski. Legislation as logic programs. In G. Comyn, N.E. Fuchs, and M. Ratcliffe, editors. *Logic Programming in Action, Second International Logic Programming Summer School*, Lecture Notes in Computer Science, vol. 636, pages 203–230. Springer, Berlin, 1992.

[43] R.A. Kowalski and F. Sadri. The situation calculus and event calculus compared. In M. Bruynooghe, editor. *Logic Programming: The 1994 International Symposium*, pages 539–553. MIT Press, Cambridge, MA, 1994.

[44] R.A. Kowalski and F. Sadri. Reconciling the event calculus with the situation calculus. *Journal of Logic Programming*, 31(1–3):39–58, 1997.

[45] R.A. Kowalski and M.J. Sergot. A logic-based calculus of events. *New Generation Computing*, 4(1):67–95, 1986.

[46] F. Lévy and J.J. Quantz. Representing beliefs in a situated event calculus. In H. Prade, editor, *Proceedings of the Thirteenth European Conference on Artificial Intelligence*, pages 547–551, Chichester, UK, 1998. John Wiley.

[47] V. Lifschitz. Computing circumscription. In *Proceedings of the Ninth International Joint Conference on Artificial Intelligence*, pages 121–127, Los Altos, CA, 1985. Morgan Kaufmann.

[48] V. Lifschitz. Formal theories of action. In F.M. Brown, editor, *The Frame Problem in Artificial Intelligence: Proceedings of the 1987 Workshop*, pages 35–57, Los Altos, CA, 1987. Morgan Kaufmann.

[49] V. Lifschitz. Pointwise circumscription. In M.L. Ginsberg, editor. *Readings in Nonmonotonic Reasoning*, pages 179–193. Morgan Kaufmann, Los Altos, CA, 1987.

[50] V. Lifschitz. Frames in the space of situations. *Artificial Intelligence*, 46(3):365–376, 1990.

[51] V. Lifschitz. Circumscription. In D.M. Gabbay, C.J. Hogger, and J.A. Robinson, editors. *Nonmonotonic Reasoning and Uncertain Reasoning, Handbook of Logic in Artificial Intelligence and Logic Programming*, vol. 3, pages 298–352. Oxford University Press, Oxford, 1994.

[52] V. Lifschitz. Book review: M. Shanahan, Solving the frame problem. *Artificial Intelligence*, 123(1–2):265–268, 2000.

[53] F. Lin. Embracing causality in specifying the indirect effects of actions. In *Proceedings of the Fourteenth International Joint Conference on Artificial Intelligence*, pages 1985–1993, San Mateo, CA, 1995. Morgan Kaufmann.

[54] F. Lin and R. Reiter. State constraints revisited. *Journal of Logic and Computation*, 4(5):655–678, 1994.

[55] N.C. McCain and H. Turner. A causal theory of ramifications and qualifications. In *Proceedings of the Fourteenth International Joint Conference on Artificial Intelligence*, pages 1978–1984, San Mateo, CA, 1995. Morgan Kaufmann.

[56] J. McCarthy. Epistemological problems of artificial intelligence. In R. Reddy, editor, *Proceedings of the Fifth International Joint Conference on Artificial Intelligence*, pages 1038–1044, Los Altos, CA, 1977. William Kaufmann.

[57] J. McCarthy. Circumscription—a form of non-monotonic reasoning. *Artificial Intelligence*, 13(1–2):27–39, 1980.

[58] J. McCarthy. Applications of circumscription to formalizing common sense knowledge. In *Proceedings of the Non-Monotonic Reasoning Workshop*, pages 295–324, Menlo Park, CA, 1984. AAAI Press.

[59] J. McCarthy. Applications of circumscription to formalizing common-sense knowledge. *Artificial Intelligence*, 28:89–116, 1986.

[60] J. McCarthy. Generality in artificial intelligence. *Communications of the ACM*, 30(12):1030–1035, 1987.

[61] J. McCarthy. Elaboration tolerance. In R. Miller and M. Shanahan, editors, *Fourth Symposium on Logical Formalizations of Commonsense Reasoning*, London, 1998. Queen Mary and Westfield College.

[62] J. McCarthy and P.J. Hayes. Some philosophical problems from the standpoint of artificial intelligence. In B. Meltzer and D. Michie, editors. *Machine Intelligence*, vol. 4, pages 463–502. Edinburgh University Press, Edinburgh, Scotland, 1969.

[63] R. Miller and M. Shanahan. Narratives in the situation calculus. *Journal of Logic and Computation*, 4(5):513–530, 1994.

[64] R. Miller and M. Shanahan. Reasoning about discontinuities in the event calculus. In L.C. Aiello, J. Doyle, and S.C. Shapiro, editors, *Proceedings of the Fifth International Conference on Principles of Knowledge Representation and Reasoning*, pages 63–74, San Francisco, 1996. Morgan Kaufmann.

[65] R. Miller and M. Shanahan. The event calculus in classical logic—Alternative axiomatisations. *Linköping Electronic Articles in Computer and Information Science*, 4(016), 1999.

[66] R. Miller and M. Shanahan. Some alternative formulations of the event calculus. In A.C. Kakas and F. Sadri, editors. *Computational Logic: Logic Programming and Beyond: Essays in Honour of Robert A. Kowalski, Part II, Lecture Notes in Computer Science*, vol. 2408, pages 452–490. Springer, Berlin, 2002.

[67] L. Missiaen, M. Bruynooghe, and M. Denecker. Chica, an abductive planning system based on event calculus. *Journal of Logic and Computation*, 5(5):579–602, 1995.

[68] L. Morgenstern. Mid-sized axiomatizations of commonsense problems: A case study in egg cracking. *Studia Logica*, 67:333–384, 2001.

[69] E.T. Mueller. Story understanding through multi-representation model construction. In G. Hirst and S. Nirenburg, editors, *Text Meaning: Proceedings of the HLT-NAACL 2003 Workshop*, pages 46–53. Association for Computational Linguistics, East Stroudsburg, PA, 2003.

[70] E.T. Mueller. Event calculus reasoning through satisfiability. *Journal of Logic and Computation*, 14(5):703–730, 2004.

[71] E.T. Mueller. A tool for satisfiability-based commonsense reasoning in the event calculus. In V. Barr and Z. Markov, editors, *Proceedings of the Seventeenth International Florida Artificial Intelligence Research Society Conference*, pages 147–152, Menlo Park, CA, 2004. AAAI Press.

[72] E.T. Mueller. Understanding script-based stories using commonsense reasoning. *Cognitive Systems Research*, 5(4):307–340, 2004.

[73] E.T. Mueller. Event calculus answer set programming. http://www.signiform.com/csr/ecas/, 2005.

[74] E.T. Mueller. *Commonsense Reasoning*. Morgan Kaufmann, San Francisco, 2006.

[75] E.T. Mueller. Event calculus and temporal action logics compared. *Artificial Intelligence*, 170(11):1017–1029, 2006.

[76] E.T. Mueller. Modelling space and time in narratives about restaurants. *Literary and Linguistic Computing*, 22(1):67–84, 2007.

[77] E.T. Mueller and G. Sutcliffe. Discrete event calculus deduction using first-order automated theorem proving. In B. Konev and S. Schulz, editors. *Proceedings of the Fifth International Workshop on the Implementation of Logics,* number ULCS-05-003, pages 43–56. Department of Computer Science, University of Liverpool, Liverpool, UK, 2005.

[78] E.T. Mueller and G. Sutcliffe. Reasoning in the event calculus using first-order automated theorem proving. In I. Russell and Z. Markov, editors. *Proceedings of the Eighteenth International Florida Artificial Intelligence Research Society Conference*, pages 840–841. AAAI Press, Menlo Park, CA, 2005.

[79] I. Niemelä and P. Simons. Smodels—an implementation of the stable model and well-founded semantics for normal logic programs. In J. Dix, U. Furbach, and A. Nerode, editors. *Proceedings of the Fourth International Conference on Logic Programming and Nonmonotonic Reasoning, Lecture Notes in Computer Science*, vol. 1265, pages 420–429. Springer, Berlin, 1997.

[80] A. Nonnengart and C. Weidenbach. Computing small clause normal forms. In J.A. Robinson and A. Voronkov, editors. *Handbook of Automated Reasoning*, vol. 1, pages 335–367. Elsevier and MIT Press, Amsterdam and Cambridge, MA, 2001.

[81] E.P.D. Pednault. ADL: Exploring the middle ground between STRIPS and the situation calculus. In R.J. Brachman, H.J. Levesque, and R. Reiter, editors, *Proceedings of the First International Conference on Principles of Knowledge Representation and Reasoning*, pages 324–332, San Mateo, CA, 1989. Morgan Kaufmann.

[82] J.A. Pinto and R. Reiter. Temporal reasoning in logic programming: A case for the situation calculus. In D.S. Warren, editor. *Logic Programming: Proceedings of the Tenth International Conference*, pages 203–221. MIT Press, Cambridge, MA, 1993.

[83] D.A. Plaisted and S. Greenbaum. A structure-preserving clause form translation. *Journal of Symbolic Computation*, 2:293–304, 1986.

[84] R. Reiter. Circumscription implies predicate completion (sometimes). In D.L. Waltz, editors, *Proceedings of the National Conference on Artificial Intelligence*, pages 418–420, Menlo Park, CA, 1982. AAAI Press.

[85] R. Reiter. *Knowledge in Action: Logical Foundations for Specifying and Implementing Dynamical Systems*. MIT Press, Cambridge, MA, 2001.

[86] J.A. Robinson and A. Voronkov. *Handbook of Automated Reasoning, vols. 1 and 2*. Elsevier and MIT Press, Amsterdam and Cambridge, MA, 2001.

[87] F. Sadri. Three recent approaches to temporal reasoning. In A.P. Galton, editor. *Temporal Logics and their Applications*, pages 121–168. Academic Press, London, 1987.

[88] F. Sadri and R.A. Kowalski. Variants of the event calculus. In L. Sterling, editor, *Logic Programming: The Twelfth International Conference*, pages 67–81, Cambridge, MA, 1995. MIT Press.

[89] E. Sandewall. Filter preferential entailment for the logic of action in almost continuous worlds. In N.S. Sridharan, editor, *Proceedings of the Eleventh International Joint Conference on Artificial Intelligence*, pages 894–899, San Mateo, CA, 1989. Morgan Kaufmann.

[90] E. Sandewall. *Features and Fluents: The Representation of Knowledge about Dynamical Systems*, vol. I. Oxford University Press, Oxford, 1994.

[91] L.K. Schubert. Monotonic solution of the frame problem in the situation calculus: An efficient method for worlds with fully specified actions. In H.E. Kyburg Jr., R.P. Loui, and G.N. Carlson, editors. *Knowledge Representation and Defeasible Reasoning*, pages 23–67. Kluwer, Dordrecht, 1990.

[92] B. Selman, H.A. Kautz, and D.A. McAllester. Ten challenges in propositional reasoning and search. In *Proceedings of the Fifteenth International Joint Conference on Artificial Intelligence*, pages 50–54, San Mateo, CA, 1997. Morgan Kaufmann.

[93] M. Shanahan. Prediction is deduction but explanation is abduction. In N.S. Sridharan, editor, *Proceedings of the Eleventh International Joint Conference on Artificial Intelligence*, pages 1055–1060, San Mateo, CA, 1989. Morgan Kaufmann.

[94] M. Shanahan. Representing continuous change in the event calculus. In L.C. Aiello, editor, *Proceedings of the Ninth European Conference on Artificial Intelligence*, pages 598–603, London, 1990. Pitman.

[95] M. Shanahan. A circumscriptive calculus of events. *Artificial Intelligence*, 77:249–284, 1995.

[96] M. Shanahan. Robotics and the common sense informatic situation. In W. Wahlster, editor, *Proceedings of the Twelfth European Conference on Artificial Intelligence*, pages 684–688, Chichester, UK, 1996. John Wiley.

[97] M. Shanahan. Event calculus planning revisited. In S. Steel and R. Alami, editors. *Recent Advances in AI Planning, Lecture Notes in Computer Science*, vol. 1348, pages 390–402. Springer, Berlin, 1997.

[98] M. Shanahan. *Solving the Frame Problem*. MIT Press, Cambridge, MA, 1997.

[99] M. Shanahan. A logical formalisation of Ernie Davis's egg cracking problem. In R. Miller and M. Shanahan, editors, *Fourth Symposium on Logical Formalizations of Commonsense Reasoning*, London, 1998. Queen Mary and Westfield College.

[100] M. Shanahan. The event calculus explained. In M.J. Wooldridge and M.M. Veloso, editors. *Artificial Intelligence Today: Recent Trends and Developments, Lecture Notes in Computer Science*, vol. 1600, pages 409–430. Springer, Berlin, 1999.

[101] M. Shanahan. The ramification problem in the event calculus. In *Proceedings of the Sixteenth International Joint Conference on Artificial Intelligence*, pages 140–146, San Mateo, CA, 1999. Morgan Kaufmann.

[102] M. Shanahan. What sort of computation mediates best between perception and action? In H.J. Levesque and F. Pirri, editors. *Logical Foundations for Cognitive Agents: Contributions in Honor of Ray Reiter*, pages 352–369. Springer, Berlin, 1999.

[103] M. Shanahan. An abductive event calculus planner. *Journal of Logic Programming*, 44(1–3):207–240, 2000.

[104] M. Shanahan. Abductive event calculus planners [Computer software], 2000.

[105] M. Shanahan. The frame problem. In L. Nadel, editor. *Encyclopedia of Cognitive Science*, vol. 2, pages 144–150. Nature Publishing Group, London, 2002.

[106] M. Shanahan. An attempt to formalise a non-trivial benchmark problem in common sense reasoning. *Artificial Intelligence*, 153:141–165, 2004.

[107] M. Shanahan. Perception as abduction: Turning sensor data into meaningful representation. *Cognitive Science*, 29:103–134, 2005.

[108] M. Shanahan and D.A. Randell. A logic-based formulation of active visual perception. In D. Dubois, C.A. Welty, and M.-A. Williams, editors, *Proceedings of the Ninth International Conference on Principles of Knowledge Representation and Reasoning*, pages 64–72, Menlo Park, CA, 2004. AAAI Press.

[109] M. Shanahan and M. Witkowski. Event calculus planning through satisfiability. *Journal of Logic and Computation*, 14(5):731–745, 2004.

[110] G. Sutcliffe and C.B. Suttner. The TPTP problem library for automated theorem proving, 2005.

[111] M. Thielscher. Ramification and causality. *Artificial Intelligence*, 89:317–364, 1997.

[112] K. Van Belleghem, M. Denecker, and D. De Schreye. On the relation between situation calculus and event calculus. *Journal of Logic Programming*, 31(1–3):3–37, 1997.

[113] M. van Lambalgen and F. Hamm. *The Proper Treatment of Events*. Blackwell, Malden, MA, 2005.

[114] J. Wilk. Dynamic workflow pulling the strings. Distinguished Project (MEng). Department of Computing, Imperial College London, London, 2004.

[115] P. Yolum and M.P. Singh. Reasoning about commitments in the event calculus: An approach for specifying and executing protocols. *Annals of Mathematics and Artificial Intelligence*, 42(1–3):227–253, 2004.

Handbook of Knowledge Representation
Edited by F. van Harmelen, V. Lifschitz and B. Porter
© 2008 Elsevier B.V. All rights reserved
DOI: 10.1016/S1574-6526(07)03018-0

Chapter 18

Temporal Action Logics

Patrick Doherty and Jonas Kvarnström

18.1 Introduction

The study of frameworks and formalisms for reasoning about action and change [67, 58, 61, 65, 70, 3, 57] has been central to the knowledge representation field almost from the inception of Artificial Intelligence as a general field of research [52, 56].

The phrase "Temporal Action Logics" represents a class of logics for reasoning about action and change that evolved from Sandewall's book on *Features and Fluents* [61] and owes much to this ambitious project. There are essentially three major parts to Sandewall's work. He first developed a narrative-based logical framework for specifying agent behavior in terms of action scenarios. The logical framework is state-based and uses explicit time structures. He then developed a formal framework for assessing the correctness (soundness and completeness) of logics for reasoning about action and change relative to a set of well-defined intended conclusions, where reasoning problems were classified according to their ontological or epistemological characteristics. Finally, he proposed a number of logics defined semantically in terms of definitions of preferential entailment[1] and assessed their correctness using his assessment framework.

Several of these logics were intended to correspond directly to existing logics of action and change proposed by others at the time, while the rest were new and were intended to characterize broad classes of reasoning problems which subsumed some of the existing approaches. Each of these definitions of preferential entailment were then analyzed using the assessment framework, giving upper and lower bounds in terms of the classes of reasoning problems for which they produced exactly the intended conclusions. Much insight was gained both in terms of advantages and limitations of previously proposed logics of action and change and in how one might go about proposing new logics of action and change in a principled manner with formal assessments included.

---

[1] Preferential entailment reduces the set of classical models of a theory by only retaining those models that are minimal according to a given preference relation, a strict partial order over logical interpretations [66].

The starting point for Temporal Action Logics was one of the definitions of preferential entailment in Sandewall's book called PMON (Pointwise Minimization of Occlusion with Nochange premises). It was one of the few preferential entailment methods that were assessed correct for the $\mathcal{K}$–**IA** class of action scenario descriptions, where $\mathcal{K}$ is an epistemological characteristic stating approximately that explicit, correct and accurate knowledge is provided (with no requirements on complete knowledge in the initial state and no restrictions on knowledge about other states), and **IA** is an ontological characteristic stating approximately that discrete integer time is used together with plain inertia (without ramification constraints, delayed effects, or other complicating factors).

Thus, PMON solved the frame problem relative to an explicit statement of assumptions ($\mathcal{K}$–**IA**) under which it could be assessed correct. The nature of the definition of preferential entailment was somewhat related to explanation closure [64, 19], although a partitioning of action scenario theories was used where only parts of the theory were minimized and other parts used as filters on the preferred model set for the theory. Though ramifications and qualifications to actions were not allowed in $\mathcal{K}$–**IA**, the class is in fact quite broad, permitting the use of conditional effects, non-deterministic effects, incomplete specification of states and the timing of actions, actions with duration and specification of dynamics within action durations.

18.1.1 PMON and TAL

While the original PMON was characterized semantically in terms of a preferential entailment method, Doherty later developed an equivalent syntactic characterization in classical 2nd-order logic (also called PMON), using a circumscription axiom to formalize the PMON definition of preferential entailment [7, 14]. In these papers, he also showed that the 2nd-order circumscription axiom was equivalent to a 1st-order pointwise circumscription axiom, enabling the use of standard first-order theorem proving techniques to reason about PMON action narratives. In extended versions of PMON which led to TAL, it has also been shown that quantifier elimination techniques or predicate completion techniques (Definition 7.3.6 in Chapter 7 of this Handbook) can be used to reduce TAL circumscribed theories to logically equivalent 1st-order theories under certain assumptions.

Doherty's PMON logic used two languages for representing and reasoning about narratives. The surface language $\mathcal{L}$(SD), Language for Scenario Descriptions, provided a convenient high-level notation for describing narratives, and could be described as a set of macros easily translated into a base language $\mathcal{L}$(FL), which was initially a many-sorted first-order language and was later altered to be an order-sorted[2] first-order language. The $\mathcal{L}$(SD) language was later renamed to $\mathcal{L}$(ND), Language for Narrative Descriptions.

The logic was further extended and generalized in several steps in order to deal with such issues as the ramification and qualification problems, use of concurrent actions, use of structured object-oriented action theories, and use as a specification formalism for TALplanner. Each extension generally implied adding new macros to $\mathcal{L}$(ND), adding additional predicates to $\mathcal{L}$(FL), extending the translation definition to

---

[2]Essentially, an order-sorted language allows the use of sub-sorts; for example, CAR and BICYCLE may be sub-sorts of the VEHICLE sort.

$\mathcal{L}$(FL) and providing slight modifications to the circumscription policies used. It is important to observe that all extensions proposed have been made in a manner which preserves the property of reducibility of the 2nd-order circumscription theory to a 1st-order theory. This is essential for practical reasons.

A number of the main extensions to PMON which led to the TAL family of logics include:

- **PMON-RC** [25], which provides a solution to the ramification problem for a broad, but as yet unassessed class of action scenarios. The main idea is the addition of a new statement type for causal constraints, where changes taking place in the world can automatically trigger new changes at the same time or at a specified delay from the original change. The solution is very fine-grained in the sense that one can easily encode dependencies between individual objects in the domain, work with both boolean and non-boolean fluents and represent both Markovian and non-Markovian dependencies [21]. PMON-RC also correctly handles chains of side effects.

- **TAL 1.0 (PMON^{+})** [8], which is an extended version of the original PMON logic incorporating the changes made in PMON-RC together with other useful extensions. This logic was originally called PMON^{+}, but was later renamed TAL 1.0 and provided the first stable kernel for the TAL family of logics.

- **TAL-C** [35], which uses fluent dependency constraints (an extended form of causal constraints) as a basis for representing concurrent actions. A number of phenomena related to action concurrency such as interference between one action's effects and another's execution, bounds on concurrency, and conflicting, synergistic, and cumulative effects of concurrent actions are supported.

- **TAL 2.0** [10], which provides a basic stable kernel of TAL. It is essentially TAL-C with some useful extensions and includes a tutorial on TAL and how it is used.

- **TAL-Q** [11, 42], which introduces the idea of combining an encoding of default values for features using persistence statements together with dependency constraints for representing qualifications to actions.

TAL 2.0 (TAL-C), extended with additions from TAL-Q, has been used as the basis for much of the recent work with Temporal Action Logics and will be described in some detail in this chapter. In the remainder of the chapter, we will use "TAL" as a term to denote the latest stable kernel of this family of logics.

18.1.2 Previous Work

There has been a great deal of previous work in the development of the material described in this chapter. We briefly summarize this work chronologically.

The root node from which TAL originated is the Features and Fluents (F&F) monograph [61]. Later developments with F&F are summarized in Sandewall [63]. Doherty [7] provides a syntactic characterization of PMON using pointwise circumscription and shows how a particular class of narratives can be characterized as first-order theories. Doherty [6] contains a detailed account of PMON circumscription theories and provides additional characterizations of PMON in terms of predicate circumscription and predicate completion, where syntactic transformations are defined on narratives to provide a definition of the *Occlude* predicate. Doherty and Łukaszewicz [14] provide syntactic characterizations of 7 out of the 9 definitions of preferential entailment considered in F&F, using different forms of circumscription. Doherty and Peppas [18] incorporate the use of primary and secondary fluents in PMON to model a subclass of indirect effects of actions. A framework is also introduced for comparing linear time logics such as PMON with branching time logics such as the situation calculus. Karlsson [29] considers how to formally characterize different modal truth criteria used in planning algorithms such as TWEAK and NONLIN using PMON. Karlsson [31, 30] extends this work. Doherty [8] provides a detailed description of TAL 1.0 used as a basis for early implementations of TAL. Doherty, Łukaszewicz and Szałas [16, 17] develop a quantifier elimination algorithm which constructively generates logically equivalent 1st-order formulas for a certain class of 2nd-order formulas. The intent with the work was to study the possibility of reducing other logics for action and change characterized in terms of circumscription theories, thus making them amenable to classical theorem proving techniques. Gustafsson and Doherty [25] extend TAL to deal with ramifications of actions by introducing causal constraints, which have later been subsumed by the use of dependency constraints in TAL-C. In addition, they show how to represent delayed effects of actions in TAL. Doherty, Łukaszewicz and Szałas [19] consider the relation between the automatic generation of a definition for the *Occlude* predicate using circumscription and quantifier elimination, with the manual generation of Explanation Closure axioms considered in Schubert [64]. Karlsson [32] investigates a number of weaknesses in situation calculus and provides an alternative semantics grounded in intuitions derived from work with TAL. Bjäreland and Karlsson [5] investigates the use of regression operators as a means of doing inference in TAL related formalisms. Bjäreland [4] provides a detailed presentation of the approach in [5] and other approaches using tractable temporal logics. Karlsson, Gustafsson and Doherty [9, 36] examine the use of delayed effects of actions and various problems of interference which arise with their introduction. Doherty and Kvarnström [11] present an initial solution to simple forms of qualification to actions. Kvarnström and Doherty [42] provide a more detailed solution to the qualification problem described in this chapter. Karlsson and Gustafsson [35] consider the problem of modeling concurrent actions in TAL and the variety of interactions that may ensue between actions executing concurrently. Gustafsson [23] provides a detailed study of extensions to TAL involving dependency constraints, concurrency, and delayed effects of actions. Karlsson [33] studies the possibility of introducing narratives as 1st-class objects in the object language of a logic whose semantics is related to that of TAL. Doherty, Łukaszewicz and Madalińska-Bugaj [15] study the relation between TAL and belief update. Karlsson [34] provides detailed accounts of narratives as 1st-class citizens in action logic, concurrent actions and additional extensions to TAL. Gustafsson [24] provides a detailed description of many of the extensions to TAL up to 2001. Gustafsson and Kvarnström [26, 27] provide a novel means of structuring large TAL narratives based on the use of intuitions from object-oriented programming.

Doherty and Kvarnström [12] present a new forward chaining planner which uses TAL as a semantic framework for its development. In Kvarnström and Doherty [43], an early detailed account of TALplanner is provided. Kvarnström, Doherty and

Haslum [44] provide an extension to TALplanner which integrates concurrent actions and resources. Doherty and Kvarnström [13] provide a concise overview of TALplanner. Kvarnström and Magnusson [45] provide a description of some of the control rules used in TALplanner in the Third International Planning Competition (IPC-2002), and the reasoning underlying these rules. Kvarnström [40] discusses application of domain analysis techniques to control rules in TALplanner. Kvarnström [41] provides the most recent and most detailed description of TALplanner.

The thesis work of both Karlsson [34] and Gustafsson [24] provide excellent references to much of the later extensions to TAL. The thesis work of Kvarnström [41] provides an excellent description of TALplanner. A software system VITAL [39] for reasoning about action and change using TAL is available for download and on-line use.

18.1.3 Chapter Structure

In Section 18.2, the main concepts and ideas used in the development of TAL are presented. In Section 18.3, action narratives used in TAL are defined and a complex scenario, the Russian Airplane Hijack (RAH) scenario, is presented. This will be used throughout the chapter to explain the different features provided by TAL. Section 18.4 considers the relation between the high level macro language $\mathcal{L}(ND)$ used to specify action narratives and the base logical language $\mathcal{L}(FL)$ which it is translated to. In Section 18.5, we provide a formal description of the language $\mathcal{L}(ND)$, and in Section 18.6, we provide a formal definition of the base logical language $\mathcal{L}(FL)$. In Section 18.7, the circumscription policy used to specify the definition of preferential entailment used in TAL is presented. In addition, we show how the resulting 2nd-order circumscription theories which characterize action narratives can be reduced to logically equivalent 1st-order theories under certain conditions. Section 18.8 proposes a solution to the ramification problem which is used in TAL. The RAH scenario is modified to incorporate this solution. Section 18.9 proposes a solution to the qualification problem which is used in TAL. The RAH scenario is again modified to incorporate this solution. Section 18.10 provides further examples of the expressivity of TAL actions. Section 18.11 presents an extension to TAL which models the use of concurrent actions where complex types of interaction between such actions may occur. Section 18.12 presents an application of TAL to planning where it is shown how TAL can be used as a semantic framework in the development and implementation of TALplanner, an award winning automated planner. In Section 18.13, we conclude.

18.2 Basic Concepts

When using TAL, we assume there is an *agent* interested in reasoning about a specific *world*. This world might be formally defined, or it might be the "real world", in which case the agent can only reason about a formally defined abstraction of the real world. In either case, it is assumed that the world is dynamic, in the sense that the various properties or *features* of the world can change over time. Conceptually, any feature has a fluent function associated with it representing the stream of values associated with the feature at each state or temporal entity used in the formalism.

The TAL framework also permits the use of multiple *value domains*, which can be used for modeling different types of *objects* that might occur in the world which is being modeled. For example, the well-known blocks world contains blocks that can be stacked on top of each other. The blocks world can then be modeled using a value domain for blocks, containing values such as A, B and C, together with parameterized boolean-valued features representing relations such as on($block_1$, $block_2$), which holds iff $block_1$ is on top of $block_2$, and clear($block$), which holds iff there is no block on top of $block$. Of course, values can also be used to represent properties of objects rather than the objects themselves. For example, if the color of each block should be modeled, then this could be done using a value domain for colors containing values such as red, green and blue, together with a color-valued (non-boolean) feature color($block$). In summary, instantiated parameterized features take specific values (boolean or non-boolean) at specific times. In this manner, both relations and properties are capable of being represented.

Time itself can be viewed differently depending on the nature of the world being reasoned about and the reasoning abilities of the agent. TAL offers a modular means of choosing the temporal structure to be used. Currently, TAL uses linear time structures, as opposed to branching time structures. Research within the TAL framework has been focused on discrete non-negative integer time structures, and such a structure will be used throughout this chapter, though most concepts should carry over directly or with little modification to a real-valued time structure using ideas from [59, 60, 65].

The development of the world over a (possibly infinite) period of discrete time can be viewed in two different ways. Fig. 18.1 shows what would happen in a simple blocks world scenario where block A is initially on top of B, which is on the table, and where one unstacks A from B, places it on the table, picks up B, and finally stacks this block on top of A. The information about this scenario can be viewed as a sequence of *states*, where each state provides a value to all features (or "state variables") for a single common timepoint, or as a set of *fluents*, where each fluent is a function of time which specifies the development of a single feature. We sometimes use the terms "feature" and "fluent" interchangeably to refer to either a specific property of the world or the function specifying its value over time.

Consequently, a logical model in TAL is a sequence of states indexed by time, where each state contains a value for each feature in the vocabulary at the timepoint

	time 0	time 1	time 2	time 3	time 4	
on(A,A)	false	false	false	false	false	
on(A,B)	true	false	false	false	false	
on(B,A)	false	false	false	false	true	**fluent**
on(B,B)	false	false	false	false	false	
ontable(A)	false	false	true	true	true	
ontable(B)	true	true	true	false	false	
clear(A)	true	false	true	true	false	
feature clear(B)	false	true	true	false	true	
handempty	true	false	true	false	true	
			state			

Figure 18.1: Viewing a development as fluents or states.

associated with the state. In the logical language, the assertion that a feature has a value at a specific time is denoted as $[\tau]\ f(\bar{\omega}) \hat{=} \omega$ in the macro language $\mathcal{L}(ND)$ and $Holds(\tau, f(\bar{\omega}), \omega)$ in the logical language $\mathcal{L}(FL)$, where τ is a temporal expression, $f(\bar{\omega})$ is a parameterized feature and ω is a value from the feature's value domain.

Since there is an agent, there is usually also a set of *actions* that the agent can perform. Such actions can only be performed when the requisite *preconditions* are satisfied. Performing an action changes the state of the world according to a set of given rules. Such rules are not necessarily deterministic. For example, the action of tossing a coin can be modeled within the TAL framework, and there will be two possible result states. TAL offers a highly expressive language for specifying actions where non-deterministic, context-dependent, concurrent and durational actions are expressible, among other types of actions.

Background knowledge associated with a reasoning domain can be modeled in a number of ways in TAL. *Observation statements* represent observations made by an agent. *Domain Constraint statements* represent facts true in all scenarios associated with a particular reasoning domain. *Dependency Constraint statements* can be used to represent causal theories or assertions which model intricate dependencies describing how and when features change relative to each other.

All of these concepts are modeled in a narrative specified in the language $\mathcal{L}(ND)$. $\mathcal{L}(ND)$ is a high-level extendable macro language which provides support to the knowledge engineer when constructing narratives and permits specification of narratives at a higher level of abstraction than logical statements. An extendable translation function is provided which translates narratives specified in $\mathcal{L}(ND)$ into 1st- and 2nd-order logical theories.

One of the fundamental problems in developing logics for reasoning about action and change has been in finding both representational and computationally efficient ways to encode the fact that there is a great deal of invariant structure in the world at a particular level of abstraction in which agents often describe and reason about the world. Even though the world is often dynamic and changing, from the perspective of an agent functioning in the world, properties and relations among entities are more often than not inert. On the other hand, there are often reasons for features in the world to change or reasons that provide the possibility for change. Many of these are obvious. For example, if an agent executes a physical action, the intent is usually to change some aspect of the world to the agent's advantage in completing a task. Others are less obvious, for example the subtle ramifications and aftereffects of an action. Developing theories of action and change is very much about identifying and representing normative rules which capture invariant and non-invariant epistemic and physical structure in environments in which agents are embedded and in which they operate.

Many of the representational and computational problems associated with modeling action and change have been given names, such as the frame, ramification and qualification problems, while others have not. Many useful techniques for capturing normative behavior have also been developed such as default reasoning. The principal intuition used in the development of TAL to deal with many of these issues is very simple to state, but quite difficult to make operational in an efficient manner in a logical formalism such as TAL.

In any TAL model, a time series is implicitly associated with any feature in the vocabulary. Whether a feature may change value or not in a transition from one time-point to another in the time series is specified by occluding or marking that feature as being given the *possibility* of changing value relative to other constraints in the theory. Policies for occluding features at timepoints are both contextually and temporally dependent on a number of factors and done for a number of reasons. The definitions of the frame, ramification and qualification problems specify some of these reasons. For whatever reason this is done, to the greatest extent possible, this labeling process should be achieved in a principled manner and remain more or less hidden from the knowledge engineer via the use of macro mechanisms in the $\mathcal{L}(\text{ND})$ language and the translation into the base logical language $\mathcal{L}(\text{FL})$.

At the level of $\mathcal{L}(\text{ND})$, there are a number of ways to incrementally provide an occlusion policy for a feature, some more explicit than others. At the $\mathcal{L}(\text{FL})$ level, the policies result in a set of labels for each feature represented as $Occlude(\tau, f(\bar{\omega}))$. The generation of such policies provide sufficient conditions for features being given the possibility to change value in state transitions (from $\tau - 1$ to τ). A circumscription policy then provides the necessary conditions and a definition of the occlusion predicate in the logical theory. An additional specification of whether and when a feature is persistent, durational, or dynamic in nature is also provided. These statements provide a means of filtering "bad" models out of the model set for a particular narrative, such as models where persistent features change value without being occluded.

If one uses this technique in a principled manner and restricts the generation of such policies to only include positive occurrences of the predicate *Occlude* in the theory, then a reduction of the 2nd-order circumscription theory to a logically equivalent 1st-order theory is always guaranteed. It is in this manner we provide partial solutions to the frame, ramification and qualification problems in the context of TAL.

18.3　TAL Narratives

A narrative in $\mathcal{L}(\text{ND})$ can be said to consist of two parts: The *narrative background specification* (NBS), which provides background information that is common to all narratives for a particular domain, and the *narrative specification* (NS), which provides information specific to a particular instance of a reasoning problem. Most of this information is represented as a set of labeled narrative statements in the surface language $\mathcal{L}(\text{ND})$.

Before providing a formal definition of the $\mathcal{L}(\text{ND})$ language, we will introduce most of the macros, formula types and statement classes using a rather complex example scenario called the *Russian Airplane Hijack* (RAH) scenario, which in order to be adequately represented in any logical formalism would require robust solutions to the frame, ramification and qualification problems. We say robust because a complete description of the RAH world requires the representation of concurrent actions, incomplete specifications of states, ramification with chaining, the use of non-boolean features, fine-grained dependencies among objects in different feature value domains, actions with duration, two types of qualification (*weak* and *strong*) and the use of explicit time, in addition to other features.

The RAH narrative description will be used as a vehicle for considering different facets of Temporal Action Logics and demonstrating how various aspects of a domain can be modeled in TAL. This will be done in stages. In this section, we will represent the narrative without the use of side effects and under the assumption that actions always succeed if their basic preconditions are satisfied. In other words, we will omit solutions to the ramification and qualification problems.[3] After having provided formal specifications of the $\mathcal{L}$(ND) and $\mathcal{L}$(FL) languages (Sections 18.5 and 18.6), we will once more return to the RAH scenario in order to consider how ramification constraints (Section 18.8) and qualification constraints (Section 18.9) can be modeled in TAL.

18.3.1 The Russian Airplane Hijack Scenario

The Russian Airplane Hijack scenario[4] can be described as follows.

Example 18.1 *(Russian Airplane Hijack scenario).* A Russian businessman, Boris, travels a lot and is concerned about both his hair and safety. Consequently, when traveling, he places both a comb and a gun in his pocket. A Bulgarian businessman, Dimiter, is less concerned about his hair, but when traveling by air, has a tendency to drink large amounts of vodka before boarding a flight to subdue his fear of flying. A Swedish businessman, Erik, travels a lot, likes combing his hair, but is generally law abiding.

One ramification of moving between locations is that objects in your pocket will follow you from location to location. Similarly, a person on board a plane will follow the plane as it flies between cities.

Generally, when boarding a plane, the only preconditions are that you are at the gate and you have a ticket. However, if you try to board a plane carrying a gun in your pocket, which will be the case for Boris, this should qualify the action. Also, a condition that could sometimes qualify the boarding action is if you arrive at the gate in a sufficiently inebriated condition, as will be the case for Dimiter. When the boarding action is qualified, attempting to board should have no effect.

Boris, Erik and Dimiter already have their tickets. They start (concurrently) from their respective homes, stop by the office, go to the airport, and try to board flight SAS609 to Stockholm. Both Erik and Boris put combs in their pockets at home, and Boris picks up a gun at the office, while Dimiter is already drunk at home and may or may not already have a comb in his pocket. Who will successfully board the plane? What are their final locations? What will be in their pockets after attempting to board the plane and after the plane has arrived at its destination?

Let us assume that the scenario is encoded correctly in TAL and that we agree on our commonsense intuitions regarding what solutions to the frame, ramification and qualification problems would imply. Then the following inferences should be entailed by the logical theory associated with the RAH scenario[5]:

---

[3]This will initially result in a scenario where it is assumed that any attempt to board a plane always succeeds, regardless of whether a person carries a gun or is drunk. In addition, ramifications of action effects will be included in action specifications rather than being specified separately.

[4]This scenario is an elaboration and concretization of a sketch for a scenario proposed by Vladimir Lifschitz in on-line discussions in the Electronic Transactions on Artificial Intelligence (ETAI/ENAI), and was previously published in [11, 42].

[5]Assume that Boris, Erik and Dimiter own the combs comb1, comb2 and comb3, respectively.

1. Erik will board the plane successfully, eventually ending up at his destination.

2. An indirect effect of flying is that a person ends up at the same location as the airplane he is on. In addition, because items in pockets follow a person, a transitive effect results where items in a person's pocket are at the same location as the plane which that person is on. Consequently, Erik's comb, comb2, will also end up at his destination.

3. Boris will get as far as the airport with a gun and comb1 in his pocket. He will be unable to board the plane.

4. Dimiter will get as far as the airport, and may or may not be able to board the plane. If he is able to board the plane, he will eventually end up at his destination. Otherwise, he will remain at the airport. In any case, if he initially carried a comb, it will end up in the same location.

18.3.2   Narrative Background Specification

A narrative background specification contains a collection of statements of the following types:

- *Persistence statements* (labeled **per**[6]) allow each fluent to be specified as being persistent (normally retaining its value from the previous timepoint), durational (normally reverting to a default value), or dynamic (varying freely, subject to other constraints involving this fluent).

- *Domain constraint statements* (labeled **dom**) characterize acausal information which is always true in the world being modeled.

- *Action type specifications* (labeled **acs**) provide generic definitions of action types.

- *Dependency constraint statements* (labeled **dep**) characterize causal and directional dependencies among features.

A narrative background specification also contains a vocabulary for the narrative. In the following subsections, each of the statement types and the vocabulary specification will be described in detail and correlates to the RAH scenario will be listed.

Vocabulary

The vocabulary of an $\mathcal{L}$(ND) narrative defines the constant symbols, feature symbols, action symbols, and other symbols that are available for use in narrative formulas. Since narrative examples used in the literature have traditionally been quite simple, the vocabulary has usually either been considered to be implicit in the remainder of the narrative specification or has been described informally in the main text of the article. Here, however, vocabularies will be described in terms of labeled narrative

---

[6]A number is often suffixed to each label, as in **per3**. These numbers are used to disambiguate references in the text and have no semantic meaning.

declaration statements using a syntax borrowed from the software tools VITAL [39] and TALplanner [41].

For the Russian Airplane Hijack scenario, we define a domain LOCATION for locations, and a domain THING containing everything that has a location. We also define the subdomains RUNWAY for LOCATIONs that are runways, PLANE for THINGs that are airplanes, PERSON for THINGs that are people, and PTHING for THINGs that people can pick up.

> **domain** LOCATION :elements { home1, home2, home3, office, airport, run609, run609b, air }
> **domain** THING :elements { gun, comb1, comb2, comb3, boris, dimiter, erik, sas609 }
> **domain** RUNWAY :parent LOCATION :elements { run609, run609b }
> **domain** PLANE :parent THING :elements { sas609 }
> **domain** PERSON :parent THING :elements { boris, dimiter, erik }
> **domain** PTHING :parent THING :elements { gun, comb1, comb2, comb3 }

We also use the boolean domain, which is present by default in all narratives and behaves as if it had been specified in the following manner:

> **domain** BOOLEAN :elements { true, false }

Note that the domain specification in $\mathcal{L}$(ND) describes a type hierarchy. This will translate into the order-sorted vocabulary in the base logic $\mathcal{L}$(FL).

Finally, four fluents and four actions are used where the arguments to these are typed relative to the domain specification above.

> **fluent** loc(THING) :domain LOCATION
> **fluent** inpocket(PERSON, PTHING) :domain BOOLEAN
> **fluent** onplane(PLANE, PERSON) :domain BOOLEAN
> **fluent** drunk(PERSON) :domain BOOLEAN
>
> **action** pickup(PERSON, PTHING)
> **action** travel(PERSON, LOCATION, LOCATION)
> **action** board(PERSON, PLANE)
> **action** fly(PLANE, RUNWAY, RUNWAY)

Persistence statements

Persistence statements are a novel feature of TAL and offer a very powerful and fine-grained mechanism for specifying inertia and default value assumptions for individual features when used together with the occlusion labeling mechanism mentioned previously. The majority of existing formalisms for action and change build in an assumption that a property or relation is either *always* assumed to be inert and subject to nochange by default or to be dynamic and subject to change by default. Through the use of persistence statements TAL permits the specification of contextually and temporally dependent inertia assumptions and default value assumptions per feature and down to the feature object level. This is an important feature of any action and change formalism since the inertial granularity of physical and other objects differs greatly. For example, a mountain will remain in place much longer than a ball on the ground which under certain weather conditions is in fact not inert at all.

Persistence statements can be used to classify features as being *persistent, durational*, or *dynamic*. In fact, a specific instantiated feature or set of features may be classified differently in the same scenario relative to context.

A feature declared as *persistent* at a timepoint is only allowed to change value when an action or dependency constraint in the scenario explicitly allows it to change, by labeling the feature at that timepoint as being occluded using a reassignment macro (Section 18.5.2, subsection *Formulas*). Otherwise, it retains the same value it had at the previous timepoint (the *persistence assumption* or *inertia assumption*). For example, the persistence statement below declares that all instantiated features of the form loc(*thing*) are inert at all timepoints:

per $\forall t, thing\ [Per(t, \text{loc}(thing))]$

The translation from $\mathcal{L}(\text{ND})$ to $\mathcal{L}(\text{FL})$ is performed using the *Trans* function defined in Section 18.6.1. If the timeline is infinite in both directions, the following translation could be used for the *Per* predicate, stating that unless a feature is occluded at τ, it will retain its previous value.

$$Trans(Per(\tau, f)) = \neg Occlude(\tau, f) \supset Holds(\tau, f, v) \equiv Holds(\tau - 1, f, v)$$

However, TAL is generally used with a non-negative time structure, where this translation would lead to problems at the boundary where $\tau = 0$, where $\tau - 1$ does not exist. Thus, the translation has to be changed to the following, where for $\tau = 0$ there exists no t such that $\tau = t + 1$ and the antecedent of the implication will be false, which correctly models the intuition that persistence should not affect the possible values of a fluent at the beginning of time:

$$Trans(Per(\tau, f)) = \forall t.\tau = t + 1 \wedge \neg Occlude(t + 1, f) \supset$$
$$\forall v[Holds(t + 1, f, v) \equiv Holds(t, f, v)]$$

A feature declared as *durational* is associated with a default value, and can only take on another value when an action, dependency constraint, or other constraint allows it to (the *default value assumption*). At timepoints when no action or dependency constraint explicitly allows it to take on another value, it will immediately revert back to its default value. Through the use of durational features, TAL can encode simple types of default rules and assumptions. For instance, one may model the presence of noise using a durational fluent with default value false, capturing the intuition that there is no noise unless an action is currently generating it. An action generating noise would then use a suitable reassignment operator to exempt the noise fluent from its default value assumption during the appropriate temporal interval. This is especially important in the presence of concurrent actions, where an alternative solution that sets noise to true at the beginning of the action and explicitly sets it to false at the end does not work properly with partially overlapping actions, potentially generating the conclusions that when one action ends, it cancels the noise generated by another action.

For example, the persistence statement below declares that the fluent noise should have the default value false at all timepoints. Further examples will be given when qualification is discussed (Section 18.9).

per $\forall t\ [Dur(t, \text{noise, false})]$

The translation of a *Dur* declaration in $\mathcal{L}(ND)$ into $\mathcal{L}(FL)$ would be:

$$Trans(Dur(\tau, f, \omega)) = \neg Occlude(\tau, f) \supset Holds(\tau, f, \omega)$$

Unless the feature is occluded at τ, it will take on its default value.

Finally, a TAL feature can also be *dynamic* if it is not declared to be persistent or durational. Since no persistence or default value assumption is applied, dynamic fluents can vary freely over time to satisfy observations and domain constraints.

Note that some earlier TAL logics (including PMON) used a fixed *nochange axiom* instead of persistence statements, forcing all fluents to be persistent. Using persistence statements provides a more flexible and fine-grained approach to controlling the default behavior of fluents and is currently the technique used in TAL to specify inertia and default value assumptions.

Intuitively, the features used in the Russian Airplane Hijack scenario describe properties that do not change unless something changes them. These features are all declared to be persistent. The declarations for the RAH scenario are as follows:

per1 $\forall t, thing\ [Per(t, \text{loc}(thing))]$
per2 $\forall t, person, pthing\ [Per(t, \text{inpocket}(person, pthing))]$
per3 $\forall t, person\ [Per(t, \text{drunk}(person))]$
per4 $\forall t, plane, person\ [Per(t, \text{onplane}(plane, person))]$

Domain constraints

Domain constraints represent knowledge about logical feature dependencies which are not specific to a particular reasoning problem instance but which are known to hold in every possible scenario taking place within a domain. An even stronger assumption often made in other formalisms is that these are formulas true in all states (universally quantified over all timepoints, situations or states) and behave much as a classical logical formula would behave in a standard theory. In domain constraints, as well as other TAL formulas, the fact that a feature f takes on a particular value ω is denoted by the elementary fluent formula $f \hat{=} \omega$. For the boolean domain, the formula $f \hat{=} \text{true}$ ($f \hat{=} \text{false}$) can be abbreviated as f ($\neg f$). Elementary fluent formulas can be combined using boolean connectives and quantification over values to form fluent formulas. The fixed fluent formula $[\tau]\ \phi$ states that the fluent formula ϕ holds at the timepoint τ.

For the Russian Airplane Hijack scenario we will define three domain constraints: No PTHING can be carried by two PERSONs at the same time, no PERSON can be on board two PLANEs at the same time, and any PTHING in a PERSON's pocket must be at the same location as that PERSON.

dom1 $\forall t, pthing, person_1, person_2\ [person_1 \neq person_2 \wedge [t]\ \text{inpocket}(person_1, pthing) \supset$
$[t]\ \neg\text{inpocket}(person_2, pthing)]$
dom2 $\forall t, person, plane_1, plane_2$
$[plane_1 \neq plane_2 \wedge [t]\ \text{onplane}(plane_1, person) \supset [t]\ \neg\text{onplane}(plane_2, person)]$
dom3 $\forall t, person, pthing\ [[t]\ \text{inpocket}(person, pthing) \supset$
$[t]\ \text{loc}(pthing) \hat{=} value(t, \text{loc}(person))]$

Action types

Actions can be invoked by the agent in order to change some properties in the world. If *person* picks up a thing *pthing* in the Russian Airplane Hijack scenario, then this should cause inpocket(*person*, *pthing*) to become true, for example. But since the inpocket feature is persistent, simply stating the fact that inpocket(*person*, *pthing*) will be true at the end of the action invocation is not sufficient. Instead, it is necessary to use a *reassignment macro* to explicitly release this feature from the persistence assumption at the specific point in time where it should change values from false to true.

There are three different reassignment macros: X, R and I. They can all be used with a temporal interval, for example, $R((\tau, \tau'] \alpha)$, or a single timepoint, for example $I([\tau] \alpha)$. Each of these operators has the effect of releasing the features occurring in α from the persistence and default value assumptions during the given interval or at the given timepoint. However, the operators differ in whether they place further constraints on the values of these features, and if so, at what time.

The X operator is used for *occlusion*. Its purpose is simply to allow the value of the features in the formula α to vary at a timepoint or during an interval, and therefore it does not further constrain the features occurring in α. Intuitively, the X operator occludes (hides) any changes in a feature value from the persistence or default value constraints generated by the persistence statements in the narrative.

The R operator is used for *reassignment*, and ensures that α will hold at the final timepoint in the interval. During the rest of the interval, the features occurring in α are allowed to vary freely, unaffected by the persistence or default value assumption (but still subject to other constraints that may also be present in the narrative).

The I operator is used for *interval reassignment* and ensures that α will hold during the entire interval. Note that if α is a disjunctive formula, features occurring in α may still vary during the interval as long as the formula remains satisfied throughout the interval.

An *action type specification* uses reassignment macros to define what will happen if and when a particular action is invoked. Note that it does not state that an action does occur. This is specified in the narrative specification using action occurrence statements.

In many existing action formalisms, actions do not have duration and are essentially single step. If actions with duration are introduced, it is often the case that during the duration nothing can happen or be specified to happen. TAL offers highly expressive action types. They can be single-step or durational, inert during the duration or highly dynamic. Additional constraints specifying what goes on during the execution of an action can easily be included in the action specification.

In the Russian Airplane Hijack scenario, four actions were declared in the narrative background specification. Here, those actions will be defined without taking qualifications into account and without making use of ramification constraints to specify side effects, resulting in a narrative where guns do not qualify the boarding action and where the fact that people inside an airplane move when the airplane moves must be expressed explicitly in the action definition. These action definitions will later be modified in Section 18.8.

acs1 $[t_1, t_2]$fly(*plane*, *runway*$_1$, *runway*$_2$) $\leadsto$ ($[t_1]$ loc(*plane*) $\hat{=}$ *runway*$_1$ $\supset$
$\quad I((t_1, t_2)$ loc(*plane*) $\hat{=}$ air) $\land R([t_2]$ loc(*plane*) $\hat{=}$ *runway*$_2$) $\land$
$\quad \forall person[[t_1]$ onplane(*plane*, *person*) $\supset$
$\quad\quad I((t_1, t_2)$ loc(*person*) $\hat{=}$ air) $\land R([t_2]$ loc(*person*) $\hat{=}$ *runway*$_2$) $\land$
$\quad\quad \forall pthing[[t_1]$ inpocket(*person*, *pthing*) $\supset$
$\quad\quad\quad I((t_1, t_2)$ loc(*pthing*) $\hat{=}$ air) $\land R([t_2]$ loc(*pthing*) $\hat{=}$ *runway*$_2$)]])

acs2 $[t_1, t_2]$pickup(*person*, *pthing*) $\rightsquigarrow$ $[t_1]$ loc(*person*) $\hat{=}$ *value*(t_1, loc(*pthing*)) $\supset$
  $R((t_1, t_2]$ inpocket(*person*, *pthing*))

acs3 $[t_1, t_2]$travel(*person*, *loc$_1$*, *loc$_2$*) $\rightsquigarrow$ $[t_1]$ loc(*person*) $\hat{=}$ *loc$_1$* $\supset$
  $R([t_2]$ loc(*person*) $\hat{=}$ *loc$_2$*) $\wedge$
  $\forall$*pthing*[$[t_1]$ inpocket(*person*, *pthing*) $\supset$ $R([t_2]$ loc(*pthing*) $\hat{=}$ *loc$_2$*)]

acs4 $[t_1, t_2]$board(*person*, *plane*) $\rightsquigarrow$ $[t_1]$ loc(*person*) $\hat{=}$ airport $\supset$
  $R([t_2]$ loc(*person*) $\hat{=}$ *value*(t_2, loc(*plane*)) $\wedge$ onplane(*plane*, *person*))

For reasons of representational efficiency, it is quite clear from observing these action specifications that a solution to the ramification problem is really necessary.

18.3.3 Narrative Specification

In the narrative specification, *observation statements* (labeled **obs**) represent observations of feature values at specific timepoints while *action occurrence statements* (labeled **occ**) specify which instances of the generic action types occur and during which time intervals.

Observation statements

Observation statements are intended to describe specific facts that have been observed to hold in the world, permitting complete or incomplete specifications of the initial state or any other state in the world development corresponding to a narrative. They provide information about a particular reasoning problem instance within a domain, and are therefore part of the narrative specification.[7]

For this scenario, we define the initial locations of all THINGs, as well as who is drunk in the initial state. On the other hand, we do not observe which things are in whose pockets.

obs1 $[0]$ loc(boris) $\hat{=}$ home1 $\wedge$ loc(gun) $\hat{=}$ office $\wedge$ loc(comb1) $\hat{=}$ home1 $\wedge$ ¬drunk(boris)
obs2 $[0]$ loc(erik) $\hat{=}$ home2 $\wedge$ loc(comb2) $\hat{=}$ home2 $\wedge$ ¬drunk(erik)
obs3 $[0]$ loc(dimiter) $\hat{=}$ home3 $\wedge$ loc(comb3) $\hat{=}$ home3 $\wedge$ drunk(dimiter)
obs4 $[0]$ loc(sas609) $\hat{=}$ run609

Action occurrence statements

Action occurrence statements specify which actions actually do take place in a narrative. Like observations, they are part of the narrative specification—the instance-specific part of the narrative.

For the Russian Airplane Hijack scenario, the following action occurrences are also required. The exact timepoints used below were not specified in the RAH scenario, but have been chosen arbitrarily. Alternatively, exact timepoints could have been avoided by using non-numerical temporal constants. Note, however, that many of the actions are concurrent, sometimes with partially overlapping intervals.

---

[7]In some earlier versions of TAL, an explicit *Observe* predicate was introduced in the base logical language $\mathcal{L}$(FL) to which observation statements are translated. Distinguishing sensor-generated facts about the world from other facts is useful when interfacing such logics to robotic systems. One might choose to view observation statements as perception statements, although this is not done in the current version of TAL.

occ1 [1,2] pickup(boris, comb1)	**occ8** [7,9] travel(erik, office, airport)
occ2 [1,2] pickup(erik, comb2)	**occ9** [8,10] travel(boris, office, airport)
occ3 [2,4] travel(dimiter, home3, office)	**occ10** [9,10] board(dimiter, sas609)
occ4 [3,5] travel(boris, home1, office)	**occ11** [10,11] board(boris, sas609)
occ5 [4,6] travel(erik, home2, office)	**occ12** [11,12] board(erik, sas609)
occ6 [6,7] pickup(boris, gun)	**occ13** [13,16] fly(sas609, run609, run609b)
occ7 [5,7] travel(dimiter, office, airport)	

Note that this action scenario has been simplified for expository purposes. A number of additional extensions to the scenarios would in fact make it more realistic. For example, one could add more realistic timing actions, perhaps by explicitly modeling distances between locations and dividing by expected speed. In addition, upon introducing truly concurrent actions, one must be aware that there may be different types of interactions and these would have to be dealt with in an appropriate manner. TAL allows such extensions and we refer the interested reader to Section 18.11 where a summary of concurrent actions in TAL is provided.

18.4　The Relation Between the TAL Languages $\mathcal{L}$(ND) and $\mathcal{L}$(FL)

In order to reason about a particular narrative, it is first mechanically translated into the base language $\mathcal{L}$(FL), an order-sorted classical first-order language with equality using a linear discrete time structure (Fig. 18.2). A circumscription policy is applied to the resulting theory, foundational axioms are added, and quantifier elimination techniques are used to reduce the resulting second order theory to first order logic. This is possible only under certain assumptions pertaining to the use of the *Occlude* predicate and the nature of the temporal structure used.

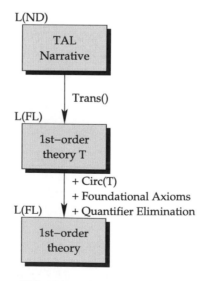

Figure 18.2: The relation between $\mathcal{L}$(ND) and $\mathcal{L}$(FL).

In Section 18.5, we will present the TAL surface language $\mathcal{L}$(ND). In Section 18.6, we will present the TAL base language $\mathcal{L}$(FL), and in Section 18.7, we will consider the circumscription policy used in TAL and reducibility results.

18.5 The TAL Surface Language $\mathcal{L}$(ND)

This section defines the surface language $\mathcal{L}$(ND). The translation to the first-order language $\mathcal{L}$(FL) is presented in Section 18.6.1. In the following, the overline is used as an abbreviation for a sequence, when the contents of the sequence is obvious. For example, $f(\bar{x}, \bar{y})$ means $f(x_1, \ldots, x_n, y_1, \ldots, y_m)$.

18.5.1 Sorts, Terms and Variables

Definition 18.1 (Basic sorts). *There are a number of sorts for values $\mathcal{V}_i$, including the boolean sort $\mathcal{B}$ with the constants {true, false}. TAL is order-sorted, and a sort may be specified to be a subsort of another sort. The sort $\mathcal{V}$ is a supersort of all value sorts.*

There are a number of sorts for features $\mathcal{F}_i$, each one associated with a value sort $dom(\mathcal{F}_i) = \mathcal{V}_j$ for some j. The sort $\mathcal{F}$ is a supersort of all fluent sorts.

There is also a sort for actions $\mathcal{A}$ and a temporal sort $\mathcal{T}$.

The sort $\mathcal{T}$ is often assumed to be interpreted and semantic attachment is used in implementations, but it can be axiomatized in various ways. For example, in first-order logic, it can be axiomatized as a subset of Presburger arithmetic [38] (natural numbers with addition), or in second-order logic as Peano arithmetic.

Definition 18.2 (Terms). *A value term, often denoted by ω, is a variable v or a constant v of sort $\mathcal{V}_i$ for some i, an expression value(τ, f) where τ is a temporal term and f is a fluent term, or an expression $\mathsf{g}(\omega_1, \ldots, \omega_n)$ where $\mathsf{g} : \mathcal{V}_{k_1} \times \cdots \times \mathcal{V}_{k_n} \to \mathcal{V}_i$ is a value function symbol and each ω_j is a value term of sort $\mathcal{V}_{k_j}$.*

A temporal term, often denoted by τ, is a variable t or a constant $0, 1, 2, 3, \ldots$ or $\mathsf{s}_l, \mathsf{t}_l, \ldots$, or an expression of the form $\tau_1 + \tau_2$, all of sort $\mathcal{T}$.

A fluent term, often denoted by f, is a feature variable or an expression $\mathsf{f}(\omega_1, \ldots, \omega_n)$ where $\mathsf{f} : \mathcal{V}_{k_1} \times \cdots \times \mathcal{V}_{k_n} \to \mathcal{F}_i$ is a feature symbol and each ω_j is a value term of sort $\mathcal{V}_{k_j}$.

An action term Ψ is an expression $A(\omega_1, \ldots, \omega_n)$ where $A : \mathcal{V}_{k_1} \times \cdots \times \mathcal{V}_{k_n} \to \mathcal{A}$ is an action symbol and each ω_j is a value term of sort $\mathcal{V}_{k_j}$.

Variables are typed and range over the values belonging to a specific sort. Although the sort is sometimes specified explicitly in narratives, it is more common to simply give the variable the same name as the sort but (like all variables) written in italics, possibly with a prime and/or an index. For example, the variables *plane*, *plane'* and *plane₃* would be of the sort PLANE. Similarly, variables named t or τ are normally temporal variables, and variables named n are normally integer-valued variables.

The function *value*(τ, f) returns the value of the fluent f at the timepoint τ, where $[\tau]\ f \hat{=} v$ iff *value*$(\tau, f) = v$. The expression $[\tau]\ f \hat{=} g$, where f and g are fluent terms, is shorthand notation for $[\tau]\ f \hat{=} value(\tau, g)$.

18.5.2 Formulas

Definition 18.3 (Temporal and value formulas). *If τ and τ' are temporal terms, then $\tau = \tau'$, $\tau < \tau'$ and $\tau \leqslant \tau'$ are temporal formulas. A value formula is of the form $\omega = \omega'$ where ω and ω' are value terms, or $r(\omega_1, \ldots, \omega_n)$ where $r\colon \mathcal{V}_{k_1} \times \cdots \times \mathcal{V}_{k_n}$ is a relation symbol and each ω_j is a value term of sort $\mathcal{V}_{k_j}$.*

We will sometimes write $\tau \leqslant \tau' < \tau''$ to denote the conjunction $\tau \leqslant \tau' \wedge \tau' < \tau''$, and similarly for other combinations of the relation symbols $\leqslant$ and $<$.

Definition 18.4 (Fluent formula). *An elementary fluent formula, sometimes called an isvalue expression, has the form $f \,\hat{=}\, \omega$ where f is a fluent term of sort $\mathcal{F}_i$ and ω is a value term of sort $dom(\mathcal{F}_i)$. A fluent formula is an elementary fluent formula or a combination of fluent formulas formed with the standard logical connectives and quantification over values.*

The elementary fluent formula $f \,\hat{=}\, \mathsf{true}$ ($f \,\hat{=}\, \mathsf{false}$) can be abbreviated f ($\neg f$).

Definition 18.5 (Timed formulas). *Let τ and τ' be temporal terms and α a fluent formula. Then:*

- $[\tau, \tau']\,\alpha$, $(\tau, \tau']\,\alpha$, $[\tau, \tau')\,\alpha$, $(\tau, \tau')\,\alpha$, $[\tau, \infty)\,\alpha$, $(\tau, \infty)\,\alpha$ *and* $[\tau]\,\alpha$ *are* fixed fluent formulas,

- $C_T([\tau]\,\alpha)$, $C_F([\tau]\,\alpha)$ *and* $C([\tau]\,\alpha)$ *are* fluent change formulas,

- $R([\tau, \tau']\,\alpha)$, $R((\tau, \tau']\,\alpha)$, $R([\tau, \tau')\,\alpha)$, $R((\tau, \tau')\,\alpha)$ *and* $R([\tau]\,\alpha)$ *are* reassignment formulas,

- $I([\tau, \tau']\,\alpha)$, $I((\tau, \tau']\,\alpha)$, $I([\tau, \tau')\,\alpha)$, $I((\tau, \tau')\,\alpha)$ *and* $I([\tau]\,\alpha)$ *are* interval reassignment formulas, *and*

- $X([\tau, \tau']\,\alpha)$, $X((\tau, \tau']\,\alpha)$, $X([\tau, \tau')\,\alpha)$, $X((\tau, \tau')\,\alpha)$ *and* $X([\tau]\,\alpha)$ *are* occlusion formulas.

Fixed fluent formulas, fluent change formulas, reassignment formulas, interval reassignment formulas and occlusion formulas are called timed formulas.

Definition 18.6 (Static formula). *A static formula is a temporal formula, a value formula, a fixed fluent formula, a fluent change formula,* true*,* false*, or a combination of static formulas formed using the standard logical connectives together with quantification over values and time.*

Note that the formulas true and false are not the same as the boolean values true and false.

Definition 18.7 (Change formula). *A change formula is a formula that is rewritable to the form $Q\bar{v}(\alpha_1 \vee \cdots \vee \alpha_n)$ where $Q\bar{v}$ is a sequence of quantifiers with variables, and each α_i is a conjunction of static, occlusion and reassignment formulas. The change* *formula is called* balanced *iff the following two conditions hold.* (a) *Whenever a feature* $f(\bar{\omega})$ *appears inside a reassignment or occlusion formula in one of the* α_i *disjuncts, it must also appear in all other* α_i *'s inside a reassignment or occlusion formula with exactly the same temporal argument.* (b) *Any existentially quantified variable* v *in the formula, whenever appearing inside a reassignment or occlusion formula, only does so in the position* $f \hat{=} v$.

Definition 18.8 (Application formula). *An application formula is any of the following:* (a) *a balanced change formula;* (b) $\Lambda \supset \Delta$, *where* Λ *is a static formula and* Δ *is a balanced change formula; or* (c) *a combination of elements of types* (a) *and* (b) *formed with conjunction and universal quantification over values and time.*

Application formulas will be used in dependency constraints and action type specifications. The structural constraints on balanced change formulas and application formulas guarantee the proper generation of the occlusion predicate in the translation from $\mathcal{L}(\text{ND})$ to $\mathcal{L}(\text{FL})$. Restricting the structure of these formulas will guarantee first-order reducibility of the circumscription policy applied to the narrative.

Definition 18.9 (Occurrence formula). *An occurrence formula has the form* $[\tau, \tau']\ \Psi$, *where* τ *and* τ' *are temporal terms and* Ψ *is an action term.*

Definition 18.10 (Persistence formula). *A persistence formula is an expression of the form* $Per(\tau, f)$ *where* τ *is a temporal term and* f *is a fluent term, an expression of the form* $Dur(\tau, f, \omega)$ *where* τ *is a temporal term,* f *is a fluent term and* ω *is a value term, or a combination of persistence formulas formed with conjunction and universal quantification over values or time.*

18.5.3 Statements

Definition 18.11 (Narrative statements). *The following types of narrative statements are available in the current version of TAL.*

An action type specification or action schema (labeled **acs**) *has the form* $[t, t']\ \Psi \rightsquigarrow \phi$, *where* t *and* t' *are temporal variables,* Ψ *is an action term and* ϕ *is an application formula.*

A dependency constraint (labeled **dep**) *consists of an application formula.*

A domain constraint (labeled **dom**) *consists of a static formula.*

A persistence statement (labeled **per**) *consists of a persistence formula.*

An observation statement (labeled **obs**) *consists of a static formula.*

An action occurrence statement (labeled **occ**) *consists of an occurrence formula* $[\tau, \tau']\ \Psi$ *where* τ *and* τ' *are ground temporal terms and* Ψ *is a ground action term.*

All of these statement types have been provided with intuitive meanings in Section 18.3 except dependency constraints, which will be used to model side effects of actions (Section 18.8) and qualifications to actions (Section 18.9).

18.6   The TAL Base Language $\mathcal{L}$(FL)

This section defines the current base language $\mathcal{L}$(FL) used in TAL. The translation from $\mathcal{L}$(ND), which has already been described, to the first-order language $\mathcal{L}$(FL) is presented in Section 18.6.1. The base language $\mathcal{L}$(FL) is an order-sorted classical first-order language with equality. We assume familiarity with standard ways to define vocabulary and variable types in sorted logics. Additionally, a temporal structure must be chosen for the temporal sort $\mathcal{T}$. This would include a domain such as the natural numbers or integers and associated operators. It was mentioned previously that a number of choices as to temporal structure could be made.

$\mathcal{L}$(FL) currently uses the following predicates where $\mathcal{T}$ is the temporal sort, $\mathcal{F}$ is a supersort of all fluent sorts and $\mathcal{V}$ is a supersort of all value sorts.

- *Holds*: $\mathcal{T} \times \mathcal{F} \times \mathcal{V}$—The *Holds* predicate expresses what value a feature has at each timepoint, and is used in the translation of fixed fluent formulas; for example, the formula [0] loc(boris) $\hat{=}$ home1 $\wedge$ loc(gun) $\hat{=}$ office can be translated into *Holds*(0, loc(boris), home1) $\wedge$ *Holds*(0, loc(gun), office).

- *Occlude*: $\mathcal{T} \times \mathcal{F}$—The *Occlude* predicate expresses the fact that a persistent or durational feature is exempt from its persistence or default value assumption, respectively, at a given timepoint. It is used in the translation of the R, I and X operators, which are intended to change the values of features.

- *Occurs*: $\mathcal{T} \times \mathcal{T} \times \mathcal{A}$—The *Occurs* predicate expresses that a certain action occurs during a certain time interval, and is used in the translation of action occurrence statements and action type specifications.

18.6.1   Translation from $\mathcal{L}$(ND) to $\mathcal{L}$(FL)

The following translation function is used to translate $\mathcal{L}$(ND) formulas into $\mathcal{L}$(FL).

Definition 18.12 (*Trans* Translation function). *Trans is called the* expansion transformation, *and is defined as follows. All variables occurring only on the right-hand side are assumed to be fresh variables.*

The formulas true *and* false *need no translation*:

$$Trans(\texttt{true}) = \texttt{true}$$
$$Trans(\texttt{false}) = \texttt{false}$$

Basic macros are translated into $\mathcal{L}$(FL) predicates:

$$Trans([\tau]\ f(\bar{\omega})) = Holds(\tau, f(\bar{\omega}), \text{true})$$
$$Trans([\tau]\ f(\bar{\omega}) \hat{=} \omega) = Holds(\tau, f(\bar{\omega}), \omega)$$
$$Trans(X([\tau]\ f(\bar{\omega}))) = Occlude(\tau, f(\bar{\omega}))$$
$$Trans(X([\tau]\ f(\bar{\omega}) \hat{=} \omega)) = Occlude(\tau, f(\bar{\omega}))$$
$$Trans([\tau, \tau']\ \Psi) = Occurs(\tau, \tau', \Psi), \quad \text{where } \Psi \text{ is an action term}$$

In some versions of TAL, the $\mathcal{L}$(ND) functions Per and Dur are also translated into $\mathcal{L}$(FL) predicates. Here, they are translated directly into constraints on fluent values *and occlusion.*

$$Trans(Per(\tau, f)) = \forall t. \tau = t + 1 \wedge \neg Occlude(t + 1, f) \supset$$
$$\forall v[Holds(t + 1, f, v) \equiv Holds(t, f, v)]$$
$$Trans(Dur(\tau, f, \omega)) = \neg Occlude(\tau, f) \supset Holds(\tau, f, \omega)$$

Top-level connectives and quantifiers are left unchanged:

$$Trans(\neg \alpha) = \neg Trans(\alpha)$$
$$Trans(\alpha \mathcal{C} \beta) = Trans(\alpha) \mathcal{C} Trans(\beta), \quad where\ \mathcal{C} \in \{\wedge, \vee, \supset, \equiv\}$$
$$Trans(\mathcal{Q}v[\alpha]) = \mathcal{Q}v[Trans(\alpha)], \quad where\ \mathcal{Q} \in \{\forall, \exists\}$$

Action type specifications use $\leadsto$ to denote the definition of an action. For this version of TAL, it is simply translated into an implication.

$$Trans([\tau, \tau']\ \Psi \leadsto \phi) = Trans([\tau, \tau']\ \Psi) \supset Trans(\phi)$$

Fixed fluent formulas can contain nested connectives and quantifiers, which are transferred outside the scope of the temporal context $[\tau]$.

$$Trans([\tau]\ \mathcal{Q}v[\alpha]) = \mathcal{Q}v[Trans([\tau]\ \alpha)], \quad where\ \mathcal{Q} \in \{\forall, \exists\}$$
$$Trans([\tau]\ \neg \alpha) = \neg Trans([\tau]\ \alpha)$$
$$Trans([\tau]\ \alpha \mathcal{C} \beta) = Trans([\tau]\ \alpha) \mathcal{C} Trans([\tau]\ \beta),$$
$$where\ \mathcal{C} \in \{\wedge, \vee, \supset, \equiv\}$$

Nested connectives and quantifiers can also occur within occlusion formulas. However, the translation of these formulas has to be modified somewhat to take into account the fact that any occlusion formula should occlude all fluents occurring within the scope of the occlusion operator: Even a disjunctive formula such as $X([\tau]\ \alpha \vee \beta)$ should occlude all fluents in α and all fluents in β and is therefore not equivalent to $X([\tau]\ \alpha) \vee X([\tau]\ \beta)$ but to $X([\tau]\ \alpha) \wedge X([\tau]\ \beta)$. The translation procedure takes this into account by removing negations inside the X operator, translating connectives occurring inside X into conjunctions, and converting all quantifiers inside X into universal quantification.

$$Trans(X([\tau]\ \neg \alpha)) = Trans(X([\tau]\ \alpha))$$
$$Trans(X([\tau]\ \alpha \mathcal{C} \beta)) = Trans(X([\tau]\ \alpha) \wedge X([\tau]\ \beta)),$$
$$where\ \mathcal{C} \in \{\wedge, \vee, \supset, \equiv\}$$
$$Trans(X([\tau]\mathcal{Q}v[\alpha])) = \forall v[Trans(X([\tau]\alpha))], \quad where\ \mathcal{Q} \in \{\forall, \exists\}$$

Fixed fluent formulas can contain infinite temporal intervals. This is a shorthand notation; infinity is not part of the temporal sort and disappears in the translation.

$$Trans([\tau, \infty)\ \alpha) = \forall t[\tau \leqslant t \supset Trans([t]\alpha)]$$
$$Trans((\tau, \infty)\ \alpha) = \forall t[\tau < t \supset Trans([t]\alpha)]$$

Finite temporal intervals are permitted both in fixed fluent formulas and in the occlusion operator. Only one form of interval is shown; the extension to allow open, closed and semi-closed intervals is trivial.

$$Trans([\tau, \tau'] \alpha) = \forall t[\tau \leqslant t \leqslant \tau' \supset Trans([t]\alpha)]$$

$$Trans(X((\tau, \tau'] \alpha)) = \forall t[\tau < t \leqslant \tau' \supset Trans(X([t]\alpha))]$$

The R and I operators are defined as follows. Again, one form of interval is shown.

$$Trans(R((\tau, \tau'] \alpha)) = Trans(X((\tau, \tau'], \alpha)) \wedge Trans([\tau']\alpha)$$

$$Trans(R([\tau] \alpha)) = Trans(X([\tau] \alpha)) \wedge Trans([\tau] \alpha)$$

$$Trans(I((\tau, \tau']\alpha)) = Trans(X((\tau, \tau'] \alpha)) \wedge Trans((\tau, \tau'] \alpha)$$

$$Trans(I([\tau] \alpha)) = Trans(X([\tau] \alpha)) \wedge Trans([\tau] \alpha)$$

Finally, the C_T "changes to true" operator is defined as follows, with the operators C_F (changes to false) and C (changes) added for symmetry.

$$Trans(C_T([\tau] \alpha)) = \forall t[\tau = t + 1 \supset Trans([t] \neg\alpha)] \wedge Trans([\tau] \alpha)$$

$$Trans(C_F([\tau] \alpha)) = \forall t[\tau = t + 1 \supset Trans([t] \alpha)] \wedge Trans([\tau] \neg\alpha)$$

$$Trans(C([\tau] \alpha)) = Trans(C_T([\tau] \alpha) \vee C_F([\tau] \alpha))$$

Example 18.2 *(Narrative translation)*. The following is a translation of several of the $\mathcal{L}(ND)$ statements in the Russian Airplane Hijack scenario into $\mathcal{L}(FL)$. For brevity, the translation is limited to one statement of each statement class; the remaining formulas are translated in a similar manner.

per1	$\forall t, thing, t' \ [t = t' + 1 \wedge \neg Occlude(t' + 1, \mathsf{loc}(thing)) \supset$
	$\forall v[Holds(t' + 1, \mathsf{loc}(thing), v) \equiv Holds(t', \mathsf{loc}(thing), v)]]$
dom1	$\forall t, pthing, person_1, person_2 \ [\neg(person_1 = person_2) \wedge$
	$Holds(t, \mathsf{inpocket}(person_1, pthing), \mathsf{true}) \supset$
	$\neg Holds(t, \mathsf{inpocket}(person_2, pthing), \mathsf{true})]$
acs2	$\forall t_1, t_2, person, pthing \ [Occurs(t_1, t_2, \mathsf{pickup}(person, pthing)) \supset$
	$(Holds(t_1, \mathsf{loc}(person), value(t_1, \mathsf{loc}(pthing))) \supset$
	$Holds(t_2, \mathsf{inpocket}(person, pthing), \mathsf{true}) \wedge$
	$\forall t \ [t_1 < t \wedge t \leqslant t_2 \supset Occlude(t, \mathsf{inpocket}(person, pthing))])]$
obs1	$Holds(0, \mathsf{loc}(boris), home1) \wedge Holds(0, \mathsf{loc}(gun), office) \wedge$
	$Holds(0, \mathsf{loc}(comb1), home1) \wedge \neg Holds(0, \mathsf{drunk}(boris), \mathsf{true})$
occ1	$Occurs(1, 2, \mathsf{pickup}(boris, comb1))$

18.7 Circumscription and TAL

The commonsense intuition one would like to capture and formally model in TAL is the fact that at a particular level of abstraction, relations between and properties of objects generally have reasons for changing and if not, we can assume, unless observed otherwise, that these are the only *possible* changes we need to be concerned about when reasoning about the specific environment around us and knowledge associated with that environment. So far, we have shown how one can encode in a principled manner sufficient reasons for the possibility of change by using a combination of the *Occlude* predicate and automatic translations from the surface language $\mathcal{L}(ND)$ to the base language $\mathcal{L}(FL)$. When specifying narratives in TAL, all sufficient reasons for the possibility of change are specified using the reassignment macros *R*, *I* and *X* in dependency constraints and action type definitions. When translated, these statements result in constraints on the *Occlude* predicate. Unfortunately, what has been achieved so far under-constrains our notion of normative change, for we would also like to state that these are the only, or necessary, reasons for *possible* change.

In order to add this additional constraint to our action theories, we will appeal to the use of circumscription (Section 6.4 in Chapter 6 of this Handbook; [54, 55]) with an additional twist. Rather than applying a circumscription policy to the whole action theory, the theory will be partitioned and we will apply circumscription selectively to different partitions. Although this technique, which we call filtered circumscription [14], is now commonly used in other action theories [65, 48], in the context of action and change, it was first proposed in Sandewall [60]. Here, it was called filtered preferential entailment and was used as a basis for several of the definitions of preferential entailment in [61].

The basic idea will be to first circumscribe the predicate *Occlude* in that part of the action theory containing action occurrence statements and dependency constraint statements. This will result in a set of preferred or minimal models for the action theory providing a definition of all timepoints and features where it is possible for them to change value based on the constraints in the theory. Of course, these models will also contain spurious change since we have only provided sufficient and necessary conditions for the definition of *Occlude*. To rule out spurious change, we will then filter the resulting circumscriptive sub-theory with that part of the theory containing persistence statements. Persistence statements specify when features should not change value, assuming a predefined definition of *Occlude* which circumscription provides. In this manner, any model containing feature change not mandated by the implicit occlusion policy in the action theory will be excluded as a model of the action theory. For example, the Yale Shooting Problem [28] involves loading a gun, waiting, and shooting. Since waiting occludes no fluents, interpretations where the gun becomes unloaded while waiting are filtered out, yielding the intended conclusion that the gun remains loaded at the start of the shooting action. A separate circumscription policy will be used for that part of the action theory containing action occurrence statements, where the predicate *Occurs* will be circumscribed. Finally, all partitions will be conjoined.

Due to the structural syntactic constraints built into statement definitions in $\mathcal{L}(\text{ND})$, we can show that the two circumscribed sub-theories which are 2nd-order due to the use of circumscription, can be reduced to logically equivalent first-order theories. In fact, since only positive occurrences of the predicates *Occlude* and *Occurs* occur in the two circumscribed partitions of the action theory, respectively, a standard syntactic transformation on formulas may be used to generate the necessary conditions for both predicates. This in fact is a form of predicate completion, and it is related to Definition 7.3.6 in Chapter 7 of this Handbook.

The formal definition of the circumscription policy used in TAL will use the following terminology:

- Let $\mathcal{N}$ denote the collection of narrative statements contained in a narrative in $\mathcal{L}(\text{ND})$, and let $\mathcal{N}_{\text{per}}$, $\mathcal{N}_{\text{obs}}$, $\mathcal{N}_{\text{occ}}$, $\mathcal{N}_{\text{acs}}$, $\mathcal{N}_{\text{dom}}$, and $\mathcal{N}_{\text{dep}}$ denote the sets of persistence statements, observation statements, action occurrence statements, action type specifications, domain constraint statements, and dependency constraint statements in $\mathcal{N}$, respectively.

- Let Γ denote the translation of $\mathcal{N}$ into $\mathcal{L}(\text{FL})$ using the *Trans* translation function, and let Γ_{per}, Γ_{obs}, Γ_{occ}, Γ_{acs}, Γ_{dom}, and Γ_{dep} denote the persistence formulas, observation formulas, action occurrence formulas, action type specifications, domain constraint formulas, and dependency constraint formulas in Γ, respectively.

- Let Γ_{fnd} denote the set of foundational axioms in $\mathcal{L}(\text{FL})$, containing unique names axioms, unique values axioms, etc.

- Let Γ_{time} denote the axiomatization of the particular temporal structure used in TAL.

In the following, we assume familiarity with circumscription [54, 55] and common notation used to denote circumscription policies [47]. Let

$$\Gamma = \Gamma_{\text{per}} \wedge \Gamma_{\text{obs}} \wedge \Gamma_{\text{dom}} \wedge \Gamma_{\text{occ}} \wedge \Gamma_{\text{dep}} \wedge \Gamma_{\text{acs}}$$

be the translation of an action narrative in $\mathcal{L}(\text{ND})$ into a first-order theory in $\mathcal{L}(\text{FL})$ as described previously. Based on the discussion above, we use circumscription to minimize *Occurs* in Γ_{occ} and *Occlude* in $\Gamma_{\text{dep}} \wedge \Gamma_{\text{acs}}$ as follows:

$$\Gamma_1 = \Gamma_{\text{per}} \wedge \Gamma_{\text{obs}} \wedge \Gamma_{\text{dom}} \wedge CIRC[\Gamma_{\text{occ}}; Occurs] \wedge$$
$$CIRC[\Gamma_{\text{dep}} \wedge \Gamma_{\text{acs}}; Occlude]$$

In addition, let

$$\Gamma_2 = \Gamma_{\text{fnd}} \wedge \Gamma_{\text{time}}$$

For any narrative $\mathcal{N}$ in TAL, a preferred narrative theory in the base logic $\mathcal{L}(\text{FL})$ is defined as

$$\Delta_{\mathcal{N}} = \Gamma_2 \wedge \Gamma_1$$

We say that a formula α in the base logic $\mathcal{L}(\text{FL})$ is preferentially entailed by the narrative $\mathcal{N}$ whose translation into $\mathcal{L}(\text{FL})$ is Γ iff

$$\Delta_{\mathcal{N}} \models \alpha$$

Observe that there are several equivalent formalizations of $\Delta_{\mathcal{N}}$ due to the following general property of circumscription (p. 311, [47]): for any sentence B not containing P, Z (where P is minimized and Z is varied),

$$CIRC[\Gamma(P, Z) \wedge B; P; Z] \equiv CIRC[\Gamma(P, Z); P; Z] \wedge B \tag{18.1}$$

and the observation that

$$CIRC[\Gamma_{\text{occ}}; Occurs] \wedge CIRC[\Gamma_{\text{dep}} \wedge \Gamma_{\text{acs}}; Occlude]$$
$$\equiv CIRC[\Gamma_{\text{occ}} \wedge \Gamma_{\text{dep}} \wedge \Gamma_{\text{acs}}; Occurs, Occlude]$$

From this, it follows that $\Delta_{\mathcal{N}}$ is equivalent to

$$\Delta' = \Gamma_2 \wedge \Gamma_{\text{per}} \wedge \Gamma_{\text{obs}} \wedge \Gamma_{\text{dom}} \wedge CIRC[\Gamma_{\text{occ}} \wedge \Gamma_{\text{dep}} \wedge \Gamma_{\text{acs}}; Occurs, Occlude]$$

and since $\Gamma_2 \wedge \Gamma_{obs} \wedge \Gamma_{dom}$ does not contain *Occurs* or *Occlude*, this is equivalent to

$$\Delta' = \Gamma_{per} \wedge CIRC[\Gamma_2 \wedge \Gamma_{obs} \wedge \Gamma_{dom} \wedge \Gamma_{occ} \wedge \Gamma_{dep} \wedge \Gamma_{acs}; Occurs, Occlude]$$

Note that it is important that Γ_{per} is outside the circumscriptive theory due to the fact that it contains occurrences of the predicate *Occlude*. Consequently, filtered circumscription is fundamental to the approach used in TAL.

As it stands, Δ_N is in fact, a second-order theory due to the fact that Γ_1 contains two second-order circumscription formulas, $CIRC[\Gamma_{occ}; Occurs]$ and $CIRC[\Gamma_{dep} \wedge \Gamma_{acs}; Occlude]$. Due to structural syntactic constraints in the narrative N in $\mathcal{L}(ND)$ which are carried over to its translation Γ in $\mathcal{L}(FL)$, it can be shown that both $CIRC[\Gamma_{occ}; Occurs]$ and $CIRC[\Gamma_{dep} \wedge \Gamma_{acs}; Occlude]$ are reducible to logically equivalent first-order formulas. We now show this. First some preliminaries.

An occurrence of a predicate symbol in a formula is *positive* if it is in the range of an even number of negations (this is assuming that the connectives $\supset$ and $\equiv$ have been eliminated and replaced by other connectives in some equivalent normal form). A formula $A(P)$ is *positive* (relative to P) if all occurrences of P in $A(P)$ are positive.

Based on Definitions 18.7 and 18.8 for change and application formulas in $\mathcal{L}(ND)$ and the definition of the translation function *Trans* from $\mathcal{L}(ND)$ into $\mathcal{L}(FL)$, it is straightforward to show that the predicate *Occurs* can only appear positively in Γ_{occ} and that the predicate *Occlude* can only appear positively in $\Gamma_{dep} \wedge \Gamma_{acs}$. The following proposition can then be applied to show that both $CIRC[\Gamma_{occ}; Occurs]$ and $CIRC[\Gamma_{dep} \wedge \Gamma_{acs}; Occlude]$ are reducible to logically equivalent first-order formulas [17]:

Proposition 18.1. *(See p. 316, [47].) If $A(P, Z)$ is positive relative to P, then the circumscription $CIRC[A(P, Z); P; Z]$ is equivalent to*

$$A(P, Z) \wedge \neg \exists x, z[P(x) \wedge A(\lambda y(P(y) \wedge x \neq y), z)]$$

In fact, it can be shown that predicate completion can be applied to Γ_{occ} and $\Gamma_{dep} \wedge \Gamma_{acs}$, respectively. The following proposition will be of use. Let $\bar{x}$ be a tuple of variables, and $F(\bar{x})$ be a formula with all parameters explicitly shown.

Proposition 18.2. *(See p. 309, [47].) If $F(\bar{x})$ does not contain P, then the circumscription $CIRC[\forall \bar{x}(F(\bar{x}) \supset P(\bar{x})); P]$ is equivalent to $\forall \bar{x}(F(\bar{x}) \equiv P(\bar{x}))$.*

This proposition generalizes to conjunctions of formulas of the form $\forall \bar{x} F(\bar{x}) \supset P(\bar{x})$. Using a number of syntactic transformations [8, 10], it can be shown that

$$\Gamma_{occ} = \bigwedge_{i=1}^{n} \forall \bar{x}(F_i(\bar{x}) \supset Occurs(\bar{x})) \tag{18.2}$$

where n is the number of *Occurs* formulas in Γ_{occ}. By the generalization of Proposition 18.2 and (18.2), it follows that

$$CIRC[\Gamma_{occ}; Occurs] = \forall \bar{x}\left[\left(\bigvee_{i=1}^{n} F_i(\bar{x})\right) \equiv Occurs(\bar{x})\right] \tag{18.3}$$

In addition it can be shown [8, 10] that

$$\Gamma_{\text{dep}} \wedge \Gamma_{\text{acs}}$$

$$= \left[\bigwedge_{i=1}^{n} B_i \wedge \bigwedge_{j=1}^{k} C_j \wedge \forall \bar{x} \left[\left(\bigvee_{i=1}^{n} F_i(\bar{x}) \vee \bigvee_{j=1}^{k} G_j(\bar{x}) \right) \supset Occlude(\bar{x}) \right] \right]$$

(18.4)

where B_i and C_i contain no occurrences of the $Occlude$ predicate.
    By (18.1), it follows that,

$$CIRC[\Gamma_{\text{dep}} \wedge \Gamma_{\text{acs}}; Occlude]$$

$$= \bigwedge_{i=1}^{n} B_i \wedge \bigwedge_{j=1}^{k} C_j \wedge$$

$$CIRC\left[\forall \bar{x} \left[\left(\bigvee_{i=1}^{n} F_i(\bar{x}) \vee \bigvee_{j=1}^{k} G_j(\bar{x}) \right) \supset Occlude(\bar{x}) \right]; Occlude \right] \quad (18.5)$$

By the generalization of Proposition 18.2 and (18.5), it follows that

$$CIRC[\Gamma_{\text{dep}} \wedge \Gamma_{\text{acs}}; Occlude]$$

$$= \bigwedge_{i=1}^{n} B_i \wedge \bigwedge_{j=1}^{k} C_j \wedge \forall \bar{x} \left[\left(\bigvee_{i=1}^{n} F_i(\bar{x}) \vee \bigvee_{j=1}^{k} G_j(\bar{x}) \right) \equiv Occlude(\bar{x}) \right] \quad (18.6)$$

Consequently, one can reduce Γ_1 in $\Delta_{\mathcal{N}}$ to a logically equivalent first-order formula. Under the assumption that Γ_2 in $\Delta_{\mathcal{N}}$ is also first-order (the temporal structure has a first-order axiomatization), for any narrative $\mathcal{N}$, its translation into a preferred narrative in $\mathcal{L}(\text{FL})$, $\Delta_{\mathcal{N}}$, is a first-order theory.

Example 18.3 (*Circumscription of the RAH scenario*). Though the circumscription of the $Occlude$ predicate can be translated into a single first order formula, we have instead chosen for expository purposes to generate a separate formula for each ground fluent in the narrative, where the conjunction of these formulas is entailed by the original 2nd-order circumscription axiom. Here, we show a subset of these formulas for the Russian Airplane Hijack scenario.

    First, the following are the necessary and sufficient conditions for loc(boris) to be occluded at any given point in time. For example, if boris is at home at time 3, which is a precondition for the action occurrence [3,5] travel(boris, home1, office), then his location will be occluded at time 5, when the final effects of the travel action take place.

$\forall t \; [Occlude(t, \text{loc(boris)}) \equiv t = 5 \wedge Holds(3, \text{loc(boris)}, \text{home1}) \vee$
$t = 10 \wedge Holds(8, \text{loc(boris)}, \text{office}) \vee t = 11 \wedge Holds(10, \text{loc(boris)}, \text{airport}) \vee$
$14 \leqslant t \wedge t \leqslant 15 \wedge$
$Holds(13, \text{loc(sas609)}, \text{run609}) \wedge Holds(13, \text{onplane(sas609, boris)}, \text{true}) \vee$
$t = 16 \wedge Holds(13, \text{loc(sas609)}, \text{run609}) \wedge$
$Holds(13, \text{onplane(sas609, boris)}, \text{true})]$

The conditions for occlusion of loc(dimiter) are quite similar, but differ in certain time-points given that boris and dimiter do not travel at the same time.

$\forall t$ [*Occlude*(*t*, loc(dimiter)) ≡ *t* = 4 ∧ *Holds*(2, loc(dimiter), home3) ∨
t = 7 ∧ *Holds*(5, loc(dimiter), office) ∨ *t* = 10 ∧
Holds(9, loc(dimiter), airport) ∨
14 ≤ *t* ∧ *t* ≤ 15 ∧ *Holds*(13, loc(sas609), run609) ∧
Holds(13, onplane(sas609, dimiter), true) ∨
t = 16 ∧ *Holds*(13, loc(sas609), run609) ∧
Holds(13, onplane(sas609, dimiter), true)]

The fluent inpocket(boris,gun) may be occluded at time 7 if boris is at the required location when attempting to pick it up, but inpocket(dimiter,gun) can never be occluded.

$\forall t$ [*Occlude*(*t*, inpocket(boris, gun)) ≡ *t* = 7 ∧ *Holds*(6, loc(boris), loc(gun))]
$\forall t$ [*Occlude*(*t*, inpocket(dimiter, gun)) ≡ false]

18.8   Representing Ramifications in TAL

The ramification problem [46, 20, 37, 48, 51, 21, 62, 25, 68] states that it is unreasonable to explicitly specify all the effects of an action in an action specification itself. One would rather prefer to state the direct effects of actions in the action specification and then use deductive machinery to derive the indirect effects of actions using the direct effects of actions together with general knowledge of *directional* dependencies among features specified in some background theory. The feature dependencies specified do not necessarily have to be based solely on notions of physical or other causality, but often are. A solution to the ramification problem is important from the representational perspective, where one strives for incremental, modular and intuitive characterizations of action and change. When one thinks of actions at a certain level of abstraction, one normally thinks of actions in terms of their direct effects and one would like to represent actions as such. On the other hand, causality plays an important role in any type of reasoning about action and change, therefore modular and incremental theories of causal and other dependencies among features is equally important to represent as is the interaction between actions and causal theories.

Some earlier approaches to solving the ramification problem made use of pure domain constraints (essentially logical implication) in order to infer side effects of actions. For the Russian Airplane Hijack scenario, for example, one might specify that everyone onboard an airplane is always in the same physical location as the airplane. Should one fly the airplane to another location, a direct effect would constrain the airplane to be in the new location, and the locations of everyone onboard would have to change location to the airplane's new location in order to still satisfy the domain constraint. This type of solution is non-directional, which may sometimes be of advantage but may also lead to unexpected or unintended results. For example, in some representations, invoking an action that moves a single person would also cause the airplane and everyone else onboard to move.

The key insight in providing a good solution to the ramification problem is that of finding appropriate and representationally efficient ways of encoding directionality in dependencies among features which cause change in addition to allowing longer chains of directional feature change. Logical implication, for example, is one way to encode a dependency constraint among features, but it under-constrains the directionality of a dependency due to the fact that the contrapositive to an implication formula is logically equivalent to that formula. Another important point to keep in mind is the way in which dependencies are triggered. This is highly contextual and though it is often the case that change triggers change, it is also the case that state triggers change. Both types of context and combinations of both should be expressible in action theories.

The TAL solution to the ramification problem involves the use of dependency constraints, which were formally specified in Definition 18.11. In this definition, the similarity between action type specifications and dependency constraints may be noted. Whereas an action type specification is an application formula conditionalized by the occurrence of an action ($[t, t']\ \Psi$ where Ψ is an action term) and then a precondition once that action is invoked, a dependency constraint consists of an application formula without such an action occurrence precondition. In a sense, while actions must be explicitly invoked, dependency constraints are constantly active. In both cases, there is an explicit directionality of feature change implicit in the representation. Technically, this is achieved by noting that features are occluded via assignment operators on the right hand side of implications, whereas they are not on the left hand side. This together with the minimization policy for occlusion and persistence statements permits the encoding of directionality of change in a fine-grained manner.

This solution to the ramification problem can be directly applied to the Russian Airplane Hijack scenario. Recall that the definition of the travel and fly actions included formulas explicitly causing anything a person was carrying to move to the same destination (Section 18.3.2). Clearly it would be better if such a formula could be factored out and modeled as a side effect of a person moving between two locations in any manner, rather than having to be specified for every action that causes a person to move. This can be represented using the following feature dependency constraint, stating that if the fact that *person* is at *loc* becomes true (changes to true)—in other words, if the person has just moved to *loc*—then anything the person carries in his pockets will also move to the same location. The use of explicit reassignment with the R operator ensures that such changes are permitted despite the general persistence assumption for the loc fluent.

> **dep1** $\forall t, person, pthing, loc\ [[t]\ \mathsf{inpocket}(person, pthing) \land C_T([t]\ \mathsf{loc}(person) \hat{=} loc) \supset$
> $R([t]\ \mathsf{loc}(pthing) \hat{=} loc)]$

With this change, the travel action can be simplified as follows:

> **acs3** $[t_1, t_2]\mathsf{travel}(person, loc_1, loc_2) \rightsquigarrow [t_1]\ \mathsf{loc}(person) \hat{=} loc_1 \supset$
> $R([t_2]\ \mathsf{loc}(person) \hat{=} loc_2)$

The fly action can be simplified in a similar manner. Before showing the new definition of this action though, we will consider one more indirect effect: people on board an airplane move when the airplane moves.

> **dep2** $\forall t, plane, person, loc\ [[t]\ \mathsf{onplane}(plane, person) \land C_T([t]\ \mathsf{loc}(plane) \hat{=} loc) \supset$
> $R([t]\ \mathsf{loc}(person) \hat{=} loc)]$

Note that the context for the dependency constraint in **dep2** has both a triggering condition (C_T) and a standard state condition. This is useful for encoding chaining of indirect effects.

Though this is quite similar to the previous indirect effect, it serves to illustrate an important property of fluent dependency constraints: It is possible to trigger not only a single indirect effect but a *chain* of indirect effects, which can be utilized to further modularize the specification of a narrative. In this particular scenario, causing an airplane to move will cause all people on board the airplane to move, which in turn will cause anything they are carrying to move, allowing the fly action to be modeled as follows:

acs1 $[t_1, t_2]$fly($plane, runway_1, runway_2$) $\rightsquigarrow [t_1]$ loc($plane$) $\hat{=} runway_1 \supset$
       $I((t_1, t_2)$ loc($plane$) $\hat{=}$ air) $\land R([t_2]$ loc($plane$) $\hat{=} runway_2$)

18.9   Representing Qualifications in TAL

The qualification problem [67, 46, 20, 49, 51, 65, 11, 42, 69] was identified by McCarthy [53, 54] while developing systems for representing general commonsense knowledge. McCarthy showed a way to deal with the representational problem by using circumscription. In his own words,

> The "qualification problem" immediately arose in representing general commonsense knowledge. It seemed that in order to fully represent the conditions for the successful performance of an action, an impractical and implausible number of qualifications would have to be included in sentences expressing them. [54]

A solution to the qualification problem would involve a normative representation of an action which would model the fact that an action can be invoked unless *something* prevents it from being invoked, where that *something* is assumed by default not to exist unless explicitly represented in an action theory. Additionally, when qualifications to actions are learned, the representation should permit an incremental and elaboration tolerant means of adding such qualifications to the action theory.

We have now modeled most of the Russian Airplane Hijack scenario in TAL, but we have not provided a means for modeling qualifications to actions in a representationally efficient, incremental and elaboration tolerant manner. Some examples of qualifications to actions in the RAH scenario would be: someone who carries a gun cannot board a plane, or someone who is drunk may or may not be able to board a plane. In fact, it may be the case that there are qualifications to qualifications. For example, security personnel should be able to board a plane with a gun.

There are already a number of solutions to various aspects of the qualification problem in the literature, some of which would be applicable in TAL. However, many of these solutions are dependent on the assumption of highly constrained action types, where (for example) actions must correspond to simple state transition with a precondition state and an effect state with no description of what happens in the duration of an action. As we have shown, actions in TAL go far beyond this limited form of representation. We would like to provide a solution that retains at least the following features of TAL:

- Any state, including the initial state, can be completely or incompletely specified using observations and domain constraints.

- Actions can be context-dependent and non-deterministic. They can have duration and internal state, and the duration may be different for different executions of the action. There may be concurrent actions with partially overlapping execution intervals.

- There can be dynamic processes continuously taking place independently of any actions that may occur.

- Domain constraints can be used for specifying logical dependencies between fluents generally true in every state or across states. They may vary over time.

- Actions can have side effects, which may be delayed and may affect the world at multiple points in time. They may in turn trigger other delayed or non-delayed side effects.

We would also like to retain the first-order reducibility of the circumscription axiom in any solution to the qualification problem in TAL. In order to do this, the following restrictions and assumptions will apply. First, we will be satisfied with a solution where invoking a qualified action either has no effect or has some well-defined effect. Secondly, we will restrict the solution to the off-line planning and prediction problems and not claim a complete solution for the post-diction problem, which would require being able to conclude that an action was qualified because its successful execution would have contradicted an observation of some feature value after that action was invoked.

18.9.1   Enabling Fluents

To handle the qualification problem, we use a solution based on defaults where each action type in a narrative is associated with an *enabling fluent*, a boolean durational fluent with default value true and with the same number and type of arguments as the action type. This fluent will be used in the precondition of the action and will usually be named by prefixing "poss-" to the name of the action. For example, the boarding action in the RAH scenario will be associated with an enabling fluent poss-board(*person, plane*). We also add a persistence statement for this fluent stating that it is a durational fluent. Recall that a durational feature retains its default value unless an additional constraint specifies that there is an exception to that value at a particular point or points in time. **acs4** is then modified as follows:

per5 $\forall t, person, plane \ [Dur(t, \text{poss-board}(person, plane), \text{true})]$
acs4′ $[t_1, t_2] \ \text{board}(person, plane) \rightsquigarrow$
          $[t_1] \ \text{poss-board}(person, plane) \wedge \text{loc}(person) \hat{=} \text{airport} \supset$
          $R([t_2] \ \text{loc}(person) \hat{=} value(t_2, \text{loc}(plane)) \wedge \text{onplane}(plane, person))$

The other action types are modified in a similar way. Note that the existing precondition that loc(*person*) $\hat{=}$ airport remains in the action definition and will not be moved to the definition of poss-board. This is a modeling issue, where some conditions are identified as "ordinary" preconditions whereas others are identified as qualifications which are moved outside the action type specification. A similar modeling issue already arose in the case of ramifications, where some effects are considered "ordinary" action effects whereas others are considered to be indirect effects modeled using dependency constraints.

Now, suppose that board(*person*, *plane*) is executed between timepoints t_1 and t_2. If poss-board (*person*, *plane*) is false at t_1 for some reason, the action is qualified, or *disabled*. On the other hand, if the fluent is true at t_1, the action is *enabled*. Of course, it can still be the case that the action has no effects, if other parts of its precondition are false.

To generalize this, a context-independent action that should have no effect at all when qualified can be defined using a simple action definition of the form[8]

acsm $[t_1, t_2]$ action $\rightsquigarrow$ $[t_1]$ poss-action $\wedge \alpha \supset R([t_2] \beta)$

where α is the precondition and β specifies the direct effects of the action (context-dependent actions are defined analogously). However, we also wanted to be able to define actions that do have some effects when they are qualified. This can be done by defining a context-dependent action that defines what happens when the enabling fluent is false:

acsn $[t_1, t_2]$ action $\rightsquigarrow$ $([t_1]$ poss-action $\wedge \alpha_1 \supset R([t_2] \beta_1)) \wedge$
       $([t_1] \neg$ poss-action $\wedge \alpha_2 \supset R([t_2] \beta_2))$

For example, suppose that whenever anyone tries to board a plane but the action is qualified, they should try to find new transportation. In order to model this, we would add a new persistent fluent find-new-transportation(PERSON) : BOOLEAN and modify the boarding action from Section 18.3.2 as follows:

acs4″ $[t_1, t_2]$ board(*person*, *plane*) $\rightsquigarrow$
       $([t_1]$ poss-board(*person*, *plane*) $\wedge$ loc(*person*) $\hat{=}$ airport $\supset$
         $R([t_2]$ loc(*person*) $\hat{=}$ value(t_2, loc(*plane*)) $\wedge$ onplane(*plane*, *person*))) $\wedge$
       $([t_1] \neg$poss-board(*person*, *plane*) $\wedge$ loc(*person*) $\hat{=}$ airport $\supset$
         $R([t_2]$ find-new-transportation(*person*)))

In this alternative scenario, if anyone is at the airport and tries to board a plane, and the action is qualified, they will have a goal of finding new transportation. If they are at the airport but the action is not qualified, they will board the plane. If they are not at the airport, none of the preconditions will be true, and invoking the action will have no effect. Note that it may very well be the case that they can not board for a more serious reason such as carrying a gun. This is a case where the original qualification might have to be qualified.

Regardless of whether a qualified action has an effect or not, its enabling fluent is a durational fluent with default value true. Therefore, the fluent will normally be true, and the action will normally be enabled. In the remainder of this section, we will examine some of the ways in which we can disable an action using strong and weak qualification.

---

[8]Note that due to the regularity of the solution, such extensions could be implicit in an action macro, thus avoiding unneeded clutter in the representation and delegating representation responsibility to the system rather than the knowledge engineer.

18.9.2   Strong Qualification

When there is sufficient information to conclude that an action will definitely not succeed, it is *strongly qualified*. This can be modeled by forcing its enabling fluent to be
false at the timepoint at which the action is invoked.

For example, suppose that when a person has a gun in his pocket, it should be
impossible for that person to board a plane. Then, whenever inpocket(*person*, gun)
holds, poss-board(*person*) necessarily becomes false. This can be represented using a
dependency constraint:

dep3 $\forall t, person, plane$ [[t] inpocket(*person*, gun) $\supset$ I ([t] ¬poss-board(*person*, *plane*))]

At any timepoint t when a person has a gun in his pocket, we use the I macro both
to occlude poss-board(*person*, *plane*) for all airplanes, thereby releasing it from the
default value axiom, and to make it false. This implies that as long as a person has
a gun in his pocket, poss-board will be false for that person on all airplanes. If the
gun is later removed from the pocket, this dependency constraint will no longer be
triggered. At that time, assuming no other qualifications affect the enabling fluent, it
will automatically revert to its default value, true.

18.9.3   Weak Qualification

Although strong qualification can often be useful, we may sometimes have enough
information to determine that an action *may* fail, even though we cannot conclusively
prove that it will. We call this *weak* qualification.

For example, we may want to model the fact that when a person is drunk, he *may or
may not* be able to board an airplane, depending on whether airport security discovers
this or not. We may not be able to determine within our model of the RAH scenario
whether airport security does discover that any given person is drunk. In this case,
whenever drunk(*person*) holds, we must release poss-board from the default value
assumption, which would otherwise have forced poss-board to be true:

dep4 $\forall t, person$ [[t] drunk(*person*) $\supset$ $\forall plane$ [X ([t] poss-board(*person*, *plane*))]]

At any timepoint t when a person is drunk, we occlude poss-board(*person*, *plane*) for
all airplanes, but since we do not state anything about the *value* of the enabling fluent,
it is allowed to be either true or false.

Although being able to state that an action *may* fail is useful in its own
right, it is naturally also possible to restrict the set of models further by adding
more statements to the scenario which could make it possible to infer whether
poss-board(dimiter, sas609) is true or false at some or all timepoints. For example,
we may know that people boarding sas609 are always checked more carefully, so that
it is impossible for anyone who is drunk to be on board that airplane, which could
be expressed using an additional domain constraint. In the context of postdiction,
observation statements could be used in a similar manner. For example, adding the
observation statement **obs5** [13] onplane(sas609, boris) to the narrative would allow
us to infer that Boris did in fact board the plane and that poss-board(boris, sas609)
was in fact true. He would then end up at his intended destination. If instead we added

the observation statement **obs6** [13] ¬onplane(sas609, boris), we could infer that he was unable to board the plane and he did not end up at his destination.

It should be noted that this approach to modeling qualification has similarities to a standard default solution to the qualification problem, but with some subtle differences. For example, it permits more control of the enabling precondition, even allowing it to change during the execution of an action. More importantly, it involves no changes to the minimization policy already used in TAL to deal with the frame and ramification problems, consequently the circumscription theory is still first-order reducible.

18.9.4 Qualification: Not Only For Actions

As we have shown, this approach to qualification is based on general concepts such as durational features and fluent dependency constraints, instead of introducing new predicates, entailment relations or circumscription policies specifically designed for dealing with the qualification problem. This is appealing not only because we avoid introducing new complexity into the logic, but also because reusing these more general concepts adds to the flexibility of the approach. In fact, exactly the same approach can be used for specifying qualifications to any rule or constraint. Most notably, one can provide qualifications for ramification constraints, thereby introducing defeasible side effects—or one can even qualify qualification constraints themselves.

As an example, when we initially considered the boarding action, the "natural" preconditions were that one had to be at the airport; this is the precondition encoded in the definition of board (**acs4**). Later, we found another condition that should qualify the action: No one should be able to board a plane carrying a gun. Now, however, we may discover that this qualification does not always hold: Airport security *should* be able to board a plane carrying a gun.

Assuming that there is a fluent is-security(person) : BOOLEAN, this exception to the general qualification rule could of course be modeled by changing the dependency constraint **dep3** in the following way:

> **dep3′** $\forall t, person, plane$ [[t] inpocket(*person*, gun) $\land$ ¬is-security(*person*) $\supset$
> I ([t] ¬poss-board(*person*, *plane*))]

However, we may later discover additional conditions under which it should be possible for a person to board a plane with a gun, and we do not want to modify **dep3** each time. Instead, the qualification itself should be qualified. This can easily be done using the same approach as for actions. A new enabling fluent guns-forbidden(PERSON, PLANE) : BOOLEAN is added for the qualification constraint, and **dep3** is modified as follows:

> **dep3″** $\forall t, person, plane$ [[t] inpocket(*person*, gun) $\land$ guns-forbidden(*person*, *plane*) $\supset$
> I ([t] ¬poss-board(*person*, *plane*))]

Now, we can qualify the qualification **dep3** simply by making guns-forbidden false for some person and airplane. In order to do this, we add a new dependency constraint:

> **dep5** $\forall t, person, plane$ [[t] is-security(*person*) $\supset$
> I ([t] ¬guns-forbidden(*person*, *plane*))]

18.9.5   Ramifications as Qualifications

A problem related to the qualification problem occurs in formalisms where ramification constraints and qualification constraints are expressed as domain constraints [20, 49]. Assume, for example, that we are reasoning about the blocks world, and that we have the following domain constraint (expressed using TAL syntax), stating that no two blocks can be on top of the same block:

dom $\forall t, x, y, z \, [[t] \, \mathsf{on}(x, z) \wedge \mathsf{on}(y, z) \supset x = y]$

Now, suppose that the direct effect of the action put(A, C) is on(A, C), and the action is executed in a state where on(B, C) is true. Then, we cannot determine syntactically whether the domain constraint should be interpreted as a ramification constraint (since no two blocks can be on top of C, B must be removed) or as a qualification constraint (since no two blocks can be on top of C, the action should fail).

In TAL, however, all indirect effects of an action must be expressed as *directed* dependency constraints. Therefore, this problem simply does not arise. For example, if a ramification constraint is required, the following dependency constraint can be used:

dep $\forall t, x, y, z \, [[t] \, \mathsf{on}(x, z) \wedge C_T([t + 1] \, \mathsf{on}(y, z)) \wedge x \neq y \supset R([t + 1] \, \neg\mathsf{on}(x, z))]$

If x is on z, and we then place y on z, then an indirect effect is that x is removed from z. On the other hand, if a qualification constraint is required, an enabling fluent poss-put(BLOCK, BLOCK) can be used and the following qualification condition would then be added:

dep $\forall t, x, y, z \, [[t] \, \mathsf{on}(x, z) \wedge x \neq y \supset I([t] \, \neg\mathsf{poss\text{-}put}(y, z))]$

Clearly, the problem of determining whether a constraint should be implicitly interpreted as a qualification or a ramification does not arise in this approach. One could criticize such a solution as over-constraining the action theory model, but then again, use of domain constraints could equally well be criticized for under-constraining the model.

A description of the TAL representation of the Russian Airplane Hijack scenario is now complete and the general methods used to resolve the frame, ramification and qualification problems have been described. The partial translations into $\mathcal{L}(\text{FL})$ were done using VITAL [39], a research tool that can be used to study problems involving action and change within TAL and generate visualizations of action scenarios and preferred entailments.

18.10   Action Expressivity in TAL

For the sake of brevity, narratives used as examples in the literature are generally modeled at a rather high level of abstraction. This is especially true when a narrative is used for the purpose of demonstrating the properties of a solution to a specific problem; for example, the Russian Airplane Hijack scenario was explicitly designed for the demonstration of qualification constraints. This, however, should not be taken to mean that this is the *only* level of abstraction possible in TAL. We briefly illustrate this point by adding more realistic timing to several action types in the RAH scenario and by introducing effects at inner timepoints during the execution of the fly action.

As shown in previous examples, the timing of an action occurrence has often been completely specified in the corresponding action occurrence statement:

occ $[1, 2]$ pickup(boris, comb1)

In many cases, the duration of the action is better specified in the action itself. An action specification can contain arbitrary constraints on its parameters, which can be used to constrain the time required for boarding as well as the amount of time required when boarding fails:

acs $[t_1, t_2]$ board(*person, plane*) $\rightsquigarrow$
$([t_1]$ poss-board(*person, plane*) $\wedge$ loc(*person*) $\hat{=}$ airport $\supset$
$R([t_2]$ loc(*person*) $\hat{=}$ value(t_2, loc(*plane*)) $\wedge$ onplane(*plane, person*) $\wedge$
$t_2 = t_1 + 100)) \wedge$
$([t_1]$ ¬(poss-board(*person, plane*) $\wedge$ loc(*person*) $\hat{=}$ airport) $\supset$
$t_2 = t_1 + 10)$

This also illustrates the use of contextually dependent effects, where the exact outcome of the action is determined by the state of the world when it is invoked (though non-deterministic and incompletely specified effects are also possible). An arbitrary number of conditions (mutually exclusive or not) can be used to specify the effects of an action.

The timing in the action occurrence statements is then relaxed by introducing a number of temporal constants. Here, boris begins picking up comb1 at time 1. He does not know when he will finish, but at the next timepoint (boris1 + 1), he will begin traveling to the office.

occ $[1, \text{boris1}]$ pickup(boris, comb1)
occ $[\text{boris1} + 1, \text{boris2}]$ travel(boris, home1, office)
occ ...

Of course, action durations do not have to be defined using a constant. If distances between locations are modeled using a dist fluent, one can specify the duration of a fly action as follows:

acs $[t_1, t_2]$ fly(*plane, runway*$_1$, *runway*$_2$) $\rightsquigarrow$
$[t_1]$ loc(*plane*) $\hat{=}$ *runway*$_1$ $\supset$
$I((t_1 + 200, t_2)$ loc(*plane*) $\hat{=}$ air) $\wedge$ $R([t_2]$ loc(*plane*) $\hat{=}$ *runway*$_2$) $\wedge$
$t_2 = t_1 + 200 + \text{dist}(runway_1, runway_2)/200$

Here, flying between two locations takes an initial 200 timepoints for taxiing, plus time proportional to the distance between the two locations. This more accurate model of the fly action can be further extended by modeling the remaining distance at any given time when the plane is in the air, by conjoining the following formula to the effects given above:

$$\forall t \ [t_1 + 200 < t \wedge t \leqslant t_2 \supset I([t] \text{ remaining-distance}(plane) \hat{=}$$
$$\text{dist}(runway_1, runway_2) \cdot (t - t_1 - 200)/(t_2 - t_1 - 200))]$$

At any timepoint within the interval $(t_1 + 200, t_2]$, the remaining distance is assigned a new value. Further elaborations to effects and timing can be added as required by the task to which the model will be applied.

18.11   Concurrent Actions in TAL

Much work in reasoning about action and change has been done under the (sometimes implicit) assumption that there is a single agent performing sequences of non-overlapping actions. The use of explicit metric time in TAL clearly enables the specification of narratives where action execution intervals are partly or completely overlapping, whether those actions are performed by a single agent or by multiple cooperating or adversarial agents. Similarly, the fact that actions can have non-unit duration and that one can specify in detail what happens during the execution interval enables richer domain models where a larger class of phenomena related to concurrency can be modeled. However, a complete treatment of concurrency also requires the ability to model interactions between concurrent effects of multiple actions. Such interactions can be *synergistic*, where two actions must be executed concurrently in order to achieve the desired effect. For example, moving a table requires lifting both sides of the table simultaneously in order to avoid the undesired side effects of everything on the table sliding off onto the floor. Interactions may also be *accumulative*, as when a number of agents are placing packages in a vehicle for transportation, or *harmful*, where one action provides the desired effect unless certain other actions are executed concurrently.

In each of these cases, the composite effect of executing several actions is not equivalent to the logical conjunction of the individual effects. For example, lifting the left side of the table causes the table to tilt, as does lifting the right side of the table, but lifting both sides at once cancels this effect. Though this could in theory be handled by modeling all possible interactions within each action definition, this would clearly be an extremely non-modular solution and would suffer from a combinatorial explosion in the number of conditional effects required in each action definition. This is especially true when dealing with actions with duration, where the number of combinations is determined not only by the number of actions but also by the number of ways two or more actions can overlap in time. The use of ramification constraints also complicates the issue by introducing interactions between actions and chains of (potentially delayed) ramification effects.

For these reasons, a more principled and indirect solution was proposed by Karlsson and Gustafsson [35], where actions do not directly change the state of the world but instead produce a set of influences. Fluent dependency constraints can then be used to model how the world is affected by a combination of influences.

18.11.1   Independent Concurrent Actions

The use of independent concurrent actions involving disjoint sets of features is unproblematic in TAL. This is illustrated in the following narrative, describing a world with two types of actions (LightFire and PourWater), and a number of agents (bill and bob) and other objects (wood1 and wood2). All variables appearing free are implicitly universally quantified.

acs1 $[s, t]$ LightFire(a, *wood*) $\supset$ ($[s]$ dry(*wood*) $\supset$ $R((s, t]$ fire(*wood*)))
acs2 $[s, t]$ PourWater(a, *wood*) $\supset$ $R((s, t]$ ¬dry(*wood*) $\wedge$ ¬fIre(*wood*))
obs1   [0] dry(wood1) $\wedge$ ¬fire(wood1) $\wedge$ wood(wood1)
obs2   [0] dry(wood2) $\wedge$ ¬fire(wood2) $\wedge$ wood(wood2)
occ1   [2, 7] LightFire(bill, wood1)
occ2   [2, 7] LightFire(bob, wood2)
occ3   [9, 12] PourWater(bob, wood1)

The first action law states that if an agent a lights a fire using a piece of wood, and the wood is dry, then the wood will be on fire. The second action law states that if somebody pours water on an object, then the object will no longer be dry, and will cease being on fire. There are two pieces of wood (wood1 and wood2) which are initially dry and not burning. Two fires are lit by bill and bob during the temporal interval [2, 7], and then bob pours water on bill's fire at [9, 12]. Since no concurrency is involved, the expected effects will take place: Both pieces of wood will be on fire at 7, and wood1 will no longer be burning at 12.

18.11.2   Interacting Concurrent Actions

Now consider the case where actions affecting the same fluents occur concurrently. For example, suppose bob pours water on wood1 while bill is still lighting the fire. Intuitively, the wood should not be on fire at 7. We formalize this in TAL by modifying **occ3**.

     occ3   [3, 5] PourWater(bob, wood1)

From the modified narrative one can still infer that wood1 is on fire at time 7, because the effects of LightFire(bill, wood1) are only determined by whether the piece of wood is dry at time 2, whereas in reality the effects of any action may also be altered by the direct and indirect effects of other concurrent actions. A slight modification of the narrative above illustrates another problem. Assume that **occ3** is replaced with the following:

     occ3   [3, 7] PourWater(bob, wood1)

Now, the lighting and pouring actions end at the same time. From **acs1** and **occ1** one can infer the effect [7] fire(wood1) and from **acs2** and **occ3** one can infer [7] ¬fire(wood1). Both effects are asserted to be direct and indefeasible. Thus, the narrative becomes inconsistent. The conclusion one would like to obtain is again that the wood is not on fire.

18.11.3   Laws of Interaction

Karlsson and Gustafsson [35] considers two solutions to these problems.

In the first solution, action laws are extended to allow references to other action occurrences and the effects of LightFire are made conditional on the fact that there is no interfering PourWater action. As noted in the introduction, this solution makes action descriptions less modular and there may be a combinatorial explosion in the number of conditional effects for each action. Other problems include the fact that a concurrent action might only interfere with part of an action's effects, leading to further complexity in action laws.

The second solution is based on the assumption that interactions resulting from concurrency are best modeled not on the level of actions but on the level of features. Action laws encode the influences that an action has upon the environment of the agent; in the fire example, $[s, t]$ LightFire$(a, wood)$ would have the effect $I((s, t]$ fire*$(wood, \text{true}))$ where fire*$(wood, \text{true})$ is a fluent representing an influence to make the feature fire$(wood)$ true. This example follows the convention of representing the influences on an actual fluent f$(\bar{\omega})$ with f*$(\bar{\omega}, v)$, where v is a value in the domain of f. Similarly, dependency constraints are modified to result in influences rather than actual fluent changes. The actual effects that these influences have on the environment are then specified in a special type of dependency laws called influence laws. Applying this solution to the fire example yields the following narrative:

dom1	$Per(\text{fire}(wood)) \wedge Dur(\text{fire}^*(wood, v), \text{false})$
dom2	$Per(\text{dry}(wood)) \wedge Dur(\text{dry}^*(wood, v), \text{false})$
acs1	$[s, t]$ LightFire$(a, wood) \supset I((s, t]$ fire$^*(wood, \text{true}))$
acs2	$[s, t]$ PourWater$(a, wood) \supset I((s, t]$ dry$^*(wood, \text{false}))$
dep1	$[s]\ \neg\text{dry}(wood) \supset I([s]$ fire$^*(wood, \text{false}))$
inf1	$[s, s + 3]$ fire$^*(wood, \text{true}) \wedge \neg\text{fire}^*(wood, \text{false}) \supset R([s + 3]$ fire$(wood))$
inf2	$[s]$ fire$^*(wood, \text{false}) \supset R([s]\ \neg\text{fire}(wood))$
inf3	$[s, s + 3]$ dry$^*(wood, \text{true}) \wedge \neg\text{dry}^*(wood, \text{false}) \supset R([s + 3]$ dry$(wood))$
inf4	$[s]$ dry$^*(wood, \text{false}) \supset R([s]\ \neg\text{dry}(wood))$
obs1	$[0]\ \neg\text{fire}(wood1) \wedge \text{dry}(wood1)$
occ1	$[2, 6]$ LightFire(bill, wood1)
occ2	$[3, 5]$ PourWater(bob, wood1)

The action laws **acs1** and **acs2** and dependency law **dep1** produce influences; for example, **dep1** states that the fact that the wood is not dry produces an influence fire*$(wood, \text{false})$ to extinguish the fire (if there is one). The effects of these influences, alone and in combination, are specified in **inf**x; for example, in order to affect the feature fire$(wood)$, the influence fire*$(wood, \text{true})$ for starting the fire has to be applied without interference from fire*$(wood, \text{false})$ for an extended period of time. In the preferred models of this narrative, wood1 will be wet at $[4, \infty)$, implying that fire*$(wood1, \text{false})$ will hold at $[4, \infty)$; consequently there is no interval $[s, s + 3]$ where fire*$(wood1, \text{true}) \wedge \neg\text{fire}^*(wood1, \text{false})$, and fire$(wood1)$ will never become true.

The case when an effect of one action enables the effect of another action can also be handled with conditional influence laws. For instance, the following influence law states that opening a door requires initially keeping the latch open (the example is originally due to Allen [1]):

inf1 $[t]$ latch-open $\wedge [t, t + 5]$ open$^*(\text{true}) \supset R([t + 5]$ open$)$

Though not explicitly shown here, it is possible to use separate modular influence laws to specify the result of arbitrary combinations of influences, including combinations that lead to no effect at all. Influences can naturally also be combined with the TAL approach to ramification, both in the sense that ramifications may lead to influences and in the sense that influences may cause chains of ramifications. One can also use influence laws to model resource conflicts, with either deterministic, non-deterministic or prioritized outcomes when two agents attempt to use the same resource [35, 24]. This results in a highly flexible and modular solution to many problems associated with concurrency, regardless of whether that concurrency is due to actions, ramifications or delayed effects.

18.12   An Application of TAL: TALplanner

The flexibility of TAL as a language for describing and modeling actions with concurrent effects, dependencies between fluents and other commonly occurring aspects of dynamic domains also makes it eminently suitable for modeling planning domains. This is especially true for planners that make extensive use of domain knowledge in various forms. For this reason, TAL has been used as the semantic basis for a planner called TALplanner [12, 13, 41], where TAL is used for modeling not only actions, initial states and standard state-based goals but also a set of control formulas acting as constraints on the set of valid plans. This latter use of logical formulas was initially inspired by the planner TLPLAN [2].

One of the intended uses of TAL in TALplanner is as a specification language providing a declarative semantics for planning domains and plans. This is an important difference from TLPLAN where only control formulas are based on the use of logic and actions are instead modeled using an operational semantics. But unlike Green's approach [22], which involved not only representing planning domains in logic but also *generating* plans using a resolution theorem prover, the declarative semantics of TAL currently serves mainly as a specification for the proper behavior of the planning algorithm. The TALplanner implementation generates plans using a procedural forward-chaining search method together with a search tree which is pruned with the help of temporal control formulas.

Given that performance is of paramount importance in a planner, the full expressivity of TAL is intended to be introduced into the planner implementation in stages; the full power of the language, including non-deterministic actions, chains of ramifications and arbitrary interactions between concurrent actions, must be approached carefully. Having the specification of the proper semantics of such constructs available from the beginning is useful even in the initial phase, providing a better view of what extensions will be desired in the future, which sometimes affects the basic framework of an implementation. Nonetheless, the language currently used for domain specifications in TALplanner is a subset of the full language for TAL described previously in this chapter.

Planning domains and planning problems also require the specification of certain types of information that were not originally supported in TAL or its predecessors. This required a set of new additions to the language which will be described.

Thus, both extensions and limitations relative to TAL are in order. This falls neatly within the TAL policy of providing macro languages adapted to specific tasks together with a translation into a single unified first-order base language $\mathcal{L}(FL)$ with a well-defined semantics and circumscription policy. While the details of the new macro language $\mathcal{L}(ND)^*$ are beyond the scope of this chapter (see Kvarnström [41] for a

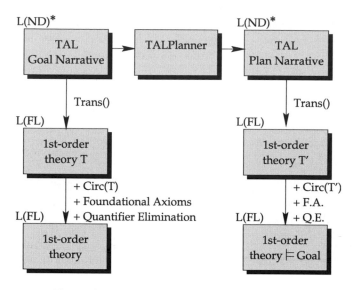

Figure 18.3: The relation between TAL and TALplanner.

complete definition), most of the extensions are used in the example planning domain discussed below.

Planning as narrative generation

TAL is based on the use of narratives, and automated planning can be viewed as a form of narrative generation where an initial narrative, specifying an initial state as well as various forms of domain knowledge, is incrementally extended by adding new action occurrences—in other words, new steps in the plan. The intention, then, is to generate a suitable set of action occurrences such that the desired goals are satisfied in the resulting complete narrative.

Fig. 18.3 contains an extended version of the diagram previously shown in Fig. 18.2. As seen in the top row of this figure, the input to TALplanner is a narrative in the extended macro language $\mathcal{L}(ND)^*$. This narrative is sometimes called a *goal narrative*, emphasizing the fact that it specifies a planning problem instance, and is usually denoted by $\mathcal{N}$. The goal narrative consists of two parts: A domain description, defining among other things the operators that are available to the planner, and a problem instance description, defining the initial state and the goal. TALplanner uses this high-level description of a planning problem to search for a set of TAL action occurrences (plan steps) that can be added to this narrative so that in the corresponding logical model, a goal state is reached. If this succeeds, the output is a new TAL narrative in $\mathcal{L}(ND)^*$ where the appropriate set of TAL action occurrences has been added. This narrative is sometimes called a *plan narrative*, emphasizing the fact that it represents a solution to a planning problem. Both goal narratives and plan narratives can be translated into $\mathcal{L}(FL)$ (the second row in the figure). As in pure TAL, a number of foundational axioms are required, and a standard TAL circumscription policy is applied, yielding complete definitions of the *Occlude* and *Occurs* predicates (the third row). Further details are available in Kvarnström [41].

Adding action occurrences to a standard TAL narrative is a non-monotonic operation, in the sense that conclusions entailed by the original narrative may have to be retracted once a new action occurrence is added. However, at each step in the planning process, one would also prefer to be able to determine whether a certain conclusion will remain valid regardless of what new actions may be added to a plan. This is especially important in the context of temporal control formulas, where a candidate plan should not necessarily be discarded for violating a control formula if this violation might be "repaired" by adding new actions.

The key to solving this problem lies in the flexibility of the TAL solution to the frame problem. By selecting a search space where new action occurrences are constrained not to begin before any of the actions already present in the plan—that is, if there are actions beginning at times 0, 10 and 273, one cannot add a new action beginning at 272—one can guarantee that along any branch of the forward-chaining search tree, there is a monotonically increasing temporal horizon such that any new effects introduced by future actions will take place strictly after this horizon.[9] Then, the standard definition of inertia can be altered to ensure that persistence is applied up to and including this temporal horizon, while leaving fluents unconstrained at all later timepoints. This is easily done by changing the TAL translation function while retaining the same circumscription policy.

It should be noted that this approach is not equivalent to assuming a complete lack of knowledge after the temporal horizon. On the contrary, any fluent constraints resulting from action effects or (in a future implementation) domain constraints are still equally valid after the temporal horizon; only the persistence assumption has been relaxed at those timepoints where the complete set of effects is unknown. Thus, depending on the effects that have been applied so far, it can still be possible to prove that a control formula has been definitely violated after the temporal horizon, which is essential for the performance of the concurrent version of TALplanner.

An example planning domain

We will now show some examples of the use of $\mathcal{L}(ND)^*$ in modeling the timed version of the ZenoTravel domain, originally used in the AIPS 2002 International Planning Competition [45, 50]. Due to space limitations, the complete domain description will not be provided. Nevertheless, the most pertinent aspects of the modeling language will be presented in sufficient detail.

The ZenoTravel domain contains a number of aircraft that can fly people between cities. There are five planning operators available: Persons may board and debark from aircraft, and aircraft may fly, zoom (fly quickly, using more fuel), and refuel. There are no restrictions on how many people an aircraft can carry. Flying and zooming are equivalent except that zooming is generally faster and uses more fuel. Fig. 18.4 shows a tiny example problem, with arrows pointing out goal locations.

Objects in a planning problem are modeled using standard TAL values, and state variables are modeled using TAL fluents.

---

[9]Note that this does not rule out the generation of plans with concurrent actions and one version of TALplanner does generate actions concurrently.

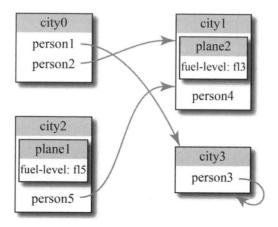

Figure 18.4: A ZenoTravel problem instance.

domain	THING :elements { ... }	
domain	AIRCRAFT :parent THING :elements { ... }	
domain	PERSON :parent THING :elements { ... }	
domain	CITY :elements { ... }	
feature	at(THING, CITY), in(PERSON, AIRCRAFT) :domain BOOLEAN	
feature	fuel(AIRCRAFT) :domain INTEGER	

...

Operators are modeled using a new form of operator statement, which uses a new syntax with explicit preconditions, prevail conditions, durations and effects. As specified by the competition organizers, the time required to board a plane is specified using the boarding-time fluent, which is here multiplied by 1000 in order to provide higher precision timing. Note also that the plane is required to remain at its location during boarding. The time required to fly between two cities is proportional to the distance and inversely proportional to the speed of the aircraft.[10]

operator	board($person$, $aircraft$, $city$) :at s
:duration	$value(t, 1000 *$ boarding-time) :as dur
:precond	$[s]$ at($person$, $city$) $\wedge$ at($aircraft$, $city$)
:prevail	$[s+1, s+dur]$at($aircraft$, $city$)
:effects	$[s+1]$at($person$, $city$) := false, $[s+dur]$in($person$, $aircraft$) := true
operator	fly($aircraft$, $city_1$, $city_2$) :at s
:duration	$value(t, 1000 *$ distance($city_1$, $city_2$) / slow-speed($aircraft$)) :as dur
:precond	$[s]$ at($aircraft$, $city_1$) $\wedge$ $city_1 \neq city_2$ $\wedge$
	$[s]$ fuel($aircraft$) $\geqslant$ distance($city_1$, $city_2$) * slow-burn($aircraft$)
:effects	$[s+1]$ at($aircraft$, $city_1$) := false,
	$[s+dur]$ at($aircraft$, $city_2$) := true,
	$[s+dur]$ fuel($aircraft$) := $value(s,$ fuel($aircraft$)) $- 1$

---

[10]We appeal to the use of *semantic attachment* [71] techniques in the implementation of TAL and TALplanner by liberal use and invocation of built in mathematical and other functions associated with value domains for features.

Control formulas specify constraints that must be satisfied in the logical model corresponding to a solution plan. In some respects, the central use of explicit control formulas is really what stands out from other automated planning paradigms. Control formulas are intended to represent the high-level heuristics or commonsense smarts that one usually assumes a human might use when faced with specific planning problems in well-defined domains. Initially, a person may not have sufficient competence about a domain. Consequently, the plans generated may not be the best and will certainly take longer to generate. As a person acquires a feel for a domain, certain constraints are then applied when generating plans which in turn minimize the search space. It is this intuition which is behind the use of control formulas as a domain dependent means of limiting the huge search space of action combinations one is faced with when using a forward chaining planner. The technique is also incremental in nature. Control formulas may be added incrementally as one learns more about the domain in question thus improving the efficiency of the planner.

The following two control formulas used in the ZenoTravel domain state that passengers should only board an aircraft when they desire to be in another city, and that they should only debark when they have reached their destination. Free variables are assumed to be universally quantified.

control :name "only-board-when-necessary"
$[t]$ ¬in($person, aircraft$) ∧ $[t + 1]$ in($person, aircraft$) ⊃
∃$city, city_2$ [$[t]$ at($person, city$) ∧ goal(at($person, city_2$)) ∧ $city \neq city_2$]

control :name "only-debark-when-in-goal-city"
$[t]$ in($person, aircraft$) ∧ $[t + 1]$ ¬in($person, aircraft$) ⊃
∃$city$ [$[t]$ at($aircraft, city$) ∧ goal(at($person, city$))]

In addition to these statements, which are valid in an entire planning domain, the planner also needs a complete specification of the initial state (using TAL observation statements) and a specification of the state-based goals that should be achieved. The latter is specified using goal statements, consisting of TAL fluent formulas that must hold in the final state resulting from executing a solution plan.

The following are possible goal and initial state statements for the example in Fig. 18.4:

goal at(person1, city3) ∧ at(person2, city1) ∧ at(person3, city3) ∧ at(person5, city1)
obs ∀$city$ [$[0]$ at(person1, $city$) ≡ $city =$ city0]
obs ∀$city$ [$[0]$ at(person2, $city$) ≡ $city =$ city0]
obs ∀$city$ [$[0]$ at(plane1, $city$) ≡ $city =$ city2]
obs $[0]$ fuel(plane1) $\hat{=}$ 5

The main statement types for goal and plan narratives have now been introduced. A goal narrative is input to the forward-chaining TALplanner system and if possible, a TAL plan narrative is generated by the planner which contains action occurrence statements and timings for such statements which entail the goal and control statements originally included in the goal narrative.

It was stated that the strategy used in TALplanner is not "planning as theorem-proving", but using TAL as a specification language for developing planners. Perhaps a better way to describe TAL and its relation to TALplanner is not only as a specification framework, but as "theorem-proving as an aid to plan generation". One can clearly see from Fig. 18.3 that in the plan generation process, one can use TAL to reason about partial plans being generated. In fact, during plan generation, a simple form of inference is currently used to verify that control formulas are satisfied in theories associated with partial plans. In the plan execution process, one can use TAL to verify and monitor the plan execution process by querying the current state of a robotic system with TAL formulas. This is a form of on-line model-checking similar to the progression algorithms used in TALplanner and TLPLAN. TALplanner also uses a limited form of resolution to reason about control formulas and operators during the initial (preprocessing) phase of the planning process, inferring a set of facts that must necessarily be true during the invocation of an operator and thereby improving the performance of checking control formulas during the planning phase. The flexible framework described in this section offers great potential for leveraging the use of logic with planning in a pragmatic and efficient manner.

18.13   Summary

This chapter provides a presentation of the latest stable version of TAL, a temporal action logic for reasoning about action and change. In the article, we present the basic narrative framework for specifying action scenarios using two languages $\mathcal{L}(\text{ND})$ and $\mathcal{L}(\text{FL})$. A definition of the circumscription policy used for TAL is provided in addition to proposals for partial solutions to the frame, ramification and qualification problems. Solutions are obviously dependent on the nature of the application domains to which they are applied. We say the solutions are partial because it is unclear whether such solutions would hold up practically unless one had specifications of the environments in which TAL would be used and a means of assessing whether the formalism would cover the spectrum of reasoning problems associated with a particular domain. Such a qualification would apply to any action and change formalism and assessments should be done using either formal assessment frameworks such as that described in the introduction to this chapter or empirical testing. TAL has been partially assessed for a particular type of application domain but much remains to be done in terms of assessing many of the newer extensions to TAL. That being said, TAL is one of the most expressive logical formalisms for reasoning about action and change, the underlying semantic framework is highly intuitive and TAL has been shown to correctly model the majority of benchmark problems proposed in the action and change research community. In the chapter, we have also provided a description as to how one could deal with the very complex problem of true concurrent actions and their interactions. We have concluded with an application of TAL to an award winning automated planner, TALplanner.

Acknowledgements

The TAL framework described in this chapter is very much a team effort and has continued with spurts and lags beginning in 1994. We acknowledge contributions by the following members of the Knowledge Processing Lab at the Department of Computer and Information Science, Linköping University: Marcus Bjäreland, Joakim Gustafsson, Lars Karlsson, Martin Magnusson, Andrzej Szałas and Witold Łukaszewicz.

The writing of this article and research included in it has been supported by funding from the Wallenberg Foundation under the WITAS UAV Project, Swedish Research Council grants (50405001, 50405002) and a Swedish National Aeronautics Research grant (NFFP4-S4203).

Bibliography

[1] J. Allen. Temporal reasoning and planning. In Allen, Kautz, Pelavin, and Tenenberg, editors. *Reasoning about Plans*. Morgan Kaufmann, 1991.

[2] F. Bacchus and F. Kabanza. Using temporal logics to express search control knowledge for planning. *Artificial Intelligence*, 116 (1–2):123–191, 2000.

[3] C. Baral and M. Gelfond. Logic programming and reasoning about actions. In M. Fisher, D.M. Gabbay, and L. Vila, editors. *Handbook of Temporal Reasoning in Artificial Intelligence*. Elsevier Publications, 2005.

[4] M. Bjäreland. Two aspects of automating logics of action and change: Regression and tractability. Master's thesis, Linköping University, 1998. Thesis No 674. LiU-Tek-Lic 1998:09.

[5] M. Bjäreland and L. Karlsson. Reasoning by regression: Pre- and postdiction procedures for logics of action and change with nondeterminism. In *Proceedings of the 15th International Joint Conference on Artificial Intelligence (IJCAI'97)*, Nagoya, Japan, August 1997. Morgan Kaufmann, 1997.

[6] P. Doherty. Notes on PMON circumscription. Technical Report LITH-IDA-94-43, Dept. of Computer and Information Science, Linköping University, Linköping, Sweden, December 1994.

[7] P. Doherty. Reasoning about action and change using occlusion. In A.G. Cohn, editor. *Proceedings of the Eleventh European Conference on Artificial Intelligence (ECAI-1994)*, Amsterdam, The Netherlands, 1994, pages 401–405. John Wiley and Sons, Chichester, England, 1994.

[8] P. Doherty. PMON$^+$: A fluent logic for action and change, formal specification, version 1.0. Technical Report LITH-IDA-96-33, Department of Computer and Information Science, Linköping University, Linköping, Sweden, December 1996.

[9] P. Doherty and J. Gustafsson. Delayed effects of actions = direct effects + causal rules. *Linköping Electronic Articles in Computer and Information Science*, 3, 1998.

[10] P. Doherty, J. Gustafsson, L. Karlsson, and J. Kvarnström. TAL: Temporal Action Logics—language specification and tutorial. *Electronic Transactions on Artificial Intelligence*, 2(3–4):273–306, September 1998.

[11] P. Doherty and J. Kvarnström. Tackling the qualification problem using fluent dependency constraints: Preliminary report. In L. Khatib and R. Morris, editors. *Proceedings of the Fifth International Workshop on Temporal Representation and Reasoning (TIME-1998)*, Los Alamitos, CA, USA, May 1998, pages 97–104. IEEE Computer Society Press, 1998.

[12] P. Doherty and J. Kvarnström. TALplanner: An empirical investigation of a temporal logic-based forward chaining planner. In C. Dixon and M. Fisher, editors. *Proceedings of the Sixth International Workshop on Temporal Representation and*

Reasoning (TIME-1999), Orlando, Florida, USA, May 1999, pages 47–54. IEEE Computer Society Press, 1999.

[13] P. Doherty and J. Kvarnström. TALplanner: A temporal logic-based planner. *AI Magazine*, 22(3):95–102, 2001.

[14] P. Doherty and W. Łukaszewicz. Circumscribing features and fluents: A fluent logic for reasoning about action and change. In D.M. Gabbay and H.J. Ohlbach, editors. *Proceedings of the First International Conference on Temporal Logic (ICTL-1994), Lecture Notes in Artificial Intelligence*, vol. 827, pages 82–100. Springer-Verlag, London, 1994.

[15] P. Doherty, W. Łukaszewicz, and E. Madalińska-Bugaj. The PMA and relativizing change for action update. In *Proceedings of the 6th International Conference on Principles of Knowledge Representation and Reasoning (KR'98)*, 1998.

[16] P. Doherty, W. Łukaszewicz, and A. Szałas. Computing circumscription revisited: Preliminary report. In *Proceedings of the 14th International Joint Conference on Artificial Intelligence (IJCAI'95)*, vol. 2, pages 1502–1508, 1995.

[17] P. Doherty, W. Łukaszewicz, and A. Szałas. Computing circumscription revisited: A reduction algorithm. *Journal of Automated Reasoning*, 18:297–336, 1997.

[18] P. Doherty and P. Peppas. A comparison between two approaches to ramification: PMON(R) and $\mathcal{AR}_0$. In X. Yao, editor. *Proceedings of the 8th Australian Joint Conference on Artificial Intelligence*, pages 267–274. World Scientific, 1995.

[19] P. Doherty, W. Łukaszewicz, and A. Szałas. Explaining explanation closure. In *Proceedings of the 9th International Symposium on Methodologies for Intelligent Systems (ISMIS'96)*, 1996.

[20] M.L. Ginsberg and D.E. Smith. Reasoning about action II: The qualification problem. *Artificial Intelligence*, 35(3):311–342, 1988.

[21] E. Giunchiglia and V. Lifschitz. Dependent fluents. In *Proceedings of the Fourteenth International Joint Conference on Artificial Intelligence (IJCAI-1995)*, Montréal, Québec, Canada, pages 1964–1969. Morgan Kaufmann Publishers, San Mateo, CA, USA, 1995.

[22] C. Green. Applications of theorem proving to problem solving. In *Proceedings of the First International Joint Conference on Artificial Intelligence (IJCAI-1969)*. Morgan Kaufmann, 1969.

[23] J. Gustafsson. Extending temporal action logic for ramification and concurrency. Master's thesis, Linköping University, 1998. Thesis No 719. LiU-Tek-Lic 1998:54.

[24] J. Gustafsson. Extending temporal action logic. PhD thesis, Linköping Studies in Science and Technology, Dissertation No. 689, 2001.

[25] J. Gustafsson and P. Doherty. Embracing occlusion in specifying the indirect effects of actions. In L.C. Aiello, J. Doyle, and S.C. Shapiro, editors. *Proceedings of the Fifth International Conference on Principles of Knowledge Representation and Reasoning (KR-1996)*, pages 87–98. Morgan Kaufmann Publishers, San Francisco, CA, USA, 1996.

[26] J. Gustafsson and J. Kvarnström. Elaboration tolerance through object-orientation. In *Proceedings of the Fifth Symposium on Logical Formalizations of Commonsense Reasoning (Common Sense-2001)*, 2001.

[27] J. Gustafsson and J. Kvarnström. Elaboration tolerance through object-orientation. *Artificial Intelligence*, 153:239–285, March 2004.

[28] S. Hanks and D.V. McDermott. Default reasoning, nonmonotonic logics, and the frame problem. In *Proceedings of the Fifth National Conference on Artificial Intelligence (AAAI-1986)*, Philadelphia, Pennsylvania, USA, August 1986, pages 328–333. Morgan Kaufmann Publishers, Los Altos, CA, USA, 1986.

[29] L. Karlsson. Specification and synthesis of plans using the Features and Fluents framework. Master's thesis, Linköping University, 1995. Thesis No 469. LiU-Tek-Lic 1995:01.

[30] L. Karlsson. Causal links planning and the systematic approach to action and change. In *Proceedings of the AAAI 96 Workshop on Reasoning about Actions, Planning and Control: Bridging the Gap*, Portland, OR, August 1996. AAAI Press, 1996.

[31] L. Karlsson. Planning, truth criteria and the systematic approach to action and change. In *Proceedings of the 9th International Symposium on Methodologies for Intelligent Systems (ISMIS'96), Lecture Notes for Artificial Intelligence*. Springer-Verlag, 1996.

[32] L. Karlsson. Reasoning with incomplete initial information and nondeterminism in situation calculus. In *Proceedings of the 15th International Joint Conference on Artificial Intelligence (IJCAI'97)*, 1997.

[33] L. Karlsson. Anything can happen: on narratives and hypothetical reasoning. In *Proceedings of the 6th International Conference on Principles of Knowledge Representation and Reasoning (KR'98)*. Morgan Kaufmann, 1998.

[34] L. Karlsson. Actions, interactions and narratives. PhD thesis, Linköping Studies in Science and Technology, Dissertation No. 593, 1999.

[35] L. Karlsson and J. Gustafsson. Reasoning about concurrent interaction. *Journal of Logic and Computation*, 9(5):623–650, October 1999.

[36] L. Karlsson, J. Gustafsson, and P. Doherty. Delayed effects of actions. In H. Prade, editor. *Proceedings of the Thirteenth European Conference on Artificial Intelligence (ECAI-1998)*, Brighton, UK, August 1998, pages 542–546. John Wiley and Sons, Chichester, England, 1998.

[37] G.N. Kartha and V. Lifschitz. Actions with indirect effects. In *Proceedings of the International Conference on Knowledge Representation and Reasoning (KR)*, pages 341–350. Morgan Kaufmann, 1994.

[38] M. Koubarakis. Complexity results for first-order theories of temporal constraints. In J. Doyle, E. Sandewall, and P. Torasso, editors. *Proceedings of the Fourth International Conference on Principles of Knowledge Representation and Reasoning (KR-1994)*, pages 379–390. Morgan Kaufmann Publishers, San Francisco, CA, USA, 1994.

[39] J. Kvarnström. VITAL. An on-line system for reasoning about action and change using TAL. 1997–2006.

[40] J. Kvarnström. Applying domain analysis techniques for domain-dependent control in TALplanner. In M. Ghallab, J. Hertzberg, and P. Traverso, editors. *Proceedings of the Sixth International Conference on Artificial Intelligence Planning and Scheduling (AIPS-2002)*, Toulouse, France, April 2002, pages 101–110. AAAI Press, Menlo Park, CA, USA, 2002.

[41] J. Kvarnström. TALplanner and other extensions to temporal action logic. PhD thesis, Linköpings universitet, April 2005. Linköping Studies in Science and Technology, Dissertation no. 937.

[42] J. Kvarnström and P. Doherty. Tackling the qualification problem using fluent dependency constraints. *Computational Intelligence*, 16(2):169–209, May 2000.

[43] J. Kvarnström and P. Doherty. TALplanner: A temporal logic based forward chaining planner. *Annals of Mathematics and Artificial Intelligence*, 30:119–169, 2000.

[44] J. Kvarnström, P. Doherty, and P. Haslum. Extending TALplanner with concurrency and resources. In W. Horn, editor. *Proceedings of the Fourteenth European Conference on Artificial Intelligence (ECAI-2000), Frontiers in Artificial Intelligence and Applications*. Berlin, Germany, August 2000, pages 501–505. IOS Press, Amsterdam, The Netherlands, 2000.

[45] J. Kvarnström and M. Magnusson. TALplanner in the Third International Planning Competition: Extensions and control rules. *Journal of Artificial Intelligence Research*, 20:343–377, December 2003.

[46] V. Lifschitz. Formal theories of action. In F.M. Brown, editor. *The Frame Problem in Artificial Intelligence: Proceedings of the 1987 Workshop*, Lawrence, Kansas, USA, April 1987, pages 35–58. Morgan Kaufmann Publishers, Los Altos, CA, USA, 1987.

[47] V. Lifschitz. Circumscription. In D.M. Gabbay, C.J. Hogger, and J.A. Robinson, editors. *Handbook of Artificial Intelligence and Logic Programming*, vol. 3, pages 297–352. Oxford University Press, 1991.

[48] F. Lin. Embracing causality in specifying the indirect effects of actions. In *Proceedings of the Fourteenth International Joint Conference on Artificial Intelligence (IJCAI-1995)*, Montréal, Québec, Canada, August 1995. Morgan Kaufmann Publishers, San Francisco, CA, USA, 1995.

[49] F. Lin and R. Reiter. State constraints revisited. *Journal of Logic and Computation*, 4(5):655–678, 1994.

[50] D. Long and M. Fox. The third international planning competition: Results and analysis. *Journal of Artificial Intelligence Research*, 20:1–59, December 2003.

[51] N. McCain and H. Turner. A causal theory of ramifications and qualifications. In *Proceedings of the International Joint Conference on Artificial Intelligence (IJCAI)*, pages 1978–1984, 1995.

[52] J. McCarthy. Programs with common sense. In *Proceedings of the Teddington Conference on the Mechanization of Thought Processes*, London, pages 75–91. Her Majesty's Stationary Office, 1959.

[53] J. McCarthy. Epistemological problems of artificial intelligence. In R. Reddy, editor. *Proceedings of the Fifth International Joint Conference on Artificial Intelligence (IJCAI-1977)*, Cambridge, MA, USA, pages 1038–1044. William Kaufmann, 1977.

[54] J. McCarthy. Circumscription—a form of non-monotonic reasoning. *Artificial Intelligence*, 13(1–2):27–39, 1980. Reprinted in [56].

[55] J. McCarthy. Applications of circumscription to formalizing common sense knowledge. *Artificial Intelligence*, 28(1):89–116, 1986. Reprinted in [56].

[56] J. McCarthy. *Formalization of Common Sense, papers by John McCarthy edited by Vladimir Lifschitz*. Ablex, 1990.

[57] E.T. Mueller. *Commonsense Reasoning*. Morgan Kaufmann, 2006.

[58] R. Reiter. *Knowledge in Action*. MIT Press, 2001.

[59] E. Sandewall. Combining logic and differential equations for describing real-world systems. In R.J. Brachman, H.J. Levesque, and R. Reiter, editors. *Proceedings of the International Conference on Knowledge Representation and Reasoning (KR)*, pages 412–420. Morgan Kaufmann, 1989.

[60] E. Sandewall. Filter preferential entailment for the logic of action and change. In N.S. Sridharan, editor. *Proceedings of the Eleventh International Joint Conference on Artificial Intelligence (IJCAI-1989)*, San Francisco, August 1989. Morgan Kaufmann Publishers, San Mateo, CA, USA, 1989.

[61] E. Sandewall. *Features and Fluents: A Systematic Approach to the Representation of Knowledge about Dynamical Systems*, vol. 1. Oxford University Press, 1994.

[62] E. Sandewall. Assessments of ramification methods that use static constraints. In *Proceedings of the International Conference on Knowledge Representation and Reasoning (KR)*, pages 99–110. Morgan Kaufmann, 1996.

[63] E. Sandewall. Cognitive robotics and its metatheory: Features and fluents revisited. *Electronic Transactions on Artificial Intelligence*, 2(3–4), 1998.

[64] L.K. Schubert. Monotonic solution of the frame problem in situation calculus. In H.E. Kyburg, R.P. Loui, and G.N. Carlson, editors. *Knowledge Representation and Defeasible Reasoning*, pages 23–67. Kluwer, 1990.

[65] M. Shanahan. *Solving the Frame Problem: A Mathematical Investigation of the Common Sense Law of Inertia*. The MIT Press, Cambridge, MA, USA, 1997.

[66] Y. Shoham. Nonmonotonic logics: Meaning and utility. In J.P. McDermott, editor. *Proceedings of the Tenth International Joint Conference on Artificial Intelligence (IJCAI-1987)*, Milan, Italy, August 1987, pages 388–393. Morgan Kaufmann Publishers, Los Altos, CA, USA, 1987.

[67] Y. Shoham. *Reasoning about Action and Change*. MIT Press, 1987.

[68] M. Thielscher. Ramification and causality. *Artificial Intelligence*, 89(1–2):317–364, 1997.

[69] M. Thielscher. The qualification problem: A solution to the problem of anomalous models. *Artificial Intelligence*, 131(1–2):1–37, 2001.

[70] M. Thielscher. *Reasoning Robots—The Art and Science of Programming Robotic Agents*. Springer, 2005.

[71] R.W. Weyhrauch. Prolegomena to a theory of mechanized formal reasoning. *Artificial Intelligence*, 13(1–2), 1980.

Handbook of Knowledge Representation
Edited by F. van Harmelen, V. Lifschitz and B. Porter
© 2008 Elsevier B.V. All rights reserved
DOI: 10.1016/S1574-6526(07)03019-2

Chapter 19

Nonmonotonic Causal Logic

H. Turner

This chapter describes a nonmonotonic causal logic designed for representing knowledge about the effects of actions. A causal rule

$$\phi \Leftarrow \psi$$

where ϕ and ψ are formulas of classical logic, is understood to express that (the truth of) ψ is a sufficient condition for ϕ's being caused. A causal theory T is a set of causal rules, and is assumed to describe all such sufficient conditions. Thus, given an interpretation I, the set of formulas

$$T^I = \{\phi \mid \phi \Leftarrow \psi \in T \text{ and } I \models \psi\}$$

can be understood to describe everything caused in a world such as I (according to T). The *models* of causal theory T are those interpretations for which what is true is exactly what is caused: that is, the interpretations I such that I is the unique model of T^I. This fixpoint condition makes the logic nonmonotonic; adding causal rules to T may produce new models.

Causal theories allow for convenient formalization of such challenging phenomena as indirect effects of actions (ramifications), implied action preconditions, concurrent interacting effects of actions, and things that change by themselves. These capabilities stem from a robust solution to the frame problem [33]: one can write causal rules

$$F_{t+1} \Leftarrow F_{t+1} \wedge F_t$$
$$\neg F_{t+1} \Leftarrow \neg F_{t+1} \wedge \neg F_t \tag{19.1}$$

saying that a sufficient cause for fluent F's being true (respectively, false) at time $t + 1$ is its being so at time t and remaining so at time $t + 1$. In this way, persistent facts are effectively said to have inertia as their cause. On the other hand, the fixpoint definition of a model of a causal theory T requires that everything have a cause (according to T), and so any facts not explained by inertia must have some other explanation. Consequently, in the context of the fixpoint condition, the inertia rules (19.1) capture the commonsense notion that things do not change unless they are made to. (The frame problem is briefly discussed in Chapter 6 as one of the motivations for nonmonotonic logics, and other solutions to the frame problem are presented in Chapters 16–18.)

In a causal theory, one easily describes not only direct effects of actions, but also their indirect effects, and even interacting effects of concurrent actions. For example, suppose there is a large bowl of soup, with left and right handles. We can describe the direct effect of lifting each side as follows.

$$up(left)_{t+1} \Leftarrow lift(left)_t$$
$$up(right)_{t+1} \Leftarrow lift(right)_t \tag{19.2}$$

More interestingly, we can then describe, without reference to any action, that if only one side of the bowl is up, then there is a cause for the soup's being spilled.

$$spilled_t \Leftarrow up(left)_t \neq up(right)_t \tag{19.3}$$

Under this description, if the soup is not already spilled and both sides of the bowl are lifted at once, the soup will remain unspilled. But if only one side is lifted, the soup will be spilled. Let us consider these two scenarios in more detail. Assume that initially neither side is up and the soup is unspilled. In the first scenario, both handles are lifted concurrently, and at the next time: by (19.2) there is a cause for both sides' being up, and by inertia—that is, by (19.1) with *spilled* in place of F—there is a cause for the soup's being unspilled. For the second scenario, suppose instead that only the left handle is lifted. Then, at the next time: by (19.2) there is a cause for the left side's being up, by inertia there is a cause for the right side's remaining down, and by (19.3) there is a cause for the soup's being spilled. Notice that the formalization does not support the incorrect alternative outcome in which, after lifting only the left handle, both sides are up and the soup remains unspilled. Why not? By (19.2) there would be a cause for the left side's being up, and by inertia there would be a cause the soup's remaining unspilled, but there would be *no* cause for the right side to be up (and the definition of a model requires that everything have a cause).

The prior example is meant to help with intuitions about the fixpoint definition of a model and its role in the expressive possibilities of causal theories. In the interest of clarity, it is important to emphasize that the example causal theory is incompletely specified. Indeed, the fixpoint definition requires that *everything* have a cause according to the theory. Accordingly, about occurrences and nonoccurrences of actions A, we often write that they are caused in either case, as follows.

$$A_t \Leftarrow A_t$$
$$\neg A_t \Leftarrow \neg A_t \tag{19.4}$$

That is, if A occurs at time t, there is a cause for this, and if, on the other hand, A does not occur at time t, there is a cause for that. Similarly, we typically say that initial facts about fluents F are caused.

$$F_0 \Leftarrow F_0$$
$$\neg F_0 \Leftarrow \neg F_0 \tag{19.5}$$

So, although everything in a model must be caused, it is convenient to take the view that some causes are exogenous to our description, and we can simply stipulate their existence, by writing rules such as those in (19.4) and (19.5). Moreover, this is only the most extreme version of the general case. After all, the nonmonotonic logic described here is *causal* only in a limited sense: causal rules allow a distinction between being true and having a cause. Causal theories do not grapple with the question of what a cause may be, and do not support direct reasoning about what causes what. Fortunately, many questions related to reasoning about actions require only that we be able to determine what are the causally possible histories (of the world being described), and for this purpose it seems enough to be able to describe the conditions under which facts are caused.

This strategic emphasis on the distinction between what is caused and what is (merely) true can be understood to follow Geffner [14, 15], whose work was influenced by Pearl [35]. (Pearl's ideas on causality have been extensively developed since then. See, for instance, [36].) In the reasoning about action community, this line of work was motivated primarily by the ramification problem—the problem of representing and reasoning about indirect effects of actions. For some time there were attempts to describe relationships like those described by (19.3) through the use of "state constraints": formulas of classical logic such as

$$(up(left)_t \not\equiv up(right)_t) \supset spilled_t. \tag{19.6}$$

It seems that the crucial shortcoming of a formula like (19.6), for the purpose of reasoning about ramifications, is that it simply does not say enough about what can (and cannot) cause what. Indeed, it is equivalent to its contrapositive

$$\neg spilled_t \supset (up(left)_t \equiv up(right)_t).$$

In the last 15 years, there have been *many* reasoning about action proposals incorporating more explicitly causal notions. The nonmonotonic causal logic described in this chapter was introduced in [30]. The most relevant prior work appears in [28, 29, 44]. A much fuller account of causal theories was published in 2004 [18], although a number of results presented in this chapter do not appear there. Causal theories have been studied, applied and extended in [24, 25, 17, 31, 45, 22, 27, 47, 2–4, 6, 7, 11, 20, 1, 5, 10, 21, 46, 13, 9, 42].

An implementation of causal theories—the Causal Calculator (CCALC)—is publicly-available, and many of the above-cited papers describe applications of it. The key to this implementation is an easy reduction from (a subclass of) causal theories to classical propositional logic, by a method introduced in [30], closely related to Clark's completion [8] for logic programs (discussed in Chapter 7). Thus, automated reasoning about causal theories can be carried out via standard satisfiability solvers. (The initial version of CCALC was due primarily to Norm McCain, and is described in his PhD thesis [32]. Since then it has been maintained and developed by Vladimir Lifschitz and his students at the University of Texas at Austin.)

Subsequent sections of this chapter are organized as follows.

- Section 19.1 defines causal theories (more adequately), considers a few examples, and remarks on several easy mathematical properties.

- Section 19.2 presents a "strong equivalence" result, which justifies a general replacement property, despite the nonmonotonicity of the logic.

- Section 19.3 specifies the reduction to classical propositional logic that makes automated reasoning about causal theories convenient.

- Section 19.4 demonstrates further expressive possibilities of causal theories, such as nondeterminism and things that change by themselves.

- Section 19.5 briefly describes the high-level action language $C+$ that is based on causal theories.

- Section 19.6 characterizes the close mathematical relationship between causal theories and Reiter's default logic, and notes the remarkable fact that inertia rules essentially like (19.1) appear already in Reiter's 1980 paper.

- Section 19.7 presents Lifschitz's reformulation of causal theories in higher-order classical logic, somewhat in the manner of circumscription.

- Section 19.8 presents the modal nonmonotonic logic UCL that includes causal theories as a special case.

19.1   Fundamentals

We first define a slight extension of usual (Boolean) propositional logic, convenient when formulas are used to talk about states of a system. Then we define the syntax and semantics of causal theories, make some observations, and consider a few examples, including a more precise account of the soup-bowl example already discussed.

19.1.1   Finite Domain Propositional Logic

A (finite-domain) *signature* is a set σ of symbols, called *constants*, with each constant c associated with a nonempty finite set $Dom(c)$ of symbols, called the *domain* of c. An *atom* of signature σ is an expression of the form

$$c = v$$

("the value of c is v") where $c \in \sigma$ and $v \in Dom(c)$. A *formula* of σ is a propositional combination of atoms.

To distinguish formulas of usual propositional logic from those defined here, we call them "classical".

An *interpretation* of σ is a function mapping each element of σ to an element of its domain. An interpretation I *satisfies* an atom $c = v$ (symbolically, $I \models c = v$) if $I(c) = v$. The satisfaction relation is extended from atoms to arbitrary formulas according to the usual truth tables for the propositional connectives.

Also as usual, a *model* of a set Γ of formulas is an interpretation that satisfies all formulas in Γ. If Γ has a model, it is said to be *consistent*, or *satisfiable*. If every model of Γ satisfies a formula F, then we say that Γ *entails* F and write $\Gamma \models F$. Formulas, or sets of formulas, are *equivalent* if they have the same models.

A *Boolean* constant is one whose domain is the set {t, f} of truth values. A *Boolean* signature is one whose constants are all Boolean. If c is a Boolean constant, we sometimes write c as shorthand for the atom $c = $ t. When the syntax and semantics defined above are restricted to Boolean signatures and to formulas that do not contain f, they turn into the usual syntax and semantics of classical propositional formulas. Even when the signature is not Boolean, there are easy reductions from finite domain propositional logic to classical propositional logic. (For more on this, see [18].)

19.1.2 Causal Theories

Syntax

A *causal rule* (of signature σ) is an expression of the form

$$\phi \Leftarrow \psi \tag{19.7}$$

where ϕ and ψ are formulas (of σ). We call ϕ the *head* of the rule, and ψ the *body*. The intuitive reading of (19.7) is "ϕ is caused if ψ".

A *causal theory* (of σ) is a set of causal rules (of σ).

Semantics

Consider any causal theory T and interpretation I (of σ). We define

$$T^I = \{\phi \mid \phi \Leftarrow \psi \in T, I \models \phi\}.$$

Intuitively, T^I describes what is caused in a world like I, according to T.

An interpretation I is a *model* of a causal theory T if I is the only model of T^I.

Observation 1. *For any causal theory T and interpretation I, I is a model of T iff, for all formulas ϕ,*

$$I \models \phi \text{ iff } T^I \models \phi.$$

This observation corresponds precisely to the informal characterization we began with—the models of a causal theory T are the interpretations for which what is true is exactly what is caused (according to T).

Observation 2. *If I is a model of a causal theory T, then $I \models \psi \supset \phi$ for every $\phi \Leftarrow \psi \in T$.*

Examples. Take

$$\sigma = \{p\}, \quad Dom(p) = \{1, 2, 3\}, \quad T_1 = \{p = 1 \Leftarrow p = 1\}.$$

There are three interpretations (of σ), as follows: $I_1(p) = 1$, $I_2(p) = 2$, $I_3(p) = 3$. Notice that $T_1^{I_1} = \{p = 1\}$. Clearly $I_1 \models T_1^{I_1}$, while $I_2 \not\models T_1^{I_1}$ and $I_3 \not\models T_1^{I_1}$, which shows that I_1 is a model of T_1. On the other hand, $T_1^{I_2} = T_1^{I_3} = \emptyset$. So I_2 is not the unique model of $T_1^{I_2}$, nor is I_3 the unique model of $T_1^{I_3}$. Consequently, neither I_2 nor I_3 is a model of T_1.

Consider the causal theory T_2 obtained by adding the causal rule $p = 2 \Leftarrow p = 2$ to T_1. One easily verifies that both I_1 and I_2 are models of T_2, which shows that causal theories are indeed nonmonotonic: adding a rule to T_1 produced a new model.

Now let us reconsider the soup-bowl domain, discussed somewhat informally in the introductory remarks. Take the Boolean signature

$$\sigma = \{upL_0, upR_0, sp_0, upL_1, upR_1, sp_1, liftL_0, liftR_0\}.$$

Then following causal theory T represents the soup-bowl domain, with constants abbreviated: upL_0 for $up(left)_0$, sp_1 for $spilled_1$, $liftL_0$ for $lift(left)_0$, and so forth.

$$
\begin{array}{lll}
upL_0 \Leftarrow upL_0 & upL_1 \Leftarrow upL_1 \wedge upL_0 & \\
\neg upL_0 \Leftarrow \neg upL_0 & \neg upL_1 \Leftarrow \neg upL_1 \wedge \neg upL_0 & liftL_0 \Leftarrow liftL_0 \\
upR_0 \Leftarrow upR_0 & upR_1 \Leftarrow upR_1 \wedge upR_0 & \neg liftL_0 \Leftarrow \neg liftL_0 \\
\neg upR_0 \Leftarrow \neg upR_0 & \neg upR_1 \Leftarrow \neg upR_1 \wedge \neg upR_0 & liftR_0 \Leftarrow liftR_0 \\
sp_0 \Leftarrow sp_0 & sp_1 \Leftarrow sp_1 \wedge sp_0 & \neg liftR_0 \Leftarrow \neg liftR_0 \\
\neg sp_0 \Leftarrow \neg sp_0 & \neg sp_1 \Leftarrow \neg sp_1 \wedge \neg sp_0 & (19.8)
\end{array}
$$

$$
\begin{array}{ll}
upL_1 \Leftarrow liftL_0 & sp_0 \Leftarrow upL_0 \not\equiv upR_0 \\
upR_1 \Leftarrow liftR_0 & sp_1 \Leftarrow upL_1 \not\equiv upR_1 \qquad\qquad (19.9)
\end{array}
$$

Most of the causal rules in T are of the "standard" kinds already discussed: the first column of (19.8) says that facts about the initial time are exogenous, the second column of (19.8) says that fluents upL, upR, sp are inertial, and the third column says that causes of occurrence and nonoccurrence of the actions $liftL, liftR$ are exogenous. The "interesting" rules appear in (19.9): the two on the left describe the direct effects of lifting the left and right handles of the bowl, and the other two say that, at both times 0 and 1, if only one side of the bowl is up, then there is a cause for the soup's being spilled.

Without much difficulty, one can verify that the models of this formalization are as previously described. For instance, consider the interpretation in which both sides are initially down, the soup is initially unspilled, the left handle is lifted at time 0, and at time 1 the left side is up, the right side is not, and the soup is spilled. That is, take

$$I = \{\neg upL_0, \neg upR_0, \neg sp_0, liftL_0, \neg liftR_0, upL_1, \neg upR_1, sp_1\}.$$

Then

$$T^I = \{\neg upL_0, \neg upR_0, \neg sp_0, liftL_0, \neg liftR_0, upL_1, \neg upR_1, sp_1\},$$

and so I is a model of T. (That is, I is the unique model of T^I.) By comparison, consider the interpretation

$$I = \{\neg upL_0, \neg upR_0, \neg sp_0, liftL_0, \neg liftR_0, upL_1, upR_1, \neg sp_1\}.$$

Then

$$T^I = \{\neg upL_0, \neg upR_0, \neg sp_0, liftL_0, \neg liftR_0, upL_1, \neg sp_1\},$$

and so this interpretation I is not a model of T, since it is not the unique model of T^I. (Intuitively, there is no explanation for the right side's being up at time 1.)

Constraints

A causal rule with head $\bot$ is called a *constraint*. A constraint

$$\bot \Leftarrow \phi \qquad (19.10)$$

can be understood to say that $\neg\phi$ must be the case, but without asserting the existence of a cause for $\neg\phi$. Constraints behave monotonically. That is, adding (19.10) to a causal theory simply rules out those models that satisfy ϕ.

Definitional extensions and defaults

It is straightforward to add a new Boolean constant d to the signature σ and define it using a formula ϕ of the original signature: simply add the rule

$$d \equiv \phi \Leftarrow \top. \qquad (19.11)$$

Indeed, let T be a causal theory (of σ), with T_d the causal theory (of $\sigma \cup \{d\}$) obtained by adding (19.11) to T. For any interpretation I of σ, let I_d be the interpretation of $\sigma \cup \{d\}$ such that (i) $I_d(c) = I(c)$, for all $c \in \sigma$, and (ii) $I_d(d) = \mathsf{t}$ iff $I \models \phi$. Then, I is a model of T iff I_d is a model of T_d. Moreover, every model of T_d has the form I_d, for some interpretation I of σ.

More generally, we can add to σ a new constant d with $Dom(d) = \{v_1, \ldots, v_n\}$ and define d using formulas $\phi_2, \ldots, \phi_n$ of σ, no two of which are jointly satisfiable, by adding the following causal rules.

$$\begin{aligned}
&d = v_1 \Leftarrow d = v_1 \\
&d = v_2 \Leftarrow \phi_2 \\
&\quad\vdots \\
&d = v_n \Leftarrow \phi_n
\end{aligned} \qquad (19.12)$$

Indeed, let T be a causal theory (of σ), with T_d the causal theory (of $\sigma \cup \{d\}$) obtained by adding the rules (19.12) to T. For any interpretation I of σ, let I_d be the interpretation of $\sigma \cup \{d\}$ such that (i) $I_d(c) = I(c)$, for all $c \in \sigma$, and (ii) for all $i \in \{2, \ldots, n\}$, $I_d(d) = v_i$ iff $I \models \phi_i$. Then, I is a model of T iff I_d is a model of T_d. Moreover, every model of T_d has the form I_d, for some interpretation I of σ.

Notice that this latter technique can also be understood as a way of giving new constant d a default value which is overridden just in case one of $\phi_2, \ldots, \phi_n$ is true.

19.2 Strong Equivalence

Equivalence of causal theories is defined in the usual way—as having the same models—but since the logic is nonmonotonic, equivalence does not yield a replacement property. That is, it is not generally safe to replace a subset of the rules of a causal theory with an equivalent set of rules. For example, assume that the signature is Boolean, with two constants, p and q. Let S be the causal theory with rules

$$\begin{aligned}
&p \Leftarrow q, \\
&q \Leftarrow p
\end{aligned}$$

and let T be the causal theory with rules

$$p \Leftarrow p,$$

$$q \Leftarrow q.$$

Causal theories S and T are equivalent, for each the unique model is $\{p, q\}$. Now, let R consist of the single rule

$$\neg p \Leftarrow \neg p.$$

Notice that $S \cup R$ still has only the model $\{p, q\}$, while $T \cup R$ has a second model, $\{\neg p, q\}$. Thus, in the context of $S \cup R$ it is not safe to replace S with T, even though S and T are equivalent.

Of course it is clear that we can always safely replace a rule $\phi \Leftarrow \psi$ with a rule $\phi' \Leftarrow \psi'$ if ϕ is equivalent to ϕ' and ψ is equivalent to ψ'. But we can do better.

The crucial notion is "strong equivalence", introduced (for logic programming) in [23]. (See Chapter 7.) We say causal theories S and T are *strongly equivalent* if, for every causal theory R, $S \cup R$ is equivalent to $T \cup R$.

It is clear that strong equivalence yields the replacement property we want. If S and T are strongly equivalent, we can safely replace S with T no matter the context: doing so will not affect the set of models. But the definition is inconvenient to check, since it requires reasoning about all possible contexts $S \cup R$. For convenience, we want a rather different characterization of strong equivalence.

An *SE-model* of causal theory T is a pair (I, J) of interpretations such that

- $I \models T^I$, and

- $J \models T^I$.

Strong Equivalence Theorem. *(See [46].) Causal theories are strongly equivalent iff their SE-models are the same.*

While deciding equivalence of causal theories is a Π_2^P-complete problem, deciding *strong* equivalence is co-NP-complete.

19.3 Completion

A causal theory is *definite* if

- the head of every rule is either an atom or $\bot$, and

- no atom occurs in the head of infinitely many rules.

We say an atom $c = v$ is *trivial* if $Dom(c) = \{v\}$. If a causal theory is definite, its *completion* consists of the following formulas.

- For each constraint $\bot \Leftarrow \phi$, include the formula $\neg\phi$.

- For each nontrivial atom A of the signature, include the formula

$$A \equiv (\phi_1 \vee \cdots \vee \phi_n)$$

where $\phi_1, \ldots, \phi_n$ are the bodies of the rules with head A. (If $n = 0$, the right-hand side is $\perp$.)

Completion Theorem. *(See [30, 18].) If a causal theory is definite, its models are exactly the models of its completion.*

Assume that the signature has three atoms, p_0, p_1, and a_0, with $Dom(p_0) = Dom(p_1) = \{1, 2, 3\}$ and $Dom(a_0) = \{\text{t}, \text{f}\}$. Consider the following (definite) causal theory.

$$\begin{aligned}
&p_0 = 0 \Leftarrow p_0 = 0 \\
&p_0 = 1 \Leftarrow p_0 = 1 && a_0 \Leftarrow a_0 \\
&p_0 = 2 \Leftarrow p_0 = 2 && a_0 = \text{f} \Leftarrow \neg a_0 \\
&p_1 = 0 \Leftarrow p_1 = 0 \wedge p_0 = 0 && p_1 = 1 \Leftarrow p_0 = 0 \wedge a_0 \\
&p_1 = 1 \Leftarrow p_1 = 1 \wedge p_0 = 1 && p_1 = 2 \Leftarrow p_0 = 1 \wedge a_0 \\
&p_1 = 2 \Leftarrow p_1 = 2 \wedge p_0 = 2 && p_1 = 0 \Leftarrow p_0 = 2 \wedge a_0
\end{aligned}$$
$$(19.13)$$

Its completion is as follows.

$$\begin{aligned}
&p_0 = 0 \equiv p_0 = 0 && a_0 \equiv a_0 \\
&p_0 = 1 \equiv p_0 = 1 && a_0 = \text{f} \equiv \neg a_0 \\
&p_0 = 2 \equiv p_0 = 2 \\
&p_1 = 0 \equiv (p_1 = 0 \wedge p_0 = 0) \vee (p_0 = 2 \wedge a_0) \\
&p_1 = 1 \equiv (p_1 = 1 \wedge p_0 = 1) \vee (p_0 = 0 \wedge a_0) \\
&p_1 = 2 \equiv (p_1 = 2 \wedge p_0 = 2) \vee (p_0 = 1 \wedge a_0)
\end{aligned}$$

All but three of these formulas are tautological. Those three together can be simplified as follows.

$$p_0 = 0 \supset (p_1 = 0 \wedge \neg a_0) \vee (p_1 = 1 \wedge a_0)$$

$$p_0 = 1 \supset (p_1 = 1 \wedge \neg a_0) \vee (p_1 = 2 \wedge a_0)$$

$$p_0 = 2 \supset (p_1 = 2 \wedge \neg a_0) \vee (p_1 = 0 \wedge a_0)$$

The Completion Theorem would not be correct if we did not restrict the completion process to nontrivial atoms. Consider, for instance, the causal theory with no rules whose signature σ has only one constant c, with $Dom(c) = \{0\}$. This causal theory has one model—the only interpretation of σ. But if the definition of completion did not exclude trivial atoms, then the completion of this theory would be $c = 0 \equiv \perp$, which is unsatisfiable.

The Completion Theorem implies that the satisfiability problem for definite causal theories belongs to class NP. In fact, it is NP-complete. Indeed, given any formula ϕ of Boolean signature σ, the causal theory $\{\perp \Leftarrow \neg\phi\} \cup \{c = v \Leftarrow c = v \mid c \in \sigma, v \in \{\text{t}, \text{f}\}\}$ is definite and has the same models as ϕ.

As mentioned previously, the Causal Calculator uses completion to automate reasoning about definite causal theories via standard satisfiability solvers for propositional logic. In relation to this, there are two complications to consider: (i) the completion formulas are not in clausal form, and (ii) the completion formulas are not Boolean. Both these obstacles can be efficiently overcome, as long as we are willing to modify and extend the signature, with the result that all models of the resulting set of clauses correspond to models of the definite causal theory, and vice versa. (For more detail, see [18].)

19.4 Expressiveness

We have already seen an example involving conditional (direct) effects of actions (19.13), and have discussed at some length an example with indirect effects of actions and interacting effects of concurrent actions (19.8), (19.9). We have mentioned other possibilities, such as nondeterminism, implied action preconditions, and things that change by themselves. A few examples follow. Many additional examples, of these and other kinds, can be found in the cited papers on causal theories, including some developing the theme of "elaboration tolerance", which is crucial to the long-term success of approaches to reasoning about action, but beyond the scope of this chapter.

19.4.1 Nondeterminism: Coin Tossing

The nondeterminism of coin tossing is easily represented. Let the signature consist of three constants—$coin_0$, $coin_1$, $toss_0$—where the first two constants have domain $\{heads, tails\}$ and the third constant is Boolean. Let T be as follows.

$$coin_0 = v \Leftarrow coin_0 = v$$

$$toss_0 \Leftarrow toss_0$$

$$\neg toss_0 \Leftarrow \neg toss_0$$

$$coin_1 = v \Leftarrow coin_1 = v \wedge coin_0 = v$$

$$coin_1 = v \Leftarrow coin_1 = v \wedge toss_0$$

(Each line above in which v appears represents two causal rules, one for each appropriate value of the metavariable v.) As discussed previously, the first line expresses that causes for initial facts are exogenous; the next two that causes for action occurrences (and nonoccurrences) are exogenous; the fourth that the value of *coin* is inertial. The two rules represented by the fifth line rather resemble the inertia rules, except that they say: if the coin is heads after toss, then there is a cause for this, and, on the other hand, if the coin is tails after toss, then there is a cause for that. One easily verifies that T has six models. In two of them, the coin is not tossed and so remains either heads or tails. In the other four, the coin is initially heads or tails, and after being tossed it is again either heads or tails.

19.4.2 Implied Action Preconditions: Moving an Object

There are k Boolean constants $put(v)_0$, for $v \in \{1, \ldots, k\}$ $(k > 1)$, along with two additional constants, loc_0, loc_1, whose domains are $\{1, \ldots, k\}$.

$$loc_0 = v \Leftarrow loc_0 = v$$

$$put(v)_0 \Leftarrow put(v)_0$$

$$\neg put(v)_0 \Leftarrow \neg put(v)_0$$

$$loc_1 = v \Leftarrow loc_1 = v \wedge loc_0 = v$$

$$loc_1 = v \Leftarrow put(v)_0$$

(Here, v is a metavariable ranging over $\{1, \ldots, k\}$, so the five lines above represent $5k$ causal rules.) The first three lines express the exogeneity of initial facts and actions in the standard way; the fourth line expresses inertia; the fifth says that putting the object in location v causes it to be there. This causal theory has $k(k + 1)$ models: there are k possible initial locations of the block, and for each of these, there are $k + 1$ possible continuations—either zero or one of the k put actions occurs, with the appropriate outcome at time 1. Although concurrent actions are, in general, allowed in causal theories, in this case the conflicting outcomes of the k put actions make it impossible to execute two of them at once. It is not necessary to include the $\frac{k(k-1)}{2}$ causal rules that would be required to explicitly state these impossibilities. Instead, they are implied by the description.

19.4.3 Things that Change by Themselves: Falling Dominos

We wish to describe the chain reaction of k dominos falling over one after the other, after the first domino is tipped over at time 0. In this description, for simplicity, we will stipulate that all dominos are initially up, and we will describe only the possibility of the tip action occurring at time 0. So the signature consists of tip_0 along with $up(d)_t$ for $d \in \{1, \ldots, k\}$ and $t \in \{0, \ldots, k\}$.

$$up(d)_0 \Leftarrow \top \qquad\qquad (1 \leqslant d \leqslant k)$$

$$tip_0 \Leftarrow tip_0$$

$$\neg tip_0 \Leftarrow \neg tip_0$$

$$up(d)_{t+1} \Leftarrow up(d)_{t+1} \wedge up(d)_t \qquad (1 \leqslant d \leqslant k, 0 \leqslant t \leqslant k - 1)$$

$$\neg up(d)_{t+1} \Leftarrow \neg up(d)_{t+1} \wedge \neg up(d)_t \qquad (1 \leqslant d \leqslant k, 0 \leqslant t \leqslant k - 1)$$

$$\neg up(1)_1 \Leftarrow tip_0$$

$$\neg up(d + 1)_{t+2} \Leftarrow \neg up(d)_{t+1} \wedge up(d)_t \qquad (1 \leqslant d \leqslant k - 1, 0 \leqslant t \leqslant k - 2)$$

The first line says that initially all dominos are up; the second and third that the tip action may or may not occur at time 0; the fourth and fifth lines posit inertia for the dominos' being up or down; and the sixth line describes the direct effect of the tip action (executed at time 0). The seventh and last line is of particular interest. It says that if domino d is up at time t and down at time $t + 1$, then there is a cause for domino $d + 1$ to be down at time $t + 2$. Notice that this rule mentions three successive time points, but no actions. Once the first domino is tipped, the others fall successively with no further action taken. This causal theory has two models. In the first, the tip action does not occur at time 0 and all dominos are up at all times. In the second, all dominos are initially up, and at each time point i ($1 \leqslant i \leqslant k$) the ith domino has fallen. (That is, in this model I, for all $t \in \{0, \ldots, k\}$ and $d \in \{1, \ldots, k\}$, $I \models up(d)_t$ iff $d > t$.)

19.4.4 Things that Tend to Change by Themselves: Pendulum

So far all examples have postulated commonsense inertia in the standard way: things do not change unless made to. But we can easily take a more general view: some things will change unless made not to. For example, we can describe a pendulum that, if left alone, will oscillate between being on the left and not being on the left. But if held, the pendulum will not change position.

$$left_0 \Leftarrow left_0$$

$$\neg left_0 \Leftarrow \neg left_0$$

$$hold_t \Leftarrow hold_t$$

$$\neg hold_t \Leftarrow \neg hold_t$$

$$left_{t+1} \Leftarrow left_{t+1} \wedge \neg left_t$$

$$\neg left_{t+1} \Leftarrow \neg left_{t+1} \wedge left_t$$

$$left_{t+1} \Leftarrow hold_t \wedge left_t$$

$$\neg left_{t+1} \Leftarrow hold_t \wedge \neg left_t$$

The first four lines express the usual assumptions about exogeneity. The next two lines express that the pendulum will tend to change position from one time to the next. That is, if it changes position between times t and $t + 1$, then there is a cause for its position at time $t + 1$. The last two lines say that when the pendulum is held, it will not change position. In all models of this causal theory, the pendulum changes position between times t and $t + 1$ iff it is not held at time t.

19.5   High-Level Action Language $\mathcal{C}+$

High-level action languages feature a concise, restricted syntax for describing the effects of actions, and often benefit from a relatively simple, well-understood semantics, typically defined in terms of a transition system whose nodes are the possible states and whose directed edges are labeled with the actions whose execution in the source state can result in the target state. STRIPS [12] and ADL [37, 38] can be seen as the first high-level action languages.

Language $\mathcal{C}+$ [18] is a descendant of the action language $\mathcal{A}$ [16]. The semantics of $\mathcal{C}+$ is given by reduction to causal theories: for each action description D of $\mathcal{C}+$ and each natural number n, there is a corresponding causal theory $T(D, n)$. The states of the transition system described by D are given by the models of $T(D, 0)$, and the possible transitions are given by the models of $T(D, 1)$. The paths of length n in the transition system correspond to the models of $T(D, n)$. For instance, the causal theory (19.13) is $T(D, 1)$ for the following domain description D

inertial p

exogenous a

a causes $p = 1$ if $p = 0$

a causes $p = 2$ if $p = 1$

a causes $p = 0$ if $p = 2$

where p is designated a "simple fluent constant" with domain $\{0, 1, 2\}$ and a a Boolean "action constant". Similarly, the causal theory (19.8), (19.9) for the soup bowl example corresponds to the domain description

> inertial *upL*, *upR*, *sp*
>
> exogenous *liftL*, *liftR*
>
> *liftL* causes *upL*
>
> *liftR* causes *upR*
>
> caused *sp* if *upL* $\not\equiv$ *upR*

where *upL*, *upR* and *sp* are Boolean "simple fluent constants" and *liftL* and *liftR* are Boolean "action constants". Here, as elsewhere, the high-level action language provides an especially nice syntax for representing action domains. Indeed, many of the published applications of the Causal Calculator use $\mathcal{C}+$, or its immediate predecessor $\mathcal{C}$ [17], as the "input language".

19.6 Relationship to Default Logic

A causal theory of a Boolean signature can be viewed as a default theory in the sense of Reiter [41]. (The syntax and semantics of propositional default theories are reviewed in Chapter 6.) Let us agree to identify a causal rule $\phi \Leftarrow \psi$ with the default

$$\frac{: \psi}{\phi}.$$

In the statement of the following theorem, we identify an interpretation I with the set of formulas satisfied by I.

Default Logic Theorem. *Let T be a causal theory of a Boolean signature. An interpretation I is a model of T iff I is an extension of T in the sense of default logic.*

This theorem shows that causal rules are essentially prerequisite-free defaults with a single justification, so long as we are interested only in those extensions that correspond to interpretations (that is to say, in the extensions that are consistent and complete).

For instance, the causal theory

$$\{p \Leftarrow q, q \Leftarrow q, \neg q \Leftarrow \neg q\} \tag{19.14}$$

corresponds to the default theory

$$\left\{ \frac{: q}{p}, \frac{: q}{q}, \frac{: \neg q}{\neg q} \right\},$$

which has two extensions: the set of all consequences of p, q, and the set of all consequences of $\neg q$. The first extension is complete, and corresponds to the only model of (19.14).

Remarkably, the causal rules (19.1) used in the solution to the frame problem that has been adopted in causal theories were, in essence, proposed already in Reiter's original 1980 paper on default logic. But an account of how to successfully "use" such default rules to express commonsense inertia in reasoning about action did not appear until [43, 44]. (This use of such default rules was derived from a similar application in the setting of knowledge update [39, 40].) In this connection, it may be helpful to mention the historically important "Yale Shooting" paper of Hanks and McDermott [19], who argued that neither default logic nor circumscription were suitable formalisms for reasoning about action. The Yale Shooting paper considered a rather different attempt to solve the frame problem in default logic, and demonstrated that *that attempt* was unsatisfactory. A brief account of this appears in [26]. For more detail, see [44].

19.7 Causal Theories in Higher-Order Classical Logic

Lifschitz [24] extended causal theories to the nonpropositional case using higher-order classical logic to express the fixpoint condition on a model, much in the manner of circumscription. His definition can be understood to provide a general method for translating finite Boolean causal theories into classical propositional logic.

Begin with a signature of classical logic, with a finite subset of the nonlogical constants designated "explainable". A *nonpropositional causal rule* is an expression of the form

$$\phi \Leftarrow \psi$$

where ϕ and ψ are classical formulas. A *nonpropositional causal theory* is a finite set of nonpropositional causal rules.

The special case of nonpropositional causal theories in which all nonlogical constants are explainable propositional constants coincides with the special case of the previously defined (finite-domain propositional) causal theories in which all constants are Boolean and causal theories are assumed to be finite.

In what follows, let $\overline{N}$ be a list of all explainable nonlogical constants. We say that a list of nonlogical constants or variables is *similar* to $\overline{N}$ if it has the same length as $\overline{N}$ and each of its members is of the same sort as the corresponding member of $\overline{N}$. We can denote a formula (in which none, some, or all explainable nonlogical constants appear) by $\phi(\overline{N})$. Then for any list $\overline{M}$ that is similar to $\overline{N}$, we can write $\phi(\overline{M})$ to denote the formula obtained by simultaneously replacing each occurrence of each member of $\overline{N}$ by the corresponding member of $\overline{M}$.

Consider a nonpropositional causal theory T with rules

$$\phi_1(\overline{N}, \overline{x_1}) \Leftarrow \psi_1(\overline{N}, \overline{x_1})$$
$$\vdots$$
$$\phi_k(\overline{N}, \overline{x_k}) \Leftarrow \psi_k(\overline{N}, \overline{x_k})$$

where $\overline{x_i}$ is the list of all free variables for the ith causal rule. Let $\overline{n}$ be a list of new variables that is similar to $\overline{N}$. By $T^*(\overline{n})$ we denote the formula

$$\bigwedge_{1 \leq i \leq k} \forall \overline{x_i}(\psi_i(\overline{N}, \overline{x_i}) \supset \phi_i(\overline{n}, \overline{x_i})).$$

An interpretation is a *model* of T if it is a model of

$$\forall \overline{n}(T^*(\overline{n}) \equiv \overline{n} = \overline{N}) \tag{19.15}$$

where $\bar{n} = \overline{N}$ stands for the conjunction of the equalities between members of $\bar{n}$ and the corresponding members of $\overline{N}$.

Where the definitions overlap syntactically, this definition of model of a causal theory agrees with the definition given earlier.

Notice that for finite Boolean propositional causal theories the corresponding sentence (19.15) is a quantified Boolean formula, from which quantifiers can be eliminated (with worst-case exponential increase in size). Thus this approach yields a general translation of finite Boolean propositional causal theories into classical propositional logic.

The completion method from Section 19.3 can be extended to "definite" nonpropositional causal theories, so that a "first-order" causal theory T has the same models as the corresponding completion (which is a classical first-order formula) [24].

19.8   A Logic of Universal Causation

UCL is a modal nonmonotonic logic obtained from standard S5 modal logic (see Chapter 15) by imposing a simple fixpoint condition that reflects the "principle of universal causation"—the requirement that everything true in a model have a cause. In [45], UCL was defined not only in the (Boolean) propositional case, but also for nonpropositional languages, and was shown to subsume the nonpropositional causal theories described in the previous section. Here, we consider a different extension of (Boolean) propositional UCL, introduced in [46], built from finite-domain propositional formulas.

The fundamental distinction in UCL—between propositions that have a cause and propositions that (merely) obtain—is expressed by means of the modal operator C, read as "caused". For example, one can write

$$\psi \supset C\phi \tag{19.16}$$

to say that ϕ is caused whenever ψ obtains. UCL formula (19.16) corresponds to the causal rule $\phi \Leftarrow \psi$. This claim is made precise in the UCL Theorem below.

UCL formulas are obtained by extending the recursive definition of a formula with an additional case for the modal operator C, in the usual way for modal logic:

- If ϕ is a UCL formula, then so is $C\phi$.

A *UCL theory* is a set of UCL formulas.

An *S5-structure* is a pair (I, S) such that I is an interpretation and S is a set of interpretations (all of the same signature) to which I belongs. *Satisfaction* of a UCL formula by an S5-structure is defined by the standard recursions over the propositional connectives, plus the following two conditions:

- if ϕ is an atom, $(I, S) \models \phi$ iff $I \models \phi$,

- $(I, S) \models C\phi$ iff for all $J \in S$, $(J, S) \models \phi$.

For a UCL theory T, if $(I, S) \models T$, we say that (I, S) is an *I-model* of T, thus emphasizing the distinguished interpretation I.

We say that I is *causal model* of T if $(I, \{I\})$ is the unique I-model of T.

UCL Theorem. *For any causal theory* T, *the models of* T *are precisely the causal models of the corresponding UCL theory*

$$\{\psi \supset C\phi : \phi \Leftarrow \psi \in T\}.$$

It is possible to characterize strong equivalence for UCL theories, much as was done in Section 19.2 for causal theories. Interestingly, this requires a slight strengthening of S5. The SE-models of a UCL theory are a subset of the S5 models: those S5 models (I, S) such that $(I, \{I\})$ is also an S5 model [46].

Acknowledgement

Many thanks to my collaborators on this topic: Enrico Giunchiglia, Joohyung Lee, Vladimir Lifschitz, and Norm McCain. This work partially supported by NSF CAREER Grant #0091773.

Bibliography

[1] V. Akman, S. Erdoğan, J. Lee, V. Lifschitz, and H. Turner. Representing the Zoo World and the Traffic World in the language of the Causal Calculator. *Artificial Intelligence*, 153:105–140, 2004.

[2] A. Artikis, M. Sergot, and J. Pitt. An executable specification of an argumentation protocol. In *Proc. of Artificial Intelligence and Law (ICAIL)*, pages 1–11, 2003.

[3] A. Artikis, M. Sergot, and J. Pitt. Specifying electronic societies with the Causal Calculator. In F. Giunchiglia, J. Odell, and G. Weiss, editors. *Proc. of Workshop on Agent-Oriented Software III (AOSE)*, *LNCS*, vol. 2585, pages 1–15. Springer, 2003.

[4] A. Bochman. A logic for causal reasoning. In *Proc. IJCAI-03*, pages 141–146, 2003.

[5] A. Bochman. A causal approach to nonmonotonic reasoning. *Artificial Intelligence*, 160(1–2):105–143, 2004.

[6] J. Campbell and V. Lifschitz. Reinforcing a claim in commonsense reasoning. In *Logical Formalizations of Commonsense Reasoning: Papers from 2003 AAAI Spring Symposium*, pages 51–56, 2003.

[7] A. Chopra and M. Singh. Nonmonotonic commitment machines. In F. Dignum, editor. *Workshop on Agent Communication Languages*, *Lecture Notes in Computer Science*, vol. 2922, pages 183–200. Springer, 2004.

[8] K. Clark. Negation as failure. In H. Gallaire and J. Minker, editors. *Logic and Data Bases*, pages 293–322. Plenum Press, New York, 1978.

[9] R. Craven and M. Sergot. Distant causation in C+. *Studia Logica*, 79:73–96, 2005.

[10] S. Dogandag, P. Ferraris, and V. Lifschitz, Almost definite causal theories. In *Logic Programming and Nonmonotonic Reasoning: Proc. of Seventh Internat. Conf.*, pages 74–86, 2004.

[11] T. Eiter and T. Lukasiewicz. Probabilistic reasoning about actions in nonmonotonic causal theories. In *Proceedings of the 19th Conference on Uncertainty in Artificial Intelligence (UAI-2003)*, pages 192–199, 2003.

[12] R. Fikes and N. Nilsson. STRIPS: A new approach to the application of theorem proving to problem solving. *Artificial Intelligence*, 2(3–4):189–208, 1971.

[13] A. Finzi and T. Eiter. Game-theoretic reasoning about actions in nonmonotonic causal theories. In *Logic Programming and Nonmonotonic Reasoning: 8th International Conference, LNCS*, vol. 3662, pages 185–197. Springer, 2005.

[14] H. Geffner. Causal theories of nonmonotonic reasoning. In *Proc. of AAAI-90*, pages 524–530, 1990.

[15] H. Geffner. *Reasoning with Defaults: Causal and Conditional Theories*. MIT Press, Cambridge, MA, 1992.

[16] M. Gelfond and V. Lifschitz. Representing action and change by logic programs. *Journal of Logic Programming*, 17:301–322, 1993.

[17] E. Giunchiglia and V. Lifschitz. An action language based on causal explanation: Preliminary report. In *Proc. AAAI-98*, pages 623–630, 1998.

[18] E. Giunchiglia, J. Lee, V. Lifschitz, N. McCain, and H. Turner. Nonmonotonic causal theories. *Artificial Intelligence*, 153(1–2):49–104, 2004.

[19] S. Hanks and D. McDermott. Nonmonotonic logic and temporal projection. *Artificial Intelligence*, 33(3):379–412, 1987.

[20] J. Lee and V. Lifschitz. Describing additive fluents in action language C+. In *Proc. IJCAI'03*, pages 1079–1084, 2003.

[21] J. Lee. Definite vs. nondefinite causal theories. In *Logic Programming and Nonmonotonic Reasoning: Proc. of Seventh Internat. Conf.*, pages 141–153, 2004.

[22] V. Lifschitz, N. McCain, E. Remolina, and A. Tacchella. Getting to the airport: the oldest planning problem in AI. In *Logic-Based Artificial Intelligence*, pages 147–165. Kluwer, 2000.

[23] V. Lifschitz, D. Pearce, and A. Valverde. Strongly equivalent logic programs. *ACM Transactions on Computational Logic*, 2:526–541, 2001.

[24] V. Lifschitz. On the logic of causal explanation. *Artificial Intelligence*, 96:451–465, 1997.

[25] V. Lifschitz. Situation calculus and causal logic. In *Proc. of the Sixth Internat. Conf. on Principles of Knowledge Representation and Reasoning*, pages 536–546, 1998.

[26] V. Lifschitz. Success of default logic. In H. Levesque and F. Pirri, editors. *Logical Foundations of Cognitive Agents: Contributions in Honor of Ray Reiter*, pages 208–212. Springer-Verlag, 1999.

[27] V. Lifschitz. Missionaries and cannibals in the Causal Calculator. In *Proc. of the 7th Internat. Conf. on Principles of Knowledge Representation and Reasoning*, pages 85–96, 2000.

[28] F. Lin. Embracing causality in specifying the indirect effects of actions. In *Proc. of IJCAI-95*, pages 1985–1991, 1995.

[29] N. McCain and H. Turner. A causal theory of ramifications and qualifications. In *Proc. of IJCAI-95*, pages 1978–1984, 1995.

[30] N. McCain and H. Turner. Causal theories of action and change. In *Proc. of AAAI-97*, pages 460–465, 1997.

[31] N. McCain and H. Turner. Satisfiability planning with causal theories. In *Principles of Knowledge Representation and Reasoning: Proc. of the Sixth Internat. Conference*, pages 212–223, 1998.

[32] N. McCain. Causality in commonsense reasoning about actions. PhD Dissertation, University of Texas at Austin, Department of Computer Sciences, 1997.

[33] J. McCarthy and P. Hayes. Some philosophical problems from the standpoint of artificial intelligence. In B. Meltzer and D. Michie, editors. *Machine Intelligence*, vol. 4, pages 463–502. Edinburgh University Press, Edinburgh, 1969, Reproduced in [34].

[34] J. McCarthy. *Formalizing Common Sense: Papers by John McCarthy*. Ablex, Norwood, NJ, 1990.

[35] J. Pearl. Embracing causality in default reasoning. *Artificial Intelligence*, 35:259–271, 1988.

[36] J. Pearl. *Causality: Models, Reasoning and Inference*. Cambridge University Press, 2000.

[37] E. Pednault. ADL: Exploring the middle ground between STRIPS and the situation calculus. In R. Brachman, H. Levesque, and R. Reiter, editors, *Proc. of the First Internat. Conf. on Principles of Knowledge Representation and Reasoning*, pages 324–332, 1989.

[38] E. Pednault. ADL and the state-transition model of action. *Journal of Logic and Computation*, 4:467–512, 1994.

[39] T. Przymusinski and H. Turner. Update by means of inference rules. In *Proc. of the 3rd Internat. Conf. on Logic Programming and Nonmonotonic Reasoning*, pages 156–174, 1995.

[40] T. Przymusinski and H. Turner. Update by means of inference rules. *Journal of Logic Programming*, 30(2):125–143, 1997.

[41] R. Reiter. A logic for default reasoning. *Artificial Intelligence*, 13(1,2):81–132, 1980.

[42] M. Sergot and R. Craven. Some logical properties of nonmonotonic causal theories. In *Logic Programming and Nonmonotonic Reasoning: 8th International Conference, LNCS*, vol. 3662, pages 198–210. Springer, 2005.

[43] H. Turner. Representing actions in default logic: A situation calculus approach. In *Working Papers of the Third Symposium on Logical Formalizations of Commonsense Reasoning*, 1996.

[44] H. Turner. Representing actions in logic programs and default theories: A situation calculus approach. *Journal of Logic Programming*, 31(1–3):245–298, 1997.

[45] H. Turner. A logic of universal causation. *Artificial Intelligence*, 113:87–123, 1999.

[46] H. Turner. Strong equivalence for causal theories. In *Logic Programming and Nonmonotonic Reasoning: Proc. of Seventh Internat. Conf.*, pages 289–301, 2004.

[47] G. White. A modal formulation of McCain and Turner's theory of causal reasoning. In *Logics in Artificial Intelligence: Proc. 8th European Conference (JELIA'02)*, pages 211–222, 2002.

Part III

Knowledge Representation
in Applications

Handbook of Knowledge Representation
Edited by F. van Harmelen, V. Lifschitz and B. Porter
© 2008 Elsevier B.V. All rights reserved
DOI: 10.1016/S1574-6526(07)03020-9

Chapter 20

Knowledge Representation and Question Answering

Marcello Balduccini, Chitta Baral, Yuliya Lierler

20.1 Introduction

Consider an intelligence analyst who has a large body of documents of various kinds. He would like answers to some of his questions based on the information in these documents, general knowledge available in compilations such as fact books, and commonsense. A search engine or a typical information retrieval (IR) system like Google does not go far enough as it takes keywords and only gives a ranked list of documents which may contain those keywords. Often this list is very long and the analyst still has to read the documents in the list. Other reasons behind the unsuitability of an IR system (for an analyst) are that the nuances of a question in a natural language cannot be adequately expressed through keywords, most IR systems ignore synonyms, and *most IR systems cannot reason*. What the intelligence analyst would like is a system that can take the documents and the analyst's question as input, that can access the data in fact books, and that can do commonsense reasoning based on them to provide answers to questions. Such a system is referred to as a question answering system or a QA system. Systems of this type are useful in many domains besides intelligence analysis. Examples include a Biologist who needs answers to his questions, say about a particular set of genes and what is known about their functions and interactions, based on the published literature; a lawyer looking for answers from a body of past law cases; and a patent attorney looking for answers from a patent database.

A precursor to question answering is database querying where one queries a database using a database query language. Question Answering takes this to a whole other dimension where the system has increasing body of documents (in natural languages, possibly including multimedia objects and possibly situated in the web and described in a web language) and it is asked a query in natural language. It is expected to give an answer to the question, not only using the documents, but also using appropriate commonsense knowledge. Moreover, the system needs to be able to accommodate new additions to the body of documents. The interaction with a question answering system can also go beyond a single query to a back and forth exchange where the system may ask questions back to the user so as to better understand and answer the user's original question. Moreover, many questions that can be asked in English can be proven to be inexpressible in most existing database query languages.

The response expected from a QA system could also be more general than the answers expected from standard database systems. Besides yes/no answers and factual answers, one may expect a QA system to give co-operative answers, give relaxed answers based on user modeling and come back with clarifying questions leading to a dialogue. An example of co-operative answering [31] is that when one asks the question "Does John teach AI at ASU in Fall'06", the answer "the course is not offered at ASU in Fall'06", if appropriate, is a co-operative answer as opposed to the answer "no". Similarly, an example of relaxed answering [30] is that when one asks for a Southwest connection from Phoenix to Washington DC National airport, the system realizing that Baltimore is close to DC, and Southwest does not fly to DC, offers the flight schedules of Southwest from Phoenix to Baltimore.

QA has a long history and [53] contains an overview of that as well as various papers on the topic. Its history ranges from early attempts on natural language queries for databases [39], deductive question answering [40], story understanding [19], web based QA systems [4], to recent QA tracks in TREC [72], ARDA supported QA projects and Project Halo [29]. QA involves many aspects of Artificial Intelligence ranging from natural language processing, knowledge representation and reasoning, information integration and machine learning. Recent progress and successes in all of these areas and easy availability of software modules and resources in each of these areas now make it possible to build better QA systems. Some of the modules and resources that can be used in building a QA system include natural language parsers, WordNet [54, 26], document classifiers, text extraction systems, IR systems, digital fact books, and reasoning and model enumeration systems. However, most QA systems built to date are not strong in knowledge representation and reasoning, although there has been some recent progress in that direction. In this chapter we will discuss the role of knowledge representation and reasoning in developing a QA system, discuss some of the issues and describe some of the current attempts in this direction.

20.1.1   Role of Knowledge Representation and Reasoning in QA

To understand the role of knowledge representation and reasoning in a QA system let us consider several pairs of texts and questions. We assume that the text has been identified by a component of the QA system from among the documents given to it, as relevant to the given query.

1.   *Text*: John and Mike took a plane from Paris to Baghdad. On the way, the plane stopped in Rome, where John was arrested.

   Questions: Where is Mike at the end of this trip? Where is John at the end of this trip? Where is the plane at the end of this trip? Where would John be if he was not arrested?

   Analysis: The commonsense answers to the above questions are Baghdad, Rome, Baghdad and Baghdad respectively. To answer the first and the third question the QA system has to reason about the effect of the action of taking a plane from Paris to Baghdad. It has to reason that at the end of the action the plane and its occupants will be in Baghdad. It has to reason that the action of John getting arrested changes his status as an occupant of the plane. To reason about John's status if he was not arrested, the QA system has to do counterfactual reasoning.

2. *Text*: John, who always carries his laptop with him, took a flight from Boston to Paris on the morning of Dec 11th.

   Questions: In which city is John's laptop on the evening of Dec 10th? In which city is John's laptop on the evening of Dec 12th?

   Analysis: The commonsense answers to the above questions are Boston and Paris respectively. Here, as in the previous case, one can reason about the effect of John taking a flight from Boston to Paris, and conclude that at the end of the flight, John will be in Paris. However, to reason about the location of John's laptop one has to reason about the causal connection between John's location and his laptop's location. Finally, the QA system needs to have an idea about the normal time it takes for a flight from Boston to Paris, and the time difference between them.

3. *Text*: John took the plane from Paris to Baghdad. He planned to meet his friend Mike, who was waiting for him there.

   Question: Did John meet Mike?

   Analysis: To answer the above question, the QA systems needs to reason about agent's intentions. From commonsense theory of intentions [18, 22, 74], agents normally execute their intentions. Using that one can conclude that indeed John met Mike.

4. *Text*: John, who travels abroad often, is at home in Boston and receives a call that he must immediately go to Paris.

   Questions: Can he just get on a plane and fly to Paris? What does he need to do to be in Paris?

   Analysis: The commonsense answer to the first question is 'no'. In this case the QA system reasons about the precondition necessary to perform the action of flying and realizes that for one to fly one needs a ticket first. Thus John cannot just get on a plane and fly. To answer the second question, one needs to construct a plan. In this case, a possible plan is to buy a ticket, get to the airport and then to get on the plane.

5. *Text*: John is in Boston on Dec 1. He has no passport.

   Question: Can he go to Paris on Dec 4?

   Analysis: With the general knowledge that it takes more than 3 days to get a passport the commonsense answer to the above is 'no'.

6. *Text*: On Dec 10th John is at home in Boston. He made a plan to get to Paris by Dec 11th. He then bought a ticket. But on his way to the airport he got stuck in the traffic. He did not make it to the flight.

   Query: Would John be in Paris on Dec 11th, if he had not gotten stuck in the traffic?

   Analysis: This is a counterfactual query whose answer would be "yes". The reasoning behind it would be that if John had not been stuck in the traffic, then he would have made the flight to Paris and would have been in Paris on Dec 11th.

The above examples show the need for commonsense knowledge and domain knowledge; and the role of commonsense reasoning, predictive reasoning, counterfactual reasoning, planning and reasoning about intentions in question answering. All these are aspects of knowledge representation and reasoning. The examples are not arbitrarily contrived examples, but rather are representative examples from some of the application domains of QA systems. For example, an intelligence analyst tracking a particular person's movement would have text like the above. The analyst would often need to find answers for what if, counterfactual and intention related questions. Thus, knowledge representation and reasoning ability are very important for QA systems. In the next section we briefly describe attempts to build such QA systems and their architecture.

20.1.2 Architectural Overview of QA Systems Using Knowledge Representation and Reasoning

We start with a high level description of approaches that are used in the few QA systems [1, 57, 71, 62] or QA-like systems that incorporate knowledge representation and reasoning.

1. Logic Form based approach:
   In this approach an information retrieval system is used to select the relevant documents and relevant texts from those documents. Then the relevant text is converted to a logical theory. The logical theory is then added to domain knowledge and commonsense knowledge resulting in a Knowledge Base KB. (Domain knowledge and common-sense knowledge will be together referred to as "background knowledge" and sometimes as "background knowledge base".) The question is converted to a logic form and is posed against KB and a theorem prover is then used. This approach is used in the QA systems [1, 20] from *Language Computer/LCC*.[1]

2. Information extraction based approach:
   Here also, first an information retrieval system is used to select the relevant documents and relevant texts from those documents. Then with a goal to extract relevant facts from these text, a classifier is used to determine the correct script and the correct information extractor for the text. The extracted relevant facts are added to domain knowledge and commonsense knowledge resulting in

---

[1] http://www.languagecomputer.com.

the Knowledge Base KB. The question is translated to the logical language of KB and is then posed against it. An approach close to this is used in the story understanding system reported in [62].

3. Using logic forms in information extraction:
   A mixed approach of the above two involves processing the logic forms to obtain the relevant facts from them and then proceed as in (2) above.

We now describe the above approaches in greater detail. We start by examining various techniques to translate English to logical theories. Next, we describe COGEX and DD, two systems that perform inference starting from the logic form of English sentences. Section 20.5 presents an approach where the output of a semantic parser is used directly in obtaining the relevant facts, and background knowledge is employed to reduce semantic ambiguity. In Section 20.6, we describe Nutcracker, a system for recognizing textual entailment based on first-order representation of sentences and first-order inference tools. Section 20.7 examines an approach based on the use of Event Calculus for the semantic representation of the text. Finally, in Section 20.8 we draw conclusions.

20.2 From English to Logical Theories

An ambitious and bold approach of doing reasoning in a question answering system is to convert English (or any other natural language for that matter) text to a logical representation and then use a reasoning system to reason with the resulting logical theory. Here, we discuss some of the attempts [1, 20] in this direction.

The most popular approach for the translation from English to a logical representation is based on the identification of the *syntactic structure* of the sentence, usually represented as a tree (the "parse tree") that systematically combines the phrases in which the English text can be divided and whose leaves are associated with the lexical items. As an example, the parse tree of the sentence "John takes a plane" is shown in Fig. 20.1. Once the syntactic structure is found, it is used to derive a logical representation of the discourse.

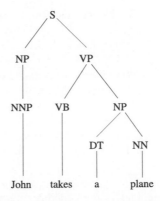

Figure 20.1: Parse tree of *"John takes a plane"*.

The derivation of the logical representation typically consists of:

- Assigning a logic encoding to the lexical items of the text.

- Describing how logical representations of sub-parts of the discourse are to be combined in the representation of larger parts of it.

Consider the parse tree in Fig. 20.1 (for the sake of simplicity, let us ignore the determiner "a"). We can begin by stating that lexical items "John" and "plane" are represented by constants *john* and *plane*. Next, we need to specify how the verb phrase is encoded from its sub-parts. A possible approach is to use an atom $p(x, y)$, where p is the verb and y is the constant representing the syntactic direct object of the verb phrase. Thus, we obtain an atom *take*$(x, plane)$, where x is an unbound variable. Finally, we can decide to encode the sentence by replacing the unbound variable in the atom for the verb phrase with the constant denoting the syntactic subject of the sentence. Hence, we get to *take*$(john, plane)$.

Describing formally how the logical representation of the text is obtained is in general a nontrivial task that requires a suitable way of specifying how substitutions are to be carried out in the expressions.

Starting with theoretical attempts in [59] to a system implementation in [7], attempts have been made to use *lambda calculus* to tackle this problem. In fact, lambda calculus provides a simple and elegant way to mark explicitly where the logical representation of smaller parts of the discourse is to be inserted in the representation of the more complex parts. Here we describe the approach from [14].

Lambda calculus can be seen as a notational extension of first-order logic containing a new *binding operator* λ. Occurrences of variables bound by λ intuitively specify where each substitution has to occur. For example, an expression

$$\lambda x.plane(x)$$

says that, once x is bound to a value, that value will be used as the argument of relation *plane*. The application of a lambda expression is denoted by symbol @. Hence, the expression

$$\lambda x.plane(x) \ @ \ boeing767$$

is equivalent to *plane*$(boeing767)$. Notice that, in natural language, nouns such as plane are preceded by "a", "the", etc. In the lambda calculus based encoding, *the representation of nouns is connected to that of the rest of the sentence by the encoding of the article*.

In order to provide the connection mechanism, the lambda expressions for articles are more complex than the ones shown above. Let us consider, for example, the encoding of "a" from [14]. There, "a" is intuitively viewed as describing a situation in which an element of a class has a particular property. For example, "a woman walks" says that an element of class "woman" "walks". Hence, the representation of "a" is parameterized by the class, w, and the property, z, of the object, y:

$$\lambda w.\lambda z.\exists y.(w \ @ \ y \wedge z \ @ \ y).$$

In the expression, w is a placeholder for the lambda expression describing the class that the object belongs to. Similarly, z is a placeholder for the lambda expression denoting the property of the object. Notice the implicit assumption that *the lambda expressions substituted to w and z are of the form* $\lambda x.f(x)$—that is, they lack the "$@ \ p$" part. This assumption is critical for the proper merging of the various components of a sentence: when w, in $w \ @ \ y$ above, is replaced with the actual property of the object, say $\lambda x.plane(x)$, we obtain $\lambda x.plane(x) \ @ \ y$. Because of the use of parentheses, it is *only at this point* that the $@ \ y$ part of the expression above can be used to perform a substitution. Hence, $\lambda x.plane(x) \ @ \ y$ is simplified into $plane(y)$, as one would expect.

To see how the mechanism works on the complete representation of "a", let us look at how the representation of the phrase "a plane" is obtained by combining the encoding of "a" with the one of "plane" (which provides the class information for "a"):

$$\lambda w.\lambda z.\exists y.(w \ @ \ y \wedge z \ @ \ y) \ @ \ \lambda x.plane(x) =$$

$$\lambda z.\exists y.(\lambda x.plane(x) \ @ \ y \wedge z \ @ \ y) =$$

$$\lambda z.\exists y.(plane(y) \wedge z \ @ \ y).$$

Note that this lambda expression encodes the assumption that the noun phrase is followed by a verb. This is achieved by introducing z as a placeholder for the verb.

The representation of proper names is designed, as well, to allow the combination of the name with the other parts of the sentence. For instance, "John" is represented by:

$$\lambda u.(u \ @ \ john),$$

where u is a placeholder for a lambda expression of the form $\lambda x.f(x)$, which can be intuitively read (if $f(\cdot)$ is an action) "an unnamed actor x performed action f". So, for example, the sentence "John did f" is represented as:

$$\lambda u.(u \ @ \ john) \ @ \ \lambda x.f(x).$$

As usual, the right part of the expression can be substituted to u, which leads us to:

$$\lambda x.f(x) \ @ \ john.$$

The expression can be immediately simplified into:

$$f(john).$$

The encoding of (transitive) verb phrases is based on a relation with both subject and direct object as arguments. The subject and direct object are introduced in the expression as placeholders, similarly to what we saw above. For example, the verb "take" is encoded as:

$$\lambda w.\lambda z.(w \ @ \ \lambda x.take(z, x)),$$

where z and x are the placeholders for subject and direct object respectively. The assumption, here, is that *the lambda expression of the direct object contains a placeholder for the verb*, such as z in $\lambda z.\exists y.(plane(y) \wedge z \ @ \ y)$ above. Hence, when the representation of the direct object is substituted to w, the placeholder for the verb can be replaced by $\lambda x.take(z, x)$. Consider how this mechanism works on the phrase "takes a plane". The lambda expressions of the two parts of the phrase are directly combined into:

$$\lambda w.\lambda z.(w @ \lambda x.take(z, x)) @ \lambda w.\exists y.(plane(y) \wedge w @ y).$$

As we said, the expression for the direct object is substituted to w, giving:

$$\lambda z.(\lambda w.\exists y.(plane(y) \wedge w @ y) @ \lambda x.take(z, x)).$$

Now, the placeholder for the verb, w, in the encoding of the direct object is replaced by (the remaining part of) the expression for the verb.

$$\lambda z.(\exists y.(plane(y) \wedge \lambda x.take(z, x) @ y) =$$
$$\lambda z.(\exists y.(plane(y) \wedge take(z, y))).$$

At this point we are ready to find the representation of the whole sentence, "John takes a plane". "John" and "takes a plane" are directly combined into:

$$\lambda u.(u @ john) @ \lambda z.(\exists y.(plane(y) \wedge take(z, y)))$$

which simplifies to:

$$\lambda z.(\exists y(plane(y) \wedge take(z, y))) @ john$$

and finally becomes:

$$\exists y(plane(y) \wedge take(john, y)).$$

It is worth stressing that the correctness of the encoding depends on the proper identification of subject, verb, and objects of the sentences. If, in the example above, "John" were to be identified as direct object of the verb, the resulting encoding would be quite different.

As this example shows, lambda calculus offers a simple and elegant way to determine the logical representation of the discourse, in terms of first-order logic formulas encoding the meaning of the text. Notice, however, that the lambda calculus specification alone does not help in dealing with some of the complexities of natural language, and in particular with *ambiguities*. Consider the sentence "John took a flower". A possible first-order representation of its meaning is:

$$\exists y(flower(y) \wedge take(john, y)).$$

Although in this sentence verb "take" has a quite different meaning from the one of "take a plane", the logical representations of the two sentences are virtually identical. We describe now a different approach that is aimed at providing information to help disambiguate the meaning of sentences.

This alternative approach translates the discourse into logical statements that we will call *LCC-style Logic Forms* (LLF for short). Logic forms of this type were originally introduced in [44, 45], and later substantially extended in, e.g., [42, 21]. (Note that as mentioned in Chapter 8 of [6], there have been many other logic form proposals, such as [73, 60, 66].) Here, by LLF, we refer to the extended type of logical representation of [42, 21]. In the LLF approach, a triple $\langle base, pos, sense \rangle$ is associated with every noun, verb, adjective, adverb, conjunction and preposition, where *base* is the base form of the word, *pos* is its part-of-speech, and *sense* is the word's sense in the classification found in the WordNet database [54, 26]. Notice that such tuples provide richer information than the lambda calculus based approach, as they contain sense information about the lexical items (which helps understand their semantic use).

In the LLF approach, logic constants are (roughly) associated with the words that introduce relevant parts of the sentence (sometimes called *heads of the phrases*). The association is obtained by atoms of the form:

$$base\_pos\_sense(c, a_0, \ldots, a_n),$$

where *base*, *pos*, *sense* are the elements of the triple describing the head word, c is the constant that denotes the phrase, and $a_0, \ldots, a_n$ are constants denoting the sub-parts of the phrase. For example, "John takes a plane" is represented by the collection of atoms:

$$John\_NN(x1), take\_VB\_11(e1, x1, x2), plane\_NN\_1(x2).$$

The first atom says that $x1$ denotes the noun (NN) "John" (the sense number is omitted when the word has only one possible meaning). The second atom describes the action performed by John. The word "take" is described as a verb (VB), used with meaning number 11 from the WordNet 2.1 classification (i.e., "travel or go by means of a certain kind of transportation, or a certain route"). The corresponding part of the discourse is denoted by $e1$. The second argument of relation *take_VB_11* denotes the syntactic subject of the action, while the third is the syntactic direct object.

The relations of the form *base_pos_sense* can be classified based on the type of phrase they describe. More precisely, there are six different types of predicates:

1. verb predicates

2. noun predicates

3. complement predicates

4. conjunction predicates

5. preposition predicates

6. complex nominal predicates

In recent papers [56], verb predicates have been used with variable number of arguments, but no less than two. The first required argument is called *action/eventuality*. The second required argument denotes the subject of the verb. Practical applications of logic forms [1] appear to use the older *fixed slot allocation* schema [58], in which verbs always have three arguments, and dummy constants are used when some parts of the text are missing. For sake of simplicity, in the rest of the discussion, we consider only the fixed slot allocation schema.

Noun predicates always have arity one. The argument of the relation is the constant that denotes the noun.

Complement relations have as argument the constant denoting the part of text that they modify. For example, "run quickly" is encoded as (the tag RB denotes an adverb):

$$run\_VB\_1(e1, x1, x2), quickly\_RB(e1).$$

Conjunctions are encoded with relations that have a variable number of arguments, where the first argument represents the "result" of the logical operation induced by the conjunction [65, 58]. The other arguments encode the parts of the text that are connected by the conjunction. For example, "consider and reconsider carefully" is represented as:

$and\_CC(e1, e2, e3), consider\_VB\_2(e2, x1, x2),$

$reconsider\_VB\_2(e3, x3, x4), carefully\_RB(e1).$

One preposition atom is generated for each preposition in the text. Preposition relations have two arguments: the part of text that the prepositional phrase is attached to, and the prepositional object. For example, "play the position of pitcher" is encoded as:

$play\_VB\_1(e1, x1, x2), position\_NN\_9(x2),$

$of\_IN(x2, x3), pitcher\_NN\_4(x3).$

Finally, complex nominals are encoded by connecting the composing nouns by means of the *nn_NNC* relation. The *nn_NNC* predicate has a variable number of arguments, which depends on the number of nouns that have to be connected. For example, "an organization created for business ventures" is encoded as:

$organization\_NN\_1(x2), create\_VB\_2(e1, x1, x2),$

$for\_IN(e1, x3),$

$nn\_NNC(x3, x4, x5), business\_NN\_1(x4), venture\_NN\_3(x5).$

An important feature of the LLF approach is that the logic forms are also augmented with *named-entity tags*, based on *lexical chains among concepts* [43]. Lexical chains are sequences of concepts such that adjacent concepts are connected by an hypernymy relation.[2] Lexical chains allow to add to the logic forms information *implied by the text*, but not explicitly stated. For example, the logic form of "John takes a plane" contains a named-entity tag:

$human\_NE(x1),$

stating that John (the part of the sentence denoted by $x1$) is a human being. The named-entity tag is derived from the lexical chain connecting name "John" to concept "human (being)".

A recent extension of this approach consists in further augmenting the logic forms by means of *semantic relations*—relations between two words or concepts that provide a somewhat deeper description of the meaning of the text.[3] More than 30 different types of semantic relations have been identified, including:

---

[2]Recall that a word is a hypernym of another if the former is more generic or has broader meaning than the latter.

[3]Further information can be found at:
http://www.hlt.utdallas.edu/~moldovan/CS6373.06/IS_Knowledge_Representation_from_Text.pdf,
http://www.hlt.utdallas.edu/~moldovan/CS6373.06/IS_SC.pdf, and
http://www5.languagecomputer.com/demo/polaris/PolarisDefinitions.pdf.

- Possession (*POS_SR(X, Y)*): *X* is a possession of *Y*.

- Agent (*AGT_SR(X, Y)*): *X* performs or causes the occurrence of *Y*.

- Location, Space, Direction (*LOC_SR(X, Y)*): *X* is the location of *Y*.

- Manner (*MNR_SR(X, Y)*): *X* is the way in which event *Y* takes place.

For example, the agent in the sentence "John takes a plane" is identified by:

$$AGT\_SR(x1, e1).$$

Notice that the entity specified by *AGT_SR* does not always coincide with the subject of the verb.

The key step in the automation of the generation of logic forms is the construction of a parse tree of the text by a syntactic parser. The parser begins by performing word-sense disambiguation with respect to WordNet senses [54, 26] and determines the parts of speech of the words. Next, grammar rules are used to identify the syntactic structure of the discourse. Finally, the parse tree is augmented with the word sense numbers from WordNet and with named-entity tags.

The logic form is then obtained from the parse tree by associating atoms to the nodes of the tree. For each atom, the relation is determined from the triple ⟨*base, pos, sense*⟩ that identifies the node. For nouns, verbs, compound nouns and coordinating conjunction, a fresh constant is used as first argument (*independent argument*) of the atom and denotes the corresponding phrase. Next, the other arguments (*secondary arguments*) of the atoms are assigned according to the arcs in the parse tree. For example, in the parse tree for "John takes a plane", the second argument of *take_VB*_11 is filled with the constant denoting the sub-phrase "John", and the third with the constant denoting "plane".

Named-entity tagging substantially contributes to the generation of the logic form when the parse tree contains ambiguities. Consider the sentences [56]:

1. They gave the visiting team a heavy loss.

2. They played football every evening.

Both sentences contain a verb followed by two noun phrases. In (1), the direct object of the verb is represented by the second noun phrase. This is the typical interpretation used for sentences of this kind. However, it is easy to see that (2) is an exception to the general rule, because there the direct object is given by the *first* noun phrase.

Named-entity tagging allows the detection of the exception. In fact, the phrase "every evening" is tagged as an indicator of time. The tagging is taken into account in the assignment of secondary arguments, which allows to exclude the second noun phrase as a direct object and correctly assign the first noun phrase to that role.

Finally, semantic relations are extracted from text with a pattern identification process:

1. Syntactic patterns are identified in the parse tree.

2. The features of each syntactic pattern are identified.

3. The features are used to select the applicable semantic relations.

Although the extraction of semantic relations appears to be at an early stage of development (the process has not yet been described in detail by the LCC research group), preliminary results are very encouraging (see Section 20.4 for an example of the use of semantic relations).

The approach for the mapping of English text into LLF has been used, for example, in the LCC QA system *PowerAnswer* [1, 20].

In the next section, we turn our attention to the reasoning task, and briefly describe the reasoning component of the LCC QA system.

20.3   The COGEX Logic Prover of the LCC QA System

The approach used in many recent QA systems is roughly based on detecting matching patterns between the question and the textual sources provided, to determine which ones are answers to the question. We call the textual sources available to the system *candidate answers*. Because of the ambiguity of natural language and of the large amount of synonyms, however, these systems have difficulties reaching high success rates (see, e.g., [20]). In fact, although it is relatively easy to find fragments of text that possibly contain the answer to the question, it is typically difficult to associate to them some kind of measure allowing to select one or more *best answers*. Since the candidate answers can be conflicting, the inability to rank them is a substantial shortcoming.

To overcome these limitations, the LCC QA system has been recently extended with a prover called COGEX [20]. In high-level terms, COGEX is used to analyze the connection between the question in input and the candidate answers obtained using traditional QA techniques. Consider the question "Did John visit New York City on Dec, 1?" and assume that the QA system has access to data sources containing the fragments "John flew to the City on Dec, 1" and "In the morning of Dec, 1, John went down memory lane to his trip to Australia". COGEX is capable of identifying that the connection between question and candidate answer requires the knowledge that "New York City" and "City" denote the same location, and that "flying *to* a location" implies that the location will be visited. The type and number of these differences is used as a measure of how close a question and candidate answer are—in our example, we would expect that the first answer will be considered the closest to the question (as the second does not describe an *actual* travel on Dec, 1). This measure gives an ordering of the candidate answers, and ultimately allows the selection of the best matches.

The analysis carried out by COGEX is based on world knowledge extracted from WordNet (e.g., the description of the meaning of "fly (to a location)") as well as knowledge about natural language (allowing to link "New York City" and "City"). In this context, the descriptions of the meaning of words are often called *glosses*.

To be used in the QA system, glosses from WordNet have been collected and mapped into logic forms. The resulting pairs ⟨*word, gloss_LLF*⟩ provide definitions of *word*. Part of the associations needed to link "fly" and "visit" in the example above are encoded in COGEX by axioms (encoding complete definitions, from WordNet, of those verbs with the meanings used in the example) such as[4]:

---

[4]To complete the connection, axioms for "travel" and "go" are also needed.

$\exists x_3, x_4 \forall e_1, x_1, x_2$

   $fly\_VB\_9(e_1, x_1, x_2) \equiv$

     $travel\_VB\_1(e_1, x_1, x_4) \wedge in\_IN(e_1, x_3) \wedge airplane\_NN(x_3),$

$\exists x_3, x_4, x_9 \forall e_1, x_1, x_2$

   $visit\_VB\_2(e_1, x_1, x_2) \equiv$

     $go\_VB\_1(e_1, x_1, x_9) \wedge to\_IN(e_1, x_3) \wedge certain\_JJ(x_3) \wedge place\_NN(x_3) \wedge$

     $as\_for\_IN(e_1, x_4) \wedge sightseeing\_NN(x_4).$

(As discussed above, variables x_2, x_4 in the first formula and x_9 in the second are placeholders, used because verbs "fly", "travel", and "go" are intransitive.)

The linguistic knowledge is aimed at linking different logic forms that denote the same entity. Consider for instance the complex nominal "New York City" and the name "City". The corresponding logic forms are

   $New\_NN(x_1), York\_NN(x_2), City\_NN(x_3), nn\_NNC(x_4, x_1, x_2, x_3)$

and

   $City\_NN(x_5).$

As the reader can see, although in English the two names sometimes denote the same entity, their logic forms alone do not allow to conclude that $x5$ and $x4$ denote the same object. This is an instance of a known linguistic phenomenon, in which an object denoted by a sequence of nouns can also be denoted by one element of the sequence. In order to find a match between question and candidate answer, COGEX automatically generates and uses axioms encoding instances of this and other pieces of linguistic knowledge. The following axiom, for example, allows to connect "New York City" and "City".

   $\forall x_1, x_2, x_3, x_4$

     $New\_NN(x_1) \wedge York\_NN(x_2) \wedge$

     $City\_NN(x_3) \wedge nn\_NNC(x_4, x_1, x_2, x_3) \rightarrow City\_NN(x_4).$

Another example of linguistic knowledge used by COGEX is about equivalence classes of prepositions. Consider prepositions "in" and "into", which are often interchangeable. Also usually interchangeable are the pairs "at, in" and "from, of". It is often important for the prover to know about the similarities between these prepositions. Linguistic knowledge about it is encoded by axioms such as:

   $\forall x_1, x_2 \ (in\_IN(x_1, x_2) \leftrightarrow into\_IN(x_1, x_2)).$

Other axioms are included with knowledge about appositions, possessives, etc.

From a technical point of view, for each candidate answer, the task of the prover is that of refuting the negation of the (logic form of the) question using the candidate answer and the knowledge provided. If the prover is successful, a correct answer has been identified. If the proof fails, further attempts are made by iteratively *relaxing* the question and finding a new proof. The introduction of the two axioms above, allowing the matching of "New York City" with "City" and of "in" with "into", provides two examples of relaxation. Other forms of relaxation consist of uncoupling arguments in the predicates of the logic form, or removing prepositions or modifiers (when they are not essential to the meaning of the discourse). The system keeps track of how many relaxation steps are needed to find a proof. *This number is the measure of how close an answer and a question are*—the higher the value, the farther apart they are. If no proof is found after relaxing the question beyond a given threshold, the procedure is assumed to have failed. This indicates that the candidate is *not* an answer to the question.

Empirical evaluations of COGEX have given encouraging results. [20] reports on experiments in which the LCC QA system was tested, with and without COGEX, on the questions from the 2002 Text REtrieval Conference (TREC). According to the authors, the addition of COGEX caused a 30.9% performance increase.

Notice that, while the use of the prover increased performance, it did not bring any significant addition to the *class of questions* that can be answered. These systems can do a reasonable job at matching parts of the question with other text to find candidate answers, but they are not designed to perform inference (e.g., prediction) *on the story that the question contains*.

That is why the type of reasoning carried out by these QA systems is sometimes called *shallow reasoning*. Systems that can reason on the domain described by the question are instead said to perform *deep reasoning*. Although the above mentioned systems do not use domain knowledge and common-sense knowledge (recall that together they are referred to as background knowledge) that is needed for deep reasoning, they could do so. However it is not clear whether the 'iterative relaxing' approach would work in this case.

In the following two sections we describe two QA systems capable of deep reasoning, which use extraction of relevant facts from natural language text as a first step. We start with the DD system that takes as input a logical theory obtained from natural language text, as was described in this section.

20.4   Extracting Relevant Facts from Logical Theories and its Use in the DD QA System about Dynamic Domains and Trips

The DD system focuses on answering questions in natural language about the evolution of dynamic domains and is able to answer the kind of questions (such as reasoning about narratives, predictive reasoning, planning, counterfactual reasoning, and reasoning about intentions) we presented in Section 20.1.1. Its particular focus is on travel and trips. For example, given a paragraph stating *"John is in Paris. He packs the laptop in the carry-on luggage and takes a plane to Baghdad"*, and a query *"Where is the laptop now?"*, DD will answer "Baghdad".

Notice that the task of answering questions of this kind requires fairly deep reasoning, involving not only logical inference, but also the ability to *represent and reason about dynamic domains and defaults*.

To answer the above question, the system has to know, for instance, that whatever is packed in the luggage normally stays there (unless moved), and that one's carry-on luggage normally follows him during trips. An important piece of knowledge is also that the action of taking a plane has the effect of changing the traveler's location to the destination.

In DD, the behavior of dynamic domains is modeled by *transition diagrams* [37, 38], directed graphs whose nodes denote states of the domain and whose arcs, labeled by actions, denote state transitions caused by the execution of those actions. The theory encoding a domain's transition diagram is called here *model of the domain*.

The language of choice for reasoning in DD is AnsProlog [33, 9] (also called A-Prolog [35, 36, 32]) because of its ability to both model dynamic domains and encode commonsense knowledge, which is essential for the type of QA task discussed here. As usual, problem solving tasks are reduced to computing models, called answer sets, of suitable AnsProlog programs. Various inference engines exist that automate the computation of answer sets.

20.4.1 The Overall Architecture of the DD System

The approach followed in the DD system for understanding natural language consists of translating the natural language discourse, in various steps, into its *semantic representation* (a similar approach can also be found in [14]), a collection of facts describing the semantic content of the discourse and a few linking rules. The task of answering queries is then reduced to performing inference on the theory consisting of the semantic representation and model of the domain.

More precisely, given a discourse *H* in natural language, describing a particular history of the domain, and a question *Q*, as well in natural language, the DD system:

1. obtains logic forms for *H* and *Q*;

2. translates the logic forms for *H* and *Q* into a *Quasi-Semantic Representation* (*QSR*), consisting of AnsProlog facts describing properties of the objects of the domain and occurrences of events that alter such properties. The representation cannot be considered fully semantic, because some of the properties are still described using syntactic elements of the discourse (hence the attribute *quasi*). The encoding of the facts is independent of the particular relations chosen to encode the model of the domain;

3. maps the QSR into an *Object Semantic Representation* (*OSR*), a set of AnsProlog atoms which describe the contents of *H* and *Q* using the relations with which the domain model is encoded. The mapping is obtained by means of AnsProlog rules, called *OSR rules*;

4. computes the answer sets of the AnsProlog program consisting of the OSR and the model of the domain and extracts the answer(s) to the question from such answer sets.

Although, in principle, steps 2 and 3 can be combined in a single mapping from *H* and *Q* into the OSR, their separation offers important advantages. First of all, separation of concerns: step 2 is mainly concerned with mapping *H* and *Q* into AnsProlog facts, while 3 deals with producing a semantic representation. Combining them would significantly complicate the translation. Moreover, the division between the two steps allows for a greater modularity of the approach: in order to use different logic form generators, only the translation at step 2 needs to be modified; conversely, we only need to act on step 3 to add to the system the support for new domains (assuming the vocabulary of H and Q does not change). Interestingly, this multi-layered approach is also similar to one of the most widely accepted text comprehension models from cognitive psychology [48].

20.4.2   From Logic Forms to QSR Facts: An Illustration

Consider

- a history H consisting of the sentences "*John is in Paris. He packs the laptop in the carry-on luggage and takes a plane to Baghdad*",

- a query, Q, "*Where is the laptop at the end of the trip?*"

The first step consists in obtaining logic forms for H and Q. This task is performed by the logic form generator described in Section 20.2, that here we call LLF generator. Recall that LLFs consist of a list of atoms encoding the syntactic structure of the discourse augmented with some semantic annotations. For H, the LLF generator returns the following logic form, H_{lf}:

```
John_NN(x1)      &  _human_NE(x1)   &  be_VB_3(e1,x1,x27) &
in_IN(e1,x2)     &  Paris_NN(x2)    &  _town_NE(x2) &
AGT_SR(x1,e1) & LOC_SR(x1,x2)    &

pack_VB_1(e2,x1,x9)      &
laptop_NN_1(x9)          &  in_IN(e2,x11)               &
carry-on_JJ_1(x12,x11)   &
luggage_NN_1(x11)        &  and_CC(e15,e2,e3)           &
take_VB_11(e3,x1,x13)    &  plane_NN_1(x13)
&  to_TO(e3,x14)          &  Baghdad_NN(x14)             &
_town_NE(x14)            &

TMP_SR(x5,e2)   &  AGT_SR(x1,e2)   &  THM_SR(x9,e2) &
PAH_SR(x12,x11) &  AGT_SR(x1,e3)   &
THM_SR(x13,e3) & LOC_SR(x14,e3)
```

Here, *John_NN*($x1$) says that constant $x1$ will be used in the logic form to denote noun (NN) "John". Atom $be\_VB\_3(e1, x1, x27)$ says that constant $e1$ denotes a verb phrase formed by "to be", whose subject is denoted by $x1$. Hence, the two atoms correspond to "John is".[5]

One feature of the LLF generator that is important for the DD system is its ability to insert in the logic form simple semantic annotations and ontological information, most of which are extracted from the WordNet database [54, 26]. Recall that, for example, the suffix _3 in $be\_VB\_3(e1, x1, x27)$ says that the third meaning of the verb from the WordNet classification is used in the phrase (refer to Section 20.2 for more details). The availability of such annotations helps to identify the semantic contents of sentences, thus substantially simplifying the generation of the semantic representation in the following steps. For instance, the logic form of verb "take" above, *take_VB*_$11(e3, x1, x13)$ makes it clear that John did not actually *grasp* the plane.

---

[5] As this sense of verb "to be" does not admit a predicative complement, constant $x27$ is unused.

The logic form, Q_{lf}, for Q is:

```
laptop_NN_1(x5) & LOC_SR(x1,x5)
```

It can be noticed that the LLF generator does not generate atoms representing the verb. This is the feature that distinguishes the history from *where is/was/...* and *when is/was/...* queries at the level of logic form.[6] In the interpretation of the logic form of such queries, an important role is played by the *semantic relations* introduced by the LLF generator. Semantic relations are intended to give a rough description of the semantic role of various phrases in the discourse. For example, $LOC\_SR(x1, x5)$ says that the location of the object denoted by $x5$ is $x1$. Notice, though, that $x1$ is not used anywhere else in Q_{lf}: $x1$ is in fact a placeholder for the entity that must be identified to answer the question. *In general, in the LCC Logic Forms of this type of questions, the object of the query is identified by the constant that is not associated with any lexical item.* In the example above, $x2$ is associated to John by $John\_NN(x2)$, while $x1$ is not associated with any lexical item, as it only occurs in $LOC\_SR(x1, x5)$.

The second step of the process consists in deriving the QSR from H_{lf} and Q_{lf}. The steps in the evolution of the domain described by the QSR are called *moments*. Atoms of the form *true_at(FL, M)* are used in the QSR to state that property *FL* is true at moment *M* of the evolution. For example, the phrase corresponding to $be\_VB\_3(e1, x1, x27)$ (and associated atoms) is encoded in the QSR as:

```
true_at(at(john,paris), m(e1)).
```

where $at(john, paris)$ ("John is in Paris") is the property that holds at moment $m(e1)$. In fact, the third meaning of verb "to be" in the WordNet database is "occupy a certain position or area; be somewhere". Property $at(john, paris)$ is obtained from the atom $in\_IN(e1, x2)$ as follows:

- *in_IN* is mapped into property *at*;

- the first argument of the property is obtained by extracting from the LLF the actor of $e1$: first, the constant denoting the actor is selected from $be\_VB\_3(e1, x1, x27)$; next, the constant is replaced by the lexical item it denotes, using the LLF $John\_NN(x1)$.

Events that cause a change of state are denoted by atoms of the form *event (EVENT_NAME, EVENT_WORD, MEANING, M)*, stating that the event denoted by *EVENT_NAME* and corresponding to *EVENT_WORD* occurred at moment *M* (with *MEANING* being the index of the meaning of the word in WordNet's classification). For instance, the QSR of the phrase associated with $take\_VB\_11(e3, x1, x13)$ is:

```
event(e3,take,11,m(e3)). actor(e3,john). object(e3,plane).
parameter(e3,to,baghdad).
```

---

[6]Yes/no questions have a simpler structure and are not discussed here to save space. The translation of the LLFs of *Where-* and *When-*queries that do not rely on verb "to be" (e.g., "where did John pack the laptop") has not yet been fully investigated.

The first fact states that the event of type "take" occurred at moment $m(e3)$ (with the meaning "travel or go by means of a certain kind of transportation, or a certain route") and is denoted by $e3$. The second and third fact specify the actor and the object of the event. Atom *parameter*($e3$, *to*, *baghdad*) states that the parameter of type *to* of the event is Baghdad.

A default temporal sequence of the moments in the evolution of the domain is extracted from H_{lf} by observing the order in which the corresponding verbs are listed in the logic form. Hence, the QSR for H_{lf} contains facts:

```
next(m(e1),m(e2)). next (m(e2),m(e3)).
```

The first fact states that the moment in which John is said to be in Paris precedes the one in which he packs. Notice that the actual order of events may be modified by words such as "after", "before", "on his way", etc. Although the issues involved in adjusting the order of events have not been investigated in detail, we believe that the default reasoning capabilities of AnsProlog provide a powerful way to accomplish the task.

Finally, the QSR of Q_{lf} is obtained by analyzing the logic form to identify the property that is being queried. Atom $LOC\_SR(x1, x5)$ tells us that the query is about the location of the object denoted by $x5$. The corresponding property is *at*(*laptop*, C), where variable C needs to be instantiated with the location of the laptop as a result of the QA task. All the information is condensed in the QSR:

```
answer_true(C) :- eventually_true(at(laptop,C)).
```

The statement says that the answer to the query is C if *at*(*laptop*, C) is predicted to be true at the end of the story.

20.4.3   OSR: From QSR Relations to Domain Relations

The next step consists in mapping the QSR relations to the domain relations. Since the translation depends on the formalism used to encode the transition diagram, the task is accomplished by an *interface module* associated with the domain model. The rules of the interface module are called Object Semantic Representation rules (OSR rules for short).

The domain model used in our example is the *travel domain* [11, 34], a common-sense formalization of actions involving travel. The two main relations used in the formalization are h—which stands for holds and states which fluents[7] hold at each time point—and o—which stands for occurs and states which actions occur at each time point.

The key object of the formalization is the *trip*. Properties of a trip are its origin, destination, participants, and means of transportation. Action *go_on*(*Actor*, *Trip*) is a compound action that consists in embarking in the trip and departing.

Hence, the mapping from the QSR of event "take", shown above, is obtained by the following OSR rules (some rules have been omitted to save space):

---

[7]Fluents are relevant properties of the domain whose truth value may change over time [37, 38].

```
o(go_on(ACTOR,trip(Obj)), T) :- event(E,take,11,M),
                                 actor(E,ACTOR),
                                 object(E,Obj),
                                 time_point(M,T).

h(trip_by(trip(Obj),Obj),T) :- event(E,take,11,M),
                                object(E,Obj),
                                time_point(M,T).

dest(trip(Obj),DEST) :- event(E,take,11,M),
                        parameter(E,to,DEST),
                        object(E,Obj).
```

The first rule states that, if the QSR mentions event "take" with sense 11 (in the WordNet database, this sense refers to travel), the actor of the event is *ACTOR* and the object is *Obj*, then the reasoner can conclude that action *go_on(ACTOR, trip(Obj))* occurs at time point *T*. In this example, the time point is computed in a straightforward way from the sequence of moments encoded by relation *next* described in the previous section.[8] Notice that the name of the trip is for simplicity obtained by applying a function *trip* to the means of transportation used, but in more realistic cases this need not be.

Explicit information on the means of transportation used for the trip is derived by the second rule. The rule states that the object of event "take" semantically denotes the means of transportation. Because, in general, the means of transportation can change as the trip evolves, *trip_by* is a fluent.

The last rule defines the destination of the trip. A similar rule is used to define the origin.[9]

Atoms of the form *true_at(FL, M)* from the QSR are mapped into domain atoms by the rule:

```
h(FL,T) :- true_at(FL,M),
           time_point(M,T).
```

The mapping of relation *eventually_true*, used in the QSR for the definition of relation *answer_true*, is symmetrical:

```
eventually_true(FL) :- h(FL,n).
```

where *n* is the constant denoting the time point associated with the end of the evolution of the domain.

Since the OSR rules are written in AnsProlog, the computation of the OSR can be combined with the task of finding the answer given the OSR: in our approach, the answer to *Q* is found by computing, in a single step, the answer sets of the AnsProlog program consisting of the QSR, the OSR rules, and the model of the travel domain.

---

[8]Recall that, in more complex situations, the definition of relation *time_point* can involve the use of defaults, to allow the assignment of time points to be refined during the mapping.

[9]Since in the travel domain the origin and destination of trips do not change over time, the formalization is designed to allow to specify the origin using a static relation rather than a fluent. This simplification is not essential and can be easily lifted.

A convenient way of extracting the answer when SMODELS[10] is used as inference engine, is to add the following two directives to the AnsProlog program:

```
#hide. #show answer_true(C).
```

As expected, for our example SMODELS returns[11]:

```
answer_true(baghdad).
```

20.4.4   An Early Travel Module of the DD System

As mentioned earlier, and as is necessary in any QA system performing deep reasoning, the DD system combines domain knowledge and common-sense knowledge together with information specific to the instance, extracted from text, questions, and the mapping rules (of the previous subsection). As a start the DD system focused on domain knowledge about travels and trips (which we briefly mention in the previous subsection) and contained rules for commonsense reasoning about dynamic domains. In this section we briefly describe various parts of an early version of this background knowledge base, which is small enough to be presented in its entirety, but yet shows various important aspects of representation and reasoning.

Facts and basic relations in the travel module

The main objects in the travel modules are *actions*, *fluents* and *trips*. In addition there are various domain predicates and a Geography module.

1. Domain predicates: The predicates include predicates such as *person*(X), meaning X is a person; $l(Y)$, meaning Y is a possible location of a trip; *time_point*(X), meaning X is a time point; *travel_documents*(X), meaning X is a travel document such as passports and tickets; *belongings*(X), meaning X is a belonging such as a laptop or a book; *luggage*$(carry\_on(X))$, meaning X is a carry-on luggage; *luggage*$(lugg(X))$, meaning X is a regular (non-carry-on) luggage; *possession*(X), meaning X is a possession; *type_of_transp*(X), meaning X is a type of transportation; *action*(X) meaning X is an action; *fluent*(X) meaning X is a fluent; and *day*(X) meaning X is a day.

2. The Geography module and related facts: The DD system has a simple geography module with predicates *city*(X) denoting X is a city; *country*(X) denoting X is a country; *union*(X) denoting X is a union of countries such as the European Union; and *in*$(XCity, Y)$ denoting *XCity* is in the country or union Y. In addition it has facts such as *owns*(P, X), meaning person P owns luggage X; *vehicle*(X, T) meaning X is a vehicle of type T; $h(X, T)$ meaning fluent X holds at time point T; and *time*(T, day, D) meaning the day corresponding to time point T is D.

3. The Trips: The DD system has the specification of an activity "trip". Origins and destinations of trips are explicitly stated by the facts *origin*$(j, C1)$ and *dest*$(j, C2)$.

4. Actions and actors: The DD system has various actions such as *depart*(J), meaning trip J departs from its origin; *stop*(J, C), meaning trip J stops at city C; *go_on*(P, J), meaning person P goes on trip J; *embark*(P, J), meaning person P

---

[10]http://www.tcs.hut.fi/Software/smodels/.

[11]The issue of translating the answer back into natural language will be addressed in future versions of the system.

embarks on trip J; and *disembark*(P, J), meaning person P disembarks from trip J. In each of these actions J refers to a trip. Other actions include *get*(P, PP), meaning person P gets possession PP; *pack*(P, PP, C), meaning person P packs possession PP in container C; *unpack*(P, PP, C), meaning person P packs possession PP in container C; and *change_to*(J, T), meaning trip J changes to the type of transportation T. The domain contains facts about actions and actors. For example, the fact *action*$(depart(j))$ means that *depart*(j) is an action; and the fact *actor*$(depart(j), j)$ means that j is the actor of the action *depart*(j).

5. *Fluents:* The DD system has various fluents such as *at*(P, D), meaning the person P is at location D; *participant*(P, J), meaning the person P is a participant of trip J; *has_with_him*(P, PP), meaning person P has possession PP with him; *inside*(B, C), meaning B is inside the container C; and *trip_by*(J, T), meaning the trip J is using the transportation type T.

The rules in the travel module

We now present various rules of the travel module. We arrange these rules in groups that have a common focus on a particular aspect.

6. *Inertia:* The following two rules express the commonsense law of inertia that normally fluents do not change their value.

```
h(Fl,T+1)   :- T < n,   h(Fl,T),   not -h(Fl,T+1).
-h(Fl,T+1)  :- T < n,   -h(Fl,T),  not  h(Fl,T+1).
```

7. *Default values of some fluents:* The following two rules say that, normally, people have their passport and their luggage with them at the beginning of the story.[12] Here, 0 denotes initial time point. (A different number could have been used with minor changes in few other rules.)

```
h(has_with_him(P,passport(P)),0) :-
                not -h(has_with_him(P,passport(P)),0).
h(has_with_him(P,Luggage),0) :-
                owns(P,Luggage),
                not -h(has_with_him(P,Luggage),0).
```

8. *Agent starting a journey:* The following two rules specify that normally people start their journey at the origin of the journey.

```
h(at(J,C),0)  :- o(go_on(P,J),0), origin(J,C),
                not -h(at(J,C),0).
h(at(P,C),0)  :- o(go_on(P,J),0), origin(J,C),
                not -h(at(P,C),0).
```

9. *Direct and Indirect effect of the action embark:* The effects of the action *embark* and its executability conditions are expressed by the rules given below.

The following rule expresses that a person after embarking on a journey on a plane no longer has his luggage with him.

---

[12]Obviously these defaults are meaningful only in the context of travel-related stories, and can be suitably qualified in AnsProlog . We omit the qualification to simplify the presentation.

```
-h(has_with_him(P,lugg(P)),T+1)  :- o(embark(P,J),T),
                                     h(trip_by(J,plane),T).
```

The following three rules express conditions under which a person can embark on a journey: he must be a participant; he must be at the location of the journey and he must have all that he needs to embark on that journey.

```
-o(embark(P,J),T)  :- -h(participant(P,J),T).
-o(embark(P,J),T)  :- h(at(P,D1),T), h(at(J,D2),T),
                      neq(D1,D2).
-o(embark(P,J),T)  :- need(P,TD,J),
                      -h(has_with_him(P,TD),T).
```

The following rules define what person needs to go embark on a trip. The first rule says he normally needs a passport if he is traveling between two different countries. The third rule states an exception that one traveling between two European Union countries does not need a passport. The fourth rule states that one normally needs a ticket for a journey. The fifth rule states an exception that for a car trip one does not need a ticket. The last two rules define a car trip as a trip which started as a car trip and which has not changed its mode of transportation.

```
need(P,passport(P),J)    :- place(embark(P,J),C1),
                            dest(J,C2), diff_countries(C1,C2),
                            not -need(P,passport(P),J).
diff_countries(C1,C2)    :- in(C1,Country1), in(C2,Country2),
                            neq(Country1,Country2).
-need(P,passport(P),J)   :- citizen(P,eu),
                            place(embark(P,J),C1),
                            dest(J,C2), in(C1,eu), in(C2,eu).

need(P,tickets(J),J)     :- not -need(P,tickets(J),J).
-need(P,tickets(J),J)    :- car_trip(J).
-car_trip(J)             :- h(trip_by(J,TypeOfTransp),T),
                            neq(TypeOfTransp,car).
car_trip(J)              :- h(trip_by(J,car),0),
                            not -car_trip(J).
```

10. Direct and Indirect effect of the action disembark: The direct and indirect effects of the action *disembark* and its executability conditions are expressed by the rules given below.

The first two rules express that by disembarking a person is no longer a participant of a trip and unless his luggage is lost, he has his luggage with him. The third and fourth rules specify that one cannot disembark from a trip at a particular time if he is not a participant at that time, or if the journey is en route at that time.

```
-h(participant(P,J),T+1)  :- o(disembark(P,J),T).
 h(has_with_him(P,lugg(P)),T+1)  :-
                          o(disembark(P,J),T),
                          o(embark(P,J),T1),
                          h(has_with_him(P,lugg(P)),T1),
                          not h(lost(lugg(P)),T+1).
```

```
-o(disembark(P,J),T) :- -h(participant(P,J),T).
-o(disembark(P,J),T) :-  h(at(J,en_route),T).
```

11. Rules about the action go_on: The action *go_on* is viewed as a composite action consisting of first embarking and then departing. This is expressed by the first two rules below. The third rule states that a plane trip takes at most a day.

```
o(embark(P,J),T)   :-  o(go_on(P,J),T).
o(depart(J),T+1)   :-  o(go_on(P,J),T).

time(T2,day,D) | time(T2,day,D + 1) :- o(go_on(P,J),T1),
                                       o(disembark(P,J),T2),
                                       time(T1,day,D),
                                       h(trip_by(J,plane),T1).
```

12. Effect of the action get: The first rule below states that if one gets something then he has it. The second rule states that getting a passport could take at least three days. Rules that compute the duration of an action are discussed later in item 16.

```
h(has_with_him(P,PP),T+1) :- o(get(P,PP),T).
:- duration(get(P,passport(P)),Day), Day < 3.
```

13. Effect axioms and executability conditions of the actions pack and unpack:
The first two rules below state the effect of packing and unpacking a possession inside a container. The third and fourth rule state when one can pack a possession and the fifth and sixth rules state when one can unpack a possession.

```
h(inside(PP,Container),T+1)   :- o(pack(P,PP,Container),T).
-h(inside(PP,Container),T+1)  :- o(unpack(P,PP,Container),T).

-o(pack(P,PP,Container),T)    :- -h(has_with_him(P,PP),T).
-o(pack(P,PP,Container),T)    :- -h(has_with_him(P,Container),T).
-o(unpack(P,PP,Container),T)  :- -h(has_with_him(P,Container),T).
-o(unpack(P,PP,Container),T)  :- -h(inside(P,Container),T).
```

14. Direct and Indirect effects (including triggers) of the actions depart and stop:
The first two rules below express the impact of departing and stopping. The third rule says that a stop at the destination of a journey is followed by disembarking of the participants of that journey. The fourth rule says that a stop in a non-destination is normally followed by a depart action. The fifth and sixth rules give conditions when departing and stopping is not possible. The seventh rule says that normally a trip goes to its destination. The eighth rule says that after departing one stops at the next stop. The last rule states that one can stop at only one place at a time.

```
h(at(J,en_route),T+1)  :- o(depart(J),T).
h(at(J,C),T+1)         :- o(stop(J,C),T).

o(disembark(P,J),T+1)  :- h(participant(P,J),T),
                          o(stop(J,D),T), dest(J,D).
```

```
o(depart(J),T+1)           :- o(stop(J,C),T), not dest(J,C),
                              not -o(depart(J),T+1).

-o(depart(J),T)            :- h(at(J,en_route),T).
-o(stop(J,C),T)            :- -h(at(J,en_route),T).
o(stop(J,C),T)             :- h(at(J,en_route),T), dest(J,C),
                              not -o(stop(J,C),T).

o(stop(J,C2),T+1)          :- leg_of(J,C1,C2), h(at(J,C1),T),
                              o(depart(J),T).
-o(stop(J,C),T)            :- o(stop(J,C1),T), neq(C,C1).
```

15. Effect of changing the type of transportation:

```
h(trip_by(J,Transp),T+1) :- o(change_to(J,Transp),T).
```

16. State constraints about the dynamic domain: The following are rules that encode constraints about the dynamic domain. The first rule states that an object can only
be in one place at a particular time. The second rule states that a trip can only have
one type of transportation at a particular time. The third rule states that if a person is
at a location then his possessions are also at the same location. The fourth rules states
that a participant of a trip is at the same location as the trip. The fifth rules states that
if a person has a container then he also has all that is inside the container. The last rule
defines the duration of an action based on the mapping between time points and days.
(It assumes that all actions occurring at a time point have the same duration.)

```
-h(at(O,D1),T)             :- h(at(O,D2),T), neq(D1,D2).
-h(trip_by(J,Transp2),T) :- h(trip_by(J,Transp1),T),
                              neq(Transp1,Transp2).

h(at(PP,D),T)    :- h(has_with_him(P,PP),T), h(at(P,D),T).
h(at(P,D),T)     :- h(participant(P,J),T), h(at(J,D),T).

h(has_with_him(P,PP),T) :- h(inside(PP,Container),T),
                              h(has_with_him(P,Container),T).
duration(A,D)  :- action(A), o(A,T), time(T,day,D1),
                  time(T+1,day,D2), D = D2 - D1.
```

20.4.5   Other Enhancements to the Travel Module

The module in the previous section is only sufficient with respect to some of the text
question pairs of Section 20.1.1. For others we need additional modules, such as planning modules, modules for reasoning about intentions, and modules that can map time
points to a calender.

Planning

Planning with respect to a goal can be done by writing rules about whether a goal is
satisfied at the desired time points; writing rules that eliminate models where the goal
is not satisfied and then writing rules that enumerate possible action occurrences. With
respect to the example in Section 20.1.1 (fifth item), the following rules suffice.

```
answer_true :-    o(go_on(john,j,T)), origin(j,boston),
                  dest(j,paris), time(T,day,4).
yes :-answer_true.

:- not yes.

{o(Act,T) : action(Act) : actor(Act,P)}1 :- T < n-1.
```

The first rule states that the answer to query q is "true" if John performs the action of going to Paris on day 4. The next two rules say that it is impossible for the answer not to be "true". Finally, the last rule states that any action can occur at any time step.

Reasoning about intentions

To reason about intentions one needs to formalize commonsense rules about intentions [10]. One such rule is that an agent after forming an intention will normally attempt to achieve it. Another rules is that an agent will not usually give up on its intentions without good reason; i.e., intentions persist. We now give a simple formalization of these. We assume that intentions are a sequence of distinct actions.

In the following *intended_seq*(S, I) means that the sequence of actions S is intended starting from time point I. Similarly, *intended_action*(A, I) means that the action A is intended (for execution) at time point I.

```
intended_action(A,I)    :- intended_seq(S,I), seq(S,1,A).

intended_action(B,K+1)  :- intended_seq(S,I), seq(S,J,A),
                           occurs(A,K), time_point(K),
                           seq(S,J+1,B).

occurs(A,I) :- action(A), intended_action(A,I),
               time_point(I), not -occurs(A,I).

intended_action(A,I+1)  :- action(A), time_point(I),
                           intended_action(A,I),
                           not occurs(A,I).
```

The first rule above encodes that an individual action A is intended for execution at time point I, if, A is the first action of a sequence which is intended to be executed starting from time point I. The second rule encodes that an individual action B is intended for execution at time point $K + 1$, if B is the $(J + 1)$th action of a sequence intended to be executed at an earlier time point and the Jth action of that sequence is A which is executed at time point K. The third rule encodes the notion that intended actions occur unless they are prevented. The last rule encodes the notion that if an intended action does not occur as planned then the intention persists.

20.5   From Natural Language to Relevant Facts in the ASU QA System

In the previous section relevant facts and some question-related rules were obtained from natural language by processing a logic form of the natural language. In this section we briefly mention an alternative approach from [71] where the output of a semantic parser is used directly in obtaining the relevant facts. In addition we illustrate the use of knowledge in reducing semantic ambiguities. Thus knowledge and reasoning is not only useful in obtaining answers but also in understanding natural language.

In the ASU QA system to extract the relevant facts from sentences, Link Grammar [70] is used to parse the sentences so that the dependent relations between pairs of words are obtained. Such dependent relations are known as *links*. The Link Grammar parser outputs labeled links between pairs of words for a given input sentence. For instance, if word a is associated with word b through the link "S", a is identified as the subject of the sentence while b is the finite verb related to the subject a. From the links between pairs of words, a simple algorithm is then used to generate AnsProlog facts. A simplified subset of the algorithm is presented as follows:

Input: Pairs of words with their corresponding links produced by the Link Grammar parser.

Output: AnsProlog facts.

Suppose e_i is the current event number[13] and the event is described in the jth sentence of the story.

1. Form the facts *in_sentence*(e_i, j) and *event_num*(e_i).

2. If word a is associated with word b through the link "S" (indicating a is a subject noun related to the finite verb b), then form the facts *event_actor*(e_i, a) and *event_nosense*(e_i, b). If a appears in the name database, then form the fact *person*(a).

3. If word a is associated with word b through the link "MV" (indicating a is a verb related to modifying phrase b), and b is also associated with word c through the link "J" (indicating b is a preposition related to object c), then form the fact *parameter*(e_i, b, c). If c appears in the city database, then form the fact *city*(c).

4. If word a is associated with word b through the link "O" (indicating a is a transitive verb related to object b), then form the facts *noun*(b) and *object*(e_i, b).

5. If word a is associated with word b through the link "ON" (indicating a is the preposition "on" related to certain time expression b) and b is also associated with word c through the link "TM" (indicating b is a month name related to day number c), then form the fact *occurs*(e_i, b, c).

6. If word a is associated with word b through the link "Dmcn" (indicating a is the clock time and b is AM or PM), then form the fact *clock_time*(a). (Here a is a time as one reads in a clock and hence is more fine grained than the information in the earlier used predicate *time_point*.)

---

[13] We use a complex sentence processer that processes complex sentences to a set of simple sentences. Thus we assume that there is one event in each sentence. We assign event numbers sequentially from the start of the text. This is a simplistic view and there have been some recent work on more sophisticated event analysis, such as in [47].

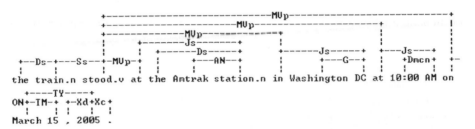

Figure 20.2: Output of the Link Grammar Parser for *"The train stood at the Amtrak station in Washington DC at 10:00 AM on March 15, 2005"*.

7. If word a is associated with word b through the link "TY" (indicating b is a year number related to date a), then form the fact *occurs_year*(e_i, b).

8. If word a is associated with word b through the link "D" (indicating a is a determiner related to noun b), then form the fact *noun*(b).

To illustrate the algorithm, the Link Grammar output for the sentence "The train stood at the Amtrak station in Washington DC at 10:00 AM on March 15, 2005." is shown below in Fig. 20.2.

The following facts are extracted based on the Link Grammar output:

```
event_num(e1).                          in_sentence(e1,1).
event_actor(e1,train).                  event_nosense(e1,stood).
parameter(e1,at,amtrak_station).
parameter(e1,in,washington_dc).
parameter(e1,at,t10_00am).
occurs_year(e1,2005).                   occurs(e1,march,15).
city(washington_dc).                    person(\mathit{john}).
noun(train).                            verb(stood).
clock_time(t10_00am).                   noun(amtrak_station).
```

In the above extracted facts, the constant $e1$ is an identifier that identifies related facts extracted from the same sentence. Atoms such as *noun*(*train*), *verb*(*stood*) are event independent and thus no event number is assigned to such facts. The atom *event_nosense*($e1$, *stood*) indicates that word sense has yet to be assigned to the word *stood*.

After extracting the facts from the sentences, it is necessary to assign the correct meanings of nouns and verbs with respect to the sentence. The process of identifying the types utilizes WordNet hypernyms. Word a is a hypernym of word b if a has a "is-a" relation with b. In the travel domain, it is essential to identify nouns that are of the types transportation (denoted as *tran*) or person (denoted as *person*). Such identification is performed using predefined sets of hypernyms for both transportation and person. Let H_t be a set of hypernyms for type t. Noun a belongs to type t if a is a hypernym of $h \in H_t$, and a AnsProlog fact $t(a)$ is formed. The predefined sets of hypernyms of transportation and person are: $H_{tran} = \{travel, public\ transport, conveyance\}$ and $H_{person} = \{person\}$. For instance, the hypernym of the noun *train* is *conveyance*. So we assign a AnsProlog fact *transportation*(*train*).

A similar process is performed for each extracted verb by using the hypernyms of WordNet. The component returns all possible senses of a given verb. Given the verb v and v has hypernym v', then the component returns the fact $is\_a(v, v')$. From the various possible senses of verbs, the correct senses are matched by utilizing the extracted facts related to the same event. AnsProlog rules are written to match the correct senses of verbs. The following rule is used to match the correct senses of a verb that has the meaning of *be*:

```
event(E,be)  :- event_actor(E,TR),
                is_a(V,be), event_nosense(E,V),
                parameter(E,at,C), parameter(E,at,T).
```

The intuition of the above AnsProlog rule is that verb V has the meaning of *be* if event E has transportation TR as the actor and E involves city C, clock time T and V has the hypernym *be*. With the extracted facts, we can assign the meaning of *stood* to have the meaning of *be* in our example sentence.

Using the extracted facts together with verbs and nouns with their correct senses, reasoning is then done with an AnsProlog background knowledge base similar to the one in the DD system described in the previous section.

20.6   Nutcracker—System for Recognizing Textual Entailment

In the problem of recognizing textual entailment, the goal is to decide, given a text *Text* and a hypothesis *Hypothesis* expressed in a natural language, whether a human reasoner would call the hypothesis *Hypothesis* a consequence of the text. The following example is part of *Text\Hypothesis* pair No. 633 in the collection of problems proposed as the Second PASCAL Recognizing Textual Entailment Challenge [8]:

Text: Yoko Ono unveiled a statue of her late husband, John Lennon.

Hypothesis: Yoko Ono is John Lennon's widow.

Expected entailment: Yes

We can see recognizing textual entailment (RTE) as a special case of the question answering problem. It is a textual answering task that covers only some aspects of general QA problem. Most of the systems that are designed to solve this problem [24, 8] reason directly on a natural language input by applying various statistical methods. These methods generally encounter problems when reasoning involves background knowledge. To recognize the fact that *Hypothesis* is "entailed" by *Text*, we often need to use some background commonsense knowledge. For instance, in the example above it is essential that "being a late wife" is a the same as "being a widow".

One approach to the RTE problem is to use first-order reasoning tools to check whether the hypothesis can be derived from the text conjoined with relevant background knowledge, after expressing all of them by first-order formulas. Bos and Markert employ this method in [17] and implemented in the system Nutcracker.[14] Related work is described in [5, 28].

---

[14]http://www.cogsci.ed.ac.uk/~jbos/RTE/.

We can summarize the approach to recognizing textual entailment employed by Bos and Markert as follows:

1. *Text* and *Hypothesis* are represented first by discourse representation structures [46] and then by first-order formulas T and C, respectively,

2. potentially relevant background knowledge is identified and expressed by a first-order formula *BK*,

3. an automated reasoning system, first-order logic theorem prover or model builder, is used to check whether the implication

$$T \wedge BK \rightarrow C$$

is logically valid.

Step 1 of this approach employs similar ideas as described in Section 20.2 where lambda calculus is used to build semantic representation of a text in the form of first-order logic formula. Instead, lambda calculus is used to build semantic representation of a text in the form of discourse representation structure (DRS) [16]. Next, discourse representation structure is translated into first-order logic formula as described in [15]. The intermediate step of building DRS for the text, for instance, allows the Nutcracker system to use the anaphora resolution mechanism that discourse representation theory [46] about DRSs provides. Consider

Text: Yoko Ono unveiled a statue of her late husband, John Lennon.

It has the following first-order logic representation produced by Nutcracker

$$\exists x \ y \ z \ e \ (p\_ono(x) \wedge p\_yoko(x) \wedge r\_of(z, x) \wedge$$

$$n\_statue(y) \wedge r\_of(y, z) \wedge$$

$$a\_late(z) \wedge n\_husband(z) \wedge p\_lennon(z) \wedge p\_john(z) \wedge$$

$$n\_event(e) \wedge v\_unveil(e) \wedge r\_agent(e, x) \wedge r\_patient(e, y)).$$

It is interesting to note different prefixes $a\_$, $n\_$, $v\_$, $r\_$, $p\_$ that intuitively stand for adjective, noun, verb, relation, and person. The fact that Yoko Ono is a person or statue is a noun is available to Nutcracker from a syntax parse tree of a sentence produced by Combinatorial Categorial Grammar (CCG) parser[15] employed by the system. On the other hand unary predicates n_event, r_agent and $r\_patient$ are fixed symbols that are generated during the semantic analysis of the sentence by associating the transitive verb *unveil* with the event whose agent is Yoko Ono and patient is the statue.

Nutcracker approach benefits by choosing first-order logic as the formal language for representing semantic meaning of the sentence. First-order logic allows occurrence of negation, disjunction, implication, universal and existential quantifiers in the formula with arbitrary nesting. This provides a possibility to formally express various natural language phenomena. For example, for sentence "John has all documents"., Nutcracker produces the following first-order logic formula

---

[15]http://svn.ask.it.usyd.edu.au/trac/candc/wiki/.

$\exists x (p\_john(x) \land$

$\qquad \forall y \ (n\_document(y) \rightarrow$

$\qquad\qquad \exists e \ (n\_event(e) \land v\_have(e) \land r\_agent(e, x) \land r\_patient(e, y))))$.

To the best of our knowledge logic form employed by the LCC method described in Section 20.2 is not capable of properly representing the sentences of such type. I.e., the information about generalized quantifier *all* used in the sentence will be lost.

Unlike the LCC method that performs word sense disambiguation while producing logic form of the sentence, Nutcracker disregards this issue.

Step 2 of Nutcracker system that identifies potentially relevant background knowledge is based on the following principles. Words occurring in *Text* and *Hypothesis* are used as triggers for finding necessary background knowledge that is represented as a set of first-order logic axioms *BK*. Nutcracker generates the formula *BK* using hand coded database of background knowledge and automatically generated axioms.

Hand coded knowledge is of two types. One is domain specific, as for example, first-order logic formula

$\forall x \ y \ (n\_husband(x) \land a\_late(x) \land r\_of(x, y) \rightarrow$

$\qquad (n\_widow(y) \land r\_of(y, x)))$

that encodes the fact that if x is a late husband of y then y is a widow of x.[16] Other hand coded axioms represent the generic knowledge that cover the semantics of possessives, active-passive alternation, and spatial knowledge. Bos and Markert in [17] present the axiom

$\forall e \ x \ y \ (n\_event(e) \land r\_agent(e, x) \land f\_in(e, y) \rightarrow f\_in(x, y))$

as an example. It states that if an event occurs in some location then the agent of this event is at the same location. Note that restating this axiom as "*normally* if an event occurs in some location then the agent of this event is at the same location" is a nontrivial task for the first-order logic formalism. On the other hand, the approach described in Sections 20.4 and 20.5 where nonmonotonic AnsProlog language is used to represent the background knowledge suits well for representing such axioms.

Automatically generated knowledge is created by two means. One uses hypernym relations of WordNet to create an ontology for the nouns and verbs occurring in the text that corresponds to some snapshot of the general WordNet database. Such ontology is called MiniWordnet and its construction mechanism is described in [16]. Its general structure is a tree whose nodes represent the words and the edges stand for the hypernym relations between the words. For example, MiniWordnet will, among others, contain the following hypernym relation for the sentence "Yoko Ono is John Lennon's widow.": *n_widow* is a hypernym of *n_person*. Nutcracker produces two kinds of first-order logic formulas that encode the knowledge represented by the Mini-Wordnet. First, it creates the implication for each hypernym relation that occurs in

---

[16]In fact such an axiom has a flaw. Consider a following pair *Text*: "Abraham is the husband of Sarah. Abraham is the father of Isaac. Isaac is the husband of Rebecca." and *Hypothesis*: "Abraham is the husband of Rebecca." Given a first-order logic representation of the pair and this axiom, *Text* entails *Hypothesis*. Resolving such issues is the problem of farther investigation.

the ontology. If MiniWordnet contains information that *n_widow* is a hypernym of *n_person* then the corresponding first-order formula is generated

$$\forall x \ (n\_widow(x) \rightarrow n\_person(x)).$$

It naturally can happen that one of the nodes in MiniWordnet has several children, i.e., several words are in hypernym relation with the node. Linguistic evidence suggests that the concepts (nonsynonyms) that are in hypernym relation with the same word are mutually exclusive. For instance, node that contains *n_person* might have two children that stand for *n_widow* and *n_husband*. In such case, Nutcracker generates the following two implications for *BK*

$$\forall x \ (n\_widow(x) \rightarrow \neg n\_husband(x)),$$

$$\forall x \ (n\_husband(x) \rightarrow \neg n\_widow(x)).$$

The second type of background knowledge automatically generate by the Nutcracker uses the syntax and lexical information provided by the parser. For instance, when the parser recognizes that *Yoko* is a person, the system will generate the following first-order logic formula

$$\forall x \ (p\_yoko(x) \rightarrow n\_person(x)).$$

The last step of the Nutcracker approach involves the use of an automated reasoning system, first-order logic theorem prover or model builder, to check whether the implication

$$T \wedge BK \rightarrow C \tag{20.1}$$

is logically valid. The formulas T and C are created during the Step 1 and correspond to *Text* and *Hypothesis* respectively. Formula *BK*, on the other hand, is the conjunction of the first-order formulas construction of which is described above.

Bos and Markert [17] propose the use of first-order logic tools in the following manner:

1. if a theorem prover finds a proof for the formula (20.1), Nutcracker concludes that *Text* entails *Hypothesis*.

2. if a theorem prover finds a proof for the formula

$$\neg(T \wedge BK) \wedge C,$$

   then Nutcracker concludes that *Text* does not entail the *Hypothesis* due to the fact that they are inconsistent.

3. if a model builder finds a model for the negation of the formula (20.1)

$$T \wedge BK \wedge \neg C \tag{20.2}$$

   then the system concludes that there is no entailment.

It is interesting to note that if the formula (20.2) belongs to the class of "effectively propositional", or "near-propositional" formulas [67] then it would be sufficient to only use, so-called, effectively propositional reasoning (EPR) solvers to find an entailment. Effectively propositional formula is the universal closure of a quantifier-free formula in conjunctive normal form. On the class of such formulas the above three invocations of first-order tools can be reduced to one. For instance, model builder PARADOX[17] can also be seen as an EPR-solver, as it always recognizes a formula that can be converted into effectively propositional formula and is able to either find its models or state that the formula has no model. Furthermore, for effectively propositional formulas logic programming under stable model semantics can be used to verify the entailment.

This approach to RTE is related to QA approach described in Sections 20.4 and 20.5. First, Bos and Markert also consider the step of acquiring the related background knowledge as a vital element of a successful system for solving the RTE problem. Second, this method uses the first-order logic as the semantic representation language for the texts and background knowledge. Similarly, the systems described in Sections 20.4, 20.5 translate the natural language input and background knowledge into the AnsProlog rules. In both cases the representations have a formal model-theoretic semantics. Afterwards the approaches use general-purpose inference mechanisms designed for first-order logic and answer set programming inference, respectively.

20.7 Mueller's Story Understanding System

A different technique for obtaining a semantic representation of the discourse is described by Mueller in [62]. The technique uses *Event Calculus* [69, 55, 61] (which originated from [49] and evolved through [68]) for the semantic representation of the text. There, the discourse is initially mapped into a collection of *templates*—descriptions of the events consisting of frames with slots and slot fillers. Consider the text (this example is taken from [62]):

> *Bogota, 15 Jan 90—In an action that is unprecedented in Colombia's history of violence, unidentified persons kidnapped 31 people in the strife-torn banana-growing region of Uraba, the Antiouqia governor's office reported today. The incident took place in Puerto Bello, a village in Turbo municipality, 460 Km northwest of Bogota [. . .].*

Information extraction systems [2, 3] can be used to generate a template such as:

0. MESSAGE:ID DEV-MUC3-0040 (NNCOSC)

1. MESSAGE:TEMPLATE 1

2. INCIDENT:DATE – 15 JAN 90

---

[17]http://www.math.chalmers.se/~koen/paradox/.

3. INCIDENT: LOCATION COLOMBIA: URABA (REGION):

                    TURBO (MUNICIPALITY):PUERTO BELLO (VILLAGE)

4. INCIDENT: TYPE KIDNAPPING

5. INCIDENT: STAGE OF EXECUTION ACCOMPLISHED

[...]

8. PERP: INCIDENT CATEGORY TERRORIST ACT
9. PERP: INDIVIDUAL ID "UNIDENTIFIED PERSONS"/[...]
[...]

19: HUM TGT:NAME –

20. HUM TGT:DESCRIPTION: "VILLAGERS"

21. HUM TGT:NUMBER 31: "VILLAGERS"

22. HUM TGT:FOREIGN NATION –

23. HUM TGT:EFFECT OF INCIDENT –

24. HUM TGT:TOTAL NUMBER –

Next, each template is analyzed to find the *script* active in the template. The script determines the type of commonsense knowledge that the reasoner will use to understand the discourse. The above template is classified as matching the *kidnapping* script.

The pair consisting of the template and the script is then mapped into a *commonsense reasoning problem* encoding the initial state and narrative of events that take place in the story. Differently from what happens in the DD system, the commonsense reasoning problems for a particular script have a rather rigid structure: events listed in the script are *always* assumed to occur (apparently, even in the presence of contrary evidence from the text), while events mentioned in the story but not in the script are disregarded.

For the kidnapping script, the initial state and sequence of events are:

1. Initially the human targets are at a first location and the perpetrator is at a second location.

2. Initially the human targets are alive, calm, and uninjured.

3. The perpetrator loads a gun.

4. The perpetrator walks to the first location.

5. The perpetrator threatens the human targets with the gun.

6. The perpetrator grabs the human targets.

7. The perpetrator walks to the second location with the human targets.

8. The perpetrator walks inside a building.

9. The perpetrator lets go of the human targets.

10. For each human target:

(a) If the effect on the human target (from the template) is *death*, the perpe-trator shoots the human target resulting in death.

(b) Otherwise, if the effect on the human target is *injury*, the perpetrator shoots the human target resulting in injury.

(c) Otherwise if the effect on the human target is *regained freedom*, the human target leaves the building and walks back to the first location.

Finally, reasoning is reduced to performing inferences on the theory formed by the commonsense reasoning problem and the commonsense knowledge selected based on the active script. The commonsense knowledge consists of Event Calculus axioms such as:

% An object can be only in one location at a time.

*HoldsAt(At(object, location*1*), time)* $\wedge$

*HoldsAt(At(object, location*2*), time)* $\Rightarrow$

*location*1 = *location*2.

% For an actor to activate a bomb, he must be holding it.

Happens(BombActivate(actor, bomb), time) $\Rightarrow$

HoldsAt(Holding(actor, bomb), time).

Next, we describe how Event Calculus theories can be used for question answering. Notice that the approach described in [62] does not explain how the questions are to be mapped into their logical representation.

For yes–no question answering about space:

Was actor "a" present when event "e" occurred?

- If for every time point t at which e occurs, the locations of a and that of the actor of e coincide, *the answer is "yes"*.

- If for every time point t at which e occurs, the two locations differ, *the answer is "no"*.

- Otherwise, *the answer is "some of the times"*.

For yes–no question answering about time:

Was fluent f true before event e occurred?

- If f is true for all time points less than or equal to t, *the answer is "yes"*.

- If f is false for all time points less than or equal to t, *the answer is "no"*.

It is also possible to deal with more complex questions whose answer is a phrase, such as "Where is the laptop?" Given an event or a fluent g whose ith argument is the one being asked, one can return an answer consisting of the conjunction of the ith arguments of all the events of fluents in the model that match g in all the arguments except the ith. To answer the question about John's laptop, for example, the reasoner will return a conjunction of all the fluents of the form $at(laptop, L)$ that occur in the model of the theory.

20.8   Conclusion

To answer natural language questions posed with respect to natural language text, one either needs to develop a reasoning engine directly in natural language [52, 24, 41, 25] or needs a way to translate natural language to a formal language for which reasoning engines are available. While the first approach is commonly used for textual answering tasks such as in PASCAL [24] where the system needs to determine if a certain text H follows from a text T, at this point it is not developed enough to be used for answering the questions of the kind in Section 20.1.1. For questions of this kind there is an additional issue besides translating natural language to formal language; the need for commonsense knowledge, domain knowledge and specific reasoning modules. These are needed because often to answer a question with respect to a given text one needs to go beyond the text. The only exception is when the answer is a fact that is directly present or contradicted by the text.

In this paper we discussed two approaches to go from natural language to a formal representation. The first approach converts natural language to particular representations in classical logic. We discussed two such attempts: one does a syntactic parsing of the text, disambiguates the meaning of sentences using WordNet, creates a logic form, and uses a specialized reasoning engine; the second uses parsing but does not disambiguate, constructs first-order representations of knowledge and then uses first-order reasoning tools.

The second approach extracts relevant facts from the natural language. We discussed three such attempts: one that obtains relevant facts from the logic form mentioned earlier; the second that uses the semantic parser Link Grammar, the WordNet database and background knowledge to obtain relevant facts; and the third that uses an information extraction system to fill slots in templates.

In regards to background knowledge (domain knowledge plus commonsense knowledge) and specific reasoning modules, we illustrated their use in the DD QA system. In that system the knowledge representation language AnsProlog [32] is used for the most part. Recently, [63] also uses AnsProlog for natural language question answering. Mueller in [62] uses event calculus while LCC uses LLF and COGEX-based inference in their various QA systems. In this regard, one system that we did not cover so far is the CYC QA system. We are told that they use Link Grammar for understanding natural language and the CYC knowledge base [50, 23] for expressing domain knowledge. Since details of the CYC language, especially its semantics, are not available to us, we were not able to discuss the CYC system in more detail. However secondary sources such as [64] mention that the CYC system did not have axioms for reasoning about action and change, a very important component of commonsense reasoning. (It did have a rich ontology of actions and events.)

In the DD QA system and in general, by domain knowledge we refer to knowledge about specific topics such as the calendar, and world geography. By commonsense knowledge we refer to axioms such as the rule of inertia. By reasoning modules we refer to modules such as planning module, and reasoning about intentions module. The

DD QA system is a prototype and at present focuses only on a few types of domain knowledge, commonsense knowledge and reasoning modules.

To develop a broad QA system one needs a much larger background knowledge base than is in the DD system. In this regard CYC and its founders could be considered as pioneers. However by limiting its development to be within the company and by using a proprietary unvetted (outside CYC) language its usefulness to the general research community has become limited. This is despite CYC's effort to release ResearchCYC and other subsets of CYC. Thus what is needed is a community wide effort to build a knowledge repository that is open and to which anyone can contribute. To do that several sociological and technical issues still remain. Some of these issues are:

1. Which formal language(s) should be used by the community?

   While many are more comfortable with propositional and first-order logic, others prefer nonmonotonic logics that are more appropriate for knowledge representation. In this regard a recent development [51], whereby algorithms have been developed to translate theories in nonmonotonic knowledge representation languages such as AnsProlog and circumscriptive theories to propositional theories, is useful. It allows one to write knowledge in the more suitable and compact nonmonotonic logics, while the models can be enumerated using the efficient and ever improving propositional solvers.

2. How do we organize knowledge modules and how do we figure out which modules (say from among the travel module, calendar module, etc.) are needed to answer a particular question with respect to a particular text collection? For example in languages like JAVA there exists a large library of classes and methods. A programmer can include (i.e., reuse) these classes and methods in their program and needs to write much less code than if she had to write everything from scratch. Currently most knowledge bases outside CYC are written from scratch.

   A start in this regard has been made in the AAAI06 Spring Symposium on Knowledge repositories. It includes several papers on modular knowledge representation. We hope the community pursues this effort and similar to linguistic resources such as the WordNet [54, 26], FrameNet [27], the various large scale biological databases, and the large libraries of various programming languages, it develops an open knowledge base about everything in the world. A step in this direction would be to combine existing open source knowledge bases. Several of them are listed in http://www.cs.utexas.edu/users/mfkb/related.html.

3. If more than one logic needs to be used how do modules in different logics interact seamlessly?

   It seems to us that no single logic or formalization will be appropriate for different kinds of reasoning or for representing different kinds of knowledge. For example, while it is easier to express inertia axioms in AnsProlog, to deal with large numbers and constraints between them it is at present more efficient to use constraint logic programming. Thus there is a need to develop methodologies that would allow knowledge modules to be written in multiple logics and yet one will be able to use them together in a seamless manner. An initial attempt in this direction, with respect to AnsProlog and Constraint logic programming is made in [13].

Finally, two other large research issues loom. First, to answer questions about calculating probabilities, one needs to be able to integrate probabilistic reasoning with logical reasoning without limiting the power and expressiveness of one or the other. Most existing approaches, except [12], limit the power of one or the other. Second, one needs to be able to develop ways to automatically learn some of the domain knowledge, commonsense knowledge and reasoning modules. While there has been some success in learning domain knowledge (and ontologies), learning commonsense knowledge and reasoning modules is still in its infancy.

Acknowledgements

We would like to thank Michael Gelfond, Richard Scherl, Luis Tari, Steve Maiorano, Jean-Michel Pomarede and Vladimir Lifschitz for their feedback on drafts of this paper. Section 20.5 was mostly written by Luis. The second reader Erik Mueller's comments were extremely insightful and improved the paper substantially. This research was supported by DTO contract ASU-06-C-0143 and NSF grant 0412000.

Bibliography

[1] The Language Computer Corporation Web Site, http://www.languagecomputer.com/.

[2] *Proceedings of the Third Message Understanding Conference (MUC-3)*. Morgan Kaufmann, 1991.

[3] *Proceedings of the Fourth Message Understanding Conference (MUC-4)*. Morgan Kaufmann, 1992.

[4] http://www.askjeeves.com, 1996.

[5] E. Akhmatova. Textual entailment resolution via atomic propositions. In *Proceedings of the PASCAL Challenges Workshop on Recognising Textual Entailment*, 2005.

[6] J. Allen. *Natural Language Understanding*. Benjamin Cummings, 1995.

[7] H. Alshawi, editor. *The Core Language Engine*. MIT Press, Cambridge, MA, 1992.

[8] R. Bar-Haim, I. Dagan, B. Dolan, L. Ferro, D. Giampiccolo, B. Magnini, and I. Szpektor. The second PASCAL recognising textual entailment challenge. In *Proceedings of the Second PASCAL Challenges Workshop on Recognising Textual Entailment*, Venice, Italy, 2006.

[9] C. Baral. *Knowledge Representation, Reasoning and Declarative Problem Solving*. Cambridge University Press, 2003.

[10] C. Baral and M. Gelfond. Reasoning about intended actions. In *Proceedings of AAAI 05*, pages 689–694, 2005.

[11] C. Baral, M. Gelfond, G. Gelfond, and R. Scherl. Textual inference by combining multiple logic programming paradigms. In *AAAI'05 Workshop on Inference for Textual Question Answering*, 2005.

[12] C. Baral, M. Gelfond, and N. Rushton. Probabilistic reasoning with answer sets. In *Proceedings of LPNMR-7*, pages 21–33, Jan 2004.

[13] S. Baselice, P. Bonatti, and M. Gelfond. Towards an integration of answer set and constraint solving. In *Proc. of ICLP'05*, pages 52–66, 2005.

[14] P. Blackburn and J. Bos. *Representation and Inference for Natural Language. CSLI Studies in Computational Linguistics.* CSLI, 2005.

[15] J. Bos. Underspecification, resolution, and inference. *Logic, Language, and Information*, 12(2), 2004.

[16] J. Bos. Towards wide-coverage semantic interpretation. In *Proceedings of Sixth International Workshop on Computational Semantics (IWCS-6)*, pages 42–53, 2005.

[17] J. Bos and K. Markert. Recognising textual entailment with logical inference. In *Proceeding of the Conference on Empirical Methods in Natural Language Processing (EMNLP)*, pages 628–635, 2005.

[18] M.E. Bratman. *Intention, Plans, and Practical Reason.* Harvard University Press, Cambridge, MA, 1987.

[19] E. Charniak. Toward a model of children's story comprehension. Technical Report AITR-266, MIT, 1972.

[20] C. Clark, S. Harabagiu, S. Maiorano, and D. Moldovan. COGEX: A logic prover for question answering. In *Proc. of HLT-NAACL*, pages 87–93, 2003.

[21] C. Clark and D. Moldovan. Temporally relevant answer selection. In *Proceedings of the 2005 International Conference on Intelligence Analysis*, May 2005.

[22] P.R. Cohen and H.J. Levesque. Intention is choice with commitment. *Artificial Intelligence*, 42:213–261, 1990.

[23] J. Curtis, G. Matthews, and D. Baxter. On the effective use of CYC in a question answering system. In *Proceedings of the IJCAI Workshop on Knowledge and Reasoning for Answering Questions*, 2005.

[24] I. Dagan, O. Glickman, and M. Magnini. The PASCAL recognizing textual entailment challenge. In *Proc. of the First PASCAL Challenge Workshop on Recognizing Textual Entailment*, pages 1–8, 2005.

[25] R. de Salvo Braz, R. Girju, V. Punyakanok, D. Roth, and M. Sammons. An inference model for semantic entailment in natural language. In *Proc. of AAAI*, pages 1043–1049, 2005.

[26] C. Fellbaum, editor. *WordNet: An Electronic Lexical Database.* MIT Press, 1998.

[27] C. Fillmore and B. Atkins. Towards a frame-based organization of the lexicon: The semantics of risk and its neighbors. In A. Lehrer and E. Kittay, editors. *Frames, Fields, and Contrast: New Essays in Semantics and Lexical Organization*, pages 75–102. Lawrence Erlbaum Associates, Hillsdale, 1992.

[28] A. Fowler, B. Hauser, D. Hodges, I. Niles, A. Novischi, and J. Stephan. Applying COGEX to recognize textual entailment. In *Proceedings of the PASCAL Challenges Workshop on Recognising Textual Entailment*, 2005.

[29] N.S. Friedland, P.G. Allen, M. Witbrock, G. Matthews, N. Salay, P. Miraglia, J. Angele, S. Staab, D.J. Israel, V. Chaudhri, B. Porter, K. Barker, and P. Clark. Towards a quantitative, platform-independent analysis of knowledge systems. In D. Dubois, C.A. Welty, and M.-A. Williams, editors. *Proceedings of the Ninth International Conference on Principles of Knowledge Representation and Reasoning*, pages 507–515. AAAI Press, Menlo Park, CA, 2004.

[30] T. Gaasterland, P. Godfrey, and J. Minker. Relaxation as a platform for cooperative answering. *Journal of Intelligent Information Systems*, 1(3–4):293–321, Dec 1992.

[31] T. Gaasterland, P. Godfrey, and J. Minker. An overview of cooperative answering. *Journal of Intelligent Information Systems*, 1(2):123–157, 1992.

[32] M. Gelfond. Answer set programming. In V. Lifschitz, F. van Hermelen, and B. Porter, editors. *Handbook of Knowledge Representation*. Elsevier, 2006.

[33] M. Gelfond and V. Lifschitz. The stable model semantics for logic programming. In R. Kowalski and K. Bowen, editors. *Logic Programming: Proc. of the Fifth Internat. Conf. and Symp.*, pages 1070–1080. MIT Press, 1988.

[34] M. Gelfond. Going places—notes on a modular development of knowledge about travel. In *AAAI Spring 2006 Symposium on Knowledge Repositories*, 2006.

[35] M. Gelfond and V. Lifschitz. The stable model semantics for logic programming. In *Proceedings of ICLP-88*, pages 1070–1080, 1988.

[36] M. Gelfond and V. Lifschitz. Classical negation in logic programs and disjunctive databases. *New Generation Computing*, pages 365–385, 1991.

[37] M. Gelfond and V. Lifschitz. Representing action and change by logic programs. *Journal of Logic Programming*, 17(2–4):301–321, 1993.

[38] M. Gelfond and V. Lifschitz. Action languages. *Electronic Transactions on AI*, 3(16), 1998.

[39] B. Green, A. Wolf, C. Chomsky, and K. Laughery. BASEBALL: An automatic question answer. In *Computers and Thought*, pages 207–216. 1963.

[40] C. Green. The application of theorem proving to question-answering systems. PhD thesis, Stanford University, 1969.

[41] A. Haghighi, A. Ng, and C. Manning. Robust textual inference via graph matching. In *Proc. of HLT-EMNLP*, 2005.

[42] S. Harabagiu, G.A. Miller, and D. Moldovan. WordNet 2—A morphologically and semantically enhanced resource. In *Proceedings of SIGLEX-99*, pages 1–8, Jun 1999.

[43] S. Harabagiu and D. Moldovan. A parallel inference system. *IEEE Transactions on Parallel and Distributed Systems*:729–747, Aug 1998.

[44] J. Hobbs. Ontological promiscuity. In *Proceedings of the 23rd Annual Meeting of the Association for Computational Linguistics*, pages 61–69, Jul 1985.

[45] J. Hobbs. *The Logical Notation: Ontological Promiscuity*, 1985.

[46] H. Kamp and U. Reyle. *From Discourse to Logic, vols. 1, 2*. Kluwer, 1993.

[47] G. Katz, J. Pustejovsky, and F. Schilder, editors. *Annotating, Extracting and Reasoning about Time and Events*, 10–15 April 2005. *Dagstuhl Seminar Proceedings, Dagstuhl Seminar Proceedings*, vol. 05151, 2005.

[48] W. Kintsch. *Comprehension: A Paradigm for Cognition*. Cambridge University Press, 1998.

[49] R. Kowalski and M. Sergot. A logic-based calculus of events. *New Generation Computing*, 4:67–95, 1986.

[50] D. Lenat and R. Guha. *Building Large Knowledge Base Systems*. Addison-Wesley, 1990.

[51] F. Lin and Y. Zhao. ASSAT: computing answer sets of a logic program by SAT solvers. *Artificial Intelligence*, 157(1–2):115–137, 2004.

[52] H. Liu and P. Singh. Commonsense reasoning in and over natural language. In M.Gh. Negoita, R.J. Howlett, and L.C. Jain, editors. *Knowledge-Based Intelligent Information and Engineering Systems, Lecture Notes in Computer Science*, vol. 3215, pages 293–306. Springer, Berlin, 2004.

[53] M. Maybury. *New Directions in Question Answering*. AAAI Press/MIT Press, 2004.

[54] G.A. Miller. WordNet: A lexical database for English. *Communications of the ACM*:39–41, 1995.

[55] R. Miller and M. Shanahan. Some alternative formulations of the event calculus. In A.C. Kakas and F. Sadri, editors. *Computational Logic: Logic Programming and Beyond, Essays in Honour of Robert A. Kowalski, Part II*, vol. 2408, pages 452–490. Springer-Verlag, Berlin, 2002.

[56] A. Mohammed, D. Moldovan, and P. Parker. Senseval-3 logic forms: A system and possible improvements. In *Proceedings of Senseval-3: The Third International Workshop on the Evaluation of Systems for the Semantic Analysis of Text*, pages 163–166, July 2004.

[57] D. Moldovan, S. Harabagiu, R. Girju, P. Morarescu, A. Novischi, F. Lacatusu, A. Badulescu, and O. Bolohan. Lcc tools for question answering. In E. Voorhees and L. Buckland, editors. *Proceedings of TREC 2002*, 2002.

[58] D. Moldovan and V. Rus. Transformation of WordNet glosses into logic forms. In *Proceedings of FLAIRS 2001 Conference*, May 2001.

[59] R. Montague. The proper treatment of quantification in ordinary English. In *Formal Philosophy: Selected Papers of Richard Montague*, pages 247–270, 1974.

[60] R. Moore. Problems in logical form. In *Proc. of 19th ACL*, pages 117–124, 1981.

[61] E. Mueller. Event calculus. In V. Lifschitz, F. van Hermelen, and B. Porter, editors. *Handbook of Knowledge Representation*. Elsevier, 2006.

[62] E.T. Mueller. Understanding script-based stories using commonsense reasoning. *Cognitive Systems Research*, 5(4):307–340, 2004.

[63] F. Nouioua and P. Nicolas. Using answer set programming in an inference-based approach to natural language semantics. In *Proc. of Inference in Computational Semantics (ICoS-5)*, Buxton, England, 20–21 April, 2006.

[64] A. Parmar. The representation of actions in KM and Cyc. Technical Report FRG-1, Department of Computer Science, Stanford University, Stanford, CA, 2001. http://www-formal.stanford.edu/aarati/techreports/action-reps-frg-techreport.ps.

[65] V. Rus. Logic forms for Wordnet glosses. PhD thesis, Southern Methodist University, May 2002.

[66] L. Schubert and F. Pelletier. From English to logic: Context free computation of conventional logical translation. *AJCL*, 1:165–176, 1982.

[67] S. Schulz. A comparison of different techniques for grounding near-propositional CNF formulae. In *Proceedings of the 15th International FLAIRS Conference*, pages 72–76, 2002.

[68] M. Shanahan. A circumscriptive calculus for events. *Artificial Intelligence*, 75(2), 1995.

[69] M. Shanahan. *Solving the Frame Problem: A Mathematical Investigation of the Commonsense Law of Inertia*. MIT Press, 1997.

[70] D.D. Sleator and D. Temperley. Parsing English with a link grammar. In *Third International Workshop on Parsing Technologies*, 1993.

[71] L. Tari and C. Baral. Using AnsProlog with link grammar and WordNet for QA with deep reasoning. In *AAAI Spring Symposium Workshop on Inference for Textual Question Answering*, 2005.

[72] E. Voorhees. Overview of the TREC 2002 Question Answering Track. In *Proc. of the 11th Text Retrieval Evaluation Conference*. NIST Special Publication 500-251, 2002.

[73] W. Woods. Semantics and quantification in natural language question answering. In M. Yovitz, editor. *Advances in Computers*, vol. 17. Academic Press, 1978.

[74] M. Wooldridge. *Reasoning about Rational Agents*. MIT Press, 2000.

© 2008 Elsevier B.V. All rights reserved
DOI: 10.1016/S1574-6526(07)03021-0

Chapter 21

The Semantic Web: Webizing Knowledge Representation

Jim Hendler and Frank van Harmelen

Abstract
The World Wide Web opens up new opportunities for the use of knowledge representation: a formal description of the semantic content of Web pages can allow better processing by computational agents. Further, the naming scheme of the Web, using Universal Resource Indicators, allows KR systems to avoid the ambiguities of natural language and to allow linking between semantic documents. These capabilities open up a raft of new possibilities for KR, but also present challenges to some traditional KR assumptions.

21.1 Introduction

The web-page http://www.cs.rpi.edu/~hendler is not much different than most other pages in many ways. Besides content, it contains many links to other pages: links to pages of students, links to downloadable files, links to various digital libraries, links to the Web resources used in classes and to University pages that describe when the classes were given, what the prerequisites were, etc. In short, a great deal of the information "on" this page is not actually on the page at all, it is provided by the linking mechanisms of the Web. It is, in fact, exactly this network effect of gaining advantage by linking to information created by other people, rather than recreating it locally, that makes the Web so powerful.

Now consider knowledge representation. When trying to create a machine-readable KR page that would contain similar information, we could not get this kind of network effect using the KR techniques described in most of the chapters in this book. First, even if we were to use a particular representation technique, and even if it is a well-defined technique like FOL, there is still the issue of using information defined by someone else. One author might write:

ForAll(x)(Advisor(x, Hendler) → StudentOf(Hendler,x).

while another might put

> Advisor(_x,_ y) :- PhDAdvisor(_y,_x).
> PhDAdvisor(Hendler,Smith).

Try to unify these KBs. Even though there is no logical mismatch, the mere syntactic differences between the representations makes it impossible to simply re-use the knowledge between KBs. The problem would be even worse when the two KBs were using different forms of KR, say some particular subset of FOL, some particular temporal logic, or some kind of modal operators.

Even when using the same exact logical language, say the Conceptual Graphs that John Sowa describes in Chapter 5, and even when using the same implementation (so syntax matters go away), we still do not have the kind of linking we have on the Web. Most KR systems do not have a mechanism by which to specify that a KB living somewhere else should be included at query time so as to make use of the knowledge defined by someone else. In short, we do not have a way to get the network effect in KR that we get in the Web world.

In fact, in many KR systems the notion of knowledge not directly under the control of a single mechanism, and not incorporated at what would be the equivalent of compile time, is anathema to the design. It can lead to inconsistency in all sorts of nasty ways. For example, one KB might be using knowledge in a way that is incompatible or inconsistent with another via unexpected interactions. If one KB said "man" implies "male" where the other was using the term in the non-gendered "all men are mortals" sense, then, when our KBs are linked a mother from one system becomes a male in the other system, but mothers are known to be female, and thus we have a contradiction from which all manner of improper things could be inferred in many systems, requiring belief revision at the least. Or consider even if the terms are used correctly, but at query time the other KB's server is down, and thus the list of students varies, depending on the uptime of the server, again leading to potential problems.

Traditionally, the field of knowledge representation has faced these potential problems by either ignoring them (by assuming people are using the same KR system, or doing all merging at "compile" time), by addressing them as special cases (such as in the design of temporal reasoners (cf. Chapter 12) or belief revision systems (cf. Chapter 8)) or by defining the problem away. This latter is generally done by using inexpressive languages that do not allow inconsistency, or defining inconsistency as an "error" that will be handled offline.

Additionally, there is another issue that KR systems in AI have tended to ignore: the issue of scaling. KR often talks of algorithmic complexity, or even performance issues, but compared to the size of a good database system, or an incredible information space like the World Wide Web, KR systems have lagged far behind. The engineering challenges proposed by KBs that could be linked together to take advantage of the network effect that could be achieved thereby, are beyond the scaling issues explored in most AI work today.

In short, there is a set of KR challenges that have not been widely explored until recently. First, solving syntactic interoperability problems demands standards: not just at some kind of KR logic level, but all the way down to the nitty-gritty syntactic details. Second, linking KR systems requires "extra-logical" infrastructure that can be exploited to achieve the network effect. Third, the languages designed need to be scalable, at least in some sense thereof, to much larger sizes than traditional in AI work. Fourth, and finally, achieving such linkage presents challenges to current KR formulations demanding new kinds of flexibility and addressing issues that have largely been previously ignored.

From a KR perspective, designing systems to overcome these challenges, using the Web itself for much of the extra-logical infrastructure, is the very definition of what has come to be known as the "Semantic Web". It was this thinking that the authors of a widely cited vision paper on the Semantic Web [2] to conclude that

> Knowledge representation is currently in a state comparable to that of hypertext before the advent of the web: it is clearly a good idea, and some very nice demonstrations exist, but it has not yet changed the world. It contains the seeds of important applications, but to unleash its full power it must be linked into a single global system.

Other articles have been written that explain how Semantic Web systems are like traditional KR systems (cf. Chapter 3 which describes the correspondence of the Semantic Web language OWL to description logics), and thus this article will concentrate on the other side of this: the things that make Semantic Web KR different from traditional systems.

However, before we go on, it is important to note one way in which this chapter differs from many of the others in this Handbook. The KR languages that we will discuss here are not academic efforts aimed at extending the philosophical reach of computational reasoning. They are languages that were designed as standards with an eye towards widespread use. The languages RDF, RDFS and OWL, which we will discuss in the remainder of this chapter, are without question the most widely used KR languages in history. A web search performed around the beginning of 2007 finds millions of RDF and RDFS documents, and tens of thousands of OWL ontologies. The user community goes way beyond the traditional AI users, and these languages form the basis of a new phase of commercial development going forward under the name "Web 3.0". This article discusses these languages from a KR perspective, but a realization of the scale of the deployment, the wide range of users, and the power that has been achieved through the standardization of these KR languages is crucial to an understanding of their design.

21.2   The Semantic Web Today

The Semantic Web is an extension of the current World Wide Web in which information is tied to machine-readable metadata, making it easy to exchange, integrate and process data in a systematic, machine-automated manner. Using standardized languages, published as World Wide Web Consortium (W3C) recommendations, Semantic Web data cannot only explicitly describe the knowledge content underlying HTML pages, but also specify the implicit information contained in media like images and videos, or be a publicly accessible and usable representation of an otherwise inaccessible database or other resource.

The standardized languages which are the basis of the Semantic Web form a layered stack, at the bottom of which lies the Resource Description Framework (RDF)

[16]. RDF is a simple assertional language that is designed to represent information in the form of triples, i.e., statements of the form: subject, predicate, object. RDF predicates may be thought of as attributes of resources and in this sense correspond to traditional attribute-value pairs. $p(s, o)$: resource s has resource o as value for attribute p. The arguments to RDF predicates must always be ground values except for the possibility of local existential variables to represent anonymous objects: *colleague(Jim, _1)*, *hometown(_1, Amsterdam)* states that Jim has some (otherwise unknown) colleague whose hometown is Amsterdam.

RDF however, contains no mechanisms for describing these predicates, nor does it support description of relationships between predicates and other resources. This is provided by the RDF vocabulary description language, RDF Schema (RDFS [6]). RDFS allows the specification of classes (generalized categories or unary relations) and properties (predicates or binary relations), which can be arranged in a generalization hierarchy: a hierarchy for classes, and a hierarchy for properties. In addition, it allows simple typing of such properties, by stating the classes to which subject and object of a particular property must belong. This allows simple inferencing of the following forms: inferring class membership and subclass relations through transitive inference in the subclass hierarchy, inferring class membership through occurrence in typed property-positions, and inferring property values and subproperty relations through transitive inference in the subproperty hierarchy.

From an AI perspective, RDFS is similar to some of our early frame systems in its representational capabilities. Notably, RDF and RDFS lack any notion of negation or disjunction and (as mentioned above) have only a very limited notion of existential quantification. Together this makes for a language with very limited expressive power. One illustration of this limited expressivity is the fact that (barring the use of XML datatypes), it is not possible to express inconsistencies in RDF. Also, it has turned out to be practical to perform exhaustive forward inferencing, i.e., to compute the entire deductive closure of an RDF graph. In fact, some of the most widely used RDF storage and query engines (e.g., Sesame [4]) work in this way. This is clearly only possible with a sufficiently weak language which does not in practice cause the exponential blow-up that deductive closures of richer languages suffer from.

The Web Ontology Language (OWL) [7], released in February 2004 as a W3C recommendation, is a more expressive ontology language that is layered on top of RDF and RDFS. OWL can be used to define classes and properties as in RDFS, but in addition, it provides a rich set of constructs to create new class descriptions as logical combinations (intersections, unions, or complements) of other classes; define value and cardinality restrictions on properties (e.g., a restriction on a class to have only one value for a particular property) and so on. OWL's expressivity is sufficient to cover most of the well-known Description Logic formalisms, and some of its representational characteristics largely resemble those of DL. However, OWL is unique in two ways. First, it is the first reasonably expressive ontology language to become a standard recognized by a major standards body. This is very important for tool interoperability and ontology reuse, which we discuss below. In addition, OWL is the first widely-used ontology language whose design is based on the Web architecture, i.e., it is open (non-proprietary); it uses Universal Resource Identifiers (URIs) to unambiguously identify resources on the Web (similar to RDF and RDFS); it supports the linking of terms across ontologies making it possible to cross-reference and reuse information; and it has an XML syntax (RDF/XML) for easy data exchange.

OWL provides three increasingly expressive sub-languages: OWL Lite, OWL DL, and OWL Full, each with a different intended audience based on scope and complexity of the application domain. For example, the goal of OWL Lite is to provide a language that is viewed by tool builders to be easy enough and useful enough to support, thereby acting as an entry ontology language for semantic web application developers, whereas OWL Full provides more freedom in domain modeling at the cost of a higher learning curve. At the time of this writing, an effort is underway to define another sublanguage, sometimes referred to as RDFS+ and other times as OWL Very Lite, which is intended to be a much simpler version that provides only simple reasoning extensions to RDFS to allow for very efficient scalability. A second effort [5] has identified a number of subsets of OWL that have polynomial reasoning performance.

Within the KR community, the most used form of OWL is OWL DL, due to its support for automated reasoning. OWL DL has a formal model-theoretic semantics [18] providing a rigorous and provably decidable semantics for the language. As discussed in Chapter 3, DLs are a decidable subset of First Order Logic (FOL), being restricted to the 2-variable fragment of FOL. The decidability of the logic ensures that sound and complete DL reasoners can be built to check the consistency of an OWL DL ontology, i.e., verify whether there are any logical contradictions in the ontology axioms. Furthermore, reasoners can be used to derive inferences from the asserted information, e.g., infer whether a particular concept in an ontology is a subconcept of another, or whether a particular individual in an ontology belongs to a specific class. Popular existing DL reasoners in the OWL community include Pellet [21] and FaCT [13] which are available for free download and use, as well as several commercial products.

In addition to reasoners, numerous OWL ontology browsers/editors such as Protégé [17], SWOOP [14] and KAON [3] have been built to aid in the design and construction of OWL ontology models. Most of these OWL tools have expanded their functionality beyond basic editing to include features such as change management and query handling, and in a lot of cases included a reasoner for consistency checking of the ontology. For example, Protégé allows integration of any DIG-compliant reasoner and has plug-ins for collaborative ontology development, ontology change-management, ontology visualization, import and export to and from various representation formats. SWOOP provides the ability to automatically partition, collaboratively annotate and version control OWL ontologies. For example, Fig. 21.1 shows some of the features of the Swoop editor being used to browse an OWL ontology.

While tools such as these are familiar to many in the AI community, the need for wider deployment and ontology development by non-AI-experts (for example, subject matter experts in some domain), requires that these tools explore making the AI concepts available to others. Current efforts include using the "cultural metaphors" of the online culture, such as hypertext links, expandable menus, Web-browser-like look and feel, etc. to make these tools more comfortable to users who are familiar with the Web but not with AI.

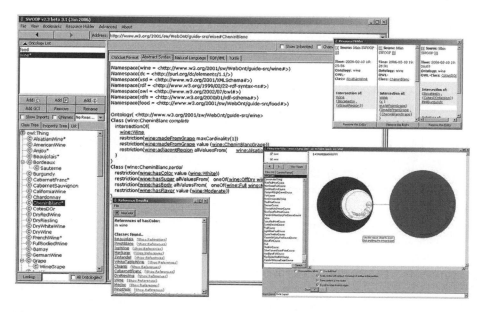

Figure 21.1: The standard syntax, and Web features, of OWL have led to the development of a number of new, Web-based, tools. SWOOP, shown in this figure, is an example of an ontology browser/editor developed for the Semantic Web.

21.3   Semantic Web KR Language Design

Despite these primary similarities to traditional AI work, there are some key differences in the design of OWL, and of current efforts to build new languages adding features missing from OWL, from traditional AI work. These differences are in many ways similar to the ways in which the World Wide Web was different from traditional Hypertext systems, and thus the term Semantic Web is most correctly applied to systems which focus on these features. In the remainder of this article we describe some of these differences, focusing on

- The importance of standards based on the Web infrastructure.

- The "Webization" of ontology language.

- The emphasis on scalability.

We will then discuss some of the emerging trends on the Semantic Web including work on bringing rule languages and FOL to the Semantic Web. We conclude by discussing some of the challenges to traditional AI reasoning that we will need to overcome if we are going to "unleash KR's full power".

21.3.1   Web Infrastructure

There are two reasons why the decision to build OWL and other Semantic Web languages based on Web standards, as opposed to other attempts to standardize knowledge exchange [9, 15], are so critical to the uptake of this technology. One is the importance of being able to exploit the Web infrastructure for wider deployment, which we discuss in this section, and one is more important to the technical under-pinnings of KR, the grounding of assertions and definitions dereferencably.

The building of the Semantic Web on top of the Web infrastructure is largely moti-vated by a lesson learned from the efforts to more widely disseminate expert systems technology in the mid-1980's. Often seen as a failure, despite wide use today of rule-based technologies, one of the reasons expert systems had trouble with uptake is that, especially in the early days, they did not "play nice" with the rest of a user or orga-nization's computer infrastructure. The need for special languages and machines, and the difficulty in embedding rule-bases into existing code was a major impediment. For a web of KR to succeed, it must be deployable via existing infrastructure, and the Web infrastructure is the mostly widely deployed and used in the world today.

Underlying the web is the Hypertext Transfer Protocol [8], the ubiquitous HTTP typed into web pages. For the facts and axioms of the Semantic Web to be sharable on the Web infrastructure, it is clearly crucial that they must be encoded in an HTTP friendly way, mandating use of HTML, XML, RDF or some other widely used web format (MIME type) for exchange. The Semantic Web is built largely on RDF, for reasons discussed in the next section. However, Web embedding is more than using these languages: simply HTTP-GETting a document to display in the browser is not akin to putting KR on the Web.

Most Web applications today use a three-tiered architecture in their client–server communication. The client sends the HTTP-GET request to the server which is to return a document in HTML or other specified MIME type (XML is becoming much more prevalent, and many applications are switching to that today). The server, rather than just serving up the document as would be done for static HTML, generates the document by using a database or other backend which keeps the base information in whatever proprietary form the provider uses. The "middle tier" issues queries (or similar) to find the relevant information and transform it into the requested document format, and this is in turn returned to the client as the response to the GET request.

For a KR infrastructure to live on the Web, it is important that it can be integrated into such applications. The Semantic Web infrastructure was designed with this in mind. While proprietary knowledge bases and knowledge base languages could un-derlie the applications, without standards for the exchange formats, what is requested by one cannot be generated by another. So a major aspect of the Semantic Web lan-guages is simply this: that it can coexist with other web applications, be made to work through server modifications, and to integrate well into current and future Web based architectures. This is also an important economic incentive to wider adoption of Se-mantic Web KR by industry, the deployed infrastructure for information exchange, web servers and clients, does not require replacement to get any reasoning benefits the Semantic Web can offer, and many end-users will see the benefit of the Semantic Web solely as new functionality delivered to them through their Web browser.

21.3.2 Webizing KR

With the advent of the Web, the neologism "webize" has come into being to refer to bringing new resources to the Web in a way that allows them to be integrated into the existing infrastructure, as described above, but also to be linked to one another to achieve the network effect that makes the Web succeed. In the words of Tim Berners-Lee, the inventor of the Web

> The essential process in webizing is to take a system which is designed as a closed world, and then ask what happens when it is considered as part of an open world. Practically, this effect on a computer language is to replace the names/tokens/identifiers for URIs. Thus, where before reference could only be made to something in the same document/program/module one can with equal ease make reference to something in a different one somewhere in that abstract space which is the Web. (Berners-Lee, 2001)

In essence, we make something a first-class citizen of the web by assigning it its own Universal Resource Identifier (URI). This is an identifier obeying a set of rules of web access, but essentially is equivalent to providing a pointer into a near infinite name space. Thus, the URI http://www.w3.org/2003/08/owlfaq.html is the identifier for the W3C OWL FAQ, as a pointer into Web space.

There are a number of important aspects of URIs with respect to making the Web work: the definition of URI scheme, the convention that the first element is the server at which the resource named can be found, etc. From the KR point of view, however, there is another feature that is very crucial: any resource on the Web can be given an identifier, and any Web server pointed at that name will retrieve the same underlying representation of the resource. Using RDF as the basis of Semantic Web KR ensures that any term defined in a Web-based ontology is given a globally recognized identifier.

In a traditional KR system we can generally assert a new class or predicate or formula, and within the KB it resides the name is unique. However, if we want to refer to it from outside that KB, there is generally not a way to do so. So if we want to say "the concept **Student** which is used by **Jim Hendler's Web Page**" or "the concept **person** as defined in **CYC**" there needs to be an identifier for the concept, and traditional KR has not provided an externally addressable referent.

On the Web, URIs provide this function, and RDF was designed precisely to take advantage of this. The URI

http://www.cs.umd.edu/users/hendler/onts/Research.owl#student

is an identifier that cannot be used for other definition but the student concept. This URI thus provides a label that could be used anywhere in "web space" and remains unambiguous—two different KBs that each refer to this term must be referring to the same thing by definition.

The ability to have global names is a very powerful concept in and of its own right, and there are a number of philosophical issues in KR to be discussed in this respect (a couple of which we touch on later in this chapter). The most important, however, is the notion of *dereferencability*. On the Web, a URI can be used not only to name a document, but as a reference to a document—in your browser when you click on an HTTP URI, a document is fetched and typically a presentation is displayed by your browser.

RDFS and OWL are defined so that the concepts created in the ontology definition documents are assigned URIs that dereference to a representation of the document that defined them. So, for example, the student URI defined above not only gives a precise name to the student concept, but also if an HTTP-GET is performed on the URI, an OWL document containing the definition will be returned to the client performing the GET. Thus, while simply by examining the name there is no way to tell whether the definition of "student" is a class name, a predicate, or an individual, by retrieving the document and parsing it into RDF, an assertion will be found that answers this question. Thus, we would find a piece of OWL that entails that

> http://www.cs.umd.edu/users/hendler/onts/Research.owl#student
> rdf:type owl:class

(RDF statements are comprised of triples read as object predicate object, thus this says that the binary relation "rdf:type" holds between the subject URI and the URI "Owl:class"—for details on the RDF representation as both triples and as XML documents, see [7].)

Typically, when dealing with OWL as a KR language we use an XML rendering, or other presentation syntax, to remove the details of the RDF triples and provide a level of abstraction. For example, the triple above could be rendered in the N3 presentation syntax as

> @prefix: "http://www.cs.umd.edu/users/hendler/onts/Research.owl".
> : student a owl:class.[1]

Other, more complex relations can also be similarly shortened, for example, the OWL specification [7] also contains an "abstract syntax" so that a statement such as

> Ontology(<http://www.cs.umd.edu/users/hendler/onts/Research.owl>
> Class (Research:CS_Course partial
> restriction(Research:offeredIn someValuesFrom(Research:CS_Department))
> Research:Course))

which states that the concept defined at the URI

> http://www.cs.umd.edu/users/hendler/onts/Research.owl#CS_Course

is a subclass of those things which are in the intersection of Courses and those things which are existentially quantified as being offered in a CS_Department (and further that CS_Department, CS_Course, Course and offeredIn are also defined). This statement would be rendered in XML as the much less readable (but nicely Web compatible)

```
<owl:Class rdf:about="#CS_Course">
  <rdfs:subClassOf>
    <owl:Class rdf:about="#Course"/>
  </rdfs:subClassOf>
  <rdfs:subClassOf>
    <owl:Restriction>
      <owl:onProperty>
        <owl:ObjectProperty rdf:about="#offeredIn"/>
      </owl:onProperty>
      <owl:someValuesFrom>
        <owl:Class rdf:about="#CS_Department"/>
      </owl:someValuesFrom>
    </owl:Restriction>
```

---

[1] rdf: and owl: are common abbreviations for actual deferencable URIs that link to the standards documents that define RDF and OWL, respectively.

```
    </rdfs:subClassOf>
    </owl:Class>
```

which in turn would "compile" into a large number of RDF triples, forming a labeled, directed graph of URIs, that could be stored in an RDF datastore and used by RDF, RDFS and or OWL tools.

Regardless, however, of the representation syntax used, the semantics of the expression are defined in the OWL Model Theory [18] and the URIs for the classes, individuals, and predicates defined in such expressions are uniquely and globally assigned to allow Semantic Web systems to use each others' data and domain descriptions in a clean, Web-accessible, and distributed (open) manner.

There are other interoperability advantages which we will not go into here. For example, the is an emerging standard for an RDF-based query language (SPARQL [19]) which can be used for querying data (or Abox) assertions that have been defined against RDFS and OWL ontologies. For more about the Semantic Web from the perspective of interoperability, see the W3C Semantic Web Activity Web page (http://www.w3.org/2001/sw).

21.3.3 Scalability and the Semantic Web

There are two aspects of scalability that apply to the design of Semantic Web KR systems, one is the scalability of the underlying reasoning itself, as is a concern in most KR work, and the other is a scalability in the sense that the Web is scalable, the creation of an open and distributed KR world. This latter puts some constraints on the requirements for OWL, and any successor languages, and is a point where Web and AI research come very much into contact (and sometimes conflict).

The first kind of scalability on the Web is the one that is usually discussed, the fact that the Web itself is massive, with hundreds of billions of documents of many different kinds, some open and accessible, some of limited access (sometimes called the deep web). In addition, with one of the goals of the Semantic Web being to bring significantly more data resources to the Web, and to make these more accessible via linking to ontological knowledge, the scale of the emerging Semantic Web Knowledge Bases dwarfs just about anything tried in AI before now.

For one example, a number of people in the "Health Care and Life Sciences Interest Group"[2] are working to develop ontologies in biological areas and to link these to sets of data coming out of various datasources to better integrate these data sources. As one example, the Uniprot (Universal Protein Resource) Web site offers access to protein sequencing data being produced at a number of sites. Knowledge Bases, containing hundreds of millions of triples have been developed, and these are being tied to OWL ontologies that range in size from tens to thousands of classes. Scaling AI reasoning techniques, even when using the decidable fragment of OWL, to these sorts of scales is a major engineering challenge for Semantic Web researchers.[3] At the time of writing, the most scalable RDFS system can handle up to a few tens of billions of RDF triples

---

[2] http://www.w3.org/2001/sw/hcls/.

[3] It is worth noting that a number of large OWL ontologies also exist without instances, for example, the National Cancer Institute maintains a metathesaurus that is released in OWL. At the time of this writing it has over 50,000 class definitions [10].

while still complying with the standard semantics. For the various OWL variants, these numbers are significantly smaller. In particular reasoning with very large numbers of instances has traditionally imposed significant problems for DL reasoners.

The other scaling challenge to Semantic Web KR, and one of the key challenges in the design of OWL, was designing a language that would fit into the overall Web architecture and its constraints. Consider again the example of the introduction, where we consider linked knowledge documents as analogous to linked Web pages. It may seem like it is simple to talk about the contents of a Web page, but in reality it is extremely difficult (and still not well defined). Is the content just what is returned by a single HTTP-Get (i.e., the "page" you see in your browser), is it all possible renderings of that page in different MIME types, is it the page plus all the documents it is linked to directly, or all the pages on the same site? In fact, if we consider the "transitive closure" of the link space, then the content associated with any particular page is, in the worst case, the entirety of World Wide Web!

In creating a knowledge representation for the Web, it was important to keep in mind that it too would include documents (cf. ontologies), linked to datasets (cf. RDF triple stores), linked to possibly other documents, other datasets, and to regular web resources (for example, it is useful to say that the person described in the Web page http://www.cs.umd.edu/~hendler is named "Jim Hendler"—combining an HTML referent and a KB referent in a smooth way). If one assumed that such knowledge sources were being created dynamically, for example, via a web crawl or dynamic mapping from multiple databases to a triple store, then it appeared that full knowledge of all the assertions associated with a fact on the Web, would essentially map to the problem of finding all the content linked to a particular web page—in the worst case, the entire Semantic Web.

Given this notion of Web KR being amenable to applications like crawlers, which might at any point in time have an "incomplete" view of the word, the design of Semantic Web languages has favored the open-world semantics of FOL to the closed-world semantics of databases. In addition, assuming an incremental addition of information (i.e., a crawler accreting knowledge over time) a monotonic logic ended up being favored. For example, in the design of the OWL language, an original objective was to have the language include default reasoning, motivated by many AI applications, but no non-monotonic solution amenable to Web architecture concerns was found. This debate continues at the time of this writing in the design of a rules language for the Semantic Web (cf. [12]) where the need for negation as failure is recognized as important to many applications, but no mechanism for closing the world of discourse, compatible with open and distributed Web principles, has been developed.

21.4 OWL—Defining a Semantic Web KR Language

The best example of a current KR language for the Web, which meets the requirements above but still meets the needs of many KR projects is the Web Ontology Language OWL, which became a World Wide Web Consortium recommendation in February of 2004. OWL was designed to be expressive enough for many practical problems, simple enough for "real users" to get a start without taking an AI course, and designed to meet the needs of companies interested in deploying AI-related applications on the

Web. As we will discuss, OWL comes in three "dialects" known as OWL Lite, OWL DL, and OWL Full. As we shall see, the rationale behind having these three dialects helps explains how OWL supports the different needs of different user communities.

To start with, OWL is designed as an extension to the Resource Description Framework (RDF) and RDF Schema (RDFS) language developed by earlier standards efforts. RDF and RDFS provide several useful KR concepts, roughly corresponding to the ISA-hierarchy and simple slot definitions of early frame-based KR languages. One difference, however, is that RDF is designed such that several important aspects of the Web are built in. RDF provides a mechanism for assigning URIs to class names (thus giving them the global addressing property described previously), it provides a mechanism for the internationalization of terms (based on Unicodes), and it provides a mechanism for accessing the "XML Schema Datatypes" that are used on the Web for providing standard definitions for common datatypes such as strings, integers, dates, etc. In short, by building OWL on RDF the needs for web embedding are largely met.

However, embedding on RDF was something of a struggle for designing a Web KR language. Traditional KR languages have not provided mechanisms for external references, externally defined datatypes ad the like. In addition, some common features of KR languages (cf. variables in arguments, closed lists, and mechanisms for asserting equivalence of terms) were not provided in the original RDF. The working group thus had to provide a design that either avoided the problems, created solutions at the OWL level, or required working with those updating the RDF standard to provide common solutions.

In addition, the designers of OWL inherited some constraints from the Web domain. Some of the designers felt that a Web ontology language should be monotonic and without defaults, given that new information is often discovered on the Web and reinferencing in the presence of new information. Some designers felt that it was crucial the language be decidable, others argued that there should be a well-designed decidable fragment of the language. In addition, although RDF allowed properties on classes, these were always universal, and the designers of OWL felt it was crucial on the Web to be able to have class descriptions that could be restricted to only some subset of a class as this would mean that if definitions from multiple documents were merged, there would be means to separate aspects of the class definitions. Note that from these definitions it becomes clear why OWL resembles a Description Logic language—DLs largely meet these KR design goals.

However, there were also KR design goals of OWL that could not be met within standard approached to DL, but which use cases mandated for OWL necessitated. A good example of this is inverse functional datatypes. One of the features of OWL that is very important in many Web applications is the ability to designate two individuals or classes to be equivalent. OWL provides mechanisms for directly asserting this, but very important in many cases was the use of an "Inverse Functional Property" definition, which allows an OWL ontology to designate some property as being unique to individuals. That is,

$$P1 \text{ an inverseFunctionalProperty } \Leftrightarrow P1(x,y) \wedge P1(z,y) \Rightarrow \text{equivalent}(x,z).$$

(An example of the use of this feature is in FOAF, where we can designate that individuals with the same "foaf:mbox" property (i.e., same email address) should be merged into the same node in the FOAF networks.)

However, there was a problem. If, using standard DL semantics, one designated a datatypeProperty to be inverse functional, then the system becomes undecidable. On the one hand, decidability is a desirable feature, on the other hand, many use cases of OWL require that datatypes be inverse functional (in particular, database keys mapped to RDF require inverse functional datatype properties). No single design could satisfy both goals. This was one of the reasons for defining both a general form of OWL (OWL Full) which does not restrict datatypes in this way, and OWL DL, a decidable profile of OWL which does. Several other features of the use of OWL also have similar dichotomies, including using classes as instances (i.e., metamodeling) and having classes that have not been typed (Datatype, objectType, annotationType, or ontologyProperty) in the defining document. In all these cases, the semantics of OWL DL could be kept clean and decidable and the semantics of OWL Full included some features that allow undecidability, necessary for some of the webized applications.

In addition, in designing OWL one option was to choose the language to include the largest decidable subset of FOL known (i.e., the most expressive DLs known) while another option was to include only options whose value was proven important and useful. OWL Lite is a subset of OWL DL that removes some features that were felt to be outside this class, or that might be confusing to novice users.

Other challenges in the design of OWL required providing the semantics for some of the Web features of the language that were not included in many standard KR languages. For example, since OWL defines the URI mechanism, it is easy for an OWL document to refer to terms in other ontology documents. Thus, the vocabulary of OWL that can be used within a single document can be used to express relations between classes in an ontology and those defined in other ontologies. This could include simple assertions, perhaps stating that what some European document refers to as :footballTeam is different from what a US document means by the same term, or that it is equivalent to what some US document calls a :soccerTeam.

The links between documents can, however, also be more complex than this. For example, supposing we would like to say that our pet cat is a short-tailed Abyssinian cat and that we would like to use the properties of Cat that are already in CYC, but perhaps Cyc does not have all the features we need (for example, tail-length or the AbyssinianCat Class). In OWL we can simply extend the classes from CYC by creating a document that defines the CYC: namespace as pointing to CYC's URIs, and asserting, for example:

```
:AbyssinianCat a cyc:petCat.
:tailLength a owl:datatypeProperty;
    range cyc:Cat; {note that in CYC a petCat would be asserted to be a Cat}
    domain xsd:string.
:myCat a :AbyssinianCat;
    :tailLength "short".[4]
```

However, if a reasoner sees this document, what semantics should it adopt? Should the terms from CYC be expected to include all the semantics of the CYC ontology, should there be no "official" semantics for this, letting external links be defined by

---

[4]We make length a string for simplicity of this example, we leave defining and enumerated class of appropriate lengths as an exercise to the reader.

some sort of extra-logical mechanism, or could some other solution be devised and standardized at some later time. OWL provides mechanisms for declaring that one ontology "imports" another, and therefore all the semantics should be observed, and a mechanism by which this can be defined as an annotation property (or, in OWL Full, left unspecified) essentially asserting that no semantics should be assigned to the class *a priori* but rather that systems might use externally defined mechanisms to meet user expectations.

A recurring issue in the design of web-based KR languages is the choice between open world semantics and closed world semantics. A closed world semantics typically allows the derivation of conclusions from the absence of conclusions to the contrary. In programming languages such as Prolog, this is known as Negation by Failure, and is closely related to default reasoning. Although in general the Web would seem more suited to open-world reasoning (and indeed both RDFS and OWL adopt an open-world semantics) there are many use-cases where a closed-world semantics is appropriate: students in a class, customers of a company, cities in a country are all examples of closed sets: if a student is not listed as enrolled, we can safely assume she is not enrolled. Although useful in many cases, there is currently no practical mechanism in RDFS or OWL to state that a given set of individuals (or facts) is "closed".

A related, although different, issue is the unique name assumption. Typically, database systems assume a single, unique name for each individual. If we encounter two individuals with different names, we can safely assume they are indeed different individuals. Again, on the web this assumption would be too strong. In a world as large as the web, many individuals are known under multiple names ("Jim Hendler", "James Hendler", "Prof. J. Hendler", "the author of Chapter 21", etc.). When encountering two such different names, we should safely assume that they may or may not designate the same individual, until further reasoning decides the issue one way or the other. OWL contains a simple device to state that all individuals in an enumerated set are known to be different (i.e., that they are not just different names for some of the same individuals), but this language construct (`owl :allDifferent`) requires the explicit enumeration of these names, which can be either impractical, or even impossible in principle.

Traditionally, systems such as databases and logic programming systems have tended to support closed-worlds and unique names, while knowledge representation systems and theorem provers support open-worlds and non-unique names. Ontologies are sometimes in need of one, and sometimes in need of the other. This conundrum was nicely resolved in [11], which identified a fragment of OWL baptized DLP, for Description Logic Programming: this fragment is the largest fragment on which the choice for CWA and UNA does not matter as depicted in Fig. 21.2. That is to say, OWL DLP is weak enough so that the differences between the choices do not show up. The advantage of this is that people or applications that wish to make different choices on these assumptions can still exchange ontologies in OWL DLP without harm. Of course, as soon as they go outside OWL DLP, they will notice that they draw different conclusions from the same statements. In other words, they will notice that they disagree on the semantics.

Fortunately, DLP is still large enough that it can be used for useful representation and reasoning tasks. It allows the use of such OWL constructors as class and property equivalence, equality and inequality between individuals, inverse, transitive, symmet-

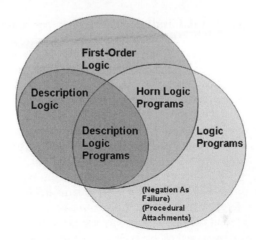

Figure 21.2: Relation of OWL-DLP to other KR languages.

ric and functional properties, and the intersection of classes. It excludes however constructors such as intersection and arbitrary cardinality-constraints. These constructors do not only allow useful expressivity for many practical cases, while guaranteeing correct interchange between OWL reasoners independent of their CWA and UNA, they also allow for a translation into efficiently implementable reasoning techniques based on databases and logic programs.

As is already clear from the above two points, RDFS and OWL do not allow any form of default reasoning, even though many years of KR applications have shown this to be a very useful device for dealing with incomplete knowledge. This would be particularly important in a world as large as the Web, where not all properties of all objects will be explicitly known, but must often be inferred by default until shown otherwise. However, a lack of concensus in the KR community on how to best formalize defaults has prevented such features from being included in the Semantic Web standardized representation languages.

Finally, a point often raised is that the large and open world of the Web will almost certainly need some forms of uncertainty and fuzziness. Again, lack of concensus has prevented such language features from being included, although it would seem clear that they will ultimately be needed in some form or other, either in the representation or in the inference mechanisms.

As time progresses, new work also continues which pushes OWL in different directions. In practical use on the Web, OWL has needed to be scaled to problems that have been much larger than those previously attempted in KR research. Very large Tboxes (thousands of class definitions) coupled with extremely larges Aboxes (millions of individuals) turned out to be relatively easy to construct, and necessary for Web uses. To this end, as we mentioned earlier, several groups are exploring tractable subsets of OWL, some of which are very close to RDFS others of which attempt to provide more functionality while remaining polynomial (cf. [20] which describes a number of these). On the other hand, some usages are exploring more expressive features that were not included in OWL including qualified restrictions, limited forms of non-monotonicity, integration with rules, mereological constructs, and others.

21.5   Semantic Web KR Challenges

Perhaps the most interesting thing about OWL, and future Semantic Web KR languages, is not what was solved in the OWL design, but what was left unsolved. For example, above we described what happens when one document imports another. However, on the Web the typical mechanism for implementing this inclusion is an HTTP-Get of the imported document. What happens if the server where that document lives is down, or if the owner of the document makes changes that remove the class I am referring to (or even worse, makes a change that subtly changes the semantics)? Or what happens if the document we link to links, in turn, to some other document which has a different semantic interpretation of some shared terms we use? For example, we may have said cyc:cat is a cyc:mammal, someone else that it is a cyc:insect, as they prefer the cat class for referring to caterpillars, and cyc: contains an assertion that mammals and insects are disjoint classes. At this point, all my instances of cats become inconsistent, a real problem especially when trying to use some typical logical reasoner that uses some form of reasoning by negation, in which case it would follow that any unasserted fact was true. Definitely not the desired behavior!

Most KR systems have been designed in the past to assume that inconsistency is a problem, and to define mechanisms to rule it out (either by limiting expressivity or defining inconsistency as an error condition) or which provide some mechanism (like a belief revision mechanism) that triggers from knowing the sources of the inconsistency. Semantic Web KR appears to mandate either some form of local consistency or the development of paraconsistent or other, some argue higher order, logics that disallow the general proof of all concepts from an inconsistency.[5]

In addition to attempts to explore semantics that handle some of the Web problems in KR, there are also attempts to explore the provision of capabilities that OWL disallows, such as providing mechanisms for scoping RDF graphs to allow default reasoning and negation as failure or to provide unifying logics in which other Web KR languages can be expressed, providing semantic interoperability without an insistence (as in the case of OWL) on syntactic uniformity.

21.6   Beyond OWL

The continued use of Semantic Web KR, beyond the OWL language, requires the design of other reasoning frameworks in ways that provide the same opportunities for interoperability standards and linking that OWL provides for basic KR vocabularies. A number of efforts have looked, for example, at bringing the power of rules to the Web for providing the linking of properties that OWL does not provide. A number of these efforts came together in the RuleML effort [12] as well as the development of Web specific rule languages like N3 [1], aimed specifically at providing support for RDF-based ontologies. At the time this chapter is being written, the World Wide Web Consortium has created the Rules Interchange Format (RIF) Working Group to explore the standardization of rules for the Web and to formalize a mapping between OWL and this emerging rules language.

---

[5]The interested reader is also directed to SCL [20] an attempt to provide a unifying logic for the Web which allows some higher-order-like reasoning within the constricts of FOL.

Other efforts are exploring other kinds of KR on the Web. Probabilistic extensions to OWL are also a current area of interest and several efforts are underway to extend OWL to provide richer expressivity ranging from extensions that aim to maintain the OWL DL guarantees to new, post OWL languages that extend the logic in many of the ways found in other chapters in this book.

A key point to note about OWL is that it was *not* intended to be the be-all and end-all knowledge representation for the Web. Like any good standard, it was designed to be a consensus language that could be used by a wide variety of users, sacrificing some of the advanced expressivity features that were not yet ready for standardization or for which there did not yet seem to be use cases compelling to the non-researchers involved in the standardization process. It is a truism in the standards community that good standards evolve, and the many activities looking to extend OWL in various directions are a healthy sign that OWL adoption is taking place.

21.7 Conclusion

At the time of this writing, subsets of the OWL language are being supported by major database vendors and RDF and RDFS are seeing wide use in both corporate and wider Web applications under the name "Web 3.0". In the academic arena, significant investment from the US and EU governments have helped to create a large community exploring many aspects of the use of Semantic Web technologies. New efforts in the standardization community are exploring adding rules to the Semantic Web, the use of semantic web ontologies in health care and life sciences, approaches to embedding Semantic annotations in traditional Web pages, adding probability to OWL, and others (See in particular the World Wide Web Consortium's Semantic Web Activity.[6]) OWL has become the most used KR language in the history of the field, not because of its particular representational power, but rather because it was designed to be a common syntax usable by many KR systems, to be webized for easier sharing of ontologies and concepts, and to be expressive enough for many problems without totally sacrificing scalability.

Acknowledgements

Funding for Dr. Hendler's research at the University of Maryland and RPI has been provided by: Fujitsu Laboratories of America—College Park, Lockheed Martin Advanced Technology Laboratory, NTT Corp., Kevric Corp., SAIC, National Science Foundation, DARPA, National Geospatial Intelligence Agency, Northrop Grumman Electronic Systems, US Army Research Laboratory, NIST, Other DoD sources and the Rensselaet Polytechnic Institute endowment. Special thanks to Guus Schreiber for comments on this article, to Vladimir Kolovski and Chris Halaschek-Weiner for their help in its preparation, and to the MINDSWAP project at Maryland where much of the foundations Semantic Web work took place.

---

[6]http://www.w3.org/2001/sw.

Bibliography

[1] T. Berners-Lee, D. Connolly, L. Kagal, Y. Scharf, and J. Hendler. N3Logic: A logic for the web. *Theory and Practice of Logic Programming*, 2007 (Special Issue on Logic Programming and the Web).

[2] T. Berners-Lee, J. Hendler, and O. Lassila. The semantic Web. *Scientific American*, 284(5):34–43, May 2001.

[3] E. Bozsak, M. Ehrig, and S. Handschub. Kaon—towards a large scale semantic web, 2002.

[4] J. Broekstra, A. Kampman, and F. van Harmelen. Sesame: A generic architecture for storing and querying rdf and rdf schema. In I. Horrocks and J. Hendler, editors. *Proceedings of the First International Semantic Web Conference, Lecture Notes in Computer Science*, vol. 2342, pages 54–68. Springer-Verlag, July 2002.

[5] B. Cuenca-Grau. Owl 1.1 web ontology language tractable fragments (editor's draft of 6 April 2007). Available at: http://webont.com/owl/1.1/tractable.html, 2007.

[6] D. Brickley and R. Guha. RDF vocabulary description language 1.0: RDF schema. http://www.w3.org/tr/rdf-schema/, February 2004.

[7] M. Dean and G.E. Schreiber. Owl web ontology language reference, w3c recommendation. Available at http://www.w3.org/TR/owl-ref/, 2004.

[8] J. Fielding, J. Gettys, H. Mogul, H. Frystyk, and T. Berners-Lee. Hypertext transfer protocol—http/1.1. IETF Network Working Group Request for Comments: 2068, 1997.

[9] M.R. Genesereth and R.E. Fikes. Knowledge interchange format, version 3.0 reference manual. Available at: http://www-ksl.stanford.edu/knowledge-sharing/kif/.

[10] J. Golbeck, G. Fragoso, F. Hartel, J. Hendler, B. Parsia, and J. Oberthaler. The national cancer institute's thesaurus and ontology, 2003.

[11] B.N. Grosof, I. Horrocks, R. Volz, and S. Decker. Description logic programs: combining logic programs with description logic. In *Proceedings of the World Wide Web Conference*, pages 48–57, 2003.

[12] D. Hirtle, H. Boley, B. Grosof, M. Kifer, M. Sintek, S. Tabet, and G. Wagner. Schema specification of RuleML 0.91. Available at: http://www.ruleml.org/0.91/, 2006.

[13] I. Horrocks. The fact system. In *TABLEAUX '98: Proceedings of the International Conference on Automated Reasoning with Analytic Tableaux and Related Methods*, pages 307–312. Springer-Verlag, London, UK, 1998.

[14] A. Kalyanpur, B. Parsia, E. Sirin, B.C. Grau, and J. Hendler. Swoop: A web ontology editing browser. *Journal of Web Semantics: Science, Services and Agents on the World Wide Web*, 4(2), June 2006.

[15] P.D. Karp, K.L. Myers, and T.R. Gruber. The generic frame protocol. In *IJCAI (1)*, pages 768–774, 1995.

[16] O. Lassila and R. Swick. Resource description framework (rdf) model and syntax specification.

[17] M. Musen, J.H. Gennari, H. Eriksson, and A.R. Puerta. Computer support for development of intelligent systems from libraries of components. *Medinfo*, 8(1):766, 1995.

[18] P. Patel-Schneider, P. Hayes, and I. Horrocks, OWL web ontology language semantics and abstract syntax w3c recommendation. http://www.w3.org/tr/2004/rec-owl-semantics-20040210/, February 2004.

[19] E. Prud'hommeaux and A. Seaborne. SPARQL query language for rdf, w3c working draft. Available at: http://www.w3.org/TR/rdf-sparql-query/, 2007.

[20] E. Prud'hommeaux and A. Seaborne. SPARQL query language for rdf, w3c working draft. Available at: http://www.w3.org/TR/rdf-sparql-query/, March 2007.

[21] E. Sirin, B. Parsia, B.C. Grau, A. Kalyanpur, and Y. Katz. Pellet: A practical owl-dl reasoner. *Journal of Web Semantics: Science, Services and Agents on the World Wide Web*, 2006.

Handbook of Knowledge Representation
Edited by F. van Harmelen, V. Lifschitz and B. Porter
© 2008 Elsevier B.V. All rights reserved
DOI: 10.1016/S1574-6526(07)03022-2

Chapter 22

Automated Planning

Alessandro Cimatti, Marco Pistore,
Paolo Traverso

22.1 Introduction

We intuitively refer to the term *Planning* as the deliberation process that chooses and organizes actions by anticipating their expected effects [24]. This deliberation aims at satisfying some pre-defined requirements and achieving some prestated objectives.

The intuition is that actions are executed in a given domain. They make the domain evolve and change its state. For instance, in a robot navigation domain, an action moving the robot changes its position; in the case of a microprocessor, an instruction can be viewed as an action that changes the value of the registers; a web service for booking flights can receive a message with a flight reservation confirmation, and this is an action that changes its state.

The deliberation process can organize actions in different ways. For instance, moving a robot to a given room and then to the corridor is an example of a sequential organization of actions; executing an instruction depending on the result of the execution of a previous one is an example of a conditional combination of actions; requesting for a flight reservation until a seat is available is an example of an iterative combination.

Actions are organized and combined with the aim to satisfy some requirements on the evolution of the domain. An example of a requirement for a mobile robot is that of "reaching a given room", while a requirement for a flight service can be that of "never exceeding a given number of overbooking".

Automated Planning is the area of Artificial Intelligence that studies this deliberation process computationally. Its aim is to support the planning activity by reasoning on conceptual models, i.e., abstract and formal representations of the domain, of the effects and the combinations of actions, and of the requirements to be satisfied and the objectives to be achieved. The conceptual model of the domain in which actions are executed is called the *planning domain*, combinations of actions are called *plans*, and the requirements to be satisfied are called *goals*. Intuitively, given a planning domain and a goal, a *planning problem* consists in determining a plan that satisfies the goal in a given domain.

In this Chapter, we provide a general formal framework for Automated Planning. The framework is defined along the three main components of the planning problem: domains, plans, and goals.

- **Domains.** We allow for *nondeterministic domains*, i.e., domains in which actions may have different effects, and it is impossible to know at planning time which of the different possible outcomes will actually take place. We also allow for *partial observability*. It models the fact that in some situations the state of the domain cannot be completely observed, and thus cannot be uniquely determined. A model with partial observability includes the special cases of *full observability*, where the state can be completely observed and thus uniquely determined, and that of *null observability*, where no observation is ever possible at run time.

- **Plans.** We define plans where the action to be executed in a given state can depend on available information about the history of previous execution steps. The definition is general enough to include *sequential plans*, i.e., plans that are simply sequences of actions, *conditional plans*, i.e., plans that can choose a different action depending on the current situation at execution time, *iterative plans* that can execute actions until a situation occurs. We can have plans that depend on a finite number of execution steps (*finite-memory plans*), as well as plans that do not depend on the previous execution steps (*memory-less plans*). In general, plan executions result in trees (called execution trees) whose nodes correspond to states of the domain.

- **Goals.** We define goals as sets of acceptable trees that corresponds to desired evolutions of a planning domain. They can represent classical *reachability goals* that express conditions on the leaves of execution trees, which determine the final states to be reached after a plan is executed. More in general, they can represent more complex forms of "extended goals", like *temporally extended goals*, that express conditions on the whole execution tree.

Our framework is general enough to represent a relevant and significant set of planning problems. *Classical planning* (see, e.g., [22, 40]) can be modeled with deterministic domains, plans that are sequences of actions, and reachability goals. In addition, our framework is well suited for modeling certain forms of planning under uncertainty and incomplete information, which are being recently addressed in the research literature and are relevant to several real-world applications. Indeed, nondeterministic domains model uncertainty in action effects, while partial observability models uncertainty in observations. For instance, the so-called *conformant planning* (see, e.g., [14, 9]) can be modeled with nondeterministic domains, null observability, sequential plans, and reachability goals. *Contingent planning* (see, e.g., [13, 32, 5]) can be modeled with nondeterministic domains, conditional plans, and reachability goals. *Planning for temporally extended goals* (see, e.g., [44, 1, 35]) can be modeled with nondeterministic domains, history dependent plans, and goals that represent desired evolutions of the domain.

For practical reasons, the framework cannot be so general to include all the different planning problems that have been addressed in the literature so far. For instance, a difference with respect to planning based on Markov Decision Processes (MDP) [8] is that we do not represent probabilities of action outcomes in action domains, and goals represented as utility functions.

A final remark is in order. We define the planning framework model theoretically, independently of the language that can be used to describe the three components of a planning problem. For instance, different languages can be used to describe planning domains and plans, see, for instance [39, 26, 23, 38, 27]. This is the case also for goals. For instance, propositional logic can be used to represent reachability goals, while different temporal logics, such as LTL or CTL [21], or specialized goal languages (see, e.g., [17]) can express temporally extended goals.

In this Chapter, we start by defining a general framework that can model domains, plans and goals. In the next sections, we instantiate the framework to some specific cases along the different dimensions of the planning components: domains, plans, and goals. We conclude by reporting on state-of-the-art techniques in the field, and discussing some future research challenges.

22.2 The General Framework

In this section we define a general, formal framework for Automated Planning, which is able to capture a wide variety of planning problems addressed by the literature. In the next sections, we will show how the framework can by applied to capture the different specific problems.

22.2.1 Domains

A planning domain is defined in terms of its *states*, of the *actions* it accepts, and of the possible *observations* that the domain can exhibit. Some of the states are marked as *initial states* for the domain. A *transition function* describes how (the execution of) an action leads from one state to possibly many different states. Finally, an *observation function* defines what observations are associated to each state of the domain.

Definition 22.2.1 (Planning domain). *A nondeterministic planning domain with partial observability is a tuple* $\mathcal{D} = \langle \mathcal{S}, \mathcal{A}, \mathcal{O}, \mathcal{I}, \mathcal{R}, \mathcal{X} \rangle$, *where*:

- $\mathcal{S}$ *is the set of* states.

- $\mathcal{A}$ *is the set of* actions.

- $\mathcal{O}$ *is the set of* observations.

- $\mathcal{I} \subseteq \mathcal{S}$ *is the set of* initial states; *we require* $\mathcal{I} \neq \emptyset$.

- $\mathcal{R} : \mathcal{S} \times \mathcal{A} \to 2^{\mathcal{S}}$ *is the* transition function; *it associates to each current state* $s \in \mathcal{S}$ *and to each action* $a \in \mathcal{A}$ *the set* $\mathcal{R}(s, a) \subseteq \mathcal{S}$ *of next states*.

- $\mathcal{X} : \mathcal{S} \to 2^{\mathcal{O}}$ *is the* observation function; *it associates to each state* s *the set of possible observations* $\mathcal{X}(s) \subseteq \mathcal{O}$.

We say that action a is executable *in state s if* $\mathcal{R}(s, a) \neq \emptyset$. *We require that in each state* $s \in \mathcal{S}$ *there is some executable action, that is some* $a \in \mathcal{A}$ *such that* $\mathcal{R}(s, a) \neq \emptyset$. *We also require that some observation is associated to each state* $s \in \mathcal{S}$, *that is,* $\mathcal{X}(s) \neq \emptyset$.

We say that $\mathcal{D}$ *is* finite state *if sets* $\mathcal{S}$, $\mathcal{A}$, $\mathcal{O}$ *are finite.*

Technically, a domain is described as a nondeterministic Moore machine, whose outputs (i.e., the observations) depend only on the current state of the machine, not on the input action. Uncertainty is allowed in the initial state and in the outcome of action execution. Also, the observation associated to a given state is not unique. This allows modeling noisy sensing and lack of information.

22.2.2 Plans and Plan Executions

A *plan* is a definition of the next action to be performed on a planning domain in a specific situation. A situation can be defined as the past history of the interactions of the (executor of the) plan with the planning domain. In the initial situation, the only information available to the executor is the initial (nondeterministic) observation o_0, and the executor reacts triggering action a_1. This leads to a new (nondeterministic) observation o_1, to which the executor reacts with an action a_2, which leads to a new (nondeterministic) observation o_2. This alternation of observations and actions can go on infinitely, or can stop when the executor stops triggering new actions.

Formally, we will define a plan as a partial function $\pi : \mathcal{O}^+ \rightharpoonup \mathcal{A}$ that associates an action $\pi(w)$ to a sequence of observations $w = o_0 o_1 \dots o_n$. This way, the alternation of outputs and actions just described is $o_0 a_1 o_1 a_2 \dots o_n$, where $a_{i+1} = \pi(o_0 o_1 \dots o_i)$.

Definition 22.2.2 (Plan). *A* plan *for planning domain* $\mathcal{D} = \langle \mathcal{S}, \mathcal{A}, \mathcal{O}, \mathcal{I}, \mathcal{R}, \mathcal{X} \rangle$ *is a partial function* $\pi : \mathcal{O}^+ \rightharpoonup \mathcal{A}$ *such that*:

- *if* $o_0 o_1 \dots o_n \in \mathrm{dom}(\pi)$ *with* $n > 0$, *then* $o_0 o_1 \dots o_{n-1} \in \mathrm{dom}(\pi)$.

If $\pi(w)$ *is defined for some* $w = o_0 o_1 \dots o_n$, *then we denote with* $\pi^*(w)$ *the sequence of outputs and actions* $o_0 a_1 o_1 a_2 \dots o_n$ *such that* $a_{i+1} = \pi(o_0 o_1 \dots o_i)$ *for* $i = 1..n$.

Notice that the previous definition ensures that, if a plan defines an action to be executed for a sequence of observations, then an action is defined also for all the nonempty prefixes of the sequence.

Since we consider nondeterministic planning domains, the execution of an action may lead to different outcomes, and observations associated to these outcomes are also nondeterministic. Therefore, the execution of a plan on a planning domain can be described as a tree, where the branching corresponds to the different states reached by executing the planned action, and by the observations obtained from these states.

Formally, we define a *tree* τ with nodes labeled on set Σ (or Σ-labeled tree) as a subset of Σ^+ such that, if $\omega \cdot \sigma \in \tau$, with $\omega \in \Sigma^+$ and $\sigma \in \Sigma$, then also $\omega \in \tau$. Notice that tree τ can have finite branches—corresponding to strings ω that cannot be further extended in τ—as well as infinite branches—whenever there are sequences of strings $\omega_1, \omega_2, \dots, \omega_n, \dots$ such that ω_i is a strict prefix of ω_{i+1}.

We can now define an execution tree as a $(\mathcal{S} \times \mathcal{O})$-labeled tree, where component Σ of the label of the tree corresponds to a state in the planning domain, while component $\mathcal{O}$ describes the observation obtained from that state.

Definition 22.2.3 (Execution tree). *The execution tree for domain $\mathcal{D} = \langle \mathcal{S}, \mathcal{A}, \mathcal{O}, \mathcal{I}, \mathcal{R}, \mathcal{X} \rangle$ and plan π is the $(\mathcal{S} \times \mathcal{O})$-labeled tree τ defined as follows*:

- $(s_0, o_0) \in \tau$, *where $s_0 \in \mathcal{I}$ and $o_0 = \mathcal{X}(s_o)$*;

- *if $(s_0, o_0)(s_1, o_1) \ldots (s_n, o_n) \in \tau$, $\pi(o_0 o_1 \ldots o_n) = a_n$, $s_{n+1} \in \mathcal{R}(s_n, a_n)$ and $o_{n+1} \in \mathcal{X}(s_{n+1})$, then $(s_0, o_0)(s_1, o_1) \ldots (s_n, o_n)(s_{n+1}, o_{n+1}) \in \tau$.*

Not all plans can be executed on a given domain. Indeed, it might be possible that the actions prescribed cannot be executed in all the states. We now define *executable* plans as those for which the triggered action is always executable on the domain.

Definition 22.2.4 (Executable plan). *Let $\mathcal{D} = \langle \mathcal{S}, \mathcal{A}, \mathcal{O}, \mathcal{I}, \mathcal{R}, \mathcal{X} \rangle$ be a planning domain and π be a plan for $\mathcal{D}$. We say that π is* executable *if the following condition holds on the execution tree τ for $\mathcal{D}$ and π*:

- *if $(s_0, o_0)(s_1, o_1) \ldots (s_n, o_n) \in \tau$ and $\pi(o_0 o_1 \ldots o_n) = a_n$ then $\mathcal{R}(s_n, a_n) \neq \emptyset$.*

22.2.3 Goals and Problems

A *planning problem* consists of a planning domain and of a goal g that defines the set of desired behaviors. In the following, we assume that goal g defines a set of execution trees, namely the execution trees that exhibit the behaviors described by the goal (we say that these execution trees satisfy the goal).

Definition 22.2.5 (Planning problem). *A planning problem is a pair $(\mathcal{D}, g)$, where $\mathcal{D} = \langle \mathcal{S}, \mathcal{A}, \mathcal{O}, \mathcal{I}, \mathcal{R}, \mathcal{X} \rangle$ is a planning domain and g is a set of $(\mathcal{S} \times \mathcal{O})$-labeled trees. A solution to planning problem (D, g) is a plan π such that the execution tree for π satisfies goal g.*

22.3 Strong Planning under Full Observability

The first problem we address is the problem of strong planning under full observability. This problem can be defined restricting the framework with two assumptions, one on the planning domain, and one on the goal.

The first assumption is that the domain is fully observable. This means that we can assume that execution will have no run-time uncertainty whatsoever on the reached state: before attempting an action, the executor will know precisely the state of the domain. Intuitively, this can be modeled by letting the set of observations to coincide with the set of states, and by assuming that the observation relation is actually an identity function. Formally,

Definition 22.3.1 (Fully observable domain). *A planning domain $\mathcal{D} = \langle \mathcal{S}, \mathcal{A}, \mathcal{O}, \mathcal{I}, \mathcal{R}, \mathcal{X} \rangle$ is fully observable iff $\mathcal{O} = \mathcal{S}$ and $\mathcal{X}(s) = s$.*

For simplicity, in the following we will assume that fully observable planning domains are defined as tuples $\mathcal{D} = \langle \mathcal{S}, \mathcal{A}, \mathcal{I}, \mathcal{R} \rangle$.

The second assumption is that we are interested in *strong* solutions, that guarantee that a set of target states will be reached in a finite number of steps, regardless of initial uncertainty in the initial states, and of nondeterministic action effects.

Definition 22.3.2 (Goal for strong planning). *Let $\mathcal{G}$ be a set of states. An execution tree π is a solutions to the strong planning problem $\mathcal{G}$ iff every branch of π is finite and ends in a state in $\mathcal{G}$.*

In this setting, we can restrict our solutions to a very specific form of plans, i.e., memoryless policies. Memoryless policies are plans where the selection of actions depends on the last observation only.

Definition 22.3.3 (Memoryless plans). *Let $\mathcal{D} = \langle \mathcal{S}, \mathcal{A}, \mathcal{O}, \mathcal{I}, \mathcal{R}, \mathcal{X} \rangle$ be a finite state domain. Plan π for domain $\mathcal{D}$ is memoryless if, for all ω, ω', and o, $\pi(\omega o) = \pi(\omega' o)$.*

Intuitively, memoryless plans are enough to solve the problem due to full observability, and to the simplicity of the goal.

Memoryless plans can be described in a compact way as a partial function, called state-action table, mapping states to the actions to be executed in such states. More precisely, a state-action table SA is a subset of $\mathcal{S} \times \mathcal{A}$, and a deterministic state-action table is a state-action table SA such that $\langle s, a \rangle \in$ SA and $\langle s, a' \rangle \in$ SA imply $a = a'$. The definition of a plan corresponding to a deterministic state-action table is trivial.

We now describe an algorithm for strong planning. The algorithm operates on the planning problem: the sets of the initial states $\mathcal{I}$ and of the goal states $\mathcal{G}$ are explicitly given as input parameters, while the domain $\mathcal{D} = \langle \mathcal{S}, \mathcal{A}, \mathcal{I}, \mathcal{R} \rangle$ is assumed to be globally available to the invoked subroutines. The algorithm either returns a solution state-action table, or a distinguished value for state-action tables, called $\perp$, used to represent search failure. In particular, we assume that $\perp$ is different from the empty state-action table, that we will denote with $\emptyset$.

The algorithm, presented in Fig. 22.1, is based on a breadth-first search proceeding backwards from the goal, towards the initial states. At each iteration step, the set of states for which a solution has been already found is used as a target for the expansion preimage routine at line 5, that returns a new "slice" to be added to the state-action table under construction. Functions STRONGPREIMAGE is defined as follows:

$$\text{STRONGPREIMAGE}(S) \doteq \big\{ \langle s, a \rangle \colon \emptyset \neq \mathcal{R}(s, a) \subseteq S \big\}.$$

STRONGPREIMAGE(S) returns the set of state-action pairs $\langle s, a \rangle$ such that the execution of a in s is guaranteed to lead to states inside S, regardless of nondeterminism. We contrast the definition of STRONGPREIMAGE with the WEAKPREIMAGE function (that will be used in the following sections):

$$\text{WEAKPREIMAGE}(S) \doteq \big\{ \langle s, a \rangle \colon \mathcal{R}(s, a) \cap S \neq \emptyset \big\}.$$

Intuitively, WEAKPREIMAGE(S) returns the set of state-action pairs $\langle s, a \rangle$ such that the execution of a in s *may* lead inside S, but it is not guaranteed to do so.

```
1   function STRONGPLAN(I, G);
2       OldSA := ⊥;
3       SA := ∅;
4       while (OldSA ≠ SA ∧ I ⊄ (G ∪ STATESOF(SA))) do
5           PreImage := STRONGPREIMAGE(G ∪ STATESOF(SA));
6           NewSA := PRUNESTATES(PreImage, G ∪ STATESOF(SA));
7           OldSA := SA;
8           SA := SA ∪ NewSA;
9       done;
10      if (I ⊆ (G ∪ STATESOF(SA))) then
11          return SA;
12      else
13          return ⊥;
14      fi;
15  end;
```

Figure 22.1: The algorithm for strong planning.

In the strong planning algorithm, function STRONGPREIMAGE is called using as target the goal states G and the states that are already in the state-action table SA: these are the states for which a solution is already known. The returned preimage PreImage is then passed to function PRUNESTATES, defined as follows:

$$\text{PRUNESTATES}(\pi, S) \doteq \{\langle s, a \rangle \in \pi : s \notin S\}.$$

This function removes from the preimage table all the pairs $\langle s, a \rangle$ such that a solution is already known for s. This pruning is important to guarantee that only the shortest solution from any state appears in the state-action table. The termination test requires that the initial states are included in the set of accumulated states (i.e., $G \cup \text{STATESOF}(SA)$), or that a fix-point has been reached and no more states can be added to state-action table SA. In the first case, the returned state-action table is a solution to the planning problem. In the second case, no solution exists.

Notice that the state-action table SA computed by the algorithm is not necessarily deterministic. However, a deterministic state-action table can be obtained from SA associating to state s an arbitrary action from set $\{a: \langle s, a \rangle \in SA\}$, whenever this set is notempty.

22.4 Strong Cyclic Planning under Full Observability

Strong cyclic planning can be defined in the same setting as strong planning: domains are fully observable, and plans are memoryless policies. The variation is in the set of acceptable executions: here, in addition to executions that terminate in the goal, we also accept infinite executions (e.g., that can loop for ever), with the proviso that the chance of reaching the goal is retained.

Definition 22.4.1 (Goal for strong cyclic planning). *Let G be a set of states. Then an execution tree π is a solution to the strong cyclic planning problem G iff every path in π either ends in a state in G, or each of its finite prefixes has a suffix that ends in G.*

We now present an algorithm for strong cyclic planning. The main difference with the algorithm presented in previous section is that here the resulting plans allow for infinite behaviors: loops must no longer be eliminated, but rather controlled, i.e., only certain, "good" loops must be kept. Infinite executions are accepted only if they correspond to "unlucky" patterns of nondeterministic outcomes, and if a goal state can be reached from each state of the execution under different patterns of nondeterministic outcomes.

The strong cyclic planning algorithm is presented in Fig. 22.2. The algorithm starts to analyze the universal state-action table with respect to the problem being solved, and eliminates all those state-action pairs which are discovered to be source of potential "bad" loops, or to lead to states which have been discovered not to allow for a solution. With respect to the algorithms presented in previous section, here the set of states associated with the state-action table being constructed is reduced rather than being extended: this approach amounts to computing a greatest fix-point.

The starting state-action table in function STRONGCYCLICPLAN is the universal state-action table UnivSA. It contains all state-action pairs that satisfy the applicability conditions:

$$\mathrm{UnivSA} \doteq \big\{ \langle s,\, a \rangle \colon \mathcal{R}(s, a) \neq \emptyset \big\}.$$

The "elimination" phase, where unsafe state-action pairs are discarded, corresponds to the while loop of function STRONGCYCLICPLAN. It is based on the repeated application of the functions PRUNEOUTGOING and PRUNE UNCONNECTED. The role of PRUNEOUTGOING is to remove all those state-action pairs which may lead out of $G \cup \mathrm{STATESOF(SA)}$, which is the current set of potential solutions. Because of the elimination of these actions, from certain states it may become impossible to reach the set of goal states. The role of PRUNEUNCONNECTED is to identify and remove such states. Due to this removal, the need may arise to eliminate further outgoing transitions, and so on. The elimination loop is quit when convergence is reached. The resulting state-action table is guaranteed to generate executions which either terminate in the goal or loop forever on states from which it is possible to reach the goal. Function STRONGCYCLICPLAN then checks whether the computed state-action table SA defines a plan for all the initial states, i.e., $\mathcal{I} \subseteq \mathcal{G} \cup \mathrm{STATESOF(SA)}$. If this is not the case a failure is returned.

The state-action table obtained after the elimination loop is not necessarily a valid solution for the planning problem. Indeed, it may contain state-action pairs that, while preserving the reachability of the goal, still do not perform any progress toward it. In the strong cyclic planning algorithm, function REMOVENONPROGRESS on line 9 takes care of removing all those actions from a state whose outcomes do not lead to any progress toward the goal. This function is similar to the strong planning algorithm: it iteratively extends the state-action table by considering states at an increasing distance from the goal. In this case, however, a weak preimage is computed at any iteration step, since it is sufficient to guarantee progress towards the goal for *some* outcome of action execution. Moreover, the computed weak preimage is restricted to the state-action pairs that appear in the input state-action table, and hence that are "safe" according to the elimination phase.

```
1   function STRONGCYCLICPLAN(I, G);
2       OldSA := ∅;
3       SA := UnivSA;
4       while (OldSA ≠ SA) do
5           OldSA := SA;
6           SA := PRUNEUNCONNECTED(PRUNEOUTGOING(SA, G), G);
7       done;
8       if (I ⊆ (G ∪ STATESOF(SA))) then
9           return REMOVENONPROGRESS(SA, G);
10      else
11          return ⊥;
12      fi;
13  end;
```

```
1   function PRUNEUNCONNECTED(SA, G);
2       NewSA := ∅;
3       repeat
4           OldSA := NewSA;
5           NewSA := SA ∩ WEAKPREIMAGE(G ∪ STATESOF(NewSA));
6       until (OldSA = NewSA);
7       return NewSA;
8   end;
```

```
1   function PRUNEOUTGOING(SA, G);
2       NewSA := SA \ COMPUTEOUTGOING(SA, G ∪ STATESOF(SA));
3       return NewSA; ;
4   end;
```

```
1   function REMOVENONPROGRESS(SA, G);
2       NewSA := ∅;
3       repeat
4           PreImage := SA ∩ WEAKPREIMAGE(G ∪ STATESOF(NewSA));
5           OldSA := NewSA;
6           NewSA := NewSA ∪ PRUNESTATES(PreImage, G ∪ STATESOF(NewSA));
7       until (OldSA = NewSA);
8       return NewSA;
9   end;
```

Figure 22.2: The algorithm for strong cyclic planning.

Functions PRUNEOUTGOING, PRUNEUNCONNECTED, and REMOVENONPRO-GRESS, also presented in Fig. 22.2, exploit primitives WEAKPREIMAGE and PRUNE STATES, already defined in Section 22.3, and the primitive COMPUTEOUTGOING, that takes as input a state-action table SA and a set of states S, and returns those state-action pairs which are not guaranteed to result in states in S:

$$\text{COMPUTEOUTGOING}(\text{SA}, S) \doteq \big\{ \langle s, a \rangle \in \text{SA} : \mathcal{R}(s, a) \nsubseteq S \big\}.$$

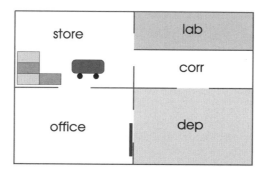

Figure 22.3: A simple nondeterministic planning domain.

22.5 Planning for Temporally Extended Goals under Full Observability

We now extend the problem of planning in fully observable domains by considering temporal goals. Under the hypothesis of full observability, the planning domain is still the same as the one formalized in Section 22.3. Plans cannot instead be limited to memoryless policies. In order to satisfy temporal goals, the plan function needs to select actions depending on the previous execution steps. Intuitively, this is due to the fact that plans need to keep track of which part of the temporal goal has been satisfied, and which one is still open. Consider for instance the following example.

Example 22.5.1. A simple domain is shown in Fig. 22.3. It consists of a building of five rooms, namely a store, a department dep, a laboratory lab, an office, and a corridor corr. A robot can move between the rooms. The laboratory is a dangerous room it is not possible to exit from. For the sake of simplicity, we do not model explicitly the objects, but only the movements of the robot. Between rooms office and dep, there is a door that the robot cannot control. Therefore, an *east* action from room office successfully leads to room dep only if the door is open. Another nondeterministic outcome occurs when the robot tries to move *east* from the store: in this case, the robot may end nondeterministically either in room corr or in room lab. The transition graph for the domain is represented in Fig. 22.4.

Consider now the goal of going from the corridor corr to room dep and then back to room store. The action to execute in room corr depends on whether the robot has already reached room dep and is going back to the store.

Plans are therefore *regular plans* that take into account previous execution steps and that are instantiated to the case of fully observable domains.

Definition 22.5.2 (Regular plan). *Plan π for finite state domain $\mathcal{D} = \langle \mathcal{S}, \mathcal{A}, \mathcal{O}, \mathcal{I}, \mathcal{R}, \mathcal{X} \rangle$ is regular if there is a finite set of contexts C and a function $f : \mathcal{O}^+ \to C$ such that*:

- *if $f(\omega) = f(\omega')$ then $\pi(\omega) = \pi(\omega')$,*

- *if $f(\omega) = f(\omega')$, then $f(\omega o) = f(\omega' o)$.*

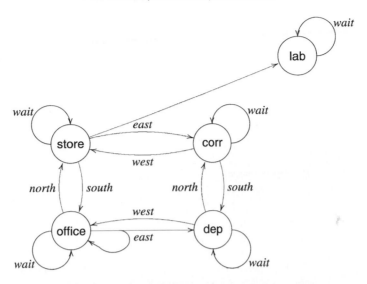

Figure 22.4: The transition graph of the navigation domain.

It is easy to see that regular plans can be defined specifying: (1) the finite set of contexts C, (2) an initialization function *init* : $\mathcal{O} \rightharpoonup C$ defining the initial context given the initial observation, and (3), an evolution function *evolve* : $C \times \mathcal{O} \rightharpoonup C$, defining the next context, given the current context and the observation.

In the following, we prefer a different alternative characterization of regular plans for fully observable domains, which is more adequate for the planning algorithm that we are going to define. More precisely, a regular plan can be defined in terms of an *action function* that, given a state and an *execution context*, specifies the action to be executed, and in terms of a *context function* that, depending on the action outcome, specifies the next execution context.

Definition 22.5.3 (Regular plans (for temporally extended goals)). *A plan for a fully observable domain D is a tuple $\langle C, c_0, act, ctxt \rangle$, where*:

- *C is a finite set of (execution) contexts,*

- *$c_0 \in C$ is the initial context,*

- *act : $\mathcal{S} \times C \rightharpoonup \mathcal{A}$ is the action function,*

- *ctxt : $\mathcal{S} \times C \times \mathcal{S} \rightharpoonup C$ is the context function.*

We require that a plan satisfies the following conditions:

1. *$act(s_0, c_0)$ is defined for each $s_0 \in \mathcal{I}$;*

2. *whenever $act(s, c) = a$ and $ctxt(s, c, s') = c'$, then $\mathcal{R}(s, a) \neq \emptyset$ and $s' \in \mathcal{R}(s, a)$;*

$$act(\text{store}, c_0) = south \qquad ctxt(\text{store}, c_0, \text{office}) = c_0$$
$$act(\text{office}, c_0) = east \qquad ctxt(\text{office}, c_0, \text{dep}) = c_1$$
$$ctxt(\text{office}, c_0, \text{office}) = c_0$$
$$act(\text{dep}, c_1) = west \qquad ctxt(\text{dep}, c_1, \text{office}) = c_1$$
$$act(\text{office}, c_1) = north \qquad ctxt(\text{office}, c_1, \text{store}) = c_1$$
$$act(\text{store}, c_1) = wait \qquad ctxt(\text{store}, c_1, \text{store}) = c_1$$

Figure 22.5: An example of plan.

3. *whenever* $act(s, c) = a$ *and* $s' \in R(s, a)$, *then there is some context* c' *such that* $ctxt(s, c, s') = c'$ *and* $act(s', c')$ *is defined.*

If we are in state s and in execution context c, then $act(s, c)$ returns the action to be executed by the plan, while $ctxt(s, c, s')$ associates to each reached state s' the new execution context. Functions act and $ctxt$ may be partial, since some state-context pairs are never reached in the execution of the plan. We require plans to be defined in all the initial states (Condition 1 in Definition 22.2.2), to be *executable*, i.e., the actions should be applicable and contexts should be defined over states that are the results of applying the actions (Condition 2), and to be *complete*, i.e., a plan should always specify how to proceed for all the possible outcomes of any action in the plan (Condition 3).

Example 22.5.4. An example of a plan is shown in Fig. 22.5. The plan leads the robot from room store to room dep going through the office, and then back to the store, again going through the office. Two contexts are used, namely c_0 when the robot is going to the dep and c_1 when the robot is going back to the store. This allows the plan to execute different actions in state office and in state store.

As discussed in Section 22.2, the execution of a plan can be described as a labeled tree. In the case of a fully observable domain, observations are not important, and the execution of a plan can be simply described as a S-labeled tree.

Definition 22.5.5 (Execution tree (in a fully observable domain)). *The execution tree for a fully observable domain* D *and regular plan* π *is the* S-*labeled tree* τ *defined as follows:*

- $s_0 \in \tau$, *where* $s_0 \in I$;

- *if* $s_0 s_1 \ldots s_n \in \tau$, $\pi(s_0 s_1 \ldots s_n) = a_n$, $s_{n+1} \in R(s_n, a_n)$, *then* $s_0 s_1 \ldots s_n s_{n+1} \in \tau$.

Notice that, due to Condition 3 in Definition 22.2.2, execution trees obtained from regular plans do not contain finite paths.

We describe temporally extended goals by means of formulae in a temporal logic. In this setting, we use Computation Tree Logic (CTL) [21] that enables us to characterize the corresponding set of trees.

Definition 22.5.6 (CTL goal). *A CTL goal is defined by the following grammar, where s is a state of the domain* $\mathcal{D}^1$:

$$g ::= p \mid g \wedge g \mid g \vee g \mid \text{AX}\, g \mid \text{EX}\, g$$
$$\text{A}(g\, \text{U}\, g) \mid \text{E}(g\, \text{U}\, g) \mid \text{A}(g\, \text{W}\, g) \mid \text{E}(g\, \text{W}\, g)$$
$$p ::= s \mid \neg p \mid p \wedge p$$

CTL combines temporal operators and path quantifiers. "X", "U", and "W" are the "next time", "(strong) until", and "weak until" temporal operators, respectively. "A" and "E" are the universal and existential path quantifiers, where a path is an infinite sequence of states. Formulas AF g and EF g (where the temporal operator "F" stands for "future" or "eventually") are abbreviations of $\text{A}(\top\, \text{U}\, g)$ and $\text{E}(\top\, \text{U}\, g)$, respectively. AG g and EG g (where "G" stands for "globally" or "always") are abbreviations of $\text{A}(g\, \text{W}\, \perp)$ and $\text{E}(g\, \text{W}\, \perp)$, respectively. A remark is in order. Even if negation $\neg$ is allowed only in front of basic propositions, it is easy to define $\neg g$ for a generic CTL formula g, by "pushing down" the negations: for instance, $\neg\text{AX}\, g \equiv \text{EX}\, \neg g$ and $\neg\text{A}(g_1\, \text{W}\, g_2) \equiv \text{E}(\neg g_2\, \text{U}\, (\neg g_1 \wedge \neg g_2))$.

We now define valid plans, i.e., plans that satisfy CTL goals, i.e., we define $\tau \models g$, where τ is the execution tree of a plan π for domain $\mathcal{D}$, and g is a CTL goal. The definition of predicate $\models$ is based on the standard semantics of CTL [21].

Definition 22.5.7 (Valid plan for a CTL goal). *Let* π *be a plan for domain* $\mathcal{D}$. *Let* τ *be the execution tree of* π *in domain* $\mathcal{D}$. *Let* n *be a node of* τ.
We define $\tau, n \models g$ *as follows.*

- $\tau, n \models s$ *iff* $n = s$.

- $\tau, n \models \neg s$ *if* $n \neq s$.

- $\tau, n \models g \wedge g'$ *if* $\tau, n \models g$ *and* $\tau, s \models g'$.

- $\tau, n \models g \vee g'$ *if* $\tau, n \models g$ *or* $\tau, n \models g'$.

- $\tau, n \models \text{AX}\, g$ *if for all* n' *that are successors nodes of* n *in* τ, *then* $\tau, n' \models g$.

- $\tau, n \models \text{EX}\, g$ *if there is some successor node* n' *of* n *in* τ *such that* $\tau, n' \models g$.

- $\tau, n \models \text{A}(g\, \text{U}\, g')$ *if for all paths* $n_0 n_1 n_2 \ldots$ *in* τ *with* $n = n_0$ *there is some* $i \geqslant 0$ *such that* $\tau, n_i \models g'$ *and* $\tau, n_j \models g$ *for all* $0 \leqslant j < i$.

- $\tau, n \models \text{E}(g\, \text{U}\, g')$ *if there is some path* $n_0 n_1 n_2 \ldots$ *in* τ *with* $n = n_0$ *and some* $i \geqslant 0$ *such that* $\tau, n_i \models g'$ *and* $\tau, n_j \models g$ *for all* $0 \leqslant j < i$.

- $\tau, n \models \text{A}(g\, \text{W}\, g')$ *if for all paths* $n_0 n_1 n_2 \ldots$ *of* τ *with* $n = n_0$, *either* $\tau, n_j \models g$ *for all* $j \geqslant 0$, *or there is some* $i \geqslant 0$ *such that* $\tau, n_i \models g'$ *and* $\tau, n_j \models g$ *for all* $0 \leqslant j < i$.

---

[1] Here we chose to identify each state of the domain with a basic Boolean proposition of CTL formulas. Actually, we would need only $\lceil \log_2 |S| \rceil$ basic propositions, using a boolean encoding of the states.

- $\tau, n \models E(g \, W \, g')$ *if there is some path* $n_0 n_1 n_2 \ldots$ *in* τ *with* $n = n_0$ *such that either* $\tau, n_j \models g$ *for all* $j \geqslant 0$, *or there is some* $i \geqslant 0$ *such that* $\tau, n_i \models g'$ *and* $\tau, n_j \models g$ *for all* $0 \leqslant j < i$.

We define $\tau \models g$ *if* $\tau, n_0 \models g$ *for all the initial states* $n_0 = s_0 \in \mathcal{I}$ *of* $\mathcal{D}$.

A planning algorithm can search the state space by progressing CTL goals. A CTL goal g defines conditions on the current state and on the next states to be reached. Intuitively, if g must hold in s, then some conditions must be projected to the next states. The algorithm extracts the information on the conditions on the next states by "progressing" the goal g. For instance, if g is $EF \, g'$, then either g' holds in s or $EF \, g'$ must still hold in some next state, i.e., $EX \, EF \, g'$ must hold in q. One of the basic building blocks of the algorithm is the function *progr* that rewrites a goal by progressing it to next states. *progr* is defined by induction on the structure of goals.

- $progr(s, s') = \top$ if $s = s'$, $\bot$, otherwise;

- $progr(s, \neg s') = \neg progr(s, s')$;

- $progr(s, g_1 \wedge g_2) = progr(s, g_1) \wedge progr(s, g_2)$;

- $progr(s, g_1 \vee g_2) = progr(s, g_1) \vee progr(s, g_2)$;

- $progr(s, AX \, g) = AX \, g$ and $progr(s, EX \, g) = EX \, g$;

- $progr(s, A(g \, U \, g')) = (progr(s, g) \wedge AX \, A(g \, U \, g')) \vee progr(s, g')$;

- $progr(s, E(g \, U \, g')) = (progr(s, g) \wedge EX \, E(g \, U \, g')) \vee progr(s, g')$;

- $progr(s, A(g \, W \, g')) = (progr(s, g) \wedge AX \, A(g \, W \, g')) \vee progr(s, g')$;

- $progr(s, E(g \, W \, g')) = (progr(s, g) \wedge EX \, E(g \, W \, g')) \vee progr(s, g')$.

The formula $progr(s, g)$ can be written in a normal form. We write it as a disjunction of two kinds of conjuncts, those of the form $AX \, f$ and those of the form $EX \, h$, since we need to distinguish between formulas that must hold in all the next states and those that must hold in some of the next states:

$$progr(s, g) = \bigvee_{i \in I} \left(\bigwedge_{f \in A_i} AX \, f \wedge \bigwedge_{h \in E_i} EX \, h \right),$$

where $f \in A_i$ ($h \in E_i$) if $AX \, f$ ($EX \, h$) belongs to the ith disjunct of $progr(s, g)$. We have $|I|$ different disjuncts that correspond to alternative evolutions of the domain, i.e., to alternative plans we can search for. In the following, we represent $progr(s, g)$ as a set of pairs, each pair containing the A_i and the E_i parts of a disjunct:

$$progr(s, g) = \big\{ (A_i, E_i) \mid i \in I \big\}$$

with $progr(s, \top) = \{ (\emptyset, \emptyset) \}$ and $progr(s, \bot) = \emptyset$.

Given a disjunct (A, E) of $progr(s, g)$, we can define a function that assigns goals to be satisfied to the next states. We denote with assign-progr$((A, E), S)$ the set of all the possible assignments $i : S \rightarrow 2^{A \cup E}$ such that each universally quantified goal is assigned to all the next states (i.e., if $f \in A$ then $f \in i(s)$ for all $s \in S$) and each existentially quantified goal is assigned to one of the next states (i.e., if $h \in E$ and $h \notin A$ then $f \in i(s)$ for one particular $s \in S$).

Given the two basic building blocks *progr* and assign-progr, we can now describe the planning algorithm build-plan that, given a goal g_0 and an initial state s_0, returns either a plan or a failure.[2] The algorithm is reported in Fig. 22.6. It performs a depth-first forward search: starting from the initial state, it picks up an action, progresses the goal to successor states, and iterates until either the goal is satisfied or the search path leads to a failure. The algorithm uses as the "contexts" of the plan the list of the active goals that are considered at the different stages of the exploration. More precisely, a context is a list $c = [g_1, \ldots, g_n]$, where the g_i are the active goals, as computed by functions *progr* and assign-progr, and the order of the list represents the *age* of these goals: the goals that are active since more steps come first in the list.

The main function of the algorithm is function build-plan-aux(s, c, pl, open), that builds the plan for context c from state s. If a plan is found, then it is returned by the function. Otherwise, $\perp$ is returned. Argument pl is the plan built so far by the algorithm. Initially, the argument passed to build-plan-aux is pl $= \langle C, c_0, act, ctxt \rangle = \langle \emptyset, g_0, \emptyset, \emptyset \rangle$. Argument open is the list of the pairs state-context of the currently open problems: if $(s, c) \in$ open then we are currently trying to build a plan for context c in state s. Whenever function build-plan-aux is called with a pair state-context already in open, then we have a loop of states in which the same sub-goal has to be enforced. In this case, function is-good-loop((s, c), open) is called that checks whether the loop is valid or not. If the loop is good, plan pl is returned, otherwise function build-plan-aux fails.

Function is-good-loop computes the set loop-goals of the goals that are active during the whole loop: iteratively, it considers all the pairs (s', c') that appear in open up to the next occurrence of the current pair (s, c), and it intersects loop-goals with the set setof(c') of the goals in list c'. Then, function is-good-loop checks whether there is some strong until goal among the loop-goals. If this is a case, then the loop is bad: the semantics of CTL requires that all the strong until goals are eventually fulfilled, so these goals should not stay active during a whole loop. In fact, this is the difference between strong and weak until goals: executions where some weak until goal is continuously active and never fulfilled are acceptable, while the strong until should be eventually fulfilled if they become active.

If the pair (s, c) is not in open but it is in the plan pl (i.e., (s, c) is in the range of function *act* and hence condition "defined pl.$act[s, c]$" is true), then a plan for the pair has already been found in another branch of the search, and we return immediately with a success. If the pair state-context is neither in open nor in the plan, then the algorithm considers in turn all the executable actions a from state s, all the different possible progresses (A, E) returned by function *progr*, and all the possible assignments i of (A, E) to $\mathcal{R}(s, a)$. Function build-plan-aux is called recursively for each destination state in $s' \in \mathcal{R}(s, a)$. The new context is computed by function order-goals($i[s'], c$): this function returns a list of the goals in $i[s']$ that are ordered by

---

[2] It is easy to extend the algorithm to the case of more than one initial state.

```
 1   function build-plan(s₀, g₀): Plan
 2       return build-plan-aux(s₀, [g₀], ⟨∅, g₀, ∅, ∅⟩, ∅)
 3
 4   function build-plan-aux(s, c, pl, open): Plan
 5       if (s, c) ∈ open then
 6           if is-good-loop((s, c), open) then return pl
 7               else return ⊥
 8           if defined pl.act[s, c] then return pl
 9           foreach a ∈ A(p) do
10               foreach(A, E) ∈ progr(s, c) do
11                   foreach i ∈ assign-progr((A, E), R(s, a)) do
12                       pl' := pl
13                       pl'.C := pl'.C ∪ {c}
14                       pl'.act[s, c] := a
15                       open' := conc((s, c'), open)
16                       foreach s' ∈ R(s, a) do
17                           c' := order-goals(i[s'], c)
18                           pl'.ctxt[s, c, s'] := c'
19                           pl' := build-plan-aux(s', c', pl', open')
20                           if pl' = ⊥ then next i
21                       return pl'
22           return ⊥
23
24       function is-good-loop((s, c), open): boolean
25           loop-goals := setof(c)
26           while(s, c) ≠ head(open) do
27               (s', c') := head(open)
28               loop-goals := loop-goals ∩ setof(c')
29               open := tail(open)
31           if ∃g ∈ loop-goals: g = A(_U_) or g = E(_U_) then
32               return false
33           else
34               return true
```

Figure 22.6: A planning algorithm for CTL goals.

their "age": namely those goals that are old (they appear in $i[s']$ and also in c) appear first, in the same order as in c, and those that are new (they appear in $i[s']$ but not in c) appear at the end of the list, in any order. Also, in the recursive call, argument pl is updated to take into account the fact that action a has been selected from state s in context g. Moreover, the new list of open problems is updated to conc((s, c), open), namely the pair (s, c) is added in front of argument open.

Any recursive call of build-plan-aux updates the current plan pl'. If all these recursive calls are successful, then the final value of plan pl' is returned. If any of the recursive calls returns ⊥, then the next combination of assign decomposition, progress component and action is tried. If all these combinations fail, then no plan is found and ⊥ is returned.

22.6 Conformant Planning

The problem of conformant planning is the result of the assumption that no observation is available at run time. In such a setting, the execution will have to proceed blindly, without the possibility to acquire any information. Intuitively, we model the absence of information by associating each state to the same observation.

Definition 22.6.1 (Unobservable domain). *A planning domain* $\mathcal{D} = \langle \mathcal{S}, \mathcal{A}, \mathcal{O}, \mathcal{I}, \mathcal{R}, \mathcal{X} \rangle$ *is unobservable iff* $\mathcal{O} = \{\bullet\}$ *and* $\mathcal{X}(s) = \bullet$.

Since only one observation is available, it conveys no information at all. Therefore, plans can only depend on the length of the history, since $\mathcal{O}^*$ is a sequence of bullets. In this setting, meaningful plans can be presented as sequences of actions.

Definition 22.6.2 (Sequential plan). *Let* $a_1, \ldots, a_n$ *be a sequence of actions. Then, the corresponding plan is defined for any history of length* $i \leqslant n$, *and returns* a_i.

The problem of conformant planning requires to find a *strong* solution, that guarantees goal achievement for all initial states, and for nondeterministic action effects.

Definition 22.6.3 (Goal for conformant planning). *Let* $\mathcal{G}$ *be a set of states. An execution tree* π *is a solution to a conformant planning problem* $\mathcal{G}$ *iff all the branches are finite and of the same length, and they all end in* $\mathcal{G}$.

At this point, it should be clear that the problem we are tackling is much harder than the classical planning problem. Suppose we are given a possible conformant plan, having a run from one initial state to the goal; we still have to check that it is a valid conformant plan, i.e., it is applicable in each state in $\mathcal{I}$, and that the final state of each run is in $\mathcal{G}$. In fact, conformant planning reduces to classical planning if the set of initial states is a singleton and the domain is deterministic.

We notice that the branching in the execution tree of a sequential plan is only due to the nondeterminism in the action effects, since the same action is executed regardless of the activity of the system. Therefore, the ith level in the tree represents all the possible system states which can be reached by the domain after the execution of the first n actions in the plan. We also notice that such states are in fact "indistinguishable". Based on this observation, conformant planning can be tackled as search in the space of *belief states*. A belief state is a nonempty set of states, intuitively expressing a condition of uncertainty, by collecting together all the states which are indistinguishable. Intuitively, a belief state can be used to capture the ith level of the execution tree associated with a sequence of actions.

Belief states are a convenient representation mechanism: instead of analyzing all the traces associated with a candidate plan, the associated set of states can be collected into a belief state. In this setting, conformant planning reduces to deterministic search in the space of belief states, called the *belief space*. The belief space for a given domain is basically the power-set of the set of states of the domain. For technical reasons, we explicitly restrict our reasoning to nonempty belief states, and define the belief space as $Pow^+(\mathcal{S}) \doteq Pow(\mathcal{S}) \setminus \emptyset$.

```
1   function HEURCONFORMANTFWD(I, G)
2       Open := {⟨I, ε⟩};
3       Closed := ∅;
4       Solved := False;
5       while (Open ≠ ∅ ∧ ¬Solved) do
6           ⟨Bs, π⟩ := EXTRACTBEST(Open);
7           INSERT(⟨Bs, π⟩, Closed);
8           if Bs ⊆ G then
9               Solved := True; Solution := π;
10          else
11              BsExp := FWDEXPANDBS(Bs);
12              BsPList := PRUNEBSEXPANSION(BsExp, Closed);
13              for ⟨Bsᵢ, aᵢ⟩ in BsPList do
14      INSERT(⟨Bsᵢ, π; aᵢ⟩, Open)
15              endfor
16          fi
17      done
18      if Solved then
19          return Solution;
20      else
21          return ⊥;
22      fi
23  end
```

Figure 22.7: The forward conformant planning algorithm.

The execution of actions is lifted from states to belief states by the following definition.

Definition 22.6.4 (Action applicability, execution). *An action a is applicable in a belief state Bs iff a is applicable in every state in Bs. If a is applicable in a belief state Bs, its execution in Bs, written Exec(a, Bs), is defined as follows*:

$$Exec(a, Bs) \doteq \{s' : s \in Bs \text{ and } s' \in \mathcal{R}(s, a)\}.$$

Definition 22.6.5 (Plan applicability, execution). *The execution of plan π in a belief state Bs, written Exec(π, Bs), is defined as follows*:

$Exec(ε, Bs) \quad \doteq Bs,$
$Exec(π, ⊥) \quad \doteq ⊥,$
$Exec(a; π, Bs) \doteq ⊥, \text{ if } a \text{ is not applicable in } Bs,$
$Exec(a; π, Bs) \doteq Exec(π, Exec(a, Bs)), \text{ otherwise.}$

⊥ *is a distinguished symbol representing violation of action applicability. Plan π is applicable in a belief state Bs iff Exec(π, Bs) ≠ ⊥.*

Fig. 22.7 depicts an algorithm for conformant planning. The algorithm searches the belief space, proceeding forwards from the set of initial states $\mathcal{I}$ towards the goal $\mathcal{G}$, and can be seen as a standard best-first algorithm, where search nodes are (uniquely indexed by) belief states. *Open* contains a list of open nodes to be expanded, and *Closed* contains a list of closed nodes that have already been expanded. After the initialization phase, *Open* contains (the node indexed by) $\mathcal{I}$, while *Closed* is empty. The algorithm then enters a loop, where it extracts a node from the open list, stores it into the closed list, and checks if it is a success node (line 8) (i.e., it a subset of $\mathcal{G}$); if so, a solution has been found and the iteration is exited. Otherwise, the successor nodes are generated, and the ones that have already been expanded are pruned. The remaining nodes are stored in *Open*, and the iteration restarts. Each belief state *Bs* is associated with a plan π, that is applicable in $\mathcal{I}$, and that results exactly in *Bs*, i.e., $Exec(\pi, \mathcal{I}) = Bs$.

The algorithm loops (lines 5–17) until either a solution has been found (*Solved* = *True*) or all the search space has been exhausted (*Open* = ∅). A belief state *Bs* is extracted from the open pool (line 6), and it is inserted in closed pool (line 7). The belief states *Bs* is expanded (line 11) by means of the FWDEXPANDBS primitive. PRUNEBSEXPANSION (line 12) removes from the result of the expansion of *Bs* all the belief state that are in the *Closed*, and returns the pruned list of belief states. If *Open* becomes empty and no solution has been found, the algorithm returns with $\bot$ to indicate that the planning problem admits no conformant solution. The expansion primitive FWDEXPANDBS takes as input a belief state *Bs*, and builds a set of pairs $\langle Bs_i, a_i \rangle$ such that a_i is executable in *Bs* and the execution of a_i in *Bs* is contained in Bs_i. Notice that a_i is a conformant solution for the planning problem of reaching Bs_i from any nonempty subset of *Bs*.

$$\text{FWDEXPANDBS}(Bs) \doteq \{\langle Bs_i, a_i \rangle \colon Bs_i = Exec(a_i, Bs) \neq \bot\}.$$

Function PRUNEBSEXPANSION takes as input a result of an expansion of a belief state and *Closed*, and returns the subset of the expansion containing the pairs where each belief state has not been expanded. The PRUNEBSEXPANSION function can be defined as:

$$\text{PRUNEBSEXPANSION}(BsP, Closed) \doteq$$
$$\{\langle Bs_i, a_i \rangle \colon \langle Bs_i, a_i \rangle \in BsP, \text{ and } \langle Bs_i, \pi \rangle \in Closed \text{ for no plan } \pi\}.$$

When an annotated belief state $\langle Bs, \pi \rangle$ is inserted in *Open*, INSERT checks if another annotated belief state $\langle Bs, \pi' \rangle$ exists; the length of π and π' are compared, and only the pair with the shortest plan is retained.

Obviously, the algorithm described above can implement several search strategies, e.g., depth-first or breadth-first, depending on the implementation of the functions EXTRACTBEST (line 6) and INSERT (line 14). Variations based on backward search have been explored, but are not reported here for lack of space.

22.7 Strong Planning under Partial Observability

We consider now the problem of strong planning under partial observability. The problem is characterized by a generic domain, without constraints on the observations.

As in the case of strong planning under full observability, the acceptable execution trees can be presented by a set of goal states, that must be reached regardless of the initial condition and of nondeterministic action effects.

Definition 22.7.1 (Goal for strong planning under partial observability). *Let G be a set of states. An execution tree π is a solution to a problem of strong planning under partial observability G iff all the branches are finite, and they all end in G.*

The availability of observations enables us to use richer plans than sequences: it is possible to delay at execution time the choice of the next action, depending on the observation, even in presence of uncertainty due to lack of full observability. Tree-shaped plans are needed, that define sequential courses of actions, which however depend on the observation that will arise at run time. Such tree-shaped plans correspond to the generic model of plans defined in Section 22.2, where observation histories identify specific courses of actions, with the only constraint that plans should not contain infinite branches.

Similarly to conformant planning, strong planning under partial observability can be solved by means of a search in the space of beliefs. In fact, conformant planning can be seen as a special case of planning with partial observability, where the observations are disregarded. The new element (with respect to conformant planning) is that the information conveyed by observations can be used to limit the uncertainty: the belief state modeling the current set of uncertainty can be reduced by ruling out the states that are incompatible with the observation. However, since the value of the observations that will occur during execution is not available at planning time, all possible options have to be taken into account: therefore, an observation "splits" a belief state in two belief states. These two belief states must both be solved in order to find a strong solution: for this reason, an AND/OR search in the space of beliefs is required (rather than a deterministic search).

Strong planning under full observability can also be seen as a special case of the problem addressed in this section. In fact, a memoryless policy can be mapped directly into a tree-shaped plan; however, the tree-shaped representation of the plan is potentially much more expensive than the memoryless policy representation (which is in essence a compact representation of a DAG). As far as the search algorithms are concerned, it would be possible to solve strong planning under full observability with an AND/OR search in the space of beliefs; however, full observability enables us to rule out uncertainty at execution time, so that all the belief states degenerate into singletons. In addition, the regressive search algorithm used with full observability is more amenable to deal with the branching factor due to nondeterminism than the progressive AND/OR search used with partial observability.

Finally, we notice that it would be in principle possible to reduce a problem of strong planning under partial observability to a problem of strong planning under full observability so that a regressive algorithm can be applied. However, this approach would results in an exponential blow up, due to the fact that a state would be required for every belief state in the original problem.

22.8 A Technological Overview

In this section, we overview the technologies underlying the main approaches to planning. Most of the work has been developed within the setting of classical planning. The first remark is that most of the planners work at the level of the language describing the domain, rather than explicitly manipulating an explicit representation of the domain, which is in principle exponentially larger. Historically, the first classical planners were based on techniques such as regression and partial order planning, trying to exploit the causal connection between (sub)goals and action effects. The first computation breakthrough is due to the introduction of Planning Graphs [7], that enable for a "less intelligent" but efficient and compact overapproximation of the state space. Planning based on satisfiability decision procedures [36] is based on the generation of a propositional satisfiability problem, that is satisfiable only if the planning problem admits a solution (of given bound); the problem is then solved by means of efficient propositional SAT solvers, that are typically able to solve structured problem with large number of variables. Each of the problems is limited to bounded-length, i.e., it looks for a strong solution of specified length l. When this does not exist, the bound is iteratively increased l until a solution is found or a specified limit is reached. More recently, classical planning has been tackled by means of the integration of planning graphs with heuristic search techniques [31].

Some of the techniques developed in the setting of classical planning have also been used to tackle the problems described in this paper. The work in [54, 41, 45] pioneered the problem of generating conditional plans by extending the seminal approaches to classical planning (e.g., regression, partial order planning). These works address the problem in the case of partial observability by exploiting the idea of "sensing actions", i.e., actions that when executed acquire information about the state of the domain. The proposed solutions never demonstrated experimentally the ability to scale up to nontrivial cases. Conformant and Sensorial Graphplan (CGP and SGP, resp.) [52, 55] were the first planners to extend planning graph techniques [7] to planning for reachability goals in the case of null observability and partial observability, respectively. These planners allowed for significant improvements in performance compared with previous extensions of classical planners. However, a practical weakness of this approach lies in the fact that algorithms are enumerative, i.e., a planning graph is built for each state that can be distinguished by observation. For this reason, both CGP and SGP are not competitive with more recent planners that address the same kind of problems. More recently, planning graphs used in cooperation with propositional satisfiability techniques in the CFF system, and efficient extension of the FF to deal with Conformant and Conditional planning [9, 32]. In CFF, planning graphs are used to compute heuristic measures and an AO*-like search is performed based on satisfiability techniques.

Among the planners based on reduction to a satisfiability problem, QBFPLAN [47] can deal with partial observability and reachability goals. The (bounded) planning problem is reduced to a QBF satisfiability problem, which is given in input to an efficient solver [48]. The approach exploits its symbolic approach to avoid exponential blow up caused by the explicit enumeration of states, but seems unable to scale up to large problems. Extensions to satisfiability techniques that can deal with conformant planning are reported in [11, 25].

A different approach to the problem of planning under partial observability is the idea of "Planning at the Knowledge Level", implemented in the PKS planner [42]. This approach is based on a representation of incomplete knowledge and sensing at a higher level of abstraction. The extension presented in [43] provides a limited solution to the problem of deriving complete conclusions from observations.

Situation Calculus [46] provides a rather expressive formalism that has been used to do automated planning by reasoning in first order logic. In situation calculus it is possible to reason about actions with nondeterministic effects, which can be represented with disjunctive formulas. Partial observability has also been represented through knowledge or sensing actions [51, 53]. The problem of making situation calculus competitive in terms of performance with other more automated planning techniques has been addressed by providing the ability to specify a plans as programs (see, e.g., the work on Golog [37]).

DLVK [20] reduces conformant planning to answer set programming, by exploiting the Disjunctive Datalog-based system DVL. The produced answer set is to be interpreted as a (parallel) plan. The domain description language of DLVK is $\mathcal{K}$, where it is possible to express incomplete information, action nondeterminism, and initial uncertainty; in particular, in $\mathcal{K}$ it is possible to express transitions between knowledge states, where predicates can be three-valued (known true, known false, unknown). DLVK can produce conformant plans by requiring the underlying DLVK engine to perform "secure" reasoning, which amounts to iteratively producing weak plans, i.e., plans that are not guaranteed to reach the goal, and checking their security. DLVK tackles bounded conformant planning problems, i.e., the length of plans must be provided to the system.

Several approaches are based on the extension of techniques developed in model checking [16]. Among these, SIMPLAN [35] adopts an explicit-state representations, which limits its applicability to large state spaces. It was however the first planners to deal with nondeterministic domains and goals expressed in LTL, in the case of full observability. [18] presents an automata based approach to formalize planning in deterministic domains. The work in [28, 30, 29] presents a method where model checking with timed automata is used to verify that generated plans meet timing constraints.

A more recent approach is the one based on symbolic model checking. The work on the MBP planner has addressed the problem of planning for reachability goals under full observability [13], conformant planning [14], planning for reachability goals under partial observability [5], and planning for temporally extended goals [44, 17]. The underlying idea of symbolic model checking that is exploited in MBP is the following: sets of states are represented as propositional formulas, and search through the state space is performed as a set of logical transformations over propositional formulas. Such logical transformations are implemented in planning algorithms by exploiting Binary Decision Diagrams (BDDs) [10], that allow for a compact representation and effective manipulation of propositional formulae. MBP accepts as input languages for the description of the domain the $\mathcal{AR}$ action language [26]. A description of how $\mathcal{AR}$ is used as an input language for the MBP planner is given in [12, 15]. Several experimental comparisons show that symbolic model checking techniques are very competitive for planning under uncertainty.

Other BDD-based approaches to the problem of strong planning under partial observability have been proposed in the YKA [49] and JUSSIPOP planners [50]. These planners perform a backward search in the space of beliefs. As such, observations are used to recombine beliefs, according to a fixed cardinality-based heuristics. Some planners that are based on symbolic model checking techniques restrict to the case of full observability, see, e.g., UMOP [33, 34], or to classical planning, see, e.g., MIPS [19].

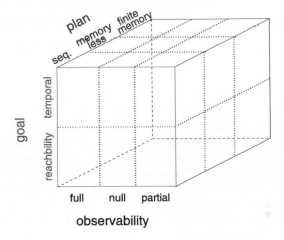

Figure 22.8: The different dimensions of a planning problem.

22.9 Conclusions

In this Chapter, we have proposed a general framework for planning, and instantiated it to some interesting planning problems. This is by no means exhaustive. Given the three planning components, domains, plans, and goals, one can think of different possible combinations (see Fig. 22.8).

We have started considering the case of *full observability*, and analyzing reachability and temporally extended goals. We have shown that memory-less plans are enough in the case of reachability goals, while finite-memory (or regular) plans are instead needed in the case of temporal goals. Of course, it would be possible to study the case in which we restrict acceptable solutions to memory-less plans, or plans with bounded memory. In fact, for temporally extended goals, some planning problems that can be solved with plans with finite but unbounded memory may have no solutions that are memory-less or bounded memory plans.

In addition, we have shown how *temporally extended goals* can be expressed in CTL. Different temporal logics can be used to express temporally extended goals, like Linear Time Logic (LTL), which has incomparable expressive power with respect to CTL (see [21] for a comparison), or more expressive temporal logics like CTL* or μ calculus, or specific languages for extended goals (see, e.g., [17, 2]).

In the case of *null observability*, we have just limited the analysis to reachability goals and sequential plans. We have not explored the case of null observability with temporally extended goals.

In the case of *partial observability*, the analysis is restricted to the case of reachability goals. Providing effective planning algorithm for the general case of partial observability and extended goals is a research challenge for the future. Some preliminary results in this directions are presented in [4, 6, 3].

Bibliography

[1] F. Bacchus and F. Kabanza. Using temporal logic to express search control knowledge for planning. *Artificial Intelligence*, 116(1–2):123–191, 2000.

[2] C. Baral and J. Zhao. Goal specification in presence of non-deterministic actions. In R.L. de Mántaras and L. Saitta, editors. *Proceedings of the 16th European Conference on Artificial Intelligence (ECAI-04)*, pages 273–277. IOS Press, 2004.

[3] P. Bertoli, A. Cimatti, and M. Pistore. Strong cyclic planning under partial observability. In *Proceedings of the 17th European Conference on Artificial Intelligence (ECAI-06)*, pages 580–584, Riva del Garda, Italy, August 2006. IOS Press.

[4] P. Bertoli, A. Cimatti, M. Pistore, and P. Traverso. A framework for planning with extended goals and partial observability. In *Proceedings of the International Conference on Automated Planning and Scheduling (ICAPS-03)*, June 2003.

[5] P. Bertoli, A. Cimatti, M. Roveri, and P. Traverso. Strong planning under partial observability. *Artificial Intelligence*, 170(4–5):337–384, 2006.

[6] P. Bertoli and M. Pistore. Planning with extended goals and partial observability. In *Proceedings the International Conference on Automated Planning and Scheduling (ICAPS-04)*, June 2004.

[7] A.L. Blum and M.L. Furst. Fast planning through planning graph analysis. *Artificial Intelligence*, 90(1–2):279–298, 1997.

[8] C. Boutilier, T. Dean, and S. Hanks. Decision-theoretic planning: structural assumptions and computational leverage. *Journal of Artificial Intelligence Research (JAIR)*, 11:1–94, 1999.

[9] R. Brafman and J. Hoffmann. Conformant planning via heuristic forward search: a new approach. In *Proceedings of the International Conference on Automated Planning and Scheduling (ICAPS-04)*, June 2004.

[10] R.E. Bryant. Graph-based algorithms for Boolean function manipulation. *IEEE Transactions on Computers*, C-35(8):677–691, August 1986.

[11] C. Castellini, E. Giunchiglia, and A. Tacchella. SAT-based planning in complex domains: Concurrency, constraints and nondeterminism. *Artificial Intelligence*, 147:85–118, 2003.

[12] A. Cimatti, E. Giunchiglia, F. Giunchiglia, and P. Traverso. Planning via model checking: a decision procedure for $\mathcal{AR}$. In *Proceeding of the Fourth European Conference on Planning (ECP-97)*, September 1997. Springer-Verlag.

[13] A. Cimatti, M. Pistore, M. Roveri, and P. Traverso. Weak, strong, and strong cyclic planning via symbolic model checking. *Artificial Intelligence*, 147(1–2):35–84, July 2003.

[14] A. Cimatti, M. Roveri, and P. Bertoli. Conformant planning via symbolic model checking and heuristic search. *Artificial Intelligence*, 159(1–2):127–206, November 2004.

[15] A. Cimatti, M. Roveri, and P. Traverso. Automatic OBDD-based generation of universal plans in non-deterministic domains. In *Proceeding of the Fifteenth National Conference on Artificial Intelligence (AAAI-98)*, Madison, WI, 1998. AAAI-Press.

[16] E.M. Clarke, E.A. Emerson, and A.P. Sistla. Automatic verification of finite-state concurrent systems using temporal logic specifications. *ACM Transactions on Programming Languages and Systems*, 8(2):244–263, 1986.

[17] U. Dal Lago, M. Pistore, and P. Traverso. Planning with a language for extended goals. In *Proceedings of the Eighteenth National Conference on Artificial Intelligence (AAAI-02)*, pages 447–454, Edmonton, Alberta, Canada, July 2002. AAAI-Press/The MIT Press.

[18] G. De Giacomo and M.Y. Vardi. Automata-theoretic approach to planning for temporally extended goals. In *Proceeding of the Fifth European Conference on Planning (ECP-99)*, September 1999. Springer-Verlag.

[19] S. Edelkamp and M. Helmert. On the implementation of MIPS. In *AIPS-Workshop on Model-Theoretic Approaches to Planning*, pages 18–25, 2000.

[20] T. Eiter, W. Faber, N. Leone, G. Pfeifer, and A. Polleres. A logic programming approach to knowledge-state planning, II: The DLVK system. *Artificial Intelligence*, 144(1–2):157–211, 2003.

[21] E.A. Emerson. Temporal and modal logic. In J. van Leeuwen, editor. *Handbook of Theoretical Computer Science, Volume B: Formal Models and Semantics*, pages 995–1072. Elsevier, 1990 (Chapter 16).

[22] R.E. Fikes and N.J. Nilsson. STRIPS: A new approach to the application of theorem proving to problem solving. *Artificial Intelligence*, 2(3–4):189–208, 1971.

[23] M. Gelfond and V. Lifschitz. Representing actions and change by logic programs. *Journal of Logic Programming*, 17(2–4):301–321, 1993.

[24] M. Ghallab, D. Nau, and P. Traverso. *Automated Planning: Theory and Practice*. Morgan Kaufmann Publishers, Inc., 2004.

[25] E. Giunchiglia. Planning as satisfiability with expressive action languages: Concurrency, constraints and nondeterminism. In *Proceedings of the Seventh International Conference on Principles of Knowledge Representation and Reasoning (KR-00)*, 2000.

[26] E. Giunchiglia, G.N. Kartha, and V. Lifschitz. Representing action: Indeterminacy and ramifications. *Artificial Intelligence*, 95(2):409–438, 1997.

[27] E. Giunchiglia and V. Lifschitz. An action language based on causal explanation: Preliminary report. In *Proceedings of the 15th National Conference on Artificial Intelligence (AAAI-98)*, Menlo Park, July 26–30 1998. AAAI Press.

[28] R.P. Goldman, D.J. Musliner, K.D. Krebsbach, and M.S. Boddy. Dynamic abstraction planning. In *Proceedings of the Fourteenth National Conference on Artificial Intelligence (AAAI-97) and Ninth Innovative Applications of Artificial Intelligence Conference (IAAI-97)*, pages 680–686. AAAI Press, 1997.

[29] R.P. Goldman, D.J. Musliner, and M.J. Pelican. Using model checking to plan hard real-time controllers. In *Proceeding of the AIPS2k Workshop on Model-Theoretic Approaches to Planning*, Breckeridge, CO, April 2000.

[30] R.P. Goldman, M. Pelican, and D.J. Musliner. Hard real-time mode logic synthesis for hybrid control: A CIRCA-based approach, March 1999. Working notes of the 1999 AAAI Spring Symposium on Hybrid Control.

[31] J. Hoffmann. FF: The fast-forward planning system. *AI Magazine*, 22(3):57–62, 2001.

[32] J. Hoffmann and R. Brafman. Contingent planning via heuristic forward search with implicit belief states. In *Proceedings of the International Conference on Automated Planning and Scheduling (ICAPS-05)*, 2005.

[33] R.M. Jensen and M.M. Veloso. OBDD-based universal planning for synchronized agents in non-deterministic domains. *Journal of Artificial Intelligence Research (JAIR)*, 13:189–226, 2000.

[34] R.M. Jensen, M.M. Veloso, and M.H. Bowling. OBDD-based optimistic and strong cyclic adversarial planning. In *Proceedings of the Sixth European Conference on Planning (ECP-01)*, 2001.

[35] F. Kabanza, M. Barbeau, and R. St-Denis. Planning control rules for reactive agents. *Artificial Intelligence*, 95(1):67–113, 1997.

[36] H.A. Kautz and B. Selman. Pushing the envelope: Planning, propositional logic, and stochastic search. In *Proceedings of the Thirteenth National Conference on Artificial Intelligence (AAAI-96) and Eighth Innovative Applications of Artificial Intelligence Conference (IAAI-96)*, 1996.

[37] H.J. Levesque, R. Reiter, Y. Lesperance, F. Lin, and R. Scherl. Golog: a logic programming language for dynamic domains. *Journal of Logic Programming*, 31:59–83, 1997.

[38] D. McDermott. PDDL—the planning domain definition language. Web page: http://www.cs.yale.edu/homes/dvm, 1998.

[39] E. Pednault. ADL: Exploring the middle ground between STRIPS and the situation calculus. In *Proceedings of the 1st International Conference on Principles of Knowledge Representation and Reasoning (KR-89)*, 1989.

[40] J.S. Penberthy and D.S. Weld. UCPOP: A sound, complete, partial order planner for ADL. In B. Nebel, C. Rich, and W. Swartout, editors, *Proceedings of the 3rd International Conference on Principles of Knowledge Representation and Reasoning (KR-92)*, pages 103–114, Cambridge, MA, October 1992. Morgan Kaufmann.

[41] M. Peot and D. Smith. Conditional nonlinear planning. In J. Hendler, editor, *Proceedings of the First International Conference on AI Planning Systems (ICAPS-92)*, pages 189–197, College Park, MD, June 15–17 1992. Morgan Kaufmann.

[42] R. Petrick and F. Bacchus. A knowledge-based approach to planning with incomplete information and sensing. In *Proceedings of the Sixth International Conference on Artificial Intelligence Planning and Scheduling (AIPS-02)*, 2002.

[43] R. Petrick and F. Bacchus. Extending the knowledge-based approach to planning with incomplete information and sensing. In *Proceedings of the International Conference on Automated Planning and Scheduling (ICAPS-04)*, pages 2–11, 2004.

[44] M. Pistore and P. Traverso. Planning as model checking for extended goals in non-deterministic domains. In *Proceedings of the Seventeenth International Joint Conference on Artificial Intelligence (IJCAI-01)*. AAAI Press, 2001.

[45] L. Pryor and G. Collins. Planning for contingency: A decision based approach. *J. of Artificial Intelligence Research*, 4:81–120, 1996.

[46] R. Reiter. The frame problem in the situation calculus: a simple solution (sometimes) and a completeness result for goal regression. In V. Lifschitz, editor. *Artificial Intelligence and Mathematical Theory of Computation: Papers in Honor of John McCarthy*, pages 359–380. Academic Press, 1991.

[47] J. Rintanen. Constructing conditional plans by a theorem-prover. *Journal of Artificial Intelligence Research*, 10:323–352, 1999.

[48] J. Rintanen. Improvements to the evaluation of quantified Boolean formulae. In T. Dean, editor, *Proceedings of the 16th International Joint Conference on Artificial Intelligence (IJCAI-99)*, pages 1192–1197. Morgan Kaufmann Publishers, August 1999.

[49] J. Rintanen. Backward plan construction for planning as search in belief space. In *Proceedings of the International Conference on AI Planning and Scheduling (AIPS-02)*, 2002.

[50] J. Rintanen. Research on conditional planning with partial observability: The Jussi-POP/BBSP planning system. Web page: http://www.informatik.uni-freiburg.de/rintanen/planning.html, 2004.

[51] R.B. Scherl and H.J. Levesque. Knowledge, action, and the frame problem. *Artificial Intelligence*, 144(1–2):1–39, 2003.

[52] D.E. Smith and D.S. Weld. Conformant Graphplan. In *Proceedings of the 15th National Conference on Artificial Intelligence (AAAI-98) and of the 10th Conference on Innovative Applications of Artificial Intelligence (IAAI-98)*, pages 889–896, Menlo Park, July 26–30, 1998. AAAI Press.

[53] T.C. Son and C. Baral. Formalizing sensing actions—a transition function based approach. *Artificial Intelligence*, 125(1–2):19–91, 2001.

[54] D. Warren. Generating conditional plans and programs. In *Proceedings of the Summer Conference on Artificial Intelligence and Simulation of Behaviour (AISB-76)*, 1976.

[55] D.S. Weld, C.R. Anderson, and D.E. Smith. Extending Graphplan to handle uncertainty and sensing actions. In *Proceedings of the 15th National Conference on Artificial Intelligence (AAAI-98) and of the 10th Conference on Innovative Applications of Artificial Intelligence (IAAI-98)*, pages 897–904, Menlo Park, July 26–30, 1998. AAAI Press.

Handbook of Knowledge Representation
Edited by F. van Harmelen, V. Lifschitz and B. Porter
© 2008 Elsevier B.V. All rights reserved
DOI: 10.1016/S1574-6526(07)03023-4

Chapter 23

Cognitive Robotics

Hector Levesque and Gerhard Lakemeyer

This chapter is dedicated to the memory of Ray Reiter. It is also an overview of cognitive robotics, as we understand it to have been envisaged by him.[1] Of course, nobody can control the use of a term or the direction of research. We apologize in advance to those who feel that other approaches to cognitive robotics and related problems are inadequately represented here.

23.1 Introduction

In its most general form, we take *cognitive robotics* to be the study of the knowledge representation and reasoning problems faced by an autonomous robot (or agent) in a dynamic and incompletely known world. To quote from a manifesto by Levesque and Reiter [42]:

"Central to this effort is to develop an understanding of the relationship between the knowledge, the perception, and the action of such a robot. The sorts of questions we want to be able to answer are

- to execute a program, what information does a robot need to have at the outset vs. the information that it can acquire *en route* by perceptual means?

- what does the robot need to know about its environment vs. what need only be known by the designer?

- when should a robot use perception to find out if something is true as opposed to reasoning about what it knows was true in the past?

- when should the inner workings of an action be available to the robot for reasoning and when should the action be considered primitive or atomic?

and so on. With respect to robotics, our goal (like that of many in AI) is *high-level robotic control*: develop a system that is capable of generating actions in the world that are appropriate

---

[1] To the best of our knowledge, the term was first used publicly by Reiter at his lecture on receiving the IJCAI Award for Research Excellence in 1993.

as a function of some current set of beliefs and desires. What we do *not* want to do is to simply engineer robot controllers that solve a class of problems or that work in a class of application domains. For example, if it turns out that online reasoning is unnecessary for some task, we would want to know what it is about the task that makes it so."

We take this idea of knowledge representation and reasoning *for the purpose of* high-level robotic control to be central to cognitive robotics [71]. This connects cognitive robotics not only to (traditional, less cognitive) robotics but also, as discussed later, to other areas of AI such as planning and agent-oriented programming.

To illustrate the knowledge representation and reasoning issues relevant to high-level robotic control, we will use Reiter's variant of the situation calculus. There are several reasons for this: we, the authors, have worked with the situation calculus and hence feel most comfortable with it; the situation calculus is a very expressive formalism which can be used to model many of the features relevant to cognitive robotics; it was already introduced at length in a chapter of this volume (which we assume as a prerequisite), so that we do not need to present it from scratch; and last but not least, it is a tribute to Ray Reiter. For a book length treatment of cognitive robotics *not* based on the situation calculus, see [81].

The structure of the this chapter is as follows. In Section 23.2, we discuss some of the knowledge representation issues that arise in the context of cognitive robotics. In Section 23.3, we turn to problems in automated reasoning in the same setting. In Section 23.4, we examine how knowledge representation and reasoning come to bear on the issue of high-level agent control. Finally, in Section 23.5, we briefly draw conclusions and suggest a direction for future research.

23.2   Knowledge Representation for Cognitive Robots

As a special sort of knowledge-based system, cognitive robots need to represent knowledge about relevant parts of the world they inhabit. What makes them special is the emphasis on knowledge about the *dynamics* of the world, including, the robot's own actions. In currently implemented systems, knowledge about objects in the world can be very simple, as in robotic soccer [21], where little is known beyond their position on a soccer field, to the very complex, involving knowledge about the actual shape of the objects [56, 67]. Likewise, knowledge about actions can be as simple as taking an action to be a discrete change of position from *A* to *B*, or fairly involved with probabilistic models of success and failure [23, 22].

But whatever the application, the key feature of cognitive robotics is the focus on a changing world. A suitable knowledge representation language must at the very least provide *fluents*, that is, predicate or function symbols able to change their values as a result of changes in the world. For our purposes, we will use the situation calculus; but there are many other possible choices, modal vs. nonmodal, state-based vs. history-based, time-based vs. action-based, and so on.[2] Each of these will need to address similar sorts of issues such as the frame, qualification, and ramification problems, discussed in the Situation Calculus chapter, and in [66].

---

[2] While planning languages like STRIPS [28] or PDDL [53] also qualify and have been used to control robots [51, 57, 20], they are more limited in that they only specify planning problems, but do not lend themselves to a general representation and reasoning framework for cognitive robots as advocated by Reiter.

23.2.1 Varieties of Actions

In its simplest setting, the situation calculus is used to model actions that change the world in a discrete fashion and instantaneously. For robotic applications, this is usually far too limited and we need much richer varieties. Let us begin with actions which are continuous and have a duration. A simple idea to accommodate both is due to Pinto [54], who proposed to split, say, a *pickup* action into two (instantaneous) *startPickup* and *endPickup* actions with an additional time argument and a new fluent *Pickingup* with the following successor state axiom:

$$Pickingup(x, t, do(a, s)) \equiv \exists t'(a = startPickup(x, t') \wedge t' \leqslant t) \vee$$
$$Pickingup(x, t, s) \wedge \neg \exists t'(a = endPickup(x, t') \wedge t' \leqslant t).$$

While this works fine for some applications,[3] having to explicitly specify time points when an action starts and ends is often cumbersome if not impossible. An alternative approach, first introduced by Pinto [54] and later adapted by Grosskreutz and Lakemeyer [30] is to define fluents as continuous functions of time. For example, a robot's location while moving may be approximated by a linear function taking as arguments the starting time of the moving action and the robot's velocity. Using the special action called *waitFor*(ϕ) time advances until the condition ϕ becomes true. The use of *waitFor* was actually inspired by robot programming languages like RPL [49]. For an approach to continuous change in the event calculus see [68].

The situation calculus also deals with actions whose effects are deterministic, that is, where there is no doubt as to which fluents change and which do not. In practice, however, the world is often not that clear cut. For example, the robot's gripper may be slippery and the *pickup* action may sometimes fail, that is, sometimes it holds the object in its gripper afterwards and sometimes it does not. There have been a number of proposals to model nondeterministic effects such as [78, 27, 4]. On a more fine-grained level, which is often more appropriate in robotics applications, one also attaches probabilities to the various outcomes. Reiter's stochastic situation calculus [62], for example, achieves this by appealing to nature choosing among various deterministic actions according to some probability distribution. For example, imagine that when the robot executes a *pickup* action, nature actually chooses one of two deterministic actions *pickupS* and *pickupF*, which stand for a successful and failed attempt and which occur, say, with probabilities 0.95 and 0.05, respectively. A nice feature of this approach is that successor state axioms can be defined as usual because they only appeal to nature's choices, which are then deterministic.

23.2.2 Sensing

In the situation calculus, actions are typically thought of as changes to the world, in particular, those which are due to a robot's actuators. Sensing actions, which provide the robot with information about what the world is like but leave the world unchanged otherwise, are of equal importance from a robot's perspective. Various ways to model sensing in the situation calculus have been proposed. One is to introduce a special

---

[3]Thinking of *all* actions as instantaneous in this way also has the advantage of reducing the need for true action parallelism, allowing us to use the much simpler variant of interleaved concurrency [17].

fluent $SF(a, s)$ (for *sensed fluent value*) and axioms describing how the truth value of SF becomes correlated with those aspects of a situation which are being sensed by action a [41]. For example, suppose we have a sensing action $senseRed(x)$, which registers whether the color of object x is red. This can be captured by the following axiom:

$$SF(senseRed(x), s) \equiv Colour(x, red, s).$$

The idea is that, when the robot executes $senseRed$, its sensors or perhaps more concretely, its image processing system, returns a truth value, which then tells the robot whether the object in question is red. We can use this predicate to define what the robot learns by doing actions $a_1, a_2, \ldots, a_n$ in situation s and obtaining binary sensing results $r_1, r_2, \ldots, r_n$:

$$Sensed(\langle\rangle, \langle\rangle, s) \overset{\text{def}}{=} True;$$

$$Sensed(\vec{a} \cdot A, \vec{r} \cdot 1, s) \overset{\text{def}}{=} SF(A, do(\vec{a}, s)) \wedge Sensed(\vec{a}, \vec{r}, s);$$

$$Sensed(\vec{a} \cdot A, \vec{r} \cdot 0, s) \overset{\text{def}}{=} \neg SF(A, do(\vec{a}, s)) \wedge Sensed(\vec{a}, \vec{r}, s).$$

In general, of course, sensing results are not binary. For example, reading the temperature could mean returning an integer or real number. See [75] on how these can be represented. Noisy sensors can be dealt with as well, as shown in [3, 69]. For the distinction between sensing and perception, see [55].

Sensing the color of an object is usually deliberate, that is, the robot chooses to actively execute an appropriate sensing action. There are, however, cases where sensing results are provided in a more passive fashion. Consider, for example, a robot's need to localize itself in its environment. In practice, this is often achieved using probabilistic techniques such as [82], which continuously output estimates of a robot's pose relative to a map of the environment. Grosskreutz and Lakemeyer [32] show how to deal with this issue using so-called *exogenous* actions. These behave like ordinary nonsensing actions, which change the value of fluents like the robot's location. The only difference is that they are not issued by the robot "at will", but are provided by some external means. See also [15, 64] for how passive sensors can be represented by other means. Exogenous actions are not limited to account for passive sensing. In general, they can be used to model actions which are not under the control of the robot, including those performed by other agents.

23.2.3 Knowledge

When a robot has a model of its environment in the form of, say, a basic action theory, this represents what the agent *knows* or *believes* about the world. Yet so far there is no explicit notion of knowledge as part of the theory, and this may not be necessary, if we are interested only in the logical consequences of that theory. However, this changes when we need to refer to what the robot does *not* know, which is useful, for example, when deciding whether or not to sense. We need an explicit account of knowledge also when it comes to knowledge about the mental life (including knowledge) of other agents. In the situation calculus, knowledge is modeled possible-world style[4] by introducing a special fluent $K(s', s)$, which is read as "situation s' is (epistemically)

---

[4]Modeling knowledge using possible worlds is due to Hintikka [35].

accessible from s". Let $\phi[s]$ be a formula that is uniform in s. Then knowing ϕ at a situation s, written as $Knows(\phi, s)$, means that ϕ is true in all accessible situations:

$$Knows(\phi, s) \stackrel{\text{def}}{=} \forall s'. K(s', s) \supset \phi[s'].$$

This idea of reifying possible worlds was first introduced by Moore [50]. Later, Scherl and Levesque [75] showed that the way an agent's knowledge changes as a result of actions can be captured by a successor state axiom for the fluent K:

$$K(s'', do(a, s)) \equiv \exists s'. s'' = do(a, s') \wedge K(s', s) \wedge [SF(a, s') \equiv SF(a, s)].$$

In words: a situation s'' is accessible after action a is performed in s just in case it is the result of doing a in some other situation s' which is accessible from s and which agrees with s on the value of SF. The effect of this axiom is, roughly, that it eliminates from further consideration all those situations which disagree with the result of sensing. For example, if a $senseRed(A)$ action returns the value $true$, only those situations remain accessible after performing the action where A is red. Note that this notion of epistemic alternatives generalizes the situation calculus discussed in the chapter of this volume in that we now assume that there are initial situations other than S_0.[5] One nice feature of the successor state axiom for K is that general properties of the accessibility relationship like reflexivity or transitivity only need to be stipulated for initial situations, as they are guaranteed to hold ever after [75]. For a treatment of knowledge and sensing in the fluent calculus, see [79]. For approach to knowledge in the situation calculus that avoids using additional situations, see [19].

Besides knowledge, there are many other mental attitudes that a cognitive robot may find useful to model. Proposals exist, for example, to model *goal* or *ability*, also using a possible-world semantics [74, 39, 47, 36]. The issue of belief change after receiving information that conflicts with what is currently known about the world has also been addressed [72, 73]. Here a preference relation over situations plays an essential role.

23.3 Reasoning for Cognitive Robots

The research problems in cognitive robotics are not limited to problems in representation seen in the previous section. We are fundamentally concerned with how these representations are to be *reasoned* with, and furthermore, as we will see in the next section, how this reasoning can be used to control the behavior of the robots.

23.3.1 Projection via Progression and Regression

There are two related reasoning tasks that play a special role in cognitive robotics. The main one is called the (temporal) *projection task*: determining whether or not some condition will hold after a sequence of actions has been performed starting in some initial state. The second one is called the *legality task*: determining whether a sequence of actions *can* be performed starting in some initial state. Assuming we have access to the preconditions of actions, legality reduces to projection, since we can

---

[5] Instead of a single tree rooted at S_0, we now have a forest of trees each with their own initial situation.

determine legality by verifying that the preconditions of each action in the sequence are satisfied in the state just before the action is executed. Projection is a very basic task since it is necessary for a number of other larger tasks, including planning and high-level program execution, as we will see in the next section.

We can summarize the definition of projection from the Situation Calculus chapter as follows: given an action theory $\mathcal{D}$, a sequence of ground action terms, $a_1, \ldots, a_n$, and a formula $\phi[s]$ that is uniform in s, the task is to determine whether or not

$$\mathcal{D} \models \phi[do(\vec{a}, S_0)].$$

As explained in that chapter, one of the main results proved by Reiter in his initial paper on the frame problem [61] is that the projection problem can be solved by *regression*: when $\mathcal{D}$ is a basic action theory (as defined in the earlier chapter), there is a regression operator $\mathcal{R}$, such that for any ϕ uniform in s,

$$\mathcal{D} \models \phi[do(\vec{a}, S_0)] \quad \text{iff} \quad \mathcal{D}_{una} \cup \mathcal{D}_{S_0} \models \phi'[S_0],$$

where $\mathcal{D}_{S_0}$ is the part of $\mathcal{D}$ that characterizes S_0, and $\phi' = \mathcal{R}(\phi, \vec{a})$. So to solve the projection problem, it is sufficient, to regress the formula using the given actions, and then to determine whether the result holds in the initial situation, a much simpler entailment.

Regression has proven to be a powerful method for reasoning about a dynamic world, reducing it to reasoning about a static initial situation. However, it does have a serious drawback. Imagine a long-lived robot that has performed thousands or even millions of actions in its lifetime, and which at some point, needs to determine whether some condition currently holds. Regression involves transforming this condition back through the thousands or millions of actions, and then determining whether the transformed condition held initially. This is not an ideal way of staying up to date.

The alternative to regression is *progression*. In this case, we look for a progression operator $\mathcal{P}$ that can transform an initial database $\mathcal{D}_{S_0}$ into the database that results after performing an action. More precisely, we want to have that

$$\mathcal{D} \models \phi[do(\vec{a}, S_0)] \quad \text{iff} \quad \mathcal{D}_{una} \cup \mathcal{D}'_0 \models \phi[S_0],$$

where $\mathcal{D}_{S_0}$ is the part of $\mathcal{D}$ that characterizes S_0, and $\mathcal{D}'_0 = \mathcal{P}(\mathcal{D}_{S_0}, \vec{a})$. The idea is that as actions are performed, a robot would change its database about the initial situation, so that to determine if ϕ held after doing actions $\vec{a}$, it would be sufficient to determine if ϕ held in the progressed situation (with no further actions), again a much simpler entailment. Moreover, unlike the case with regression, a robot can use its *mental idle time* (for example, while it is performing physical actions) to keep its database up to date. If it is unable to keep up, it is easy to imagine using regression until the database is fully progressed.

There are, however, drawbacks with progression as well. For one thing, it is geared to answering questions about the *current* situation only. In progressing a database forward, we effectively lose the historical information about what held in the past. It is, in other words, a form of *forgetting* [45, 38]. While questions about a current situation can reasonably be expected to be the most common, they are not the only meaningful ones.

A more serious concern with progression is that it is not always possible. As Lin and Reiter show [46], there are simple cases of basic action theories where there is no operator $\mathcal{P}$ with the properties we want. (More precisely, the desired $\mathcal{D}'_0$ would not be first-order definable.) To have a well-defined projection operator, it is necessary to impose further restrictions on the sorts of action theories we will use.

23.3.2 Reasoning in Closed and Open Worlds

So far, we have assumed like Reiter, that $\mathcal{D}_{S_0}$ is any collection of formulas uniform in S_0. Regression reduces the projection problem to that of calculating logical consequences of $\mathcal{D}_{S_0}$. In practice, however, we would like to reduce it to a much more tractable problem than ordinary first-order logical entailment. It is quite common for applications to assume that $\mathcal{D}_{S_0}$ satisfies additional constraints: domain closure, unique names, and the closed-word assumption [60]. With these, for all practical purposes, $\mathcal{D}_{S_0}$ does behave like a database, and the entailment problem becomes one of database query evaluation. Furthermore, progression is well defined, and behaves like an ordinary database transaction.

Even without using (relational) database technology, the advantage of having a $\mathcal{D}_{S_0}$ constrained in this way is significant. For example, it allows us to use Prolog technology directly to perform projection. For example, to find out if $(\phi \lor \psi)$ holds, it is sufficient to determine if ϕ holds or if ψ holds; to find out if $\neg\phi$ holds, it is sufficient to determine if ϕ does not hold (using negation as failure), and so on. None of these are possible with an unconstrained $\mathcal{D}_{S_0}$.

This comes at a price, however. The unique name, domain closure and closed-world assumptions amount to assuming that we have *complete knowledge* about S_0: anytime we cannot infer that ϕ holds, it will be because we are inferring that $\neg\phi$ holds. We will never have the status of ϕ undecided.

This is obviously a very strong assumption in a cognitive robotic setting, where it is quite natural to assume that a robot will not know everything there is to know about its world. Indeed we would expect that a cognitive robot might start with incomplete knowledge, and only acquire the information it needs by actively *sensing* its environment as necessary.

A proposal for modifying Reiter's proposal for the projection problem along these lines was made by de Giacomo et al. [15]. They show that a modified version of regression can be made to work with sensing information. They also consider how closed-world reasoning can be used in an open world using what they call *just-in-time queries*. In a nutshell, they require that queries be evaluated only in situations where enough sensing has taken place to give complete information about the query. Overall, the knowledge can be incomplete, but it will be locally complete, and allow us to use closed-world techniques.

Another independent proposal for dealing effectively with open-world reasoning is that of Liu and Levesque [48]. (A related proposal is made by Son and Baral [76] and by Amir and Russell [1].) They show that what they call *proper knowledge bases* represent open-world knowledge. They define a form of progression for these knowledge bases that provides an efficient solution to the projection problem that is always logically sound, and under certain circumstances, also logically complete. The restrictions involve the type of successor-state axioms that appear in the action theory $\mathcal{D}$: they require action theories that are *local-effect* (actions only change the properties of the objects that are parameters of the action) and *context-complete* (either the actions are context-free or there is complete knowledge about the context of the context-dependent ones).

23.4 High-Level Control for Cognitive Robots

As noted earlier, one distinguishing characteristic of the area of cognitive robotics is that the knowledge representation and reasoning are for a particular purpose: the control of robots or agents. We reason about a world that is changing as the result of actions taken by agents *because* we are attempting to decide what to do, what actions to take towards some goal. This is in contrast, for example, to reasoning for the purposes of answering questions or generating explanations.

23.4.1 Classical Planning

Perhaps the clearest case of this application of knowledge representation and reasoning is in *classical planning* [29]. As discussed in the Situation Calculus chapter, we are given an action theory $\mathcal{D}$ of the sort discussed above and a goal formula, $\phi[s]$ that is uniform in some situation variable s. The task is to find a sequence of ground actions terms $\vec{a}$ such that

$$\mathcal{D} \models \phi[do(\vec{a}, S_0)] \wedge \textit{Executable}(do(\vec{a}, S_0)).$$

Thus, we are looking for a sequence of actions which, according to what we know in $\mathcal{D}$, can be legally executed starting in S_0 and result in a state where ϕ holds.

Think of having a robot, and wanting it to achieve some goal ϕ. Instead of simply programming it directly, we get the robot to use what is known about the initial state of the world and the actions available to figure out what to do to achieve the goal. This has the very desirable effect that if information about the world changes, that is, if we learn something new, or discover that something old was incorrect, it will not be necessary to reprogram the robot. All we need do is revise its beliefs. Using the terminology of Zenon Pylyshyn [58], we have an architecture that is *cognitively penetrable* in that the behavior of the robot can be altered by simply changing its beliefs about the world.

In practice, very little of the actual research in classical planning is formulated using the situation calculus in this way. Rather, it is expressed in the more restrictive notation of STRIPS [28]. Instead of an action theory, we have an the initial database formulated as a set of atomic formulas (with an implicit closed-world assumption), and a collection of actions formulated as operators on databases, with preconditions and effects characterized by the additions and deletions they would make to a current database. Although STRIPS has a very operational flavor, it is possible to reconstruct its logical basis in the situation calculus [44, 46].

Despite the restrictions imposed by STRIPS, the classical planning task remains extremely difficult. Even in the propositional case (and with complete knowledge about the initial world state), the problem is NP-hard [10]. While many optimizations exist for many special cases, nobody would consider planning as a *practical* way of generating the millions of action that might be required of a long-lived robot to achieve long-term goals starting from some initial state.

But this is an unreasonable picture anyway. Nobody would expect *people* to deal with their long-term goals by first closing their eyes and computing a sequence of millions of action, and then blindly carrying out the sequence to achieve the goal, even assuming such a sequence were to exist. This is an *offline* view of how to decide what to do. We need to consider a much more *online* view of high-level control, where as actions are taken, new information that is acquired gets to contribute to the decision-making. Instead of planning in advance for all possible long-term contingencies, we need to be able to get a robot to achieve some part of a goal, assess its current situation, and plan for the rest with the new information taken into account.

23.4.2 High-Level Offline Robot Programming

In an attempt to come up with a more flexible sort of control, one of the directions that has proven to be quite fruitful is the *high-level programming* [42] found in languages such as those in the Golog family [43, 17, 16, 62] and variants like FLUX [80]. Virtually all of the high-level control currently considered in cognitive robotics is of this sort. This brings cognitive robotics closer to the area of *agent-oriented programming* or AOP (see [33, 59], for example).[6]

By a high-level program, we mean a program that contains the usual programming features (like sequence, conditional, iteration, recursive procedures, concurrency) and some novel ones:

- the *primitive statements* of the program are the actions that are characterized by an action theory;

- the *tests* in the program are conditions about the world formulated in the underlying knowledge representation language;

- programs may contain *nondeterministic* operations, where a reasoned choice must be made among alternatives.[7]

Instead of planning given a goal, we now consider program execution given a high-level program. In the situation calculus, Levesque et al. [43] make this precise as follows: they define an operator $Do(\delta, s, s')$ that maps any high-level program δ into a formula of the situation calculus with two free variables s and s'. Intuitively $Do(\delta, s, s')$ is intended to say that if program δ starts in situation s, one of the situations it may legally terminate in (since the program need not be deterministic) is s'. This is defined inductively on the structure of the program:

Primitive action: $Do(A, s, s') \stackrel{\text{def}}{=} Poss(A, s) \wedge s' = do(A, s)$;

Test: $Do(\phi?, s, s') \stackrel{\text{def}}{=} \phi[s] \wedge s' = s$;

Sequence: $Do(\delta_1; \delta_2, s, s') \stackrel{\text{def}}{=} \exists s''.Do(\delta_1, s, s'') \wedge Do(\delta_2, s'', s)$;

Nondeterministic branch: $Do(\delta_1|\delta_2, s, s') \stackrel{\text{def}}{=} Do(\delta_1, s, s') \vee Do(\delta_2, s, s')$;

---

[6]This is perhaps a difference of emphasis only: cognitive robotics tends to emphasize the robotic interaction with the world, whereas AOP tends to emphasize the mental state of the agent executing the program.

[7]In many applications, we can preserve the effectiveness of an essentially deterministic situation calculus by pushing the nondeterminism into the programming.

Nondeterministic value: $Do(\pi x.\ \delta, s, s') \overset{\text{def}}{=} \exists x.\ Do(\delta, s, s')$;

Nondeterministic iteration: $Do(\delta^*, s, s') \overset{\text{def}}{=} \forall P[\forall s_1 P(s_1, s_1) \wedge \forall s_1 s_2 s_3 (P(s_1, s_2) \wedge Do(\delta, s_2, s_3)) \supset P(s_1, s_3)) \supset P(s, s')].$

Other programming common constructs can be defined in terms of these:

if ϕ **then** δ_1 **else** $\delta_2 \overset{\text{def}}{=} (\phi?; \delta_1)|(\neg\phi?; \delta_2)$;

while ϕ **do** $\delta \overset{\text{def}}{=} (\phi?; \delta)^*; \neg\phi?.$

The *offline high-level program execution task* then is the following: given a high-level program δ find a sequence of actions $\vec{a}$ such that

$$\mathcal{D} \models Do(\delta, S_0, do(\vec{a}, S_0)).$$

As with planning, we solve this task and then give the resulting action sequence to the robot for execution.

While this is still completely offline like planning, it does allow for far more flexibility in the specification of behavior. Consider, for example, a high-level program like the following

$$A_1;\ A_2;\ A_3;\ \ldots A_n;\ \phi?$$

where each A_i is a primitive action and ϕ is some condition. This program can only be executed in one way, that is, by performing the A_i in sequence and then confirming that ϕ holds in the final state (or fail otherwise). We would naturally expect that solving the execution task for this program would be trivial, even if n were large, since the program already contains the answer. At the other extreme, consider a program like the following:

while $\neg\phi$ **do** $\pi a.\ a.$

This is a very nondeterministic program. It says: while ϕ is false, pick an action a and do it. A correct execution of this program is a sequence of actions that can be legally executed and such that ϕ holds in the final state. But finding such a sequence is precisely the planning task for ϕ. So the execution task for this program is no different than the general planning task. However, it is between these two extremes that we can see advantages over planning. Consider this variant:

while $\neg\phi$ **do** $\pi a.\ Acceptable(a)?;\ a.$

In this case, we have modified the previous program to include a test that the nondeterministically selected action a must satisfy. Assuming we have appropriate domain-dependent knowledge (represented in $\mathcal{D}$) about this *Acceptable* predicate, we can constrain the planning choices at each stage anyway we like, such as in the forward filtering of [2]. Similarly, we can generalize the first example as in the following:

$$A_1;\ A_2;\ A_3;\ [\textbf{while}\ \neg\psi\ \textbf{do}\ \pi a.a];\ A_4;\ (A_5|B_5);\ \phi?.$$

In this case, we begin the same way, but then we must solve a (presumably easier) subplanning problem to achieve ψ, then perform A_4, followed by either A_5 or B_5 as appropriate. In a nutshell, what we see here is that the high-level program can provide as much or as little procedural guidance as deemed necessary for high-level robot control.

This strategy has proven to be very effective. Among some of the applications built in this way, we mention an automated banking agent that involved a 40-page Golog program [63]. This is an example of high-level specification that would have been completely infeasible formulated as a planning problem.

When a program contains nondeterministic actions, all that matters about the actual choices is that they lead to a successful execution of the entire program. There is no reason to prefer one execution over another. However, real decision making often involves determining which choices are *better* than others. One way to address this issue is to attach numerical *rewards* to situations. Consider, for example, a robot whose only job is to collect objects, but with a preference for red ones. We might use the following successor state axiom for *reward*:

$$reward(do(a, s)) = r \equiv$$

$$\exists x (a = pickup(x) \land Colour(x, red, s) \land r = reward(s) + 10) \lor$$

$$\exists x (a = pickup(x) \land \neg Colour(x, red, s) \land r = reward(s) + 5) \lor$$

$$\neg \exists x (a = pickup(x) \land r = reward(s)).$$

The operator $Do(\delta, s, s')$ introduced above is then replaced by $BestDo(\delta, s, s')$ which selects sequences of actions that maximize accumulated reward. Note that, in the above example, this does not necessarily mean that the robot will always pick up a red object if one is available, as even higher rewards may be unattainable if a red object is picked up now. When combining the idea of maximizing rewards with probabilistic actions, we obtain a decision-theoretic version of Golog, which was first proposed in [8].

23.4.3 High-Level Online Robot Programming

The version of high-level programming we have considered so far has been *offline*. A more online version is considered by de Giacomo et al. [16, 65]. Instead of using *Do* to define the complete execution of a program, they consider the single-step method first-used to define the offline execution of ConGolog [17]. This is done in terms of two predicates, $Final(\delta, s)$, and $Trans(\delta, s, \delta', s')$. Intuitively, $Final(\delta, s)$ holds when program δ can legally terminate in situation s, and $Trans(\delta, s, \delta', s')$ holds when program δ can legally take one step resulting in situation s', with δ' remaining to be executed. It is then possible to redefine the *Do* in terms of these two predicates[8]:

$$Do(\delta, s, s') \stackrel{\text{def}}{=} \exists \delta' (Trans^*(\delta, S_0, \delta', s') \land Final(\delta', s')),$$

where $Trans^*$ is defined as the reflexive transitive closure of $Trans$.[9]

---

[8]Much of the work with *Trans* and *Final* requires quantifying over and therefore reifying programs. Some care is required here to ensure consistency since programs may contain formulas in them. See [17] for details.

[9]To talk about reflexitivity and transitivity, we can consider *Trans* to be a binary relation over configurations, where a configuration is a pair consisting of a program and a situation.

Now imagine that we started with some program δ_0 in S_0, and that at some later point we have executed certain actions $a_1, \ldots, a_k$, and that we have obtained sensing results $r_1, \ldots r_k$ from them, with program δ remaining to be executed. The *online high-level program execution task* then is to find out what to do next, defined by:

- stop, if $\mathcal{D} \cup Sensed(\vec{a}, \vec{r}, S_0) \models Final(\delta, do(\vec{a}, S_0))$;

- return the remaining program δ', if

$$\mathcal{D} \cup Sensed(\vec{a}, \vec{r}, S_0) \models Trans(\delta, do(\vec{a}, S_0), \delta', do(\vec{a}, S_0)),$$

  and no action is required in this step;

- return action b and δ', if

$$\mathcal{D} \cup Sensed(\vec{a}, \vec{r}, S_0) \models Trans(\delta, do(\vec{a}, S_0), \delta', do(b, do(\vec{a}, S_0))).$$

So the online version of program execution uses the sensing information that has been accumulated so far to decide if it should terminate, take a step of the program with no action required, or take a step with a single action required. In the case that an action is required, the robot can be instructed to perform the action, gather any sensing information this provides, and the online execution process iterates.

The online execution of a high-level program has the advantage of not requiring a reasoner to determine a lengthy course of action, requiring perhaps millions of actions, before executing the first step in the world. It also gets to use the sensing information provided by the first n actions performed so far in deciding what the $(n + 1)$ action should be. On the other hand, once an action has been executed in the world, there may be no way of backtracking if it is later found out that a nondeterministic choice was resolved incorrectly. In other words, an online execution of a program may fail where an offline execution would succeed.

To deal with this issue, de Giacomo et al. propose a new programming construct, a *search operator*. The idea is that given any program δ the program $\Sigma(\delta)$ executes online just like δ does offline. In other words, before taking any action, it first ensures using offline reasoning that this step can be followed successfully by the rest of δ. More precisely, we have that

$$Trans(\Sigma(\delta), s, \Sigma(\delta'), s') \equiv Trans(\delta, s, \delta', s') \wedge \exists s^*.Do(\delta', s', s^*).$$

If δ is the entire program under consideration, $\Sigma(\delta)$ emulates complete offline execution. But consider $[\delta_1; \delta_2]$. The execution of $\Sigma([\delta_1; \delta_2])$ would make any choice in δ_1 depend on the ability to successfully complete δ_2. But $[\Sigma(\delta_1); \delta_2]$ would allow the execution of the two pieces to be done separately: it would be necessary to ensure the successful completion of δ_1 before taking any steps, but consideration of δ_2 is deferred. If we imagine, for example, that δ_2 is a large high-level program, with hundreds of pages of code, perhaps containing Σ operators of its own, this can make the difference between a scheme that is practical and one that is only of theoretical interest.

The idea of interleaving execution and search has also been applied to decision-theoretic Golog [77, 21]. Here, instead of just searching for a successful execution of a sub-program, an optimal sub-plan is generated which maximizes the expected accumulated reward.

Being able to search still raises the question of how much offline reasoning should be performed in an online system. The more offline reasoning we do, the safer the execution will be, as we get to look further into the future in deciding what choices to make now. On the other hand, in spending time doing this reasoning, we are detached from the world and will not be as responsive. This issue is very clearly evident in time-critical applications such as robot soccer [21] where there is very little time between action choices to contemplate the future. Sardina has cast this problem as the choice between deliberation and reactivity [64], and see also [6].

Another issue that arises in this setting is the form of the offline reasoning. Since an online system allows for a robot to acquire information during execution (via sensing actions, or passive sensors, or exogenous events), how should the robot deal with this during offline deliberation [12]. The simplest possibility is to say that it ignores any such information in the plan for the future that it is constructing. A more sophisticated approach would have it construct a plan that would prescribe different behavior depending on the information acquired during executing. This is *conditional planning* (see, for example, [7, 52]) and one form of this has been incorporated in high-level execution by Lakemeyer [37]. Another possibility is to attempt to *simulate* what will happen external to the robot, and use this information during the deliberation [40]. In [31], this idea is taken even further: at deliberation time a robot uses, for example, a model of its navigation system by computing, say, piece-wise linear approximations of its trajectory; at execution time, this model is then replaced by the real navigation system, which provides position updates as exogenous actions.

Another issue arises whenever a robot performs at least some amount of lookahead in deciding what to do. What should the robot do when the world (as determined by its sensors) does not conform to its predictions (as determined by its action theory)? First steps in logically formalizing this possibility were taken by de Giacomo et al. [18] in what they call *execution monitoring*. In [21], a simple form of execution monitoring is implemented for soccer-playing robots. Here, the assumptions made by the decision-theoretic planner are explicitly encoded in the generated plan. During execution, these assumptions are re-evaluated against the current world model and, in case of a disagreement, the plan is discarded and a new one generated. See also [26, 34, 22–24] for related approaches.

23.5 Conclusion

Cognitive robotics is a reply to the criticism that knowledge representation and reasoning has been overly concerned with reasoning in the abstract and not concerned enough with the dynamic world of an embodied agent. It attempts to address the sort of representation and reasoning problems an autonomous robot would face in trying to decide what to do. In many ways, it has only scratched the surface of the issues that need to be dealt with.

A number of cognitive robotic systems have been implemented on a variety of robotic platforms, using the sort of ideas discussed in this chapter, based either on the situation calculus or on one of the other related knowledge representation formalisms. For a sampling of these systems, see [14, 13, 5, 70, 21, 11, 25]. Perhaps the most impressive demonstration to date was that of the museum tour-guide robot reported in [9].

A fundamental question in the area of cognitive robotics (that Reiter had begun to examine) is the relationship between pure logical representations of incomplete knowledge and the more numerical measures of uncertainty. A start in this direction is the work on the stochastic situation calculus [62] as well as that on noisy sensors and effectors and decision-theoretic Golog, noted above.

On an even broader scale, a much tighter coupling of the high-level control program and other parts of a robot's software, like mapping and localization, or even vision, is called for. For example, when localization fails and a robot gets lost, it should be possible to use high-level control to do a reasoned failure recovery. Making progress along these lines requires a deep understanding of both cognitive and more traditional robotics, and should help to reduce the gap that currently exists between the two research communities.

Bibliography

[1] E. Amir and S. Russell. Logical filtering. In *Proc. of the IJCAI-03 Conference*, pages 75–82, Acapulco, 2003.

[2] F. Bacchus and F. Kabanza. Using temporal logics to express search control knowledge for planning. *Artificial Intelligence*, 116(1–2):123–191, 2000.

[3] F. Bacchus, J. Halpern, and H. Levesque. Reasoning about noisy sensors and effectors in the situation calculus. *Artificial Intelligence*, 111:171–208, 1999.

[4] C. Baral. Reasoning about actions: non-deterministic effects, constraints, and qualification. In *Proc. of the IJCAI-95 Conference*, pages 2017–2026, Montreal, 1995.

[5] C. Baral, L. Floriano, A. Hardesty, D. Morales, M. Nogueira, and T.C. Son. From theory to practice: the UTEP robot in the AAAI 96 and AAAI 97 robot contests. In *Proc. of the Agents-98 Conference*, pages 32–38, 1998.

[6] C. Baral and T. Son. Relating theories of actions and reactive control. *Electronic Transactions of Artificial Intelligence*, 2(3–4):211–271, 1998.

[7] P. Bertoli, A. Cimatti, M. Roveri, and P. Traverso. Planning in nondeterministic domains under partial observability via symbolic model checking. In *Proc. of the IJCAI-01 Conference*, pages 473–478, Seattle, 2001.

[8] C. Boutilier, R. Reiter, M. Soutchanski, and S. Thrun. Decision-theoretic, high-level agent programming in the situation calculus. In *Proc. of the AAAI-00 Conference*, pages 355–362, 2000.

[9] W. Burgard, A.B. Cremers, D. Fox, D. Hähnel, G. Lakemeyer, D. Schulz, W. Steiner, and S. Thrun. Experiences with an interactive museum tour-guide robot. *Artificial Intelligence*, 114(1–2):3–55, 1999.

[10] T. Bylander. The computational complexity of propositional STRIPS planning. *Artificial Intelligence*, 69:165–204, 1994.

[11] A. Carbone, A. Finzi, A. Orlandini, F. Pirri, and G. Ugazio. Augmenting situation awareness via model-based control in rescue robots. In *Proc. of IROS-2005 Conference*, Edmonton, Canada, 2005.

[12] M. Dastani, F. de Boer, F. Dignum, W. van der Hoek, M. Kroese, and J.-J. Meyer. Programming the deliberation cycle of cognitive robots. In *Proc. of the 3rd International Cognitive Robotics Workshop*, Edmonton, 2002.

[13] G. de Giacomo, L. Iocchi, D. Nardi, and R. Rosati. Moving a robot: the KR & R approach at work. In *Proc. of the KR-96 Conference*, pages 198–209, 1996.

[14] G. de Giacomo, L. Iocchi, D. Nardi, and R. Rosati. Planning with sensing for a mobile robot. In *Proc. of the ECP-97 Conference*, Toulouse, France. 1997.

[15] G. de Giacomo and H. Levesque. Projection using regression and sensors. In *Proc. of the IJCAI-99 Conference*, Stockholm, Sweden, pages 160–165, August 1999.

[16] G. de Giacomo, Y. Lespérance, H. Levesque, and S. Sardiña. On the semantics of deliberation in Indigolog. *Annals of Mathematics and Artificial Intelligence*, 41(2–4):259–299, 2004.

[17] G. de Giacomo, Y. Lespérance, and H. Levesque. ConGolog, a concurrent programming language based on the situation calculus. *Artificial Intelligence*, 121:109–169, 2000.

[18] G. de Giacomo, R. Reiter, and M. Soutchanski. Execution monitoring of high-level robot programs. In *Proc. of the KR-98 Conference*, Trento Italy, 1998.

[19] R. Demolombe and M. Pozos Parra. A simple and tractable extension of situation calculus to epistemic logic. In *Proc. of the ISMIS-2000 Conference*, pages 515–524, 2000.

[20] P. Doherty, G. Granlund, K. Kuchcinski, E. Sandewall, K. Nordberg, E. Skarman, and K. Wiklund. The WITAS unmanned aerial vehicle project. In *Proc. of the ECAI-00 Conference*, pages 747–755, Berlin, 2000.

[21] A. Ferrein, C. Fritz, and G. Lakemeyer. On-line decision-theoretic Golog for un-predictable domains. In *Proc. of 27th German Conference on AI*, pages 322–336, 2004.

[22] A. Finzi and F. Pirri. Diagnosing failures and predicting safe runs in robot control. In *Proc. of the Commonsense 2001 Conference*, pages 105–113, New York, 2001.

[23] A. Finzi and F. Pirri. Combining probabilities, failures and safety in robot control. In *Proc. of the IJCAI-01 Conference*, Seattle, August 2001.

[24] A. Finzi and F. Pirri. Representing flexible temporal behaviors in the situation calculus. In *Proc. of the IJCAI-05 Conference*, pages 436–441, 2005.

[25] A. Finzi, F. Pirri, M. Pirrone, and M. Romano. Autonomous mobile manipulators managing perception and failures. In *Proc. of the Agents-01 Conference*, pages 196–201, Montreal 2001.

[26] M. Fichtner, A. Großmann, and M. Thielscher. Intelligent execution monitoring in dynamic environments. *Fundamenta Informaticae*, 57:371–392, 2003.

[27] E. Giunchiglia, J. Lee, V. Lifschitz, N. McCain, and H. Turner. Nonmonotonic causal theories. *Artificial Intelligence*, 153:49–104, 2004.

[28] R. Fikes and N. Nilsson. STRIPS: A new approach to the application of theorem proving to problem solving. *Artificial Intelligence*, 2:189–208, 1971.

[29] M. Ghallab, D. Nau, and P. Traverso. *Automated Planning: Theory and Practice*. Morgan Kaufmann, 2004.

[30] H. Grosskreutz and G. Lakemeyer. Turning high-level plans into robot programs in uncertain domains. In W. Horn, editor, *Proc. of the ECAI-2000 Conference*, pages 548–552, 2000.

[31] H. Grosskreutz and G. Lakemeyer. ccGolog: An action language with continuous change. *Logic Journal of the IGPL*, 2003.

[32] H. Grosskreutz and G. Lakemeyer. On-line execution of cc-Golog plans. In *Proc. of the IJCAI-01 Conference*, pages 12–18, 2001.

[33] K. Hindriks, F. de Boer, W. van der Hoek, and J.-J.Ch. Meyer. A formal semantics for an abstract agent programming language. In *Proc. of the ATAL-97 Conference*, June 1998.

[34] K. Hindriks, F. de Boer, W. van der Hoek, and J.-J.Ch. Meyer. Failure, monitoring and recovery in the agent language 3APL. In *Proc. of the AAAI-98 Fall Symp. on Cognitive Robotics*, pages 68–75, 1998.

[35] J. Hintikka. *Knowledge and Belief*. Cornell University Press, Ithaca, 1962.

[36] W. van der Hoek, J.J. Meyer, and B. Linder. On agents that have the ability to choose. *Studia Logica*, 66(1):79–119, 2000.

[37] G. Lakemeyer. On sensing and off-line interpreting in GOLOG. In *Logical Foundations for Cognitive Agents, Contributions in Honor of Ray Reiter*, pages 173–187. Springer, Berlin, 1999.

[38] G. Lakemeyer. Relevance from an epistemic perspective. *Artificial Intelligence*, 97(1–2):137–167, 1997.

[39] Y. Lespérance, H. Levesque, F. Lin, and R. Scherl. Ability and knowing how in the situation calculus. *Studia Logica*, 66:165–186, October 2000.

[40] Y. Lespérance and H.-K. Ng. Integrating planning into reactive high-level robot programs. In *Proc. of the Second International Cognitive Robotics Workshop*, Berlin, Germany, pages 49–54, 2000.

[41] H. Levesque. What is planning in the presence of sensing? In *Proc. of AAAI-96 Conference*, pages 1139–1146, Portland, OR, Aug. 1996.

[42] H. Levesque and R. Reiter. Beyond planning. In *AAAI Spring Symposium on Integrating Robotics Research*, Working notes, Palo Alto, CA, March 1998.

[43] H. Levesque, R. Reiter, Y. Lespérance, F. Lin, and R. Scherl. GOLOG: A logic programming language for dynamic domains. *Journal of Logic Programming*, 31:59–84, 1997.

[44] V. Lifschitz. On the semantics of STRIPS. In *Proc. of the 1986 Workshop Reasoning about Actions and Plans*, pages 1–9. Morgan Kaufmann, 1987.

[45] F. Lin and R. Reiter. Forget it! In *Proc. of the AAAI Fall Symposium on Relevance*, New Orleans, USA, November 1994.

[46] F. Lin and R. Reiter. How to progress a database. *Artificial Intelligence*, 92(1–2):131–167, 1997.

[47] B. Linder, W. van der Hoek, and J.J. Meyer. Formalizing motivational attitudes of agents: On preferences, goals and commitments. In *Proc. of the ATAL-96 Conference*, pages 17–32, Berlin, 1996.

[48] Y. Liu and H. Levesque. Tractable reasoning with incomplete first-order knowledge in dynamic systems with context-dependent actions. In *Proc. of the IJCAI-05 Conference*, Edinburgh, August 2005.

[49] D. McDermott. Robot planning. *AI Magazine*, 13(2):55–79, 1992.

[50] R. Moore. A formal theory of knowledge and action. In *Formal Theories of the Commonsense World*, pages 319–358. Ablex, Norwood, NJ, 1985.

[51] N. Nilsson. Shakey the robot. SRI Technical report, 1984.

[52] F. Bacchus and R. Petrick. Modeling an agent's incomplete knowledge during planning and execution. In *Proc. of the KR-98 Conference*, Trento, Italy, 1998.

[53] M. Fox and D. Long. PDDL2.1: An extension of PDDL for expressing temporal planning domains. *Journal of AI Research*, 20:61–124, 2003.

[54] J. Pinto. Integrating discrete and continuous change in a logical framework. *Computational Intelligence*, 14(1), 1997.

[55] F. Pirri and A. Finzi. An approach to perception in theory of actions: Part I. *Electronic Transaction on Artificial Intelligence*, 3(41):19–61, 1999.

[56] F. Pirri and M. Romano. A situation-Bayes view of object recognition based on symgenons. In *Proc. of the Third International Cognitive Robotics Workshop*, Edmonton, 2002.

[57] F.F. Ingrand, R. Chatila, R. Alami, and F. Robert. PRS: A high level supervision and control language for autonomous mobile robots. In *Proc. Int. Conf. on Robotics and Automation*, 1996.

[58] Z. Pylyshyn. *Computation and Cognition: Toward a Foundation for Cognitive Science*. MIT Press, Cambridge, MA, 1984.

[59] A. Rao. AgentSpeak(L): BDI agents speak out in a logical computable language. In *Agents Breaking Away*. Springer-Verlag, 1996.

[60] R. Reiter. On closed world data bases. In *Logic and Databases*, pages 55–76. Plenum Press, New York, 1987.

[61] R. Reiter. The frame problem in the situation calculus: A simple solution (sometimes) and a completeness result for goal regression. In *Artificial Intelligence and Mathematical Theory of Computation: Papers in Honor of John McCarthy*, pages 359–380. Academic Press, New York, 1991.

[62] R. Reiter. *Knowledge in Action: Logical Foundations for Specifying and Implementing Dynamical Systems*. MIT Press, Cambridge, MA, 2001.

[63] S. Ruman. GOLOG as an agent-programming language: experiments in developing banking applications. MSc, Dept. of Computer Science, University of Toronto, January 1996.

[64] S. Sardina. Deliberation in agent programming languages. PhD thesis, Dept. of Computer Science, University of Toronto, June 2005.

[65] S. Sardiña. Indigolog: Execution of guarded action theories. MSc Thesis, Dept. of Computer Science, University of Toronto, April 2000.

[66] M.P. Shanahan. *Solving the Frame Problem*. MIT Press, 1997.

[67] M.P. Shanahan. A logical account of perception incorporating feedback and expectation. In *Proc. of the KR-02 Conference*, pages 3–13, 2002.

[68] M.P. Shanahan. Representing continuous change in the event calculus. In *Proc. of the ECAI-90 Conference*, 1990.

[69] M.P. Shanahan. Noise and the common sense informatic situation for a mobile robot. In *Proc. of the AAAI-96 Conference*, pages 1098–1103, 1996.

[70] M.P. Shanahan. Reinventing Shakey. In J. Minker, editor. *Logic-Based Artificial Intelligence*, pages 233–253. Kluwer Academic, 2000.

[71] M.P. Shanahan and M. Witkowski. High-level robot control through logic. In *Proc. of the ATAL-2000 Conference*, pages 104–121, 2001.

[72] S. Shapiro, M. Pagnucco, Y. Lespérance, and H. Levesque. Iterated belief change in the situation calculus. In *Proc. of the KR-2000 Conference*, pages 527–538, Breckenridge, CO, April 2000.

[73] S. Shapiro and M. Pagnucco. Iterated belief change and exogenous actions in the situation calculus. In *Proc. of the ECAI-04 Conference*, pages 878–882, 2004.

[74] S. Shapiro, Y. Lesperance, and H. Levesque. Goal change. In *Proc. of the IJCAI-05 Conference*, Edinburgh, August 2005.

[75] R. Scherl and H. Levesque. Knowledge, action, and the frame problem. *Artificial Intelligence*, 144:1–39, 2003.

[76] T. Son and C. Baral. Formalizing sensing actions—A transition function based approach. *Artificial Intelligence*, 125(1–2):19–91, 2001.

[77] M. Soutchanski. An on-line decision-theoretic Golog interpreter. In *Proc. of the IJCAI-01 Conference*, Seattle, Washington, 2001.

[78] M. Thielscher. Modeling actions with ramifications in nondeterministic, concurrent, and continuous domains—and a case study. In *Proc. of the AAAI-00 Conference* pages 497–502, 2000.

[79] M. Thielscher. Representing the knowledge of a robot. In *Proc. of the KR-2000 Conference*, Breckenridge, pages 109–120, 2000.

[80] M. Thielscher. FLUX: A logic programming method for reasoning agents. *Theory and Practice of Logic Programming*, 5(4–5):533–565, 2005.

[81] M. Thielscher. *Reasoning Robots: The Art and Science of Programming Robotic Agents*. Springer, 2005.

[82] S. Thrun. Robotic mapping: A survey. In G. Lakemeyer and B. Nebel, editors. *Exploring Artificial Intelligence in the New Millennium*. Morgan Kaufmann, 2002.

Handbook of Knowledge Representation
Edited by F. van Harmelen, V. Lifschitz and B. Porter
© 2008 Elsevier B.V. All rights reserved
DOI: 10.1016/S1574-6526(07)03024-6

Chapter 24

Multi-Agent Systems

Wiebe van der Hoek and Michael Wooldridge

We review the state of the art in knowledge representation formalisms for multi-agent systems. We divide work in this area into two categories. In the first category are approaches that attempt to represent the cognitive state of rational agents, and to characterize logically how such a state leads a rational agent to act. We begin by motivating this approach. We then describe four of the best-known such logical frameworks, and discuss the possible roles that such logics can play in helping us to *engineer* artificial agents. In the second category are approaches based on representing the strategic structure of a multi-agent environment, and in particular, the *powers* that agents have, either individually or in coalitions. Here, we describe Coalition Logic, Alternating-time Temporal Logic (ATL), and epistemic extensions.

24.1 Introduction

The discipline of knowledge representation focuses on how to represent and reason about environments with various different properties, usually with the goal of making decisions, for example about how best to act in this environment. But what are the things that are actually *doing* this representation and reasoning? The now-conventional terminology is to refer to these entities as *agents*. The agents may be computer programs (in which case they are called *software agents*) or they may be people like you or I. The case where there is only assumed to be one agent in the environment (for example, a single autonomous robot operating in a warehouse) is usually the simplest scenario for knowledge representation, and often does not require techniques beyond those described elsewhere in this book. However, where there are *multiple* agents in the environment, things get much more interesting—and challenging. This is because it becomes necessary for an agent to represent and reason about *the other agents in the environment*. Again there are two possibilities. The first is that all the agents in the environment can be assumed to *share a common purpose*. This might be the case, for example, if we are designing a multi-robot system to operate in a warehouse environment. Here, we can assume the robots share a common purpose because we can design them that way. However, the second case is again much more interesting, and presents many more challenges for knowledge representation. This is where the agents comprising the system do *not* share the same purpose. This might be the case, for example, in e-commerce systems, where a software agent is attempting to buy some particular item for as low a price as possible, while a seller agent tries to sell it for as high a price as possible. While in one sense the agents share a common goal of engaging in trade, there is obviously a fundamental difference with respect to their more specific goals.

How should we go about representing and reasoning about environments containing multiple agents? That is, what aspects of them should we be attempting to represent? Within the multi-agent systems community, one can distinguish two distinct trends:

Cognitive models of rational action: The first main strand of research in representing multi-agent systems focuses on the issue of representing the *attitudes* of agents within the system: their beliefs, aspirations, intentions, and the like. The aim of such formalisms is to derive a model that predicts how a *rational agent* would go from its beliefs and desires to actions. Work in this area builds largely on research in the philosophy of mind.

Models of the strategic structure of the system: The second main strand of research focuses not on the internal states or attitudes of agents, but on the strategic structure of the environment: what agents can accomplish in the environment, either together or alone. Work in this area builds on models of effectivity from the game theory community, and the models underpinning such logics are closely related to formal games.

Inevitably, the actual divisions between these two categories are more blurred than our rather crisp categorization suggests.

24.2   Representing Rational Cognitive States

In attempting to understand the behavior of agents in the everyday world, we frequently make use of *folk psychology*:

> Many philosophers and cognitive scientists claim that our everyday or "folk" understanding of mental states constitutes a theory of mind. That theory is widely called "folk psychology" (sometimes "commonsense" psychology). The terms in which folk psychology is couched are the familiar ones of "belief" and "desire", "hunger", "pain" and so forth. According to many theorists, folk psychology plays a central role in our capacity to predict and explain the behavior of ourselves and others. However, the nature and status of folk psychology remains controversial. [117]

For example, we use statements such as *Michael intends to write a paper* in order to explain Michael's behavior. Once told this statement, we expect to find Michael shelving other commitments and developing a plan to write the paper; we would expect him to spend a lot of time at his computer; we would not be surprised to find him in a grumpy mood; but we *would* be surprised to find him at a late night party. The philosopher Dennett coined the phrase *intentional system* to refer to an entity that is best understood in terms of folk-psychology notions such as beliefs, desires, and the like [25]. This was also what Hofstadter was referring to already in 1981, when he sketched "coffee house conversation on the Turing test to determine if a machine can think" [55], in which several students discuss AI and in which one of them states that "you AI advocates have far underestimated the human mind, and that there are things a computer will never, ever be able to do". Sandy, a philosophy student puts the following forward:

> But eventually, when you put enough feelingless calculations together in a huge coordinated organization, you'll get something that has properties on another level. You can see it—in fact you *have* to see it—not as a bunch of little calculations, but as a system of tendencies and desires and beliefs and so on. When things get complicated enough, you're forced to change your level of description. To some extend that's already happening, which is why we use words such as "want", "think", "try", and "hope", to describe chess programs and other attempts at mechanical thought.

The intentional stance is essentially nothing more than an abstraction tool. It is a convenient shorthand for talking about certain complex systems (such as people), which allows us to succinctly predict and explain their behavior without having to understand or make claims about their internal structure or operation. Note that the intentional stance has been widely discussed in the literature—let us just remark here that Sandy of the Coffeeshop Conversation claims that the really interesting things in AI will only begin to happen, 'when the program *itself* adopts the intentional stance towards itself'—and it is not our intention to add to this debate; see [112] for a discussion and references.

If we accept the usefulness of the intentional stance for characterizing the properties of rational agents, then the next step in developing a formal theory of such agents is to identify the components of an agent's state. There are many possible mental states that we might choose to characterize an agent: beliefs, goals, desires, intentions, commitments, fears, hopes, and obligations are just a few. We can identify several important categories of such attitudes, for example:

Information attitudes: those attitudes an agent has towards information about its environment. The most obvious members of this category are knowledge and belief.

Pro attitudes: those attitudes an agent has that tend to lead it to perform actions. The most obvious members of this category are goals, desires, and intentions.

Normative attitudes: including obligations, permissions and authorization.

Much of the literature on developing formal theories of agency has been taken up with the relative merits of choosing one attitude over another, and investigating the possible relationships between these attitudes. While there is no consensus on which attitudes should be chosen as primitive, most formalisms choose knowledge or belief together with at least goals or desires.

24.2.1   A Logical Toolkit

In attempting to axiomatize the properties of a rational agent in terms of (say) its beliefs and desires, we will find ourselves attempting to formalize statements such as the following

> Wiebe believes Ajax are great.   (24.1)

> Wiebe desires that Ajax will win.   (24.2)

This suggests that a logical characterization of these statements must include constructions of the form

$$i \begin{Bmatrix} \text{believes} \\ \text{desires} \end{Bmatrix} \varphi$$

where i is a term denoting an agent, and φ is a sentence. We immediately encounter difficulties if we attempt to represent such statements in first-order logic. First of all, the constructs mentioned above should definitely not be *extensional*—even if "it rains in Utrecht" and "it rains in Liverpool" may accidentally both be true, one can believe one without the other, desire the second but not the first, even try to achieve one while hindering the other. Apart from this, representing such statements in first-order logic— as binary predicates of the form $Bel(i, \varphi)$ and $Desire(i, \varphi)$—will not work, because the second term is a sentence, and not a term. By fixing the domain of the first-order language to be itself a language, we can get around this problem, thereby obtaining a first-order meta-language. The meta-language approach has been successfully adopted by a number of researchers, for example, [106]. However, meta-language approaches have also been criticized for representing mental states (see, e.g., [63] for a detailed critique). Instead of choosing a meta-language approach, most researchers opt for a *modal* approach, whereby an agent's beliefs, desires, and the like are represented by an indexed collection of modal operators. The semantics of these operators are generally given in terms or Kripke structures, in the by-now familiar way [19, 86, 13]. The use of Kripke structures and their associated mathematics of correspondence theory makes it possible to quickly generate a number of soundness results for axiomatizations of these logics. However, the *combination* of many modalities into a single framework presents a significant challenge from a logical point of view. Completeness, expressivity and complexity results for logics that incorporate multiple modalities into a single framework are typically complex, and this area of research is much at the leading edge of contemporary modal logic research [34]. Moreover, reasoning in such enriched systems is typically computationally very hard [39]. Despite these problems, modal approaches dominate in the literature, and in this article, we focus exclusively on such approaches.

   In addition to representing an agent's attitudes, logics of rational agency also typically incorporate some way of representing the *actions* that agents perform, and the effects of these actions. Many researchers adapt techniques from *dynamic* logic in order to represent actions and their effects [42], whereas others confine themselves to a *temporal* set-up. Although there is some work in establishing the exact relation between the two approaches, this issue still deserves a better investigation.

   In the next four sections, we review some of the best-known formalisms for reasoning about the cognitive states of rational agents:

- Dynamic Epistemic Logic (DEL);

- Cohen and Levesque's seminal intention logic [22];

- Rao and Georgeff's BDI framework [91]; and

- the KARO framework of Linder et al. [70].

24.2.2 Dynamic Epistemic Logic

The first formalism we deal with, dynamic epistemic logic, is intended to capture the interaction between the actions that an agent performs and its knowledge. Elsewhere in this handbook is a full treatment of logics for knowledge, and we pre-suppose some familiarity with this subject. The idea is simply to take the logical machinery of epistemic logic [30] and augment it with a dynamic component [43], for referring to actions. The origins of such logics for knowledge representation lie in the work of Robert Moore [77]. Moore's chief concern was to study the ways that knowledge and action interact, and he identified two main issues. The first is that some actions *produce knowledge*, and therefore their effects must be formulated in terms of the epistemic states of participants. The second is that of *knowledge preconditions*: what an agent needs to know in order to be able to perform an action. A simple example is that in order to unlock a safe, one must know the combination for the lock. Using these ideas, Moore formalized a notion of *ability*. He suggested that in order for an agent to be able to achieve some state of affairs φ, the agent must either:

- know the identity of an action α (i.e., have an "executable description" of an action α) such that after α is performed, φ holds; or else

- know the identity of an action α such that after α is performed, the agent will know the identity of an action α' such that after α' is performed, φ holds.

The point about "knowing the identity" of an action is that, in order for me to be able to become rich, it is not sufficient for me simply to know that *there exists some action* I could perform which would make me rich; I must either know what that action is (the first clause above), or else to be able to perform some action which would furnish me with the information about which action to perform in order to make myself rich. This apparently subtle distinction is rather important, and it is known as the distinction between knowledge *de re* (which involves knowing the identity of a thing) and *de dicto* (which involves knowing that something exists) [30, p. 101]. We will see later, when we review more recent work on temporal logics of ability, that this distinction also plays an important role there.

Nowadays, the term *Dynamic Epistemic Logic* (DEL) [11, 108] is used to refer to formalisms that add a special class of actions—*epistemic actions*—to the standard logic S5 for knowledge. The term "epistemic action" is used to refer to an action with an epistemic component, such as learning or announcing something. Thus, in DEL, actions themselves have an epistemic flavor: they denote an announcement, a private message, or even the act of "suspecting" something.

There are several variants of dynamic epistemic logic in the literature. In the language of [108], apart from the static formulas involving knowledge, there is also the construct $[\alpha]\varphi$, meaning that after execution of the epistemic action α, statement φ is

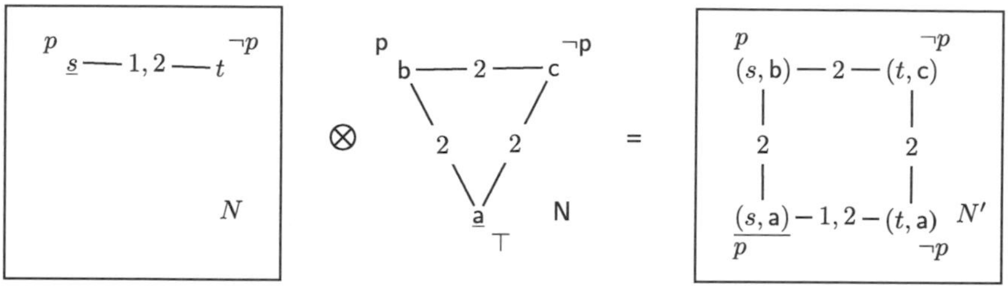

Figure 24.1: Multiplying an epistemic state N, s with the action model (N, a) representing the action $L_{12}(L_1?p \cup L_1?\neg p \cup !\top)$.

true. Actions α specify who is informed by what. To express "learning", actions of the form $L_B\beta$ are used, where β again is an action: this expresses the fact that "coalition B learns that β takes place". The expression $L_B(!\alpha \cup \beta)$, means the coalition B learns that either α or β is happening, while in fact α takes place.

To make the discussion concrete, assume we have two agents, 1 and 2, and that they commonly know that a letter on their table contains either the information p or $\neg p$ (but they do not know, at this stage, which it is). Agent 2 leaves the room for a minute, and when he returns, he is unsure whether or not 1 read the letter. This action would be described as

$$L_{12}(L_1?p \cup L_1?\neg p \cup !\top)$$

which expresses the following. First of all, in fact nothing happened (this is denoted by $!\top$). However, the knowledge of *both* agents changes: they commonly learn that 1 might have learned p, and he might have learned $\neg p$.

Although this is basically the language for DEL as used in [108], we now show how the example can be interpreted using the appealing semantics of [11]. In this semantics, both the uncertainty about the state of the world, and that of the action taking place, are represented in two independent Kripke models. The result of performing an epistemic action in an epistemic state is then computed as a "cross-product", see Fig. 24.1. Model N in this figure represents that it is common knowledge among 1 and 2 that both are ignorant about p. The triangular shaped model N is the *action model* that represents the knowledge and ignorance when $L_{12}(L_1?p \cup L_1?\neg p \cup !\top)$ is carried out. The points a, b, c of the model N are also called *actions*, and the formulas accompanying the name of the actions are called *pre-conditions*: the condition that has to be fulfilled in order for the action to take place. Since we are in the realm of *truthful information transfer*, in order to perform an action that reveals p, the pre-condition p must be satisfied, and we write pre(b) $= $ p. For the case of nothing happening, only the precondition $\top$ need be true. Summarizing, action b represents the action that agent 1 reads p in the letter, action c is the action when $\neg p$ is read, and a is for nothing happening. As with 'static' epistemic models, we omit reflexive arrows, so that N indeed represents that p or $\neg p$ is learned by 1, or that nothing happens: moreover, it is commonly known between 1 and 2 that 1 knows which action takes place, while for 2 they all look the same.

Now let $M, w = \langle W, R_1, R_2, \ldots, R_m, \pi \rangle$, w be a static epistemic state, and M, w an action in a finite action model. We want to describe what $M, w \oplus M, w = \langle W', R'_1,$

$R'_2, \ldots, R'_m, \pi'$, w', looks like—the result of 'performing' the action represented by M, w in M, w. Every action from M, w that is executable in any state $v \in W$ gives rise to a new state in W': we let $W' = \{(v, \mathsf{v}) \mid v \in W, M, v \models \mathrm{pre}(\mathsf{v})\}$. Since epistemic actions do not change any objective fact in the world, we stipulate $\pi'(v, \mathsf{v}) = \pi(v)$. Finally, when are two states (v, v) and (u, u) indistinguishable for agent i? Well, he should be both unable to distinguish the originating states ($R_i uv$), and unable to know what is happening ($\mathsf{R}_i \mathsf{uv}$). Finally, the new state w' is of course (w, w). Note that this construction indeed gives $N, s \oplus \mathsf{N}, \mathsf{a} = N', (s, \mathsf{a})$, in our example of Fig. 24.1. Finally, let the action α be represented by the action model state M, w. Then the truth definition under the action model semantics reads that $M, w \models [\alpha]\varphi$ iff $M, w \models \mathrm{pre}(\mathsf{w})$ implies $(M, w) \oplus (\mathsf{M}, \mathsf{w}) \models \varphi$. In our example: $N, s \models [L_{12}(L_1?p \cup L_1?\neg p \cup !\top)]\varphi$ iff $N', (s, \mathsf{a}) \models \varphi$.

Note that the accessibility relation in the resulting model is defined as

$$R_i(u, \mathsf{u})(v, \mathsf{v}) \Leftrightarrow R_i uv \,\&\, \mathsf{R}_i \mathsf{uv}. \tag{24.3}$$

This means that an agent cannot distinguish two states after execution of an action α, if and only if he could not distinguish the 'sources' of those states, and he does not know which action exactly takes place. Put differently: if an agent knows the difference between two states s and t, then they can never look the same after performing an action, and likewise, if two indistinguishable actions α and β take place in a state s, they will give rise to new states that can be distinguished.

Dynamic epistemic logics provide us with a rich and powerful framework for reasoning about information flow in multi-agent systems, and the possible epistemic states that may arise as a consequence of actions performed by agents within a system. However, they do not address the issues of how an agent *chooses* an action, or whether an action represents a *rational choice* for an agent. For this, we need to consider pro-attitudes: desires, intentions, and the like. The frameworks we describe in the following three sections all try to bring together information-related attitudes (belief and knowledge) with attitudes such as desiring and intending, with the aim of providing a more complete account of rational action and agency.

24.2.3 Cohen and Levesque's Intention Logic

One of the best known, and most sophisticated attempts to show how the various components of an agent's cognitive makeup could be combined to form a logic of rational agency is due to Cohen and Levesque [22]. Cohen and Levesque's formalism was originally used to develop a theory of intention (as in "I intended to...''), which the authors required as a pre-requisite for a theory of speech acts (see next chapter for a summary, and [23] for full details). However, the logic has subsequently proved to be so useful for specifying and reasoning about the properties of agents that it has been used in an analysis of conflict and cooperation in multi-agent dialogue [36, 35], as well as several studies in the theoretical foundations of cooperative problem solving [67, 60, 61]. This section will focus on the use of the logic in developing a theory of intention. The first step is to lay out the criteria that a theory of intention must satisfy.

When building intelligent agents—particularly agents that must interact with humans—it is important that a *rational balance* is achieved between the beliefs, goals, and intentions of the agents.

For example, the following are desirable properties of intention: An autonomous agent should act on its intentions, not in spite of them; adopt intentions it believes are feasible and forego those believed to be infeasible; keep (or commit to) intentions, but not forever; discharge those intentions believed to have been satisfied; alter intentions when relevant beliefs change; and adopt subsidiary intentions during plan formation. [22, p. 214]

Following [15, 16], Cohen and Levesque identify seven specific properties that must be satisfied by a reasonable theory of intention:

1. Intentions pose problems for agents, who need to determine ways of achieving them.

2. Intentions provide a "filter" for adopting other intentions, which must not conflict.

3. Agents track the success of their intentions, and are inclined to try again if their attempts fail.

4. Agents believe their intentions are possible.

5. Agents do not believe they will not bring about their intentions.

6. Under certain circumstances, agents believe they will bring about their intentions.

7. Agents need not intend all the expected side effects of their intentions.

Given these criteria, Cohen and Levesque adopt a two tiered approach to the problem of formalizing a theory of intention. First, they construct the logic of rational agency, "being careful to sort out the relationships among the basic modal operators" [22, p. 221]. On top of this framework, they introduce a number of derived constructs, which constitute a "partial theory of rational action" [22, p. 221]; intention is one of these constructs.

Syntactically, the logic of rational agency is a many-sorted, first-order, multi-modal logic with equality, containing four primary modalities; see Table 24.1. The semantics of Bel and Goal are given via possible worlds, in the usual way: each agent is assigned a belief accessibility relation, and a goal accessibility relation. The belief accessibility relation is euclidean, transitive, and serial, giving a belief logic of KD45. The goal relation is serial, giving a conative logic KD. It is assumed that each agent's goal relation is a subset of its belief relation, implying that an agent will not have a goal of something

Table 24.1. Atomic modalities in Cohen and Levesque's logic

Operator	Meaning
(Bel i φ)	agent i believes φ
(Goal i φ)	agent i has goal of φ
(Happens α)	action α will happen next
(Done α)	action α has just happened

it believes will not happen. Worlds in the formalism are a discrete sequence of events, stretching infinitely into past and future. The system is only defined semantically, and Cohen and Levesque derive a number of properties from that. In the semantics, a number of assumptions are implicit, and one might vary on them. For instance, there is a fixed domain assumption, giving us properties as $\forall x(\text{Bel } i \ \varphi(x)) \rightarrow (\text{Bel } i \ \forall x\varphi(x))$. Also, agents 'know what time it is', we immediately obtain from the semantics the validity of formulas like $2 : 30\text{PM}/3/6/85 \rightarrow \text{Bel } i 2 : 30\text{PM}/3/6/85$.

The two basic temporal operators, Happens and Done, are augmented by some operators for describing the structure of event sequences, in the style of dynamic logic [41]. The two most important of these constructors are " ; " and " ? ":

$\alpha; \alpha'$ denotes α followed by α'

$\varphi?$ denotes a "test action" φ

Here, the test must be interpreted as a test by the system; it is not a so-called 'knowledge-producing action' that can be used by the agent to acquire knowledge.

The standard future time operators of temporal logic, " $\Box$ " (always), and " $\Diamond$ " (sometime) can be defined as abbreviations, along with a "strict" sometime operator, Later:

$$\Diamond \alpha \hat{=} \exists x \cdot (\text{Happens } x; \alpha?)$$

$$\Box \alpha \hat{=} \neg \Diamond \neg \alpha$$

$$(\text{Later } p) \hat{=} \neg p \wedge \Diamond p$$

A temporal precedence operator, $(\text{Before } pq)$ can also be derived, and holds if p holds before q. An important assumption is that *all* goals are eventually dropped:

$$\Diamond \neg (\text{Goal } x \ (\text{Later } p))$$

The first major derived construct is a *persistent* goal.

$$(\text{P-Goal } i \ p) \hat{=} (\text{Goal } i \ (\text{Later } p)) \qquad\qquad \wedge$$
$$(\text{Bel } i \ \neg p) \qquad\qquad \wedge$$
$$\begin{bmatrix} \text{Before} \\ \quad ((\text{Bel } i \ p) \vee (\text{Bel } i \ \Box \neg p)) \\ \quad \neg(\text{Goal } i \ (\text{Later } p)) \end{bmatrix}$$

So, an agent has a persistent goal of p if:

1. It has a goal that p eventually becomes true, and believes that p is not currently true.

2. Before it drops the goal, one of the following conditions must hold:
   (a) the agent believes the goal has been satisfied;

   (b) the agent believes the goal will never be satisfied.

It is a small step from persistent goals to a first definition of intention, as in "intending to act". Note that "intending that something becomes true" is similar, but requires a slightly different definition; see [22]. An agent i intends to perform action α if it has a persistent goal to have brought about a state where it had just believed it was about to perform α, and then did α.

(Intend i α) $\hat{=}$ (P-Goal i

[Done i (Bel i (Happens α))?; α]

)

Cohen and Levesque go on to show how such a definition meets many of Bratman's criteria for a theory of intention (outlined above). In particular, by basing the definition of intention on the notion of a persistent goal, Cohen and Levesque are able to avoid overcommitment or undercommitment. An agent will only drop an intention if it believes that the intention has either been achieved, or is unachievable.

A critique of Cohen and Levesque's theory of intention is presented in [102]; space restrictions prevent a discussion here.

24.2.4 Rao and Georgeff's BDI Logics

One of the best-known (and most widely misunderstood) approaches to reasoning about rational agents is the *belief-desire-intention* (BDI) model [17]. The BDI model gets its name from the fact that it recognizes the primacy of beliefs, desires, and intentions in rational action. The BDI model is particularly interesting because it combines three distinct components:

- A *philosophical foundation.*

  The BDI model is based on a widely respected theory of rational action in humans, developed by the philosopher Michael Bratman [15].

- A *software architecture.*

  The BDI model of agency does not prescribe a specific implementation. The model may be realized in many different ways, and indeed a number of different implementations of it have been developed. However, the fact that the BDI model *has* been implemented successfully is a significant point in its favor. Moreover, the BDI model has been used to build a number of significant real-world applications, including such demanding problems as fault diagnosis on the space shuttle.

- A *logical formalization.*

  The third component of the BDI model is a family of logics. These logics capture the key aspects of the BDI model as a set of logical axioms. There are many candidates for a formal theory of rational agency, but BDI logics in various forms have proved to be among the most useful, longest-lived, and widely accepted.

Intuitively, an agent's *beliefs* correspond to information the agent has about the world. These beliefs may be incomplete or incorrect. An agent's *desires* represent states of affairs that the agent would, in an ideal world, wish to be brought about. (Implemented BDI agents require that desires be *consistent* with one another, although *human* desires often fail in this respect.) Finally, an agent's *intentions* represent desires that it has *committed* to achieving. The intuition is that an agent will not, in general, be able to achieve *all* its desires, even if these desires *are* consistent. Ultimately, an agent must therefore fix upon some subset of its desires and commit resources to achieving them. These chosen desires, to which the agent has some commitment, are intentions [22]. The BDI theory of human rational action was originally developed by Michael Bratman [15]. It is a theory of *practical reasoning*—the process of reasoning that we all go through in our everyday lives, deciding moment by moment which action to perform next. Bratman's theory focuses in particular on the role that *intentions* play in practical reasoning. Bratman argues that intentions are important because they constrain the reasoning an agent is required to do in order to select an action to perform. For example, suppose I have an intention to write a book. Then while deciding what to do, I need not expend any effort considering actions that are incompatible with this intention (such as having a summer holiday, or enjoying a social life). This reduction in the number of possibilities I have to consider makes my decision making considerably simpler than would otherwise be the case. Since any real agent we might care to consider—and in particular, any agent that we can implement on a computer—must have resource bounds, an intention-based model of agency, which constrains decision-making in the manner described, seems attractive.

The BDI model has been implemented several times. Originally, it was realized in IRMA, the Intelligent Resource-bounded Machine Architecture [17]. IRMA was intended as a more or less direct realization of Bratman's theory of practical reasoning. However, the best-known implementation is the Procedural Reasoning System (PRS) [37] and its many descendants [32, 88, 26, 57]. In the PRS, an agent has data structures that explicitly correspond to beliefs, desires, and intentions. A PRS agent's beliefs are directly represented in the form of PROLOG-like facts [21, p. 3]. Desires and intentions in PRS are realized through the use of a *plan library*.[1] A plan library, as its name suggests, is a collection of plans. Each plan is a recipe that can be used by the agent to achieve some particular state of affairs. A plan in the PRS is characterized by a *body* and an *invocation condition*. The body of a plan is a course of action that can be used by the agent to achieve some particular state of affairs. The invocation condition of a plan defines the circumstances under which the agent should "consider" the plan. Control in the PRS proceeds by the agent continually updating its internal beliefs, and then looking to see which plans have invocation conditions that correspond to these beliefs. The set of plans made active in this way correspond to the *desires* of the agent. Each desire defines a possible course of action that the agent may follow. On each control cycle, the PRS picks one of these desires, and pushes it onto an execution stack, for subsequent execution. The execution stack contains desires that have been chosen by the agent, and thus corresponds to the agent's *intentions*.

The third and final aspect of the BDI model is the logical component, which gives us a family of tools that allow us to reason about BDI agents. There have been several versions of BDI logic, starting in 1991 and culminating in Rao and Georgeff's 1998 paper on systems of BDI logics [92, 96, 93–95, 89, 91]; a book-length survey was published as [112]. We focus on [112].

Syntactically, BDI logics are essentially branching time logics (CTL or CTL*, depending on which version you are reading about), enhanced with additional modal

---

[1] In this description of the PRS, we have modified the original terminology somewhat, to be more in line with contemporary usage; we have also simplified the control cycle of the PRS slightly.

operators Bel, Des, and Intend, for capturing the beliefs, desires, and intentions of agents respectively. The BDI modalities are indexed with agents, so, for example, the following is a legitimate formula of BDI logic

$$\text{(Bel } i \text{ (Intend } j \text{ A } \Diamond \, p)) \rightarrow \text{(Bel } i \text{ (Des } j \text{ A } \Diamond \, p))$$

This formula says that if i believes that j intends that p is inevitably true eventually, then i believes that j desires p is inevitable. Although they share much in common with Cohen–Levesque's intention logics, the first and most obvious distinction between BDI logics and the Cohen–Levesque approach is the explicit starting point of CTL-like branching time logics. However, the differences are actually much more fundamental than this. The semantics that Rao and Georgeff give to BDI modalities in their logics are based on the conventional apparatus of Kripke structures and possible worlds. However, rather than assuming that worlds are instantaneous states of the world, or even that they are linear sequences of states, it is assumed instead that worlds are themselves branching temporal structures: thus each world can be viewed as a Kripke structure for a CTL-like logic. While this tends to rather complicate the semantic machinery of the logic, it makes it possible to define an interesting array of semantic properties, as we shall see below.

Before proceeding, we summarize the key semantic structures in the logic. Instantaneous states of the world are modeled by *time points*, given by a set T; the set of all possible evolutions of the system being modeled is given by a binary relation $R \subseteq T \times T$. A *world* (over T and R) is then a pair $\langle T', R' \rangle$, where $T' \subseteq T$ is a non-empty set of time points, and $R' \subseteq R$ is a branching time structure on T'. Let W be the set of all worlds over T. A pair $\langle w, t \rangle$, where $w \in W$ and $t \in T$, is known as a *situation*. If $w \in W$, then the set of all situations in w is denoted by S_w. We have belief accessibility relations B, D, and I, modeled as functions that assign to every agent a relation over situations. Thus, for example:

$$B : Agents \rightarrow \wp(W \times T \times W).$$

We write $B_t^w(i)$ to denote the set of worlds accessible to agent i from situation $\langle w, t \rangle$: $B_t^w(i) = \{w' \mid \langle w, t, w' \rangle \in B(i)\}$. We define D_t^w and I_t^w in the obvious way. The semantics of belief, desire and intention modalities are then given in the conventional manner:

- $\langle w, t \rangle \models \text{(Bel } i \; \varphi)$ iff $\langle w', t \rangle \models \varphi$ for all $w' \in B_t^w(i)$.

- $\langle w, t \rangle \models \text{(Des } i \; \varphi)$ iff $\langle w', t \rangle \models \varphi$ for all $w' \in D_t^w(i)$.

- $\langle w, t \rangle \models \text{(Intend } i \; \varphi)$ iff $\langle w', t \rangle \models \varphi$ for all $w' \in I_t^w(i)$.

The primary focus of Rao and Georgeff's early work was to explore the possible interrelationships between beliefs, desires, and intentions from the perspective of semantic characterization. In order to do this, they defined a number of possible interrelationships between an agent's belief, desire, and intention accessibility relations. The most obvious relationships that can exist are whether one relation is a subset of another: for example, if $D_t^w(i) \subseteq I_t^w(i)$ for all i, w, t, then we would have as an interaction axiom $\text{(Intend } i \; \varphi) \rightarrow \text{(Des } i \; \varphi)$. However, the fact that worlds themselves have structure in BDI logic also allows us to combine such properties with relations on the *structure* of worlds themselves. The most obvious structural relationship that can exist between two worlds—and the most important for our purposes—is that of one world being a *subworld* of another. Intuitively, a world w is said to be a subworld of world w' if w has the same structure as w' but has fewer paths *and is otherwise identical*. Formally, if w, w' are worlds, then w is a subworld of w' (written $w \sqsubseteq w'$) iff $paths(w) \subseteq paths(w')$ but w, w' agree on the interpretation of predicates and constants in common time points.

The first property we consider is the *structural subset* relationship between accessibility relations. We say that accessibility relation R is a structural subset of accessibility relation $\bar{R}$ if for every R-accessible world w, there is an $\bar{R}$-accessible world w' such that w is a subworld of w'. Formally, if R and $\bar{R}$ are two accessibility relations then we write $R \subseteq_{sub} \bar{R}$ to indicate that if $w' \in R_t^w(i)$, then there exists some $w'' \in \bar{R}_t^w(i)$ such that $w' \sqsubseteq w''$. If $R \subseteq_{sub} \bar{R}$, then we say R is a *structural subset* of $\bar{R}$.

We write $\bar{R} \subseteq_{sup} R$ to indicate that if $w' \in R_t^w(i)$, then there exists some $w'' \in \bar{R}_t^w(i)$ such that $w'' \sqsubseteq w'$. If $R \subseteq_{sup} \bar{R}$, then we say R is a *structural superset* of $\bar{R}$. In other words, if R is a structural superset of $\bar{R}$, then for every R-accessible world w, there is an $\bar{R}$-accessible world w' such that w' is a subworld of w.

Finally, we can also consider whether the *intersection* of accessibility relations is empty or not. For example, if $B_t^w(i) \cap I_t^w(i) \neq \emptyset$, for all i, w, t, then we get the following interaction axiom:

$$(\text{Intend } i \; \varphi) \rightarrow \neg(\text{Bel } i \; \neg\varphi).$$

This axiom expresses an *inter-modal consistency* property. Just as we can undertake a more fine-grained analysis of the basic interactions among beliefs, desires, and intentions by considering the structure of worlds, so we are also able to undertake a more fine-grained characterization of inter-modal consistency properties by taking into account the structure of worlds. We write $R_t^w(i) \cap_{sup} \bar{R}_t^w(i)$ to denote the set of worlds $w' \in \bar{R}_t^w(i)$ for which there exists some world $w'' \in R_t^w(i)$ such that $w' \sqsubseteq w''$. We can then define $\cap_{sub}$ in the obvious way.

Putting all these relations together, we can define a range of BDI logical systems. The most obvious possible systems, and the semantic properties that they correspond to, are summarized in Table 24.2.

24.2.5 The KARO Framework

The KARO framework (for Knowledge, Actions, Results and Opportunities) is an attempt to develop and formalize the ideas of Moore [76], who realized that dynamic and epistemic logic can be perfectly combined into one modal framework. The basic framework comes with a sound and complete axiomatization [70]. Also, results on automatic verification of the theory are known, both using translations to first order logic, as well as in a clausal resolution approach. The core of KARO is a combination of epistemic (the standard knowledge operator $\mathbf{K}_i$ is an S5-operator) and dynamic logic; many extensions have also been studied.

Along with the notion of the result of events, the notions of ability and opportunity are among the most discussed and investigated in analytical philosophy. Ability plays an important part in various philosophical theories, as, for instance, the theory of free

Table 24.2. Systems of BDI logic

Name	Semantic condition	Corresponding formula schema
BDI-S1	$B \subseteq_{sup} D \subseteq_{sup} I$	(Intend i E(φ)) $\to$ (Des i E(φ)) $\to$ (Bel i E(φ))
BDI-S2	$B \subseteq_{sub} D \subseteq_{sub} I$	(Intend i A(φ)) $\to$ (Des i A(φ)) $\to$ (Bel i A(φ))
BDI-S3	$B \subseteq D \subseteq I$	(Intend i φ) $\to$ (Des i φ) $\to$ (Bel i φ)
BDI-R1	$I \subseteq_{sup} D \subseteq_{sup} B$	(Bel i E(φ)) $\to$ (Des i E(φ)) $\to$ (Intend i E(φ))
BDI-R2	$I \subseteq_{sub} D \subseteq_{sub} B$	(Bel i A(φ)) $\to$ (Des i A(φ)) $\to$ (Intend i A(φ))
BDI-R3	$I \subseteq D \subseteq B$	(Bel i φ) $\to$ (Des i φ) $\to$ (Intend i φ)
BDI-W1	$B \cap_{sup} D \neq \emptyset$	(Bel i A(φ)) $\to$ $\neg$(Des i $\neg$A(φ))
	$D \cap_{sup} I \neq \emptyset$	(Des i A(φ)) $\to$ $\neg$(Intend i $\neg$A(φ))
	$B \cap_{sup} I \neq \emptyset$	(Bel i A(φ)) $\to$ $\neg$(Intend i $\neg$A(φ))
BDI-W2	$B \cap_{sub} D \neq \emptyset$	(Bel i E(φ)) $\to$ $\neg$(Des i $\neg$E(φ))
	$D \cap_{sub} I \neq \emptyset$	(Des i E(φ)) $\to$ $\neg$(Intend i $\neg$E(φ))
	$B \cap_{sub} I \neq \emptyset$	(Bel i E(φ)) $\to$ $\neg$(Intend i $\neg$E(φ))
BDI-W3	$B \cap D \neq \emptyset$	(Bel i φ) $\to$ $\neg$(Des i $\neg\varphi$)
	$D \cap I \neq \emptyset$	(Des i φ) $\to$ $\neg$(Intend i $\neg\varphi$)
	$B \cap I \neq \emptyset$	(Bel i φ) $\to$ $\neg$(Intend i $\neg\varphi$)

Source: [91, p. 321].

will and determinism, the theory of refraining and seeing-to-it, and deontic theories. Following Kenny [62], the authors behind KARO consider ability to be the complex of physical, mental and moral capacities, internal to an agent, and being a positive explanatory factor in accounting for the agent's performing an action. Opportunity, on the other hand, is best described as circumstantial possibility, i.e., possibility by virtue of the circumstances. The opportunity to perform some action is external to the agent and is often no more than the absence of circumstances that would prevent or interfere with the performance. Although essentially different, abilities and opportunities are interconnected in that abilities can be exercised only when opportunities for their exercise present themselves, and opportunities can be taken only by those who have the appropriate abilities. From this point of view it is important to remark that abilities are understood to be *reliable* (cf. [18]), i.e., having the ability to perform a certain action suffices to take the opportunity to perform the action every time it presents itself. The combination of ability and opportunity determines whether or not an agent has the (practical) possibility to perform an action.

Let i be a variable over a set of agents $\{1, \ldots, n\}$. Actions in the set Ac are either atomic actions (Ac $= \{a, b, \ldots\}$) or composed ($\alpha, \beta, \ldots$) by means of confirmation of formulas (confirm φ), sequencing ($\alpha; \beta$), conditioning (if φ then α else β) and repetition (while φ do α). These actions α can then be used to build new formulas to express the possible *result* of the execution of α by agent i (the formula $[do_i(\alpha)]\varphi$ denotes that φ is a result of i's execution of α), the *opportunity* for i to perform α ($\langle do_i(\alpha)\rangle \top$) and i's *capability* of performing the action α ($\mathbf{A}_i\alpha$). The formula $\langle do_i(\alpha)\rangle\varphi$ is shorthand for $\neg[do_i(\alpha)]\neg\varphi$, thus expressing that one possible result of performance of α by i implies φ.

With these tools at hand, one has already a rich framework to reason about agent's knowledge about doing actions. For instance, a property like *perfect recall*

$$\mathbf{K}_i[do_i(\alpha)]\varphi \to [do_i(\alpha)]\mathbf{K}_i\varphi$$

can now be enforced for *particular actions* α. Also, the core KARO already guarantees a number of properties, of which we list a few:

1. $\mathbf{A}_i \, \text{confirm} \, \varphi \leftrightarrow \varphi$.

2. $\mathbf{A}_i \alpha_1 ; \alpha_2 \leftrightarrow \mathbf{A}_i \alpha_1 \wedge [do_i(\alpha_1)] \mathbf{A}_i \alpha_2$ or $\mathbf{A}_i \alpha_1 ; \alpha_2 \leftrightarrow \mathbf{A}_i \alpha_1 \wedge \langle do_i(\alpha_1) \rangle \mathbf{A}_i \alpha_2$.

3. $\mathbf{A}_i \, \text{if} \, \varphi \, \text{then} \, \alpha_1 \, \text{else} \, \alpha_2 \, \text{fi} \leftrightarrow ((\varphi \wedge \mathbf{A}_i \alpha_1) \vee (\neg \varphi \wedge \mathbf{A}_i \alpha_2))$.

4. $\mathbf{A}_i \, \text{while} \, \varphi \, \text{do} \, \alpha \, \text{od} \leftrightarrow (\neg \varphi \vee (\varphi \wedge \mathbf{A}_i \alpha \wedge [do_i(\alpha)] \mathbf{A}_i \, \text{while} \, \varphi \, \text{do} \, \alpha \, \text{od}))$
   or $\mathbf{A}_i \, \text{while} \, \varphi \, \text{do} \, \alpha \, \text{od} \leftrightarrow (\neg \varphi \vee (\varphi \wedge \mathbf{A}_i \alpha \wedge \langle do_i(\alpha) \rangle \mathbf{A}_i \, \text{while} \, \varphi \, \text{do} \, \alpha \, \text{od}))$.

For a discussion about the problems with the ability to do a sequential action (the possible behavior of the items 2 and 4 above), we refer to [70], or to a general solution to this problem that was offered in [48].

Practical possibility is considered to consist of two parts, viz. correctness and feasibility: action α is *correct* with respect to φ iff $\langle do_i(\alpha) \rangle \varphi$ holds and α is *feasible* iff $\mathbf{A}_i \alpha$ holds.

$$\mathbf{PracPoss}_i(\alpha, \varphi) \langle do_i(\alpha) \rangle \varphi \wedge \mathbf{A}_i \alpha.$$

The importance of practical possibility manifests itself particularly when ascribing —from the outside—certain qualities to an agent. It seems that for the agent itself practical possibilities are relevant in so far as the agent has knowledge of these possibilities. To formalize this kind of knowledge, KARO comes with a Can-predicate and a Cannot-predicate. The first of these predicates concerns the knowledge of agents about their practical possibilities, the latter predicate does the same for their practical impossibilities.

$$\mathbf{Can}_i(\alpha, \varphi) \stackrel{\triangle}{=} \mathbf{K}_i \mathbf{PracPoss}_i(\alpha, \varphi) \quad \text{and}$$

$$\mathbf{Cannot}_i(\alpha, \varphi) \stackrel{\triangle}{=} \mathbf{K}_i \neg \mathbf{PracPoss}_i(\alpha, \varphi).$$

The Can-predicate and the Cannot-predicate integrate knowledge, ability, opportunity and result, and seem to formalize one of the most important notions of agency. In fact it is probably not too bold to say that knowledge like that formalized through the Can-predicate, although perhaps in a weaker form by taking aspects of uncertainty into account, underlies all acts performed by rational agents. For rational agents act only if they have some information on both the possibility to perform the act, and its possible outcome. It therefore seems worthwhile to take a closer look at both the Can-predicate and the Cannot-predicate. The following properties focus on the behavior of the *means*-part of the predicates, which is the α in $\mathbf{Can}_i(\alpha, \varphi)$ and $\mathbf{Cannot}_i(\alpha, \varphi)$.

1. $\mathbf{Can}_i(\text{confirm} \, \varphi, \psi) \leftrightarrow \mathbf{K}_i(\varphi \wedge \psi)$.

2. $\mathbf{Cannot}_i(\text{confirm} \, \varphi, \psi) \leftrightarrow \mathbf{K}_i(\neg \varphi \vee \neg \psi)$.

3. $\mathbf{Can}_i(\alpha_1 ; \alpha_2, \varphi) \leftrightarrow \mathbf{Can}_i(\alpha_1, \mathbf{PracPoss}_i(\alpha_2, \varphi))$.

4. $\mathbf{Can}_i(\alpha_1 ; \alpha_2, \varphi) \rightarrow \langle do_i(\alpha_1) \rangle \mathbf{Can}_i(\alpha_2, \varphi)$ if i has perfect recall regarding α_1.

5. $\mathbf{Can}_i(\text{if} \, \varphi \, \text{then} \, \alpha_1 \, \text{else} \, \alpha_2 \, \text{fi}, \psi) \wedge \mathbf{K}_i \varphi \leftrightarrow \mathbf{Can}_i(\alpha_1, \psi) \wedge \mathbf{K}_i \varphi$.

6. $\mathbf{Can}_i(\texttt{if } \varphi \texttt{ then } \alpha_1 \texttt{ else } \alpha_2 \texttt{ fi}, \psi) \wedge \mathbf{K}_i\neg\varphi \leftrightarrow \mathbf{Can}_i(\alpha_2, \psi) \wedge \mathbf{K}_i\neg\varphi.$

7. $\mathbf{Can}_i(\texttt{while } \varphi \texttt{ do } \alpha \texttt{ od}, \psi) \wedge \mathbf{K}_i\varphi \leftrightarrow \mathbf{Can}_i(\alpha, \mathbf{PracPoss}_i(\texttt{while } \varphi \texttt{ do } \alpha \texttt{ od}, \psi)) \wedge \mathbf{K}_i\varphi.$

In *Actions that make you change your mind* [69], the authors of KARO look at specific atomic actions. At that the agents can perform, i.e., doxastic actions of expanding, contracting or revising its beliefs (we have now both knowledge ($\mathbf{K}_i$) and belief ($\mathbf{B}_i$)). Those actions are assumed to have the following general properties:

- $\models \langle do_i(\alpha)\rangle\top$ realizability
- $\models \langle do_i(\alpha)\rangle\chi \rightarrow [do_i(\alpha)]\chi$ determinism
- $\models \langle do_i(\alpha;\alpha)\rangle\chi \leftrightarrow \langle do_i(\alpha)\rangle\chi$ idempotence

Realizability of an action implies that agents have the opportunity to perform the action regardless of circumstances; determinism of an action means that performing the action results in a unique state of affairs, and idempotence of an action implies that performing the action an arbitrary number of times has the same effect as performing the action just once.

Then, specific definitions for the three actions are given, and related to the AGM framework of belief revision [4]. As an illustration, we list some properties, written in one object language, of the action of revising one's beliefs (here, φ is an objective formula):

- $[do_i(\texttt{revise } \varphi)]\mathbf{B}_i\varphi.$

- $[do_i(\texttt{revise } \varphi)]\mathbf{B}_i\vartheta \rightarrow [do_i(\texttt{expand } \varphi)]\mathbf{B}_i\vartheta.$

- $\neg\mathbf{B}_i\neg\varphi \rightarrow ([do_i(\texttt{expand } \varphi)]\mathbf{B}_i\vartheta \leftrightarrow [do_i(\texttt{revise } \varphi)]\mathbf{B}_i\vartheta).$

- $\mathbf{K}_i\neg\varphi \leftrightarrow [do_i(\texttt{revise } \varphi)]\mathbf{B}_i\bot.$

- $\mathbf{K}_i(\varphi \leftrightarrow \psi) \rightarrow ([do_i(\texttt{revise } \varphi)]\mathbf{B}_i\vartheta \leftrightarrow [do_i(\texttt{revise } \psi)]\mathbf{B}_i\vartheta).$

In [74], the KARO-authors show how motivational attitudes can be incorporated in their framework. The most primitive notion here is that agent i *wishes* φ ($\mathbf{W}_i\varphi$), from which it has to *select* some (if so, $\mathbf{C}_i\varphi$ becomes true). In order to define what a goal is, a higher order notion of *implementability* is first defined:

$$\Diamond_i\varphi \leftrightarrow \exists k \in \mathbb{N} \exists a_1, \ldots, a_k \in \mathbf{AtPracPoss}_i(a_1; \ldots; a_k, \varphi)).$$

Now the notion of a goal in KARO is as follows:

$$\mathbf{Goal}_i\varphi \overset{\triangle}{=} \mathbf{W}_i\varphi \wedge \neg\varphi \wedge \Diamond_i\varphi \wedge \mathbf{C}_i\varphi.$$

It is easily seen that this definition of a goal does not suffer from effects as being closed under consequence. In [74], these motivational attitudes are also 'dynamized', in the sense that actions, like committing and decommitting are added, with which an agent can change its motivational attitudes. Semantically, this is supported by letting the agents maintain an "agenda". Space does not permit us to investigate this issue further.

24.2.6 Discussion

Undoubtedly, formalizing the informational and motivational attitudes in a context with evolving time, or where agents can do actions, have greatly helped to improve our understanding of complex systems. At the same time, admittedly, there are many weaknesses and open problems with such approaches.

To give one example of how a formalization can help us to become more clear about the interrelationship between the notions defined here, recall that Rao and Georgeff assume the notion of *belief-goal compatibility*, saying

$$\mathbf{Goal}_i \varphi \rightarrow \mathbf{B}_i \varphi$$

for formulas φ that refer to the future.

Cohen and Levesque, however, put a lot of emphasis on their notion of *realizability*, stating exactly the opposite:

$$\mathbf{B}_i \varphi \rightarrow \mathbf{Goal}_i \varphi.$$

By analyzing the framework of Cohen and Levesque more closely, it appears that they have a much weaker property in mind, which is

$$\mathbf{Goal}_i \varphi \rightarrow \neg \mathbf{B}_i \neg \varphi.$$

To mention just one aspect in which the approaches mentioned here are still far from completed, we recall that the three frameworks allow one to reason about many agents, but are in essence still one-agent systems. Where notions as distributed and common knowledge are well understood epistemic notions in multi-agent systems, their motivational analogues seem to be much harder and are yet only partially understood (see Cohen and Levesque's [24] or Tambe's [104] on teamwork).

24.2.7 Cognitive Agent Logics in Practice

Broadly speaking, logic has played a role in three aspects of software development.

- as a *specification language*;

- as a *programming language*; and

- as a *verification language*.

In the sections that follow, we will discuss the possible use of logics of rational agency in these three processes.

Specification

The software development process begins by establishing the client's requirements. When this process is complete, a *specification* is developed, which sets out the functionality of the new system. Temporal and dynamic logics have found wide applicability in the specification of systems. An obvious question is therefore whether logics of rational agency might be used as specification languages.

A specification expressed in such a logic would be a formula φ. The idea is that such a specification would express the desirable behavior of a system. To see how this might work, consider the following formula of BDI logic (in fact from [112]), intended to form part of a specification of a process control system.

(Bel *i* *Open(valve32)*) → (Intend *i* (Bel *j* *Open(valve32)*)).

This formula says that if *i* believes valve 32 is open, then *i* should intend that *j* believes valve 32 is open. A rational agent *i* with such an intention can select a speech act to perform in order to inform *j* of this state of affairs. It should be intuitively clear how a system specification might be constructed using such formulae, to define the intended behavior of a system.

One of the main desirable features of a software specification language is that it should not dictate *how* a specification should be satisfied by an implementation. It should be clear that the specification above has exactly these properties. It does not dictate how agent *i* should go about making *j* aware that valve 32 is open. We simply expect *i* to behave as a rational agent given such an intention.

There are a number of problems with the use of such logics for specification. The most worrying of these is with respect to their semantics. The semantics for the modal connectives (for beliefs, desires, and intentions) are given in the normal modal logic tradition of possible worlds [19]. So, for example, an agent's beliefs in some state are characterized by a set of different states, each of which represents one possibility for how the world could actually be, given the information available to the agent. In much the same way, an agent's desires in some state are characterized by a set of states that are consistent with the agent's desires. Intentions are represented similarly. There are several advantages to the possible worlds model: it is well studied and well understood, and the associated mathematics of correspondence theory is extremely elegant. These attractive features make possible worlds the semantics of choice for almost every researcher in formal agent theory. However, there are also a number of serious drawbacks to possible worlds semantics. First, possible worlds semantics imply that agents are logically perfect reasoners (in that their deductive capabilities are sound and complete), and they have infinite resources available for reasoning. No real agent, artificial or otherwise, has these properties.

Second, possible worlds semantics are generally *ungrounded*. That is, there is usually no precise relationship between the abstract accessibility relations that are used to characterize an agent's state, and any concrete computational model. As we shall see in later sections, this makes it difficult to go from a formal specification of a system in terms of beliefs, desires, and so on, to a concrete computational system. Similarly, given a concrete computational system, there is generally no way to determine what the beliefs, desires, and intentions of that system are. If temporal modal logics of rational agency are to be taken seriously as *specification* languages, then this is a significant problem.

Implementation

Once given a specification, we must implement a system that is correct with respect to this specification. The next issue we consider is this move from abstract specification to concrete computational system. There are at least two possibilities for achieving this transformation that we consider here:

1. somehow directly execute or animate the abstract specification; or

2. somehow translate or compile the specification into a concrete computational form using an automatic translation technique.

In the subsections that follow, we shall investigate each of these possibilities in turn.

Directly executing agent specifications. Suppose we are given a system specification, φ, which is expressed in some logical language L. One way of obtaining a concrete system from φ is to treat it as an *executable specification*, and *interpret* the specification directly in order to generate the agent's behavior. Interpreting an agent specification can be viewed as a kind of constructive proof of satisfiability, whereby we show that the specification φ is satisfiable by *building a model* (in the logical sense) for it. If models for the specification language L can be given a computational interpretation, then model building can be viewed as executing the specification. To make this discussion concrete, consider the Concurrent METATEM programming language [33]. In this language, agents are programmed by giving them a temporal logic specification of the behavior it is intended they should exhibit; this specification is directly executed to generate each agent's behavior. Models for the temporal logic in which Concurrent METATEM agents are specified are linear discrete sequences of states: executing a Concurrent METATEM agent specification is thus a process of constructing such a sequence of states. Since such state sequences can be viewed as the histories traced out by programs as they execute, the temporal logic upon which Concurrent METATEM is based has a computational interpretation; the actual execution algorithm is described in [12]. A somewhat related language is the IMPACT framework of Subrahmanian et al. [103]. IMPACT is a rich framework for programming agents, which draws upon and considerably extends some ideas from logic programming. Agents in IMPACT are programmed by using rules that incorporate deontic modalities (permitted, forbidden, obliged [75]). These rules can be interpreted to determine the actions that an agent should perform at any given moment [103, p. 171].

Note that executing Concurrent METATEM agent specifications is possible primarily because the models upon which the Concurrent METATEM temporal logic is based are comparatively simple, with an obvious and intuitive computational interpretation. However, agent specification languages in general (e.g., the BDI formalisms of Rao and Georgeff [90]) are based on considerably more complex logics. In particular, they are usually based on a semantic framework known as *possible worlds* [19]. The technical details are somewhat involved but the main point is that, *in general*, possible worlds semantics do not have a computational interpretation in the way that Concurrent METATEM semantics do. Hence it is not clear what "executing" a logic based on such semantics might mean.

In response to this issue, a number of researchers have attempted to develop executable agent specification languages with a simplified logical basis, that has a computational interpretation. An example is Rao's AgentSpeak(L) language, which although essentially a BDI system, has a simple computational semantics [88]. The 3APL project [45] is also an attempt to have a agent programming language with a well-defined semantics, based on transition systems. One advantage of having a thorough semantics is that it enables one to compare different agent programming languages, such as AgentSpeak(L) with 3APL [44] or AGENT-0 and 3APL [46]. One complication in bridging the gap between the agent programming paradigm and the formal systems of Sections 24.2.3–24.2.5, is that the former usually take goals to be procedural (a plan), whereas goals in the latter are declarative (a desired state). A programming language that tries to bridge the gap in this respect is the language GOAL [64].

GOLOG [66, 97] and its multiagent sibling CONGOLOG [65] represent another rich seam of work on logic-oriented approaches to programming rational agents. Essentially, GOLOG is a framework for executing a fragment of the situation calculus; the situation calculus is a well known logical framework for reasoning about action [73]. Put crudely, writing a GOLOG program involves expressing a logical theory of what action an agent should perform, using the situation calculus; this theory, together with some background axioms, represents a logical expression of what it means for the agent to do the right action. Executing such a program reduces to constructively solving a deductive proof problem, broadly along the lines of showing that there is a sequence of actions representing an acceptable computation according to the theory [97, p. 121]; the witness to this proof will be a sequence of actions, which can then be executed.

Compiling agent specifications.   An alternative to direct execution is *compilation*. In this scheme, we take our abstract specification, and transform it into a concrete computational model via some automatic synthesis process. The main perceived advantages of compilation over direct execution are in run-time efficiency. Direct execution of an agent specification, as in Concurrent METATEM, above, typically involves manipulating a symbolic representation of the specification at run time. This manipulation generally corresponds to reasoning of some form, which is computationally costly. Compilation approaches aim to reduce abstract symbolic specifications to a much simpler computational model, which requires no symbolic representation. The 'reasoning' work is thus done off-line, at compile-time; execution of the compiled system can then be done with little or no run-time symbolic reasoning.

Compilation approaches usually depend upon the close relationship between models for temporal/modal logic (which are typically labeled graphs of some kind), and automata-like finite state machines. For example, Pnueli and Rosner [85] synthesize reactive systems from branching temporal logic specifications. Similar techniques have also been used to develop concurrent system skeletons from temporal logic specifications. Perhaps the best-known example of this approach to agent development is the *situated automata* paradigm of Rosenschein and Kaelbling [99]. They use an epistemic logic to specify the perception component of intelligent agent systems. They then used a technique based on constructive proof to directly synthesize automata from these specifications [98].

The general approach of automatic synthesis, although theoretically appealing, is limited in a number of important respects. First, as the agent specification language becomes more expressive, then even offline reasoning becomes too expensive to carry out. Second, the systems generated in this way are not capable of *learning* (i.e., they are not capable of adapting their "program" at run-time). Finally, as with direct execution approaches, agent specification frameworks tend to have no concrete computational interpretation, making such a synthesis impossible.

Verification

Once we have developed a concrete system, we need to show that this system is correct with respect to our original specification. This process is known as *verification*, and it is particularly important if we have introduced any informality into the development process. We can divide approaches to the verification of systems into two broad classes: (1) *axiomatic*; and (2) *semantic* (model checking). In the subsections that follow, we shall look at the way in which these two approaches have evidenced themselves in agent-based systems.

Axiomatic approaches. Axiomatic approaches to program verification were the first to enter the mainstream of computer science, with the work of Hoare in the late 1960s [47]. Axiomatic verification requires that we can take our concrete program, and from this program systematically derive a logical theory that represents the behavior of the program. Call this the program theory. If the program theory is expressed in the same logical language as the original specification, then verification reduces to a proof problem: show that the specification is a theorem of (equivalently, is a logical consequence of) the program theory. The development of a program theory is made feasible by *axiomatizing* the programming language in which the system is implemented. For example, Hoare logic gives us more or less an axiom for every statement type in a simple PASCAL-like language. Once given the axiomatization, the program theory can be derived from the program text in a systematic way.

Perhaps the most relevant work from mainstream computer science is the specification and verification of reactive systems using temporal logic, in the way pioneered by Pnueli, Manna, and colleagues [72]. The idea is that the computations of reactive systems are infinite sequences, which correspond to models for linear temporal logic. Temporal logic can be used both to develop a system specification, and to axiomatize a programming language. This axiomatization can then be used to systematically derive the theory of a program from the program text. Both the specification and the program theory will then be encoded in temporal logic, and verification hence becomes a proof problem in temporal logic.

Comparatively little work has been carried out within the agent-based systems community on axiomatizing multi-agent environments. We shall review just one approach. In [111], an axiomatic approach to the verification of multi-agent systems was proposed. Essentially, the idea was to use a temporal belief logic to axiomatize the properties of two multi-agent programming languages. Given such an axiomatization, a program theory representing the properties of the system could be systematically derived in the way indicated above. A temporal belief logic was used for two reasons. First, a temporal component was required because, as we observed above, we need to capture the ongoing behavior of a multi-agent system. A belief component was used because the agents we wish to verify are each symbolic AI systems in their own right. That is, each agent is a symbolic reasoning system, which includes a representation of its environment and desired behavior. A belief component in the logic allows us to capture the symbolic representations present within each agent. The two multi-agent programming languages that were axiomatized in the temporal belief logic were Shoham's AGENT0 [101], and Fisher's Concurrent METATEM (see above). Note that this approach relies on the operation of agents being sufficiently simple that their properties can be axiomatized in the logic. It works for Shoham's AGENT0 and Fisher's Concurrent METATEM largely because these languages have a simple semantics, closely related to rule-based systems, which in turn have a simple logical semantics. For more complex agents, an axiomatization is not so straightforward.

Also, capturing the semantics of concurrent execution of agents is not easy (it is, of course, an area of ongoing research in computer science generally).

Semantic approaches: model checking.   Ultimately, axiomatic verification reduces to a proof problem. Axiomatic approaches to verification are thus inherently limited by the difficulty of this proof problem. Proofs are hard enough, even in classical logic; the addition of temporal and modal connectives to a logic makes the problem considerably harder. For this reason, more efficient approaches to verification have been sought. One particularly successful approach is that of *model checking* [20]. As the name suggests, whereas axiomatic approaches generally rely on syntactic proof, model checking approaches are based on the semantics of the specification language.

The model checking problem, in abstract, is quite simple: given a formula φ of language L, and a model M for L, determine whether or not φ is valid in M, i.e., whether or not $M \models_L \varphi$. Model checking-based verification has been studied in connection with temporal logic. The technique once again relies upon the close relationship between models for temporal logic and finite-state machines. Suppose that φ is the specification for some system, and π is a program that claims to implement φ. Then, to determine whether or not π truly implements φ, we take π, and from it generate a model M_π that corresponds to π, in the sense that M_π encodes all the possible computations of π; determine whether or not $M_\pi \models \varphi$, i.e., whether the specification formula φ is valid in M_π; the program π satisfies the specification φ just in case the answer is 'yes'. The main advantage of model checking over axiomatic verification is in complexity: model checking using the branching time temporal logic CTL [20] can be done in polynomial time, whereas the proof problem for most modal logics is quite complex.

In [95], Rao and Georgeff present an algorithm for model checking BDI logic. More precisely, they give an algorithm for taking a logical model for their (propositional) BDI agent specification language, and a formula of the language, and determining whether the formula is valid in the model. The technique is closely based on model checking algorithms for normal modal logics [40]. They show that despite the inclusion of three extra modalities (for beliefs, desires, and intentions), into the CTL branching time framework, the algorithm is still quite efficient, running in polynomial time. So the second step of the two-stage model checking process described above can still be done efficiently. However, it is not clear how the first step might be realized for BDI logics. Where does the logical model characterizing an agent actually come from—can it be derived from an arbitrary program π, as in mainstream computer science? To do this, we would need to take a program implemented in, say, JAVA, and from it derive the belief, desire, and intention accessibility relations that are used to give a semantics to the BDI component of the logic. Because, as we noted earlier, there is no clear relationship between the BDI logic and the concrete computational models used to implement agents, it is not clear how such a model could be derived.

One approach to this problem was presented in [113], where an imperative programming language called MABLE was presented, with an explicit BDI semantics. Model checking for the language was implemented by mapping the language to the input language for the SPIN model checking system [56], and by reducing formulae in a restricted BDI language to the Linear Temporal Logic format required by SPIN. Here, for example, is a sample claim that may be made about a MABLE system, which may be automatically verified by model checking:

```
claim
[]
((believe agent2
          (intend agent1
                  (believe agent2 (a == 10)))))
   ->
   <>(believe agent2 (a == 10))
);
```

This claim says that it is always ([ ]) the case that if agent 2 believes that agent 1 intends that agent 2 believes that variable *a* has the value 10, then subsequently (<>), agent 2 will itself believe that *a* has the value 10. MABLE was developed primarily as a testbed for exploring possible semantics for agent communication, and was not intended for large-scale system verification.

Several model checkers for logics combining knowledge, time, and other modalities have become developed in recent years. For example, using techniques similar to those used for CTL model checkers [20], Raimondi and Lomuscio implemented MCMAS, a model checker that supports a variety of epistemic, temporal, and deontic logics [87, 71]. Another recent approach to model checking multi-agent systems is [49], which involves model checking temporal epistemic logics by reducing the model checking problem to a conventional LTL model checking problem.

24.3 Representing the Strategic Structure of a System

The second main strand of research that we describe focuses not on the cognitive states of agents, but on the *strategic structure* of the environment: what agents can achieve, either individually or in groups. The starting point for such formalisms is a model of *strategic ability*.

Over the past three decades, researchers from many disciplines have attempted to develop a general purpose logic of strategic ability. Within the artificial intelligence (AI) community, it was understood that such a logic could be used in order to gain a better understanding of planning systems [31, 68, 5]. The most notable early effort in this direction was Moore's dynamic epistemic logic, described above [76, 77]. Moore's work was subsequently enhanced by many other researchers, perhaps most notably, Morgenstern [78, 79]. These distinctions also informed later attempts to integrate a logic of ability into more general logics of rational action in autonomous agents [115, 112] (see [114] for a survey of such logics).

In a somewhat parallel thread of research, researchers in the philosophy of action developed a range of logics underpinned by rather similar ideas and motivations. A typical example is that of Brown, who developed a logic of individual ability in the mid-1980s [18]. Brown's main claim was that modal logic was a useful tool for the analysis of ability, and that previous—unsuccessful—attempts to characterize ability in modal logic were based on an over-simple semantics. Brown's account of the semantics of ability was as follows [18, p. 5]:

> [An agent can achieve *A*] at a given world iff *there exists* a relevant cluster of worlds, at *every* world of which *A* is true.

Notice the ∃∀ pattern of quantifiers in this account. Brown immediately noted that this gave the resulting logic a rather unusual flavor, neither properly existential nor properly universal [18, p. 5]:

> Cast in this form, the truth condition [for ability] involves *two* metalinguistic quantifiers (one existential and one universal). In fact, [the character of the ability operator] should be a little like each.

More recently, there has been a surge of interest in logics of strategic ability, which has been sparked by two largely independent developments: Pauly's development of Coalition Logic [83, 82, 81, 84], and the development of ATL by Alur, Henzinger, and Kupferman [8, 38, 27]. Although these logics are very closely related, the motivation and background to the two systems is strikingly different.

24.3.1 Coalition Logic

Pauly's Coalition Logic was developed in an attempt to shed some light on the links between logic—and in particular, modal logic—and the mathematical theory of games [80]. Pauly showed how the semantic structures underpinning a family of logics of cooperative ability could be formally understood as games of various types; he gave correspondence results between properties of the games and axioms of the logic, gave complete axiomatizations of the various resulting logics, determined the computational complexity of the satisfiability and model checking problems for his logics, and in addition, demonstrated how these logics could be applied to the formal specification and verification of social choice procedures. The basic modal operator in Pauly's logic is of the form $[C]\varphi$, where C is a set of agents (i.e., a subset of the grand coalition Σ), and φ is a sentence; the intended reading is that "C can cooperate to ensure that φ".

The semantics of cooperation modalities are given in terms of an *effectivity function*, which defines for every coalition C the states that C can cooperate to bring about; the effectivity function $\mathsf{E} : S \rightarrow (\mathcal{P}(\Sigma) \rightarrow \mathcal{P}(\mathcal{P}(S)))$, gives, for any state t and coalition C a set of sets of end-states $\mathsf{E}_C(t)$, with the intended meaning of $S \in \mathsf{E}_C(t)$ that C can enforce the outcome to be in S (although C may not be able to pinpoint the exact outcome that emerges with this choice; this generally depends on the choices of agents outside C, or 'choices' made by the environment). This effectivity function comes on a par with a modal operator $[C]$ with truth definition

$$t \models [C]\varphi \text{ iff for some } S \in \mathsf{E}_C(t) \colon \text{ for all } s(s \models \varphi \text{ iff } s \in S).$$

In words: coalition is effective for, or can enforce φ if there is a set of states S that it is effective for, i.e., which it can choose, which is exactly the denotation of φ: $S = [\![\varphi]\!]$. It seems reasonable to say that C is also effective for φ if it can choose a set of states S that 'just' guarantees φ, i.e., for which we have $S \subseteq [\![\varphi]\!]$. This will be taken care of by imposing monotonicity on effectivity functions: we will discuss constraints on effectivity in the end of this section.

In games and other structures for cooperative and competitive reasoning, effectivity functions are convenient when one is interested in the *outcomes* of the game or the encounter, and not so much about *intermediate states*, or *how* a certain state is reached. Effectivity is also a level in which on can decide whether two interaction scenarios are

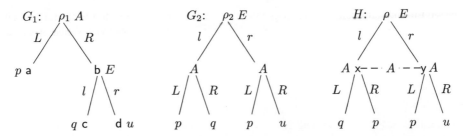

Figure 24.2: Two games G_1 and G_2 that are the same in terms of effectivity. H is an imperfect information game: see Section 24.3.3.

the same. The two games $G1$ and $G2$ from Fig. 24.2 are "abstract" in the sense that they do not lead to payoffs for the players but rather to states which satisfy certain properties, encoded with propositional atoms p, q and u. Such atoms could refer to which player is winning, but also denote other properties of an end-state, such as some distribution of resources, or "payments". Both games are two-player games: in $G1$, player A makes the first move, which he choses form L (Left) and R (Right). In that game, player E is allowed to chose between l and r, respectively, but only if A plays R: otherwise the game ends after one move in the state satisfying p. In game $G2$, both players have the same repertoire of choices, but the order in which the players choose is different. It looks like in $G1$ player A can hand over control to E, while the converse seems to be true for $G2$. Moreover, in $G2$, the player who is not the initiator (i.e., player A), will be allowed to make a choice, no matter the choice of his opponent.

Despite all these differences between the two games, when we evaluate them with respect to what each coalition can *achieve*, they are the same! To become a little more precise, let us define the powers of a coalition in terms of effectivity functions E. In game G_1, player A's effectivity gives $E_A(\rho_1) = \{\{a\}, \{c, d\}\}$. Similarly, player E's effectivity yields $\{\{a, c\}, \{a, c\}\}$: he can enforce the game to end in a or c (by playing l), but he can also force be the end-state among a and d (by playing r). Obviously, we also have $E_{\{A, E\}}(\rho_1) = \{\{a\}, \{c\}, \{d\}\}$: players A and E together can enforce the game to end in any end-state. When reasoning about this, we have to restrict ourselves to the properties that are true in those end states. In coalition logic, what we have just noted semantically would be described as:

$$G_1 \models [A]p \wedge [A](q \vee u) \wedge [E](p \vee q) \wedge [E](p \vee u) \wedge$$
$$[A, E]p \wedge [A, E]q \wedge [A, E]r.$$

Being equipped with the necessary machinery, it now is easy to see that the game G_2 verifies the same formula, indeed, in terms of what propositions can be achieved, we are in a similar situation as in the previous game: E is effective for $\{p, q\}$ (by playing l) and also for $\{p, u\}$ (play r). Likewise, A is effective for $\{p\}$ (play L) and for $\{q, u\}$ (play R). The alert reader will have recognized the logical law $(p \wedge (q \vee u)) \equiv ((p \wedge q) \vee (p \wedge u))$ resembling the 'equivalence' of the two games: $(p \wedge (q \vee u))$ corresponds to A's power in G_1, and $((p \wedge q) \vee (p \wedge u))$ to A's power in G_2. Similarly, the equivalence of E's powers is reflected by the logical equivalence $(p \vee (q \wedge u)) \equiv ((p \vee q) \wedge (p \vee u))$.

At the same time, the reader will have recognized the two metalinguistic quantifiers in the use of the effectivity function E, laid down in its truth-definition above. A set of outcomes S is in E_C iff *for some* choice of C, we will end up in S, under *all* choices of the complement of C (the other agents). This notion of so-called α-effectivity uses the $\exists\forall$-order of the quantifiers: what a coalition can establish through the truth-definition above, their α-ability, is sometimes also called $\exists\forall$-ability. Implicit within the notion of α-ability is the fact that C have *no knowledge* of the choice that the other agents make; they do not see the choice of $\overline{C}$ (i.e., the complement of C), and then decide what to do, but rather they must make their decision *first*. This motivates the notion of β-ability (i.e., "$\forall\exists$"-ability): coalition C is said to have the β-ability for φ if for every choice $\sigma_{\overline{C}}$ available to $\overline{C}$, there exists a choice σ_C for C such that if $\overline{C}$ choose $\sigma_{\overline{C}}$ and C choose σ_C, then φ will result. Thus C being β-able to φ means that no matter what the other agents do, C have a choice such that, if they make this choice, then φ will be true. Note the "$\forall\exists$" pattern of quantifiers: C are implicitly allowed to make their choice while being aware of the choice made by $\overline{C}$. We will come back to information of other player's moves in Section 24.3.3, and to the pairs of α and β ability in Section 24.3.4.

We end this section by mentioning some properties of α-abilities. The axioms for $[C]\varphi$ based on α-effectivity (or effectivity, for short) are summarized in Fig. 24.3; see also Pauly's [83]. The two extreme coalitions $\emptyset$ and the grand coalition Σ are of special interest. $[\Sigma]\varphi$ expresses that some end-state satisfies φ, whereas $[\emptyset]\varphi$ holds if no agent needs to do anything for φ to hold in the next state.

Some of the axioms of coalition logic correspond to restrictions on effectivity functions $E\colon S \to (\mathcal{P}(\Sigma) \to \mathcal{P}(\mathcal{P}(S)))$. First of all, we demand that $\emptyset \notin E_C$ (this guarantees axiom $\perp$). The function E is also assumed to be monotonic: For every coalition $C \subseteq \Sigma$, if $X \subseteq X' \subseteq S$, $X \in E(C)$ implies $X' \in E(C)$. This says that if a coalition can enforce an outcome in the set X, it also can guarantee the outcome to be in any superset X' of X (this corresponds to axiom (M)). An effectivity function E is *C-maximal* if for all X, if $\overline{X} \notin E(\overline{C})$ then $X \in E(C)$. In words: If the other agents $\overline{C}$ cannot guarantee an outcome outside X (i.e, in $\overline{X}$), then C is able to guarantee to be it in X. We require effectivity functions to be Σ-maximal. (This enforces axiom (N—Pauly's symbol for the grand coalition is N): if the empty coalition can not enforce an outcome satisfying φ, the grand coalition Σ can enforce φ. The final principle governs the formation of coalitions. It states that coalitions can combine their strategies to (possibly) achieve more: E is *superadditive* if for all X_1, X_2, C_1, C_2 such that $C_1 \cap C_2 = \emptyset$,

$(\perp)$	$\neg[C]\perp$
(N)	$(\neg[\emptyset]\neg\varphi \to [\Sigma]\varphi)$
(M)	$[C](\varphi \wedge \psi) \to [C]\psi$
(S)	$([C_1]\varphi_1 \wedge [C_2]\varphi_2) \to [C_1 \cup C_2](\varphi_1 \wedge \varphi_2)$
	where $C_1 \cap C_2 = \emptyset$
(MP)	from φ and $\varphi \to \psi$ infer ψ
(Nec)	from φ infer $[C]\varphi$

Figure 24.3: The axioms and inference rules of Coalition Logic.

$X_1 \in \mathsf{E}(C_1)$ and $X_2 \in \mathsf{E}(C_2)$ imply that $X_1 \cap X_2 \in \mathsf{E}(C_1 \cup C_2)$. This obviously corresponds to axiom (S).

24.3.2 Strategic Temporal Logic: ATL

In Coalition Logic one reasons about the powers of coalitions with respect to final outcomes. However, in many multi-agent scenarios, the strategic considerations continue during the process. It would be interesting to study a representation language for interaction that *is* able to express the temporal differences in the two games G_1 and G_2 of Fig. 24.2. *Alternating-time Temporal Logic* (ATL) is intended for this purpose.

Although it is similar to Coalition Logic, ATL emerged from a very different research community, and was developed with an entirely different set of motivations in mind. The development of ATL is closely linked with the development of branching-time temporal logics for the specification and verification of reactive systems [29, 28, 109]. Recall that CTL combines path quantifiers "A" and "E" for expressing that a certain series of events will happen on all paths and on some path respectively, and combines these with tense modalities for expressing that something will happen eventually on some path ($\Diamond$), always on some path ($\Box$) and so on. Thus, for example, using CTL logics, one may express properties such as "on all possible computations, the system never enters a fail state" (A $\Box$ ¬*fail*). CTL-like logics are of limited value for reasoning about *multi-agent* systems, in which system components (agents) cannot be assumed to be benevolent, but may have competing or conflicting goals. The kinds of properties we wish to express of such systems are the powers that the system components have. For example, we might wish to express the fact that "agents 1 and 2 can cooperate to ensure that the system never enters a fail state". It is not possible to capture such statements using CTL-like logics. The best one can do is either state that something will inevitably happen, or else that it may possibly happen: CTL-like logics have no notion of agency.

Alur, Henzinger, and Kupferman developed ATL in an attempt to remedy this deficiency. The key insight in ATL is that path quantifiers can be replaced by cooperation modalities: the ATL expression $\langle\langle C \rangle\rangle \varphi$, where C is a group of agents, expresses the fact that the group C can cooperate to ensure that φ. (Thus the ATL expression $\langle\langle C \rangle\rangle \varphi$ corresponds to Pauly's $[C]\varphi$.) So, for example, the fact that agents 1 and 2 can ensure that the system never enters a fail state may be captured in ATL by the following formula: $\langle\langle 1, 2 \rangle\rangle \Box$ ¬*fail*. An ATL formula true in the root ρ_1 of game G_1 of Fig. 24.2 is $\langle\langle A \rangle\rangle \bigcirc \langle\langle E \rangle\rangle \bigcirc q$: A has a strategy (i.e., play R in ρ_1) such that in the next time, E has a strategy (play l) to enforce u.

Note that ATL generalizes CTL because the path quantifiers A ("on all paths...") and E ("on some paths...") can be simulated in ATL by the cooperation modalities $\langle\langle \emptyset \rangle\rangle$ ("the empty set of agents can cooperate to...") and $\langle\langle \Sigma \rangle\rangle$ ("the grand coalition of all agents can cooperate to...").

One reason for the interest in ATL is that it shares with its ancestor CTL the computational tractability of its model checking problem [20]. This led to the development of an ATL model checking system called MOCHA [9, 6]. With MOCHA, one specifies a model against which a formula is to be checked using a model definition language called REACTIVE MODULES [7]. REACTIVE MODULES is a guarded command language, which provides a number of mechanisms for the structured specification of

models, based upon the notion of a "module", which is basically the REACTIVE SYS-
TEMS terminology for an agent. Interestingly, however, it is ultimately necessary to
define for every variable in a REACTIVE MODULES system which module (i.e., agent)
controls it. The powers of agents and coalitions then derive from the ability to control
these variables: and as we noted in the introduction, this observation was a trigger for
[54] to develop a system for propositional control, CL-PC, as a system in its own right.
We will come briefly back to this idea in Section 24.3.4.

ATL has begun to attract increasing attention as a formal system for the specification and verification of multi-agent systems. Examples of such work include formalizing the notion of role using ATL [100], the development of epistemic extensions to
ATL [50, 52, 51], and the use of ATL for specifying and verifying cooperative mechanisms [84].

To give a precise definition of ATL, we must first introduce the semantic structures
over which formulae of ATL are interpreted. An *alternating transition system* (ATS)
is a 5-tuple

$$S = \langle \Pi, \Sigma, Q, \pi, \delta \rangle, \text{ where:}$$

- Π is a finite, non-empty set of *Boolean variables*;

- $\Sigma = \{a_1, \dots, a_n\}$ is a finite, non-empty set of *agents*;

- Q is a finite, non-empty set of *states*;

- $\pi : Q \to 2^{\Pi}$ gives the set of Boolean variables satisfied in each state;

- $\delta : Q \times \Sigma \to 2^{2^Q}$ is the system transition function, which maps states and
  agents to the choices available to these agents. Thus $\delta(q, a)$ is the set of choices
  available to agent a when the system is in state q. We require that this function
  satisfy the requirement that for every state $q \in Q$ and every set $Q_1, \dots, Q_n$ of
  choices $Q_i \in \delta(q, a_i)$, the intersection $Q_1 \cap \dots \cap Q_n$ is a singleton.

One can think of $\delta(q, a)$ as the possible moves agent a can make in state q. Since
in general he cannot determine the next state on his own, each specific choice that a
makes at q yields a set of possible next states Q_a, which can be further constrained
by the choices of the other agents. Indeed, the constraint that $Q_1 \cap \dots \cap Q_n$ gives a
singleton $\{q'\}$ resembles that the system as a whole is deterministic: once every agent
a has made a decision Q_a at q, *the* next state q' of q is determined.

The games G_1 and G_2 of the previous section can be conceived of as special cases
of alternating transition system: *turn based synchronous* systems, where, at every decision point (state) of the system, exactly one agent is responsible for the next state. For
instance, we have, in G_1 that $\delta(\rho_1, A) = \{\{a\}, \{b\}\}$, and $\delta(\rho_1, E) = \{\{a, b\}\}$, denoting
that E leaves the choice in ρ_1 to A. To make G_1 a real transition system, the transition
function should specify choices for every state, also for the leaves a, c and d. One could
do this for instance by looping those states to themselves: $\delta(a, A) = \delta(a, E) = \{\{a\}\}$.
In order to reason about them as leaves, one could add a proposition *end* that is true
in exactly those states. Turn based systems satisfy the following property (cf. [52]),

which is not valid in ATL in general:

$$\langle\langle \Sigma \rangle\rangle \bigcirc \varphi \to \bigvee_{a \in \Sigma} \langle\langle a \rangle\rangle \bigcirc \varphi.$$

An ATL formula, formed with respect to an alternating transition system $S = \langle \Pi, \Sigma, Q, \pi, \delta \rangle$, is then defined by the following grammar:

$$\varphi ::= \top \mid p \mid \neg\varphi \mid \varphi \vee \varphi \mid \langle\langle C \rangle\rangle \bigcirc \varphi \mid \langle\langle C \rangle\rangle \Box \varphi \mid \langle\langle C \rangle\rangle \varphi \mathcal{U} \varphi$$

where $p \in \Pi$ is a Boolean variable, and $C \subseteq \Sigma$ is a set of agents. We assume the remaining connectives ("$\bot$", "$\to$", "$\leftarrow$", "$\leftrightarrow$", "$\wedge$") are defined as abbreviations in the usual way, and define $\langle\langle C \rangle\rangle \Diamond \varphi$ as $\langle\langle C \rangle\rangle \top \mathcal{U} \varphi$.

To give the semantics of ATL, we need some further definitions. For two states $q, q' \in Q$ and an agent $a \in \Sigma$, we say that state q' is an *a-successor* of q if there exists a set $Q' \in \delta(q, a)$ such that $q' \in Q'$. Intuitively, if q' is an *a*-successor of q, then q' is a possible outcome of one of the choices available to a when the system is in state q. We denote by $succ(q, a)$ the set of a successors to state q, and say that q' is simply a *successor* of q if for all agents $a \in \Sigma$, we have $q' \in succ(q, a)$; intuitively, if q' is a successor to q, then when the system is in state q, the agents Σ can cooperate to ensure that q' is the next state the system enters.

A *computation* of an ATS $\langle \Pi, \Sigma, Q, \pi, \delta \rangle$ is an infinite sequence of states $\lambda = q_0, q_1, \ldots$ such that for all $u > 0$, the state q_u is a successor of q_{u-1}. A computation $\lambda \in Q^\omega$ starting in state q is referred to as a *q-computation*; if $u \in \mathbb{N}$, then we denote by $\lambda[u]$ the uth state in λ; similarly, we denote by $\lambda[0, u]$ and $\lambda[u, \infty]$ the finite prefix $q_0, \ldots, q_u$ and the infinite suffix $q_u, q_{u+1}, \ldots$ of λ, respectively.

Intuitively, a *strategy* is an abstract model of an agent's decision-making process; a strategy may be thought of as a kind of plan for an agent. Formally, a strategy f_a for an agent $a \in \Sigma$ is a total function $f_a : Q^+ \to 2^Q$, which must satisfy the constraint that $f_a(\lambda \cdot q) \in \delta(q, a)$ for all $\lambda \in Q^*$ and $q \in Q$. Given a set $C \subseteq \Sigma$ of agents, and an indexed set of strategies $F_C = \{f_a \mid a \in C\}$, one for each agent $a \in C$, we define $out(q, F_C)$ to be the set of possible outcomes that may occur if every agent $a \in C$ follows the corresponding strategy f_a, starting when the system is in state $q \in Q$. That is, the set $out(q, F_C)$ will contain all possible q-computations that the agents C can "enforce" by cooperating and following the strategies in F_C. Note that the "grand coalition" of all agents in the system can cooperate to uniquely determine the future state of the system, and so $out(q, F_\Sigma)$ is a singleton. Similarly, the set $out(q, F_\emptyset)$ is the set of all possible q-computations of the system.

We can now give the rules defining the satisfaction relation "$\models$" for ATL, which holds between pairs of the form S, q (where S is an ATS and q is a state in S), and formulae of ATL:

$S, q \models \top$;

$S, q \models p$ iff $p \in \pi(q)$ (where $p \in \Pi$);

$S, q \models \neg\varphi$ iff $S, q \not\models \varphi$;

$S, q \models \varphi \vee \psi$ iff $S, q \models \varphi$ or $S, q \models \psi$;

$S, q \models \langle\!\langle C \rangle\!\rangle \bigcirc \varphi$ iff there exists a set of strategies F_C, such that for all
$\lambda \in out(q, F_C)$, we have $S, \lambda[1] \models \varphi$;

$S, q \models \langle\!\langle C \rangle\!\rangle \square \varphi$ iff there exists a set of strategies F_C, such that for all
$\lambda \in out(q, F_C)$, we have $S, \lambda[u] \models \varphi$ for all $u \in \mathbb{N}$;

$S, q \models \langle\!\langle C \rangle\!\rangle \varphi \mathcal{U} \psi$ iff there exists a set of strategies F_C, such that for all
$\lambda \in out(q, F_C)$, there exists some $u \in \mathbb{N}$ such that $S, \lambda[u] \models \psi$, and for all
$0 \leqslant v < u$, we have $S, \lambda[v] \models \varphi$.

Pauly's Coalition Logic is then the fragment of ATL in which the only cooperation modalities allowed are of the form $\langle\!\langle C \rangle\!\rangle \bigcirc$ [81, 82, 38]. The truth of a Coalition Logic formula is determined on an ATS by using the first five items of the definition for satisfaction above. The satisfiability problem for ATL is EXPTIME-complete [27, 110], while for Coalition Logic it is PSPACE-complete in the general case [81, p. 63].

A number of variations of ATL have been proposed over the past few years, for example, to integrate reasoning about obligations into the basic framework of cooperative ability [116], to deal with quantification over coalitions [3], adding the ability to refer to strategies in the object language [107], and adding the ability to talk about preferences or goals of agents [2, 1]. In what follows, we will focus on one issue that has received considerable attention: the integration of *knowledge and ability*.

24.3.3 Knowledge in Strategic Temporal Logics: ATEL

The semantics of Coalition Logic and of ATL assume that agents have *perfect information* about the game. This is immediately apparent in the notion of strategy in ATL: by having an agent decide his next action given an element of Q^+, this makes two strong assumptions. First of all the agents have perfect information about the state they are in, which obviously is an idealized assumption: typically, agents do not know exactly what the state is. They may be unsure about certain facts in the state they are in, but also about the mental states of other agents, which is crucial in any strategic decision making. Secondly, the definition of a strategy assumes that the agents have *perfect recall*: they remember exactly what has happened in reaching the current state, so that they can make different decisions even in identical states.

We first address the issue of imperfect information. The paper [52] adds modalities for knowledge to ATL to obtain ATEL (Alternating-time Temporal Epistemic Logic). For every individual i, add an operator K_i to the language ($K_i \varphi$ is read as "i knows φ"), and for every coalition G, add operators E_G (everybody in G knows), D_G (it is distributed knowledge in G), and C_G (it is common knowledge in C).[2] The following examples of what can be expressed in ATEL are taken from [52].

Performing actions and knowledge interfere in at least two ways: for some actions, in order to be able to do them properly, some knowledge is required, and, on the other hand, actions may add to an agent's knowledge. We have already mentioned knowledge pre-conditions in Section 24.3. We can formulate knowledge pre-conditions quite naturally using ATEL and its variants, and the cooperation modality naturally and elegantly allows us to consider knowledge pre-conditions for *multi*-agent plans. The requirement that, in order for an agent a to be able to eventually bring about state

---

[2]A more detailed exposition on epistemic logic is given in Chapter 15 of this Handbook.

of affairs φ, it must know ψ, might, as a first attempt, be specified in ATEL as: $\langle\langle a \rangle\rangle \lozenge \varphi \rightarrow K_a \psi$. This intuitively says that knowing ψ is a *necessary* requirement for having the ability to bring about φ. However, this requirement is too strong. For instance, in order to be able to ever open the safe, I do not necessarily in general have to know the key right *now*. A slightly better formulation might therefore be $\langle\langle a \rangle\rangle \bigcirc \varphi \rightarrow K_a \psi$. As an overall constraint of the system, this property may help the agent to realize that he has to possess the right knowledge in order to achieve φ. But taken as a local formula, it does not tell us anything about what the agent should know if he wants to bring about φ the day after tomorrow, or "sometime" for that matter. Taken as a local constraint, a necessary knowledge condition to bring about φ might be $(\neg\langle\langle a \rangle\rangle \bigcirc \varphi)\mathcal{U}K_a\psi$. This expresses that our agent is not able to open the safe until he knows its key. The other way around, an example of an ability that is generated by possessing knowledge is the following, expressing that if Bob knows that the combination of the safe is s, then he is able to open it (o), as long as the combination remains unchanged.

$$K_b(c = s) \rightarrow \langle\langle b \rangle\rangle(\langle\langle b \rangle\rangle \bigcirc o)\mathcal{U}\neg(c = s). \tag{24.4}$$

One of the properties of the most widely embraced systems for knowledge is introspection, of which the positive variant says $K_a\varphi \rightarrow K_a K_a \varphi$. Another well-accepted principle of knowledged has it that from $K_a\varphi$ and $K_a(\varphi \rightarrow \psi)$ it follows that $K_a\psi$. Such idealized properties have been criticized since they assume agents to be perfect reasoners who know all consequences of their knowledge in a blow. One may also use ATEL-formulas to model limited reasoners, i.e., reasoners that do not make all inferences in one strike, but where this behavior can be approximated over time. Positive introspection might then look like

$$K_a\psi \rightarrow \langle\langle a \rangle\rangle \bigcirc K_a K_a \psi. \tag{24.5}$$

As a final example, in security protocols where agents a and b share some common secret (a key S_{ab}, for instance), what one typically wants is (24.6), expressing that a can send private information to b, without revealing the message to another agent c:

$$K_a\varphi \wedge \neg K_b\varphi \wedge \neg K_c\varphi \wedge \langle\langle a, b \rangle\rangle \bigcirc (K_a\varphi \wedge K_b\varphi \wedge \neg K_c\varphi). \tag{24.6}$$

Semantically, ignorance of the agents is usually modeled by specifying that each agent is unable to distinguish certain states: the more states he considers undistinguishable from a given state, the weaker his knowledge in that state. In game theory, such an indistinguishibility relation is often called a partition [10]. Take the game H in Fig. 24.2, for example. The dashed line labeled with agent A denotes that this agent does not know what E's move was: A cannot distinguish state x from y. It seems reasonable that do require strategies of agents to be *uniform*: if an agent does not know whether he is in state s or s', he should make the same decision in both. But there is more to adding knowledge to decision making. Let us assume that atom p in game H denotes a win for A. Then, in the root ρ we have that $[\![E]\!] \bigcirc \langle\langle A \rangle\rangle \bigcirc p$: saying that whichever strategy E plays in ρ, in the next state A will be able to reach a winning state in the next state. Note that this is even true if we restrict ourselves to uniform strategies! We even have $H, x \models K_A \langle\langle A \rangle\rangle \bigcirc p$, saying that A knows that he has a winning strategy in x. This, of course, is only true in the *de dicto* reading of knowledge of A: he knows in x that he has a uniform strategy to win, but he does not know which one it is! To obtain a *de re* type of reading of knowledge of strategies, work is still in progress, but we refer to [58] and the recent [105, 59].

Having discussed the issue of imperfect information in a state of the game, there is also the question how to represent what an agent knows about the past: in order to relate this to the example of DEL in Section 24.2.2, we present this for a system with operators for knowledge and change, not necessarily cooperation modalities. In a *synchronous system*, agents are aware of a clock and they know what time it is: in a game, this would mean that they know how many moves have played. In a game with *perfect recall*, agents recall what they have experienced: however, they need not be aware of the time, and also not aware of moves that does not have an impact on their information. In a logical language for knowledge and time one might expect that perfect recall corresponds to

$$K_i \varphi \rightarrow \Box K_i \varphi. \tag{24.7}$$

But this can in general not be. First of all, φ might refer to some specifics of the moment of evaluation. For instance, knowing that it is Wednesday should not imply that I always know that it is Wednesday. Moreover, φ might refer to i's ignorance, i.e., φ might be $\neg K_i \varphi$. Then, if (24.7) would hold, the agent would for ever know that he does not know φ. Since in most logics of knowledge, $\neg K_i \varphi$ is equivalent to $K_i \neg K_i \varphi$, scheme (24.7) would give $\neg K_i \psi \rightarrow \Box \neg K_i \psi$, a rather pessimistic principle! It appears that the proper characterization for perfect recall is

$$K_i \bigcirc \varphi \rightarrow \bigcirc K_i \varphi.$$

For a further discussion about this scheme and perfect recall, we refer to [30]. Let us finally mention that Bonanno [14] studies a property about memory in games that is weaker than perfect recall. He calls a game a *Von Neumann game* if for every two states that an agent cannot distinguish in a game, the number of predecessors in that game must be the same. This would mean that an agent knows how many moves have been played, but not necessarily which ones. Let P be a temporal operator denoting 'always in the past', and $\Box$ 'always in the future', then the epistemic temporal property characterizing Von Neumann games is

$$K_i \varphi \rightarrow \Box K_i P K_i \varphi.$$

Going back to DEL of Section 24.2.2, our example of Fig. 24.1 is rich enough to show that DEL in general does not satisfy perfect recall. To see this, let α be $L_{12}(L_1?p \cup L_1?\neg p \cup !\top)$. We then have $N, s \models K_2[\alpha]\neg(K_1 p \vee K_1 \neg p)$ (2 knows that if nothing happens, 1 will not find out whether p), but not $N, s \models [\alpha]K_2\neg(K_1 p \vee K_1 \neg p)$. We *do* have in general the following weaker form of perfect recall, however. Let M, w be a static epistemic state, and α an action, represented by some action state M, w. Let A be the set of actions that agent i cannot distinguish from M, w. Then we have

$$M, w \models \bigwedge_{\beta \in A} K_i[\beta]\varphi \rightarrow [\alpha]K_i\varphi. \tag{24.8}$$

In words, in order for agent i to 'remember' what holds after performance of an action α, he should already now in advance that it will hold after *every epistemically possible execution* of that action.

24.3.4 CL-PC

Both ATL and Coalition Logic are intended as *general purpose* logics of cooperative ability. In particular, neither has anything specific to say about the *origin* of the powers that are possessed by agents and the coalitions of which they are a member. These powers are just assumed to be implicitly defined within the effectivity structures used to give a semantics to the languages. Of course, if we give a specific *interpretation* to these effectivity structures, then we will end up with a logic with special properties. In [54], a variation of Coalition Logic was developed that was intended specifically to reason about *control* scenarios, as follows. The basic idea is that the overall state of a system is characterized by a finite set of variables, which for simplicity are assumed to take Boolean values. Each agent in the system is then assumed to control some (possibly empty) subset of the overall set of variables, with every variable being under the control of exactly one agent. Given this setting, in the Coalition Logic of Propositional Control (CL-PC), the operator $\Diamond_C \varphi$ means that there exists some assignment of values that the coalition C can give to the variables under its control such that, assuming everything else in the system remains unchanged, then if they make this assignment, then φ would be true. The box dual $\Box_C \varphi$ is defined in the usual way with respect to the diamond ability operator $\Diamond_C$. Here is a simple example:

Suppose the current state of the system is that variables p and q are false, while variable r is true, and further suppose then agent 1 controls p and r, while agent 2 controls q. Then in this state, we have, for example: $\Diamond_1(p \wedge r)$, $\neg\Diamond_1 q$, and $\Diamond_2(q \wedge r)$. Moreover, for any satisfiable propositional logic formula ψ over the variables p, q, and r, we have $\Diamond_{1,2}\psi$.

The ability operator $\Diamond_C$ in CL-PC thus captures *contingent* ability, rather along the lines of "classical planning" ability [68]: ability under the assumption that the world only changes by the actions of the agents in the coalition operator $\Diamond_C$. Of course, this is not a terribly realistic type of ability, just as the assumptions of classical planning are not terribly realistic. However, in CL-PC, we can define α effectivity operators $\langle\!\langle C \rangle\!\rangle_\alpha \varphi$, intended to capture something along the lines of the ATL $\langle\!\langle C \rangle\!\rangle \bigcirc \varphi$, as follows:

$$\langle\!\langle C \rangle\!\rangle_\alpha \mathrel{\hat{=}} \Diamond_C \Box_{\bar{C}} \varphi.$$

Notice the quantifier alternation pattern $\exists\forall$ in this definition.

One of the interesting aspects of CL-PC is that, by using this logic, it becomes possible to explicitly reason in the object language about who controls what. Let i be an agent, and let p be a system variable; let us define $ctrl(i, p)$ as follows:

$$ctrl(i, p) \mathrel{\hat{=}} (\Diamond_i p) \wedge (\Diamond_i \neg p).$$

Thus $ctrl(i, p)$ means that i can assign p the value true, and i can also assign p the value false. It is easy to see that if $ctrl(i, p)$ is true in a system, then this means that the variable p must be under the control of agent i. Starting from this observation, a more detailed analysis of characterizing control of arbitrary formulae was developed, in terms of the variables controlled by individual agents [54]. In addition, [54] gives a complete axiomatization of CL-PC, and shows that the model checking and satisfiability problems for the logic are both PSPACE-complete. Building on this basic formalism, [53] investigates extensions into the possibility of *dynamic* control, where variables can be "passed" from one agent to another.

24.3.5   Applications of Strategic Cooperation Logics

One of the fascinating aspects of coalition logic is its use in social choice theory, and in particular in the specification, development, and verification of *social choice procedures*. Consider the following scenario, adapted from [81].

> Two individuals, *A* and *B*, are to choose between two outcomes, *p* and *q*. We want a procedure that will allow them to choose that will satisfy the following requirements. First, we definitely want an outcome to be possible—that is, we want the two agents to bring about either *p* or *q*. We do not want them to be able to bring about both outcomes simultaneously. Similarly, we do not want either agent to dominate: we want them both to have equal power.

The first point to note is that we can naturally axiomatize these requirements using coalition logic:

$$\langle\langle A, B \rangle\rangle \bigcirc x, \quad x \in \{p, q\}$$

$$\neg \langle\langle A, B \rangle\rangle \bigcirc (p \wedge q)$$

$$\neg \langle\langle x \rangle\rangle \bigcirc p, \quad x \in \{A, B\}$$

$$\neg \langle\langle x \rangle\rangle \bigcirc q, \quad x \in \{A, B\}$$

It should be immediately obvious how these axioms capture the requirements as stated above. Now, given a particular voting procedure, a model checking algorithm can be used to check whether or not this procedure implements the specification correctly. Moreover, a constructive proof of satisfiability for these axioms might be used to *synthesize* a procedure; or else announce that no implementation exists.

24.4   Conclusions

In this paper, we have motivated and introduced a number of logics of rational agency; moreover, we have investigated the role(s) that such logics might play in the *development* of artificial agents. We hope to have demonstrated that logics for rational agents are a fascinating area of study, at the confluence of many different research areas, including logic, artificial intelligence, economics, game theory, and the philosophy of mind. We also hope to have illustrated some of the popular approaches to the theory of rational agency.

There are far too many research challenges open to identify in this article. Instead, we simply note that the search for a logic of rational agency poses a range of deep technical, philosophical, and computational research questions for the logic community. We believe that all the disparate research communities with an interest in rational agency can benefit from this search.

Bibliography

[1] T. Agotnes, W. van der Hoek, and M. Wooldridge. On the logic of coalitional games. In *Proceedings of the Fifth International Joint Conference on Autonomous Agents and Multiagent Systems (AAMAS-2006)*, Hakodate, Japan, 2006.

[2] T. Agotnes, W. van der Hoek, and M. Wooldridge. Temporal qualitative coalitional games. In *Proceedings of the Fifth International Joint Conference on Autonomous Agents and Multiagent Systems (AAMAS-2006)*, Hakodate, Japan, 2006.

[3] T. Agotnes, W. van der Hoek, and M. Wooldridge. Quantified coalition logic. In *Proceedings of the Twentieth International Joint Conference on Artificial Intelligence (IJCAI-07)*, Hyderabad, India, 2007.

[4] C.E. Alchourrón, P. Gärdenfors, and D. Makinson. On the logic of theory change: partial meet contraction and revision functions. *Journal of Symbolic Logic*, 50:510–530, 1985.

[5] J.F. Allen, J. Hendler, and A. Tate, editors. *Readings in Planning*. Morgan Kaufmann Publishers, San Mateo, CA, 1990.

[6] R. Alur, L. de Alfaro, T.A. Henzinger, S.C. Krishnan, F.Y.C. Mang, S. Qadeer, S.K. Rajamani, and S. Taşiran. MOCHA user manual. University of Berkeley Report, 2000.

[7] R. Alur and T.A. Henzinger. Reactive modules. *Formal Methods in System Design*, 15(11):7–48, July 1999.

[8] R. Alur, T.A. Henzinger, and O. Kupferman. Alternating-time temporal logic. *Journal of the ACM*, 49(5):672–713, September 2002.

[9] R. Alur, T.A. Henzinger, F.Y.C. Mang, S. Qadeer, S.K. Rajamani, and S. Taşiran. Mocha: Modularity in model checking. In *CAV 1998: Tenth International Conference on Computer-aided Verification, LNCS*, vol. 1427, pages 521–525. Springer-Verlag, Berlin, Germany, 1998.

[10] R.J. Aumann. Interactive epistemology I: Knowledge. *International Journal of Game Theory*, 28:263–300, 1999.

[11] A. Baltag and L. Moss. Logics for epistemic programs. *Synthese*, 139(2):165–224, 2004 (In the section 'Knowledge, Rationality and Action').

[12] H. Barringer, M. Fisher, D. Gabbay, G. Gough, and R. Owens. METATEM: A framework for programming in temporal logic. In *REX Workshop on Stepwise Refinement of Distributed Systems: Models, Formalisms, Correctness, LNCS*, vol. 430, pages 94–129. Springer-Verlag, Berlin, Germany, June 1989.

[13] P. Blackburn, M. de Rijke, and Y. Venema. *Modal Logic*. Cambridge University Press, Cambridge, England, 2001.

[14] G. Bonanno. A characterisation of von Neumann games in terms of memory. *Synthese*, 139(2):281–295, 2004 (In the section 'Knowledge, Rationality and Action').

[15] M.E. Bratman. *Intention, Plans, and Practical Reason*. Harvard University Press, Cambridge, MA, 1987.

[16] M.E. Bratman. What is intention? In P.R. Cohen, J.L. Morgan, and M.E. Pollack, editors. *Intentions in Communication*, pages 15–32. The MIT Press, Cambridge, MA, 1990.

[17] M.E. Bratman, D.J. Israel, and M.E. Pollack. Plans and resource-bounded practical reasoning. *Computational Intelligence*, 4:349–355, 1988.

[18] M.A. Brown. On the logic of ability. *Journal of Philosophical Logic*, 17:1–26, 1988.

[19] B. Chellas. *Modal Logic: An Introduction*. Cambridge University Press, Cambridge, England, 1980.

[20] E.M. Clarke, O. Grumberg, and D.A. Peled. *Model Checking*. The MIT Press, Cambridge, MA, 2000.

[21] W.F. Clocksin and C.S. Mellish. *Programming in Prolog*. Springer-Verlag, Berlin, Germany, 1981.

[22] P.R. Cohen and H.J. Levesque. Intention is choice with commitment. *Artificial Intelligence*, 42:213–261, 1990.

[23] P.R. Cohen and H.J. Levesque. Rational interaction as the basis for communication. In P.R. Cohen, J. Morgan, and M.E. Pollack, editors. *Intentions in Communication*, pages 221–256. The MIT Press, Cambridge, MA, 1990.

[24] P.R. Cohen and H.J. Levesque. Teamwork. *Nous*, 25(4):487–512, 1991.

[25] D.C. Dennett. *The Intentional Stance*. The MIT Press, Cambridge, MA, 1987.

[26] M. d'Inverno, D. Kinny, M. Luck, and M. Wooldridge. A formal specification of dMARS. In M.P. Singh, A. Rao, and M.J. Wooldridge, editors. *Intelligent Agents IV, LNAI*, vol. 1365, pages 155–176. Springer-Verlag, Berlin, Germany, 1997.

[27] G. van Drimmelen. Satisfiability in alternating-time temporal logic. In *Eighteenth Annual IEEE Symposium on Logic in Computer Science (LICS 2003)*, pages 208–217, Ottawa, Canada, 2003.

[28] E.A. Emerson. Temporal and modal logic. In J. van Leeuwen, editor. *Handbook of Theoretical Computer Science Volume B: Formal Models and Semantics*, pages 996–1072. Elsevier Science Publishers B.V., Amsterdam, The Netherlands, 1990.

[29] E.A. Emerson and J. Srinivasan. Branching time logic. In J.W. de Bakker, P. de Roever, and G. Rozenberg, editors. *REX School-Workshop on Linear Time, Branching Time and Parial Order in Logics and Models for Concurrency, LNCS*, vol. 354, pages 123–172. Springer-Verlag, Berlin, Germany, 1988.

[30] R. Fagin, J.Y. Halpern, Y. Moses, and M.Y. Vardi. *Reasoning About Knowledge*. The MIT Press, Cambridge, MA, 1995.

[31] R.E. Fikes and N. Nilsson. STRIPS: A new approach to the application of theorem proving to problem solving. *Artificial Intelligence*, 2:189–208, 1971.

[32] K. Fischer, J.P. Müller, and M. Pischel. A pragmatic BDI architecture. In M. Wooldridge, J.P. Müller, and M. Tambe, editors. *Intelligent Agents II, LNAI*, vol. 1037, pages 203–218. Springer-Verlag, Berlin, Germany, 1996.

[33] M. Fisher. A survey of Concurrent METATEM—the language and its applications. In D.M. Gabbay and H.J. Ohlbach, editors. *Temporal Logic—Proceedings of the First International Conference, LNAI*, vol. 827, pages 480–505. Springer-Verlag, Berlin, Germany, July 1994.

[34] D.M. Gabbay, A. Kurucz, F. Wolter, and M. Zakharyaschev. *Many-Dimensional Modal Logics: Theory and Applications*. Elsevier Science Publishers B.V., Amsterdam, The Netherlands, 2003.

[35] J.R. Galliers. A strategic framework for multi-agent cooperative dialogue. In *Proceedings of the Eighth European Conference on Artificial Intelligence (ECAI-88)*, pages 415–420, Munich, Federal Republic of Germany, 1988.

[36] J.R. Galliers. A theoretical framework for computer models of cooperative dialogue, acknowledging multi-agent conflict. PhD thesis, Open University, UK, 1988.

[37] M.P. Georgeff and A.L. Lansky. Reactive reasoning and planning. In *Proceedings of the Sixth National Conference on Artificial Intelligence (AAAI-87)*, pages 677–682, Seattle, WA, 1987.

[38] V. Goranko. Coalition games and alternating temporal logics. In J. van Benthem, editor, *Proceeding of the Eighth Conference on Theoretical Aspects of Rationality and Knowledge (TARK VIII)*, pages 259–272, Siena, Italy, 2001.

[39] J.Y. Halpern and M.Y. Vardi. The complexity of reasoning about knowledge and time. I. Lower bounds. *Journal of Computer and System Sciences*, 38:195–237, 1989.

[40] J.Y. Halpern and M.Y. Vardi. Model checking versus theorem proving: A manifesto. In V. Lifschitz, editor. *AI and Mathematical Theory of Computation—Papers in Honor of John McCarthy*, pages 151–176. The Academic Press, London, England, 1991.

[41] D. Harel. *First-Order Dynamic Logic. LNCS*, vol. 68. Springer-Verlag, Berlin, Germany, 1979.

[42] D. Harel. Dynamic logic. In D. Gabbay and F. Guenther, editors. *Extensions of Classical Logic, Handbook of Philosophical Logic*, vol. II, pages 497–604. D. Reidel Publishing Company, Dordrecht, The Netherlands, 1984 (*Synthese Library*, vol. 164).

[43] D. Harel, D. Kozen, and J. Tiuryn. *Dynamic Logic*. The MIT Press, Cambridge, MA, 2000.

[44] K. Hindriks, F.S. de Boer, W. van der Hoek, and J.-J.Ch. Meyer. A formal embedding of agentspeak(l) in 3APL. In G. Antoniou and J. Slaney, editors. *Advanced Topics in Artificial Intelligence, LNAI*, vol. 1502, pages 155–166. Springer, 1998.

[45] K.V. Hindriks, F.S. de Boer, W. van der Hoek, and J.-J.Ch. Meyer. Agent programming in 3APL. *Autonomous Agents and Multi-Agent Systems*, 2(4):357–402, 1999.

[46] K.V. Hindriks, F.S. de Boer, W. van der Hoek, and J.-J.Ch. Meyer. A formal semantics for the core of AGENT-0. In E. Postma and M. Gyssens, editors, *Proceedings of Eleventh Belgium–Netherlands Conference on Artificial Intelligence*, pages 27–34, 1999.

[47] C.A.R. Hoare. An axiomatic basis for computer programming. *Communications of the ACM*, 12(10):576–583, 1969.

[48] W. van der Hoek, J.-J.Ch. Meyer, and J.W. van Schagen. Formalizing potential of agents: The Karo framework revisited. In M. Falle, S. Kaufmann, and M. Pauly, editors. *Formalizing the Dynamics of Information, CSLI Lecture Notes*, vol. 91, pages 51–67. CSLI Publications, Stanford, 2000.

[49] W. van der Hoek and M. Wooldridge. Model checking knowledge and time. In D. Bošnački and S. Leue, editors. *Model Checking Software, Proceedings of SPIN 2002, LNCS*, vol. 2318, pages 95–111. Springer-Verlag, Berlin, Germany, 2002.

[50] W. van der Hoek and M. Wooldridge. Tractable multiagent planning for epistemic goals. In *Proceedings of the First International Joint Conference on Autonomous Agents and Multiagent Systems (AAMAS-2002)*, pages 1167–1174, Bologna, Italy, 2002.

[51] W. van der Hoek and M. Wooldridge. Model checking cooperation, knowledge, and time—a case study. *Research in Economics*, 57(3):235–265, September 2003.

[52] W. van der Hoek and M. Wooldridge. Time, knowledge, and cooperation: Alternating-time temporal epistemic logic and its applications. *Studia Logica*, 75(1):125–157, 2003.

[53] W. van der Hoek and M. Wooldridge. On the dynamics of delegation and cooperation, and control: A logical account. In *Proceedings of the Fourth International Joint Conference on Autonomous Agents and Multiagent Systems (AAMAS-2005)*, pages 701–708, Utrecht, The Netherlands, 2005.

[54] W. van der Hoek and M. Wooldridge. On the logic of cooperation and propositional control. *Artificial Intelligence*, 164(1–2):81–119, May 2005.

[55] D.R. Hofstadter. Metamagical themas: A coffeehouse conversation on the Turing test to determine if a machine can think. *Scientific American*, pages 15–36, May 1981 issue.

[56] G. Holzmann. The Spin model checker. *IEEE Transactions on Software Engineering*, 23(5):279–295, May 1997.

[57] M. Huber. JAM: A BDI-theoretic mobile agent architecture. In *Proceedings of the Third International Conference on Autonomous Agents (Agents 99)*, pages 236–243, Seattle, WA, 1999.

[58] W. Jamroga and W. van der Hoek. Agents that know how to play. *Fundamenta Informaticae*, 63(2–3):185–219, 2004.

[59] W. Jamroga and T. Ågotnes. Constructive knowledge: What agents can achieve under incomplete information. Technical Report IfI-05-10, Clausthal University of Technology, 2005. *Journal of Applied Non-Classical Logics*, Submited for publication. Full paper downloadable at http://www.in.tu-clausthal.de/fileadmin/homes/techreports/ifi0510jamroga.pdf. Short version to appear in *Proc. AAMAS 2006*

[60] N.R. Jennings. On being responsible. In E. Werner and Y. Demazeau, editors. *Decentralized AI 3—Proceedings of the Third European Workshop on Modelling Autonomous Agents in a Multi-Agent World (MAAMAW-91)*, pages 93–102. Elsevier Science Publishers B.V., Amsterdam, The Netherlands, 1992.

[61] N.R. Jennings. Towards a cooperation knowledge level for collaborative problem solving. In *Proceedings of the Tenth European Conference on Artificial Intelligence (ECAI-92)*, pages 224–228, Vienna, Austria, 1992.

[62] A. Kenny. *Will, Freedom and Power*. Basil Blackwell, Oxford, 1975.

[63] K. Konolige. *A Deduction Model of Belief*. Pitman Publishing/Morgan Kaufmann, London/San Mateo, CA, 1986.

[64] W. van der Hoek, K.V. Hindriks, F.S. de Boer, and J.-J.Ch. Meyer. Agent programming with declarative goals. In C. Castelfranchi and Y. Lespérance, editors. *Intelligent Agents VII, Proceedings of the 6th workshop on Agent Theories, Architectures, and Languages (ATAL), LNAI*, vol. 1986, pages 228–243. Springer, 2001.

[65] Y. Lésperance, H.J. Levesque, F. Lin, D. Marcu, R. Reiter, and R.B. Scherl. Foundations of a logical approach to agent programming. In M. Wooldridge, J.P. Müller, and M. Tambe, editors. *Intelligent Agents II, LNAI*, vol. 1037, pages 331–346. Springer-Verlag, Berlin, Germany, 1996.

[66] H. Levesque, R. Reiter, Y. Lespérance, F. Lin, and R. Scherl. Golog: A logic programming language for dynamic domains. *Journal of Logic Programming*, 31:59–84, 1996.

[67] H.J. Levesque, P.R. Cohen, and J.H.T. Nunes. On acting together. In *Proceedings of the Eighth National Conference on Artificial Intelligence (AAAI-90)*, pages 94–99, Boston, MA, 1990.

[68] V. Lifschitz. On the semantics of STRIPS. In M.P. Georgeff and A.L. Lansky, editors. *Reasoning About Actions & Plans—Proceedings of the 1986 Workshop*, pages 1–10. Morgan Kaufmann Publishers, San Mateo, CA, 1986.

[69] B. van Linder, W. van der Hoek, and J.-J.Ch. Meyer. Actions that make you change your mind. In A. Laux and H. Wansing, editors. *Knowledge and Belief in Philosophy and AI*, pages 103–146. Akademie-Verlag, 1995.

[70] B. van Linder, W. van der Hoek, and J.J.-Ch. Meyer. Formalizing abilities and opportunities of agents. *Fundamenta Informaticae*, 34(1–2):53–101, 1998.

[71] A. Lomuscio and F. Raimondi. MCMAS: a tool for verifying multi-agent systems. In *Proceedings of The Twelfth International Conference on Tools and Algorithms for the Construction and Analysis of Systems (TACAS-2006)*. Springer-Verlag, Berlin, Germany, 2006.

[72] Z. Manna and A. Pnueli. *Temporal Verification of Reactive Systems—Safety*. Springer-Verlag, Berlin, Germany, 1995.

[73] J. McCarthy and P.J. Hayes. Some philosophical problems from the standpoint of artificial intelligence. In B. Meltzer and D. Michie, editors. *Machine Intelligence 4*, pages 463–502. Edinburgh University Press, 1969.

[74] J.-J.Ch. Meyer, W. van der Hoek, and B. van Linder. A logical approach to the dynamics of commitments. *Artificial Intelligence*, 113:1–40, 1999.

[75] J.-J.Ch. Meyer and R.J. Wieringa, editors. *Deontic Logic in Computer Science—Normative System Specification*. John Wiley & Sons, 1993.

[76] R.C. Moore. Reasoning about knowledge and action. In *Proceedings of the Fifth International Joint Conference on Artificial Intelligence (IJCAI-77)*, Cambridge, MA, 1977.

[77] R.C. Moore. A formal theory of knowledge and action. In J.F. Allen, J. Hendler, and A. Tate, editors. *Readings in Planning*, pages 480–519. Morgan Kaufmann Publishers, San Mateo, CA, 1990.

[78] L. Morgenstern. A first-order theory of planning, knowledge, and action. In J.Y. Halpern, editor. *Proceedings of the 1986 Conference on Theoretical Aspects of Reasoning About Knowledge*, pages 99–114. Morgan Kaufmann Publishers, San Mateo, CA, 1986.

[79] L. Morgenstern. Knowledge preconditions for actions and plans. In *Proceedings of the Tenth International Joint Conference on Artificial Intelligence (IJCAI-87)*, pages 867–874, Milan, Italy, 1987.

[80] M.J. Osborne and A. Rubinstein. *A Course in Game Theory*. The MIT Press, Cambridge, MA, 1994.

[81] M. Pauly. Logic for social software. PhD thesis, University of Amsterdam, 2001. ILLC Dissertation Series 2001-10.

[82] M. Pauly. A logical framework for coalitional effectivity in dynamic procedures. *Bulletin of Economic Research*, 53(4):305–324, 2002.

[83] M. Pauly. A modal logic for coalitional power in games. *Journal of Logic and Computation*, 12(1):149–166, 2002.

[84] M. Pauly and M. Wooldridge. Logic for mechanism design—a manifesto. In *Proceedings of the 2003 Workshop on Game Theory and Decision Theory in Agent Systems (GTDT-2003)*, Melbourne, Australia, 2003.

[85] A. Pnueli and R. Rosner. On the synthesis of a reactive module. In *Proceedings of the Sixteenth ACM Symposium on the Principles of Programming Languages (POPL)*, pages 179–190, January 1989.

[86] S. Popkorn. *First Steps in Modal Logic*. Cambridge University Press, Cambridge, England, 1994.

[87] F. Raimondi and A. Lomuscio. Symbolic model checking of multi-agent systems via OBDDs: an algorithm and its implementation. In *Proceedings of the Third International Conference on Autonomous Agents and Multiagent Systems (AAMAS-04)*, pages 630–637, New York, NY, 2004.

[88] A.S. Rao. AgentSpeak(L): BDI agents speak out in a logical computable language. In W. Van de Velde and J.W. Perram, editors. *Agents Breaking Away: Proceedings of the Seventh European Workshop on Modelling Autonomous Agents in a Multi-Agent World, LNAI*, vol. 1038, pages 42–55. Springer-Verlag, Berlin, Germany, 1996.

[89] A.S. Rao. Decision procedures for propositional linear-time Belief-Desire-Intention logics. In M. Wooldridge, J.P. Müller, and M. Tambe, editors. *Intelligent Agents II, LNAI*, vol. 1037, pages 33–48. Springer-Verlag, Berlin, Germany, 1996.

[90] A.S. Rao and M. Georgeff. BDI Agents: from theory to practice. In *Proceedings of the First International Conference on Multi-Agent Systems (ICMAS-95)*, pages 312–319, San Francisco, CA, June 1995.

[91] A.S. Rao and M. Georgeff. Decision procedures for BDI logics. *Journal of Logic and Computation*, 8(3):293–344, 1998.

[92] A.S. Rao and M.P. Georgeff. Asymmetry thesis and side-effect problems in linear time and branching time intention logics. In *Proceedings of the Twelfth International Joint Conference on Artificial Intelligence (IJCAI-91)*, pages 498–504, Sydney, Australia, 1991.

[93] A.S. Rao and M.P. Georgeff. Modeling rational agents within a BDI-architecture. In R. Fikes and E. Sandewall, editors. *Proceedings of Knowledge Representation and Reasoning (KR&R-91)*, pages 473–484. Morgan Kaufmann Publishers, San Mateo, CA, April 1991.

[94] A.S. Rao and M.P. Georgeff. An abstract architecture for rational agents. In C. Rich, W. Swartout, and B. Nebel, editors, *Proceedings of Knowledge Representation and Reasoning (KR&R-92)*, pages 439–449, 1992.

[95] A.S. Rao and M.P. Georgeff. A model-theoretic approach to the verification of situated reasoning systems. In *Proceedings of the Thirteenth International Joint Conference on Artificial Intelligence (IJCAI-93)*, pages 318–324, Chambéry, France, 1993.

[96] A.S. Rao, M.P. Georgeff, and E.A. Sonenberg. Social plans: A preliminary report. In E. Werner and Y. Demazeau, editors. *Decentralized AI 3—Proceedings of the Third European Workshop on Modelling Autonomous Agents in a Multi-Agent World (MAAMAW-91)*, pages 57–76. Elsevier Science Publishers B.V., Amsterdam, The Netherlands, 1992.

[97] R. Reiter. *Knowledge in Action*. The MIT Press, Cambridge, MA, 2001.

[98] S. Rosenschein and L.P. Kaelbling. The synthesis of digital machines with provable epistemic properties. In J.Y. Halpern, editor, *Proceedings of the 1986 Conference on Theoretical Aspects of Reasoning About Knowledge*, pages 83–98. Morgan Kaufmann Publishers, San Mateo, CA, 1986.

[99] S.J. Rosenschein and L.P. Kaelbling. A situated view of representation and control. In P.E. Agre and S.J. Rosenschein, editors. *Computational Theories of Interaction and Agency*, pages 515–540. The MIT Press, Cambridge, MA, 1996.

[100] M. Ryan and P.-Y. Schobbens. Agents and roles: Refinement in alternating-time temporal logic. In J.-J.Ch. Meyer and M. Tambe, editors. *Intelligent Agents VIII: Proceedings of the Eighth International Workshop on Agent Theories, Architectures, and Languages, ATAL-2001, LNAI*, vol. 2333, pages 100–114. Springer, 2002.

[101] Y. Shoham. Agent-oriented programming. *Artificial Intelligence*, 60(1):51–92, 1993.

[102] M.P. Singh. A critical examination of the Cohen–Levesque theory of intention. In *Proceedings of the Tenth European Conference on Artificial Intelligence (ECAI-92)*, pages 364–368, Vienna, Austria, 1992.

[103] V.S. Subrahmanian, P. Bonatti, J. Dix, T. Eiter, S. Kraus, F. Ozcan, and R. Ross. *Heterogeneous Agent Systems*. The MIT Press, Cambridge, MA, 2000.

[104] M. Tambe. Towards flexible teamwork. *Journal of AI Research*, 7:83–124, 1997.

[105] N. Troquard and A. Herzig. Uniform choices in STIT. In *Proceedings of the Fifth International Joint Conference on Autonomous Agents and Multi-Agent Systems (AMAS)*, 2006.

[106] R. Turner. *Truth and Modality for Knowledge Representation*. Pitman Publishing, London, 1990.

[107] W. van der Hoek, W. Jamroga, and M. Wooldridge. A logic for strategic reasoning. In *Proceedings of the Fourth International Joint Conference on Autonomous Agents and Multiagent Systems (AAMAS-2005)*, pages 157–153, Utrecht, The Netherlands, 2005.

[108] H.P. van Ditmarsch, W. van der Hoek, and B.P. Kooi. *Dynamic Epistemic Logic. Synthese Library*, vol. 337. Springer, Berlin, 2007.

[109] M.Y. Vardi. Branching vs. linear time: Final showdown. In T. Margaria and W. Yi, editors. *Proceedings of the 2001 Conference on Tools and Algorithms for the Construction and Analysis of Systems, TACAS 2001, LNCS*, vol. 2031, pages 1–22. Springer-Verlag, Berlin, Germany, April 2001.

[110] D. Walther, C. Lutz, F. Wolter, and M. Wooldridge. ATL satisfiability is indeed ExpTime-complete. *Journal of Logic and Computation*, 16:765–787, 2006.

[111] M. Wooldridge. The logical modelling of computational multi-agent systems. PhD thesis, Department of Computation, UMIST, Manchester, UK, October 1992.

[112] M. Wooldridge. *Reasoning about Rational Agents*. The MIT Press, Cambridge, MA, 2000.

[113] M. Wooldridge, M.-P. Huget, M. Fisher, and S. Parsons. Model checking multi-agent systems: The MABLE language and its applications. *International Journal on Artificial Intelligence Tools*, 15(2):195–225, April 2006.

[114] M. Wooldridge and N.R. Jennings. Intelligent agents: Theory and practice. *The Knowledge Engineering Review*, 10(2):115–152, 1995.

[115] M. Wooldridge and N.R. Jennings. The cooperative problem solving process. *Journal of Logic and Computation*, 9(4):563–592, 1999.

[116] M. Wooldridge and W. van der Hoek. On obligations and normative ability. *Journal of Applied Logic*, 3:396–420, 2005.

[117] E.N. Zalta. Stanford encyclopedia of philosophy. See http://plato.stanford.edu/.

Handbook of Knowledge Representation
Edited by F. van Harmelen, V. Lifschitz and B. Porter
© 2008 Elsevier B.V. All rights reserved
DOI: 10.1016/S1574-6526(07)03025-8

Chapter 25

Knowledge Engineering

Guus Schreiber

25.1 Introduction

The discipline of knowledge engineering grew out of the early work on expert systems in the seventies. With the growing popularity of knowledge-based systems (as these were by then called), there arose also a need for a systematic approach for building such systems, similar to methodologies in main-stream software engineering. Over the years, the discipline of knowledge engineering has evolved into the development of theory, methods and tools for developing knowledge-intensive applications. In other words, it provides guidance about when and how to apply particular knowledge-presentation techniques for solving particular problems.

In this chapter we first discuss (Section 25.2) a number of principles, that have become the baseline of modern knowledge engineering. These include the common distinction made in knowledge engineering between task knowledge and domain knowledge. In Section 25.3 we explore the notion of problem-solving tasks in detail and present typical patterns and methods user for solving such tasks. In Section 25.4 we focus on the domain perspective, in particular the representation and use of ontologies. Finally, Section 25.5 summarizes the main techniques that are being used in knowledge engineering, examples of their use.

25.2 Baseline

The early expert systems were based on an architecture which separated domain knowledge, in the form a knowledge base of rules, from a general reasoning mechanism. This distinction still is still valid in knowledge engineering practice. In the early eighties a number of key papers were published that set the scene for a systematic approach to knowledge engineering.

In 1982 Newell published a paper on "The Knowledge Level" [28] in which he argued the need for a description of knowledge at a level higher the level of symbols in knowledge-representation systems. The knowledge-level was his proposal for realizing a description of an AI system in terms of its rational behavior: why does the system (the "agent") perform this "action", independent of its symbolic representation in rules, frames or logic (the "symbol" level). Descriptions at the knowledge level has since become a principle underlying knowledge engineering.

Two other key publications came from Clancey. His "Epistemology of a rule-based system" [8] can be viewed as a first knowledge-level description of a knowledge-based system, in which he distinguished various knowledge *types*. Two tears later his article "Heuristic classification" appeared [9] which described a standard problem-solving pattern in knowledge-level terms. Such patterns subsequently became an important focus of knowledge-engineering research; these patterns typically serve as reusable pieces of task knowledge. We treat these in more depth in Section 25.3.

In the nineties the attention of the knowledge-engineering shifted gradually to domain knowledge, in particular reusable representations in the form of ontologies. A key paper, which also quite wide attention outside the knowledge-engineering community was Gruber's paper on portable ontologies [16]. During this decade ontologies are getting widespread attention as vehicles for sharing concepts within a distributed community such as the web (e.g., see Chapter 21 on the Semantic Web). Similar to task knowledge, patterns also play an important role on modeling domain knowledge. In Section 25.4 we describe in some detail the main issues in ontology engineering.

25.3   Tasks and Problem-Solving Methods

In the early expert systems task knowledge was embedded in the reasoning engine and in rules in the knowledge base. The key point of Clancey's "epistemology" paper was to explicate the underlying problem-solving method. Since then, the knowledge-engineering community has developed a range of such problem-solving methods. We can define a problem-solving method as follows:

> A problem-solving method (*PSM*) *is a knowledge-level specification of a reasoning pattern that can used to carry out a knowledge-intensive task.*

To categorize problem-solving-methods we need a typology of knowledge-intensive tasks. Various (partial) task typologies have been reported in the literature. Stefik [41] distinguishes between "diagnosis", "classification" and "configuration". Chandrasekaran [7] has described a typology of "design tasks" (including configuration). McDermott [24] describes a taxonomy of problem types. Table 25.1 shows the typology of task types distinguished by Schreiber et al. [37].

In this section we describe two problem-solving methods in more detail: one method for configuration design and one method for assessment. In general, there does not need to be a one-to-one correspondence between methods and tasks, although in practice there often is.

25.3.1   Two Sample Problem-Solving Methods

Propose-and-revise.   The propose-and-revise (P&R) method was described by Marcus and McDermott [23]. The method was used to solve a configuration-design task, namely elevator design (the so-called VT case study [22]). The data for this case

Table 25.1. Task types in CommonKADS (adapted from [37])

Task type	Input	Output	Knowledge	Features
ANALYTIC TASK TYPES				
Classification	Object features	Object class	Feature-class associations	Set of classes is predefined.
Diagnosis	Symptoms/ complaints	Fault category	Model of system behavior	Form output varies (causal chain, state, label) and depends on use made of it (troubleshooting).
Assessment	Case description	Decision class	Criteria, norms	Assessment is performed at one particular point in time (cf. monitoring).
Monitoring	System data	Discrepancy class	Normal system behavior	System changes over time. Task is carried out repeatedly.
Prediction	System data	System state	Model of system behavior	Output state is a system description at some future point in time.
SYNTHETIC TASK TYPES				
Design	Requirements	Artifact description	Functions, components, skeletal design, constraints, preferences	May include creative design of components.
Configuration design	Requirements	Artifact description	Functions, components, constraints, preferences	Subtype of design in which all components are predefined.
Assignment	Two object sets, requirements	Mapping set 1 → set 2	Constraints, preferences	Mapping need not be one-to-one.
Planning	Goals, requirements	Action plan	Actions, constraints, preferences	Actions are (partially) ordered in time.
Scheduling	Job activities, resources, time slots, requirements	Schedule = mapping activities → time slots of resources	Constraints, preferences	Time-oriented character distinguishes it from assignment.

study was subsequently used in a comparative study in which different knowledge-engineering approaches were used to solve this problem. The results of the study were published in special issue of Human-Computer Studies [38]. This issue provides a wealth of information for readers interested in details of modern knowledge engineering. We will come back to this study in the next section, as reuse of the pre-existing ontology was a prime focus of this study.

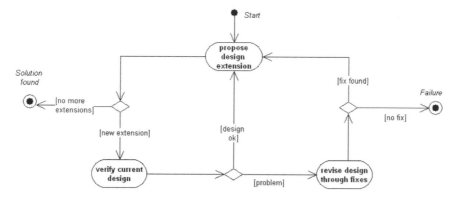

Figure 25.1: Top-level reasoning strategy of the P&R method in the form of a UML activity diagram.

Fig. 25.1 shows the top-level reasoning strategy of the P&R method. The method decomposes the configuration-design task into three subtasks:

1. Propose an extension to the existing design, e.g., add a component.

2. Verify the current design to see whether any of the constraints are violated. For example, adding a particular hoist cable might violate constraints involving the strength of the cable in comparison to other elevator components.

3. If a constraint is violated, use domain-specific revision strategies to remedy the problem, for example, upgrading the model of the hoist cable.

Unlike some other methods, which undo previous design decisions, P&R fixes them. P&R does not require an explicit description of components and their connections. Basically, the method operates on one large bag of parameters. Invocation of the propose task produces one new parameter assignment, the smallest possible extension of an existing design. Domain-specific, search-control knowledge guides the order of parameter selection, based on the components they belong to. The verification task in P&R applies a simple form of constraint evaluation. The method performs domain-specific calculations provided by the constraints. In P&R, a verification constraint has a restricted meaning, namely a formula that delivers a Boolean value. Whenever a constraint violation occurs, P&R's revision task uses a specific strategy for modifying the current design. To this end, the task requires knowledge about fixes, a second form of domain-specific, search-control knowledge. Fixes represent heuristic strategies for repairing the design and incorporate design preferences. The revision task tries to make the current design consistent with the violated constraint. It applies combinations of fix operations that change parameter values, and then propagates these changes through the network formed by the computational dependencies between parameters.

Applying a fix might introduce new violations. P&R tries to reduce the complexity of configuration design by disallowing recursive fixes. Instead, if applying a fix introduces a new constraint violation, P&R discards the fix and tries a new combination. Motta and colleagues [27] have pointed out that, in terms of the flow of control, P&R offers two possibilities. One can perform verification and revision directly after every

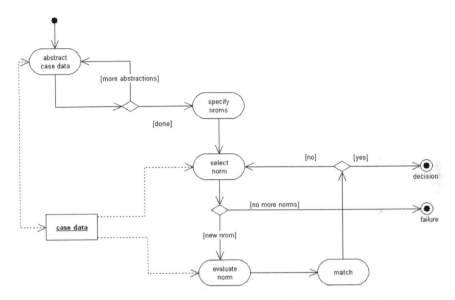

Figure 25.2: Top-level reasoning strategy of the basic assessment method in the form of a UML activity diagram.

new design or after all parameter values have been proposed. The original P&R system used the first strategy, but Motta argues that the second strategy is more efficient and also comes up with a different set of solutions. Although this method has worked in practice, it has inherent limitations. Using fix knowledge implies that heuristic strategies guide the design revisions. Fix knowledge implicitly incorporates preferences for certain designs. This makes it difficult to assess the quality of the method's final solution.

Assessment.   Assessment is a task not often described in the AI literature, but of great practical importance. Many assessment application have been developed over the years, typically for tasks in financial domains, such as assessing a loan for mortgage application, or in the civil-service area, such as assessing whether a permit can be given. The task is often confused with diagnosis, but where diagnosis is always considered with some faulty state of the system, assessment is aimed at producing a *decision*: e.g., yes/no to accept a mortgage application. During the Internet hype at the start of this decade every bank was developing such applications to be able to offer automated services on the Web.

A basic method for assessment is shown in Fig. 25.2. Assessment starts off with case data (e.g., customer data about a mortgage application). As a first step the raw case data is abstracted into more general data categories (e.g., income into income class). Subsequently, domain-specific norms/criteria are retrieved (e.g., "minimal income") and evaluated against the case data. The method then checks whether a decision can be taken or whether more norms need to be evaluated. This basic method is typically enhanced with domain-specific knowledge, e.g., select inexpensive (e.g., in terms of data acquisition) first. The resulting decision category are also domain-specific; for example, for a mortgage application this could be "accepted", "declined", or "flag for manual assessment".[1]

A detailed example of the use of this method can be found in the CommonKADS book [37, Ch. 10]. Valente and Löckenhoff [43] have published a library of different assessment methods.

25.3.2   The Notion of "Knowledge Role"

Above we showed two examples of methods for different tasks. These methods cannot be applied directly to a domain; typically, the knowledge engineer has to link the components of the method to elements of the application domain. Problem-solving methods can best be viewed as *patterns*: they provide template structures for solving a problem of a particular type. Designing systems with the help of patterns is in fact a major trend in software engineering at large, see, for example, the work of Gamma and colleagues [13] on design patterns.[2]

The knowledge-engineering literature provides a number of proposals for specification frameworks and/or languages of problem-solving methods. These include the "Generic Task" approach [6], "Role-Limiting Methods" [24], "Components of Expertise" [40], Protégé [32], KADS [48, 49] and CommonKADS [39]. Although there differences at a detailed level between these approaches, the one important commonality is: all rely on the notion of "knowledge role":

> A knowledge role *specifies in what way particular domain knowledge is being used in the problem solving process.*

Typical knowledge role in the assessment method are "case data", "norm" and "decision". These are method-specific names for the role that pieces of domain knowledge play during reasoning. From a computational perspective, they limit the role that these domain-knowledge elements can play, and therefore make problem solving more feasible, when compared to old "old" expert-systems idea of one large knowledge-vase with a uniform reasoning strategy. In fact, the assumption behind PSM research is that the epistemological adequacy of the method gives one a handle on the computational tractability of the system implementation based on it. This issue is of course a long-standing debate in knowledge representation at large (see, e.g., [4]).

Another issue that frequently comes up in discussions about problem-solving methods is their correspondence with human reasoning. Early work on KADS used problem-solving methods as a coding scheme for expertise data [47]. Over the years the growing consensus has become that, while human reasoning can form an important inspirational source for problem-solving method and while it is use to use role cognitively-plausible terms for knowledge role, the problem-solving strategy may well be different. Machines have different qualities than humans. For example, a method that requires a large memory space cannot be carried out by a human expert, but presents no problem to a computer program. In particular methods for synthetic tasks,

---

[1] Many of these assessment systems are aimed at reducing administrative workload and are not designed to solve the standard cases and leave atypical ones for manual assessment.

[2] Problem-solving methods would be called "strategy patterns" in the terminology of Gamma et al. [13].

where the solution space is usually large, problem-solving methods often have no counterpart in human problem solving.

25.3.3 Specification Languages

In order to put the notions of "problem-solving method" and "knowledge role" on a more formal footing, the mid-1990s saw the development of a number of formal languages that were specifically designed to capture these notions.

The goal of such languages was often twofold. First of all, to provide a formal and unambiguous framework for *specifying* knowledge models. This can be seen as analogous to the role of formal specification languages in Software Engineering, which aim to use logic to describe properties and structure of software in order to enable the formal verification of properties. Secondly, and again analogous to Software Engineering, some of these formal languages could be made executable (or contained executable fragments), which could be used to simulate the behavior of the knowledge models on specific input data. Most of the languages that were developed followed the maxim of *structure preserving specification* [44]: if the structure of the formal specification closely follows the structure of the informal knowledge model, any problems found during verification activities performed on the formal model can be easily translated in terms of possible repairs on the original knowledge model.

In particular the Common KADS framework was the subject of a number of formalization attempts, see [12] for an extensive survey. Such languages would follow the structure of Common KADS model into (1) a *domain layer*, where an ontology is specified describing the categories of the domain knowledge and the relationships between these categories (i.e., the boxes in Fig. 25.5); (2) *knowledge roles* link the components of the method to elements of the application domain; (3) *inference steps* that are the atomic elements of a problem solving method (i.e., the ovals in Fig. 25.2), and (4) a task definition which emposes a control structure over the inference steps to complete the definition of the problem solving method.

A simplified example is shown in Fig. 25.3, using a simplification of the syntax of $(ML)^2$ [45]:

- the *domain layer* specifies a number of declarative facts in the domain. These facts are already organized in three different modules.

- the *knowledge roles* empose a problem-solving interpretation on these neutral domain facts: any statement from the patient-data module is interpreted as data, any implication from the symptom-definition module is interpreted as an abstraction rule, and any implication from the symptomatology module is interpreted as a causal rule.

- the *inference steps* then specify how these knowledge roles can be used in a problem solving method: an abstraction step consists of a deductive (modus ponens) step over an abstraction rule, whereas a hypothesize step consists of an abductive step over a causation rule.

- finally, the *task model* specifies how these atomic inference steps must be strung together procedurally to form a problem solving method: in this a sequence of a deductive abstraction step followed by an abductive hypothesize step.

DOMAIN
> patient-data: $temp(patient1) = 38$
> symptom-definitions: $temp(P) > 37 \rightarrow fever(P)$
> sympotomatology: $hepatitis(P) \rightarrow fever(P)$

KNOWLEDGE ROLES
> **from** patient-data: $A \mapsto data(A)$
> **from** symptom-definition: $A \rightarrow B \mapsto abstraction(A, B)$
> **from** sympotomatology: $A \rightarrow B \mapsto causation(A, B)$

INFERENCE
> $abstract(A_1, A_2)$: $data(A_1) \wedge abstraction(A_1, A_2) \rightarrow observation(A_2)$
> $hypothesise(B_1, B_2)$: $observation(B_2) \wedge causation(B_1, B_2) \rightarrow hypothesis(B_1)$

TASK
> **begin** abstract(A,B) ; hypothesize(B,C) **end**

Figure 25.3: A simple problem-solving method specification in the style of $(ML)^2$.

The impact of the languages such $(ML)^2$ [45], KARL [11] and many others (see [12]) was in one sense very limited: although the knowledge modeling methods are in widespread use, the corresponding formal languages have not received widespread adaptation. Rather than direct adoption, their influence is perhaps mostly seen through the fact that they forced a much more precise formulation of the principles behind the knowledge modeling methods.

There is renewed activity in the area of formal languages for problem solving methods at the time of writing. This is causes by an interest from web services. Web-services are composed into work-flows, and these workflows often exhibit typical patterns (e.g., browse-order-pay-ship, or search-retrieve-process-report). Problem solving methods are essentially reusable workflows of reasoning-patterns, and the established lessons from problem solving methods may well be applicable to this new area.

25.4   Ontologies

During the nineties ontologies become popular in computer science. Gruber [16] defines an ontology as an "explicit specification of a conceptualization". Several authors have made small adaptations to this. A common definition nowadays is:

> *An* ontology *is an explicit specification of a shared conceptualization that holds in a particular context.*

The addition of the adjective "shared" is important, as the primary goal of ontologies in computer science was to enable knowledge sharing. Up till the end of the nineties "ontology" was a niche term, used by a few researchers in the knowledge engineering and representation field.[3] The term is now in widespread use, mainly due

---

[3] At a preparation meeting for a DARPA program in this area in 1995, the rumors were that DARPA management talked about the O-word.

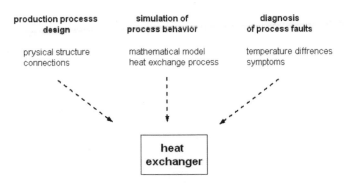

Figure 25.4: Three different viewpoints on a heat exchanger.

to enormous need for shared concepts in the distributed world of the web. People and programs need to share at least some minimal common vocabulary. Ontologies have become in particular popular in the context of the Semantic Web effort, see Chapter 21.

In practice, we are confronted with many different conceptualizations, i.e., ways of viewing the world. Even is in a single domain there can be multiple viewpoints. Take, for example, the concept of a heat exchanger as shown in Fig. 25.4. The conceptualization of a heat exchanger is can be very different, depending on whether we take the viewpoint of the physical structure, the internals of the process, or the operational management.

"Context" is therefore an important notion when reusing an ontology. We cannot expect other people or programs to understand our conceptualization, if we do not explicate what the context of the ontology is. Lenat [21] has made an attempt to define a theory of context spaces. In practice, we see most often that context is being defined though typing the ontology. We discuss ontology types in Section 25.4.2 and/or reusing an ontology.

The plural form used in the title of this section is revealing. The notion of ontology has been a subject of debate in philosophy for many ages. The study of ontology, or the theory of "that what is" (from the Greek "ontos" = being), has been a discipline in its own right since the days of Aristotle, who can be seen as founder and inspirator. The plural form signifies the pragmatic use made of the notion in modern computer science. We talk now about "ontologies" as the state of the art does not provide us with a single theory of what exists.

25.4.1 Ontology Specification Languages

Many of the formalisms can be said to be useful for specifying an ontology. An insightful article into the ontological aspects of KR languages is the paper by Davis and colleagues [10]. They define five roles for a knowledge representation, which we can briefly summarize as follows:

1. A surrogate for the things in the real world.

2. A set of ontological commitments.

3. A theory of representational constructs plus inferences it sanctions/recommends.

4. A medium for efficient computation.

5. A medium for human expression.

One can characterize ontology-specification languages as KR languages that focus mainly on roles 1, 2 and 5. In other words, ontologies are not specified with a particular reasoning paradigm in mind.

There have been several efforts to define tailor-made ontology-specification languages. In the context of the DARPA Knowledge Sharing Effort Gruber defined Ontolingua [16]. Ontolingua was developed as an ontology layer on top of KIF [15], which allowed frame style definition of ontologies (classes, slots, subclasses, . . .). Additional software was provided to be able the use of Ontolingua as a mediator between different knowledge-representation languages, such as KIF and LOOM. Ontolingua provided a library service where users share their ontologies.[4]

Other languages, in particular conceptual graphs (see Chapter 5) have been popular for specifying ontologies. Recently, OWL has gained wide popularity. OWL is the W3C Web Ontology Language [46]. Its syntax is XML based. Things defined in OWL get a URI, which simplifies reuse. OWL sails between Scylla of expressiveness and the Charybdis of computability by defining a subset of OWL (OWL DL) that is equivalent to a well-understood fragment of description logic (see Chapter 3). User who limit themselves to this fragment of OWL get some guarantees with respect to computability. The OWL user is free to step outside the bounds of OWL DL, if s/he requires additional expressive power. An overview of OWL is given in Chapter 21.

One might ask, whether the use of description logic as a basis for an ontology language does to contradict the statement of the start of this section, namely that ontologies are not specified with a reasoning mechanism in mind. It is undoubtedly true that the DL reasoning paradigm biases the way one models the world with OWL. However, subclass modeling appears to be an intrinsic feature of modeling domain knowledge. The use of a DL-style modeling in knowledge of domains has been popular since the early days of KL-ONE [5]. Also, DL reasoning is often mainly used to validate the ontology; typically, additional reasoning knowledge is needed in applications. The fact that Web community is defining a separate rule language to complement OWL is also evidence for this. Still, one could take the view that a more general first-order language would be better for ontology specification, as it introduces less bias and provides the possibility of specifying reasoning within the same language. If one takes this position, a language like KIF [15] is a prime candidate as ontology language.

25.4.2 Types of Ontologies

Ontologies exist in many forms. Roughly, ontologies can be divided into three types: (i) foundational ontologies, (ii) domain-specific ontologies, and (iii) task-specific ontologies.

---

[4]http://ontolingua.stanford.ed.

Foundational ontologies.   Foundational ontologies stay closest to the original philosophical idea of "ontology". These ontologies aim to provide conceptualizations of general notions, such as time, space, events and processes. Some groups have published integrated collections of foundational ontologies. Two noteworthy examples are the SUMO (Suggested Upper Merged Ontology)[5] and DOLCE (Descriptive Ontology for Linguistic and Cognitive Engineering).[6] An ontology of time has been published by Hobbs and Pan [20], which includes Allen's set of time relations [1]. Chapter 12 of this Handbook also addresses time representation.

Ontologies for part–whole relations have been an important area of study.   Unlike the subsumption relation, part–whole relations are usually not part of the basic expressivity of the representation language. In domains dealing with large structures, such as biomedicine, part–whole relations are often of prime importance. A simple baseline representation of part–whole relations is given by Rector and Welty [35]. Winston et al. published a taxonomy of part–whole relations, distinguishing, for example, assembly–component relations from portion–mass relations. Such typologies are of practical importance as transitivity of the part–whole relation does not hold when different part–whole relations are mixed ("I'm part of a club, my hand is part of me, but this does not imply my hand is part of the club"). Several revised versions of this taxonomy have been published [30, 2].

Lexical resources such as WordNet[7] [26], can also be seen as foundational ontologies, although with a weaker semantic structure. WordNet defines a semantic network with 17 different relation types between concepts used in natural language. Researchers in this area are proposing richer semantic structuring for WordNet (e.g., [31]). The original Princeton WordNet targets the English–American language; WordNets now exist or are being developed for almost all major languages.

Domain-specific ontologies.   Although foundational ontologies are receiving a lot of attention, the majority of ontologies are domain-specific: they are intended for sharing concepts and relations in a particular area of interest. One domain in which a wide range of ontologies has been published is biomedicine. A typical example is the Foundational Model of Anatomy (FMA) [36] which describes some 75,00 anatomical entities. Other well-known biomedical ontologies are the Unified Medical Language System[8] (UMLS), the Simple Bio Upper Ontology,[9] and the Gene Ontology.[10]

Domain ontologies vary considerably in terms of the level of formalization. Communities of practice in many domains have published shared sets of concepts in the form of vocabularies and thesauri. Such concept schemes typically have a relatively weak semantic structure, indicating many hierarchical (broader/narrower) relations, which most of the time loosely correspond to subsumption relations. This has triggered a distinction in the ontology literature between weak versus strong ontologies. The SKOS model,[11] which is part of the W3C Semantic Web effort, is targeted at

---

[5] http://ontology.teknowledge.com/.

[6] http://www.loa-cnr.it/dolce.html.

[7] http://wordnet.princeton.edu/.

[8] http://www.nlm.nih.gov/pubs/factsheets/umls.html.

[9] http://www.cs.man.ac.uk/~rector/ontologies/simple-top-bio/.

[10] http://www.geneontology.org/.

[11] http://www.w3.org/2004/02/skos/.

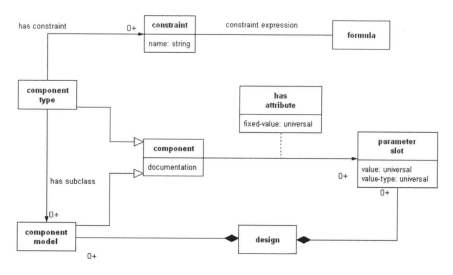

Figure 25.5: Configuration-design ontology in the VT experiment [18] (in the form of a UML class diagram).

allowing thesaurus owners to publish their concept schemes in an interoperable way, such that sharing of these concepts on the Web becomes easier. In practice, thesauri are important sources for information sharing (the main goal of ontologies in computer science). For example, in the cultural-heritage domain thesauri such as the Getty vocabularies[12] (Art & Architecture Thesaurus, Union List of Artist Names, Thesaurus of Geographic Names) and IconClass (concepts for describing image content) are important resources. Current efforts focus therefore on making such vocabularies available in ontology-representation formats and enriching ("ontologizing") them.

Task-specific ontologies.   A third class of ontologies specifies the conceptualizations that are needed for carrying out a particular task. For each of the task types listed in Table 25.1 one can specify domain conceptualizations needed for accomplishing this task. An example of a task-specific ontology for the configuration-design task can be found in Fig. 25.5. Data of configuration-design of an elevator system were used in the first ontology-reuse experiment in the nineties [38].

In general, conceptualizations of domain information needed for reasoning algorithms typically takes the form of a task-specific ontology. For example, search algorithms typically operate on an ontology of states and state transitions. Tate's plan ontology [42] is another example of a task-specific ontology.

25.4.3   Ontology Engineering

Ontology engineering is the discipline concerned with building and maintaining ontologies. It provides guidelines for building domain conceptualizations, such as the construction of subsumption hierarchies.

---

[12]http://www.getty.edu/research/conducting_research/vocabularies/.

An important notion in ontology engineering is *ontological commitment*. Each statement in an ontology commits the user of this ontology to a particular view of the domain. If a definition in an ontology is stronger than needed, than we say that the ontology is over-committed. For example, if we state that the name of a person must have a first name and a last name we are introducing a western bias into the ontology and may not be able to use the ontology in all intended cases. Ontology engineers usually try to define an ontology with a minimal set of ontological commitments. One can translate this into an (oversimplified) slogan: "smaller ontologies are better!". Gruber [17] gives some principles for minimal commitments.

Construction of subsumption hierarchies is seen as a central activity in ontology engineering. The OntoClean method of Guarino and Welty [19] defines a number of principles for this activity, based on three meta-properties of classes, namely rigidity, unity and identity. Central in the OntoClean method is the identification of so-called "backbone" classes of the ontology. Rector [33] defines also a method for backbone identification.

In addition, design patterns have been specified for frequently occurring ontology-engineering issues. We mention here the work of Noy on patterns for defining N-ary relations [29] (to be used with an ontology language that supports only binary relations, such as OWL) and the work of Rector on patterns for defining value sets [34]. Gangemi has published a set of design patterns for a wide range of modeling situations [14].

25.4.4 Ontologies and Data Models

The difference between ontologies and data models does not lie in the language being used: you can define an ontology in a basic ER language (although you will be hampered in what you can say); similarly, you can write a data model with OWL. Writing something in OWL does not make it an ontology! The key difference is not the language the intended use. A data model is a model of the information in some restricted well-delimited application domain, whereas an ontology is intended to provide a set of shared concepts for multiple users and applications. To put it simply: data models live in a relatively small closed world; ontologies are meant for an open, distributed world (hence their importance for the Web). So, defining a name as consisting of a first name and a last name might be perfectly OK in a data model, but may be viewed as incorrect in an ontology. It must be added that there is a tendency to extend the scope of data models, e.g., in large companies, and thus there is an increasing tendency to "ontologize" data models.

25.5 Knowledge Elicitation Techniques[13]

Although this entire Handbook is devoted to the formal and symbolic representation of knowledge, very few if any of its chapters are concerned with how such representations are actually obtained. Many techniques have been developed to help elicit knowledge from an expert. These are referred to as knowledge elicitation or

---

[13]Material in this section has been taken from the CommonKads book [37], the CommonKADS website at http://www.commonkads.uva.nl and the website of Epistemics, http://www.epistemics.co.uk.

knowledge acquisition (KA) techniques. The term "KA techniques" is commonly used.

The following list gives a brief introduction to the types of techniques used for acquiring, analyzing and modeling knowledge:

- Protocol-generation techniques include various types of interviews (unstructured, semi-structured and structured), reporting techniques (such as self-report and shadowing) and observational techniques.

- Protocol analysis techniques are used with transcripts of interviews or other text-based information to identify various types of knowledge, such as goals, decisions, relationships and attributes. This acts as a bridge between the use of protocol-based techniques and knowledge modeling techniques.

- Hierarchy-generation techniques, such as laddering, are used to build taxonomies or other hierarchical structures such as goal trees and decision networks.

- Matrix-based techniques involve the construction of grids indicating such things as problems encountered against possible solutions. Important types include the use of frames for representing the properties of concepts and the repertory grid technique used to elicit, rate, analyze and categorize the properties of concepts.

- Sorting techniques are used for capturing the way people compare and order concepts, and can lead to the revelation of knowledge about classes, properties and priorities.

- Limited-information and constrained-processing tasks are techniques that limit the time and/or information available to the expert when performing tasks. For instance, the twenty-questions technique provides an efficient way of accessing the key information in a domain in a prioritized order.

- Diagram-based techniques include the generation and use of concept maps, state transition networks, event diagrams and process maps. The use of these is particularly important in capturing the "what, how, when, who and why" of tasks and events.

Specialized tool support has been developed for each of these techniques. Table 25.2 briefly describes some of these techniques, and correlates them with the appropriate tool support.

This wide variety of techniques is required to access the many different types of knowledge possessed by experts. This is referred to as the Differential Access Hypothesis, and has been shown experimentally to have supporting evidence.

Fig. 25.6 presents the various techniques described above and shows the types of knowledge they are mainly aimed at eliciting. The vertical axis on the figure represents the dimension from object knowledge to process knowledge, and the horizontal axis represents the dimension from explicit knowledge to tacit knowledge. The details of these techniques are described in a number of survey articles and textbooks, such as [3], [37, Ch. 8], and [25].

Table 25.2. Summary of elication techniques

Technique	Used for	Tool support
Unstructured interview	Familiarization with organization and application domain	Markup tools; text analysis
Structured interview	Knowledge-identification activities; initial knowledge specification; completing the knowledge bases	Markup tools; rule editor (when used for completing the knowledge base)
Protocol analysis	Checking a task template Generating an inference/task specification (in case of unfamiliar application domains, for which no models exist yet)	Marking up a transcript with inference and/or task markers
Laddering	Preparatory work for domain-schema specification with respect to useful hierarchies and concept attributes	Graphical support for constructing multiple hierarchies
Concept sorting	Domain-schema specification in unfamiliar domains	Graphical support tool for creating piles and new features
Repertory grid	Domain-schema specification in unfamiliar domains	Graphical grid presentation/editing plus cluster analysis software

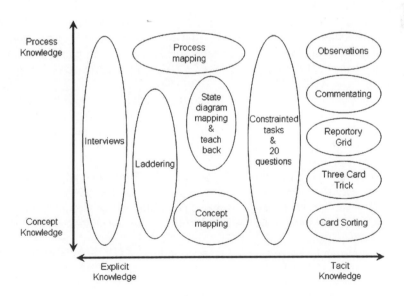

Figure 25.6: Applicability of Knowledge Acquisition techniques.

Bibliography

[1] J. Allen. Maintaining knowledge about temporal intervals. *Communications of the ACM*, 26:832–843, 1983.

[2] A. Artale, E. Franconi, and L. Pazzi. Part-whole relations in object-centered systems: An overview. *Data and Knowledge Engineering*, 20:347–383, 1996.

[3] J.H. Boose. A survey of knowledge acquisition techniques and tools. *Knowledge Acquisition*, 1(1):3–37, 1989.

[4] R.J. Brachman and H.J. Levesque. The tractability of subsumption in frame-based description languages. In *AAAI 84*, 1984.

[5] R.J. Brachman and J.G. Schmolze. An overview of the KL-ONE knowledge representation system. *Cognitive Science*, 9:171–216, 1985.

[6] B. Chandrasekaran. Generic tasks in knowledge based reasoning: High level building blocks for expert system design. *IEEE Expert*, 1(3):23–30, 1986.

[7] B. Chandrasekaran. Design problem solving: A task analysis. *AI Magazine*, 11:59–71, 1990.

[8] W.J. Clancey. The epistemology of a rule based system—a framework for explanation. *Artificial Intelligence*, 20:215–251, 1983.

[9] W.J. Clancey. Heuristic classification. *Artificial Intelligence*, 27:289–350, 1985.

[10] R. Davis, H. Shrobe, and P. Szolovits. What is a knowledge representation? *AI Magazine*:17–33, Spring 1993.

[11] D. Fensel. *The Knowledge Acquisition and Representation Language KARL*. Kluwer, ISBN-13: 978-0792396017, 1995.

[12] D. Fensel and F. van Harmelen. A comparison of languages which operationalise and formalise KADS models of expertise. *The Knowledge Engineering Review*, 9:105–146, 1994.

[13] E. Gamma, R. Helm, R. Johnson, and J. Vlissides. *Design Patterns: Elements of Reusable Object-Oriented Software*. Addison-Wesley, Reading, MA, 1995.

[14] A. Gangemi. Ontology design patterns for Semantic Web content. In *International Semantic Web Conference ISWC'05, Galway, Ireland, LNCS*, pages 262–276. Springer-Verlag, 2005.

[15] M.L. Ginsberg. Knowledge interchange format: the KIF of death. *AI Magazine*, 12(33):57–63, 1991.

[16] T.R. Gruber. A translation approach to portable ontology specifications. *Knowledge Acquisition*, 5:199–220, 1993.

[17] T.R. Gruber. Towards principles for the design of ontologies used for knowledge sharing. In N. Guarino and R. Poli, editors. *Formal Ontology in Conceptual Analysis and Knowledge Representation*. Kluwer, Boston, 1994.

[18] T.R. Gruber, G.R. Olsen, and J. Runkel. The configuration-design ontologies and the VT elevator domain theory. *Int. J. Human-Computer Studies*, 44(3–4):569–598, 1996.

[19] N. Guarino and C. Welty. Evaluating ontological decisions with OntoClean. *Comm. ACM*, 45(2):61–65, 2002.

[20] J.R. Hobbs and F. Pan. Time ontology in OWL. Technical report, Ontology Engineering Patterns Task Force of the Semantic Web Best Practices and Deployment Working Group, World Wide Web Consortium (W3C), http://www.w3.org/TR/owl-time/, 2006.

[21] D. Lenat. The dimensions of context space. Technical report, CYCORP. URL: http://www.cyc.com/doc/context-space.pdf, 28 October 1998.

[22] S. Marcus, editor. *Automatic Knowledge Acquisition for Expert Systems*. Kluwer, Boston, 1988.

[23] S. Marcus and J. McDermott. SALT: A knowledge acquisition language for propose-and-revise systems. *Artificial Intelligence*, 39(1):1–38, 1989.

[24] J. McDermott. Preliminary steps towards a taxonomy of problem-solving methods. In S. Marcus, editor. *Automating Knowledge Acquisition for Expert Systems*, pages 225–255. Kluwer, Boston, 1988.

[25] M.A. Meyer and J.M. Booker. *Eliciting and Analyzing Expert Judgement: A Practical Guide*. Academic Press, 1991.

[26] G. Miller. WordNet: A lexical database for English. *Comm. ACM*, 38(11), November 1995.

[27] E. Motta, A. Stutt, Z. Zdrahal, K. O'Hara, and N.R. Shadbolt. Solving VT in VITAL: a study in model construction and reuse. *Int. J. Human-Computer Studies*, 44(3–4):333–372, 1996.

[28] A. Newell. The knowledge level. *Artificial Intelligence*, 18:87–127, 1982.

[29] N. Noy and A. Rector. Defining *N*-ary relations on the Semantic Web. Technical report, W3C Working Group Note, http://www.w3.org/TR/swbp-n-aryRelations, 2006.

[30] J. Odell. Six different kinds of composition. *Journal of Object Oriented Programming*, 5(8):10–15, 1994.

[31] A. Oltramari, A. Gangemi, N. Guarino, and C. Masolo. Restructuring WordNet's top-level: The OntoClean approach. In *Proc. LREC 2002*, 2002.

[32] A.R. Puerta, J. Egar, S. Tu, and M. Musen. A multiple-method shell for the automatic generation of knowledge acquisition tools. *Knowledge Acquisition*, 4:171–196, 1992.

[33] A. Rector. Modularisation of domain ontologies implemented in description logics and related formalisms including OWL. In *Proc. K-CAP'03*, pages 121–128. AAAI, 2003.

[34] A. Rector. Representing specified values in OWL: "value partitions" and "value sets". Technical report, W3C Working Group Note, http://www.w3.org/TR/swbp-specified-values, 2005.

[35] A. Rector and C. Welty. Simple part–whole relations in OWL ontologies. Technical report, World-Wide Web Consortium (W3C), Working Group Note, http://www.w3.org/2001/sw/BestPractices/OEP/SimplePartWhole/, 2005.

[36] C. Rosse and J.V.L. Mejino. A reference ontology for biomedical informatics: the foundational model of anatomy. *J. Biomedical Informatics*, 36:478–500, 2003.

[37] A.Th. Schreiber, J.M. Akkermans, A.A. Anjewierden, R. de Hoog, N.R. Shadbolt, W. Van de Velde, and B.J. Wielinga. *Knowledge Engineering and Management: The CommonKADS Methodology*. MIT Press, Cambridge, MA, 1999.

[38] A.Th. Schreiber and W.P. Birmingham. The Sisyphus-VT initiative. *Int. J. Human-Computer Studies*, 43(3–4):275–280, 1996 (Editorial special issue).

[39] A.Th. Schreiber, B.J. Wielinga, R. de Hoog, J.M. Akkermans, and W. Van de Velde. CommonKADS: A comprehensive methodology for KBS development. *IEEE Expert*, 9(6):28–37, December 1994.

[40] L. Steels. Components of expertise. *AI Magazine*, Summer 1990.

[41] M. Stefik. *Introduction to Knowledge Systems*. Morgan Kaufmann, Los Altos, CA, 1993.

[42] A. Tate. Towards a plan ontology. *Journal of the Italian AI Association (AIIA)*, January 1996.

[43] A. Valente and C. Löckenhoff. Organization as guidance: A library of assessment models. In *Proceedings of the Seventh European Knowledge Acquisition Workshop (EKAW'93)*, pages 243–262, 1993.

[44] F. van Harmelen and M. Aben. Structure preserving specification languages for knowledge-based systems. *International Journal of Human Computer Studies*, 44:187–212, 1996.

[45] F. van Harmelen and J.R. Balder. $(ML)^2$: a formal language for KADS models of expertise. *Knowledge Acquisition*, 4(1), 1992. Special issue: 'The KADS approach to knowledge engineering', reprinted in A.Th. Schreiber, et al., editors, *KADS: A Principled Approach to Knowledge-Based System Development*, 1993.

[46] Web Ontology Working Group. OWL web ontology language overview. W3C recommendation, World Wide Web Consortium, http://www.w3.org/TR/owl-features/, 2004.

[47] B.J. Wielinga and J.A. Breuker. Interpretation of verbal data for knowledge acquisition. In T. O'Shea, editor, *Advances in Artificial Intelligence*, pages 41–50, Amsterdam, The Netherlands, 1984. ECAI, Elsevier Science. Also as: Report 1.4, ESPRIT Project 12, University of Amsterdam.

[48] B.J. Wielinga and J.A. Breuker. Models of expertise. In *Proceedings ECAI-86*, pages 306–318, 1986.

[49] B.J. Wielinga, A.Th. Schreiber, and J.A. Breuker. KADS: A modelling approach to knowledge engineering. *Knowledge Acquisition*, 4(1):5–53, 1992.
Reprinted In B. Buchanan and D. Wilkins, editors. *Readings in Knowledge Acquisition and Learning*, pages 92–116. Morgan Kaufmann, San Mateo, CA, 1992.

Author Index

Subject Index